**The New York Times**

**Twentieth Century in Review**

# THE BALKANS

## VOLUME I: 1875–1949

Other Titles in
The New York Times 20th Century in Review

*The Cold War*
*The Gay Rights Movement*
*Political Censorship*


Forthcoming
*The Rise of the Global Economy*
*The Vietnam War*

𝕿𝖍𝖊 𝕹𝖊𝖜 𝖄𝖔𝖗𝖐 𝕿𝖎𝖒𝖊𝖘
Twentieth Century in Review

# THE BALKANS
## VOLUME I: 1875–1949

**Editor
Ana Siljak**

**Introduction by Roger Cohen**

**Series Editor
David Morrow**

**FITZROY DEARBORN PUBLISHERS
CHICAGO  LONDON**

For information write to:

FITZROY DEARBORN PUBLISHERS
919 North Michigan Avenue, Suite 760
Chicago IL 60611
USA

or

FITZROY DEARBORN PUBLISHERS
310 Regent Street
London W1B 3AX
England

**British Library and Library of Congress Cataloging in Publication Data are available.**

ISBN 1-57958-330-X

First published in the USA and UK 2001

Typeset by Print Means, Inc., New York, New York

Printed by Edwards Brothers, Ann Arbor, Michigan

Cover Design by Peter Aristedes, Chicago Advertising and Design, Chicago, Illinois

# CONTENTS

## VOLUME I
## 1875–1949

## VOLUME II
## 1950–2000

# PREFACE

This volume brings together articles from The New York Times exemplary of the newspaper's coverage of Southeastern Europe over the past century. Defining the Balkans is a notoriously vexing task, but for the purposes of this collection, the Balkans includes the territories that constitute present-day Albania, Bulgaria, Greece, Romania and the states of the former Yugoslavia. The ever-shifting borders of this region—the tendency of states to form, collapse and reappear—explain much of its complex history. The history of any particular Balkan state cannot be narrated in isolation; the region is all but defined by cultural, political and linguistic interaction. For these reasons, the articles in this volume have been arranged chronologically. It is hoped that this will allow the reader to comprehend the broader, regional nature of Balkan history.

Conflict emerges as the central theme in this collection of articles. In part, of course, this is due to the editorial choices made by The New York Times. Conflict—military conflict in particular—sells newspapers, and wars draw correspondents to regions largely ignored during times of peace. This was particularly true during the late nineteenth and early twentieth centuries, when The Times's coverage of international affairs was scattered. But the prevalence of articles on warfare is not merely a matter of selective coverage. The history of the Balkans from 1875 (when this volume begins) has indeed been one of revolts, skirmishes, wars and assassinations, as national groups struggled to expand and defend borders or to topple despised rulers and occupiers. Seen over the long term, the 45 years of the cold war present something of an exception: a period of relative peace bounded on both sides by often bloody and brutal conflict.

If anything, this selection underrepresents the proportion of articles that The New York Times dedicated to warfare in its Balkan coverage. Particularly during the world wars, the bulk of the paper's reporting was devoted to the blow by blow of daily combat. This collection, however, tries to balance articles on political and military affairs with articles on social and cultural issues.

One of the most striking aspects of this collection is the recurrence of atrocity stories reported from the Balkans. Whether it was the Turks against the Bulgarians, the Germans against the Serbs, or the Serbs against the Albanians, articles chronicle the terrible slaughter of civilians caught between the region's warring factions. In the editorial pages of The New York Times, one finds repeated attempts to make sense of this carnage and to understand how cultures developed the capacity to wreak destruction on even the most innocent of their neighbors. Morbid atrocity stories also provided The Times with occasions for favorable and at times self-serving comparisons between Eastern Europe and the Western world.

The Balkan reporting of The New York Times consistently paid disproportionate attention to Serbia and Yugoslavia. This was dictated partly by historical circumstance and partly by editorial choice. Serbia burst onto the front page with the assassination of Archduke Ferdinand in Sarajevo in 1914, and the editorial page portrayed "Brave little Serbia" as a symbol of resistance to "Teutonic" oppression throughout the course of World War I. Yugoslavia's armed struggle against Hitler elicited the newspaper's sympathy some three decades later. Similarly, Tito's dramatic break with Stalin and his sporadic flirtation with the West earned Yugoslavia regular and usually favorable coverage. The breakup of Yugoslavia in the 1990s transformed Serbia from victim to oppressor, and yet again, The New York Times focused on the Yugoslav civil wars to the exclusion of events in neighboring nations. The selection of articles in this volume tries to correct for this privileging of Serbia and Yugoslavia by including a greater proportion of articles on Bulgaria, Greece, Romania and Albania.

The West's lack of familiarity with the Balkans was continually revealed in The Times. Over the century, correspondents repeatedly struggled to make sense of the region's bewildering diversity of languages and ethnic groups and to reconcile the mutually conflicting historical claims that animated each event or conflict. The paper offered periodic primers on the intricate history of the region. The rebellion in the province of Herzegovina in 1875 and the subsequent Russo-Turkish War of 1877 prompted The New York Times to include long articles on the history of the Balkan nations and their struggles against Turkish domination. A century later, in 1992, similar historical pieces were written on complicated subjects such as the Greek dispute over the name "Macedonia." In each article, one senses the writer's effort to untangle narratives that often stretched back to the Middle Ages and were of dubious reliability but had strong contemporary relevance.

Dominant cultural attitudes toward the Balkans were often reflected in the prejudices and sympathies in The New York Times's coverage of the region. The 1876 editorial on the brutal tendencies of "Mohammedan fanaticism," written at a time when sympathy lay with the Christians supposedly languishing under Muslim oppression, would be supplanted more than 100 years later by similar editorials denouncing Christian atrocities against Muslim victims. During the two world wars, Balkan nations were portrayed as "brave" or "treacherous" in succession, depending on their shifting status within the major alliances. And during the cold war, articles on economic misery in Bulgaria and Romania reflected U.S. fears of Soviet Communism, while articles on Tito and Yugoslavia often revealed an opposite tendency: a hope in some leftist circles that a moderate, socialist experiment might succeed and prosper.

The articles in this book are divided into eight parts, each of which discusses a particular period in the history of the Balkans. Within each section, care was taken to include a balance of articles on political, social and cultural topics. Articles were also selected to give the reader a sense of how reporting and editorial writing changed over time—from the shorter, almost dispatch-like quality of the articles in the early twentieth century to the feature-length coverage in the cold war and post-cold war decades. Occasional articles on American and European reactions to Balkan events were included to trace changing international attitudes toward the region over the course of the century.

The first part contains articles on the Balkans in the late nineteenth century, particularly articles on the uprising in Herzegovina in 1875, which eventually led to the Russo-Turkish war of 1877–1878. The period from 1875 to 1900 witnessed a decline of Ottoman and Austrian imperial control over the Balkans region and an increase in the rebelliousness of the Balkan people. These articles narrate the stirrings of Balkan nationalism and the increasingly successful struggles for independence from Ottoman rule. Within the editorial pages of The New York Times, one can see growing sympathy for what was perceived to be a fight for national independence and religious freedom.

Part II documents the continuing Balkan battles to secure statehood and expand national territory in the years from 1900 to 1913. This was a period of almost continual warfare. The Serbs, Bulgarians and Romanians finally chased the Ottoman Empire out of the region, but then they immediately turned to fight each other in dividing the spoils of war. The articles in this section also chronicle the perils each new nation encountered in trying to build its new state. Domestic unrest, including assassinations and revolts, plagued the new countries as they tried to establish stable regimes after centuries of imperial domination.

Part III covers World War I, a war that came to be seen (both within the Balkans and without) as a war of nations against empires. The Times's coverage of the conflict reflected this attitude—Serbia was second only to Belgium as the symbol of a brave nation standing up to an oppressive German empire. Other Balkan nations were viewed as potential pawns in the war, and articles reflect the hope that Greece would finally rise up against the Germans, or that Bulgaria would surrender. In the ensuing peace, the Balkans (like all of Eastern Europe) became the site of a grand European experiment: empires were dismantled and boundaries redrawn to create nation-states, in the hopes that a Europe of independent nations would become a Europe without war. One of the most daring of such experiments was the creation of the Kingdom of Serbs, Croats and Slovenes. It was believed that this Slavic kingdom would become the model for a post-imperial, democratic state, but these hopes were quickly dashed.

The short period of peace between the two world wars, the subject of Part IV, did not give the Balkan states enough time to develop stable democratic governments. Parliamentary democracy proved difficult to sustain in the face of economic difficulties and ethnic conflict. In Greece, Yugoslavia and Romania, political assassinations added to the turmoil. The West could only watch in dismay as each Balkan state abandoned all attempts to preserve democracy and installed royal dictatorships, and the articles in this section reflect U.S. disappointment in the Balkan turn to absolutism. In this section there are also frequent hints of things to come. The rise of communism and fascism are evident in the anti-Jewish riots in Romania, the arrest of communist agitators in Bulgaria and the unification of fascist parties in Yugoslavia.

Part V chronicles the tragedy of World War II as it swept through the Balkans. One by one, each Balkan country fell to the Axis powers—some were forced to sign humiliating pacts and others were simply occupied. The territories of these countries were dismembered and their populations soon divided into ideological camps. The harshest fate was reserved for Greece and Yugoslavia, the two countries that dared to resist Nazi Germany. Not only did they suffer terrible German reprisals for their resistance, but they also endured vicious internal conflicts between ideological factions. Yugoslavia descended into a particularly bloody civil war that pitted Serbs against Croats and communists against nationalists—a civil war that resulted in some of the most terrifying atrocities of the twentieth century. The articles in this section reveal that The New York Times was often puzzled by the various players in these conflicts. Reporters were not sure whether Bulgarians and Romanians were Hitler's supporters or his unwilling victims, and they were particularly perplexed by Tito and his role in the Yugoslav resistance movement. By the end of the war, the articles hint at ominous signs that fascist occupation would be replaced by Soviet Communist domination.

The slow but inexorable rise of communism in the Balkans is described in Part VI. One by one, opposition figures in Bulgaria, Romania and Yugoslavia became victims of Soviet-style purges, and the Soviet Union consolidated its hold on these countries via supposedly democratic elections. Greece became the sole exception to this trend, but not without substantial British assistance during its difficult civil war. This section also includes articles on the dramatic break between Yugoslavia and the Soviet Union in 1948. At first, this rift did little to disturb the Soviet Union's iron grip over the rest of the communist bloc. Soon, however, cold war conflict in the Balkans centered on U.S. and Soviet attempts to woo the enigmatic Yugoslav leader, Josip Broz Tito.

In the period covered by Part VII, communism was entrenched in the Balkan states, with Greece as the lone democratic country. Yugoslavia was the only country that successfully established cordial relations with both sides during the cold war, and it became the focus of Western hopes for the end of Soviet control of Eastern Europe. The New York Times began to devote more coverage to Tito and his erratic attempts to reform the Yugoslav system of government. Reporters were fascinated by the shifts in Yugoslav policy—Tito made overtures to Khrushchev and then visited President Kennedy, he liberalized the economy and then imprisoned vocal dissidents. The other countries in the Balkans received less attention, in part because information was so difficult to gather under repressive regimes. Aside from reports of economic austerity in Romania and Bulgaria, and apart from a few articles on the Albanian move to side with China against the Soviet Union, life in these countries was mostly shrouded in obscurity.

Part VIII covers the end of the century, when the old communist regimes tumbled and the Balkan countries once again endeavored to establish new states from under the rubble of the old. The articles in this section strikingly resemble those of the early part of the century—they chronicle warfare, domestic unrest and the struggle to preserve democracy. This section will be most familiar to contemporary readers, since the images of the wars in Bosnia and Kosovo are still fresh. Naturally, the coverage in this section focuses almost exclusively on the collapse of Yugoslavia and its aftermath, with its dramatic scenes of the siege of Sarajevo and the bombing of Kosovo. But an attempt was made to include articles that describe the aftermath of communism in states such as Bulgaria, Romania and Albania. The articles discuss the first euphoria that followed the collapse of communist rule and the subsequent dismay at the economic hardship and political turmoil that followed.

This last section of the book ends the story of the Balkans in the twentieth century on an enigmatic note. On the one hand, the articles demonstrate that the peace established in Bosnia and in Kosovo is still fragile, and there are hints that the Serbs, Muslims, Croats, Macedonians and Albanians are not yet ready to give up their battles over contested territories. On the other hand, the recent elections in the region prove that these states have not yet abandoned their democratic aspirations, and Yugoslavia and Croatia have even managed to oust their former dictators. It remains to be seen whether peace and democracy will continue to grow or whether the region will once again enter into the old Balkan spiral of unrest, revolt, assassination and war.

*Ana Siljak received her Ph.D. in History from Harvard University. She is currently managing editor of the "Journal of Cold War Studies" and a fellow at the Davis Center for Russian Studies. She is co-editor of the forthcoming book "Ethnic Cleansing in East-Central Europe, 1944–1948."*

# INTRODUCTION

## By Roger Cohen

In a dispatch from Bucharest dated March 24, 1956, C.L. Sulzberger noted that the Romanian capital that once had the "lovable cheek to call itself the Paris of the East" had abruptly come to resemble "a Moscow of the West." Gone were the pretentious sophistication of the city's restaurants and the ramshackle gaiety; in their place, "a drab and earnest capital, bedecked with Red placards exhorting Marxist man to fill his norm." No facelift for this city, The Times man mused. Rather, its face had been "dropped" by what he called "miraculous new methods of psychological town planning."

Such disorientation has been commonplace before the often violent transformations of the Balkans over the past 130 years. The post-war arrival of communism in Bucharest and elsewhere complicated the task, already arduous, of disentangling national identities from the legacy of sprawling empires. Economic backwardness accentuated susceptibility to autocratic leaders. As a result, no other part of Europe has proved so volatile. This instability may produce sensations of vertigo in the visitor dismayed by the speed with which the ground may shift and the living appear to fall beneath the shadow of the dead.

Winston Churchill famously remarked that the problem with the Balkans was the region's capacity to produce more history than it could consume. But instant digestion is the journalist's calling, even when the lead is as momentous as on this dispatch from Sarajevo, dated June 29, 1914: "Archduke Francis Ferdinand, heir to the throne of Austria-Hungary, and his wife, the Duchess of Hohenberg, were shot and killed by a Bosnian student here today." Within weeks, Austria-Hungary declared war on Serbia, seen as the origin of the assassination plot, and World War I began.

Wars are hell; they also make for powerful copy. So, in this volume, correspondents grapple day by day to make sense of the tumult of recent Balkan history and, in many instances, rise to convey the very taste of turmoil and suffering. Here is John. F. Burns reporting on June 8, 1992, from the besieged city of Sarajevo, under bombardment by Serb nationalists: "It is a disaster of such magnitude, and of such seeming disconnectedness from any achievable military or political goals, that those who take shelter for days in basement bunkers, emerging briefly into daylight for fresh supplies of bread and water, exhaust themselves trying to make sense of it."

But cumulatively these dispatches do help make sense of Balkan history. They place the reader at the center of events from the last spasms of the Ottoman Empire in World War I to the war NATO fought with Serbia over Kosovo. Several themes emerge: the struggle for the nation-state, the ravages of communism, the enduring nature of psychological wounds inflicted by war in states where history has often been manipulated to serve authoritarian regimes rather than confronted to serve some semblance of a truth that may console.

So the Balkan gyre sweeps round and round. Nicholas Gage, whose mother was killed by Greek communists after World War II, was the chief correspondent in Athens at the time of military rule by the colonels. In a story dated January 31, 1971, he tells of a confrontation with an aunt over the acts of the colonels, who had brutalized communists and leftists since taking power in 1967. "Who have the colonels killed?" the aunt asks him dismissively. And before Gage can answer, she reminds him: "Who killed your mother?"

Who killed your mother? Such a question is not easily laid to rest in the Balkans. The scars go deep, inflicted in significant measure by the struggle to define the borders and populaces of nation-states in areas that were for centuries under imperial Ottoman or Austro-Hungarian rule. Drawing national borders in regions so marked by the ebb and flow of peoples and religions has proved problematic and often violent.

Woodrow Wilson, the American President, thought he had a solution after World War I when he helped concoct the state that would be called Yugoslavia. Noble sentiments drove him. Because the peoples gathered within the new state had long been subjected to imperial rule, they would feel liberated by their new Yugoslav incarnation—or so Wilson reasoned. But Yugoslavia, of course, was about as multinational as the empires that preceded it, and the peoples within it—particularly Serbs and Croats—proved largely impervious to Wilsonian dreams of self-determination if two or more "selves" had to "determine" themselves on the same land.

A brief dispatch dated July 26, 1919, evokes a Croatian revolt "taking the form of a movement for separation from Serbia." That movement turned violent during World War II when Yugoslavia dissolved and a puppet-Nazi Croatian state embarked on a genocidal purge of Serbs. Tito then put the state together again under the clamp of a communist rule that chose not to dwell on these and other atrocities.

Decades later, on July 10, 1996, Chris Hedges reports on the "human skulls, grayish thigh bones and soggy black boots" discovered in a mass grave of Bosnian Muslims killed by Serbian forces near Srebrenica. The thread is constant enough—and has extended most recently into Kosovo and Macedonia. From its birth through its mid-life crisis in World War II to its violent destruction, Yugoslavia always tended toward its own unraveling, propelled by those who chose to see not the links of language and blood in this part of the Balkan peninsula but the divisions of religion and culture.

The amount of blood spilled—and the number of Catholic churches, Orthodox monasteries and Islamic mosques destroyed—provide one measure of the reality of the Yugoslav bonds that had to be broken to divide up land so mottled by migration, marriage and mixing. That process is still not entirely completed. The battles over a "Greater Serbia" that dominated the 1990s have given way to a "Greater Albanian" question as the southeastern leg of Yugoslavia's undoing proceeds, marked by further bloodshed.

But, as the dispatches gathered here make clear, breaking bonds is old Balkan business. On January 10, 1923, Edwin L. James reported from Lausanne on the conference convoked to end fighting between Greece and Turkey. "In the name of peace and justice," he wrote, "1,000,000 men, women and children are to be torn from their homes and forcibly taken to other lands. Such was the remarkable decision taken today by this remarkable Near East conference. The statesmen of the civilized nations and of Turkey this morning voted to exchange the Greek population of Turkey against the Turkish population of Greece."

So began a vast movement of human beings in what would become a familiar image of twentieth-century Europe: columns of bedraggled refugees leaving their ancestral homes in the name of nation-states conceived on principles of ethnic homogeneity or in the furtherance of some crazed act of social engineering.

The slogans then were "Turkey for the Turks" and "Greater Greece." And what then of those Christians in Turkey or Muslims in Greece who did not fit? They could no more be tolerated than those Yugoslavs of mixed descent made homeless by the nationalist discourse of Serbia's Slobodan Milosevic and Croatia's Franjo Tudjman in the 1990s.

The Greeks of Asia Minor moved west; the Turks scattered throughout Greece moved in the opposite direction; a grim peace, permeated with suspicion, took hold. Decades later, the Serbian eviction at gunpoint of several hundred thousand Muslims from a wide swathe of Bosnia in the early months of the Bosnian war in 1992 jolted a Western world made complacent by the fall of communism in Europe three years earlier. The phrase "ethnic cleansing" dominated headlines. But the term and the practice were less new than they seemed.

It is noteworthy that James's dispatch from Lausanne speaks of "the civilized nations and of Turkey." The clear implication is that Turkey is not clubbable—at least not in the best Western clubs. The Times correspondent went further: the decision to move populations forcibly was "due entirely and exclusively to the Turks's determination to expel the Greeks from their country."

Scarcely a judgment that would stand up today in the court of journalistic objectivity. Greece, after all, had sent its forces into Asia Minor—not the other way around. But The Times man was writing in a solid tradition. For example, one dispatch in the mid-1870s chronicling the uprisings of Christian Slavs against Turkish rule speaks of the "effete despotism of the Moslems" as if it were a proven and universally accepted characteristic.

Prejudice such as this flowers in the Balkans: consider the wave of the hand and the laconic "This is the Balkans, you know" with which many Western politicians dismissed the complexities of the Bosnian war between 1992 and 1995, as if savagery were somehow endemic to the region, written into the Balkan gene.

Understanding is scarcely served by such attitudes. Turkey, of course, was long "the sick man of Europe," its protracted, intermittently cruel rule of most of southeastern Europe unraveling in the late 19th century. The Ottoman stake driven through the heart of the Serb rebel is an image buried deep in the Serbian psyche; so, too, are the rampages of Turkish bashibazouks and the myriad tales of gifted Serbian children being whisked away for indoctrination at the grand vizier's court in Istanbul.

Such specters are easily summoned. Milosevic did not hesitate to do so, convincing his people that a fundamentalist Muslim or even perhaps reincarnated Ottoman threat loomed over the Serbs of Bosnia in 1992. In fact, of course, most of the Bosnian Muslims were thoroughly secular—until persecution, directed mainly from Belgrade, imbued them with a new identity.

Shifting identities, like shifting borders, have plagued the Balkans, confounding steady economic or political development. After World War II—in which 1.7 million Yugoslavs alone were killed—most of the Balkan states fell behind the Iron Curtain. The regimes endured for decades as dictators from Bulgaria's Todor I. Zhivkov to Romania's Nicolae Ceausescu sought, in different ways, to create their own versions of "Homo Sovieticus."

One partial exception was Tito's Yugoslavia where, as M.S. Handler reported on November 3, 1950, communists sought for a time "to determine the degree to which liberalism can exist within a Communist state without becoming a threat to such a state." The conclusions of the experiment: only to a very small degree. Tito's notion of an "institutionalized revolution" amounted to an oxymoron. The more-liberal communists ended up in prison. As C.L. Sulzberger remarks, "an institutionalized revolution would be like a frozen waterfall."

Elsewhere, communist idealism quickly degenerated into drudgery and the deification of despots. R.W. Apple, reporting from Romania in 1982, noted that flour, sugar, meat, tea, coffee and cooking oil were often unobtainable. Nonetheless, the "Rumanian leader's picture still adorns a wall in every office, signs praising him still stand at 500-yard intervals along country roads, and he still permits not a murmur of dissent."

The full extent of the folly became clear after 1989, a year whose revolutions—velvet and less so (as in Romania)—are chronicled here with great vividness. Long repressed truths now pour forth: Zhivkov's 30 houses and hunting lodges, the 8,000 workers and 7,000 soldiers put to work daily by Ceausescu on his 300-foot-high House of the Republic, the terrible AIDS-infested orphanages of Romania resulting from the regime's draconian policies against birth control, the ravages of Stalinism on Albania—a European country that had achieved the status of "least developed nation" by the time the regime collapsed. Only in December of 1990 did Albania tear down "East Europe's last towering statues of Stalin."

It was a time of celebration. Democracy has now taken hold in much of the region. But it was also a time when the collapse of one system—communism—left a vacuum conducive to the rise of nationalism. Henry Kamm, reporting from Belgrade in 1989, was one of the first to spot the trend. "Since Yugoslavia was formed in 1918," he wrote, "keeping Serbia from exerting its numerical and historic power has been widely considered the key to preserving national unity. Yet an appeal to Serbian nationalism has been the fuel powering Mr. Milosevic's rise." He quoted a leading Serbian intellectual, Kosta Mihailovic, arguing that "We occupied a vassal position in Yugoslavia."

The Serbian "vassals"—real or imagined, it mattered not—soon rose in a frenzy behind Milosevic and his vow to avenge trampled Serbian honor in the pursuit of a glorious—if vague—Serbian future. Within two years, Slovenia and Croatia had declared independence from what they now viewed as "Serboslavia," war had broken out and the gracious, mixed town of Vukovar on the Danube in Croatia had been razed by Serbian forces whose handiwork was a latter-day Dresden.

Chuck Sudetic was there on November 20, 1991, to witness the "liberation" of the town by the Serbs: "Only soldiers of the Serbian-dominated army, stray dogs and a few journalists walked the smoky, rubble-choked streets and the ruins of the apartment buildings, stores and hotel in Vukovar's center. Not one of the buildings seen in a daylong visit to this town could be described as habitable. In one park, shellfire had sheared thick trees in half like so many blades of grass cut by a mower. Across the street, the dome of an Orthodox Christian church had fallen onto the altar. Automatic weapons fire erupted every few minutes as the prowling Serbian soldiers, some of them drunk, took aim at land mines, pigeons and windows that had survived the fighting." So much for restored Serbian honor.

Vukovar was a name—like Omarska, Sarajevo, Mostar, Srebrenica, Racak—that would become a symbol of the bloody destruction of Yugoslavia. The concentration camps, such as Omarska, where the Serbs threw Muslims in 1992, torturing many, killing some, were the scene of atrocities not witnessed in Europe for decades. It is against such horror, and in the name of a Europe whole and free, that Western nations belatedly reacted, bombing Serbian forces at Sarajevo in 1995 and Belgrade in 1998 and helping to unseat Milosevic in 2000. They have since committed themselves to a vast program of reconstruction in the Balkans.

The challenge is enormous. Kosovo and Macedonia remain deeply unstable, the latter teetering on the brink of war. Bosnia, even years after the American-inspired Dayton peace accords, is characterized less by peace than by the absence of war. But Western nations appear to have grasped that a commitment similar to that which placed Allied troops in Berlin for decades and ultimately won the cold war will now be required to bring the nations of the Balkans into a united Europe. Only such a prolonged effort of political will may wrest the region at last from its spiral of conflict. The investment required—of money and manpower—will be huge, equaled only by the potential price of failure.

Writing on October 20, 1935, from Athens, Emil Lengyel took note of the city's importance for Western culture: "At the foot of the Acropolis, where excavators are at work exposing the remnants of the ancient Agora, western man ventured his first halting steps on the road to political self-determination. Here Solon formulated laws that have inspired many commonwealths. Here was argued whether Pericles was a man of the people or a tyrant. Here citizens plotted to overthrow Pisistratus, father of the modern dictator-demagogue. Here Demosthenes arraigned Philip of Macedon before the bar of civilization."

Europe, as this passage makes clear, is inconceivable without the Balkans, and a peaceful Europe inconceivable without a Balkans at peace. An unstable Europe is not in the American interest and so—the cries of the Washington isolationists notwithstanding—the current American commitment to the Balkans is prudent.

But not only prudent. The area holds many lessons of coexistence and religious tolerance that no nationalist gunner, however persistent, can quite blast away. It belongs in the Western clubs—the European Union, chief among them—whose values are those of liberal, open, democratic societies.

More than a century ago, on September 17, 1876, a commentary on Balkan violence by Victor Hugo, the French poet, was printed in The New York Times. "What Europe requires is a European Nationality, one Government, one immense fraternal arbitration," Hugo wrote. He called for "Democracy at peace with itself" throughout the continent before summing up his thoughts as, "In one word, the United States of Europe. There is the goal, there is the port."

If for no other reason than to bring peace and stability to the Balkans, this still seems a goal worth pursuing. A "Paris of the East"—tolerant, open, stable, gracious—would then be entirely conceivable.

*Roger Cohen is deputy foreign editor of The New York Times and is the author of "Hearts Grown Brutal: Sagas of Sarajevo." He has served as bureau chief for The Times in Berlin and Zagreb and has provided award-winning coverage of the Balkans region during the 1990s.*

# PART I

## BALKAN REBELLIONS AND THE DECLINE OF EMPIRE, 1875–1899

The Herzegovinian insurrection is assuming threatening proportions. On account of the nearness of the Province of Herzegovina to Austria, that Empire is supposed to have a deep interest in the welfare of the people, especially as Christians form a considerable element in the population. The insurrection began with troubles between the Moslems and Christians; it has gradually drifted into a rebellion against Turkish domination. Servia, a semi-independent State, sympathizes with the Herzegovinians, and the Servians are aiding the insurrectionists by subscriptions. Prince Milan, the reigning sovereign of Servia, is making a pilgrimage to Vienna for the purpose, it is said, of ascertaining what position Austria proposes to occupy in this latest complication. Austria, at the first outbreak, hastily dispatched troops to the frontier, but has preserved a strict neutrality. Servia is interested to know if this attitude is to be preserved, or if Austria will interfere in the interests of peace in case the insurrection shall long continue. Meantime, Servia, which has been under the rule of native Princes but nominally subject to Turkey since 1815, may drift into the current and become actually independent.

\* \* \*

At first sight, it is not quite obvious what interest the news of further disturbances in Herzegovina can have for the world at large. The first outbreak was due to the rapacity of the Turkish tax-gatherers who insisted on making a peasantry impoverished by bad harvests and cattle plague submit to imposts greater than they could bear. Moslem fanaticism came in to aggravate the disorders which began with official greed, and now the sentiment of a common race, and the aspirations toward a united nationality, appear to have expanded the Herzegovinian rising into a general insurrection of the Serbs who owe fealty to the Porte. When the Montenegrin subjects of Prince Nitika and the Dalmatian subjects of Austria unite with Herzegovinians in a revolt against the authority of the Sultan, there is already in existence an armed nucleus for the "Great Serbia" of the future. That constitutes an event of some importance when viewed in connection with its relations to the equilibrium of power, and the maintenance of peace in Europe.

\* \* \*

### THE SICK MAN AGAIN

It does not seem at all likely that the Herzegovinian difficulty will be settled by Turkey. It is said, to be sure, that the Sublime Porte proposes to inquire into the causes of grievance. Inquiry presumes redress, if possible. But this is precisely the way in which Turkey always goes to war with its revolted colonies. There must be a certain amount of proclamation of the benevolent intentions of the Sultan, and many assurances of pardon to repentant rebels, before the Army moves and the real fighting begins. In the end, however, foreign aid will come in to quiet the insurgent provinces. It is conceded that Turkey exists on the map of Europe only by the consent and countenance of the great powers. The integrity of the Empire is sustained so long as the powers agree; when these finally disagree, Turkey will dissolve. It is possible, indeed, that the catastrophe may be hastened by financial debility. The sick man is failing fast; it is uncertain whether this spasm is not the last.

The real complaint in Herzegovina, as in other so-called Christian provinces of the Ottoman Empire, is simple enough. It is not altogether a question of taxation, though it may sometimes take that shape. Indeed, some of the revolted districts are exempt from taxation—an immunity which they secured during the last war between Turkey and Montenegro; other districts have already paid their taxes and have no such immediate cause for commotion. The real trouble is that the race is at enmity with the Moslems. So long as Serbia, Montenegro, Croatia, Bosnia, and Herzegovina are governed by an alien tribe, and compelled to yield any form of obedience to a hated religious rule, there must be discontent and rebellion. We may grant that the instinct, if we call it by no higher name, of the Sclavic race is not political; but it is, nevertheless, hostile to Mohammedanism and Turkish domination. Moreover, there is a distinct plan of union always clearly set forth in the minds of the leaders and the more intelligent people. A restoration of that great Serbia which fell before the conquering arms of the house of Osmanli, would bring independence to the Christian provinces now in arms, or meditating revolt against Turkey.

Of the fifteen millions of population of Turkey in Europe, only four millions are reckoned as Mohammedans. Yet the crescent in all this vast domain floats above the cross. It is a patent fact that the governing race has utterly broken down in numbers and organization. What may be accomplished in a community of one compact nationality is

1

shown in Serbia, where, though political troubles have occasionally appeared, there are prosperity, harmony, and comparative order. Outside of the Serbian boundaries, the Sclavic dependencies are in a state of continual turmoil and discontent. There is no justice in their being governed by the effete despotism of the Moslems. There is no real reason why these increasing and hardy Christian nationalities should long submit to a power that rules only by the consent of distant neighbors.

Turkey has long since been practically bankrupt. Each year the budget shows a deficit; each year the expenses of the State increase. Everything possible of mortgage has been pledged in security of loans floated in European capitals. The Egyptian tribute, the general revenues of the Empire, Customs, tithes, duties, mines, and provincial excise dues, have been mortgaged one after another, until, as Karl Blind says, no tangible security is left but the bracelets and bangles of the seraglio. Nevertheless this bankrupt, incoherent, misgoverned, and depleted Empire hangs together. It is sustained by that public opinion in Europe which protects the holders of Turkish bonds, and by that ancient superstition which teaches European diplomatists that Constantinople is the gateway to India. If it were possible that a Serbian or Sclavic Empire, extending from the Adriatic to the Danube, should spring out of the political chaos in Turkey, European diplomacy would be appalled. If, as a consequence of such a change on the map, the remainder of the Turkish Empire should crumble, as it must do, we should expect that three or four great powers would instantly assume an offensive attitude. Christian nations maintain Moslem supremacy in European Turkey. What with an interest in the bonds of the moribund State, and fears of the consequences of a division of the dead man's effects, these nations agree to keep the invalid alive.

Nevertheless, the end must some time come. The new Christian empire south of the Danube may not now arise. It is possible that another Turkish loan may be negotiated. It is likely that the Sultan will make terms with the insurgents; but these things must be accomplished by the aid and active interference of Christian Governments. The money must be borrowed in London, Frankfort, and Vienna. England, Russia, Germany, and Austria will prescribe conditions of peace in Herzegovina and Bosnia, just as they did in Montenegro, and just as they secured for Serbia that *quasi* independence which now excites the envy of neighboring dependencies of Turkey. After all, it is only a shadow which remains of Turkey. Christian nations fight its battles and decide when peace shall be proclaimed. It does not much matter what formal steps Turkey may take in the troubles of the Christian provinces. The real power felt there does not reside in Constantinople.

\* \* \*

January 9, 1876

# THE EASTERN QUESTION

### THE DEMAND OF THE GREAT POWERS

*How the Porte Received It—Effect of Vigorous Measures— Reforms Promised But Suggestions Unheeded—Count Andrassy's Ultimatum*

From Our Own Correspondent

PARIS, Monday, Dec. 20, 1875—I have just received very important news from Vienna, which will be forwarded to you this evening by telegraph, via London. An arrangement has been made between the three great powers respecting the *question d'Orient,* and it has been resolved to brook no further delays. Austria will take the lead in the matter, under the direction of Russia, the latter power agreeing to support the former in all that it does, whatever the consequences may be. Upon this Count Andrassy drew up a programme indicating the reforms demanded for the vassal States of the Porte, and this was forwarded to Constantinople. The Porte, finding that resistance was useless, and that safety depended upon doing all that was required, had taken the initiative in the matter of reforms, and had gone even further in the way of reform than Count Andrassy himself. In other words, the Porte accorded more than had been demanded. A statement of this fact was returned in reply to the Austrian note accompanying the programme of the allied powers, and for a moment there was hesitation on the part of the latter. Several notes passed between Vienna and St. Petersburg upon the new situation created by the Porte, and it was more than suspected that this was a piece of cunning Oriental diplomacy. Yet when such fair words were used what could be done? The three powers had made a few simple demands, and found that the Porte had accorded them in advance, with a great many more. In the case of almost any other Government in the world this would have been regarded as satisfactory, but Turkey has always been noted for the duplicity of her policy and for the wide difference existing between her words and her acts. Hence a want of confidence was felt in these fine promises of the Porte, and it was resolved to test them. Count Andrassy prepared another note upon the subject.

Meantime, there had been a very considerable delay, and the over-cunning statesmen upon the Bosphorus began to think that they had once more been too much for the "Christian dogs." Finally they gave expression to their joy in the columns of the official journal. A small item was inserted which stated that the most eminent statesmen of the Ottoman Empire had advised the Sultan to reject the programme of the three powers for two very good reasons: 1. Because the reforms voluntarily inaugurated by the Porte were far more complete, meeting every cause of complaint; 2. Because the acceptance of a foreign programme would be badly received in Turkey—would look like coercion—and, hence, would weaken the authority of the Government. The item closed by saying that the reforms of the Porte were about to be promulgated. All this was very well, but was the Sultan serious in his promises of reform or only indulging in Oriental diplomacy for the purpose of gaining time? It was resolved to make a test, and it was soon seen that the Porte was in no hurry to carry out the programme it had announced. Count Andrassy then sent another note urging an immediate decision upon the demands of the the three powers, dwelling particularly upon the necessity of giving preference to his measures of reform rather than those announced by the Porte; for while they might go further than the three powers desired to go at this moment, the people of the Principalities would have no confidence in them, or in any promises made by the Sultan which were not guaranteed by the three powers. It was urgent, therefore, that the Vienna programme should be adopted, for it would at once restore confidence; the people of the vassal States would feel satisfied, knowing that the faithful execution of the promises would be guaranteed by the three powers.

Count Andrassy wrote in a way to demand an immediate reply; but it is not easy to get a direct answer from Ottoman statesmen. They returned a *non possumus*—that is to say, they urged the extreme difficulty of introducing the reforms that were, in a manner, imposed by a foreign power; but, in order to show its friendly feelings and its desire to do all that friendly neighbors could ask in justice and in reason, the Sultan would proceed at once to institute his promised reforms, and would go even further than he had promised. Two months had thus passed in negotiations that resulted in nothing definite, and last week Count Andrassy, upon advice from St. Petersburg, resolved to send an ultimatum. This he has done, and in language that will not be likely to be misunderstood. In the Ottoman note the proposed guarantees were mentioned, the Porte averring that it would be quite impossible to give satisfactory guarantees, other than its word, for the faithful execution of these reforms. Count Andrassy recognizes the partial truth of this assertion, but finds in the fact an additional reason for urging his own programme. He now formally demands its adoption, and unless the Porte can find some way for guaranteeing its immediate promulgation and faithful execution, Austria will take it upon herself to do so, and will immediately send a *corps d'armée* into the Herzogovina.

This time, I fancy, it will require more than Ottoman duplicity to avoid immediate action. The Austrian programme must be adopted without delay, for the Czar has lost patience at last and means to proceed with energy. What the result will be remains to be seen, but I fancy that the Porte will make all the required concessions when there is no longer a loophole for escape. But even that will not go far, for in a not very remote future other difficulties will arise of a still more serious nature, for Servia and Montenegro are only awaiting the order of the three powers to throw off the Ottoman yoke. Excuses for beginning hostilities are easily found when wanted, and they will be wanted as soon as the three powers have agreed among themselves as to the future of Turkey. I should have stated above that one of the main reasons for urging the Austrian project of reform was that it would pacify Herzegovina at once, for as soon as it was adopted, with the guarantees of the three powers, the insurgents would lay down their arms. If they refused to do so the three powers would take it upon themselves to use force; and, on the other hand, if they submitted with good grace their surrender would be to the three powers, and their persons and property fully protected.

\*    \*    \*

**April 21, 1876**

## THE DANGERS IN EASTERN EUROPE

To comprehend the telegrams which reach us daily from London and Paris in regard to the war in Eastern Europe, our readers must bear in mind the great historical facts which lie behind them. Important events are doubtless near at hand which may change the whole current of history for that portion of Europe. It is plain that things cannot continue long as they are, and there is an anxious undertone of expectation through the business world as to what this Spring may bring forth in the settlement of the long-mooted "Eastern question." A recent dispatch has reported much excitement on the Paris Bourse at the rumor that seven thousand Montenegrins had joined the insurgents, and that Servia was mobilizing her Army. To appreciate the significance of such rumors, our readers must remember that historically Eastern Europe is like a plain covered with a drift deposit, from which here and there an old granite peak arises—an indication of the earliest strata.

In the Middle Ages a considerable Sclavonic and Christian Kingdom occupied the eastern provinces of Europe. The great Turkish invasions of the fourteenth and fifteenth centuries covered these districts, and would have flowed disastrously over all Europe but for the obstacles there offered. There remain now above the level of the detritus and refuse left by this great inundation only one or two of the old landmarks of the region. Montenegro, the little country of the Black Mountains, near the Adriatic, was never fairly conquered by the Turks, and has retained its independence. It formed a barrier in the Middle Ages to the Turkish flood, and still obstructs it. The head of this little principality is, no doubt, in near relations with the Russian Government, and throughout this rebellion the refugees of Bosnia and Herzegovina have taken refuge in its mountain fastnesses. Many a Montenegrin soldier has, no doubt, served among the insurgent Christians. It has probably required incessant exertions by the Prince to keep his subjects from marching in force to drive out their long-hated enemies and oppressors from the territory of their kinsmen.

Another "survival" of ancient times is the province of "Free Servia." This region had been overwhelmed and occupied by the Turks, but seventy years ago it was substantially freed and has only paid a nominal tribute to the Porte since. Under freedom it has made a continual progress, and its independence and advancing prosperity are an unceasing model to all the Sclavonic provinces of Turkey of what they could be and ought to be. Servia, moreover, possesses a remarkably bold and war-like population, and can turn out a considerable body of hardy troops. She will naturally be the leader of these provinces, if once they are made free. Her Government, poor as it is, is borrowing money freely to purchase arms and to mobilize the Army. Servia, Montenegro, and all these provinces, it should be remembered, are animated with the traditions and passions which have been transmitted by five centuries of bloody and bitter struggle with the Turks. The passions of to-day are no new feelings. They are the same fires which have been kindled generation after generation in the hearts of a simple and free-dom-loving people. Diplomacy cannot possibly quench them. The old fire bursts forth when Turkey is singularly weak. The Government seems at its last ebb in finance. The Sultan is using his forced loans for his own pleasures, and borrowing at thirty per cent. interest, while the Army are without pay and the Administration without income. No doubt the Porte can awake the old Mohammedan fanaticism. But that is a danger-ous implement. The Russian press already report massacres of Christians, and it would need but a few occurrences of that nature to kindle a fire in the Sclavonic race which would destroy every vestige of Turkish rule in Europe. All these Sclavonic provinces, though closely connected in sympathy and blood and creed with the Russian people, yet represent the South Sclavonians, and are therefore not in entire harmony with the Russian Government.

Two powers are now silently playing their game beneath the confusion which covers the field of war. Russia supplies assistance, sympathy, perhaps promises, and will, no doubt, check all outside interference, unless of the combined pow-ers. Austria is forced to consider the Sclavonians at home, as well as those in the provinces, and has sent a Sclavonian, Baron Rodich, to induce the insurgents to accept terms from the Porte, while she is threatening Servia with armed inter-vention if the peace is broken. To Austria, the Eastern ques-tion is an intensely vital one. She would gladly possess the outlet of the Danube, but she cannot afford war, or any great discontent among her Sclavonic population. In the meantime passions are fermenting which neither Austrian nor Russian power can confine.

\* \* \*

**June 24, 1876**

## THE EASTERN COMPLICATIONS

*Atrocities by Turkish Troops in Bulgaria—Old Men, Women, and Children Massacred and Villages Burned—The Servian Military Preparations—The Sultan Ill*

LONDON, June 23—The *Daily News* this morning pub-lishes a letter from its Constantinople correspondent, dated June 16, giving details of atrocities committed in Bulgaria during the insurrection and since by the Bashi-Bazouks (Turkish irregular troops.) The writer says all movable property has been plundered, houses and villages burned, and old men, women, and children indiscriminately slaugh-tered. It is estimated that the province which heretofore yielded to the Government an annual revenue of $4,000,000 will not pay one-quarter of that sum this year or for years to come. Various estimates place the number of lives sacri-ficed at from eighteen thousand to thirty thousand. The cor-respondent names thirty-seven villages known to have been destroyed. Among the refugees, the number of whom is very small, there is not a girl over ten years of age. In the village of Serustitza, in the District of Phillippopolis, 1,500 persons are known to have been killed. This village con-sisted of 400 houses, and was prosperous and peaceful. Every house has been burned, and all the inhabitants killed except a few women and children, who took refuge in Phil-lippopolis and some women who were carried off by the Bashi-Bazouks. These cruelties have made a great impres-sion at Constantinople. The English Ambassador has inter-vened with the Government to put an end to them.

In the House of Commons this afternoon Mr. Forster gave notice that he will ask Mr. Disraeli, on Monday, whether he can give any information regarding the truth of the statements in the *Daily News*' Constantinople letter of the cruelties of the Turks in Bulgaria.

A special dispatch from Vienna, published in the second edition of The Times to-day, says that according to intelli-gence received from Belgrade, an order for the mobilization of the first contingent of the Servian militia has been issued. Each brigade is to assemble in its station to-morrow. Next week an order will be issued for the mobilization of the sec-ond contingent. At the end of that week the Army is to take its strategical positions on the frontier. At the same time Prince Milan is to issue a manifesto to the people and pro-ceed to the Army. As an intention to attack Turkey is still dis-claimed, these measures, if carried into effect, may be meant as a demonstration and pressure to promote the diplomatic success of M. Ristic, the Servian Minister.

A Berlin dispatch to the *Morning Post* reports that Prince Milan of Servia is in serious difficulty. The influence of Prince Karageorgevich, a pretender to the throne, is being used to inflame the popular sentiment, which already is decidedly in favor of war with Turkey. Karageorgevich's popularity is reported to be increasing, and it is said the Servian Government apprehends disturbances among the people.

CONSTANTINOPLE, June 23—Several Circassians have been arrested on charges in connection with the recent assas-sinations. The Police have seized a quantity of arms and ammunition. The Sultan is not well.

PARIS, June 23—La France publishes a report that the garrison of Constantinople has revolted. The report is not confirmed from any other source.

\* \* \*

July 3, 1876

# THE OUTBREAK IN THE EAST

## SERVIA'S DECLARATION OF WAR

*Prince Milan's Proclamation—The Servian Representative at Constantinople Recalled—Firing on the Frontier*

The foreign dispatches in The Times of yesterday announced war as actually declared between Servia and Turkey. A dispatch from Vienna dated July 1 said: "Prince Milan, in his proclamation, says: 'Turkey has provoked war by not satisfying Bosnia, and by threatening Servia. We enter Bosnia in the cause of humanity and nationality, and to re-establish peace without offending Turkey's integrity.' " The proclamation commences by describing the insupportable condition in which Servia has been placed since the outbreak of the insurrection, and continues: "Servia has done nothing whatever to hinder the work of pacification, while on the other hand Turkey has surrounded Servia with a belt of iron. It is impossible, therefore, to remain longer within the bounds of moderation, the Porte is responsible for any eventual bloodshed. The Montenegrins will be on our side, and it will not be long before the Herzegovinians, Bosnians, Bulgarians, and Greeks co-operate with us." Prince Milan concludes his manifesto by exhorting the troops to respect the frontier of Austria, which, he says, has a claim on their gratitude because of the benevolent protection extended to their Herzegovinian brethren.

The news from Belgrade was to the effect that the Servian representative at Constantinople had been recalled, and that it was believed that the Servian troops would commence hostilities by crossing the frontier yesterday. A dispatch by way of Constantinople, from Widden, a strongly fortified town in Bulgaria, on the Danube, near the Servian frontier, reported that the Servians had fired several shots at the Turkish frontier guards. The dispatch also stated that Servian Commissioners, to inquire into the alleged violations of the frontier, left Widden suddenly. Several of last Saturday's evening journals in Vienna stated that Turkey "is about to issue a circular to the great powers, throwing the entire responsibility of war upon Servia, and declaring Prince Milan a rebel because he seceded from the union of vassals." A Berlin dispatch stated that "the Prince of Montenegro has solemnly engaged to remain neutral in the Servo-Turkey troubles."

\* \* \*

July 3, 1876

# "TIME AND MY RIGHT"

The coat of arms of the Princes of Servia is a white cross on a red field, with a drawn sword between two dates—1389–1815—and the legend "Time and my Right." A whole history is in this heraldic device. For nearly five centuries the Servians have upheld the cross on bloody fields against the Turks. Through the Middle Ages they were the border-guard of Europe. The date "1389" represents the year of the great battle when the free Christian Empire of Servia was broken by Amurath and Bajazet, and this brave people was trodden under foot by the Turks. The intervening centuries are long periods of oppression, servitude, and suffering, under a conqueror who never knew the meaning of the word mercy to a Christian. When we recall that in this long era the best youth of Servia were taken as children to be trained for Mohammedan slaves or janissaries, and that a Christian mother often beheld her boys carried away by violence to serve the unnatural vices of Viziers and Pashas and grow up as Mohammedan servants, and that in later years no property or harvest was safe from the rapacity of Turkish tax-gatherers and Governors—that in this long history of tyranny, religion was insulted and all rights trampled on—we may understand the deep and bitter passions which lie back of the present Servian outbreak. The date "1815" is the year of Servian independence, won by the valor of the people; and, though a nominal tribute has been paid to the Porte, Servia since that year has been a free and self-governing State. Her progress and freedom, the happiness and courage of the peasantry, the advance of public improvements, are a perpetual model to the subject Sclavonic provinces in their servitude and barbarism of what they would be, freed from the tyranny of the Turks.

"Time and my right" is the legend which expresses the ambition of the Servian people, as well as of the ruling house. More than four centuries of defeat and disaster have not quenched the passion to be revenged on the Moslem and to restore the "right" of the Servian Empire. Before 1389 the Servian monarchy extended from Belgrade to the Black Sea, from the Danube to the Adriatic, and even over Macedonia and Thessaly. Montenegro is still a cliff from that primitive formation, standing over the later drift of the Mohammedan invasion. Bosnia and Herzegovina are only fragments of that ancient Sclavonic State. The Servians have waited almost five centuries to avenge Kassowa, to advance the cross again over bloody fields, and to drive the crescent from Europe.

It might be thought that a little State like Servia, with only a million and a quarter of inhabitants, could hardly thus venture to throw down the glove to a great Empire like Turkey. But it should be remembered that the population of this State is peculiarly warlike, and animated by the most bitter traditional hatred against the Turks. The militia has been trained to arms and is remarkably numerous for so small a community—numbering, it is stated, some 90,000. The whole Turkish regular force in all European Turkey, is reported to be only 60,000. Then the territory of Servia and all the surrounding provinces has been fought over and over again in the incessant wars with the Ottomans. Every feature has been studied in a strategical view. So natural are the battle-grounds that history repeats some of the battles, generation after generation. The Servians and the insurgents know their ground. Then, just outside of Servia is Bulgaria, with a population of some six millions of kindred race, flaming in insurrection and burning with resentment at the recent cruelties of the Mohammedans. To the west are Bosnia and Herzegovina, the kinsmen of Servia, and holding their own against their former master. Little Montenegro is but another Servia and we doubt if any jealousies of the princely houses can keep her brave Army from the fray when Servia declares war.

In European Turkey are eight or nine millions of Sclavonians; in Austria, close by the scene of war, four millions more of the same race. Still beyond is the great Sclavonic Empire, with millions burning with ardor to aid their southern brethren in their unequal struggle with the ancient enemy of their faith and race. Despite the inequality, we should be inclined to predict the success of the weaker combatant, if it were not for one peculiarity of the Turkish race. The Turks, in their degeneracy, preserved one of the qualities of a once commanding race, the "staying" power. They do not know when they are beaten. And, if put on the last defensive, they may hold their lines of communication with Constantinople and protract the war for years. They have repudiated practically their debt, and can now fight on with all they can wring from an oppressed people. The new softa or devotee faction ought to have something of the ancient fanaticism, and therefore should fight to the end. The European powers will counterbalance one another, and the crescent and the cross fight their own battles on the historic fields of the Danube, as they have so often done before.

\* \* \*

July 18, 1876

## THE POPULATION OF TURKEY

*Official Statistics—More Non-Moslems Than Mussulmans*

The *Pall Mall Gazette* says: "While the Exhibition of 1873 was open a society was formed at Vienna of public men, journalists, merchants, and Orientalists for the collection and publication of information relating to the East. This society issues a monthly journal, and from its pages the *Journal Officiel,* of Paris, has taken the figures which we reproduce. At the Vienna Exhibition it was found that there was not a single map which accurately represented the political division of Turkey, and the information on other matters was little more satisfactory. The society endeavored to supply the defects thus brought to light. At the capitals of most of the vilayets there are published annually *salnamés,* or official almanacs, which contain, in addition to lists of the public authorities, statistical notices of the Provinces. From these notices the information respecting the population is drawn. The first vilayet, Bosnia, contained seven sandschaks, of which the Herzegovina was one. The vilayet of Monastir comprises the greater part of Albania. The vilayet of Janina consists of

ancient Thessaly and Epirus; that of Salonica corresponds to ancient Macedonia; that of Adrianople to ancient Thrace; and the vilayet of the Danube contains all the country between the Danube and the Balkan, and between the Black Sea and the eastern frontier of Servia. Constantinople forms a division apart, and contains 680,000 inhabitants. The District of Constantinople is the most thickly peopled part of the Empire. After it comes the vilayet of Adrianople, where the density of population is not more than 168 to the square mile. The sparseness of population, indeed, is so great that there are only two other countries in Europe more thinly populated. These are Greece and Russia. But in proportion to the area the population of Spain, and even that of Sweden, is larger than that of Turkey. A point of more interest than the density of population is its amount. We get no information regarding the number of women, but the male population of each Province is given according to religious denominations. It is as follows:

|  | Mussulmans | Non-Moslem |
|---|---|---|
| Vilayet of Bosnia | 309,522 | 306,707 |
| Vilayet of Monastir | 485,993 | 417,805 |
| Vilayet of Janina | 250,749 | 467,601 |
| Vilayet of Salonica | 124,828 | 124,157 |
| Vilayet of Adrianople | 235,587 | 401,148 |
| Vilayet of Danube | 455,767 | 715,938 |
| Total | 1,862,446 | 2,433,356 |

The total male population of Turkey, excluding the vassal States, as also the islands, but including the districts of Constantinople, is, according to the official almanacs, 4,976,000, or in round numbers, about 5,000,000. Assuming that the sexes are as nearly equal as in other countries, the population would thus somewhat exceed 10,000,000. Returning to the information given by the official almanacs, we find from the above figures that the non-Mussulman population bear to the Mussulmans the proportion of 57 to 43. In Bosnia it will be seen the Mohammedans are very slightly in a majority; in the vilayet of Monastir the majority is somewhat larger, and in that of Salonica there is almost an equality. But in the three remaining vilayets the Christians very largely outnumber the Mussulmans. In the European part of the district of Constantinople, again, the proportion of Christians to the Mussulmans is in the proportion of fifty-four to forty-six. It must not be forgotten that these statistics are official, and that the officials are naturally desirous to make the number of Mussulmans appear as large as possible; and in the hope of escaping taxation the Christians would try to make their own numbers appear small. It is likely, therefore, that in these statistics the Mussulmans are overestimated. But, even if we make that allowance, the Mussulmans seem to be much more numerous than is generally supposed.

\* \* \*

September 7, 1876

## THE BULGARIAN ATROCITIES

*Mr. Gladstone's Pamphlet—Relief for the Sufferers Called For—*
*A Meeting of Protest in Plymouth*

LONDON, Sept. 6—A pamphlet by Mr. Gladstone entitled "Bulgarian Horrors and the Question of the East" has been issued. He says: "It is urgent, in addition to the termination of the war, first, to put an end to the anarchical misrule, plundering and murdering which still desolate Bulgaria; second, to make effectual provision against its recurrence by excluding the Ottoman Government from administrative control, not only in Bosnia and Herzegovina, but above all in Bulgaria. Third, to redeem by these measures the honor of the British name, which in the deplorable events of the year has been more gravely compromised than I have known it in any former period." Mr. Gladstone says he is still desirous to see the territorial integrity of Turkey upheld, though that desire should not be treated as paramount to still higher objects of policy. As an old servant of the crown and State he entreats his countrymen to require and insist that the Government, which has been working in one direction, shall work in the other, and shall apply all its vigor to concur with the other States of Europe in obtaining the extinction of Turkish executive power in Bulgaria. Mr. Gladstone concludes with an appeal for an organized collection and distribution of relief to the Bulgarians.

At a meeting held at Plymouth last night to protest against the Bulgaria atrocities, a speaker said a communication had been sent to Lord Derby expressing regret at the absence of any official declaration that the apparent apathy of Mr. Elliot, the British Ambassador at Constantinople, was undergoing investigation, and if substantiated would be appropriately dealt with, to which Lord Derby replied as follows: "Your friends may be assured that no efforts will be spared by her Majesty's Government to ascertain the exact truth as regards the occurrences in Bulgaria, and it will be ready, in common with other powers, to take such action upon them as the justice of the case may require."

\*   \*   \*

September 17, 1876

## VICTOR HUGO ON THE ATROCITIES

The following letter, headed "For Servia," appears in the Paris *Rappel:*

It becomes necessary to call the attention of the European Governments to a fact so small it seems that the Governments appear not to perceive it. The fact is this, a people is being assassinated. Where! In Europe! Has this act witnesses? One witness, the whole world. Do the Governments see it? No. The nations have above them something which is below them—the Governments. At certain moments this anomaly presents itself—civilization is in the people's barbarism. Is it willful? No it is simply professional. What the human race knows Governments are ignorant of. This is because Governments see nothing through the shortsightedness peculiar to them, while the human race looks on with another eye, the conscience. We are about to astonish European Governments by teaching them one thing—viz., that crimes are crimes; that it is no more allowable for a Government than for an individual to be an assassin; that Europe is *solidair;* that all that happens in Europe is done by Europe; that if there exists a wild-beast Government it must be treated as a wild beast; that at the present moment, quite close by us, there under our eyes, people are massacring, burning, pillaging, exterminating, cutting the throats of fathers and mothers, selling the little girls and boys; that the children too small to be sold are being cut in two by the blow of a sabre; that families are burned in their houses; that one town—Batak, for example—has been reduced in a few hours from 9,000 inhabitants to 1,300; that the cemeteries are choked with more corpses than can be buried so that to the living who have sent them carnage the dead send back the pestilence, which is only fair. We teach the Governments of Europe this, that pregnant women are being ripped open to kill the children in their wombs; that in the public squares there are heaps of the remains of women with the trace of this treatment; that dogs gnaw in the streets the skulls of outraged girls; that all this is horrible; that a gesture of the Governments of Europe would be enough to prevent it, and that the savages who commit these crimes are terrifying, and that the civilized who let them commit them are appalling. The time has come to raise one's voice. The universal indignation is being aroused. There are hours when the human conscience speaks and orders Governments to listen. The Governments stammer a reply. They have already tried this stammer. They say it is exaggerated. Yes, it is exaggerated. It was not in a few hours that the town of Batak was exterminated; it was in a few days. It is said 200 villages were burned—there were only 99. What you call pestilence is only typhus. All the women have not been outraged; all the girls have not been sold; a few have escaped. Prisoners have been mutilated, but their heads have also been cut off, which lessens the thing. The infant said to have been thrown from one pike to the other was, in reality, only placed on the point of one bayonet. Where there is one you put two; you exaggerate the two, &c. And then why has this people revolted? Why do not a flock of men let themselves be owned like a herd of animals? Why, &c. This fashion of palliating increases the horror. To quibble with public indignation, nothing more miserable. The attenuations aggravate. It is subtlety pleading for barbarism. It is Byzantium excusing Stamboul. Let us call things by their name. To kill a man at the corner of a wood called a Forest of Bonds is a crime; to kill a people at the corner of that other wood called diplomacy is a crime also, a greater one. That is all the difference. Does crime diminish in proportion to its enormity? Alas! that is, indeed, an old law of history. Kill six men you are Troppmann, kill 600,000 you are Cæsar. To be monstrous is to be acceptable. Witness the St. Bartholomew blessed by

Rome, the Dragonnades glorified by Bossuet, the 2d of December saluted by Europe. But it is time that the old law is succeeded by the new law. However black the night, the horizon must end by getting light. Yes, the night is black, we are at the rising of ghosts. After the Syllabus behold the Koran. From one Bible to the other people fraternize. *Jungamus Dextras.* Behind the Holy See stands the Sublime Porte. We are given the choice of darkness, and, seeing that Rome offered us its middle ages, Turkey has thought proper to offer us his. Hence the things happening in Servia. Where will it stop? When will finish the martyrdom of this heroic little nation? It is time there issues from civilization a peremptory prohibition to go further. This prohibition to go farther in crime we the people intimate to the Government. "But," we are told, "you forget that there are questions!" To murder a man is a crime, to murder a people is a question! Each Government has its question. Russia has Constantinople, England has India, France has Prussia, Prussia has France. We reply, "Humanity also has its question," and that question is this: It is greater than India, England, and Russia. It is the infant in its mother's womb. Let us supersede the political question by the human question. The whole future is there. Let us say no. The future, whatever is done, will exist. Everything serves it, even crimes. What is happening in Servia proves the necessity of the United States of Europe. Let the distinct Governments be succeeded by the united peoples. Let us have done with the murderous empires. Let us muzzle the fanaticisms and despotisms. Let us break the swords which are the valets of superstitions and the dogmas which have the sabre in hand. No more wars, no more massacres, no more carnage, free thought, free trade, fraternity. Is peace, then, so difficult? The Republic in Europe, the Continental Federation, there is no other political reality than that. Reasonings prove it, and events also. On this reality, which is a necessity, all the philosophers are agreed; and now the executioners join their demonstration to the demonstration of the philosophers. After its fashion, and just because it is horrible, savagery testifies for civilization. What Europe requires is a European Nationality, one Government, one immense fraternal arbitration. Democracy at peace with itself, all the sister nations having for their city and capital Paris—that is Liberty, having Light as its capital; in one word, the United States of Europe. There is the goal, there is the port. It was only truth yesterday: to-day, thanks to the executioners of Servia, it is evidence. To the thinkers are added the assassins—the proof was given by the monsters. The future is a god drawn by tigers.

*VICTOR HUGO*
*AUG. 29, 1876*

\*   \*   \*

**October 27, 1876**

# THE EASTERN WAR

There is a capacity of fanaticism in the Mohammedans which is almost unknown to European races and religions. It was this fiery impulse, along with their remarkable ability in governing, which gave the Turks such conquest, and made them the terror of Europe for so many centuries. The old fires are now burned out; the race itself is degenerated, and is probably not capable of any great and sustained passion. Still, such impulses have a certain power from association and tradition. They may be kindled again temporarily. We should not be surprised at any moment to hear of an outburst of this ancient fanaticism among the ignorant classes of Constantinople, led by their theological leaders, the Softas, which should extend through the Empire.

Our readers must remember that the masses of the Turks know nothing of modern history or of the world outside the "Empire of the Faithful." All Christians and other races are simply Giaours and infidels. To them it is only needful to advance the Crescent, and the old career of Amurath or Bajazet could be repeated among the Sclavonic tribes on the Danube. The science and progress of the world are unknown to them. They look upon themselves as the natural masters of Asia and the provinces of Europe around the Black Sea and the Adriatic. To them the talk of peace with the infidel sounds weak and cowardly, and the yielding of provinces, especially after a victorious campaign against their old enemies, as the height of treachery and feebleness. This spirit will have to be considered in all efforts at settling the Eastern question, and we should not be surprised at its yet overthrowing all the wise schemes of diplomacy. It shows itself already in the assassination of officials; it no doubt threatens the lives of the new Sultan and his Viziers; and the foreign residents at Pera, who understand its savage nature, live in terror of it. When the plans of peace fairly unfold themselves, it will not be a surprising thing to hear of another insurrection at Constantinople, the Sultan deposed, and a general massacre of Christians attempted. The Mohammedan spirit when aroused is that of a tiger; it thirsts for blood. The massacres in Bulgaria are only a foretaste of what the Ottoman Moslems would present to the world if this fanaticism broke loose. Few people who have not resided in the East or studied Oriental history can estimate the truly savage and barbaric spirit of Mohammedanism and how utterly unsuited it is to modern conditions. Except among the half-savage tribes of Africa, and perhaps in its first preaching, this faith has been an almost unmingled curse to the world.

We have no doubt that in the negotiations which must soon take place over the new political arrangements of Eastern Europe, the tone and spirit of the Turks will most injure themselves and assist Russia. There will be some terrible outbreak, some new and combined series of brutal murders, some declaration of a "holy war" against the infidels, which will reveal to the diplomatists with what savages they are dealing, and convince them that, as a governing power, Turkey cannot remain in Europe. We have not, as our readers know, believed in the imminence of a general war; and have even doubted if there would be a war this Autumn between Turkey and Russia. Appearances point now either to an armistice or to an enforced peace during the Winter, owing to the difficulty of moving armies in those stormy and mountainous regions. Full time is thus given for negotiations. Russia may forward forces so as to compel a settlement of the points in dispute. And the position of Servia and Montenegro in determined hostility to the Porte will force the European powers to intervene. It is the interest of all Europe to prevent a war between Russia and Turkey, and to "localize" the present struggle. The threatening attitude of the Czar will only be another lever in the hands of the powers to force Turkey from her present position.

The issue of the negotiations must be the yielding of the Porte to the demands of united Europe. Still, there are various eventualities which may postpone this happy result. There may be the outburst of Mohammedan fanaticism of which we have spoken. There may be a movement of Russian ambition and excitement, which will go far beyond the limits of diplomacy, and open unknown fields of war and struggle. It is, of course, probable that the popular feeling in the Muscovite Empire may force the Government into a desperate and determined effort to drive the Ottomans from Europe and gain Constantinople. But we hear already of financial embarrassment in Russia. The country is not ready for a great war. The Czar is peaceful in his inclinations. It is uncertain what allies Turkey might have. The probability seems that the whole question may be settled by negotiation, and that the final settlement will be the formation of new Sclavonic States, paying a tribute to the Porte, but self-governing. This would come the nearest to satisfying all parties in Europe, and the Government of Turkey would have to submit.

\* \* \*

January 31, 1877

## THE BULGARIAN ATROCITIES

*A Large Meeting in Association Hall to Express Sympathy with the Christians in Turkey—How Christians Are Maltreated— Resolutions Adopted*

A public meeting was held last evening at Association Hall to express sympathy for the Christian sufferers by the Turkish atrocities in Bulgaria. Hon. William E. Dodge presided and introduced Rev. Dr. Anderson, who opened the meeting with prayer. At the conclusion of the prayer Dr. William H. Thompson delivered an interesting lecture describing the condition of the Ottoman Empire and the Christians who lived under its Government. The atrocities practiced in Bulgaria were due, he said, to causes which, so long as they continued to exist, would entail a constant repetition of similar occurrences. One of the most potent of these causes was the religious differences of the Christians and Mohammedans. Not only, he said, were there a multiplicity of races in Turkey, but there was among these a separation and isolation from each other, and an inherent hatred of each other that could not but attract the attention of the visitor. In every city one would find one part assigned to the use of the

True Believers, another part to the Christians, another to the Jews, until it was finally divided and subdivided among the different sects of inhabitants bitterly opposed to each other. Individuals were never referred to as more men and women, but were always alluded to as Jews, Christians, or followers of the various other creeds of religion. The effect of this was that religion, and religion alone, determined man's status in society. In fixing the status of the Christians, the law, he said, was especially strict, even going so far as to prescribe the kind of dress to be worn by them, the manner they should be saluted on the street, the manner that letters should be addressed to them, and placing restriction on all such petty matters, merely for the purpose of injuring the feelings of the Christian inhabitants. So rigidly were these cruel restrictions enforced, that a Christian never dared to venture into the streets without being attired in black, that color being prescribed by law, to indicate that at the judgment day the Christian would be doomed to wear the robes of darkness. The speaker, on one occasion, had even seen a lady spit upon and struck in the face by Mohammedans for venturing to appear in the street with a green veil over her face. Insults of this character might be cited without number, and were due to the fact that the Mohammedan teachers always instilled into the minds of their pupils the notion that they were bound to persecute Christians, and to regard with disfavor any indications of wealth in their Christian neighbors. The Mohammedan law further enjoined that no Christian should ever stand or walk at the right side of a Mohammedan, and that no Christian should ever build a house of two stories if the house occupied by his Mohammedan neighbor was only one story. In the courts, too, the same unjust and absurd restrictions were made. There no testimony given by a Christian could be for a moment considered if it was given against that of a Mohammedan. A Christian, therefore, could never obtain justice unless he could bribe a Mohammedan witness to swear to his version of the case. As this result was generally quite easily accomplished, however, the Christians were, on most occasions, enabled to right their wrongs in spite of the disadvantages under which they labored under the law.

In referring to previous massacres by the Turks, the speaker said that once, in Syria, a priest having been so unwise as to ride to church on horseback, the Mohammedans of the city in which be dwelt arose suddenly in a mass and murdered 1,800 Christians for no other cause than the slight and unintentional affront given by the priest. The still more cruel massacre at Damascus, where 8,000 Christians were butchered in cold blood, had not even a fancied affront like this for its origin, the Turks having committed the murders without any provocation whatever. The Speaker said that the reason why so little was ascertained by Americans in relation to this atrocity was, that all accounts were filtered through the British press, which, with the English Government, considered it policy at the time to sustain the Turkish Government. He did not believe that much would have been learned of the recent atrocities in Bulgaria had it not been that an American citizen had been on the spot, and had revealed the true extent and barbarity of the crimes committed by Turkish armies. The speaker next demonstrated that the slight consulate protection that had been accorded to Christians in Turkey during the past 30 years gave them little assurance of entire safety and immunity from violence and massacre. The Government, he said, had indeed promised to institute "reform," but how little joy could such a promise convey to the Christians, knowing, as they did, that such promises had been often made, and as often broken in the past, and that absolutely no other body of people on the globe knew so well "how not to do a thing" as the Turks. The relative social position of the Mohammedans and Christians was another cause of trouble. While the former were gradually retrograding and dying out, the latter were constantly advancing and absorbing the wealth of the land; a condition of affairs that only increased the animosity of the Mohammedans, and constantly stirred into action their murderous hatred of the Christians. The repetition of such cruelties as those practiced in Bulgaria could only be rendered impossible, the speaker said, in conclusion, by the subjugation of the Turks and their removal from Turkey into Asia, where they could be kept from doing further damage.

At the conclusion of the address Rev. Dr. Washburn offered for adoption the following resolutions:

*Resolved.* That while we have no direct connection with the religious and political questions involved in the Bulgarian atrocities, we share deeply in the feeling which has awakened so many in England and on the Continent, of sympathy with the sufferers from the inhuman wrongs perpetrated by Turkish armies and unpunished by the Turkish Government; and,

*Resolved.* That whatever may be the settlement of the strife between the Porte and its outraged provinces, our earnest hope is that the European powers will secure such liberties for the sufferers as to prevent forever the repetition of these crimes against the code of the whole Christian and civilized world.

After brief addresses by Drs. Washburn and Bellows, the resolutions were unanimously adopted, and the audience were dismissed with the benediction.

\* \* \*

**April 25, 1877**

## THE CZAR DECLARES WAR

### ADVANCE OF THE RUSSIAN FORCES

*Manifesto to the Army—Protection of Christians and the Enforcement of the Porte's Reform Pledges—Prince Gortschakoff's Circular Announcing the Declaration of War—The Russian Forces Move Across the Frontier Without Opposition*

The circular of the Czar to the Army, setting forth the origin of the controversy with Turkey and ordering the Army to cross the frontier, was promulgated from Kischeneff yesterday. Simultaneously, a note from Prince Gortschakoff, the Foreign Minister, was read by the Russian representatives abroad to the foreign powers to which they are accredited, announcing the fact that an order to advance into Turkey had been issued, and giving the reasons of the Russian Government for its action. Dispatches from the Russo-Roumanian frontier indicate that Russian troops have crossed into Roumania at various points, without protest from the Roumanian authorities, and were everywhere welcomed by the inhabitants.

### The Czar's Order to Advance

ST. PETERSBURG, April 24—The Czar's manifesto to the Russian Army was promulgated to-day. Following is the text:

Our faithful and beloved subjects know the strong interest we have constantly felt in the destinies of the oppressed Christian population in Turkey. Our desire to ameliorate and assure their lot has been shared by the white Russian nation, which now shows itself ready to bear fresh sacrifices to alleviate the position of the Christians in the Balkan Peninsula.

The blood and property of our faithful subjects have always been dear to us, and our whole reign attests our constant solicitude to preserve to Russia the benefit of peace. This solicitude never failed to actuate us during the deplorable events which occurred in Herzegovina, Bosnia, and Bulgaria. Our object before all was to effect amelioration in the position of the Christians in the East by means of pacific negotiations, and, in concert with the great European powers, our allies and friends, for two years we have made incessant efforts to induce the Porte to effect such reforms as would protect the Christians in Bosnia, Herzegovina, and Bulgaria from the arbitrary measures of local authorities. The accomplishment of these reforms was absolutely stipulated by anterior engagements contracted by the Porte toward the whole of Europe.

Our efforts, supported by diplomatic representations made in common with the other Governments, have not, however, attained their object. The Porte has remained unshaken in its formal refusal of any effective guarantee for the security of its Christian subjects, and has rejected the conclusions of the Constantinople Conference. Wishing to essay every possible means of conciliation in order to persuade the Porte, we proposed to the other Cabinets to draw up a special protocol comprising the most essential conditions of the Constanipole Conference, and to invite the Turkish Government to adhere to this international act, which states the extreme limits of our peaceful commands. But our expectation was not fulfilled. The Porte did not defer to this unanimous wish of Christian Europe, and did not adhere to the conclusions of the protocol.

Having exhausted pacific efforts, we are compelled by the naughty obstinacy of the Porte to proceed to more decisive acts, feeling that our equity and our own dignity enjoin it. By her refusal Turkey places us under the necessity of having recourse to arms.

Profoundly convinced of the justice of our cause, and numbly committing ourselves to the grace and help of the Most High, we make known to our faithful subjects that the moment, foreseen when we pronounced words to which all Russia responded with complete unanimity, has now arrived. We expressed the intention to act independently when we deemed it necessary, and when Russia's honor should demand it. In now invoking the blessing of God upon our valiant armies we give them the order to cross the Turkish frontier.

ALEXANDER.

"Given at Kischeneff this the 12th day of April, (old style,) in the year of grace, 1877, and in the twenty-third year of our reign." [New style April 24.]

A dispatch from Kischeneff, dated yesterday, and officially published to-day, announces that at the review of the troops by the Czar at Tiraspol yesterday his Majesty, addressing the officers, said: "I felt grief at sending you to the field of battle, and therefore delayed action as long as possible, hesitating to shed your blood. But, now that the honor of Russia is attacked, I am convinced you will all, to the last man, know how to vindicate it. May God be with you. I wish you complete success. Farewell until you return."

\* \* \*

April 26, 1877

## RESUME OF THE EASTERN QUESTION

*The Beginning of the Hostilities—A Revolt in a Turkish Province—The Great Powers in Consultation—How the Bulgarian Atrocities Were Made Public—Stubbornness of the Porte*

The circumstances attendant upon the present controversy between Russia and Turkey are of comparatively recent date. The beginning of the strife which has just ended in a hostile demonstration of armed force on the part of the Emperor of Russia dates back no longer than 1874. Just after the harvest of that year a dispute took place in Herzegovinia between some tithe farmers and some Christian peasants, and an outbreak at once followed. The strike continued until January of 1875, when the peasants, to escape from exactions and imprisonment, fled to Montenegro. Soon after the Governor of Herzegovina, at the request of the Prince of the country in which they were refugees, agreed to let them return home, and offered them an amnesty. But they were stopped on the frontiers by Turkish troops, and two of them were killed. In justification it was claimed that the troops acted without orders; but after the people had returned, they were exposed to outrage and insult. Their houses were burned, some of them were beaten, and one was put to death. The month of June saw the beginning of a desultory contest, brought on partly by political motives. The peasants, it is claimed, listened to the promptings of Servia, and were likewise pushed on by a man named Pezzia, who, 18 years before, had been a brigand in Bosnia and had lately escaped from confinement. It is more than likely, however, that the real causes of the disturbance had long existed in the constitution of Mohammedan society and the grinding exactions

of Ottoman rule. The rebellion followed, and foul outrages and atrocious murders are charged against both sides.

A couple of months later the more prominent European Cabinets tried to quell the revolt by sending their Consular agents to confer with the insurgents, but the attempt, after weeks of negotiation, signally failed. The insurgents did not dare to lay down their arms unless assured of protection against the Agas and the Zaptiehs. Soon afterward they formally stated their grievances and demands. After complaining of the heavy advance in taxation they said that Christians were made to undergo forced labor on the public roads, that their horses were used for the service of the Army, that the Agas were tyrannical, the courts corrupt, and property, life and honor insecure, and that some Christians had been killed simply for going to see the Emperor of Austria on the occasion of his journey through Dalmatia. The Christians added that they would rather die than suffer such slavery, and begged either for a territory to which they might all emigrate, so that Bosnia and Herzegovina might be formed into an autonomous State tributary to the Sultan; or that the European powers would protect them with troops until better laws were established. Meanwhile, the Porte had sent a Commissioner, in the person of Server Pasha, to the country, and he had made numerous promises. In September, 1875, he gave a pledge that there should be no more arbitrary or vexatious acts, that justice should be given to all who had been wronged, and those unjustly imprisoned should be set free. These promises were approved of by an Imperial Hatl. The insurgents, however, refused to listen to these offers, and the Porte declared that the tithe would be lowered to the old rates; that all arrears of taxes should be abandoned; that the several religious communities should be represented in the Administrative Councils, &c. On the 11th of October, Server Pasha gave a further list of the reforms intended by the Porte, and on Dec. 13 all the principles of these reforms were set forth in an imperial firman. The rebels received the firman with indifference, and the rebellion rapidly spread throughout the country. In October, 1875, several Christians who had come back to their homes from Dalmatia were massacred, and this deepened the bitterness of the strife. Many persons took refuge in Austria. Numerous skirmishes occurred, and the insurgents were afforded secret aid by both Servia and Montenegro. Prince Milan, in a speech delivered before the National Assembly of Servia, said it was impossible longer to remain indifferent to the fate of these suffering Christians, and material as well as verbal help was furnished them. At the same time the more warlike of the Montenegrins joined in the fight against their hereditary foe.

### The Andrassy Note

In the meantime Russia, Germany, and Austria had been taking counsel together as to the better way to remove the cause of dispute. To Count Andrassy was left the task of stating the common views of the three imperial courts. The result was the famous Andrassy note, which was made public late in December, 1875. The note, so-called, established a system of reforms in the shape of specific demands, in which it was held that complete religious liberty should be established, the system of farming the taxes abolished, the revenue derived in Bosnia and Herzegovina from indirect taxation should be applied to the annual purposes of the Ottoman Empire, while the income obtained from direct taxation should be spent on the Province itself, and that the State should sell portions of its waste lands to the Christian peasantry on easy terms. This note was adopted by the powers, though England gave her support none too readily, and then only because the Porte urged her to do so. The document was presented to the Porte Jan. 31, 1876, and all of its demands accepted save the one defining the purposes to which the indirect and direct taxes of the revolted Provinces should be applied. This reply was sent out in a circular note to the powers, and little more was ever heard of the famous Andrassy document. The rebels in the meantime continued their fighting, preferring the sword to the pledges of the Porte. An amnesty was offered them by Ali Pasha, Governor General of Herzegovina, on March 24, but they refused to accept it at the price of surrender. Six days later an armistice of 10 days was agreed upon, to enable an envoy of the Austrian Government to negotiate with the insurgents. He found that their demands had grown with the rebellion. They insisted that a third of the land should become the property of the Christian peasantry, the Turkish troops should be concentrated in the garrison towns, the houses and churches destroyed by Mohammedans should be rebuilt by the Porte, the peasantry should be given food and agricultural implements for at least a year, they should be freed from taxes for three years, be permitted to keep their guns until the Mussulmans were disarmed, and, finally, that the money for the compensation of the Christians should be paid to a European commission. All these demands were promptly set aside by Count Andrassy, though Prince Gortchakoff thought that at least they might have been discussed.

The rebellion spread from one district to another. Servia and Montenegro grew daily more and more threatening. On the 6th of May, 1876, an outburst of Mohammedan fanaticism was displayed in the murder of the French and German Consuls in Salonica. The excitement spread to Constantinople, and so great was the fear that the Mussulmans would rise and massacre the Christians that Sir Henry Eliot, the British Ambassador, telegraphed to Jaffa, where the British squadron was lying, urging Admiral Drummond to bring the fleet to Besika Bay, to which point it proceeded May 24. On the 30th of May Sultan Abdul Aziz was dethroned, and was succeeded on the same day by his nephew Murad. On the 4th of June Abdul Aziz put an end to his own life, and on the 31st of August Murad, in turn, was dethroned, on the ground of hopeless mental incapacity, and was succeeded by his brother, the present Sultan. Only a short time subsequent to the dethronement of Abdul Aziz, the Turkish Minister of War and the Minister of Foreign Affairs were assassinated by an officer in the Army.

**The Berlin Note**

Once more the three imperial powers made another and bolder attempt to restore peace. On the 11th of May Gortschakoff, Bismarck, and Andrassy framed the Berlin note, so called because it was prepared and signed in that city. In brief and peremptory terms, it stated that as the Sultan had given the powers a pledge to execute the reforms specified in the Andrassy note, he had at the same time given them a moral right to insist that he should keep his word. It was essential, said the note, to "establish certain guarantees of a nature to insure beyond doubt the loyal and full application of the measures agreed upon between the powers and the Porte." Further, the imperial powers demanded a suspension of arms for two months, and it was proposed that the Porte should restore the dwelling-houses and churches which had been destroyed, and if the armistice should fail to bring peace "the three imperial courts are of opinion that it would become necessary to supplement their diplomatic action by the sanction of an agreement, with a view to such efficacious measures as might appear to be demanded in the interests of general peace to check the evil and prevent its development." France and Italy agreed to support the note, but England jealously declined to accept a plan in the preparation of which it had not been consulted, and which it was claimed would not succeed.

Meanwhile a rebellion had broken out in Bulgaria, the first authentic details of which appeared in The New York Times. One of our special European correspondents happened fortunately to be in that immediate vicinity at the time, and his letters to this journal were copied not only at home but abroad. At first it was said the danger was trivial, but the results of the investigations of The Times' correspondent, (which were subsequently confirmed by Mr. Eugene Schuyler, of the United States Legation at Constantinople, and by other reputable gentlemen,) showed it to be one of the most horrid of modern times. The public feeling everywhere, but especially in England was aroused, and this feeling was in no wise calmed by a speech made by Disraeli, in which he compared the leaders of the agitation to the authors of the massacre. Public opinion soon convinced the British Government, and on Sept. 21 Lord Derby expressed the indignation of the country in a dispatch, in which he called on the Porte to punish the chief authors of the Bulgarian atrocities. They were never punished.

On the 30th of June Prince Milan formally proclaimed that Servia's arms would be joined to those of Herzegovina and Bosnia to secure the liberation of the Slavonic Christians from the yoke of the Porte. At the same time Montenegro went to war with Turkey. The progress of the war was graphically described at length by The Times' own correspondent. From June to September there were constant skirmishes with more or less success to either army. Servia was, however, not so successful as Montenegro. Early in September England proposed an armistice, which, however, the Porte declined to grant. Instead, it offered peace on conditions so disagreeable that they were declared inadmissible by all the powers. Another basis of discussion was proposed by Lord Derby on

Sept. 21, but the proposals were promptly rejected by Prince Milan, much to the annoyance of the British Government. War broke out again; reinforcements from Russia arrived in Servia, and Gen. Tchemayeff managed to resist the Turkish troops till Oct. 31, when Alexinatz fell, and Russia intervened with an ultimatum.

### Proposals of the Powers

Before this, however, Count Schouvaloff informed Lord Derby that, in the opinion of the Czar, force should be used to stop the war and put an end to Turkish misrule. It was proposed that Russian troops should occupy Bulgaria, that Austrian soldiers should occupy Bosnia, and that the united fleets of the powers should enter the Bosphorus. On October 3, the British Government gave notice that it would not support this plan, but that it would sustain an armistice of not less than a month. On the 5th, the British Ambassador at Constantinople was instructed to press the Porte to grant such an armistice, and in case of refusal he was to leave forthwith. It was also suggested by the British Minister that the granting of an armistice should be followed by a conference. The diplomatic calculations were, however, suddenly upset by an offer on the part of Turkey for an armistice of six months, and the promulgation of a general scheme of reform. England, France, and Austria accepted this six months' truce, but Russia held that Servia could not accept so long an armistice, because she could not keep her army on the war footing for such a length of time without putting too severe a strain on her resources, hence it was insisted that the armistice should be for only a month or six weeks. In this view Russia was supported by the Kingdom of Italy. The influence of Germany was sought by England, but Prince Bismarck replied that although an armistice of six months seemed acceptable to his Government, he could not put pressure on any other power to make secure its sanction. The war continued; Alexinatz was captured, and then came Russia's ultimatum.

In an interview at Livadia with the British Ambassador, the Emperor of Russia "pledged his sacred word of honor, in the most earnest and most solemn manner, that he had no intention of acquiring Constantinople, and that if necessity should oblige him to occupy a portion of Bulgaria, it would be provisionally, and until the peace and safety of the Christian population are secured." The Czar further earnestly urged the Ambassador to do his utmost to dispel the cloud of suspicion and distrust of Russia which had gathered in England. These assurances of his Majesty were accepted by the British Cabinet with expressions of great satisfaction, notwithstanding which, Mr. Disraeli, on the evening of Nov. 9, made a speech, in which he found fault with Russia for rejecting the offer of a six months' armistice, and ridiculed the ultimatum already referred to. That this speech was telegraphed to the Czar seems certain, from the fact that the very next day, in speaking to the nobles and Communal Council of Moscow, the Emperor of Russia said he hoped that a conference would bring peace, but that "should this not be achieved, and should I see that we cannot obtain such guarantees as are necessary

for carrying out what we have a right to demand of the Porte, I am firmly determined to act independently, and I am convinced that the whole of Russia will respond to my summons should I consider it necessary, and should the honor of Russia require it." The speedy mobilization of a large part of the Russian forces followed.

### The Constantinople Conference

Meanwhile Turkey was yielding nothing. On the 22d of December Midhat Pasha was made Grand Vizier, and the next day the Porte proclaimed the new Constitution. It had been prepared by the new Grand Vizier, and intimated that the Sultan had become a constitutional monarch; that the Minister should be responsible to a Parliament composed of a Senate and a Chamber of Deputies, and that these chambers should pass all the laws requisite for the pacification of the Empire. That same day was held the first regular sitting of the famous Constantinople conference, which was attended by the representatives of all the great powers. Much also was made by this conference, but its final results were absolutely nothing. All the propositions were rejected, the conference was closed, the representatives quit Constantinople, as did the other Ambassadors, and the diplomatic business was left in the hands of Charges d'Affaires.

Then Russia at once represented to the powers that inasmuch as the demands of the conference had been rejected, it devolved upon Europe to take more forcible proceedings. The Porte sent telegrams to its Ambassadors at the various courts, informing them that while rejecting the proposals it undertook to faithfully extend the new constitutional liberties to all its subjects. About the same time Turkey began to treat for peace direct with Servia, this stroke of diplomacy being calculated to force Russia to show her hand. To this, however, Russia offered no objection, and it soon became understood that Turkey's effort was simply a desire to appear magnanimous in the eyes of Europe. Finally, however, Prince Milan accepted the conditions of the Porte, and either on the 9th or 10th of February peace between Servia and Turkey was agreed upon at Belgrade.

The complications continued. Several Christians were appointed to be Governors of Turkish provinces. The Czar expressed a pacific disposition, and for this was charged with desiring to have an excuse for not going to war. Shiploads of war material arrived in Turkey from the United States, and both armies were ready for the strife. Russia, believing that she could support the strain of mobilization longer than Turkey, kept a large force on the frontier; reinforcements were moving to the front on both sides, and the outlook was a gloomy one. Midhat Pasha, the author of the new Constitution, was dismissed as Grand Vizier, and was succeeded by Edhem Pasha, the Turkish member of the late Conference, and who in its sittings most violently opposed all the proposals of the European powers. This change was most significant, showing as it did that the promises of reform on the part of the Porte were not likely to be carried out. In the meantime peace negotiations were begun between Turkey and Montenegro. Prince Nicholas' demands were refused by the Porte. Those negotiations have never been concluded.

Early in February the Russian Prime Minister sent out another note, but it contained no suggestion of anything which properly could be called a threat. Prince Gortschakoff said: "Before deciding on a course he may think it right to follow, his Majesty the Emperor wishes to know what course will be determined upon by the Cabinets with whom Russia has acted." The circular was simply a continuation of Gen. Ignatieff's policy during the conference. The powers declined to participate in any measures of coercion against the Porte, and also declined constituting Russia their mandatory. On Feb. 26 a rumor was circulated that Russia was about to cross the Pruth, but this was soon denied. That country repeated officially that she had no wish to go to war, and would be happy to desist from hostilities were some regard paid to her feelings and to the position in which she was placed. Stock-jobbing reports continued to be circulated. One was that Russia was demobilizing her Army; another, that Prince Gortschakoff had resigned. Both of these were untrue, and the complications were still unsolved. It was officially stated that a Turkish commission had acquitted some of the more responsible agents in the Bulgarian atrocities. The Secretary of the English Legation and Mr. Schuyler both considered their acquittal contrary to the evidence. Soon afterward the London *Times* printed the following in prominent types: "Dark tales of Mussulman violence and rapine continue to reach us from many provinces, especially from Bulgaria, Macedonia, and Albania, where public security, either on the highway or in isolated houses or small hamlets, seems altogether at an end. Those who are willing to give Turkey one or three years to mature reforms may see what elements are at work for future improvement, either in the Government on among the people. Not one Ziptiech has been dismissed the service; no tithe-gatherer has been stopped in his career of unlawful exaction, and no step is made toward the establishment of public security or the administration of fair and equal justice."

### The Policy of Russia

Gen. Ignatieff, the Russian Ambassador to Turkey, who, with the others, had left Constantinople at the close of the conference, went on a tour of Europe ostensibly for his health, but in reality to give verbal explanations of the future policy of Russia. On March 3 the powers agreed to acknowledge the meritorious zeal of Russia on behalf of the Christians in Turkey; her retreat from her threatening position was made comparatively easy, and it was suggested that the Porte be granted a term for the execution of the reforms. To this, Russia offered no objections, only stipulating that the Sultan should sign a protocol, accepted by the powers, containing collective guarantees to Europe for the execution of such reforms. On the same day, the Turkish Parliament, so-called, met, and was opened by the Sultan in person. His speech from the throne repeated his promises of reform, but contained no guarantees. On the 10th of March were announced

Count Schouvaloff's definite proposals for the solution of the pending questions. These were in the shape of a protocol. The Porte offered counter proposals by issuing a note specifying 11 measures of reform which it was already putting into operation; but there was considerable difference between it and the protocol, and Russia refused to accept it. On the 13th of March the English Cabinet met to consider the terms presented by Russia. Many councils followed, and after some amendments the protocol was accepted. England, desirous of dictating terms, demanded that Russia should demobilize at once, but this was decisively rejected by the other powers. Count Andrassy proposed that Russia and Turkey should demobilize simultaneously. England did nothing, promised nothing, and exhibited only distrust and condemnation of Russia. Then Russia yielded assent to Count Andrassy's plan. Prince Bismarck signed the protocol on condition that it was first accepted by Austria. Then England consented to sign it. On the 31st of March it was officially announced that the protocol was signed by all the powers. What followed is still fresh in the minds of our readers. The protocol was presented to the Porte, and that body refused to entertain any of its demands. Turkey insisted that the lamentable events in Bulgaria were due to foreign intrigue, and refused, absolutely, to disarm until Russia had first done so. This answer of the Porte was communicated to the great powers early in the present month.

\* \* \*

April 27, 1877

## THE THEATRE OF THE WAR

### BULGARIA AND THE BALKANS

*Characteristic of the People—A Thrifty and Affectionate Race— Confusion of Nationalities—The Craving After Liberty—The Religion of the Country—The Danube River and the Railroads— A Monument of Turkish Glory*

From Our Own Correspondent

BELGRADE, Monday, April 9, 1877—The peace patched up between this Principality and the Porte has put an end to Servia's mission in the Eastern question, at least for the moment, but no one believes that a final settlement will be made without a new appeal to the patriotism of the population to take up arms again, not in defense of Slavonic aspirations, but, as the word of order has been given for the cause of Christianity. At present all the interest here is centred in Bulgaria, which is to be the theatre of the coming war, and of which, although much has been said and written, so little is really known.

Officially the name is applied only to the district north of the Balkans; in reality the whole Peninsula, from the Danube to the southern slopes of the Pindus, belongs to the Bulgarians, whose Czars, during the Middle Ages, reigned over Servia and Albania, and more than once dictated terms to the sovereigns of the Byzantine Empire. The origin of this race, which, in point of numbers, is certainly the first in European Turkey, can only be traced back to the fifth century, when the appellation of Bulgaria was given by the Greek chroniclers to a tribe of the Ougri, who, following in the wake of Attila, devastated the western shores of the Euxine. It is supposed that they came from the neighborhood of the Volga, whence they derived their name, and that they were of kindred race to the Samoyedes, as their language bore a close analogy to that now spoken by those degraded inhabitants of Polar Russia.

### The Changes Wrought by Centuries

But during the centuries which have elapsed since their invasion the Bulgarians have become completely Slavonized, and not a trace can be found among them of their ferocious ancestors, whose name, modified into "Ogre," has remained a synonym for ugliness and brutality in the jargons and nursery tales of Christendom. As early as the fourteenth century they understood the Servian tongue. Soon afterward they abandoned their own. Their dialect is less correct, and is coarser than that of their neighbors, but as they have no national literature, and are without any political cohesion, they have never been able to give any distinctive character to their idioms, and are as thoroughly Slavs as are the Serbs and Russians. Their prodigious facility of imitation, and the natural amalgamation of the conquering with the conquered races, similar to what took place in England between Normans and Saxons after the battle of Hastings, will account for this transformation. In personal appearance the Bulgarians are short in stature, with large, coarse heads set upon broad, sturdy shoulders, not unlike the peasants of Lower Brittany. Frequently a decided Kalmuck type is met with, and in the vicinity at Phillippopolis the men shave their heads and cultivate a pigtail, after the manner of John Chinaman. By the Greeks and Wallachians they are turned into ridicule as dull and unintelligent, but the reproach is undeserved. Although without the vivacity of the Wallachian and the suppleness of the Hellene, the Bulgarian is by no means stupid. Centuries of persecution have crushed his spirit, and in the southern provinces, where he is oppressed by the Turk and cheated by the Christian, he has become a mere hewer of wood and drawer of water for his masters. On the northern plains, however, and in the mountain haunts, where he has suffered less, his face has none of that sad, careworn expression which is characteristic of the Thracian rayah, his bearing is more manly, his speech less servile, and his mode of life more in accordance with what is generally conceived to be the existence of a human being. In one of the high valleys of Rhodope, south of Phillippopolis, there is a tribe—the Pomaris—whose tall stature, dark eyes, and enthusiastic temperament would seem to point them out as descendants of the ancient Thracians, a theory which gains some weight from the fact that their popular chants still celebrate the exploits of Orpheus, the divine musician, the charmer of birds and men and deities.

Elsewhere the people have lost all remembrance of the past, and their village bard, unlike his Servian brother, never sings of aught save the sufferings of some oppressed serf in a petty domestic drama where the "modest Zaptieh," in his quality of policeman, always plays a leading part. In short, the Bulgarian is a quiet peasant, with none of the would-be warlike swagger of the Servians, honest after his lights, thrifty and laborious, a good husband and father, fond of his fireside, and devoted to plum brandy, of which he can absorb an inordinate quantity without any perceptible effect. Almost the totality of Turkey's agricultural exports are due to his labors, and even with the most primitive and imperfect instruments he has converted a vast portion of the plains of the Lower Danube into fields of wheat and corn rivaling in productiveness those of Hungary and Roumania. The only flour judged worthy of the Sultan's table comes from the farms of Eskri Zagra, and the single district of Kezanlik, at the foot of the Haemus, is a parterre of roses shadowed by groves of mulberry trees, which exports annually far more than 20,000,000 francs of attar of roses and cocoons to the other provinces of the Empire. Nor are the Bulgarians deficient in the industrial arts: every village has its specialty, and there are few of the native workmen who, in the manufacture of carpets, pottery, and metallic ornaments, have not given proofs of skill and taste which would compare favorably with the productions of civilized Europeans.

### Their Yoke Too Heavy to Be Borne

But this pacific people, so well broken in to toil and slavery, have begun to weary of their yoke. Of themselves, they would never have dreamed of open revolt, and their few partial insurrections, always quenched in blood, have been the work of the mountain Heydukes, or of agents sent among them from Russia or Servia. Still the craving after liberty is there, and, after her lethargy of nearly a thousand years, Bulgaria has awakened to the fact that her sons have rights to assert as well as duties to perform. The first step toward the reconquest of her independence was religious. At the time of the Turkish invasion many of the inhabitants became Mussulmans. Some years later a few embraced the Latin creed, but the great majority remained faithful to the creed of their ancestors. Naturally, the influence of the "orthodox" clergy over their flocks was unbounded; they were their guides and comforters during long ages of persecution; their churches were the only refuge of the oppressed peasant. But, within a few years, the Bulgarians have lost confidence in these ecclesiastics, who did not deign to even speak their language, and who pretended to submit them to the direction of a nation so dissimilar to their own in customs and tradition as are the Hellenes. They would repudiate any idea of a schism, but they demanded to be freed from the control of the Patriarch of Constantinople, and at last, in spite of Phanariot opposition, and of the ill-will of the Porte, always jealous of everything tending to the emancipation of its subjects, the separation between the Greek and Bulgarian Churches became complete. It would have taken place sooner, perhaps, but for the opposition of the women, who denounced all change in the celebration of the rite or in the costume of its ministers as an abominable heresy. Leveled, apparently, against the Greeks, this pacific revolution has a most important bearing against the Osmanli. From the Danube to the Wardar the Bulgarians acted in concert, and thus, perhaps unconsciously, formed a new element of resistance to Turkish oppression, by giving a definite cohesion to the populations of Slavonic origin. That the Osmanli appreciate the danger is evident, since the first of the "reforms" (?) promised by the new Constitution is to be the reunion of the Churches under the direction of the Constantinopolitan Patriarch—a boon for which this benighted people are, I fear, not particularly grateful. There are few Turks in Western Bulgaria, except in the large towns possessing some strategic importance. They are the preponderating element in the East, where, from the Danube to the Gulf of Bourgas, their "holy places," in great odor of sanctity, abound, whereas scarcely a Christian church can be met with in a day's ride. Here the population is intensely fanatical, and may be regarded as the representative type of the Turkish nation in the Balkans; elsewhere, these masters of the country are looked upon as foreigners and intruders.

### The Confusion of the Nationalities

Next in political importance to the Turks are the Greeks, but these are neither numerous nor influential in the north. South of the Hæmus, although in feeble proportion to other races, a colony of them can be found in every village, where their cleverness, to call it by a mild name, and indefatigable activity have given them the lead in trade and finance. They have large and prosperous communities in Phillippopolis and Basardjik, and in a valley of the Rhodope possess a city, Steinmacho, of 15,000 inhabitants, where neither Turk nor Bulgarian has ever been allowed to settle. The ruins of ancient edifices, the dialect of its inhabitants—containing about 200 words of Hellenic origin, unknown, however, to modern Romaic—and a few half effaced mural inscriptions have proved to the satisfaction of archæologists that Steinmacho was built 2,000 years ago by a colony from Eubœa. North of the Balkans the preponderating element is Wallachian. The superior intelligence and enterprise of this people have gradually driven out the original natives, and the whole right bank of the Danube from Tchernavoda to the sea has become so completely "Roumanized" that in the course of another generation it will have entirely changed its customs and its language.

This confusion of nationalities becomes even greater in the district of Dobrutscha, where a tribe of Nogäi Tartars, banished from the Crimea for their sympathy with the allies during the war, lead a semi-nomadic existence under an hereditary Khan, subject to the authority of the Sultan. Toward the end of 1864 about 400,000 Circassians sought an asylum among their Turkish coreligionists, and were installed in Western Bulgaria, with the vain hope of thus breaking the ethnical cohesion between the Bulgarians and the Serbs. The peasants were obliged to cede their lands and their stock, and to build villages for the new-comers. But these, true to the predatory habits of their race, declined to work, and, planting their swords in the ground, simply took possession of such spots as pleased them, informing the inhabitants that they were the masters of the soil and must be supported. Famine, epidemics, and the climate—so different from that of their native mountains—soon made frightful ravages among them, and, at the end of the first year nearly one-fourth of their number had succumbed. Perhaps from want, more probably from ancient custom, the traffic in human flesh soon commenced, and such were the profits accruing to the local Turkish functionaries, that it is more than likely that this wretched people was designedly starved. The harems of Constantinople were glutted with Circassian girls and boys, sold at one-eighth of their ordinary price, until the traders were obliged to send over their surplus stock to be disposed of in the slave markets of Egypt and Syria. Within the last three or four years, however, these "gentle savages" have become acclimatized, and are in the same hygienic condition as the natives, with whom they are represented as living in much concord and harmony. How far the panegyrics of their admirers are justified may be judged from their eccentric conduct during the last Summer's atrocities in Bulgaria.

Still another colony, and, in this instance, a prosperous one, inhabits the extreme northeastern corner of the Dobrutscha, where some Ruthenian Tartars, of the sect known as "Old Believers," settled at the close of the last century. Driven from Russia by the persecutions of Catherine II, these people were kindly received by the more tolerant Sultan, and their descendants, although preserving their national costume, their language, and their religion, have always manifested their gratitude to their adopted country by a stanch defense of its frontiers during its wars with Russia. As a matter of course, they are an especial abomination in the eyes of their "orthodox" neighbors beyond the Pruth. A Polish colony, a few German villages along the southern branch of the Danube, a group of some thousands of Arabs, several wandering tribes of Ziganes or gypsies, and finally the individual representatives of every people of Europe and Asia who, from a spirit of speculation or in search of occupation, have flocked to the Port of Sulina, complete this species of ethnological congress established in the Dobrutscha. But the difference is very marked between the nationalities living isolated in the interior and this cosmopolitan population which swarms in the avenues of the commercial centres, where the characteristics of distinctive races are gradually blending into the common type of the Levantine.

Sooner or later, however, the mixture of Greeks and Franks, English and Armenians, Maltese and Russians, Wallachs and Bulgarians, which forms so remarkable a feature of the Delta, must be reproduced in the interior of the Peninsula, for in no other country are the main international lines of communication more distinctly traced by nature.

### Improved Facilities of Travel

For centuries the Danube has been the highway of nations in their commerce with the East, but the great river is too slow a channel for modern enterprise. The first attempt at abridgment was a railway through the Dobrutscha to Kustundji—the Pomis of Ovid, where the poet mourned in exile the splendors of the imperial city. This was followed by another from Rustchuk to Varna, where trains run regularly twice a week, in connection with the mail boats to Constantinople. Two more are in contemplation, one through the depression in the Balkans south of Shumla to Adrianople, the other by Tirnova, from the Lower Danube to the shores of Thrace. The great line destined to make Constantinople the direct port of exchange between Europe and Asia has as yet only been partially completed, but if a more healthy political and administrative régime be ever established in the country, it will connect with a railway from Belgrade to Rodosto, along the line of the military road followed by the Roman legions in their march from Pannonia to Byzantium. Thanks to their admirable geographical position upon this main artery of traffic, all the great stations of antiquity have before them a most brilliant future. Sofia, the Sardica of Constantine, once contemplated by him as the seat of his Eastern capital; beautiful Phillippopolis, with its "triple mountain," commanding the valley of the Maritza; Nisch, placed like a sentinel to guard the entrance to the Morava basin, will become prosperous commercial centres as soon as they are in definite and regular intercourse with the Western world. How far sympathy with the Moslem will increase is another question, when travelers gaze upon the hideous pyramid of Kele-Kilissi, built of the skulls of a Christian garrison, who, during the war of Servian independence, blew up their redoubt rather than fall alive into the hands of their enemies. A few years ago a Pasha, more enlightened than his predecessors, urged the demolition of this abominable relic, but Mussulman fanaticism prevailed over the dictates of humanity, and it still stands at the gates of Nisch a monument of Turkey's "glory," and of the real sentiments of Islam toward the Giaour.

A people as imitative and as malleable as the Bulgarians must necessarily soon modify its customs and its morals under the influence of Western civilization, and no one who has not visited the country can form a just idea of its need of a social regeneration. The Albanian element has been rendered savage by war, the Bulgarian has been debased by ages of servitude more terrible than were the worst days of Southern slavery in America. Their women, particularly in the large towns, presented a spectacle of the most shameful corruption, and by their immorality and their gross disregard of every law of common decency, merited the just contempt of their Mohammedan sisters. But a change for the better has even already begun. The influence of foreign missionaries has made itself felt, and, if not very successful in the way of proselytism, it has at least taught the people that without education there can be no real progress, Schools and colleges have been founded, books are published, young men are sent to European universities, and in many districts every family makes up a purse in order that its children may be rescued from the slough of ignorance. The young Bulgarians take the lead in the mixed lyceums of Constantinople, and only ask for the opportunity of turning to practical account the results of their studies. This is a sign of wonderful vitality, and if "traditional policy" does not, in its egotism, create new obstacles, this race, so long suppressed from history as a nation, will once again assume its place upon the stage of the world. In the Peninsula of the Balkans, in Austro-Hungary, from the shores of the Baltic to the Egean, there are peoples, or fragments of peoples, of common origin and creed, who demand an equality of rights and a political autonomy, and these are seeking to group themselves together according to their natural affinities; preparing themselves, as it were, by moral solidarity for the establishment of free confederations.

\*   \*   \*

June 17, 1877

## ROUMANIAN INDEPENDENCE

### A LONG-NURTURED HOPE REALIZED

*The Legislative Decision upon the Government's Policy—Official Consecration of Its Action—Hearty Unanimity in the Legislative Palace—Roumanina Ladies at Mrs. Rosetti's— Qualities of Their Beauty*

From our Special Correspondent

BUCHAREST, Wednesday, May 23, 1877—Monday, the 21st of May, according to the Greek calendar the 8th, is destined to be a great anniversary in the annals of Roumania, for then it was that she crossed the Rubicon of official neutrality and made the decisive plunge which, for weal or woe, pledges her to leave participation in the war. The milk-and-water resolution passed a week ago had satisfied, in reality, nobody, but had dissatisfied the dominant party as well as the Russians, for while establishing the existence of a state of war, it had not been sufficiently explicit to secure for the Roumanians the full rights of belligerents. Everybody felt that some more definite action must be taken, something categorical be laid down, for it was rather hard that while the Turks were raiding on Roumanian villages and bombarding Roumanian fortresses, and generally behaving in a hostile manner, that Roumamian batteries should be, by the law of nations, forbidden to sink or stop the neutral vessels which, under the Austrian flag, were daily revictualing the Moslem strongholds of Widdin, in the very teeth of the guns of Kalafat. So it was decided to insist upon a positive explanation of the Governmental policy, and all Bucharest flocked to the legislative palace to witness the solemnity. The grounds around the building were thronged with vehicles of all sorts, pedestrians toiled up the steep hill which leads to its doors, anxious faces peered from the windows of the neighboring houses, all waiting for the verdict which was to decide whether Roumania as a nation was "to be or not to be." The entrance to the house was guarded by a picket of infantry, who sternly turned back the majority of the inquisitive patriots, who were forced either to saunter about the courtyard or to flatten their noses against the windowpanes of the lobby, in hopes of gleaning some idea of the progress of affairs from the faces of those inside. Two soldiers had crossed the butts of their muskets before the doorway, but there was an usher just within, and to him I passed my card and said "Presidents." This was an "open sesame," and I was immediately admitted into the antechamber, filled with groups of politicians awaiting the arrival of Mr. Rosetti—the Speaker, as we would call him—who drove up punctually at 1 o'clock, when, without more ado, everybody went into the hall and business commenced. It is a low-ceilinged room, with tiers of seats, in the form of a horse-shoe, rising one above the other; in front is an elevated astrade for the President, with a tribune for orators in front, and a Ministerial bench on the left. The house was crowded wherever there was even standing room. All the beauty and fashion of Bucharest occupied the ladies' box, and in the *loge diplomatique* people were packed like herrings, but strange to say, when one considers the importance of the subject to be considered, all the diplomatists, *Anglice,* the Consuls-General, were conspicuous by their absence.

### Calm Debate and Almost Unanimous Vote

Rosetti took his seat, called the house to order, and then proceeded to inform it that the Honerable Mr. Felva had the floor to present to its appreciation an interpellation upon the policy of the Government. You might have heard a pin drop. The Deputy rose and read his motion, crossing over immediately afterward to the tribune to develop it. He spoke in a quiet, unimpassioned manner, without rant, and evidently with no attempt to produce oratorical effect, but every word seemed to tell, and from the bursts of applause by which he was interrupted from time to time, it was evident that his cause won before it had been pleaded. The speech lasted for about half an hour, and finished in a tempest of cheers, whereupon Mr. Cogliniceano, the Minister for Foreign Affairs, rose to reply. He, too, was as quiet, and, perhaps, more impressive, than his predecessor, and was applauded even more frequently. His discourse was a simple statement of facts, justifying the Ministerial conduct, re-enumerating Turkish outrages and Roumanian forbearance, insisting upon the great desire of the Cabinet to preserve neutrality, and ending with the cordial acceptance of Mr. Felva's resolution. Then Rosetti rose again, and informed the Assembly that in such circumstances as these the country should know the names of those who wished her well, and that the votes would be taken nominally instead of by ballot, as in ordinary cases. One after another the Deputies left their seats and walked up to the Clerk of the House, and the answer of each was *penteu,* ("for,") until their list had been exhausted, and then the Assembly was told that, of the 81 Deputies present, two had abstained from voting, but that the remaining 79 had declared that—

"Satisfied with the explanations of the Government relative to the vote of the 29th April, (12th May, according to our style,) this legislative body decides that the state of war existing between Turkey and Roumania, the rupture of all friendly relations between us and the Porte, and the absolute independence of Roumania, have received their official consecration, and, relying upon the justice of the guaranteeing powers, passes to the order of the day."

The great work had thus been accomplished for which Roumanian patriots have toiled for 30 years, their long-cherished dream had been realized and yet there was no display of either excitement or exultation. In America a similar situation would have called for unlimited whisky, in France or Italy these men would have danced a carmagnole, and shed tears, and a band would have played the Marseillaise or Garibaldi's Hymn, or some other popular melody; but here these benighted beings took it all as quietly as possible, and after passing another vote by which it was resolved that both chambers should go in a body to congratulate Prince Charles on the eleventh anniversary of his accession to the throne, separated to their respective avocations to plan and execute those measures which are necessary to the maintenance of the principles which they had just so courageously affirmed.

### The People in the Cathedral

There was little pomp about the morrow's ceremonies. The town was hung with flags of the blue, yellow, and red Roumanian tricolor, and a good many people of all classes went to the Cathedral for the *Te Deum,* but there was nothing at all imposing. The church itself has no claims to architectural merit. It is a square white building of no particular style, losing even a part of its Byzantine *cachet* by the substitution of polygonal cupolas for the ordinary onion-shaped bulbs common to nearly all the "orthodox" places of worship. The walls and ceiling of the nave are covered with frescoes, generally portraits of saints or scenes from sacred history, but rather at variance with the usual rules of perspective, although, in many instances, as delicately finished and colored as a portrait on ivory. The outer porch was ornamented in the same style, but the hands of sacrilegious little boys, and the mania possessed by some travelers of transmitting their names to posterity by scratching them in places where there is every reason that they should not be found, has greatly defaced the frescoes. One year choice subject—placed above the reach of vandalism—struck me as something quite out of the common: Our Saviour, seated upon a bank of clouds, is receiving new-comers to Heaven; the mode of access is by a pair of ladders, one resting upon the doorstep of a church, the other suspended over the mouth of a fiery dragon. Up the rounds of the ladder are clambering a number of gentlemen in long pink robes, in attitudes intended to represent the extreme difficulty of the ascent, which is still more complicated by the assaults of seven very long-legged little devils, who now and then are successful in throwing a sinner into the dragon's throat, but who are, as a rule, repulsed by seven angels in blue dresses, armed with tridents. The work is more than coarsely done, but, as it is a new method of treating the subject I have noticed it for the benefit of any of my readers who may be artists. The ceremony unattended by either the Prince or Princess, was short and not impressive, the Metropolitan, assisted by four other ecclesiastics in magnificent vestments, each holding a book in one hand and three candles tied together with a red ribbon in the other, were grouped around a small portable altar placed in the centre of the nave. Candles were lighted, some prayers and litanies intoned, with responses from the choir, the latter sung with admirable precision, the whole affair terminating in a chorus of thanksgiving which, despite the nasal twang of the chanters, was most musical. The "orthodox" Church allows no instrumental accompaniment, a circumstance which, while it possibly takes away some of the charm, certainly adds to the merits of the execution.

All the military men and strangers of distinction called and inscribed their names in the registers of the Palace between 12 and 1 o'clock; at 3 the Consuls-General were received, and at 4 the two houses of the General Assembly, some member of which will probably give vent to the legislative sentiments about the part to be taken in the war, and the possible change of title of the sovereign, who, it is said, will be proclaimed King—an innovation which is, however, discouraged by many sincere well-wishers of the Prince as being contrary to the spirit of Roumaniau traditions and institutions.

### A Party at Mrs. Rosetti's

On Sunday evening last, a party was given by Mrs. Rosetti, at which all the ladies were to appear in national costume; of course, some broke down before the time came, and preferred the latest fashions from Paris. I must add that these were the least pretty ones, for this national dress, although exceedingly effective in itself, is a terrible ordeal to a plain woman. A high-necked chemisette, with long, loose sleeves, profusely embroidered in leaves and flowers and spangles, gathered in at the waist by a broad scarlet sash; a white skirt reaching nearly to the ankles and braided at the bottom; over this two long aprons, a mass of silk and worsted parti-colored tapestry woven in with gold threads; to the belt hangs a coarse linen handkerchief stitched in patterns of blue, red, and green worsted; below the skirt peep out the miniature feet, shod with crimson stockings and high-heeled shoes. Young girls wear flowers in their hair, which is plaited into a long thick club, not unlike what one saw in Paris a year or two ago, tied with a broad ribbon to match the colors of their dress. Married women put on a veil of thin gauze, which covers the back of the head, and is draped around the neck and shoulders like a cloud, with sequins or gilt flowers in front, and glass beads and ornaments of every imaginable hue and shape disposed everywhere. The effect is very pretty, and three of the ladies, the daughter and two nieces of Mr. Rosetti, would have created a furor, even in Paris, but then these three are beauties such as one rarely meets. That they were immensely admired, especially by the foreigners, is incontestable, but they fell short of the ideal, for though they wore the peasant's dress, they did not succeed in looking like peasants. The stamp of refinement and distinction was there, and, disguise themselves as they might, they could never have been mistaken for ought save *grandes dames.* As yet I

have had no opportunity of seeing much of the ultra-fashionable society of Bucharest, for this is not the gay season, and the impending war has put a stop to all balls and parties; but so far as my experience goes, I must admit that in no other country have I met with so remarkable a combination of brilliant accomplishments and solid education. Several of the ladies sing like artists, all speak at least two foreign languages, and all are able to converse about European politics with a knowledge of their subject which would put to the blush nine out of ten of the best informed women of Europe or America. Naturally they are all intensely patriotic, and most anxious that their husbands and brothers and lovers should do something to prove that the Roumains deserve a kindlier criticism than has been inflicted upon them by some of the French and English papers. A good deal of the old Roman heroism still lies dormant—at least among the fair sex—and one little beauty told me, with her eyes flashing as she spoke, that she would rather hear that all her male relatives had fallen in battle than have them live to be known as cowards. I do not think that many Roumains will behave badly, and I am very sure that they will have an uncommonly disagreeable time at home if they do. Mrs. Rosetti herself is an English woman, said to be nearly 60 years of age, and looking about 42; her life, like that of her husband, has been a long romance. From the moment of their marriage she has been his faithful and devoted helpmate in his sufferings, his sacrifices, and his triumphs. His companion in imprisonment and exile, his friend and comforter in those days when he was hunted like an outlaw and his head set at a price, toiling barefooted through mud and snow by his side when he was expelled ignominiously from the country whose liberty he was striving to obtain, she now, after the long struggle of more than 30 years, sees the lover of her youth the virtual ruler of his nation's destinies. I had intended to give in this letter a sketch of this remarkable man, whose biography, with that of his friend and colleague, Bratiano, now the Minister of the Interior and President of the Cabinet, epitomizes the history of Roumania, and will do more to enlighten the public regarding this much and most unjustly maligned people than all the diplomatic reports and letters produced by the most able graduates of that school whose maxim is that "language was given to man to disguise his thoughts." But it is too important to be treated summarily, and I must reserve till later a subject which must be replete with interest to every true friend of progress.

### Receiving the Grand Duke's Son

The Grand Duke was expected yesterday. He was to come over to pass a few hours e*n famille,* and people were delighted with the promised visit, as they saw in it a proof that the relations between Russia and Roumania were becoming more intimate and more cordial, and that their "plunge" had not been made in vain. But the Grand Duke could not come himself, and there was not a little disappointment, until it was found out that he had sent over his son, which, after all, was the same thing, as the whole affair was strictly in the social line. Some 50 Circassians accompanied the young Prince. Thus, too, was a significant fact, for these were privates as well as officers now. In short, the situation has become clearly accentuated, and the hopes of those who have maintained the possibility of a localization of the war have been dashed to the ground. In the evening, all the streets were brilliantly illuminated; in every window was a row of candles, or a display of Chinese lanterns; all the shopfronts were open, with their goods so disposed as to show a tasteful combination of the national tri-colors; the Opera house was opened for an "extraordinary representation," at which all the beauty and fashion was present in gorgeous array, and where even those great magnates the Consuls-General were to be seen in uniform; and a procession of 4,000 persons bearing torches, and preceded by the splendid band of the Palace Guard, marched through the streets and visited the residences of the Ministers and of the chiefs of the Liberal Party to the cry, taken up by the whole population of the capital, of "Traesca Reabelni!" "Traesca Indepintas!" "Vive la Guerra, Vive l'Independance."

\* \* \*

**June 26, 1877**

## THE GREEK UPRISING

A new coalition Ministry has been formed in Athens, which is to unite all parties in a vigorous opposition to Turkey. The popular feeling is generally aroused in favor of Greece taking part in the war. A loan is about being placed, and, no doubt, an army of at least 20,000 men will soon be put on a war-footing. The Government is reported as somewhat timid, but Parliament and the nation desire to use this fresh opportunity to pay back old scores against the Ottomans, and to increase the domain and glory of the little Attic Kingdom. The French journals remind the new Cabinet at Athens that they may be only repeating the experiment of Servia, and may ruin their country without vitally injuring their enemy. Turkey, they warn the Greek leaders, is immensely stronger by sea, and they incur the danger of the bombardment of their ports, and the destruction of Greek commerce. Their ally, they allege, is in reality their greatest rival in all the region they hope to acquire, and, even if victory should follow their campaign against the Turks, the Slavonians in Macedonia, Thessaly, and Albania, would have the support of the Russians as against the Greeks. They rather counsel them to use the ancient "Greek arts" of peace, and gradually get possession of the Government of those countries (as they have of their trade) from the hands of the stupid Slavs and the barbarian Mussulmans.

Such prudent advice, however, is seldom listened to in time of revolution—nor is it by such advice that kingdoms are founded. Had the Sardinian Cabinet Ministers thus met the overtures of their French allies in the war with Austria, the Kingdom of Italy would never have been built up. It was not such a policy which enabled Bismarck to convert Prussia into the leading power of Europe, in the struggle with Austria. There are supreme moments in the destinies of people, when they must strike and risk all. To all outward observers, such a crisis seems at hand for the petty Hellenic Kingdom. Their ancient enemy is in the very struggle for life. The Greek populations on the coast of the continent, so long oppressed by the Turks, are ripe for insurrection. The Greeks can land with little difficulty a small army of men, either in Albania, on one coast, or in Thessaly or Macedonia, on the other, and thus either assist the Montenegrins and Bosnians, and increase the revolt there, or come up on the rear of the Ottoman connections behind the Balkans. With a small force they could produce a considerable effect on the fortunes of the war.

Moreover, it is clear that a new formation of the map of Europe is in progress. The Turks will in all probability be forced, as one result, to abandon their rule over a portion of their European provinces. It is not at all improbable that a new State, or new confederations or States, will be formed on the Danube or the Adriatic. The idea has often been broached that Greece should have the hegemony of any new combination of provinces between the Archipelago and the Adriatic. It is her old historic ground. She would but regain what Greek arms once held. Hers is the only civilized government in that region of the world. It would not be safe to Europe to intrust Russia with such distant conquests. Were Austria to acquire these provinces, the jealousy of Germany or England might be aroused. They could not properly be left to self-government, as the peasantry are not fit for it. It might well be that a new Grecian Kingdom, composed of the old Chersonnesus and modern Greece, might suit the European powers debating over the dismemberment of Turkey.

There is, too, a more brilliant prize among the possible rewards of daring and sacrifice. The ancient Greek metropolis, the pride of the Second Empire, the city beyond all others in the world placed and built to be the emporium of the world, filled with monuments of Greek art and crowded with a Greek population; a city which, according to both Russian and English ideas, ought to become a "free city" of Europe and Asia, but which the great powers will never consent to become the property of any one leading nation. If Constantinople be indeed captured by the Muscovites, and the Czar be ready—as he professes himself—to yield it up again, after exacting an indemnity and securities for reform, what more natural thing than for the Russians, with the consent of the great powers, to make it a Grecian free city, under the Hellenic Kingdom? This may be indeed a somewhat shadowy prize for a nation to cast in blood and treasure to struggle for. But nations have before now won more distant rewards, and with less present chances of success. Those who do not risk cannot win. The only possibility of gain to the Grecian Kingdom from the war would be by bold daring and ready sacrifices before the issue is decided. With all these glorious chances before her, we may well believe that Greece will soon throw her sword into the scales. But sober historic truth compels us to say that neither her bravery in the field nor her wisdom in peace will aid much in the final solution of the "Eastern question."

\*   \*   \*

September 1, 1877

## ALBANIAN SHARP-SHOOTERS

The last few days' fighting for the possession of the Schipka Pass has brought prominently forward, for the first time since the commencement of the war, the prowess of those far-famed Albanian riflemen, celebrated in several of his finest passages by their admirer Lord Byron, who went so far as to compliment them by having his portrait painted in Albanian costume. The deadly accuracy of aim which proved fatal to so many Russian officers in the battle of the 25th appears to be hereditary with this singular race, who have enjoyed for some generations the renown of the best marksmen in Turkey. Their dispatch to the front at this juncture, by hundreds at a time, shows how thoroughly their skill in mountain warfare is appreciated by the Turkish Generals. And well it may be. Whatever figure an Albanian "crack shot" might make at Creedmoor, his recorded feats on his own ground would appear incredible were they less fully authenticated. At the siege of Acre by Bonaparte, in 1798, a French officer, leaning his elbow on the parapet of a work considerably over a hundred yards from the nearest point of the city wall, was cautioned to remove it, lest it should offer a mark to the Albanians. "Bah!" laughed the officer, "do you think any one could hit a man's ellbow at that distance?" The words were barely uttered when a bullet completely shattered the limb, necessitating instant amputation.

It must be owned, however, that these redoubtable auxiliaries are "irregulars" in the highest sense of the word and deplorably lax in their notions of allegiance. Their "loyalty" was well exemplified in the formidable outbreak of 1821, headed by the famous Ali Tebellin, Pasha of Yanina, whose betrayal and cruel death have been immortalized by Dumas; and even now it may safely be pronounced that, provided they can enjoy their favorite pastime of fighting, they care very little whether they fight for the Sultan or against him. In fact, the Albanian mountaineer, like his rival the Montenegrin, is a born guerrilla, of the same type as the Scottish Borderer of the fifteenth century or the Circassian of the seventeenth. While regaling you with milk and half raw meat, he will tell off upon his brown, sinewy fingers the number of men whom he has slain as complacently as a sportsman vaunting a good "bag." When you meet him on his native uplands, whether tilling his ground or driving his herds to pasture, he is never without the long gun on his shoulder, the trenchant yataghan at his side, the *khanjar* (dagger) and silver-mounted pistols in his girdle. He makes, undoubtedly, a magnificent tableau on the steep hillside, with the morning sunshine lighting up his dark, handsome, brigand-like face and picturesquely barbaric costume, blending the garb of the Greek and the Scottish Highlander; but it must be admitted

that he is not exactly the kind of companion whom a nervous traveler would wish to encounter in a lonely place. There is a perceptible "swagger" in his bearing, characteristic of one who counts himself a match for any man living, and is always glad of a chance of proving it; and it is difficult to avoid reflecting how easily he might test the vaunted keenness of the blade which he is flourishing within an inch of one's face, by drawing it dexterously across one's throat. The presence of such men in the Turkish Army may well appear singular to those who remember that Turkey's deadliest enemy in the Middle Ages was an Albanian Prince, the famous George Castriot, (better known by his nickname of Iskander Bek or Scanderbeg,) whose devastating inroads gave rise to the proverb. "The Turk's riches are Scanderbeg's revenues." But the Albanian will doubtless be faithful if allowed sufficient latitude in the matter of plunder; and so long as his choice lies between Turk and Russian the former may safely count upon his allegiance.

\*   \*   \*

July 14, 1878

## PEACE SIGNED AT BERLIN

### CLOSING OF THE CONGRESS OF POWERS

*Banquet of Celebration at the White Hall Palace—A British Version of the Agreement—Lord Salisbury Declines to Hold a Supplementary Conference*

BERLIN, July 13—The congress held its last sitting to-day. All the plenipotentiaries and other members were present in full dress, as at the opening of the congress. The proceedings commenced at 2:30 and ended at 4 o'clock. The treaty was signed by all the plenipotentiaries alphabetically. The Secretaries attended previously at 1 o'clock in the afternoon to affix the plenipotentiary seals to each copy. After the signature Count Andrassy warmly eulogized Prince Bismarck's presidency. Prince Bismarck thanked the plenipotentiaries for their indulgence. The proceedings terminated with a grand court dinner this evening at the White Hall Palace. The Crown Prince Frederick William congratulated the illustrious statesmen upon the realization of his hopes that the blessing of peace crowned their efforts. He declared that Germany's cooperation can be counted on for all that tends to secure and preserve this great benefit. He drank the health of the plenipotentiaries of the sovereigns of the Governments who this memorable day signed the treaty of Berlin. The only absentees from the banquet were Lord Beaconsfield and Prince Gortschakoff.

The German semi-official press publish long pæans, rejoicing and triumphing in the signature of the treaty of peace.

LONDON, July 13—The treaty of peace contains 58 articles. The Times' version, which is declared at Berlin to be unauthentic, contains 57 articles, and makes no mention of two important questions, namely, the Dardanelles and Armenia. It is probably an early copy, obtained before final revision. Its first 12 articles relate to Bulgaria, which is constituted an autonomatic tributary principality, under the suzerainty of the Sultan, with a Christian Government and national Militia. These articles further regulate the election of the Prince, by notables at Tirnova, arrange a provisional Government previous to his election, and lay the bases of the Government after his election. Articles 13 to 21 inclusively, relate to the new province called Eastern Roumelia, south of the Balkans, which is placed under the direct military and political authority of the Sultan, with, however, a Christian Governor, and in the conditions of autonomous administration. The Governor is to be appointed by the Porte, with the assent of the powers, for five years.

Article 22 fixes the Russian occupation at nine months from the signature of the treaty of Berlin. Article 23 provides for the Austrian occupation and administration of Bosnia and Herzegovina. Articles 24 to 30, inclusively, relate to Montenegro; 31 to 39 to Servia; 40 to 54 to Roumania and the Danube; 55 and 56 to Greece and Crete; and 57 to religious equality in the Turkish dominions.

At yesterday's sitting of the congress Prince Bismarck moved that a supplementary conference be held next Autumn, either at Constantinople or Berlin, but Lord Salisbury declared his inability to accede to any proposal interfering with the immediate submission of the papers to the English Parliament, and the motion was thrown out.

\*　\*　\*

July 28, 1878

## AUSTRIA'S DIFFICULT POSITION

---

### Her Troops to Enter Bosnia Today—Armed Resistance Expected—A Conciliatory Proclamation Issued by the Austrian Government

---

LONDON, July 27—The Austrians will enter Bosnia on Sunday, though no convention has been concluded. It is expected that they will encounter armed resistance.

A dispatch to Reuter's Telegram Company says: "Austria has abandoned the idea of a convention with Turkey about Bosnia and Herzegovina, and will move the troops into Bosnia, and afterward send a note or declaration to the Porte, setting forth Austria's views and intentions."

BELGRADE, July 27—Austrian subjects residing in Servia, belonging to the Austrian Reserves, have been peremptorily summoned to join their battalions. This creates uneasiness because it indicates far larger mobilization than was originally intended for the occupation of Bosnia.

VIENNA, July 27—In view of the impending occupation of Bosnia and Herzegovina, the Austrian Government has prepared a proclamation, which has been translated into the native language and distributed. It says: "The Austrian troops come as friends to stop evils which have for many years disturbed Bosnia, Herzegovina, and the Austrian borders. The Emperor Francis Joseph could no longer look on and see the sufferings of these provinces, where force and turbulence reigned, while the Government of the country was incapable of restoring order, and want and misery were knocking at the frontiers of his own States. The Emperor, therefore, directed the eye of Europe to your position, and the council of nations decided that Austria should give you back your long-missed peace and prosperity. The Sultan commits you to the protection of his mighty friend the Emperor. The Austrian troops bring you peace, not war; they will protect all and oppress none. Established customs and institutions will be respected. The revenues will be applied solely to the wants of the country. Arrears of taxes will not be collected."

\*　\*　\*

February 11, 1880

## THE BULGARIAN PARLIAMENT

In recent numbers of the Augsburg *Allgemeine Zeitung,* some interesting details are given on the present position of Bulgaria. Of the session of the Bulgarian Parliament for November and December it says: "The Assembly at Sopha contains very few intelligent heads: even from among the mass of half-educated there are scarcely 12 persons who are the least capable of expressing an opinion on a bill, or, indeed, on any serious subject which requires some intelligence and ripe judgment. All the rest were boors, who in the sittings partly gave utterance to wretched nonsense (as the Voivode Debo Zeko) partly slept, and outside the Assembly saved 14 out of the 15 francs daily allowance for onions and bread, in order to add to their household wealth by the purchase of oxen, &e. Besides these are 15 Turkish Deputies from the east of the country, who do not understand Bulgarian, and who sit like statues, unconcerned with what is going on. These Turks also make a fine thing out of their allowance. One of these [Osman Effendl, of Tesluk,] attends his colleagues as servant, and earns daily a few piastres in addition to his 15 francs. Every morning and evening this bright specimen of a Parliamentarian could be seen with large water cans and bundles of wood, in white turban and dirty burnoose, wandering merrily through the streets of the Bulgarian capital—a representative of the people!" There was nothing like a regular debate. Each spoke as often as he wished, sometimes 30 times in a sitting. Unpopular speakers were simply howled down, and the wishes of the Ministers and other disliked individuals, summarily annulled. By a bare majority of voices were certain of the chief Opposition shouters, who had not attained the regulation 30 years of age, declared to be of that age, and thus the chamber was in a position, unconcerned before the whole of Europe, to decree the greatest nonsense by a simple majority of voices. After the foolish and thoroughly fruitless session had cost the impoverished country 120,000 francs, the Assembly was dissolved, and "many of the country Deputies were compelled to wander home on foot, since they had lost all their allowance at cards, and they had all too surely counted on the continuation of the golden time till Christmas."

* * *

May 17, 1880

## BETROTHED TO A PRINCE

### THE UNION OF GREAT RICHES AND HIGH RANK

*The Daughter of a Very Wealthy Roman to Wed Alexander of Bulgaria—Politics in Royal Marriage—Weddings in Paris*

PARIS, April 30—For the first time the notables of Bulgaria have gratified their sovereign with the title of Highness, in their address of congratulation on his return to the society of his "faithful subjects." The notables of Bulgaria are really glad to see their Prince once more, as when he left their midst the chances were decidedly against his coming back again. The Bulgarians had not been at all nice with young Alexander Von Battenberg, whose life they rendered quite miserable during the few months of his residence at Tirnova, and he told them very plainly that either they must behave themselves or seek a new ruler, and he was entirely in earnest. But, as in the case of wedded pairs on the eve of a separation, both parties reflected on the consequences, and agreed to postpone a definite rupture until some more auspicious moment. The natives are not a very intelligent race, but among their teachers and preachers are to be found a few individuals possessing a little common sense, and these were shrewd enough to take in that, if Alexander should be forced to abdicate, some worse thing might befall them. Either the Turks would come back or a Russian protectorate would be established, either hypothesis implying that Nihilo-Socialist ranting and agitation was not to be tolerated. The unexpected Liberal victory in England was a powerful lever in the hands of the Russian party, and the so-called Liberals of Bulgaria prudently fell back to bide their time for another antimonarchical demonstration, to be gotten up simply in the interests of Austria. So much for the Bulgarian politicians, who threw up the sponge as soon as a warning was sent them from St. Petersburg. For the Bulgarian Prince to be tempted back again was not nearly so easy. He is a gentleman, accustomed to the society of gentlemen, and to live among these boors is naturally very repugnant to his feelings. But imperial commands brook no disobedience; it suits Russia's policy that Bulgaria shall be an independent State, just now; Russia is not quite ready for a regular annexation of the Balkan Peninsula, and, until she be ready it is expedient that some one in her interest shall sit on the throne of Turkey's nominally vassal State, so that when the fullness of time arrives a convenient pretext for another interference can be found. This, I think, is the gist of Russian policy, which will become more accentuated now that nothing in the way of a Disraeli surprise is to be apprehended, and it is quite astonishing how rapidly Prince Gortschakoff became convalescent after it was ascertained that Mr. Glad-

stone would soon be again all potent in Downing street. However, all these remarks are merely incidental; Prince Alexander was loth to go back; the Czar, who knows the sweet people with whom this unfortunate youth is condemned to cohabit, was inexorable in sending him back, but, being of a benevolent turn of mind, has, so far as possible, gilded the bitter pill with a rich marriage. It is quite settled at last, and a daughter of Prince Youssoupoff is the destined victim. A curious personage is the old Prince, celebrated throughout all Russia for his colossal fortune and his eccentricities. His family is of Tartar origin, and became naturalized in Muscovy, under the sign of Joann Grossey, whom history has surnamed Ivan the Terrible. No one can tell how wealthy is the last scion of this race, whose ancestral palace stands on the banks of the Moïka in the great Morskaja, but his extravagances are as familiar as household words to the population of St. Petersburg. He began his career by marrying his cousin, and as unions of this kind are forbidden by the orthodox Church, the ceremony was performed in Austria, and never again did he set foot within the Russian Empire so long as Nicholas was Czar. He besought forgiveness and a dispensation; his friends reminded his Majesty that there were precedents; that other sovereigns had been less stern toward the nobles of the land; it was all in vain; the Emperor was inflexible. "Princes," he said, "are no more, in my estimation, than serfs; what is prohibited to a serf cannot be permitted to a Prince." Only when Alexander II, succeeded to the throne was Youssoupoff authorized to reside where he pleased, and even then so conditionally that, as Russian law makes all foreign marriages between Russian subjects irregular he has settled several millions of rubles on each of his two daughters, in order that they may be provided for should his will be disputed. Perhaps the greatest stock gambler in Europe, Prince Youssoupoff employs some 20 clerks on his correspondence with his broker in Paris, where he has been almost uniformly successful, and with the German bankers who manage his operations at Berlin and Vienna, on whose Bourses he lost countless sums at the moment of the famous Berliner Krach. At present he is on amicable terms with the Court, save, it may be, with the Czarewitch, in whose honor he alone in all St. Petersburg refused to illuminate his palace some years ago. He is an Imperial Chamberlain, also, and consequently has a right to the title of Excellence, which he prefers to any other, as he is not "a most serene," but only "a most illustrious," Prince, thus taking rank after the Loéven and Dolgorouki and Galitzine, whom, from the pinnacle of his golden grandeur, he affects to look down upon as parvenus—mere mushroom aristocrats. Still, he is very benevolent, a doting father, and averse to everything in the shape of politics. The contemplated marriage of his daughter will be a great gain for him socially, although, it seems, that the express command of his sovereign was needed to obtain his consent to what he calls "his child's premature interment." The young lady, they say, was less unwilling; the title which she will bear gives her precedence over all but the members of the imperial family, and, besides this consideration, Prince Alexander is anything but an undesirable match. He is young, good-looking, a nephew of the Czarina, and, even should he be sent into exile some day by the turbulent inhabitants of the new State, has very nice family connections. His history, too, is romantic, and he became a relative of the Romanoffs by a mere accident. To make amends for the massacre of M. Von Haucke, during the Polish revolution of 1831, the Emperor Nicholas sent for the two daughters of his unlucky employe, gave them the title of Countess, and attached them, as ladies of honor, to the person of the then Crown Princess, the present Empress, Marie Alexandrowna. The younger girl soon married Baron de Stackelberg, an officer of the Imperial Guard. The elder, Julie, was seduced by Prince Alexandre de Hesse-Darmstadt, a brother of the hereditary Grand Duchess. She became a mother, and escaped in disguise across the Austrian frontier, where she was joined and immediately married by her lover, for which the Czar, in his anger, deprived him of all his titles and decorations and banished him from Russia forever. After the accession of his brother-in-law he was received with his wife at Court, but their marriage was only morganatic, and not until several years afterward, as the earnest request of Alexander II., did the Emperor of Austria concede to her the title of Princess of Battenberg, transmissible to her descendants. Alexandre de Battenberg, reigning Prince of Bulgaria, is the first issue of the marriage of Prince Alexandre de Hesse-Darmstadt with Countess Julie de Haucke.

We are not yet informed of the probable date of the Prince's marriage, but, on account of the rapidly failing health of his aunt, the Czarina, it is not likely to be long postponed, especially, to use the words of one of the trans-Balkan orators, as it will be "the vital cement"—whatever that may be—"of the Russo-Bulgarian edifice." There is no doubt that its motive is political, it avoids everything like the appearance of an infraction of those clauses of the Berlin treaty by which any member of any reigning dynasty is excluded from the sovereignty of Bulgaria, but at the same time, it consolidates influence by the introduction of new elements of intrigue. Somebody has written in one of those sapient political articles for which the French press is entitled to the palm of glory that royal marriages in the nineteenth century no longer have the slightest bearing upon international relations. This may be so, up to a certain point, but I think there are cases where the matrimonial connections of sovereigns have a vast deal to do with the question of peace or war, and few who have watched the situation with attention will deny that Russia and Germany would long since have drawn the sword if their respective rulers were not nephew and uncle. I believe that there is a reciprocal influence between politics and matrimony in every sphere of foreign social life, and that from the Prince to the peasant political antipathies and sympathies are considerations which are weighed more carefully than either financial suitableness or mutual inclination. Mlle. Diane De Gallifet is about to espouse Baron de Sellière; her mother, a celebrated beauty in the days of the Empress Eugenie, has affinities by birth and alliance with the noble

Faubourg; so has the future bridegroom's sister, who is the Princess de Sagan, but the Marquis has passed over arms and baggage to the Republic, which, being the established Government of his country, he serves faithfully as commander of the Ninth Army Corps. The Princess and the Marchioness would have none but the extra cream of fashion at the ceremony; the General makes a sine qua non the extension of invitations to his Republican friends. It will be a serious spectacle should all the guests accept; and, as among the number there are many professed atheists who consider it a crying shame to enter the precincts of a church, people wonder how they will manage to conciliate the call of friendship with the stern dictates of principle.

A son of the composer Gounod was married on Monday. It might have been thought that, as the parties most nearly concerned belonged to the world of art, politics would have been left out altogether, and yet in looking through the list of literary and musical celebrities who were present, we are struck by names which indicate that the attendance at the Trinité is infected with that terrible epidemic, uncompromising Clericalism. At the same hour, at Notre Dame de Bonne Nouvelle, Dr. Vigouroux led to the hymeneal altar a daughter of the chief editor of the Patrie, where none except Bonapartists dyed in the wool assembled to add their congratulations to the benediction sent from Rome by his Holiness Pope Leo XIII. However, the crowning glory belongs, in all justice, to M. J. B. Durand (Eure) whose postscript to the wedding cards issued by him for the marriage one of his servants is a chef d'œuvre: "M. J. B. Durand (Eure) desiring to testify his gratitude to his maid-of-all-work, Citizeness Elise Picaut, in commemoration of his well-beloved wife, whom she nursed with tenderness and solicitude, will be happy if you will be present at the nuptial ceremony—strictly civil—of this young woman, in order to show to her and to the community at large that we Republicans are able to appreciate devotion and fidelity."

I might ask what Republicanism has to do with the appreciation of these two qualities which are equally prized by "vile reactionaries," but I prefer not to bias the opinions of my readers by any comments. Not many decent people in Europe are quite satisfied with a "strictly civil" marriage. The fact that M. Jules Ferry would not consent to any religious service has always been held up as a reproach to him, and even those who least put into practice the prescriptions of their creed consider the blessing of some minister of God on their union a very desirable, if not an absolutely indispensable, brevet of respectability. There is no solemnity in the performances before the Officier de l'Etat Civil, who not unfrequently is some vulgar cad quite out of keeping with the position, and who, nearly always, gallops through his task with indecent haste, as though to get rid of a business which is repugnant to his feelings. There is nothing impressive about it, and, precisely because Sardou's "Daniel Rochat" turned it into ridicule, the Radicals uncorked the vials of their wrath. "Only what is true is offensive," says the French proverb. The admirers of "strictly civil" weddings have been forced to admit that their institution was open to the sneers of their adversaries, and so M. Herold has profited by the first opportunity to read a lesson on decorum and dignity to his subordinates, of which most of them stand strongly in need. They must dress better, he tells them, their deportment must "be more solemn," and, above all, "they must not allow anybody who so pleases to pronounce an epithalamium." Citizen Clovis Hugnes and Dame Hubertine Auclerc were the immediate causes of this Prefectoral letter. Clovis is a Provençal poet, whose fruitful muse obtained the honors of a notice from the master himself on her first symptoms of fecundity; Hubertine is a French rival of Victoria Woodhull, and, although not a rhymer, is a fellow-laborer of Clovis in the great work of social regeneration. Her particular hobby is woman's rights; she believes that her sex has been put upon, and, as she considers herself to be the equal of any man, she demands her inscription on the list of voters in the Tenth Ward, where she resides, failing to obtain which privilege she proposes never more to pay taxes. Citizen Gambou sacrificed his cow in 1870 from a similar appreciation of civic rights and duties, and won name and fame thereby, as we see his patronymic in white letters on a blue ground at the corners of the street once known as the Rue de Luxembourg. Awaiting like immortality, Hubertine—whom we style Dame, because we do not know if she is married, and, therefore, entitled to a Madame, and whom we dare not call Mademoiselle, because she may have a responsible, though silent, partner—Dame Auclerc, and her collaborator, Clovis, air their sentiments on every possible occasion, declaiming fiercely against the injustice of the Civil Code, by which the man is considered to be the head of the family. Generally, their orations pass unnoticed by the authorities, but in this particular instance they were uttered at the Mayor's office of the Tenth Arrondissement, and the Prefect of the Seine was indignant that "such unseemly exhibitions should have been tolerated in the mansion of the law, which, by the introduction of the polemics of clubs, will be transformed into a theatre of trouble and agitation." M. Herold is quite right in principle, but as the dignity of civil marriages is set up in contradiction to the dignity of religious marriages, he would have done well for his cause to imitate the custom observed in churches, where no one except the officiating clergyman makes remarks, instead of permitting the Officier de l'Etat Civil to choose a spokesman among the spectators. However, everything, in France is done for effect; nobody can keep quiet; nobody seems to understand that if speech is silver silence is gold. Even Prince Napoleon—the Plon Plon of the ancients—has a bad attack of the prevailing malady. He made a fool of himself with a circular about a fortnight ago. Now, I hear, he is on the eve of another manifesto. He tried to curry favor with the cads by his claim, in the name of the Bonapartes, to the paternity of the decrees of the 29th of March; nothing but censure and ridicule was expressed for his approval of the expulsion of the Jesuits; at present he proposes to rehabilitate himself by qualifying as iniquitous M. Paul Bert's bill which makes one year's military service obligatory upon all members of the priesthood who have not yet shouldered a musket. It was so easy for the Bonapartist pretender to have held his tongue; his party was only nominal before he was seized with this *cacoethes scribendi;* two or three more such professions of faith from its official head and it will cease to exist, even upon paper.

\* \* \*

**June 1, 1880**

## ALBANIA AND THE POWERS

### HOW THE INSURGENTS DEMANDS ARE TO BE TREATED

*They Want to Set Up an Autonomous Province—Turkish Ministers Aiding Their Designs—Signs of Italian Influence—French Home Affairs*

PARIS, May 10—A fortnight ago, as soon as it was a certainty that Lord Beaconsfield had been definitely shelved, Europe was bidden to be of good cheer and assured that the political horizon was unclouded, and that the dream of a general disarmament of nations approached its realization. To-day, even the most incorrigible optimist admits that things look mixed, if not squally. Perfectly true is it that with the discomfiture of the Tories all fears of England's participation in the dual alliance are allayed, but another danger has cropped up which no one seemed to anticipate. Mr. Gladstone's well-known opinions in Eastern matters, his letter to Count Karolyi, in which, under cover of a courteous apology, more or less sincere, for language used by him when not in office, there is a very distinct warning to Austria against interference with the liberties of those provinces of Turkey which have already become emancipated, or with the aspirations of those other provinces still groaning under the yoke of Islam; and finally, Lord Granville's circular to the powers has stirred into action those elements which have been seething and fermenting in silence for nearly two years. The Albanian insurrection is the "burning question" of the day, and Continental statesmen are sorely puzzled to guess what may eventually grow out of it. The French press says very little, partly because of its limited acquaintance with the causes and theatre of the movement—in plain English, the majority of French writers do not well know where Albania is located—still more, because the situation at home is extremely critical. But the Russian and Austrian newspapers, from which last source well-nigh all the news comes that is published in London, are less reticent, and both at Vienna and at St. Petersburg do not hesitate to express apprehensions of the gravity of what should be called a revolution, not merely an insurrection. The *Golos* affirms that the very earliest intelligence received in Russia came from the Austrian capital, where the first alarming impressions have been modified, in so much that the Albanians are thought not to have proclaimed the absolute independence of their country, but only its autonomy. This the *Golos* esteems to be a question of very secondary importance to Europe, or rather concludes that it may become a cause of additional complication. Its independence cannot become an accomplished fact without the consent of all the powers which signed the Berlin treaty; on the contrary, its automony is absolutely in conformity with those clauses of this treaty which stipulated the introduction of reforms in all parts of the Ottoman Empire. The Porte would even be disposed to consent to the constitution of an autonomous State which would remain a tributary of Turkey, provided the Albanians will bind themselves to resist the advance of the Austrian troops upon Mitrovitza, and to aid in the restitution of Bosnia and Herzegovina. Europe is only interested in the Albanian question so far as the intentions of the insurgents to conform to the stipulations of Berlin are concerned. Will they or will they not agree to cede a part of their territory to Montenegro? Until this point be settled, until the delimitation of the Græco-Turkish frontiers be definitely traced, the solution of the Albanian difficulty is impracticable.

The *Gazette de St. Petersbourg* of the 14th of May is more affirmative, considering that the Albanian question has already assumed the proportions of a European question, concerning which, it is inclined to think, the British Cabinet has possibly taken the initiative, in the sense of a revision or modification of that disastrous document. Since Lord Beaconsfield's defeat, Prince von Bismarck no longer feels himself strong enough to protect the ambitious projects of his Austro-Hungarian neighbor, and it may be that the moment is at hand when the Hapsburg legions may be obliged to evacuate those provinces, which were to have been occupied only temporarily. Russia and Italy do not think it their duty to break a lance for the greater glory of Francis Joseph's monarchy, and France has no especial interest in the aggrandizement of his Empire. Whence we conclude that the example given by the Albanians may become contagious to the Herzegovinians and the Bosnians.

At Vienna great uneasiness is felt. The Government hesitates to accept the mission of conciliation which, rumor pretends, has been offered to it by the other Continental Cabinets in order to come to some compromise with the insurgents, such being as yet their official designation. But at the same time it is extremely anxious lest Italy be requested to act as the pacifier. One thing only appears to be universally admitted: the responsibility of the Porte in the movement. Turkey has everything to gain, nothing to lose, by the triumph of the Albanian cause, which will secure to her at least the tribute of a vassal State, whereas the consummation of the Montenegrin convention would be the definite loss of a certain portion of its territory. At Constantinople the progress of the movement has been carefully watched from the moment of its inception. I will say more: The movement would have been impossible without secret aid in supplies and arms from the Turkish Government. Last year was wet, the crops failed everywhere, and the Albanian would have starved to death had he neglected to till his ground, unless the Turks had given him the wherewithal to support himself and his family while he was arming for the fray. He is warlike, patriotic, his aspirations after freedom have been awakened by the spectacle of

the liberties accorded to Bulgaria and Roumelia; but he must eat, and if he had not been subsidized from Stamboul he would have been forced to sink every other consideration in that of self-preservation. This is the secret of the delays, artfully contrived by the Porte, to the arrangements of the Greek and the Montenegrin frontiers. The Turkish statesmen knew that the populations were disposed to resist annexation, whether to the Tchernagorans or to the Hellenes; all that was necessary was to gain time; time has been gained; the Albanians are now ready to defend their soil, and Eastern diplomacy has again outwitted Western diplomacy. The "energetic note" addressed by the powers to the Porte, about the non-execution of its engagements with Prince Nicholas, was, possibly, an unpleasant reminder of promises unfulfilled. But the Porte is used to "energetic notes;" it has had so many "energetic notes" more or less comminatory that it has grown quite callous, feeling pretty sure that whatever threats may be made they will not be put into execution. Still, courtesy rendered a reply necessary, and the text of this reply, as communicated by the Havas agency, shows that there is no intention to abandon the game of masterly inactivity which has always so far been successful. Another commission is proposed; the powers are even promised that they may establish the conditions of the inquest, and that the Porte will examine the report, and, in concert with the other powers, will decide upon the steps to be taken to restore order and prevent any further effusion of blood.

All this is beautifully diplomatic, but months must elapse before these steps can be taken, and while Cabinets are deliberating the insurrection is gaining ground. The Albanians are quite ready to fight at the present moment; the Tonti contingent numbers 8,000 men, those of Hoti-Gruda and Castrati are estimated at 4,000 more, within supporting distance of each other. Between these, the vanguard of the insurrection, the communications are open with All Pasha, of Gussinje, who can dispose of 10,000 warriors, from Diakova-Ipek, Gussinje, and Plava, without counting 8,000 furnished by Dibra, Tirana, and Martiria. A subscription of 80,000 florins has been raised for the purchase of arms, and a syndicate of bankers, among whom we find the names of several prominent Italians, has undertaken to supply all necessary funds, while the presence of Siesmit-Doda, a brother of the well-known Italian statesman, at Scutari is quite sufficient to show whence has come the initiative of the movement. It is indeed due to this gentleman's exertions that all religious complications have been avoided; later, the Mussulmans and the Christians may cut each others throats, but, for the present, the commandership in chief of the League is shared by a Mohammedan Mufti and the Catholic Prince of the Mirdites. From the standpoint of Italian interests this is a circumstance of capital importance, as the Catholic Albanians, now allied with the Mussulman Albanians, are precisely those who have been most actively worked upon by Italian emissaries, a fact to which I called attention in my last letter. The sympathies of the Mirdites for Italy are of very long standing; they have always been kept up unofficially by the sovereigns of Piedmont, and now we read in the semi-official press of the Peninsula advice to call for a plebiscite and a reminder of the deputation sent to ask aid of the House of Savoy, in the sixteenth century, and of the exploits of their hero, Georges Castriot, better known as Scanderbeg, who asserted and defended the independence of his nation for five and twenty years against Amurath and Mohammed II. However much Turkey may be indirectly responsible, it is Italy who must be considered as the direct instigator of the revolution, and her hand is visible in the wording of the last Albanian manifesto. "Europe," says this document, "has created a Principality for the Bulgarians; Servia and Montenegro have obtained their independence and an increase of their territory; consequently the Albanians, who were free and independent centuries ago, can justly assert their claims to form a separate State." What this State is to be the manifesto also informs us: "Thessaly, Epirus, and Albania proper are the patrimony of the Albanian nation, which numbers three million souls. Our country must be free and independent; it must be governed by a Prince of our own choice." In these last five words, I believe, may be found the whole secret; the Duke d'Aoste is intended to be the chosen vessel, who, at a given moment, will be proclaimed the sovereign of a nominal vassal of Islam, who will act under orders from the Quirinal.

As I remarked at the commencement of my letter, the French are, apparently, indifferent to this Eastern storm cloud. Their hands are full of trouble at home, and, although the Government press, very naturally, makes light of it, the Government itself is uneasy. The strikes all over the country, and especially in the Department of the North are very ugly symptoms of an approaching social conflict. For a while they had little effect except to ruin factory owners and bring nearly to starvation several thousand wretched operatives. The Minister of the Interior ordered an investigation and published his opinion that politics were entirely foreign to the question; that there was nothing to show the hand of the Internationale, or to indicate the interference of Socialist agents from abroad. This was very reassuring, or rather, ought to have been, for nobody was reassured when it became known that the garrison had been reinforced at Lille, and that detachments had gone to other manufacturing centres, "where public order had not been disturbed and would not be." Simple precautionary measures they were termed, and events proved that they were not taken any too soon, as on Friday the mob marched through the streets of Roubaix and Armentières, uttering threats of death against the factory proprietors, and only dispersed after being charged by the chasseurs and the cavalry. This display of energy had, as usual, a most salutary effect in calming down the popular effervescence, but it has not put an end to the agitation. The strike continues, the employers refuse to make concessions, the operatives to give way and go to work again, while seditious proclamations are posted in the streets, exciting the workmen to "revolt" and "revenge themselves upon those infamous capitalists of whom they too long have been the victims." Generally, the Parisian Socialist organs have kept a prudent silence; but Citizen Buffenoir's *Père Duchéne,* and poor old Louis Blanc's *Reveil Social* are doing all they can to fan the flame of rebellion by telling the mob that it has justice on its side, and that "to raise its fists [*sic*] against bayonets placed by tyranny at the service of the oppressors of the proletarian will be the assertion of a primordial right of human nature." Scarcely had the gravity of the strikes begun to be appreciated when the debate on the right of meeting came up in the Chamber, resulting in one of those victories for the Cabinet which, if repeated two or three times, will force M. De Freycinet's colleagues to retire to private life. The day after the discussion the Minister of the Interior resigned, which was only natural after the coalition of 78 members of the group represented by him in the Ministry with the 130 Legitimists and Bonapartists who opposed the Ministerial bill. M. Lepère is no loss, but his retreat is a symptom that all the Union Republican element is to be weeded out in favor of nobody can tell precisely whom, although the alternative will be either a return of reactionary or of advanced Radical Deputies when the country, tired of opportunism, shall be appealed to at the next general elections. Another cause of anxiety is the possible consequences of the manifestation in honor of the Commune, announced for the 23d of May, with which the Government may interfere. I anticipate no disturbance, but this again is an ugly symptom, and, taken in connection with the candidacy of Blanqui, at Lyons, shows that the ringleaders of the insurrection of 1871 have by no means renounced their designs, and that the returned convicts are quite as much unrepentant and unreconstructed rebels as when they were sent out to Noumea. With such affairs, then, as these at home, it is not extraordinary that French journalism should neglect foreign matters and expend all their intelligence in endeavors to prove that the tears of Continental complications, in which France may be involved ultimately, are purely chimerical.

\*   \*   \*

June 13, 1880

## THE GREEK FRONTIER QUESTION

With the conference which assembles at Berlin on the 16th of this month the long-delayed question of the Greek frontier evidently enters upon its final stage. The conference will be one of Ambassadors, including representatives of Germany. Austria, France, Great Britain, Italy, and Russia, and is summoned, under the twenty-fourth article of the treaty of Berlin, which provides for European mediation in event of the failure of Greece and the Porte to agree upon the rectification of the northern boundary of Greece, as indicated in the thirteenth protocol. The history of the long course of negotiations through which Greece has sought to enlarge her territory and secure her rights is one of praiseworthy patience and self-restraint on the part of the Government at Athens, of contemptible evasion, trickery, and double-dealing on the part of the Porte, and of studied perfidy on the part of the

Cabinet of Lord Beaconsfield. On the breaking out of the war between Russia and Turkey, in 1877, the Greek Government and people saw the long-desired opportunity to wrest Epirus and Thessaly from the control of the Turk. Those Provinces are essentially Greek, and rightly belong to Greece. The Porte begged England to restrain the Greeks from invading its territory, rightly judging that the Russians would require its undivided attention. In July, 1877, Lord Derby, then Foreign Secretary, assured the Greek Government that when the time came for settling the questions growing out of the war England would use its "best influence to secure for the Greek population in the Turkish Provinces any administrative reforms or advantages which may be conferred upon the Christian population of any other race." When the treaty of San Stefano was signed, Greece saw herself not only without hope of advantage under that instrument, but directly menaced by the creation of a new Slav State, extending to the Ægean. She, therefore, again prepared to take care of her interests in her own way, and a Greek force was sent across the Turkish frontier. There was a double purpose in this move—the conquest of Epirus and Thessaly, which was the direct object, and secondly, to put the claims of Greece before Europe upon the same footing as those of Bulgaria, Servia, and other Provinces which had actually taken part against Turkey in the war. On being assured by several powers that this last claim would be conceded, and by England that everything in its power would be done to secure to Greece the reforms and advantages which might be granted to other races, the invading force was recalled.

Greece was denied admission to the Berlin congress of 1878, but she relied upon the friendly offices of England to guard her interests, a confidence which was amply justified by the repeated assurances of the British Cabinet. Lord Beaconsfield and the Marquis of Salisbury deliberately betrayed that trust. The later manifested in the early sessions of the congress a disposition to deal generously with Greece, even to the extent of acknowledging her claim to Epirus, Thessaly, and Crete. To this Lord Beaconsfield at first seemed inclined to assent, but discovering later on, in the course of his bargaining with the representatives of the Porte, that the Sultan was alarmed at the prospect of being compelled to give up so much territory, he turned suddenly against Greece, and successfully opposed her claims, carrying with him in his change of front his pliant colleague, the Marquis of Salisbury. The Greek representatives then put their case into the hands of M. Waddington, who proposed to the congress that Epirus and Thessaly should be given up to Greece. Italy, Austria, Germany, and Russia assented to this, but the opposition of the British representatives defeated the proposition. This was, to say the least, the most modest basis on which, with any pretense of justice, the Hellenic claim could be presented, for a full recognition of the territorial and national rights of Greece would give her not only the two border Provinces and Crete, but Macedonia and Thrace as well. Yet the friendly power which had solemnly engaged to use its best influence in behalf of Greece coldly frowned

down this compromise. M. Waddington then brought forward a proposal to cut Epirus and Thessaly into two nearly equal portions, and give the southern halves to Greece, and this plan, though it violated the principle of nationalities, and in monstrous cruelty deserves to rank with the partition of Poland and the scission of Alsace and Lorraine, was adopted, and became the thirteenth protocol of the treaty of Berlin.

It was stipulated that Greece should consider this line through Epirus and Thessaly as indicating, in the opinion of the signatory powers, the extreme limit to which her aspirations could be allowed to extend; and that Turkey should accept it as a fair basis of settlement. Had Lord Beaconsfield been willing to allow the thirteenth protocol to be considered as a definite and obligatory settlement of the matter, instead of as an "invitation" to the Porte, Greece would have been spared two years of anxiety and costly negotiation, and a threatening question would have been removed from the arena of European politics. He was not so disposed, however, and now, after the two years of futile dalliance with the Porte, Greece once more appeals to the signatory powers, and the phil-Hellenic spirit of the Liberal English Cabinet, which has taken the initiative in the matter, assures a fair and just recognition of her rights under the treaty. The line indicated by the thirteenth protocol starts at the mouth of the Kalamas River, on the west coast of Epirus, and follows very nearly the course of that stream eastward to the Gulf of Janina, and at Metsovo, in the heart of the Pindus range, meets the line which divides Thessaly, following the course of the Salambria River to its mouth, on the Gulf of Salonica. This partition gives Greece half of Epirus and Thessaly, including the important cities of Janina—once a centre of Hellenic thought, aspiration, and activity, and the real Greek capital in the days when Athens was ground under the heel of the Turk—Metsovo, and Trikala. The Porte has done everything in its power to avoid the cession of these cities, and even tried to carry the western extremity of the boundary line down to the Gulf of Arta, retaining Preveza, which commands the entrance to the gulf, in its own hands. The Berlin conference will settle the political questions involved in the dispute, and will name a commission which will be charged with the technical work of delimitation, and as the Porte has been able hitherto to put off the settlement by professing its inability to protect the members of the commission, a sufficient force will be sent with it to insure its safety from attack by the Albanian league or Thessalian brigands.

\* \* \*

**January 18, 1882**

It has become each year apparent enough that the treaty of Berlin, now almost four years old, so far from ending the serious troubles of South eastern Europe, has practically been a cause of trouble which, but for it, might not have been known. No sooner is the Greek boundary defined and agreed to—in a greatly restricted form, however—than there are rumors of a grave crisis in Bocchesi, and so soon as we hear that the Bocchesi difficulty is passed, rumors come of an insurrection in Herzegovina against Austrian control. Alarm is felt at Vienna, where $10,000,000 are desired for campaign expenses, while the troops in Herzegovina and in Krivoscle are to be increased to 23,000 men. That Austria has been for months preparing to use her treaty rights in the occupied Provinces for the furtherance of ambitious schemes becomes more and more apparent from this news. She attempted early last year to levy the military conscription in the Bocchesi, and then temporarily, at least, abandoned the project in the face of the crisis, but issued soon afterward a proclamation levying the conscriptions in neighboring Bosnia and Herzegovina. Since these Provinces had not been formally annexed this act came in a very bad time, and it is no doubt the direct result of attempts to enforce it that trouble now arises. Active military works further east, on the road from Serajevo to Salonica, have been already undertaken by Austria, and are nearly finished at three important points, while at Serajevo warehouses have been filled with military stores. Early in the coming Spring Austrian sovereignty in the two Provinces will be proclaimed, and these towns—which are Sienitza, Novibazar, and Mitrovitza—will then all be garrisoned. A military roa is being pushed on to Prijepolji, the most advanced of all points yet occupied, while on the Adriatic, at Pola and Trieste naval preparations are in hand. It was conceded to Austria in the Berlin treaty that the three towns might be garrisoned, but a condition was that it should be done in order to secure the freedom of her communications. Whether her freedom in communications now requires that such steps should be taken, is, of course, an open question, and one to which she no doubt could offer a ready reply; but what real need for them there should be does not yet appear, and recent travelers in the country have been impressed with the strong contrast between the energy shown in military preparations and the general stagnation of other public works. Men will be required to garrison these towns, and from the occupied Provinces Austria will naturally expect to obtain them. Full knowledge of this must have had much to do with the present insurrection. How far it extends to Montenegro the dispatches do not say, but neither Montenegro nor Servia can view with complacency this advance into Novibazar and Mitrovitza, territory lying squarely between their respective boundaries, setting up, as it would, a dangerous enemy between the sister States. An eminent Austrian officer is credited with having said before the Russo-Turkish war that his country might leave Montenegro independent, but intended to "put a girdle round her." That, at any rate, is what she would continue still further to do by an advance to Novibazar and Mitrovitza.

\*     \*     \*

January 23, 1882

## THE BALKAN REBELLION

The insurrection in Dalmatia and Herzegovina which Austria is now taking measures to suppress bears a remarkable likeness to the uprising of the Summer of 1875 in a little Herzegovinian glen which led to the war between Russia and Turkey. That spark kindled into flame which swept through Bosnia, Herzegovina, Servia, and Bulgaria. Compelled by the pressure of the European powers to make at least an attempt to restore order in her Provinces, Turkey sent troops into Bulgaria and murdered a few thousand old men, women, and children with atrocious cruelties such as only a Turk can invent or inflict. But this, strange to say, did not suffice to pacify the Christian population of the Balkan peninsula, provoked by years of outrage and grinding taxation to take up arms against their Moslem oppressors. Lord Beaconsfield was then Prime Minister in England, and Mr. Gladstone's vehement denunciation of the Bulgarian butcheries and the historian Freeman's eloquent pleas for "south-eastern freedom" fell unheeded on the ears of a purely selfish and pro-Turkish Government. The Christian powers allowed Russia to seize the opportunity to gain certain private territorial ends under the pretext of shielding the Christians of the Balkans from the rage of the infidels.

Austro-Hungary is reported to be alarmed at the present extent and rapid spread of the uprising. Well she may be and all Europe with her. The late Foreign Minister of France was guilty of no exaggeration in declaring that a conflict originating in the Balkan territory was always a perilous affair, being liable to "spread rapidly to the neighboring countries and convulse the whole East and perhaps even the world." It is one of the territorial crimes committed in the name of the treaty of Berlin which is now crying out for vengeance. That treaty gave Bosnia and Herzegovina to Austria on conditional terms which have lately given place to those of absolute annexation. It took an army of 100,000 men to make the cession effective and fasten the iron grip of Austria on the unfortunate Provinces. In truth, they gained little in exchanging masters—the unspeakable Turk for the grim Austrian. The Austrian administration has been extremely harsh. The taxes have been as heavy as ever, and their collection has been commonly intrusted to the old Turkish tax-gatherers, many of whom, as owners of land, remained in the Provinces after the transfer. The Government has been purely military, and the people have been allowed such freedom and privileges as dogs enjoy. Armed guards are everywhere, and the meanest citizen is made to feel that he is the slave of the foreign tyrant to whom he was sold at Berlin. Last Spring there was a revolt against the Austrian conscription in the Cattaro district of Dalmatia. It was never wholly suppressed by the Austrians, as the insurgents fled to the mountains, while hundreds of families emigrated to America to escape the draft. The outbreak at Krivoscie a few weeks ago was occasioned by the conscription. Four Austrian gendarmes were killed. Lately the insurrection has spread to Herzegovina, where there have previously been one or two attempts to resist conscription. At Newesinje 1,000 insurgents overpowered the military post and captured the garrison. The native gendarmes—recruited by conscription, no doubt—were set at liberty, but the Austrian soldiers were sent to Mostar. The rising is said to be spreading into Bosnia, and in Albania and Montenegro there are smoldering embers of discontent which a sympathetic spark may at any time kindle into a very troublesome conflagration.

Austria, though professing alarm, is probably not greatly displeased at the chance her rebellious subjects have given her of undertaking military operations which may, before the recall of the troops, lead to an advance toward Salonica, a road she longs to travel. The time is propitious. Envoys of Turkey have recently visited Vienna, where a complete understanding was reached between the two powers. This understanding extends to Germany, whose influence is every day gaining ground in Constantinople, as may be seen by the frequent appointment of German officers to Turkish administrative posts. Italy has lately appeared as a suppliant for Austrian favor, and could be easily induced to consent to Austria's south-eastern designs. There remains only Russia, and she is tortured to death with her internal maladies. Besides, with Germany and Turkey favorable to her purposes, why need Austria consult Russia about her movements in the Balkans? The rumors of Russian intrigues at Cattaro and Slav agitators at work among the insurgents have a suspicious look. If Austria really proposed to strike the long intended blow toward Salonica and wished to discount in advance Russia's protests, she would go to work very much in this way. Her method is very simple. There is a revolt; the rumor is circulated that the Russians have caused it; Austrian troops go to crush it, and the insurgents scatter, some of them across the frontier into Montenegro, Servia, or Albania, where the troops pursue them. Russia protests and threatens; Germany intervenes and Russia discreetly pauses; meanwhile the Austrian Army is carrying the war on toward the Ægean. What power would venture to forcibly call to account Austria and Germany combined? When the trouble was over, and a new treaty of Vienna or Berlin was signed, it would no doubt be found that a new map of the Balkan peninsula was necessary, and Austria would be coterminous with Greece. This may prove to be a small fire, but it has in it the potentiality of a very big blaze.

\* \* \*

February 19, 1882

## THE PRINCIPLE OF NATIONALITIES

In one of his recent lectures Mr. Freeman gave a sketch of the ideal solution of the Eastern question on the principle of nationalities, a principle which the powers of Europe are too blind or too selfish to recognize. Rejecting altogether the expression "Turkey" as a word to which there is no corresponding fact, Mr. Freeman would apportion the territory which he calls enslaved Greece, enslaved Roumania, enslaved Bulgaria, and enslaved Servia among the countries to which its various divisions rightfully belong, and which the people who inhabit them acknowledge as their fatherlands. To complete the work and settle the Eastern difficulty forever, he would make Austria atone for the wrongs she has inflicted by giving up Bosnia and Herzegovina and her Adriatic possessions. Mr. Freeman is hardly a panslavist, but in the inhabitants of the Balkan peninsula, outside the Greeks and the Albanians (as the followers of the Prophet are only temporary visitors they may be disregarded), he sees the descendants of a common Slav ancestry. The people of Bosnia, Herzegovina, Dalmatia, and Montenegro are one in blood and sympathy. Freed from the grasp of Austria, the three first mentioned would unite with Montenegro, and Prince Nikita would become the ruler of a State having an area of nearly 40,000 square miles (not quite so big as Pennsylvania) and a population of two millions and a quarter.

Austria so far disagrees with the distinguished English historian as to oppose with the bayonet all movements of the subject population of her southern Provinces looking toward any other form of political existence than that of bondage to her. She is likely to go on acquiring territory rather than to lose any she now has, and the people of Dalmatia, Herzegovina, and Bosnia will never realize their dreams of unity, if they have any, until her power has crumbled. In the revolt which Austrian troops are now trying, with small success, to crush, the harsh conscription law appears as the provoking cause, but the spread of the disorder from Dalmatia into Herzegovina and Bosnia, and even into Montenegro, where Prince Nikita's subjects are arming to help their brethren over the frontier, shows that the sympathy of a kindred race easily overcomes in those little Provinces whatever sentiment of separate geographical existence the congresses and delimitation commissions of Europe have been able to create. The Montenegrins long to strike a blow in aid of their enslaved kin, but their Prince restrains them. The powers gave him Dulcigno, and he feels bound to repay them. He has been asked by Austria to use his good offices in their behalf. He tells the Herzegovinians that they ought not to resist the military law of Austria, an empire which was "just and benevolent in all its actions." It has even been said that he would allow the Austrian troops to cross and occupy his frontier in their operations against the insurgents, a move which would give them a great advantage in the struggle, cutting the rebels off from all aid and comfort or reinforcement from Russia.

If Prince Nikita has really gone over to the side of the Austrians, we may be sure he has left his subjects behind him. The Black Mountaineers will acknowledge no other international obligation than that of hatred for Austria and all other powers which refuse autonomy to their neighbors and brothers and have been or may be hostile to their own independence, which they have defended so often and with so much stubborn valor. Too much consorting with the Austrians may dethrone the Prince. His subjects will be quick to see the danger of his course. If Austria makes him a friend and ally, she will soon make him her slave and his people with him unless they again buy their freedom with blood. His interference in favor of the oppressor is unlooked for, and instead of being a help to Austria may inflame the rage of the people of her own Provinces and of Montenegro against her, in which case she would need an army large enough to destroy the rebels, that being about the only method of subduing them. At present the insurgents are formidable not so much from their numbers as from their character. In their mountain fastnesses they are practically unconquerable. Fifty men can defy a battalion of regular troops, harassing them continually, yet always eluding them when pursued. This kind of warfare is tedious and costly for Austria, even with no more than a thousand insurgents in arms. If the outbreak attains to the proportions of a general rising, it will be a long while before peace is restored, and other powers can hardly escape becoming involved in the war.

\*   \*   \*

March 8, 1882

## KING MILAN

There is a new King in Europe. Prince Milan of Servia, who, ever since the Prince of Roumania became a King, has been anxious to follow his example, has finally provided himself with a crown and announced his intention of taking his place among the crowned heads of Europe.

As everybody knows, the chief difference between a Prince and a King is that the former wears a military helmet and the latter a crown. There is no doubt that a well-made and fashionable crown is a pretty head-dress, but it has its inconveniences. If it does not fit, or if it is too heavy, the wearer is made very uncomfortable. The venerable German Emperor, who is so tenacious of his privileges as to wear his crown by night as well as by day, suffers to an extent that must seriously affect his health. His crown is a large heavy one, which fits rather loosely now that his hair has grown thin, and it can only be kept in position by a strap passing under his chin. It undoubtedly tends to give him a headache in the day time, and at night, when his uneasy movements frequently bring the sharp edges of the crown in contact with the back of his neck, it becomes really dangerous. Bismarck has repeatedly urged the Emperor to hang his crown at the head of his bed or to put it under his pillow, but the determined old man has always replied. "No, Otto. It is my duty to wear the crown, and I will never take it off for a single moment while I have a head on which to wear it."

Queen Victoria has several crowns, one of which she wears in the Winter, another in the Summer, and a third, which is the oldest and least valuable of the three, is worn in rainy weather and when she is in the misty Highlands. When she opens Parliament her crown is carried before her on a cushion. This is done because the door of the House is so low that she would be apt to knock her crown off if she tried to pass through the door with the crown on her head. Although this is the only occasion on which she is ever seen without wearing her crown, it is well known that she takes it off at night and has it locked up in the plate closet of the Tower. This habit is believed to have originated in the narrow escape from losing his eye which the late Prince Albert once had. The Prince had just said his prayers and blown the light out, and was in the act of bidding the Queen good night, when one of the sharp-pointed ornaments of the crown entered his right eye, and he exclaimed in agony. "There, my dear, you've succeeded in putting my eye out at last." Such was her Majesty's horror and remorse that she then and there vowed never to wear her crown at night—a vow which she has faithfully kept.

Much of the popularity of King Humbert is probably due to the jaunty way in which he wears his crown, a little on one side of his head, and the grace with which he lifts it when he meets an acquaintance. So courteous is this gallant young monarch that when he stops in the street to speak to a lady he always removes his crown and holds it in his right hand while the interview lasts. Instead of wearing the crown at balls and parties as is the usual, but hardly commendable, custom of other Kings, he carries it under his left arm, or, in case he is sitting down, holds it on his knee. It should be mentioned that the Italian crown is a very heavy one, made of cast iron, and that the King always puts it outside of his door, beside his boots, every night, in order to have it polished. As soon as the finances of the kingdom improve the Ministry will probably bring in a bill authorizing the King to have the crown nickle-plated, and so save the trouble and expense of so much polishing.

The Prince of Servia can, of course, buy a crown and wear it if he so desires, and he can call himself a King and be acknowledged as such in Servia, but, nevertheless, he cannot force his way into the society of other Kings any more than Bradlaugh can swear himself into the House of Commons. In order to be admitted into the circle of European crowned heads a two-thirds vote is necessary. The Prince of Roumania obtained the requisite vote—though with a good deal of difficulty—before he assumed the crown, and had he not obtained it, there is every reason to believe that he would still be only a plain Prince. It is notorious that at least two years ago Prince Milan was proposed by the King of Greece and seconded by the King of Denmark for admission to the European kingly circle, but he was defeated by a large majority, and the Emperor of Austria made a speech against him, asserting that it was time to draw a line which would forever keep petty upstart rulers from intruding into royal and imperial society. The Prince has grown tired of waiting for a reversal of this verdict, and has undertaken to make himself a King. This is a most rash and unfortunate step. It will perhaps increase his salary and increase the respect with which the Servians will treat him, but it will render the other European monarchs justly indignant. They will, one and all, refuse to associate with him, and if they accidentally meet him at an industrial exhibition, or on a steamer, they will cut him severely. He may urge that he has a moral and legal right to wear a crown if he can afford to pay for one and his people do not make any objection, but the Kings will be as deaf to his arguments as the House of Commons is to the arguments of Bradlaugh. Unless he is a man of extraordinary independence of character and indifference to public opinion, he will, before very long, bitterly regret the step he has taken, and will be ready to resign his crown and to retire to private life.

If Kings continue to increase in number as they have increased during the last century, it will be no more an honor to be a King than it is to be a German Baron. The Kings of Belgium, Italy, Greece, and Roumania have all been added to the circle within the memory of the present generation, and if to these we add the older reigning monarchs and the vast throng of ex-Kings it will be seen that we are steadily approaching the day when European Kings will be as common and as unimportant as Georgia Colonels.

\*    \*    \*

December 31, 1882

## THE SIXTH CENTENNIAL OF THE HAPSBURGERS

During the last week of 1882 the imperial house of the Hapsburg family celebrated their six hundredth anniversary. If age and imperial dignities and vast possessions can justly give family pride, the Hapsburgers may look down on all the royal and imperial lines of Europe. When the Hohenzollern were petty Princes and the Guelphs were unknown their ancestors ruled over even grander territories than now. But history, in weighing in the balance the merits of the rulers of men, looks at other matters than position and good fortune. The modern estimate of this ancient house is anything but flattering. Every historian notes indeed their good luck, but few writers, native or foreign, have chronicled their virtues. Their lucky fortune is proverbial. They seemed in modern times broken by Napoleon, but they recovered with sufficient force to bear a large share in his downfall. They were threatened with utter destruction by the Hungarian rebellion, but secured the assistance of the Russians in time to extinguish it in blood. They were beaten by the French and lost Northern Italy, but seemed only to be stronger afterward. They were overthrown by the Prussians, and the whole fabric of the empire appeared ready to fall to pieces when an early peace saved it. And later, when no power seemed able to preserve the unity of the empire, with Hungary ready to revolt and the Bohemians and Slavs discontented, and every Province divided and hostile to one another, their preserver suddenly presented himself in the person of one of their enemies—a Hungarian statesman, Deak, who framed a possible system of dual government, and Austria and the Hapsburgers had another lease of power.

But this unexampled good luck and brilliant fortune cannot cover the long and lurid line of blood and havoc which has marked the career of the family. For many years they held the fairest Provinces of Italy under the heel of their regiments, and Italian freedom was trampled to the ground. Previous to this they had assisted to drown Polish efforts for independence in blood, and had aided in the ill-famed parti-

tion. Hungary, which had enjoyed a thousand years of constitutional freedom, was crushed under the Hapsburg tyranny and her best youth exiled or brought to the scaffold. As one follows the record of this ancient family through the centuries it is a career of blood and tyranny and bitter oppression. The noble prisoners in a thousand dungeons seem to join in the great cry of execration which follows it from oppressed and desolated countries. No loyalty or affection—except among the ignorant but honest mountaineers of the Tyrol—anywhere attends it. And yet today the Hapsburg house seems one of the strongest regal houses in Europe. The source of its strength, however, lies in external circumstances, not in the qualities of the race. The Hungarians, who still despise and hate the family, have obtained from its prudence and fears the leadership of the empire, and have no motive for revolt or opposition. If independent of Austria, they are exposed to the great danger which ever looms before Eastern Europe, the Slavonic invasion, or to the other peril, the being swallowed up by united Germany. They prefer to bear the military and fiscal burdens of the "dual Government" and enjoy their local independence and their supremacy in Austrian councils. The Slavs dare not oppose the imperial family, or they might fall into the hands of a worse enemy—the Magyars. The Czechs dread absorption into Germany, and therefore are contented to stick by the Hapsburgers. The Germans of Vienna and the German Provinces thus far prefer to be apparent leaders in a great, though motley, empire to being a Province of the German Fatherland.

All the various races in that strangely populated empire hold to the Hapsburgers as a *pis-aller*. A change or revolution might give them a worse master. And it is to be confessed by all impartial judges that the Hapsburgers are now—whatever they have been in the past—mild, kindly, and wise governors. Their administration is, according to American and English ideas, too "paternal." But that is a fault on a good side. It certainly belongs to a rule which is very useful to poor and backward districts. For democratic institutions the Hapsburgers could not, of course, have sympathy, but they have had the wisdom to yield to the tide of the age. And, as a result, Austria, or rather Hungary, is now more free politically than Prussia or Germany.

How long such a disjointed structure as the Hapsburg Empire can last no one would venture to predict. It has borne the storms of six centuries. It may stand the strain of many more years. But the probability is that another generation will see an entire new constitution of Eastern Europe. The new State will be either Slavonic or German, and under its wide rule the Hapsburgers become, as the Kings of Saxony or Bavaria are now, petty princes belonging to a mighty confederation. Even the proverbial good luck and stupidity of the family cannot always save them. When they finally come to an end some future Tacitus will write their epitaph—*paucis lachrymis compositus*—"buried with few tears," and justice in the affairs of men and nations will seem satisfied.

\*    \*    \*

February 25, 1896

# PRINCE BORIS HEIR TO A FRAIL CROWN

### His Conversion to the Orthodox Greek Church Makes Ferdinand a King

Since Prince Boris, heir to the throne of Bulgaria, Prince of Tirnova, chief of a regiment of infantry, of a regiment of cavalry, and of a regiment of artillery, has been baptized as an Orthodox Greek his father, Ferdinand, has ceased to be only a tolerated King. He is an acknowledged King now, Prince Ferdinand! His master the Sultan, his master the Czar, his masters the other sovereigns of Europe, have taken him into their council. If they crush him, they crush a King.

Prince Boris does not know what all this means. He is two years of age, and to his large gray eyes everything is very big and dazzling. There are rows and rows of stars on his father's breast under epaulets that hurt the eyes. There are tall paintings on the walls of the room where he sits for his portrait, on a velvet-cushioned chair, with his hair banged in the style of the children of the English King Edward. His look of amazement may last always. He is only two years old, and it will be some time before he sees that his head is like an orange, and shudders at the thought of Salome's silver charger.

Bulgaria is still savage. Prince Ferdinand is weak and wicked. There are no refinements of kindness in the land where Stambuloff ruled and was murdered. But Prince Boris's mother will take her son, tenderly, to other lands where he may be taught the sciences, the arts, and literature that polish manners. He will play with missals and images. His little hands will be white and frail, there will be a great deal of reason in his little mind, and when he becomes a King in his turn, if he ever becomes a King, he will know that he is not a type of Bulgaria, and it will be a pity.

\*   \*   \*

February 25, 1896

# THE CONVERSION OF PRINCE BORIS

The baptism in the Greek Church of a two-year-old baby is not commonly an event to which any "political significance" can be supposed to attach. But in the baptism of Prince Boris in Sofia there is not professed or supposed to be any other than a political significance. The Russians are rather thick-skinned about such matters, and most of the Russian newspapers celebrate the conversion of the Bulgarian Prince as a triumph of Russian policy. But it is rather satisfactory to observe that even in Russia there is at least one newspaper which manifests disgust at this mummery and ventures to speak of it as a "prostitution of religion." The conversion of course implies that the baby, after maturely considering the historical and theological claims of the various branches of the Christian Church, and after strictly meditating the question of the "filloque," has concluded that it is his duty to

be baptized over again and by an Exarch instead of a mere Archbishop.

The fact is that the child's natural guardian, his father, does not pretend to have been converted. The person who actually gave the orthodox answers to the Exarch's questions was a purely official sponsor and representative of the Russian interest and of the Czar—Gen. Kutuzoff. When Henry IV discovered that "Paris was worth a mass," he at least acted on his discovery and personally assumed the responsibility of his blasphemy. He looks really heroic in comparison with Prince Ferdinand, who finds it necessary to maintain the regency of Bulgaria by sending his child to be "converted" and baptized into a church of which he himself does not profess to be an adherent. Nobody concerned in the transaction, except the helpless baby, appears to advantage, but nobody else cuts quite so contemptible a figure as the reigning Prince. Every decent person must desire that he shall not receive any advantage from his humiliation, and there are gratifying evidences that he will not be allowed to do so. The Russian semi-official statement that "the ruler of Bulgaria must be orthodox" seems to indicate that Prince Ferdinand must do his humiliation in person, and not vicariously through his child, if he is to be recognized by Russia as a lawful ruler.

There is in this miserable mockery an element of humiliation for the whole civilized world, which has already spoken out in resentment of the outrages upon the Christians in Turkey. The lives of those hapless persons, it has already been shown, were mere counters in a particularly scandalous game of politics. But this has not been so vividly shown before as in the mummery by which it has been pretended that a two-year-old baby has changed his religion, a mummery which Christian Russia instigated, and of which Mohammedan Turkey, by the presence of its official representatives, showed its approval. We have no desire to flatter Platt, but we really doubt if Platt would go quite so far as this in deference to "politics."

\*   \*   \*

March 7, 1897

# GREECE AND RUSSIA

It looks very much as if history were repeating itself in the relations between Greece and Russia. The first effective measures for Greek freedom from the Sultan were taken early in the century by an association called the Hetairia, comprising a number of influential and patriotic Greeks in Asia Minor and Greece, who were also in communication with Europe. Their centre was at Constantinople, but their treasury was at Munich, and the real head at St. Petersburg. They claimed to have the cordial support of the Czar and his Prime Minister. For a time they contented themselves with a general revolutionary propaganda, but the massacre of the Suliotes under the lead of Botzaris stirred the greatest excitement, which was fanned into a flame of revolt by various emissaries, including Russian priests, who went through the Morea, Thessaly, and Epirus. The result was an outbreak in 1821 in the north. The Hetairia had as its leader Ypsilanti, son of the famous Wallachian, and aide de camp of the Czar. He gave out that in response to a question from him as to the wisdom of an insurrection, the Czar had said: "If Greece entire rises my Cossacks shall march to second her."

The next step was a proclamation by Ypsilanti: "Hellenes, the hour has struck; it is time to shake off the yoke and to avenge our religion and our country." The Servians, the remnants of the Suliotes, the Moldavians, and the Epirotes joined in the revolt. Scarcely had Ypsilanti entered the field when the Russian Consul at Bucharest, in the name of his Government, protested against the enterprise, pronouncing it "the effect of the exaltation which characterized the epoch, as well as of the thoughtlessness and inexperience of a young man." What followed is well known. Ypsilanti was deprived of his rank. The Greeks of Constantinople who failed to secure safety by flight were massacred. The Greek Patriarch was hanged at the door of his palace, and his corpse mutilated, dragged through a sewer, and flung into the Bosporus. Thrace, Macedonia, and Thessaly were given over to pillage. The desertion of Russia, however, seemed to stir the Greeks to more heroic efforts rather than to discourage them, and but for their internal dissensions and rivalries they might possibly have carried the day at once. As it was, the fight continued, occasioning the fearful massacre at Scio, followed in its turn by heavy reprisals and the capture of Missolonghi.

Then came a European conference. The Greeks were refused a hearing, but the Sultan was invited to send a delegate. The peoples of Europe, however, would not follow their Governments, but formed societies of Philhellenes everywhere and sent money, arms, and ammunition to the revolutionists. It was at this time that Lord Byron, Col. Fabvier, and others went to give their personal support. The Turks in despair called in the aid of the Egyptian Pasha, regained Missolonghi, and besieged Athens. Another appeal to Europe was followed by the usual diplomatic bargaining. England, as mediary, wanted Greece to be divided into three principalities, subject to the suzerainty of the Sultan, a plan rejected by both Greeks and Turks. The fighting went on, although Athens had fallen. The battle of Navarino, brought about by the Egyptian fleet, resulted in a break between the Sultan and Russia, and, at last, in 1830, Greece was free.

With a slight change of words the history of seventy-five years ago is true of the past year. There is no question that Russian influence has been at the bottom of the disturbed condition in Crete and Macedonia, or that King George has had private if not official assurance of support from St. Petersburg. As in the case of Ypsilanti, he has been disowned as soon as he acted. As usual, England has been the intermediary, proposing a continued vassalage to the Sultan. It remains to be seen whether the massacre of Solo will be repeated and the Greeks of Constantinople and Smyrna suffer what the Armenians of Ersrum and Van have. That the Greeks will hold out now as they did then there is little doubt. King George and M. Delyannis have committed themselves definitely to war if war be necessary to drive the Turk from Crete. The peoples of the world are with them, as they always have been. The Governments of Europe seem to have learned nothing. Nicholas II is following in the footsteps of Nicholas I, Count Goluchewski appears to be emulating the famous Metternich, and English Admirals are doing what the Duke of Wellington did. It seems impossible for any of them to learn that peace is founded upon justice, not injustice, and that nations which defend such a barbarism as the Ottoman Government will have to pay the penalty sooner or later. Most contemptible of all is the course of Russia. A word from her and Crete would be free. It seems incredible that she should not speak the word, and eventually we believe that she will. Meanwhile her course of deception and fraud is one that must bring upon her the contempt of all right-minded people.

# PART II

## THE STRUGGLE FOR NATIONHOOD, 1900–1913

June 12, 1903

### KING AND QUEEN OF SERVIA SLAIN

**KILLED BY REVOLUTIONISTS IN BELGRADE PALACE**

*Ministers Assassinated*

**QUEEN DRAGA'S RELATIVES ALSO PUT TO DEATH**

*Prince Peter Karageorgevitch, the Pretender to the Throne,
Proclaimed King—Servians Approve the Coup d'Etat*

BELGRADE, June 11—A military conspiracy, which subsequent events show had the sympathy of the majority of the Servian people, was carried out in the early hours of this morning, and King Alexander, Queen Draga, her two brothers, and several Ministers were assassinated.

Prince Peter Karageorgevitch, the pretender to the throne, has been proclaimed King by the army, and there is every reason to believe that this decision will be confirmed by the Servian Parliament, which has been summoned to meet on June 15.

The revolution was executed without any opposition on the part of the people of Belgrade, and the capital and the country remain tranquil.

While the main outlines of the events which took place within the Royal Palace are known, the details are conflicting, owing to the extraordinary secrecy with which the plot was contrived and carried out. The chief conspirators were all men of high rank, who acted in concert with the army. The participation of the latter in the assassinations which blotted out the Obrenovitch dynasty, that has ruled Servia with a short intermission for nearly a century, is mainly due to the attitude of King Alexander and his consort toward the army officers, whom they always treated with scant courtesy. The King's desire to remove the War School from Belgrade to Shebats in particular gave the officers offense.

#### A Sinister Anniversary

To-day's date is a sinister one in the history of the Obrenovitch house, being the thirty-fifth anniversary of the assassination of King Alexander's granduncle, Michael, who was done to death by agents of Alexander Karageorgevitch, the then leading member of the house which has long disputed the throne of Servia against the Obrenovitch family, and whose head to-day, Prince Peter Karageorgevitch, has been proclaimed King. To-day a requiem mass was to be sung in memory of Prince Michael, and now the last of his race and all connected with the dynasty by his unfortunate marriage are dead.

Dissatisfaction against King Alexander's rule has been accentuated since his suspension of the Constitution, and it is from that time that the military plot dates. The organization of last night's bloody deed was carried out with consummate skill. The King for the past two months was thrown off his guard by the apparent quietude of the reception of his recent coup d'état. In the meantime the conspirators had decided on June 10 as the date for the execution of the revolution for two reasons—first, because it was the anniversary of the murder of the King's granduncle, and secondly, because it was feared that further delay would permit the Skuptachina to settle the succession to the throne according to the King's wishes, and it was believed that the brother of the hated Queen would be his choice.

The prime movers in the plot were Ljubomir Schiokovics and Vojisiav Velikovics, who have entered the new Cabinet as Ministers of Justice and Finance, respectively. M. Schiokovics was condemned to twenty years' penal servitude for an attempt to assassinate ex-King Milan.

#### The Tragedy in the Palace

The King and Queen passed the eve of their death quietly. They attended a choral festival, took supper in the Konak, and afterward retired to rest. Meanwhile the conspirators held a meeting in the Kalimegden Park. The Sixth Infantry Regiment, which was chosen to carry out the coup d'état, was punished recently for having used its weapons against a crowd of demonstrators.

About 1 o'clock in the morning the Sixth and Seventh Regiments were called to arms, and were led to the royal palace, which they entirely surrounded. A band of thirty officers, led by Col. Maschin and Col. Mischics, forced their way into the palace, shooting all who attempted to bar their passage. They were aided by treason within. The aide de camp on duty, Col. Naumovics, had been won over by the conspirators, and was intrusted with the plans for action within the royal inclosure. Several doors leading to the royal apartments were blown in by dynamite, Col. Naumovics himself bursting in the door of the royal bedchamber with a bomb. The officers had called on the King to open, but he had curtly refused.

As the door fell the King rushed to a window and appealed for assistance, but no answer came. Realizing the situation he returned to the Queen, holding her in his arms to protect her, and awaited the conspirators. Col. Naumovics and the officers then entered the room. Naumovics presented to the King a form of abdication for his signature. The document contained the statement that by marrying Queen Draga the King had degraded Servia and that he must abdicate.

The King's answer was to draw a revolver and kill Naumovics on the spot. Col. Mischics picked up the document and presented it again. King Alexander waved it from him.

The officers then with their revolvers fired a hail of bullets, and the royal couple fell together to the ground. The King lingered until 4 o'clock this morning.

The band who carried out the assassination appear to have met with great resistance on the balcony side of the palace, where the curtains are torn and the window broken as though the occupants had tried to escape into the garden. Torn gloves and articles of soldiers' clothing lie scattered below. This resistance was probably offered by two loyal aides de camp, who were killed.

### The People Joyful

A single cannon shot announced the execution of the plot, all the terrible details of which may perhaps never be accurately known. Detachments of troops immediately marched to the Bureaus of Posts and Telegraphs and the railway stations and occupied them. Other troops marched to the barracks and proclaimed Prince Karageorgevitch King. A body of mounted officers, with Lieut. Col. Gruics, the son of the present Ambassador at Constantinople, at their head, rode to the centre of the town and announced the army's choice to the people, who, now alarmed, were thronging the streets.

Enthusiastic shouts were raised of "Long live Karageorgevitch!" and "Long live the Army!" The warmest welcome was extended to Queen Draga's brother-in-law, Col. Maschin, one of the regicides. The troops at the barracks received the news with joy. There was only one objector, Gen. Nikolics, Commander of the Danube Division, who was promptly shot down and severely wounded, but not before he had shot and killed Lieut. Gagics.

All the places of business are closed and many inhabitants have left the town. Even with a pass it is difficult to obtain admission to Belgrade, so carefully guarded is the city.

The following is the official list of the killed, the time of the assassinations being given as 2 A. M.:

King Alexander.

Queen Draga.

The Queen's two brothers.

Premier Markovitch.

The Minister of War, Gen. Pavlovitch.

Two aides-de-camp and two other officers.

It is said, however, that Queen Draga's two sisters, M. Tudorovics, the Minister of the Interior, and various others were also killed.

There is intense excitement here. As the day advanced, in spite of the pouring rain, thousands of people gathered in the vicinity of the palace. Everywhere troops of all arms were posted, and field guns were placed in positions to deal quickly with any opposition to the newly formed Government's will. The soldiers discarded their cockades bearing King Alexander's cipher, and substituted for them flowers, green twigs, and leaves.

Bands of young men paraded the streets waving flags and shouting: "Long live Karageorgevitch." Flags are flying from nearly every house in Belgrade, and there is absolutely no display whatever of crape or other sign of mourning.

The royal standard has been lowered from over the palace.

Reports from places outside Belgrade indicate that the country accepts the disappearance of the Obernovitch dynasty without regret.

The newspapers forecast a better future for Servia, and the new state of things is heartily welcomed by the masses.

Nothing definite has been decided regarding the burial of the dead. It is said that a post-mortem examination of the bodies was held at 11 o'clock this morning. Afterward they were placed in coffins.

The local papers in their reports of the tragedy print all sorts of extraordinary statements. According to one of them, the bodies of the King and Queen were placed in shrouds and were lowered from a window of the palace to the gardens, whence they were carried away in a baggage wagon.

BERLIN, June 11—A dispatch from Semlin, Hungary, to the National Zeitung says:

"A party of officers proceeded to the palace by previous arrangement with Gen. Ljubasivkovics and called upon King Alexander to abdicate in favor of Prince Peter Karageorgevitch. The King refused and shot Col. Naumovics, who made the proposal. The other officers thereupon summoned the War Minister (Gen. Pavlovitch) and M. Tudorovics, (the Minister of the Interior,) and shot the King and Queen and Petrovitch, one of the King's aide-de-camps, and other loyal officers. The leader of the actual assailants was Lieut. Col. Mischics, who himself murdered the Queen. The latter, together with her brother and sisters, was struck down with an axe. The King was shot. The Queen died immediately. The King lived a few minutes after being shot.

"The immediate cause of the revolution was the return to Belgrade of Lieut. Lunjevitza, brother of the Queen, and a supposed candidate for the throne.

"The surviving Ministers have been arrested.

"The obsequies of the King and Queen will take place on June 14.

"A festal illumination of Belgrade is projected for this evening."

The dispatch concludes with stating that intense joy prevails at Belgrade.

### Bodies Thrown Into Park

A later dispatch to the National Zeitung from Semlin corroborates other reports that the bodies of the King and Queen were thrown from their bedroom window into the park. King Alexander was shot through the neck at the first fire, and the rush of blood suffocated him. Queen Draga received several shots, and after she was dead the regicides slashed her body with their swords and thrust it through and through. The rugs in the royal chamber were soaked with blood, which flowed over the inlaid floor. The window hangings were torn down and trampled under foot, the windows broken, and the objects of art shattered in wanton destruction.

The murderers afterward embraced, congratulated one another on the success of the plot, and announced joyfully to those below that the King and Queen had been disposed of.

The residence of the Queen's brothers, near the palace, was nearly wrecked. When the brothers were lying dying from their shot wounds they kissed each other.

The Ministers who were killed met their death at their homes, and in some instances the attacks on them were made in the presence of the members of their families, who had run in. Thus the daughter of Police Minister M. Todorowitch was wounded. The Minister himself escaped with some wounds inflicted while he was trying to telephone to Police Headquarters for help. He did not get the connection, as the telephone exchange was occupied by troops.

### Seat for Austrian Troops

Count Marshal Nikoljevitch escaped from the royal palace and sought refuge in the Austrian Legation. The Austrian Minister, Herr Dumba, was thus the first diplomat to learn of the assassinations. He sent a boat across the river requesting the officer commanding at Semlin to send troops to protect the legation. While the officer was deliberating whether he ought to encroach on Servian territory the Minister sent another message withdrawing the request.

Shots were fired at the Russian Legation, but it was afterward explained that they were fired by mistake.

About 150 officers were in the plot, which was kept secret astonishingly well.

This afternoon the streets of Belgrade are fairly quiet. The soldiers in force are doing police duty.

Ljubomir Schiokovics, the new Minister of Justice, has made three speeches to the populace, arguing the necessity for the deed.

Bank Director Petrovitch, Queen Draga's brother-in-law, and one of the bitterest enemies of the King and Queen, will inherit her fortune.

VIENNA, June 11—Dispatches from Belgrade say that the revolution was planned weeks ago. Secret committees were organized in the country and worked in co-operation with the army. Leaders of the revolution are said to have been the new Ministers of Justice and Finance. The Sixth Regiment of Infantry, garrisoning Belgrade, was designated to carry out the plot.

It was originally intended that the plot should be executed later, but fears that the new Servian Parliament would settle the question of the succession to the throne hastened matters.

Col. Naumovics, the Adjutant of the King, was intrusted with the execution of the plans. While on duty at 11 o'clock last night Naumovics burst in the door leading to the sleeping apartments of the royal couple with a bomb, and then entered, accompanied by Col. Mischics and a number of junior officers. Previously the palace guard had been overpowered and its commander, Capt. Pauajowics, was killed.

Naumovics presented to the King a form of abdication for his signature. The document contained the statement that by marrying Queen Draga the King had degraded Servia and that therefore he must abdicate. The King's answer was to draw a revolver and kill Naumovics on the spot.

Mischics then picked up the document and presented it again, and the King, who perceived his danger, fled with Queen Draga to the palace roof, both being in their night clothes. The officers followed, continuously firing, and ultimately shot down the royal couple. Major Luka Lazarewics, who had been under the King's displeasure for two years, is said to have fired the shot which actually killed the King.

At about 2 o'clock this morning Queen Draga's two brothers were shot at their homes, as well as Premier Markovitch and his brother-in-law, M. Milkovitz; the Minister of the Interior, M. Tudorovics and his daughter, and the War Minister, Gen. Pavlovitch.

While these events were proceeding at the palace the streets of the city were already occupied by soldiers, and an armed force surrounded the royal residence. The horses and guns of the batteries of artillery were all decorated with evergreens, as for a festival. The soldiers discarded the badge of King Alexander from their helmets.

### Tried to Save the King

An attempt was made to support the Obrenovitch dynasty by the commander of the Danube Division, who tried to march the Eighth Regiment of Infantry into the city to help the late King, but he was opposed by a body of troops under Col. Gagowits. In the fight which ensued both the officers mentioned were killed.

What purports to be an official explanation of the tragedy was issued at Belgrade to-day. It says:

"After dinner on Wednesday evening the King and Queen, with some of their relatives and several Ministers, sat on the balcony of the palace. Suddenly the King demanded that Queen Draga leave the country. She refused and was supported by some of the Ministers. When the King saw this opposition he ordered the military to occupy the palace. In the meanwhile the Queen's friends were also active, and collected her supporters. It was in a fight between the two factions that the King and Queen were killed."

\*   \*   \*

June 12, 1903

## THE MASSACRE AT BELGRADE

It is natural enough that the historic town which was for generations the outpost of Christendom against the aggressions of the Turk, and which was possessed in turn by both parties to the great struggle of the sixteenth and seventeenth centuries, should exhibit the vices both of the Orient and of the Occident. The dynasty of which the unlamented Alexander was the last has continued to exhibit these, in the persons of its representatives, down to its extinction at the beginning of the twentieth century. Both the murdered ruler and his father have combined with every variety of black-guardism known to the most frivolous royalty of Western Europe what Carlyle calls a "Samoyedic savagery" from which Western Europe is exempt.

That the sordid farce which the Government of Servia under its late ruler had become should be concluded by a horrible tragedy was not unnatural, nor was it unexpected by those who were in the best position for forecasting the future. The unspeakable Milan was luckier than he deserved in being allowed to get out alive. His equally unspeakable successor has met a fate more consonant with poetical justice. A kingdom is in a bad way which, with about two-thirds of the population of Greater New York, keeps on foot and theoretically under pay an army of something over a hundred thousand in time of peace, an army more numerous than the pupils of the public schools, although education as well as military service is compulsory. From a human and domestic point of view the luxuriousness which characterized Alexander was almost a redeeming trait. But politically it was the worst of his faults and precipitated his ruin. Solemnly to proclaim a "Constitution" in obedience to popular clamor which you find irresistible, and, within two years, to proclaim the suspension of it for a few hours, while you rearrange the Government to suit yourself, afterward proclaiming again that it is in full force and effect—this is a series of procedures which would excite the scorn and wrath of the most patient tribe of slaves on the face of the earth. These proceedings were taken, it appears, at the instigation of the Queen, who has expiated her folly with her life. She had made herself odious to the Servian people by a course of nepotism as tactless as it was shameless, resulting in gross favoritism in every branch of the public service, and culminating in the attempt to have her brother declared heir to the throne. The Servians or any other people would have endured this sort of conduct much more patiently on the part of a hereditary monarch. The Servian dynasty has at least historic claims upon the Servian people, remounting, as it does, through five generations, and connected, as it is, with the proudest of the Servian traditions, the successful effort to throw off, after four centuries, the Turkish yoke. But the marriage of the King with Queen Draga was in itself such a misalliance as created a national scandal, and that the low-born Queen should have undertaken to exert an influence which would have been shameful on the part of a Queen born in the purple was more than the Servians could stand. They seem to have taken their revenge not only by murdering the offending woman, but by extirpating her whole race, and thus making sure that none of her plots for the benefit of her kindred could be successful.

While, as a human tragedy, the massacre is thus dreadfully complete, it remains to be seen whether it is to have any important political consequences. It is evidently true that the newly proclaimed sovereign is an admirer of Russia, and it will be apprehended in Vienna that his reign will show subjection to Russian influence. Almost by the nature of the case, the ruler of one of the Balkan States must take sides with one or the other of the great empires upon their frontiers. But while Prince Karageorgevitch is doubtless a partisan of Russia, it is only fair to say that there is no evidence that the massacre that has opened his way to the throne was directly or indirectly the result of "Russian intrigue." The misbehavior of the murdered King and Queen was quite sufficient to account for the angry and murderous revolt against them. Without doubt, Belgrade will continue to be the centre of active intrigues, Russian and anti-Russian, just as Sofia and Bucharest will continue to be like centres. That is the destiny of the capital of a Balkan State. Undoubtedly, also, the Russian intriguers will gain by the presence of the new monarch, while his term lasts. But it does not follow that Belgrade will be more of a storm centre than it has been, or that the change wrought by the assassins will put in greater jeopardy the peace of Europe. And that to dwellers outside the Balkan States is the chief consideration.

\* \* \*

June 12, 1903

## THE NEW KING OF SERVIA

### PRINCE PETER HAS LIVED IN GENEVA SINCE 1891

#### It is Said He Will Start for Belgrade To-day—Russian Money Used to Aid Him?

GENEVA, June 11—Prince Peter Karageorgevitch, whom the Servian Army has proclaimed King, has been living in Geneva since 1891. He appeared greatly astonished on receiving the news from Belgrade, which he said had reached him through a private telegram from Vienna. The Prince did not leave his house all day.

Over the telephone this afternoon the Prince said he had not yet received any official notice regarding the events in Belgrade. He did not even know whether it was true that he had been proclaimed King, and said he did not know when or whether he would start for Belgrade. The new Ministry, he added, included several of his adherents, but he was unable to speak definitely on this subject, as a number of names had been mutilated in telegraphic transmission.

Through the Russian Consul, an intimate friend of Prince Karageorgevitch, the following statement was obtained:

"Prince Karageorgevitch declares himself innocent of any knowledge of the tragedy at Belgrade. He says that through his grandfather he had undoubtedly the best right to the Servian throne and intended taking it, if possible, for the sake of his son, but he expected to meet with great difficulties and hoped for assistance from Austria."

From other sources it is learned that the Prince will leave secretly to-morrow morning for Vienna, whence he will proceed to Belgrade.

Rumors have been current here for three days of expected trouble in Servia, and Prince Karageorgevitch has been receiving an enormous quantity of telegrams for a week past, many of them from the frontier of Servia.

During his residence in Geneva, the Prince went freely into society. It has been a subject of general remark among the aristocracy and the people that he has looked extremely careworn for some months.

The Prince is a widower, aged fifty-three, and appears older. He is of medium height and build, and his face, distinguished by long military mustaches, is rather fierce. He has three children: George, his heir, sixteen years old; Alexander, fourteen years old, and Helene, aged nineteen years. He lives in an extremely simple manner, and occupies a whole house, an unusual thing in Geneva, in the Rue de la Bellotte. The house is elegantly furnished, though the Prince is not rich and keeps only a woman servant and a valet. He has several times proclaimed himself heir to the Servian throne, but has no entourage, and his poverty is known and the presence of a court would have excited suspicion.

Russian money was undoubtedly used in the revolution, which, according to general belief, was planned here. It is recalled that when the Austrian Empress was murdered by an Anarchist in this city in 1898. Prince Karageorgevitch openly applauded the deed. He is extremely popular here with all classes, and is described as unassuming, sensible, and strictly honest in all private and public transactions.

The Prince usually visited Vienna and St. Petersburg every year, but recently he has been several times to Vienna and has also visited St. Petersburg.

He is still considered to be a member of the Montenegrin royal family, into which he married.

PARIS, June 11—Prince Peter Karageorgevitch is well known here. He was a member of the fashionable diplomatic set of Paris, and included among his acquaintances a number of Americans. He is described as having an agreeable personality, has been a frequenter of the leading clubs and hotels, and was a well-known figure at races and sports. The Prince was educated at the St. Cyr Military College, and entered the French army in 1870, with the rank of Captain.

A brother, Prince Arsene, is now in Paris. He received a dispatch this morning advising him that Prince Peter had been proclaimed King. Prince Arsene said he would probably join his brother and take part in the events connected with his assuming the sovereignty of Servia.

A cousin of Prince Peter, Prince Bodijar Karageorgevitch, lives in the Avenue du Bois de Boulogne. He took part in the French campaign in Tongking, and was decorated with the cross of the Legion of Honor. In an interview to-day Prince Bodijar said his cousin, the new King, had long aspired to the Servian throne, and declared that the family was closely allied to Russia, thus assuring a pro-Russian policy in Servia.

Prince Bodijar does not mix up in politics. He is well known in artistic circles, and designs tasteful cabinets and articles of stamped leather. He told a Temps reporter he did not hesitate to declare that he considered Queen Draga to have been the cause of the assassinations. On becoming Queen she made herself first feared and then hated. She brutally revenged herself for the slightest offenses and pitilessly crushed high or low who had the misfortune to displease her. The late King was only a tool in the hands of this bold, domineering woman. He was so weak-minded that a doctor who examined him at Biarritz declared that if he had been a Frenchman he would have been declared intellectually unfit for military service.

Prince Bodijar added:

"The youthful sovereign was the victim of the merited unpopularity of his consort. He could not resist her. His culpable weakness destroyed him. Moreover, 'whoso draws the sword shall perish by the sword.' My family has been tried to the utmost. My grandfather was assassinated, and seventeen of my relatives have been executed without trial, while others were tortured. Such crimes must be expiated sooner or later."

Dr. Petrovitch of the Servian Legation described the new King as a student of affairs of state, as being intensely animated by Servia's political destinies, and as an admirer of Russia. The newly proclaimed King, Dr. Petrovitch added, was sending his son to St. Petersburg, where he would be educated at the expense of the Imperial Court of Russia. Politicians had frequently sought to induce the new King to attempt to take the throne of Servia, but he always replied that he would not permit a dynastic contest to provoke a civil convulsion and that he preferred to await the result of the popular weariness resulting from the old régime.

BERLIN, June 11—A dispatch to the Vossiche Zeitung from Dresden says Prince Peter Karageorgevitch has maintained close relations with Russia, but until recently lived near the Austrian Court. The seizure of the Servian throne had long been planned, and his plans were warmly supported by his elder brother, who lives in Paris as a newspaper writer and who has close relations with the French Republicans.

It is believed here that Prince Peter enjoys much greater sympathy with high Russian Government officials than did King Alexander.

ROME, June 11—The Karageorgevitch family is well known here. Prince Peter's son visited the Italian sovereigns last Summer.

Prince Karageorgevitch entertains great esteem and deference for the King of Italy, whom he visited two years ago on the occasion of the birth of Princess Yolanda. On that occasion, by the intermediation of King Victor Emmanuel, Prince Karageorgevitch met at the Quirinal and became reconciled to Prince Nicholas of Montenegro.

BOSTON, June 11—Prince Alexis, brother of the new King of Servia, was a visitor in Boston in the Spring and Summer of 1899.

For a time he was a guest at the residence of E. C. Swift of Beverly, near here, and during the season he was prominent in the social affairs of the Summer colony in that vicinity.

Special to The New York Times

MONTREAL, June 11—Nicolas de Struve, Russian Consul General here, is a personal friend of the new King of Servia. To-day he expressed the opinion that Peter Karageorgevitch would never have taken part in such a conspiracy, in the first place because he is not that sort of a character and again because he would be unwilling to cause complications for his father-in-law, the Prince of Montenegro.

It was at Cettinge, in Montenegro, that the Russian diplomat met the new King, and was impressed with his deep affection for his country. This feeling he voiced on all occasions while he regretted the turn of affairs at that time (1890).

*   *   *

**September 2, 1903**

## REVOLT IS PROCLAIMED

---

**Macedonian Insurgents Issue Their Long-Expected Document**

**TWO TURKISH MASSACRES**

**Entire Population of Armensi and Velesi Annihilated—Malkoternovo in a State of Anarchy**

---

SOFIA, Bulgaria, Sept. 1—The Macedonian revolutionaries awaited the anniversary of the Sultan's accession to announce the long anticipated general insurrection in Northern Macedonia, the proclamation of which was issued to-day, signed by all the members of the insurgent general staff. The new outbreak is headed by the famous Macedonian leaders, Gen. Zontcheff. President of the Macedonian Committee, and Col. Jankoff, who was wounded in the rising of 1902.

The new territory covers the district in the valley of the Struma, at the base of the Rhodope Mountain chain and to the north of the River Vardar. Col. Jankoff is directing the movements of the bands in the southern part.

News of severe fighting is still coming in. At the Village of Armensi, after a day's fighting, the Turkish troops in the night massacred the entire population of 180 men and 200 women. The Turks have also massacred the inhabitant of the Village of Velesi.

It is reported that Hilmi Pacha, the Inspector General for Macedonia, fears to leave his headquarters at Monastir. The insurgent leader, Grueff, in a letter to Hilmi Pacha demanded that he prevent the barbarous acts of the Turkish soldiers and Bashi-Bazouks, otherwise the revolutionaries would massacre all the Turkish inhabitants.

The insurgents have occupied the mountain pass of Gergele on the main line from Salonika to Uskub, and Turkish troops have been sent to dislodge them.

The town of Malkoternovo is reported to be in a state of anarchy, the Turks plundering the houses and committing unspeakable atrocities on the women.

A strong force of Turkish infantry, cavalry, and artillery recently attacked the village of Stoilovo, northward of Malkoternovo, which had been occupied by insurgents. The latter retired, after which the Turks entered the place, massacred the entire population, and destroyed the village.

Prince Ferdinand of Bulgaria has arrived at Euxinograde, Bulgaria, where he has been joined by Premier Petroff. The Prince is expected to remain there for some time.

*   *   *

**October 26, 1903**

## COMPLICATIONS OF THE BALKAN PROBLEM

---

**MANY WARRING ELEMENTS IN THE MACEDONIAN PROVINCES**

**Bulgarians Wonder If Russia Will Aid Them if They Fight Turkey and Are Defeated**

---

Foreign Correspondence The New York Times

SOFIA, Oct. 12—Sofia and its vicinity have been from the remotest times the stamping ground of various races. The Ugrish barbarians, the refined Greek merchants, the Roman soldiers, the Slavic peasants, heathens, Mohammedans, Christians, and Jews all passed in kaleidoscopic array within sight of the nearby Vitosh Mountain; all lived and struggled here, the new-comer usually doing his utmost to destroy, or at least to obliterate, that which his predecessor had built.

On one of the highest eminences in the city rise the lofty ruins of the Sophia Church, which was erected by the Christians some time in the twelfth century. Between 1382 and 1877, during the Turkish dominion over Bulgaria, Sophia Church was used in turn as a Mohammedan prayer house, a refuge for dervishes, and Turkish military barracks. As soon as the first liberating Russian column entered Sofia the cross, that had not been seen on the grand old edifice for five centuries, was again reared there. Across the street from the palace stands a Turkish mosque, which has recently been converted into a museum. Another mosque serves as a place of Christian worship, and a cross has usurped the place of the half moon on the dome.

In the yard of the museum are to be seen countless marbles, some of them beautifully worked, bearing Greek and Roman inscriptions. The lettering on most of the stones is so old and weather-beaten that one can scarcely decipher it; on a few of the stones, however, the texts are as legible as if the chisel of the Greek or Roman artisan had carved them out but yesterday. A few steps from the mosque, and apparently belonging to it, is a water fountain with fine lettering in Turkish. To the Romans Sofia was known as Serdica; the Greeks called it Triaditza; the Slavs corrupted the name to Sredec.

Always a babel of tongues in miniature, Sofia houses even now a most curious mixture of people. Bulgarians, Spanish Jews, Turks, gypsies, Rumuns, Greeks, Armenians, and Western Europeans elbow for room in its busy streets and market places. But whatever public improvements you see in Sofia, such as street paving, trolley cars, electric illumination, and gardens and baths, all are of recent origin; and whatever culture or commerce has taken root here is all due to the energy and enterprise of people other than the Turks. For, aside from temples to Allah, the Mohammedans built nothing, improved nothing. A low-roofed cottage with an entrance from the garden is pointed out as the place where the Russians made their headquarters while in Sofia. At that time it was looked upon as a very pretentious house. Now the streets of the Bulgarian capital are lined with mansions, some of which would be a credit to New York. The first census, taken in 1881, showed a population of 20,500; in 1888 it had increased to 30,428, and in 1893 to 45,639. According to the census of 1900, Sofia has 67,920 inhabitants.

Summoned to an independent existence at the cost of great sacrifices on the part of Russia, Bulgaria, ever since its liberation, in 1878, has given considerable worry to European Prime Ministers. The pen which entered Bulgaria on the list of nations had hardly time to dry when one day Europe was startled by the announcement that the Bulgars, by a bold coup d'état, had annexed East Roumelia to their principality. Soon thereafter Bulgarians plunged into a fourteen-day war with Servia—a war of Slavs with Slavs.

Again the Chancellories of Europe are compelled to keep an anxious vigil over the Bulgarian frontier. One million Macedonian Bulgars, who speak the same language, who profess the same faith and cherish the same racial traditions as their kinsmen in the principality, raise a cry for help. The cruel Turk murders their brothers and assaults their women, and the natural impulse is to free them or aid them in some way. Public opinion in Bulgaria is incensed. All feel that Turkey is either impotent or unwilling to stop the lawlessness prevailing in Macedonia. But how and whence shall help come? Will the powers be able to introduce order by peaceful methods? Or can war alone clear the perplexing situation? Should war come, however, is Bulgaria strong enough in men and resources to cope single-handed with the enemy? Twenty-seven years ago, when inaugurating their rebellion, the Bulgars were led to believe that the sick man at Constantinople would capitulate, as it were, on hearing the first cannon fired by the insurgents. In the City Museum in Sofia you can see a cannon bored from the trunk of a cherry tree—a sample of the armament with which the liberation of the fatherland was to be accomplished. Subsequently it required all the might of the great Slavonic empire on the north to release the sick man's grip on the throats of the Christian rebels. Bulgaria now has 3,750,000 people, but she had less at the time of the revolution, and it cost the bones of one Russian soldier to make fifteen Bulgarians free. It was only after the tremendous slaughter at Plevna, Grivnica, and Shipka that Bulgaria obtained her freedom.

The great question which agitates all Bulgaria now is: In case of a disaster, would Russia help? The masses of the people are openly pro-Russian, yet Prince Ferdinand's Ministry is not, and the White Czar, like everybody else, is not inclined to pay a premium on ingratitude. It is not so very long time ago that he announced plainly but firmly that while the Slavic States in the Balkans can always count on the powerful protection and cordial support of Russia in all their peaceful undertakings he will not sacrifice one Russian soldier's life in a war for Macedonia.

That the situation beyond the Bulgarian frontier is intolerable all sides admit. Even the Sultan does not deny it: only he blames the Bulgarian population in both Macedonia and the principality for the recrudescent agitations. Be that as it may so much is certain, that it will be a hard problem, indeed, to reconcile the many warring elements in Macedonia. Greeks, Servians, Bulgarians, Kutsoviachs, and Turks live there in considerable numbers, and every one of these races differing in origin and faith, claims to have distinct rights and grievances. The formula which Boris Sarafof, the leader of the rebels, borrowed from the Monroe Doctrine, "Macedonia for Macedonians," sounds very well in theory, Likewise attractive appears to be the programme formulated by Michailovsky, another of the leaders: "No aspiration toward union with Bulgaria; complete equality of rights of all inhabitants of Macedonia; political autonomy, with the eventual prospect of federation of all the Balkan States." The most difficult part of all will be for Sarafof to prove that his theory will stand a practical test; and for Prof. Michailovsky to convice the various races that he means what he says. The Turks, for example, and there are over 500,000 of them, have no wish to be classed as Macedonians, They are Mohammedans, first of all, and their country is where Islam reigns supreme. The Servians still dream of reviving Old Servia, and they fear that the autonomy proposed for Macedonia would establish a second Roumelia, with the same result after the Bulgarian administration had had time to absorb it. The Greeks also have their serious misgivings. They know that the Bulgarians, who have a majority in the province, would at once, as the dominant race, take a leading part in the administration of Macedonia depriving the Greeks of the influence which they now exercise everywhere, owing more to their superior energy than to mere numbers. Add to the racial controversy another element of discord, namely, religious differences, and you will appreciate how extremely intricate the problem is.

*T. C.*

\* \* \*

October 7, 1908

## AUSTRIA TAKES TWO PROVINCES

*Bosnia and Herzegovina Are Annexed and a Lliberal Constitution Granted*

**SERVIAN ARMY MOBILIZED**

*Leaders of All Parties Angered by Austria and War Talk Is Popular*

**CONFERENCE ON BULGARIA**

*Britain, France, and Russia Acting Together—Bulgarian Minister Explains the Declaration of Independence*

LONDON, Oct. 6—The second and culminating step in the Austro-Bulgarian programme for the aggrandizement of themselves at the expense of the sttatus established by the

Treaty of Berlin was consummated to-night when Emperor Francis Joseph formally proclaimed the practical annexation of Bosnia and Herzegovina to the dual monarchy, with a pledge of a Constitution guaranteeing civic rights and a representative assembly.

The present situation is as follows: Turkey calls upon the powers to preserve to her, what they guaranteed by that treaty. Austria and Bulgaria strongly declare their determination to keep what they have taken. Servia is protesting belligerently against being hemmed in more strongly between two unpopular neighbors and against having the Servians in Bosnia absorbed into the Austria-Hungarian nationality.

The other powers concerned in the Berlin Treaty are discussing the holding of an international conference. Turkey's unexpectedly restrained policy minimizes the possibilities of war, which now is considered out of the question.

A conference of the powers is expected to be held within two or three months if it can be arranged, but no one imagines that it will undo this week's work. Austria declines even to discuss the matter of its annexation of the provinces, and the most that is expected is some arrangement that will save Turkey's pride.

Before the powers agree to enter upon a conference, they probably will be obliged to define its scope, which will be a hard task. British statesmen suggest that compensation be made to Turkey, and that guarantees be given against further disturbance of the status quo. Sir Edward Grey, the Foreign Secretary, will address his constituents to-morrow evening, when it is expected he will explain the attitude of the British Government.

The English papers unite in praising Turkey's moderation and in denouncing Austria. The Standard, in a typical utterance says: "We are sorry for the aged Emperor. We regret that so late in his long and honorable career he had chosen to sully his name with a deed which will go down in history alongside of the partition of Poland."

Several of the London newspapers question whether or not Emperor Francis Joseph is acting against his will.

\* \* \*

**January 17, 1909**

FRANCIS JOSEPH BUYS TWO MORE ARTICLES FOR HIS "HAPPY FAMILY" CURIO CABINET

August 29, 1909

## NICHOLAS NOW A KING

*Montenegro Raised to a Kingdom with Much Ceremony*

Special Cable to The New York Times
Dispatch to The London Times

CETTINGE, Aug. 28—Montenegro today has made a kingdom and a King. Since early morning Cettinge has presented a wonderful spectacle, and the streets of the village capital, which are beautifully adorned with festoons, Venetian masts and banners, have been densely crowded with a picturesque throng.

At 5 o'clock this morning the church bells began pealing and military bands and trumpeters traversed the streets. At 6:30 the Skupshtina assembled in secret session and voted an address to Prince Nicholas, requesting him to assume the royal title. An hour later a Parliamentary deputation headed by the President entered the palace, bearing a document embodying the decision of the national representatives, to which the Prince appended his signature.

As soon as this solemn act was completed the Crown Prince appeared on a balcony of the palace and proclaimed the new kingdom to the assembled army and people.

"Montenegro," he said, "has become a kingdom and your Prince a King."

The announcement was received with loud cries of "Zivio!" which were renewed when King Nicholas, himself, wearing the national costume, stepped upon the balcony, accompanied by the Queen and all the attending royal personages, and acknowledged the salutations of the multitude. In a little while the royal couple left the palace on foot and proceeded to the adjoining monastery, the new King conducting his daughter, Queen Helena of Italy, and Victor Emmanuel of Italy conducting Queen Milena.

The ancient monastery at Cettinge embodies some of the noblest traditions of Montenegro's history. It was many times besieged by the Turks and once with all its precious documents and relics was blown up by the monks, who preferred death to surrender to their traditional Moslem foe. Here the Te Deum was celebrated and the allocution delivered by the Archbishop of Cettinge.

At the conclusion of the service a salute of 101 guns was fired.

Official receptions were held this afternoon, and to-night the town resounds with the strains of military bands and with the singing of national songs. Not only the streets but the neighboring heights are illuminated and bonfires are burning on all the mountains of Montenegro.

\*　\*　\*

October 3, 1909

## CONCERN OVER NEAR EAST

*Unrest in Greece and Ambition of Bulgaria Threaten European Peace*

PARIS, Sept. 24—There is a good deal of speculation in political circles as to the turn events may take in the East during the next few months. No definite answer has yet been given to the question whether the King of Greece may or may not abdicate. At the present moment the chances are believed to be rather against his retirement from the throne, but it is understood that much will depend upon circumstances, and that it will be impossible to form a decided opinion until the Hellenic Parliament assembles, which will be at the beginning of next month.

That the feelings of King George have been deeply wounded by the attitude of the army toward his sons is a well-known fact, and as this trouble has come after quite a series of other vexations, it is perfectly natural that he should have lost heart. That Greece would be the real sufferer if the King were to depart is a truth which is generally realized, and the recognition of it may yet induce him to stay.

At the same time the situation is even now unsatisfactory in other respects. I learn, for instance, that officers who declined to sign the memorial attesting their fidelity to King George are still stationed at out-of-the-way garrisons, and there is even a grim rumor that some of them have been shot. On the other hand, an unfortunate impression has been produced in the army by the refusal of the Crown Prince to receive the officers of one garrison who had asked to be presented to him, and this on the pretext that they had been disloyal. It is argued that, as a sponge was passed over that miserable affair, the Crown Prince might have been just if he could not be generous.

These and other episodes seem to be keeping the sore open, and there are experienced authorities who doubt whether the King will be able to tolerate much longer a situation which has become extremely galling to him.

Other questions connected with the Balkans still command attention, and chief among them is the course which Czar Ferdinand may elect to adopt. The Bulgarian army contains 330,000 highly trained troops, and in the opinion of competent judges, will never be fitter for a campaign, and may deteriorate as time rolls on. Twice already has it been on the point of trying conclusions with Turkey in the last twelve months. The first was when the independence of the country was proclaimed at the beginning of last October, and there is also no doubt that if the Salonica army had not promptly repressed the military mutiny at Constantinople Bulgarian troops would have poured into Macedonia.

Czar Ferdinand is believed to be still biding his time, ready to take advantage of any fresh weakness that Turkey may display, but if he does not perceive any new opportunity in that direction he is equally prepared to invade Servia and to wrest from that little kingdom a goodly portion of its territory.

There are some who imagine that the fate of Servia is at the present moment trembling in the balance, and who are inclined to regard an alliance between Bulgaria and Austria for Servia's partition as being quite within the limits of future possibilities. At any rate it appears to be patent enough to close observers on the spot that according to circumstances Bulgaria will make an incursion into either Macedonia or Servia at no distant date, with or without support, as her sovereign has no idea of allowing the splendid force at his disposal to rust, and is, moreover, as need scarcely be added, extremely ambitious.

It is said, too, that the Austrians have of late been devoting particular attention to the study of the country in Albania, so that if they were to send an army into it they would be well acquainted with the terrain. This is a fact, although there has otherwise been nothing in their attitude to lead to the suspicion that they may contemplate any special activity in that quarter. So this may, perhaps, be set down as a simple measure of precaution.

There is, however, no doubt that, what with the unsettled state of politics in Greece, and the temptation, which is likely to prove irresistible, to launch the Bulgarian army on a career of conquest, there are sufficient elements to cause apprehension as to the maintenance of peace in the Balkans without reference to other troublesome matters such as the Cretan question, the still unsettled condition of the Turkish Empire, and the future of Macedonia and Albania.

Lastly, with regard to Roumania, there is no speculation here, as she made no sign whatever during the acute crisis in the Balkans, and seems perfectly content with the development of her own resources, while as for her agreement with Austria and Germany it is no news for those politicians who were well aware that for years she had had an understanding with those powers, a result of her dissatisfaction at the manner in which Russia repaid her for her valuable aid during the great war with Turkey in the seventies.

\* \* \*

**October 30, 1909**

## GREEKS BATTLE NEAR ATHENS

*Salamis, Where Xerxes Was Crushed, Sees Fight of Ironclads and Torpedo Boats*

**THE REBELS BEATEN OFF**

*Two of the Three Torpedo Boats of Naval Mutineers Under Tibaldos Escape*

**FLEET NOW GUARDS ATHENS**

*Tibaldos Had Seized Arsenal After Failing to Get Army League to Back Him for Marine Minister*

Special Cable to The New York Times
Dispatch to The London Times
ATHENS, Oct. 29—Athens was startled at 4:35 o'clock this afternoon by the sound of a vigorous bombardment, which lasted about a quarter of an hour and then ceased completely. I learn from a good source that Lieut. Tibaldos, leader of the naval mutineers, who quitted the capital on Wednesday and who to-day seized the Marine Arsenal at Leros on famous "sea born Salamis," attacked three ironclads with a flotilla of torpedo boat destroyers, that the attack failed and that one of the destroyers has been badly damaged by a shell and driven ashore.

The destroyers after the engagement withdrew into the harbor at Salamis, according to the information received to-night at the Ministry of Marine.

The casualties of the loyal fleet in to-day's engagement were two men wounded. The losses of the mutineers are not known, but of their three destroyers one was disabled and another took to flight in the direction of Eleusis and disappeared in the darkness. The third succeeded in reaching the Poros naval station, where, however, it met a hostile reception and was compelled to put to sea again.

The loyal fleet is cruising off the Piraeus to-night in order to prevent any attempt at landing or any attack on the town, and also with the object of closing the Straits of Salamis. No torpedoes were discharged during the fight.

### Eye Witness Describes Battle

ATHENS, Oct. 29—After almost 2,000 years from the unforgotten time when Themistocles gained his victory over the Persians, the sea beside the Island of Salamis, was again to-day the scene of a naval battle. From scaramanga on the Attic boat opposite Leros the correspondent saw twenty minutes of fighting this afternoon between field batteries and big warships on the one side and on the other the torpedo boats of the mutinous band of naval officers which quitted the capital Wednesday and to-day took possession of the arsenal on Salamis. The first shots were fired soon after 4 o'clock, and a sharp exchange of shell followed. Some of the projectiles struck the Arsenal Buildings, but the correspondent saw only one shell hit a torpedo boat— the Sphendona—which immediately was enveloped in a cloud of smoke.

During the action the torpedo boats gradually retired, steaming backward until they obtained the shelter of the headland, when the firing ceased. The rebel flotilla, while the engagement was in progress, returned the fire of the warships and field batteries, but apparently little damage was done on either side. The mutineers were led by Lieut. Tibaldos, and are reported to have numbered 300 men.

Athens remains superficially quiet tonight, but there is much excitement. An official statement has been issued stating that the arsenal, which was in the hands of the rebels, has been recaptured, and that the mutinous torpedo boats are expected to surrender.

At midnight the troops still occupied the shores opposite the arsenal and were under orders to fire upon any of the mutineers who attempted a landing. The palace and Parliament Building also are strongly guarded by troops, and throughout the evening soldiers were passing and repassing through the streets of the city. Meetings of politicians were held at the residences of all the party leaders.

Further news of the mutinous torpedo boats is still lacking.

### Leading Officer Arrested

A newspaper prints the report of the arrest of a prominent officer, who, however, is not Lieut. Tibaldos. Further reinforcements have been summoned from the provinces to the capital.

The general opinion is that the Military League has suffered a great loss in prestige by reason of to-day's events and may be compeled to proclaim a dictatorship. Ex-Premier Rallis in an interview to-night predicted that the upshot of the crisis would be the overthrow of the Government and the entrance of the Military League into office. This development, he thought, would not affect the position of King George.

Lieut. Tibaldos appears to have been actuated by his disapproval of the tactics of the Military League and the junior naval officers in consenting to negotiate a compromise in the matter of the ultimatum recently issued by the Military League demanding the enactment of an ordinance suspending all promotions for five years and the abolition of the posts of Rear Admiral, Vice Admiral, and fifteen places of lesser rank. Tibaldos took a prominent part in the military movement last August. He was the first officer to go to the camp at Goudi, outside the city, after the Premier's refusal to receive a deputation of officers, and he was subsequently appointed commander of the rebel camp.

### Tibaldos Disowned by League

At a meeting of the military league yesterday Tibaldos said:

"I led the last revolt, and without me it would have failed. Now you abandon me, but I will carry out a second revolt single-handed."

The military league's proclamation disowning Tibaldos, who was in command of a flotilla of torpedo boats and sub-marines and demanded the portfolio of Minister of Marine for himself, ascribes his pretensions to madness and the influence of outsiders, and threatens to have him court-martialed for treason. The league held a meeting late to-night to discuss what its attitude should be toward the naval officers who took part in to-day's fight. It is believed that the league is inclined to show them indulgence.

Meanwhile the position of the mutinous torpedo boats resembles that of the Russian battleship Kniaz Potemkine, which mutinied in 1905 and fired on Odessa and then roamed the Black Sea for several weeks, and the Government is apprehensive as to where it may next hear of them. It is rumored that they have gone toward the Island of Crete.

In the Chamber of Deputies this afternoon Premier Mavromichalis, after detailing the events of the day, said the Government was determined to suppress the outbreak by force. Happily the movement was very limited. The Ministers, he said, were occupied in reforms in all branches of the administration, and would not neglect the navy. Therefore, the officers' impatience was unjustified. The Premier added,

however, that if the naval officers had been led astray they still had time to rehabilitate themselves.

### Story of the Mutiny

The following shows how the revolt had its origin: The Government, in response to the demands of the naval officers for the suspension of promotion for five years and the abolition of certain high naval posts, had consented to introduce a navy purification bill, but it insisted that the bill must be absolutely impersonal, and declared that it would flatly reject any proposals aimed at individual officers. The Military League accepted this solution of the problem, but Lieut. Tibaldos spurned it as inadequate, and secretly convened a meeting of naval officers, all of whom signed a document laying down their minimum demands.

This document Lieut. Tibaldos presented Thursday night to Col. Tsorbas, head of the Military League, and at the same time appealed to the league to make him Minister of Marine. Col. Tsorbas declined to entertain the proposals, and an angry scene ensued, Lieut. Tibaldos retiring from the scene to prepare for the revolt which followed to-day, and Col. Tsorbas to inform Premier Mavromichalis.

The Government, however, displayed curious hesitation. It took no steps to arrest Lieut. Tibaldos and permitted him partly to carry out his plans before any measures in opposition were taken. Even this morning, in order to prevent the shedding of blood, the Government dispatched a friendly officer to endeavor to dissuade Tibaldos from his wild design.

The troops that had been sent to occupy coast points were able to prevent a number of Tibaldos comrades from joining him, and as he had but few officers to man his torpedo boats he commandeered the loyal fleet for his attack. It was not a very serious affair.

Vice Admiral Buduris, who had command of the arsenal, was without means of defense and was compelled to surrender when Lieut. Tibaldos threatened to employ forces.

### The Cause of the Mutiny

The ultimate cause of the naval revolt in Greece is to be found, probably, in the recent failure of the Greek cause in Crete when the powers, upon Turkey's protest, removed the Hellenic flag which had been hoisted at Canea. For this failure to secure Crete for Greece the blame was popularly laid to governmental inefficiency, and as a result several weeks ago two battalions of troops at Athens mutinied. Retiring to the suburbs, they demanded the surrender of the high places held in the army by Crown Prince Constantine, Commander in Chief of the Greek Army; Prince Andrew a Captain of cavalry, and Prince Christopher, a sub-Lieutenant in the infantry.

The cause of the malcontents was espoused by the Military League, which on Oct. 15 forced the Chamber of Deputies to vote a measure abolishing the right of the Crown Prince to hold the post of Commander in Chief and of the other Princes to hold military commands. King George earlier in the day having persuaded his sons, the Princes Constantine, George, Nicholas, and Christopher, to resign their commissions. Before the passage of the military bills in the Chamber of Deputies thirty royalist members showed their disapproval by withdrawing from the Chamber. These loyalists insisted that the Military League was determined to force the King to abdicate.

To some observers it seemed that the crisis had been postponed by the retirement of the Princes, but to all it was evident that it was likely to grow acute again if the Cretans returned deputies to the Chamber at the next election.

Meanwhile the military league, not satisfied with the humiliation of the royal family, on last Wednesday issued an ultimatum demanding the enactment within twenty-four hours of an ordinance suspending all promotion for five years, the abolition of the post of Rear Admiral, heretofore held by Prince George, together with two Vice Admiralships and fifteen positions of lesser rank. The Premier offered a compromise in the form of a bill altering the age limit for super-annuation from 65 years to 58 years. This was not satisfactory to the league, and on Wednesday night thirty naval officers retired to the Island of Salamis, upon which is situated the arsenal which today these officers seized, and where, previous to the engagement between the fleet and their torpedo boats, they in-trenched themselves.

As every schoolboy used to know in a more classical age, the island off the coast of Attica in the Aegean Sea owes its chief celebrity to the decisive victory achieved there in 480 B. C. in the strait between the long northeastern promontory and the coast of Attica by the Athenian fleet under Themistocles and Eurybiades against the much larger Persian fleet of the great King Xerxes, then upon his invasion of Greece. The small Athenian fleet was about to withdraw to the isthmus, when Themistocles persuaded Xerxes to blockade the straits at night, and in the morning to enter them for battle. The superior numbers of the Persian vessels and their huge bulk only hampered them in the narrow waters, and the Persian defeat was complete and overwhelming, checking for all time the advance upon Greece.

Salamis is within ten miles of Athens itself, lying to the west, and the bombardment yesterday suggested a possible repetition of what happened when in 1687 the city was captured from the Turks by the Venetians after a siege during which a bomb partly destroyed the Parthenon, which had been used by the Turks as a powder magazine. The ruins of that noble pile and others which crown the Acropolis seemed almost within reach of more hostile shells.

\*　\*　\*

November 14, 1909

# GREEK ARMY REVOLT AIMED AT GRAFTERS

### *Military League is Supported by the People in Fighting Corrupt Politicians*

### NO MOVE AGAINST THRONE

### *King George Realizes Need of Administrative Reforms and Has Shown Disposition to Work with Leaders*

ATHENS, Nov. 3—Recent events in Greece, though seeming natural to those acquainted with conditions, both political and social, among the Greek people, have startled the outside world to such an extent as to result in the publication of the most extraordinary stories in the columns of the European press, some wrongly condemning what is considered in Greece a national movement of restoration.

It is known, of course, that in August last a military movement broke out in Athens resulting in the resignation of the Rallis Ministry and the appointment of a Cabinet in favor of radical reforms, under the Presidency of M. Mavromichalis. It is known also that in September an imposing mass meeting, numbering 100,000 persons, urged the King to accept a programme of general reforms in spite of any opposition from the Greek Parliament. As to the last rebellious outbreak in the navy, it needs little consideration. These are the facts, but they have been insufficiently explained.

The military movement of August last, when it took place, had the misfortune of being explained by the majority of the European press as an ordinary mutiny due to the professional ambitions of certain officers of the Greek army and navy. This was not the true character of the movement. The aim of the Greek officers was higher and more unselfish. Greece, like every country which has passed from an extremely despotic regime to an extremely liberal government, has suffered, and still suffers, from the despotism of political parties and politicians.

In the first days of liberty, after the struggle of 1821–1829, Greece was subject to the rule of a Greek statesman, born in Corfu, but naturalized in Russia, where he occupied for many years a high position in the Imperial administration. This man, Kapodistria by name, was appointed by the protecting powers Governor of independent Greece, and, in accordance with his education, his ideas, and even his tastes, he thought the Greek people, before attaining a thoroughly liberal government, should receive a political education. The idea was not unreasonable, but Kapodistria wanted to enforce it by means of a foreign power. He was assassinated by Greek liberals.

Prince Otto of Bavaria followed him as the first King of Greece. Otto was an admirer of his adopted country, and cherished its ideals as much as any Greek. His political programme was internally a strong administration patterned after that of Bavaria, and internationally a vigorous policy in accordance with the aspirations of his people. In order to succeed on both lines Otto declared himself a partisan of the gradual emancipation of his people. He had studied the Greek character, and he was one of the first to foresee the disastrous influence of corrupt politicians on the future of the country.

The revolution of Sept. 12, 1843, obliged him to give a Constitution to his people. The politicians then took their revenge by forcing him to quit the soil of Greece. His abdication, however, was largely due to foreign influence, as Europe never ceased to consider his reign a danger to peace in the Near East. With a people dreaming of the old glories of the Byzantine Empire and with a King indorsing the policy of its restoration, Europe had good reason to fear for the integrity of the Turkish Empire, on which rests the solution of the Eastern question, so complicated and so dangerous at the same time.

Prince George of Denmark was elected King of Greece in succession to Otto. The powers protecting Greece—the kingdom has never ceased to have protectors—sanctioned his choice, and George I. became King of the Hellenes. The great powers, to demonstrate their good-will toward Greece, bestowed on King George the amount of a loan which the country owed them, the Government of Great Britain offering as a gift the Ionian Islands. In exchange for these favors, King George, according to the belief of a large class in Greece, repudiated any idea of a further expansion of his kingdom at the expense of the Ottoman Empire.

King George, well aware of the fate of his predecessors, took the easiest way to success by adopting the harmless policy "To reign, not to rule." For a period of forty-six years King George never took an active part in national affairs. He left the most liberal constitution in the hands of a young and inexperienced people as one might leave a razor in the hands of a baby. The result was as disastrous. The liberal constitution, instead of giving the country a good administration, gave it all kinds of politicians. The King instead of becoming involved in political intrigues, devoted himself to financial enterprises, making huge profits in stocks on the Paris, London, and New York Exchanges. His vacation trips to Aix-les-Bains and Paris for a long period of years furnished rich material to the European satirical press.

King George, however, never ceased to show his eagerness in supporting before the Courts of Europe the claims of his people. He belongs to the illustrious royal family of Denmark. His sister is Queen of England. Another sister was Empress of Russia. One of his nephews is Emperor of Russia, another King of Norway, and his brother is King of Denmark. The German Emperor, who gave his sister in marriage to the Crown Prince of Greece, is also connected with King George. In such circumstances the King of the Hellenes might well enjoy for forty-five years the confidence of the Greek people in matters concerning the national Interests of Greece. So all his vacations assumed the aspect of national and political missions of the highest importance, and every act of his in the various Courts of Europe was watched from his kingdom as bearing on it the realization of many a national dream.

Were the Greek people wrong in so doing? No, but the Government and the politicians were. All of them were clever and educated persons, most of whom had spent years studying politics in Europe, all of them knew what the King was doing,

whether in Paris or Aix-les-Bains, but they were too much bent on their personal interests to disillusionize the people.

The Cretan question arose early in 1866, again in 1868, and again in 1896. Greece, yielding to the national impulse, took an active part in the last revolt, occupying the island with its army. The Graeco-Turkish war followed. Although disastrous for Greece, this effort brought Crete its independence, but, on the other hand, it established in the kingdom the International Financial Commission, a foreign body charged with the supervision of the country's finances, dangerously affected by the $20,000,000 indemnity which Greece paid to Turkey after the war.

Immediately after the disaster Greece thought it necessary to reorganize the army and navy. The Ministers introduced many bills intended to reform the existing system. Some of them were good, but to make them effective too much money was needed. Some others were good, but affected the political interests of parties and organized grafters. The net result was that twelve years after the war Greece had accomplished little that it had intended to.

The Tukish revolution of July, 1908, came unexpectedly. As unexpectedly came the Bulgarian declaration of independence and the annexation of Bosnia and Herzegovina by Austria in October of the same year. At the same time Crete, until then an autonomous State under the High Commissionership of M. Alexander Zalmis, a deputy of the Greek Parliament, declared its union with Greece. It was in the hands of the Greek Government to accept the declaration of the Cretan people, but at the same time Turkey threatened to cross the Greek frontier with 200,000 troops. War was imminent and conditions in Greece were bad. The Greek Government did not accept the declaration of the Cretans.

The King then proposed to settle the matter through his relations with the courts of Europe. He came back to Athens full of hope in November, 1908, promising to have the union of Crete with Greece accomplished before Spring. But Spring came and went, and Summer brought a bitter disappointment to the Greek people.

In July last the Government was upset. M. Rallis succeeded M. Theotokis. A few days after its accession to power the Rallis Ministry received a deputation of officers of the army and navy. This deputation presented to the Prime Minister a memorandum including a full programme of reform in the army and navy, as well as in State affairs. M. Rallis refused to accept the memorandum, and ordered the arrest of the officers comprising the deputation. On the following day broke in Athens the military revolution which forced the Rallis Ministry out of office. The King summoned M. Mavromichalis, who formed a Cabinet and accepted the programme of the officers. Those who know little of the military movement have attributed to it an anti-dynastic character, but those who have studied conditions in Greece during the last twelve years following the Graeco-Turkish war considered the military outbreak of August last merely an armed protest of the nation against the schemes of the politicians who have ruined Greece.

This is the true character of the army movement, which has developed almost into a dictatorship. The enormous mass meetings held simultaneously in the Greek capital and in the provinces in September showed that the whole nation supported the efforts of the army in its fight against the corrupt system prevailing. The Greek nation sees no danger in the army. It has confidence in its officers. Their protest is the expression of the national protest. Their claims and their programme are the claims and the programme of the nation. Nor does the nation blame the crown for the neglects of the past, inasmuch as King George was the first to bow to the dictates of the army.

Thus originated the national movement in the army. The principal difficulty consisted in giving to its programme of general reform the form of constitutional legislation. For this purpose the Chamber was summoned in special session, but even then the military party had good reason to fear the opposition of the political parties to the programme of reform, involving many radical modifications in every branch of administration, and, therefore, affecting the most essential interests of the various politicians and grafters. The military league, insisting on its programme, decided to have it voted by the Chamber by any means, even by force.

From another point of view this action of the army was necessary. The new Cabinet possessed no majority in the Parliament, and its programme, without outside influence, was very likely to be defeated. The military league, therefore, gave the Government its full support. Parliament, from the first day of the session, found itself under the absolute power of the army. The Ministry offered its programme and presented the necessary bills, asking the vote of the national representative body. Some of the members objected to certain features of the new programme, but the military league intervened and ordered that no discussion and no objection be allowed. The bills abolishing the privileges of the royal Princes in the army and navy passed almost without discussion, as did the ensuing military, financial, educational, and administrative reforms. Not a voice was raised in protest or even in discussion. Maxim's silencer could not have been more effective.

The Greek Nation approved, and still approves the acts of the Military League. In thus humiliating their Parliamentary representatives the people took revenge for the humiliations suffered on account of their past misdeeds. The idea of a military dictatorship in place of political oppression is more popular and more in conformity with the wishes of the Greek Nation, because it means the elimination of the grafters and corrupt politicians responsible for the weakness and misery of the country.

King George is well aware of this popular sentiment. He is willing to work in favor of the reforms with his army officers and their ministry. If there are rumors of his abdication they should be attributed solely to the powerless political gang, which silenced both in Parliament and the local press, tries now to turn the world's public opinion against the military movement, which proved so disastrous to its individual and personal interests. The dismissal of the Royal Princes from their posts in the army may be counted against the military movement; there was a bit too much zeal on the part of the officers. But this has nothing to do with any rumor of the possible abdication of the King. There is no anti-dynastic sentiment in Greece.

The latest naval revolt in Salamis was of little importance. It was a movement due to the excitement of a party of young naval officers, led by an ambitious Lieutenant, who considered himself able enough to be supreme chief of the navy. The fact that the Government adopted the sane part of the claims of the mutinous naval officers is proof of the fact that there is no opposition to any honest effort for real reform.

\* \* \*

October 9, 1910

## BALKAN ALLIANCES

### Greece and Bulgaria Against Turkey and Roumania

ATHENS, Sept. 25—Although the work of the National Assembly is proceeding slowly and by no means tranquilly, it becomes more and more evident that anti-Turkish feeling predominates and that the leading statesmen of all the principal parties are looking forward to an alliance with Bulgaria, that ancient enemy of Greece, as a war measure.

In these circumstances the news that the Government of Constantinople and Bucharest had signed a treaty for cooperative military action in the Balkans serves only to hasten the project for a Graeco-Bulgar alliance.

The common belief that the treaty does not tend toward peace may be explained as follows: The situation in the Balkans, though unrestful, does not call for any special military agreement. Even the military convention which some time ago was said to have been signed between Greece and Bulgaria did not place Turkey in a grave danger. The new treaty between Turkey and Roumania may be said to be an answer to such a convention, whether it existed or is in prospective. But so far from balancing the Graeco-Bulgarian combination, it makes the equilibrium still more uncertain.

Therefore, in itself it is held that the treaty provides a danger, and the aims of the signatory powers, if they can be explained at all, point to a similar fear. Not being called for by the existing situation, it is agreed that the treaty is aimed against some power or powers, and there is not much hesitation in designating the quarter that it is aimed against. Bulgaria is the power aimed at, and there are fears that the agreement will also affect other nations with whom Turkey has direct contact—namely, Great Britain in Cyprus and in Egypt, and Russia in the Black Sea and in the Caucasus.

The arrangement meets so entirely with the only half-hidden desires of German and Austro-Hungarian newspapers that there is but slight hesitation here to couple it with Hakki Pasha's last visit to Count von Aehrenthal at Marienbad.

Austro-Hungarian policy, moreover, has persistently been directed toward turning Roumanian attention away from the Carpathians. By encouraging it against Bulgaria this idea is given effect. Similarly, and at the same time, the menace to Bulgaria is an indirect setback to Russia.

Recognizing, in consequence, that the treaty is partly if not wholly due to the policy of Count von Aehrenthal, it is asked what assurance he can have given to Turkey to persuade her to fall in with his plans. They perhaps concern Greece quite as much as Russia.

\* \* \*

**April 4, 1912**

## LOSE CROATIA CONSTITUTION

### *Drastic Action Follows an Election That Favors Secession*

VIENNA, April 3—Telegrams from Ogram, capital of Croatia, announce that owing to the elections to the Landtag or Diet, which resulted in an overwhelming majority in favor of the severance of Croatia from Hungary, absolute government has been proclaimed there.

The constitution has been suspended and all authority is vested in a royal commission.

Croatia and Slavonia have an area of 16,423 square miles and a population of about 2,500,000, about one-seventh of the population of Hungary proper. It has had an autonomous provincial government, consisting of three departments, with a ban who is responsible to the provincial Diet of 90 members and the Hungarian Prime Minister.

\* \* \*

**September 4, 1912**

## BULGARIANS WANT TO FIGHT

### *If the Powers Do Not Aid Macedonia War with Turkey is Likely*

Special Cable to The New York Times
LONDON, Wednesday, Sept. 4—A telegram to The Daily Mail from Sofia says:

"Unless the powers succeed without delay in securing self-administration for Macedonia, even the present Bulgarian Government will become convinced of the necessity for war with Turkey. The Cabinet, its supporters, and a few Socialists are the only people opposed to an immediate campaign.

"Autonomy is the one form of government possible in Macedonia. Turkey will concede autonomy only under compulsion. Either the powers must exert that compulsion or Bulgaria must be allowed to exert it.

"This presents the true attitude of Bulgaria at the present moment."

The Times's Vienna correspondent says: "A note, not indeed of alarm, but of disquietude, continues to be struck by all trustworthy reports on the Balkan outlook. Bellicose agitation in Bulgaria persists and is causing some doubt whether the Cabinet will be able indefinitely to resist it.

"The Bulgarian desire that some guarantee be established for the better treatment of the Macedonian Christians is insistent. As is natural, it is believed to find a sympathetic echo in Russia, however much the Russian Government may urge upon Bulgaria the expediency of keeping the peace."

The Times prints a dispatch from a correspondent who visited Berano, a village a few miles from the Montenegro border, the scene of recent Turkish atrocities.

"Djavid Pasha told me," says the correspondent, "that now, as always, the Turkish Government acts with justice and goodness, that peace reigns everywhere, and that no Moslems are permitted to possess weapons.

"I next heard from Christians piteous tales of suffering and barbarism. Three unarmed men were dragged from a house and shot without trial by Nizams, who then sacked the Christian quarter. A woman of 70 was beaten with rifles and shut, bleeding, in a filthy outbuilding.

"Many villages were completely annihilated, and even orchards were burned up. Very many people are destitute. The whole appears to be a violent attempt to exterminate the Christian population. A state of siege has been proclaimed.

"One wounded woman in the hospital says the Nizams ordered her to leave her home and fired at her as she was running out. Seventeen women and children were butchered."

\* \* \*

**October 9, 1912**

## WAR DECLARED;
## BATTLE RAGING IN THE BALKANS

### *Montenegrins Attack Berani, Turkey—Said to Have Been Defeated Elsewhere*

### A MASSACRE IN BULGARIA

### *Mob Kills Nearly All the Turks in Turtukai—Not Even Women and Children Spared*

### KING NICHOLAS WITH ARMY

### *People of Skutari Hail Him as Their Ruler and Ask Him to Take the City*

### TO EXTEND WAR TO-MORROW

### *Belief That the Other Balkan States Will Then Join Montenegro in Attacking Turkey*

Special Cable to The New York Times
LONDON, Wednesday, Oct. 9—G. Ward Price, The Daily Mail's special correspondent at Constantinople, telegraphs:

"The report of a Montenegrin attack on Berani, Albania, is confirmed. The town has been the centre of a brisk engagement since last (Monday) night.

"A report is current that Servian troops have crossed the frontier near Samdos, but this is entirely without confirmation at the Porte.

"The Ministers of the Balkan States are hourly expecting instructions from their Governments ordering them to leave.

"Montenegro's precipitation of the long-awaited Balkan conflict by her sudden declaration of war has destroyed all the faint hopes of peace which had been reviving here as a result of the action of the powers.

"A declaration of solidarity with Montenegro from the other three States is expected hourly, or even the opening of hostilities without a declaration of war.

"At last Turkey stands at bay, fighting the long-delayed fight which will settle whether she is to retain the last traces of her once mighty position in Europe.

### Relentless War Expected

"It will be one of the most relentless campaigns in history. The war spirit of the Turkish people is worked up to fight desperately in defense of their territory from joint attack by neighboring States. In no crisis in the recent chaotic history of Turkey has her position, not only without her gates but also within, been so marked by grave possibilities, and, above and beyond all, is the grim fact that the scourge of war may only too easily spread to the rest of Europe.

"A council of war has been sitting all day at the Porte. Mahmud Shefket, the ex-War Minister, was called in as an adviser.

"The fall in Turkish funds on the Exchange has been very heavy.

"The spirit of war fills the excited streets, which are thronged with marching columns of soldiers, from whose cartridge belts peep bright nickel bullets, which in a week will probably be singing through the air in the deadly earnest of battle.

"It is debated here whether Montenegro's declaration of war was intended to precipitate a general conflict by making it incumbent on the rest of the Balkan Confederation to support their city. The promised reforms in Macedonia would, it is needles to say, not affect Montenegro's own grievances against the Porte.

"The Government has countermanded the contracts for barley for the army made last week. On the other hand, all the trains in Turkey in Europe, even those of the Constantinople suburban service, have been suspended in order to facilitate military transport. Horses are still being commandeered. Troops and mounted batteries, fully supplied with ball ammunition, march constantly through the streets to the station."

The Daily Telegraph's Belgrade correspondent says:

"King Nicholas of Montenegro today (Tuesday) arrived at the army headquarters at Podgoritza. The inhabitants of Skutari, who at once proclaimed Nicholas their King, begged his Majesty to occupy the town.

"In Belgrade a lady named Jubitza Yovanovitch, aged 22, entered the army as a volunteer. She had cut off her hair and dressed as a man. She threatened to commit suicide if she were not allowed to serve. She is an excellent shot."

### Balkan States' Solidarity

The Daily Mail's Belgrade correspondent wires:

"The Parliaments of the Balkan States have exchanged cordial telegrams containing assurances of their mutual solidarity.

"The advance of the Turkish army seems to be the immediate reason for the declaration of war by the Montenegrins, who wish to prevent Turkey from occupying a strategical position near the Montenegrin frontier.

"The news of the declaration of war was received here with unexpected calm.

"The enrolling of volunteers has been stopped. Instead of the required 300,000 men, 400,000 responded to the mobilization summons, and for the third line, for which 30,000 are required, there were 80,000 applicants. It is now only with the utmost difficulty that any one can join the colors. Applications from foreign volunteers are being refused.

"News has reached the Servian Government that the Turkish authorities are distributing arms to every one without distinction, even to criminals."

### Bulgarians Massacre Turks

The Daily Mail's Vienna correspondent quotes the following dispatch from Oltenitza, Roumania, to the Neues Wiener Tagblatt:

"A massacre occurred yesterday (Monday) at Turtukai, Bulgaria, near the Roumanian frontier.

"Egged on by agitators from Rustchuk, armed Bulgarians attacked the Turkish inhabitants at the dead of night, pillaged their houses, and started appalling slaughter, even women and children being sacrificed.

"The Turkish quarter presents an awful spectacle to-day. Piles of corpses are lining the streets. Only a few Turks succeeded in escaping to Oltenitza, which is just across the Roumanian border. A witness of the massacre states that Bulgarian police participated in the slaughter and pillage."

The Daily Mail's correspondent adds:

"The action of Montenegro in declaring war has completely nonpulsed diplomatic circles in Vienna. It is asked whether the rupture of negotiations between Montenegro and Turkey is an individual move on the part of the Montenegrins, and therefore to be interpreted as a mark of dissension in the Balkan league, or whether Montenegro is acting in accordance with a plan previously made by the Balkan States.

"I have also found a disposition in some quarters to believe that the Montenegrin action is intended to bring pressure to bear on the powers and to force on their attention the urgent need of the introduction of reforms in the Turkish European provinces.

"The semi-official Allgemeine Zeitung says that Montenegro's action appears the more inexplicable inasmuch as she is very dependent on Russia financially and otherwise, and it is difficult to understand how Montenegro could act against the intentions of M. Sazonoff in so striking a fashion.

"The same journal says it learns that the alliance between the Balkan States is only a defensive one, and, therefore, as Montenegro has taken the offensive, the other three States are not obliged to go to her help or support her by breaking off diplomatic relations with Turkey themselves."

### "The Chances All for War"

Bennet Burleigh, the well-known war correspondent, wires to The Daily Telegraph from Sofia:

"The greater powers may arrange to keep the ring, but the Balkan peoples, with bitter memories in their minds and accumulated sorrows in their hearts, persist in declaring for war. The Balkans are resolved at all costs henceforth to be absolutely free from Turkish control direct or indirect.

"The foregoing may be accepted as true of public opinion and partly true of official opinion. The chances are all for war within ten days. There will be no retreat.

"Let me emphasize that Europe in general overestimates the military power in action of the Turks. For defense they are excellent. For attack they are faulty and weak.

"Nor have you known or counted the strength and character of the allied forces—the Bulgars, Serbs, Greeks, and Montenegrins. Bulgaria puts over 300,000 men into the field—60,000 more than was estimated; Servia has over 300,000, also an increase of strength, while Greece and Montenegro have larger numbers than was expected."

M. H. Donohoe, The Daily Chronicle's correspondent in Constantinople, says:

"I was at the Sublime Porte in the morning when the Montenegrin Minister left, having had a final interview with the Foreign Minister. He had presented an ultimatum to Turkey on behalf of King Nicholas and had demanded his passports.

"The storm is expected now to break in all its fury. Greece, Servia and Bulgaria are expected to follow the example of Montenegro at any moment, and war on all hands will follow as a matter of course.

"The Montenegrin Minister walked from the Sublime Porte down the steps leading to the courtyard with bowed head and the air of a man who had taken a momentous, history-making decision.

"Outside the Sublime Porte a very large crowd had assembled anxious for news of any developments. The Montenegrin Minister was recognized by the populace and there were attempts at manifestations of the ill-feeling which is entertained against all four of the States ranged against Turkey. A rush was made toward the Minister, but the police on duty were too quick for the people, and his Excellency was able to pass through the excited crowd without molestation."

### London is Pessimistic

Though in some quarters the hope is still expressed that Montenegro's declaration of war against Turkey may be an independent move and that the extension of hostilities to Bulgaria, Servia, and Greece may yet be prevented, the prevalent opinion in London is pessimistic.

No official information has reached here as to the exact relations of the four countries, but The Times's correspondent at Sofia, who is particularly well acquainted with Balkan affairs, states that the Balkan League ought to be called a Quadruple Entente rather than a Quadruple Alliance, as Montenegro is not bound by any definite engagement toward the other States. From this it is deduced that the other States in the league are not bound by any formal engagement to follow the example set by Montenegro. There is considered to be little chance, however, that Bulgaria and Servia will not do so.

The Times thinks it likely that the Montenegrin move was part of a concerted plan. The other Balkan States, which have no plausible pretext for declaring war at this moment, may have feared that they might, before such a pretext could be provided by the presentation and rejection of their demands be entangled in protracted negotiations with the powers concerning the extent of the projected reforms and the nature of the guarantees for their execution. If such negotiations were once begun it might be difficult to prevent them from dragging on indefinitely, and the States may have wished to confront the powers with an accomplished fact and to hurry on a conflict.

Montenegro was already engaged in difficult negotiations with the Porte arising out of the frontier disputes and incidents. She had some sort of pretext for declaring war and her geographical situation made it comparatively safe for her to do so. It may also have been hoped that, by taking the offensive before the others she might draw away part of the Turkish forces from the main theatre of war and disorganize the war plans of the Turkish staff. The comparatively easy mobilization of her peasant soldiery made it possible for her to strike more quickly than her allies.

Mobilization in Montenegro, as a military correspondent points out, consists in doling out cartridges from magazines, for every man has always with him his rifle and equipment. It had always been supposed that the whole available fighting strength of the country could be collected in six days, and the declaration of war coincides with the date when readiness to act was to be assumed.

Far-reaching operations by the mountaineers cannot be anticipated. Skutari is their probable objective, but a good deal will depend upon the attitude of the Albanians. It is doubtful whether the Turks will waste their strength upon an invasion of Montenegro. It would be necessary to employ not fewer than 100,000 men and to use a system of converging columns, whose operations would be exceedingly arduous and would require time.

Such strategy would scarcely be permissible until the Servian army was struck down, and in a Macedonian campaign it would be the Servian army that must primarily be dealt with. Assuming that the other Balkan allies will follow the example of Montenegro when they are ready, the Turkish operations against the little State will probably be defensive, and should not require the services of more than 30,000 Turks.

By Marconi Transatlantic Wireless Telegraph to
The New York Times

BERLIN, Oct. 8—The visit to Berlin of M. Sazonoff, the Russian Foreign Minister, who has now departed after conferences lasting sixteen hours with Russian, German, Italian, Bulgarian, and Greek diplomats, has been completely overshadowed by the announcement that Montenegro has declared war on Turkey.

M. Sazonoff declined to receive foreign correspondents, who besieged him in force, asking for interviews, but in a statement made to the editor of the National Zeitung, who is a personal friend, M. Sazonoff, it is said, "gave the impression of bitter anger when apprized of Montenegro's action."

M. Sazonoff is reported to have said:

"If there is nothing else to be done, the powers will quietly observe developments. As the localization of the war is absolutely decided upon, a final settlement between the belligerents cannot in any event be made without the approval and co-operation of the powers, who are in a position to give effect to their agreements.

"I have told representatives of the Balkan States with whom I have spoken that the whole situation is a simple matter of arithmetic, Now that the powers are agreed, there may be no alteration of the territorial status quo. The States themselves can make the calculation—on the one side is the cost of mobilization, on the other side the cost and risk of war. The result will be the same in both cases—reforms in Macedonia, to which Turkey has already given us her assent.

"The Balkan States know that even in case of victory they have no hope of territorial gains. Turkey, of course, has also no such hope. If, in these circumstances, they still care to go to war, it is their affair and their responsibility."

VIENNA, Oct. 8—War declarations by Bulgaria and Servia are expected to-morrow, according to authoritative diplomatic information.

Roumania is reported to have ordered from the Creusot Works in France 150 mountain guns, for delivery in a week.

### Montenegro's Declaration

CONSTANTINOPLE, Oct. 8—The Montenegrin Charge d'Affaires, M. Plamenatz, today asked for his passports from the Turkish Government, and to-night left Constantinople.

Russia has assumed charge of Montenegrin Interests in Turkey.

The Bulgarian, Servian, and Greek Ministers are arranging to depart on Thursday.

Prior to receiving his passports M. Plamenatz handed the following note on behalf of his Government to the Porte:

I regret that Montenegro has exhausted without avail all amicable means of settling the numerous misunderstandings and conflicts which have constantly arisen with the Ottoman Empire.

With the authorization of King Nicholas, I have the honor to inform you that from today the Government of Montenegro ceases all relations with the Ottoman Empire, leaving it to the arms of the Montenegrins to obtain recognition of their rights and the rights, which have been ignored for centuries, of their brothers in the Ottoman Empire.

I am leaving Constantinople.

The Royal Government will hand his passports to the Ottoman representative at Cettinje.

PLAMENATZ

An official dispatch from the Montenegrin frontier says that Montenegrins yesterday attacked the blockhouse at Kalava, but were repulsed with heavy losses. Fifteen Turks were wounded.

The same day a large detachment of the Montenegrin Army crossed the northern frontier and attacked Berani. A battle ensued, which, according to the latest reports, still continues.

It is also reported that the Turks surrounded and annihilated one body of Montenegrin soldiers.

Skirmishes are reported on the Servian frontier and with Greek bands in the neighborhood of Dhisikata.

An exchange of shots has occurred near Djamabala on the Bulgarian frontier.

M. Plamenatz received instructions on Sunday to declare war to-day which, according to the Russian calendar, is the birthday of the King of Montenegro.

The opinion is deepening here that Montenegro was used as a cat's paw by the other Balkan States in order to forestall European intervention and to confront the Powers with a fait accompli. It is believed that the representations of the Powers to Bulgaria, Servia, and Greece, will now receive the reply: "It is too late: we must go to the succor of our ally."

Turkish troops have been placed on board all the Greek vessels in Turkish waters, which have been seized by the Ottoman Government. The Greek Legation here has ordered the masters of the vessels to land the crews.

The publication of news concerning the mobilization of the army and military movements as well as attacks on the internal and external policy of the Government are prohibited. A ban has also been placed on the carrying of arms. Martial law has been proclaimed here.

The Minister of War, in bidding farewell to officers proceeding to the front, is quoted as saying: "Dear comrades, don't forget to take your gala uniforms with you, as they will be useful on parade in Sofia."

### King Nicholas with His Army

CETTINJE, Oct. 8—King Nicholas, with his second son, Prince Mirko, left the capital at noon to-day for the army headquarters at Podgoritza, to the accompaniment of guns thundering, bells pealing, and crowds cheering.

The Ministers of the allied Balkan States saw the King off.

Before his departure the King received the Russian and Austrian Ministers, who jointly made a last effort for the maintenance of peace.

SOFIA, Oct. 8—The Austrian and Russian Ministers made joint representations to the Bulgarian Government on behalf of the powers at noon to-day.

BELGRADE, Oct. 8—The Austrian and Russian Ministers called at the Foreign Office this afternoon and made representations on behalf of the powers. The Premier and the Foreign Minister received them in a friendly spirit, but gave no reply.

Reports reached here to-day that Montenegrin troops had crossed the Turkish frontier.

The Servian Parliament to-day voted an extra credit of $8,900,000 for military purposes, while the merchants of this city are making large donations to the funds that are being raised for the assistance of poor families whose breadwinners have been called out for military service.

Three hundred beds, with seven doctors and forty-five nurses, sent here by the Russian Red Cross Society, arrived today.

ATHENS, Oct. 8—Gen. Ricciotti Garibaldi, who fought for Greece against Turkey in 1897, has again offered his services to the Hellenic Government.

### General Conflagration Expected

PARIS, Oct. 8—A general conflagration in the Balkans is expected by officials here within forty-eight hours.

Montenegro's move is considered in Paris to be part of a prearranged plan. It is asserted that Greece was first selected by the Balkan confederation to force the issue and inaugurate the war. This could easily have been done by Greece seating in the Greek Parliament the Deputies from Crete, which would be certain to prove a casus belli to Turkey. Greece, however, declined to accept responsibility for starting the flame of battle.

Montenegro was then picked for the task. She had a long-standing quarrel with Turkey over the boundary question, and Turkey's refusal to grant satisfaction was seized upon as justification for Montenegro's resort to arms. A well-known diplomat said to-night.

"It looks as if our fine European diplomacy had been beaten by the cleverness of the Balkan States. These States have grown weary of Ottoman promises. Turkey's recent decision to inaugurate reforms was considered unsatisfactory, and the slowness and hesitancy of certain powers to join in urgent intervention led the Balkan peoples to feel that the battlefield was the only sure means of exacting what they felt to be justice."

Despite the Russians' sympathy for their Slav brethren of the Balkans, whose political welfare Russia has fostered, no complications are anticipated between Russia and Austria, and both these nations have assured the other powers of their determination not to be drawn into any Balkan imbroglio.

Official circles in France greatly regret the criticism of certain French newspapers that Great Britain's slowness in agreeing to the phraseology of the powers' note embarrassed and retarded the representations. This criticism, it is averred, does not represent the official French view. It is pointed out that such criticism is liable to cause a false impression abroad, and that it has furnished ammunition for an attack by the German press on Great Britain.

The real story of how the Balkan Powers forestalled and outwitted European intervention is told in official advices from Cettinje. The Austrian and Russian representatives presented the note in the name of the Powers, warning the Balkan States against war, at 11 o'clock in the morning; but two and a half hours earlier the Montenegrin Government had handed his passports to the Ottoman Charge. Thus the Montenegrin Cabinet was in a position to say that the representations of the Powers came too late, a rupture of diplomatic relations having already taken place. The note was as follows:

The Governments of Russia and Austria declare to the Balkan States:

First—That the powers energetically reprove any measure susceptible of causing a rupture of the peace

Second—That, leaning on Article XXIII, of the Treaty of Berlin, they 'will take in hand in the interest of the Balkan peoples the realization of reforms in the administration of European Turkey, it being understood that these reforms shall not affect the sovereignty of the Sultan or the territorial integrity of the Ottoman Empire. The powers reserve to themselves liberty of action for a collective ulterior study of these reforms.

Third—That if, nevertheless, war breaks out between the Balkan States and the Ottoman Empire, they will permit at the end of the conflict no modification of the territorial status quo in European Turkey.

The powers will make collectively to the Sublime Porte representations similar to the above declaration.

In declining to concur in the views of the two powers, the Montenegrin Government declared that its patience was exhausted. For over two months it had been protesting in vain to Turkey, and resort to arms was the logical sequence. Even if Montenegro stood alone, it was added she was unable to act differently.

### Loan Refused to Bulgaria

The Bulgarian Government was not discouraged by the recent refusal of France to grant a loan, for she has again applied for financial help, and has asked a Parisian bank to advance $1,000,000. The bank in question immediately informed Finance Minister Klotz, who conferred with Premier Poincare, with the result that Bulgaria did not get the money.

Belgrade has been placed in a state of siege according to a dispatch from Nish, Servia, to La Liberia. All the trains running through Servia except the Orient Express have been held up at Belgrade. The Orient Express itself has been requisitioned as a military train. Its speed has been reduced by the authorities to six miles an hour. All the railroad tracks are guarded by aged peasants armed with rifles. None but women and sick men are now left in the villages.

LONDON, Wednesday, Oct. 9—A brigade of nine battalions of Turkish infantry proceeding from Skutari to Tusi on the Montenegrin frontier was attacked on Monday evening by a large force of Mallisori tribesmen just before reaching Tusi. The battle continued throughout the night and fighting, according to a dispatch received here, was still proceeding yesterday.

Dispatches from Constantinople say that military patrols are going round the city requisitioning all the horses. The military authorities have placed troops on board the large number of Greek vessels which were seized in Turkish waters, and it is understood that these are to be used for the transport of troops.

### PANIC NOT NOW FEARED
#### Effect of War on European Bourses Apparently Discounted

LONDON, Wednesday, Oct. 9—The Times, in an article discussing the effect of the Balkan situation on the Stock Exchange account, which ends to-day, says:

"London has for a long time held few foreign bonds that would be affected directly by war in the Balkans or even over a wider area in Europe. Turkish, Egyptian, Austrian, Hungarian, Russian, Bulgarian, Servian, and Greek securities are held chiefly abroad.

"London, however, is considerably interested in a number of important inter-Bourse securities, such as Rio Tinto, Peruvian Corporation, Shell Transport, leading South African gold shares, and De Beers and other diamond shares, all of which were more or less unfavorably affected by the heavy fall in Paris yesterday week.

"French holders of Russian industrial shares and other securities which are difficult to sell when market conditions are bad were free sellers of Rio Tinto and also to a less extent, of other shares which enjoy an international market in order to provide funds to meet leases on their other holdings. Since the heavy break a week ago, with its accompanying liquidation, the position has become safer. The securities sold from Paris were well taken here, and it may be assumed that Paris is now in better condition for receiving bad news.

"As regards Berlin, its sales of Canadian Pacific and several American railroad shares were largely met by purchases on New York account. The measures taken by the Reichsbank and the leaders of the Berlin money market to reduce the volume of speculation in order that Sept. 30 might pass off without serious trouble appear to have been almost too effective, for it is evident that there must have been quite a large total of bull accounts open in several departments at the end of last month in Berlin, and it is probable that this was so because operators felt satisfied that there would be no money squeeze owing to the arrangements made by the banking authorities.

"Moreover, there were no bear positions, and but for the fact that London and New York, especially the latter, were ready to buy what was offered, the results in the German capital would have been much worse than they actually were.

"Since that fateful Tuesday both Paris and Berlin have been in a sounder position than they were before, but they have displayed considerable uneasiness. Small rises in prices brought in prompt sales, and any buying has been of a very cautious character.

"In London visible results of a fear of war which had such a serious effect on the two leading Continental Bourses have not been considerable except in the foreign market, where the stocks of countries which will be actually engaged in war with Turkey unless diplomacy averts the catastrophe have given way considerably, Bulgarians falling 3, while Turkish bonds dropped from 1 to 3 points. Some Russian issues have also given way, and Hungarian, German, French and Spanish securities are also lower. These movements were in consequence of the receipt of lower prices from the Continent, the dealings here being few in all of them, but the effect of their fall has been to weaken prices generally here, partly by the market's sympathy but also by creating a feeling that as the Continent took a gloomy view of the situation, this was no time to indulge in operations for a rise.

"American securities show small irregular changes, with Atchison, Milwaukee and Reading rather higher."

### PEACE WITH ITALY
#### Turkey Instructs Her Delegates to Sign the Preliminaries

CONSTANTINOPLE, Oct. 8—The Council of Ministers has designated Rechad Pasha and Assim Bey to sign the peace preliminaries with Italy.

\* \* \*

**October 10, 1912**

## THE BALKAN "WAR"

Prince Nicholas of Montenegro seems to be playing the part of "an old man in a hurry"—a rôle for which he has shown no bent in the past. Naturally the query arises: Is he serving the interests of his son-in-law, the King of Italy, and pricking the sides of the Turks, who are a little slow in coming to terms on Tripoli? In any case he has injected a new element of complexity into a situation already very mixed.

There are, however, two general facts that stand out fairly clear in this situation. One is that the Powers of Europe are formally agreed that no more territory shall at present be taken from Turkey, and have so notified the Governments both of Turkey and of the four States—Bulgaria, Servia, Montenegro, and Greece. The other is that these four Governments are united in demanding reforms in European Turkey, especially in Macedonia, Albania, and Crete, amounting to practical autonomy, under a Christian Governor General. If the Powers are sincere, and if they can maintain united action, it would be reasonable to infer that the integrity of Turkey would, in form, be observed, and that substantial reforms—if not autonomy, a long step in that direction—would be the outcome. Nor would the hasty action of Montenegro, even if it were followed by a war between the confederation and Turkey, necessarily prevent this outcome. If in the war either side should gain a decided success—a result probable for Turkey alone—or if it should prove a drawn game, the Powers could still intervene, whenever they could agree to do so, and dictate terms.

The difficulty is in the agreement. It is now thirty-four years since the Powers met in conference and tried to fix upon a policy which they would enforce in the Near East. In the interval nearly every important provision of that policy has been violated. Eastern Roumelia has been added to Bulgaria and Bulgaria has become independent. Bosnia and Herzegovina have been annexed by Austria-Hungary. Nearly one-fourth of the European territory embraced within the sovereignty or the suzerainty of the Sultan has been lopped off by his powerful neighbors, or with their connivance. At no one of the crises leading to this series of losses have the Powers which framed the Treaty of Berlin been able to unite in enforcing it. They now face a new and formidable attack on Turkey. What reason is there to suppose that they can shape its ultimate outcome? Not, we fear, very much.

Bulgaria has invoked the Twenty-third Article of the Treaty of Berlin, and it is on that basis that the note of the Powers rests. What does this article require or permit? Very little. The Sublime Porte engages to apply to Crete, with some changes, a plan ten years old at the time, and never acted on. "Analogous regulations, adapted to local requirements," are to be "introduced into other parts of Turkey in Europe." Before any of these plans are promulgated the "Sublime Porte shall take the advice of the European Commission appointed for Eastern Roumelia." It all reads like very ancient history. The commission whose "advice" is the only means of controlling Turkish action went out of existence years ago. If the Powers are really to influence the course of Turkey it must be on grounds not connected with the Treaty of Berlin, on grounds of actual duty or interest. The chances that they will do so are not good. Undoubtedly they will localize whatever war takes place, if they can. If they succeed they will, at the proper time, interpose and secure from Turkey new promises of reform. Whether these promises will be any better kept than those made from time to time in the last forty years is extremely doubtful. The real interest of the Powers, the only thing they care very much about, the thing that is most needful to them until their plans develop elsewhere, is to maintain the statu quo in the Near East. To secure this they are likely, for the present, to take the promises Turkey is ready to make and not trouble themselves needlessly with enforcing their performance.

\* \* \*

October 14, 1912

## BALKAN STATES GIVE SULTAN ULTIMATUM

*Uncompromising Demand for Reforms Voiced by Bulgaria for the Allies*

**POWERS ALSO REBUFFED**

*Reply Milder Than Expected, but Servia Rejects Proposals— Montenegrins Capture Town*

Special Cable to The New York Times

LONDON, Monday, Oct. 14—Bulgaria preserved a note to Turkey last night and a separate note to Austria and Russia in behalf of the 'Balkan States.'

While the declaration is described in some quarters as an ultimatum, no time limit is imposed for the reply from Turkey, and in some quarters there is a disposition to think this not only leaves the door still open for peace but also that it is an indication that the Balkan league is far from being so ready to proceed to the last extremity of war as has been generally supposed.

An eminent financier expressed the opinion yesterday that Bulgaria had been bluffing but at the same time it was stated that the bluff had been carried so as that it would be difficult to close the game without bloodshed.

According to a dispatch to The Times from Sofia the note presented to Turkey says that notwithstanding the promise of the great powers to take in hand the realization of reforms in European Turkey the Governments of the allied States feel bound to address themselves directly to the Sublime Porte and declare that only radical reforms, sincerely and integrally applied, can improve the miserable condition of the Christian population of European Turkey, guarantee order and tranquillity in that country, and assure durable peace between Turkey and the Balkan States.

The three States regretting that Montenegro cannot join them owing to recent events invite Turkey to apply the reforms indicated in Article XXIII of the Berlin treaty, on the basis of the principle of nationality, with administrative autonomy of the provinces, Belgian or Swiss Governors, elective Assemblies, their own gendarmerie and militia, and free education, the reforms to be applied by a council composed of an equal number of Christians and Moslems, under the superintendency of the Ambassadors of the powers and the Ministers of the four States in Constantinople.

The note finally demands an undertaking on the part of the Porte to execute the reforms within six months and to recall the order for mobilization.

With reference to Bulgaria's answer to Austria and Russia, who acted for the powers, the Sofia correspondent says:

"In it the three Governments express their gratitude at the interest shown by the great powers in the condition of the populations of European Turkey and takes cognizance of their promise to undertake the realization of the reforms in administration on the basis of Article XXIII of the Berlin treaty.

"After so many promises made by Turkey and recorded in international documents, it would be cruel to these populations not to endeavor to obtain more radical and definite reforms in order to ameliorate their condition.

"Three States, therefore, have addressed themselves directly to Turkey, indicating the general nature of these reforms and the necessary guarantees for their application. Should the Turkish Government act as proposed, order and tranquility will be established in the Ottoman dominions and durable peace will be assured between Turkey and the Balkan States, toward which Turkey has so often assumed an arbitrary and provocative attitude."

The Times commenting on these notes, takes a pessimistic view of the situation and declares there is no chance that the Porte will grant these concessions and war may be expected at any moment.

A dispatch to The Daily Mail from Podgoritza, Montenegro, says:

"No permits have been issued to leave Podgoritza for the front, the order of the Minister of War being that until the revolutionary fighting is over and the regular plan of campaign is entered upon no war correspondents or military attaches may witness the operations.

" 'The Minister of the Interior kindly received me and explained the general outline of this plan.

"The Montenegrin forces are split up into three armies,' he said—'one, consisting of three columns, which is now surrounding seventeen battalions of Turks at Tushi; another army is moving on Scutari, on the west side of Lake Scutari and a third is lying near by. The three columns will move on Scutari, on the east side of the lake, supported in the rear by some of the troops from Berane.' "

### Trying to Halt Panic

A Paris dispatch to the Times says:

"Strenuous efforts, which are vigorously seconded by the well informed press, are being directed to calming the excited state of European feeling and the alarm which was reflected at the close of the week on the European Boursen.

"Simultaneous endeavors at Vienna and Berlin in the same directions show that grave as the situation and its prospective consequences must appear, there has undoubtedly been some exaggeration with regard to the danger of immediate dissensions among certain great powers.

"As one of the ablest and best informed of the French writers points out to-night, the real danger from the point of view of European peace in the larger sense will arise, not during the impending Balkan war but at the conclusion of peace when the war is over."

The Daily Telegraph's Vienna correspondent reports that the Queen of Roumania ("Carmen Sylva") has sent this telegram to Baron Destournelles de Constant, who in a vehement letter attacked King Nicholas of Montenegro:

"The entire moral and fair-minded world will envy you the virile courage, of which you have given such a brilliant example in your admirably written letter. I congratulate you on this proof of loftiness of soul."

LONDON, Monday, Oct, 14—Imminence of war in the Balkans is increasingly indicated by all the advices from the Near East capitals.

In accordance with agreement, Servia, Bulgaria, and Greece have drafted replies to the powers' note. Bulgaria's reply, handed to the diplomatic representatives in Sofia last night, is said to be moderate in tone, and asks an explanation of a certain clause in the communication.

Servia's reply, however, which will be delivered at the various capitals to-day with that of her allies, is a refusal to accept the powers' suggestions or intervention, while simultaneously a demand for Macedonian autonomy will be presented to Turkey.

The latter demand will be made the ultimatum of the Balkan league. According to a dispatch from Rome, the States, will make such a demand as it will be impossible for the Porte to accept, namely, that the reforms in Macedonia be executed under the supervision of the European powers and the Balkan States, and that the Porte as a pledge of good faith assent to the immediate demobilization of the Turkish forces.

It is understood that the Porte will have only until Tuesday to make answer to this demand, and there is every expectation that it will be followed by immediate hostilities.

The movement of the Bulgarian army began yesterday, according to a Sofia dispatch for The Daily Telegraph, trains proceeding toward the frontier every two hours.

It is reported that Christian soldiers have deserted the Turkish army in a body and that large numbers are arriving at Sofia. The Servian troops, says the same dispatch, are now in position and will move next week.

The hitch in the negotiations between Italy and Turkey, the Constantinople correspondent of The Telegraph asserts, is not serious, and a peace settlement is believed to be imminent.

The noted Macedonian leader, Todor Lazaroff, committed suicide Friday, says a Sofia dispatch to the Chronicle, because the military doctors refused to enroll him in the army because he has tuberculosis. He left a letter, saying that he could not remain behind to die in bed, while his brothers were fighting for liberty. The incident has acted as a spur to patriotism.

An official account of the operations on the Montenegrin frontier, reaching The Daily Telegraph by way of Constantinople, says the Montenegins massacred every man, woman and child in the villages around Akova. After severe fighting the Turks recaptured Akova and drove the enemy back in disorder. They also captured Mojkovac, a village on the border.

The Montenegrin offensive campaign, says the dispatch, may already be considered at an end.

\*   \*   \*

**October 18, 1912**

# BALKAN NATIONS PROCLAIM WAR; FIGHTING BEGUN

*A Million Men Under Arms in Five Nations—Three Kings at the Front*

### GREEK BOATS PASS FORTS

*Break Blockade in Gulf of Arta—Turkish and Greek Outposts on the Frontier Clash*

### SERVIANS CLAIM A VICTORY

*Report in Vienna That Montenegrins Have Been Routed— Movements on Bulgarian Frontier Hidden*

### BANK RATES ALL GOING UP

*Bank of England and Bank of France Take Action—German and Austrian Banks to Follow*

Special Cables to The New York Times

PARIS, Friday, Oct. 18—The Matin publishes an Athens telegram, dispatched at 1 o'clock this morning, stating that the Greek Government has ordered the Greek Minister at Constantinople to deliver this morning a declaration of war against Turkey.

LONDON, Friday, Oct. 18—Turkey's declaration of war against Bulgaria and Servia was speedily followed by the proclamation of hostilities by King Peter, while King Ferdinand has also declared war and has left Sofia to join the headquarters of his army.

Turkey refrained from declaring war on Greece, who, it was hoped at the Sublime Porte, might, even at the last moment, dissociate herself from nationalities with which she had no common racial, religious, or economic ties. Turkish hopes in this particular were belied, for Greece has opened hostilities.

Thus five States are at war, three Kings at the front, and a million men in arms. The greatest conflict that Europe has known since the Franco-Prussian war has opened under conditions which make the struggle likely to be one of the blood-thirstiest and bitterest in modern history.

The area of conflict is enormous. Fighting is already in progress on four frontiers. There was a tendency to believe that so far in the fighting on the Montenegrin frontier the Turks had not displayed the qualities with which in past wars they had showed themselves endowed, particularly in stubborn defense behind intrenchments, and the Montenegrins' capture of Berana was hailed as a great feat of arms.

Last night, however, a Vienna dispatch stated that a report had just been received there that the Montenegrins had suffered a decisive defeat near Podgoritza, by Essad Pasha's division, reinforced by several thousand Mohammedan Albanians. The Montenegrin advance on Scutari is thus declared to be checked.

Operations in that district in any case are of relatively little importance. Scutari is only worth winning for prestige. Its strategical value as a factor in an advance on Uskub is small.

That the Montenegrins allowed the defenders of Berana to escape means that its capture was more spectacular than useful, militarily speaking.

### Big Battles Expected Soon

On the other frontiers hostilities as yet are of no great military importance. Turkish regulars and Albanians crossed the Servian frontier at Prepolats, but, allowing for the usual process of exaggeration at Belgrade, the encounter which followed was of little consequence.

On the Greek frontier mobilization is well advanced, and Capt. Butler, a British army officer acting as The Daily Mail's correspondent with the Greek forces, telegraphs from Larissa that the Greeks, fighting in the region where they were so easily defeated by the Turks in 1897, are likely to give a much better account of themselves now.

From Bulgaria no news beyond reports of continued concentration of troops is yet to hand. It cannot now be long before big battalions come into contact. A military writer in The Daily Mail says:

"To Greece and Servia will fall the artistry of the campaign, to Bulgaria the bludgeon work, and, were history to recall from the shadows her masters for every post in the field, she would place this morning Napoleon himself at Nish, having under him Leo at Vrania and Nogi at Mustapha-Pasha, while Wellington, at first at Salonika, would handle Murat and Craufurd at Uskub, Massena at Monastir, and, in his own Adrianople, Osman Pasha."

### War Forced on Us, Says Sultan

The Daily Mail's correspondent at Constantinople has been received in audience by the Sultan, who said he had heard from Kiam Pasha that public sympathy in England was on the Turkish side in the war adding:

"I greatly appreciate the good wishes of the people, and thank them from my heart. War has been forced upon us. Turkey would never have attacked if she had been left at peace. We have grasped the sword solely to defend our territory and our just rights."

A telegram from Belgrade says that before leaving that city for the military headquarters, King Ferdinand signed a declaration of war, which will be read by the monarch himself in the presence of the troops at Starazagora, who will be blessed by ecclesiastical dignitaries and sprinkled with holy water.

BELGRADE, Oct. 17—War against Turkey was formally declared to-night by the Servian Government. The declaration was transmitted to the Servian Minister at Constantinople this afternoon, with instructions to present it to the Porte to-morrow. The Minister will then leave Turkey immediately for Belgrade.

The great powers will also receive notification to-morrow of Servia's declaration.

Immense crowds paraded the streets, singing and cheering after the announcement of Servia's determination to fight. The crowds are increasing hourly, and an enthusiastic war spirit prevails.

Two hundred Aritaut tribesmen were killed this morning in a battle with Servian troops on the frontier near Priepoll in the northern part of the Sanjak of Novi-Bazar. The tribesmen attacked and were repulsed by the Servians.

King Peter left here to-day for Nish.

### King Ferdinand Joining His Army

SOFIA, Oct. 17—King Ferdinand is on his way to the headquarters of the Bulgarian Army near the Turkish frontier.

The King's manifesto to the people proclaiming war will be published to-morrow. A special service will be held in the Cathedral, at which the Archbishop will invoke a blessing on the holy war on which the country is embarking. Similar services will be held throughout the country.

Premier Guechoff issued a statement to-day on the attitude of Turkey, saying:

"With pride which ill accords with the miserable role she plays in the European concert Turkey has just declared that the identical note of the three Balkan States does not merit an answer."

The Premier characterizes this as comical in view of Lord Salisbury's definition of Turkey at the Berlin Conference as "a power dependent upon the protection of others for its existence," and adds:

"Turkey also accuses the Balkan States of being lacking in difference to the great powers. It is ridiculous that a Government which, since the Crimean war, has done nothing but trample under foot its pledges to the great powers upon whose protection it depends, should accuse us of failure to show respect for its protectors."

ATHENS, Oct. 17—Fighting between the Greek Army and the Turkish forces stationed along the frontier began early to-day.

A daring feat was accomplished this morning by the commanders of the Greek gunboats A and D.

At 2 o'clock they made a dash to force the Turkish blockade at the narrow entrance to the Gulf of Arta, one side of which is Turkish and the other Greek. They were observed from the Turkish fort at Prevesa which dominates the entrance, and a heavy fire was directed on them, which they returned with spirit.

They succeeded in fighting their way through, and at 4:30 A. M. reached the Greek town of Nonitza, on the southern shore of the bay, with very little damage.

There is great jubilation over what is described as the almost miraculous feat of the two gunboats. Unnoticed by the Turkish gunners they passed within 240 yards of the Turkish fortress of Pantokrator, and then through the narrow channel between the new fortress at Prevesa and the coast batteries. They saw the Turkish troops busily engaged in completing defensive works in the full blaze of electric lights. A Turkish gunboat and destroyer are shut up in Prevesa, where they sought refuge at the beginning of the Italian war.

The Turkish Minister to Greece left Athens to-day without complying with the formalities usual in such cases and without asking for his passports.

The Governor of the National Bank announces that the cash reserves and deposits abroad are so large that there is no fear of a rise in the rate of exchange or of exceptional measures on behalf of commercial interests.

### Convoying Greeks from America

ALGIERS, Oct. 17—An escort of four Greek destroyers is convoying the Greek steamer Macedonia which has on board a number of Greeks, Bulgarians, and Servians, who are returning from America to join their regiments to fight against the Turks. She carries also a large cargo of ammunition.

The Macedonia arrived here last night from New York and found the four destroyers, recently purchased by Greece in England, waiting to accompany her on her voyage.

PODGORITZA, Oct. 17—The fighting ceased this afternoon temporarily. The troops of the Montenegrin centre column are concentrating around Tushi preparatory to a general advance against Scutari. Strong bodies of Turks have been dispatched from that city against them and a great battle is imminent on ground most unfavorable to the Montenegrin Army—the marshy eastern shore of Lake Scutari.

In the event of their defeat, the Montenegrins will be left with their rear unprotected, the small Lake of Houms lying behind them rendering communication with the other columns difficult.

King Nicholas has awarded to Gen. Vukotitch the highest military distinction, the Oblica Medal, for his victory at Berana.

Over 300 wounded from the northern column have been brought here, and the lack of doctors is already making itself felt. Crown Princess Militza is personally directing the work at the provisional hospitals.

CONSTANTINOPLE. Oct. 17—A formal declaration of war against Servia and Bulgaria was published by the Turkish Government to-day.

Hostilities were opened at half past two this morning by the Turkish troops at various points on the Bulgarian and Servian frontiers.

The divisions of the Turkish army were ordered to make a simultaneous forward movement.

In giving the order for a general advance, the War Minister mentioned only that the movement was to be made against the frontiers of Bulgaria and Servia.

There is a powerful Turkish army concentrated near the Greek frontier, but this has not yet been put into motion.

All reports received here to-night indicate that serious fighting is proceeding at various points, including the district north of Gusiago, on the Montenegrin frontier.

According to official information, large numbers of Pemaks, fanatical tribes of Mussulman Bulgars, who in past times have massacred Christian Bulgarians wholesale, crossed the frontier at Kirdchali, about forty miles to the west of Mustapha Pasha, penetrating several miles into Bulgarian territory, the Bulgarians retiring.

The Ottoman Government this morning handed their passports to the Servian and Bulgarian Ministers, and they will probably depart to-morrow as will also the Greek Minister.

A note addressed by the Turkish Government this morning to the Bulgarian and Servian legations here said it was impossible to maintain peace any longer, although it was the ardent desire of the Porte to do so. The Government was, therefore, obliged to put an end to the missions of the Bulgarian and Servian Legations and the diplomats were invited to withdraw their passports and leave Constantinople at the earliest moment.

The note stated that the step was taken in consequence of the recent note handed to the Turkish-Government by the Balkan States, which Turkey considered as constituting interference with her internal affairs. A second factor was the mobilization undertaken by Servia and Bulgaria, and the third reason was the daily skirmishes on the frontier.

The Cabinet assembled to-day to consider the note sent by Greece, which had only just been received, as the Turkish Minister at Athens refused to transmit it.

Similar action to that taken against Servia and Bulgaria will probably be taken against Greece, as the note was found to be identical with those received from Sofia and Belgrade. The Council of Ministers was still engaged to-night in debating the attitude to be taken toward Greece.

The decision of the Government to declare war is welcomed with enthusiasm by the Turkish people as the action of a strong and confident Cabinet.

### Turkey Using Old War Fund

BERLIN, Oct. 17—Turkey has withdrawn a large sum of money, reported to be $17,500,000, from Germany, according to a dispatch from Bucharest.

The money was deposited in Germany in the course of the reign of Sultan Abdul Hamid, and was earmarked exclusively for a war fund.

Germany has consented, says the correspondent, to the delivery of the money to the Ottoman Government, and the gold is now on the way from Kustendji, Rumania, to Constantinople on board the steamer Regele Carol I.

LONDON, Friday, Oct. 18—While Turkey and the Balkan States are carrying out the last formalities connected with the declaration of war, interest has been transferred to the prospects of the campaign.

Two influences will, it is expected, make the war short and sharp. The first is the approach of Winter; the second is financial pressure.

None of the belligerent States is in a position to stand the strain of prolonged military operations. Bulgaria was disappointed recently in her efforts to raise even a small loan in Paris, while Turkey has been endeavoring both in New York and Paris to borrow money, up to the present without success. The financial resources of the other States concerned are very limited.

Little is likely to be heard of the proposed European conference until some decisive action has been fought, when doubtless the European Concert will renew its efforts to bring about peace on broad lines.

The war will, it is expected, develop into a land campaign between Bulgaria and Turkey and a naval struggle between Turkey and Greece: It is believed that Turkey will concentrate her strength and attack the Bulgarians separately before the Servians can come to their aid. Much will depend on whether Turkey gains command of the sea, which would facilitate the transport of her Asiatic troops to the theatre of war.

How far preparations have gone is largely a matter of conjecture, as neither Military Attachés nor correspondents are allowed anywhere near the armies. The troops may, in fact, be ready for an immediate big battle, but military authorities do not expect one for some days.

Little is known as to how far the allied Balkan States have concerted their strategic plans. The independent action of Montenegro seems to indicate that a settled course is being followed.

The Bulgarian Cabinet was sitting last night in continuous session, but was having difficulty in communicating with Belgrade and Athens.

The news of actual fighting is indefinite and conflicting. The Turks claim a substantial victory over the Montenegrins.

The Greek people are rejoicing over their first naval victory, the forcing by two gunboats of Prevesa Strait. This feat gives the Greeks command of the Gulf of Arta and secures a supply of stores to the army in Epirus.

### Greece Cannot Now Buy Cruisers

The official declaration of war deprives Greece of the services of a Chinese cruiser she had arranged to buy at Newcastle, as she has been obliged to abandon the purchase for fear of diplomatic complications The four destroyers which Greece purchased at Liverpool shipped naval crews at Algiers and have started for Greece, convoying the steamer Macedonia, which has on board Greek reservists from New York. These sea wasps will prove serviceable if they succeed in reaching a Greek port without being intercepted by Turkish warships.

There is an inclination among military men to think that the importance of the Montenegrin victories has been exaggerated and that much has been made of them in order to screen the struggle that is going on for the possession of the forts guarding the Turkish town of Scutari.

The Montenegrins are fighting desperately, but they neglect the commissariat service and the hospitals, which are essential in such a campaign.

\*　\*　\*

## BLUNTSCHLI NOT IN THIS WAR

Who remembered that the scene of Bernard Shaw's "Arms and the Man" is laid in the Balkan country, and that the hero, Bluntschli, though a mercenary, is a Balkan warrior? We can remember the plots and scenes of Shakespeare's plays, but not of Shaw's. But the production of the musical version of the play, "The Chocolate Soldier," in Paris just at this moment is ill-timed. The Slavs in Paris are angry. The world is not in a mood to sneer at Balkan soldiers or to make fun of them. None of the Bulgars, Serbs, or Montenegrins have been carrying chocolate drops instead of cartridges.

We shall hear from Shaw on this matter before long. He will tell us that the satire of his play has reformed Balkan military methods. It will turn out to be Shaw who whipped the Turks. This is an aspect of the new Balkan question which the Chancelleries have not considered.

*   *   *

## HOSTILITIES END IN TURKEY TO-DAY

---

*Terms of Armistice Are Formally Accepted by the Ottoman Cabinet*

### APPLIES TO WHOLE WAR AREA

*It Will Continue in Force While the Negotiations for Peace Are in Progress*

### AUSTRIAN DANGER FADING

*Events of Past Weak Have Materially Helped to Lessen the Tension Between Great Powers*

---

Special Cable to The New York Times

LONDON, Sunday, Dec. 1—With all the omens pointing to early peace, the week has come to a better ending than any since the first shot was fired in the Balkan war. Even in regard to the Baghtch negotiations for an armistice the fears that Turkey would once more try the issue of combat rather than accept the allies' conditions seem to have been dissipated.

Confident reports come from both Constantinople and Sofia that the armistice will be signed soon. The Turkish capital asserts that the agreement will be signed this afternoon, probably in the Sultan's palace car, where the delegates have been meeting.

A dispatch to a Sunday paper from Constantinople says:

"The situation in regard to peace negotiations, as described to me this morning at official headquarters, is as follows:

"The Bulgarians have shown a considerable tendency toward conciliation during the last few days and are coming to realize that they are too much exhausted to ever break through the Tchatalja lines.

"The allies are beginning to dispute among themselves, which is an additional reason for their wishing to end the war quickly.

"An armistice will almost certainly be signed to-day or to-morrow on the basis of nothing more than a cessation of hostilities and a revictualing of the besieged towns.

"In the meanwhile all reports sent from here regarding frontier delimitations and other peace terms are absolutely unfounded. The peace negotiations are such that they will begin only when the Greek delegate, who is now due, has arrived with instructions from his Government.

"Everything looks very promising for a speedy end of the war."

The chief danger of the Austro-Russian-Servian situation has been removed, according to general agreement, by the openings for discussion supplied by the course of events the past week.

As Winston Churchill said yesterday, there is no point of difference between Austria and Russia which patience and good feeling cannot adjust and smooth away.

One of the most satisfactory features of the situation which has arisen from the Balkan difficulties has been the demonstration that Great Britain and Germany have been working together for the common end of peace.

### TURKISH CABINET APPROVES
*Sofia Expects Agreements and Seems Inclined to Yield a Bit*

CONSTANTINOPLE, Nov. 30—The Cabinet has approved the protocol of an armistice, which will be signed at 2 o'clock to-morrow afternoon. An irade has been issued sanctioning the protocol.

The armistice will be signed by the Turks on the one hand and the Bulgarians on the other, in behalf of the four allies. It will thus apply not merely to Tchatalja, but to all Turkey in Europe.

The armistice will last as long as the preliminary negotiations for peace continue.

It is stipulated that the position of the belligerents shall remain exactly as at the time of signature.

Up to the present there have been no pourparlers on the subject of the terms of peace.

SOFIA, Nov. 30—According to the latest information, the negotiations at Tchatalja are progressing favorably, and it is even hoped that an armistice may be agreed upon by Sunday. The discussion of the terms of peace will then be taken up.

One of the chief difficulties of the armistice negotiations is the question of the surrender of Adrianople, which the Turks have positively refused to agree to.

The allies may consent that the investment of Adrianople shall remain as at present, as has already been arranged with respect to the positions of the two armies at the Tchatalja lines.

It is understood here that the proposed armistice will not fix any definite term, but that both sides will be free to resume hostilities at any time.

## GREEK OUTRAGES REPORTED
*Berlin Gets Stories of Maltreatment of Jews in Macedonia*

Special Cable to The New York Times

BERLIN, Nov. 30—The Central Jewish Relief League of Germany, which acts for American Jews in European and Oriental philanthropic work, is receiving circumstantial accounts of the maltreatment of Jews by the conquering Greek soldiers at Salonika and other points in European Turkey.

Robbery, pillage, and worse seems to have occurred at many points to a degree which recalls the horrors of Kishineff, and fears are expressed in prominent German Jewish circles that the regime of the Greek Catholic Church in the conquered provinces may not be as pleasant even as under the Moslems.

### SAYS TURKS SLEW 180 GREEKS
*Salonika Dispatch to Athens Tells of Slaughter in Mosque*

ATHENS, Nov. 30—According to a semi-official statement from Salonika 180 Greeks, who took refuge in a mosque in the village of Mavrova, were killed by Turkish troops, who had retreated through Florina. The Turks also destroyed many villages.

The Bulgarian Army which left Salonika on nineteen Greek transports, has landed at Dedeaghaten.

### The Montana at Port Said

PORT SAID, Nov. 30—The United States cruiser Montana arrived here today to coal preparatory to leaving for the Syrian coast.

\*   \*   \*

March 19, 1913

# KING OF GREECE MURDERED AT SALONIKA; SLAYER MAD; POLITICAL RESULTS FEARED

---

*Shot While Walking in Captured City—Dies in Half an Hour*

### THE ASSASSIN IS A GREEK
*Said to be a Socialist—Declares After Arrest He Is Against Governments*

### QUEEN ALEXANDRA STRICKEN
*Collapses on Being Told by Princess Victoria of the Death of Her Favorite Brother*

### KING IGNORED WARNINGS
*With Full Confidence in His People, He Walked About with Only One Attendant*

### KILLED WHILE VERY HAPPY
*His Last Words Were of Delight at the Success of the Greek Arms in the Balkan War*

---

By Marconi Transatlantic Wireless Telegraph to
The New York Times
Dispatch to The London Times

SALONIKA, March 18—The King of the Hellenes was shot while walking in the principal street of Salonika at about 5:15 o'clock this afternoon. Half an hour later his Majesty was dead.

Since his triumphal entry into Salonika the King had been accustomed to take an afternoon walk, either to the famous White Tower or to the cavalry barracks.

The King's confidence in the people was so great that he went about freely attended by a single equerry. The dangers of this habit were apparent to his entourage, who repeatedly but without avail requested his Majesty to permit the presence of civil guards.

A few days ago four gendarmes were ordered to follow the King, but their presence was considered so objectionable by his Majesty and so out of keeping with that affection which he felt for his subjects, old and new, that the number was reduced to two, who followed at a long distance.

With Col. Frankoulis, he was returning to-day after a walk to the White Tower. He was in a happy, contented mood, and as he walked along talked of the war, of the success of the Greek arms, of the capture of Yanina and Salonika, and of this fitting climax to his fifty years' reign.

#### The King's Last Words

"To-morrow," continued the King, "when I pay my formal visit to the dreadnought Goeben, it is the fact that a German battleship is to honor a Greek King here in Salonika that will fill me with happiness and contentment."

These proved the monarch's last words, for at that moment a shot rang out from behind.

Col. Frankoulis sprang around and seized the hand of the assassin, which was already pointed at him. Covering his royal master with his body he grabbed the assailant by the throat and held him fast until passing soldiers ran to his aid, but the first shot had found its mark, for King George had already sunk to the earth.

His Majesty was placed in a carriage, his head resting on his arm. He continued to breathe a short time, but before a hospital was reached life was extinct.

The bullet, fired at a distance of two paces, had entered the King's back below the shoulder blade and made its exit from the stomach. There was a great hemorrhage, the jeweled cross which the King always wore being smothered with blood.

The assassin is Aleko Schinas, a Greek of feeble intellect, who states that he was driven to desperation by sickness and want. The crime, therefore, was without motive.

As the tidings spread, groups of grief-stricken people gathered at street corners and conversed in muffled accents.

The troops were recalled to barracks, the shop and cafes were closed, the tramways were stopped, lights extinguished, and Salonika to-night has a dead and deserted appearance that fittingly expresses the sorrow at the loss of a ruler who in so short a time had made himself beloved by one and all.

As I write, the church bells are tolling and the shrill call of the Last Post echoes along the deserted street.

### Died Before Reaching Hospital

SALONIKA, March 18—King George was assassinated while walking in the streets. The assassin was a Greek of low mental type, who gave his name as Aleko Schinas. He shot the King through the heart.

The King was accompanied only by an aide-de-camp, Lieut. Col. Francoulis. The assassin came suddenly at him and fired one shot from a seven-chambered revolver.

The King fell into the arms of his aid. Two soldiers ran up on hearing the firing and helped to support him.

The tragedy caused intense excitement. Schinas was seized immediately and overpowered.

The wounded King was lifted into a carriage and taken to the Papation Hospital. He was still breathing, but died within half an hour.

Prince Nicholas, the King's third son, and other officers hurried to the hospital. Arriving first, Prince Nicholas summoned the officers, and, speaking in a voice choked with sobs, said:

"It is my deep grief to have to announce to you the death of our beloved King, and to invite you to swear fidelity to your new sovereign, King Constantine."

The officers responded by shouting:

"Long live the King!"

Prince Nicholas is the only member of the royal family in Salonika.

The Greek Governor at once issued a proclamation announcing that the oath of fealty had been taken.

Crown Prince Constantine, who succeeds King George, is at Yanina, recently captured by the Greeks. He will, it is expected, come here with all possible speed.

George I., King of Greece

The assassin of the King is an evil-looking fellow, about 40 years of age. On being arrested he refused to explain his motive for the crime. He declared that his name was Aleko Schinas, and, in reply to an officer who asked him whether he had no pity for his country, announced that he was against Governments.

Schinas maintained a perfectly impassable demeanor, his manner suggesting that he is not responsible for his actions.

Notwithstanding the rapidity with which the King received attention, he was found to be dead on his arrival at the hospital.

Precautions were at once taken throughout the city, and perfect order is being maintained.

King George, who had taken personal command of his troops during the earlier period of the war, had been here since December, when the Turkish fortress was occupied by the Greeks after a short siege.

Queen Olga has also been here and has paid great attention to the case of the sick and wounded.

King George in December had a meeting here with King Ferdinand of Bulgaria, at which, it is supposed, they discussed the fate of the captured Turkish territory after the war.

## QUEEN ALEXANDRA OVERCOME
### *King Her Favorite Brother—Political Results of Murder Feared*

By Marconi Transatlantic Wireless Telegraph to
The New York Times

LONDON, Wednesday, March 12—Late last evening dispatches were received in London confirming the report of the assassination of the King of Greece. A message was received at the Foreign Office soon after 9 P. M. and was immediately communicated to the King, while the sad news was also conveyed to Queen Alexandra, the dead King's sister, at Marlborough House.

Queen Alexandra had been informed of the tragedy by an earlier unofficial report. She was almost unable to credit it, and to the last minute cherished the hope that it would prove incorrect. Shortly before 10 o'clock, however, an official message, stating briefly that the King had been shot and killed, was received at Marlborough House.

The painful duty of communicating the intelligence to her mother was undertaken by Princess Victoria. Queen Alexandra broke down completely, and had to be helped to bed in a state of collapse.

The sympathy of the English people will go out to Queen Alexandra in her latest sorrow. In the short space of a few years her eldest brother, the King of Denmark; her husband, King Edward; her son-in-law, the Duke of Fife; her nephew, Prince George of Cumberland; a near relative, Prince Francis of Teck, and now her brother the King of Greece, have been taken from her by death.

The news of the assassination was received in the House of Commons with great concern, much uneasiness being expressed regarding its political consequences. It is not yet known whether it was the work of a lunatic or of one politically distraught. If it was inspired by political design it may, as the Daily News points out, react very seriously on the Balkan situation, already sufficiently troubled without such a disturbance.

It was taken for granted, in view of the King's physical and mental vigor that he would occupy the throne during the restoration of peace and the subsequent reconstruction of a larger and stronger Greece. His death is regarded as a great calamity for the Balkan League and for Europe.

### Rigid Censorship on News

LONDON, Wednesday, March 19—The official world of London and the general public were startled last evening by a terse message from Salonika announcing the assassination of the King of Greece.

Interest in the troubled Balkans had been waning of late days, but the news of this tragedy erected an instant and immense situation. It was not generally known that the King of Greece was still at Salonika, as nothing had been heard of his movements for several days.

Concern regarding the details of the assassination was intense but as hours passed and no further news reached London it became evident that a rigid censorship was being maintained by army administration. The strained relations between the Greek and Bulgarian contingents at Salonika gave grounds for some that the assassination of King George might have been incident to a clash between the allies, but a message received at midnight dispelled such apprehensions by identifying the assassin as a Greek degenerate. Another dispatch referred to him as demented.

The British Foreign Office, Marlborough House, where Queen Alexandra, sister of the dead King, is residing, and the Greek Legation were besieged by reporters, but no one at these places had any information except the newspaper bulletins until nearly 10 o'clock.

The King and Queen of England are at Windsor Castle. The first official confirmation of the tragedy came to the Foreign Office in a dispatch from Prince Nicholas at Salonika. It was transmitted to Windsor and to Marlborough House, and then given to the public. This dispatch announced that the King had been shot and had died in half an hour. Another telegram reporting similarly, was received from the Greek Administrator at Salonika.

Earlier in the evening the press message had been communicated to the King and the Queen mother as a rumor.

The greatest sympathy is felt for Queen Alexandra. The King of Greece was her favorite brother. King George and Queen Mary will come from Windsor this morning to give her what consolation they can.

### Will Hurt the London Season

Even if the dead King's close relationship with the British royal family did not exist, the circumstances of his death would debar the court for a time from social functions. It is expected that court mourning will be announced for three months, and that all official engagements, except the most necessary ones, will be cancelled.

The London social season, which begins after Easter, will therefore suffer an eclipse, and several branches of retail business will lose heavily.

It is expected that the body of the murdered King will be taken to Athens on board a warship for burial.

King George of Greece was a frequent visitor to London, his last visit being on the occasion of King Edward's funeral, when he met Col. Theodore Roosevelt and became exceedingly friendly with the ex-president whom he impressed as one of the most democratic characters among the European sovereigns assembled here. He remained as a guest at Buckingham Palace for several days and with his brother, King Frederick of Denmark, walked about the streets entirely unattended and unrecognized. Several times they joined the crowds which gathered in front of the palace to cheer the new English King, their identity wholly unsuspected by the workingmen with whom they rubbed elbows.

In the course of a former visit to this city the London Corporation entertained the King at the Guildhall and presented an address of welcome. Of all the crowned heads of Europe, King George of Greece and his Danish brother, King Frederick, who was overtaken by a fatal illness while strolling in the streets of Hamburg alone, were among the most unostentatious. The Greek King had many friends among the diplomats of the various nations, and some of his warmest friendships were with untitled persons.

### King George's Courage

The King in the course of his reign, and particularly in the latter years of it, passed through many dangers, but always went about either alone or attended by one or two aids. When be was struck down arrangements were being completed for his jubilee, and it seemed that this celebration would take place in a period of national triumph.

Personal courage was a marked characteristic of him. On one occasion, when an attempt was made to assassinate him while he was driving with Princess Marie, he rose in the carriage and, shielding his daughter with his body, furiously shook his cane at two men who were firing at him at close range.

King George had a particular fondness for a good dinner and a game of cards, and was known to all the foremost restaurateurs in the Continental capitals and watching places. He was popularly credited with being rather easy-going in the matter of hard work.

At a meeting of Moslems and Turkish sympathizers here last night the announcement of the assassination was greeted with cries of "Shame!" although there were some cheers. The audience rose as a token of respect for the King's memory.

The Earl of Selborne, presiding at a meeting of the Royal Colonial Institute, announced the death of the King, and said that all would wish to express their deep sympathy for Queen Alexandra in her bitter loss.

The Greek Legation had received no official word of the death of the King up to a late hour last night, but the two members of the peace delegation remained in London and many other Greeks called to express their sympathy. The Lord Mayor of London sent a message to the Greek Minister, saying. "The citizens of London sympathize with the Greek royal family and the Greek Nation in their bereavement and express their horror at the crime."

The Lord Mayor also telegraphed condolence to King George and to Queen Alexandra, while the Lord Mayor of Windsor called at the Castle to offer condolence.

### Why He Was at Salonika

The long stay of the Greek King at Salonika was made with the object of showing Greece's title to the permanent possession of the city. When the war with Turkey began each of the Allies made for territory in which its interests lay. Salonika was a point at which individual interests were focussed, and the Greeks, Bulgars, and Serbs alike coveted the prosperous port.

The Greek army won the race to the city, and, unaided, received the submission of the Turkish garrison. The Bulgarians, however, who were not far behind, sent in a portion of their army, and since then there has been considerable friction and even fighting.

The Greeks, nevertheless, established an administration, and the King hurriedly left Athens for Salonika. He played host to King Ferdinand of Bulgaria and afterward to the Crown Prince of Servia on their visits to the city. He realized that his presence there was not without peril, for he was surrounded by malcontents—Turks who had lost one of their most cherished cities, and Servians and Bulgarians who envied the Greeks their possession of the place.

\* \* \*

**March 20, 1913**

# KING'S MURDERER IS EDUCATED ANARCHIST

*Once Worked in New York—Started School Which Greek Government Closed*

**HIS CRIME PREMEDITATED**

*King George's Body Embalmed and Taken to Palace at Salonika—Priests Chant Prayers Continually*

By Marconi Transatlantic Wireless Telegraph to
The New York Times

LONDON, March 19—According to a telegram received by the Greek Minister in London, Aleko Schinas, the murderer of the King of the Hellenes, is a victim of alcoholism.

It is added that the assassination cannot be ascribed to any political motive.

SALONIKA, March 19—The assassin of King George of Greece is still held in close confinement. At various periods throughout last night he was forced to undergo examinations, which failed to elicit any facts to show that other persons were implicated in the crime.

Aleko Schinas, it is now said, is not a madman, but apparently is weak-minded. He lived by begging, and three weeks ago came to Salonika by way of Athens. He stopped for a few days at his birthplace, Volo, Thessaly, where he delivered harangues, in which he declared that in a short time he would succeed in establishing equality, that there would no longer be either rich or poor, and that work which was now accomplished in one hour would be spread out over two.

Interrogated as to why he assassinated the King, Schinas replied:

"I had to die somehow, as I suffer from neurasthenia and therefore wished to redeem my life."

He appears to have led a wretched existence, subsisting almost entirely on milk. His family have long ceased to acknowledge him.

Schinas for a time was an instructor in the medical department of the University of Athens. He refuses to give any explanation of his crime beyond the fact that two years ago he applied for assistance at the palace and was driven away by an aide-de-camp.

The premeditation of the regicide appears to be established by the fact that Schinas lurked in hiding. He rushed out when his royal victim was within six feet of him and fired pointblank into the back of the King, who at the time was only a few yards from Police Headquarters.

The body of King George was embalmed to-day, and removed from the hospital to the palace on a stretcher borne by his son, Prince Nicholas; several of the dead monarch's aids de camp, and other superior officers of the Greek Army, who took turns in carrying the stretcher.

It was a strangely diversified procession, consisting of regular troops in their campaign outfit, officers in brilliant uniforms, clergy, civilians, Cretans, Greeks, Mussulmans, and members of the various Balkan races in a kaleidoscopic variety of costumes.

Soldiers of the Greek Light Infantry, in their quaint kilts, closely surrounded the humble military stretcher which was in the middle of the procession, and which traversed the spot where King George was shot down yesterday afternoon.

On the arrival of the procession at the Palace, military honors were rendered. The body was then placed on a bier in the main chamber, the Greek Metropolitan offered prayer, and the civil and military authorities filed past. Many of the spectators burst into tears.

A guard of honor, consisting of Greek Captains and priests, the latter continually chanting prayers, will remain permanently stationed around the body until it is removed for burial.

* * *

**May 15, 1913**

## THE FUTURE OF THE BALKANS

The occupation of Scutari by an international force, which began yesterday, may be regarded as the first important step by Europe toward taking under its control the final settlement, so far as possible, of the future of the Balkan Peninsula. It is a sign of the assent of Austria to the general plan of the European concert and equally of the practical harmony into which Russia has been brought with the other Powers. Two tasks now await the Powers. One to arrange the more or less conflicting claims of the members of the Balkan alliance to the territory that has been wrested from Turkey; the other the erection and administration of Albania as a semi-independent State. The former will be the most immediately vexatious; the latter is likely to offer the more lasting difficulties. Whatever may be the heartburnings which the Bulgarians, the Greeks, and the Serbs may feel if they do not get all that they respectively desire, it is practically certain that each Government in the long run will yield to the "advice" which the Powers present, if the Powers be united.

In connection with this state of affairs, the recent utterances of Field Marshal Von Der Golz, the military adviser to the Turkish Government for a dozen years after 1883, are interesting. He is of the opinion that the Balkan allies, so soon as they have recovered from the strain of the recent war, will undertake further expansion, and, since there is nothing more to be got from the Turks, they will direct their efforts northward across the southern frontier of Austria, and in this will be aided indirectly by Russia. As there are some seven millions of Serbs in Austria, along the border of the Balkans, the work of the allies would be based on the principle of nationality. This does not afford a very cheerful view of the prospects of lasting peace, since, in the judgment of the Field Marshal, Germany would be bound by interest and honor to come to the help of her ally, Austria.

It does not follow, however, that the expansive tendencies of the Balkan allies must lead to expansion by force. There must remain the alternative of a change of policy in the Austrian Government, and of an attempt at organizing a coalition that will satisfy both the Slavs already in Austrian dominions and those along the southern border. It is believed that a change of this sort is favored by the Crown Prince, who will succeed to the throne on the death of the aged Emperor, as it is by some of the most influential of the Austrian statesmen. If it should be tried in good faith, it would tend powerfully toward peace and progress throughout all Europe. We are persuaded that it will seem more practicable as time passes.

* * *

**May 19, 1913**

## FORESEE NEW BALKAN WAR

*Daily Chronicle Says Greece and Servia May Fight Bulgaria*

Special Cable to The New York Times

LONDON, Monday, May 19—The Daily Chronicle says that the situation in the Near East has gone from bad to worse and that there is great danger of that troubled region being the theatre of another war. The Chronicle's special Balkan correspondent says he has excellent authority for stating that Greece and Servia, which did not sign the preliminaries of peace, have concluded an agreement which, it is believed, takes the definite form of a treaty, the main points of which are a common policy regarding the conquered territories and an alliance against Bulgaria. There is even danger, says the correspondent, of an immediate ultimatum to Bulgaria.

LONDON, Monday, May 19—All the delegates to the Balkan peace conference are new in London and will be formally welcomed to-day by Sir Edward Grey, Secretary of Foreign Affairs. The first meeting of the conference will probably be held on Tuesday.

Whether a preliminary peace treaty will be signed this week, as was expected, is still doubtful. The Greek and Servian delegates have not received authority to sign a treaty, and it is supposed that Greece and Servia are pursuing a policy of delay in order to keep the Bulgarian forces before the Tchatalja lines and Bulair, while the territorial disputes with Bulgaria are still unsettled.

It is believed, however, that the powers will be able to influence Greece and Servia to sign.

*   *   *

**May 31, 1913**

## BALKAN FOES SIGN TREATY OF PEACE

*Proceedings in London Concluded Quietly in an Hour's Time*

### SIR EDWARD GREY PRAISED

*Bulgarian Delegate Expresses Gratitude to Him—Montenegro Signs, but Accuses Britain*

Special Cable to The New York Times

LONDON, May 30—The treaty of peace between Turkey and the Balkan allies was signed at St. James's Palace at 12:40 P. M. to-day. Thanks to the firm action of Sir Edward Grey, the trusted and respected spokesman of the European concert, the Balkan war, after a duration of nearly eight months, was definitely terminated by a ceremony lasting exactly one hour.

Five copies of the treaty, one for each of the belligerent States, on plain printed sheets, with blanks left for signatures, lay on the polished mahogany table when Sir Edward opened the proceedings by inviting the delegates to sign the treaty. Thereupon the copies of the treaty were passed from hand to hand by the different delegates for signature as they sat around a long table.

The proceedings were businesslike and brisk. The only jarring note, from the point of view of the Servians and Greeks, was the discovery of an annexe to the treaty, believed to have been drafted by the Bulgarians, proposing that the treaty should come in force without further ratification. This annexe was not signed.

LONDON, May 30—Dr. S. Danoff, the Bulgarian peace delegate, in the course of an interview after the signature of the preliminary treaty of peace, said:

"I am rejoiced. It means not only Balkan peace, but general peace, for Europe is saved from one of the most thorny problems of the Near East. We owe a deep debt of gratitude to Sir Edward Grey, whose enduring and untiring mastery in treating diplomatic problems has brought about peace much sooner than some of us had expected."

The first meeting of the peace conference has been fixed for Monday, June 2.

M. Popovitch, the Montenegrin chief delegate, after signing the preliminary treaty on behalf of Montenegro, delivered a short speech, in which be said:

"We have signed the preliminary treaty because nothing else remained for us to do. We are said to have peace but are profoundly dissatisfied with the terms we have been obliged to accept. We have been despoiled of the fruits of our victories. We have been made the whipping boy of Europe. Great Britain took the leading part in depriving us of Soutari. We look here to secure a modification of the Albanian frontier, so as to give us lands for cultivation and a natural route between Podgoritza and Ipek."

The Bulgarian and Turkish peace delegates also signed a protocol providing for the immediate removal of their respective armies from the scene of operations.

After informing the Ambassadorial Conference of the signing of the peace draft Sir Edward Grey suggested that the conference limit its discussions to three questions—a Constitution for Albania, the delimitation of the southern frontier of Albania, and the status of the Aegean Islands. The Ambassadors are now awaiting further instructions from their Governments regarding a Constitution for Albania, but the conference is working in greater harmony and expects to conclude its labors by the end of June.

The relations between the Balkan Allies show a distinct improvement. The postponed meeting between the Servian and Bulgarian Premiers is now definitely fixed to take place on the frontier to-morrow evening. The latest suggestion for a settlement of the quarrel between the two countries is that Servia and Bulgaria denounce the old treaties and conclude a new alliance providing for a joint administration of Macedonia.

ROME, May 30—The signing, in London to-day of the preliminary peace treaty between the Balkan Allies and Turkey caused great satisfaction both at the Quirinal and the Vatican, and the hope was expressed that further complications between the Balkan States might be avoided. In Government circles it was said that Greece should understand that Italy held no hostile feelings against her, but was merely desirous of protecting her own interests in the Adriatic.

ATHENS, May 30—Artillery fire was opened on the Greek positions in the direction of Eleuthora yesterday by the Bulgarian troops stationed at Prawa, to the east of Salonika. The Bulgarian commander refused to enter into negotiations with the Greek commander for the purpose of stopping the firing. Details of the engagement have not yet been received.

Owing to this aggression by the Bulgarians a position of the Greek fleet has been sent to Eleuthora.

BELGRADE, May 30—The Pravda says that Bulgaria is ready to negotiate with Servia for a revision of the treaty of alliance on condition that all the Balkan Governments order a demobilization of their forces.

### HOW THE WAR WAS FOUGHT
*Turks' Power Crushed at Kirk Kilissch, Salonkia, and Adrianople*

The Balkan war was expected by those who studied European affairs closely as soon as the Turco-Italian war began, but it was not till Sept. 30 last year that it was learned that the forces of Bulgaria, Servia, Montenegro, and Greece were actually mobilizing.

It was the occurrence of a series of massacres in Macedonia and Thessaly, almost on the frontiers of the Balkan States which gave the final impetus to the alliance between them, which had for so long been regarded as an impossibility. At Otchana in August the Turks had massacred a number of Bulgarians and at Philipopolis the people held large gatherings to demand the liberation of Macedonia. The Montenegrins were stirred by the news of other atrocities at Berase, and a mutiny occurred at Monastir.

The great powers, which always watch the Balkans with the keenest anxiety and were conscious that their own subjects might force them to observe the responsibilities they had assumed for decent government in European Turkey became seriously alarmed and addressed many exhortations to the Balkan States on the danger and folly of upsetting the status quo.

Mr. Venizelos, the Premier of Greece, however, was at work, and through his ability Bulgaria, Greece, Servia, and Montenegro agreed to forget their mutual hatreds and to advance together against the common foe. On Oct. 13 Bulgaria, Servia, and Greece sent Turkey a note demanding an autonomous Macedonia, and four days later Turkey handed the Balkan Ministers at Constantinople their passports.

Considering the interior position, which Turkey occupied, the military strength of that empire and of the allies was not unequally matched. Turkey could muster, it was estimated, 500,000 men. Bulgaria 300,000, Servia 200,000, Greece 80,000, and Montenegro 50,000. Montenegro struck the first blow and carried on independent operations which led her to Scutari, but the decisive operations of the war were conducted by Bulgaria, with Servia acting as an invaluable ally on her right.

The Servians were making for Durazzo, which they actually reached on Nov. 28, and the Greeks were pressing forward to both Janina and Salonika. Those operations hampered the Turks by distracting their attention, but the mistake which cost them their European dominions was committed in not appreciating the strategy of Bulgaria. The army of this kingdom, as expected, moved at once upon Adrianople and invested it; but instead of stopping there it threw forward one army corps on the left, and in rapid succession drove the Turks back from the Kirk Kilisseh and Lule Burgas positions in disastrous retreat upon Constantinople.

The Bulgarians had, however, outrun their strength and supplies, and seem also to have been infected to some extent by the cholera, which had appeared in the Turkish ranks. So, when they reached the lines of Tchatalja, they were unable to force them and on Dec. 3 an armistice was signed between the Turks and the Allies.

Though operations were still carried on by the Greeks, the negotiations for peace were undertaken in London. Nothing was accomplished, as the demand of the Allies for a large indemnity was refused by the Turks. The result was that the war was renewed on Feb. 4 and on March 27 Adrianople at last fell before the Bulgarians and Servians. Still the Allies were held back by the lines of Tchatalja, and the result was a second armistice.

On the western frontier of the Turkish Empire, however, King Nicholas of Montenegro, fearing for his throne, refused to lay down his arms, and on April 24, in spite of the protest of the Great Powers and the presence of their fleets in demonstration against him conquered Scutari. A few days later,

however, he was forced to evacuate it in the face of the enormous diplomatic pressure put upon him.

\* \* \*

**June 11, 1913**

## RUSSIA MAY FORCE PEACE IN BALKANS

*Asks the Powers to Take Joint Action for Demobilization*

### SERBS FIGHT WITH BULGARS

*Many Killed in Serious Encounter—Servian Minister May Leave Bulgarian Capital*

By Marconi Transatlantic Wireless Telegraph to
The New York Times

VIENNA, June 10—All news from Belgrade and Sofia tends to show that war between Servia and Bulgaria is inevitable, and that on both sides military preparations are nearly perfected.

In diplomatic circles, however, some confidence is shown that war will be averted. Russia has made a proposal to the powers to take joint action in regard to the Balkan States, summoning them to demobilize. There seems to be a chance that all the powers may adopt Russia's suggestion. It is said that a joint note embodying it will be transmitted to Sofia and Belgrade to-morrow.

LONDON, June 10—Many Servians were killed to-day in a serious encounter between Servian and Bulgarian troops near the small town of Makres, to the north of Istip, according to a special dispatch to the Belgrade Mall Journal, forwarded here by the Exchange Telegraph Company.

Further conflicts are expected in the same neighborhood, as the Servians on Monday sent a note to the Bulgarian commander giving him until 7 o'clock in the evening to evacuate the small town of Volodan, failing which the Servian General declared that he would bombard Istip, now occupied by the Bulgarians.

The great powers are exerting every effort to prevent the Balkan States from flying at each others throats and, reports from Vienna indicate, with some success. Russia and Germany particularly are busy counseling peace and moderation, and the French Government is supporting them, and as the principal creditor is giving both Servia and Bulgaria clear warning that in the event of war no financial assistance will be forthcoming either before or after hostilities.

Since Servia has definitely declared that she will avoid all provocations toward Bulgaria, even should the latter refuse revision of the treaty of alliance, and will wait before proclaiming annexation of the occupied territories, and since Bulgaria has also expressed readiness to do anything possible to maintain peace. It is still hoped that war may be averted.

The Neue Freie Presse learns that Dr. Daneff will soon form a new cabinet at Sofia, no military reasons for further delay existing, as the Bulgarian army is ready for action on the Servian and Macedonian frontiers.

A Bucharest dispatch to The Daily Telegraph says that if war occurs Rumania will mobilize her army, but at present has no understanding with any of the allies.

The official Mir at Sofia says that the Servians want war, and that, this being so, no middle course is open to Bulgaria, which must demand the immediate evacuation of the territories in the uncontested zone while awaiting the judgment of the arbitrator and must send to all parts of the disputed zone as many troops as the Servians have there.

A Belgrade dispatch says that the Russian Emperor has addressed telegrams to King Peter and King Ferdinand, imploring them to avoid a fratricidal war and expressing the hope that they will accept the intervention of arbitrators.

\* \* \*

July 15, 1913

## GREY SAYS BALKANS MUST FIGHT IT OUT

*War Deplorable, but Combatants Will Soon Be Exhausted— No Complications Feared*

**COLD COMFORT FOR BULGARS**

*They Are Informed That Gen. Ivanoff's Retreat Was "Splendid"— More Details of Atrocities*

LONDON, Tuesday, July 15—That the Balkan struggle will end by a process of mutual exhaustion seems the only hope that Sir Edward Grey is able to hold out. In the House of Commons last night the Foreign Secretary, replying to a suggestion that an armistice should be forced on the Balkan States, said it was impossible to exaggerate the horror of the war, but mere words were not likely to affect the situation, and it would be most difficult for the concert of Europe to resort to force to impose peace.

Bulgaria had asked Russia to aid her in arranging peace, and Servia and Greece had agreed to cease hostilities upon certain conditions. As to Turkey, no exception could be taken to her action, so long as she adhered to the Enos-Midia line.

The essential thing for the powers, said the Secretary, was to perfect and maintain an agreement. The war was so exhausting that it could not be of long duration, and no complication ought to arise endangering the European concert. There was every reason to believe that matters would be brought to a satisfactory termination.

Neither Servia nor Greece has paid any attention to Russia's proposal that they cease hostilities. They appear determined to negotiate peace with Bulgaria only on the field, without intervention by any third party, and, unless Bulgaria prove amenable, it is believed that an advance will be made upon Sofia to enforce acceptance of the Servian-Greek terms.

Serious fighting for the time being is suspended, but the advance of the Turkish and Rumanian troops continues without opposition. A Belgrade report says that the Servians on Sunday captured an important position eight miles west of Kostendil.

According to the Athens correspondent of The Daily Telegraph, Greece and Servia signed a secret treaty last May binding them to prosecute a war, which was then foreseen, with Bulgaria until the Bulgars acquiesced in the territorial arrangements laid down in the treaty. By these arrangements the eastern boundaries of Greece would be extended to the Mesta River, considerably to the east of Drama, and Servia would have access to the Aegean Sea at two points.

A Salonika dispatch to The Times says:

"Greece is prepared to sign an armistice only on condition that the frontier questions, the payment of indemnity by Bulgaria, and guarantees for the welfare of the Greeks under Bulgarian rule shall be settled on the battlefield. The Greek and Servian Premiers are meeting at Nish to discuss the situation.

"Premier Venizelos is now of the opinion that the creation of three numerically equal States is the only way to secure lasting peace in the Balkans. Greece was previously prepared to admit that Bulgaria might have a population one million in excess of Greece.

"The Greek Premier, further, refuses to oppose the annexation of Thrace to Bulgaria, although many of his countrymen consider that this attitude sacrifices the interests of his country. But he says that he has no desire to create difficulties for the great powers, and will be content with adequate guarantees for the future of Greeks in Thrace.

"King Constantine agrees with M. Venizelos on these points."

### Ferdinand Accuses Foes

King Ferdinand of Bulgaria, in a long message dispatched from Sofia on July 12 to The Evening News, says:

The stories and reports which the Greeks and Servians have been circulating in Europe concerning so-called outrages committed by my troops upon the Greek and Servian populations in Macedonia are absolutely unfounded and are published with the object of creating a bad impression.

King Ferdinand proceeds to tell of the liberties enjoyed by the people of Adrianople without regard to their nationality, and closes with the allegation:

Systematic attacks and persecutions have been directed against the Bulgarian element in Macedonia by the Servians and the Greeks. The Districts of Kastoria, Florina, and Vodena have been cleared of all well-educated men and the prisons of Salonika are overflowing with innocent Bulgarians. Great numbers of Bulgarians have been transported from their homes to the country to Greece and to the islands in the Aegean Sea . . . The same cruel regime has been applied to the Bulgarians in the regions occupied by the Servians The purely Bulgarian town of Kakesh has been completely burned by the Greek troops.

Thousands of refugees, King Ferdinand concludes, on arriving in Sofia "gave terrifying accounts of the horrible deeds committed by the Servians and Greeks. The Bulgarian Government is ready to come to an international inquiry which will enlighten the world concerning the stories of these excesses."

### A "Splendid Retreat"

SOFIA, July 14—The report that Gen. Ivanoff has effected a splendid retreat is confirmed.

Semi-official statements have been issued accusing the Greeks of setting fire to the town of Seres and declaring that the Bulgarians attempted vainly to get the fire under control. Other statements charge the Greeks with wholesale massacres and atrocities at Seres and elsewhere in Macedonia.

The Mayor of Drama reports that irregular Greeks have landed at Leftera and occupied the town of Pravi. The Greeks, he declares, massacred the whole Bulgarian and Mussulmans population.

BELGRADE, July 14—Only outpost engagements along the frontier occurred to-day.

It is reported that Bulgaria has made direct overtures to Servia for an armistice.

SALONIKA, July 14—The reports of the sacking and burning of the town of Seres by the defeated Bulgarian Army, and the accompanying outrages on women and atrocities on men were fully confirmed to-day in a dispatch from a well-known Greek correspondent.

The retreating Bulgarian soldiers, he telegraphs, opened a cannonade with four field guns from a hill above the town last Friday. At the same time bands of Bulgarian soldiers led by their officers scoured the streets, first pillaging the stores and houses and then drenching them with petroleum and setting them alight until the greater part of the town was blazing.

The Austro-Hungarian, and Italian Consuls stationed in this city have gone to Seres to verify officially the stories concerning atrocities committed by the Bulgarian troops and to aid their nationals.

Greek troops to-day occupied the town of Melnik, fifty-five miles to the northeast of Salonika, and are advancing toward the Bulgarian frontier. The Bulgarians have further retreated to Djumbala, close to the famous pass. The Greek commanders anticipate that the next big fight will take place on Bulgarian territory.

The soldiers were accompanied by the notorious revolutionary Colonel Yankoff, who, with other former officers of the Bulgarian Army, was very active in Macedonia in 1903.

Even the foreign Consulates in Seres were not spared, according to the correspondent. The Austro-Hungarian consular offices were plundered and burned. Vice Consul George C. Zlatko was carried off by the marauders, but subsequently ransomed. The Italian Consulate was also sacked, but the Consul bought off the incendiaries.

The Bank of Athens, the Oriental Bank, the Palace of the Metropolitan, the Great Synagogue, all the schools, the tobacco warehouses of the American, Austrian, and German companies, and the hospitals were burned after they had been pillaged. The American Tobacco Company alone suffered to the extent of $1,000,000.

Many persons were crucified, hacked to pieces, or burned alive by the maddened Bulgarians, who committed incredible outrages on women of all ages, many of whom died.

The condition of those who escaped is lamentable. Rich merchants are dying from hunger, while wretched mothers, trembling with cold, are trying to find covering and food for their naked and starving children.

The situation is desperate, as all the pharmacies were burned down, and there is a total lack of medicine for the sick and bandages for the wounded.

The Greek authorities in Salonika are rushing foodstuffs, clothing, and medicines to the stricken town.

Two thousand Bulgarians of the Kavala garrison have been induced to evacuate the town by a ruse of the commander of the Greek fleet, who manoeuvred in a manner to lead the Bulgars to believe that a large force of Greeks was being landed.

### The Rumanians' Advance

BUCHAREST, July 14—The Bulgarian Minister to Rumania and the staff of the legation left here to-day on a special train for Sofia.

It is officially stated that detachments of Rumanian cavalry have occupied Dobritch, Baltchik, and the surrounding villages.

CONSTANTINOPLE, July 14—The Turkish delegates to the Balkan Financial Commission at Paris have been recalled.

The Turkish armies are continuing their advance and have arrived at the Silivri-Belgrade forest line. Enver Bey's forces have occupied Rodosto.

It is understood that a Servian-Turkish agreement has been reached, but is awaiting ratification from Belgrade before being signed.

\*   \*   \*

**August 7, 1913**

## BALKANS AT PEACE; BULGARIA YIELDS

*Rumanian Threats to Occupy Sofia Compel Her Acquiescence*

**TURKEY STILL DEFIANT**

*Says She Will Hold Adrianople to the Last Extremity—*
*Demobilization Expected*

By Marconi Transatlantic Wireless Telegraph to
The New York Times

LONDON, Aug. 6—Peace has been concluded in the Balkans, so far as the former allies are concerned; but Turkey has regained Adrianople, and declares that she will resist to the last extremity any attempt to dislodge her from the city which the Bulgarians captured.

Bulgaria's submission to Servia, Greece, and Montenegro is due to Rumania's interference. Up to yesterday King Ferdinand's Government struggled to continue the negotiations, but Rumania threatened to occupy Sofia on Saturday unless Bulgaria gave way on all points at issue.

Gen. Nelson A. Miles arrived in London yesterday from Sofia. He will return to the United States in ten days. He reiterated his statements made to The New York Times that Bulgaria did not declare war upon Greece and Servia, but was invaded; also that she committed no atrocities, and could have coped successfully with Greece and Servia but for the interference of Rumania.

In Gen. Miles's opinion, Great Britain should take the initiative in forcing Turkey to adhere to the treaty of London and evacuate Adrianople; but there is a strong current of opinion in this country in favor of letting some other powers pull the chestnuts out of the fire.

BUCHAREST, Aug. 6—Peace was concluded to-night among the Balkan States, and the preliminary treaty will be signed to-morrow by the delegates of Servia, Greece, Montenegro, Rumania, and Bulgaria. The agreement was arrived at only after another exhibition of the utter helplessness of Bulgaria to face her ring of enemies.

The new frontier, as agreed upon, starts at a point on the old frontier west of the Struma River, follows the watershed to the west of the town of Strumitza, thence runs almost through the Struma Valley to the Belesh Mountains, and thence easterly in almost a straight line to the Mesta River. This leaves the town of Strumitza, the port of Lagos, and Xanthi to Bulgaria, and the port of Kavala to Greece. The establishment of the new frontier is a deep disappointment to the Bulgarians, who still nurse hopes for its eventual revision by the powers.

It is believed that an agreement for the demobilization of the various armies will be signed to-morrow. The news that peace had been arranged caused great rejoicings here.

LONDON, Thursday, Aug. 7—The second Balkan peace conference having concluded peace on a basis of compromise which is unsatisfactory to all the States concerned, except possibly Rumania, the question is being asked how soon before a third Balkan war will break out.

Bulgaria has obtained under the agreement arrived at in Bucharest to-day a considerable portion of Northern Macedonia—much more than the allies were at first inclined to give her—and also about sixty miles of the Aegean seaboard, which will enable her to build her projected railway from Philippopolis to the sea.

Bulgaria, however, deeply resents being deprived of Kavala a port on Kavala Bay, which goes to Greece under the agreement. Also she is confronted with the task of expelling the Turks from Adrianople, it being clear that the powers will do nothing in this direction. Bulgaria will seek to introduce in the peace protocol to be signed at Bucharest to-morrow a reservation practically appealing to the European powers for a subsequent revision of the peace treaty.

Full details of the new frontier line are still unknown, but apparently the whole of the disputed country between the northly courses of the Vardar and Struma Rivers goes to Servia, including Ovchepolye, Veles, Istip, and Kotchana, while Demirhissar, Seres, Drama, and Kavala fall to Greece.

The Times says to-day that Montenegro will receive from Servia an extension of territory east and south corresponding to the aid Montenegro rendered Servia in the war with Bulgaria. It adds that Vodena and Florina will be Greek, as also will be the Salonika-Monastir Railway to within about eight miles of its head.

### Bryan Admits Balkan Snub

Special to The New York Times

WASHINGTON, Aug. 6—Secretary Bryan this afternoon confirmed the dispatches telling of the efforts of the United States to insert in the Balkan peace treaty a clause safeguarding the civil and religious liberty of all persons in the territory affected by its provisions. Publication of the rejection of Mr. Bryan's suggestion caused great surprise among public men here, as the action of the State Department had been kept entirely a secret.

Mr. Bryan said that the request was a perfectly natural one on the part of this Government, inasmuch as many of the inhabitants of the countries concerned had emigrated to the United States, and as citizens here desired to secure protection for themselves and their kin.

For months protests have been coming to the State Department against the treatment of the Jews in Rumania. It has been charged that Jews in that country are deprived of their civil rights as guaranteed under the Treaty of Berlin. When asked if the refusal of the delegates to the Balkan Peace Conference to comply with the request would lead to further action by this Government, the Secretary of State declined to discuss the matter.

The suggestion rejected yesterday was conveyed indirectly from the State Department to the plenipotentiaries through the Rumanian and Greek Foreign Offices. The American Ministers to Greece and Rumania, it is said, could not deal officially with the peace conference.

The State Department acted as the result of strong pressure brought to bear from various quarters by Jewish individuals and organizations in this country. This agitation also found expression in Congress, where Senator Penrose and Representative J. Hampton Moore of Pennsylvania introduced resolutions calling upon the State Department for information as to what had been or would be done to cause the Government of Rumania to respect the rights of Jews guaranteed by the Treaty of Berlin.

\*   \*   \*

**August 11, 1913**

# ALLIES SIGN PEACE; TURKEY OBSTINATE

*Rumanians to Evacuate Bulgaria in Fifteen Days, Allies in Three*

## PROVIDES FOR ARBITRATION

*Frontier Disputes May Be Referred to Belgium, Holland, or Switzerland*

BUCHAREST, Aug. 10—The Balkan peace treaty was signed at 10:30 o'clock this morning. In honor of the occasion the city was decorated with flags, guns were fired, bells were rung, and the bands played.

A solemn Te Deum in the cathedral at noon was attended by King Charles, Queen Elizabeth, (Carmen Sylva,) and other members of the royal family and the delegates to the peace conference. King Charles conferred high decorations upon all the delegates, except the Bulgarians, who declined to receive them.

The peace treaty provides that the Rumanian Army shall evacuate Bulgarian territory in fifteen days after its signature and the Servian and Greek Armies in three days. It also provides for arbitration by Belgium, Holland, or Switzerland in the event of a disagreement over the delimitation of the new frontier. Bulgaria engages in the treaty to begin demobilization immediately.

CONSTANTINOPLE, Aug. 10—The Porte to-day made an evasive reply to the recent note of the powers, in which a threat was made that the latter would withdraw their moral and financial support from Turkey unless the Ottoman Government ordered its troops to retire within the Enos-Midia line, in accordance with the treaty of London.

## MORE OF BULGARS' MASSACRES
*Letter Tells of Terrified Greeks and Slaughter of 2,000 Villagers*

Partial confirmation of the stories of atrocities committed by the retiring Bulgarian forces upon the Greek inhabitants of Macedonian towns is contained in a private letter just received in New York from an American employee of the American Tobacco Company, stationed at Kavala, European Turkey. Under date of July 27, he writes:

"You have no doubt seen in the papers that the Greeks have taken Kavala and that their fleet was here in the harbor. The few days prior to the evacuation of the town by the Bulgars and the arrival of the Greek fleet were about the most thrilling that I ever spent. When it was reported on June 30 that war had commenced, the Bulgars arrested about thirty of the most prominent Greeks in town, and removed them to a farm just over the mountains from Kavala. They were to be killed if there was the least sign of an uprising among the Greek population.

"From this time on Comitadji swarmed into town. These men have to be seen to be appreciated. They are nothing less than brigands, and their arrival in a town is usually the signal for a little fancy killing. When they began to come in the Greeks were of course panic-striken, and became more excited every day until Monday, the 7th, when they lost their heads completely. On the morning of that day we had a number come in with the news that the Bulgars were quitting the town that night, and would burn the place and massacre everybody before they left. We didn't put much faith in this report until the afternoon, when more arrests of prominent Greeks were made. One of the American Tobacco Company's men was among the number that they tried to get, but he hid in the Italian consulate. On our arrival home that afternoon we found his whole family, consisting of his wife, sister-in-law, a 3-year-old girl, a month-old baby, and a nurse, all of them yelling murder as only these people can.

"By this time the town looked as if it were deserted, all gates being barred, as well as windows and doors. You can take it from me that there was mighty little sleep in town for the people that night, but after all the excitement nothing really happened. The excitement kept up all the next day, though, and at 7 o'clock in the evening the Bulgars marched out. A boat was sent to Thasos that night to notify the Greek fleet, and on the following morning four Greek boats steamed into the harbor. There really wasn't as much enthusiasm as one would have expected, for everybody had a feeling that the Bulgars had a card up their sleeved; but so far nothing has happened.

"The Bulgars in their flight have done some awful things in the nearby villages, though. Seres was completely destroyed, we having lost about half a million dollars, and our men there having had to walk all the way to Salonika to escape with their lives.

"Another American, an Englishman and I rode out to Doxat, a village about twenty miles from here, to see the ruins yesterday and I hope I will never see such a sight again. Doxat was a Greek town with a population of 10,000, and when we got there yesterday we didn't find a house standing. About 2,000 men, women and children had been butchered, some of the children being impaled on the pickets of iron fences. This happened about five days ago, and a few of the people had ventured back from the mountains, and it was a pitiful sight to see them. I was riding down one of the streets and had to guide my horse around a man who was standing in the middle of the road with a blank look on his face and who didn't even see me. Women were sitting around among the ruins—some crying, others just talking to themselves as if their minds were gone. Nearly all the villages have been treated in the same way, and the country is absolutely desolate.

"I haven't begun to tell you of the awful things that have happened and that I have seen, but they would certainly fill a book. I don't think you people so far away realize how bad it is, otherwise there would have been a warship here long ago. We are out of communication either by telegraph or post with the outside world, so we can't notify our consul at Salonika. I don't know when this will get away, but thought I would write you while I had the time, business of course being at a standstill."

# PART III

## WORLD WAR I, 1914–1919

June 29, 1914

### HEIR TO AUSTRIA'S THRONE IS SLAIN WITH HIS WIFE BY A BOSNIAN YOUTH TO AVENGE SEIZURE OF HIS COUNTRY

---

*Francis Ferdinand Shot During State Visit to Sarajevo*

#### TWO ATTACKS IN A DAY

*Archduke Saves His Life First Time by Knocking Aside a Bomb Hurled at Auto*

#### SLAIN IN SECOND ATTEMPT

*Lad Dashes at Car as the Royal Couple Return from Town Hall and Kills Both of Them*

#### LAID TO A SERVIAN PLOT

*Heir Warned Not to Go to Bosnia, Where Populace Met Him with Servian Flags*

#### AGED EMPEROR IS STRICKEN

*Shock of Tragedy Prostrates Francis Joseph—Young Assassin Proud of His Crime*

---

Special Cable to The New York Times

SARAJEVO, Bosnia, June 28, (By courtesy of the Vienna Neue Freie Presse.)—Archduke Francis Ferdinand, heir to the throne of Austria-Hungary, and his wife, the Duchess of Hohenberg, were shot and killed by a Bosnian student here today. The fatal shooting was the second attempt upon the lives of the couple during the day, and is believed to have been the result of a political conspiracy.

This morning, as Archduke Francis Ferdinand and the Duchess were driving to a reception at the Town Hall a bomb was thrown at their motor car. The Archduke pushed it off with his arm.

The bomb did not explode until after the Archduke's car had passed on, and the occupants of the next car, Count von Boos-Waldeck and Col. Morizzi, the Archduke's aide de camp, were slightly injured. Among the spectators, six persons were more or less seriously hurt.

The author of the attempt at assassination was a compositor named Gabrinovics, who comes from Trebinje.

After the attempt upon his life the Archduke ordered his car to halt, and after he found out what had happened he drove to the Town Hall, where the Town Councillors, with the Mayor at their head, awaited him. The Mayor was about to begin his address of welcome, when the Archduke interrupted him angrily, saying:

"Herr Burgermeister, it is perfectly outrageous! We have come to Sarajevo on a visit and have had a bomb thrown at us."

The Archduke paused a moment, and then said: "Now you may go on."

Thereupon the Mayor delivered his address and the Archduke made a suitable reply.

The public by this time had heard of the bomb attempt, and burst into the hall with loud cries of "Zivio!" the Slav word for "hurrah."

After going around the Town Hall, which took half an hour, the Archduke started for the Garrison Hospital to visit Col. Morizzi, who had been taken there after the outrage.

As the Archduke reached the corner of Rudolf Street two pistol shots were fired in quick succession by an individual who called himself Gavrio Princip. The first shot struck the Duchess in the abdomen, while the second hit the Archduke in the neck and pierced the jugular vein. The Duchess became unconscious immediately and fell across the knees of her husband. The Archduke also lost consciousness in a few seconds.

The motor car in which they were seated drove straight to the Konak, where an army Surgeon rendered first aid, but in vain. Neither the Archduke nor the Duchess gave any sign of life, and the head of the hospital could only certify they were both dead.

The authors of both attacks upon the Archduke are born Bosnians. Gabrinovics is a compositor, and worked for a few weeks in the Government printing works at Belgrade. He returned to Sarajevo a Servian chauvinist, and made no concealment of his sympathies with the King of Servia. Both he and the actual murderer of the Archduke and the Duchess expressed themselves to the police in the most cynical fashion about their crimes.

#### ARCHDUKE IGNORED WARNING
#### Servian Minister Feared Trouble if Heir Went to Bosnia

Special Cable to The New York Times
[Dispatch to The London Daily Mail]

VIENNA, June 28—When the news of the assassination of the Archduke Francis Ferdinand and the Duchess was broken to the aged Emperor Francis Joseph he said: "Horrible, horrible! No sorrow is spared me."

The Emperor, who yesterday left here for Ischl, his favorite Summer resort, amid acclamations of the people, will return to Vienna at once, in spite of the hardships of the journey in the terrible heat.

The Archduke, who was created head of the army, went to Bosnia to represent the Emperor at the grand manoeuvres there. This was the first time the Archduke had paid an official visit to Bosnia. The Emperor visited the provinces immediately after their annexation, in 1908, and the manner in which he mixed freely with the people was much criticised at the time, as those in his party were always afraid lest some Slav or Mohammedan fanatic might attempt the monarch's life. The Emperor's popularity, however, saved him from all danger of this kind.

Before the Archduke went to Bosnia last Wednesday the Servian Minister here expressed doubt as to the wisdom of the journey, saying the country was in a very turbulent condition and the Servian part of the population might organize a demonstration against the Archduke. The Minister said if the Archduke went himself he certainly ought to leave his wife at home, because Bosnia was no place for a woman in its present disturbed state.

The Minister's word proved correct. The people of Sarajevo welcomed the Archduke with a display of Servian flags, and the authorities had some difficulty in removing them before the Archduke made his state entry into the city yesterday, after the conclusion of the manoeuvres. In these manoeuvres were the famous Fifteenth and Sixteenth Army Corps, which were stationed on the frontier throughout the recent Balkan war, and they carried out the evolutions before the Archduke.

### Greeted with Cheers

The details of the tragedy, as received in Vienna, were as follows: The Archduke was driving in a motor car, toward the Town Hall in Sarajevo, with the Duchess of Hohenberg by his side. A large crowd assembled to watch them go by. The Archduke, raising his hand to his military cap, acknowledged the cheers, while the Duchess was smiling and bowing, her pretty face framed by her blonde hair.

Suddenly the Archduke's sharp eye caught sight of a bomb hurling through the air. His first thought was for his wife, and he threw up his arm in time to catch the bomb, which thus was turned aside from its course and fell on the pavement and exploded. The Archduke's motor car hastened on its way, its occupants unharmed, but the two Adjutants who were seated in the next motor car were injured by splinters from the bomb. Several persons on the pavement were very seriously hurt by the explosion of the bomb, which was thrown by a young man named Tabrinovitch (Gabrinovics) who is a typist from Trebenje. In Herzegovina, and is of Servian nationality. He was arrested some twenty minutes later.

The Archduke and his wife left the Town Hall, intending to visit those who had been injured by the bomb, when a schoolboy 19 years old, named, Prinzip, who came from Grahovo, fired a shot at the Archduke's head. The boy fired from the shelter of a projecting house.

### Wore Bullet-Proof Coat

The boy must have been carefully instructed in his part, for it was a well-guarded secret that the Archduke always wore a coat of silk strands which were woven obliquely, so that no weapon or bullet could pierce it. I once saw a strip of this fabric used for a motor-car tire, and it was punc-

ture-proof. This new invention enabled the Archduke to brave attempts on his life, but his head naturally was uncovered.

The Duchess was shot in the body. The boy fired several times, but only two shots took effect. The Archduke and his wife were carried to the Konak, or palace, in a dying condition.

Later details show that the assassin darted forth from his hiding place behind a house and actually got on the motor car in which the Archduke and his wife were sitting. He took close aim first at the Archduke, and then at the Duchess. The fact that no one stopped him, and that he was allowed to perpetrate the dastardly act indicate that the conspiracy was carefully planned and that the Archduke fell a victim to a political plot. The aspiration of the Servian population in Bosnia to join with Servia and form a great Servian kingdom is well known. No doubt today's assassination was regarded as a means of forwarding this plan.

### Break News to Children

The Archduke's children are at Glumex, in Bohemia, and relatives already have left Vienna to break the news to them. The Duke of Cumberland motored to Ischl immediately upon receipt of the news and was received by the Emperor, who will arrive in Vienna at 6 o'clock tomorrow. The bodies of the Archduke and his wife will not be brought to Vienna until tomorrow a week.

The Archduke Charles Francis Joseph, the new heir to the throne, is at Reichenau, near Vienna with his wife. Princess Zita of Parma and their little son and daughter. He is expected in Vienna tonight.

When the first news of the assassination became known in Vienna, early this afternoon, crowds collected in solemn silence and discussed the report, which was not credited at first. Every one connected with the press was stormed by crowds asking whether confirmation had been received, and on hearing the truth they said. "How awful!" and then dispersed, to go about their ordinary business or pleasure. The newspapers are getting out extra editions, and the whole city talks of nothing else.

### New Heir Popular

The Archduke Charles Francis Joseph, who is now heir to the throne, always has enjoyed great popularity. He was trained for the throne from the first, although he was kept somewhat in the background, being sent to country garrisons. He was not allowed to undertake to act as the representative of the Duchy of Vienna to as great an extent as the Viennese would have wished. This, however, did not detract from his popularity, while the Princess Zita, his wife, won all hearts before she married the heir to the throne, and the birth of a son two years ago completed her popularity, if, indeed, anything was lacking.

General opinion here connects the assassins with the Servian faction, and it is feared that it will lead to serious complications with that unruly kingdom, and may have far-reaching results. The future of the empire is a subject of general discussion. It is felt that the Servians have been

Archduke Francis Ferdinand and his Consort the Duchess of Hohenberg Slain by Assassin's Bullets.

treated too leniently, and some hard words are being said about the present foreign policy.

All the public buildings are draped in long black streamers and the flags are all at half-mast.

### BRAVERY OF ARCHDUKE
#### Gave First Aid to Those Wounded by the Bomb

SARAJEVO, Bosnia, June 28—Archduke Francis Ferdinand, heir to the Austro-Hungarian throne, and the Duchess of Hohenberg, his morganatic wife, were shot dead in the main street of the Bosnian capital by a student today while they were making an apparently triumphant progress through the city on their annual visit to the annexed provinces of Bosnia and Herzegovina.

The Archduke was hit full in the face and the Duchess was shot through the abdomen and throat. Their wounds proved fatal within a few minutes after they reached the palace, whence they were hurried with all speed.

Those responsible for the assassination took care that it would prove effective, as there were two assailants, the first armed with a bomb and the other with a revolver. The bomb was thrown at the royal automobile as it was proceeding to the Town Hall, where a reception was to be held, but the

Archduke saw the deadly missile coming and warded it off with his arm. It fell outside the car and exploded slightly wounding two aids de camp in a second car, and half a dozen spectators. It was on the return of the procession that the tragedy was added to the long list of those that have darkened the pages of the recent history of the Hapsburgs.

As the royal automobile reached a prominent point in the route to the palace an eighth grade student, Gavrio Prinzip, sprang out of the crowd and poured a fusillade of bullets from an automatic pistol at the Archduke and the Duchess. Both fell mortally wounded.

Prinzip and a fellow-conspirator, a compositor from Trebinje, Nedeijo Gabrinovics, barely escaped lynching by the infuriated spectators and were finally seized by the police, who afforded them protection. Both men are natives of the annexed province of Herzegovina.

#### Wards Off the Bomb

The first attempt against the Archduke occurred just outside the Girls' High School. The Archduke's car had restarted after a brief pause for an inspection of the building when Gabrinovics hurled the bomb. This was so successfully warded off by the Archduke that it fell directly beneath the following car, the occupants of which, Count von Boos-Waldeck and Col. Merizzo, were struck by splinters of iron.

Archduke Francis Ferdinand stopped his car and after making inquiries as to the injuries of his aids and lending what aid he could, continued his journey to the Town Hall. There the Mayor began the customary address, but the Archduke sharply interrupted and snapped out, "Herr Burgomeister, we have come here to pay you a visit and bombs have been thrown at us. This is altogether an amazing indignity."

After a pause, the Archduke said: "Now you may speak."

On leaving the hall the Archduke and his wife announced their intention of visiting the wounded members of their suite at the hospital on their way back to the palace. They were actually bound on their mission of mercy when, at the corner of Rudolf Street and Franz Josef Street, Prinzip opened his deadly fusillade.

A bullet struck the Archduke in the face. The Duchess was wounded in the abdomen and another bullet struck her in the throat, severing an artery. She fell unconscious across her husband's knees. At the same moment the Archduke sank to the floor of the car.

### Plunges Into River

After his unsuccessful attempt to blow up the imperial visitors Gabrinovics sprang into the River Miljaka in an effort to escape, but witnesses plunged after him and seized him.

A few yards from the scene of the shooting an unexploded bomb was found which, it is suspected, was thrown away by an accomplice after he had noted the success of Prinzip's attack.

The assassins were questioned by the police during the course of the afternoon, and both seemed to glory in their exploit. Prinzip said he had studied for a time at Belgrade. He declared he had long intended to kill some eminent person from nationalist motives. He was awaiting the Archduke at a point where he knew the automobile would slacken speed, turning into Franz Josef Street. The presence of the Duchess in the car caused him to hesitate, but only for a moment. Then his nerve returned and he emptied his pistol at the couple. He denied that he had any accomplices.

Prinzip is 18 years old and Nedeijo Gabrinovics is 21. Gabrinovics told the police that he had obtained the bomb from Anarchists at Belgrade, whose names he did not know. He similarly denied that he had accomplices and treated the whole tragedy with cynical indifference.

Anti-Servian demonstrations began tonight. The crowds knelt in the streets and sang the national anthem. The Mayor of Sarajevo issued a proclamation to the inhabitants of the city denouncing the crime, and declaring that by the concessions of the assassins it was shown beyond all doubt that the bomb thrown at the Archduke's car came from Belgrade.

It is said that after the attempt with the bomb the Duchess tried to dissuade the Archduke from venturing in the motor car again. To allay her fears M. Potiorek, Governor of Bosnia, said: "It's all over now. We have not more than one murderer in Sarajevo," whereupon the Archduke decided to go on.

At a meeting of the provincial Diet tonight the President of the Chamber expressed Bosnia's profound sorrow and indignation over the outrage and paid a glowing tribute to the Archduke and the Duchess. He also declared his devotion to the Emperor and the ruling house.

### FRANCIS JOSEPH PROSTRATED
#### Aged Emperor Takes to His Room on Hearing of the Tragedy

ISCHI, June 28—Emperor Francis Joseph suffered a profound shock when he was informed of the assassination of the Archduke Francis Ferdinand and the Duchess, and retired immediately to his private apartment after giving orders that everything should be in readiness for his return to the palace of Schoenbrunn on Monday. The Duke of Cumberland paid a visit of condolences this afternoon.

The three young children of the Archduke and the Duchess who remained here with the aged Emperor when their parents went to Bosnia, were playing in the gardens of the palace when the news came. Nobody had the heart to inform them of their bereavement.

The succession, if no change is made hereafter, now passes to Archduke Charles Francis, son of the late Archduke Otto, and a nephew of Francis Ferdinand, who married Princess Zita of Parma. They have one son and one daughter.

VIENNA, June 28—The assassination of Archduke Francis Ferdinand and the Duchess of Hohenberg caused a profound sensation here. The streets were quickly thronged, and anxious inquiries were made regarding the details of this, the latest addition to the list of tragedies that have befallen some of the most prominent members of the imperial family during the present reign.

Immediately the assassination became known, the authorities took possession of all telegraphic and telephonic facilities at Sarajevo and shut off unofficial communications.

The utmost sympathy is expressed everywhere for the venerable Emperor Francis Joseph, who only yesterday left Vienna for Ischi, upper Austria, to recuperate after a serious illness.

Archduke Francis Ferdinand and his wife left the capital on Wednesday in the best of health and spirits for a tour of Bosnia and Herzegovina, where the Archduke was also to take command of important manoeuvres. According to reports received here they had met with an enthusiastic reception everywhere. Rumors of a plot against the life of the heir to the throne had been in circulation for the past few days and the police thought they had taken effective precautions to safeguard the Archduke and the Duchess.

It is feared that the Sarajevo tragedy will still further embitter the none too friendly relations existing between Austria and Servia. Both the youth who fired the fatal shots and the bomb thrower are Servians with close associations with Belgrade. The bombs also came from Belgrade. It is likewise remarkable that the first news of the assassination received at Budapest came from the Servian capital.

The effect of the tragedy on the stock market was the subject of discussion by brokers, but tomorrow being St. Peter's and St. Paul's Day, and a holiday, will give the Boerse an opportunity to recover before the opening on Tuesday.

Telegrams are being received tonight from all parts of the kingdom announcing the immense sensation caused by the crime. All public festivities have been canceled.

Anti-Servian demonstrations occurred tonight outside the Servian Legation, and stones were thrown at the residences of prominent Servians. Troops were ordered out to suppress the disorders.

It is reported here that several Bosnians and Serbs have been arrested at Sarajevo for complicity in the plot, which is said to have wide ramifications. The newspapers have issued special editions with black borders, expressing abhorrence at the crime.

The Wiener Zeitung pays high tribute to the extraordinary zeal and devotion to the empire displayed by the Archduke, to whose indefatigable care, it says, were due the great developments of recent years in the Austrian army and navy.

### POPE MUCH DEPRESSED
#### Spends a Long Time in Prayer—Italian Foreign Office Anxious

Special Cable to The New York Times

ROME, June 28—The terrible crime at Sarajevo, though not a personal grief to the Italian sovereigns as they did not know the Archduke Ferdinand, is causing considerable anxiety at the Foreign Office. Although the Archduke was considered unfriendly to Italy, being very clerical and also under the influence of the military party, his successor is an unknown quantity, and might not be such a stanch supporter as the aged Emperor of the Triple Alliance.

The Pope was much depressed by the crime. At first his entourage intended to withhold the news, but Cardinal Merry del Val broke it as gently as possible to the Pope who every year is less able to withstand the shock of such news.

The deep impression made by the news was shown by the Pope's melancholy today. He spent a long time at the altar, praying for the repose of the souls of the Archduke and the Duchess.

### WILL SEND CONDOLENCES
#### United States Government Notified of Assassination by Embassy

Special to The New York Times

WASHINGTON, June 28—Secretary Bryan said this evening that the American Embassy at Vienna had notified him of the assassination of Archduke Francis Ferdinand.

He said official condolences to the aged Emperor of Austria would be sent promptly.

\*    \*    \*

June 29, 1914

# AUSTRIA TO BLAME, SAYS PROF. PUPIN

*Policy of Repression of Serbs, He Says, Is Cause of Assassinations*

**A RACE 'DRIVEN TO FERMENT'**

*Tragedy Was Inevitable, He Asserts, Because of the Domineering Tactics Adopted by Austria*

"Austria's policy of repression of the Serb peoples is responsible for this calamity," said Prof. Michael I. Pupin of Columbia University at the University Club last night. Prof. Pupin comes of Servian stock and typifies the big, dark-haired and dark-eyed men of his race.

"There are two recent movements that really foreshadowed some disaster to anyone familiar with the temperament of the Servian people," he said. "These are the strike of the students in the Government schools in Bosnia and Herzegovina that began several months ago, and has not been settled; and second, that probably of greater importance, the military manoeuvres of the Austrian army that have been going on in these two countries under the direction of the Crown Prince.

"The student strike began, you remember, when a Government professor in the school at Mostar, Herzegovina, made violent attacks on the Serb race. The students of his class rose in a body and asked him to retract. He refused. They pitched him out of the class room and used him rather roughly. These fifty Serb students went on strike. They are only high school students really, boys about 16 to 19 years old. But their patriotism is inflammable. They refused to return till the professor was dismissed. They were expelled. Then throughout Herzegovina and Bosnia the students struck in sympathy. The Government sent troops and officers to restore order. The students refused to give in. And so the fight stands deadlocked.

"With all Servian people smarting under the oppression of Austria, that country's policy toward the provinces she has annexed is criminally foolish. Nothing could be more calculated to provoke the people of Herzegovina and Bosnia to rage than to have Austrian troops thrown across their borders to execute manoeuvres along the Servian frontier. They are Serbs, of the same stock as the people of Servia proper, and to see the Archduke massing his forces in mimic war preparatory to the war which all feel must come some day between Austria and Servia when the former tries to seize Servia—this was maddening.

#### A Tragedy Inevitable

"It does not surprise me to learn of today's tragedy. By that I do not mean to condone assassination. And yet knowing the temperament of the people it seems to have been inevitable. Years of Austria's domineering repression of the Serb instinct for independence has got the race in a ferment. This morning I was reading the life of the Serb, D. Obradovich, who was the first man to introduce the influence of modern literature among the Servian people.

"He was the apostle of Servian education and culture. After traveling all over the world he returned to Servia in 1803 at the call of Black George, grand-father of the present King Peter, to fight for Servia's freedom from Turkey. That war lasted twenty-five years.

"Obradovich was born under the Austrian flag. But he was a Servian. In spite of this Austria has always called him a traitor, a renegade, a hypocrite, a sneak and accused him of inciting the Austrians against their Emperor. In truth he was one of the noblest men who ever lived. And when I read the story of the oppressions he suffered, the persecution, and the blackening of his name, it stirred me so that I felt if there was one thing bred in my bones it was hatred of Austria.

"I cite this to show how systematic has been Austria's vilification of the Serbs for generations. In the press and by every possible means she has tried to blacken their name. In that fight for independence she tried to weaken Servia by refusing to sell her grain or any munitions. She had ships of grain lying in the Danube, but the merchants of Belgrade could not buy it. Faced with starvation, the Servian soldiers crept up one night, cut the anchor ropes, and floated the ships down stream, and gave the grain to the hungry people.

"Today, the same as a hundred years ago, Austria is trying to obstruct every movement that will lead to the complete national independence of the Servian people. Why? Because of Austria's economic greed. She needs a seaport on the Adriatic that will make her mistress of that and the Aegean Seas. The Grecian capture of Salonica was a bitter pill for her. That is why she is spreading slanders against the Greeks.

### Hints at Austrian Intrigue

"I firmly believe that it was an Austrian intrigue which resulted in the Carnegie commission's findings which represented the 'Greeks and Servians' conduct as so barbarous in the Balkan war, I don't credit those reports, of course. No man who is informed can. But it has served to blacken the Servian name throughout the civilized world.

"Ever since the outbreak of the Balkan war Austria's hostility to Servia and Montenegro has been most marked. It was she who insisted that the Servians must evacuate Albania. Austria expects to gobble up Albania herself and so finally acquire the opening on the Adriatic for which she longs. It was she who insisted that Montenegro should evacuate Scutari. There she intends to plant her foot on the border or the sea.

"In her conduct with all the countries and provinces inhabited by Serbs her conduct has been unbearably high-handed and insolent. Bosnia, Herzegovina, Dalmatia, Croatia, Slavonia, and Banat, all of them have suffered from her arrogance and greed. There is an ambiguity in calling the natives of these countries Servians—they are Serbs. The young student by whose hand the Archduke and Duchess fell was a Servian in this sense. He was undoubtedly a native of Bosnia, not of Servia.

"Imagine how the sense of their country's wrongs works on the minds of these impressionable boys. They feel the sufferings of their people—the economic oppression, the burden of taxes, &c. Before Austria secured Bosnia and Herzegovina by the treaty of Berlin in 1878 the people were better off. Then they were allowed some little liberty with the land.

"Now an old woman cannot go into the forests and gather up an apronful of sticks for her fire without making herself liable to arrest and heavy punishment. No, the wood is first shipped to Vienna and then brought back to Bosnia and sold to the peasant at ten or fifteen times the price it should bring.

"To men of mature years it is plain that nothing can be accomplished by murder, and such acts of lawlessness. But as that young lad stands in his cell tonight in Sarajevo he is smiling, he is happy. His instinct was to strike a blow for his country. And with his single arm he struck as high as he could hope to reach.

"His act is not to be compared with that by which McKinley lost his life. McKinley was the victim of a maniac. This boy was doubtless supported by companions all in the plot. The way in which the deed is said to have been done would seem to prove that it was not the act of a single individual, but the result of combined effort. It is regrettable, but I can only repeat that it gives me no surprise.

"I have myself experienced the unfair methods by which Austria works and inflames those whom she oppresses. About two years ago a native of Bosnia, who was working in Chicago, went back home and made an attempt on the life of the Austrian Governor of Bosnia. To my surprise I found that in the Reichspost of Vienna the official organ to the Crown Prince, I was accused of being the instigator of that deed. And furthermore it stated that I was the head of a Servian organization in this country fomenting revolutions in the Austrian provinces.

"I can say with absolute conviction that this attack on the Archduke was not made at the instigation of the Servian capital. In Belgrade and throughout Servia, it is recognized by everyone of intelligence, and certainly by the students, that it would hurt their country in the eyes of the whole world to have the responsibility for such a deed laid at their doors."

\* \* \*

**June 30, 1914**

## SEE SERB PLOT IN ROYAL MURDERS

*Killing of the Archduke and His Wife Believed to Have Been Planned in Belgrade*

**MARTIAL LAW IS DECLARED**

*Fatal Anti-Serb Riots at Sarajevo—Much Property Destroyed*

**FUNERAL TO BE HURRIED**

*Decision Due to Desire to Spare the Aged Emperor as Much as Possible and to Avert Clashes*

Special Cable to The New York Times
VIENNA, June 29—The youth Prinzip, who yesterday killed the Archduke Francis Ferdinand and the latter's wife,

the Duchess of Hohenberg, and Gabrinovics, who had previously thrown a bomb at the Archduke, deny the existence of a plot, but the authorities nevertheless believe that both outrages were the results of a far-spread conspiracy with its origin in Belgrade.

Several dozen persons, including a couple of women, who are suspected of complicity, have been arrested.

Prinzip declared that he was an enemy of imperialism and had decided to kill the Archduke as its embodiment. Gabrinovics has confessed that the bomb he threw was made in the Servian arsenal at Kraguyevatz. He said that as a convinced Servian Nationalist he had planned to kill an enemy of Servia.

A military personage who saw the assassination of the Archduke and his wife says neither of them appeared to know he or she was wounded until the Duchess fell into her husband's arms. The Archduke said, "What is the matter." By this time his uniform was covered with blood from a wound in his own neck. The chauffeur could not bring the motor car to a standstill for some seconds.

### Tried to Close Husband's Wound

The Duchess clutched at her husband's neck with her fingers as if trying to close his terrible wound. As she saw that the blood continued to flow she screamed "My God! my God!" and sank backward in the car. She was removed from the car to the Konak, where she died without recovering consciousness.

As the Archduke was being carried upstairs in the Konak he opened his eyes several times and his hands seemed to clutch at the air.

Francis Kaner, a monk, who was in the neighborhood of the Konak, hastened to the scene and gave the pair the last benediction. Six doctors hurried up, but it was too late to do anything.

The fatal shots were fired by Prinzip from a distance of three paces. One bullet, piercing the side of the automobile, mortally wounded the Duchess. The Governor of Bosnia, who was sitting opposite the Archduke and the Duchess in the car, declares that the Archduke had hardly time to utter the words, "Sophie, remain alive for our children!" when he also was mortally wounded by another bullet, which struck him in the neck, rupturing an artery and the windpipe.

The chauffeur of the Archduke's car made the mistake of driving down Franz Josef Strasse instead of going straight on as he had been ordered to do. In consequence he was compelled to stop and turn the car. It was while he was doing this that the fatal shots were fired.

In describing to a representative of the press the throwing of the bomb by Gabrinovics, Count Waldeck, who was driving in a car immediately following the Archduke, states that he saw a black package fall on the opened hood of the Archduke's car. The Archduke picked it up and threw it out of the car. As it touched the ground it exploded close to the front wheel of Count Waldeck's car. It is a miracle, the Count says, that all the occupants were not killed.

### Would Punish the Serbs

In military and clerical circles the feeling aroused by the assassination of Archduke Francis Ferdinand and his wife borders on frenzy. A punitive war upon Servia is advocated by advanced sections of the Military and Clerical Parties, who looked to the murdered Archduke to carry out their political aims.

A typical expression of this feeling, is found in the Reichspost, the journal which the late Archduke specially favored, and the leading organ of the Military and Clerical Parties. The Reichspost says editorially:

"With bleeding hearts we have to announce that the murderer belongs to that race which has ever enjoyed the especial attention and greatest good-will and care of our reigning house.

"We have here to deal with a carefully planned blow, with a plot which, through the person of the Heir Apparent, was aimed at the State itself. The band of conspirators pushed mere youths into the foreground and incited them to the murder. A 19-year-old madman pulled the trigger of the revolver, instead of the thousands who for decades have been active in trying to tear Bosnia and Herzegovina from the empire.

### A "Murderous Propaganda"

"Were not the plots against the Governor of Bosnia, Varzeni; against Jianusse, Cuvaj and Skeriecz; against Vizebanus and Grazkowits forerunners of this present diabolical murderous propaganda? Nothing that is sacred can restrain these mad pan-Servian fanatics from bloodshed and murder. It is inconceivable—this piling up of political insanity which has found expression in such a horrible way.

"The future hope of Austria-Hungary was murdered by the pan-Servian idea. It is only a few days since the heir to the throne walked arm-in-arm with the Kaiser Wilhelm in the rose gardens of Konopischt, Bohemia, and at a critical time gave the world renewed proof of the close relations between the two allied nations. At the very time when the Czar was exchanging brotherly kisses with King Charles of Rumania at Costanza there was given to the world at Konopischt proof of the unshakable firmness of the alliance between two mighty Continental nations, and from Konopischt the Archduke traveled via Vienna direct into that territory where the enemy must be met in future—the enemy who must be regarded as the puppet of that great power whose rancor and hostility we learned from the wording of the first Balkan alliance.

"The blood of the Austrian heir and of the Duchess of Hohenberg were shed by a young Servian, but this blood had to flow because of those aggressive tendencies which for years have been inspired from another side in the Servian consciousness.

"Alone, like a tree stripped of its foliage, our Kaiser stands today in his responsible position. Closer than ever will the peoples of Austria now range themselves about the throne of the Hapsburgs. With sorrowing hearts, but with an undaunted, manly spirit, will they renew their loyal pledge to aid with their riches and blood the Hapsburg crown and the honor of the empire."

The bodies of the Archduke and the Duchess will be interred at the Archduke's seat at Artstetten. The Archduke arranged this long ago, because he wished the whole family to be buried together, although there is no doubt now that his morganatic wife would be admitted to the Capuchin vault in Vienna, kept sacred to members of the imperial family, after her bravery in attempting to shield her husband's body with her own.

In the obituary notices published here it is freely admitted that the Archduke Francis Ferdinand was not popular, and probably would never have been so in that sense in which the Emperor is popular. It is generally supposed that he was somewhat embittered by the difficulties attending his marriage with the woman of his choice and the anomalous position given to his consort and children.

\* \* \*

June 30, 1914

## BRUTAL REVENGE FOR BOSNIA

Some weeks since, when the life of the Emperor Francis Joseph was daily despaired of, the whole world, in spite of its sympathy with the courageous old ruler of Austria-Hungary, felt that there would be compensation for his loss in the likelihood that his successor, the Archduke Francis Ferdinand, would be able to hold together the various States united under Austrian rule. He was accounted a popular Prince, a sagacious and resourceful man, and he was known throughout the empire. Today the situation is changed. The heir to the throne is dead, the chief victim of one of the most horrible assassinations ever shamefully associated with the sacred cause of liberty. The old Emperor's failing health is rendered still more precarious by the shock of this murder, and the prospect that the tremendous responsibilities of his kingship may shortly fall upon a young man whose capacity for rule has never been proved must disturb all Europe.

For the present, however, the unutterable brutality of the slaughter of the Archduke and the wife for whose sake he risked all his kingly prospects, and the wounding of some members of their escort, absorbs the attention. No political murder was ever more deliberately performed. It was a festal day in Sarajevo, and there was no suspicion that the heir to the throne and the lady who has been looked upon throughout all Austria and its dependencies as a popular idol were in any danger. The event proves that the successor to Francis Joseph's throne will have a task set before him which might bewilder the most heroic mind. This murder was inspired not by the spirit of anarchy, but by revenge. The seizure by Austria of Bosnia and Herzegovina was high-handed and in defiance of the concert of Europe. The act has been punished in a manner which reflects no credit on Bosnia.

\* \* \*

July 5, 1914

## IDEALS OF PAN-GERMANISM AND PAN-SLAVISM

Twenty years ago the late Prof. Mommsen predicted that Germany's isolation and the defects of German diplomacy would have their revenge at Vienna on the death of Francis Joseph. About the same time the late Constantinis Pobedonostev, former tutor of Czar Alexander II and Procurator of the Holy Synod, prophesied that the same event would find Russia in Constantinople. Pan-Germanism, speaking broadly, means the absorption of the Austrian Germans by the German Empire. Added to the self-evident fact that Germany needs raw materials for her manufactures and agricultural products for her rapidly growing population is the firm belief in Berlin that the Austrian Germans are not as happily governed as they would be under the German Kaiser. Besides, Germany desires a port on the Adriatic. If Pan-Germanism is thus consummated, Alsace, Lorraine, and Luxembourg are to be returned to France; Italy is to have Triest and possibly Dalmatia; Russia, Galicia and Bukowina, and perhaps a strip along the Black Sea leading to Constantinople, and independence would be given to Hungary.

Pan-Slavism is partly religious—to bring under the Holy Synod all the Balkan communicants of the Greek Church; partly racial—to bring all Slavonic peoples under the Czar; and partly commercial—to give Russia a southern port within easy access to markets. Between 1709 and 1877 Russian armies made five unsuccessful attempts to reach Constantinople. Therefore there developed from the original Pan-Slavism a policy of conciliation toward the Slavs of Austria-Hungary and one of encouragement toward the nations of the Balkans. This was intended to disrupt the Austro-Hungarian Empire and inspire the Slav nationalities of the Balkans with material and spiritual support to drive the Turk out of Europe.

The Austrian policy, of which the late Archduke Francis Ferdinand was a formidable exponent, consisted in keeping the Turk in Europe as a force to be counted on against Russian expansion, to add territory to the Slav portion of the Empire, and then gradually to turn the dual monarchy into a German, Magyar, and Slav federation. Although the recent successes of the Balkan nations and the strengthening of Russia's influence among them have caused more or less disaffection among the Slavs of Austria-Hungary, the idea of federation is still strong among them. Although they may be Pan-Slav they are not Pan-Russian. It probably will be found, however, when the venerable Austrian Kaiser dies, that both Pan-Germanism and Pan-Slavism have become mere academic questions, and that the policy of a great German-Magyar-Slav federation cannot be shattered by either.

\* \* \*

**July 24, 1914**

## AUSTRIA READY TO INVADE SERVIA, SENDS ULTIMATUM

---

*Demands by 6 P. M. Tomorrow Disavowal of Anti-Austrian Propaganda*

**SUPPRESSION OF SOCIETIES**

*Also Punishment of All Accomplices in Murder of Archduke Francis Ferdinand and Wife*

**SERVIA MAY NOT COMPLY**

*Will Resist Requirements for the Suppression of Political Organization, Berlin Hears*

**7 ARMY CORPS AT TEMESVAR**

*Fleet of Danube Monitors Gathering at Semlin, Opposite the City of Belgrade*

**GERMANY AND ITALY TO AID**

*Prepared to Prevent at All Cost Interference on Behalf of the Little Kingdom*

---

Special Cable to The New York Times

BERLIN, July 23—A note from Austria couched in the peremptory terms of an ultimatum and demanding a reply by 6 o'clock Saturday evening was delivered to the Servian Government at Belgrade this evening at 6 o'clock.

It demands the punishment of all accomplices in the murder of the Archduke Francis Ferdinand and the suppression of all the societies which have fomented rebellion in Bosnia. The Servian Government must publish on Sunday an official disavowal of its connection with the anti-Austrian propaganda.

It is understood here that Belgrade will refuse to comply with the demand for the suppression of the societies.

Grave importance is attached to the fact that Baron Hoetzendorf, Chief of the Austrian General Staff, yesterday visited Temesvar, from where the Austrian army would invade Servia. Seven corps have been ordered to be held in readiness and several monitors have proceeded to Semlin.

In case of Servia's non-compliance with the ultimatum the army will invade the kingdom without further parley.

Germany and Italy have expressed full approval of the Austrian programme and announced their readiness to go to extremes to "keep the ring" for their ally in case interference in support of Servia is offered from any quarter.

German officers, it is learned from an authoritative quarter, have been able to obtain leave during the last few days only on condition that they will return instantly to their posts on telegraphic notice.

BELGRADE, July 23—The Servian Government received tonight a note from the Austro-Hungarian Government bearing on the relations between the two countries and dealing directly with the assassination at Sarayevo on June 28 of Archduke Francis Ferdinand, heir to the Austrian throne.

The note reviews the relations with Servia since 1907, and complains that, although the Servian Government promised loyalty to the Austro-Hungarian Government, it has failed to suppress subversive movements and agitations by the newspapers, and that this tolerance has incited the Servian people to hatred of the Austro-Hungarian monarchy and contempt for its institutions.

This, says the note, culminated in the Sarayevo assassinations, which are proved by depositions and confessions of the perpetrators to have been hatched at Belgrade, the arms and explosives having been supplied by the connivance of Servian officers and functionaries.

"The Austro-Hungarian Government," continues the note, "is unable longer to pursue an attitude of forbearance, and sees the duty imposed upon it to put an end to the intrigues which form a perpetual menace to the monarchy's tranquillity. It therefore demands from the Servian Government formal assurance that it condemns the dangerous propaganda whose aim is to detach from the monarchy a portion of its territory, and also that the Servian Government shall no longer permit these machinations and this criminal, perverse propaganda."

The note then gives the terms of a long formal declaration which the Servian Government is required to publish in its official journal on the front page, condemning the subversive propaganda, deploring its fatal consequences, regretting the participation of Servian officers in this propaganda, repudiating any further interference with Austro-Hungarian interests, and warning all Servian officers and functionaries, and the whole Servian population, that rigorous proceedings will be taken in the future against any persons guilty of such machinations.

This declaration must also be proclaimed officially to the Servian Army and the Servian courts must undertake to suppress subversive publications and dissolve immediately the Pan-Servian society styled "Narodna Odbrana," confiscating all its means of carrying on a propaganda, and suppress all similar societies having anti-Austrian tendencies.

Servia is further enjoined to eliminate from the educational system such tendencies, to remove all officers and functionaries guilty of anti-Austrian propaganda, whose names and deeds the Austrian Government reserves to itself the right of communicating to the Servian Government; to accept the assistance of representatives of the Austro-Hungarian Government in this work of suppression; to prosecute the accessories to the Sarayevo plot; to arrest Major Tankavitch and a Servian State employe, Giganovitch, who were compromised by the Sarayevo magisterial inquiry; to stop the illicit traffic of arms and explosives across the frontier, to dismiss and punish the Servian officials in the frontier service guilty of assisting the assassins across the frontier; to furnish the Austrian Government with explanations of anti-Austrian utterances, credited to high Servian officials since the Sarayevo crime, and finally to notify the Austrian Government promptly of the execution of all the foregoing demands.

Appended to the note is a long memorandum detailing all the facts of Servian complicity elicited by the magisterial inquiry at Sarayevo.

## NATIONS LONG AT ODDS
### Archduke's Murder Precipitated Crisis in
### Austro-Servian Relations

The demands of Austria upon Servia are based in part on the confession of Nedeijo Gabrinovics who threw the bomb at the Archduke Francis Ferdinand on June 28, shortly before Gabrio Prinzip shot him, Gabrinovics said that he had formed in Belgrade a conspiracy with Prinzip and four others to kill the Archduke. One of the four, a Belgrade student named Grabes has been arrested; but the others are still at large.

The Pan-Servian union is the society aimed at in the ultimatum. This organization aspires to unite the entire Servian race. Its Secretary, Major Milan Pribitchevitch formerly an officer in the Austrian Army, was appealed to by Gabrinovics and his accomplices, according to the confession, and through him they obtained bombs and revolvers from the Servian arsenal at Kraguyevatz.

The feeling between the two nations, however, goes back much further. Only a minority of the Servian race live in Servia and the Macedonian territory recently won from the Turks. Montenegro is inhabited by people ethnically and linguistically the same, so are Bosnia and Herzegovina, so is much of the hinterland of Dalmatia and large districts in Hungary. In other words a hundred years ago part of the Servian race was subject to Turkey and part to the Hapsburg monarchy. The part under Turkish domination has won its freedom; the other has not.

Bosnia and the Herzegovina rose against Turkey in 1876, as did Servia proper. After the Congress of Berlin had settled the Balkan question in 1878 these two countries, so far from receiving their freedom, were handed over to Austria, though remaining under nominal Turkish suzerainty. They promptly revolted, and were subdued only after four years of guerrilla warfare. Ever since then there has been much bitter feeling and a strong army of occupation has been maintained.

### Annexed to Austria

Austria spent large sums on public improvements, and felt that she had a property interest in the territory. When, therefore, the Turkish constitutional revolution in 1908 led to a call for representatives to come to a Parliament from all parts of the empire, including Bosnia and the Herzegovina. Austria had a good excuse for announcing the annexation of these countries. Servia protested violently, and was backed by Russia, but Germany's support of Austria led to the withdrawal of the opposition of the Slav powers and the annexation was completed.

This inflamed the feeling of the Servians, which the promise of an autonomous diet for the two provinces did nothing to allay. Austria's ambitions still looked toward the ultimate acquisition of Salonika and Servian and Turkish territory lay squarely in the way. The first Balkan war made the situation more acute, for Servian troops easily conquered Western Macedonia and forced their way through Albania to the Adriatic by a series of brilliant Winter campaigns.

Then Austrian diplomacy won another victory. In the conferences of the powers which followed the war Montenegro was deprived of Scutari, and Servia was compelled to withdraw her troops from Albania. There was a vague premise that the country should be allowed commercial access to the Adriatic through an unfortified port, but it went no further than words. Austria, seeing her pathway to the Aegean closed for the time, was in no mood to allow the Servian race, which consciously or unconsciously has been striving for union for the last century, to gain a foothold on the other sea.

The second Balkan war, in which Servia, Greece, Turkey, and Rumania defeated Bulgaria, has been usually ascribed to the machinations of Austrian diplomats, who are said to have worked upon Ferdinand of Bulgaria to attack the Servians. The Servian victories in the war were largely neutralized by the fact that Austria seized the occasion to occupy the Sanjak of Novi Bazar a strip of territory between Montenegro and Servia which belonged to Turkey till the war of 1912, thus thrusting herself in between the Servians and their Montenegrin kinsmen. And so another blow was dealt to the unification of the Serbs, which if ever carried through, would cut off the entire southwestern corner of the Hapsburg Empire.

Since then a strong army has been at all times maintained by Austria within striking distance of the Servian frontier. The troubles became more acute last Winter when a students' strike in Bosnia brought all the latent hatred to a head and started the train of events which led to the assassination of the Archduke Francis Ferdinand and his wife.

### Where War Would Start

Semlin, where the fleet of monitors is assembling, lies on the west bank of the Danube just above the point where the Sava joins it. In the intersection of the two rivers rises the lofty butte which is the core of the City of Belgrade, the Servian capital, which thus juts out into Hungarian territory. Semlin is only two or three miles away, and is easily commanded by guns placed on the heights of Belgrade, as the land lying in the neighborhood is very low. At the intersection of the two rivers is War Island a marshy expanse formed by the silt brought down by the Save. Around this the Austrian transports would have to go to take troops down the river, but the guns of warships at Semlin could easily bombard the City of Belgrade itself.

Semlin has a population of about 17,000, but is a town of no special importance, except as a customs station and the starting point of military operations below the Danube. It is almost surrounded by low-lying swampy ground, through which the railroad goes on to the southeast and crosses the Save into Belgrade at a point about three or four kilometres distant.

Temesvar is an important railroad centre and garrison town of about 40,000 inhabitants, about fifty miles east of the Danube as it flows south through the plain of Hungary, and seventy-five miles northeast of Belgrade. From it diverge several railroad lines, which could carry troops down to the Danube so as to commence an invasion all along the northern frontier of Servia.

One of these lines striking off to the southeast, reaches the river, just after crossing the Rumanian frontier, at Verclorova. Another leads to the southwest and ends at Panesova, on the Danube, only a few miles below Belgrade. A third, running southward, forks at Versecz, about twenty miles from the frontier. One branch runs to Panesova on the southwest, another east to Bazias, on the Danube, about forty, miles below Belgrade, and the third to Kubin, midway between Belgrade and Bazias.

Opposite Kubin is the Servian town of Semendria, formerly a fortress of great strength. It is still a town of considerable importance, and, as the end of a branch line of railroad, could be used as the starting point of manoeuvres to cut off Belgrade from the rest of Servia.

*   *   *

**July 25, 1914**

## AMERICAN INTEREST IN SERVIA

It was an American statesman who asked what the United States "had to do with Abroad." No economist or financier could have been guilty of such an imbecility. The assassinations in Sarajevo were directly related to this week's export of gold from New York, and have equally close associations with the price of the wheat partially harvested on the prairies of this continent. Finance and commerce ignore political subdivisions and are as much single as the ocean, which has many waves but only one true level. The money markets of the world are under such a strain that it seems as though no money could be found for war. But that is an economic objection merely. Military finance is a thing apart from economies or logic.

If reason ruled the minds of commanders or followers, Norman Angell's "Great Illusion" would have demonstrated that war does not pay and that it mattered not who ruled a country in a business sense. For if either prevails commerce will find its way to a profit equally in a mother-land or a colony, equally in a republic or a monarchy. But war is rage, not reason. It may spring from dynastic lust for power, or from racial avarice for territory, but whatever its motive lack of money has never yet stopped it. Those who have money must part with it to those who want it enough to pay the price. The comparative strength of this country is no defense against its being drained of its resources, so much needed at home for trade and so much more needed abroad for war.

Those who fancy that it is possible to protect themselves because they owe nothing to any foreigner will find that money is borrowed away from the American at an auction at which he must bid, if his defense is to be maintained. The process is the opposite of that at auctions with which most are familiar. Prices are offered down rather than up, until a price is found attractive to buyers. In world finance it matters little what is offered down. All prices are relative in the money market, and when prices get "out of line" investments are shifted and the operator who does not avail himself of the opportunities offering loses a profit; or even loses a percentage of his capital. Just now American securities are being offered down as a means of bidding a premium for our gold. It suits our statesmen and politicians of a sort to associate the export of gold with our tariff rather than with foreign politics. No doubt that is a contributory factor, but the main factor is the almost unprecedented bid for capital indicated by the depression in the best sort of foreign Government bonds. In the world auction for money a tariff is a trivial thing in comparison with the fall of rentes to the lowest price for a generation twenty-six years, to be exact. The sale of a new French loan the other day was said to promise relief to the world, but that loan is now at a discount, an unprecedented incident in French finance. In England the situation is similar. The fall of consols recently to the lowest price for a century is only another way of saying that capital is dear to every borrower in the world's financial capital, where we are favored customers.

The German battalions recently were held in check for a moment by financial considerations, and the Kaiser said it should not happen again. Since then the Reichsbank has raised its gold reserves by $141,838,000. We know where some of it came from, and none too willingly. If the Servian ultimatum should precipitate Armageddon it is very much an affair of ours. The money must come from here, in large part, because no other source of supply can provide it with less sacrifice. We must pay such debts as we owe, we must take such American securities as are offered down, and we may be induced to buy fresh foreign securities if they are offered at prices which show a profit on comparison of prices with what we have refused to sell. It is a thousand pities. The money might as well be thrown into the sea, or even better, for then bloodshed would be averted. The best hope of peace is the tension already in the world's money markets, but that reliance alone is a broken reed.

*   *   *

**July 26, 1914**

# AUSTRIAN MINISTER RECALLED AS REPLY TO ULTIMATUM IS REJECTED

### SERB ARMY CHIEF CAUGHT

*Was Trying to Return to Belgrade from Gratz, Where He Had Been Staying*

### "TO BERLIN!" CRY IN PARIS

*Popular Belief There That Germany Engineered Vienna Coup Against Servia*

### DISSATISFACTION IN ITALY

*Attitude of Austrian Ally Not to the Liking of the Press, Which Is Opposed to War*

### BRITAIN TO WORK FOR PEACE

*Hope Entertained That Trouble Can Be Adjusted by Means of Mediation*

Diplomatic relations between Austria-Hungary and Servia were broken off at 6 o'clock last evening, and war is considered certain. Martial law has been proclaimed throughout the Austro-Hungarian Empire.

Servia's reply to the Austrian ultimatum was delivered to the Austrian Minister at Belgrade at 10 minutes before 6 o'clock, the limit of time for a reply set by the Dual Monarchy. It was judged unsatisfactory, and Emperor Francis Joseph's representative with the entire legation staff and their families, left on a special train for Vienna.

King Peter and his Governments thereupon withdrew from Belgrade, which is on the frontier, to Kragouyevatz, in the heart of the kingdom, where there is an arsenal and an arms and ammunition factory. The funds of the various banks in Belgrade also were removed to the new capital.

Gen. Putnik, Chief of Staff of the Servian Army, who has been staying at Gratz, is reported to have been arrested while trying to return to Servia.

Orders to mobilize the Russian Army have been issued by the Czar.

Emperor William is hurrying back to Berlin from Norway.

In Vienna and Berlin the war fever is at its height, and last night crowds thronged the streets of each capital, where the national anthems of both countries were sung and played amid intense enthusiasm.

Crowds paraded the Paris boulevards shouting, "To Berlin!"

General panic prevailed on the bourses of Europe.

### WAR CONSIDERED CERTAIN
**Austrian Troops Said to be Already Massing on Servian Frontier**

Special Cable to The New York Times
VIENNA, July 25—That war with Servia is certain is the feeling throughout Vienna tonight. Thousands of people are marching through the streets cheering with wild enthusiasm.

Servia's reply to the Austrian ultimatum is announced to be unsatisfactory, and the Austrian Government has recalled its Minister from Belgrade.

It is expected that the Emperor will issue a manifesto to the Austro-Hungarian people tomorrow in which he will declare the firm determination of the Government to exact the reparation foreshadowed in the ultimatum communicated to Servia.

Simultaneously the concentration of troops on the Servian frontier will begin. In fact, it is generally believed here that orders have been given for such a military movement. A strict censorship over all military news already has been established.

According to special information received by The New York Times the Servian Army is not expected to offer serious resistance to the Austrian invasion, and the Austrian General staff count on occupying Belgrade without difficulty.

The idea at military headquarters here is that the Servians will concentrate in the direction of the Bulgarian frontier.

Efforts at mediation are expected from various powers, but Austria is determined to brook no interference.

By The Associated Press
VIENNA, July 25—Diplomatic relations between Austria-Hungary and Servia were formally broken off tonight, and it is reported that partial mobilization of the Austrian Army has been ordered. Martial law has been proclaimed throughout the Empire.

The Servian Minister and his staff left Vienna tonight. A military censorship has been established in the telegraph offices here.

The Servian Government waited until the last moment left it by terms of the note, and only ten minutes before the hour of 6, when the Austro-Hungarian ultimatum expired, did the Servian Premier appear at the legation and present his Government's reply to the Austrian Minister, Baron Giesl von Gieslingen.

No details of the tenor of reply have been revealed here, but the terse statement was made that it was "unsatisfactory."

Immediately upon receiving the note the Austrian Minister informed the Foreign Office, and diplomatic relations were broken off. Half an hour later the Minister and his staff, with their families, had boarded a train for Austria territory. The train was in readiness to depart as an unfavourable reply to the Austrian demands had been expected.

According to newspaper messages received here the mobilization of the Servian Army was ordered at 3 o'clock in the afternoon. King Peter, who had hurriedly returned to Belgrade when the Austrian ultimatum was announced, left the capital this evening on a special train with the principal members of the Government, in the realization that the Austrians could capture Belgrade without difficulty. The temporary seal of the Government will be established at Kragouyevatz where there is an arsenal and an arms and ammunition factory.

The portentous news of Servia's decision was made known to the public by extra editions of the evening papers, and at 8 o'clock tonight half the population of the city seemed to be on the streets. They fought eagerly for the papers and processions were formed which marched through all the thoroughfares, singing national hymns and cheering for Emperor Francis Joseph, Emperor William and the army.

Everywhere throughout the country similar demonstrations are being held.

Count Leopold Berchfold the Austro-Hungarian Minister of Foreign Affairs visited Ischi early in the afternoon and had a long audience with the Emperor. Later he conferred with the Minister of War, Gen. Krobatin, and the Emperor's chief military adviser, Gen. Baron de Bolfras von Ahnenburg, and the Minister of Finance.

Count Berchfold had another audience at 7 o'clock with the Emperor, to whom he communicated the Servian note.

Gen. R. Putnik, Chief of Staff of the Servian Army, stated from Gratz on his return to Servia this afternoon:

A high official of the Austro-Hungarian Foreign Office made the following statement tonight:

"Should Servia at this stage of affairs take military measures against Austria every penny of the cost of Austrian mobilization will have to be paid by Servia."

An official communication issued late tonight points out that the foreign situation has assumed a development which makes regard for military necessities the supreme law. It proclaims a series of ordinances applicable to the whole empire including Hungary.

These ordinances include the transfer of the civil administration of Bosnia-Herzegovina and Dalmatia to the commander in chief, the suspension throughout the empire of the constitutional laws on liberty of assembly of private correspondence of the press, the suppression of juries, the restriction of the issue of passports, the submission of civilians accused of reprehensible acts against the army to military jurisdiction, the partial prohibition of the export and import of products, the enforcement of military jurisdiction generally, and the closing of the provincial diets and the Reicharath.

The communication trusts that all Austro-Hungarian subjects will appreciate the grave necessity which compels the Government in the exercise of a heavy responsibility to take exceptional measures.

The health of Emperor Francis Joseph is good in spite of the excitement of the last few days. The Emperor will remain at Ischl. No arrangements have been made for his departure.

\*　　\*　　\*

**July 29, 1914**

## AUSTRIA FORMALLY DECLARES WAR ON SERVIA

*Notice Sent to the Powers of the Opening of Hostilities*

**SERVIAN VESSELS SEIZED**

*Sharp Fighting Begins Along the River Drina on the Bosnian Frontier*

**COUNTER INVASION PLAN**

*Montenegrin and Serb Armies to Invade Bosnia and Start a Rebellion There*

**GREY'S PEACE PLAN FAILS**

*Kaiser Declines to Join in Conference to Exert Pressure on Austrian Ally*

**BUT REPLY IS CONCILIATORY**

*And London Still Has Faith That His Influence Will Avert General Conflict*

Special Cable to The New York Times

LONDON, Wednesday, July 29—Austria-Hungary declared war on Servia yesterday. The declaration was made at noon to the Servian Government by means of an open telegram. The Austro-Hungarian forces followed up the declaration by seizing two Servian vessels at Orsova, on the Danube, together with a number of boats.

The question whether the Austro-Servian war can be localized and a European Armageddon can be avoided now depends, so far as anything can depend on one man, upon Emperor William.

The New York Times correspondent referred yesterday to the hopes of the British Foreign Office that the Kaiser's personal influence would be exercised for peace. Now that Germany has refused to accept Sir Edward Grey's suggestion of an ambassadorial conference and Austria has declared war on Servia, the only hope of avoiding that greater conflict, which the whole world apprehends, lies in the conversations that are proceeding directly between Vienna and St. Petersburg, and particularly the turn which can be given them by the German monarch.

### The Kaiser's Role

The Times correspondent is informed on the best authority that great hopes are based on Emperor William's influence in this direction. This information is reflected in The Times editorial this morning which says:

"There is reason to believe that in the most exalted quarter of Germany the maintenance of European peace is warmly and honestly desired. The pressure from all manner of influential personages and groups is doubtless being exerted to overcome the pacific leanings of the Emperor. It may tax his powers of resistance severely, but in foreign affairs he is the undoubted master and he has often shown that he has a will and judgment of his own. We still hope with some confidence that they will be exerted on the side of that peace which it has often been his honorable boast he helped to keep for six and twenty years.

"Our Paris correspondent repeats that grounds exist for the belief that Germany has already given a better proof of her wish for peace than is known to France."

In London Germany's reply to Sir Edward Grey's proposal is not looked upon as a diplomatic rebuff. The tone of the reply was conciliatory, and Prince Lichnowsky, the German Ambassador here, explained that Germany, while most anxious to co-operate with Great Britain in the attempt to find a settlement, was unable to accept the role of a mediator so far as the Austro-Servian dispute was concerned, as she must eschew anything calculated to create the impression that she was not in entire harmony with her Austrian ally. The German Ambassador particularly insisted on the weight which Germany attaches to co-operation with Great Britain with a view to localizing the conflict.

The conversations at St. Petersburg between Count Szapary, the Austrian Ambassador, and Premier Sazonoff, are understood to be proceeding on a tone which gives good hope that it will be found possible to prevent the conflagration spreading beyond the present limits.

Up to a late hour this morning no definite confirmation had been received here of the various reports that Russia had begun a general mobilization.

Statements that the army corps in the west and southwest of Russia were being brought up to their war strength were accepted without hesitation as part of the precautionary measures which every country in Europe, big or small, with the exception of Spain, Portugal, and Switzerland, considered necessary. The news of the issue of orders for a general mobilization of Russian forces would mean that a great European conflict would be precipitated.

### May Strike First at France

Berlin dispatches state that Germany has made it quite clear in St. Petersburg that even "a partial mobilization" will be answered immediately by the mobilization of the German Army, which, according to one dispatch, "nothing could then hold back."

This is in accordance with what is known of the German war policy. The German General Staff does not contemplate simultaneous campaigns on a great scale against both France and Russia. France can mobilize nearly as quickly as herself. Russia takes some weeks to mobilize and more weeks to move her armies from mobilization centres to the frontier.

Germany's safety lies in taking advantage of the slowness of Russian mobilization. She will content herself with a comparatively slight screen of troops along her Eastern frontier to hold back the Russians and will launch all her striking force against the French lines of defense, hoping to pierce them and break the back of the French armies before Russia is ready to act.

The next few hours is likely to show whether Germany thinks the extensive military movements which are taking place along the Russian side of the German-Austrian frontiers constitutes a partial mobilization.

In this connection extreme importance attaches to the statement made in a special dispatch to The New York Times from St. Petersburg that Russia will declare a general mobilization if Austria occupies Belgrade.

A military expert who is acquainted with the European situation said, when shown the dispatch, that he hoped the correspondent's forecast was incorrect, for such a step would precipitate an Armageddon, as Germany could not afford to throw away the advantage which the slowness of Russian mobilization, the chief weakness of the Dual Alliance, gave her, and would immediately strike at France.

### Probable Plans of Opposing Armies

The Servians are reported to have formed a division in the Sanjak of Novi Bazar and to be concentrating strong forces on the River Lim, which runs through the Sanjak. Montenegrin troops are stated to be in close contact with the Servian forces.

The object of these movements, according to The London Times, is apparently to threaten Herzegovina and Bosnia, where the nature of the ground is favorable for guerrilla operations.

Rumors of fighting on the Drina River that forms the frontier between Bosnia and Servia, were circulated in Vienna and Berlin. Part of the Austro-Hungarian forces is expected to advance across the Drina in the direction of Kraguoyevatz. The Servian forces, on the other hand, are expected to cross into Bosnian territory with the object of raising an insurrection among the Bosnian Serbs.

It is stated on Austrian authority that the object of Austria-Hungary is to crush and disarm Servia and, in particular, capture the Servian artillery and compel Servia to reduce her army in future to inoffensive proportions.

Austria-Hungary also is determined to seize Mount Lovteben, a Montenegrin stronghold, which commands the important naval base of Bocche di Cattaro, despite the opposition which Italy is expected to offer to this proceeding.

Three Italian training ships now on a visit to the Clyde have been recalled.

Austrian naval concentration has been ordered at Fiume.

### Black Sea Lights Out

The Russian authorities have ordered all lights along the Russian Black Sea coast extinguished, with the exception of the Chersonesf Lighthouse near Sebastopol harbor. Sebastopol itself is open only to Russian warships.

Russia has ordered the mobilization of fourteen army corps in the neighborhood of the Austrian frontier, but these orders are understood to be merely preparatory, not final. In diplomatic circles it is stated that Germany will not reply to this partial mobilization unless a Russian army is mobilized also in the north.

Two French Cabinet councils were held yesterday. No mobilization order has been issued, but considerable military preparations are being made. All officers and men on leave have been recalled to the colors. The French Socialists have issued a manifesto calling upon the Government to use its influence in Russia in favor of peace.

Military preparations are proceeding in Holland and Belgium, with the view of maintaining the neutrality of those countries against an attack by the great powers.

### Hungarian Diet Enthusiastic

Great enthusiasm prevailed in the Hungarian Chamber when Count Tiza, the Prime Minister, announced the outbreak of war and declared the situation demanded a deed of arms, not words. Count Apponyl, leader of the Opposition, supported the Premier. The Parliament was prorogued by royal decree.

Patriotic demonstrations took place in St. Petersburg, the crowds cheering the friendly embassies and legations, including those of Great Britain and Servia.

The Times St. Petersburg correspondent reports the growth of pessimism in official circles. News of the Austro-Hungarian occupation of Belgrade would inflame public feeling. Russian statesmen are convinced that England alone can save the situation, and that Sir Edward Grey's proposals by no means exhaust all his possibilities of persuasion.

### Captured Passengers Detained

BELGRADE, July 28, (by Indirect Route.)—The Servian steamers Deligrad and Morava were seized today at Orsova, on the Danube, by Austrians. The Servian colors were hauled down and the Austrian flag hoisted. The passengers were detained.

Many Servian families have left the capital for the country districts in spite of the advice of the authorities, while there has been a great exodus of Austrians and Hungarians from Belgrade and other parts of Servia.

Perfect order prevails in the capital, the police duties having been undertaken by a corps of volunteers composed of students.

Military preparations are being carried out with feverish activity. The troops have been concentrated in fortified positions. The headquarters of the army has been established at Kragouyevatz, but in the event of necessity will be transferred to Krushevatz, ninety miles southeast of Belgrade.

### Two Army Corps at the Border

BERLIN, July 28—Reports from the Austrian border today state that the transport of the Eighth and Ninth Austrian Army Corps from Bohemia toward the Servian frontier began yesterday, and that there was no other traffic on the Bohemian railroads except troop trains. The two army corps in Bohemia consist of thirty-two battalions of infantry with a large number of quick-firing machine guns, six regiments of cavalry, two regiments of field artillery, and two regiments of the Army Service Corps.

An unconfirmed dispatch from Gumbinnen, Eastern Prussia, to the Taegliche Rundschau, today says Russia has occupied Wirballen. Russian Poland, with a force of engineers,

cavalry, artillery, and two regiments of infantry while Russian guards have been placed along all roads on the frontier. The dispatch adds that a squadron of German Uhlans has advanced to Eydtkuhnen on the Russian frontier.

### AUSTRIA MAY PAUSE
#### Suggestion in Paris That She May Take Some Territory and Wait

PARIS, July 28—According to what is believed to be responsible opinion, there remains the possibility that when Austria has occupied some Servian territory she will in a day or two announce her intention not to proceed further, but to hold what she has taken until Servia gives competent guarantees that she will observe Austria's wishes. Russia would not then be likely to intervene, it is argued, except diplomatically, and negotiations appear to be going on at the present time between Austria and Russia.

On the announcement of war tonight Paris became animated. There were patriotic demonstrations in the capital and many other cities throughout the republic, but there were also demonstriations against the war.

A large number of noted French aviators, led by Roland Garros, in a letter to the Minister of War, have offered their services.

Maurice Barros, member of the Chamber of Deputies and President of the League of Patriots, has issued a call for a big demonstration on the arrival at Paris of President Poincaré to signify affirmation of the Triple Entente and readiness for the service of France.

\*  \*  \*

July 30, 1914

## HEAVY BOMBARDMENT OF BELGRADE FAILED TO PROVOKE RESPONSE

---

### MANY BUILDINGS DAMAGED
*Two Banks Hit and a Banker Wounded—Protest Lodged at German Legation*

### SEMLIN BRIDGE BLOWN UP
*Big Gun Duel at Vichnitza—Serbs in Dual Monarchy Held as War Prisoners*

### TWO ARMIES OF INVASION
*Gen. Von Hoetzendorf, In Chief Command, to Attack Servia and Gen. Ermoly, Montenegro*

---

### By MARTIN H. DONOHUE
New York Times—London Chronicle Special Cable Dispatch
SEMLIN, Hungary, July 29—The Austrians began hostilities this morning by bombarding Belgrade.

Three monitors took up their positions at the confluence of the Danube and the Save, but close to shore, and opened fire. The monitors' guns were directed on the Belgrade barracks, and no pains were taken to avoid hitting the public buildings, some of which were seen, even from here, to be damaged. The Servians made no reply to the Austrian gunfire, but have destroyed the railway bridge between Semlin and Belgrade. The bombardment was bloodless, so far as the imperial forces were concerned.

### Banks Damaged, Banker Wounded

Special Cable to The New York Times

ATHENS, July 29—The Servian Legation has received the following telegram from Nish, dated July 29:

"During the night Belgrade was bombarded. Shells fell in various quarters of the town, causing great damage. Several fell on the Franco-Servian and the Androvitch banks. M. Androvitch, of the banking firm, was wounded. Both banks have lodged a protest at the German Legation.

"An artillery duel is proceeding at Vichnitza, about 8½ miles down the river from Belgrade."

LONDON, Thursday, July 30—It was stated in connection with the blowing up of the railway bridge across the River Save by Servians, that the Austrians have another bridge in sections on their side of the river, which they can put up in a few days.

Dispatches from Servian points yesterday indicated that the Bosnian frontier was looked upon as the most likely point of attack of the Austrian troops, and thither the soldiers of King Peter were being hurried in great numbers.

Strong forces were dispatched to the fortified towns of Vaiyevo and Uzhitza, on the frontier, and to Svilajnatz, in the eastern part of the country, while strong divisions of volunteers reinforced by regulars were gathering along the River Drina, near Losnitz.

The Montenegrin soldiery, evidently preparing to support their brother Serbs, have also concentrated along the Bosnian frontier. A brigade with a mountain battery was stationed near Priboj, where the women were busy building earthworks.

Servian and Austrian aviators at the same time were flying along the frontiers, trying to locate the positions of the opposing forces.

VIENNA, July 29—The Servians at 1:30 o'clock this morning blew up the bridge spanning the River Save between the Austrian town of Semlin and Belgrade. The Austrian infantry and artillery stationed at Semlin, in conjunction with monitors on the Danube, fired on the Servian positions beyond the bridge. The Servians retreated after a short engagement, with trifling losses.

The shells wrought havoc in the exposed part of the city, damaging the King's Palace, the fortification walls and the barracks and other buildings.

A small detachment of pioneers, in co-operation with the customs officers, yesterday captured two Servian steamers laden with ammunition and arms. The pioneers and revenue guards, after a short, sharp encounter overcame the Servian crews and took possession of the vessels and their dangerous cargoes. The captured ships were towed away by one of the Danube steamers.

### Emperor to Go to Budapest

Emperor Francis Joseph will return to Vienna from Ischl tomorrow and may then go to Budapest in order to be near the scene of action. Popular enthusiasm is growing since the Emperor's manifesto, and patriotic demonstrations are being held all over the country. Runs on the savings banks are diminishing.

All Servians liable to military service residing in Austria-Hungary are being arrested and handed over to the military as prisoners of war.

Special Cable to The New York Times

BERLIN, July 29—The Berliner Tagoblatt learns that the Austrian plan of campaign consists of operations by two great armies under the general command of Gen. Baron von Hoetzendorf, Chief of General Staff. The larger army, under the command of Field Marshal Potiorek, is to carry out the invasion of Servia, while the smaller army, commanded by Cavalry Gen. Ermoly, will attack Montenegro.

\* \* \*

**July 30, 1914**

# TROUBLE IN EUROPE A WAR OF TONGUES

*Struggle for Supremacy Between Germanism and Slavism, Says Prof. Dorsey*

**CASE OF BIG AND LITTLE DOG**

*Servia Likened to a Mongrel Roused to Spunk After 500 Years and Promptly Pounced Upon*

Special to The New York Times

CHICAGO, July 29—Prof. George A. Dorsey, formerly of the University of Chicago and now Curator of Ethnology at the Field Museum, recently returned from a long sojourn in that part of Europe where war is now threatened, and in a signed article, which will appear in The Chicago Herald tomorrow, gives his views of the cause which led up to the present crisis between Austria-Hungary and Servia. He says:

"An orphan, mongrel cur, having for the first time in 500 years got up enough spunk to take, his tail from between his legs to wag it and feel growing pains. Along comes a great big dog and says:

" 'Put that ball down—and gimme that bone.'

"We see this sort of thing nearly every day.

"Once upon a time little old Servia was an empire, and very nearly over-came the Byzantine Empire, which probably would have changed the whole of European history. There might have been no Turkey in Europe. That was in the fourteenth century, under the mighty Dushan. Servia is now a poor, wretched little peasant kingdom, not half as big as Illinois in size, with less people than the City of New York. And the house of Hapsburg would wipe little Servia off the map.

Even though the process involve more lives and money than any war of any time.

"That is the life. You or I in the house of Hapsburg's shoes would do the same thing. It is the law of existence. Nature works today as in the stone age or when sabre-toothed tiger fought with mastodon.

"Why does Austria-Hungary, the dual monarchy, want poor peasant Servia? Hasn't the dual monarchy, with its internal babel of confusion, enough trouble already?

"Suppose the dual monarchy does want Servia, what is it to Russia? Suppose Russia does object, what is it to Germany? Suppose Germany objects to Russia's objecting, what business it is of France or England? Balance of power. Human nature. Life.

### Germanism vs. Slavism

"I propose to analyze this whole situation. And right here let us clearly recognize the fact—two facts. The contest now impending is not based on economic laws. To put it in another way, the desires which lead to action in Eastern Europe are not based on Christian ethics or national procedure, but on certain thoughts. Things are what we think they are, and thinking depends on the point of view. Pan-Germanism versus Pan-Slavism. If we understand this, we have traveled far. First let me give an illuminating illustration:

"In Prague, an important city of Austria, I was warned I would get along much better in shops and otherwise if I employed English first. Of course English is not generally understood in that city, but German is. We naturally think of German as the language of Austria, and proud as the ancient capital of Bohemia was once, to all intents and purposes a German city, it now tries to forget, and won't talk German if it can possibly help it.

"The term Pan-Germanism stands for a movement which seeks the common welfare of the Germanic peoples of Europe at the expense of Pan-Slavism, or common weal of Slavs. Before we can understand the significance of these two movements, we must consider the question of the 'nationals' or of the 'races,' as it is sometimes called. In fact, this is not a question either or nations or races, but of tongues.

"German is spoken by 80,000,000 people, of which 10,000,000 are in Austria and 2,000,000 in Hungary. There are 140,000,000 Slavs in Europe. From this it appears that the present political boundaries are not coterminous with linguistic groups.

"Right here in this fact we have the seeds of present and future troubles and a clew to the causes of most of the wars in Eastern Europe through 2,000 years. Russia is a veritable hodge-podge of tongues, but of her Slav population alone we have at least two distinct elements today bitterly opposed to each other, with the possibility, if not the probability, of a third, which will seek recognition. As against Russians proper there are over 10,000,000 Poles, and of the remaining Slavs there are 8,000,000 Ruthenians.

"In Germany there are over 3,000,000 Slavs, chiefly Polish. Of Austria's 30,000,000 population only about a third is Ger-

man, the remainder being Slav, of which there are 6,000,000 Czechs or Bohemians, 5,000,000 Poles, 3,500,000 Ruthenians, and a million and a quarter Slovenes.

### Hungary a Babel of Tongues

"Hungary is even more diversified in tongue. The Magyar element (10,000,000) is equaled by the non-Magyar, made up roughly of 2,000,000 Germans, 2,000,000 Slovaks, 500,000 Ruthenians, 3,000,000 Serbo-Croats, all of the Slavic tongue and about 3,000,000 Rumanians, who do not speak Slav at all.

"The population of Montenegro about half a million, are Slavs of the Servian branch. Rumanians are of mixed origin, but the Rumanian tongue is spoken by 12,000,000, of which 5,500,000 are in Rumania, (92 per cent, of its total population.) The remaining millions are found in the dual monarchy, Servia, Bulgaria, and Russia.

"Millions of people today speak Polish whose ancestors a few generations ago were not conscious of the fact that they spoke any language at all. Today there is a Slovene literature: fifty years ago no one even thought of such a thing. The millions of Bohemians had become almost entirely Germans, and never before have they been so thoroughly Slavic as today.

"Bohemian hostility to Germany has been called a passion. It was not so very long ago that the language of the Hungarian Parliament was Latin. Magyar was held fit only for peasant talk. Today the bitterness between Magyar and Slav is as strong as between German and Pole.

"A few years ago there was no consciousness in Galicia of linguistic distinction between Poles and Ruthenians. Ruthenian peasants were content to remain serfs of Polish nobility. There was no Ruthenian literature: Ruthenian was not a polite language. Today there are distinguished scholars who seek to found a Ruthenian university.

"The sympathies of the Rumanians of Hungary are not so much with the flag of their country or their loyalty so much for the Emperor of the Dual Monarchy as for the flag and the King of Rumania."

Prof. Dorsey, then goes into the familiar history of the Poles and continues:

"The house of Hapsburg has had the foresight to avoid the mistake of Russia. By holding their sympathy, the Poles of Galicia have been placed in the position of preferring to remain subjects of Austria, rather than suffer the fate of Poles in Prussia or Russia, they do not care to jump from the frying pain into the fire. But the hope of a reunited Poland is not less strong in Galicia than among other Poles.

"Germany, for Germany, has acted with amazing stupidity. Because of their attractive qualities, perhaps as many as 100,000 Germans in Eastern Prussia had become Polarized in the nineteenth century. It was simply a natural process. That was followed by a period when the Polish population of Prussia was on the road to Germanization. That process was going on nicely, and if let alone might have resulted in complete obliteration of the Poles of Prussia as Poles. Then Bismarck decided to push matters.

"Bismarck said he was afraid of the Polish woman—she was so prolific. Beginning in 1873 and continuing up to the present there has been a systematic attempt on the part of Prussia to Germanize their Poles. This attempt has failed ignominiously, utterly.

"In Russia Catholic Poles are in conflict with the Greek religion. In Prussia, Catholic Poles are in conflict with Protestants. In Austria there is no question of religion.

### Germanization of Bohemia

"Bohemia, too, had an ancient and honorable history as a national entity. But for 200 years she had to surrender most of her historic privileges, and later on succumbed to an insidious process of Germanization.

"This Germanization process was hastened enormously by the Jesuists. The German language was placed on the same footing as the Czech in 1627. And German emigrants who poured into Bohemia after the Thirty Years War hastened the process of Germanization.

"With the beginning of the eighteenth century Austria and Bohemia, long bound by common ties, began the process of fusion, which was completed before the end of the century.

"The Magyar population forms a wedge between North and South Slavia. The latter group comprises the Croats, Serbs, Bulgars, and Slovenes. The southern Slavs are allied by a common tongue, though they are divided in their allegiance between the Catholic and orthodox churches.

"The Slovenes had almost ceased to exist as Slavs, so rapid and continuous had been the process of Germanization. But in 1908 there were Slovene riots at Libach against the Germans. They succeeded in their demand for a high school in their mother tongue and are now demanding a university. The Croats are the last Slavs that need be considered in the review.

"Croatia—that long arm that stretches across the southern end of Hungary is said to hold the key to the reconstruction which is believed will take place sooner or later in the dual monarchy.

### Servia Under Turkey

"And now for Servia. Duchan's empire, though brilliant, did not last long. Within 100 years the whole Serb people including those of present Servia, Bosnia. Herzegovina, Montenegro, and Macedonia, passed into the hands of Turkey, where they suffered and struggled against oppression for 400 years.

"The part that Servia proper played in throwing off Turkish oppression was important. Practically autonomy was secured in 1816. By the Berlin Congress the Servian principality was declared independent, and in 1882 the principality became a kingdom.

"For more than forty years Servia's aspirations, both politically and economically, have been blocked systematically and persistently by the dual monarchy. With a persistence which must seem to Servia maddening. Austria-Hungary has tried to deny her direct access to the coast or even railway connection with the Adriatic.

"Compared with the Servians, Bulgarians have been called 'doers and workers,' the former 'talkers and loungers,' and this description it seems to me is not entirely inappropriate. The Servian peasant is the best of his country. He is essentially a man of vision.

"Servia considers herself the natural centre for the South Slav kingdom. At any rate, having fought her way to the sea, she wants a seaport for her plums and her pigs, and she certainly doesn't want, nay, she will fight bitterly to prevent being absorbed, as she recently saw Bosnia absorbed by Austria.

"The pan-Germanism movement in Austria began in 1871. Since then there has been a growing desire on the part of much of its German element for union with the German Empire, between 1800 and 1804 there were many appeals urging the union of all Germanic peoples.

"In 1894 was founded the Alldeutscher Verband, thus crystallizing a movement already 100 years old. According to the league, the 1870 war with France only made it plain that it was Germany's desire to enter into closer economic and political connection with the other German States, Austria, The Netherlands and Switzerland.

"For twenty years this Pan-German movement has conducted a propaganda throughout the German world and has had adherence in the Austrian Parliament. Austria herself once was willing, but now there are difficulties in the way.

### Emperor William's Hope

"It is just fourteen years since the German Emperor expressed the hope that the Fatherland would become as powerful, as strongly united, and as extraordinary as the Roman Empire. Pan-Germanism is an ideal, an inspiration, a sentiment. But it is very real and perhaps furnishes us with a sufficient clue to German's interest in the impending struggle between the dual monarchy and little Servia.

"Pan-Slavism, too, is an ideal, but much less capable of fulfillment than Pan-Germanism. As a movement it has contributed to the social, economic and political advance of the Slavs, but as a political movement it seems an impossibility.

"Pan-Slavism with a less definite political programme than Pan-Germanism can be turn into a mighty force but before there can be a free and united Slav federation based on mutual willingness to federate there must be a change in Russia's attitude toward the Poles and in the position of the Croats to the Orthodox Church and the Czechs to their aspirations of nationality.

"The little Slav groups naturally look to Russia as their protector though they would hesitate to place themselves in the hands of the Russian dynasty. But in the Pan-Slav movement in general we find the answer to the question of why Russia is interested in the preservation of the autonomy of poor little Servia."

\* \* \*

August 2, 1914

# SLAVS HERE PLEDGE ALL AID TO SERVIA

*In Big Mass Meeting They Utter Piercing Battle Cries and Denounce Austrian Rule*

**WILD CHEERS FOR PUPIN**

*Columbia Professor Stirs Throng to Frenzy by Arraignment of the Hapsburgs*

Servians, Bohemians, Herzegovinians, Bosnians, Montenegrins, Croatians, Greeks, and others of Slavic origin held a mass meeting in the Central Opera House, in East Sixty-seventh Street, near Third Avenue, last night, and pledged support in money and blood, if need be, to the cause of Servia and the nations that have come to the assistance of that little kingdom in the present crisis. It was a wonderful meeting in many ways. For enthusiasm it could hardly be surpassed, while every one noted the deep-rooted hatred of Austria-Hungary that seemed to pervade the meeting, every denunciation of Franz Josef and his monarchy being greeted with great outbursts of frantic cheering and singing.

The crowd that packed the Opera House was one of well-dressed, prosperous-looking men and women. Hundreds of those present, it was said, were born in Austria or Hungary. But in the present crisis they were Slavs first, they said, and as such were bound to assist in every way possible their Serb and Russian brethren. On the stage were many of the leading New York members of the nationalities represented, while back of them and held aloft by strong young men, all of them veterans of the Balkan wars, were the flags of Servia, Greece, Montenegro, and Russia.

As the Greek emblem was brought on the stage, 400 Greek veterans of the Balkan wars, all in the field service uniform of the Greek Army, marched into the hall while the crowd stood up and yelled itself hoarse, sang the national anthem of the Greeks, and after that ended the demonstration with a weird, piercing rendition of the battle cry of the Slavs, a cry the English spelling of which is "Ibeel," and if you can pronounce that word you know how it sounded.

## Always the Battle Cry

Before the speaking started, there was demonstration after demonstration, each ending with the battle cry of the Slavs, while interspersed with the cheering were the national anthems of the peoples represented, and the "Hej Slavoni," the national song of all the Slav people. It was noted that everybody present seemed to know the words of the national songs of all the other Slavic nations represented.

One of the noisiest of the demonstrations was that which greeted the appearance of Prof. Michael I. Pupin of Columbia University, the honorary Consul General of Servia to the United States. Everybody present appeared to know Prof. Pupin personally and they cheered him a full five minutes before they would permit him to take his seat.

Engelbert Svehla, editor of the New Yorske Listy, the Bohemian daily, presided at the meeting, and the other speakers were Prof. Pupin, Bret G. Gregr, Milan Geting, and O. Grecev, the last named representing the Slavs of Russian birth resident in New York. Mr. Gregr, who is a Bohemian, was the first speaker.

"At this time of great European conflict," he said, "and while waiting the commencement of a war that is to change the map of Europe, we the Bohemians of the United States, who number half a million, and most of us former subjects of Austria-Hungary, raise our voices not to protest against the hazardous war upon which Austria-Hungary has embarked, but also to condemn the cowardly act of Austria-Hungary in attacking Servia, when the Servs are just recovering from the exhaustion of the bloody Balkan wars in which they bore so splendid a part. Since the first Hapsburg ascended the throne of Bohemia our people have suffered persecution and political and economic exploitation, and it has continued from the day of Ferdinand II, in 1621, to the present time.

Milan Geting, a Slovak, spoke next. He too condemned the attitude of Austria-Hungary in the present conflict in bitter terms.

"When the despotic monarchy of Austria-Hungary," said Mr. Getting, "calls the Slovaks to its defense in its interests, the Slovaks remember that it was Austria-Hungary that has permitted the destruction of the national life of the Slovaks, and so it is that the Slovaks before the civilized world give answer that they will not permit themselves to be used as ammunition for Austria-Hungary cannon."

## The Curse of Austria

Prof. Pupin was the next speaker. Every few minutes he was interrupted with wild applause.

"Austrian rule and Austrian influence," said Prof. Pupin, "were always a curse to every nation. National sentiments, lofty ideals, and noble aspirations cannot flourish in a soil which is saturated with the poisons of Austrian corruption. Freedom shrieks at the sight of the Austrian eagle. King Peter of Servia is a St. George of Servia; he killed the Austrian dragon, and during his reign the Servians removed the poisons of this pestiferous beast from the fair banks of the Save and the Morava, and from that on Servia became a happy and prosperous country.

"Gladstone asked once, 'Can any one put his finger on any spot of the map where Austria has done any good?' He could have asked also, 'Was there ever a man, an institution, or a State whom Austria has not deceived and betrayed?'

"The Serbs of Austria settled along her southern frontier over two hundred years ago; they were forced to do so by the Emperor, Leopold I of Austria, because he knew that they could defend that frontier against the Turks. They agreed to perform that gigantic task in return for definite political and economic privileges which the Emperor granted to them.

"Not only did they live up to their original agreement, but, moreover, for over 200 years they were the bravest and most loyal part of the Austrian Army, and they defended the

Austrian Empire against France, Prussia, Italy, and against every other enemy of the Austrian Emperor. But the Empire betrayed them: it annulled all the privileges granted to them 200 years ago and persecuted them as no other race was ever persecuted in a civilized state.

"The Austrian government makes a charge against the Serbs in Servia, that they are fomenting trouble and dissatisfaction among the Serbs in Austria, but he who knows what has been going on for years in the Southern Provinces of Austria understands perfectly well that the Serbs and Croatians in Austria do not need any outside influence to stir them up to the highest pitch of bitterness against the Austrian Empire. Besides, who is responsible for the bitter hostility of the Bohemians, of the Slovaks, the Ruthenians, and the Rumanians?

"It is not Servia, and, therefore, according to Austrian logic, it must be Russia. But why should I go on describing Austria when she is doing it herself just now in most eloquent language? He who never before understood the methods of Austria understands them now. The language of Austria and her political methods are written down in the Austrian ultimatum to Servia and in the history of Europe during the last ten days. The world rings with righteous indignation as it listens to Austrian language and gets a clear view of Austrian political methods.

"The blackest crime is being committed today on the banks of the lower Danube. Austria is the criminal. The world is dumbfounded and stands against at the sight. The Austrian black eagle soars way up among the blackest clouds, holding a blazing torch in its bloody claws, threatening to set the world afire. The stoutest of human hearts are trembling; a hell on earth is being prepared for helpless humanity.

### An Empire Crumbling

"An impotent empire is tumbling down under the weight of its own wickedness; I hear already the thundering crash of its rotten structure, and it will be a miracle if its ruins do not destroy and bury forever the toil of modern civilization. The spirit of mediaeval Austria is the real menace to the peace of Europe; it is the modern Beelzebub who is leading on his black and yellow host against modern civilization. Let us hope that modern civilization will come out victorious and that it will banish forever this fearful spirit of evil. Not a single one among the 25,000,000 Slavs in Austria will shed a mourning tear when this Beelzebub is carried to his grave."

At the close of the meeting resolutions were offered and adopted condemning the methods which were described as "tyrannical, high-handed, and criminal" by which the Government of Austria is "conspiring to deprive the free and independent people of Servia of their independence." The resolution ended with an appeal to the people of the United States to "raise a voice of protest against the criminal acts of Austria . . . "

\*   \*   \*

September 13, 1914

## CAPTURE OF SEMLIN GREAT AID TO SERBS

*Success of Offensive Operations Against Austrians Continues—*
*Headed for Budapest*

**WOMEN HURL GRENADES**

*Thousands of Men Left Behind in Retreat—Austrian Slavs*
*Refuse to Fight*

Special Cable to The New York Times

ROME, Sept. 12. (Dispatch to The London Morning Post)—Military writers attach great importance to the capture by Servians of Semlin.

The Tribune considers that the Servians leaving the Montenegrins to conduct guerrilla warfare in Bosnia intend to march toward Budapest in concert with Russian action from the north.

In Servian circles special satisfaction is expressed at the humiliation of the proud Hungarians.

One reason for the Servian successes is the refusal of Austrian Slavs to fight against them. In fact, most of the prisoners taken by the Servians are Croats and Dalmatians.

It is officially stated that the Servian attacking force is getting on satisfactorily, but in view of military operations in progress details cannot at present be communicated.

The Germans are flooding Italian universities with partisan literature on the causes and the result of the war, begging professors to communicate the contents to students and press. Against this attempt to influence opinion Prof. Rossi of Genoa has protested.

A German letter has fallen into my hands asking for names and addresses of any persons having relations with leading Italian papers.

Antonio Cippico, translator of "King Lear," who is well known in London, states that a German postcard is in circulation bearing inscription, "Rome, 1870; Nice, Savoy, Africa, 1914."

LONDON, Sept. 13, 2:30 A. M.—A dispatch to Lloyds' News from Milan quotes a statement by the Servian Legation in Rome describing the passage of the River Save and the taking of Semlin, Austria-Hungary, by the Servians.

"The Servians made the difficult passage of the Save from the south," says the statement, "with all their wagons and munitions in two days and nights, during which time the attention of the Austrian artillery was cleverly diverted. Thus the Servians crept up to the rear of Semlin and burst into the city. When the Austrians realized what had happened a desperate combat began. Many Serbs perished in the waters of the Danube and the Save, owing to the terrific fire to which they were subjected while crossing. Nevertheless they obtained a firm lodging in Semlin."

ROME, Sept. 12. (via London)—The Nish correspondent of the Messaggero states that the Austrians lost 500 killed and 500 wounded at Mitrovitza, Servia. The Austrians continue to retreat, leaving behind hundreds of pieces of artillery and thousands of prisoners.

\*     \*     \*

**September 23, 1914**

## BOSNIAN CAPITAL OCCUPIED BY SERVIANS

*Austrians Abandon Sarajevo After Overwhelming Defeat—Meet Disaster Also on River Drina*

LONDON, Sept. 22—In a dispatch from Rome the correspondent of The Star says Servian and Montenegrin forces have occupied Sarajevo, the capital of Bosnia, which was abandoned by the Austrians after an overwhelming defeat.

NISH, Servia, Sept. 22—The battle which has been in progress for several days near Krupani, on the Drina River, has, according to an official announcement made today, ended in complete disaster for the Austrian army.

The announcement declared that 100,000 Austrian troops were engaged in this encounter, while the Servian forces included various bodies of men who had been concentrated along the Drina, reinforced by troops hastily recalled from Semlin and Slavonia. The fighting was very sanguinary.

The Austrian attempt on Shabatz was repulsed with heavy loss.

Prince George of Servia, who for the second time has been wounded while leading a charge of a Servian battalion, is doing well, and it is the opinion of his physician that his life is in no danger. A rifle bullet penetrated the trunk of his body.

Prince George was wounded first at Belgrade in the early part of August by a fragment of a shell when that city was being bombarded by the Austrians.

PARIS, Sept. 22—In a dispatch from Nish, Servia, dated Sunday, Sept. 20, the correspondent of the Havas News Agency says:

"The Austrians have been forced to retreat along the entire front between Lioubovia, Svornik, and Losnitza, and they are being hotly pursued by the Servian forces near Kouriatcitza. The Servians destroyed the bridges over the River Drina, but after suffering heavy losses the Austrians succeeded in gaining the opposite bank.

"The Austrian attempt to cross the River Save between Mitrovitza and Shabatz has failed.

"In Bosnia yesterday the Servians occupied the heights west of Rogatnitza."

\*     \*     \*

**October 6, 1914**

## A WAR FOR NATIONALITIES

*Hilaire Belloc Says it is in Aid of the Smaller Peoples*

Special Cable to The New York Times

LONDON, Oct. 5—Addressing a meeting in London tonight, Hilaire Belloc declared that the whole issue of the present war was the re-edification of the smaller nationalities in Europe. Future historians would say that the war was fought to discover whether free nationalities should or should not continue to exist in Europe.

Mr. Belloc warned his hearers not to underestimate the German forces. But, he said, suppose the war went in favor of the Allies, what measures would be taken to produce a Europe in which local feelings would be satisfied? If a long cycle of wars was to be avoided, the populations of smaller nationalities would have to be consulted as to their mode of government.

Far from England or France desiring to annex the country of an unwilling population, said Mr. Belloc, they would be ready to pay the people £10 ($50) per head to govern themselves. But certain other countries were not like them in this respect. By a vote of the populations, Great Britain should discover what the will of smaller nationalities was, and their wishes should guide her in re-establishing them.

\*     \*     \*

**December 20, 1914**

## BRAVE LITTLE SERVIA'S VICTORY

*Their Soldiers Fine Specimens of a People Who Know How to Make History and Fight Up to It*

Written for The New York Times
By ADAMANTIOS TH. POLYZOIDES
*Editor of the Greek Newspaper Atlantis*

Ten days ago most of the people who get their everyday impressions from the more or less official statements of the warring European countries thought that Servia's end was at hand. The big battle of Vaijovo, where superior Austrian forces overwhelmed the exhausted Servian Army, was considered on the strength of the Vienna statements, as the closing chapter of the Teutonic campaign in that part of Europe. Already the Austrian strategists were considering the possibility of reaching the Bulgarian frontier by taking Kraguyevatz and Nish. Such a scheme would give the Austrians and their allies a direct line of railroad communication from the North Sea down to the Persian Gulf. It is true that part of this line runs through Bulgarian territory, but it must be borne in mind that for all practical reasons Bulgaria must be regarded as an ally of the Central European coalition, and this holds good as long as convincing evidence to the contrary is not forthcoming. But things somehow went against the Austrians, to the utter surprise of all those not thoroughly acquainted with the tactics and the spirit of Servian strategy. The Servian Government from Nish was vainly protesting on Dec. 6, 7, and 8 that the withdrawal of the Servian Army from Valjevo instead of being the result of a rout was, on the contrary, a strategic move of the first magnitude. No-where since the beginning of this war was the Servian Army routed. Although fighting against tremendous odds with everything against them, the Servians kept continuously on the aggressive, as their leaders knew beforehand that a defensive campaign was against the character of the Servian soldier, and, therefore, doomed to failure from the outset.

Only once in the last thirty years did the Servians make a defensive war, and that was in 1885 against the Bulgarians, when the results were in such a degree disastrous for Servia that the European powers had to step in and force peace at any price on the belligerents.

The Servian offensive had showed itself in all its splendid qualities in the first Balkan war, when the fighters of Peter Karageorghewitz and Volvoda Putnik swept over the Macedonian plains like a flood of iron and fire and won the brilliant victories of Kumanowa, Islip and Monastir. The same story was repeated at the second Balkan war with the battles of the Bregolnitso and Krivolak, and the system was followed in the third war against Austria, this time when the Servian troops inaugurated their campaign by invading Bosnia and engaging successfully the enemy at Vishegrad Bogatitsa and Fotscha, with the assistance of the Montenegrins in the latter place.

Undoubtedly the Servians counted much on the assistance of the Russians, which, however, has not been of much aid to them up to the present date.

Had the Russian Army mastered Galicia and pushed on in Hungary the Servian Army would have to it all Bosnia and Herzegovina today. But the gallant little people of the Balkans were left to their own resources, which at best cannot be much above eight army corps, in addition to one Montenegrin or 360,000 men all told. And still these 360,000 soldiers, fighting for a principle which is the liberation of their brethren in Austria, under competent officers and an intelligent staff, have performed wonders.

With only one railway line to depend upon for communications with the rear, with supplies reduced to the minimum, with a commissariat service far from perfect, lacking hospital facilities, fighting in the heart of a hard Balkan Winter to say nothing of the natural exhaustion which comes to every people who had fought two successive wars, the Servians have proven themselves to be a fine specimen of a people who know how to make history and fight up to it.

The first Russian reverses in Poland and Hungary, insignificant in their relation to the entire European war, had a most momentous bearing on the Servian campaign, because Austria, temporarily immune from the Russian danger, had thrown all her strength against the Servians in order to deal them a severe blow and put them out of the way once for all. In this enterprise Austria was assisted by a whole Bavarian corps, sent there by express order of Emperor William of Germany.

But the Vienna strategists did not make a secret of their plans, which somehow reached the Servians. Against the advancing Austro-German masses only one course was open to the Servian Army, and that was to fall back on their bases and their magazines, supplies, and reinforcements, and this is what they did, while the distance between the Austro-German hosts and their bases was becoming daily greater.

In this way the Servians, having retired to the south of Kolubora River, fortified themselves in strong positions and awaited the enemy who was advancing on their heels. Eventually the two opposing armies clashed, the Servians taking a tremendously vigorous offensive, which drove the foe out of Servian territory in the space of four days which worked an Austrian rout comparable with only that of Lemberg, and the utter collapse of the campaign against Servia.

The result is unique in the history of this European war. And as it was in the beginning of it with Belgium, so now it is little brave Servia that towers above all its strong foes and allies as the winner of the most significant victory in the entire five months of the European campaign.

\* \* \*

January 16, 1915

## BELGRADE WAS TERRORIZED

### *Austrians Hanged Respectable Citizens—1,000 Sent Into Captivity*

Special Cable to The New York Times

NISH, Servia, Jan. 1, (Dispatch to The London Morning Post)—It is now known that there has been more plundering and terrorism in Belgrade than was at first supposed.

The inhabitants were menaced by threats of punishment and death. More than 1,000 citizens were seized by the Austrians and sent away into captivity, and, to increase the fear and horror of the populace one man was hanged on a gallows in a square in the most frequented part of the town and exposed all day to the public gaze.

According to information recently obtained, it was in consequence of the intervention of the chief doctor of the United States Red Cross Society at Belgrade that the gallows was removed from the public square and no more executions took place there. But it was only a change of scene. Thirteen more executions took place in the grounds of the fortress and in each case a respectable citizen was hanged like a common felon.

\* \* \*

February 15, 1915

## ALBANIANS INVADE SERVIA IN FORCE

*King Peter's Troops Are Forced to Retreat Before Overwhelming Numbers*

**RAIDERS STILL ADVANCING**

*New Complication in the Eastern War Area May Involve Italy or Greece*

PARIS, Feb. 14—Albanians in force have crossed the Servian frontier, forcing the Servian troops and local authorities to withdraw.

News of this new complication in the eastern war situation reached here in a telegram from Nish to the Havas News Agency, quoting this official statement of the Servian Government.

"Large numbers of Albanians broke through our lines yesterday, crossing the frontier in the Department of Prisrend. Before superior forces of the enemy our troops, as well as the municipal authorities, were forced to retreat.

"The Albanians continue to advance in the direction of Zapod, Topoliana, and Glavotchnitz.

"The enemy succeeded in certain places in cutting the telephone and telegraph communications."

### May Involve Italy or Greece

Aside from strategic considerations, the principal interest aroused by the Albanian invasion of Servia is in the possibility of this incident leading to the entrance of Greece or Italy into the war. Since the outbreak of the great war in August conditions in Albania have been more disorganized than ever.

Nominally Albania is still a kingdom, and after Mpret, William of Wied, fled, the Diet elected on Sept. 29 Prince Burhan Ed-Din, a son of the former Sultan, Abdul Hamid, as ruler of the country. He never took his seat however, and on Oct. 4 Essad Pasha one of the principal Albanian noblemen, who had been Minister of War and the Interiors under William, was elected Provisional President.

Upon the Turkish declaration of war against the Allies. Essad was named Governor of Albania and commander of the Turkish Army in the province, but this was hardly more than a form, as he already held the chief power in the country. It is uncertain whether he now regards himself as a Turkish Governor or an independent President.

Albanian hostility to the Servo-Montenegrins, a matter of long standing, was intensified when Servians occupied Durazzo early in 1913 and Montenegrins captured Scutari. The creation of Albania into an independent Kingdom was a direct blow by Austria at Servian aspirations, and the Albanians (two-thirds of whom are Mohammedan and one-seventh Roman Catholics) have felt that the Serbs and Greeks are only waiting for a chance to divide up their territories. This hatred was further intensified by a certain lingering loyalty to the Sultan, by memories of the previous wars and the

Greek incursions on the south, and since the present war began, by the fact that food has trebled in price owing to the difficulties of import.

Should the Albanians capture Prisrend which, though just over the Servian border is largely Albanian in population, they would be within thirty-five miles of Skoplje, an important junction point on the railroad from Nish to Salonica, and thus could cut off many Servian supplies as well as threaten the yet undevastated districts of that country.

\* \* \*

April 5, 1915

## SERBIA PROTESTS ON BULGARIAN RAID

*Asks That Those Responsible Be Punished—Fifth Outbreak of the Kind*

**GREEKS FIRE ON RAIDERS**

*Bulgars Blame Macedonian Revolutionists Operating Within Serbian Territory*

PARIS, April 4—The Petit Journal says that Serbia has protested to Bulgaria because of the invasion of Serbian territory by a force described as Hungarian irregulars. While couched in moderate terms, the protest is said to request the arrest and imprisonment of the persons responsible for the raid.

Further details of the incident received today confirm the report that the invaders were driven away from the railroad station at Strumitsa, the Serbian town near the Bulgarian border where the attack was made. The railway stationmaster at Strumitsa reports that the line to Ghevghell is now clear of the raiders, and apparently has not been damaged.

Serbian frontier guards who pursued the fleeing irregulars retook the two cannon which had been captured.

Six bodies were found in the railway station at Strumitsa. The extent of the losses inflicted upon the attacking force is unknown, but is believed to be large. Thirty bodies were found, and the raiders themselves picked up and buried a number of others.

This is said to be the fifth incident of its kind since the beginning of the European war, and there is much speculation in Paris as to their exact significance. It is felt that the attitude of Bulgaria on this occasion will indicate what policy she intends to pursue.

The Havas Agency received today from Nish, Serbia, a dispatch saying that the losses of the Serbian troops were sixty killed and fifty-three wounded, including five officers.

### Serbian Legation's Statement

LONDON, April 4—The Serbian Legation in London received today the following official dispatch from Nish:

"The Bulgarian irregulars were driven back from Strumitsa. The fight was short. When reinforcements arrived our advanced posts cleared the Strumitsa station, and the invaders fled in the direction of Bulgaria.

"Our troops, pursuing the enemy, found thirty of their dead, and it is presumed that others were carried away. We lost fifty killed."

A semi-official communication from Nish to Reuter's Telegram Company states that the invading force scattered among the Serbian frontier villages and compelled the inhabitants to remove to Bulgaria, taking their goods and cattle with them. It is also stated, although not confirmed, that the invaders set fire to the Serbian blockhouses at Flauvoton and Borakli.

### Blame Put on Macedonians

ROME, April 4 (via Paris)—D. Rizow, Bulgarian Minister to Rome, expressed the opinion today that the incident on the Serbo-Bulgarian border was the work of Macedonian revolutionists in Serbia, who are opposed to the Serbian regime in the territory gained in the Balkan wars, in which the fighting occurred. M. Rizow asserted that the Bulgarian Government was in no way responsible for the affair and that its only desire was to preserve neutrality.

M. Ristach, the Serbian Minister, took issue with M. Rizow's statement. He said that, having spent thirty years in the region concerned, he knew it thoroughly and could affirm that the Macedonians in this part of Serbia had no desire to oppose the present order of things. Responsibility for the incident he asserted, might be determined by considering to whose interests it would be to provoke such an outbreak. This, he said, pointed clearly to Bulgaria, which by occupying the left bank of the Vardar River could threaten to cut Serbian communications with Saloniki, the only source from which the country could bring in its supply. Already, he said, communication by telegraph and telephone had been cut.

ROME, April 4 (Dispatch to The London Daily News)—The prevailing impression in official centres here, undoubtedly based on direct and confidential information from the Balkans is that the Bulgarian attack on Serbia although sufficiently serious, still will not exceed the proportions of a frontier incident. Its importance is due to the well-known fact that the raid was instigated by a German agent who is striving to persuade the Bulgarians that their aspirations in Macedonia are hopeless unless they avail themselves of the present favorable conditions to compel Serbia and Greece to come to terms and make concessions. The result of the German intrigue, however, is disappointing since Bulgaria probably has been warned that Italy and Rumania will not tolerate war against Serbia, which Greece is determined to defend. Hence she now fully realizes that it will be a blunder to follow the Austro-German policy. It is believed that the frontier incident may be amicably settled shortly.

### London's View of the Clash

LONDON, Monday, April 5—The Chronicle's main editorial on the Bulgar-Serb frontier incident says:

"Though this opens on serious possibilities against which Serbia now our ally must be duly guarded one can hardly believe in another Serb-Bulgarian rupture. By treaty both Greece and Rumania would be bound in that event to come into the conflict on Serbia's side and therefore German and Austrian statesmanship has a motive for not provoking it. The attitude of the Greek Government however, continues somewhat enigmatic and the political struggle now developing between Gounaris, the King's nominee in the Premiership and ex-Premier Venizelos will have to be watched with attention."

The Chronicle's diplomatic correspondent says:

"Diplomatic quarters in London do not expect any serious developments from the Macedonian raid incident. The disquieting feature of the affair, it is admitted, however, is the absence of any official dementi from Sofia. Bulgarian opinion here is inclined to look upon the whole thing as a mere frontier incident. There have been a series of such incidents lately. Bulgarian peasants fleeing from Serbian Macedonia have, it is declared, been fired on by Serbian frontier guards. Representations have been made at Nish and an inquiry asked for but the Serbian Government has refused to take any action. Although no official information has yet come through from Sofia it is surprised that this latest incident does not differ very much from other recent incidents. On the other hand, it may be pointed out, first, that this raid is no mere frontier affair; second, that Bulgarian troops are said to have been engaged; third, that the Vardar was crossed and the railway that is Serbia's only tie with the outside would occupied and, fourth, that the fighting seems to have been severe.

"By the Serbo-Greek alliance, it should be added. Greece is bound to come to Serbia's assistance in the event of an attack by Bulgaria."

The Times says:

"In point of time the Bulgarian raid upon Serbia comes too soon after the visit of von der Goltz Pasha to Sofia to seem altogether fortuitous. Bulgaria is at liberty to choose her course, but she would sadly err were she to suppose that the allied powers will remain indifferent should she continue to allow the 'strict neutrality' so recently proclaimed by her Premier to be so strangely practiced by her citizens."

### Urges Allies to Act

By Marconi Transatlantic Wireless Telegraph to
The New York Times

LONDON, Monday, April 5—The Daily News editorial, discussing the Serbo-Bulgarian affair, says:

"It is no accident that this incident should take place simultaneously with the rather bitter controversy between the present Greek Premier Gounaris and his predecessor, Venizelos, as to the proper policy for Greece to adopt toward Bulgaria. If Serbia has sinned in taking by force Macedonian territory unquestionably Bulgarian in character, the Greeks have also committed the same sin. They are both suffering for it now. Serbia, instead of having the help of a group of Balkan, allies in her struggle with Austria, finds herself alone, and in her hour of most urgent need is in danger of being attacked in the rear. Greece is paying for taking a few hundred square miles more than her due by being checkmated in far more ambitious schemes of expansion. The Allies who permitted this unjust division of Macedonia, are also learning that political offenses sometimes avenge themselves."

The paper proceeds to urge the Bulgarian claims be satisfied. Hitherto, it says, the diplomacy of the Allies toward the question seems to have lacked firmness and clearness, but the blow now struck at the Saloniki railway by the Bulgarian irregulars ought to bring them to a decision.

### Divergent Views in Paris

Special Cable to The New York Times

PARIS, Monday, April 5—The press expresses divergent views on the Serbian frontier affair. The majority likes to consider the attack similar to the recent Albanian raid, purely by irregulars bribed by Austria in the hope of causing complications. The Temps says:

"Such incidents cause bad feeling between neighbors, but the Sofia Cabinet will make the final decision with a wider outlook. It is further east that Bulgaria seeks a reason for decisive action. We do not expect the consequences to be serious."

The Journal des Débats, however, maintains it is an impossibility that Bulgaria was not implicated. It says:

"The presence of regular Bulgarian troops shows the intentions are serious, nothing indicates they tried to suppress the raid, rather, contrariwise, they seem to have protected the raiders. It looks as it they meant to invade Serbia if the raid was successful. The Allies are mistaken in trying to influence friendly Balkans to make sacrifices to Bulgaria. If the latter does not disavow and punish the comitadjis promptly we ought to regard her an enemy. She has refused the opportunity of our friendship. Will she risk our hostility?"

\* \* \*

April 21, 1915

# VENIZELOS'S PLEA FOR WAR BY GREECE

*Text of Memorandum to the King Advising Participation with Entente Powers*

**A GREAT EMPIRE HIS AIM**

*Co-operation of Bulgaria and Rumania Through Territorial Concessions—Feared Turkey's Revenge*

Special Cable to The New York Times

LONDON, Wednesday, April 21—The Daily Chronicle publishes the full text of the memorandum to the King of Greece in which former Premier Venizelos urged the participation of Greece in the war on the side of Servia against Germany and Austria and outlined his plan of obtaining the co-operation of Bulgaria and Rumania by offering territorial concessions.

The memorandum was contained in a dispatch dated Athens, April 11, and received yesterday. As a result of this memorandum, M. Venizelos avers, the King authorized him

to obtain the co-operation of Bulgaria and Rumania in the war on the basis of territorial concessions, an assertion which the King, through the present Government, flatly denied. In consequence of this denial, which M. Venizelos regarded as an insult, he withdrew from politics altogether and quitted Greece. The memorandum reads:

"Sire: Up till today our policy has consisted of the maintenance of neutrality as long as our obligations as allies of Serbia do not demand that we should depart from it; but now we are requested to enter into the war not only to fulfill our simple moral obligations but for concessions which, if realized, would create a great and powerful Greece such as even the most optimistic would not have imagined a few years ago.

"If we by continuing to remain neutral allow Serbia to be annihilated by a new Austro-German invasion we have no guarantee that Austro-German troops will stop before they reach the Macedonian frontier, and they might be attracted to come south as far as Saloniki.

"But even if Austria were content at annihilating Serbia and did not enter into Macedonia, is there any doubt that Bulgaria, instigated by Austria, would attack Serbia for the purpose of occupying Serbian Macedonia?

"It is necessary for us to strive for the co-operation not only of Rumania, but, if possible, also for that of Bulgaria. Should such co-operation be brought into existence all the Christian States of the Balkan peninsula, would be confederated. Thus not only would the chances of local defeat be avoided, but the new co-operation would very seriously strengthen the side of the Entente.

### Concessions to Bulgaria

"Therefore I think it essential to make important concessions to Bulgaria, which up to the present we have declined even to discuss. At the moment, however, in which our national aspirations in Asia Minor are on the point of being realized, it is necessary to make some sacrifices in the Balkans. Chiefly we ought to withdraw our objections already raised concerning concessions on the part of Serbia to Bulgaria, even if these concessions extend as far as the right bank of the River Axios.

"In the event of the concessions offered on such a scale not proving sufficient to attract Bulgaria to co-operate toward her late allies, or at least getting her to maintain a friendly neutrality toward them, I would not hesitate, much as the operation would be painful to me, to suggest the sacrifice of Cavalla to save Hellenism in Turkey and secure the creation of a really great Greece, embracing almost all the countries over which Hellenism, during its history of centuries, hold sway.

"This sacrifice would be made, not to purchase Bulgaria's neutrality, but as an exchange for her active co-operation in the war on the side of our allies. At the same time, as a partial exchange for this cession, we would require that, in case Bulgaria should extend over the Axios River, Serbia ought to cede to us the Dalrani-Gevaghill district, so as to have a fairly important frontier on the north opposite Bulgaria, as we are at present deprived of such a good frontier on the east.

"Unfortunately, on account of Bulgaria's avidity, it is almost sure that whatever concessions may be made to her she will not consider them satisfactory enough to induce her to enter into co-operation with her former allies. Then in this connection it would be indispensable to secure at least the cooperation of Rumania, because without the co-operation of that State our participation in the war would be very dangerous to us assuming the war will end without giving predominance to any one side; but with the return of the status quo, as before the war began, then the end of all Hellenism in Turkey would be sure and sudden.

### Turkey's Probable Action

"Turkey would come out of the war unharmed, although she had dared the great powers, and audacious in a sense of security which her alliance with Germany would command, an alliance which would certainly continue after the war as serving Germany's ends. These facts would complete without delay the work of destruction of Hellenism in Turkey, which would expel systematically, without any pretext and on a large scale, masses or population and confiscate their property. Germany would certainly not prevent or oppose such a course. In fact, she would encourage it, as it would be the means of ridding Asia Minor of another claimant of the country which she covets herself. Expulsion in masses of the millions of Greeks from Turkey would not only ruin individuals but would mean for Greece financial shipwreck.

"Finally in the event of unsuccess we would continue to enjoy the friendship and appreciation of the powerful nations of the Entente, which nations created Greece and so often since that time have helped and supported her. On the other hand, our refusal to fulfill our obligations as allies toward Serbia would not only ruin our moral prestige as a State, not only would it expose us to the dangers above mentioned, but it would leave us without any friends and without any political credit in the future." (Signed)

*"ELEFTHERIOS VENIZELOS"*

After the King had considered the above memorandum, Venizelos, the Chronicle's correspondent says, had an audience with his Majesty, and as a result the Premier was authorized to approach Rumania in order to ascertain if she were favorable to an alliance.

In his second memorandum to the King the then Premier stated that he had found Rumania would refuse all military co-operation unless Bulgaria participated. Rumania would have been content with a declaration of neutrality on the part of Bulgaria, but M. Venizelos adds that it was absolutely improbable that such a declaration could be obtained.

The Greek General Staff could not be persuaded that it was safe to act on the assurance of Bulgarian neutrality, as that might be broken when it appeared to suit the interests of that country.

\* \* \*

May 9, 1915

# SERBIA BATTLES WITH TYPHUS

*Young American Sculptor, Working with the Red Cross, Writes of Conditions in the Fighting Zone*

*The article which follows, is a portion of a letter written by Cecil Howard, a young American sculptor well known in Paris, to a friend in the French capital. The letter is dated at Vrnjatchka Banja, Serbia, on March 26. Mr. Howard who is now with the British Red Cross in Serbia, is a sociétaire of the Salon des Beaux Arts. His sister is Miss Kathleen Howard of the Century Opera Company.*

### By CECIL HOWARD

We have seen something of the Serbian soldier. He is a well-built and rather handsome fellow dressed in all sorts of outlandish garments, unless he is a more recent recruit, in which case he has a very neat uniform of a particularly good warm gray color. From the time our train crossed the frontier we heard a good deal of scrambling about and talking going on outside on the steps and on top of the cars, and later discovered that, while we had spent a sleepless and shivering night in our overcoats and blankets inside the train, fifty or sixty Serbian soldiers had been hanging on outside, and showed up smiling and cheerful in the morning.

As we stopped at dawn, I went down the platform the length of the train and saw that we had several trucks of artillery on behind, also filled with soldiers. One had two rifles on his back and was guarding three Austrian prisoners, one of whom had his arms bound behind his back. This is really all we have seen of troops on the move in Serbia, and we have heard less.

At Gevgelija, however, we first heard of some other troubles of Serbia. We met at the station some American doctors who are working there. They told us of crowded hospitals and the difficulties of caring for thousands of sick and wounded without nurses and in filthy old buildings, We were duly warned against the great enemies—lice and overwork. Five of their staff were down with "it" and one was dead. Their last words to us as the train pulled out were: "Remember, the treatment is five drops of tincture of iodine twice daily." "It" is typhus.

We reached Nish, were formally received by representatives of the Serbian Government and the Service de Santé, &c., and spent a day sightseeing. It is a place of wide mud streets and low whitewashed houses with a few shops where you can buy most things you don't want and some that you do. The sights are chiefly bullock carts—the eternal Serbian bullock carts, driven by peasants in brown sacking and weird footgear, consisting of socks outside the trousers, and sandals. The socks are a great feature and one of the most remarkable things in Serbia. They are half an inch thick and have color schemes like the Salon des Indépendents in all its glory.

Another great feature is the Austrian prisoner, whose acquaintance we made at Nish. There are some 60,000 of

Convalescent Soldiers Being Transported in an Ox Cart in Serbia.

them and they seem to do most of the hard work of the country—cleaning streets, mending roads, building and working as orderlies in the hospitals. They are most convenient but a mixed blessing, as the Serbs say it is they who brought the great trouble into Serbia—typhus, which has been on the rampage all Winter.

Typhus is a disease of dirt, overcrowding, and underfeeding, and is carried from the sick to the well by lice. This sounds soft enough for clean people, but in Serbia it is not always easy to keep clean, and a louse or two is almost unavoidable when nursing dirty patients in old and filthy buildings.

The death rate has been rather high at Nish and Ouskoub, particularly among the prisoners. Some English and American doctors have also succumbed. The great trouble is that the various hospital staffs are much too small to tackle the thousands of patients or to undertake thorough cleansing of the hospital buildings. On the main street of Nish is a coffin-maker's shop doing a humming trade, with dozens of plain board coffins out in front on the sidewalk. On the hill outside the town we saw rows and rows of little wooden crosses and picked up plenty of cartridge cases, mostly Turkish ones. These are being used by the Serbian Army now and were captured in the last war.

On arriving at Vrnjatchka Banja, after another night in the train, changing at Kruchevatz, which is about thirty miles from here, the first thing we did after the official reception was to visit all the available buildings in the town and pick out the Sanatorium, a new building with water supply, bath tubs, and electric light, for our main hospital. In time of peace this village is a Thermal station and health resort. There are hot springs and big hotels, so is well adapted for a hospital town.

When our sanatorium was in running order and filled with about sixty cases taken from the numerous native hospitals in the village, we took over three other buildings which we

fumigated and cleaned and made into two convalescent hospitals and a clearing house. The last is for the purpose of receiving and sorting out the newly arriving patients—bunches of 150 or so, usually—where the typhus suspects are kept till the disease declares itself fully, or the incubation period, two weeks, has elapsed, when they are sent on to the other hospitals or the typhus barracks, which are now taken over by the Bennet party, (Sir Thomas Lipton's crowd,) and made clean and efficient.

Now that all new patients arriving in the village are bathed and cleanly clothed and the typhus cases are sorted out, the epidemic is on the wane, and very few cases have been contracted here. Two Greek doctors, who were running a hospital here when we arrived, have fallen victims, and one died. One of the Bennet party also developed a slight case soon after arrival, but is now well. Most of the present cases are Austrians recently arrived with the infection on them.

There are two English missions here in Vrnjatchka Banja now—ours, which is organized and directed by Dr. Berry of the Royal Free Hospital, London, and consists of twenty-six members, and Captain Bennet's, which was sent out by the British Red Cross Society on Lipton's yacht. Their mission is chiefly medical, while ours is surgical, and we generally divide work. They run two surgical hospitals and the typhus barracks.

We have taken over the bathhouse of the village—a large pool filled by the hot springs—for a washing house for new patients, and it is a great sight to see them arriving through the snow in bullock carts to be put through the mill of clipping and scrubbing in batches of fifteen or twenty at once. The bad cases are washed on tables and the light ones are pushed into the pool to soak.

We couldn't do half what we do without the Austrians. With the Bennets, we have about sixty of them. It was a fine sight when we picked them out from a bunch of about 150 lined up for our inspection, like a slave market, asking searching questions and feeling muscles. Most of the prisoners seem to be

Convalescent Soldiers Dancing Before Going Home.

Bohemians, Bosnians, Tzchecks, Croats, &c., and I imagine they were easy captures. Half of them speak Serbian and few speak good German. One of ours, a Bohemian, was a waiter at the Carlton in London before the war, has also been in America, and speaks good English, French, Italian and German. We also have carpenters, stone masons, engineers, &c. The engineers of the sanatorium were taken prisoners by the director of the sanatorium in person during the great Austrian retreat.

The Serbs are very proud of their success over Austria and say that with 500,000 men they would be in Vienna in a month. Maybe they would. They seem a fine lot of men and are renowned for being able to take care of themselves and for not bothering the Government about food or clothing. Give a Serbian soldier a loaf of bread and he will march and fight for two days. Give him nothing at all and he will say it is hard luck, but he will march and fight just the same. This is their boast, and it seems to be no more than the truth.

Some of them are very brave fellows, as we can see in hospital, many preferring even rather serious operations without anaesthetic and standing it without a wink.

The man who is in charge of the commissariat post of the hospitals of this district—Neuhut by name—is a great card. He found it convenient to spend five years in America after the assassination of the late King and his wife, so speaks broken American most fluently.

The Serbs about here think us all rather mad, and can't understand why we work so hard. They are especially astounded by our willingness to do hard labor. One day we were digging a ditch for drainage and a Serb who was driving an ox-cart stopped and sat down to watch us for an hour or two. Finally he said: "You work too hard," and went on down the road with his oxen, playing a half tune on a sort of double flute, like you see in Greek drawings of fauns.

There are many funerals, of course. The coffin shop in the backyard of one of the hospitals is a busy spot, and on the hillside beyond the village there are rows and rows of wooden crosses with names and dates painted on them. A fresh row of graves is dug every day and usually filled the next.

The Serbians are great on going out in bands of fifty or sixty, working independently almost, and foraging for themselves. They are very fond of hand grenades and bayonet fighting and seem brave as lions. One can quite believe that in their own rather wild country they are practically invincible. They are a cheerful and sympathetic lot, and we find them very easy patients to handle. The Government and military authorities fall in with all our plans, making every thing as easy as possible for us.

One thing you may not have heard: I have it on good authority that there are English, French, and Russian soldiers in Belgrade, and have been for some time. They are gunners sent out with their own guns, about fifty each of English and French, and a good many more Russians.

\* \* \*

June 15, 1915

### RUMANIA AGREES WITH ALLIES TO JOIN THE WAR; BULGARS' ACCESSION BALKED BY GREECE AND SERBIA

ROME, (via Paris,) June 14—A dispatch to the Giornale d'Italia from Sofia says:

"M. Filipesco, leader of the Rumanian Conservatives, stated today that the quadruple entente powers (Great Britain, France, Russia, and Italy) had agreed to the demands of Rumania. Therefore, a definite conclusion of an understanding for the intervention of Rumania in the war is imminent.

"Greece and Serbia will send an identical note to the Bulgarian Premier, M. Radoslavoff, and his Cabinet, declining the proposals of the quadruple entente powers for the cession of Macedonian territory to Bulgaria."

The correspondent adds:

"I am assured that Greece and Serbia are sending a note of protest to the great powers, stating that it is impossible to accept a Balkan understanding on such terms.

"M. Radoslavoff and his Cabinet will use pressure on Serbia and Greece, because in the end the conception of the quadruple entente is based on right, and a just consideration of national aspirations in the Balkans must prevail."

With a population of 8,000,000 in her 53,489 square miles, (a little more than the area of New York State,) Rumania will be a formidable addition to the ranks of the Allies. Her strategic position to the west and southwest of Hungary, on which she borders for 375 miles, stretching from the Serbian frontier clear to Bukowina, will make her an uncomfortable antagonist for the harassed forces of Francis Joseph. And her capacity for causing trouble is not diminished by the fact that if the Allies win she will expect as compensation large slices of Austrian territory, including probably Bukowina, which has 900,000 Rumanians among its population, and Transylvania, which has 3,000,000 Rumanians. She may also be seeking from Russia the Province of Bessarabia with its 3,000,000 Rumanians.

\* \* \*

**July 22, 1915**

# THREE BALKAN KINGS TO MEET IN ATHENS

*Budapest Hears Rulers of Rumania, Bulgaria, and Greece Are Soon to Confer*

**KING OF SERBIA LEFT OUT**

*Coming Meeting May Mean a Speedy Decision to Join the Allies in War*

Special Cable to The New York Times

BUDAPEST, July 21 (Dispatch to The London Morning Post.)—Private reports from three different sources reaching Budapest state that the Kings of Rumania. Bulgaria, and the Hellenes are to meet in Athens shortly. At first, says a Berlin telegram, it was arranged that the meeting should take place at Bucharest, but later the place of meeting, considering the illness of King Constantine, was decided in favor of Athens. A Bucharest telegram to the same effect adds that the foreign Ministers of the three countries will accompany their rulers.

A Sofia message says: "Rumors of a meeting of three neutral sovereigns of the Balkans are neither confirmed nor denied in Sofia, yet political circles attach little credit to them for the present at least."

The Hungarian papers also doubt the truth of the rumor. Az Ujsaz says:

"The rumors are most probably untrue, simply because the Serbian monarch is not included. A meeting of this nature would not be undertaken by Balkan rulers with the exclusion of the King of Serbia, as the questions to be discussed affect Serbia as much and more deeply than any of the other three countries. If any meeting of the three Kings were to be held without the King of Serbia taking part. It would be interpreted in Belgrade as an unfriendly act and would create the impression that the entente powers were hostile toward Serbia."

The meeting of the three Balkan monarchs has significance at this time, and in the allied capitals, at least, is likely to be regarded as an omen of a speedy decision as to entrance of those nations into the war, probably on the allied side.

Bulgaria, at the end of the second Balkan war of 1913, felt bitter toward Serbia and Greece, to whom had been allotted territory she thought she should have had; toward Rumania which, by invasion, had obtained the price of the neutrality she had maintained during the first Balkan war of 1912–13, and toward Russia, whom she believed had conspired to prevent her having a dominant influence in Balkan affairs.

Thus, when the great war began her sympathies, looking to practical advantages, were pro-Teutonic, and if Austria had succeeded in taking Nish with the command of the Orient Railway to Constantinople, it is believed that she would have been forced to enter the war on the side of Germany and Austria.

Her uncertain attitude for a long time served to enforce neutrality in Rumania and Greece, when there was a growing clamor to enter the war on the side of the Entente Powers, lest Bulgaria, after their intervention, might attack them on their flank in order to obtain the territory in Macedonia, of which they had been deprived in 1913.

First England tried her hand at bringing about a Balkan modus vivendi, by which Rumania, Greece, and Serbia were to make territorial concessions to Bulgaria. The agreement was almost reached when the fall of the Venizelos Government at Athens rendered void all arrangements. Then Italy, having denounced the Triple Alliance on May 4, tried her hand and agreements were reached with Serbia, Rumania, and Bulgaria, only Greece still hanging fire.

Serbia, in lieu of certain territory in Macedonia, which was to go to Bulgaria, agreed to accept the guarantee of the Entente Powers that she should have compensation in Bosnia and in Dalmatia, with a foothold on the Adriatic. Rumania was to have Bukowina and Transylvania, with their Rumanian populations, with promised concessions for the Rumanians of Bessarabia from Russia. It was believed that if Italy entered the war, followed by Rumania Greece would then come in, all fears of Bulgarian aggression having been removed.

Italy entered the war on May 24, but Rumania lacked ammunition to do so and her agents in the United States reported that her promised allies had contracted for everything in sight. Rumania, therefore, with the strong Francophile and Italophile sympathies of her people, still holds the key to the situation. She has placed an embargo on all munitions sent from Germany through her territory for Turkey and has obtained from England as Serbia had already done, some 6-inch naval guns on mobile carriages.

Meanwhile, the Interventionists of Greece have triumphed in general elections with the return to power of M. Venizelos—a power, however, he cannot exercise until the convening of the new parliament on Aug. 18.

\* \* \*

**September 24, 1915**

## THE BALKAN RESURGENCE

A Balkan crisis is no new thing. It is only now and then more acute than chronic. It happens at this instant to wear an aspect crucial to the issues of the internecine warfare going on in Europe. Between the Central Teutonic Powers on the one hand and the Allies on the other, each side bidding for their aid, Bulgaria, Rumania, and Greece have wavered, balked, and counteracted, higgling hopelessly with each other, apparently unable to decide anything above the principle of immediate and petty national aggrandizement. Bulgaria, for instance, has wanted as a price for siding with the Allies, an area that temporarily is in Serbia's possession. This the Allies could not barter, because they stand as Serbia's protectors. Bulgaria also wanted something on the other side from Turkey, a strip of ground on which she had built a railroad to the sea, and this Turkey was persuaded by her German ally to cede. In the meantime Greece has wanted territory the Bulgars wished her not to have. Rumania has maintained a kind of tentative neutrality, apparently wishing first, to see which way the victory leaned and sell her strength accordingly. Serbia meanwhile has been obdurate, unwilling to yield anything. She wants more herself, a "window" on the Adriatic, and, by a very curious twist of things, Italy, her friend, would perhaps regret to see her have it, because if she got it her command of the Adriatic Sea at the only point where her window could be cut through might in time, for geographical reasons, embarrass the Italian aspiration.

The fact is that the Balkan peoples distrust the Powers of Europe almost as much as they distrust each other which makes it very hard to deal with them. For that Europe has itself to thank. For nearly 500 years the Balkan States have been a buffer work between Christian Europe and the Turk. After the fall of Constantinople in 1453 the whole Balkan Peninsula that terminates in Greece was submerged by the Turkish inundation. Mohammedanism threatened to overwhelm all Christendom. It was checked at last: its highest water mark was Vienna. Christian Europe saved itself, but never rescued from the Turk the conquered Balkan people. They were abandoned to the Turk's misrule. That was not the worst. The Powers of Europe used the Balkan Peninsula as a twilight trading ground. Unable or unwilling to put the Turk back into Asia, they made treaties with him. They needed thoroughfare in the Dardanelles. It was easier to bargain for it than to take it, hence the spectacle of Christian Europe treating with Mohammedan and lending distant ears to the appeals of the Christians he oppressed in its own backyard.

From the first of the nineteenth century the Turkish power, for reasons inherent in itself, declined in Europe, the Turkish population in the Balkan Peninsula diminished, and correspondingly the Christian population increased. For all that time it has been refractory, unassimilable, unmalleable. But for the petty jealousies of the European Powers, which led England in the Crimean war to side with Mohammedan against Christian Slavs, the Turkish rule in Europe would have decayed even faster than it did. It was indeed, for a long time fostered, in order to keep a state of equilibrium in Europe, and the Balkan peoples paid the price in religious, racial, and economic oppression.

In 1829 the Greeks, alone, won their independence from the Turks by fighting for it. A year later the partial independence of Serbia was declared. In 1877 Russia moved against Turkey, and was stayed by Europe. There was then the treaty of San Stefano, which created the Principality of Bulgaria. This was followed by the treaty of Berlin, which reduced Bulgaria, whose strength had begun seriously to alarm the Turks; and which also gave final independence to Serbia, Rumania, and Montenegro. And so it went, Europe and Turkey both together agreeable to a course in the Balkan Peninsula baffling to the racial aspirations of its native people, who are at last the kind of people in habits and temperament, naturally evolved by centuries of political neglect, ill-usage, and disappointed expectations.

When at last, in 1912, Bulgaria, Serbia, Greece, and Montenegro forgot their separate quarrels in their hatred of the Turk and formed the Balkan League to fight him, the Powers

of Europe were aghast. The Chancelleries of Europe reminded the Balkan peoples of the reforms proposed peaceably to be extracted from the Turks on their behalf, but it was then too late. Promises had never been fulfilled: they perhaps would never be. At any rate, the Balkan States would fight for what they wanted. And in the first European war of the twentieth century they did more to put the Turk back into Asia than the Powers of Europe all together had done in several hundred years. They left him but a toehold. Then, unfortunately, they fell out over a division of the spoils of war and went to fighting with each other. That weakened them with Europe, which now interfered to limit Balkan aspirations, especially those of Serbia. Between her and the Adriatic was created the new State of Albania, purposely to prevent her gaining a window on the sea. Austria was mainly responsible for that, supported by her allies, Germany and Italy.

The reasons the Balkan peoples cannot trust each other are not hard to understand. They are mainly blood reasons, complicated by artificial national boundaries, fixed by Europe arbitrarily. An ethnographical map of the Balkans differs very markedly from a map showing the political divisions of nationality. Here is the most conglomerate blood caldron in the world. Across the Balkan Peninsula went the Crusaders to the Holy Land and back a thousand years ago, and then came the Turkish wave, which, receding, left the submerged people to a further race confusion. But the racial ego was very vital to begin with, and now yearns for self-expression.

What price the Turco-Teutonic allies have offered Bulgaria is yet unknown. But her assistance would be worth a very high one. She could open to the Germans the pathway the Crusaders used from Europe to the Holy Land, across a little neck of Serbia, which is all that separates Bulgaria from Hungary. With thoroughfare across Bulgaria, the Teutonic forces could match directly to the assistance of the Turk.

\* \* \*

**October 9, 1915**

## KING OF THE GREEKS TALKS FOR AMERICA

*Receives Associated Press Correspondent at His Summer Palace Outside Athens*

**KEEN INTEREST IN THE WAR**

*Believes Central Empires Cannot Be Defeated—Losses of Greeks Who Emigrate to the United States*

ATHENS, Sept. 10 (Correspondence of The Associated Press)—The King of the Greeks received The Associated Press correspondent at the Chateau of Dekeleia, the Summer residence of the royal family, at Tatoi, some sixteen miles northeast of Athens, this noon. The road to Tatoi lies through the almost barren Attic Valley, with its low, square, infrequent adobe houses set in the dusty sun-parched plain.

Gradually, however, the way extricates itself from the furnace of the valley, climbing through a prepared park where well-tended trees freshen the air. The Summer place of Constantine I. is at hand. A gate is passed; a quick turn of the drive and before a building that might be a chalet in the Harz Mountains, the motor stops. A butler shows the visitor away from the main building to a sort of guard house to one side. Here Colonel Lewidis, Aide de Camp to the King, chats with the correspondent until his Majesty's pleasure is expressed by telephone.

When the summons came, the Colonel preceded the correspondent around one corner of the chateau—in reality the residence of the "diadochos," or Crown Prince George, Duke of Sparta, and his wife, the Princess Marie Bonaparte. The King is occupying it temporarily, while a much more imposing Summer palace in the same wooded park is being made ready for him.

Down a shady side alley covered by a trellis a tall, rather slim man in gray flannels, hatless, and quite bald, was making signs to some one in the house. Discovering the Colonel and the correspondent, the man in gray flannels hastened out of sight around an angle of the pergola. When seen again he was seated in a pleasant little retreat beside a wicker table covered with books and magazines—German, French, English. Tucked away in this quiet shelter, the King of the Greeks might have been a college professor on vacation.

### The King's Military Views

Constantine I is just turned 47—an affable, pleasant-looking, fine-mannered gentleman, whose principal business is that of a soldier, albeit he does not look it. After his father's unfortunate war with the Turks in 1898, when the then Prince Constantine received his baptism of fire, the 30-year-old "diadochos" set resolutely to work to create a Greek army capable of achieving victory.

It has been the work of his life. He studied in the War College in Berlin, where he became thoroughly trained in the Prussian theory of modern warfare—a theory which he is generally believed to regard as by far the best. From 1898 to 1902, Prince Constantine and the General Staff worked out plans for an entirely renovated military establishment in Greece. In 1904 his plans were adopted. Two years later, however, they had to be partially abandoned for lack of funds to continue them. But in 1910, Eleutherios Venizelos, aided by his Secretary of the Treasury, Lambros A. Coromilas, now Greek Minister in Rome, effected reforms in the internal affairs of Greece that enabled the Government to complete its plans for military preparedness.

Then came the two Balkan wars and the truly remarkable performance of Greece in putting more armed men into the field than her agreement with Bulgaria called for. This is the pride of King Constantine—this achievement and the army that it represents.

On March 5, 1913, his father was assassinated at Saloniki, and Constantine I. came to the throne. With all the increase of responsibilities the position brought the army has been his first care. He is said to be convinced, as indeed are most of his subjects, that a decisive struggle between Bulgaria and Greece is still on the cards. He does not propose that the opening of that struggle, should it come, shall find Greece unprepared.

### People Disagree with Him

As a soldier who has led his armies to two victories and who permits his subjects to dream of further conquests, Constantine I. is immensely popular with his countrymen. They do not share the belief, with which he is generally credited, that the armies of the central empires in the present European war are unconquerable. They feel, on the contrary, that should their King be right about this their dream of a greater Greece is over.

They do not always approve the active part which he is said to have taken in politics, and are quite frank in their expressed desire that he stick more strictly to his constitutional prerogatives. His Court is not altogether favorably regarded, despite an active cult of royalism long fostered in Greece. But for the man himself—the soldier and the thorough Greek he has become—they have nothing but admiration.

The King rose at the approach of The Associated Press correspondent. There was a warm handshake and an invitation to be seated. Straightway the Ring plunged into the subject uppermost in his mind—the war. With unquestioning confidence in the correspondent's pledge not to quote him, he expressed his views with the utmost frankness; he asked questions which revealed that he followed, daily, the movements of all the armies, and followed with especial interest the campaign in Russia. He speaks English perfectly, but with a slight lisp. On the whole he is an agreeable, versatile, delightful talker and interested listener, taking keen pleasure in conversation.

Slowly the talk veered through Greek foreign politics to the sovereign's own subject—the Greek army. And from that, by a natural enough traverse, to the Greeks everywhere. For after all Constantine I. is, officially, not King of Greece, but "King of the Greeks," a distinction which he shares with his wife's cousin, Albert, King of the Belgians. And he takes the distinction seriously. He feels himself King of the Greeks whether they be in Greece or not. It was thus that he came to speak of the Greeks in the United States, and to permit The Associated Press to print his views on the subect of Greek emigration.

### The Greeks in America

"For, you see," said the King, "the question of Greek emigration to the United States is a most important one. There are something over 300,000 Greeks in your country. But it is, in great measure, a temporary population. Before the Balkan wars there were probably even more Greeks in America. At that time something like 45,000 returned to Greece to fight in the Greek armies for the freedom of those of their blood who were not free. I believe that, if the occasion were to arise again, as many would again return for the same purpose.

"Since then, however, many of the Greeks who came home at that time have gone back to America. But this time the emigration has been with a signal difference. At the first emigration the men went alone. Their idea was to make a modest fortune, return to their families in Greece, buy a little farm or a shop in one of the cities, and live in comfort to the end of their days, among their own people.

"But a great many of those who returned to America after a first trial and after they had served their country nobly in the Balkan wars took their families with them on the second trip. For them it was no longer an experiment, fraught with the risks and dangers of unknown adventure. They had been to America once. They had learned where and how to live. They knew where to go and how to get there, even when encumbered with their families and their household goods. So when they sailed for the West the second time it was with all their belongings, not so much in the spirit of the ancient Greeks, going into the world in search of fortune and adventure, as has been the habit of Greeks for thirty-five centuries, but rather as prospective Americans, almost all of them quitting their mother country forever.

"And I cannot believe that this is, or indeed that it has proved, an unmixed good for Greece or for the Greeks who have so left Greece. Greece is not overpopulated. There is plenty of room here for the population to spread out and develop the land for many years—for generations—without being in any wise crowded. On the other hand, in going to America, the emigrant Greek runs very considerable risks over which he himself, as a Greek, has little or no control.

"Just the other day, a trans-Atlantic Greek liner brought back to Greece more than a thousand Greeks who had embarked in New York. This is happening constantly, these days. Less than two years after a Greek has emigrated with all his family to establish himself in the United States, he comes back again with all his family to Greece.

"On account of the war, industrial conditions in the United States would seem to be inferior to industrial conditions in Greece. At home the Greek finds that he is proportionately more prosperous than in America. But he has lost something in making the double voyage. He has lost the cost of the venture in actual outlay of money—no little matter for a poor man—and, what is more important still, he has lost virtually three years, in this instance, in the continuity of his employment, in which time he might well have been establishing himself on a firm foundation in his native country, among his own people, building up those relationships which would constitute the most important element in his capital.

"The loss is a serious one. It reveals a serious problem. This matter of Greek emigration to the United States is one well worth thinking about for us here in Greece. It is a problem which we must handle for the future of Greece. And it is one which Greece must have time and calm in which to reach a proper solution."

*   *   *

October 10, 1915

## TEUTONIC FORCES CAPTURE BELGRADE AND DRIVE SERBS BACK ALONG DANUBE; BULGARS ARE ADVANCING TOWARD NISH

### CONCERTED DRIVE NOW ON

*Serb Capital Easily Taken by Main Army Under Von Mackensen*

### DEFENDING FORCE RETIRES

*And Will Await the Invaders in Prepared Positions in the Mountains*

### ALLIES RUSHING UP TROOPS

*14,000 Men Are Being Landed Daily at Saloniki to Go to Serbia's Aid*

LONDON, Sunday, Oct 10—Belgrade, the old capital of Serbia, or the greater part of it, has been occupied by the advancing host of Austro-German troops. Other bodies of Teutonic forces have crossed the Danube at four points below Semendria, and are reported to be driving the Serbians southward.

Announcement of these successes in the Balkan War area was contained in the German Army Headquarters bulletin, which said concerning these operations:

The main sections of two armies of the newly formed army group under Field Marshal von Mackensen have crossed the Save and Danube Rivers.

After the German troops of the army of the Royal and Imperial Infantry, under General von Koevess, had captured Ziguner Island and the hills southwest of Belgrade, the army succeeded in bringing the greater part of the city of Belgrade into the hands of the allies. Austrian troops stormed the citadel and the northern section of the town of Belgrade. German troops stormed the New Konak, (the Royal Palace.) The troops are penetrating further through the southern part of the town.

The army of Artillery General von Gallwitz has forced crossings over the Danube at four points on the section below Samandria, and is driving the enemy in front of it toward the south.

The Austrian official statement concerning the operations says:

The Austro-Hungarian troops of the army of General von Koevess yesterday penetrated the northern part of Belgrade and stormed the citadel. Early this morning German troops from the west cut a path to the Konak (the royal palace.) Austro-Hungarian and German flags are flying from the castle of the Serbian kings.

Both above and below Belgrade the enemy watching the banks could nowhere resist the allies.

The capture of Belgrade had been expected, as it was not thought that the Serbians would make any serious attempt to defend the city, which lies on a point of land at the junction of the Save and Danube, jutting toward Austria, and could be attacked from three sides.

The real test of strength will come when the invaders reach the main Serbian positions in the mountains, where the Austrians were so severely defeated in December. The present, however, is a more formidable attack, a new army group having been organized under command of Field Marshal von Mackensen for that purpose. Its strength is not exactly known, but it is supposed that it is composed chiefly of Austro-Hungarians, with a stiffening of Germans, and is largely commanded by German officers.

### Bulgar Army is Moving

The Bulgarians, acting in concert with their new allies, are advancing from Sofia toward Pirot, on the Serbian frontier, the fortress which covers the road to Nish, the Serbian war capital.

No definite information is available yet as to the campaign plans of the Serbian commanders, but a Rome dispatch quotes the Military Attaché of the Serbian Legation there as saying that the Serbians would take the offensive against the Austro-German forces as soon as the Entente Allies' reinforcements came up. Even without the allied reinforcements, he asserted, the Serbians were quite able to meet the Austro-German invasion.

The French and British are now landing troops at the rate of 14,000 daily at Saloniki to send by railway to the assistance of Serbia.

With the Balkans thus taking their place with the Russian and western fronts as a centre of war interest, the Black and Aegean Seas will also be the scenes of activity, for as soon as Bulgaria strikes at Serbia the allied fleets will give the Bulgarian ports their attention.

Although the Bulgarian Minister at London, who has not received or asked for his passports, stated yesterday that Bulgaria had no quarrel with England, an attack on Serbia would be regarded by England as sufficient reason for a quarrel.

Turkey, according to a dispatch from Saloniki, is sending 50,000 men to Varna and Dedeaghatch to help in the defense of those Bulgarian ports.

### Greece Assailed by Both Sides

Greece's attitude is still somewhat obscure. The Greek Minister at Paris yesterday reiterated that Greece's neutrality would continue to be one of benevolence toward the Entente Powers. But more than that was expected, and the allied capitals are awaiting a definite statement from the new Greek Cabinet.

Meanwhile, Bulgaria through her Premier, is reported to have warned Greece that she cannot continue to be regarded as neutral if she permits the landing of allied troops at Saloniki. On the other hand, the allied envoys at Athens are said to have told the Greek King that the landing of troops would go on.

\* \* \*

October 15, 1915

# ITALY TO JOIN IN BALKAN CAMPAIGN; CZAR ASKS PASSAGE THROUGH RUMANIA, BULGARIA SUMMONS TURKS TO RESIST IT

### PRESSURE ON RUMANIA

*Germany Stops Her Traffic and Asks Her Intentions*

### ALLIES BUSY IN GALLIPOLI

*Bulgaria, After Defeat at Frontier, Accuses Serbia of Starting Hostilities*

### SERBS HOLDING GERMANS

*But Capture of Pozarevec is Near—Said to Have Taken a Bulgarian Division*

LONDON, Friday, Oct. 15—Three pieces of news stand out prominently in the latest developments in the Balkan situation—an intimation by Premier Viviani in the French Senate that Italy would take part in the campaign; a report from Rome, in which there is an inclination here to believe that Petrograd has asked Rumania to allow Russian troops to pass through her territory on the way to Bulgaria, and a statement from Bucharest by way of Switzerland that Germany has suspended the postal service to Rumania and is holding up all foodstuffs consigned over German railways until Bucharest defines more clearly its atitude toward the central powers.

There is naturally much speculation as to how Italian and Russian assistance will be afforded. Italy has a large number of troops available and the means of moving them to the desired spot, but Russia is handicapped in this respect. For Rumania to grant the Czar's request to allow his army to cross into Bulgaria would be construed by Germany as tantamount to a definite alliance with the entente and would doubtless result in Austro-German troops attacking Rumania. This, it is thought, might happen anyway, as previous to her present action Germany had shown her displeasure at Rumania's refusal to allow munitions to pass through to Turkey.

### Turkish Troops for Bulgaria

A special dispatch from Rome to The Daily Telegraph says that Bulgaria has asked Turkey for two army corps to dispatch to the Rumanian frontier to meet the eventual Russian attack. Two Turkish army corps already are concentrated at Adrianople and Kirk Kilisse.

The same dispatch says that up to yesterday the Bulgarians had not occupied any point of Serbian territory, having been repulsed everywhere. In an attack on Kniazevatz they lost a whole division, which fell into an ambuscade.

An Amsterdam dispatch says semi-official announcement that a Turco-Bulgarian military agreement has been signed is made in the Lokal Anzeiger. Under the terms of the agreement Turkey places two army corps and her munitions factories at the disposal of Bulgaria, while the latter country agrees to supply Turkey with coal and railway materials. It is agreed that Turkey shall have free use of Bulgarian harbors.

According to the Universul of Bucharest Russian troops have been withdrawn from Bessarabia, near the Rumanian frontier, and are being concentrated at Odessa. From this point, the Universul says, a movement will be undertaken against Bulgarian ports.

Meanwhile the Russians are continuing their attacks in Galicia in an effort to clear the Austrians from the Rumanian frontier and prevent them from sending any further reinforcements against Serbia, while the French and British have resumed the offensive in the Dardanelles to keep the Turks busy.

Although under constant attack since Oct. 8, the Serbians are giving ground only foot by foot. The Teuton troops which forced the passage of the Danube, occupied Belgrade and Semendria, and pushed on to Pozarevac in their attempt to drive through the Morava Valley, have got no further, though the capture of the town is imminent. The Berlin War Office announcement yesterday of the operations was embodied in a couple of sentences. It said:

Our troops continue to advance south of Belgrade. The works on the west, northeast, and southeast fronts of Pozarevac, which are of a fortified character, have been taken.

Pozarevac is about ten miles southwest of Semendria and, as the crow flies, five miles south from the Danube.

The Vienna official bulletin covered the advance further west from the neighborhood of Belgrade as follows:

Our troops yesterday stormed from the region of Belgrade, advancing to the southeast to the fortress-like intrenched positions on Brino, Brdo, Cunak, and Stawaras. The enemy, who, according to statements made by prisoners, had been ordered to stand to the last man, fled to the Avala Mountains and the region to the east. His losses were extraordinarily heavy.

Our big artillery, as is always the case in such operations, won the greatest part of the success.

The attacks of our allies on the lower Morava River are also progressing favorably. They have captured from the enemy fortifications on the western, northern, and eastern fronts of Posarevac.

No mention is made of the armies which have been trying to break into Serbia over the Save and Drina Rivers, so apparently the operations there, in which the invaders have suffered terrible losses have made no progress whatever.

Further south the small but efficient army of Montenegro is holding the line successfully on enemy territory.

The extent of the Bulgarian invasion up to the present, according to a dispatch from Nish, consists of an advance over the frontier at one point of a mile. With this exception says the report, the fighting line remains intact and the railways have not yet been reached. This contradicts a report from Athens that communications had been cut between Nish and Trahmva (Vranya?) for a distance of five miles.

An assertion that Serbian troops were the aggressors against Bulgarian forces was printed Wednesday in the Ministerial organ, Napodni Prava, according to a Sofia dispatch to The London Times. The Bulgarian newspaper's statement follows:

"Near Belogradchik Monday morning Serbian troops without cause attacked our forces. In reply to this foolish provocation our troops, in order better to defend themselves, captured, after a sharp conflict, the heights of Kitka in Serbian territory. The fighting lasted from 7 A. M. until 6. P. M."

A Reuter dispatch from Sofia says it is officially announced that Bulgaria will protest to the legations of the neutral States against this violation of her territory by Serbian troops, and that a royal manifesto has been issued calling upon the Bulgarian people and army to defend the national soil, "violated by a perfidious neighbor and deliver their brethern, oppressed beneath the Serbian yoke." The manifesto refers to the great efforts made by the King and Government to preserve the peace and make both groups of belligerents realize the injustice done to Bulgaria by the division of Macedonia.

The whereabouts of the Anglo-French expedition, which landed at Saloniki, and what it is doing, remain a dark secret as far as the press and public are concerned.

\* \* \*

**November 10, 1915**

## LARGE BRITISH FORCES ARE LANDED IN SERBIA

### *And Decisive Move Is Near—Berlin Reports 300,000 Allies Are There*

Special Cable to The New York Times

SALONIKI, Nov. 9 (Dispatch to The London Daily Telegraph)—There are good grounds for hoping that the misfortunes of the Serbians have ended and that the tide which has been running against them has reached its high-water mark and that what is left of their sorely tried country will be saved from invasion.

Large British forces have arrived and more are expected.

The Allies will soon be in a position to take a decisive offensive.

LONDON, Wednesday, Nov. 10—Newspapers of Berlin, as quoted by the correspondent at Copenhagen of the Exchange Telegraph Company, say that the Allies already have landed 300,000 men at Saloniki.

In spite of this, however, every hour adds to the peril of the Serbian armies, which are fighting desperately to hold back the Austro-Germans pressing them from the north and the Bulgarians, invading their country from the east, until the assistance their allies are sending can reach them.

The Bulgarians have extended their grip on the Belgrade-Saloniki Railway north and south of Nish, and have occupied Leskovac, south of the captured capital, and Aleksinac, to the north. At the latter point they are in close touch with the German Army, which, after occupying Krusevac, extended its left wing as far as Gyunis, on the left bank of the Bulgar Morava.

The Austro-Germans, advancing southward, are making progress except in the west, where they are being held by the Montenegrins. The invading forces are now reaching the most difficult part of Serbia, the mountainous region, where the natives, knowing every hill and gully, can offer the strongest resistance. The Austrians and Germans, however, are plentifully supplied with mountain guns, with which they expect to drive the defenders from their fastnesses.

### Allies Clear Railroad to Veles

In the south the ever-growing strength of the French and British forces is beginning to tell. They are carrying on an energetic offensive against the Bulgars, have managed to keep the railway clear as far as Veles, and are barring the Bulgars' route to Monastir.

A Paris Havas dispatch from Athens filed on Monday says the French have reached Gradsko on the railroad from Krivolak to Veles. A Bulgarian attack against Krivolak, with heavy forces of infantry and artillery, is reported to have been repulsed, after which the French occupied the village of Komental.

On the Anglo-French front, northwest of Guevgeli, the advance of the Allies continues, and the Bulgarians now occupy only the village of Ourmandi in Serbian territory.

A dispatch from Rome tends to confirm the recent reports that Italy will send troops to Albania to aid the Serbs. It states, that a semi-official note has been issued which says that while Italy did not participate in the recent expedition of the Allies to assist Serbia she has found a better way to oppose the Austro-German-Bulgarian attack upon Serbia.

This way, the note says, was opened by the Bulgarians themselves when they threatened to invade Albania to reach the Adriatic, a design so dangerous to Italy's interest that "the mere threat must oblige Italy to take appropriate measures to frustrate it immediately."

A Bucharest dispatch by way of Geneva says that 60,000 Albanians are preparing to attack the Serbians in the rear at Monastir and Prisrend.

### Official Reports of Operations

The text of yesterday's German official statement concerning the operations follows:

South of Kraijevo and southwest of Krusevac the enemy has been driven out of his rear-guard positions. Our troops are continuing the advance. The heights near Gyunis, on the left bank of the Morava, were stormed.

The booty taken at Krusevac was increased to about 50 cannon, including 10 heavy pieces. The number of prisoners was increased to 7,000.

The army (Bulgarian) of General Boyadjieff on the evening of Nov. 7 had reached the Morava at a point northwest of Aleksinac, which is to the northwest of Nish. Southwest of Nish, in conjunction with other Bulgarian troops advancing from the south, this army has taken Leskovac.

The Austrian War Office version of the advance says:

On the Montenegrin frontier the situation is unchanged.

One group of Austro-Hungarian troops fighting in Serbia has occupied Ivanjica, and another group has ejected the enemy from height positions on the road from Ivanjica to Kraljevo. The German forces have dislodged the enemy from an intrenched position south of Kraljevo.

South of Trsnick our battalions are engaged in battle. On the sector of Kraljevo a German division is advancing southward. The Bulgarians have captured Leskovac.

Repulse of Austrian attacks was reported in the official statement issued by the Montenegrin War Office at Cettinje yesterday as follows:

Important artillery engagements occurred along the entire front on Nov. 7. The enemy threw forward his infantry in attacks at various points without attaining successes.

A delayed dispatch from Sofia, dated Sunday, says:

"The booty, captured at Nish consisted of forty-two guns, thousands of rifles, much ammunition, 700 railway cars, and automobiles. The retreating Serbians abandoned guns, machine guns, and rifles which have not been counted. Thus far [several thousand] prisoners taken at Nish have been counted."

Members of the Rumanian Parliament who are being interviewed by Premier Bratiano to obtain their views upon the international situation have been told that the hypothesis of action against Russia need not be considered, says the Bucharest correspondent of the Petit Parisien of Paris.

"The prohibition of the transit of ammunition to Bulgaria," the Prime Minister is quoted as having said, "proves our sympathy for the Entente. I repudiate any policy which expects profits without corresponding sacrifices, but neither will I make sacrifices without the probability of success."

There is no change in the attitude of Greece, although it is considered significant that at the moment that Bulgaria has again protested against the hospitality accorded the allied troops at Saloniki the Greek Government has applied to the Allies for financial assistance—an application which is receiving favorable consideration. The Greek Government has also renewed to the Allies an expression of its firm determination to maintain neutrality and of its sincere goodwill toward the Entente powers.

\* \* \*

## WOMEN HURL BOMBS AT BULGAR INVADERS

*Children and Old Men in Serb Towns Also Fight Enemy Desperately*

LONDON, Thursday, Nov. 4—Fighting in Bulgaria has been far more desperate than in any former Balkan war, according to telegrams from the Bulgarian front, received at Budapest by way of Sofia and forwarded by the correspondent of The Post. M. Montchllow, President of the Sobranje, who has just returned from the front, is quoted as saying.

"In all Serbian towns, and even in the trenches, our soldiers found women, children, and old men who had been trained as bomb throwers and were generally quite expert. The civil population is taking a large share in the fighting and is even more desperate than the soldiers.

"There was not one Serbian village which Bulgarian soldiers entered, except in Macedonia, where they were not received with bombs and hand grenades from the hands of the civil population. Great numbers of bombs were found in almost every Serbian house. In many cases the Bulgarians were obliged to annihilate whole villages, the residents of which after apparently having surrendered, threw bombs into the streets at the entering soldiers. Even Serbian officers, after being taken prisoner, frequently hurled bombs into the faces of their captors. In Macedonia the civil population has not taken any part in the fighting."

Special Cable to The New York Times

LONDON, Thursday, Nov. 4—Dr. Svetozar Grgitch, the Serbian State physician with the Montenegrin Army, has arrived in London on his way to the United States. To a Daily News representative he said: "When I left my country the spirit of the army was splendid. Every Serb feels that he is fighting not only for his independence but for the existence of the nation. There are over a thousand women between the ages of 18 and 28 fighting with the Serbian Army.

"Their presence has an ennobling effect among soldiers. They are of course, not officially attached to the army, but those who are wives live with their husbands at the front and have their own mess rooms. Many of the young girls are dressed as soldiers and they all carry arms.

"Now that the army has retreated, the question of food supply becomes more serious. The enemy has invaded rich agricultural districts and the Serbs have less opportunities of replenishing their supplies in the mountainous districts to which they have retreated.

"If the Allies can lend a strong hand in the Balkans I have little doubt that Rumania and Greece will join up against the common enemy, but it must be a strong hand."

\*   \*   \*

## LAST STAND OF THE SERBS

*Driven Into a Corner in a Way That Once Menaced Washington*

The precarious position of the Serbian army is similar to that which seemed likely to be the position of the American army in the early Summer of 1781, when the French troops and fleet arrived and made the investment of York-town possible. Field Marshal Putnik is using the strategy which Washington had in mind to employ if the French reinforcements had not come, and if Clinton from New York had attempted to cut off his retreat to the middle Hudson.

The American commander had completed plans to take the Continental Army into the mountains of Western Virginia and there make a last stand. Putnik is now making his last stand in the mountains of western Serbia, and his area of occupation, bounded by Albania, Montenegro, and a bit of Bosnia on the west and the pressing foe on the north, east, and south represents a territory of 850 square miles.

Nature has formed in the Serbian mountains three practically impregnable fortresses, similar to those on the slopes of the Selva di Ternova, north and east of Gorizia, which the Italians have been pounding in vain for many weeks.

In the eastern centre of the area, between Mitrovitsa and Pristina, is the Kossovo Polye, or Plain of the Blackbirds. This plain, a natural battlefield, is now being pierced by the Bulgars. It can be swept from the north, west, and south, and an army entering far can be annihilated by a force of one-twentieth its numbers.

It is west of the Kossovo Polye that the Serbian found refuge from the Turks in 1889 and formed the little principality of Crnagora, which later became Montenegro.

In the south the importance of the Vardar is equal for both Bulgars and the Anglo-French reinforcements for the Serbs. This area also has its natural battlefield, the plateau between the upper Vardar and the Treska, which the Bulgars have just crossed.

In the north, almost in the angle formed by the frontiers of Bosnia and Montenegro, is the Krusevica Plateau. Lines drawn so as to connect Nish, Aleksinac and Krusevica form an inviting entrance from either north or east—whence are coming the Germans and Austrians, respectively. Once in occupation of the Krusevica plain, the army there is shut in and may be attacked from three sides.

\*   \*   \*

**December 4, 1915**

# BULGARS ALONE MAY FIGHT ALLIES

*London Thinks Germans Will Face Russians, Leaving Montenegro to Austrians*

**TEUTONS OCCUPY MONASTIR**

*Retreat of Serb Forces to the South Said to Have Been Cut Off*

**ALBANIANS JOINING FOE**

*Vienna Reports Capture of 3,500 Prisoners in Two Days Near Montenegrin Border*

**VON MACKENSEN WOUNDED BY A SERBIAN BULLET**

PETROGRAD, Dec. 3, (via London, Dec. 4)—Field Marshal von Mackensen was slightly wounded by a Serbian bullet during the recent operations, says a Copenhagen dispatch to the Novoe Vremya.

LONDON, Saturday, Dec. 4—The second phase of the Balkan campaign is developing slowly. It is expected, however, that the operations against Serbia having been concluded and Monastir occupied, the whole Bulgarian Army, when the weather permits, will attempt to drive the British and French forces out of Southern Serbia, while the Austrians continue their efforts to overrun Montenegro, and the Germans, with the aid of the Turks, and what Bulgarians and Austrians can be spared, turn their attention to the Russians, who again are reported to have entered Rumanian territory on their way to Bulgaria.

It is reported from France that part of the German Army is going to the Gallipoli Peninsula to assist the Turks in a great effort to drive the Entente Allies from the peninsula. This is hardly credited in military circles here, where it is not believed that they can spare the men, guns, and ammunition for such a venture. The Turks, it is true, have been displaying more activity recently in the Dardanelles, but this they are believed to have been doing more with ammunition which they have been collecting during the quiet period than with any fresh supplies from Germany.

### Germans to Mass at Rustchuk

Rustchuk, on the Danube west of the Rumanian border, in the opinion of well-advised persons here, is to be the point of concentration for the Germans, both as a warning to Rumania that it would be dangerous for her to join the Entente Allies and to meet any Russian advance.

There is conflict in the speculation regarding the position of Greece. Some dispatches say a satisfactory agreement has been reached between the Entente Allies and the Hellenic Kingdom, while others aver that the situation is so unsatisfactory that the Entente Allies have re-established their restrictions on Greek commerce. The Daily Mail this morning, however, says this is denied by the Foreign Office.

Detachments of Mohammedans and Albanians have joined the Austro-Hungarian Army attempting to invade Montenegro, according to the official bulletin covering the operations in the Balkans issued yesterday by the Austrian War Office. It says:

West and south of Novibabar Austro-Hungarian detachments, strengthened by many armed Mohammedans, captured yesterday and the day before 3,500 prisoners. In the fighting on the frontier district between Mitrovitza and Ipek numerous Arnauts (Albanians) joined us.

Following is the text of the German official statement:

In the mountains southwest of Mitrovitza successful engagements took place yesterday with detached enemy divisions, during which more than 1,200 Serbians were taken prisoner.

### Admit Loss of Plevije

The Montenegrin General Staff admits the evacuation of Plevije in the following statement made public in Paris yesterday:

Following the arrival of strong columns of the enemy from the vicinity of Pribolie and Metalka, our troops on Dec. 1 received orders to evacuate the city of Plevije and to retire on their defensive positions.

The Bulgarians have dropped a few shells on the railway station at Krivolak, on the allied front. Reuter's Saloniki correspondent, wiring yesterday, says there have been artillery duels on the Strumitza line, where the Bulgars have abstained from resuming the offensive since Nov. 3, when they suffered heavy losses.

Two thousand Bulgarian rifles were found in a trench taken Wednesday by French troops, according to a Paris Havas dispatch from Saloniki. The French are strongly intrenched before Krivolak, 150 yards from the Bulgar advanced posts. The British troops also are well dug in in their sector.

Members of the Serbian Chamber of Deputies and the Minister of War have arrived at Saloniki, while the Minister of Finance is at Florina, Greece, fifteen miles southeast of Monastir. Other Serbian governmental offices now at Elbassan and Koritsa, in Albania, will be removed to Avlona.

In a dispatch from Saloniki The Daily Telegraph's correspondent says:

"The situation at Saloniki is certainly not satisfactory. The effort so far made is not one from which results can be expected, and if we are to continue some other factor must appear to render progress possible and bring security.

"The present uncertainty must not be allowed to continue."

Regarding the field of operations, the correspondent says:

"Owing mainly to the intense cold the troops from certain advanced positions have been withdrawn and a slight concentration to the rear is taking place."

\* \* \*

December 6, 1915

## THE STAND AT THE "BLACK MOUNTAIN"

When the Serbian Empire fell in the great battle on the plains of Kossovo, those Serbians who thought it better to live free men in a barren and forbidding country than to hold their fertile fields under a hated Turkish rule fled to the hills of Montenegro. That was five centuries ago, and their children are the Montenegrins of today. A proud people, they have always held fighting to be their chief business: industry and commerce have never to this day received their serious attention. They alone of the Balkan peoples held off the Turk and built up their little country with Russia's help and with the support of France and Great Britain.

The Montenegrin is now pitted against the Bulgar and they are nearly opposite in character. It is said that in a drawing room the Montenegrin, for centuries a free man, is at once recognized as a gentleman, while the Bulgar as long a bondsman of the Turk, is apt to appear otherwise. But put the two into the field and the Bulgar will work and thrive while the Montenegrin does nothing.

Again the "Black Mountain" has become the refuge of the Serbians, their last stand. Great forces are assembling in the Sanjuk of Novi Razar for a thrust at the heart of the little mountain kingdom. Huge German cannon and motor transport give the Austro-Germans and the Bulgars a tremendous advantage over the Turks, who failed time and time again to conquer the country. But the Allies will look to the Montenegrins for a defense of their country, in the highest degree heroic. They will recall Tennyson's words:

> O smallest among peoples! rough rock-throne
> Of Freedom! warriors beating back the swarm
> Of Turkish Islam for five hundred years.
> Great Tsernagora! never since thine own
> Black ridges drew the cloud and broke the storm.
> Has breathed a race of mightier mountaineers.

And there is Gladstone's famous speech of 1895, in which he said: "In my deliberate opinion the traditions of Montenegro . . . exceed in glory those of Marathon and Thermopylae and all the war traditions of the world."

It is to such a people that the eyes of the world are now turned in the great test of their history.

\*   \*   \*

January 5, 1916

## THE PLIGHT OF GREECE

M. Gounaris, who is expected to succeed M Skouloudis as Premier of Greece when the highly constitutional King Constantine speaks the word upon the reassembling of Parliament, naturally disagrees with M. Venizelos as to the recent elections. The supporters of M. Venizelos abstaining, and the army of some 300,000 men unable to vote, M. Venizelos pointed to the small vote as a proof of national sympathy with his policy. M. Gounaris in his statement of a few days ago "denies that there was any considerable number of abstentions." M. Gounaris is not a mathematician but a poet. He is sure that the result would have been the same if the soldiers had voted. The policy of Greece is "unchanged." And "Germanophiles do not exist in Greece." M. Gounaris has a pretty fancy. Greece is tenderly attached to Russia, England, France, especially the last. She has a singular way of showing it. "Greece is a "small State which does not want to "be dragged into the war." She fears a fate like Belgium's and Serbia's.

A prudent resolution for a nation in a tight place. But has M. Gounaris forgotten that only the other day M. Skouloudis admitted that the model of neutrality had been ready to go to war on the side of the Allies, wouldn't have "hesitated" if they had offered her booty enough and smiled upon the "On to Byzantium" movement?

A concordance of the Constantinists seems to be necessary. Here is M. Gounaris saying that he doesn't know what Greece will do if her old enemies, the Bulgarians and the Turks, come over the border. On the other hand, M. Rhallis, the Minister of Justice, is sure that neither Turk nor Bulgarian will be allowed to set foot on the soil of Hellas. That will depend on Germany. Meanwhile, the Allies must be wondering how much Germany is depending upon the Greek Army.

Italy, we are told, has made "satisfactory explanations" of the presence of her expeditionary force at Avlona. What explanation other than military and naval necessity could be given of the Italians at Avlona and at Durasso? It is curious to recall that Italy, holding up the hands of Austria, forced the Montenegrins to evacuate Soutari, after King Nicholas's somewhat theatrical proceedings there. It was required as a capital for the new Albania. Italy's interest, it was said, was in having a weak Power on the east side of the Adriatic. Albania as a part of Greater Hellas when the work of "rectification" comes is on the Hellenic program. The Albanians, if one can apply the word to a lot of wild clans and tribes, have often fought for Greek independence and are said to consider themselves Hellenes, rather queerly, if, as some ethnologists tell us, they are of Illyrian-Thracian stock with an admixture of Serbo-Croat and Gothic. At any rate, Albania as a State is an Austrian idea, a buffer against the Slavs of Montenegro and Serbia.

Scarcely pleasant for Greece, Italian occupation of those harbors, in connection with Italian ambitions on the east shore of the Adriatic further north; but there is nothing but bitterness in the Greek prospect at present, unless Germany has made large promises to Constantine and can keep them. Austria has long wanted to come through Serbia to the Aegean. Saloniki, the best port and most thriving city, is Greek, with the stretch of Thracian littoral to the Mesta, since the war with Turkey and Bulgaria. Bulgaria, which got her own littoral on the Aegean and the hinterland from the Maritza to the Mesta, casts longing eyes on Greece's share in the spoils. Bulgaria wants Serbian Macedonia, too, and cannot but sulk at Germany's restraining hand and the appointment of a German Governor General. Monastir is "Greek," according to the

Greeks, if not given to her by the treaty of Bucharest. Rumania, which believes itself a "Latin" State, "sits tight," nursing her finances and her army, ready to fall upon Bulgaria's back again, bound to have compensation, a share in the swag. The balance of power in the Balkans is threatened again, and by Bulgaria. If the great Powers had not been called in by the raid into Serbia, what a lovely shindy, remarkable even in the ferocious peninsula of the mountains, the "Christians" and Moslems of the Balkan States, the choicest cutthroats of the world, would be treating themselves to! Very likely it is brewing. It is always brewing.

The preponderance of Greek sympathy, so far as the Greeks sympathize with anybody but themselves, seems to be on the side of the Allies, in spite of the German Court. Those bundles of women's ears cut off for the earrings by the Bulgarians in the last war may be legendary, and the Bulgars have a counterlegend of a bundle of noses cut off by the Greeks. The stories paint the deep affection of the two nations. And if the Germans win, must not the little corner to which Turkey in Europe has been reduced be enlarged at Greek as well as Bulgarian expense? Greeks have their preferences, but as yet the Government—which is the Kaiser's brother-in-law—doesn't dare to make a bet.

\* \* \*

January 27, 1916

## BULGARS FIGHTING ESSAD'S ARMY NOW

*Advance Guard Reported to Have Been Defeated by the Albanians Near Elbassan*

### MONTENEGRINS TO DISARM?

*Austrians Report Agreement to Sign—Italians Fought on Mt. Lovcen*

LONDON, Thursday, Jan. 27—Bulgarian forces are said to have advanced into Central Albania and come in contact with Albanian troops under Essad Pasha, Provisional President of Albania, who is co-operating with the Entente Allies.

Dispatches from Tirana, Albania, to Brindisi, Italy, as forwarded by the Exchange Telegraph Company, say that an advance guard of the Bulgarians has been defeated near Elbassan by Essad Pasha's forces.

### Surrender Articles Signed

BERLIN, Jan. 26, (by Wireless to Sayville.)—The delegates of the Montenegrin Government at 6 o'clock last night, signed articles providing for the laying down of the arms of the Montenegrin forces, according to an announcement made today by the Austro-Hungarian headquarters. The text of the statement follows:

Yesterday at 6 P. M. the delegates of the Montenegrin Government signed articles regarding the laying down of the arms of the Montenegrin Army. The disarming is

going on without difficulty and has extended to the districts of Kolasin and Andriyevica.

The Overseas News Agency today gave out the following information regarding the Montenegrin situation:

"Detailed reports state that the Montenegrins on Jan. 7 were still celebrating the Greek New Year as though nothing was happening, but as the day dawned the Austro-Hungarian forces advancing on Mount Lovcen encountered among its defenders 500 Italians, who were the first to flee.

On Jan. 10 Major Lyumovic and First Lieutenant Popovic of the Montenegrin Army, arrived at Nyegus. They carried white flags and brought a letter signed by the Montenegrin Prime Minister, Lazare Miouchekovitch, asking for a day's truce of arms. They also sought to open negotiations with regard to future peaceful and neighborly relations, but this was declined. Instead, the Austro-Hungarian commander asked for the unconditional surrender of the Montenegrin forces.

"On Jan. 11, the Montenegrin authorities left Cettinje for Podgoritza. On Jan. 13, a Bosnian detachment, under the command of a young First Lieutenant, entered Cettinje, and was welcomed ceremoniously by the 100-year-old Iliva Plamerac, the hero of many fights against the Turks in former years. The Lieutenant ordered the inhabitants to surrender their arms.

"On the same day two Montenegrin officers, with a flag of truce, and bearing a letter written personally by King Nicholas, arrived in Cettinje. The officers were escorted to a hotel, where they were guarded by Bosnian sentries.

"In the meantime, an Austro-Hungarian brigade arrived, and the commander was received in the hotel by a delegation composed of citizens, and the formal surrender of the capital took place.

"Martial law was declared in Cettinje by the Austro-Hungarian authorities on Jan. 14.

"The letter sent by King Nicholas asked Emperor Francis Joseph for graceful conditions for the unhappy country.

"On Jan. 16 Austro-Hungarian troops occupied the district between Cettinje and Rieka. On the same day three delegates appointed by the Montenegrin Government arrived, bringing with them a written declaration signed by all the Ministers and stating that the unconditional surrender of the army had been accepted. Hostilities consequently ceased on Jan. 17.

"Street riots broke out in several Montenegrin districts after the Montenegrin troops had left, and these were only quelled by the arrival of Austro-Hungarian troops.

"In Antivari a mob stormed and looted the Italian Consulate.

"The worst scenes took place in Podgoritza, where the Albanians fought in the streets against the Montenegrins.

"King Nicholas was last seen by his people at Podgoritza, where he arrived on a white horse in the midst of a silent population. As the King was passing through the town one man stepped forward and said: 'Sire, we have no bread.' The King then left almost unnoticed."

### Italians Still Puzzled

Special Cable to The New York Times

ROME, Jan. 26—The mystery of the attitude of Montenegro grows daily more impenetrable, and the conviction is gaining ground here that further surprises are impending.

Meanwhile Austria officially declares that disarmament is proceeding normally, while from other sources it is known that numerous Montenegrin prisoners have been captured, whom there would have been no reason to take had an agreement been arrived at. The Austrian explanation is that they preferred to be made prisoners to returning to their homes, which is regarded here as hardly convincing. The truth, Italians think, probably lies in the frank admission of the Deutsche Tageszeitung that hostilities have recommenced.

The general feeling is that while the Montenegrin interlude has delayed Austria, her descent upon Albania is inevitable, and that it is only a question of time until they arrive before Avlona.

ROME, Jan. 25, (via Paris, Jan. 26.)—A dispatch from San Giovanni di Medua to the Idea Nazionale says that the Montenegrins made a determined stand on Mount Tarabosch in an effort to save the City of Scutari, but that the approach of a strong Austrian column forced the garrison to evacuate the place and the detachment on the mountain to retreat. The women, it is stated, conducted themselves as heroically as the men, carrying on their backs during the retreat everything that was necessary to continue the struggle.

Military experts affirm that no immediate anxiety is felt for Durazzo, which is understood to be defended satisfactorily by Essad Pasha, nor for Avlona, which is believed to be safe from a sudden blow.

### BATTLE IN ALBANIA NEAR
#### Austrians and Bulgars Nearing Italian Army There

The occupation of the little village of San Giovanni di Medua reported on Tuesday brings the Austrians to within twenty-five miles of Durasso, where a strong Italian force has been gathering for some months. The occupation was evidently brought about by forces marching along the coast south from the Montenegrin ports of Antivari and Duicino, as the roads from Scutari could hardly be traversed at this time of year.

Moreover, it has recently been announced from Vienna that the Austrians along a ragged line from Scutari to Prisrend, fifty miles, were pressing south, following up the remnant of the Montenegrin Army and making a fresh invasion via Dibra on the eastern frontier, and that the Bulgarians marching along the old Roman road, which leads from Monastir to Durasso, had actually captured Elbassan and occupied Berat, thirty miles south of Elbassan and thirty north of the Avlona-Monastir highway.

Avlona, like Durazzo, is also believed to be occupied by a strong Italian army. Indeed, advices from Rome repudiate the alleged capture of Elbassan and Bernt by the Bulgarians. It is near Elbassan that Essad Pashas with the Albanians is, this morning reported to have defeated an advance guard of Bulgarians.

In any event military operations are so tending that a formidable engagement between Austro-Hungarian troops and those of King Victor Emmanuel cannot long be avoided, if Italy is to make the effort expected of her to dispute Austria's dominance of the eastern Adriatic littoral—Dalmatia, Montenegro, and Albania—which would instantly expose the low-lying coasts of Italy opposite.

Two considerations have governed Italy and her allies in whatever moves they may have made, one, the political has almost disappeared by the virtual occupation of Serbia and Montenegro by Austria—that is, these nations cannot at present be considered factors in any idea that Italy may have in regard to an Adriatic hegemony. There remains the military consideration, the struggle to be fought out by Italy and her allies against Austria and hers for the supremacy of the Adriatic, Serbia and Montenegro offering what aid they can so as to maintain a claim to a hegemony in the congress after the war.

The Italian army in Albania, recently augmented by a division (22,000) of veterans from Libia Italiana, in North Africa, is under the command of General Giovanni Ameglio, the conqueror of Libya. It is believed that, all told, he has over 170,000 troops placed at different strategic positions which have been long in preparation.

### CZAR'S LETTERS FOUND IN SERBIA URGED WAR
#### Promised Aid of Russian Armies to Resist Austria, According to German Version

BERLIN, Jan. 26, (via London.)—Telegraphing from Budapest the correspondent of the Tageblatt says that according to a Sofia dispatch two letters and one telegram signed by the Russian Emperor were found among the archives of the Serbian Crown Prince Alexander which were recently captured by the Bulgarians.

All the documents were dated just before the outbreak of the war. The first letter advises the Crown Prince under no circumstances to yield to the demand of Austria-Hungary for the dissolution of the Marodni Ochrana, a Serbian political society.

In the telegram Emperor Nicholas is said to have instructed the Serbians to reject the Austro-Hungarian ultimatum because Russia was ready to support Serbia with force of arms.

In the second letter the Russian Emperor is declared to have pointed out the advantages which Serbia would derive in following Russia's orders. His Majesty added that Russia's armed power was being held in readiness and he urged Serbia to resist to the last drop of blood.

LONDON, Thursday, Jan. 27—Diplomatic circles in London showed little surprise at the Berlin Tageblatt's publication of the correspondence between the Russian Emperor and Crown Prince Alexander of Serbia, but declined to comment until convinced of the authenticity of the letters and telegram.

The Russian Embassy stated that the Russian Orange Book embraced all the correspondence of which it had knowledge.

It is pointed out by some of the diplomats that actual events prove that there was no conspiracy between Russia and Serbia, as Serbia gave way completely to the Austrian demands for the dissolution of the Narodni Ochrana, the Serbian political society, and stood out only against the clauses in the Austrian ultimatum which threatened the sovereignty of Serbia.

\* \* \*

January 27, 1916

## MOUNT ATHOS MONKS FIGHT ONE ANOTHER

### Bulgar Monks Attack Monastery Occupied by Serbians and Set Fire to It

LONDON, Thursday, Jan. 27—A dispatch to The Times from Bucharest says:

"The war has invaded the peaceful seclusion of Mount Athos, where Bulgarian monks from the Monastery of Zographu endeavored to oust their Serbian brethren from the neighboring Monastery of Chiliandmari. The attack failed, owing to the defenses of the Serbian monastery, whereupon the Bulgarians set fire to a portion of the structure. All the monasteries on the holy mountain were fortified in the Middle Ages in order to resist pirates."

Athos Mountain is on the easternmost of the three Macedonian peninsulas projecting into the Aegean Sea southwest of Saloniki. The peak rises 6,350 feet. Many monasteries are built on it, some dating back to the fourteenth century.

\* \* \*

February 12, 1916

## RUMANIA DRIFTING TO WAR BESIDE ALLIES

### Interventionists Now Unopposed, It Is Said, and Military Preparations Are Made Openly

Special Cable to The New York Times

MILAN, Feb. 11 (Dispatch to The London Daily Telegraph)—A dispatch from Bucharest to the Neue Zurcher Zeitung declares that Rumania appears to be definitely on the point of entering the war on the side of the Allies. This is rather remarkable as coming from a paper with noted pro-German sympathies.

The correspondent says the Rumanian question was seriously discussed between the Kaiser and Czar Ferdinand at their meeting. He repeats also what is already known, that M. Take Jonescu is having daily conferences with the Russian Envoy, which is giving great annoyance to the German and Austrian representatives.

Everything really tends, he says, to create the impressions that big events are preparing, and that the Government no

longer is offering the slightest opposition to the interventionist agitation. Quite the contrary, it rather favors it.

From a military point of view, he goes on, there are still greater reasons for apprehension on the part of the Central Empires. Military preparations are in progress openly which no longer leave any doubt as to their ultimate object. The Ministers of War and Finance are taking deliberate steps which tend systematically to a declaration of war. The credits asked for by the Government for the army are increasing daily and the country finds itself in a latent state of war. The preparations are far in excess of what is needed for armed neutrality.

\* \* \*

March 21, 1916

## RUMANIA AND THE WAR

The reports of Rumania's intention to enter the war multiply in numbers and definiteness. To some extent, no doubt, they are the reflex of the growing confidence among the Allies—a confidence greatly strengthened by the failure, so far, of the German assault upon Verdun—that the Spring will see them on the high road to victory. Next May is now specifically indicated as the date when Rumania may lay aside her neutrality. After the experience of the last eighteen months one becomes skeptical about all such forecasts. Rumania has disappointed already many and equally explicit prophecies as to the time and manner of her intervention. She may do so again. A year ago she seemed on the very verge of a decision. After the death of King Charles, and Turkey's plunge into the war, and the Russian occupation of Bukowina, further hesitation appeared impossible. Yet the statesmen of Bucharest have contrived to hold aloof, even though the war since then has raged along their very frontiers. Why now should the Allies be entertaining such strong hopes that at last she is about to move?

The reasons are to be found partly in the accumulating signs of Turkey's prostration and of Russia's renewal of strength, partly in the success of the Allies in establishing around Saloniki a position which will fully engage the whole power of the Bulgarian Army, and partly in the belief that neither Germany nor Austria can undertake another Balkan expedition. What does all this amount to? It amounts to something like a pledge of security. The situation has so far changed that it is now much more possible for Rumania to take a hand in it without incurring the fate of Belgium and Serbia. What up to now has held her back has been simply a prudent care for her own safety. Germany last year had by far the better of the diplomatic struggle in the Balkans because she could inspire fear by force, while the Allies could hold out only promises and a future they were powerless to guarantee. What was the use of Russia's offering to restore Bessarabia if at the end of the war there was no Rumania to receive it? What was the use of dwelling on the ill-treatment of the 8,000,000 Rumanians in Transylvania if the effort to rescue them were to cost the life of the Rumanian State?

There is no doubt where the bulk of the Rumanian people stand in this war. Their sympathies are strongly with the Allies. There is no doubt, either, that to regain Bessarabia and to unite in a single State the 12,000,000 Rumanians who at present live under three different rulers are ambitions that powerfully appeal to Rumanian sentiment. But the statesmanship of Bucharest has long been noted for a cautious opportunism. It has never shown any fondness for taking long changes. If now, as seems not unlikely, the Rumanian leaders are coming around to the opposite view, it is because they are convinced that the tide has turned, that the Central Powers cannot win and that Rumania may gain all on which her heart is set without any excessive sacrifice. Should that indeed prove to be her estimate of the situation and should she then throw in her lot with the Allies, it would be a development of the utmost significance.

*   *   *

April 19, 1916

## VENIZELOS OPENLY DEFIES KING CONSTANTINE; WANTS TO SETTLE QUESTION OF DIVINE RIGHT

LONDON, April 18—Following the breaking up by agents of the Greek Government, as the Liberals allege, of the meeting in Athens on Sunday of Venizelos adherents, the former Premier, who heretofore has been careful to base his antagonism on questions of policy, has come out openly in opposition to King Constantine personally.

A dispatch from Athens contains the following interview given by M. Venizelos on Monday to the representative in the Greek capital of The Associated Press:

"I beg you to bring the events of yesterday and the earnest protest of a majority of Greeks to the knowledge of the American people, who have struggled for so long to establish free speech as the fundamental right of free peoples.

"Here in Greece we are confronted by the question whether we are to have a democracy presided over by a King or whether at this hour in our history we must accept the doctrine of the divine right of Kings.

"The present Government represents in no sense the majority of the Hellenic people. We Liberals twice in the course of a year received the vote of the majority. At the last election, which was nothing more than a burlesque of the free exercise of the right of suffrage, we were not willing to participate in a farcical formality.

"The present Government of Greece is, therefore, nowise representative, and we Liberals have left us only our right of free speech and free assemblage, guaranteed by the Constitution, as the sole means of taking counsel among ourselves; of trying to enlighten the opinion of the country, and, perhaps, of exercising a pacific pressure of the will of the majority upon a Government not representing the majority.

"Now it is even sought to deny us this. The meetings organized by the Liberal Party were not even those free and open ones to which we have every right. Our meetings were held in inclosed buildings. Those who came to them were invited, but the police threw out our doorkeepers, put in their own and let enter whomsoever they, the police, wanted to be present at our meetings.

"It is a denial of every constitutional liberty.

"The moment has come when the position of the highest functionary, which every King of the Hellenes ought to occupy, must so strictly be defined that it will forever be impossible to raise again the question of the divine right of Kings in Greece; it will forever be impossible for any Government hiding behind the person of the sovereign to arrogate to itself rights which reside only in the whole Hellenic people.

"Understand me. I am not talking in any sense of the possibility of a republic in Greece. I insist only on our rights—our constitutional rights, our rights as free people which ourselves we have gained by the force of arms, and which we have no intention to abandon."

It is announced, according to another Athens dispatch, that Liberal meetings will be resumed after Easter, the Liberal Party meanwhile taking action against the police authorities for allowing, as they charge, the presence at their meetings of agents whose object was to provoke riotous events.

*   *   *

April 29, 1916

## GREEK REVOLUTION REPORTED IMMINENT

*Sentiment in Favor of Venizelos and War Said to be Sweeping the Country*

**SOLDIERS QUIT THE ARMY**

*General Staff Fears to Treat Them as Deserters—Many Officers Also Disaffected*

ATHENS, April 23, via Rome and Paris, April 28, (Delayed.)—An impartial observer who has just returned from a tour of all the mainland of Greece reports an amazing spread of sentiment in favor of Eleutherios Venizelos, the former Premier, even in conservative Peloponnesus. The recent efforts of the Government to suppress the demonstrations and meetings of the Venizelos adherents has awakened deep resentment among the people, and there is a growing determination to oust the present Government even if it be necessary to resort to arms.

The Associated Press learns from incontestable authority that several leaders of the revolution of 1909 are actively engaged in planning a similar attempt, although Venizelos deprecates this, and advises instead the practice of patience and use of legal methods. On the other hand the recent plot against him failed only by a hair's breadth, owing to the extraordinary devotion and watchfulness of his followers.

Frequent talks with King Constantine have convinced The Associated Press correspondent that the monarch honestly is persuaded that a policy of inaction is approved by a majority of the Greek people. The King persists in regarding the recent demonstrations of the growing popularity of Venizelos as mere political manoeuvres.

The weakness of the opponents of the former Premier lies in the discontent among the rank and file of the army, who largely attend the meetings of the Venizelos followers, and who are openly dissatisfied, and declare that a purposeless mobilization is depriving their families of their support. It is stated in well informed quarters that so many soldiers have returned to their homes without permission that the General Staff is unable to treat them as deserters and is obliged to grant to them leave which they already have taken. Even the officers of the army, with the exception of those in higher command, are discontented, notwithstanding that an increase of pay has been granted to them by Royal decree.

Neutral diplomatic observers who are in a position to judge declare that the present situation cannot last sixty days longer and that unless an Allied offensive against Bulgaria relieves the tension by sweeping the Greeks into war with their ancient enemies a political cataclysm in Greece is inevitable. The time for a compromise between the Liberals and the adherents of the Ministry has passed.

A most rigid, triple censorship of all press telegrams keeps the world generally ignorant of actual conditions in Greece.

* * *

**May 29, 1916**

## 25,000 BULGARS INVADE GREECE

---

*Push On to Demir-Hissar After Occupying Forts Commanding the Struma Valley*

**KAVALLA MAY BE OBJECTIVE**

*Athens Protests to Sofia—Population, Aroused, Plans Demonstration at Saloniki*

---

Special Cable to The New York Times

SALONIKI, May 28 (Dispatch to The London Daily Chronicle)—The frontier movement of the Bulgarian forces, according to the latest official and other reliable news, is on a considerable scale, the force employed being estimated at 25,000 men. The Bulgarian advance did not end with the occupation of Fort Rupel and the earthworks around it. They also took possession of Fort Dragotin, and patrols have been pushed forward and are now occupying Demir-Hissar station beside the destroyed railway bridge as well as points in the surrounding neighborhood. All the Greek covering forces are reported to have been withdrawn.

Fort Rupel is about six miles inside Greek territory and situated on the river Struma. It commands the defile leading from Bulgaria to Demir-Hissar and Seres. Rupel is one of a chain of forts erected by the Greeks along the Bulgo-Greek frontier after the Balkan wars, and it would seem to be the intention of the Bulgars to occupy all the forts on that defensive line.

What adds to the importance of this movement on the part of the Bulgars is the fact that at Xanthi in Eastern Macedonia there is no little activity. On the left bank of the Mesta River, which for some distance from its mouth forms the Bulgar-Greek frontier line, the Bulgars have collected material for bridging the stream. In military circles there is a general belief that Kavallo on the coast east of Saloniki is the objective of the Bulgars.

ATHENS, May 28, (Dispatch to The London Morning Post.)—The invasion of Greek territory by Bulgarian forces through the Rupel defile has created much excitement here and will doubtless not be without repercussion on public opinion throughout the country.

The Government press today pleads that the invasion was effected by overwhelming German forces before which the Greek frontier force was powerless. The main reason for representing the invasion as being by Germans and not by Bulgarians is that neither the Greek Army nor public opinion would remain passive if the Bulgars were known to be invaders. Hatred of Bulgarians and horror of their reappearance in the Macedonian provinces which they misgoverned and in which they massacred and burned during the few months of their occupation are feelings too strong for any fine-drawn distinctions of foreign policy.

It will be remembered that months ago Colonel Phallis made formal declaration to General Sarrail that Greece would not place any obstacles in the way of Bulgarians entering Greek territory at any point in pursuit of their operations against the Allies. Events now prove this to be the policy of the Greek Government, and it will place the issue clearly before public opinion.

The press favorable to the Government lay much emphasis on the fact that to have refused to evacuate Fort Rupel would have been tantamount to war with Germany, which, of course, it is argued, would have brought untold disasters upon Greece.

LONDON, May 28—The correspondent at Athens of the Exchange Telegraph Company says he learns from Saloniki that the Bulgarians gave the Greeks two hours to surrender Rupel Fort, which is six miles from the Demir-Hissar Bridge, recently blown up by the French in anticipation of this attack.

Athens newspapers say that the deputation of German and Bulgarian officers in demanding the surrender of Fort Rupel explained that its occupation was necessary to secure the Bulgarian left wing against an eventual Entente allied attack.

The surrender of the fort was affected at 3 o'clock Friday morning and the protocol signed by the German. Bulgarian, and Greek officers. The Germans and Bulgarians, the newspapers say, undertook to restore the fort to Greece so soon as the reasons for its occupation no longer existed.

Another dispatch from Salonika says that as an outgrowth of the popular indignation resulting from the violation of Greek territory a big meeting has been called there for tomorrow to protest against the action of the German and Bulgarian troops.

ATHENS, May 28—Greece's protest against the military operations undertaken by the Central Powers and Bulgaria in

Greek Macedonia was forwarded last night to the Ministers of Greece at Berlin, Vienna, and Sofia.

The Bulgarians entered Greek territory virtually unopposed, and this has caused violent comment in the press and considerable agitation among the population.

"Whoever dreamed to see the Bulgarian flag supplant the Greek flag in Macedonia. Just for this we have maintained mobilization at the cost of the economic ruin of the country." M. Venizelos, the former Premier, thus writes in The Herald, the Venizelist organ. The Herald appeared today with a black border as a token of national mourning.

The Greek military authorities here claim they were unable to communicate with their troops in Eastern Macedonia. The belief is general here that it is the intention of the Greek Government to confine its action to a protest.

AMSTERDAM, May 28, (via London.)—The following official communication issued at Sofia Saturday was received here today.

Today detachments of our troops operating in the Struma Valley occupied the southern exit of Rupel Pass, together with the heights east and west of the river Struma.

\* \* \*

May 30, 1916

## RIOTING AT ATHENS OVER BULGAR INVASION

### Greece Aroused Over Occupation of Forts and Territory by Traditional Foe

PARIS, May 29—A news dispatch from Athens says that grave trouble has broken out there following the news of the invasion of Macedonia by the Bulgarians.

#### Italians Suspicious of Greece

Special Cable to The New York Times
ROME, May 29—News from Greece is awaited with great interest, as any advance of the Bulgarians in Greece affects the Allies position at Saloniki. It is considered here that converging pressure on the valley of the Struma and Xanthi can only mean the Bulgarians have Kavala as an object, while it is pointed out the Greek Government only protested after the event.

Military circles are inclined to believe that George has a secret understanding with the central powers, who naturally promised that the occupation to Greek territory would be only temporary while Germany would support Greek pretentions in Epirus. Otherwise it is asked, how can Greek complaisance be explained to her hereditary enemy Bulgaria, who hitherto has been as a red rag to a bull to every Greek?

On May 26 the Bulgarians, in five regiments, occupied Fort Rupel, on the Struma, the most exposed outwork of Greece, north of Demir-Hissar, and then Forts Spatovo, Kanivo, and Dragotin, flanking it on the west, south, and east. Kanivo and Dragotin are new forts, constructed in 1913–14.

This occupation had been expected ever since May 13, when the Bulgars first crossed the border. It has been reported from Athens, via Paris, that the garrisons at these places had received orders to evacuate—at least, that is what the Bulgar commanders told the Greek commanders. While awaiting confirmation of these orders, it is said that shots, without serious casualties, were exchanged between the Bulgars and the Greeks.

\* \* \*

August 27, 1916

## ALBANIA IN REVOLT AGAINST AUSTRIANS

### Rome Papers Hear Rising Has Spread to Serbia and Montenegro, Urge Italy to Strike

Special Cable to The New York Times
ROME, Aug. 21—News from Albania indicates, that there is a rising there against the Austrians which is extending to Montenegro and Serbia.

The Italian press is unanimous in declaring that now is the moment for Italy to act, both politically and by means of the army.

The Idea Nazionale says "Italy has made many mistakes in Albania since the war began. Now is moment to correct them by issuing from her attitude of passiveness into military activity. The moment is, most propitious, when Austria's occupation is seriously menaced. We could thus block her from two sides, making an attack which perhaps, would decide the war for Italy."

\* \* \*

August 29, 1916

## RUMANIA IN WAR, ATTACKS AUSTRIA; GERMANY DECLARES WAR IN ANSWER; EUROPE EXPECTS GREECE TO FIGHT

#### RUMANIANS ENTER PASSES
Army Begins the Invasion of Transylvania in Two Directions
#### HOPES TO SHORTEN WAR
Also to Realize National Ideal, Vienna Is Told in Declaration of Hostilities
#### TWO CITES ARE MENACED
Hermannstadt and Kronstadt the Immediate Objectives of King Ferdinand's Forces
#### ALL RUMANIA'S ARMY MOVING; GERMANY SHIFTING TROOPS

Special Cable to The New York Times
LAUSANNE, Switzerland, Aug. 28 (Dispatch to The London Daily News)—I learn from a high diplomatic source

in Berne that almost the entire Rumanian Army is moving rapidly.

The Swiss frontier is closed.

The closing of the Swiss frontier obviously indicates that movements of German troops are in progress to meet the new situation, created by the entry of Rumania into the war.

LONDON, Tuesday, Aug. 20—Rumania has declared war against Austria-Hungary, Germany has retaliated by declaring war against Rumania, and fighting has already begun on the frontier of Transylvania.

The note declaring that Rumania, from 9 o'clock Sunday evening, considered herself in a state of war with Austria-Hungary was presented to the Austro-Hungarian Foreign Minister last night by the Rumanian Minister at Vienna, who personally visited the Ministry of Foreign Affairs.

The note was a lengthy document, in which Rumania set forth her grievances. The Paris newspaper La Liberté has received a summary as telegraphed from Geneva. According to this the persecution of Rumanians by Austro-Hungarian officials is alleged and it is charged that agreements which existed between Rumania and the former members of the Triple Alliance have been broken in letter and spirit from the time Germany and Austria entered the war. Italy, the declaration says, was obliged to detach herself from Austria and Germany.

#### Motives for Declaring War

In conclusion, the communication sets forth as follows the motives in compelling Rumania to enter the war:

First—The Rumanian population in Austrian territories is exposed to the hazards of war and of invasion.

Second—Rumania believes that by intervening she can shorten the world war.

Third—Rumania places herself on the side of those Powers which she believes can assist her most efficaciously in realizing her national ideal.

An official statement issued in Berlin and forwarded by Reuter's correspondent at Amsterdam says:

After Rumania, as already reported, disgracefully broke treaties concluded with Austria-Hungary and Germany she declared war yesterday against our ally.

The Imperial German Minister to Rumania has received instructions to request his passports and to declare to the Rumanian Government that Germany now likewise considers herself at war with Rumania.

Rumania's decision to enter the war was reached at a meeting of the Crown Council held Sunday morning at the Controcent Palace, Bucharest. King Ferdinand presided, and the session was prolonged over a period of several hours. The Council consists of nineteen members, of which number it is believed that four to six opposed intervention.

Besides conferring with the council, with whom the final decision rested, King Ferdinand had conferences with the leaders of all Rumanian political parties, including those favorable to intervention in the great war and those who had been the strongest supporters of Rumania continuing her neutrality.

The Rumanian military officials had discussed for some days what probably would be the first step taken when war was declared and had dismissed all alien employes many of whom were Germans. An especially large number of Germans were employed in the technical services.

General Averescu, former Minister of War, will have, it is said, chief command of the Rumanian Army.

The Bucharest newspaper, Adeverul, commenting on the council meeting, said.

"At last the decisive hour has struck. Events have dictated to the Government intervention and the realization of Rumania's national claims. The King, in view of the recent events, like the late King Carlos, convoked the Crown Council. The politicians when they leave it will have to bow to its decision. The union of all parties must be effected before the greatness of the cause."

\* \* \*

September 1, 1916

### RUMANIANS ENTER BULGARIA; CZAR'S FLEET AND ARMY ON WAY; AUSTRIANS GIVE UP WIDE AREA

**WAR COUNCIL IN VIENNA**

*Kaiser, Francis Joseph and Bulgarian King to Discuss Situation*

**REPORT RUSTCHUK SEIZED**

*Bulgarian Danube Town Opposite Giurgevo Taken by Ferdinand's Troops*

**FIGHTING IS NOW GENERAL**

*From Bukowina to Orsova Rumanians Are Engaged with Teuton Armies*

LONDON, Friday, Sept. 1—Fighting has become general over the 400-mile Transylvanian front, according to the correspondent of the Bund of Geneva at Austro-German headquarters. The Austro-Hungarians, he says are finding it impossible to hold on to the political boundary and are retreating to the second fortified line of defense.

It is reported that a council of war will assemble shortly at Vienna, at which Emperor William of Germany, Emperor Frances Joseph of Austria-Hungary and King Ferdinand of Bulgaria will be present.

An important factor in the new war situation is the closing of the Danube which has been the principal route for the shipment of munitions from Germany to Turkey and the shipping of supplies to Germany.

The Rumanian official announcement, issued on Tuesday, follows:

General mobilization of the Rumanian Army began Thursday night, Aug. 24. On the same night (?) Rumanian troops crossed the Austro-Hungarian frontier.

[This appears to be an erroneous rendition of the official announcement, as Rumania did not declare war on Austria until Aug. 27.]

Russian troops, beginning to cross the Dobrudia were welcomed enthusiastically by our population.

Austrian monitors and batteries are firing on the towns of Orsova, Turhu-Severin, and Giurgevo.

A dispatch from Bucharest to The Times says that it was on Sunday night that the Rumanian forces surrounded the slopes of the Carpathians and occupied the district around Kronstadt.

### Manifesto to Troops

King Ferdinand has issued the following order of the day, addressed to the army:

"I have called upon you who are stout-hearted and full of hope. The spirits of the great Rumanian chieftains, Michael the Brave and Stephen the Great, interred in the provinces you are about to deliver, exhort you to victories worthy of them and of our heroic and victorious allies.

"Terrific fighting awaits you, but you will endure its rigors as did your ancestors. In future ages, the entire race will bless and glorify you."

A report received in Paris says the Rumanians have occupied the Bulgarian town of Rustchuk on the Danube opposite the Rumanian town of Giorgeva. No confirmation of the report has been received.

The Munich Nachrichten says that the Central Powers do not doubt Bulgaria's loyalty, but are alarmed at her obscure attitude and the lack of news from that country. Rome reports that Bulgaria requires insurance by a reinforcement of 200,000 Turkish troops before she will declare war on Rumania.

### What Hindenburg May Do

Chief speculation regarding Field Marshal von Hindenburg's policy is whether and in what direction he will change Germany's plan of campaign, which to the moment he assumed authority has been a plain, straightforward one. Military experts here believe that vital military need of the Central Powers was the shortening of their line of defense, even before it was extended more than three hundred miles by the addition of the Rumanian boundary to the fighting front.

Whether public opinion and political interest, in view of Chancellor von Bethmang Hollweg's declaration that peace should be made on the basis of the present map of Europe, will permit any sacrifice of the territory the Central Powers have gained is questioned. Heretofore the German Government has discussed victory and defeat chiefly in terms of the continental territory gained and lost by the belligerents.

Field Marshal von Hindenburg has been regarded here as a fighting General rather than a strategist. His success in the northeast is attributed largely to his intimate knowledge of the country.

Von Hindenburg is credited with the unshakable conviction that the war must be won by pounding Russia, whereas General von Falkenhayn was apparently committed to forcing a verdict on the western front.

Some influentiaal British experts, notably the military correspondent of The Times, have hitherto criticised the establishment of an army at Saloniki as a dissipation of energy on sideshows. They contended that the Anglo-French forces should have been concentrated on the western front. Premier Briand, on the other hand, is credited with insisting on the Saloniki enterprise and with forcing his views upon the British staff. Opinion here has now swung entirely to the French strategy in occupying Saloniki.

### BERLIN IS NOT ALARMED

#### Says Austrians Have Adopted Favorite Strategy to Check Rumanians

From a Staff Correspondent
Special Cable to The New York Times

BERLIN, Aug. 31—The first news from the Rumanian theatre of war indicates that the Austrians are repeating their favorite strategy of retreating systematically as at the outbreak of war with Italy. In military circles this first Austrian move in the campaign arouses no alarm; it is even hinted to be one link of a great, painstakingly worked out plan about which nothing further may be said at this time.

How thoroughly the Rumanians prepared their offensive is indicated by the speed with which their operations developed along the whole line. The Rumanian concentric attack is proceeding on the entire front from Orsova, near the Iron Gate of the Danube, to where the wooded Carpathians on the southern boundary of the Bukowina join the Gyergyr mountain range. For public consumption a parallel is pointed out here by military critics between the Russian invasion of Transylvania, and the public is reassured by experts that the first news of the Rumanians continuing to gain ground in Transylvania need cause no anxiety, being justified by the military necessity of economizing troops by taking up a shorter straight line across Transylvania. Vienna issues a report hinting hopefully that "the enemy columns will not be able to rejoice long in their initial successes."

\* \* \*

September 5, 1916

## MACEDONIAN REBELS CALL UPON ALL FELLOW-GREEKS TO JOIN ALLIES AND DRIVE BULGARS FROM THE COUNTRY

Special Cable to The New York Times
LONDON, Saturday, Sept. 2—Ward Price, in a dispatch from Saloniki dated Wednesday, writes:

"The authority of the Central Government has been repudiated. The intention of Macedonia to undertake independent political action has been asserted. A Provisional Government has been organized, a parade of revolutionary troops has taken place, and an offer of their services has been made to the leaders of the Committee of National

Defense, consisting of a Colonel of Artillery, a Colonel of Cavalry, the Venizelist Deputy for Seres, and half a dozen less important personages.

"They are distributing in town today a long double-page proclamation, of which one side is addressed to the Greek people, and the other to the Greek Army. A summary of what they say is that the present state of affairs has lasted long enough. The surrender of Greek forts and territories is a grievous misdeed on the part of the King and the Government, and the time has come for Greece to place herself at the side of the Entente Powers, who have always been her friends.

"The proclamation urges Greek soldiers to pay no attention to orders from Athens, to ally themselves with the Entente forces and drive the Bulgarians off Greek soil.

"There are three regiments of Greek troops in Saloniki. Their officers held a meeting to discuss their attitude. Three-quarters of them are said to be pro-Entente in sentiment.

"Gendarmes, who are the best drilled in town and over 1,000 strong, many of them being Cretans, and consequently staunch Venizelists paraded this afternoon in front of their barracks in the midst of a large crowd, and affirmed their acceptance of the authority of the Committee of National Defense, at whose head stands Colonel Zimbrakakis and Colonel Mazarakis, commanding the artillery brigade of the Eleventh Division, stationed here.

"Two hours later a number of officers, chiefly of artillery and auxiliary services, met at the Church of Dimetrieff and took the oath of adhesion to the committee and to the project of driving the Bulgarians from Greek territory.

"In the afternoon a parade, which should be at once an assertion and demonstration of the committee's power, was decided upon. Cavalry and infantry soldiers of the garrison have not yet joined the movement, but Colonel Zimbrakakis put himself at the head of a capable-looking column of over 1,000 gendarmes, with whom were mingled a rather nondescript detachment of volunteers, supplied with rifles from the police armory.

"Zimbrakakis, whose brother is the well-known Ententophile General who commanded a division here till recently, when he went to take up an administrative post at Athens, rode at the head of the column.

"The procession made for French Headquarters and filled the space in front of it with much cheering. After a while General Sarrail appeared at an upper window, saluted, and withdrew again. Then Zimbrakakis went into the building and came out a quarter of an hour later and started to make a speech.

" 'I told General Sarrail' he said, 'that we have come to offer ourselves to shed the last drop of our blood fighting at the side of the Allies, and to free the invaded soil of Greece from our enemies, the Bulgarians. Is this true?'

"Shouts of 'yes,' 'yes,' came from the gesticulating crowd.

" 'General Sarrail said to me,' Zimbrakakis went on, " 'Can I count on your men?' " I told him to the last one.'

"Amid cheers for the Allies the gendarmes then marched off and the crowd broke up. It is alleged that General Paraskevopoulos, recently appointed to command the Third Army Corps, will arrive at Saloniki from Veria shortly to take over the leadership of the movement."

\*   \*   \*

September 5, 1916

## GREECE IN THE WAR

In acceding to the demands of the Entente Allies, published yesterday. Greece will be at war with the Central Allies whether she declares it or not. To give the enemies of Germany control of the mails and telegraphs, including the wireless system; to expel from Greek soil German agents indicated by the Entente; these are acts of unneutrality, practically acts of war, against Germany, Austria, and Bulgaria. When the Greek Government issues its belated declaration of war it will be a declaration after the event.

Greece must enter the war; it is the only way she can save herself now. Unfortunately for her, she will enter it without dignity or honor. She will have been taken by the back of the neck and thrown into it. And yet Greece is not the object of the scorn and ridicule which might be expected to be the portion of a nation in such a plight. The reason is that Greece herself is so plainly not guilty. She is the Greece of Venizelos, not the Greece of Constantine. Her opportunities for self-expression have been limited, but she has made use of them all to show where her desires lie. It is not the Greek people, but Constantine, who has brought her to this pass. The elections were Venizelist, but Constantine overruled the will of the people and kept his country passive and leaning to the wrong side—the wrong side from the standpoint of Greece's interests, Greece's future, even Greece's safety.

The Greek people did everything they could short of rebellion to show their desire for a different policy, and now they have thrown down even that last card. The ignoble part their country has been forced to play is not their fault. This is the reason why there are so few harsh words for them, a people betrayed, misrepresented, and misled. The policy of cowardice has once again been proved to lead not to peace but to disaster. But the policy of cowardice was not, never was, the policy of Greece. She is forced into the war she would have entered with dignity if her King had not nullified her will. Constantine himself is not a coward; he adopted the policy of cowardice because he thought it was sagacious, farseeing, cunning. Venizelos, who counseled the straightforward and evident path, was the statesman; the man who looked so far ahead, the man with the intricate mind, was so superhumanly sagacious that he committed his kingdom to the path of dishonor and of peril. And his country is paying for his blunder.

\*   \*   \*

September 16, 1916

# BULGARS ROUTED AND LINE SMASHED

*Serbians Pursue Them for Nine Miles, Capturing 25 Guns and Many Prisoners*

### FRENCH PIERCE DEFENSES

*Storm Positions Half a Mile Deep—British Take Town and Russians Join the Fighting*

LONDON, Sept. 15—Under smashing blows delivered by the Entente forces, all the Allies on this front now being represented with the entry of Russian troops in the Fighting, the Bulgar-Teuton defense line is rapidly crumbling.

The Serbians, after several days of brilliant fighting have overwhelmed the Bulgar positions in front of them, capturing twenty-five guns and a large number of prisoners, causing the enemy to retreat precipitately for more than nine miles; the French have captured positions half a mile deep over a front of a mile to the east of Vardar, while the British, west of that river, near the centre of the allied front, took by assault the town of Makukovo from a mixed Bulgar and German force as well as two points north of this locality. These successes are announced officially. Unofficial advices say Russian troops have captured villages north of Kastoria, which town southwest of Fiorina has been evacuated by the Bulgars, who, however, have occupied and fortified the heights of Coryba to the north of it.

Following is the report of operations made public today by the French War Office:

From the Struma to Lake Dolran the cannonade continues everywhere on both sides. It is rather spirited in the mountainous region of Belles.

On the left bank of the Vardar British troops delivered a violent attack against the Bulgarians, who were supported by contingents of German infantry. This terminated to the advantage of the British. Makukovo was taken by assault, as well as two points north of this locality, where the British established themselves solidly. One hundred prisoners and about ten machine guns were captured by them.

To the right of the Vardar the French troops took enemy trenches along a front of 1,300 meters, to a depth of about 800 meters.

East of the Cerna the Serbians continue to advance toward Vetrenik and Kajeckalan, west of Lake Ostrovo. The battle was under way for several days between the Serbian army and important Bulgarian forces. It resulted in a very brilliant success for our allies. Gornizevo was carried at the point of the bayonet, as well as the greater portion of Malkanidze crest.

Serbian cavalry, pursuing the Bulgarians as they retired in disorder, captured the village of Eksisu, thus compelling their adversaries to make a precipate

retreat of more than 15 kilometers, (9.3–10 miles.) During these actions the Serbians captured twenty-five cannon and took a great number of prisoners, the number of which has not yet been ascertained.

On our left wing Franco-Russian forces completely cleared out Bulgarian comitadje bands, which had advanced as far as Koyani, from the entire region south of Lake Ostrovo for a distance of sixty kilometers.

Four French aeroplanes dropped numerous bombs on Sofia and then, continuing their voyage, landed at Bucharest.

A version of this aeroplane attack received in a Reuter dispatch from Bucharest says: Noel and Lesueur, French aviators, dropped five bombs on Sofia on their way from Saloniki to the Rumanian capital, where they landed after a flight of about 400 miles.

British naval aircraft raided railways and troop concentrations within the Bulgarian lines of communication beyond Kavala between Aug. 25 and Aug. 31, according to a report issued by the Admiralty tonight. Considerable damage, the report states, was done to the railways, rolling stock, petrol and other depots and troop concentrations at Berk Drama, Ckuilar, Kavala, Porna, and Angista.

SOFIA, Sept. 15, (via London.)—An official communication issued today says:

Two enemy aeroplanes coming from the south dropped nine bombs of small calibre on Sofia Thursday, causing slight damage. The machines fled northward.

BERLIN, Sept. 15, (via London.)—Concerning the fighting on the Macedonian front the War Office statement today tells of the repulse of the Entente attacks on the Moglenica sector and east of the Vardar. The statement follows:

After violent fighting Malkanidze, east of Florina, was conquered by the enemy. In the Moglenica sector the enemy's attacks were repulsed. East of the Vardar, British detachments having obtained a footing in German trenches, were ejected again.

### RUSSIANS TAKE A HAND
#### Drive Bulgars from Two Villages North of Kastoria

*Special Cable to The New York Times*

ATHENS, Sept. 15 (Dispatch to The London Daily Chronicle)—The Crown Prince of Serbia reached the Serbian front during Wednesday night. Since then he has inspected the whole line, and held a conference with the divisional leaders.

On this front the offensive began with the first light and continued all day Thursday, the Serbians victoriously attacking along the whole front. Great success attended this determined offensive, and one after another the Bulgarian positions fell. Thus the enemy is being steadily and continuously driven back toward Florina.

On the left the Serbians pierced those Bulgar lines which resisted. Prisoners report heavy enemy losses caused be the accurate fire of the Serbian artillery.

Further reliable news from the northwest reports that a detachment of Russians has reached the neighborhood of Kastoria and taken villages north of Kastoria—Zagoritsani and Zoritsani—where prisoners fell into their hands.

French forces advancing south of Kastoria via Krupitsa, Ksepini, Makukovo, and Teapanitsa arrived within a very short distance of Kastoria. The Bulgars retreated before the French forward move to heights running to the north of the town. Here the enemy is obviously avoiding battle, and is said to be retreating to the fortified line of Roulias-Kanobiltioru.

\* \* \*

## GREEK KING POINTS TO PERIL OF WAR

*Says a Million Greeks in Turkey Would Share the Fate of the Armenians*

### IS BOUND BY NO PLEDGE

*Nation Ready to Join Entente Whenever Definite and Certain Advantage in Doing So is Seen*

On Sept. 1 the staff correspondent of The Associated Press obtained the interview from King Constantine of Greece that follows. It is impossible to say which of the censorships through which it passed held the dispatch at the time. Various reports concerning the attitude of Greece and King Constantine were afloat in the first days of the present month, but even London received no official dispatches for several days. The interview was given about the time the Entente Allied fleets was taking position at Piraeus, the port of Athens, and revolutionary outbreaks were reported taking place in Macedonia.

TATOL, Greece, Sept. 1, (via Paris, Sept. 15)—King Constantine received the correspondent of The Associated Press in his Summer palace here just previous to a visit from the British Minister at Athens. The King spoke of the present situation with the utmost frankness, although refusing to be directly quoted. He said that Greece was ready to join the Entente Allies whenever she could see her definite and certain advantage in so doing.

The King expressed indignation that it could be thought by any one, much less published, that he was bound by any pledge to any one not to make war, or that he had been moved in his course hitherto by any reasons save those he conceived to be for the greatest good of his country. He declared that the situation up to the Bulgarian invasion of Greek Macedonia and Rumania's entry into the war had not revealed with sufficient certainly the advantage to be gained by Greece to compensate for the risks and unquestionable cost in lives and property bound to follow Greek participation in the war.

King Constantine referred with particular feeling to the fate almost certain to overtake more than a million Greek living in Assia Minor and Thrace in the event of Greece finding herself engaged in hostilities with Turkey, and he pointed out that while those who judged Greece and himself harshly for what was regarded as inaction, they gave no thought to the prospect of condemning to the lot of the Armenians Greek women and children caught in the foils of the Turks.

The King said the world regarded with callousness due to ignorance, the real situation concerning the attitude of Greece, criticizing the country and the Government for bargaining when the Greeks alone could know and estimate the frightful cost of a war to Greece. He laid stress on the difference between Greece's situation and Rumania's in this respect.

Quite frankly the King admitted that the presence of Bulgarians in Macedonia and Rumania's entry into the war would greatly complicate the situation, constituting a new element which might easily alter the premises upon which the policy of Greece hitherto had been based. The King declared that all these new elements had to be duly considered and weighed before Greece would be justified in changing her position, but he added that they were now being thought over, and the course of Greece would depend on the result of that consideration and on nothing else.

With profound earnestness King Constantine stated it was not the moment to talk of his deciding the fate of Greece, nor of the Government deciding, nor of any political party in Greece indicating the action the country must take, but, as he put it, "the hour will come when we want the voice of the soul of Hellas to dictate the future of our race."

The King received the correspondent while lying on a sofa in a darkened room. Physicians and nurses are still in attendance upon him on account of the fever and continual irritation of the wound which keeps the King confined and in a state of constant physicial annoyance when not in actual pain.

Despite his mental anguish, the Greek sovereign apparently is trying to see clearly the way leading to the salvation of his country under circumstances which are altering hourly.

\* \* \*

## VENIZELOS HEADS GREEK REVOLUTION, WILL ISSUE MOBILIZATION CALL

*Ex-Premier Goes to Crete Accompanied by Head of Navy and His Former Cabinet—Country's Richest Man Offers His Entire Fortune for the Cause*

Special Cable to The New York Times

ATHENS, Sept. 25 (Dispatch to The London Daily Chronicle)—During the night former Premier Venizelos left Athens for Crete, in order to place himself at the head of the National movement, accompanied by a small band of supporters, including Admiral Condouriotis, Chief Admiral of the Greek Navy. Athens as yet is quite unaware of this dramatic step.

On arriving at Crete, M. Venizelos, in the name of his followers, will issue a proclamation in which he will state that he places himself at the head of the National movement to provide a last opportunity for the Crown and Government to place themselves in line with the majority of the Greek people.

There will be no declaration of dethronement of the monarch. M. Venizelos will call for a general mobilization throughout all the islands for the purpose of national defense. He will afterward visit Mitylene, Chios, and Samos, proceeding from the latter place to Saloniki.

I learn that Leonidas Embericos, owner of the National Steam Navigation Company of Greece, a millionaire, said to be the richest man in the country, has informed Admiral Cordouriotis that he places the whole of his great fortune at the disposal of the National movement.

Special Cable to The New York Times

LONDON, Tuesday, Sept. 26—Former Premier Venizelos of Greece, who left Athens yesterday for Crete and Saloniki, is coming to London, it is stated in well-informed circles here, and interesting deductions are drawn.

LONDON, Tuesday, Sept. 26—Former Premier Venizelos, accompanied by Rear Admiral Condouriotis, Commander in Chief of the Greek Navy, a number of superior officers, and all the members of his former Cabinet with the exception of M. Raktavin, who was Minister of Justice, left Athens early yesterday bound for Crete, whence they are expected to go to Saloniki, advises from Athena state.

According to one dispatch Mr. Venizelos took his departure from the capital at 5 o'clock in the morning. On reaching the coast he and his party put off in an open boat, from which they were picked up by the merchant ship Hesperia.

It is understood that in Crete M. Venizelos, in a proclamation, will invite King Constantine to put himself at the head of a national defense movement.

Fully armed Cretan insurgents, numbering 30,000, are reported as being in complete control of the island. Canea, Heraelion and other coast towns are in their possession.

The Greek authorities have turned over all Government buildings to the leaders of the separatist movement. Only eleven out of eighty members of King Constantine's famous Cretan Guard remain loyal. The guard has disbanded.

It is reported in political circles in Athens that a renewed effort to learn from the diplomatic representatives of the Entente Powers what Greek Ministerial changes would mollify the Entente and enable negotiations to proceed more regularly met with this unofficial suggestion: "The unacceptable members of the Cabinet know they are not acceptable without being told. If the Greek Government be sincere it will clean its own house."

Mgr. Agathangelos, Greek Metropolitan of Drama, was arrested on board the steamer Ohio on its arrival at Saloniki from Piraeus by order of the National Defense Committee, according to a Saloniki dispatch to the Paris Matin. Bishop Agathangelos constantly attacked the Entente in speeches and writings, and is also accused, the dispatch says, of acting as a spy.

\* \* \*

# RUMANIANS FLANK MACKENSEN BY CROSSING DANUBE

*Army Lands in Bulgaria Between the Fortress of Rustchuk and Tutrakan*

### DRIVE BEGUN IN DOBRUJA

*Russo-Rumanian Forces There Attack the Bulgar-Turk-German Line*

### BATTLES RACE IN NORTH

*Rumanians in Transylvania Gain Ground on Both Sides of Great Kukel River*

LONDON, Oct. 3—Rumanian troops crossing the Danube and invading Bulgaria between the fortress of Rustchuk and Tutrakan, have flanked Field Marshal Mackensen's army. Simultaneously with the landing of this force, the strength of which is not divulged in official dispatches from Bucharest and Berlin, announcing this feat, the Russo-Rumanian army stretched across Dobrudja attacked their Bulgar-Turk-German foes along the whole line. Tutrakan, which was recently captured by Mackensen, is situated where the river leaves Bulgarian territory and flows northeast through Rumania.

The morning newspapers hail the manoeuvre as a dramatic counterstroke against the Bulgarians for the defeat the Rumanians suffered at Hermannstadt.

The Times says it hopes Rumanians did not cross with small forces, "because the river is wide and the southern bank higher than the northern," so that all disadvantages of position are against the Rumanians. In any case, the crossing threatens the rear of Field Marshal von Mackensen's force in Dobrudja."

The official bulletin from Bucharest received here yesterday follows:

On the north and northwestern fronts fighting continues. In the mountains at Ghurgill and Ierghitzel we captured four machine guns and made prisoners of 11 officers and 500 men.

Southern Front—Our troops crossed the Danube between Rustchuk and Tutrakan.

In Dobrudja we attacked along the whole front and repulsed the enemy on his centre and right flank.

Berlin admits that in Transylvania, the Rumanians have gained ground on both sides of the Great Kukel River, north of Fagaras. Teutonic troops, the official statement adds, have gained successes in the Strehl Valley, also in Transylvania. The statement follows:

Transylvania Theatre: On both sides of the Great Kukel River the Rumanians have won ground. Near and north of Orsova (on the Danube) successful attacks have been made by our allies. In the Hatzeg Mountains enemy attacks on both sides of the Strehl (Sztrigy) Valley were repulsed. Oboroca height was taken by Austro-Hungarian troops.

Army Group of Field Marshal von Mackensen: South of Bucharest enemy troops have gained a footing on the right bank of the Danube. Southwest of Toprai Sari (Dobrudja) enemy attacks were repulsed.

SOFIA, Oct. 2, (via London.)—Army Headquarters today gave out the following bulletin:

Rumanian Front: The situation is unchanged and calm. We felled an enemy aeroplane in the environs of the village, Reybouner, in the Koutbounor region. Both men in the machine were saved.

VIENNA, Oct. 2, (via London.)—The official communication from General Headquarters, issued today, reads:

Rumanian Front: In the Orsova sector we captured some heights, and west of Petroseny seized Mount Oboroca. Rumanian counterattacks were repulsed. On the Great Kukel River our advanced posts were obliged to retire to Kokoli.

\*    \*    \*

**November 28, 1916**

## THE RUMANIAN FAILURE

The joining of Falkenhayn's with Mackensen's forces seems to make inevitable the speedy fall of Bucharest. The Entente Powers can only hope for a miracle. When we remember the jubilation with which the Rumanian declaration of war against Austria in August was received by them, the happy influence which it was going to exert upon Greece, the rapid military collapse of Rumania seems one of the bitterest ironies of the war. The German General Staff must have been thoroughly prepared long before the declaration. Rumania had been coaxed and bullied long by both sides. At the beginning of the war King Carol had vainly tried to range her with the Central Powers, with whom her relations had been close—till the Balkan wars—since Russia at the Congress of Berlin had robbed her of fertile Bessarabia with its Rumanian population and given her barren Dobrudja with its Turks and Bulgars.

King Carol could not make headway against the popular desire. He died a disappointed man. The war offered a prospect of realizing the old ambition of uniting to the Kingdom Transylvania, with its 1,500,000 Rumanians, to be won from the Austrians, while Russia would give back Bessarabia with its 1,750,000. The Central Powers could offer Bessarabia, but Transylvania was the richer prize. King Ferdinand was ready to take advantage of any opportunity of acquiring territory the war might bring. With Russia and the Central Powers, Rumania might be said to be quits. She had taken from Bulgaria, as the price of her intervention in the second Balkan war, which Austria lured Bulgaria into, Silistria and a rich agricultural region with a preponderant Bulgar population from the Black Sea to the Danube. The entrance of Bulgaria into the war naturally strengthened the Rumanian purpose to come in on her own hand, keep what she had of

Bulgarian territory, and get what plunder she could. Her conduct was directed by self-interest, but behind it was a background of nationalism, of "Greater Rumania" aspiration, of racial solidarity.

We do not know too much of what has been going on in Rumania since August, 1914, but we have been told of extensive military preparation. The regular army of 125,000 was mobilized at once. The reserve was ready to be called. Large credits for military purposes were voted. The Government was authorized to declare martial law whenever it should be necessary. Even since King Ferdinand came to the throne it was said to be his steady policy to provide his army with heavy artillery and to pick the best time for coming into the conflict. Until that moment he would be neutral, keep both sides guessing which he would espouse, and let his people prosper by supplying grain to both. Premier Bratiano was too slow for ardent friends of the Allies like Mr. Jonescu and Mr. Filipescu. Politicians like Mr. Marghiloman insisted that Russia was the chief enemy, that Rumania must join the Central Powers, or she wouldn't "have a friend on earth after the war." The King waited, toyed with the status quo, and finally made the plunge, apparently after inadequate preparation, which the Allies should have assured to him or kept him out.

Well, the "ring" was complete. The Germans proceeded to break a piece of it easily, to give another warning to small peoples, to chasten Rumania, insufficiently warned by the fate of Serbia and Montenegro. Nobody can help the Rumanians but the Russians, and the Russians seem to be taking a breathing spell waiting for munitions.

It is natural to look for a connection between their failure and the German influence in Russia, lately conquered, in part at least, by the retirement of Stuermer. On Greece the effect of the Rumanian disasters is only too evident. King Constantine guessed right, after all, his followers say. While the German forces cannot reach Greece, their exploits in Rumania are a threat over the heads of the Venizelists, a terror to all the timid. In Germany, however, the effect will be the most sinister. Carried to its utmost stretch, the Rumanian expedition will be, like the Serbian campaign, only a brilliant triumph over inadequately prepared enemies. It is a tour de force, it decides nothing. It touches no vital spot. But it will hearten the Germans at home. It will encourage the dying legend of German invincibility. It will postpone the day when the German people see that they have been deceived. It is a dying gleam, a flare-up of the old victorious confidence. It is no more than that.

Just as the French were led by a sentimentality to the militarily unwise adventure in Alsace-Lorraine, so the Rumanians, greedy for "Greater Rumania," began their campaign with the folly of a Transylvania invasion.

\*    \*    \*

# RUMANIANS HAVE LOST BUCHAREST; SECOND ARMY IN PERIL OF CAPTURE

*Teutons Are Closing In from North and South on Lines of Retreat—Defenders Demoralized by Foe's Swift Advance— Russian Drive Gains Northeast of Kronstadt*

LONDON, Dec. 6—The fall of Bucharest and Ploechti is announced in the German official communication tonight. It has not been confirmed from other sources, but the position revealed by the previous German and Russian communiques left little hope that the Rumanian capital could be saved.

No official Rumanian statements have been received in London since Sunday, but the Russian official reports today recorded the steady retirement of the Rumanians before the victorious Teuton forces. The rapidity of the advance of the Central Powers seems to show that no attempt was made to defend the capital, and the actions fought have probably been only of a delaying nature.

The fall of Ploechti, perhaps, is of even greater importance than that of Bucharest. Ploechti is a railway junction and the centre of the great oil district of Prahova Valley. Unless the Rumanians have been able to destroy or disable the oil wells, machinery, and stores of oil the Germans will get a much-needed prize. Moreover, in the Prahova Valley they are on the line of retreat of a portion of the Rumanian second army.

It is believed that the Rumanians will be compelled to retire until they can secure a shorter line between the Carpathians and the lower Danube, which will be within easier reach of Russian reinforcements.

A wireless dispatch from Berne says:

"The Frankfurter Zeitung warns Germans against expecting double rations as a result of the invasion of Rumania. It says the Russo-Rumanians may save their harvests and granaries, which are situated mainly on the lower Danube, in territory which has not been invaded."

Commander Locker Lampson, who has been in three actions on the Dobrudja front with British naval armored cars, has been wounded, says Reuter's Petrograd correspondent. The dispatch adds that six British petty officers are missing, but that none of the cars has been lost.

## German Announcement of Victory

BERLIN, Dec. 6 (By Wireless to Sayville)—Bucharest, the capital of Rumania, has been captured, it was officially announced today. Ploechti, the important railway junction town, thirty-six miles northwest of Bucharest, also has been taken.

Russian troops again attacked yesterday in the Carpathian forest, north of Tartar Pass, and on the Ludova, but these new assaults brought them no success. In the Trotus Valley,

(northeast of Kronstadt,) however, they made a strong attack and succeeded in reaching the German second positions. North of Oituz Pass a Russian point of support was captured.

These last operations are reported in the following statement, which preceded the brief announcement of the fall of Bucharest and Ploechti:

Front of Archduke Joseph: The Russians attacked in the wooded Carpathians, north of Tartar Pass, and four times on the Ludova. These new sacrifices of men brought the enemy no success.

The number of prisoners taken in the engagements on the Verchdebry, which were favorable for us has increased to 275 men and the booty to five machine guns and four mine throwers.

In the Trotus Valley strong pressure by the Russians against our most advanced line was parried in a prepared second position situated nearby in the rear. North of Oituz Pass a Russian point of support was captured. Our losses were small. Sixty prisoners remained in the hands of the German attacking forces.

In the Bazska Valley, southwest of the basin of Kezdi Vasarhely, a raid carried out by German and Austro-Hungarian troops, brought a considerable section of a Rumanian position, with two officers and more than eighty of the rank and file and much accumulated ammunition into our possession.

Army Group of Field Marshal von Mackensen: The Ninth Army, advancing victoriously, is approaching fighting its way forward, the Bucharest-Ploechti-Campina railroad. Under the influence of this movement the enemy evacuated his positions north of Sinaia, which town was captured by the Austro-Hungarian groups after an attack in the evening.

The Danube Army cleared the towns on the south bank of the Argechu, still occupied by the Rumanians and is advancing toward Bucharest.

On the Danube Russian attacks from the east were repulsed.

German and Austro Hungarian troops under Colonel von Szive are pursuing in Southwestern Wallachia Rumanian forces which are retreating in utter confusion. Our troops retain the enemy on the Alt to accept battle. The enemy, whose way has been blocked on the east bank of the river, lost yesterday 26 officers and 1,600 men in prisoners and four cannon. In addition to this number, more than 4,400 other Rumanians were taken prisoner on Dec. 5.

On the railroad northwest of Bucharest considerable stores of wheat bought by the British Government and labeled as such by signs fell into our hands.

On the front in Dobrudja there was calm.

\* \* \*

January 6, 1917

## RUMANIA DEFIES HER INVADING ENEMIES

*Government Manifesto to be Placarded in All Towns Says Army Is Not Conquered*

JASSY, Rumania, Jan. 5—In response to a unanimous vote of the Chamber of Deputies, the Rumanian Government has ordered that a "declaration of defiance" be placarded in every town. The declaration, which was read in the Chamber by Deputy Jorga, is in part as follows:

"To indulge at this moment in petty recriminations and personalities would be to fail to comprehend the great and tragic majesty of the time. This war will cause to arise here, as elsewhere, a new moral harvest in the soul of every one who aspires to serve the interests of the country. We see close at hand the grimacing spectre of the invader, greedy for the suffering of those whom he hopes to make his victims. But the rallying of our moral forces will show the world all the intelligence, energy, and devotion that the nation possesses.

"We are no longer party against party or personality against personality. The country absorbs us in its sorrows and hopes. . . . Two figures hitherto have been dominant in Rumanian history—Stephen the Great and Michael the Brave. Now is added the great figure of Ferdinand, who, before conquering the enemy, conquered himself by sacrificing, in order to become really King of Rumania, all the ties which attached him to his first fatherland, to the years of his youth and to his race for those among whom he had come to live, so as to become one of us. . . .

"The Rumanian Army is not conquered. It is unconquered in that which constitutes the sole value of an army even in this age of cowardly, sterile technique, namely, to the consciousness of having generously offered itself in order to save the country and to secure the triumph of its race. Its long resistance does honor to its flag. The spirit of thousands who have perished has passed, with the heroic power of that supreme moment, to those who survived and who carry with them the spirit of their lost comrades.

"The most important and most devoted part of this army is composed of peasants. Once again, solemnly and by the word of the King himself, their economic and political liberty was promised them a few days ago. At the moment of victory they shall not be rewarded only by flowers, while the fruits are reaped by others. . . .

"Does the enemy seek a reply from us? We give it here. He may have burned our harvests, ruined our resources, sent to the grave the flower of our youth: he may have destroyed the treasures of our ancient art; he may have had the glory of loosing Magyar malice and the ignoble hordes of Turkey, as well as the greedy, covetous Bulgars; but to make a theatrical play of our humiliated spirit—that pleasure he shall never have.

"We have driven many enemies from this land, and we still are able to conquer. The little church in the forest may still be seen where Basil the Wolf, after he was beaten by the Tartars, was sheltered in misfortune until he emerged to purify Moldavia. His faith and hope we have also and we await with absolute confidence the hour when we shall again become what we have been and even more than that."

\*   \*   \*

February 3, 1917

## SLAV PLEA FOR FREEDOM

*Subjects of Dual Monarchy Urge Unification with Serbs*

The Southern Slav Committee, with headquarters in London, has issued a long manifesto apropos of "King Charles of Hapsburg taking the oath on the Austrian Constitution."

The document's first paragraph is entirely taken up with the titles of the new Austro-Hungarian monarch, including "Lord of the Slovene March" and "Volvode of the Serbian Volvodina." It then proceeds to show how the Hapsburgs came into their "illegal" possessions, to fling defiance at the Emperor, and to pledge the faith of the Southern Slavs to the cause of the Allies:

"Under the pressure of the war-terror 7,000,000 members of the Southern Slav nation are unable to exercise free speech. Therefore, the Southern Slav Committee, as the only free representative body of this nation and the fully authorized mandatory of the independent southern Slav colonies in the two Americas and Australasia has both the right and the duty to define the position of the nation toward the Hapsburg dynasty.

"The Hapsburg dynasty acquired our lands on the strength of mutual treaties and solemn promises on the part of the Sovereign, which have been trampled upon, and from the standpoint of international treaties they have been broken. The violation of the law went so far that Francis Joseph I permitted Hungary to seize the croatian town of Rijeka by a falsification of the text of the very Act of the Compromise of 1868, which that Sovereign had already sanctioned.

"The Slovene lands have been compelled to wage a superhuman struggle to repel the pressure of Germanization, exercised ruthlessly with the full power of the State, with the object of carrying Germanism through these lands to the shores of the Adriatic.

"In 1908, Francis Joseph, against the nation's will, under the threat of war, proclaimed the annexation of Bosnia and Herzegovina, thereby violating an international treaty.

"Thus the occupation of these provinces by the abuse of the Mandate of Europe, was perverted into an act of political conquest and became one of the causes of the present war. Our nation, torn asunder by the Dual system, was subjected to the hegemony of the Germans and Magyars. With iron consistency the State applied itself to the systematic destruction of the strength of our national life by the sowing of internal discord, by politico-administrative subjection, and the breaking up of our territory, the hindering of intellectual development, and the exploitation of the national wealth against the interests of the nation.

"Finally, the dynasty became frankly pan-German; excluded from Germany, it cast itself with avidity upon the Balkans and evoked this horrible war in order to destroy first of all Serbia, the standard-bearer of the idea of the unification and independence of the Southery Slav race.

"While official circles are preparing to celebrate the coronation of the new Emperor and King, the Southern Slav Committee solemnly declares that our nation is released from its allegiance to the dynasty and all further ties with its Monarchy, and it protests in advance against any combination whatsoever of a reconstituted Hapsburg Monarchy, within whose framework our nation would be included. This would merely be a new betrayal by which to its own undoing, our nation would be made to serve the policy of German expansion toward the Balkans. The committee repeats that the only way in which the legitimate aspirations of our nation can be fulfilled and an enduring peace can be established in southeastern Europe, especially in the Adriatic and the Balkans, is definitely to sever all those lands, at present subject to Austria-Hungary and inhabited by a nation of one blood, called the Serbs Croats, and Slovenes, from the Hapsburg-Lorraine dynasty, and to unite them with Serbia under the glorious dynasty of the Karageorgevitch.

"We await the realization of these our just aspirations from the certain victory of the arms of the Allies, who are fighting for national freedom, for right and civilization."

\* \* \*

**June 13, 1917**

# CONSTANTINE GIVES UP GREEK THRONE; ALEXANDER, SECOND SON, IS NOW KING; RULER AND HIS HEIR OUSTED BY ALLIES

### ANGLO-FRENCH TROOPS LAND

*Occupy Corinth and Take Control of the Harvest in Thessaly*

### PREMIER HEEDS JONNART

*Told Powers' Purpose is to Re-establish Greek Unity and Protect Allied Army*

### EX-KING TO LEAVE COUNTRY

*Will Start for Italy, En Route to Switzerland, with the Crown Prince on British Warship*

### TEXT OF PREMIER'S LETTER ANNOUNCING KING'S ABDICATION

ATHENS, June 12—King Constantine's decision to accede to the demands of the protecting powers and abdicate in favor of his second son was made known to M. Jonnart, Commissioner of France, Great Britain, and Russia, by Premier Zaimis this morning in the following letter:

The Minister and High Commissioner of France, Great Britain, and Russia: Having demanded by your note of yesterday the abdication of his Majesty, King Constantine, and the nomination of his successor, the undersigned, Premier and Foreign Minister, has the honor to inform your Excellency that his Majesty the King, ever solicitous for the interests of Greece, has decided to leave the country with the Prince Royal, and nominates Prince Alexander as his successor.

*(Signed) ZAIMIS.*

ATHENS, June 12—The fall of Constantine I., King of the Hellenes, has come. In response to the demand of the protecting powers—France, Great Britain and Russia—he abdicated today in favor of his second son, Prince Alexander.

This climax in the affairs of Greece was brought about through the agency of the French Senator, M. Jonnart, who has held posts in several French Cabinets and who arrived at Athens only a day or two ago on a special mission as the representative of France, Great Britain and Russia. M. Jonnart had previously visited Saloniki and other points, and he lost no time in getting into conference with the Greek Premier, Alexander Zaimis.

The demands of the powers respecting the abdication of King Constantine also specifically eliminated Crown Prince George as his successor, the Crown Prince being included among those Greeks in official life who were considered strongly pro-German. Both the former King and Prince George, it was announced today by Premier Zaimis, intend to leave the country immediately. It is reported that they will embark on a British warship and proceed to Switzerland by way of Italy.

It is presumed that Prince Alexander will take his kingly duties with full acceptation of the ideas which the protecting powers desire to be put into effect in the Government of Greece during the present war. He is twenty-four years of age and has been free from anti-Entente proclivities.

### Appeal to Premier Heeded

Affairs in Greece, which several times since the outbreak of the war had seemed on the verge of a settlement, recently have taken on such an aspect of uncertainty that it became necessary for the powers to act with decision. M. Jonnart was selected to proceed to Athens for the purpose of laying before the Premier the aims which France, Great Britain, and Russia had with respect to establishing unity or feeling among the Greeks and greater security for the Entente forces engaged in operations in the East. While he informed the Premier that troops had been placed at his disposal, he appealed to that official to use his influence toward a peaceful settlement. The troops, according to M. Jonnart's instructions, were not to land until the King had given his answer.

M. Jonnart called upon Premier Zaimis on Monday morning and demanded in the name of the protecting powers the abdication of King Constantine and the nomination of his successor to the exclusion of the Diaboque, (Crown Prince).

M. Zaimis recognized the disinterestedness of the powers, whose sole object was to reconstitute the unity of

THE ROYAL FAMILY OF GREECE. Upper Row–King Alexander, the new ruler, Prince George, Duke of Sparta, former heir to the throne, and Princess Helene. Lower Row—Prince Paul, Queen Sophie, (sister of the German Kaiser,) Constantine the deposed King, and Princess Irene.

Greece under the Constitution, but he pointed out to M. Jonnart that a decision could only be taken by the King after a meeting of the Crown Council, composed of former Premiers. It was not until 9:30 o'clock this morning that the Premier communicated in a letter to the Commissioner of the allied powers the King's decision to accede to their demands.

### Adherents Wanted to Defend King

Prior to the announcement of the King's decision many Greeks, loyal to the crown, gathered for the protection of the sovereign. On Monday night 2,000 reservists formed a cordon around the palace in his defense. If that should be necessary, and a delegation headed by Naval Commander Mavro-michaelis was received by Constantine and pledged the devotion of the army and the people to his cause. The King's only reply was an appeal that they should remain calm.

All efforts of agitators to start a manifestation failed, and the army officers announced their intention to obey the order of the Government to take no part in any demonstrations and to maintain peace.

Agitators were still attempting to operate in the streets of Athens tonight, but there were no disorders, and everything leads to the belief that there will be none.

### French and British Troops Landed

Special Cable to The New York Times

LONDON, Wednesday, June 13—An Exchange Telegraph dispatch from Paris says French and British troops have been landed in Thessaly and Corinth.

PARIS, June 12—The War Office tonight announced the landing of troops in Thessaly in the following bulletin.

The troops charged with control of the harvests in Thessaly have penetrated that province without difficulty as far as the region of Elassona.

A dispatch to the Havas Agency from Athens says:

"M. Jonnart in a conference with Premier Zaimis announced that military forces had been placed at his disposition to establish control of the Isthmus of

Corinth and to maintain order in Athens. These forces were landed Monday without incident."

### ROYALISTS LOST LAST PROP
#### Had Told Greeks the United States Would Intervene for King

Special to The New York Times

WASHINGTON, June 12—While the State Department is without official confirmation of the Athens report that Constantine, the King of Greece, has abdicated in favor of his second son, Prince Alexander, and will soon leave the country accompanied by Crown Prince George, the announcement carried in press dispatches came as no surprise to official and diplomatic Washington.

It has been alleged and pretty substantially proved that the Greek King has been in close touch with Berlin by wireless from his headquarters in Greece, and that German submarines have been using Greek islands as a base of submarine operations against Entente shipping with the approval if not the secret connivance of the King.

It is known that a message reached the State Department yesterday which indicated that something was going to happen involving the Greek royal family and that a member of the family probably would become Regent of Greece. If the King has abdicated in favor of his son, it is interpreted here as a last attempt to save the throne to the Constantine dynasty.

As the protectors of Greek independence the Governments of Great Britain, France, and Russia claim treaty rights to interfere in the internal affairs of Greece if the independence of the kingdom and the liberties of the people are threatened. This right of the Entente is declared to be somewhat similar to the right of the United States under the Platt amendment to intervene in Cuba for the protection of Cuban independence and the preservation of public order.

The entry of the United States Government in the war against Germany placed King Constantine in an isolated and not enviable plight among his own people. The Royalist papers of Greece had been feeding the people with stories that the United States would intervene in Greece in support of the Constantine Government. Since the entry of this country into the war it has been out of the question for this Government to take any course that would strengthen the position of the Greek King as long as his sympathies and actions were favorable to the Teutonic allies.

### CAUSES THAT LED TO CRISIS
#### Ex-King an Implacable Opponent of Entente's Policy

Rumors that King Constantine would abdicate have been periodical. There was a meeting of the allied Ministers to Switzerland in the middle of April—at St. Jean de Maurienne—when, it is said, full powers were given France as a negotiator to present this alternative to the King: either he must abdicate in favor of his second son, Alexander, or the Entente Powers would recognize the Venizelos Provisional Government as pertaining to the whole of Greece instead of, as some of them had already

done, as a war Government identified only with Saloniki. Immediately all the Governments of the Allies were sounded on this proposition—the United States on April 23. Since then it had been semi-officially stated that France would conduct negotiations at Athens tending to clear up the difficult situation.

A significant dispatch was sent out of Greece to London on May 2. It read:

"The King is steadily losing followers. Fifty-seven officers recently left Athens in one day for Saloniki, and the stream is continuing. Since the Provisional Government declared that the population on any territory seceding hereafter to the National Government will not be mobilized the last plank was knocked from under the King's feet, and it is at least most doubtful if any of the rank and file will be found to stand between him and his fate."

Neither of King Constantine's elder sons is married. Prince George, the Duke of Sparta, and hitherto heir to the throne, was born July 19, 1800. He accompanied his father on his campaigns in the two Balkan wars of 1912–18, and since the Summer of 1815, together with his uncle George, has been engaged in propaganda work in order to set the policy of his father right before the Chancelleries of the Entente. Last Winter he was reported to have been in Berlin and Vienna on important missions.

Just prior to the outbreak of the war it was announced that a marriage had been arranged between Prince George and Princess Elizabeth of Rumania. The Princess is the eldest daughter of the present King Ferdinand of Rumania and the grandniece of the late King Carol. Another claimant for her hand—she is now 23—was the Czarovitch of Russia. The Kaiser, it was reported, was prepared to press the claim of his Greek nephew.

#### Alexander a Venizelist

His younger brother, Prince Alexander, the new King, is nearly three years his junior, having been born Aug. 1, 1893. He is known to have an unrestrained admiration for Venizelos and is believed to be intensely pro-Entente. A year ago it was reported that he had thrown up his commission as Captain in the first regiment of artillery in order to join Venizelos's volunteers, but was either restrained or was advised by the veteran statesman to remain where he was.

"The difficult situation" between King Constantine and the Allies has developed from three distinct causes: The alleged pro-German attitude of the King, the fact that three of the Entente Powers are guarantors of Greek constitutional liberty, the fact that the Greek-Serbian treaty of March, 1913, which he violated, pledged the support of either power if the other were attacked by Bulgaria.

The King either personally or through his spokesmen has explained his case as follows:

"When the war began the guarantors of Greek integrity insisted that we should remain neutral, although we were then ready to fulfill our destiny in the East. When Bulgaria attacked Serbia we could not carry out the treaty of 1913 for two reasons: Serbia was not only attacked by Bulgaria, but by Austria and Germany, and to attempt to aid Serbia then would have meant for Greece the fate of Belgium."

As to the King's alleged personal pro-Germanism, that arises from the fact that his wife is the sister of the German Kaiser. For several years, soon after the marriage, there were strained relations between the families at Berlin and Athens, and they continued until the present war brought the Hellenic couple directly under the influence of the Kaiser's agents at Athens.

The marriage of Princess Sophie of Prussia to the then Duke of Sparta in October, 1889, was one of the last diplomatic feats of Bismarck. The Kaiser himself attended the wedding and was seen to be on most intimate terms with his brother-in-law. He even purchased an estate on Corfu to be near him. The break came two years later, when Sophie joined the Orthodox Church of Greece. The Kaiser is said to have been so furious over his sister's apostasy that his grandmother, Queen Victoria, felt compelled to intervene and ask him to treat Sophie with more consideration, as she doubtless had acted "from the inspiration of pure and lofty ideals."

### Grievances of the Entente

The Entente, it is understood, do not hold King Constantine particularly to task for repudiating the Greek-Serbian treaty—that is a matter between Greece and her ally—but they charge that he has constantly acted against the liberties of the Greek people in a manner to call for their intervention. The constitutional liberties of the Greek people were guaranteed by England, France, and Russia in 1868.

Aside from the fact that all through the negotiations it has been proved that responsible Ministers and officers of King Constantine have aided the Central Powers—establishing submarine bases, surrendering forts and men to Bulgaria, declining to remove the menace of the Greek army from the rear of the allied force at Saloniki, or to end the pro-German propaganda at Athens, and, finally, attacking French marines in Athens who were there to maintain the peace—the principal charges against him as a monarch whose acts are more or less sanctionable by England, France, and Russia, are as follows:

In contempt of the guarantors and the Constitution the King is alleged to have dismissed the Liberal Government and dissolved the Chamber in February, 1915, under the pretext that both Government and Chamber which were prointerventionist, did not represent the country.

After the succeeding May election, which returned a still greater Liberal majority, he did not convoke the Chamber in order to keep in office a Cabinet formed to do his bidding. This Chamber was dismissed also.

Forced at length to obey the Liberal majority, he ordered a mobilization of troops when Bulgaria entered the war in September, and then a new election, at which the troops under the colors, the majority of who were Liberal, could not vote. Then again he dismissed the Government and dissolved the Chamber in response to the cries against his unconstitutional

acts, and held still another election under the auspices of his loyal troops. At this election the Liberal Party declined to vote. Since then King Constantine had governed according to his own will.

The ultimatums lodged by the Entente against the King for these acts and acts growing out of them have been numerous; numerous, too have been his acceptances and evasions.

### Growing Power of Venizelos

Meanwhile the power of Venizelos and the Provisional Government grew and attracted volunteers; more than 60,000 had assembled on the little strip of territory across Northern Greece, and practically all the Greek islands were under him. His policy, which had attempted to differentiate between the King as the hero of the Balkan wars and the King who was "unconsciously" acting in an unconstitutional manner, has been outlined by Alexander Diomedes, the representative of Venzelos in London.

Two guiding principles, he said, had ruled M. Venizelos: fidelity to the Serbian alliance and co-operation with the Entente. Fidelity to Serbia was necessary for Greece in order to secure a balance of power in the Balkans; and by a balance of power he understood not a division of the Balkans into two opposing camps, but a system which would automatically prevent any one of the Balkan States from obtaining in the Balkans such a military hegemony as Germany was attempting to obtain in Europe. Such a balance of power was the aim of the Greco-Serbian alliance.

The second principle, that of co-operation with the Entente, was founded not only on geographical reasons, but the traditional friendship of the Hellenic nation with England and France, the community of social and political interests, and the genuine harmony of Greek ideas with the English and Latin mentalities, all of which combined to dispose Greece to common action with the Western powers.

While the Entente, the King, and Venizelos, with the Kaiser more than an interested spectator, have been trying to settle the status of Greece the people outside of the zone occupied by the Entente have suffered severely. There have been blockades by the Allies and embargoes by the King—the former in retaliation for the aid given Teutonic submarines; the latter to prevent Greeks from trading with the Allies.

On May 4, during a period free from rumors of the King's inevitable abdication, Alexander Zaimis succeeded in forming a new Ministry. Zaimis had several times before tided the King over a crisis. It was a question, on account of the meeting of the allied Ministers at St. Jean de Maurienne the previous month, whether he would still aid the King or would advise the latter to yield, not only to the demands of the Allies, but to the voice of the people, which the thousands joining Venizelos were making louder and more threatening.

### The Deposed King's Career

Prior to the war King Constantine, not only in Greece, but throughout the world, had borne a very different reputation. Born on Aug. 3, 1868, Constantine was educated largely by private tutors from Leipsic, which was said to have stamped upon him a permanent German influence. His military education was furthered by attendance at manoeuvres in Germany.

One interesting chapter of his life is the way in which he became the people's idol. After having been dismissed as commander of the Greek Army in 1909 because of popular clamor, Constantine, then Crown Prince, decided to accept a command in the Russian Army, but the opposition to him at home lost its rancor and he was restored to his former dignities. He finally became a national hero in the Balkan war of 1912, when he led an army of 10,000 Greeks to the capture of Saloniki, causing 30,000 Turks to lay down their arms. His popularity was such, as a result of this feat, that Greeks in America raised several thousand dollars with which to purchase a gift sword inscribed "To Constantine, the Liberator."

When Constantine came to the throne it was said he aimed to restore the former grandeur of the ancient Hellenic Empire, and that he was a believer in the old national prophecy that under the reign of a Constantine and a Sophia the Eastern empire would be called into life again and the cross restored on St. Sophia at Constantinople in place of the crescent.

By the peace treaties signed after the Balkan wars, Greece added a considerable stretch of Turkish territory to her domain, and in December, 1913, the long-desired annexation of the island of Crete was carried out. King Constantine hoisting the Hellenic flag over the fort.

\*　\*　\*

June 14, 1917

## SETTING SARRAIL FREE

If the Kaiser's brother-in-law, Constantine, had been forced to abdicate two years ago, Serbia and Montenegro might have been saved. If he had been forced to abdicate one year ago Rumania probably would have been saved. The British and French had a strong army in the Balkans, under General Sarrail, but it could not move to Rumania's aid because Constantine's army was ready to strike in its rear the moment it did so. At the moment when the doom of Rumania became visible, King Ferdinand issued an appeal to the Allies to be less careful of Greece's interests and more of Rumania's; but there was a paralyzing hand on the arm of the Allies, and all the world believes it was that of Czar Nicholas. The Czar stood Constantine's friend, and under his shadow the clever Greek politician defied the French and British and gave the aid of an ally to his brother-in-law in Berlin.

The fall of Constantine is the first good result that has come to the war from the Russian revolution. The Czar is no longer at hand to protect him. Therefore he is removed out of Sarrail's way. Under the Czar's arm he has been making war upon the Allies; for his constant threat of war was as effective as actual fighting could have been in putting Sarrail's army out of commission. It is too late to save Rumania; but Constantine's abdication puts the Allies at last in a fighting position in the Balkans.

The power which Constantine exercised, and by which he was able to inflict actual military damage upon the Allies, even though he was nominally not at war with them, was illegally obtained. He suspended the Constitution and ruled as a dictator. The people voted twice in favor of the Venizelist, or allied, policy, but Constantine ignored them. The direction in which he exercised it was that of national treachery. Greece was bound by treaty to support Serbia, and Greece would have kept her faith, but Constantine would not permit it and kept her helpless while Serbia went down to destruction. National treachery and royal lawlessness have been the marks which Constantine has left on Greece's history, against her will and against her Constitution and laws. The marks are deep, for Constantine's influence on the war has been great and often disastrous. A man of strong character and no scruples, he fought for his own hand under pretense of serving his country. The effect of his departure on the military situation in the Balkans should appear soon, and the recent announcement that the Rumanian army is ready for the field may take on a new meaning.

\*　\*　\*

June 27, 1917

## DEMOCRACY WINS IN GREECE

Nine months after Eleutherios Venizelos left Athens to put himself at the head of a revolutionary movement he returns to head the Government. His object in both cases is and was the same, to obtain and secure for Greece a constitutional Government. His return puts an end to the separation of Greece into two countries which has been her state during most of his absence from Athens. The Entente obliged King Consantine, or rather the Czar, by laying its hand on Venizelos and holding his revolutionary movement still, but not until Venizelos had cut off from the royal Government the islands of Greece and a strip of territory across the northern part. In that awkward and impossible state of affairs Greece remained until the Entente at last found itself able to carry out the duty to which it was treaty-bound—the duty to insure a constitutional Government to the nation it had established a century ago.

When it finally composed its own internal differences and carried out this pledge, Bonar Law was asked in the House of Commons what the Entente expected to gain by its dismissal of Constantine. "What we hope to gain," he replied, "is a constitutional Government representing the whole of Greece." This constitutional Government has been denied her since Constantine overruled the elections and installed his own Parliament instead of the elected one. It will be Venizelos's first duty to expel this unconstitutional Parliament and call to their seats the men whom the people elected. "The whole of Greece" has never had a single Government, either constitutional or unconstitutional, since Venizelos began the revolution which the Allies, under pressure from the Czar, interrupted. The constitutional Government which Venizelos will restore will represent, at last, "the whole of Greece."

In September, 1915, Venizelos waited upon the King to urge that monarch to keep his treaty obligation to come to the rescue of his ally, Serbia. Constantine replied:

I am prepared to leave the internal affairs of Greece to the Government, but in international relations I consider myself alone responsible before God for their direction.

To which Venizelos answered:

You are enunciating the doctrine of the divine right of Kings, with which we have nothing to do in Greece. Your father was freely elected by the Greek people to be their King, and you are his successor. There is no divine right in that title, it is based on the mandate of the people.

This conversation is a nutshell in which can be found the whole subsequent history of Greece. Acting on his own theory of divine right, Constantine became "responsible before God" for the betrayal of his Serbian ally and the tearing up of the scrap of paper which bound him to go to her rescue. So she fell. He became "responsible before God" for the overriding of the Greek people even in those "internal affairs" which he was so magnanimously willing to leave to them, for he canceled their elections and made his own. The Greek people may feel proud, and the rest of the world may congratulate them today, that it is not they who are "responsible before God" for these typical, characteristic acts, these illustrative outgrowths of the theory of divine right.

That theory ended its short life in Greece yesterday. It had lived not two years altogether. It ended when Venizelos came back to Athens, to restore to the people the Government which had been taken from them, to prove that with that theory "we have nothing to do in Greece." If King Alexander ever said he was going to carry out "the brilliant policy of my revered father," he was only indulging in pious rhodomontade. His revered father would never have restored to power the man who went the length of revolution to save democratic Government from falling a victim to the doctrine of divine right. If he did say it, and it is doubtful if he did, his acts are better than his words, and liberty is restored to Greece.

\* \* \*

**June 30, 1917**

## GREECE NOW AT WAR WITH TEUTON ALLIES; HOSTILITIES ON GREEK SOIL MOTIVE GIVEN

ATHENS, June 29—The Greek Government has broken diplomatic relations with Germany, Austria-Hungary, Bulgaria, and Turkey.

Though war has not yet been declared, the Government considers that a state of war exists since its advent into power yesterday. The recall of the Greek diplomatic representatives to the Central Powers and their allies is imminent.

PARIS, June 29—Telegraphing from Athens under today's date the correspondent of Le Temps says:

"The Greek Government has directed its Minister to Switzerland, G. Caradja, to communicate to the Greek Legations at Berlin, Vienna, Sofia and Constantinople, instructing the Ministers to break diplomatic relations between the Greek Kingdom and the Governments of Germany, Austria-Hungary, Bulgaria, and Turkey.

"The Greek Ministers at these capitals are instructed to leave their posts with their staffs and to place their archives with the Netherlands Legations.

"The rupture is based on the incompatibility of maintaining diplomatic relations with Governments that are carrying on war in Greek territory."

The declaration of the Government of Greece that a state of war exists with the Teutonic Allies, ranges on the side of the Entente the fourteenth nation, and the twenty-first which has broken off diplomatic relations with Berlin. It also adds 3,000,000 people to the 943,100,000 already arrayed against Germany, Austria-Hungary, Bulgaria, and—Turkey with their 160,300,000.

Since King Constantine abdicated in favor of his second son, Alexander, on June 12, things have moved rapidly in Greece. Eleutherios Venizelos was recalled. French troops entered Athens to keep order. Venizelos again Premier after nearly two years, formed a Cabinet and will restore the Chamber elected in May, 1915, and illegally dissolved by King Constantine in the following November.

Premier Venizelos in his speech to the Crown, after taking the oath of office at the palace yesterday, said that Greece's place was beside democracy. The nation was struggling for freedom of the world against the two Central Powers with whom Greece's hereditary enemies were allied.

"We realize," the Premier said, "that unless we drive the Bulgarians from Eastern Macedonia that part of Greek territory will be always exposed to great danger. Before, however, thinking of mobilizing that part of Greece which has not shared in our movement, we must vitalize its military organization, which has fallen into such decay, and bring about a fusion of the two armies in brotherly co-operation. Therefore, we shall now call out the untrained classes of 1916 and 1917."

\* \* \*

**June 30, 1917**

## OUR ALLY, RUMANIA

The Rumanian mission to the United States, which arrived in Washington yesterday, is the second to come from the smaller nations that are endeavoring to stem the tide of Caesarism. When the United States entered the war Premier Bratiano sent by cable a welcome to us, in which he said:

Rumania is happy and proud to be by the side of the United States in the fight against those who imagined they could violate and warp, as their strength and selfish interests might dictate, the normal and democratic development of the great human family.

When the Italian mission was in New York Dr. Nicholas Murray Butler said, in his speech at the dinner given to them: "No indemnities?" Certainly not! "No annexations?" Certainly not! But restoration, restitution, and a return home of stolen and scattered children!

The "stolen and scattered children" whom German autocracy has parted and kept apart from their motherlands are many, from France's children in Alsace to Italy's in Istria. Among them are Serbia's children in Bosnia and Rumania's in Transylvania. There can be no permanent peace in Europe until the stolen and scattered children are restored. That is why Rumania entered the war; to liberate the Rumanians kept in Austrian bondage and reunite them with their own people. When this war ends, all the wrongs made by the ancient belief that kidnapping and homicide were legitimate national objects—a belief no longer entertained by any nations but those of Mitteleuropa—must be righted, that the world may be at peace thenceforth, and to right one of them Rumania fights.

Her army, according to recent dispatches, is ready to take the field. Rumania, though defeated last year, was not put out of action, for her army was left practically intact, and it is not the taking of territory but the destruction or capture of armies that counts. To that defeat two things contributed—Rumania's own inadequate conception of the size of the task and the failure of the Russian Court to give her the expected support. Both of these things have disappeared from the situation; Rumania has no reason to fear high-placed Russian treachery and has no illusions about her own task She is to be counted on for good work whenever Brusiloff shall be able to give the signal; perhaps earlier than that. And whatever blows she strikes will be struck not only negatively against autocracy, but actively for liberty, the liberation of her "stolen and scattered children."

*  *  *

## BULGARS ANGLE FOR PEACE

*Ferdinand's Emissaries Seek to Ascertain Entente's Terms*

Special Cable to The New York Times

ROME, July 20—Information coming from Switzerland reports active underground work by emissaries of King Ferdinand of Bulgaria, who appears to be throwing out feelers with a view of ascertaining what, if any, advantage would result from an offer to the Entente of a separate peace.

They are seeking to prove that Bulgaria threw in her lot with Germany and made an alliance with her age-long enemy, Turkey, only because she feared Russia's proprietorship of Constantinople and consequent disruption of the South Balkan States, but that, the Russian revolution having rendered this impossible, Bulgaria has no interest in continuing the war if the territory in Macedonia she covets is ceded to her.

*  *  *

## ALLIED CHIEFS SEEK BALKAN AGREEMENT

*America Not Represented at Paris Conference—Sims to Attend Naval Meeting*

**SERBIA PLANS A PROTEST**

*Wants, with Rumania, More Than Consulative Powers in the Assembly*

PARIS, July 24—The conference of members of the Entente concerned with the military and political situation in the Balkans will be begun here tomorrow. Premier Lloyd George, Foreign Secretary Balfour, and General Sir William Robertson, Chief of the Imperial Staff at Army Headquarters, are here from England, and Baron Sonnino, Foreign Minister, General Cadorna, Commander in Chief, and others have come from Italy. France will be represented strongly. Premier Ribot will preside.

Russia's views will be presented by the Chargé d'Affaires, M. Sevastepoulo. The Rumanian Minister, M. Lahovary, and the Greek Minister, M. Romanos, will represent their Governments.

The invitations to the conference were sent out by the British Government. Among them was one to the United States, accompanied by the explanation that it would be a small conference to consider specific objects, and saying that as the United States had no troops in the Balkans it would perhaps not care to participate, although its representatives would be welcomed. Washington replied that it did not wish to take part in the gathering.

A conference of naval authorities also will be held. Vice Admiral Sims, commander of the American naval forces in the war zone, has arrived for this meeting. Great Britain will be represented by Admiral Jellicoe, First, Sea Lord, France by Rear Admiral Lacaze, Marine Minister, and Italy by Vice Admiral Thaon di Revel, former Chief of the Naval Staff.

The Temps in an editorial today headed "Russia and the Conference," says: "Before their conference, which opens tomorrow, the allied Governments and the members of their staffs today were engaged in preliminary conversations which necessarily were influenced, as the conference itself will be, by the unprecedented crisis which Russia is traversing. No plans for military operations in the Balkans can be studied without preoccupation with regard to the Russian Army now retiring in Galicia. The diplomatic situation cannot be examined into without taking into account the new initiative of the Russian Ministry, which would fix a date for a conference as regards the war aims of the Allies for next month."

The article concludes by warning Russia that the way to end the bloodshed is not convince the Allies but to conquer their adversaries within and without Russia.

WASHINGTON, July 24—Serbia and Rumania are preparing to protest against the present plan of the Allies of allowing them only consultative powers at the forthcoming general Allies conference in Paris on the Balkan situation. They will insist vigorously, it was learned here today, on being admitted as full members, especially since the subject discussed is so vital to them.

Greece also has been invited to attend in a consultative status, but has not yet indicated her attitude. The United States declined some time ago to take part because officials did not deem the questions under discussion of immediate interest to this country. France, Italy, Russia, and England are the four main powers moving for the conference, and it is understood there is some difference of opinion even among them; with Russia opposing the recent allied policy in Greece as inconsistent with her revolutionary policies.

Just what details will be taken up is uncertain, but it is understood here the conference will discuss the feasibility of an allied advance on the Macedonian front, now that the Allies' rear has been secured by the entry of Greece into the war. In a diplomatic way it will discuss the new adjustment of power necessitated by Greece's presence among the belligerents and attempt to harmonize conflicting interests between Italy, Greece, and Serbia.

The allied control of Greece's internal situation has been formally abandoned, according to an Athens cable to the Greek Legation here today. While details are lacking, it is assumed this means complete withdrawal of the allied supervision of such governmental activities as railroads, telegraphs, and Post Office and the restoration of the sovereignty of the Greek Government.

\*    \*    \*

**July 28, 1917**

## ALLIES TO END BALKAN MENACE BY PUSHING WAR

*Paris Conference Resolves Not to Lay Down Arms
Until Object is Attained*

**TROOPS TO QUIT GREECE**

*Occupation of Thessaly and Epirus Abandoned Since Venizelos
Is Now an Ally*

**SALONIKI NOT AFFECTED**

*Macedonian Front Will Be Maintained by Sarrall—Corfu to
Remain a Naval Base*

PARIS, July 27—The allied powers yesterday concluded their conference after announcing a decision to continue the war until the object for which they are fighting is attained.

Their declaration, which was made unanimously before separating, reads:

"The allied powers, more closely united than ever for the defense of the peoples' rights, particularly in the Balkan Peninsula, are resolved not to lay down arms until they have attained the end which in their eyes dominates all others—to render impossible a return of the criminal aggression such as that wherefor the Central Empires bear the responsibility."

There was unanimous agreement on all decisions reached during the meetings. The Ministers of departments affected will meet in London to draw up the executive measures.

The Entente Powers decided to withdraw their troops as soon as possible from ancient Greece, Thessaly, and Epirus.

The following announcement respecting the decision of the Allies concerning Greek territory now occupied by their military forces was published today:

"France, Great Britain, and Italy, simultaneously and as soon as possible, will end the occupations they have been obliged to make in ancient Greece, Thessaly, and Epirus. Military occupation of the triangle formed by the Santi Quaranta road and the Epirus frontier will be maintained provisionally as a measure of security. Italy and Greece to agree as regards re-establishment of the civil administration under a commissioner appointed by Greece.

"France, Great Britain, and Italy will preserve during the war a naval and military base on the Island of Corfu, the island remaining under the sovereignty of Greece."

This withdrawal of troops will not affect the status of military operations on the Macedonian front. The dethronement of King Constantine and the entrance of Greece into the war have relieved the Entente Allies of the necessity of maintaining troops in Athens and elsewhere in old Greece to prevent an attack from the rear, and it is these forces which are to be withdrawn. Entente troops have been sent to Epirus, to Thessaly, to protect the grain fields, and to several other points, as well as Athens. Italian troops have been penetrating Epirus, in Northwestern Greece, and Italy was credited in some quarters with aspirations to retain control of this territory, although the Italian Government said that it merely desired to maintain order. This source of friction between Italy and Greece has been removed by the Paris agreement, providing for the evacuation of all Greek Epirus, with the exception of the small triangle designated opposite the island of Corfu.

The fighting front is in Greek Macedonia and Southern Serbia, to the north of the districts affected by the Allies' decision.

\*    \*    \*

## BULGARIA'S SUPPORT OF BERLIN'S PLANS

*All Parties, Including the Socialists, Solidly Behind Czar Ferdinand and the German Program*

By VOYSLAV M. YOVANOVITCH
Professor in the University of Belgrade

*To the Editor of The New York Times:*

The excellent leading article "What Bulgaria Wants," which you published in your issue of July 23, needs neither contradiction nor the slightest correction. It is a real pleasure for us Serbians (who, having been condemned during twelve centuries to be Bulgaria's neighbors, and who must know them,) to observe that America from the very beginning of the war is not going to repeat the blunder our European allies paid so dearly for, after having disregarded our warnings. It is a matter of common knowledge to those (unfortunately not numerous) who have closely studied the political situation in the Balkans during the last four years that Bulgaria, as you say justly, "by means of the alliance with Germany and Austria, hopes or has hoped, to be the chief power economically and politically in the Balkans."

In spite of the eloquence of your article I believe, therefore, that there will be a certain amount of interest in supplementing it with some details not so much for your information as for that portion of American public opinion which is still inclined to believe in the possibility of a separate peace with the Bulgarian nation, which they imagine to be an innocent victim of their foreign King and of their bad Government, who enticed them into the war against their will.

1. Bulgaria joined the Central Powers in October, 1915. Her resolution to attack Serbia was not a hasty resolution made in an excess of excitement which she may later repent. Her resolution was being deliberately planned during fifteen months prior to her entrance into the war. Indeed, Bulgaria's crime was premeditated.

2. It is not exactly true that Bulgaria attacked Serbia solely with the aim to "liberate" their "brethren" in Macedonia. Their ultimate aim was the crushing of Serbia as a whole and the establishing of a powerful Bulgarian Czardom which would rule "between three seas." During Bulgaria's neutrality Serbia had proved her goodwill by offering to settle amicably with her all pendiing questions, having, in April, 1915, on advice from France, Russia, and Great Britain, consented to give up to Bulgaria a large part of Serbian Macedonia, even Monastir. The Government of Sofia refused to discuss the Serbian overtures.

3. From the beginning of the war until today the Bulgarian Parliament sat regularly. It voted all war credits asked by the Government. All political parties, without exception, orthodox Socialists included, voted their confidence in Radoslavoff.

4. The Bulgarian Socialists have been, and still are, in the direct service of the Government of "Czar" Ferdinand. Their delegates for the Stockholm conference before leaving Bulgaria received instructions from the Ministers. The Sofia paper, Balkanska Poshta announced in its issue of April 25 that "Yanko Sakazoff, leader of the Socialist Party, had conferred for two hours with the Prime Minister, Radoslavoff, before he left for Stockholm." The same paper on the 8th of May published a statement to the effect that "the Prime Minister, M. Radoslavoff, and the Minister for Education. M. Pesheff, had yesterday an interview at the Sofia railroad station with the second group of representatives of Bulgarian socialism who left for Stockholm."

5. With regard to the relations between the Bulgarian Governmental Socialists and their friends in Berlin, may I be allowed to quote from Narod, (the official organ of the Bulgarian Socialist Party.) a telegram from Berlin published in its issue of May 12 announcing the arrival in that town of the Bulgarian delegation on their journey to Stockholm:

Our delegation had in the Reichstag Building two meetings with the Central Committee of the German Socialist-Democratic Party. Afterward we had a meeting with the fraction of independent Socialists discussing the program of the Stockholm Congress and especially the Balkan question. Bulgarian delegates have presented their viewpoint, which was accepted with approval.

And the Narod adds this commentary:

For us Bulgarian Socialists it is highly important that the point of view of our delegation has been approved by our Berlin comrades.

Of course there is no more mystery for anybody, and a mistake is impossible. The whole of Bulgaria is actually at war against us, the Allies; her King and her army, her Ministers and her Parliament, her fourteen political parties, and her Socialists, too. They are on the German side, all of them, not only because they believed and believe the victory will be a German one, but also, and chiefly, because their criminal ambitions have a deep root in their national character and their national education. There is only one way to rid them, "the Prussians of the Balkans," of their ambition and make them no more dangerous for the world's peace, namely, to beat them in the field.

*VOYSLAV M. YOVANOVITCH.*
*Washington, July 23, 1917.*

\* \* \*

## AUSTRIAN SLOVENES AND CROATS AGITATING FOR A REVOLUTION

LONDON, April 30—A dispatch sent out today by Reuter's Agency says that it has been learned from Serbian sources that signs of an approaching revolution in Austria-Hungary are becoming daily more evident.

A plebiscite is being held among the Serbs. Croats, and Slovenes in favor of union with Serbian and Montenegro in one independent State under King Peter of Serbia. The Prince Archbishop of Carniola is at the head of this movement.

"Demonstrations of a very serious character are taking place in the Jugoslav provinces." says the dispatch. "Now comes the news that at the request of the Austrian Government, and with the sanction of the Pope, the Nuncio at Vienna has opened a disciplinary inquiry against the Archbishop of Carniola for placing himself at the head of this revolutionary movement. Great developments are expected."

\* \* \*

**May 20, 1918**

## ITALY'S AGREEMENT WITH JUGOSLAVS

### *Alliance Against Austria Said to be One of Its Basic Considerations*

### LARGE CONCESSION BY ROME

#### *Belief Here That This Development Is Embodied in New Treaty With Entente Allies*

The new treaty which, according to a statement published yesterday by The Manchester Guardian, has been concluded between Italy and her allies to replace the agreement of April, 1915, under which Italy went into the war, is believed in Jugoslav circles here, to embody in definite form the results of the recent agreement between Italy and the Jugoslavs inhabiting the Adriatic provinces of Austria Hungary.

The exact terms of the agreement, which was confirmed at the Conference of Oppressed Austrian Nationalities held in Rome early in April, have not been worked out yet in entire detail, the spirit of both sides being strongly against endangering the newly won harmony by possibilities of conflict over details. Much of the matter in dispute may not be finally settled till after the peace treaty.

But according to Professor Pietro Silva, who recently discussed the agreement in The New Europe, the basic considerations were alliance of the two nations against Austria, recognition by Italy of the right of the Serbs, Croats, and Slovenes to a united and independent national State to be united with Serbia and Montenegro at the pleasure of its people; recognition by the Jugoslavs of Italy's right to the districts where the Italians are in a majority, this comprising Gorizia, Trieste, and the western half of the Istrian peninsula, together with certain islands off the Dalmatian coast, the constitution of the ports of Flume and Zara as free cities, and the recognition by each nation of the rights of freedom of culture and judicial equality of Italian minorities in Slav territory and Slav minorities in Italian territory. All disputed questions are to be settled by arbitration.

The treaty of April, 1915, was dictated by the necessity of getting Italy into the war on the side of the Entente, and in Italy by the necessity of bringing the extreme imperialists to the side of the liberals and irredentists who formed the centre of the war party, as well as by fear of foreign consequences. Premier Orlando has lately defended this treaty under the cir-

cumstances of those days, for Russia was still imperial, America was not in the war, and even the free stations had to consider strategic guarantees of security.

At that time the agitation in the Jugoslav provinces had not attained its present form of practically unanimous demand for complete separation from Austria and unity with Serbia, and there was a party in Italian public opinion which doubted if the whole movement were not supported by the Hapsburgs to counteract Italian ambitions. At the same time there was fear that if Italy did not obtain the eastern shore of the Adriatic after defeat of the Central Powers Russian influence, through Serbia or otherwise, would, dominate there and would give Italy another militaristic and imperialistic neighbor. So the treaty, the substance of which was known at the time, but which was not published in full until Trotsky gave it to the world from the Russian archives last January, gave Italy very wide liberty of annexation in the Jugoslav provinces, including nearly all of Dalmatia.

A natural reaction of this was to make the Jugoslav troops in the Austrian Army fight hard against the Italians, although they usually surrendered in battalions when opposed to the Russians or the Serbs. In the last year, however, Italian public opinion has undergone a distinct change of heart, and in her new treaty, it is understood, has receded from extreme demands.

#### SOP TO CROATS A RUSE
#### Austria Seeks to Set Backfire Against Southern Slav Movement

Recent cable dispatches telling of the proposal to unite with Croatia-Slavonia, which now enjoys a very limited measure of autonomy under the Magyar crown. Dalmatia, at present a province of Austria but inhabited by Serbo-Croats, are elucidated by extracts from Southern Slav papers sent to this country by the Serbian Press Bureau of Geneva.

The object was apparently to set a backfire against the Southern Slav movement for the unification of Serbs, Croats, and Slovenes with Serbia and Montenegro by trying to make concessions to the Croats alone. There was a tendency to promise some sort of reconstitution of the old kingdom of Croatia, united personally with the Magyar crown, the rights of which have been overriden in more recent times by the Magyars, the object being apparently to isolate the Slovenes further up the Adriatic, work up antagonism between the Catholic Croats and the orthodox Serbs, and thus break up the Jugoslav movement.

The leaders of the national movement in Croatia are anxious lest the populace, provoked by the Government's machinations and by the general starvations, should rise at a time when any revolt would easily be put down and would only result in useless slaughter. The local authorities have been doing their best to maintain a sort of working relation with the national Government to ameliorate conditions so far as possible, in order to prevent popular dissatisfaction from rising to the flash point.

\* \* \*

May 26, 1918

## SAYS 'FREE BALKANS' OR NO WORLD PEACE

*Dr. Masaryk, Leader of Suppressed Nationalities in Austria, Speaks Here*

**SEES 10,000 SLAVS PARADE**

*Demands Freedom for 19 Small Nations—Germans Want Balkans for Bridge to Asia*

The nineteen nations in the Balkans must be free and independent because the German push toward the East is directed toward the smaller nations of the Balkans, which it desires to use as a bridge to Asia and Africa; therefore, only the organization and freedom of these nations will give lasting peace to Europe and to mankind.

This was the declaration made last night by Dr. Thomas G. Masaryk, head of the Czechoslovak revolutionary movement against Austria-Hungary. Dr. Masaryk spoke at a meeting in Carnegie Hill held in his honor by the Bohemian National Alliances and the Slovak League. He received an ovation when he took the platform and was greeted with cries of "Nech Zye!" (Long live!) and "Na Zdar," (Success!)

Dr Masaryk first reviewed a parade of about 10,000 members representing all the Slavic societies in New York. When he arose to speak, following an enthusiastic reception, his voice vibrated with emotion as he thanked his countrymen for their appreciation, which he accepted in behalf of their common land.

He denounced Austria-Hungary as "an organization of violence," where the minority of two nations ruled a majority of seven nations. Speaking of Russia, from which he has just come, he said that the aim of the United States and its Allies ought to be the organisation of a democratic Russia.

A nation of 100,000,000 must not be allowed to become a prey to Germany, he declared. "Your President says you must be generous. I say that, with respect to Russia, you must be generous." Every mention by the speaker and by the Chairman, Nicholas Murray Butler, of the name of President Wilson was loudly cheered.

Professor Masaryk told proudly of the Slavs, who at the first opportunity deserted from the armies of the Central Powers and enrolled under the banners of France and of Italy. In Russia, he said, 50,000 Slav prisoners of war had been organised to fight against the country where they were oppressed, and he hoped that as many more would soon be ready for the same purpose.

### Must Get Rid of Hapsburgs

"We are forced—we must get rid of Austria-Hungary and the Hapsburgs," asserted the speaker to a roar of applause. "A leader of the Polish Socialists in the Austria-Hungary Reichsrat said that at least 30,000, and perhaps 60,000 civilians alone and many more thousands of soldiers, all Slavs, had been executed in the first year of the war. In the face of such Austrian atrocities, we not only have the right but the duty to sever all our connections with the Austrian House of Hapsburg.

"We will not be satisfied if Austria-Hungary grants us national autonomy. No, we will be independent. We must be independent."

"We nations of the east of Europe are bound together for life and death against the Germans," he said. "Bosnia, if she is free, will have the South Slav nation as its ally. Not only the Slavs in Austria, but the Rumanians and the Italians must be free. Count Czernin at Brest-Litovsk accepted the Russia formula of no annexations. We now see Austria annexing part of Rumania. Germany is trying to subjugate the nations of the east. The plan involves the absolute absorption of Austria, which today is only independent nominally. In fact it is governed by Berlin. Germany calls Austria the bridge to Asia. The German plan is to unite the old world. Europe, Asia, and Africa. The expression Berlin to Bagdad should now read, Berlin to Cairo."

\* \* \*

June 7, 1918

## JUGOSLAVS GET TOGETHER

*Leaders Start Move to Unite in One Big Political Party*

LONDON, June 6—A new political organization has been started in the Jugoslav lands aiming at the unity of all political groups, "a single organization and a single people," according to information received by Reuters. The most notable political representatives of the Croatians, Slovenes and Serbians are participating in the movement. Bosnia, Herzegovina, Croatia, and Dalmatia are represented.

The first manifesto issued declared that national unity is the sole aim of the movement and that the new organization will be better able than the old political parties to support its representatives in the Vienna Parliament.

\* \* \*

June 10, 1918

## MORE LIGHT

To some twenty millions of people who have done all that they could, short of a suicidal armed revolt, to right the Austrians, the Magyars, and the Germans, the indications that the nationalistic aspirations of the Czechoslovaks and Jugoslavs for "freedom" as Secretary Lansing puts it, are to have some help at last, make about the best news that could be brought. But it is good news for the rest of us, too, and that aside from any sympathies which may be felt for these particular nationalities. For the methods by which Czechoslovaks and Jugoslavs have won recognition here, where recognition was most valued and where, strangely, it has been hardest to get, are an indication that there is something in the principle which lies at the back of the whole struggle against Germany, the idea that truth itself has a certain force which may at least help it to prevail.

These Slav peoples have furnished hundreds of thousands of troops to the Allies; they have a huge roll of martyrs both of the battlefield and the scaffold; their leaders, meeting in the shadow of the gallows, have adopted downright declarations of independence behind which the peoples stand without division. Yet their cause, one of thorough loyalty to the Allies and one which is a part of the whole principle of freedom and justice for small nations as well as for great, has had hard progress against the slowness and irresolution of those who should have been their friends.

France, to whose light the intellectuals of the two races have always looked, has stood by them through thick and thin; Russia has never been against them, and was actively for them as long as Russia was still an entity; Italy had her conflicts of aspiration with the Jugoslavs, which have lately been settled in a manner highly creditable to both nations. But England and America, where geographical conditions have made possible a more disinterested view of foreign politics than can be held on the Continent, where idealism and political altruism have always grown most thrivingly, have been fields of hard endeavor for Czechoslovaks and Jugoslavs.

In the Allies' reply to President Wilson in January, 1917, they declared that "the liberation of the Italians, Slavs, Rumanians, and Czechoslovaks from foreign domination" was a part of their war aims. On Flag Day of last year the President said: "They" (the peoples in the Dual Monarchy) "would be satisfied only by undisputed independence." But in December, demanding a declaration of war on Austria-Hungary, he disclaimed any desire "to impair or rearrange the Austro-Hungarian Empire. It is no affair of ours what they do with their own life."

A few weeks later there was a shift to talk of federalization in Austria, and both Lloyd George and President Wilson talked of autonomy coupled with reiterated denials of intent to break up the Hapsburg monarchy.

Some of the reasons for this playing with the second partner in the enemy firm are still dark. A very large reason, it is now apparent, was the possibility of detaching Austria held forth by the Emperor's letter to Siztus, which was long cherished by persons who apparently failed to consider whether such a detachment at the sacrifice of principle, even if possible, would be either edifying or ultimately profitable.

Some of the causes, too, are to be found in propaganda of respectable provenance but somewhat dubious character, which has operated to devious purpose in this country, and apparently still more strongly in England. But in so far as national policy is responsive to national sentiment, which is apt to be more than appears on the surface, the reluctance of England, and more particularly of America, to respond to the claims of Czechoslovaks and Jugoslavs can be attributed to lack of information.

We in particular have been uninformed on European politics, but the American people seem to have a capacity for learning quickly in matters that touch their interest. They are beginning to learn about foreign affairs, and to learn a good deal. And when the Czechoslovaks and Jugoslavs laid their case before the American people, when they set about a campaign of information, the merits of their cause did their own talking. Probably thirty people have heard today of the prospective Czechoslovak republic and kingdom of the Serbs, Croats, and Slovenes, where one knew a year ago. Till lately most Americans thought of Austria as the country where pleasant waltzes grow; and with Hungary, even more distant and consequently more unknown, our relations had been of an uninformed pleasantness. Now the American people are beginning to learn just what Austria-Hungary is as a political organism, and especially as a political organism ruling over subject peoples; and phantasms of buying off the Hapsburgs and their Janizaries are not likely to prevail very far when that knowledge is spread.

We cannot win the war merely by letting our case rest on its merits, to be sure. But by making every people of this awkwardly large alliance aware of the merits of every other people's case we can go a long way toward winning it more quickly, and winning it so that it will stay won. To this end the example by which the Czechoslovaks and Jugoslavs have won friends for their cause is an example that should bring good cheer. For, as an American of Czech origin said lately regarding Russia: "If we only tell the truth the Germans will lose ground, for the truth is all against the Germans."

\* \* \*

June 16, 1918

## TODAY IS KOSSOVO DAY, GREAT SERBIAN ANNIVERSARY

*Date of Defeat of Serbia's Christian King Sacred Still to His People—Visit to Historic Plain Where the Battle Was Fought Five Centuries Ago*

*This is Kossovo Day. Churches of all denominations in New York will hold special services to observe the Serbian national anniversary. What the Battle of Kossovo means to the little Balkan nation, and what the associations are that cling about the plain where it was fought are told in the following article:*

### By MME. SLAVKO GROUITCH

Every one you talk with about this war will tell you it began on July 28, 1914, when Austria attacked Serbia, everybody, that is except, a Serb. He will tell you, it began in 1380, when the Turks, who had already established themselves in Thrace with their capital at Adrianople, under the leadership of their Sultan, Murad I, sent a challenge to the Serbian Tsar to come out and meet him in decisive battle on the plain of Kossovo.

It was on that plain in October, 1912, that the Serbian troops under King Peter avenged the defeat of 1380, thereby liberating from Turkish rule that part of Old Serbia and

Macedonia which had not been reached in the earlier Serbian wars for independence—which, beginning in 1804 under the grandfather of the present King, were finally successful in 1878—including Bosnia and Herzegovina, which, however, were unjustly wrested from Serbia by the Treaty of Berlin.

The legends which overlie the historical facts of the battle of Kossovo are among the most beautiful of the poems of chivalry. Their elevation of tone, their Christian and martial idealism are unsurpassed. The fact that the battle was a defeat seems only to have quickened the Serbian soul to greater intellectual efforts. The Serbians themselves explain this by a legend. It and the other poems in this article are from Noyee's and Bacon's "Heroic Ballads of Serbia." On the morning preceding the battle Tsar Lazar took communion at the Church of Grachenitsa, where at the moment of consecration an angel appeared unto him, saying:

> "O King, whom the Serbs revere,
> Wilt thou choose for thine own the Kingdom of God
> Or an earthly empire here?
> If instead of a heavenly rule,
> Thou choosest an earthly realm
> Leap astride thy steed,
> Belt about thee the girdle of war,
> Tighten in the girth of thy steed,
> And sheer shalt thou slaughter the Turk
> Till he beg of thee to share with him the conquest
>     of this world.

> But if thou choosest the Kingdom of God's own,
> Take of Christ the white bread and the wine
> And marshal thy army of Serbs to a Life Everlasting.
> And upon that dreadful day in the van of the war
>     thou shalt die, O Tsar
> With the whole of thine array."

> When the Tsar heard the holy words
> His thoughts came two and two.
> "Dear God, what is the whole Thine heart and
>     what is the deed to do?
> Which shall I hold for the better realm?
> Man's sovereignty may die,
> But the Kingdom of the living God,
> Its power goes on for aye.

> The Turks smote down Tsar Lazar
> With the edges of the brand.
> Seven and seventy thousand men lay dead upon
>     the sod,
> All valiant Serbs,
> And their pure blood was dear unto their God.

The scene in which Tsar Lazar accepts defeat and raises his sword in the form of a cross to the Most High has been most admirably represented in a medallion. "The Spirit of Serbia," by Anna Coleman Ladd an American sculptress.

Those who have wondered at the noble resignation and poise of the Serbian nation under defeat ever since their country was invaded in 1915 by the Austro-German and Bulgarian forces, during which Kossovo was again the scene of a great battle, in which the Serbians were defeated by overwhelming odds, should have witnessed their serenity in the Autumn of 1912, in those days of national rejoicing, when hourly bulletins brought news of victories over regions which ever since the first battle of Kossovo the Serbian people had mourned the loss of; every child, male or female, had been pledged at birth by parents, Church, and State to liberate from Turkish rule the lands where for centuries before their overthrow on Kossovo their people had prospered in learning and magnificence under Christian rulers with whom French Kings and Venetian doges sought alliances and treaties, sealed by the hands in marriage of Princesses of the royal blood.

To the Serbian of 1912 the overwhelming success of his armies in the first battle of that war, while hoped for, was considered miraculous in its completeness of revenge for Kossovo. The dismay and chagrin of the Turks was shared by their present allies, who yet waited until better prepared to join in the attack. The positions for the battle had been chosen by the Turks themselves, or their German Commander in Chief, General Liman von Sanders. The Turkish Army was equipped entirely with German small arms, artillery, and ammunition. The Serbian armament was as French as it is today, but its leaders had been trained in all the military schools and universities of Europe, its army being officered by the flower or the intellectual classes of the whole kingdom, to which were added many volunteers from all the Macedonian and Jugoslav provinces. The plain of Kumanovo where the Turkish Army attacked the Serbian frontiers, corresponds to the plain of Kossovo as one end of a long tunnel to the other, and the plain of Monastir where the Serbians and their allies are now fighting, may be described as a continuation of that tunnel only the first section of which is yet built (being the railway line from Skoplye to Ferisovitch), the second section being lengthened by snowcapped mountains, high plateaus, and unnavigable rivers, whose basins in Autumn are lakes and bogs of mire, into which horsemen and artillery sink as in a Hindenburg dream.

The battle of Kumanovo raged from Oct. 20 to 26, date of the triumphal entry into Skoplye, Serbian's ancient imperial capital. Ten days later King Peter, at the head of his victorious army, accompanied by his officers of State, made a solemn pilgrimage to the battlefield of Kossovo, whither they were followed by hundreds of Serbian women and children singing national songs, strewing flowers, there where in the springtime grow the wild peonies which, pure white, have been red ever since that day, June 15, 1389, when they were dyed crimson with the blood of Serbian heroes fallen in battle. Behind the army came the priests of the Orthodox Church, bearing crosses and banners and great church bells with which to rededicate the ancient church and monastery of Grachenitsa.

One who lives in a Serbian house will soon become familiar with the legends of Kossovo and of Marco Kralijevich, a contemporary of Lazar and his knights, but who for some reason which the ancient chronicles do not explain was not among the Dukes and Princes who led their hosts to Kossovo. None the less, he seems to have carried on a private war of his own until his death. Even then, the legend says, he went to sleep promising to wake again when Serbia should strike to free herself from Turkish rule.

Marco's domain was at Prilip on the Shar Mountains, above Monastir. Ruins of his castle still exist, and in 1912 the Serbian troops battling for the capture of Prilip suddenly made a dash right at the enemy under the fire of their own barrage, unheeding the signal from the officers to fall back, because, they said, Prince Marco on his white horse had appeared and was commanding them to advance.

The compelling influence of these legends over the Serbian mind and character was demonstrated to me in the early days of October, 1912, in my own home, then the Serbian Legation in London. For weeks the war cloud, that had been dispelled after the Agadir incident, again darkened the horizon of diplomatic chancelleries, and those who knew whispered that Turkey was being urged by Germany and Austria to attack the Balkan Block which France and Russia had built up for the greatest safety of Europe from a monarch mad with desire for Mediterranean conquest.

One day a party of Serbian officers who were in London on a mission for the Government came to our legation to say good-bye before leaving for the front war with Turkey being inevitable. My husband then told me for the first time that as an officer in the Reserve Guards he had applied for leave to join his regiment. That afternoon the answer came. It was that he was to remain at his diplomatic post. Upon reading the telegram he burst into tears and kept repeating over and over the lines of Czar Lazar's curse on those who went not to battle on Kossovo:

Who springeth of a Serbian house, in whom Serb blood
   doth run,
Who cometh not to battle at Kossovo, may he never
   have a son.
And no child of his heart whatever! May naught grow
   under his hand,
Neither the yellow liquor, nor the white wheat in
   the land!
May he like iron be rusted, and his stock dwindle
   away!

Victory succeeded victory in the triumphal progress of the Serbian Army, from Kumanovo to Kossovo, past Pristina, Mitrovitza, and Ferisovitch, up to Prizend the Magnificent, with its noble castle, as imposing as Windsor and Carcassonne, thence across the Albanian Alps to Durazzo on the Adriatic, while another army operating from Skoplyo drove the routed Turks through Veles up over the Babouna past Prilip and Bacra na Gumno down to Monastir, on to Ochrida, Struga, Mistra to

Scutari on the Boiana, where the tired Turks surrendered after a siege of several months.

As I watched the little flags which my husband after each successful battle pinned on the map hanging over his desk grow in number, the strangeness of all those geographical names, known to me only through the legends of Kossovo, and the recent events, stirred within me a sense that something remarkable which concerned me vitally was happening without my being there to see it. So one day I announced to my husband that I was going on a pilgrimage to Kumanovo, Kossovo, and all the other names on his map. It seemed unfair, because he was still tied to his post by the sessions of the Peace Conference, of which he was Secretary, and at the later sittings of which the Bulgarian delegates had been uttering jealous protest because Serbia dared to claim as her own the Macedonian regions which her own army had liberated without the aid of a single Bulgar, while, on the other hand, 50,000 Serbian troops had aided Bulgaria to capture Adrianople from the Turks after a long siege. The irresistible call of the legends was in my blood, and so early in April I left London for Belgrade on route to Kossovo. In company with several friends, one of them a distinguished English writer on Serbian historical and political matters, arriving in the Serbian capital just in time to witness the celebration of the fall of Scutari. The celebration consisted principally in the whole population parading in front of the King's palace and acclaiming the leaders of the army with shouts of "Long live Kossovo" so indissolubly linked was their past with their present.

It is a night's Journey from Belgrade to Kumanovo by train. At that time we were unaccustomed to the sight of many men in military uniform, and the throngs of them that lined the railway station gave it an unfamiliar air. Beyond, on the plain, were hundreds of tents, with men lying about on the grass or starting off with agricultural implements to cultivate the fields, April being the planting season. General Rasich, who visited America this last Winter as a member of the Royal Serbian Mission, was in command. As guests of the nation, the English visitors were asked to review the 60,000 troops . . . . Splendid looking men they were, smiling and satisfied with the victories they had won over their hereditary enemy. His Royal Highness, our Crown Prince, received our party in his tent, looking every inch a veteran in spite of his only 22 years. When congratulated upon the splendid success of the armies, of which he was Commander in Chief, he answered simply: "My men were all soldiers, and Kossovo was the prize for which they fought."

A number of officers volunteered to show us over the battlefield explaining the wonders of the machine gun, of which every one in my party heard for the first time, so unfamiliar in those days was the lay mind with military matters. The delight of the conversation was a boy Lieutenant's description of the accuracy of the "Srbska brzometha poochka"—in plain English, a Serbian quick-firing rifle. With map in hand all talking at once, they described the action during the days and nights when they battled, sometimes in the fog and at other times by moonlight, against an enemy of whose numbers they could only guess, so sudden had been the contact of the two advancing armies. They realized only when the battle was over that they had met and conquered the main body of the Turkish-Macedonian forces. Colonel Nedelkovitch, one of the heroes of the combat, told us it was a battle of Lieutenants by which he meant that many officers directed an individual battle of equal importance unconnected with the main action through lack of communication and contact with the higher command.

From Kumanovo to Skoply by train is but an hour in distance; in difference it is a continent. The great square about the railway station was crowded with Turkish fezzes and veiled women, many of them with packs on their backs or bundles in their hands, waiting for the train for Saloniki, whence by ship they would depart for Constantinople in search of the son or husband who, having departed with the army months before had not since been heard of. It was my first glimpse of what an invaded country is like, for, in claiming her own from the Turks, Serbia had dispossessed many of the latter, who felt it as great a hardship for them to live under Christian rule as it had been for Christians to live under Moslem rule. Here were the headquarters of the high command.

Field Marshal Gen. Michiton and his command received us with the greatest cordiality, holding a banquet for us in what had been until recently a Turkish palace. When we arrived we passed to our places at the head of the table between rows of bowing, smiling officers upon the breasts of most of whom glittered the medals and decorations of orders won in the battles of the preceding months. Some of them still bore traces of wounds, but all looked generally healthy, and the contented expression on their faces made one feel that it was a grand thing to belong to a victorious army.

The next day we took the train for Kossovo, the railway station of which is some little distance from the town of Pristina, where is a beautiful mosque in commemoration of the winning of the battle in 1359. My first exclamation was that I had been told that Kossovo was a plain, but it looked like an ocean—an ocean of billowy, flowering grasses and plants in which the blood-red peony predominated, with the yellow mustard, the white jonquil, and a kind of dwarf delphinium for contrast, a veritable Turkish carpet as far as the eye could see. Snow-capped mountains bordered the horizon beyond which lie Prizrond and the black Albanian Alps.

We had brought a volume of the poems of Kossovo with us. Sometimes the young Serbian diplomat who had been attached to our party by the Foreign Office at Belgrade read aloud from the original, translating what we could not understand. Sometimes, impatient to verify the scene for ourselves, we eagerly scanned the lines of Elodie Mijatovitch's translation, or the later one of Noyes and Bacon, all three American poets having succeeded in making beautiful drawings from themes which yet seem inexhaustibly richer in the original. All three writers speak of "level" Kossovo, and certainly a

flatter stretch of land was never seen than this illimitable prairie guarded by high mountains.

Along the land of Kossovo flow Lab and Sitnitsa,
Onward from the mountain to the wood,
From the maple to Sazhaya, bridged over by the arch,
Through Zvechan and Chechan, to the wood round
    Kossovo they march.

Farms, villages, and churches are lost in its vast expanse, and one comes upon them wondering why one had not perceived them from the distance.

The tomb of Murad, the Sultan, is watched over by dervishes, whose ancestors have lived on Kossovo since the days of the conquest. We visited a harem filled with women of every age and drowsy, crying children. Late in the afternoon we approached Grachenitsa. No words can describe the beauty of this pearl of Byzantine architecture, the frescoed walls of which are as fresh as yesterday, thanks to the white plaster with which the Turks had covered them to shut out the images of saints and Saviour, forbidden by the Moslem religion.

\*   \*   \*

June 17, 1918

## SLAVS MUTINOUS IN AUSTRIAN ARMY

*Troops Infected with Bolshevist Propaganda Shoot Their German Officers*

**POLES BREAK WITH CABINET**

*Cracow Conference Dissipates the Government's Hope of Controlling Reicherat*

By JULIUS WEST
Copyright, 1918, by The New York Times Company
Special Cable to The New York Times
ZURICH, June 16—Once again the Austrian frontier has been closed, and news of the internal state of affairs in that empire arrives only by round-about ways.

Two Munich papers simultaneously print telegrams from their Vienna correspondents which suggest one highly probable reason for the Austrian Government's disinclination to let the whole truth appear. According to the Münchner Neueste Nachrichten. Bolshevist propaganda among the Austrian prisoners now returned to their own country has been successful to the extent of producing a highly mutinous feeling which is now confined to any portion of the Dual Monarchy. The Münchner Augaberger Abend Zeitung says that mutinies are actually occurring, especially among Slav units commanded by German officers.

A battalion of the 7th Infantry Regiment, consisting of Slovenes, went on a strike at Oudenburg, shot their officers, and committed excesses in the town. The mutiny was only suppressed after several days of systematic trench warfare.

### Czech Rebels in Pitched Battle

This was followed by a mutiny at Rumburg, where Czech soldiers revolted and fought a pitched battle before being crushed. Some escaped into Saxony and there surrendered.

Lastly a regiment of Hungarian Serbs mutinied at Funfkirchen, but details are not known. All these cases are ascribed to Bolshevist propaganda, and the question of refusing to continue the exchange of prisoners is being considered. In all three cases German officers were the first and principal victims.

The political crisis in Austria is rapidly developing. On June 9 and 10 the Polish representatives in the Reichsrath held a conference at Cracow and decided to ask the Government for certain guarantees. Galicia must not be partitioned, and the Polish districts annexed from Russia must be placed under Polish protection, and not German. Further, as von Seidler, the Premier, is unfavorable to such measures, his resignation was demanded and the Reichsrath must be summoned forthwith.

### Poles in Definite Break

The last two points contain the sum of the situation. They mean that the Polish Deputies now definitely pass into the opposition, together with the other Slav parties already aligning with the Socialist opposition in the Vienna Parliament. A majority of the Deputies are now definitely against the Government, but the Government can hardly call a general election just now, as it would be courting disaster, nor can the Government accede to the Polish demands, as apparently a secret clause in the treaty of Austria-Hungary with the Ukraine makes the latter subsequently the master of Eastern Galicia.

Although yet unratified, the treaty has already been signed, Austria cannot protect Poland against Germany. The only solution of the difficulty, in Seidler's opinion, is a Government without Parliament and with the mailed fist.

If we bear in mind the fact that Austria and Hungary are having a little quarrel apart on the question where does Hungary come in on the Austro-Polish arrangement, it will be realized that the position of the Austrian Government is very uncertain. Everything points to the beginning of a new period of repression, and repression has a habit of urging the Government which practices it down a steep place to a sudden end.

\* \* \*

June 17, 1918

## KOSSOVO

That America and the other allies join with Serbia this year in the celebration of her national festival, the anniversary of Kossovo, is surely no undeserved tribute. For Serbia has suffered—suffered loss of life in battle, by epidemic, in the hardships of the epic retreat of her armies to the Adriatic, and in massacre, starvation, and pestilence under the conqueror; suffered loss of property by requisitions, by devastation, by the theft of everything movable by Magyars and Bulgars—more than any other of the Allies, even Belgium. Moreover, her sufferings were in large measure due to the ineptitude of allied diplomats who believed to the last that Ferdinand of Bulgaria could be trusted; and Serbia and her Jugoslav kindred who have demanded union with her and liberation from Austria have been exposed to the most vigorous attacks of certain peculiarly persistent and malevolent forms of enemy propaganda.

Kossovo Day deserves to be celebrated, for that matter, as a tribute to the spirit of a race which did not die under five centuries of oppression. From the day in 1389 when the mediaeval Serbian Empire, standing between the Turk and a divided and unready Europe, fell in the battle on the Field of Blackbirds, but in falling lamed the Turk so grievously that Europe gained a respite of half a century in which to make ready, no Serb has ever forgotten the battle. The triumph and the death of the national heroes lived in the song of scores of unknown or forgotten poets until Kara George led the rebellion that freed a fragment of the race. From that revolt in 1804 Serbia moved steadily forward until the battle of Kumanovo, in 1912, when the armies of Karageorgeovitch drove the Turk out of Macedonia and avenged Kossovo. But, as a French correspondent with the Serbian Army observed, Turkey was defeated, but the blow fell on Austria and Germany. For two-thirds of the Jugoslav race, blood brothers of the free Serbs, were still under Austrian oppression; and a powerful Serbia was something that Austria could never tolerate.

The Austrian ultimatum which began the present war quite evidently was never meant to be acceptable or accepted. Its acceptance, indeed, would have wiped out the free Serbian nation; so Serbia chose to fight, and until a Bulgarian attack in the rear reinforced Mackensen's blow from the front, while allied diplomats debated whether or not to offend Bulgarian sensibilities and Constantine of Greece did what he could to betray his ally and help his nation's worst enemy, Serbia held out. The disaster that fell upon her then was as complete as that of Kossovo; it might have crushed almost any nation. But a remnant of the army survived the flight over the mountains; this remnant was reorganized, and for the last two years it has been fighting, and with success, on the Saloniki front.

In the meantime, those brothers of the Turk, the Bulgar and the Magyar, have been holding carnival in Serbia. By methods well known in the Balkans they are doing their best to stamp out the national culture, the national language, the national consciousness, the national religion among the women, children, and old men who have survived the epidemics and the military executions. It is only elementary justice to demand the restoration of Serbia. But Serbia as we knew her before the war is only a third of the Jugoslav race. Serbs, Croats, and Slovenes in Austria-Hungary have kept the torch of national consciousness alight through a longer servitude than that of their brothers under the Turk. American sympathy will be appreciated; American contributions to Serbian relief can save some lives; but the only real evidence of appreciation of the Serbian people's persistent struggle for existence will be found in a determination that the end of this war shall bring the liberation of the whole Jugoslav people from Austria-Hungary, which has taken the place of the Turk as the conqueror and oppressor of a people devoted to freedom.

\*    \*    \*

July 11, 1918

## FRANCO-ITALIAN GAINS

*Foe Forced from Tomorica Valley and Austrian Attacks Fail*

**BULGARS ALSO MENACED**

*Allied Successes in Albania Cause Nervousness in Ferdinand's Forces at Monastir*

**AIM AT KEY ROAD TO SERBIA**

*Combined Forces Have as Objective the Old Roman Highway to Byzantium*

ROME, July 10—The Italian troops on the offensive in Albania are continuing their advance, the War Office announced today. The enemy in yesterday's fighting was beaten back on both sides of the Osum River.

Following is the text of the official statement:

In Albania our troops having reached ground west of the lower middle Semini and having extended to the eastward their occupation of the heights at the head of the Tomorica Valley, are advancing, repulsing the enemy at the centre, astride the Osum.

### Bulgarian Right Is Threatened

LONDON, July 10—Successes won by the allied troops in Albania will add seriously to the troubles of the Austrians. They were won by a fresh, determined action in the Balkan area, where any military success must always have immediate and valuable political reaction.

The line on which fighting is going on at present runs from the River Devoli to the Adriatic, a distance of over sixty miles. In addition to the French and Italian troops engaged in the battle, Albanian troops, under Essad Pasha, are fighting against the Austrians, and, because of their familiarity with the country, are in a position to give valuable assistance.

Although the region of the allied advance is seventy miles from the Saloniki front, there are already signs of nervousness among the enemy troops in that area. The advance in Albania is a serious threat to the right flank of the Bulgarian armies in the region of Monastir. This is evidently appreciated by the enemy, and it will also have the effect of bringing to the side of the Allies many from the hill tribes, who are among the finest fighters in the world. Every fresh success of the Allies will hearten the South Slav races, who are already in revolt against their Austrian rulers.

A further short advance will bring the Allies to Berat, the chief town of Southern Albania, and it is significant that Austrian official statements admit the progress of the French and Italians.

### Many Bulgarian Deserters

Desertions from the Bulgarian army on the Macedonian front are increasing greatly, French Headquarters in Macedonia informs the Saloniki correspondent of *The Times.*

All the deserters say that conditions in Bulgaria have become unbearable, and that hopes of an ultimate victory have vanished insubordination has increased in the Bulgarian Army, and many units recently have refused to obey orders to attack.

The submarine danger in the Mediterranean is declining the correspondent adds. Supplies needed in Greece are arriving with greater regularity.

PARIS, July 10—An official statement on the operations in the Balkans, under date of July 9, says:

There was artillery and patrol activity west of the Vardar. Notwithstanding the costly checks of yesterday at the Cerna bend, the enemy today again launched his assault troops against our positions north of Monastir and was again repulsed with appreciable losses. In the region south of the Devoli River our troops continued their advance in conjunction with the Italian troops and occupied Cafa Guriprere, the highest point of Kosnica Crest, which extends in a direction northwest of that of Bosnia. The Austrians, after having offered vigorous resistance in the course of the preceding days, retired in disorder into the Tomoriga Valley, into which we pursued them. We captured 210 Austrian prisoners and important material. Two enemy airplanes were brought down.

### Vienna Admits Retreat in Albania

VIENNA, July 10 (via London)—The following official report has been issued on the operations in Albania.

In the face of pressure from strong enemy forces, our Southern Albanian front has been withdrawn across the Berat-Fieri line. Since yesterday morning the fighting activity there has been very moderate.

### ALLIES' ALBANIAN OBJECTIVE
#### It Is the Road to Monastir, Regarded as the Key to Southern Serbia

The positions reached by the Italian Army in southern Albania, as indicated in this morning's dispatches, reveal Berat almost enveloped—on the west by the positions reached on the lower and middle Semeni River and on the east by those occupied on the Osum and the heights of Tomorica.

The advance was begun on July 6 between the coast and the Tomorica Valley, with the French on the right wing between the upper Devoli River and the Tomorica. The middle and lower, Voyusa was the scene of the principal Italian advance. By the 9th they had captured the town of Fieri,

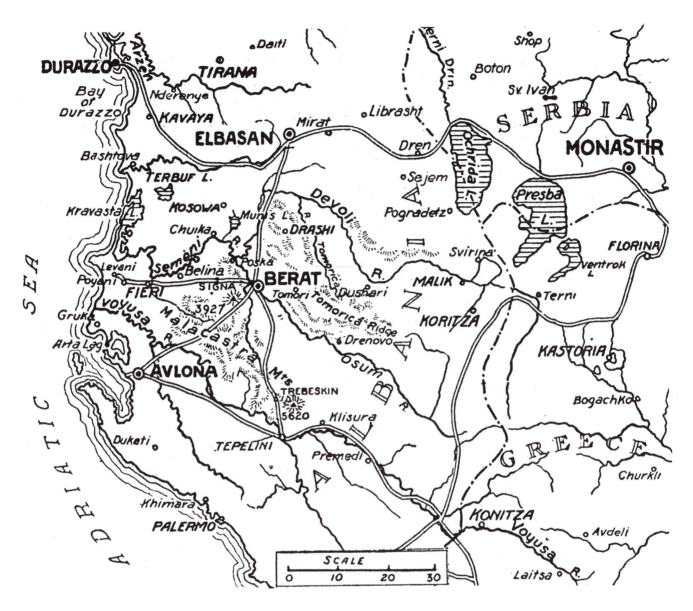

Scene of the New Offensive in the Balkans

which lies between the Semeni and the Voyusa, about eight miles from the sea. In this operation the Italians, assisted by British monitors, which served as a bridgehead, were able to cross the Voyusa and to carry the heights on the northern bank between Levani and the Pohani monastery. They also captured the Austrian strongholds of Cafa Grava and Corocop. Meanwhile, the French had taken the ridge of Bofina between Cafa Recit and Mali Gjarperit.

According to all strategic precedent in this region the Shumbi River, along which runs, from Durazzo to Lake Ochrida, the old Roman road, the Via Egnatia, is the Allies' objective. In December, 1915, the Italians tried to hold this road, which reaches Monastir, but only succeeded in rescuing the Serbian Army. They then evacuated Durazzo and concentrated at Avlona and built the railroad which a year later was to form a junction with the left wing of the Allies in Macedonia after their occupation of Monastir.

Between these two roads, the northern one, via Elbasan, in the possession of the Austrians and the southern, via Tepeleni, and Koritza, lies Berat, partly on the floor and partly on the mound of a plateau, thirty miles northeast of Avlona, and with a population of 10,000. From the Austrian side it is reached by two roads—the one from Levani, now crossed by the Italians, and the other due south from Elbasan. From the Italian side it is also reached by two roads—from Avlona and from Tepelini.

The Via Egnatia used the Shkumbi and Vardar Valleys on its way to Saloniki via Monastir (Heraklela) in the Roman and crusading days as the shortest route to Byzantium, (Constantinople.) Military critics, long before the Italian railroad was built and the Allies occupied Monastir, wondered why the Austrians did not put this road on a military footing, particularly as the Shkumbi Valley is considered not only the most vulnerable point of Albania, but actually the key to lower Serbia. From it the Allies could easily flank the enemy north of Monastir, who would be forced north toward Uskub and Koprülu on the Vardar. Such a retreat, it has been pointed out many times, would open the way up the Vardar and Struma for the long-expected advance of the Allies in both river valleys.

\*    \*    \*

July 26, 1918

# CORRESPONDENT FLIES ACROSS THE ADRIATIC

### *Ward Price Takes Part in a British Air Expedition Into Albania*

By WARD PRICE
Copyright, 1918, by The New York Time Company
Special Cable to The New York Times

BRINDISI, July 23—Since Icarius, the pioneer airman of classical times, crashed in his first attempt to fly across the Adriatic, aerial activity across this 100-mile strip of blue water between Italy and Albania has developed considerably.

Such, indeed, are the conditions of speed, action, and energy that characterize the campaign which the Italians, with their British naval and aerial allies, are carrying on against the Austrians in Albania that it has been possible for me during the last twenty and a half hours to:

(1) Fly across the Adriatic from Brindisi to Valona.

(2) Motor out to the new Italian front line in Albania.

(3) Visit Fieri, taken from the Austrians in the last advance, to cross the Semeni by the new bridge alongside the Ponte de Metalli that the Austrians blew up in their flight and see the captured piles of war material and the admirable work of development and civilization that the Italians are carrying on in Albania.

(4) Visit the Admiral and General commanding the Italian forces in Albania.

(5) Call on the British senior naval officer at Valona.

(6) Swim in the Vojusa River, which was the old Italian front line.

(7) Lunch and dine in the fairy Summer palace overlooking Valona Bay, built as a mess for the Italian Headquarters Staff at Valona.

(8) Take part in a moonlight bombing raid on Durazzo.

(9) Fly back across the Adriatic to Brindisi.

The last event of this program was not arranged beforehand. Flying out to sea at Durazzo after dropping four bombs, with the Austrian anti-aircraft fire close behind us, my pilot found himself over a low-lying fog, through which it was impossible to pick up his bearings. A strong wind also blew us further and further off our homeward course for Valona, and at last, finding himself in sight of Brindisi, the pilot decided to come down there instead of struggling back across the Adriatic against the wind with his petrol running low.

### What Flights to Cattaro Mean

About eight times in the last five months the bald statement has appeared in the English press that "British airplanes have bombed the Austrian dockyard at Cattaro," and, in addition to this, there have been half a dozen photographic reconnaissance flights as well. Few people who read these stilted official statements realize what they mean.

The flight which the airplanes make to Cattaro are only just a little shorter than that made by the airmen who go to bomb Constantinople, and the Cattaro flight is made by land machines without any ship escort beneath them across 125 miles of sea on the outward journey and 100 miles on the return, which with a detour in Albania that is usually made brings the total distance flown up to 330 miles. The air defenses of Cattaro are formidable, as the importance of the base there warrants. There is a tremendous anti-aircraft fire, and besides that a force of fast Austrian airplanes are ready to attack hostile fliers under conditions of great advantage to themselves.

This flight, indeed, which is one of the most important defensive measures against enemy submarines which we possess, is also among the most risky enterprises undertaken anywhere by the Royal Air Force. The machines go over the Gulf of Cattaro generally four at a time. They carry about three-quarters of a ton of bombs and not content with dropping these, they take some of the best airplane photographs I have ever seen as illustration of their work.

\*    \*    \*

August 15, 1918

# WHO ARE OUR FRIENDS?

The influence of the friends of Bulgaria is still powerful in Washington. Bulgarian agents from time to time make approaches to representatives of the Entente, in Switzerland or elsewhere; and now and then the news brings vague rumors of peace with Bulgaria. More than once we have heard that high officials hope to get Bulgaria out of the war.

Bulgaria, as The Times has said before, cannot be gotten out of the war without a price and a price that must be exacted from Serbia, Greece, and Rumania. Rumania has been forced out of the war, but Serbia and Greece will never acquiesce in Bulgarian occupation of their territories unless the Allies compel them to, which is unthinkable. But so long as the Bulgarian Minister stays in Washington there is an easy way open for peace offensives from the Central Powers; so long as America does not declare war on Bulgaria our position lends itself easily to the misconstruction which is even now being placed upon it by German propaganda in the Balkans.

The Germans point to our official relations of peace and friendship with Bulgaria as an indication that we care nothing for the fate of Serbia; and there is some reason to fear that the behavior of individual Americans in the conquered districts of Serbia has given corroboration to this. Serbia was attacked by Austria without justification; after reprising

Austria she was attacked by Bulgaria in the rear, a Bulgarian Premier lately boasted that Serbia had ceased to exist. Serbia exists, but only in the faith of her army and the surviving population of the conquered districts that the Allies will restore her. Our friendship with Bulgaria deals a daily blow to that faith.

The policy of Greece is guided by Elegtherios Venizelos, one of the great statesmen of Europe, a man who represents the ideals which inspire America in the war. He has his enemies in Greece; his enemies are the friends of Germany. Venizelos allowed himself to be unconstitutionally driven from power in 1915, because the Allies would not back him up, and allied fortunes in the Balkans were at their worst during his eclipse. He has now returned to power, but his enemies are doing their best to convince the people that again the Allies will not back him up. If, this man, who represents liberty and democracy, should be overthrown by a revolution, it would represent a real disaster to the allied cause. And the friends of Constantine. the friends of Germany, are busily telling the Greek people about America's friendship for Bulgaria, the traditional enemy of Greece.

It is known that the Anglo-French forces at Saloniki have been greatly reduced, that the bulk of the allied army in the Balkans is now Greek and Serbian. Do we want to convince these men, holding a front where victory may be incidental but where defeat would be extremely serious, that America loves the enemy in the opposite trenches? Are we to continue to accord the same treatment to the victim of an unprovoked attack, and to the hero of a stab from behind? Are we to continue to accord the same treatment to a King who served the Germans well and to one of the great democrats of our time? If one can sincerely love God while worshipping Mammon, it may be possible to hold to Ferdinand and Venizelos at the same time; but whatever the casuls morals of the situation, it is doing harm to the cause of America and the Allies. Persons whose democratic sensibilities were affronted by the Italian secret treaty, with its claim on comparatively small districts of Greek and Jugoslav territory, may well be asked what they think of a conqueror who has carried massacre and pillage through several Greek districts and half of Serbia.

\*   \*   \*

August 25, 1918

## BIG CONGRESS OF SLAVS SHOWS A FIRM FRONT

---

### Forms People's Council as Link in Organization Hostile to Austria

---

By GEORGE RENWICK
Copyright, 1918, by The New York Times Company
Special Cable to The New York Times
AMSTERDAM, Aug. 24 (via London)—The Cologne Gazette publishes a very interesting message from its Vienna

correspondent regarding the great Slav Congress at Laibach. Slav, Croatian, Serbian, Czech, and Polish delegates were present and the immediate purpose was the establishment of a People's Council as the first member of a future Southern Slav People's Council.

News regarding the event, the correspondent says, has been very heavily censored in Austria, but it is now clear that the meeting was "carefully prepared and skillfully carried out as a demonstration of the solidarity of the whole of the Slavdom of Austria hostile to the Austrian State."

Great speeches were delivered and greetings poured in from all quarters. Bishop Eglitch of Laibach sent a message of support and received members of the conference in audience. He allowed himself "to be hailed as the future Southern Slav primate," and said that, as a true son of Jugoslavia, he placed himself in the ranks of the people fighting for their rights.

The Polish members of the Parliament, says the message, took part in the proceedings, and the Congress "showed the Slav peoples of Austria to be possessed of a firm will not to be thwarted in their efforts to reach the goal of political, national, and economic freedom."

\*   \*   \*

September 8, 1918

## PAN-SLAV MEETING IN OHIO

One of the most important Pan Slav meetings held recently in this country took place at Lorain, Ohio, celebrating the fourth anniversary of Austria's declaration of war on Serbia. From all Northeastern Ohio Poles, Czechs, Slovaks, Ruthenians, Serbs, Croats, and Slovenes with Rumanians, gathered for a demonstration which was referred to by Professor H. A. Miller of Oberlin College, one of the speakers, as a prototype of the league of nations. In the parade which preceded the meetings of the day volunteers who are in training for the Polish Army in France, and veterans who have served with Polish, Czechoslovak, Jugoslav, and Rumanian forces were in line, with the Sokol societies which have played a part in promoting the national movements.

"The western front will be taken care of," said Professor Miller. "We have the upper hand there. But on the eastern front we need Slavic unity and solidarity to raise a barrier of united democracies against Prussian and Austrian aggression. The Czechoslovak armies and their exploits in Siberia, the wholesale going over of Slavs and Rumanians in the Austro-Hungarian armies to the Italians, shows that the idea of unity is already producing results. The Germans and Austrians are trying to keep up their old policy of stirring up strife between the small nationalities to serve the purposes of German and Austrian imperialists but in the last few months the nations have realized that by standing together in defense of the liberties of all they can break this plan and erect across Eastern Europe a line of free nations which will be a real bulwark of peace."

Alois Zuzek for the Slovenes, Professor A. Mamatey for the Czechoslovaks, Captain Paul Klieczenski for the Poles, Professor A. Bogdanovich for the Serbs, and Lieutenant Vasile Stoica for the Rumanians, recounted from the point of view to their peoples the impossibility of finding any modus vivendi with Austria, Hungary, and Germany, and the declaration that safety for the Slavs was only to be found in independence and co-operation. The speakers also praised the Slavic legions already fighting in France.

This meeting is one of a series within the last few months in the industrial cities and mining districts of Eastern Ohio and Western Pennsylvania, where the Slavic element is strong and where the Slavic nationalist movements found some of their ablest leaders.

*  *  *

## BUT WHO IS AUSTRIA?

On the very day that saw the peace invitation from the Government of Austria-Hungary given to the world, there was held in New York City a mass meeting representing the races—three-fifths of Austria-Hungary's population who for centuries past have been oppressed by that Government. These people were able from experience to recognize the truth in the saying of a Polish poet, quoted by the Czech leader, Professor Masaryk; "Austria is a sort of East India Company exploiting her peoples in the interests of a few hundred noble families." That is one of several things about Austria that should be remembered in the consideration of Count Buren's peace proposals. Another as the remark of Mr. De Lanux of the French High Commission: "The Austrian resolution is already going on. This very meeting is one of its episodes." When it is considered that hardly less than half a million nominal subjects of the Emperor-King Charles have actually enrolled in the armies fighting against him, that there have been at least two serious mutinies in his fleet and that in provincial capitals of his empire there are almost daily declarations in favor of complete independence from Hapsburg rule, one can understand the eagerness for peace of the Government which would not hear of putting off the invasion of Serbia in the last week of July, 1914.

"The only peace which could righteously adjust the still divergent conceptions of the opponents," says the Austrian note with unexpected accuracy, "would be a peace desired by all of the peoples." Is Austria ready to make a peace that would free the Czechoslovaks and Poles and give to Ruthenians, Rumanians, Jugoslavs, and Italians the opportunity to unite with the other parts of their divided races? Should the Allies abandon this demand, it would be an admission that they are unable or unwilling to win the war. The Allies have not abandoned the subject peoples of Austria. The Austrian note rather absurdly recalls some of the Austrophile declarations issued by allied statesmen in the unhappy discussions of last Winter but the world will not be deceived into forgetting

that the Czechoslovaks have been recognized as a nation by all the major Allies, and that the other Powers have backed up America's declared purpose to fight for the liberation of all the Slavs from German and Austrian rule.

*  *  *

## BRITISH INVADE BULGARIA

*Marching with Greeks on Fortress of Strumnitza North of Lake Doiran*

### VELES CAPTURED BY SERBS

*Neighboring Base of Ishtib Also Falls in Great Allied Sweep Northward*

### FOE'S WHOLE ARMY IN PERIL

*Large Force in West Cut Off in Mountains May Have to Surrender*

LONDON, Sept. 26—Veles, twenty-five miles southeast of Uskub, (the principal railroad centre of Old Serbia,) on the Uskub-Saloniki Railroad, has been captured by the Serbians.

The fall of Ishtib, eighteen miles due east toward the Serbian border, and another valuable base, which is linked with Veles by a branch line, is also reported unofficially.

British and Greek troops forming the right wing of the allied army have invaded Bulgaria, from the Doiran region. They are forcing their way over the Belachista Mountain range, while British units have crossed the border opposite Kosturino, about six miles from the Fortress of Strumnitza, which is the enemy base on this section of the front.

A British official statement from Saloniki says:
Our cavalry and infantry continue to advance into Bulgaria. The Anglo-Greeks are advancing over the steep Belachista range. The Greeks are approaching the crest of the mountains north of Lake Doiran. Our troops have reached Dzuma Obasi.

### Plight of First Bulgar Army

On the allied left the cutting at Isvor, fifteen miles north of Prilep, of the Prilep-Veles highway, the only road northward between Prilep and the Vardar River, both of which are held by the Allies, has isolated the First Bulgarian Army, under General Geshof, from its main line of communication. This places large bodies of enemy troops in an extremely dangerous position, which is rendered still more precarious by the fact that Italian cavalry has reached the road running from Prilep westward toward the Albanian frontier, which affords the only avenue of escape through the mountains, and it can be reached only by the trails through the mountainous area between.

In fact, it is pointed out that the entire Bulgarian Army, estimated to aggregate 300,000 men, is in a very dangerous position, but the victory will not be decisive, in the opinion of the military experts, until Uskub, the centre of all the enemy's communication lines, is captured. If that is accomplished, it is believed the victory will be numbered among the few decisive ones of the war.

The reports received today emphasize the demoralization of the Bulgarians, who, routed by the Serbian, French, British, Italian, Greek, and Jugoslav troops from either side of the great salient which now stretches far into Serbia, are retreating in confusion, leaving behind an enormous amount of material, and probably many thousands of prisoners, as the allied troops strain every energy, to get to Uskub, and thereby make the victory complete. The renewed resistance of the Bulgarian rearguards and the arrival of German reinforcements in Macedonia have nowhere succeeded in stemming the great allied advance.

It is pointed out that prior to the beginning of this push the Allies had no great superiority in numbers, and that they face a stupendous task in maintaining communications through the fifty miles they have penetrated. Some of this country is extremely rough.

Even should the Allies not take Uskub, or if there should be some other development which would prevent the making of the victory a decisive one, the experts believe that the Bulgarians have suffered so heavily in men and material that it is doubtful if the army will be able to recover without the aid of the Central Powers, and that contingency is viewed as unlikely. Meanwhile the Serbians have regained the greater part of Serbian Macedonia.

### Prilep May Be Serb Capital

A dispatch from Paris says that Monastir or Prilep will become the seat of the Serbian Government as soon as the allied lines north of those cities have been definitely established, according to Dr. M. R. Vesnitch, Serbian Minister to France.

The following official report, dated Wednesday, was received from Serbian Army Headquarters today:

On Sept. 24 Serbian troops achieved a very important success on the left bank (east) of the Vardar. We reached Krivolak and the outskirts of Ishtib. In this region we captured a Colonel commanding a Bulgarian regiment and a considerable number of prisoners, as well as four howitzers, three mountain guns, 100 horse wagons with teams, and other material.

Gradsko Station, which was defended by Germans, has fallen into our hands with enormous quantities of supplies, including nineteen guns, mostly heavy ones of 210 millimetres. To the number of prisoners we already had taken we added two German officers and several soldiers.

On the right of Prilep our troops have obtained very fine results. Near Izvor we are pursuing the enemy, who is completely, routed and in retreat. There, too, a great number of wagons with material has fallen into our hands.

An enemy battery which attempted to take up a position in order to come into action was attacked by our machine guns. The men were killed and the guns were captured. A complete German machine gun section also was made prisoners. These Germans complained that the Bulgarians had abandoned them intentionally and said that the Germans had continually compelled the Bulgarians by threats of opening fire on them to return to the fighting line.

At Troyatsi the Bulgarians burned their depots, and the fires spread to a hospital, with the result that more than 150 Bulgarian wounded perished. A horse hospital also was destroyed in the fire.

We have liberated more than fifty Greeks and ten Italian soldiers who had been captured.

It is confirmed that the Bulgarians continue to commit atrocities on our soldiers when they fall into their hands. One of our patrols of four men was found near the village of Veputchana horribly done to death.

Our aviators have used their machine guns very effectively against the retreating enemy troops.

### Hard Fighting on Right Wing

The review of the first day's fighting in the great offensive shows that it is not a case of the Allies chasing an enemy who was willing to retreat. On Sept. 18 Greek and British forces attacked on either side of Lake Doiran, which lies almost at the eastern extremity of the present line. West of the lake the Allies captured the ridge running from Doiran town westward, but the Allies' left was driven back. Some Bulgarian outposts east of the lake were captured, but all attacks against the Bulgarian main line were fruitless.

The next day the allied troops gained a little more ground west of the lake, but were unable to hold all their gains. The Bulgarians are described as having put up a determined resistance in the fierce fighting.

On the 20th, however, the Serbs, French, and Italians broke the Bulgarian front further westward, and the enemy began a general retreat along the whole line, which since has developed into rout. The reports of prisoners and guns taken are not surprising owing to the rapid advance of the Allies and the centring of all the allied energies in getting to their objectives.

### Asks Mackensen to Save Bulgaria

PARIS, Sept. 20—King Ferdinand of Bulgaria has asked Field Marshal Mackensen, who is now in Bucharest, to take the command of his armies so as to block the advance of the Allies in Old Serbia, and preserve Bulgaria from invasion, according to information received here from Switzerland.

"Fresh dispositions made by General Franchet d'Esperey, who has passed through Prilep justify the belief that there will be an energetic exploitation of the great inter-allied victory in Macedonia" says Marcel Hutin, editor of the Echo de Paris.

Advices received in Serbian diplomatic circles here today show that the Bulgarian troops in the region of Lake Ochrida, toward the western end of the Macedonian front, are virtually encircled by the Italians, advancing in the direction of Kichevo, and the Franco-Serbian forces moving from Monastir toward Krushevo. The fall of Krushevo is expected hourly.

The only means of exit for the Bulgarians here is a narrows passage between Kichevo and Krushevo. The army seems doomed to destruction or surrender, or to a retreat into. Albania, as the allied heavy artillery now installed northwest of Monastir commands the passes in the other direction.

Army headquarters today issued the following communication concerning the operations:

EASTERN THEATRE, Sept. 24—In spite of the arrival of new German troops, the enemy continues his retreat toward the north. Strong rearguard detachments are resisting strongly.

Northwest of Monastir, on the left wing of the allied forces, we have passed Prilep and advanced on the roads toward Krushevo, Kichevo and Veles.

In the centre, Serbian forces have taken the massif of Popadija, to the east of Habuna, and have gained ground to the west of the Cerra River.

We have enlarged the bridgehead north of the Vardar and are on the heights between the Vardar and the Kriva Lake vitsa, which the enemy is hastily crossing.

On the right wing French, British, and Greek troops have launched strong advance guards northward along the Vardar toward Gradets and Hudova. They have taken the massif of Kara Ball, north of Lake Doiran.

Booty captured is being augmented incessantly. During Sept. 23 more than thirty new cannon were captured and also a large amount of railway material.

\*   \*   \*

September 27, 1918

## TURKS AND BULGARS CLAMOR FOR PEACE

*Reports of Bulgar Cabinet Crisis and Impending Regency Under Prince Boris*

**MARTIAL LAW IN SOFIA**

*Rumanian Peasants, Excited by Allied Victories, Start Revolts Against Teuton Soldiery*

PARIS, Sept. 26—In well-informed circles there are reports that a new Ministerial crisis and a complete change in Bulgaria's foreign policy are impending.

Martial law has been proclaimed in Sofia, according to reliable news printed in the German press says the Journal of Zurich. It is said that the Bulgarian cabinet is in continuous session and King Ferdinand had a long consultation with premier Malinoff yesterday.

Pacifist manifestations were held at Sofia on Sunday, Monday, and Tuesday it is reported.

The German Government, according to advices to the Havas Agency from Zurich, is very uneasy over the pacifist

demonstrations in Bulgaria and the German Minister has conferred with King Ferdinand.

In some Bulgarian political circles it is believed that Crown Prince Boris will become regent in the present crisis.

\*   \*   \*

October 1, 1918

## ENVOYS SIGN AT SALONIKI

*Agreement Hailed in Entente Capitals as Sealing Teutons' Doom*

**OPENS ROAD TO RUMANIA**

*Rising of the Slavs of Southern Austria Also Expected to Follow*

**GERMANS REACH SOFIA**

*Field Marshal Mackensen Rushes Teuton Troops to Fortify and Defend Nish*

PARIS, Sept. 30—Bulgaria has surrendered unconditionally to the Allies and hostilities ceased officially at noon, following the signing of an armistice at Saloniki last night. General Franchert d'Esperey, the allied Commander in Chief in Macedonia, signed for the Allies, and the Bulgarian delegates for their Government.

Instructions have been given by the Government to General d'Esperey to proceed immediately to the execution of the conditions of the convention.

The armistice, La Liberté declares editorially, was signed with the full consent of King Ferdinand. It prints a denial of a report that he had taken refuge in Vienna. The King, it declares, has not left Sofia.

The announcement of the signing of the convention followed the return of Premier Clemenceau from the front, where he inspected the troops and had an opportunity of talking with General Pétain and General Pershing on the military situation.

### No Political Conditions

While the nature of the conditions is not announced, an official statement says:

"No diplomatic negotiation is actually in progress with Bulgaria and consequently no political conditions have been laid down for her."

With respect to the conditions of the armistice, it is added: "These conditions have been submitted by General Franchet d'Esperey to the allied Governments, who approved them. They are of purely military character designed to guarantee in a complete manner the security and liberty of the allied army in the Orient and to furnish every guarantee for the development of eventual pourparlers."

While the actual suspension of hostilities immediately followed the signing of the armistice, it is noted that this suspension applies only to Macedonian hostilities against Bulgaria and that it in no way affects Macedonian hostilities which the allied armies will continue against Austria-Hungary, Turkey and the German contingents sent to that locality.

The capitulation of Bulgaria, says the Journal des Débats, is the beginning of the end for the Central Powers. Germany will have the greatest difficulty in concentrating forces upon the Belgrade-Nish line in an attempt to save her communications with the Orient, and the Central Powers are incapable of occupying Bulgaria or setting up there a Government to resist the Allies.

"Ferdinand is doomed," it continues, "as his subjects will never pardon this disaster.

"Formerly the Central Powers threatened to dominate the Balkans and the Eastern Mediterranean, but the present Bulgarian debacle finds the Central Powers menaced on all the Balkan fronts. The feeble Austrian garrisons remaining in Serbia after Bulgaria's withdrawal will be annihilated.

"With the capitulation of the Bulgarians the Austrian Slavs will rise against their despotic rulers, and the fate of the Hapsburgs will be accomplished. An uprising in Bosnia and Herzegovina is a necessary sequel to the freeing of Serbia.

"Turkey must follow the example of Bulgaria and thus the Berlin-Bagdad dream disappears."

### Fatal Blow to Turkey

The Temps says that Bulgaria capitulated, knowing that Germany could no longer help her, and she did not wish to see her own country a field of battle. In 1913 Radoslavoff (then Bulgarian Premier) avenged the ambush of General Savoff, (Minister of War in the Radoslavoff Cabinet) and now the Malinoff-Savof Cabinet avenges the ambush of Radoslavoff.

"While it is too soon to appreciate the full political consequence of Bulgaria's abandonment of the Central Powers," the newspaper concludes, "yet it is plain that Bulgaria's action gives a fatal blow to Turkey, and perhaps, renders a service to Austria, as Austria now possesses an excuse for capitulation which previously it wanted."

Take Jonescu, former Minister without portfolio in the Rumanian Cabinet, in a statement made to the Intransigeant today, said that the effect of Bulgaria withdrawing from the war would be considerable in Romania. where the entire nation hates the Central Powers. M. Jonescu said be was convinced that before the end of the war the Rumanian Army would have once more the opportunity of fighting against the common enemy.

### London's View of Collapse

Special Cable to The New York Times

LONDON, Tuesday, Oct. 1—The exact terms of the Bulgarian armistice have not yet been published, but information shows that they are of a most comprehensive kind. They include demobilization of the Bulgarian Army, the surrender of all arms and ammunition, the evacuation of all foreign territory occupied by the Bulgarians, control by the Allies of railways and of transport on the Danube, and allied occupation of all strategic points, as well as control of ports.

These facilities taken together signify that Bulgaria can stand by the Allies in case of necessary as a theatre of war. The fact that the Bulgars are to be deprived of arms disposes,

at least momentarily, of the question whether they could now be enrolled against the Turk. They cease to be belligerents indeed, except with permission of the Allies.

Territorial questions are left to the peace conference, as well as the position of Czar Ferdinand. "If they like their Ferdinand they can keep him," a diplomat remarked today. It is apparent that the introduction of such controversial matters at the present time would be inadvisable, both as impeding military operations and in arousing passions.

In other terms, there is no interference with the internal Government of Bulgaria. The right of self-determination operates here, and such reserve offers an excellent prospect of a peaceful solution of the whole Balkan controversy—at the proper moment. The armistice remains in force until final and general peace is concluded.

Discussing the military effect which the Bulgarian armistice will have upon the German position in the Balkans The Daily Chronicle says it is very unlikely that any of Mackenson's army of ten divisions in Rumania will be employed south of the Danube, since it will be needed to consolidate the Danube line and in order to keep the Rumanians down. The most the Germans can do is utilize such footholds as they possess in Bulgaria.

Their control of the railways and rolling stock, for instance, is to delay the allied advance and deprive the Allies of as many as possible of the immediate Bulgarian resources.

The Chronicle estimates that it will be two months or more before the Bulgarian Army is demobilized and the railways, boats, and territories transferred to the Allies, and that it will be at least that time before a new war front is effectively constituted on the Danube.

The Daily News says it is true that Germany can still communicate with Turkey by the Black Sea, but that is a poor alternative to the corridor through the Balkans. It may safely be assumed therefore that Turkey is for effective purposes out of the war.

"Nor is this all," adds The Daily News. "The re-emergence of Rumania, if only in guerrilla warfare may be confidently anticipated and it can hardly be doubted that Austria is privy to the Bulgarian surrender. In any case that country is so eager for peace on any terms that it may be expected to welcome the impetus which Bulgaria has given to the movement which has so long been engineered from Vienna."

The Daily News says there is reason to believe that King Ferdinand has been the chief agent in securing the armistice, and finds significance in the fact that both the King of Saxony and the King of Bavaria have recently been in Sofia, and that Ferdinand himself is now in Vienna.

"These circumstances," it says, "point to very formidable possibilities for Prussia. They suggest that a phase of the war that is imminent may leave the Hohensollern dynasty isolated with the lesser Kings who have been its more or less unwilling feudatories combined against it in order to save themselves from the disaster that now seems unavoidable. That would be a fitting overture to the final humiliation of the despotism of Potsdam.

"There has been a tendency in this direction ever since the death of Emperor Francis Joseph and the catastrophic happenings of the last two months have now brought it to the surface. Suave qui peut has become the cry of the little Kings."

\* \* \*

October 1, 1918

## BULGARIA'S SURRENDER

The success of Marshal Foch's strategy on the western front has convinced Bulgaria that a most serious mistake was made in her manifesto of Oct. 8, 1915, in which it was declared that "Bulgaria must fight at the victors' side." It matters not if Czar Ferdinand secretly pledges loyalty to the Central Powers. His people have decided that Bulgaria has had enough of war. They have thrown themselves upon the mercy of the Western Allies and accepted the terms imposed for an armistice. As to Ferdinand's fidelity to principle or ally, he is notoriously false-hearted, a dissembler, a trickster. It is reported from Paris that Bulgarian representatives signed the armistice with "the full consent of King Ferdinand," He will bear watching, but in the present temper of his people he is impotent to betray them again. Bulgaria is out of the war.

By the terms arranged with General d'Espenet, as announced in London, Bulgaria has yielded control of her railways and waterways to the Western Allies and allows them to occupy strategic positions in Bulgaria. Thus Turkey will be cut off from communication with Berlin, and her submission becomes inevitable. Austria and Germany were rushing reinforcements to the aid of the Bulgarians in Macedonia a few days ago, and these troops will now be unable to proceed further than Nish, on the Oriental Railway in Central Serbia. In some quarters it is intimated that Bulgaria's collapse will release the French and British forces in Macedonia for service on the western front, but the Easterners are now going to be vindicated a campaign to recover all of Serbia and to invade Austria-Hungary by way of Belgrade is in order.

The Teutonic Powers have lost both their allies, for with Bulgaria's surrender the troops of Turkey, if the Ottomans remain in the war, will no longer be available. Simultaneously with the advance of the Allies in Macedonia upon the flank of the Austrians the renewal of the offensive by the Italians in Veneti may be expected. Obliged to send reinforcements to hold Belgrade and the Danube, the Austrians would be in dire plight in the Italian territory now occupied by them. A retreat to the Isonzo could not be avoided and ultimately the Italians would strike across that river toward Trieste and Laibach. This undoubtedly would be their plan of campaign. Austria, doubly menaced, would be inclined, in fact might be obliged, to follow the example of Bulgaria, unless reinforced on both fronts by the Germans. Such aid will become more impracticable every day. Indeed, Germany, in desperate straits in France and Belgium, must put every available man on the line there. No attention or consideration can be given to her ally, unless the far-flung offensive of Foch, extending from the North Sea to Switzerland, can be stopped and this seems to be out of the question.

There can no longer be a doubt that the whole German line in the west is giving way under the strategic pressure of the French, British, Belgian, and American armies. The German hold on the Belgian coast will be shaken if Roulers, a railway centre of great value as a base, has been taken, as reported, by Belgian and British troops. The British are now fighting in the environs of Cambral, and its capture or isolation may be looked for at any hour. With Roulers and Cambral both in the hands of the Allies, it would soon because a grave question whether the Germans would not have to evacuate the industrial metropolis of Lille. In view of the number of prisoners taken by the western allies, more than 200,000 by the latest calculation, and the spoil of guns and war material of all kinds, the Germans nowhere being able to make a stand for any length of time, there can be only one conclusion—the German Army has lost faith in its chiefs and is becoming a prey to demoralization.

If Germany entertains the hope that Marshal Foch may overreach himself and expose one of his armies to a successful counterattack it is a forlorn hope, because it is evident that in the American troops behind his lines which have not yet been sent into action he has reserves ready to deal with any drive the enemy may attempt. How else could his "hammer blows," constantly falling, be accounted for? It is not extravagant to expect an unrelaxing pressure by the Allies upon the German front day after day and week after week, with the purpose of forcing the enemy to evacuate both France and Belgium.

Meeting with continuous defeats in the west, Germany, abandoned by Bulgaria, with nothing to hope for from Turkey, and realizing that Austria may at any time herself collapse confronts disastrous failure of her plans in Russia from the Baltic to the Black Sea. With Turkey out of the war, as now seems to be a question of days, the Sea of Marmora would be opened to the fleets of the western allies, and passing into the Black Sea, they would be welcomed by the Rumanians and the people of the Ukraine, both mutinous against their oppressors. Supplied with arms, the Rumanians could join with Russians opposed to Bolshevist misrule and savagery in re-establishing in some measure an eastern front. It no longer appears to be a fantastical project.

So obvious is it that the military power of Germany is crumbling to ruin that the allies she claims in Finland and the Russian Baltic provinces must see their interest in rising against her. To provide garrisons was a great strain upon her war resources. It now becomes impossible. With the light of hope and redemption breaking for the Russian people, the horror of Bolshevism must be approaching its end. Germany at last knows what it is to have the whole civilized world in battle array against her. Her doom as an insatiate military power has sounded. Her policy of dominating the world is toppling like a house of cards.

\* \* \*

**October 19, 1918**

# CHARLES PROMISES A FEDERAL AUSTRIA

### *Manifesto Forecasts Autonomy for Each Nationality in the Empire*

VIENNA, Oct. 18 (via Basle)—Steps for the organization of Austria on a federalized basis were proclaimed by Emperor Charles today. The plan does not include the union of Austrian Poland with "the independent Polish State," the Emperor declared. The City of Trieste and the Trieste region will be treated separately, "in conformity with the desire of its population."

The manifesto is addressed "to my faithful Austrian peoples." It reads:

"Since I have ascended the throne I have tried to make it my duty to assure to all my peoples the peace so ardently desired and to point the way to the Austrian peoples of a prosperous development unhampered by obstacles which brutal force creates against intellectual and economic prosperity.

"The terrible struggles in the world war have thus far made the work of peace impossible. The heavy sacrifices of the war should assure to us an honorable peace, on the threshold of which, by the help of God, we are today.

"We must, therefore, undertake without delay the reorganization of our country on a natural, and, therefore, solid basis. Such a question demands that the desires of the Austrian peoples be harmonized and realized.

"I am decided to accomplish this work with the free collaboration of my peoples in the spirit and principles which our allied monarchs have adopted in their offer of peace.

"Austria must become, in conformity with the will of its people, a confederate State in which each nationality shall form on the territory which it occupies its own local autonomy.

"This does not mean that we are already envisaging the union of the Polish territories of Austria with the independent Polish State.

"The City of Trieste with all its surroundings shall, in conformity with the desire of its population, be treated separately."

Emperor Charles addressed the Austrian land and sea forces at the same time he issued his message to the people. In his order to the sailors and soldiers, the Emperor expressed firm confidence that the concord which has existed in the army and the navy until now will exist for the future for the well-being of the new confederated Austria.

LONDON, Oct. 18—The version of the manifesto of Emperor Charles as received here contains this concerning reconstruction of the Fatherland:

"This Reconstruction, which in no way affects the integrity of the countries under the holy crown of Hungary, will guarantee the independence of each individual national state. It will, however, also effectively protect common interests and will bring them to bear wherever community is a condition of vital importance for individual states.

"A union of all our forces will be especially necessary for a just and rightful solution of the great tasks resulting from the reaction of the war. Until legislation for the reconstruction is completed, existing institutions will remain in force unaltered. In order to safeguard the general interest of the country the Government is charged to prepare everything for the reconstruction of Austria.

The manifest appeals to the people to "co-operate in the great task with the national councils formed from the ranks of Reichsrat Deputies of each nationality, whose task it will be to assist the interests of the people to each other and toward my Government.

\*   \*   \*

**October 20, 1918**

# REFUSES AUSTRIA'S PLEA

### *President "Cannot Entertain Present Suggestions" for Peace*

#### CITES CHANGED SITUATION

### *Says Czechoslovaks, Jugoslavs, and Other Oppressed Peoples Must Have Independence*

#### MERE 'AUTONOMY' WON'T DO

### *Answer Expected to Further Unsettle Political Conditions in the Dual Monarchy*

Special to The New York Times

WASHINGTON, Oct. 19—President Wilson today replied to the Austro-Hungarian note of Oct. 7, and refused that Government's proposals for peace negotiations and an armistice. His refusal is based on events which have altered the attitude and responsibility of the American Government, and carries with it plain notice to the Vienna Government that mere "autonomy" for the Czechoslovaks, the Jugoslavs, and other oppressed peoples of the Dual Monarchy will no longer be regarded by the American Government and its allies as a basis for durable peace.

The Czechoslovaks yesterday issued their declaration of independence. The Jugoslavs have likewise declared their national aspiration for freedom. The Poles also want independence. The President insists that these peoples "and not he, shall be the judges of what action on the part of the Austro-Hungarian Government will satisfy their aspirations and their conception of their rights and destiny as members of the family of nations."

The President's answer to Austria-Hungary, by declaring that the Vienna Government must now deal with these peoples, and declaring that "mere autonomy" will no longer meet the situation, closes the door to further representations from the Dual Monarchy to the Allies for peace on any other basis. The action of the President, especially when viewed in the light of developments in Austria and Hungary, and in connection with the declared independence of the Czechoslovaks and the refusal of the Poles and the Jugoslavs to accept anything less than complete independence, makes it very plain that the American Government and its allies will themselves now be satisfied with nothing less than such a dissolution of the Dual Monarchy as will be necessary to give these oppressed peoples their freedom.

### Full Surrender Only

President Wilson's note is regarded as indicating that the Central Powers must surrender unconditionally to the terms laid down in his prior messages, and that the American and allied Governments do not intend to tolerate any compromise with Berlin and Vienna over the interpretation and application of the terms laid down. President Wilson, after a most careful consideration of the issues involved in the war, and following exchanges of views with the allied Governments, has very definite views regarding the application of his peace terms. The rapid progress of events is bringing out very positively these views and decisions.

In his recent note to Germany, to which the military and political masters at Berlin appear to be desperately endeavoring to find an answer short of complete surrender, the President gave his interpretation of that one of his terms which called for the destruction, or reduction to virtual impotency, of military autocracy. He interpreted this as meaning that the autocratic powers in the German Imperial Government should be destroyed as a condition precedent to peace.

It can be stated on the very highest authority that what the President meant in another of his terms, when he insisted that the wrong done by Germany to France, in 1871, "should be righted," means nothing less than the return by Germany to France of the lost provinces of Alsace and Lorraine. The President himself will soon make this point very plain in some public utterance.

In his note today to the Austrian Government, the President makes it plain that what he said on Jan. 8 last regarding granting opportunity for autonomous development to the oppressed peoples of Austria-Hungary must be interpreted not in the light of the situation as it stood then, but by the rule of altered events.

President Wilson's reply to the Austro-Hungarian Government is held to be well calculated to render the internal political situation in the Dual Monarchy untenable for the Hapsburgs. At the very time when the Austro-Hungarian Emperor is trying to save something out of the wreckage for his dynasty by laying plans for a fantastic federalized and autonomous makeshift for the oppressed peoples of the Dual Monarchy President Wilson sends to Vienna a note serving notice in advance that "antonomy" will not do.

The President informs the Austro-Hungarian Government that the United States Government has recognized the existence of a state of belligerency between the Czechoslovaks and the German and Austro-Hungarian Empires, and that the Czechoslovak National Council, of which Professor Masaryk,

now in Washington, is president, has been recognized as a "de facto belligerent Government clothed with proper authority to direct the military and political affairs of the Czechoslovaks." This means that the President has recognized the belligerency of the people of part of the Austro-Hungarian Empire as against the Central Powers. The President also takes his stand for full "freedom" for the Jugoslavs.

### Means All the Oppressed

When Secretary Lansing's attention was called to the fact that the note referred especially to the Czechoslovaks and Jugoslavs, without mentioning other nationalities oppressed by the Hapsburgs, he replied that the position of the United States was the same toward the latter as toward those subject peoples who were mentioned by name in the communication. Altogether, the dispatch of the note to Vienna is held to serve as a prompt and unmistakable reply to the action of Emperor Charles in proclaiming the federalization of the Austrian half of the empire, which, Secretary Lansing remarked, was a step taken too late.

No attempt was made in official circles today to explain the delay in sending the answer to the Vienna Governments note, which bore date of Oct. 7 and the official text of which was made public for the first time today. During the intervening days the President is believed to have exchanged views with the allied Governments, which have also recognized the aspirations of the Czechoslovaks and Jugoslavs for independence.

The assertion in the President's note that he cannot entertain "the present" suggestions of the Vienna Government is interpreted as meaning that before the President will think of talking peace or an armistice Austria-Hungary would have to accept, as a condition precedent, the new situation, calling for the independence of Bohemia Monrovia, and Slovakia, and also grant the Jugoslavs, comprising the Croats, Slovenes, and Serbs of Austria-Hungary, the right to determine their own condition and place in the society of nations.

It is expected here that the President's report will cause an outburst in Vienna, and especially in Budapest, the Hungarian capital, where there is evidence that the Hungarians are preparing the way for desertion of Emperor Charles, Austria, Germany and Turkey as the representatives of a lost and repudiated cause.

The President's recognition of the aspirations of the Czechoslovaks and Jugoslavs for independence means that both Austria and Hungary will lose territory and important peoples. It is expected that the ultimate effect of the President's decision, in association with the Allies, will be the reduction of Austria to a second-class power.

The formation of new and important States in Central Europe, which President Wilson's note assures, is expected to have a most vital bearing on the future peace of the world. These new free States will bar the road to the East, deprive Berlin of a former powerful ally, and rob Germany of paternal elements of autocratic power that might be used in a future war of conquest.

In its note of Oct. 7, to President Wilson, the Austro-Hungarian Government addressed itself to him as "His Lordship, the President of the United States." This is an unusual phrase for use in a diplomatic document. It was learned tonight that the Austro-Hungarian Government's communication was dispatched in French to the Swedish Foreign Office, which forwarded it in French to its Legation at Washington. The Swedish Legation delivered the communication in French. The translation was made in the State Department. The French word in the communication was "Monsigneur," an ecclesiastical tile, very difficult of translation. This word was translated as "His Lordship."

\* \* \*

**October 24, 1918**

# PEOPLES WIDENING SPLIT IN AUSTRIA

*Committee Takes Over Political Direction of Slovenes, Croatians, and Serbs*

## GERMANS FORM NEW STATE

*Teuton Deputies Begin Separatist Action—Andrassy May Be Hungarian Foreign Minister*

BASLE, Oct. 23—The Central Executive Committee elected on Oct. 5 by the National Council of Slovenes, Croatians, and Serbians at Agrani has issued a statement that the committee will at once assume the political direction of those nationalities, and declaring for the creation of a sovereign State on a democratic basis.

The following principles have been enunciated by the committee:

First, to bring about a reunion of all the Slovenes, Croatians, and Serbians on a racial basis, without reference to their present political frontiers.

Second, to create a sovereign State on a democratic basis.

Third, to see that the nationalities represented by the Council have a delegate at the peace conference.

The committee rejects the plan contained in the imperial manifesto for the settlement of nationalistic problems in Austria. It will guarantee the free development of all national majorities which may form a part of the State organized by it. Neighboring States will be assured free access to the sea, provided that they make no attempts on the constitutional rights of the State and on its territorial integrity.

The committee finally urges concord among all the nationalities in order to create a great national State.

### German Group Forms a State

The German-Austrian Deputies in the Austrian Reichsrath have formed an assembly for the purpose of conducting the affairs of the Germanic people in Austria and have issued a declaration announcing the creation of the "German State of Austria." Karl Seitz, leader of the German Socialists in

Austria, has been elected President of the new Assembly. The Deputies have announced their desire to bring about the autonomy of the Germans in Austria and to establish relations with other nations.

The Assembly has drawn up a resolution respecting the form of government of the territory occupied by Germans. The "German State of Austria" will seek access to the Adriatic Sea, in agreement with other nations. Pending the establishment of a constitution, according to this program the people will be represented by the Reichsrath Deputies constituted as a Provisional National Assembly.

This body will represent the Germans in Austria in negotiations for peace and will exercise legislative powers. The executive branch will consist of twenty members who will have power to contract State debts and administer interior affairs.

"We are able and must act in favor of peace," said Herr Seitz in taking the Presidency. "We must do all possible to lessen the misery of the German-Austrian people. The new German-Austria for which we will lay the foundation will be constituted in conformity with the free will expressed by the German-Austrian people."

Deputy Waldner in opening the Assembly announced that he had been commissioned by the German Deputies in the Reichsrath to convoke the Assembly as the representative Assembly of the German-Austrians. The organization would have the right of free speech and would proclaim solemnly an independent political State for German-Austria.

There has been evidence for some time that the German people in Austria, distrusting the wavering policy of the Austro-Hungarian Empire and fearing its dissolution on that it might draw away from Germany, were desirous of insuring their own close unity with the German Empire.

The German population in Austria is the largest of the many ethnical elements in the kingdom. The census of 1910 gave the German-speaking population as 9,950,000 out of a total of 28,325,000.

### Releasing Hungary and Poland

PARIS, Oct. 23—Measures are being taken to carry into effect the proclamation of Emperor Charles conferring independence on Hungary, says a Zurich, dispatch to the Petit Parisian. It is reported that Count Julius Andrassy will be Hungarian Foreign Minister.

Hitherto Austria and Hungary, although having separate cabinets for the administration of internal affairs, have had one minister in common for each of the departments of foreign affairs, war and finance.

Count Andrassy is a former Premier of Hungary, and has figured prominently in efforts toward peace.

AMSTERDAM, Oct. 23—The Austrian authorities in the part of Poland occupied by the Austrian Army have formally handed over the administration to Polish authorities, says a Vienna dispatch to the Vossiche Zeitung of Berlin.

The German and Austrian Governments early in the year agreed to give independence to former Russian Poland. The step now taken by Austria probably is in keeping with the agreement. Germany and Austria appointed a regency council of three members to rule Poland. The council, to which the cabinet is responsible, has had limited authority in Poland for several months.

The portion of Russian Poland occupied by Austrian troops probably is not very great. Most of Poland has been held by the Germans, Austrian occupation affecting only the territory nearest Galicia.

\* \* \*

October 27, 1918

## SERBIANS HAILED LIBERATING ARMY

*Lighted Cressets, Kneeled Praying Around Ikons, and Showered Troops with Flowers*

**IN DIRE NEED OF FOOD**

*Bulgarians, Although Defeated, Carried Off Grain Supplies— Retreated Shamefacedly*

VRANJE, Serbia, Oct. 7, (by Mail to Salonika, thence by Cable to the Serbian Press Bureau in Washington.)—I have now been in Vranje for forty-eight hours. The scene of the arrival of the troops was a most touching one. There were tears in the eyes of both the liberators and the population they had freed. Although I arrived in the town twenty-four hours after the advance guard, I had all the trouble in the world to escape being covered with flowers, as our Serbian Army and the armies of the Allies have been.

After having spent three years in the trenches on the summits of the Moglena Mountains, this town of 30,000 seems to me the most beautiful and the largest in the world. But it is Serbia, our beloved Serbia! The white houses in the brilliant sunshine seem wonderfully beautiful to me, in spite of the fact that there are everywhere visible traces of the Bulgarian robbers. The inhabitants, poor and humble though they be, barefoot old men, women, and children, are full of kindness, constancy, and patience. After having awaited our arrival for three long years, they are full of burning patriotism.

The army, both our own and that of our Allies, was received with indescribable enthusiasm. All, well-to-do or poor and humble, have come out, many in rags and barefoot, to welcome the army, their Serbian army. An old peasant woman, clothed in rags, went up to and old priest who had put on his best robe for the occasion and called out to him, "Father, long live liberty!"

An old wounded soldier who had been a prisoner and had been left behind by the Bulgarians, went to the commandant and asked that a rifle be given him to join the army in its advance. A rifle was given him, and he stuffed the cartridges into his pockets and began to hasten after the troops. But his pockets were full of holes, and the cartridges rolled all over the pavement.

I could cite a score of such incidents, but I must not forget one which touched the heart of every soldier. The day the army was awaited in the town the cressets in front of the holy Ikons in every house were lighted, and the old men and the women kneeled around them praying for the victory of the Serbian Army.

They were sure that our army would arrive as soon as it had beaten the Bulgarians and had traversed the Babuna Pass. The German soldiers in Vranje, who had begun to detest the Bulgarians for their cowardice, told the people confidentially that the Serbs would arrive in five days.

"We know the Bulgarians," they said, "and we also know how the Serbs march."

On hearing this the women began in secret to make Serbian flags for the reception of the troops.

I was at Skoplie, (Uskub,) the day an army of Bulgarians traversed the town. All of them were disarmed, but they had been allowed to keep their baggage wagons and riding horses. They were driving herds of goats, pigs, and oxen. Such was the "triumphal" passage of the Bulgarians through the town of Skoplie, in which they had created a reign of terror during the three years they had been masters of it. The inhabitants regarded these cowards with hatred, with which was mingled a feeling of joy that they were once more free. The Bulgarians had the air of bandits and robbers beaten and humiliated by their capture. Not a single one of them had the air of an honest man. All they had with them, except their uniforms of wretched quality, was booty stolen from Serbs.

Near Staro Negoritchane the First Serbian Army disarmed 20,000 Bulgarians. And this was not a surrender as the result of the signing of the military convention, but, on the contrary, they only gave up their arms when they saw the Serbian soldiers before them ready to open fire upon them. It was then that these "Prussians of the Balkans" threw away their arms and began a wild flight, like frightened sheep, toward the Bulgarian frontier.

The officers commanding the divisions and the regiments begged the Serbian military authorities to leave them a number of rifles so that they could defend themselves against their own soldiers, who, furious with rage, wanted to massacre them. The request was granted, and they were given a certain number of rifles.

Black misery reigns everywhere in Serbia, although, thank God, there are, for the time being at least, no epidemics. In Serbian Macedonia, when the Bulgarians, in the first days of our offensive, were forced to retire in haste, they had not time to carry off with them the depots of provisions. But more to the north, especially to the north of Skoplie, as they had two weeks, they were able to carry off nearly the whole of the food. The greater part of the last harvest was requisitioned, and the population left to starve. Our liberators should feel a certain shame that they have not been able to prevent this. Serbia enslaved, has received her liberty, but she still awaits bread!

\* \* \*

## SERBIA RESTORED

On the very day which saw the abject surrender of the "great Power" whose brutal and merciless attack on Serbia precipitated the war the Serbian Army re-entered Belgrade. With this reoccupation of the capital came the recovery of practically all the territory of the kingdom, and already millions of Serbs and their kinsmen are turning from the ruins of the Hapsburg monarchy to unite themselves with the state which carried the banner in the rational movement toward liberty.

Twice in the first six months of the war Austrian armies invaded Serbia; the second of these attacks even compelled the evacuation of Belgrade but eventually Serbia, alone and unaided, repelled them both. Not till a German General and German troops stiffened the third Austrian attack, with Bulgaria striking in the rear when the Serbian armies were occupied in the defense of the northern border, did the little kingdom collapse. At the moment its collapse seemed to be complete. Three years ago every foot of Serbian soil was in the hands of the enemy, the remnants of the army, survivors of the terrible retreat over the mountains, were grouped at Corfu, and the Government was the somewhat unwelcome guest of King Constantine. The losses of three wars and of the typhus epidemic had cut down the population; the starvation, executions and deportations which accompanied Bulgarian and Magyar rule reduced it still more. Nearly half of the population of the Serbia of July, 1914, is dead. There was some plausibility in the argument of the Bulgarian Premier who said last Summer that Serbia had ceased to exist.

But Serbia lived, in the remnants of an army with much to avenge, in a national consciousness that no misfortune could extinguish, and in the consciousness before the world of a just cause. It was the Serbian Army that broke the Bulgarian line in September and began the work which has just been completed. The unusual emotion which breaks out in the statement of the French War Office is fully justified:

> This army (the First Serbian Army) participated in all the fighting, marching without cease and without repose, always in contact with the enemy, whom it held by the throat, very often badly provisioned but knowing no fatigue and no hunger. It pushed ever forward by the will to conquer at any price.

It was what might be expected of the army whose recent achievements include Kumanovo and the Bregalnitza, Shabata Valjero, Monastir and Kaimakchalan. Behind the Serbian people lies a long and gloomy history of oppression, war, and hope deferred; but the spirit which has carried it through to victory is the spirit which may be relied on to inform the new unified kingdom of Serbs, Croats, and Slovenes which shall give the Southern Slav race the opportunity to live its own unhampered life.

\* \* \*

## CZECHS AND JUGOSLAVS ESTABLISH REPUBLICS

*Kramarz to be President at Prague and Pogacnik Installed at Agram*

GENEVA, Nov. 3—A new republic came into being when the conference here of Czechoslovak leaders ended yesterday. The constitution of the new government is patterned after that of the United States.

Dr. Karl Kramarz, former leader of the Hungarian Czech party, who spent several years in prison on a charge of treason, having been released in July, 1917, was chosen first President of the new republic.

A majority of the delegates left today for Prague where a Czechoslovak national parliament will be formed at once. The new government, a Vienna dispatch says, has placed in circulation stamps . . .

PARIS, Nov. 3—The new government of the Jugoslavs took the oath of office yesterday in the Cathedral at Agram, according to Vienna advices. The President of the new government is Josef Pogacnik, former Vice President of the Austrian Lower House.

The Slovenian National Assembly has taken charge of the government of Laibach: Carniola.

\* \* \*

## UNION OF THE JUGOSLAVS

The political problems involved in the task of rearranging the map of Europe so that the peoples will enjoy a better chance of self-development, and the dangers of a future war will be reduced to the minimum, are now before the allied nations. These problems are numerous and difficult, and they will not solve themselves any more than the war won itself. Their proper solution calls for the same qualities which brought the great alliance to victory over Germany—moderation, co-operation, willingness to sacrifice individual or local interests for the general good.

Already there is need for the application of these qualities in considering the question of the union of the Jugoslavs—a great and inspiring cause, for which many men have died on the battlefield and on the scaffold, and which now appears to be in some danger through the machinations of persons not well disposed to it and the ineptitude of some of its friends. A dispatch from Washington yesterday, evidently originating in a source anything but friendly to the unity of the Jugoslav peoples, strove to insinuate that the Declaration of Corfu, in which the Serbian Government and the Jugoslav Committee of London and Paris embodied the demand for a united kingdom of the Serbs, Croats, and Slovenes, with full equality for all races and religions, was only the pleasing hallucination of a few visionaries. So might the unity of Italy have seemed a few years before Magenta and Solferino, but it was accomplished: and the differences between the three branches of the Jugoslav race hardly offer more problems than the difference between the peoples of the Kingdom of Sardinia, and the Kingdom of the Two Sicilies.

This Washington dispatch suggests that the Croats and Slovenes have been cold toward the idea of unity; it would reduce the proposed Jugoslav kingdom merely to a greater Serbia, including Bosnia and Herzegovina, and the territories of Southern Hungary where the Serbs predominate. There are certain Serbian politicians, jealous of the intrusion of Croat and Slovene populations into the united kingdom, who would prefer this smaller State in which the dominant elements of the present Serbia could remain dominant; but the most progressive Serbian opinion is strongly in favor of union. Besides, what would become of the Croats and Slovenes?

The Slovenes took a popular vote on the question of union early in the Spring, and despite the Austrian police it showed an overwhelming majority in favor of it. In Croatia union sentiment is weakest, but the recently reported vote of the Croatian Diet in favor of staying with Hungary could hardly be accepted by itself as indicating the desire of the Croatian people. If Croatia should do this, the Slovenes, a million and a quarter Slavs would be left alone between Germans and Italians. And this suggestion leaves out Dalmatia, where Serbo-Croat population has a strong Slav consciousness.

Moreover, there is Montenegro King Nicholas, who delivered little indeed to win the war, now pours out congratulations "to our dear brother" Jugoslavs from their old and tried "and today happiest Jugoslav." He is an enthusiast for Jugoslavia, but a federated Jugoslavia, in which there will still be an independent throne for his sons. It is not without reason that two successive Montenegrin Premiers resigned because they favored Jugoslav unity and the King did not. The problem of union cannot be solved without renunciation; and it is to be hoped that its solution will not be made harder by the attitude of outsiders who have the strongest reason to sympathize with a people struggling toward liberty and unity.

*   *   *

December 2, 1918

## JUGOSLAVS DECLARE FOR FULL FREEDOM

*Sound Warning of War and Massacre Should Italy Encroach on the Adriatic*

### ASK WILSON FOR SUPPORT

*Mass Meeting, Made Up Mostly of American Citizens, Cheers Demand for a Plebiscite*

Nearly a thousand Americans of Jugoslav birth gathered last night in the Amsterdam Opera House at 340 West Forty-fourth Street and passed, amid wild shouting and cheering, resolutions "to combat with all means" what they call the "unjustified claims of certain Italian circles to Gorizia, Gradiska, Trleste, Dalmatia, Istria, and the eastern part of Carniola." Ilija Despot Viderske, a member of the Jugoslav National Council at Washington, made the claim that the Italians had spent millions in this country for propaganda but that, although the Jugoslavs had 10 millions they still had shoulders upon which to put their guns. Both he and Ignatius Kudek, publisher of the Glas Glasharoda in this city, declared that not a foot of the disputed territory would be taken from them by the Italians unless it were over the dead bodies of the Jugoslavs.

The meeting was held under the auspices of the Jugoslav Information Bureau, which was formed after the Signing of the armistice by the officers of all the Jugoslav, societies in New York City. Between the speeches an orchestra of girls played upon native instruments and a chorus of men sang Slovenian songs. Spiro Kuchich, head of the Information Bureau, presided.

The Jugoslavs contend that the disputed territories are inhabited by Jugoslavs to the extent of 85 per cent. of the total population. Especially is this so, they say, in the districts outside the cities: On these grounds they passed the following resolutions:

Whereas, We are in perfect accord with the just principles of our great president Wilson who has repeatedly stated and emphasized that the rights of any nation must not be curtailed, that no one can force upon it a ruler or government which it does not desire, and that States which already exist or will be created must represent national units, respectively peoples who of their own motives aspire for mutual unity, and

Whereas, We as citizens of the United States have during the war, sacrificed more than was demanded of us by our adopted country, be it either in blood or materially, and fully conscious of the unselfish principles and causes for which our great Republic entered into the war and which it so gloriously won, and

Whereas, We are fully prepared to give our lives and shed our blood for the safeguarding of the principles for which America fought, and

Whereas, We are firmly convinced that there will be no lasting peace unless the principle of the "Balkans to the Balkan peoples" be completely followed and as we fear that due to dissatisfaction and injustice another such conflagration, as raged over almost the whole world during the past four years will break out and

Whereas, Our hatred towards our former Government which enslaved us and denied as our rights is known to every one, it must be concluded that this very same hatred will be renewed against any Government or any nation which would endeavor to deprive the Jugoslav nation of its rights and territory; we

Resolve in our name and in the name of the free Jugoslav people in the old country to combat with all means the unjustified claims of certain Italian circles who support their claims with falsehoods when they state that Gorizia, Gradiska, Trieste, Dalmatia, Istria and the eastern part of Carniola are according to population and character Italian territory.

We respectfully petition our great and just President and the people of the United States to use their influence to have a plebiscite in all those lands which Italy wishes to annex in order that the inhabitants thereof may be permitted to make known their wishes as to whether they desire to be free and independent or whether they desire to be annexed to Italy.

The other provinces which the Jugoslavs hope to include in a republic, but about which there is no dispute, are Corinthia, Syria, Croatia, Slavonia, Bosnia, Herzegovina, Serbia, and Montenegro.

The principal speaker of the evening was Mr. Viderske who spoke in the Croatian language, and again and again aroused the audience to loud applause and shouts of approval. He outlined the bases of the claims which the Italians are making to territory, and declared that all of them were false, whether based upon historical, ethnological or geographical grounds. "For instance," he said, the Italians have to go back in history to the time of the Romans to prove their rights to territory along the Adriatic, but there is no validity in that because, even though Dalmatia was under foreign rule (that of Austria) for 400 years, she still retained Slav identity. The Italians say that half of Dalmatia is Italian, but that is a lie, for the statistics of the Austro-Hungaian Government proved that only 2 per cent were Italian." At this point there came shrill cries from the audience of "Down with the Italians!" and the crowd applauded lustily. "We have absolute confidence in President Wilson," continued the speaker, "for we know that with him our cause is safe. We are here now to tell him the truth of the situation, and the truth is that the Italians will know it with a vengeance if they take from us one foot of our territory. The land of the Jugoslav is living and will yet live. If the enemy should succeed in grabbing from us any land that is rightfully ours, inevitably another war will come. There will be another St. Bartholomew's massacre.

"Italy has pointed out that there are factions among the Croatians, and, of course, that is true, for there are factions among all peoples, but the Italians cannot use that as an excuse for occupation of our territory by allied troops.

"We should respect the American flag, the flag of the country that has received us so hospitably," said the speakers, and the audience heartily assented. "We have confidence in American, because she will protect our rights."

Mr. Kudek said that the Jugoslav republic was formed before the armistice was signed, and that its formation was primarily the cause of the Austrian collapse. He maintained that as soon as the republic was formed members of the National Council arranged to go to Paris to inform the Allies of the action that had been taken, but on their way through Italy they were arrested by the Italian authorities and interned, to be released only upon the protest of Great Britain.

A collection was taken for the promotion of the cause, and it was announced that the money received at the meeting and from outside sources had already reached $7,000.

\* \* \*

**December 3, 1918**

## MONTENEGRIN KING FORMALLY DEPOSED

*Family of Nicholas I. Ousted From Succession—Union with Serbia Sought*

LONDON, Dec. 2—King Nicholas of Montenegro has been deposed by the Skupshtina, the Montenegrin National Assembly, according to a message received here from Prague today.

The dispatch was sent from Prague by the Czechslovak Press Bureau by way of Copenhagen. It says that the Skupshtina voted the deposition on Friday last and declared for a union of Montenegro with Serbia under King Peter.

The family of the Montenegrin King was included in the act of deposition.

Nicholas I has been on the Montenegrin throne since Aug. 1860. He was born in 1841, and his title was that of Prince until August, 1910, when, on the occasion of the fiftieth anniversary of his accession, the National Assembly proclaimed him King.

He is the father of three sons and five daughters. His second daughter is married to Grand Duke Nicholas Nicholaievitch, former commander of the Russian armies, and his third daughter to King Victor Emmanuel of Italy.

The present Montenegrin dynasty, that of Petrovitch Njegosh, has been on the throne since 1697.

King Nicholas, his family, and his Government fled from Montenegro in December, 1915, when the country was overrun by Austro-Germans. Since that time he has been in France and the Montenegrin Government has been at Neilly-sur-Seine.

On Nov. 8, in an interview with The Associated Press, King Nicholas declared himself in favor of a union of Montenegro with the new State of Jugoslavia, with each component State independent as to religion, education, and territorial integrity.

\* \* \*

## WANT ITALY TO QUIT JUGOSLAV TERRITORY

### Complaint Made That Far More Is Occupied Than the Armistice Terms Provided For

WASHINGTON, Dec. 8—Formal notice has been given to the American Government of the purpose of Serbs, Croats, and Slovenes, formerly held by the Austro-Hungarian Government, to unite with the Kingdom of Serbia in a single Jugoslavic State and to insist upon the evacuation of Jugoslav territory now occupied by Italy.

Official texts were presented to the State Department of addresses by Prince Regent Alexander of Serbia and a delegation of twenty-seven members from the National Council of Zagreb, delivered at Belgrade Dec. 1. The Prince Regent accepted the proposal of the Zagreb Council for union under a Parliamentary Government, the delegation to sit provisionally at Belgrade as representatives of their people until a Constituent Assembly could be held within six months after the conclusion of peace.

After submitting the proposal for union, the Zagreb delegation said:

"We are profoundly grieved to be obliged to place on record that a great part of our natural soil is occupied by the troops of the Kingdom of Italy, which is allied with the powers of the Entente, and with which we desire to live in friendly relations, but we cannot recognize the opportuneness of any treaty, not even that of London, the virtue of which is in violation of the principles of nationality.

"We desire to draw the attention of your Royal Highness to the fact that the extent of the Italian occupation greatly exceeds the limits and regions foreseen in the clauses of the armistice concluded with the Commander in Chief of the Austro-Hungarian Army."

The Prince Regent in his address said: "The Government will have as its first duty to trace together with you the ethnographical frontiers of our entire nation. I have the right to hope that our great allies will judiciously appreciate our point of view, for it corresponds to the principles they have themselves proclaimed, and for which they have poured out so much blood. I further hope that this point of view will also be admitted by the Italian Government."

\* \* \*

## PROCLAIMS UNION OF ALL RUMANIANS

### Action of Transylvanian National Assembly Celebrated at Gyula-Fehervar

### SOCIALIST PARTY WON OVER

### Rumanian Troops Expected to Occupy at Once Twenty-six Provinces of Hungary

Copyright, 1918, by The New York Times Company
Special Cable to The New York Times
BERNE, Dec. 11—A great festival of Transylvanian Rumanians was held at Gyula Fehervar, or Klausenburg, north of Hermanstadt, on Dec. 1, when the National Assembly solemnly proclaimed the union of Transylvania with Rumania. According to Magyar papers a crowd of 100,000 people in all sorts of picturesque costumes filled the military training ground and enthusiastically acclaimed the speeches of the national leaders. Perfect order was maintained by the National Guard and armed peasants and there was no drunkenness.

The National Assembly of 200 members met in the offices of the Casino, among the guests being a Rumanian General and French airmen. National Leader Pop presided. A resolution was unanimously passed declaring the union of all Rumanian people in all the territories they inhabit, and affirming the inalienable right of Rumanians to all the Banat Territory between Murin Theiss and the Danube. Full liberties are to be guaranteed to all national minorities in respect to language and administration.

Other points of the declaration are universal suffrage, religious equality, radical reform of labor legislation, and the formation of a National Council with full authority to represent the nation internally and externally during the preliminary negotiations.

The Socialists said they would vote for the union only on condition that the Rumanian Kingdom was democratized but on hearing from Ernest Cogu, who had just arrived from Bucharest, that universal suffrage and land reform were guaranteed in Rumania, the Socialists withdrew their opposition, and the union was voted unanimously amid great cheering. The Socialist leader Sarmanka, declared that the Socialists would not forsake their Magyar brothers in their class struggle, but nationals must be with their own people. The National Council was elected, among its members being Octavian Goga and Lucacis, who is now in Paris.

A Cabinet was formed, with Pop as Premier and Foreign Minister Manin Minister of the Interior and War and Goldis Minister of Religion and Education.

The seat of the Government for the present is Hermannstadt. Later it will possibly be Klausenburg. It is expected that Rumanian troops will occupy within the next fortnight twenty-six Hungarian provinces claimed by the Rumanians.

Negotiations between the Magyar Government and the Czechoslovak Envoy, Hodja, have been interrupted owing to the issue in the Prague press of a communique stating that Hodja is not empowered to act as plenipotentiary, but only to liquidate all relations between the Budapest Government and the Slovak Nation. Hodja states that this is probably a misunderstanding caused by the fact that his interviews have reached Prague before his official reports. He will explain everything to President Masaryk when he arrives.

### KRAMARZ TELLS CZECH AIM
#### Premier Outlines New Republic's Plans for Future

PRAGUE, Dec. 8 (Associated Press)—"There are people who believe the world must come to an end because the Austrian and German empires no more exist, but I know we will all be happier, and especially you in America. It is the first time in the history of nations that generosity has ever conquered selfishness, and when the news came to me within my prison walls that America had entered the war, I was unable to believe it," said Dr. Karl Kramars, Premier of Czechoslovakia, to a representative of The Associated Press today.

Dr. Kramarz for many years fought for the rights of the Czech people. He was arrested at Prague on July 1, 1915, and, following his trial at Vienna, was sentenced to death. King Alfonse of Spain appealed in his behalf and the death sentence was commuted to fifteen years' imprisonment. Dr. Kramarz was released under Emperor Charles's amnesty proclamation on July 14, 1917. He was named Premier of Czechoslovakia on Nov. 19 last.

"Our sole ambition is to live peacefully and prosperously and to become a strong friend of the Entente against the Germans," Dr. Kramarz continued. "It is probable that Germany will remain a menace, since it is impossible to destroy such a strong nationality. As for our political future, we do not see a way to tie up Austrians or Hungarians.

"It is certain that we will try to maintain commercial relations with the Jugoslavs and the Rumanians. Regarding the tariff, it is certain we must maintain a protective wall against Germany or our industries will be ruined.

"We also desire to establish the frontiers of ancient Bohemia. However, we will be fairer with the Germans than they were with us. We will not oppress those within our borders. We will give them every liberty, their own schools and language, but the Government must be ours."

\*    \*    \*

December 15, 1918

## THE ADRIATIC PUZZLE CONFLICTING CLAIMS

One of the most serious danger points in European international relations at present is the conflict between Italians and Jugoslavs regarding the proper boundary between the two nations east of the Adriatic. The antipathy between the two races in the Dual Monarchy was fostered by Austro-Hungarian agents before the war, and such agents have undoubtedly had a large part in disturbing the good relations which were attained for a short time last year but the conflict goes further than that.

The Treaty of London in April, 1915, on the basis of which Italy entered the war, allotted to Italy, if she could get it, the annexation of Austrian territory east of the Adriatic, including all of Gorizia-Gradisca and Istria, with the City of Trieste, together with the coastal province of Dalmatia as far as a line just north of Spalato, and most of the Dalmation Islands. (See map.) In this region there were several hundred thousand Italians and nearly a million Jugoslavs-Slovenes and Croats in Istria and Gorisia-Gradisca, Serbo-Croats in Dalmatia. Each side claims that the Austrian census figures are falsified in favor of the other, and there is dispute as to geographical distribution of the races. Generally, however, it may be said that the Italian population predominates in the western part of Gorizia-Gradisca and Istria, and in several of the chief seaports. The population of the back country and of the islands is almost wholly Slav.

Knowledge of the Italian aspirations excited many Jugoslav troops in the Austro-Hungarian Army to fight willingly against the Italians; but many thousands of them, placed against the Russians or Serbs, surrendered without fighting and were presently formed into Jugoslav legions which fought hard in the allied armies. The fact that the Serbian people were to be included in the proposed unified State of Jugoslavia, and that they were deeply interested in the welfare of all parts of the race, made the question very largely one between two allies. A large section of the liberal Italian press, most notably the Corriere della Sera of Milan, protested against the annexation program whose most active official supporter was the Foreign Minister, Baron Sydney Sonnino; and when Trotzky published the text of the London treaty last Winter further protests followed.

This favored the movement toward cooperation between the two nations, which would divide the coast of the Adriatic between them in the event of the defeat of Austria-Hungary; it was argued by many of their leaders that they were natural allies, threatened by the common Austro-Hungarian danger. So, after the Italian defeat at Caporetto an agreement was signed between Dr. Ante Trumbitch, President of the Jugoslav Committee, and Andrea della Torre, a well-known Italian journalist representing the elements friendly to the Jugoslavs, which suggested as a solution that territorial questions should be settled on the basis of self-determination, "with due regard to the vital interests of the two peoples." and that full rights should be granted by each race to minorities of the other that might be included within its borders. This agreement was reaffirmed at the Congress of Oppressed Nationalties held at Rome last April, which though not official so far as the Italian Government was concerned, was held under the Presidency of Premier Orlando and was generally regarded as having at least semi-official standing.

There was soon a reaction, however. Last Summer the Italian press was engaged in a sharp controversy over the relations with the Jugoslavs, most of the liberal papers supporting Premier Orlando and Professor Nitti the Minister of Finance

Shaded Area Represents Extreme Jugoslav Claims. Black Line Is Limit of Italian Claims.

who favored a policy of conciliation with the Jugoslavs, while the conservative papers backed up Sonnino, whose influence, it was claimed, was manifested in several ways opposed to Jugoslav aspirations. And the Treaty of Osden was never formally repudiated by the Italian Government.

This Fall, insurrections broke out in the Jugoslav country, as in the rest of Austria, and these insurrections undoubtedly made somewhat easier the task of the Italian Army in its overwhelming final victory over the Austrians in October and November. There promptly developed on both sides, however, an unwillingness to admit that there was glory enough for all or territory enough for all. The armistice concluded with the Austro-Hungarian Government just as that Government was passing out of existence gave the Italians the right to occupy territory up to a line practically identical with that marked off for Italian annexation in the Treaty of London. This caused very bitter feeling among the Jugoslavs, who protested further

that the military occupation in some places was followed by the introduction of Italian civil administration.

Italian troops also occupied Fiume and Cattaro, seaports not included in the London treaty: it was said, however, that the occupation of Fiume had been requested by the Italian population. Another sore point was the Austro-Hungarian fleet, manned chiefly by Jugoslavs from the Dalmatian islands. In the collapse of Austria coincident with the final Italian victory on the Piave the sailors revolted and turned over the fleet to the Jugoslav National Council, newly chosen as the Provisional Government of the Jugoslav provinces pending ultimate union with Serbia and Montenegro. The armistice terms, however, provided that the fleet must be surrendered. The Jugoslavs expressed their willingness to surrender the fleet provisionally to Americans or to a joint allied commission, and some of their leaders asked for American instead of Italian occupation of the allied territory.

However, the fleet was surrendered without trouble, and to an allied force under Italian command, but including representatives of the other navies. Apparently also the army of occupation is to include contingents from all the Allies, though the command and the major portion of the troops are Italian, for the General Staff has announced that of the American troops in Italy some will be stationed in Trieste, some in Fiume, and some in Cattaro pending the final settlement.

The feeling, however, continues very bitter, the Jugoslavs contending that the Italians were willing to compromise when their armies had just been defeated at Caporetto, but insisted on extreme demands after their troops had won great victories. The Italians, on the other hand, assert that the victories of the Italian Army are chiefly responsible for the liberation of the Jugoslavs and object to the attitude of the latter as ungrateful.

The above statement is an attempt to present an impartial summary of the principal events in the controversy which is now a serious menace to peace on the Adriatic. Below are presented arguments for each side in the case, presented by official representatives of the two nations.

## ITALIAN CLAIMS

### By DR. FELICE FERRERO
*Director of the Italian Bureau of Information*

We are all agreed that the era of secret diplomacy has come to an end; let us therefore speak with complete frankness and perfect candor. Is there a question of the Adriatic? I think not.

Italy might, to begin with, raise two points of order and ask that the whole subject be ruled out without further talk:

First, the Treaty of London. Italy entered the war with a certain contract. She has faithfully performed her part of it, persisting through heavy sacrifices of blood and money when the house seemed to be falling around the ears of the Allies, and finally clinching the victory with her unrivaled success of a little more than a month ago. What honest man, which honest nation, would now dare come out and say, "You did your part, it is true, but conditions have changed and we are not going to do ours"?

Second, the military success. Let us not forget that when the Austrian commander surrendered on the battlefield to the Italian commander he did not surrender the Austrian Army, because the Austrian Army had passed, with its complete equipment, into the possession of the Italian Army. He surrendered the Austrian Empire. Italy has, therefore, much to say as to what disposition should be made of the Austrian Empire. Nothing could have prevented or could prevent her armies from marching anywhere they saw fit and occupying whatever land they considered advisable in the Austrian Empire. The very fact that Italy was content with the lands assigned to her by the Treaty of London is a sign of very high moderation.

But let us waive the two points of order and discuss the matter if it seems useful to point out the justice and reasonableness of Italy's claims.

It is rather unfortunate that a not indifferent part of the Austrian Army which was made prisoner was composed of Croatians, a part possibly larger than it ought to have been according to the proportions of the Austrian populations. It is also unfortunate that the Croatians should have distinguished themselves for ferocity in the treatment of the occupied lands in Italy and of the wounded. It is also unfortunate that among the prisoners taken by the Italians there should have been some Bosnians who disported necklaces made of ears cut off from fallen Italian soldiers—dead, we hope—and strung on a string. I am sure that Italy will forgive this, even though it may be hard to forget and be ready to be quite fair and neighborly to the young nation that is trying to rise to the east of her. These are, however, a few of several reasons why it would be advisable for the Jugloslavs to consider the situation and the claims of Italy with moderation and good-will.

These claims are based on two very solid causes. The first one is of a military nature. If the Italian Adriatic coast is to be made safe against outside aggression, only the continued possession of the points occupied on the eastern coast can insure this end. We do not need to expand on the labor of ceaseless application and devotion that was necessary for the Italian Navy to protect the Adriatic against aggression from the Austrian fleet. Even so, it could not always prevent bombardments of open towns and slaughter of innocent people. The fact is so evident that the War Council at Versailles, which passed upon the conditions of armistice dictated by the Italian commander to the Austrian commander, recognised the necessity of the occupation of the Adriatic lands as a protection against the possibility of the renewal of hostilities, and the consent of the council was in this unanimous, including the votes of the American military representatives.

It might be said that the Jugoslav State will be a small, weak State, of no danger to Italy, and that, besides, if a League of Nations is formed there will not be any need of military action of any kind. To which it might be objected that the Jugoslav nation is a small nation, it is true, but for the very reason that it is small is subject to outside influences, the nature of which is for the present entirely unforeseeable. Nor do we know what the future may bring in the way of the readjustment of States and nationalities in Eastern Europe. Italy cannot run again the risk of anxious years, as she has gone through for the last generation, with her frontiers open to a neighbor. And as for the League of Nations, that may come or may not. For the moment it is not here and must be left out of the reckoning.

Lastly, we come to the question of nationality, which I left until the end as it is a most delicate one and a rather unpleasant one to deal with in some details. The Croatians claim that the Adriatic coast is a Slavic country. This is plainly not true. What they can say with fairness of the Adriatic coast is that it is a country of mixed nationalities of which the Slavic element is prevalent in some parts and the Italian in others. Under the circumstances we cannot assign those countries to either Italy or Jugoslav without including within the limits of such lands very strong minorities of a foreign population. Now, which of the two has a right to be considered first?—you see I am speaking plainly. Let me quote from the "Frontiers of Language and Nationality in Europe" by L. Dominian, published for the American Geographical Society:

"Linguistically the eastern shore of the Adriatic is Serbian or Albanian; but the history of this coastal land is Italian in spite of the census returns. . . . The period of its subjection to Venice is one of the most brilliant in its history; all the civilization it received came from the west. The fact is that the Italian element has always been predominant. . . . Dalmatia has always greeted Italian thought as the heritage of Rome and Venice."

Let me also state that in Istria, where the population in the interior is in majority Slav, the Italian element pays five-sixths of the rent tax, three-quarters of the industrial tax, four-fifths of the income tax.

Let us not forget that Fiume, with a population 65 per cent Italian, has absolutely refused to remain under Croatian rule and has proclaimed its annexation to Italy.

Do these facts not mean anything? We are here in the presence of two races of vastly different accomplishments, of which one, the race of slower development, has been put in control of the other one, in many places, through a policy of violence of the Austrian central authority. Let me say here that while the fact that the Slavic race is the race of lower development—a self-evident fact—by saying this I do not in this way mean to reflect upon it. It may be due to the lack of opportunities more than to any other reason that the Slavic races of the Balkans are behind in the ways of civilization, or it may be due to other causes; I am not trying to judge. I am taking the fact as it is. Can any one without a feeling of partisanship actually say that the better developed race must go under the rule of the less developed race whether they desire it or not, simply because the less developed race happens to be half plus one of the population? And I leave out of consideration here the point barely touched upon of how the less developed population happened to become the majority, which is of itself a chapter that would make very interesting reading as an illustration of the political methods of the Austrian Government in dealing with its composite makeup. The passages quoted from the book by Dominian are quite eloquent on this point.

I have all through this article purposely used the word Croatian instead of Jugoslav, because the word Jugoslav is a very recent creation by which it is attempted to cover a state of affairs that is not at all promising for the young Balkanic nation. Within my recent recollections as a newspaper man there is that of a sojourn in Austria at a very troublous time, when most of the nationalities of Austria were apparently in arms against one another. At that time we used to hear a great deal, in Austria about a Pan Serbian movement and a Pan Croatian movement, each one striving to get control of the Serbo-Croatian race, one for the aggrandisement of Serbia the other one for the aggrandisement of Austria, and therefore strongly antagonistic to each other. As far as we can judge from the surface, the word Jugoslav is a new word for the Pan Serbian movement, and the recent events, with the formation of a republic at Lalbach (Lublana) and another one at Agram, and Montenegro insisting on its independence seem to prove that the unity of a Serbo-Croatian State is still to be attained. It is true that we hear from Paris that all differences have been settled and the Croatians have accepted the idea of joining Serbia, but whether this agreement will be permanent or not no one can say, although every one wishes it. This state of affairs, however, means without possibility of contradiction that it would be in the best interests of the Jugoslavs to be in the most friendly relations possible with Italy. In a place like the Balkan peninsula, or, in fact, with a political arrangement of Balkanic character extended to most of Central Europe, the friendship of one of the Great Powers would, I should think, be a very valuable asset for a small state like Jugoslavia, and Italy, I doubt not, is quite willing to extend a friendly hand to its weaker neighbor. All that is necessary for this is that the Jugoslavs show on their part a suitable amount of good will and the modesty that is requisite as a people half of which was, until a few days ago, one of the strongest supports of our common enemy.

It is plain that no satisfactory arrangement can be reached in the Adriatic except by an amicable and voluntary agreement of the interested populations, if such a thing is possible. Italy has already shown her willingness to be generous to the neighboring Slavs by allowing them to retain all the coast of Dalmatia from Spalato down to Cattaro—Spalato, the best port of Dalmatia, and a city where the Croatians for many years past have entirely ignored the formal pledge of the Austrian Government to maintain Italian schools. Italy was even willing to leave out of her claims the Italian city of Fiume, and it is no fault of hers if the Fiumans refused to try the experiment of a straight Croatian domination. Now it is the turn of the Jugoslavs to show their willingness by recognising the justice and reasonableness of Italian claims.

I know there are in this city some Jugoslav jingoes of the fire-eater brand who have expressed their intention "to throw the Italians out into the sea by force of arms if they attempt to enter Trieste." As luck would have it, inside of two weeks of the great threat the Austrian Army had disappeared, and the King of Italy was entering Trieste amidst great scenes of enthusiasm, and now the Italian Government is sharing the scanty rations of the Italian people with all the Slavs of Istria and Dalmatia, delivering them food by airplanes, so that they may not suffer. This ought to be a lesson for nationalists. Suppose we pair off the Jugoslav nationalists with the Italian nationalists who would like to occupy all the coast of Croatia, all of Dalmatia, and several other things besides, and give both a leave of absence. Then we can sit down and settle the matter in the light of reason and mutual concession, sealing the pact with a handshake for the good of us all.

### JUGOSLAV CLAIMS

#### By Dr. BOGUMIL VOSNJAK
*Member of the Jugoslav Committee*

Those parts of the territory of the former Illyrian kingdom partially inhabited by Italians include the town of Trieste, with its territory, and the counties of Gorica-Gradiska and Istria.

An examination of the figures of the official statistics will show that the majority of the population in these districts is Jugoslav. According to the latest census, that taken in 1910, the littoral is inhabited by 437,385 Slavs and only 354,495 Italians. In Gorica-Gradiska there is a majority of 154,750 Jugoslavs opposed to a minority of 90,119 Italians. In Istria the Jugoslavs number 220,382 and the Italians only 215,525. It is only in Trieste that the Italians are in a minority. The town has 118, 959 Italian and 60,074 Jugoslav inhabitants.

Official statistics distinctly tend to understate the true number of the Slavs in favor of that of the Italians. The Italians, although well aware that the result of every census is calculated to the detriment of the Slavs, maintain that the Government, in taking the census, magnifies the number of the Slavs. Nothing could be further from the truth than such a statement. If the Government were to deal justly, it would order a census in which not only the language of daily intercourse but the native tongue of the individual would be taken into account, and the Italians would probably be far from satisfied with the result of a census taken on such just and reasonable lines.

In the number of votes recorded in the Reichsrat elections for the Slovene candidate, however, we possess an excellent means of checking whether the results of the census are false or accurate. As the vote for the Reichsrat is universal and direct, it is an easy matter to obtain the statistics of the voting.

In the Reichsrat elections of 1911 the Slovene Nationalist Party polled a total of 10,859 votes in the town and territory of Trieste, and the Italian Nationalist candidates a total of 14,337 votes. In the City of Trieste the Italians polled 13,145 votes (or 10 per cent.) and the Jugoslavs 3,647 votes, (or 30 per cent.) In the territory of Trieste the Jugoslavs polled 5,906 votes (or 81 per cent.) and the Italians only 1,192, (or 19 per cent.)

Apart from Trieste there are two other towns in the Illyrian littoral where the struggle between Italians and Jugoslavs is exceedingly keen. These are the towns of Gorica and Pola. In Gorica, which lies in Slav territory, 10,792 Jugoslavs are opposed to 14,812 Italians. The latter are, however scarcely in an absolute majority today, because the town has several thousand German inhabitants as well. During the last elections for the Viennese Parliament, 1911, the Italian candidate polled in Gorica 1,792 votes and the Jugoslav candidate 1,166 votes. In Pola the elections yielded a similar result. The Jugoslav candidate polled 2,428 votes and the Italian candidate 3,877. According to the official census Pola has 15,931 Jugoslav, 29,108 Italian and 9,046 German inhabitants.

In several elections shortly before the war the German-Austrian votes supported the Italian candidates. The true preserver of the Italian element in the littoral had been the Austrian Government, which by means of an anti-democratic electoral system prevented the Italians from being politically swamped.

There is something very true and significant in the dictum that the Italian element represents the buttons on the Slav coat. The great mass of the rural population is Slav. These Slav masses were neglected, not only under the Venetians, but even more so under the political tyranny of the Italian "signori." The Slavs were given no schools.

The problems of Trieste and the Slovene littoral are only part of the general problem of the Adriatic. A closer analysis soon reveals that it is a mistake to try to keep these two problems separate, as people unfortunately sometimes attempt to do, Italy's endeavor to make the Adriatic into a mare clausum is only an extension of Italy's aspirations to the littoral.

Most certainly Italy possesses important economic interests in the Aegean and in Asia Minor but surely it is not necessary for her to close a whole sea in order to have a base for military operations. The great colonial peoples of the West, such as the English, have acted quite differently. First, the trader entered the country, then the soldier and the official.

The strategic argument advanced by Italy shows even less sound common sense. In order to protect the east coast of Italy, the greater part of the Dalmatian coast is to become Italian, and Split (Spalato) and Dubrovnik (Ragusa) are to lie within range of Italian guns. The foundation upon which this argument rests is as weak as that other, demanding that Italy should occupy the littoral for strategic reasons. But a glance at an orographic map will suffice to show that the Illyrian coast-land is not separated from the orographic system of the Balkans, the Loca (Isonso) is the real natural frontier of the Balkans.

It is always best to be frank. Let the Italians confess that they need the sole control over the Adriatic in order to economically dominate the Jugoslav State of the future. Jugoslavia is to be a dumping ground for Italian industry and Italian trade is to have the monopoly in the Balkans, so that the development of a native industry may be checked from the very outset. Perhaps they even think of directing the stream of Italian emigration toward the Balkans and dotting the country with Italian colonies.

It is never wise to tell tales out of school. An Italian political economist, Mario Alberti by name, has explained why Italy must be sole mistress of the Adriatic. If Italy possesses the Adriatic it will be the leading power in the Meditteranean and other worlds. Italy requires the Adriatic as an Italian lake, in order to obtain the hegemony in the Meditteranean.

The Convention, a secret diplomatic treaty, whereby the Adriatic was handed over to Italy, was concluded at a time when (the Spring of 1915) the Russian front (in Poland) had already begun to give way. It was extorted from Russia at the moment of a national and military catastrophe. But shall a treaty by which the fate of a million human beings is decided not be amenable to the same laws which apply to every ordinary private contract?

Is it not an immensurable tragedy that by the signature under a secret treaty more than a million human beings are to be annexed against their will, and the Jugoslav State be exposed to a position of constant economic and political peril? Do not these considerations bring us back to the idea that secret diplomatic treaties are a disease in politics. Can

European and American democracy permit this abrogation of the sovereign rights of nations?

The resolution of the Rome congress of oppressed nationalities of Austria-Hungary in April, 1918, had far-reaching results, as their paramount ideas have been taken as leading principles of the policy of the American Government toward Austria-Hungary. This point of the Rome resolution is expressed in the statement of Secretary Lansing, in which the Czechoslovaks and Jogoslavs have been granted the right to establish independent commonwealths.

It is a wrong assertion, which appears only too often in the American press, that the Rome congress finally settled the future boundary between Italy and the Jugoslavs. Both parties laid down only the general principles which will conduct them when peace comes. "They undertake to settle particular territorial controversies amicably and in the interest of future good and sincere relations between the two peoples on the basis of nationality and the right of peoples to decide their own destiny, in such a way as not to damage the vital interests of the two nations which shall be defined at the moment of peace. The two leading principles are here those of nationality and those of self-determination. Both imply the plebiscite as the way to ascertain the will of the people of a country. Every other assertion, for instance that behind the Rome resolution is still another secret agreement about the settlement of territorial claims, is absolutely incorrect. The question of territorial settlement has not yet been decided in the discussions between the committee and representatives of Italian public opinion, but only general principles have been laid down.

Prime Minister Orlando accepted the Rome resolution, every man was convinced he did it in the name of the Italian Government. Nevertheless Sonnino, the Foreign Secretary, remained a champion of the old Italian policy. The London treaty is by Italy still considered valid and the Italian Government insists that this treaty has to be the basis of the settlement.

In spite of the spirit and letter of the Rome resolution, the Austro-Italian armistice creates a line of occupation which is the same as the London treaty: It seems that allied and American occupation changed into an Italian occupation. The Italians occupied places beyond the line of the armistice. This action, first of all the occupation of Reka, (Fiume,) ancient historical Croatian territory, stirred up the population to the utmost; and we do not yet know what happened in the Jugoslav cities of the eastern shores of the Adriatic.

Serious difficulties were created also by the naval terms of the armistice concluded with the military agents of the Austro-Hungarian Government which no longer existed. Before the armistice was concluded the Jugoslav Government in Zagreb (Agram) took possession of the Austro-Hungarian fleet and has to be considered as its legal commander.

This amazing imbroglio has been created by the policy of the London treaty, which is the negation of the principle of nationality and self-determination.

But the Jugoslav program is clear and simple. The unique, fair and just solution of the Jugoslav-Italian problem in Gorica-Gradiska, Trieste, and Istria is a plebiscite taken by the authorities of the United States during the occupation of these countries by the American Army.

\*   \*   \*

December 26, 1918

## JUGOSLAV CLAIMS SET FORTH IN DETAIL

*They Include Gorizia, Trieste, Istria, and Dalmatia, National Council Says*

**WILL NOT ACCEPT LESS**

*Settlement by Force Would Result In Far-Reaching Future Troubles, It Is Declared*

Special to The New York Times
WASHINGTON, Dec. 25—A statement was issued at the headquarters of the Jugoslav National Council today in which it is asserted that the Allies had seriously contemplated according recognition to Jugoslavia but that this had been delayed by the "violent opposition of Italy."

"The dissolution of the Austrian Empire," the statement issued by the council says, "and the formation of new independent States in its stead of which Czechoslovakia and Jugoslavia have already assumed definite lines, has to a great extent given prominence to the question, 'who is to represent the former empire at the Peace Conference'?

"The two formerly dominant races of Austria-Hungary, the Germans and the Magyars, have been abandoned by all their subject races and have shrunk to a negligible minority. It is out of the question to have them representing all the different peoples formerly under their sway. There is no doubt that an opportunity must be given to the Czechoslovaks, Jugoslavs. Poles, and Rumanians to bring their wishes and claims directly and by themselves before the Peace Conference.

"But there is some reluctance on the part of the Allies. These new States, excepting Czechoslovakia, have not been recognized as yet by the Allies. The recognition of Jugoslavia, which was seriously contemplated, has until now been delayed by Italy's violent opposition. But recently such momentous events have taken place in the development of the new Jugoslav State that the Jugoslav representation at the Peace Conference may be considered as assured.

"From now on the Jugoslavs of former Austria-Hungary do not appear as a single political organization. They have proclaimed and organized a common State with Serbia and Montenegro—two of the recognized allies—and the functions of this new State began the moment when a common Ministry was formed. The Vice Premier and the Foreign Minister in this new Ministry are Jugoslavs from former Austria-Hungary. Dr. Trumbich, the new Foreign Minister does not represent the Jugoslavs from Austria-Hungary only, but Serbia as well. To ban the Jugoslavs from the Peace Conference would mean to ban Serbia and Montenegro also. The unification of all the Jugoslavs in one single State means, of course, the cessation of a separate Serbian or Montenegrin State, the new organization adopting the name State of the Slovenes, Croats and Serbs.

"The delegation which will represent the new State at the peace conference will certainly include Dr. Trumbich, the new Foreign Secretary, and this means a very strong representation of the Jugoslav cause. The delegation will lay before the conference all Jugoslav claims as a single demand of the former Serbian and Montenegrin States and of the redeemed Jugoslavs.

"Territorial questions in Macedonia will be treated in the same spirit of unity and indivisibility as the Adriatic question. There is no preponderance of Serbia in the new State, all parts of Jugoslavia being put on an absolutely equal footing without any one's demand for an aegis or whatever kind of domination and consequently there are no more separate Serbian and separate Jugoslav claims.

"The first thing the delegation will ask will be the full political and territorial recognition of the new State. The territorial claims, based upon the principle of justice and national self-determination include in the new State all those territories where Jugoslavs are in compact masses and where they have formed since time immemorial an undisputed territorial continuity. These territories are Serbia and Montenegro, Bosnia and Herzegovina, Croatia and Slovania, Dalmatia, Carniola, Istria and Trieste, Gorizia, parts of Southern Slovia, parts of Carinthia, Baoska, and parts of Banat and Megjumurje.

"Except in the Adriatic coast lands there is no dispute about the righteousness of the Jugoslav claims. Trieste and the western part of Istria have a majority of Italians but Trieste is a component and invisible part of the whole Jugoslav hinterland, whereas the proportion of the population in the whole of Istria shows 224,000 Jugoslavs as against 145,516 Italians. But Italy claims besides Istria and Trieste the whole of Chrizia, and the greater part of Dalmania where the Italian population is negligible, being 108,147, as against 767,708 Jugoslavs.

"Between Italian imperialistic and Jugoslav national claims there cannot be any compromise whatever. Only force can impose upon the Jugoslavs acceptance, for the moment, of a decision contrary to their rights. Any unjust settlement would unavoidably result in far-reaching future trouble. The Jugoslav peace delegation will have to make this point clear to the Peace Conference and to induce the Allies and America to arrange a settlement such as will assure not only peace in the Adriatic, but the very necessary good relations between Italy and the Jugoslavs."

\*   \*   \*

January 17, 1919

## NEW JUGOSLAV PROTEST

*Croats and Slovenes Want to Sit in the Peace Congress with Serbs*

PARIS, Jan. 16—Serbia cannot take part in the Peace Conference unless represented in a delegation from the combined Serbo-Croatian-Slovene State, the Jugoslav Committee here declares in a protest issued against the decision of the Supreme Council to admit delegates from the Kingdom of Serbia, but not of the United Kingdom of the Serbs, Croats, and Slovenes.

The committee says that this action threatens to provoke a conflict which may have serious consequences, and that the refusal to accept the delegates of the United States would make it impossible for Serbia herself to participate in the conference.

The protest concludes by saying that the Council, in arriving at its decision, did not take into account the new situation in Serbia, and thus will be obliged to examine the question anew.

\*   \*   \*

February 9, 1919

## CLAIMS OF THE NATIONS THAT MUST BE SETTLED AT VERSAILLES

*Map of the World Will Show Changes Not Only in Europe but in Asia, Africa, and Oceanica—Aspirations of the Belligerents and Others—Where Rival Ambitions Clash—New Nations Already at Loggerheads*

The object of these two maps is to show the parts of the world affected by the aims of the European nations, as summarized in an Associated Press dispatch from Paris published last Monday.

The section marked "AA" on the map of Europe, Asia, Africa, and Oceanica is dealt with in detail on the large map of Europe underneath.

Asterisks indicate territories dealt with on the upper map.

Each number after the headings, in the General Key, refers to a claim. Thus F-1 is Alsace-Lorraine, claimed by France as a result of the victory over Germany. In cases where there is a conflict of claims between nations, different headings will be found grouped close together—as, for instance, along the Eastern Adriatic coast, claimed both by Italy and Jugoslavia, (or Serbia). Another similar instance is that of the Aegean Islands, now in dispute between Italy and Greece.

No attempt has been made to show those territories in dispute which were not specifically mentioned in the dispatch from Paris on which these maps have been based. For this reason, the only parts of the former Russian Empire dealt with are

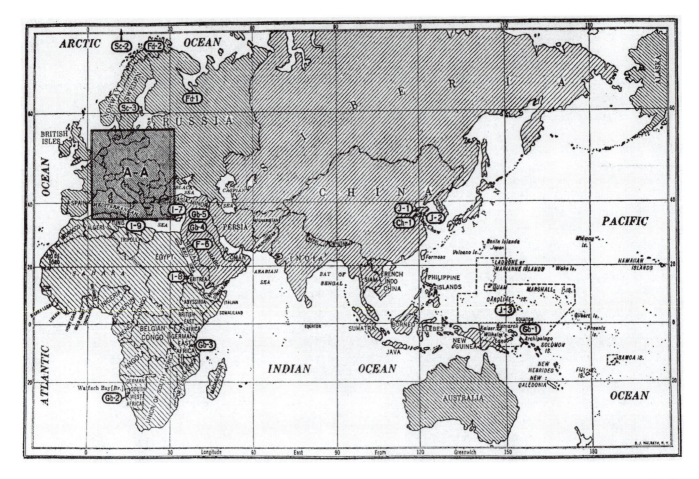

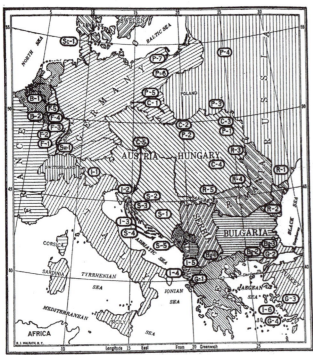

Russian Poland, Lithuania, &c., over which controversy is raging between Poles, Ukrainians, and others. Similarly, no
attempt has been made to show the various States into which
Germany and Austria-Hungary have split up.

Some of the former German colonies not specifically
mentioned in the dispatch are likewise not denoted on the
maps.

### General Key to Maps

AA—Central Europe. All territories comprised in this
part of the world are dealt with on the map of Europe on
this page. Asterisks denote the territories shown on the
upper map.

### FRENCH CLAIMS

F-1—Alsace-Lorraine. Claimed by France unconditionally.

F-2—Serre Basin. France desires also to annex this region.

F-3—Rhonish Palatinate. If the French idea of buffer States
between France and Germany becomes a reality, this may
become such a State.

F-4—Rhonish Prussia. May become a buffer State between
France and Germany, like the Palatinate.

F-5—Left Bank of the Rhine Not Comprised in F-3 and F-4.
France insists that the Peace Conference shall forbid
military works of any kind—barracks, bridgeheads forts,
fortresses—in this zone. The French feeling is that the
people inhabiting this zone should be free to decide for
themselves whether they wish to join France, form an
independent State, or return to Germany.

*F-6—Syria. The French Government does not ask for a
protectorate in Syria in the ordinary sense, because it

considers that the population there is too advanced to make a protectorate necessary; but France on account of her traditional interests in that country, feels that she should be called upon to exercise some sort of guardianship or guidance until Syria is fully able to govern herself.

## BRITISH CLAIMS

*Gb-1—German Island South of the Equator. Great Britain proposes to take mandatory power over these island for Australia.

*Gb-2—German Southwest Africa. Great Britain proposes to take mandatory power over this territory for the Union of South Africa.

*Gb-3—German East Africa. Great Britain expects to have the mandate over this region.

*Gb-4—Arabia, (parts). Great Britain expects to have mandate here. Over what part of Arabia this will extend has not been specified as yet.

*Gb-5—Mesopotamia. Great Britain has "particular claims" here. They have not been specified as yet.

## ITALIAN CLAIMS

I-1—Prentine. Claimed by Italy as part of "Italia Irredenta."

I-2—Trieste and Istria. Claimed by Italy.

I-3—Fiume, Zara, Sebenico and Dalmatian Islands. Claimed by Italy, in conflict with Jugoslavs.

I-4—Avlone and Its Hinterland. Here Italian claims of annexation conflict with Albanian claims.

I-5—Albania Proper. Italy wants a protectorate over this region.

I-6—Aegean Islands. These were taken by Italy from Turkey in the Tripolitan War. Italy wants to annex them. So does Greece.

*I-7—Province of Adalia. This section of Asia Minor is claimed by Italy if France and Great Britain take territory in Asia Minor.

*I-8—Eritrea. This colony of Italy in Africa, Italy claims, should be enlarged if France and England enlarge the African possessions.

*I-9—Tripoli. Italian holdings here should be enlarged, Italy claims, if France and Great Britain enlarge their colonial possessions in Africa.

## RUMANIAN CLAIMS

R-1—Bessarabia. This was turned over in part to Rumania by the Central Powers under the canceled treaty of Bucharest (1917) Rumania wishes to retain it.

R-2—Southern Debrudja. Ceded to Rumania by Bulgaria after the second Balkan war. Rumania wishes to retain this region, which, with Bessarabia, would give her command of the mouth of the Danube.

R-3—Bukovina. This former Austro-Hungarian crownland is claimed by Rumania.

R-4—Transylvania. Formerly Austro-Hungarian territory, now claimed by Rumania.

R-5—Banat of Temesvar. Hitherto part of Hungary, now claimed by Rumania and also by Serbia (Jugoslavia.)

## SERBIAN (JUGOSLAVIC) CLAIMS

S-1—Bosnia and Hersegovias. Seized by Austria-Hungary in 1908 and now claimed as part of the Jugoslavic nation.

S-2—Croatia (Inland). Claimed by Jugoslavia.

S-3—Fiume and Croatian Seaboard. Here Jugoslavic and Italian claims are in sharp conflict.

S-4—Dalmatian and Albanian Islands. Here Italian and Jugoslavic claims also conflict.

S-5—Montenegro. The union of Montenegro and Serbia as part of a greater Jugoslav State has been voted by the Montenegrin Parliament, but the faction representing King Nicholas of Montenegro and his adherents protests against a union which shall not leave to Montenegro entire local self-government.

## GREEK CLAIMS

G-1—Northern Epirus. Claimed by Greece.

G-2—Thrace. Claimed by Greece with the exception of Constantinople and the shores of the Bosporus and Dardanelles. (Greek extreme claims, however, include Constantinople.)

G-3—Vilayet of Smyrna. Former Turkish territory in Asia Minor claimed by Greece.

G-4—Former Turkish Islands in Eastern Mediterranean. Claimed by Greece. They include the islands known as the Dodecanesus, claimed by Italy.

## BULGARIAN CLAIMS

Bg-1—Southern Macedonia. Although Bulgaria capitulated without conditions, she has not abandoned hope of national expansion. Bulgarian ambitions include parts of Southern Macedonia.

Bg-2—Aegean Coast. Bulgaria hopes to get some territory here, despite her abject surrender.

Bg-3—Thrace. Here, too, Bulgaria has hopes, in conflict with Greece.

## CZECHOSLOVAK CLAIMS

C-1—German Saxony and German Silesia. In addition to the territories formerly of the Austro-Hungarian Empire, comprising Bohemia, Moravia, and the Slovak regions of Northern Hungary, now constituting the new republic of Czechoslovakia, the Czechoslovaks also want parts of German Saxony and German Silesia, in conflict with the Poles.

C-2—Galicia (Western). Czechoslovaks and Poles are presenting rival claims to this region.

C-3—Galicia (Eastern). In this territory Czechoslovak and Ruthenian claims conflict.

C-4—Transylvania. Fringes of the sphere claimed here by the Rumanians are also wanted by the Czechoslovaks.

C-5—"The Corridor Southward." Some Czechoslovaks want their country to have expansion southward over a frontage on the Danube and a corridor to the Adriatic.

## POLISH CLAIMS

P-1—Galicia (About Lemberg). Polish troops have been actually fighting for possession of this region with Ruthenians and Ukrainians.

P-2—Galicia (Western.) In dispute between Poles and Czechoslovaks.

P-3—Province of Chelm. In dispute between Poles and Ukrainians.

P-4—Vilna Region. In dispute between Poles, Lithuanians, and Russian Bolsheviki.

P-5—German Silesia. Polish and German troops are fighting for possession of it.

P-6—Posen and West Prussia. In dispute between Poland and Germany. Actual fighting between their troops has occurred here.

P-7—Danzig. Important German Baltic port, formerly Polish, claimed by Poland as her outlet to the sea.

## BELGIAN CLAIMS

B-1—Left Bank of Scheldt and Peninsula of Maastricht (Limbug). This territory, now Dutch, is claimed by Belgium.

B-2—Luxemburg. The independent grand duchy of Luxemburg, occupied by Germany from 1914 to November, 1918, is claimed by Belgium. Some Frenchmen, too, want it for France.

## JAPANESE CLAIMS

*J-1—Tsing Tao. Formerly German. Baron Makino, Senior Japanese delegate to the Peace Conference, is quoted as saying that Japan will hand Tsing Tao back to China under the terms of the notes exchanged between China and Japan in May, 1915.

*J-2—Shantung Peninsula. Japan interprets her rights to mean that she can retain former German concessions here.

*J-3—Southern Pacific Islands North of the Equator. Formerly German and now occupied by Japan, who desires to keep them.

## CHINESE CLAIMS

*Ch-1—Kiaochow (Tsing Tao). The Chinese want it returned to them by Japan, who captured it from Germany.

## SWISS CLAIMS

Sw-1—Neutral Rhine. Switzerland wishes to have the Rhine declared a neutral stream, thus gaining an outlet to the sea. This is in accord with French desires since, if Alsace-Lorraine becomes French from Basle northward and an independent buffer State is erected out of the Palatinate and Rhonish Prussia as suggested by Marshal Foch, it will be necessary to neutralize the Rhine.

## SCANDINAVIAN NATIONS

Sc-1—Northern Schleswig. Seized by Prussia from Denmark in 1864. Denmark wants it back. She has not asked for the rest of Schleswig and Holstein, also taken by Prussia at the same time.

*Sc-2—Spitzbergen. Norway, it is stated, has "certain aspirations" to Spitzbergen, or a part of it, but is not pressing those claims energetically.

*Sc-3—Aland Islands. A strong movement in Sweden favors the union with Sweden of the Aland Islands (formerly Russian), which are regarded by the Swedes as the naval key to Stockholm, the Swedish capital. Swedish interests here are in conflict with those of Finland.

## FINLAND

*Fd-1—Russian Karelia. Nothing has been heard since the collapse of Germany of earlier Finnish plans to obtain an outlet by the annexation of parts of this region, lying between Finland and the Alurman coast.

*Fd-2—Finmark. The Finnish plans of expansion mentioned under Fd-1 even contemplated annexation to Finland of parts of Finmark, which belongs to Norway.

\* \* \*

**February 19, 1919**

# ITALIANS REJECT JUGOSLAV PLAN

*Decline to Have Wilson Mediate, Holding it is a Conference Matter*

### ALBANIA'S CASE PRESENTED

*Conference Asked to Rectify 1913 Awards Made to Neighboring Balkan States*

PARIS, Feb. 18—The Italian delegation to the Peace Conference, according to an official note, has informed the Secretary of the conference that it cannot accept the proposal for the arbitration of Italian and Jugoslav claims in Dalmatia as urged by the Jugoslavs.

The Italian plenipotentiaries, in their letter to the Secretary, explain that all territorial claims are being submitted to the Peace Conference, and they do not believe that recourse should be had to any exceptional procedure.

The territorial claims of the Serbs, Slovenes, and Croatians were submitted to the Supreme Council at its meeting this afternoon by M. Voanitch, M Trumbitch, and M. Zolger, according to an official announcement. It was decided to submit the questions of the frontiers claimed, except those in which Italy in directly interested, to the commission already charged with the question of the frontiers of the Banat of Temesvar.

The official statement on the work of the Special Committee on Territorial Claims says:

The special committee for the study of territorial questions relating to Greece met Tuesday at 10 A. M. at the Foreign Office. This committee is composed of the following delegations. Representing America, W. L.

Westermann and Clive Day; Great Britain, Sir Robert L. Borden and Sir Eyre Crowe; France, Jules Cambon and Jean Gout; Italy, M. de Martino Castolidi.

The committee is making an examination of the conditions to be considered in determining the northern boundary of Greece and Northern Epirus. The different delegations presented their tentative proposals.

A memorandum on the claims of Albania has been presented to the conference. The Albanians asked it to acknowledge their rights, which it is said were sacrificed in Berlin in 1878 and in London in 1918.

It is recalled that the Albanians revolted at the beginning of the war against a Government under control of the Central Powers, and that they permitted the retiring Serbian Army to reach the Adriatic in 1915. The Albanians claim all territory given to Montenegro, Serbia, and Greece after the London Conference of 1913, and assert that most of the people inhabiting these territories are Albanians. Reparation for damage done in Albania by the Greeks and by the armies of the Central Powers also is asked by the Albanian Government.

Early last week the Jugoslav delegates to the Peace Conference asked President Wilson to act as arbitrator in the differences with Italy regarding the eastern coast of the Adriatic. President Wilson suggested that the Italians and Jugoslavs discuss their differences. The Italians declined to make a decision at that time. Later the Jugoslav delegates appealed to Premier Clemenceau, as President of the conference, to act as arbitrator, but there have been no reports that he took any action on the subject.

\* \* \*

**April 1, 1919**

## BESSARABIANS OBJECT TO RUMANIAN RULE

*Paris Delegation Says a Plebiscite Would Show Determination to Remain Russian*

By CHARLES H. GEASTY
Copyright 1919, by The New York Times Company
Special Cable to The New York Times

PARIS, March 30—Alexander Kronpensky and Alexander Schmidt have arrived in Paris to present Bessarabia's protest against Rumanian occupation. Their two delegates come to Paris with a direct mandate from the Bessarabian people, having been elected delegates by popular vote.

Their protest rests upon the principles of self-determination. Owing to its agricultural wealth, Bessarabia is considered a rich prize. It occupies the southwestern corner of Russia, between the Dneister, which divides it from Moldavian Rumania and the Pruth on the east; and, as it is largely Moldavian in

blood and language, Rumania has set a claim to its 7,000,000 acres of land and 2,500,000 people.

Bessarabia has at no time been Bolshevist, although succeeding waves of retreating enemies have caused considerable devastation. The peasants, however, remained at work, and the country continued to do a large business through Odessa. The Bolshevist advance at the end of 1917 gave the Rumanians a chance to enter Bessarabia, and for the last year, the delegates say, they have tried to establish control over the whole country, though they were permitted to come in on the Allied assurance, extended through the French Ambassador, that they would withdraw as soon as order was restored.

The Rumanian occupation is causing deep indignation and unrest, the delegates assert. They say the Bessarabians are Russians, and will never accept Rumanian rule. Kronpensky and Schmidt are urging a plebiscite for Bessarabia, and they say that if self-determination were confined to the Moldavian element only, which constitutes 47 per cent of the whole population, the vote would be overwhelmingly in favor of Russian sovereignty, while naturally the other 53 per cent., comprising Slavs, Greeks, Armenians, Bulgarians, and Jews, would oppose Rumanian annexation.

The delegates say that there could not be a more extreme violation of Wilsonian principles than to subject this industrious, well-intentioned people, cultivating a rich territory, to alien rule, the effect of which would be to foment discontent and disorder and to drive Bessarabia to Bolshevism against her natural inclinations. They charge that the Rumanians are co-operating with the Bolsheviki to make trouble in Bessarabia. They have put out all the native judges and other Bessarabian officials, installing Rumanians instead, thus unsettling the existing order and causing conditions favorable to anarchy.

Kronpensky is a large Bessarabian landowner, but in talks with me expresses more fear of Rumanian rule than of Russian Bolshevism: and he makes the emphatic assertion that if the Rumanians can be got rid of, the Bessarabians will successfully resist the Bolsheviki. He further asserts that if the announced plans are carried out, of permitting the Rumanian armies to push eastward in the Ukraine, their rapacity and intriguing propensities will result disastrously to the Allies.

\* \* \*

**April 15, 1919**

## OVID IN BULGARIA

It was a bitter blow to Publius Ovidius Naso, the best selling poet of Augustan Rome, when the Emperor exiled him to a desolate town on the barren shores of the Black Sea as a punishment for too faithfully reflecting the manners of his time. There he lived his last years and there he died; nor did a gentleman used to the luxurious life of the capital of the world ever quite reconcile himself to the society of barbarous Scythians.

Two thousand years later Ovid would have liked it better. By that time the town of Tomi had become Constantza, one of the principal ports of Rumania and the Summer resort of the wealthy and ease-loving society of Bucharest. And every day gentlemen very much like Ovid, and ladies whom Ovid would have liked very much, passed through the Platza Ovidiu, where a statue of the poet commemorated the first incursion, if an unwilling one, of the leisure class. In due course of time, however, Constantza fell into the hands of Scythians more ungracious than those among whom Ovid had lived. When the Bulgarian Army overran the Dobrudja in 1916 it was followed by the expropriators whom all the Central Powers sent into occupied territory. The Bulgars, like the Germans, were acquisitive; they would take anything from factory machinery to first editions and Japanese prints. Among the plunder shipped back into Bulgaria from Constantza was the statue of Ovid, once more an exile.

Malicious Rumanians have said that the Bulgars did not know who Ovid was, that they thought the statue was that of the Mayor of Constantza. Whether this be true or not, the Bulgars have been considerably more careless about the preservation of classical remains than the Rumanians. Some years ago a great heap of stones with Roman inscriptions lay in a museum yard in Sofia, with grass growing among them; nobody had cared to take the trouble to carry them indoors. Perhaps Ovid was thrown in among them to await such time as the Bulgar had leisure from his forays into other lands and could arrange his monuments of classical culture to suit himself; at any rate, Ovid escaped the ignominy of being melted and turned into shell cases, for after vigorous protests from Rumania and the Allies the Bulgarian Government finally shipped him back to Constantza.

One could wish that all the wrongs suffered by Rumania could be so easily redressed, but a correspondent who has just finished a trip through the country reports great suffering—food shortage, disorganization of business, governmental financial difficulties, and misery among the peasantry. "Rumania is passing through a critical stage," is his conclusion. "She may survive or she may go down." The decision does not rest wholly with the outer world: unless the Rumanian Government has the strength to put into force the agrarian and political reforms which have long been urgent, the fabric of Rumanian society may be unable to stand the strain. But food relief is the first necessity; starving men are not able to do very much in the way of reform. Mr. Hoover was able to deliver 26,000 metric tons of bread-stuffs to Rumania last month, and if this can be increased, and an equitable distribution assured, the Rumanian State may be able to correct its own shortcomings. One thing is certain, that Rumania has done a very considerable service to the rest of the world in holding back Bolshevism; and if Rumania goes down the chances of the democracies will be that much worse.

\*    \*    \*

June 1, 1919

## BULGARIA MUST PAY

*Her Position in the Balkans Like 'That of Germany Before the Great Powers*

By CARROL N. BROWN
College of the City of New York
May 29, 1919
*To the Editor of The New York Times:*

In reply to Mr. Sugareff's letter of last Sunday, impugning the accuracy of my statistics as to the population of Cavalla and Serres, may I state that these were drawn from the Greek University Report on the Atrocities in Eastern Macedonia, which has recently been translated and published by the American-Hellenic Society of New York. (Rapport de la Commission Universitaire Grecque sur les Atrociés et Dévastations commises par les Bulgares en Macedoine Orientale, Berger-Levrault, Nancy-Paris.)

The Greek census to which Mr. Sugareff makes reference, as giving far smaller populations, was taken immediately after the Treaty of Bucharest, and the population of Drama, Cayalla, and Serres was later enormously increased by thousands of Greek refugees driven out of Thrace by the Bulgarians. Of this fact Mr. Venizelos speaks in his memorandum presented to the Peace Conference:

"Bulgaria had scarcely taken possession of Western Thrace, when she immediately expelled the Greek population, en masse." The figure 55,000 is derived from the number of bread cards distributed in 1916.

In a brief article in the Balkan Review (March, 1919) Anatole France says:

"When the victorious English and Greek troops penetrated into Eastern Macedonia, they found the Greek towns and villages reduced to one-sixth of their population. The rest had died of hunger. Famine, carefully organized, had destroyed more than 100,000 men."

It will be noticed that Mr. Sugareff does not deny the facts; they are indisputable. He attempts to prevent the formation of anti-Bulgarian sentiment by bidding us suspend judgment and pleads that the Bulgarians did as well as could be expected is a war-torn country where modern sanitation is unknown. If Germany is, by the conscience of all mankind, held accountable for the distress and misery brought upon the world by the war of aggression which she let loose in 1914, shall not Bulgaria, which entered into the war after months of most treacherous negotiation with the Entente, and then took advantage of the traitor Constantine's pro-Germanism to gain possession of Eastern Macedonia, (even imprisoning thousands of the soldiers of her quondam ally, and ostensible friend, Greece,) be held strictly to account for the lives and property so wantonly destroyed in that all too evident attempt to change the national complexion of these regions from Greek to Bulgarian?

It must be hard for an educated Bulgarian, whose heart revolts against barbarity to accept, and believe, what even we

Americans can grasp only when repeated evidence is thrust before us. I can only advise Bulgarian propagandists in this country to cease their tactics of camouflage, and to try to convince their friends at home that the way of the transgressor is hard, and that the world wants of them, as of Germany, only deeds meet for repentance. May I, if further space be granted me, quote from an excellent book that has just appeared, "Greece Before the Conference," by Polybius, with a preface by T. P. O'Connor, M. P., and an ethnological map (Metheuen & Co., London)?

"But the Bulgarian Nation evinced none of the symptoms of dissent in the matter of joining forces with Germany. It is therefore sheer casuistry and misguided sentimentality to try to 'whitewash' Bulgaria's record in this war, and to plead that she should be forgiven.

"She has once more appealed to the sword and should abide by its decision. Even to let her off from the punishment due to her would be a travesty of justice and an injury and insult to the Entente's Balkan allies. Just as Germany will be required to yield up all alien territories that she wrested generations ago from other nations, and to repair the havoc and destruction she has wrought in her neighbors' territories during this war, so Bulgaria must relinquish that portion of Western Thrace, to which she has no ethnological claim, and must make good the terrible desolation she has left behind her in Greek Macedonla and in Serbia. There cannot be two standards of right and wrong—one for Germany and one for Bulgaria.

"Frightfulness in warfare; callousness to all sentiments of justice toward the unarmed populations of occupied districts, the endeavor to falsify the ethnological character of such districts by wholesale deportations and the most inhuman treatment of the inhabitants, are common characteristics of the Prussians of the North and the Prussians of the Balkans—with this difference—in the case of Greek Macedonia, that the Bulgarians came into its possession for two years, not by any war-like operations, but without firing a shot, being invited to enter and received as friends by the Greek Royalist authorities, thanks to King Constantine's treachery. They had therefore absolutely no excuse for the ghastly misrule which left these once fair and prosperous provinces a waste and desolation.

"As for Bulgaria, there will never be peace in the Balkans until she is rendered impotent to attack her neighbors and acknowledges once for all that the hegemony of the Balkans is not for her, nor, indeed, for any other Balkan State. This war will have been in vain if it does not establish beyond all dispute the right of every nation to its independence and its free development in the arts of peace and civilization. This right is not denied to Bulgaria by her neighbors. All that is required of her is to abandon her designs upon the rights of other peoples. She has had ample opportunity of showing how she understands government over alien races, and civilization will not permit of her giving any further such demonstrations. And, after all, this is a matter that concerns Greece, Serbia, and Rumania, above all other powers, for they alone are affected by Bulgarian imperialism. Hence in the settlement of the Balkan questions they should have the chief voice."

CARROLL N. BROWN

\*    \*    \*

**June 7, 1919**

## MACEDONIANS APPEAL TO WILSON

LAUSANNE, Switzerland, June 6—The General Council of Macedonian societies in Switzerland has sent a cablegram to the United States Senate, repeating an appeal already made to President Wilson and the Peace Conference, to "rescue the Macedonian people from misery by establishing an independent Macedonia under the direct protectorate of the great American democracy."

# PART IV

## THE INTERWAR YEARS, 1919–1939

### KUN PROPOSES CONFERENCE

*Wants All States of Former Austrian Empire to Get Together*

Copyright, 1919, by The Chicago Tribune Co.

VIENNA, June 24, (via Paris, July 1.)—Bela Kun, head of the Bolshevist Government at Budapest, recently proposed a conference of all the States of the former Austrian Empire in order to settle the status of questions existing among them and to reach a harmonious understanding. His suggestion is in line with a solution which has been in the minds of other persons interested in bringing about the same result, but who have no sympathy with the Bolsheviki.

I have asked Bela Kun for a statement of his ideas on this subject with special reference to how the conference may be called, how constituted, and other practical details. His answer, just telephoned from Budapest, is not as specific as desired, but it is an appeal to the Entente to indorse such a conference. The statement says:

"The soundness of the idea of discussing a settling of affairs in all of the States of the former Austro-Hungarian monarchy at a meeting in which the delegates of these States will take part is obvious. It is a consistent practice of the much-discussed principle of the sovereign right of nations to decide their own fate. The war has rent asunder the former monarchy, and consequently has put an end to the association of the various nations which has lasted for centuries.

"It is natural the dismemberment of the century old bonds should cause a disturbance of the functions of the newly formed States. It seems just as natural that these disturbances might be done away with by a direct exchange of views. It is not only the best but the only possible way of removing disagreements which have turned up among those States.

"Only direct negotiations of the interested States could bring about an understanding, as it concerns mostly the internal affairs of these States, questions which regard them alone.

"It is truly no mere accident that the Hungarian Communist Republic suggested the idea of such a meeting for this Government, which deems the interest of the workingman to be uppermost. It thinks it is its duty to solve all questions peacefully, and it wishes to put an end to the terrible bloodshed. We feel sure the Entente is greatly interested in the re-establishment of the States of the former empire, and will therefore not refuse to consent to such a conference."

\* \* \*

### CROATIAN TROOPS RISE AGAINST SERBIA

*Officers and Men Leave Their Units and Demand Establishment of Separate Republic*

PARIS, July 25—Dispatches from Agram and Gratz report a serious military revolt in Croatia. The revolt is taking the form of a movement for separation from Serbia and the formation of a republic.

Troops are leaving their units, officers and subalterns are tearing off their insignia and the army is in a state of dissolution, the advices say.

The railroads and telegraphs are tied up from Casktoinys southward. The Serbians are trying to suppress the revolution by the use of troops, both Serbian and Croatian.

The Agram advices do not record any disorder in that city, the Croatian capital. They state, however, that the independent Croatian republic, according to information reaching Agram, has been proclaimed by soldiers in several of the Croatian towns.

GRATZ, Styria, (via Basle) July 25—Violent combats occurred Tuesday evening at Marburg, thirty-six miles south-southeast of Gratz, where a large part of the garrison revolted as a result of dissatisfaction over demobilization. Thirty persons were killed and many wounded.

\* \* \*

### CROATS' UPRISING PLEASES ITALIANS

*They See in It an Argument Enforcing Their Claims to Fiume*

**OTHER SLAVS OPPOSE SERBS**

*Slovenes and Montenegrins Also Resent Subjection to a Serbian Monarch*

By CHARLES A. NELDEN
Copyright, 1919, by The New York Times Company
Special Cable to The New York Times

PARIS, July 26—Although absolute confirmation of the reports of demonstrations by Croats against Serbia have not been received, everybody concerned here gives them credence, except the Serbs themselves. Furthermore, they cause no surprise, because there has been discord from the outset among the three parts of the new State of Jugoslavia, the official title of which is the Kingdom of the Serbs, Croats, and Slovenes.

One of the chief difficulties of the situation, from the Croatian point of view, is indicated by that title itself. They desire a republic, and have never been enthusiastic about being made part, under a Serbian dynasty, of a kingdom in which they are greatly outnumbered by the Serbs.

Although the three groups in the Kingdom are of the same Southern Slav race, the Croatians are Catholics, despising the Serbs, who for the most part are members of the Orthodox Greek Church. Also, the Croatians consider themselves far superior, because, they assert, in the past, as part of Austria-Hungary, they had a better administrative system, laws, schools, &c., than Serbia.

The Slovenes are also Catholics and former subjects of the Hapsburgs, and have the same feeling toward the Serbs; but they are more scattered than the Croatians and not so well equipped for trouble making in the new kingdom as their neighbors.

The first intimation of what might be feared as one of the obstacles in the way of putting this new Slav State into existence came before the end of the war, when the project was first suggested. As originally proposed by the Serbs, the new nation was constantly referred to by them as "Greater Serbia." It was proposed to include all the Southern Slavs of Slavonia, Croatia, Dalmatia, Montenegro, Bosnia, and Herzegovina. This was before the break up of Austria-Hungary.

Eager as they were to free themselves from the Hapsburgs, the Croatians and Slovenes then resented the suggestion that the new State be known as "Greater Serbia." So the Serbs yielded the point, thereafter talking of "Jugoslavia" and finally adopting an official titale, including the names of Croats and Slovenes, but also the unfortunate word "kingdom."

Now the Croatians, with the sympathy of the Slovenes, are fighting to get rid of King Peter and the whole Serbian dynasty and make the new State a republic. At the same time the adherents of the King of Montenegro are trying their best to upset the new State by opposing its rule in their own small mountain kingdom.

Of course all this news of disturbances in Montenegro and Croatia pleases the Italians, who have always made part of their argument for Fiume the statement that the Serbs were a backward people who would never be able to rule the new State placed in their keeping by the great powers, and that Jugoslavia would continue to be the plague spot of Europe and to menace general peace.

Fiume itself is within the borders of Croatia and was specifically assigned to that province by the London Treaty of 1915. In their original demands upon France, England, and Russia for promises of territory as a reward for entering the war, the Italians asked for Fiume. France and England, thinking that Italy was asking too much, left the decision as to Fiume to Russia as the traditional friend and protector of Slav interests. Russia ruled against Italy, so in the Treaty of 1915, under the terms of which Italy entered the war and which has been one of the chief causes of contention

throughout the Peace Conference, Fiume was specifically reserved as a port for Croatia, then part of Hungary and, so far as the Allies could then foresee, always to be a part of Hungary.

Croatia now would prefer to be set up as a small republic, with this port on the Adriatic as its own. It prefers that even to being part of the large republic, including Serbia, and the Croats declare that they will fight for it rather than be part of a monarchical State ruled by King Peter.

When I asked a member of the Peace Conference this morning about this new difficulty made by the Croatians he shrugged his shoulders and replied: "I suppose we can send a commission to investigate."

\* \* \*

August 21, 1919

## ALBANIANS CABLE APPEAL TO SENATE

*Ask Its Protection Against "Imperialism" of Italians, Greeks and Serbs*

PARIS, Aug. 20, (Associated Press)—The Albanian delegation to the Peace Conference, headed by Monsignor Louis Bunca, has sent by cable an appeal to "the President of the United States Senate" and Senators Lodge and Hitchcock, asking for protection against the "imperialism" of their neighbors.

The Greeks, Italians, and Serbs are constantly encroaching on Albanian territory, according to the Albanian representatives, who urge that a plebiscite be granted to determine the boundaries of Albania. The appeal reads as follows:

"In this critical period of Albania's history its delegation addresses itself to the sentiments of justice of the United States Senate, imploring its powerful support of the rights of the Albanian people. Albania, after struggles to recover its liberty and after being deprived of half of its territory in favor of its neighbors, in 1913 established an independent State. Just as Belgium's neutrality guaranteed by the great Powers was violated, so was Albania's from the beginning of the war, first by Allied troops, then by enemy armies.

"Albania was transformed into a battlefield and knew the horrors of war. It saw itself covered with ruins, and thousands of its children perishing with hunger. At the proclamation of the principle of the rights of peoples, issuing from America, the Albanians took up arms to fight alongside of the Allies in an effort to save their country.

"After the Entente victory, which signified the triumph of right and justice, the Albanians formulated and presented to the Peace Conference their national claims. They had the certainty of seeing the restoration to their country of the Albanian territories incorporated into the neighboring States as a result of the Balkan war.

"For the inhabitants of these territories who went through the horrors of the Greek invasion, and who today are still delivered, as they were in the past, to premeditated massacres of extermination by the Serbs, the Albanian delegation asked several times from the Peace Conference the right of a plebiscite under the guarantee of American troops; but, instead, they see their country today menaced with dismemberment.

"In the application of the secret treaty of London of 1915, Italy insists, with force, upon annexing Valona, with the large hinterland; Greece claims northern Epirus, and Serbia claims the northern part of Albania. Thus, when the Jugoslavs, the Italians, and the Greeks deal with Fiume, Dalmatia and Thrace, the right of the principle of nationality prevails, but they refuse to acknowledge the same when they deal with their pretensions in Albania.

"The cry of distress of the Albanian people is smothered by the powerful imperialism of their neighbors. The hope which the Albanians have fixed their eyes upon is America, and from her again they expect salvation. All Albanians prefer American assistance to guide them in their political life.

"In the name of this martyred people, the Albanian delegation prays that you raise your voice to save their country from catastrophe and secure their independence."

\* \* \*

September 9, 1919

## CALL ON BULGARIA FOR $446,000,000

*Peace Terms to be Presented Today Take Western Thrace and Other Territory*

**ARMY CUT TO 20,000 MEN**

*All Loot Must Be Given Up and 250,000 Tons of Coal Delivered to Serbia*

By EDWIN L. JAMES
Special Cable to The New York Times
Copyright, 1919, by The New York Times Company

PARIS, Sept. 18—The Bulgarian delegation will be handed the Peace Treaty at 10:30 o'clock tomorrow morning and will be given twenty days to consider it. The ceremony will not be grand. The head of the delegation of each power will be present, the five great powers being represented by the members of the Supreme Council. The press representation will be limited to ten correspondents.

The conditions of the treaty follow closely those laid down for Germany and Austria, and give promise of putting the "bad boy" of the Balkans in a position where he will have to behave for some years to come. The treaty terms call for the abolition of compulsory military service in Bulgaria. A force to maintain order is permitted up to a strength of 20,000, and the Gendarmesir and the police forces may not exceed 10,000 additional. Arms and ammunitions exceeding the amounts laid down by the terms shall be deposited at the order of the Allies. An interallied commission is established to see that the conditions are carried out.

Another commission composed of representatives of England, France, Italy, Greece, Rumania, and Serbia, will deal with repatriation, allied prisoners still in Bulgaria, and will take steps to punish crimes committed by Bulgaria during the war.

Bulgaria must surrender all works of art and valuables stolen from allied countries and must pay as indemnity of 2,250,000,000 francs in periods of thirty-seven years. As for territorial changes Bulgaria is deprived of Thrace, although she is promised an outlet to the Agean Sea under the League of Nations.

Bulgaria also loses Strumitsia, a small triangle of territory, to Serbia. The boundary between Bulgaria and Rumania is left as before the war with very minor exceptions.

\* \* \*

November 2, 1919

## RUMANIA PROCLAIMS BESSARABIAN UNION

*Offers a New Defiance to the Wishes of the Peace Conference*

**ALL WARNINGS DISREGARDED**

*She Had Been Told That Allies Would Not Aid Her If Russia Attacked Her*

By EDWIN L. JAMES
Copyright, 1919, by The New York Times Company
Special Cable to The New York Times

PARIS, Nov. 1—The Peace Conference has had another serious trouble thrust upon it. Rumania announced to the Supreme Council today that she had annexed Bessarabia.

Since the armistice Rumanian troops have occupied this territory, and during the entire history of the Peace Conference Rumania has been trying to get it allotted to her. The conference favored a plebiscite, which never appealed strongly to the Rumanians, who seemed to doubt their success under such a plan.

While the conference had not taken final action on Bessarabia, it had warned the Rumanians that if they took the territory they would not please the other powers, and that if Russia ever attempted to take it back Rumania would find no helpers among them. Rumania was also warned that the League of Nations would not approve the seizure.

But, evidently heartened by her success in occupying Hungarian territory in defiance of the Peace Conference. Rumania has decided to make the best of her opportunity. Bessarabia is about the size of Ireland.

For two months the Supreme Council has been struggling with four vexing situations constituting open disregard of its authority—the presence of the Rumanians in Budapest, that of d'Annunzio in Fiume, its inability to get rid of the Hungarian treaty, and Germany's stand-pat attitude in the Baltic provinces. Now a fifth perplexity confronts it. Rumania can thus be credited with two of the five disagreeable situations before the peacemakers. Rumania is also delinquent in that she has not signed the Austrian treaty.

When the news of the annexation of Bessarabia arrived the Supreme Council was occupied in addressing a friendly note to Rumania, telling her that it was her duty to sign the Austrian treaty and warning her that otherwise she might not be allowed to sign the Bulgarian treaty.

\* \* \*

December 14, 1919

## RUMANIA'S PARLIAMENT

*Eye Witness Describes First Congress in Bucharest of New State as Big as Italy*

### By CHARLES UPSON CLARK

Nov. 20, 1919, will always remain a historic date in Bucharest. Three years ago the union of all the Rumanian lands seemed a distant vision. Germany held Wallachia, Bulgaria, the Dobrudja; Transylvania and the Banat were suffering under Hungarian tyranny. Bucovina, scourged by the Russians, was returning to Austria, and Bessarabia was enduring the horrors of civil war; only Jassy and part of Moldavia seemed saved to Rumania. What a contrast to the brilliant scene that has just been staged in the Bucharest Athenaeum: King Ferdinand takes his place in Rumanian history beside Stephen the Great and Michael the Brave; Rumania becomes a country the size of Italy and the seventh in population in Europe, with infinite possibilities.

Rumania's Parliament buildings are too small to seat the Deputies from the new provinces; so the members and guests gathered in the vast assembly hall of the Athenaeum with the proud inscription running about the bare wall under the great dome, to the effect that the space is reserved for frescoes to immortalize the union of Rumania. The box to the left before the stage was filled with a brilliant group of diplomats and military attaches, in full uniform; the Polish Minister, an English Member of Parliament, Cozzens Hardy, and our own Minister, Mr. Vopicka, were conspicuous in dress suits and white gloves, which were also worn by the civil members of the Cabinet and by a number of the Senators and Deputies in the audience.

Promptly at noon, the hour set, long lines of Generals filed upon the platform; one noticed General Prezan, Chief of Staff; General Vaitoianu, the retiring Prime Minister, and many other distinguished figures. Suddenly a loud "Hurrah" resounds from one corner of the hall; they have caught sight of the King and Queen as they come upon the stage from the wings, and wild enthusiasm breaks loose and lasts for several minutes, while they both bow and bow and smile with obvious gratification. It is the great moment in their lives.

King Ferdinand is dressed in the blue uniform with red facings of a Rumanian General, and his breast is resplendent with orders; Queen Marie wears a gray cloak trimmed with gray fur, and a tall black and white fur cap—a proud and dignified figure. Finally the cheering lets up enough for the King to start reading his message: he is evidently a little nervous; his hand trembles, but his voice carries through the room, and his first sentence, that he is proud to stand in the midst of representatives of the former kingdom, of Bessarabia, Bucovina, Transylvania, Maramuresh, Crishana, and the Banat, lets loose another storm of cheers, while Deputies lead hurrahs for each of the provinces mentioned. Other "braves" follow his tribute to the heroic dead, and his promise that the first care of the new Rumania will be the widows and orphans and cripples of the war; Professor Jorga, the historian, leads a cheer for "the King of the peasants," and one of the peasant party responds by shouting "Long live Queen Marie, mother of the wounded," at which the whole room goes wild, and the Queen blushes and bows time and again.

Ferdinand and Marie went through all the horrors of the Winter at Jassy with their soldiers, and nobody forgets it, especially the Queen's work with the Red Cross. A few sentences later a graceful reference to the Allies starts another series of cheers, and everybody waves to the diplomatic box; Minister Vopicka smiles and can hardly keep from waving back. The King's reference to the problems that confront Rumania in her relations to the Paris Conference and his hope that with good-will on both sides a solution may be found honorable to both brought forth earnest "bravos" on all sides. No one here quite understands why Rumania may not sign with reservations, and the United States may; and there is a determined desire to thrash the matter out to the end, as a matter of national pride. Rumania may be small, but she is certainly spunky.

The message is short. Another wild shout breaks loose when the King bows and gives the message over to the Prime Minister; many are overcome by the emotion called forth by the historic event; an archbishop near me, in brilliant purple robe and purple cap gives full rein to his tears. We all rush downstairs to see the brilliant cortege leave the hall. First the Generals form a line of honor, and then the King and Queen, radiant after the reception they have received, step into the quaint old high-springed State carriage, with red postillons, and high-plumed footmen behind, and the day has passed into history.

\* \* \*

December 28, 1919

## RUMANIAN ELECTION RESULT

*Bratiano's Party Won in Old Kingdom—Socialists Broke Into Chamber*

Details of the outcome of the November general elections in Rumania found in German newspapers show that in old Rumania, i.e., the kingdom as it existed before the World War, the Liberals, headed by ex-Premier J. C. Bratiano, won a decided victory, electing 183 Deputies to the Chamber, against 87 Nationalists, 58 Agrarians, 12 Socialists, 7 Progressives, and 6 followers of Avarescu. There were no Socialists in the old Parliament.

In the new annexed territory, embracing Transylvania and parts of old Hungary, 146 Nationalists and 46 opposition delegates were elected. In Bukovina 12 Nationalists, including 2 Germans, 1 Jew and 1 Ruthenian, won, while in Bessarabia 86 Nationalists, 28 Agrarians and 1 Socialist were chosen.

\* \* \*

**August 11, 1920**

## ENDING SOME WARS

With war apparently once more the natural state of man, it is comforting to find peace prevailing in certain quarters. The ratifications of the Bulgarian treaty were exchanged yesterday, so there is one war ended for the time being. Bulgaria is entirely unreconstructed in the spiritual sense, to be sure, but so long as the hard-headed Stamboliski is in power she is hardly likely to upset the Balkans by any new adventures.

Meanwhile Paris dispatches state that the Greeks and Italians have come to an agreement on the Dodecanesus, so that the Turkish treaty could be signed also. Mere signing of the treaty will not advance the solution of the Turkish question very much, for even the gentlemen who will put their names to the document are most probably in sympathy with Mustapha Kemal. But it is something if the Dodecanesus has been disposed of. Mr. Giolitti has denied the policy attributed to him by a correspondent of holding the Dodecanesus to be exchanged for wheat, raw materials and credits, and the reported agreement goes back in general to the terms of last Spring. Greece will get all the islands except Rhodes; Italy will hold that, apparently, to be given back to Greece whenever England gives up Cyprus which, like Rhodes, is predominantly Greek in population. There still seems to be some disagreement over the plebiscite in Rhodes, but if the Greeks sign the treaty it may be presumed that this is settled. The Italo-Greek agreement, in which the Dodecanesus was only an item, was one of the most creditable accomplishments of Mr. Nitti's Government, and if Giolitti goes back to it conditions in the Mediterranean will begin to encourage hopefulness.

\* \* \*

**August 13, 1920**

## VENIZELOS SHOT, TWICE WOUNDED BY GREEKS IN PARIS

*Premier Fired At Eight Times Before Police Put an End to the Fusillade*

### ASSAILANTS BADLY BEATEN

*They Are Identified as Two Former Officers, One in Army, the Other in Navy*

### ACTED "TO FREE GREECE"

*Premier's Condition Reported Satisfactory at Midnight—Paris Aroused by the Attack*

PARIS, Aug. 12 (Associated Press)—Eleutherios Constantine Venizelos, Prime Minister of Greece, narrowly escaped assassination at the hands of fellow-countrymen tonight as he was entering the Lyons railway station here.

He was shot in the left shoulder and the right thigh.

At midnight at the hospital where he was taken it was said his condition was as satisfactory as possible.

Copyright Harris & Ewing

"Maker of Modern Greece," Twice Wounded in an Attempt on His Life.

The assailants of the Premier were two former Greek officers. George Thyriakis and Apostolos Iserpris, both Lieutenants, the former in the engineers and the latter in the navy.

It had been rumored that an attempt was to be made on the life of M. Venizelos, and as a consequence the police were on the watch. They were successful in overpowering the assassins before they were able to empty their revolvers. The miscreants were badly beaten by the crowd in the station after the shooting.

### Eight Shots Fired

Eight shots were fired at the Premier. The shooting occurred at 9:45 P. M.

The assailants are said by the police to have admitted that they planned the attack. They said they acted with the object of freeing Greece from its oppressor.

After the shooting M. Venizelos was placed in the automobile of the Greek Minister and conveyed to a private hospital in the Rue Bizet, where his wounds were dressed.

The news of the attack on M. Venizelos aroused profound indignation in Paris, where the Greek Premier was held in high esteem.

President Deschanel sent an officer to the hospital where he was taken to inquire as to his condition, and Mr. Paleologue called at the hospital on behalf of Premier Millerand.

### Plots Against Venizelos

Ever since the dethronement of King Constantine of Greece there has been a conspiracy operated from a small place in Switzerland to have him return to the throne at the expense of the life of Venizelos.

At first in Athens the plot gained some adhesion from the admirers of the ex-King, who still remembered with gratitude the part he had played in the Balkan wars. But with the diplomatic success of Venizelos at Paris the plot gradually dissolved until the remnant was last Spring arrested, tried and convicted. Some Generals wre imprisoned, some exiled and a few were executed. Still, it was known from the pro-Constantine propaganda which still flourished that assassins were being encouraged to remove the maker of modern Greece.

Eleutherios Venizelos only a few days ago had seen in diplomacy and on the field of battle the finishing touches given which made his country a power with the material for future greatness.

The Turks on Aug. 10 had signed the Treaty of Sevres, which by actual sovereignty and mandate more than doubled the 30,000-odd square miles of Greece as she was before the war and quadrupled the population of 3,000,000 then brought under the Government of Athens. In Eastern Thrace and in Anatolia Greek armies, under General Paraskevopoulos, had, in the first instance, forced the Nationalist commander, Jafer Tayar, to surrender, clearing the territory between Constantinople and the Bulgar border, and in the second, fought the armies of Mustapha Kemal Pasha to a stand-still.

All this as planned by the wonderful Cretan, some have said from the inception of the Paris Peace Conference, others have said from the moment he had King Constantine dethroned on June 12, 1917.

For over two years he had been out of office, while Constantine the brother-in-law of the German Kaiser, having denounced the Serbo-Grecian Treaty of mutual defense, tried in vain to keep Greece neutral with secret sympathy and active underground aid to the Germans. With the return of Venizelos came the Chamber elected on May 31, 1915, but which had been dissolved as soon as the King bad found it would not permit him to infringe its constitutional powers. Already the "Venizelos volunteers" had been fighting with the allied army in Macedonia when on July 2 the new Government, with Constantine's second son. Alexander, as King and Venizelos again as Prime Minister, formally declared war on Germany, Austria-Hungary, Turkey and Bulgaria.

### Gained Most for His Country

At the Peace Conference, when it came together in January, 1919, some correspondents were not slow in predicting that the delegate who would gain most for his country was Venizelos. To be sure he had a clear case for the Greeks on the ground of self-determination: but so did others. That claim alone might not have gone very far in the complex problems which confronted the conference had it not been for the Cretan's personality—never out of patience, never forced into long argument over inconsequentialities, firm, good-natured, asking for nothing, but quietly insisting on much, in this way within the last few days he quietly solved the Dodecanese question with Italy.

About fifty-five years ago two Moslem hodjas and two Greek priests were earnestly praying for the safe deliverance of the wife of a rich Cretan merchant and for the long life of her child, the fourth to be born to her and the first to survive birth. The child that came safely into the world became the man who was shot in Paris yesterday. As a youth he was fortunately allowed to forsake commerce for law and at the age of 21 became a member of the Cretan Assembly, then under Turkish rule. In 1897 his eloquence persuaded Greece to declare war on Turkey. It was an unfortunate adventure save that it left Crete, his birthplace, under the guardianship of the powers, which in 1821, had become the protectors of Greek independence.

Still, he continued to have confidence in his fellow-countrymen, and his triumph came in 1913, when, after having previously declared its independence of Turkey, in 1908, Crete became annexed to Greece. This triumph was the result of the first Balkan war, for which Venizelos had united Bulgaria, Serbia, and Montenegro with Greece in order to free their nationals in Europe from the Turkish yoke. In the second Balkan war of a few days in July, 1913, he managed to unite with Greece, Serbia, and Rumania against the territorial claims of Bulgaria.

\*   \*   \*

November 6, 1920

## ALBANIA

Order reigns in Albania, at least by contrast with other days; and an Albanian Government, controlling nearly all the country, hopes for recognition by other Powers. Naturally, it looks first to America. Everybody looks first to America, but Albania has special reasons. Chief among them is the defense of Albanian territorial integrity in President Wilson's Adriatic correspondence last Winter, when the French and British Governments attempted to settle the Fiume question in Italy's favor and buy off the Serbs with Albanian territory.

The Peace Conference decided that Italy, whose armies of occupation had done some excellent work in the building of roads and the introduction of orderly administration, should have a mandate for Albania. Assuming that the mandate had been carried out disinterestedly, and not used as a lever for intrigue against other Balkan States, that would probably have been the best thing. But the Albanians would not have it. Last Summer they rose against the Italian troops of occupation and drove them down to Avlona, where they held on precariously while the Italian Socialists "demonstrated" against sending any more men and money across the Adriatic. Giolitti had no choice. He made the best of the situation by an agreement which gives Italy permission to fortify some islands off Avlona, thus adding to the strategic security of the Adriatic, and affords special economic openings to Italian enterprise. More than that Italy could not take, and the Albanians calculated shrewdly that Italian aid could always be relied on in case of Serbian or Greek aggression.

Hardly was this question out of the way when there was a little border war with the Serbs, started, apparently, by Albanians in territory that has been Serbian since 1913. At Belgrade, Italian influence was seen in this, just as in Rome Serbian influence was believed to be behind the rising three months earlier. But Serbia and Albania appealed to the Powers to settle the dispute and hostilities for a time have been suspended.

Then there is the dispute with Greece over Northern Epirus. It has not been settled, but apparently the two Governments have come to some sort of working agreement, so for the moment Albania is at peace with her neighbors. Internal affairs, too, seem quieter; the faction which supported that stormy but tenacious character Essad Pasha has apparently been broken up, Essad himself having been assassinated. For the moment the Government of Tirana seems to be pretty well obeyed throughout the country; but the record of Albanian civil turbulence will incline the cautious to wait and see. If the new Government continues the policy of trying peaceful arrangement with its neighbors instead of fighting out disputes, one of the sorest spots in the Balkans may be healed.

\*   \*   \*

November 17, 1920

## VENIZELOS RESIGNS WITH HIS CABINET; TWO DEAD IN RIOTS

*Regent Summons Ex-Premier Rhallis, Who is Expected to Form New Ministry*

### CONSTANTINE AWAITS CALL

*Must Answer It, He Says, if the Greeks "Choose to Continue Their Allegiance to Me"*

### LONDON AND PARIS AGHAST

*British and French Foreign Offices Foresee Embarrassment for Cherished Policies*

ATHENS, Nov. 16 (Associated Press)—Premier Venizelos's Cabinet resigned early today, and Admiral Coundouriotis, the Regent of Greece, has sent for George Rhallis, to whom, it is is expected, will be intrusted the formation of a new Ministry.

M. Rhallis, a former Premier, is 80 years old. His last public office was that of Minister of Finance in the Zalmis Cabinet in 1916.

The latest returns from the election give the supporters of M. Venizelos 118 Deputies against 220 Royalists. M. Venizelos and all but two of his Ministers were beaten. None of the Venizelist candidates were elected in Greece and Macedonia, with the exception of Epirus and the Aegean Islands.

The complete victory of the Opposition seemed almost certain last night, although final results were still lacking. Even the leaders of the elements opposed to Premier Venizelos in the elections held on Sunday were surprised by the showing their candidates had made in Macedonia and Attica.

It is said that M. Venizelos will leave the country, and that he has advised Liberals to abide by the verdict of the people.

Demetrios Gounaris, leader of the Opposition, has declared that the foreign policy of Greece will not be changed.

#### Two Killed in Post-Election Fights

Two persons were killed by shots fired from houses facing the Foreign Office yesterday. It was declared that reactionary elements were responsible for the firing. Armed police rushed to the scene, and a lively fusillade resulted.

Troops fired from a number of points on several occasions yesterday to disperse after-election trouble-makers. There is said to be danger that the army may get out of hand.

The disorders began with a parade of Opposition adherents to attack the Liberal Club. Troops stationed within the club quarters fired upon the marchers.

The military later attacked the Opposition headquarters, from which a few shots came. For two hours the headquarters were besieged and bombarded by the troops. A number of bystanders were wounded.

Troops are guarding the public places and the homes of the leaders of both sides.

CANEA, Island of Crete, Nov. 16—The Venizelists were uniformly successful in the elections in Crete. No Opposition candidate was returned.

### Report That Rhallis Has Accepted

LONDON, Nov. 16—George Rhallis, former Greek Premier and Minister of Finance, has been asked by the Regent to form a Cabinet succeeding that of Eleutherios Venizelos, which resigned this morning, says a Reuter dispatch from Paris.

The Athens Bourse has been closed because of the fear of a panic, it is said.

Another Reuter message from Athens said M. Rhallis had accepted the task of forming a cabinet. The former Opposition leaders, it was added, were expected to meet today, to decide whether they would recognize Admiral Coundouriotis as Regent.

### Constantine Hopes to Return

LUCERNE, Nov. 16—Ex-King Constantine of Greece, and Professor Georgios Streit, former Greek Foreign Minister, who is with the ex-King here, spent a wakeful night last night receiving hourly telegrams on the result of the Greek elections from Athens. They were greatly pleased at the defeat of their arch-enemy, Premier Venizelos.

Constantine, it is known, hopes to return to the throne, but he is still doubtful whether the Opposition will call him.

Meanwhile congratulatory telegrams, especially from monarchist countries, are pouring into Lucerne.

The ex-King has refused to make any statement regarding his plans. He said, however:

"I will abide by the will of my people. It is a question of the right of self-determination. If the Greek people choose to continue their allegiance to me I must answer their call."

WASHINGTON, Nov. 16—State Department officers declined today to discuss the report that Great Britain and France might prevent the return of King Constantine to the throne of Greece, further than to say that those countries had a peculiar relation with Greece, in that they exercised a certain supervision over the Bank of Greece, the sole bank of issue in the country.

As to the American position with respect to a change of Government in Greece, officials said this would be defined when there arose the question of recognition of the new Government, if one were set up.

### PARIS DISMAYED BY OVERTURN
#### This, with Wrangel's Collapse, Deals Blow to Foreign Policy

By WALTER DURANTY
Special Cable to The New York Times

PARIS, Nov. 16—The news of the defeat of Venizelos comes as a great shock to the French press and public opinion. But the better-informed Foreign Office has been uneasy ever since. King Alexander's death. The French diplomats attribute the result chiefly to the adverse vote of the farmers, owing to their hostility to the Smyrna adventure, which has prevented the demobilization of their sons. The failure of the Greeks to subdue the Turkish Nationalists, despite the brilliant beginning of the campaign, militated strongly against Venizelos. The heavy drain on the finances of the small nation led a great many people to wonder whether "Greater Greece" was not being bought too dearly. In the phrase of a French writer, Philippe Millet, "Venizelos fell because he tried to inflate the Greek frog into an ox."

The victory of Constantine's party—for it is no less—greatly embarrasses the French Government, which has repeatedly declared through its inspired press that it would oppose any attempt to put the ex-King or his eldest son on the throne. I was informed today, however, that the latter might be accepted, since it is understood that the British advocate his selection as a compromise. But there is no disguising the fact that French policy has received a marked setback, as France had supported Venizelos to the extent of suggesting that he appeal to the country to oust the monarchy altogether and proclaim a republic. That he declined to listen to the proposal shows that he was less sure of the result than his optimistic statements made it appear.

The Greek situation, with the simultaneous utter defeat of Wrangel, is making the French Foreign Office take a rather gloomy view of European affairs. It is pointed out that the Adriatic agreement, which was received with universal relief, is gravely compromised by the chauvinism of d'Annunzio, whose forces have occupied territory assigned to the Jugoslavs. Further east there is the ominous announcement of an offensive and defensive alliance between the Czechoslovaks and Jugoslavs against Hungarian aggression, which the former profess to expect at any moment. The press of both countries is full of complaints against France for having allowed Hungary—whom they bluntly call France's protégé—to maintain an army far larger than that authorized by the Peace Treaty. The high-handed action of the Serbs in prematurely occupying Bulgarian territory does not tend to improve the unfavorable impression here.

Meanwhile news has reached Paris that the Bolshevik, encouraged by their victory over Wrangel, are openly preparing for a new drive against Poland. As a pendant to this come sinister rumors of an anti-Polish alliance being negotiated between Germany, Russia and Lithuania.

In Asia Minor the state of affairs is going from bad to worse. Mustapha Kemal seems to have thrown in his lot definitely with the Bolsheviki, whose control in Russia is in a fair way to extend right to the shores of the Mediterranean, for it is hardly to be expected that the Greeks will now do more than hold the area around Smyrna.

Not the least alarming feature to France is her growing isolation. The British have withdrawn their troops from Persia and again seem inclined to open commercial relations with the Bolsheviki, which is generally believed here to portend British recognition of the Bolshevist régime as a de facto government.

With the Allied Supreme Council little more than a makeshift of conflicting policies, the French have the further embarrassment of growing financial difficulties. The opponents of the Government in the Finance Committee of the Chamber threw a bombshell yesterday in the shape of the publication of the fact that there would be a deficit of more than 2,000,000,000 francs in the forthcoming budget, most of it due to expenditures on French forces in the Near East, for whose curtailment there is sure to be a pressing demand.

### Gounaris Would Call Prince George

PARIS, Nov. 16 (Associated Press)—News of the resignation of the Cabinet of Premier Venizelos of Greece was received today by the Greek Legation in Paris, which accepted it as accurate, although its information was not official.

The Legation said its advices stated that ex-Premier Gounaris, after having requested George Rhallis to form a Cabinet and having received a refusal from the latter, would form a Cabinet himself.

The program of Gounaris it was added, called for an invitation to the former Crown Prince George, the Duke of Sparta, to ascend the throne of Greece.

The Legation declared that the defeat of Premier Venizelos was due to domestic questions and not to animosity or antipathy toward the Allies, and that Greece would show herself anxious to continue amicable relations with the Entente.

A dispatch to the Temps from Athens today says M. Venizelos is requesting the Liberals to accept the popular verdict, and that he has decided to leave Greece. M. Gounaris is quoted as declaring that the foreign policy of Greece will undergo no change. It is probable, the newspaper adds, that M. Venizelos will take up his home in France.

It is said that the position of France and Great Britain with regard to ex-King Constantine is very clearly against his return and that both powers are determined to do everything possible to prevent it. They will probably act together, but will await some indication of Constantine's intention to return. Should that be manifested they will then do whatever may be necessary.

It was declared today at the Foreign Office that France would take all possible steps to keep the ex-King off the throne. The question of the return of George, the former Crown Prince, had not yet been raised, it was added.

"The defeat of Premier Venizelos," a Foreign Office statement said, may be termed a display of gross ingratitude by the Greeks for the man who brought the country to the Allies side and greatly increased its size, power and influence, and this view is shared by the Allies. It was a great shock to the Allies.

Hope is expressed by "Pertinax," political editor of the Echo de Paris, that even a compromise placing Prince George on the throne will not be sanctioned by the Entente.

### GREECE SHOCKS LONDON
#### Newspapers Intimate That Ex-King's Restoration Will Be Opposed

Special Cable to The New York Times

LONDON, Wednesday, Nov. 17—The news of the downfall of Venizelos came as a surprise and shock to the British Government. The strength of the anti-Venizelist movement in

Greece had been greatly underestimated. For the present, however, the British Foreign Office is taking a waiting and observant attitude, holding that the results of the election may be regarded as a matter solely concerning Greece and not necessarily affecting the allied powers unless they should lead to developments which would conflict with the allied policy.

Any steps to restore Constantine to the throne would probably be regarded here as a dangerous move which in the interest of Europe as a whole would call for intervention. There is, however, no disposition to draw conclusions and in any event Great Britain would not take action without reference to her allies. Any representations that may be addressed to Greece will be made by the Supreme Council of the Allies.

"Decidedly, luck is against the Allies," is the comment of the Radical Star, which adds: "Ever since the armistice they have had a succession of disappointments, reverses and setbacks. Some were the fault of their own folly, others were due to sheer bad luck. So at this hour the sequence goes on. General Wrangel, whom they have been foolish enough to subsidize and encourage, is being driven out of the Crimea by the Bolshevists, and Venizelos, who has been always linked with allied policy, appears to be driven out of Greece. One by one the great figures of the allied statesmen pass away into the cold shades of defeat. Clemenceau, Wilson, Venizelos—only Lloyd George, like a cork, floats where others sink."

For the personal downfall of Venizelos there is universal regret. The Standard says:

"The tragedy of a great man condemned to work with bad tools is sufficiently poignant; but that is not the main interest of the Greek elections for this country. The points are:

"Is Constantine to be restored? If so, is he to be King of the Greater Greece, which was created on the assumption that Venizelos and his policy would remain? If the Greeks really want Constantine they will be allowed to have him. The Allies will probably not feel justified in interfering with this most undesirable manifestation of self-determination, despite the fact that this monarch stabbed his ally, Serbia, in the back, cost this country and her allies many millions of pounds and many thousands of lives, and subserved in every possible way the interests of the ex-Kaiser.

"Is a monarch or is a people so disposed to be given unrestricted enjoyment of the advantages secured to Greece under the peace? Greece can have whichever she likes, Constantine or the new territory; she cannot have both."

So far as can be ascertained in Greek Constitutional circles it is considered probable that Constantine will take French leave from Lucerne and make his way back to Greece. He is known to be highly elated at the result of the elections. It is pointed out that a Greek destroyer could convey him from Brindisi to the Greek coast in a few hours, and it is thought that in that event he would land at Patras, which is a royalist stronghold and the field of his ardent champion Gounaris.

The Chronicle says editorially:

"On the assumption that Greece had cut herself off from the sordid past which the ex-King symbolizes we cooperated during the peace negotiations in making her the leading power in the Levant; but at their earliest opportunity the Greek electorate have turned our assumption inside out. It is not merely that they have rejected the champions of pro-allied statesmanship; it is that by their abrupt reversal they have gone far to re-establish the evil reputation of their country's politics for fickleness and unreliability.

"The extent of the latter evil will depend upon how the Gounarists use their victory. They have issued a statement that the foreign policy of Greece will be unchanged. If this statement is sincere, it will preclude them from sanctioning or abetting any restoration which would encounter the strongest objections from the protecting powers. Their action under this head will therefore afford a touchstone. If it proves unsatisfactory, the Allies have many ways of defending their interests. Greek prosperity depends wholly on their good-will."

### PREDICTS EX-KING'S RETURN
#### Supporter in London Says Allies Need Not Fear Constantine

Special Cable to The New York Times

LONDON, Wednesday, Nov. 17—The Daily Chronicle publishes a statement concerning the political situation in Greece by a Greek who held high office at the Court of King Constantine when the latter was in the heyday of this power.

"The Entente Powers need feel no alarm," this authority declares. "Constantine is and always has been a constitutional sovereign. He has already declared his readiness to work in harmony with Venizelos and to insist upon his continuing in office provided the electors of the country wished it. But very decisively, it seems to me, Greece has intimated to Venizelos that it has had enough of his regime." As regards the possibility of allied intervention, The Chronicle's informant says:

"The Greek nation surely has the right to decide for itself whether it is to be ruled by Venizelos or King Constantine. The issue of the elections has been a clear-out one. The adherents of the dethroned King expressed their willingness to submit the question of the King's return to a plébiscite, but Venizelos very arrogantly and full of belief in his assured triumph at the polls waived this question of a plébiscite and said: 'Let the general elections decide. We don't want any plébiscite.' He has been taken at his word. Greece has called back her exiled King, and I take it that he will lose no time in responding to the unanimous appeal of his subjects."

The Chronicle's informant admitted the possibility of international complications, or rather, difficulties, with certain of the Entente powers in the event of Constantine immediately taking ship for Athens, but said he felt convinced that an arrangement would speedily be arrived at which would be satisfactory alike to the Greek people and the allied powers.

"Italy, we know," he said, "will not oppose the return of Constantine to Greece, especially in view of the election results. France at the moment is hostile, but that may be overcome. As to the attitude of England, I feel sure that Premier Lloyd George would not look coldly or unfavorably upon an appeal addressed to him by United Greece asking for the restoration of her King."

\* \* \*

November 17, 1920

## VENIZELOS AND HIS OPPONENTS

Eleutherios Venizelos found Greece a petty peninsular State, discredited by an unsuccessful war, paralyzed by partisan intrigue, weak and poor and discouraged by the apparent impossibility of reuniting the scattered fragments of a once great nation. In ten years he won Crete and Northern Epirus and half of Macedonia, the whole north coast of the Aegean, Thrace down to Rodosto and a great strip of Western Anatolia. He recovered Canea, Janina, Saloniki, Cavalla, Adrianople, Smyrna, he brought Greece within reach of Constantinople. Under him the national morale was restored by three successful wars, and hardly less by the successful revolt against a faithless monarch who was trying to put Greece on the wrong side in the great war, and the nation's standing in Europe was raised high by his brilliant diplomacy at Bucharest and Paris.

And now after ten years he is as overwhelmingly defeated in the general elections as the party of Woodrow Wilson was defeated two weeks ago, and for very much the same reasons. The pro-German elements voted against him as they voted against Cox, but there as here they were only one of many varieties of opposition. Macedonians and Turks in Thrace to whom the Opposition had held out tempting if vague promises; peasants in the Heloponnesus who stand by their King; solders of the Balkan wars who still admire the victorious General of Kilkis, forgetting the betrayer of Rupel; merchants who are tired of wars, even glorious and triumphant wars, and want business started up again: quiet citizens restive under the domestic strain and restrictions of wartime; above all, no doubt, men who are tired of "progress, glory and expansion," as an Athens dispatch puts it—who revolt against the mental and spiritual effort required to make a small provincial State into a considerable Mediterranean Power, and are tired of hearing Venizelos called the Just.

This is a powerful combination in an election, but a very poor support for an alternative Government. In this medley of voters who do not like Venizelos's foreign policy, or his domestic policy, or his dynastic policy, or his personality, or his fame there is no strong individual or group around which a new Government can be built. Mr. Gounares has had a sort of leadership thrust upon him, but he cannot command the allegiance of this heterogeneous Opposition very long. The Greek system makes it possible to vote against Venizelos without voting for Gounares or Dragoumes; most of all, without voting for Constantine.

Mr. Venizelos now goes into the Opposition, but, unless his opponents should be so unwise as to permit a recurrence of the violence which broke out during the internal troubles of 1916, he will be better off than the man who has to take up the leadership of the Government. Will that man take the responsibility of recalling Constantine? Constantine surrendered Greek soil to the Bulgars; Venizelos has since won many thousands of square miles that the Bulgars either had or wanted. Will Constantine be called back to show once more what royal complaisance can do for his friends in Sofia? Will the Greek Government want to give so much encouragement to the old Bulgarian leaders who fought Greece and unsettle the position of Stamboliwsky, the friend of the Allies who is loyally executing the Treaty?

Constantine stood idle while Greeks in Turkey were massacred or deported. Under Venizelos Turkey has been reduced to an array of refugees in the mountains. Will the new Government tell the Greeks of Asia Minor that their hopes are vain, that they must prepare to be sacrificed to the personal policy of a vengeful exile?

Whether France and England still retain the right of interference to guarantee to Greece a constitutional Government, which they exercised in 1917, is a delicate question of international law. To exercise that right now would be a serious mistake; if Greece should call back Constantine, it would be an exercise of self-determination proper to a sovereign State. But will a Greek Government, supported by an insecure majority elected by a protest vote, affront governmental and popular sentiment in England, France and America by taking a step which can gratify none but the irreconcilable dreamers of revenge in Berlin and Budapest?

Greece has voted for a return to the golden age, when every man is an famous as every other man, nobody has to pay taxes, and the sun is always shining. But, the millennium does not always come when you whistle for it. It would not be surprising to see Venizelos back in office after a few months of experiment with these various beneficiaries of the voters' desire to get something off their minds.

\* \* \*

December 18, 1920

## ITALIAN SENATE PASSES TREATY WITH SLAVS

### Vote Is 262 to 22 in Favor of the Settlement—Fighting Breaks Out in Zara

ROME, Dec. 17—The Senate today passed the Treaty of Rapallo, settling the Adriatic question between Italy and Jugoslavia. The vote was 262 in favor of and 22 against the proposal.

Addressing the Senators before the adoption of the treaty, Count Sforza, the Foreign Minister, followed the main lines of the speech he made before the Chamber of Deputies on the same subject recently. He declared Italy was emerging from war through the Treaty of Rapallo a great power, having secure boundaries, and being free to dispose of her own future and proceed along her own road, which was the road of peace.

"But," he continued, "this is so not only because we obtained a wonderful natural frontier, which makes Italy a sort of continental England, but also because we had the courage not to annex land or a population which would have created irredentism against us."

Dispatches from Zara report that 200 troops, by order of Rear Admiral Millo, commander of the Italian naval forces in Dalmatia, marched to the barracks of the Dalmatian Volunteer Corps for the purpose of disarming the volunteers. The Dalmatians resisted. Rifle shots were exchanged and several on both sides were wounded. The commander of the carabineers intervened and the troops were withdrawn.

\* \* \*

May 16, 1922

## ON THE ADRIATIC

Albania has become almost the classical instance of a small nation unable to govern itself, but unwilling to be governed by another. From the practical viewpoint, it would probably have been a good thing for the country if the Italian protectorate had been continued, for Italy had done a great work of development in Albania during the war. But the Albanians rebelled against the protectorate and Italy prudently refused to reimpose it by force. A new effort is now made to meet the difficulty by what seems to amount to a protectorate under the League of Nations.

This proposal, in the form of the appointment of a number of outside experts to help the Albanian Government, was made in response to a request from that Government itself. Whether, prodded to action by the recent unsuccessful uprising, it is more eager for foreign aid than the people remains to be seen: but aid from the League ought to be free from the objections which could be raised against the intervention of any single Power. If the plan works, it may offer a hopeful example for other nations which fear the helping hand of powerful neighbors, but which have so far been unable to manage their own affairs.

The Italian insistence that Italy's special interests should be safeguarded in this tentative solution of the Albanian problem is reasonable enough, and seems to have been met to Italy's satisfaction by the promise of the League Council to allow Italy a special degree of participation in the appointment of the experts. Now comes a story that Italy will raise the Montenegrin question at the League meeting, backed up by assurances—from Montenegrin sources—that the Montenegrin delegation which has been trying to get some consolation at Genoa has been received with full honors by the Italians. Whatever has or has not happened at Genoa, it is inconceivable that the Italians will bring up this question at Geneva. They would hardly take it as a friendly act if a foreign Power should support the claims of the Bourbons to the crown of the Two Sicilies; and the two questions are on almost precisely the same footing. Since Senator Schanzer took over the Ministry of Foreign Affairs, Italian foreign policy has been directed toward European harmony. It is incredible that, with Italian-Jugoslav relations strained by the troubles in Fiume, an Italian Government should raise the Montenegrin issue now. The Treaty of Rapallo was supposed to pave the road to peace between the two countries, and, despite the failure of both sides to complete the work by the supplementary agreements which were expected, it does lay the foundation on which a durable peace can be erected on the Adriatic. To suppose that the Italians would destroy this prospect by intervention in favor of the exiled and discredited dynasty of Petrovitch-Niegosh is to credit Facta and Schanzer with far less intelligence than they have consistently shown.

There is no evidence that the Montenegrin question really disturbs anybody but the exiles. A more serious problem for the Jugoslav State is the continued hostility of Stephen Raditch and his Croatian Separatist Party, whose formidable memorandum on the "Neutral Republic of Croatia" was published on Sunday. Raditch is a politician of a familiar type. He and his supporters wanted a federated Jugoslavia, but the Constituent Assembly, by a narrow majority, voted for a unitary State. Thereupon Raditch refuses to play if the majority won't play his way. His party undoubtedly is the strongest in Croatia, among the people as well as among the politicians; but the fact remains that the authority of the Kingdom of the Serbs, Croats and Slovenes does prevail in Croatia; its officials rule, reservists come willingly to the colors when the Belgrade Government calls them, and the "Neutral Republic of Croatia" exists only on paper. That the conciliation of Croatian Separatists is one of the most important and most difficult problems of the Belgrade Government is true enough; yet the wild tales coming from Italy of Croatian secession seem to have little foundation but the undying hope of unofficial Italians who are not yet reconciled to the prospect of Adriatic peace.

\* \* \*

**July 31, 1922**

## GREECE THREATENS PEACE IN NEAR EAST BY MOVE IN SMYRNA

---

*Plans to Proclaim Autonomous State, Declaring Against Restoring Conquests to Turks*

**LANDS TROOPS AT RODOSTO**

*25,000 Men With Big Guns Now at Port, Seventy Miles West of Constantinople*

**TCHATALJA PATROLS CLASH**

*British Troops Are Moved Up There—Athens, Discouraged, Fears Desperate Move*

---

Copyright, 1922, by The New York Times Company
Special Cable to The New York Times
PARIS, July 30—As a reply to the Allies refusal of his request that he be allowed to occupy Constantinople with Greek troops and to their warnings that they will meet his armed attempt to do so with all the forces at their disposal, King Constantine has today had it announced in Smyrna that the occupied districts of Asia Minor will never be given back by Greece to the Turks, but will be created into an autonomous State under the protection of the Greek Army.

To the already tangled situation this new action has added a tangle which seems at first sight to have no less consequence than a terrible new outbreak of war in the Near East. But at the same time a settlement is rendered extremely difficult from the fact that no one really knows how serious are the intentions of any one else.

In its simplest consequences Constantine's action knocks the bottom out of the allied proposals for peace, as drafted in Paris last March. These proposals called for the evacuation of the whole of Asia Minor by Greek troops within three months of the date on which an agreement had been reached, and the re-establishment of Turkish sovereignty over the whole district. The Greek Government was then thought to be agreeable to this course; but with his declaration of autonomy Constantine has declared also that he refuses absolutely to hand back to the Turks any of the territory now under Greek control. He has preferred, on the eve of the conference which was to decide the fate of the country's colonial aspirations, to play for all or nothing.

Probably his request for the Greek occupation of Constantinople and his debarking of troops at Rodosto, where some skirmishing with the Turks is reported, were only a smoke screen for his real intentions. What he has done is enormously more effective; for, while his threat to invade the Turkish capital served only for once to unite all the Allies against him, his proclamation of autonomy for Smyrna is almost certain to divide allied opinion.

It was at the invitation of Great Britain that the Greek troops originally went to Asia Minor, and it is reasonably probable that British interests would far prefer a weak autonomous State at the western end of Asia Minor, with many proclamations of its intention to protect all religions and offend none to the complete handing back of what Venizelos won to the power or abuse of the Turks.

On the other hand, the French will just as vigorously oppose the creation of a new State whose autonomy is certain to stir up new nationalist aspirations in Syria. Already the French are calling on the British fleet to cut off supplies to the Greek Army in the disputed territory, and so end all prospects of war and all prospects of a settlement favorable to Constantine.

"If England wished it, there could be peace in the Near East tomorrow," says the Temps. But the question is, What sort of peace?

### Greeks Awaiting the Allied Reply

Special Cable to The New York Times
LONDON, July 30—The Daily Herald's Athens correspondent, telegraphing today, says:

"I am officially informed that the Greek Government is fully prepared to withhold all action in connection with the proposed occupation of Constantinople pending a reply from the Allies to the Greek notes. If the reply is not satisfactory the whole Greek nation, without exception, unanimously considers the occupation of Constantinople by a Greek army to be the only means of securing lasting peace in the Near East."

The Daily Chronicle editorially blames the Allies for the fresh trouble in the Near East. It says:

"The crisis that has arisen is the direct consequence or the inactivity of the Allies. We need not, however, affirm or exaggerate the wrongdoing of the Greeks until it has happened. What they have asked permission to do and what they will do without such permission are probably very different things, though in Paris there is some disposition to identify them. We must not forget that when the Allies composed their differences last March and made peace proposals to the Greek and Turkish Nationalist Governments the Greeks accepted the terms, but the Turks have given no satisfactory reply; that the commission of inquiry to Asia Minor proposed long ago has not yet started; that the Turks have used the interval when regular hostilities have been suspended for pursuing a policy of exterminating Christians—when we remember all these things we are bound to recognize that the Allies have assumed a responsibility which they have culpably neglected. So far from helping forward the peace negotiations the Allies have been actually a drag on the wheel.

"We cannot now be surprised if the Greeks are attempting to take matters into their own hands—politically in outlining their own scheme for the Government of Ionia, militarily in preparing their forces for action. But we cannot allow that action to materialize; we ought not to tolerate the resumption of war."

### Immediate Declaration of Autonomy

LONDON, July 30—A Reuter dispatch from Athens says autonomy for Smyrna and adjacent territory under Greek occupation is to be proclaimed immediately. Under the new regime the people will have extensive self-Government.

The dispatch adds that it is rumored Prince Nicholas will be appointed Governor of Smyrna and that elections will be held in the new State, these to be followed by application for recognition by the Powers.

According to the dispatch, the understanding is the Greek Government's decision outlined in Saturday's note to the Allies will not be put into execution for the present.

ATHENS, July 30—A note sent by the Greek Government to the Allies respecting the intentions of Greece in Asia Minor emphasizes the view that the occupation of Constantinople is the only means of bringing about peace and says Greece has made arrangements with that purpose in view.

The note begs the Allies to issue the necessary orders to the army of General Sir Charles Harington, Commander of the allied forces in Constantinople, and says it is confident difficulties will not be imposed in the way of Greece. It adds that by the neutralization of Constantinople the Allies are protecting, instead of coercing, Turkey, and thus depriving Greece of means for imposing peace.

The Turkish atrocities, the note continues, make it vital for Greece to adopt more energetic measures against the Turks, but is says the Greek Government is willing to discuss the matter with the Allies.

General Harington's declaration that he will oppose by force any move toward Constantinople has caused deep discouragement and disappointment in Greece, as the newspapers had been leading the people to believe Greek occupation of Constantinople would not be resisted by the Allies.

There was a three hours' session of the Cabinet on Saturday. At its conclusion the Government handed a supplementary note to the allied diplomats. The contents of this note have not been disclosed.

An announcement that the Greek Government is prepared to extend the war against the Turks beyond the already extensive borders caused intense excitement on the Bourse and further aggravation of Greece's financial and commercial crisis. The drachma fell today to nearly fifty to the dollar.

The Greek army of 300,000 men in Asia Minor, Macedonia and Thrace is costing $7,000,000 monthly. It is realized that this expenditure cannot be kept up indefinitely in the present parlous state of the Treasury. The remittances of $50,000,000 from Greeks in America during the last year have been of immense assistance to the Government. The Greeks are still hopeful that the American Government may release the balance of the $50,000,000 credits established in the regime of Premier Venizelos. This balance amounts to $33,000,000.

The steadily increasing cost of living, the continued calling to the colors of breadwinners of families and the failure of the Government to obtain financial assistance abroad are causing complaints among the populace generally, who are war-weary after ten years of almost continuous strife. The feeling seems to prevail, however, that the Government has been driven to a desperate expedient and a majority of the people apparently are disposed loyally to support it.

### Shots Fired by Tchatalja Patrols

CONSTANTINOPLE, July 30 (Associated Press)—A movement of British troops on the Asiatic side toward Tchatalja began today.

The Tchatalja region is quiet, but a few shots were exchanged today between the Turkish gendarmerie and a Greek patrol, three men on each side being wounded.

Considerable importance is attached here to an interview which General Sir Charles Harington, commander of the allied forces in Constantinople, has had at Sinekli with General Hadjanestis, Commander-in-Chief of the Greek Army in Asia Minor. The effect of such a military movement as that of today was discussed at length by the two Generals.

The allied powers, in reply to a protest from the Sublime Porte against the concentration of Greek forces on the frontier in Thrace, have assured the Turkish Government that Constantinople is safe from attack, and that all dispositions have been taken for its defense.

Greek troops continue to land at Rodosto. It is reported that their numbers have now reached 25,000. The Greeks yesterday landed heavy batteries at that port, having transferred the guns from their front in Asia Minor.

Rodosto, which is in Thrace, is seventy miles west of Constantinople on the Sea of Marmora.

The Greek newspapers hint at important military decisions, calculated to bring about a speedy settlement of the Near Eastern problem, but in well-informed allied circles it is generally believed the Athens Government will abandon its designs on the Turkish capital in case the allied powers, as expected, oppose their formal veto.

A Constantinople dispatch to The Associated Press Saturday night said that the Greek Government had informed the allied commission that it did not intend to send an army against Constantinople without the permission of the Allies. The military movements in Thrace, it explained, were in preparation for such a step, should the Allies approve.

Paris and London dispatches represented allied Government circles as strenuously opposed to Greece's plans, and the French Government, it was announced, had informed the Greek Chargé d'Affaires that France formally refused authorization for an attack upon the stronghold of the Sublime Porte.

GENEVA, July 30 (Associated Press)—Although Eleutherios Venizelos, the former Greek Premier, refused today to make a public statement with regard to the Greco-Turkish situation, it was said by one of his entourage at St. Moritz that Venizelos considered that any Greek attack at Constantinople would be national suicide, politically and diplomatically.

\* \* \*

August 29, 1922

## JUGOSLAVIA'S KING DEFIES 'BLACK HAND'

*Alexander Refused to Be Tool of Junta*
*That Put His Father on Throne*

### 'WHITE HAND' DEFENDS HIM

*Possibility That Prince George, Who Renounced Succession,*
*May Yet Be Claimant for Throne*

Copyright, 1922, by The New York Times Company
Special Cable to The New York Times

MILAN, Aug. 28—A background recalling a dark tragedy lies behind the present dispute between King Alexander of Jugoslavia, and his brother, Prince George, regarding certain rights claimed by the Prince and refused by the King. It is the old story of a dynasty refusing to pander to the Junta which raised it to the throne, according to a narrative appearing in a Roman newspaper.

This particular Junta called the "Black Hand" was formed during the reigns of King Alexander Obranovitch and his Queen Draga, it being one of the first secret societies to resolve on the removal of these two royalties by assassination and to substitute for their dynasty their historic rivals the Karageorgevitches. The ostensible reasons for their opposition to Alexander and Draga were that their rule was reactionary and that they were merely tools of the Austrian Foreign Office.

Regicide was duly committed by the Junta, Alexander and Draga being murdered one night in 1903, and it was some time before certain European States accorded diplomatic recognition to the new dynasty. The first monarch under the revived Karageorgevitch dynasty was the late King Peter, who was in Switzerland at the time of the murders and always denied any complicity in them.

Both he and his second son when the latter assumed the regency were regarded by the Black Hand as not only their creations but also as their tools, and the new dynasty began to feel it would have to fight for its own liberty. A new secret society was formed called the "White Hand," and soon the army was, and still is, divided between the two.

Then came the great war, in which both the Prince Regent, now King Alexander, and his elder brother, Prince George, did splendid service. George suffering wounds which would have precluded his hoping to ascend the throne even had he not renounced the succession.

In 1916 at Saloniki an attempt was made on the life of the present King Alexander. It was at once assumed that the Black Hand was responsible. Several arrests were made and after a summary trial two of its members holding high commands in the army, were shot and others were sentenced to long terms of imprisonment.

When the new triune Kingdom of the Serbs, Croats and Slovenes came into being King Alexander granted amnesty to all prisoners in the kingdom as a mark of rejoicing, the imprisoned members of the Black Hand being of course included. They at once rejoined the army and these two societies, Black and White, still carry on their secret purposes.

The Whites are for the present dynasty, for whose defense they were formed. The Blacks are opposed to King Alexander, whom they raised to power, but who refuses to be their tool, and they support George's claims against his brother in the hope that should he ever reach the throne—for he may yet become a claimant—he will be what Alexander has refused to become. They have succeeded in dividing the army, and that is bad.

\* \* \*

September 12, 1922

## WHAT TO DO WITH THE TURKS

The Parisian politicians who had their three or four days of joy over the Turkish victories are beginning to temper their hilarity with reflection. It was all very fine for the Turks to beat the Greeks and take Smyrna, which, if not Turkish, would have been either Greek or Italian. But the Turks are feeling their oats. They insist on getting and holding Constantinople, Adrianople, Eastern Thrace; they want an equal share in the government of Western Thrace; they demand a contiguous frontier with Bulgaria; they tell Europe that Bulgaria must have her promised outlet to the Aegean. What is going to be done about it? The allied fleets, if they could be induced to work together, could probably keep the Turkish army in Anatolia. But the Turks are good waiters; the Allies would probably tire of keeping strong and expensive squadrons in the Straits before the Turks would tire of waiting for the warships to move away.

The Turkish victory will undoubtedly have its reactions in Bulgaria, where there will probably be a louder demand for the outlet to the Aegean that has been promised, as well as for certain things that were not promised. In India, street crowds have been cheering for the Turkish victories; France is also a great Mohammedan Power, and the feelings of French Mohammedans may conceivably be Mohammedan rather than French in the immediate future. In other words, Europe is once more face to face with the Turk, who has been kept off for the past three years by the shock-absorbing Greek army. To be sure, he is not the Turk of old; if strong in spirit, he is weak in force. But Europe is weak too, weak and divided. The Turks want certain things and are willing to work for them much harder than any European Power— except Greece, now beaten—will work to stop them.

The last stages of the Greek retreat seem to have been an utter rout; the army that fought so well last year simply collapsed when it realized that all its efforts had gone for nothing. It is significant that the Government is trying to divert the escaping troops to the islands instead of letting them come to Athens. Even so, some of them have insisted on being taken to the Piraeus and have been making demonstrations against the Government. One Ministry follows another, though the rumors of an intended abdication seem premature.

Greece now passes into the background. The Asiatic conquests must be given up; possibly even Thrace will be lost. But the responsibility of dealing with the Turks now lies on the three Powers whose dissensions and backstairs intrigue have brought the Turk back to the threshold of Europe. The Greeks were fighting for European civilization; the Turks were fighting for their own national life, a cause naturally dear to them. In the Greco-Turkish war both parties deserved the respect of outsiders. But in the prospective diplomatic conflict between the Turks and the Western Powers neutral sympathies could be wholly with the Turks but for one consideration. This is that the Western Powers do not pay their own losses. They leave that to the Christians of Anatolia. The Turks are making a great show of behaving well in Smyrna, where everybody can see them and the guns of British dreadnoughts command the town; but there is sufficient evidence as to their treatment of Greeks and Armenians when they are out of range of naval guns.

\* \* \*

December 13, 1922

## AMERICAN ENVOY ASKS GUARANTEES FOR MINORITIES

*Child Pleads at Lausanne for Creation of Territorial Refuges for Christians in Turkey*

### ISMET DEFIANT TO ALLIES

*Says There Will Be No National Home for Armenians and No Foreign Interference*

### CURZON FOR LEAGUE BOARD

*His Plan for Protecting Minorities Calls for Control Body In Constantinople*

By EDWIN L. JAMES
Copyright, 1922 by The New York Times Company
Special Cable to THE NEW YORK TIMES

LAUSANNE, Dec. 12—The United States spoke today for the Christian minorities in Turkey when Ambassador Child, expressing the vital interest of America in the problem, prayed the other nations to do something about it.

"The United States and the whole world," he said, expect and may righteously require tolerance and justice and concession on the part of the Turkish Government.

Mr. Child's prepared statement was preceded by a speech by Ismet Pasha in reply to the allied proposals in which he offered two solutions of the problem of the minorities: First, that all minorities should quit Turkey; second, that they trust in "the spirit of good-will and sense of justice which has always characterized the Turkish nation."

Lord Curzon said that the Turks failure to give any evidence of an intention of guaranteeing the safety of the minorities would cause bitter disappointment throughout the world. He assured the Turks that the Allies would not permit the concluding of peace terms which did not provide guarantees for the safety of the Greeks, Armenians and other minorities remaining under the Crescent banner. To prove the necessity for such guarantees he cited the eloquent fact that there were now in Turkey only 130,000 of the 3,000,000 Armenians who lived there a few years ago.

### Features of the Allied Plan

The allied plan is in two parts: First, that there shall be written into the Turkish treaty the general guarantees for minorities contained in the Paris Peace Conference treaties with the various Central European nations and the Allies; second, that action be taken by which a general amnesty shall be granted by both Turkey and Greece, in accordance with which Christians in Turkey and Turks in other countries shall be allowed to purchase exemption from military service, all minorities shall have freedom of movement, and the League of Nations shall establish a board in Constantinople to watch over the welfare of the minorities.

Mr. Child's statement was an eloquent exposition of America's humanitarian interest in the plight of the persecuted hordes of the Near East. But this earnest statement of America's interest, couched in the form of a recommendation of what the Allies should do, coming after Ismet's arrogant speech, lacked the "punch" which might be thought essential to obtaining the fulfilment of the American purpose. It may be taken for granted that what concessions the Turks eventually make to Lord Curzon, M. Barrere and the Marquis di Garroni will be made because behind the words of those statesmen are the naval and military forces of their respective country. Unfortunately, to help in bringing about this result Mr. Child has no such backing.

### Humanitarian Interest America's Right

In explaining his intervention Mr. Child said:

"Humanitarian interest is as much our right and duty as the right and duty of every nation." He declared that it would be in the interest of Turkey to give protection to the minorities, and that it was "unthinkable that the aspirations of Turkey for independence, for progress should not rely in part upon a generous policy of contribution to the safety and relief from suffering of mankind. The safety and relief from suffering of mankind is one of the principal concerns of Governments."

The safety of many thousands now in peril in the Near East, he said "has for the people of the United States a vital interest."

The Ambassador referred to the large sums spent by the American people in Near East relief as an earnest of their interest and added: "The people of my country ask no return for this expenditure unless it be the assurance that this conference to the full extent of its power will find a means to wipe away at once the causes of this waste of human life and human suffering."

Mr. Child then outlined the problem, saying:

"The facts are a rebuke to the world. They challenge the self-respect of civilization. They are so stupendous that pity for individuals is lost in pity for the masses."

He asked that the conference should not end without setting up machinery for permanent international labors to find a refuge for the Christians in Turkey.

"The representatives of the United States," he said in conclusion, "believe that the ends to be sought are prevention rather than mere relief, and guarantees of safety for minorities rather than mere succor to their misery, and permanent joint action rather than mere spasmodic separate activity. In this purpose the people of my country, although far removed by distance, have a profound interest and will continue to stand ready with their contributions." Mr. Child's closing words gave the impression that the United States might be willing to take a place on the commission to watch over the minorities in Turkey, although he supplies no exact information on that point.

### Curzon Presents Allied Proposals

At the opening of the session Lord Curzon presented the allied plan for the protection of minorities in a very able speech. Every one, he said should admit that the Turkish treaty must carry provisions for such protection. When the minorities in Turkey were strong there was bloodshed and carnage. Now that they were weaker the need for protection was all the more evident.

"I invite the Turkish and Greek delegations to realize that the eyes of the world are upon us," he said "as we discuss this question; and according as it is settled in an equitable and reasonable spirit or the reverse, so shall they and we be judged."

He recalled the fact that one of the war aims of the Allies was the liberation and protection of the minorities in Asia Minor. For half a century, he said, protection had been promised the Armenians.

Pointing to the provisions regarding minorities in the treaties signed by Rumania, Poland, Jugoslavia, Czechoslovakia, Austria, Hungary and Bulgaria, he said that Turkey should give no less assurances. He reviewed the various allied meetings at which the Turkish problem had been discussed, at all of which decisions to aid the minorities had been taken. He also reminded the Turks that the allied note of Sept. 23 which led to the calling of the Lausanne conference assigned Eastern Thrace to Turkey on condition that Turkey gave assurances for the safeguarding of the minorities and accept the supervision of their execution by the League of Nations. The Turkish minorities in other countries were entitled to the same guarantees as the Christian populations of Turkey. He told the Turks that they would be the gainers if they co-operated in the international plan suggested.

Turning directly to Ismet Pasha, Lord Curzon said that in the last three or four months between 600,000 and 900,000 Christians had left Turkey.

"I sometimes wonder," he said, "If the Turkish Government have fully considered the economic results of this gigantic transference of peoples, to which there is no parallel in modern history, and by which I expect Turkey will lose more than she gains."

He then made the announcement that all the Turks in Greek territory outside those in Western Thrace would be returned to Turkey. This means the migration of 350,000 Moslems. The 124,000 Turks in Western Thrace will be allowed to remain if the Turks consent to permit the Greeks in Constantinople to stay there. If the Turks refuse to do so, Greece will expel all the Turks in Western Thrace.

Lord Curzon said that the whole Greek population of Anatolia formerly more than 1,000,000 had dwindled to 50,000. The Allies and America, he said had also an interest in the Assyrian Christians in Kurdistan.

### Curzon's Plea for Armenians

"The Armenians' case is deserving of special consideration," he continued, "not merely because of the cruel sufferings which they have endured for generations and which have excited the sympathy and horror of the civilized world, but also because of the special pledges which have been made."

The old Russian Province of Erivan, now a Soviet Republic, he said has a million and a quarter Armenians, but was so crowded that it could not hold any more. The Armenian population of Kars and Ardanan, of Van, Bitlia and Erzerum had pretty well disappeared, he said, adding that in Asiatic Turkey there remained only 130,000 Armenians, where there had been 8,000,000.

Referring to the hundreds of thousands of Armenian refugees in the Causasus, Russia, Persia and other countries, Lord Curzon turned to the prospect for the establishment of an Armenian homeland. He said that circumstances rendered the execution of this plan difficult, but he would like to hear the Turkish opinion on it. Then he outlined the allied plan and invited the other delegations to speak.

Camille Barrere, head of the French delegation, and the Marquis di Garroni, head of the Italian delegation gave formal approval to the allied plan presented by Lord Curzon.

### Ismet Rejects the Allied Plan

Ismet Pasha then spoke, saying that it was impossible to judge the situation without looking at the historical background. Beginning with the capture of Constantinople by the Turks, he said, Turks and Christians had lived together in good relations until about a hundred years ago, when foreign interference changed the situation. From the Treaty of 1774, when Russia assumed the protection of Orthodox Christians in Turkey, onward, he declared, foreign nations had tried to use the situation of the Christians to work for the downfall of the Turkish Empire. He went into a long series of charges against Czarist Russia and attributed to Russian propaganda Gladstone's campaign against the Turks. The burden of his argument was an attempt to show that the Christians always started the massacres, and that the Turks were guilty only of reprisals. He charged that for many years an Armenian society in Europe provoked massacres in Turkey in order to give the Russians a chance to attack Turkey.

After 1878, when the powers collectively undertook the protection of Christians, Ismet said, the situation got worse.

"The Armenians have brought their disaster upon themselves," he declared.

"They abused the generosity of the Turks under whose régime they lived."

Arguing that the Jews, in Turkey, had never had cause for complaint, Ismet reached the conclusion that the Christians were to blame for all their troubles.

He said that the two basic causes for the troubles of the minorities in Turkey were, first, outside interference, and, second, the desire of these populations to be free.

"The safety of the minorities in future," he said, "depends upon the neutralization of these two causes of trouble."

"The League of Nations system is not acceptable because the powers would continue their interference and incite the minorities to appeal to the League. The result would be the exploitation of the minorities for political purposes behind the lying cloak of humanitarianism."

Ismet declared that there were only two solutions of the minority issue: one was the expulsion of the minorities and the other was trusting the Turks good will and sense of justice.

Answering Ismet, Lord Curzon said that the Allies could not accept the Turkish position and that they intended to do something for the distressed peoples whose misery was not open to denial. Referring to the concrete proposals by the Allies which had been furnished in advance to the Turkish delegation, he said that the Turks had made no reply except to attack the minorities in a manner which made him all the more sure they needed protection. As for Ismet's statement that all Christians should be driven from Turkey. Lord Curzon said that the answer of the world would be, "No, that is impossible."

He appealed to the Turks to approach the subject in the spirit of charity and humanity. If Ismet's speech represents all the Turks had to offer, there was a question whether there was any use going further. Ismet's speech, he said, would cause profound disappointment all over the world. "I am bitterly disappointed," Lord Curzon concluded.

Ex-Premier Venizelos recalled Article 5 of the Angora National Pact, which promised protection to the minorities and said that all the Turks had offered was the suggestion that the powers disinterest themselves in the minorities. The other powers, enemies and Allies alike, had signed treaties for the protection of minorities and Turks must do as much.

Ismet spoke again, saying that the Turkish position was: "All that the minorities have to do to be safe in Turkey is to behave themselves." He promised to give a specific reply to the allied proposals tomorrow. He added that it was not fair to accuse the Turks of being unreasonable because they were going to permit the Greeks to remain in Constantinople if the Turks were allowed to stay in Western Thrace.

The Turkish delegation tonight sent to Lord Curzon, as President of the conference, a note asking for the creation of a special subcommission to draft clauses of a treaty relating to the Straits. The purpose of this demand is to admit the Russians to the Straits discussion, which for the last few days has been conducted between the allied and Turkish experts, to the exclusion of the Russians.

### Ismet Dashes Hopes of Conference

LAUSANNE, Dec. 12 (Associated Press)—Ismet Pasha, head of the Turkish delegation, dashed the hopes of the Near Eastern conference for a speedy and satisfactory settlement for the protection of minorities in Turkey when, in an address at this afternoon's session, he insisted upon an exchange of the Greek populations in Anatolia for the Turks in Macedonia. He demanded exclusion of all foreign interference in Turkey, which he said would protect the remaining minorities as the Turks had always been able to get along with other nationals when they kept out of politics and were not stirred up by outside influences.

According to Ismet, there are now no minorities in Turkey which can claim the right to belong to any other nation, and this disposes of the Armenian claim for a national home in Turkey.

M. Spaiaikovitch speaking for Jugoslavia, denied that Russia and the Slavs generally were responsible for the unrest in Turkey, which was really caused by the sentiment of nationality that had fired so many people to free themselves from Turkish rule.

Ismet Pasha spoke again, saying that he had not had time to complete the allied plan as presented by Lord Curzon, but would study it and give a detailed reply. Lord Curzon urged him to do this tomorrow. Ismet asked for more time, but Curzon retorted. "I sat up until 2.30 this morning, and I am sure that if the Turkish delegate sits up until 2 tomorrow morning he can be prepared to speak tomorrow."

Ismet laughed and agreed. So the session will be resumed tomorrow morning.

### Empty Concession to Greeks

Turkey's official announcement at the morning session of the conference that the Greeks might remain in Constantinople under stated conditions lost much of its value to the Greeks when they learned what those conditions were. Dr. Riza Nur Bey, the second Turkish plenipotentiary, outlined them. In accordance with the desire voiced by the American and other delegations, said Riza, Turkey, inspired by high humanitarian motives, had decided to allow the Greeks to stay, but it must be understood that the Supreme Patriarch of the Greek Orthodox Church "and all his institutions" must be deported because of their hostile attitude toward Turkey.

Furthermore, all Greek residents not Turkish subjects must be deported if they were not born in Constantinople and all Greek societies and associations which had been hostile to Turkey must also go elsewhere. Permission to remain should not be understood as applying to Greeks living outside the state of the city, who should be exchanged with the Turkish element dwelling in Greece.

Riza Nur Bey made the point that the property of Greeks in Constantinople could rightfully be considered as the equivalent of the property of the Turks residing in Greece but if a general exchange were not made, Turkish refugees from Greece should be indemnified by the Greek Government: this indemnity should be calculated in accordance with any excess in the wealth of the two populations respectively. As the Greek colony in Constantinople is exceedingly prosperous, this arrangement, if carried out, would mean the payment of a considerable indemnity by the Greeks.

The conditions under which Greece will agree to renounce all ideas if the exchange of population, which remains in Anatolia numbering 300,000, shall not be deported and that the Anatolian Greeks who fled shall be permitted to return. Another condition is that former Greek residents may return to Eastern Thrace when peace is concluded and Turkey thinks the interests of the Province justify it and also that the Greek colony may remain in Constantinople without losing any rights.

In return Greece promises to refrain from coercive measures which would have the effect of driving the Turks from Greek territory and will extend the same guarantees to the Moslem minorities as the Turks extend to the Greeks.

### Soviet Delegates Walk Out

Bolshevist Russia is keeping up the pace in the way of protest at Lausanne that she set at Genoa. The Russian experts today ostentatiously walked out of the meeting which was discussing the Dardanelles and the Bosporus as a protest against the alleged exclusion of the Russians from important phases of the Straits negotiations, and tonight the Russian delegation officially notified the three Presidents of the conferences of Russia's unalterable determination to abandon none of her rights in the negotiations over the Straits directly affecting her vital interests.

In their protest the Russians condemn the Allies for dividing the Straits problem into two parts, one devoted to regulations for opening the Straits, the other concerning demilitarized zones. They assert that permission to voice their opinions on demilitarization had been denied them though this is directly connected with the Straits problem as a whole and contend that the whole basis of the conference has been laid down to the prejudice of Russia. Moreover they add the new plan for the control of the Straits presented today contained new features on which Russia had never been consulted.

The new allied project introduced in the conference gives foreign countries the right to send their warships through the Straits, each of a tonnage of 10,000 or more. The alternative plan of permitting as many foreign ships as the greatest naval power in the Black Sea is maintained in the new regulations.

\* \* \*

December 14, 1922

# HOW LEAGUE SYSTEM PROTECTS MINORITIES

*Plan Now in Operation in a Dozen Countries Is Expected to Satisfy the Turks*

WASHINGTON, Dec. 13—Allied plans for protecting minorities in Turkey are based on the system already worked out through the League of Nations for minority protection in States stretching from the Baltic to the Black Sea, according to detailed information which reached Government officials here today through unofficial channels.

The detailed scheme presented at Lausanne by Lord Curzon and upon which the conference deadlocked, it is indicated, was framed to meet the Angora Government's statement to the conference that it was willing to accept such minority protection stipulations as had been accepted by neighboring States but not willing to concur in special provisions as to Turkey, which seemed to place her in a prejudiced position.

Under the minority protection treaties applying in the States other than Turkey the nations accepting the principle of minority protection agree to certain minimum rights for religious and racial minorities within their frontiers, to recognize that these rights form a matter of international concern, and to grant to any member of the Council of the League of Nations the right to call the attention of the Council to any infraction thereof. This system, already covering a dozen nations, has now been in operation for three years and was considerably expanded in its actual method of operation at the League Assembly in September.

The allied plan would extend these same requirements to Turkey, whose acceptance had been expected as a result of her previous declarations. In addition, it was proposed to add some special clauses to fit the special situation of Turkey and in accordance with the precedent set in the other treaties. It was felt that Turkey could have no objection to this, as Poland had accepted special arrangements for the Jews, Yugoslavia, Albania and Greece, for the Moslems, Rumania for the Saxons, &c.

It was also felt essential that a high commissioner be named by the League to be present at the seat of the Turkish Government and to have the right to name investigators within Turkey to see that the minority stipulations agreed upon were carried out. Turkey, it was thought, would be willing to accept this provision, both because it was a right vested in all the minorities treaties and not in any sense special to her own, and because it would be much to her advantage to have one channel for handling all questions of this sort.

The League memorandum outlining this project in detail stresses that the League minorities protection system is already a working, existing mechanism and could offer such a permanent joint system of protection as has been urged by allied representatives at Lausanne and by Ambassador Child.

\* \* \*

January 11, 1923

## MILLION MUST QUIT HOMES IN NEAR EAST, LAUSANNE DECREES

*The Allied Conferees Accept the Turkish Proposals for the Exchange of Populations*

### CONSTANTINOPLE EXEMPTED

*200,000 Greeks There Allowed to Remain; Likewise 300,000 Turks in Western Thrace*

### PATRIARCHATE STAYS, TOO

*But New Patriarch Must Be Chosen, to Be Merely Spiritual Head of Greeks In Turkey*

By EDWIN L. JAMES
Copyright, 1923, by The New York Times Company
Special Cable to The New York Times

LAUSANNE, Jan. 10—In the name of peace and justice 1,000,000 men, women and children are to be torn from their homes and forcibly taken to other lands. Such was the remarkable decision taken today by this remarkable Near East conference.

The statesmen of the civilized nations and of Turkey this morning voted to exchange the Greek population of Turkey against the Turkish population of Greece. Excepted from the measure are the 200,000 Greeks in Constantinople, and in return the 300,000 Turks in Western Thrace, which belongs to Greece. By the terms of today's decision all other Greeks in Turkey and all other Turks in Greece must move. It is estimated that 600,000 Greeks in Turkey are affected and about 450,000 Turks in Macedonia and the rest of Greece.

Today's action is regretted by Allied diplomats, who admit its inhumanity, but defend it on the ground that it is the sole means of preventing a worse fate from overtaking the Greeks in Turkey. These same diplomats yesterday accepted the Turks' paper promises as being sufficient protection for the minorities in Turkey.

That there may be no misunderstanding, it must be made plain that this extraordinary step is due entirely and exclusively to the Turks' determination to expel the Greeks from their country. It was only after this determination became plain that the Greeks demanded that the Turks in Greece be expelled in order to make room for the Greeks who must leave Turkey, where their forefathers in many cases, had lived for many centuries.

On the other hand, the Turks today agreed to let the Greek Patriarch remain in Constantinople on condition that he be shorn of all his secular powers and retain solely his religious jurisdiction. This concession is probably part of the price paid for yesterday's surrender of the Allies in the minorities controversy, just as the Turks' consent to leave the Greeks in Constantinople was given in return for the Greek promise to leave the Turks in Western Thrace, which, by the way, the Turks hope eventually to own.

It is to be remarked that the retention of the patriarchate in Constantinople and the permission given the Greeks to remain in that city represent two solutions favored by the Americans. It should also be pointed out that the dropping of the Armenian home project and the decision to exchange populations represent the rejection of two other measures advocated by the Americans. The net result does not indicate that the influence of the Americans is predominant in the settlements made here.

It is planned that the League of Nations shall supervise the exchange of populations, providing for transportation and seeing that the Turks on the one hand and the Greeks on the other obtain a fair settlement for the property they must leave behind them. While the time limit for the transfer was not fixed, it is generally believed that it will be placed at about six or eight months.

Strange as such a decision may seem—a decision under the terms of which Greeks may live in Constantinople and not in the suburbs, under which Turks may live in Western Thrace and not in Macedonia—everyone here seems to take it seriously. In effect the move seems to mean the actual exchange of a million persons or else formal permission to the Turks to persecute Greeks who remain in Turkey.

### Exchange of Population Compulsory

The Turks sought to have the exchange made non-compulsory or voluntary, which would mean that they would chase out the Greeks, whereas the Turks would not have to leave Greece unless they chose to do so. Ex-Premier Venizelos opposed this; demanding that if an exchange were decided upon it must be compulsory. The conference adopted his point of view.

In a speech at today's session Lord Curzon expressed the deepest regret at the necessity of deciding on an exchange of populations, but declared that a week's discussion showed that no other decision was possible. Admitting that he detested the solution and deplored it, he said he thought there was nothing else to do. What he meant was that there was no way of preventing Turkey from ousting the Greeks unless the Allies were prepared to fight, and, like the Americans, the English are not ready to fight the Turks—for humanitarian ends.

In the account of today's events given by the spokesmen of the Allies great emphasis is laid on "the Patriarchate Victory," which simply represents a Turkish concession for which an ample price has been paid.

The decision was well staged-managed. Senator Montagna, Chairman of the Committee on the Exchange of Populations, reported that an agreement had been reached, except that the Turks still demanded the expulsion of the Greek Patriarch as one of the conditions of allowing the Greeks to remain in Constantinople. Lord Curzon in an eloquent speech referred to the American pronouncement against the expulsion and said that the whole world would be aroused by such a step. He suggested that the proper solution might be to take away from the Patriarch all powers and confine his activities to religious matters, allowing him to remain on these terms. Camille Barrère, speaking for France, agreed to Lord Curzon's recommendation, and so did M. Venizelos. Ismet Pasha then read a statement renouncing the Turkish demand that the Patriarch be expelled and agreeing to his remaining as a purely religious leader. Of course, it had, all been arranged beforehand.

It has been agreed that the present Patriarch, Melitos IV, shall not return to Constantinople, but shall be replaced.

### Change of British Policy Toward Turks

The Allies' action of yesterday and today under Lord Curzon's leadership brings into relief the present British policy toward the Turk. After weeks of threatening them, the British seem now to have gone back to their traditional policy of buying them off against the Russians. In the negotiations over capitulations and Mosul the Turks are still demanding a high price, and on both issues Lord Curzon has declared that he will not yield. But one must wait and see. England is more likely to give way on the capitulations issue than on that of Mosul and its oil.

But there seems little doubt that the British have shifted their Lausanne policy, and it appears to be now a question what price the British will pay for a treaty with the Turks. England has obtained a favorable solution of the Straits prob-lem, whereas the Turks have certainly won out on the minorities issue and their determination to expel the Greeks. It seems likely that the capitulations settlement will be much nearer the Turkish than the allied demands. That leaves Mosul as the big issue before the conference. The British realize that they will be criticised for giving in to the Turks on humanitarian issues, but their reply will unquestionably be that they could not be expected to fight alone for the humanitarian wishes of the world.

By the nature of their mission here the American delegates can do little more than sit by and watch the wheel spin, rejoicing when their numbers come up and remaining silent when their numbers lose. The movements of the powers that be here have given the Americans partial satisfaction in letting some warships through the Straits, and denied them satisfaction placing a League commission over the Straits. Americans may feel satisfaction because the Greek Patriarch remains in Constantinople. Satisfaction was denied them when the project of a national home for Armenians was discarded. Americans will be pleased to know that the Greeks will be left in Constantinople. They will be displeased at the decree for the exchange of populations. One may wonder if the result would have been much different had there been no American delegates here.

The belief that the conference will result in a treaty is much stronger since the Allies' surrender of yesterday and today. It is generally thought that the conference will run for several weeks, more or less, all depending on the Mosul issue.

### Greece Gets Her Minimum Demands

LAUSANNE, Jan. 10 (Associated Press)—A halt in the preparatory movement of Greek troops along the frontier of Eastern Thrace is expected to be one of the first results of the decisions in regard to the Patriarch and the Greek colony in Constantinople.

The Allies have appeared somewhat anxious over the movements of the Greek army, which was described in some reports as ready to move across the frontier if peace became clearly impossible. Maintenance of the Greek Patriarchate as a spiritual institution and permission for the Greek colony to remain in Constantinople were the minimum of the Greek demands, and today's decisions largely remove the tension between Greece and Turkey.

The change of position by the Turks on the question of the Greek Patriarchate in Constantinople has given the Armenian delegation here hope that a similar eventual agreement will make possible the establishment of a national homeland for their people in Turkey.

The Armenian delegates called on Richard Washburn Child, chief American representative, this afternoon and, after thanking him for his efforts on their behalf, requested his further personal intervention in Armenia's cause.

They were convinced, they told him, that Christian Armenia would, as a nation, never forget his humanitarian initiative, which was in consonance with the American ideal of extending a helping hand to the persecuted and suffering.

CONSTANTINOPLE, Jan. 10—The emigration of the Greek population from Angora has begun according to current Angora advices.

### CHARITY'S STAKE IN TURKEY
**"Officials Hold Aloof, Philanthropists Foot Bills," Says Burns**

The following statement was issued yesterday by the National Information Bureau:

"Officials hold aloof, Philanthropists foot the bills, sums up America's relation to the question of minorities at the Lausanne conference. This report was made yesterday to Secretary of State Hughes in Washington by Allen T. Burns, director of the National Information Bureau on country-wide relief appeals. Mr. Burns has just returned from Lausanne after a two weeks' trip among the 800,000 refugees in Greece. He made the trip to learn what the needs of these refugees were and what expenditures were necessary by the American Red Cross, which has assumed the responsibility for American relief.

"Mr. Burns reported that there are in Greece 500,000 homeless, half naked, underfed women, children and old men from Asia Minor. Their men breadwinners have all been held in Anatolia by the Turks as hostages. The reuniting of these families is the most humanly imperative feature of the minorities question at Lausanne. According to the latest news dispatches, these minorities are going to be left to the mercy of the Turks for final disposition. In this decision, momentous for these refugees and involving millions of dollars of expenditures from American relief resources the American Government takes no responsible part—is an 'observer.'

"No relief worker or giver feels that the cost to American philanthropy should be the sole factor in determining the foreign policy of the United States. But when decisions like those at Lausanne mean a charge of millions of dollars, the stake of American charity in our foreign policy becomes direct and considerable.

"The American Red Cross has undertaken to co-operate with the Greek Government in caring for these refugees. Judge John Parton Payne, National Chairman of the Red Cross, asked Mr. Burns in Washington yesterday what the cost was going to be and how long relief would be needed. The reply was:

" 'It depends absolutely on whether the Lausanne conference secures the return of the hundreds of thousands of breadwinners to their families. The possibility of putting the refugees on a self-supporting basis, and so ending the need for American charity, is indefinitely remote, unless the reuniting of the men with their women and children is secured.'

"Secretary Hughes stated to Mr. Burns that America had done all it could. He gave no reply to a question by the latter as to whether we could be more than 'observers.'

"But as the news comes from Lausanne that American 'observation' has secured no more result than a decision from the 'responsible' part of the conference to abandon the minorities to the Turks, a ghastly picture overwhelms one who has seen the victims of the decision. As one walks among these myriads of famished, shivering, bedless women and children, one hears never a word about their own condition. With one voice they plead, 'Give us back our men.' Should one go among them this morning with the news from Lausanne fresh in their ears, their tears and protestations might melt the heart of a non-participating, irresponsible Government and people. Perhaps the combined considerations of thrift and mercy would lead America to answer the refugees cry, 'How long, O Lord, how long?' with an effectual and irrepressible 'I am my brother's keeper.' "

\* \* \*

April 1, 1923

## GREECE AS TRUSTEE OF PEACE BETWEEN THE ORIENT AND EUROPE

*Her Army, Defeated by Kemal Last Year, Reorganized and Concentrated in Thrace Ready for Turks' Next Move, "Olive Branches on Its Bayonet Points"*

### By WINTHROP D. LANE

Greece, accounted a small nation, holds for the moment a place of vast importance in the peace of the world. She is the only European country today having active frontier relations with Turkey, if we omit Turkey's present occupancy of East Thrace, which gives her contact with Bulgaria but which, with the Lausanne peace unsigned, may not be permanent. Greece holds a special niche in the affections of Western peoples, her great past giving it to her. Turkey is the dominant power of the Middle East. In a peculiar sense, therefore, Greece is the trustee of European and Near East peace with the Middle Eastern world. Upon the relations of these two peoples hangs in great measure the future tranquillity of the Balkans, and the tranquillity of the Balkans is closely allied to the peace of Europe.

For three months Greece has been preparing for this "eventuality." She has made over the army that Kemal routed in Asia Minor last Fall. It is now in fighting trim; well clothed, well equipped, well armed. With a rapidity worthy of a strong Western nation she has concentrated her troops in Western Thrace, there to face along the Maritsa River whatever soldiers Kemal may muster on the other side. She has 150,000 troops in that territory. She is ready for a thrust through Eastern Thrace toward Constantinople.

"I am confident that in the near future Greece will accomplish wonders," said Pangalos, Minister of War, a few weeks ago, while negotiations were dragging at Lausanne. "Wait and hope; those are my last words." Then he added: "We come to the front holding an olive branch, but at the same time our hand rests on the hilt of the sword. We hope that we shall not be compelled to draw the sword, but if we do, then . . . ." An army with olive branches on its bayonet points! Caissons and field artillery bearing proffers of friendship! Gonatas, Prime Minister and one of the band of Colonels and Admirals who "took" Athens and set up a revolutionary government a few months ago, said at the same time: "Greece is ready for whatever may happen." To this Plastiras, "The Revolution" himself, added: "The Greek Army is now superior to the one she had during her moments of victory." Greece may not provoke war—she is too sensitive to the opinion of the world and to the necessity of retaining Great Britain's help for that—but will she be eager to go out and meet it?

### A Dream of Greater Greece

I talk to many Greeks. "Will you be sorry if Greece is forced into war?" The answer does not always come at once. "Greece has been treated badly," I am told, both by men who shine shoes on the curbstone and by members of the university faculty. "Greece wants peace; she will not take the offensive." Then there is a pause. "We cannot accept too great humiliations. We must be prepared to fight." Perhaps another pause occurs here. "If Turkey will not be reasonable . . . ." By this time the speaker's eyes are shining and he is looking past me. He is seeing that Greater Greece which has become so dear to his heart these late years "Greece has a destiny." In his mind's eye Greek territory stretches away over vast areas. He is ambitious, patriotic. Sometimes he puts his fondest hopes into words, as did the proprietor of the little seaside restaurant where I take some of my lunches who, when he heard of the threat to the warships in the Smyrna harbor, said to me: "Good. Now there will be war. We will fight Kemal. We will march through Eastern Thrace, enter Constantinople, and in fifteen days Kemal will be—nowhere!"

Sitting at a table on the sidewalk in Athens I hear these things discussed. All around me are people at other tables talking excitedly. Greek waiters shuffle in and out, bringing coffee in thick white cups, ugly little cups, to their customers, who let the coffee grow cool. Some of these waiters have been in the United States; they say to me "What will you have?" in the guttural accents to which their own language has accustomed them, and I say "ti echete?" in return. The street is aclang with automobiles and amaxis, one-seated carriages drawn by single horses, the driver sitting up high in front. Both automobiles and amaxis are likely to have three or four horns or bells, and they are kept going continuously. The Greek driver, chauffeur or amaxa, is a demon for noise. Indeed, his horn takes the place of traffic rules, for vehicles go every which-way and across every street—in Athens there ought to be a sign: "Pedestrians cross at own risk."

It is a warm day, for warm days come early in Greece. All morning men have been gathered in knots before the little bulletins pasted up by newspapers on the fronts of their buildings, jostling each other to read the small print—our large bulletin boards, legible across the street, are unknown. These men have hurried off to spread and discuss the news. Now, sitting in front of the coffee houses, they talk to each other with gestures and facial contortion; they talk with shoulders arms, elbows, necks and heads. Every man has his conversation beads, a neat string, of blue, white, yellow or brown beads, about the size of large peas, which he fingers industriously. At first these beads are taken by the stranger to be associated in some way with religion, but they are no more than something to play with, to have in one's hand when one is talking. Few Greeks would be without them; they consume nervous energy and take up too extravagant movements.

### Coffee and Politics

The Greek is political-minded. Altered though he is by racial infusions through the centuries, he has lived to justify the dictum that man is a political animal. The acts of his Government are as welcome a subject of conversation to him as to most people is the conduct of their neighbors' children, and he displays the same fertility in discussing the matter from various angles. Begin any topic with him and he will break off to ask what you think of this or that late governmental decree. "Were I dictator of Greece for one month," said an American residing in Athens, "my first act would be to make it a capital offense to discuss politics before dinner; my second would be to abolish coffee houses." The second would perhaps render the first unnecessary.

"The Lausanne Conference has broken down!" my companions at the tables are saying. "Curzon has gone home mad." "Now the Turks will find they cannot dictate to the Allies." "Ismet says he will not sign the treaty because he doesn't like the financial provisions and the decisions about capitulations." "What fools the Turks are! We conceded one thing after another and the Allies gave way at many points." "What will Angora say when Ismet gets there?" "Greece is prepared for whatever happens. Our army is strong again. It is massed in Western Thrace. If there is war, we will march through Eastern Thrace. We may go clear to Constantinople. The British will help us. Greece is a great country. She will be still greater."

Three days later the Turkish Governor of Smyrna is reported to have ordered all allied warships to leave the harbor. The British are reported to have said they would not go. It looks like war! "Now then," say the Greeks, "we are ready . . . ."

I look out of my study window at the gray and brown hills that have surrounded Athens since Themistocles defeated another Asiatic power at Salamis and Marathon. That was a war of defense against the Persians. There is another tradition in Greek history. Alexander the Great set out to conquer what was then known of the world, and one of the places that echoed to the tread of his soldiers was the country we now call Anatolia.

There is a repercussion of the enthusiasm that carried this people to the heights when Venizelos swept Lloyd George and the Council of Ten along with him at the Peace Conference in 1919. Greece had been greatly enlarged as a result of the first and second. Balkan wars. Venizelos, building a still greater Greece in his eye, demanded the whole of Western and Eastern Thrace through to the Black Sea, He demanded also the entire vilayet of Aidin in Anatolia, with the exception of one small part, and the port of Smyrna. The Erst of these meant interposing a continuous belt of Greek territory between Turkey and other European nations, and it meant shutting off Bulgaria from the Aegean. The second meant carving the richest province and principal port out of Turkey-in-Asia, bringing a large Turkish population under Greek rule, and leaving the two nations face to face over an immense land frontier.

### Venizelos Still "The Greatest Greek"

Venizelos got what he asked for. In making those demands, he probably knew the risks that he ran, but his domestic policies had threatened his political future at home and he sought strength through aggrandizement abroad. What happened is now history. The Greek army, unable to maintain itself in the Smyrna enclave, was pushed into the sea by the Turks under Kemal, and by the terms of the Mudania armistice, signed subsequently, Eastern Thrace was restored to Turkey.

Meanwhile, Venizelos is still the idol of many Greeks. His defeat in elections in 1920 came about not because of his foreign policies, but because of the very domestic measures that his foreign policies had been designed to counter-balance. The national ambitions that he evoked at that time still ring in Greece. Venizelos is the friend and inspiration of the "Revolutionary" leaders "the greatest Greek statesman," Plastiras recently called him. He gave a flare to Greek imperialism that still plays a large part in Greek psychology.

Moreover, the present Government, like Venizelos, may have to seek strength by some grandiloquent flourish. The heir of defeat after its coup d'etat in seizing control of affairs last September and driving Constantine from the throne, it has not had an easy time. Under it taxes have become heavier—every banknote in the hands of citizens was cut in two last Fall, literally clipped with a pair of scissors and one-half handed back to the owner, severe restrictions have been placed upon business and commerce, the currency has gone lower and lower in the exchange market, and the Government's pre-occupation with military preparations have prevented it from doing much to care for the three-quarters of a million refugees who are encamped on nearly every Greek's doorstep. Finally, its execution of five former Cabinet members and one General, with its prosecution of many other persons, has deepened the alienation of many Royalists. Though some of these measures may have been necessary, they do not make for political popularity. The Government has so far avoided holding elections. It, too, may find that aggrandizement abroad is the best insurance against disfavor at home.

What will Greece's aims be in a war, if there is war? To regain East Thrace, in the first place. She will not be content with anything less than the recovery of this strategic territory assigned to her in the Treaty of Sévres. That will again put her in possession of a continuous belt of land from the Aegean to the Black Sea, lying between Turkey and European nations. It will also shut off southern Bulgaria from access to the sea by its natural route of the Maritsa River; this is of great importance to the peace of the Balkans.

Bulgaria a comparatively new State in the Near East, has the impetuous nationalistic ambitions of most new States. For years she has been trying to make her diplomacy win for her what her geographical position calls for: an outlet into the Aegean. It was rivalry between Greece and Bulgaria over Macedonia and its port of Saloniki that helped to bring on the second Balkan wan. Left out in the cold there, Bulgaria regards with greater intensity than ever the outlet by the Maritsa. Passage to the Aegean along this route was accorded to her after the Balkan wars, but taken away again by the imperialist policy of Venizelos after the great war. If the second of these two policies should be followed in the future, Bulgaria and Greece will again be left fading each other over a land frontier with unfriendly feelings.

### Aspirations to Anatolia

Will Greece entertain designs on Constantinople? There are 300,000 Greeks in that city, and they are second only to Turks in number. On the ground of a historical claim Greece would perhaps aspire to the control of this metropolis, but it is not likely in the present situation that she will press her claim. To control Constantinople would involve her in menacing conflicts of interest with Russia and other nations bordering on the Black Sea, and there is little likelihood that Western powers would tolerate Greek government there now.

To the question, "Will Greece aspire again to a portion of Anatolia?" the only answer, seemingly must be: Not unless she goes mad. One must immediately make allowance, however, for the remote possibility that that disturbing thing may happen. The dream of a reconstituted Ionia, settled by Greeks in the twelfth century B. C., and the home of Greeks ever since, is always present in the minds of some Greek patriots. Moreover, Greece does not want to keep the three-quarters of a million wretched emigrants who have been lumped on her during the past few months; she would gladly see them all return tomorrow to the places they came from. Whether for that reason she would want to control the administration of a part of Turkish Asia Minor, in order that those of the emigrants who came from there might reside there in greater safety, can only be guessed.

"I am confident that in the near future Greece will accomplish wonders." Into these words of Pangalos one can read any meaning he chooses; they are strangely reminiscent of the tone of the Greek press and Greek statesmen when the soldiers from Attica were advancing toward the interior of Anatolia some time ago. The Greek is a fiery, ambitious, patriotic, political-minded person, and his ecstacies no less than his sober judgments have to be taken into account. Nevertheless, it is unlikely that Greece will today try to repeat her disastrous experiment in Asia Minor. She could do so only with the support and specific sanction of Great Britain, probably, and it is not likely that Great Britain is now in any mood to give her the same fatal backing for which Lloyd George was largely responsible three years ago. Moreover, she would first have to bring the Turkish Nationalist Government to its knees, and that is a very different matter from the temporary success she gained in her drive from Smyrna in 1920–21.

"Greece today must take the attitude of 'watchful waiting,' " says Venizelos as I write. "We accepted terms at Lausanne that are tolerable only because we desired and still desire peace . . . . At the same time we own deep gratitude to the 'Revolution,' which created a fighting army."

It is the army to which Greeks perpetually come back. The politicians in the coffee houses have their eyes fixed on it, massed away in Western Thrace, along the Maritsa River.

\* \* \*

**April 6, 1923**

## 5 KILLED AS DEPUTIES LEAD BUCHAREST RIOT

### *Rumanian Mob, Protesting Against New Constitution, Raids Prince Stirbey's Palace*

BUDAPEST, April 5 (Associated Press)—A crowd led by Deputies of the Opposition broke into the palace of Prince Stirbey near Bucharest yesterday, according to dispatches received here, and was destroying the interior of the place when the police arrived. In the fight that followed, five persons were killed, it is reported.

This is one of a series of incidents that have embittered the political controversies in the Rumanian capital between the Nationalists, led by Prime Minister Bratiano, and the minority parties. Violent opponents of the Government affirm that the minorities are deprived of their political rights under the new Constitution, and, further, that the document centralizes the powers of the Government oppressively.

Religious animosities also have been aroused, the Roman Catholics charging that the new Constitution gives ascendancy to the Greek Orthodox Church.

Student bands in the university towns, such as Jassy, Cluj, Bucharest and Czernowitz, recently organized demonstrations against the Government.

The Opposition parties have decided to continue their manifestations in an effort to arouse public opinion to such an extent that the Government will be obliged to revise the Constitution.

PARIS, April 5—A Havas dispatch from Bucharest says that the situation in Rumania remains very critical, and that throughout the country agitation continues for a revision of the new Constitution.

A state of siege is being maintained by the Government, which is resorting to a great display of military force to prevent manifestations in several cities. Disturbances have occurred with loss of life and persons wounded in Czernowitz and Jassy.

The dispatch adds that King Ferdinand has sanctioned the new Constitution, but that it is reported he has refused to take the oath again.

The Nationalists—formerly Take Jonescu's party—and the Peasant Party have issued a manifesto to the people signed "Allied Opposition," in which they denounce in violent terms the present Chamber, which, they say, was "fraudulently elected." They also protest against the Chamber's

decisions, "adopted under the protection of bayonets." The Popular Party, headed by General Fofoza Averesco, former Premier, has published a similar manifesto. These three parties represent more than 40 per cent, of the members of Parliament.

It is possible that the attack on the palace of Prince Stirbey at Buftea, a suburb of the capital, was inspired by the position he has held at court for many years, he having been an intimate friend of both King Ferdinand and Queen Marie long before they came to the throne. At Buftea, the Prince also has a fruit preserve factory which, during the war, was turned to the manufacturing of bandages for wounded soldiers. Until recently he was the administrator of the royal estates.

Ten years ago foreign correspondents at Bucharest linked the names of the Prince and the Princess Marie, a granddaughter of Queen Victoria, and the most beautiful royalty in Europe, in such a way as to create a scandal abroad, but resentment against the writers in Rumania.

The new Rumanian Constitution, voted by both houses of Parliament was formally sanctioned by King Ferdinand on March 29. Dispatches from Bucharest at the time said it insured to all Rumanians, without distinction of race or religion the same rights and liberties. The important features were nationalization of the subsoil and expropriation of wooded land for the creation of communal forests.

\* \* \*

**June 10, 1923**

## ARMY OVERTHROWS BULGAR CABINET; ARRESTS MINISTERS

### *Military Surround the Parliament Buildings and Seize Members and Deputies*

#### NO BLOODSHED IN CAPITAL

*New Government Is Formed From All the Opposition Parties Except the Communists*

#### FIGHTING IN THE COUNTRY

*Coup is a Revolt of the City People Against Rule of Stambulisky and the Agrarians*

SOFIA, Bulgaria, June 9 (Associated Press)—The Bulgarian Government was overthrown at 3 o'clock this morning by an organization of reserve officers supported by the active army.

All the Ministers were placed under arrest. A new Government has been formed by all the Opposition parties, with the exception of the Communists. The movement is supported by the provincial garrisons.

The Premiership of the new Government has been left vacant for the present, and the Ministry of Agriculture also has been left open. The other posts in the Cabinet were filled as follows:

*Minister of War* M. ZANKOFF.
*Interior*—M. HOUSSEFF.
*Public Education*—M. MOLOFF.
*Commerce and Industry*—M. BOBOSHEVSKI.
*Public Works*—M. STOENTCHEFF.
*Finance*—M. TODOROFF.
*Railways*—M. KAZASSOFF.
*Justice*—M. SMILOFF.

The new régime has proclaimed a state of siege and has issued a proclamation to the nation saying:

"Bulgarian liberty dawns again: The régime of deceit, violence and murder has collapsed under the weight of its crimes, and a new era of law, harmony and peace has arrived."

Professor Zankof, with Professor Meletieff, rector of the University of Sofia, took an active part in constituting a new Ministry which is credited with the intention of abandoning the legal proceedings carried out by the Agrarian Party against former Cabinet Ministers.

Premier Stambulisky, who has been living in semi-retirement in his native village of Slavonitz, returned to Sofia last night. On his arrival at the station he found troops drawn up and he was received in silence. When the Premier asked for an explanation the officers ignored the question. He then tried to telephone to police headquarters to obtain an explanation, but discovered the wires had been cut. Then he understood he was a prisoner.

The coup was carried out with military precision, members of the reserve officers' organization and units of the active army surrounded Parliament House and arrested the Ministers and Deputies, while those Ministers who were absent were arrested later at their homes. Among those arrested were the members of a powerful organization known as the "yellow guard" and alleged to be staunch supporters of M. Stambulisky.

All the frontiers are closed and no trains are allowed to leave the capital. The military league which led the movement issued a statement this afternoon denying rumors of a general mobilization. It said calm prevailed among the population, making such a step unnecessary.

### Deposed Ministers Face Trial

BUCHAREST, Rumania, June 9 (Associated Press)— Special editions of the newspapers here today announce the overthrow of the Agarian Government at Sofia, saying that the Military League and the opposition bloc placed themselves at the head of a popular movement. The papers report that the military elements surrounded the Parliament buildings, arresting all the Deputies and Ministers present, and later arrested the other Ministers at their homes.

No trains left Sofia today and all the frontiers were closed.

According to the advices received here no bloodshed occurred, and the revolutionaries appear to be masters of the situation, having ordered political proceedings to be taken against the former Cabinet members.

Other reports are that King Boris asked Professor Meletieff, rector of Sofia University, to form a Ministry and that the professor signed a proclamation of martial law.

LONDON, June 9—The semiofficial Bulgarian telegraph agency has issued a statement saying: "The motives for the change in government are so well known that they need no explanation. Bulgaria, which has been constitutionally independent for forty years, cannot support a government which has shown growing contempt for legality and would seem to consider violence a fundamental principle of domestic administration.

"The rapidity with which the government has been overthrown is the best proof of its unpopularity and its corruption. The new government has been received with great enthusiasm by all classes of the population."

### Revolt Against Agriculturists

The coup de main which has taken place in Bulgaria by the arrest of the peasant Premier and his colleagues and attended, so far, with no signs of general violence appears to be the revolt of the city people against the dominance of the rustics. Although before the World War 80 per cent of the Bulgars were agriculturists they were completely controlled by the industrials and capitalists of Sofia with their means of transportation and their interests in foreign markets.

The war changed all that. The Agrarian Union was formed as a politico-agricultural party and has dominated the country ever since. It has also not been without its influence amid the agricultural populations of other Balkan States and even in Central Europe—Poland and Bohemia—with its "Green International."

With the abdication of King Ferdinand and the succession of his son Boris, on Oct. 3, 1918, the military, the capitalist, the manufacturing, and even the intellectual classes have had little to say in the affairs of state. Owing to the nature of several laws passed, such as that in regard to private ownership of land and compulsory labor, the enemies of Bulgaria in the Balkans have complained to the Allies that Bulgaria was going the path of Bolshevism. Premier Stambulisky has always denied this and has pointed to the fact that in the "Zadrouga," or family Soviet government, the Bulgars ages ago tried communism and found it wanting.

Not only by popular sentiment but also by the Treaty of Neuilly of Nov. 27, 1918, the former ruling classes in the country found themselves deprived of occupation. For class satisfaction as well as to create a good impression with the Allies, reprisals were soon in order against those persons who were supposed to have been responsible for having the nation line up with Germany in the war. King Ferdinand had escaped, but his responsible ministers, including Radoslavoff, the Premier, and three generals, who had successively served as Ministers of War, were placed on trial by the High Court of Justice, convicted of treason and of personally profiting out of the war, and served with severe sentences.

The treaty entirely wiped out the old military machine and compulsory service. Its terms for disarmament, indeed, were so drastic that even the new Government resented its infliction, on the ground that it left the country not only naked to foreign enemies but helpless in case of an internal rising—such as has just taken place.

### Army Is Small

The pre-war peace strength was 56,000 men and 3,900 officers; the war strength instantly available by conscription and from the reserve was over 500,000 of all ranks. The treaty reduced the army to a volunteer service with a maximum of 20,000 men, and in order to prevent a reserve from being accumulated the men must enlist for a minimum of 12 years. Officers who were serving when the treaty was signed, if they wished to continue in the service must have pledged themselves to do so until the age of 40. New officers must serve for 20 years. Aside from the regular army of volunteers, a frontier corps was created numbering 3,000 of all ranks, while the police in general were not to be enrolled beyond 10,000.

As the pay was very small, there was few volunteers, so that when the last report of the Minister of War was made, in September last, the regular army, numbered only 7,405, including 930 officers: the frontier guards, 429; and the police, among whom the pay was higher and the perquisites more numerous, 3,834.

The country as a whole, however, has prospered, and only a few months ago Premier Stambulisky managed to make an arrangement with the Reparation Commission which was satisfactory all around. With this prosperity the power of the Agrarians increased until, at the last election April 22, they had a majority that has rarely been seen in a modern Parliament. The representation as it was by the election of March 28, 1920, and now as augmented by 18 seats, is as follows:

| Party | Now | 1920 |
|---|---|---|
| Agrarians | 212 | 110 |
| Opposition Union | 15 | — |
| Communists | 6 | 49 |
| Socialists | 2 | 8 |
| Democrats | 0 | 24 |
| Liberals | 0 | 6 |
| Radicals | 0 | 8 |
| Progressives | 0 | 8 |
| Nationalists | 0 | 14 |
| | 245 | 227 |

Since Stambulisky left the prison where the Government of Ferdinand had placed him, and, by working day and night succeeded in melding the majority class into a formidable political and industrial machine, and then assumed its control, and automatically the control of the Government in October, 1919, he has found it necessary to rebuild his Cabinet several times. His colleagues who have now been arrested assumed office on Feb. 10, 1923. Besides resuming his usual portfolio of Foreign Affairs, he also took those of Interior and War.

It is said that he administered the latter to prevent the garrison from taking up the cause of the non-agrarian classes and also to quiet resentment among their former military friends in his endeavors to meet religiously the terms of the Treaty of Neuilly and to do his best to have the Government carry them out. The pinch of reparations has not, therefore, fallen heavily upon the agrarians but upon the capitalistic, manufacturing and professional classes.

There have been periodic demonstrations with the assassination of Ministers, but no general risings until the present. Only last week a revolutionary attempt was reported, but the revolutionists had no arms to attack any more than did the Government have arms to defend, until the former apparently gained the adhesion of the miniature army, when success became inevitable.

\* \* \*

**June 12, 1923**

## BODY GUARD SEIZES DEPOSED PREMIER

*Stamboulisky Has Been Arrested by His Own Soldiers, Prague Hears*

**SERBIA IS READY TO ACT**

*It Will Not Allow Violation of Treaty—Agrarian Leaders Are Rushed to Prisons*

PRAGUE, Czechoslovakia, June 11—Former Premier Stamboulisky of Bulgaria has been arrested by his military bodyguard, according to a report published by the newspaper Prager Presse.

LONDON, June 11—The overthrow of the Stamboulisky Government in Bulgaria was planned for the end of June, according to The Times Vienna correspondent who quotes a dispatch received by the Neue Wiener Tagblatt. It was hurried, however, to forestall the great agrarian congress which Stamboulisky had arranged to be held in Sofia to impress the capital with the strength of the agrarian party.

It was intended to have 200,000 persons attend the congress and 20,000 of Stamboulisky's "Orange Guards" were to have been concentrated in Sofia, armed from the Government arsenal after having taken an oath of allegiance to the projected new constitution.

There is no independent confirmation of the report that former Premier Stamboulisky is besieged in his native village of Slavovitza, nor any reliable news of his whereabouts or his fate. Sofia has been silent today, no dispatches being received of a late date from that city, and it is inferred that a censorship is active.

Copyright, 1923, by The Chicago Tribune Co.

PARIS, June 11—The Jugoslav Minister here, M. Spalakovitz, declared tonight that the Belgrade Government has taken all necessary military measures to protect its frontiers in case the Bulgarian coup results in activities by the Sofia militarists.

The Little Entente has begun pourparlers for common action in case the Zankoff Government mobilizes, which is a violation of the Neuilly treaty.

"The situation is very grievous and peace hangs by a hair," said M. Spalakovitz.

BELGRADE, Jugoslavia, June 11—The Jugoslav Foreign Minister, Dr. Ninchitch, speaking in Parliament today, said:

"We have given proof of our desire for good relations with Bulgaria, but we could not remain indifferent if Bulgaria made any attempt to tamper with the Treaty of Neuilly."

King Alexander is interrupting his visit to Rumania owing to events in Bulgaria and is expected to return here tomorrow.

Advices from Bulgaria indicate that resistance to the new Government is becoming stronger; the Agrarians are organizing in the north, notably at Plevna and Vratza. The railroad has been out at several places and the situation is considered serious here, as the Jugoslav Cabinet is determined that the Treaty of Neuilly must be strictly observed.

Bulgaria is alleged to be violating the treaty by calling former officers into active service, and it is also announced that fresh classes are about to be called to the colors.

Copyright, 1923, by The Chicago Tribune Co.

ATHENS, June 11—Premier Stamboulisky's partisans are being arrested and imprisoned in great numbers in all parts of Bulgaria, according to dispatches from Sofia. General Lazaroff, President of the Officers Reserve Union, which is aided by Macedonian organizations, commands the revolutionary operation.

It is stated that the revolutionary forces have destroyed the rail lines to Kuystendil, Tsaribrod and the Serbian frontier, cutting off communication with Jugoslavia. Troops are constantly being brought to Sofia to protect the new régime, while bands of revolutionaries are coming from Kuystendil, Petritzi, Djoumaja and other towns.

Philippopolis is said to have been the headquarters of the revolution. Rebel troops marched from there to Sofia without discovery. They captured the Chief of Police while he was taking coffee in a café and killed him when he refused to join the revolutionaries.

SOFIA, June 11 (Associated Press)—Complete tranquillity prevailed in Sofia today. Premier Zankoff, head of the new Government, has assigned the portfolio of foreign affairs to Christo Kalloff, while Colonel Voulkoff is the new Minister of War. The Cabinet now represents all parties with the exception of the Communists and the Peasants.

CONSTANTINOPLE, June 11 (Associated Press)—Official advices received in foreign circles here say the Bulgarian revolution was conducted without strife. One American destroyer is at Varna, on the Black Sea, and another is leaving for that place tonight.

\* \* \*

June 12, 1923

## ASSERTS SOFIA COUP IS GAIN FOR GERMANY

*Radoslavoff, However, Declares Zankoff Will Carry Out Treaty and Will Not Upset Balkans*

By Wireless to The New York Times

BERLIN, June 11—"Professor Zankoff's Premiership in Bulgaria signifies a decided gain for Germany," according to Vaseil Radoslavoff, war Premier of Bulgaria, who is living, self-exiled, in Berlin, having been convicted in absentia, and sentenced to death for treason. M. Radoslavoff is jubilant at the overturn, and expects to be cleared by an amnesty, and to return to Sofia soon.

He said:

"The overturn is by no means the deed of a few radicals. It is neither a military 'putsch,' nor is a military dictatorship intended. The names of the persons who have taken power in hand guarantee that Bulgaria's intelligentsia had enough, more than enough, of Stamboulisky's régime, which was characterized by violence and lack of political understanding.

"Stamboulisky was often enough warned, but neither he nor his partisans would take heed. The urban intelligentsia won't let itself be governed any longer by one party which has only a small part of the peasantry in its following. Nothing was more false than that Stamboulisky had the entire peasantry behind him.

"No essential change in relations toward the Entente will take place.

"Premier Zankoff and his colleagues are sufficiently cool-headed to stand only on the basis of actualities. They won't aggravate the Entente, and will continue to do their best loyally to fulfill the peace treaty. But in internal politics there will be many changes for the better. The position of the King is not touched by the overturn; if anything, it is strengthened. Disorders are not to be expected, since the overwhelming bulk of the bourgeoisie and a good part of the peasantry is on the side of the new men.

"For Germany Zankoff's Premiership is a decided gain. For though he cannot brusquely oppose the Entente, he is nevertheless, in contrast to Stamboulisky, decidedly pro-German. I myself sent him, after the Balkan War, to Germany and Austria to work in co-operation with a few other men for our national cause. During the war he was a member of the Food Commission.

"His newly formed Ministry comprises all parties except Stamboulisky's and the Communists. Naturally the peasantry will in time receive representation.

"The new Interior Minister, General Rousseff, was the leader of the Seventh Army in Macedonia during the war. Professor Moloff, Minister of Agriculture and Public Education, is not to be confused with former Minister Moloff. For that matter no member of the new Ministry ever held a Cabinet post before nor was a member of the Sobranje. Minister of Justice

Smiloff was a lawyer in Varna and belongs to the National Liberal Party. Minister of Finance Theodoroff is a member of the Radical Party. Minister of Commerce Bobochevski is a member of the Progressive Party. M. Stoentcheff, the Minister of Public Works, is a lawyer and a Democrat. Minister of Transportation Kazassoff is a Socialist.

"No small part in the overturn movement is played by the Macedonian addition to the urban intelligentsia. Our Macedonian brothers were ever hostile to Stamboulisky. Finally, it became obvious to all Bulgarians that Stamboulisky took too strongly a pro-Serbian standpoint, which was not consistent with Bulgaria's well-understood interests.

"Nevertheless, Zankoff, as I know him, won't take up a hostile position against Serbia, for he is a sensible man and a politician who is absolutely not inclined to conjure up a new Balkan conflict."

There was joy in Berlin's Bulgarian colony, mostly students and expatriated politicians, over the coup. The whole German press, with the solitary exception of the Communists, views it with sympathy, while the reactionaries hail it as a triumph. Undoubtedly the reactionaries will use it as a campaign argument, a bright and shining example of how even a small, determined military force, backing a well-organized coup, could successfully overturn a republic in Germany and restore the monarchy.

\* \* \*

July 19, 1923

## URGES BULGARIAN REVOLT

### Moscow International Appeals to Communists in the Balkans

Copyright, 1923 by The New York Times Company
By Wireless to The New York Times
SOFIA, July 17—The Executive Committee of the Third [Moscow] International has addressed an appeal to all workmen and peasants of Bulgaria and other Balkan countries to use every possible means to overthrow the new Bulgarian Government.

This appeal, which is couched in violent language, is published by the Bolshevist newspaper Pravda. It puts the Bulgarian Communists in a very embarrassing position. Moscow wishes them to adopt revolutionary action, advice which they are loath to follow because they know that only a limited amount of internal support will be accorded them and they see no hope of obtaining foreign aid.

A number of Communists are much annoyed at the intervention of the Third International, which forces them to choose between Moscow and Bulgaria.

\* \* \*

September 16, 1923

## MUSSOLINI FACES AN AGED FOEMAN

### SERBIA'S PREMIER OF 80

*Quiet, Modest Demeanor Opposed to Audacity of the Italian*

### FATHER LIVED TO BE 110

*Has Guided Affairs of His Nation Through 40 Stormy Years to Present Power*

Scarcely has the curtain begun to drop on the Greco-Italian drama when, with hardly an interlude, it rises again upon a new scene and a new drama. Instead at Corfu, Fiume is the setting. Italy is still in the leading rôle, but Greece's part has been taken by Yugoslavia. As in the preceding drama, the centre of the stage is held by Italy's leading man Mussolini who with dramatic gestures has opened the play. But there now emerges a new figure on the scene, startling in contrast to Mussolini: a venerable old gentleman of great dignity, whose long, silvery beard falls far down on his black coat. He is Nicola Pashitch, Yugoslavia's leading man in the new Fiume drama—Mussolini's neighbor across the Adriatic.

In all Europe one could scarcely find a more romantic figure than that of this Serbian patriarch and, strangely enough, one less known. Prime Minister of Serbia a dozen times, probably thirty times Cabinet Minister, President of Parliament, Lord Mayor of Belgrade, Ambassador to Petrograd—for forty years, while the throne of Serbia has changed hands three times and wars have shaken his country to its foundations, Nicola Pashitch has remained the "first statesman of Serbia."

The writer met him first in Belgrade in the Spring of 1919. It was on one of those sharp stoned streets which run down the hills of Belgrade overlooking the "blue" Danube as it winds away into the distant low-lying clouds edging the former Hungarian plains. The quietness of the street, lined with shade trees, the absence of traffic, even pedestrians give an impression of tranquillity difficult to connect with the capital of a country which but recently had played so important a role in the great war.

From one of the houses in this quiet street came this old gentleman. His deep blue eyes conveyed an impression of great kindness and his long silvery hair and mustache gave him a truly patriarchal air. Some one has said that one feels with him as under an old oak tree whose shade gives a sense of great repose. It was hard to believe that this elderly scholarly looking man was the one in whose hands often had rested the destiny of his country the man into whose hands was placed that fateful Austrian ultimatum which precipitated the 1914 world catastrophe.

#### Delicate About His Age

To be with Pashitch for a short time is to realize that his venerable appearance covers an amazingly youthful and subtle spirit. That he was born in Zayetehar, a small town on the Serbo-Bulgarian frontier, is well known, but when? that is the question. He is thought to be about 80, but it is a topic he does not like to discuss. His friends told me that it was the late king Peter of Serbia's great pleasure to joke Pashitch about his age, but he got little satisfaction. Pashitch had a faculty of changing the subject in adroit fashion.

His parents, for Zayetehar, were quite well off, so that Pashitch was sent to Belgrade and later to Switzerland to study engineering. Of his abilities as an engineer there seems to be some doubt. For there is a tale of his having built a house in which he quite forgot to put a staircase.

Be that as it may from the first, political activities were Pashitch's main interest. When he was a young man King Milan was on the throne of Serbia, a young, rather autocratic ruler. Two political parties were active—the Liberals and the Progressives—and a third party, the Radicals (not "radical" in the sense that the word is used in this country), was in process of formation. Pashitch was early and vigorously connected with its activities. Soon gaining an overwhelming majority of the Serbians as followers, the new Radical Party made opponents of the reactionary régime. The conflict became so acute that in 1883 trouble broke out in that part of Serbia from where Pashitch came, known as the Zayotchar upheaval. King Milan suppressed it with military force. Ninety death sentences were imposed, among them that of Nicola Pashitch.

After several months of imprisonment spent in a jail with heavy chains on his legs (from which he still feels the effects), he escaped over the frontier into Bulgaria. Six years in exile, then a strong popular movement brought the Radical Party into power and Pashitch returned in triumph to Belgrade. It was at this time that he began his amazingly active role in the political life of Serbia.

Few statesmen of Europe have had tasks as gigantic as those he faced, tasks which involved not only the usual difficulties of every politician, but also great physical suffering. It was his hand at the helm which guided Serbia in 1912 and 1913 through two Balkan wars, and his faith and leadership which helped sustain his people in the years of the great war which saw his country invaded and occupied by the enemy, its army decimated by cold and disease, himself and his Government stranded on a foreign island. An old man over 70, he crossed the mountains of Albania on foot in the dead of the 1912 Winter, making the tragic retreat with the Serbian Army and people. With the coming of peace it was Pashitch who went to Paris to represent his country at the Peace Conference, and in the difficult days of reconstruction following the war faced by problems of the most complex order, Pashitch remained in power while one by one those once powerful war associates of his, Lloyd George, Clemenceau, Wilson, were replaced by others.

He is not a speaker of any distinction, nor has he any special literary gift. He has not the high scholarship of Mr. Wilson nor the brilliancy of Clemenceau nor the adroitness of a Lloyd George. Yet he has remained in power while they have fallen.

To get at the heart of his power one must understand the history and character of the Serbians, his people. Their story is that of the heroic struggle of a young peasant nation imbued with a touch of imagination and idealism, in their spare time singing songs of a glorious past and dreaming of great future. They have surrounded all their heroes with songs and anecdotes springing largely from their imagination. Naturally, Pashitch has come in for his share, and there is a tale which may throw some light on the secret of his power.

### The Story of the Tomcat

In 1921—so the story goes—a Radical member of the Parliament and a follower of Pashitch went to Bosnia to run a political campaign for the Radical Party. He had to spend a night in a village, and so he gathered at the inn all the prominent people of the village to talk to them about the Radical Party and Mr. Pashitch as its leader. After he had spoken at some length an old man of the village rose and said to him: "We thank you very much for the information you have given us but do not think that we are quite ignorant of this man. We have known about Mr. Pashitch and the tomcat with the candles for a long time."

"What do you mean by Mr. Pashitch and the tomcat with the candles!" asked the visitor.

"Since you have not heard about it, I will tell you," replied the old man. "There was once a German Emperor who had heard much about Mr. Pashitch and his wisdom and, wanting to talk with him, let it be known that he desired him to come to see him. Pashitch decided to go to Berlin and call upon the Emperor. Arriving there he knocked on the door of the palace and told the doorman his intention to see the Emperor. The doorman said to him: 'I can't let you in today but I will tomorrow and I warn you to be careful of the tomcat with the candles.' Pashitch turned away and after stopping at the church went home, thinking all the time of the 'tomcat with the candles.'

"The next day the doorman let him in and showed him to the Emperor, who asked him, 'Mr. Pashitch, which do you think has more power, Education or Nature.?'

"Mr. Pashitch, as a man of the people, answered right away: 'Emperor, Nature has more power than Education.'

"Then the Emperor asked him: 'If Nature has more power than Education, tell me are the people better than the Intelligentsia?' "

"Pashitch again answered as a man of the people: 'My Emperor I will tell you the truth, the People are better than the Intelligentsia.'

"The very moment Pashitch said this, the door of the court room opened and a tomcat came in walking on his hind legs and carrying two candles in his front paws. Pashitch stared in amazement, and the Emperor said to him: 'You said that Nature has more power than Education and that the People are better than the Intelligentsia, then how do you account for this?'

"But wise Pashitch who had been thinking the whole day and night about what the doorman said about the tomcat with the candles, had put a mouse in his pocket before he came to see the Emperor, and now took it out and threw it in front of the cat, which dropped the candles and ran after the mouse.

### "A Wiser Man Than I"

"When the Emperor saw that the tomcat had forgotten all about the candles he tapped Mr. Pashitch on the shoulder and said, 'I see, Mr. Pashitch, you are a wiser man than I and that Nature has more power than Education and that the People are better than the Intelligentsia and, as you are wiser than I, you should be Emperor.'

"But Pashitch answered him, 'Thank you, Emperor, for the offer of your Imperial Crown, but if I am really wise as you say, I need this wisdom for my people in Serbia.' "

Pashitch often has been reproached for his wealth. He is probably the greatest mine owner in Serbia, having used to good advantage the dowry of the rich Serbian girl he married. It is said in Belgrade that he never bought a house which did not stand on a corner, believing that corner houses have greater value.

Critics see in Mr. Pashitch a politician pure and simple, who uses his psychological understanding of the Serbian people for his own ends. Today in his country, no longer Serbia but united with its brethren, the Croats and Slovenes, often spoken of as Yugoslavia (Southern Slavs), there are some who believe Pashitch is too much Pan Serb, that the reins are held too tightly in Belgrade.

Whatever truth there is on both sides, one fact remains unchallenged. Throughout forty years Nicola Pashitch has led his country and leads it today as Prime Minister.

In the present Fiume crisis it is perhaps well that Yugoslavia has a man of such seasoned judgment and noted patience as its leader, a man who, throughout his long life, has made it a practice to reflect well on every decision to pursue his policies step by step—never precipitately. One could search the pages of history to find two national leaders of greater contrast than that presented by this venerable statesman and his dictatorial neighbor, Signor Mussolini. Theirs are leading rôles in the events immediately ahead—the consequences of which one dare not as yet venture a prophecy.

\* \* \*

**September 24, 1923**

# 100,000 PEASANTS MARCH UPON SOFIA IN BULGAR REVOLT

---

*Government Sends Troops Against Armed Agrarians and Checks Them*

### REDS CALL A BIG STRIKE

*King Decrees a State of Siege and Dismisses Parliament in Political Crisis*

---

PARIS, Sept. 23—A dispatch to the Havas Agency from Sofia says that the present insurrection in Bulgaria is spreading and gathering strength. One hundred thousand peasants, a majority of whom are armed and fairly well organized, are marching on Sofia in an attempt to overthrow the Government.

The dispatch adds that the Cabinet sat throughout Saturday night. It was presided over by King Boris.

Two regiments have been dispatched against the oncoming peasants who are reported to have halted in the face of rifle fire.

Bulgar towns along the Yugoslav frontier are showing special activity. Although it is asserted in Sofia that the movement is purely Agrarian, the Communists have taken a hand in the controversy and are directing a general strike, which is to become effective Monday.

SOFIA, Sept. 22—King Boris tonight signed three decrees—first, to reconstruct the Cabinet without M. Smiloff, Minister of Justice, a member of the National Liberal Party; second, dissolving Parliament; and, third, proclaiming a state of stage. The King is expected to sign within two weeks a decree calling elections on Nov. 4 or 11.

The Cabinet crisis has nothing to do with the present political situation, but the King was forced into action by the refusal of the Socialists to participate in the Government if the Nationalist Party was permitted representation. The main objection against the Nationalists is that they are pro-German, hence making the Government objectionable to the allied powers. The dissolution of Parliament was merely a form, as that body has not met since the overthrow of M. Stambulisky.

SOFIA, Sept. 23 (Associated Press)—The Bulgarian official agency today, after denying reports from Belgrade concerning the Serbo-Bulgarian situation, made public the following summary of the situation:

"Order never has been disturbed since the present Government obtained power. The Communists on Sept. 20 attempted to proclaim Sovietism in certain districts in Southern Bulgaria. Three hundred Communists attacked the barracks in Stara Zagora Thursday afternoon, but were dispersed, leaving five dead and ten wounded. About 200 assaulted Tchirpan. The attack failed, the assailants retiring. They removed rails from the railroad line, derailing passenger trains, but there were no casualties.

"Gendarmerie pursuing these Communists killed or wounded thirty men. Three hundred Communists attacked the sub-prefecture and city hall at Nova Zagora and proclaimed a Soviet republic, which lasted fifteen hours. The garrison at Yanboli sent troops which dislodged the revolutionists. During the pursuit the Communists lost thirty-four men killed. A majority of the others were made prisoners. Many submitted voluntarily and delivered up their arms. The Government troops lost two men killed and eight wounded.

SOFIA, Sept. 23—More than a hundred rebels were killed Thursday—some forty at Tchirpan, ten at Stara Zagora and more than fifty at or near Nova Zagora, where the Communists were almost wiped out by the cavalry sent in pursuit of them after the recapture of the town.

Steps were taken yesterday to clear the Tunja Valley of scattered bands of fugitive Communists and to protect the railways which have been under guard in several places.

All the rebels captured with arms in their possession will be dealt with by a special court-martial set up after the proclamation of martial law.

In order to guard against surprise raids, which are still considered possible, the Government with the approval of the Interallied Military Control Commission has called for temporary volunteers to strengthen the garrisons.

\*   \*   \*

December 2, 1926

## ITALY GUARANTEES STATUS OF ALBANIA

---

*Treaty of Friendship Is Signed, Adding Another to Series of Balkan Compacts*

### SOVEREIGNTY RECOGNIZED

*And Provision Is Made for Submitting Any Disputes for Conciliation and Arbitration*

---

Copyright, 1926, by The New York Times Company
By Wireless to The New York Times
ROME, Dec. 1—The network of treaties of arbitration and friendship which Italy has been casting especially over the Balkans and the countries of the Little Entente was enriched by yet another mesh on Nov. 27 when Pompeo Aloisi, the Italian Minister to Albania, and Hussein Bey Vrioni, President of Albania, signed in Durazzo an Italo-Albanian treaty of friendship and arbitration.

The treaty, as stated in the preamble, is prompted by the desire to strengthen the reciprocal relations of friendship and safety, to contribute toward the consolidation of peace and to maintain the political, juridical and territorial status quo of Albania as set down in the treaties which they have both signed and in the covenant of the League of Nations.

Article 1 contains the statement that both Italy and Albania recognize that any change in the political, juridical or territorial status quo of Albania is contrary to their reciprocal political interests.

By Article 2 the contracting parties pledge "mutual support and cordial collaboration" to safeguard the above-mentioned mutual reciprocal political interests and pledge themselves forever not to conclude with any other power political or military agreements prejudicial to the interests of the other contracting party.

Article 3 provides that any question arising between the two countries which cannot be solved through ordinary diplomatic channels shall be submitted to arbitration, according to modalities yet to be worked out in common agreement.

Article 4 states that the treaty has a duration of five years, and can be either denounced or renewed one year before its expiration.

Article 5 provides that the treaty shall be registered with the League of Nations and that ratification shall occur in Rome.

\*   \*   \*

December 3, 1926

## ALBANIA AND ITALY

A far from inconsiderable item on the credit side of the Mussolini account is the system of treaties of amity which the Italian Premier has built up with the nations of Central and Southern Europe. To these is now added a treaty of arbitration and friendship with Albania. That little republic's chief assets are harbors and rights of way to them that might be coveted by neighbors. Italy has had her temptations about the magnificent Port of Valona. Yugoslavia has had her thoughts about Scutari as a way station to the Adriatic. Such possibilities are now disposed of by the treaty in which Mussolini guarantees the present territorial and political status of Albania. As against external aggression Albania's membership in the League of Nations was sufficient protection. But the diminutive State had its internal problems and factions, exploitable by an ambitious outsider. Such meddling Italy now disavows, and there is no reason for doubting the sincerity of her intentions. Her prestige in Albania is legitimate and will survive. The country does not bulk large economically. Still, Italy holds more than one-half of such foreign trade as there is.

From 1913, when Albania got rid of the Turk and secured recognition of her independence from the Powers, up to very recently the permanent existence of the new State was not assured. Various schemes of partition were cherished in the opposite quarters. The northern part of the country seemed due to be absorbed by the Serb State, the south was coveted by Greece, and only an infinitesimal "independent" central Albania figured in the blueprints. Now it is established that if the something short of a million fighting Albanians can keep peace at home, they will have ceased to be a football of politics and become a factor in the Balkan situation. Hamilton Fish Armstrong, in "The New Balkans," regards Albania as a possible third member with Bulgaria and Yugoslavia in the Balkan Federation, which is not among the impossibilities. In the meanwhile, American missionaries in Albania report the existence of first-rate human material for molding into civilization.

\*   \*   \*

## BEGIN RUMANIA CAMPAIGN

*8,000 of National Peasant Party Hear Leader Denounce Liberals*

Copyright, 1928 by The New York Times Company

By Wireless to The New York Times

BUCHAREST, Jan. 29—A new campaign of the National Peasants against the Liberals began today with a meeting at Jassy, where 8,000 party members assembled.

The police had spread throughout the villages a rumor that the peasants were to remain at home, for Queen Marie was visiting them.

The National Peasant leader, M. Maniu, made a vigorous speech against the Government and was strongly applauded by the audience.

"The first factor in Rumania is the people itself, not the Regency Council, which only protects the Liberal regime," she said. "The Peasant Party is continuing to fight for the real interests of Rumania against the corruption of the Liberals."

\* \* \*

## CROATS AND SERBS DEEPEN BITTERNESS

*National Rivalries Bring Yugoslavia to Most Serious Crisis in Seven Years as State*

**NO HOPE IN NEW ELECTIONS**

*Distrust and Refusal to Join in Coalition Cabinet May Finally Result in Dictatorship*

Copyright, 1928, by The New York Times Company

By Wireless to The New York Times

BELGRADE, March 16—The extended political crisis of the last month has revived the animosities of three Slav peoples, the Serbs, Croats and Slovenes, who make up the Kingdom of Yugoslavia. The refusal of each national party to enter a coalition, eventually resulting in a makeshift Cabinet, brought to Yugoslavia the most serious domestic crisis she has had in the seven years of her existence.

There is a wide breach between the Serbs and the Croats, much wider than that of a few years ago which led to the abortive movement for Croatian independence. The leaders of the Croatian Peasants' Party, who include the astute Stefan Raditch, himself imprisoned for instigating the independence movement, are now frankly disgusted with affairs at Belgrade and are threatening to withdraw to Zagreb, their capital.

### Election Won't Alter Status

Though new elections will be called as soon as the Skupstina (National Assembly) passes the new budget, the Croats see little chance of relieving the present difficulty.

They openly distrust the honesty of the Vukitchivitch Cabinet in conducting elections and have refused the offers of a few Ministerial posts made to induce them to enter a new Government.

Indeed, the mistrust of these two strongest elements in the State, the Croats and the Vukitchivitch radicals, is complete and is capable of serious consequences which the coming election will probably increase instead of relieve.

The elections will not change the complexion of the present Skupstina and no elections have changed it since the formation of the new State. The Serbs, as usual, are expected to return about 140 members, about twenty short of a majority, and the Croats about ninety, while the other seats will be divided strictly on nationalistic lines among the Montenegrins, Slovenes and many other smaller elements of the kingdom. Each one is distinctly drawn from districts of the State, many of which were formerly independent countries or peoples.

### Leaning Toward Dictatorship

Each controls absolutely its own alloted election district, eliminating opposing candidates. The Croats probably would not poll ten votes in Serbia nor the Serbs ten votes in Croatia. A few independent candidates are occasionally elected, but on important questions they are found to be in the ranks of their nationals.

There does not seem to be any solution for the political problem, and in the face of the approaching crisis King Alexander is appealing to the patriotic instincts of his new subjects to support the throne and remain united.

Possibly his Majesty has an idea of instituting a dictatorship if political methods fail. It would not be a far step, and it was even suggested by some leaders when four or five attempts to form a Cabinet last month failed, but because the idea came from the Croats, who suggested that an army officer should be called for the office, it could not be sanctioned.

The army is probably the strongest element in the country, and its officers, with the support of this faction, probably could hold a Government together where a political leader would fail.

### Wider Breach With Croatia

One must remember that Yugoslavia is surrounded by dictatorships, or almost dictatorships, such as Hungary, Italy, Rumania and Albania, and that people who have spent centuries under the rule of autocratic monarchies have the instinct if not the practice of obeying an iron hand. The King himself would avoid this resort, but the opinion is held here by some leaders, especially army men, that this will be forced sooner or later.

The expulsion of Stefan Raditch, the leader of the Croats, from Parliament for his attacks on the Government and the Throne have added to the bitterness between the Serbs and the Croats. An important development last week was the resignation from office of the President of the Yugoslavian Journalists, Krezimir Kovacevitch, a Croat and an editor with considerable political influence. He retired to Zagreb, but not until he had publicly declared that the effort of the Serbs, Croats and Slovenes to live as a united nation had failed because of the Serbian leaders' selfish desire for power.

He will remain in Croatia and, in his own words, "defend it against the encroachments of Serbia." M. Kovacevitch is close to M. Raditch and his resignation is believed to have had the approval as well as the initiative of M. Raditch because with M. Kovacevitch several other prominent Croats left Belgrade for their own country.

### Clash of Three Different Peoples

Yugoslavia has always been in political ferment because the kingdom has as its basis the strong contrast of the three nations which constitute it. These peoples are all Slavs, but that is all they have in common; they differ in history, culture and customs. Their differences are elemental. They are as far separated as the Eastern and Western civilizations.

The so-called new provinces of Croatia, Slovenia, Bachka and Voyvodina, were part of the Empire of Austria-Hungary and take their culture from the West and their dominating factor is the Roman Catholic Church.

These provinces were never under Turkish rule for any long period and they developed more rapidly than Serbia or Macedonia, which until sixty years ago acknowledged the Pashas. There the Orthodox peasant was obliged to get off his horse and bow when he passed a Turk.

In Bosnia, where both Moslems and Christians lived together, they developed a different culture. It was natural that Serbia and Croatia, which had no national interests in each other, should develop along entirely different lines. Their language, alphabet, religion and ideas have been wide apart, and this fact enabled the Dual Monarchy to maintain its position among the Slavs.

### Split on Federal Capital Site

The defeat of Austria allowed the Serbs, Croats and Slovenes to unite. The plan was put forward by foreigners supported only by a few leaders of the Croats and Slovenes. The "honeymoon" lasted only a short while. It floundered when the question of establishing a Federal capital came up.

The Croats had enjoyed self-government under Hungary and wanted a Federal constitution with Zagreb, a large modern city, as the centre. Nicholas Pashitch, however, succeeded in centralizing the Government in Belgrade without allowing "State rights" and thereby abolished the traditional private institutions used by the Government of Croatia.

The Orthodox Church became the State religion and confiscated privileges which the Roman Catholic Church formerly claimed. But what rankled the Croats more was the substitution of Serbians in the army and many important State offices.

The Croats charge that they have been heavily taxed and that most of the revenue has been spent in Serbia. This is responsible for the independence movement which has

sprung up frequently. There is no such movement apparent now, though the Croats have warned the Government that there is an end to patience.

*   *   *

May 13, 1928

# A DRAMATIC STRUGGLE CENTRES IN RUMANIA

*After Years of Oppression the Peasants Demand the Rights and Liberties of Free People*

### By ROSE C. FELD

Once more Rumania, standing at the line where Orient and Occident meet and separate, is the scene of a powerful and dramatic struggle. This time the centre of the stage is held by a mass of colorful, enthusiastic peasants, suddenly grown articulate. At their head stands Juliu Maniu, demanding for them the overthrow of the Bratianu Government and the rights and liberties of a free people. Upon the answer he gets depends, also, the destiny and happiness of a royal household, already torn and disrupted by unfortunate political and domestic events.

First, there is Dowager Queen Marie, still loved by her people but no longer the powerful ruler she was during the lifetime of her husband. Second, there is Princess Hélène, mother of young King Michael, a lonely figure, respected perhaps more than she is loved by her subjects. Third, King Michael himself, a happy, normal child, seemingly unaware of the spectre of tragedy continually hovering about him. Fourth, there is Michael's father, Prince Carol, waiting in exile for a call that will bring him back to his native country, there to open battle against the rights of his own son. Action, conflict, love, jealousy, intrigue—all the elements of the theatre are here. And, as in a Greek tragedy, there is a chorus of lyric accompaniment, this time in a resounding unison of peasant voices demanding to be heard.

### Awakening of the Peasant

What is happening in Rumania today is the logical aftermath of events of the past ten years. Before the war this country was living practically under a feudal system. There were a few wealthy landowners, often absent from their estates, and hundreds of thousands of peasants who tilled their soil for them. When the war came the peasants were conscripted and left their hearths to fight on the side of the Allies. The war, according to Juliu Maniu and other leaders, did more to awaken the lumbering consciousness of the peasant than years of talking, preaching and propaganda had achieved. He rode in trains, he saw cities, he talked to men of other lands, he heard how they lived. In discovering others he discovered himself. He began to understand some of the things that men like Juliu Maniu, Vaida-Voevod and Michalache were talking about.

Maniu tells a story illustrating the peasant mind of thirty years ago. He was talking to a group of peasants in Transylvania, then under the rule of the Magyar, urging them to fight for their rights and independence as Rumanians.

"We must have our geography," he said to them, and a thousand voices answered him, "Yes, we must have our geography!" not knowing exactly what it meant.

Finally, a bolder one among them turned to his neighbor and asked:

"What is this geography he wants?"

The second peasant scratched his head, then a light dawned on his face.

"It must be the wife of Maniu!" he said.

When he came back from the war the Rumanian peasant knew what geography was.

Jon Bratianu, leader of the Liberal Party and favorite of the late King Ferdinand and Queen Marie, was in power. Jon Bratianu probably was one of the ablest statesmen Rumania has ever had. He was not unaware of the awakening consciousness of the peasant. The terms of the Peace Treaty, by adding Transylvania, Banat, Bukovina and Bessarabia, almost doubled Rumania's former population. Eighty-five per cent, of a total of 17,000,000 souls were peasants, no mean handful to keep contented. There was, in addition, great danger from the East. Bratianu knew that directly across the border Communist Russia was anxious to bring the Rumanian peasant under her colors. Jon Bratianu gave proof of his remarkable statesmanship by doing with a stroke of his pen what the peasant had not dreamed of putting into words. He convinced the King and the Liberal Party that the voice of the peasant must be stifled and that two things only would succeed in doing this—land and the franchise.

Overnight, then, the peasant became a landowner and a voter. These were the reforms that Maniu, Valda-Voevod and Michalache had told him he must fight for, and here they were given to him. He decided that his King and Queen were his little father and mother and the Bratianus were, in truth, the saviors of the country.

For a short time, a very short time, he lived in the paradise of the two Liberal reforms. Before very long, however, he awoke to the fact that they were virtually non-existent and that his condition instead of having improved had grown worse. It was true he had his few acres of land, but he had no money with which to buy the things he needed to cultivate them. When he tried to borrow, he was charged 30, 40 and 50 per cent interest. Transportation service was bad. He had to pay a tax of 3,000 lei per wagon for exporting his grain. The things he bought—seed, farm implements, fertilizer, building material, food—were high and the return for his labor was hopelessly low. Economically he was worse off than he had been when he was in service to the large landowners.

The peasant began taking an interest in the things that concerned him—the stablization of currency, the introduction of foreign capital, the floating of a foreign loan, the rehabilitation of transportation service, the proper exploitation of natural resources. He saw these things in relation to his own welfare. How to achieve them was his problem.

### His Vote Without Effect

In his franchise he saw the solution. He would vote for men who were interested in the same things as he, he would get deputies into Parliament who would reorganize the government and stabilize conditions. To his amazement, however, he discovered that he was not permitted to vote, or, if he was, that his vote made no difference. The polls were policed by members of the Liberal Party and no matter how strongly the peasant came out in numbers the results were always the same—the Bratianu Government was returned.

The Rumanian peasant is loyal and long-suffering. But the things that were happening to him continually undermined his faith. The past ten years of his life have been filled to the brim with disillusionment. He got land and the land gave him nothing but debts and hardship. He got the vote and he could do nothing with it. The Crown Prince he loved had deserted his wife, left the country with another woman, and finally had abdicated his rights to the throne. His Queen was surrounding herself with court favorites who were using her influence to rob the land. The King was a sick man and let the Bratianus rule for him. Then the King died, there was discord between Queen Marie and Princess Hélène; a child who could not rule was placed on the throne. There was misery in the land, misery in the royal household and misery at the hearth of every man. All these things became personal problems and personal tragedies to the peasant.

Throughout the years of his great travail and long before he was ready to turn to him intelligently, the peasant has had Juliu Maniu as his guide, his teacher and his leader. Maniu is a man of 55. He comes of an old Rumanian family of magistrates and lawyers. He was born in Transylvania, until ten years ago part of Hungary. Self-determination for minorities was a reality to him long before Woodrow Wilson coined the phrase. In spite of the fact that he became a member of Parliament at Budapest in his youth, he remained consistently and aggressively a Rumanian and a fighter for Rumanian rights. Hungarians feared him for the power he held over the Rumanian peasantry living in Transylvania. He never let the latter forget that they were Rumanians, that the domination of the Magyar did not make them Hungarians.

The happiest day in Maniu's life came when Transylvania, together with the other territories that had been held by neighboring countries, became part of Greater Rumania, in December, 1918. That happened at Alba Juliu, the same little city where the peasant demonstration took place last week. In 1923 Maniu became the leader of the Nationalist Party for all Rumania, and in 1926, when the Nationalist Party joined hands with the Peasant Party, Maniu was elected President of the new Nationalist-Peasant Party.

Unlike Jon Bratianu, he does not stand alone. At one side he has Vaida-Voevod, next to Maniu the greatest leader of Nationalism, and at the other side he has Jean Michalache, head of the former Peasant Party and now Vice President of

A Recent Political Demonstration in Bucharest, the Capital of Rumania

the Nationalist-Peasant Party. The three make an important and powerful group in the Opposition. Maniu, the leader, looks like a scholar—slight, retiring and silent until aroused into speech of clear and forceful logic. Vaida-Voevod is a bigger man physically, warmer and more expressive, possessing the assurance of one who knows his people and his politics. Michalache, the Peasant Deputy, comes to the House with peasant shirt hanging over his trousers, bitterly class-conscious and intensely desirous of making the peasant conscious of his power. There are in addition several minor leaders, Madgearu, Popovitch, Lugosianu. But most important of all and most feared by the Liberal Party is Maniu.

### A Demonstration of Power

The demonstration at Alba Juliu last Sunday was the culmination of Maniu's long and persistent efforts at awakening the peasant to the need of intelligent, concerted action. For years Maniu and his associates have been educating the newly enfranchised classes to the real meaning of the vote and its powers. Through the press, through schools, priests, public meetings, this work has been going on. Maniu, Vaida-Voevod and Michalache have gone to the humblest towns of Greater Rumania and have held large mass meetings to which the peasant, weary of a Government that has given him the letter but not the spirit of democracy, has trekked miles to attend.

Maniu has been described by some writers as a Mussolini. That he most assuredly is not. He is quiet, he is austere, he is puritanical almost, in a country known for its gayety, its temperament, its emotionalism. Maniu is no spellbinder in the sense that he can hold his audience rapt by an emotional or dramatic appeal. He holds them by the appeal to their intelligence, by his sanity, by his ideals and his program for reform. He has the good sense to know, however, that brain alone cannot move an audience. His co-workers make the emotional appeal. Therein, perhaps, lies Maniu's strength and his weakness. He has the sound sense to surround himself with men like Vaida-Voevod and Michalache, who complement his strength. On the other hand, a rupture with either of them would materially weaken his power.

Last February, when the writer saw him in Bucharest, he already had his reform program in print. It is made up of fourteen points. Chief among them are the strengthening of the Constitution, integrity of justice so that, as one man put it, "we shall not have to pay the judge on the bench when we are in the right in order that he may see the right." It includes the building of schools, elementary, secondary, technical and agricultural.

His program includes also economic reforms in agriculture, commerce and industry. Among other things he wants rural banks, where the peasant can borrow money at a fair rate of interest; he wants a cooperative farm movement that will facilitate for the peasant the use and purchase of farm implements and farm material; he wants to organize cooperative selling markets for the peasant; he wants to do everything, in a word, that will give the peasant the status of a self-governing farmer.

Industry he wants to take out of the hands of a few individuals interested in exploiting the wealth of the land for personal gain and put under the supervision of experts interested in the welfare of the country and its people. He wants to assure the peasant free intercourse with markets in Rumania and markets outside of Rumania. The Bratianu régime has crippled the export trade of the country by imposing large export taxes on the products of the peasant. Before the war Rumania used to supply her neighbors with wheat and grain: Today, Maniu asserts, these markets have been taken from her.

The stabilization of the leu and the introduction of foreign capital are other points in his program. Before the war the leu was 5 to the dollar. Today it is 100 and more. Everybody is in a panic. Nobody buys, nobody sells, fearful of the change the next morning will bring. Land for which the peasant paid 100,000 lei last year is worth 30,000 lei today, and the peasant is still paying interest on the 100,000 basis.

The Bratianu régime has consistently been against the introduction of foreign capital for the exploitation of the country's natural resources and its industry. A few prominent Liberals hold important options on the wealth of the country, but they do nothing to increase the wealth of the land. Last Winter the Liberals, fearful of the growing demands of the peasants, shifted a little from their position. Duca, Minister of the Interior, told the writer in an interview that the Liberal Party was now ready to welcome foreign capital. "But," he said, "we want cooperation rather than conquest. We do not wish to be a foreign colony of Germany, England, France or the United States, economically speaking."

Maniu does not see it this way. He does not believe that foreign capital wants to make a conquest of Rumania. In the hands of Rumanians, nothing is being done to give the people of the country employment, food or prosperity. In the hands of enterprising foreign capital, free of political intrigue, he believes these objects could be attained.

### Why Ford Stayed Out

"Some time ago," he told the writer, "Henry Ford let it be known he was interested in establishing a base at Constanza. He sent his men to investigate the situation here, but when they saw the obstacles in their way, placed there by men who were afraid to let a foreigner do what they would not do and could not do, they left. Henry Ford is not to be blamed. Why should he risk his wealth in a country that had no respect for justice, for constitutional rights—where men and money were juggled like beans in a bag? Yet the peasant was not unaware what Henry Ford's coming would have meant for him. Work, money, transportation, commerce, industry— everything, in a word, that meant the return of health and prosperity to the country."

Reports coming out of Rumania state that Vintila Bratianu may seek to placate the peasants by stepping out and asking Nicholas Titelescu, the Foreign Minister, to form a Cabinet. It is not improbable, but the ruse will probably not work. Such a situation occurred when Jon Bratianu stepped out and by a manipulation of the voting machine put General Averescu in power. Maniu told the writer a story which is widely circulated among the peasants. They are not unaware of what such a change means.

"The story goes this way," Maniu said. "One day the late King Ferdinand called Jon Bratianu and General Averescu to him in order to discuss affairs of State with them. The men appeared and each was wearing a dirty shirt. The King, offended, asked what they meant by coming before him in such condition.

" 'Your Majesty,' Bratianu replied, 'we were busy all night with your affairs and had no time to change.'

" 'Very well,' said the King, somewhat appeased, 'go to your chambers, change your shirts and come back to me properly clothed.'

"The men retired and in half an hour returned. The King turned to greet them and was again amazed to find that their shirts were still dirty.

" 'What does this mean?' he demanded. 'Are you playing the fool with me?'

"Bratianu respectfully inclined his head. 'Your Majesty,' he said, "we have followed your wishes. We have changed our shirts. I am wearing Averescu's and he's wearing mine.' "

"They will probably try to do the same thing again," Maniu commented, "but the peasant will not accept that kind of a change."

Maniu's position according to well-informed Rumanians, is not an enviable one. The man's strength and power every one admits. But the problem that he will have to face, should he come into power, is a tremendous one.

"He will be accused of every crime that man is capable of," said a prominent banker in Bucharest. "He will be maligned, he will be scourged, he will be crucified. When he takes over the reins of the government, he ought to be made to promise never to read a newspaper and never to attend a public meeting for five years at least. In this way only can he carry on the work he has set before him."

Not the least important problems connected with Maniu's accession of power is the possible return of Carol. Last Winter popular opinion in Rumania had it that he could not come back as King. But there was a very strong belief that should the Nationalist Peasant Party take over the government, Carol would come back as Regent. The Rumanian peasant loves his little King, but he wants to be ruled by a member of the royal house, not by a regency he mistrusts. Maniu, however, remained consistently silent on this point. According to latest reports, the Nationalist Peasant Party has disavowed any connection with Carol's attempts to return to Rumania.

\*   \*   \*

June 21, 1928

# DEPUTY'S SIX SHOTS KILL TWO, WOUND 4 IN YUGOSLAV HOUSE

*Paul Raditch Slain Protecting Gravely Wounded Uncle, Stefan, Croatian Leader*

**KILLER GIVES HIMSELF UP**

*He Fired When Accused of Dishonesty After Row on Treaties With Italy*

**TROOPS PATROL STREETS**

*Croat-Serb Bitterness Revived, Former Refusing Premier's Condolences—Political Effects Feared*

Wireless to The New York Times

BELGRADE, June 20—Punica Ratchitch, a Montenegrin deputy in the Government Party, sought to end the opposition to the Cabinet by assassinating two leaders of the Croatian Peasant Party and wounding four other Opposition Deputies, one of them the fiery peasant chief Stefan Raditch, during the full assembly of today's session of the Skuptchina.

Every bullet from the revolver which the assassin turned upon the group of opposition deputies took effect killing Paul Raditch, nephew of Stefan, and the noted Croatian author and Vice President of the Peasant Party, Dr. George Basaritchik. He also wounded Stefan Raditch, Dr. Pernar, Secretary of the party, Josip Grandja and Dr. Jelasitch.

At the hospital late tonight it was said that Raditch, who has been ill for some time, is in grave danger of death, while Pernas was not yet conscious. In the panic that swept the Chamber, crowded with Deputies, visitors and newspaper men. Ratchitch walked out of the building away from the violence of his enemies. Later in the afternoon he gave himself up to the Minister of Home Affairs. He then was handed over to the police and held without charges.

When the session opened this morning, Ratchitch, who is a Montenegrin, although he sits for a Serbian Radical district in South Serbia, was charged with misappropriation of land in his constituency by several Deputies. M. Raditch took the floor about 11 o'clock and charged the Government as a whole with dishonesty.

Ratchitch arose and shook his fist at the speaker. A general turmoil which promised to become a free for all fight followed. The President attempted to adjourn the session, but Ratchitch pulled a revolver from his pocket and pointed it at Raditch.

## Empties Pistol in One Sweep

Several members rushed toward Ratchitch while others ran away in fright, but the assassin stood still shouting:

"I'll shoot any one who tries to stop me!"

M. Pernar continued toward him and received the first shot in the chest, falling to the floor. While every one else stood in astonishment Ratchitch stepped over the body.

Dr. Basartchik fell with the next bullet and M. Grandja then stepped into his place in front of M. Raditch, when he

also received a bullet in the upper right arm. As others were running toward him Ratchitch emptied his revolver at one sweep, firing the first bullet at the then unprotected Stefan Raditch and hitting him in the stomach, and the second at Paul Raditch, who rushed toward him.

Then, almost carelessly, he fired the last one into the crowd, wounding M. Jelasitch in the hand. After he had caught six men with six bullets the Montanegrin turned and walked without hindrance out of the Chamber.

Ten minutes later news reached the public outside Parliament, with the arrival of ambulances to carry all six to the hospital, Paul Raditch dying en route. Thousands of people rushed to the Skuptchina, but guards closed the gates, while Premier Vukitchevitch left by the rear door to take the news to the King. Simultaneously troops were ordered to the main streets and all telephone and telegraph communications abroad were closed. A few hours later, when no disturbances had occurred, communications were re-established, but guards continue in the streets tonight.

### King Visits Wounded

An afternoon communique issued by the Cabinet which has been in session expressed regret at the events and promised to impose the severest penalty, death, upon the assailant and assured life pensions for dependents of the dead and indemnity for the wounded.

Less than an hour after the events, the King visited the hospital and remained there while bullets were extracted from the wounded bodies. The king since then has sent his equerry hourly to the hospital.

Relatives of Stefan Raditch and M. Pernar were admitted to their rooms tonight as the condition of these patients became worse, and they still remain with them.

Black flags were put out in the streets when the tragedy became known. The streets and cafes have been crowded with people since noon although no disorders occurred, or are reported from provinces of Zagreb, the Croatian capital.

Assassinations are not unknown in Serbia, which witnessed the killing of King Alexander and Queen Alexandra in 1903, the assassination of the Austrian Archduke Ferdinand in 1914 and the slaying of several politicians in the last two decades.

The events today may have serious consequences for the Kingdom, as the discords between the Serbians and Croats, the chief elements in the Kingdom, have increased rather than diminished since they formed a union after the war. The Croats, led by Stefan Raditch, have continually fought the Government for a share in the administration of affairs and accused the Serbians, who have almost monopolized office, with using taxes for the betterment of the old Kingdom of Serbia instead of alloting a rightful and proportionate amount to Croatia and other new provinces.

The bitterness increased when the late Pasitch, leader of the Serbian Radicals, when Premier had Stefan Raditch jailed. Against Premier Pasitch little headway could be made by the Croats but his death two years ago gave them increased power and they even attempted to take office twice.

Even in face of the romance written about Balkan States nothing in the methods supposedly used to rid them of unpopular monarchs or national enemies could reach the facts of today's tragedy, which left the King, politicians and public dazed and fearful of the possible results to the nation.

The assassinations followed the bitterest opposition of Croatians and Democrats to all proposals of the Radical coalition Government formed two months ago after many unsuccessful attempts and against the wishes of Stefan Raditch, who demanded new and free elections.

### Attacks Centred on Italian Treaties

The Opposition culminated in attacks against the ratification of the Nettuno conventions with Italy, which were seized upon because they were unpopular in the country, especially in Dalmatia. Stefan Raditch and his colleagues were accused of inciting the demonstrations in Belgrade and elsewhere, and they retaliated by interrupting all sessions of the Skuptchina in the hope of forcing the Government to abandon the program.

The Croatians, including Stefan Raditch, several times were expelled for fighting or using bad language in Parliament, only to return and accuse the Government again of dishonest appropriations.

At yesterday's session an ominous warning was uttered by one Deputy, not the assassin today, who interrupted Stefan Raditch while he was saying that his life was threatened, and shouted:

"You will have your head cut off in this Parliament. We'll see to that."

This has given Opposition circles tonight an impression of a conspiracy which is not otherwise substantiated.

### Reject Premier's Condolences

Stefan Raditch was accused by Pasitch of working for Croatian independence. These charges were revived lately following Raditch's violent attacks on the Government.

The disturbances in Parliament and throughout the country against the Nettuno treaties gave M. Raditch cause to harass the Government benches and an opportunity to demand again "free elections," backed by the threat that his party would never allow the treaty to be ratified.

Late tonight the Cabinet sent a letter of condolence to the Croatian Party headquarters which was returned to the Premier with these words written in red pencil across the envelope "not accepted."

Croatian Party leaders further showed the bitterness felt toward the Government by refusing its offer to defray funeral expenses. They declared the "fight would be kept up."

After a late Cabinet session one of the leading members announced that the Government had decided not to resign as it was not connected in any way with the action of Ratchitch. The Skuptchina has been adjourned sine die. Another Cabinet meeting has been called for Thursday morning.

It is understood that earlier in the day, leaders of the Democrats who are in the Government with the Radicals,

wanted to withdraw. It is still considered likely that a new crisis will be forced by today's happenings. The bodies of Paul Raditch and Bisaricek will be sent tonight to Zagreb for burial Friday.

### Croatians Demand Independence

Wireless to The New York Times

ZAGREB, Croatia, Yugoslavia, June 20—Less than an hour after the news reached here of the assassinations in the Skuptchina, thousands of people collected in the great public square, some carrying banners calling for a Croatian Parliament to be convoked, others demanding separation from Serbia. No serious disorders took place. The city is patrolled by police and Croatian troops.

### Upsets Little Entente Meeting

Wireless to The New York Times

BUCHAREST, June 20—News of the assassinations in the Parliament at Belgrade was received here when Foreign Ministers of the Rumania, Czechoslovakia and the Yugoslavia were at the opening session of the Little Entente conference this morning, causing a temporary suspension of the sitting. M. Marinkovich, the Yugoslavian Minister, left the room after the opening speeches were made and the session adjourned until 4 o'clock this afternoon.

The second meeting, however, did not take place until 5:30 when nothing of importance was accomplished. It is felt here that nothing will be attempted tomorrow as any decisions would be subject to possible events in Belgrade. M. Marinkovitch is not planning to return home until after the conference is closed.

The ministers declared this morning that only economic matters would be discussed at the meeting although ways of counteracting the Hungarian agitation for revision of the Treaty of Trianon undoubtedly will form an important part in the deliberations.

\* \* \*

June 22, 1928

# THREE DIE IN RIOTS FOR BELGRADE DEAD

*40 Hurt, 200 Arrested in Zagreb, Stronghold of Victims of Assassination*

### CITY PLUNGED IN DARKNESS

*Widow of Slain Deputy Urges Serbo-Croat Reconciliation—Raditch Still in Danger*

Wireless to The New York Times

ZAGREB, Croatia, Yugoslavia, Friday, June 22—Demonstrations in which three were killed, forty wounded and almost 200 arrested began here at 10 o'clock last night before the Café Corse on Ilicia Strada, one of the principal thoroughfares of the city. A crowd of 3,000 students, members of the Croatian Peasant Party, attacked the café, which is the headquarters of Serbians here.

The first hour was confined to shouting, then windows were stoned and several policemen guarding the café were hit. The crowd rushed the doors, whereupon the police fired and killed three and seriously wounded ten young men. One policeman was badly mobbed.

On reinforcements arriving the police dispersed the crowd, cleared the street, removed the dead and wounded and arrested others.

A light rain dispersed another crowd which gathered later in the park. At 1 o'clock this morning the city was quiet.

[Zagreb is the stronghold of Stefan Raditch, who was shot and seriously wounded in the Belgrade Parliament yesterday, and whose nephew, Paul, and another follower were killed.]

### Whole City In Uproar

ZAGREB, June 21 (AP)—The shooting here was continued tonight. The whole city is in an uproar and martial law probably will be proclaimed.

The student rioters, assisted by some workmen, cut the power lines. A good part of the city was in darkness, adding to the confusion and the general terror inspired by the sounds of the continuous shooting. Because of the unlighted streets, the authorities were unable to ascertain the precise number of killed and wounded.

The rioters then rushed through the streets shouting imprecations. They attacked the Jagerhof Café which is also patronized by Government officials. The smashing of this establishment caused another battle with the police.

### Cabinet Crisis Is Feared

Wireless to The New York Times

BELGRADE, June 21—The Zagreb disturbance was the only one reported here throughout the day and night, a fact that is considered a hopeful sign that no general demonstration will be made against the Government, though the work of the assassin yesterday has shaken the political foundations of the Kingdom more violently than anything since its founding.

The capital itself is in deep mourning. Most business houses are closed and draped in black. Calm prevails. Politicians and newspapers of all parties have refrained from giving vent to whatever passions the events have aroused. Extra police are watching the streets and Government buildings, but the precautions so far are unnecessary. The provisional districts, with the exception of Zagreb, the centre of the Croatian opposition, are very quiet.

Politics, suspended today, will continue so tomorrow when Paul Raditch and Georg Basaritchek, the Croatian Deputies killed in the Skupshtina, will be buried at Zagreb. After that another political crisis faces the present Radical-Democrat Coalition Cabinet, for the minority of Democrats threaten to withdraw unless the Government resigns as a show of good faith and innocence in yesterday's events.

The Cabinet held a meeting this morning and though it was secret several members later said there was no idea of resigna-tion. King Alexander, who has shown the greatest sympathy for the families of the victims, is looked to by opposition parties to take a hand and ask the Government to resign.

Opinion here is to the effect that the Government cannot withstand these attacks and will have to give up office, though there is little chance of any other combination than the present one succeeding in office. Elections can hardly be called while the excitement over the assassinations and the Nettuno treaties continues.

If the Cabinet remains in power it is not known whether it will persist in its demand for ratification of the Nettuno treaties which aroused the recent bitterness of the opposition.

### Widow Pleads for Peace

The Croatian Peasant Party continues to hold the Government responsible for the shooting in the Skupshtina. Today it announced that it would not participate further in the present Parliament nor cooperate with the Government. Many deputies who are leaving to attend the funeral at Zagreb tomorrow declared that they will never return to the Serbian city.

The Government will not be allowed to pay the funeral expenses of the victims nor to give pensions to their families, for the Croatians insist that this be borne by subscriptions already started in Croatia. The city of Zagreb has announced that it will bear the funeral expenses and erect monuments to the country's "martyrs."

The bodies of Paul Raditch and Dr. Basaritchek were moved to the Catholic Church here today where they laid in public view following a funeral mass. Thousands of people filed by the catafalques until night time. They included in the morning the widow of Paul Raditch and her seven children, who had arrived overnight from Zagreb. The widow went direct from the station to the church. She was joined there for a few moments by King Alexander, who took her hand and expressed his sorrow. Weeping, she responded with these words:

"I hope my husband will be the last victim of strife, and that Serbia and Croatia will make peace."

Escorted by members of the Croatian Party the bodies will be taken overnight to Zagreb.

Stefan Raditch and Dr. Pernar, who were severely wounded, rallied early in the day, but tonight M. Raditch developed diabetes and his condition is serious. Dr. Gustav Singer of Vienna who attended Mgr. Seipel when the Chancellor suffered diabetes after the attempt to assassinate him, has been called to Belgrade and will arrive there in the morning.

Grave anxiety is felt for M. Raditch, as his death would complicate further a complicated situation.

The assassin, Deputy Ratchitch, interviewed by the police in his cell this afternoon, said that in firing he meant to protect himself from attack. He explained:

"I am a Montenegrin and when we are insulted we fight. As Parliament did not protect me. I did so myself."

He has had published a statement to his constituency in which he writes:

"I always worked for the interests of the electorate and the King. I am sorry I shall be unable to serve you so well in the future."

### Slayer Asks No Trial

BELGRADE, June 21 (AP)—Punica Ratchitch, the Montenegrin Deputy who shot and killed two other Deputies and wounded four in the Yugoslav Parliament yesterday, lost none of his nerve when arraigned before a magistrate today on the charge of murder.

"I am ready to be taken out immediately and shot without trial," he exclaimed. "I have fulfilled my task."

All Yugoslavia is mourning the victims of yesterday's tragedy. The newspapers have appeared in black borders. Many stores, theatres, moving picture houses and cafés are closed; street cars and trains have ceased to run temporarily.

### Italians Stress Yugoslav Divisions

ROME, June 21 (AP)—The shooting affray in the Yugoslav Parliament yesterday is published prominently in the Italian newspapers.

The Popolo di Roma editorially expresses the hope that the Belgrade parties and factions will take a lesson from the fracas and practice more moderation and tolerance.

The newspaper Brillante says that the affair will weigh heavier on the young State than a military defeat.

### LITTLE ENTENTE IS RESERVED
#### Decides Not to Issue Bulletins on Conference in Bucharest

Wireless to The New York Times

BUCHAREST, June 21—The Little Entente conference which opened yesterday only to be interrupted by the assassinations in Belgrade began its discussion of Balkan political problems this morning.

The Foreign Ministers of the three nations making up the entente, Rumania, Yugoslavia and Czechoslovakia, had only time for an indefinite discussion of the problem of the negotiations among Greece, Bulgaria and Turkey for economic and friendship treaties and did not reach the question of the recent attempts of Hungary to overthrow the Treaty of Trianon which must be foremost in the minds of the conferees. The session ended after two hours and will be resumed tomorrow.

The delegates to the conference have decided not to admit the press to the meetings nor to issue the usual bulletins at the close, leaving individual members to use their discretion in dealing with the newspapers. As a result very little of the important discussions will be known to the public, certainly not that dealing with Hungary and Italy, both of which are of vital interest to all three Entente countries.

It is announced at Czech headquarters tonight that Dr. Benes would introduce his plan for a Central European economic union tomorrow. It is expected that he will propose that if it is accepted the Little Entente be enlarged later to include other States.

\*    \*    \*

June 22, 1928

## THE BELGRADE MURDERS

A madman's act like that committed on Wednesday in the legislative chamber at Belgrade ought not to lead to serious political consequences. But party passions in Yugoslavia have been running high, and if in addition to the two Croat representatives already dead it should happen that Stefan Raditch himself succumbs to his wounds, a grave situation may well arise. The elder Raditch, for whom the assassin's first bullet was intended, has been since the war the leader of the former Hapsburg South Slavs, reunited to the Serb motherland but far from contented in the new union. In the Parliament he has never been able to command a majority, but he may be regarded as the spokesman for the "redeemed" brethren, numbering two-thirds of the population of the Yugoslav kingdom. Their grievances against the dominant Serb element at Belgrade have been two: they have been denied what they consider to be a just share in the Government, and in the field of foreign policy their anti-Italian sentiments have not been taken into sufficient consideration. It was in the course of debate on ratification of the Nettuno agreements with Italy that the murderer Ratchitch ran amuck with his pistol.

Another typically Balkan episode has thus come along to aggravate a chronically difficult situation at Belgrade. The Yugoslav State badly needs foreign capital for internal development; and though international investors are not excessively sentimental, it is natural that the prospects of the big loan for which the Government has long been working should be adversely affected by another demonstration of imperfect national stability. Inevitably the royal massacre of twenty-five years ago and the tragic deed at Serajevo in 1914 come to mind. The only conceivable gain out of the latest experiment in blood-letting is that partisanship run mad may turn out to have overreached itself and that King Alexander may feel emboldened to undertake the work of reconciliation for which no political leader is at present strong enough.

\*    \*    \*

November 4, 1928

## BRATIANU RESIGNS AT REGENTS' ORDER

*Failure to Get Loan and Desire to Unify Rumania Cause Cabinet's Downfall*

### MANIU MAY GET POWER

*National-Peasant Leader Has List of Ministers Ready— Censorship Is Abolished*

Wireless to The New York Times

BUCHAREST, Nov. 4—The struggle for control of Rumania's political destiny and the multitude of office- holder plums that this mastery involves today reached a critical stage, and the result is that Vintila Bratianu is no longer Premier. At the close of a special Cabinet meeting at noon M. Bratianu tendered his resignation to the Regency, which asked for it yesterday, thus ending, at least for some time to come, it is thought, the rule of the "Bratianu dynasty" in Rumania.

On inheriting the Premiership from his brother, the late Jon Bratianu, Vintila faced the very severe opposition of the National Peasant Party, which, under the able leadership of Juliu Maniu, out-generaled him on almost every battlefield. In this fight he was greatly handicapped by the heritage from his brother of a number of mining and oil laws which were held to be unfair by foreigners, who before the war had invested money in the Rumanian petroleum industry.

Wherever he turned for the foreign loan that Rumania sorely needs, the Premier met the reply:

"Rumania will get a loan when the rights of foreigners are recognized."

American and British bankers were particularly firm in this stand. M. Maniu realized this and kept the loan failure ever before the public. M. Bratianu scored one victory when Carol was beguiled into a foolish attempt to recover the throne which ended in a fiasco for Carol and compelled M. Maniu to proclaim openly his support of the present Constitution and the régime by which the Regency reigns for Michael, the seven-year-old King.

Since the peasant congress of Alba Julia in April. M. Maniu has continually gained ground. M. Bratianu weakened, hit the toboggan slide downward a few weeks ago when it was revealed openly that a number of Liberal Deputies were guilty of the grossest corruption in the administration of the petroleum law.

### Freedom of Press Restored

The Regency wishes if possible to have a concentration Government of all parties in the country, but it is considered very unlikely that any one in Rumania will be able to form such a Cabinet, because the fight is too bitter. Under Rumania's election laws any Premier is certain of an overwhelming majority in Parliament when he holds an election. Thus former Premier Averescu had a majority till Jon Bratianu decided to force him out. At the next election, held by Jon Bratianu. General Averescu failed to return a single Deputy. Should none succeed in forming a concentration Government, it is not unlikely that M. Maniu may be empowered to form his own Government and hold elections, which would give him a majority. There are already a number of signs of defection among M. Bratianu's supporters. In the past days increasing numbers of them have intimated a wish to follow M. Titulescu's lead and break with M. Bratianu.

With Mr. Maniu as Premier, M. Titulescu is very likely to be Foreign Minister. As soon as Bratianu resigned, the Regency ordered M. Titulescu home from London.

Prince Barbu Stirbey in a press interview has declared for M. Maniu as Premier and for new elections. The official Rador News Agency tonight announced that M. Maniu is likely to become Premier.

For the first time in many months freedom of the press reigns in Rumania. Correspondents telegrah as they choose and local newspapers report freely.

### Move Favors Transylvanians

BUCHAREST, Nov. 3 (AP)—Rumania was thrown into a state of acute political turmoil today by the sudden and dramatic resignation of the Bratianu Government in the midst of his efforts to conclude a $250,000,000 stabilization loan, in which American capital was to participate.

The crisis appears to have been precipitated by the Regency Council's desire that the National-Peasant Party, backed by 80 per cent of the voters in Transylvania, should participate freely in the celebrations on Dec. 1 of Rumania's union with Transylvania. The Regency realized that without the Transylvania peasants' cooperation such celebrations would be a failure.

The National Peasants' Party executives had already served an ultimatum on the Regency that the party would have no dealings with the Government in any form and would repudiate the stabilization loan if they came into power.

### Premier Is Astonished

The Regency yesterday gave Vintila Bratianu, who succeeded to the Premiership after the death of his more famous brother, Jon, until Dec. 1 to resign. The Premier argued that the stabilization loan was paramount even to the Transylvania celebration and would go by the board if the Government resigned.

The Regency, however, which appears lately to have made up its mind that the sentiment of the country demanded a change in the régime, insisted that M. Bratianu must make a decision. The Regency Council is composed of Prince Nicholas, son of Dowager Queen Marie; Patriarch Cristea and M. Buzdugan. President of the Supreme Court. They rule Rumania in the name of seven-year-old King Michael, son of former Crown Prince Carol, now in exile.

Astonished and indignant at the Regency's change of attitude toward the powerful Liberal Party, Premier Bratianu immediately called a conference of his colleagues. This lasted most of the night and continued this morning. Some of the more recalcitrant members of the Cabinet were in favor of defying the Regency, but M. Bratianu said such a move would endanger the equilibrium of the country. Thereupon the Cabinet decided to resign.

Juliu Maniu, the suave, quiet-spoken Transylvanian lawyer and popular leader of the National Peasants Party, will probably be asked to form a Cabinet. In such an event it is thought certain that he will scrap the entire stabilization loan on the ground that its terms are too onerous for Rumania's present depleted finances.

It is thought, also, that he will make no attempt to change the present Regency, either in favor of Carol or Queen Marie, although there is considerable sentiment among the people that Queen Marie should be made a co-Regent with the present three members.

### Maniu Has Cabinet List Ready

In the meantime M. Maniu informed the Regency that the National Peasant Party was utterly opposed to forming a Cabinet together with members of the present Government, as desired by the retiring Premier, but would not be against the inclusion of M. Titulescu, Prince Barbu Stirbey, former Premier, or other neutral statesmen.

A complete deadlock therefore exists, which probably will not be relieved until the Regency Council has held further conferences with the leaders.

M. Maniu made public the Cabinet that he would form if entrusted with that duty. He would himself hold the portfolio of Foreign Minister and his associates would be M. Vaido-Voevod, Interior; M. Madgearu, Industry; Michael Popovich, Finance; M. Mihilachi, Agriculture; M. Junian, Justice; M. Joanitescu, Labor, and M. Bocu, Education. M. Maniu prefers that the Regency designate the new Minister of War.

Much of the tension engendered by the resignation was dissipated when the Regency abolished the censorship which had been maintained so rigorously under the Bratianu régime.

Bucharest remains calm, but the gendarmerie and the garrison are being held ready as a precaution against disturbances, which, however, are considered unlikely.

Fortunately the Stock Exchange was closed today before the Cabinet's resignation; otherwise the impending collapse of the stabilization loan would undoubtedly have precipitated a sharp decline in the leu. Big banking, industrial and commercial firms are apprehensive that if M. Maniu forms a Ministry he will withdraw the Liberal Government's traditional system of subsidizing big business.

\* \* \*

November 11, 1928

## RUMANIAN REGENTS DISSOLVE ASSEMBLY

*Order New Parliamentary Poll in December—Maniu Cabinet Swears Fealty to Dynasty*

**TO CONFIRM CAROL'S EXILE**

*Peasant Premier Declares War on Corruption—First Roman Catholic to Head Greek Orthodox Nation*

Wireless to The New York Times

BUCHAREST, Nov. 10—Rumania tonight has a new master, Julius Maniu, leader of the National-Peasant Party. At 4 o'clock this afternoon, with his Cabinet made up entirely from the ranks of his party, Premier Maniu drove to the palace and took the oath of office as the new Government, marking the first real break in many years in the rule of the Bratianu family and its party, Liberal by name and Conservative by policy.

From this hour, which the populace of Bucharest as well as that of the provinces celebrated with spontaneous demonstrations, a new era, and one of the most important in Rumania's national existence, began. En route to the palace to take the oath, the members of the new Government were showered with flowers and enthusiastically cheered by thousands on the street curb, these scenes being repeated when the Cabinet emerged from the palace after the ceremony of being sworn in. While the streets still echoed with jubilant shouting the Government was already at work in its first Cabinet council, following which M. Maniu received newspapermen and outlined his program. The outstanding points of it are:

First, complete freedom of the press, "my best friend because it is truthful."

Second, the slogan of equality between men and lawful procedure in Government.

Third, work in the open, not in the dark.

Fourth, the free elections which will reveal the will of the people, such elections being provided for by special decrees before the vote is polled.

Fifth, the continuation of the loan negotiations for the stabilization of the currency.

Sixth, repeal of all unfair economic laws enacted in past years, to give again to foreign capital equal rights and privileges with domestic capital in Rumania.

Seventh, revision of the customs tariff downward.

### Cabinet Represents Whole Nation

In the formation of his Cabinet M. Maniu endeavored, with almost complete success, to make the Government illustrative of the National-Peasant Party's claim to be "national." Five Ministers are Transylvanians—from M. Maniu's own province—one each from Besserabia, Bukovina and Banat, and others from that part of the country comprising pre-war Rumania, the so-called Old Kingdom.

The completed Cabinet is composed as follows:

*Premier*—JULIUS MANIU.
*Foreign Affairs*—Professor MIRONESCU.
*Interior*—A. VAIDA-VOEVOD.
*Finance*—MICHAEL POPOVICH.
*War*—General CHIKOSKI.
*Education*—M. COSTAKESCO.
*Labor*—M. RADUCANU.
*Health*—M. SEVERDAN.
*Public Works*—M. HALIPPA.
*Transportation*—M. ALEVRA.
*Agriculture*—I. MIHILACHI.
*Justice*—G. JUNIAN.
*Culture*—AUREVLAD.
*Commerce*—V. N. MADGEARU
*Without Portfolio*—Messre. NITZESCO, BOCU,
    and SAVEANU.

The personnel is regarded as a wise selection. M. Mironescu, who is not a politician, is believed to be a mere bench warmer. After the elections either M. Titulescu or M. Vaida-Voevod may get the post, M. Titulesco in the meanwhile returning to London.

The elections are scheduled for Dec. 12 for the Chamber of Deputies and Dec. 15 for the Senate.

The official gazette today issued a special edition announcing the early dissolution of the present Parliament.

M. Maniu's victory has aroused such bitterness in the Liberal Party that all the ex-Ministers left their posts today, though tradition requires them to remain to receive their successors.

### Maniu to Uphold Regency

BUCHAREST, Nov. 10 (AP)—Julius Maniu, head of the National Peasant Party who, today, as Premier took over the reins of Government, had earlier announced that the dissolution of Parliament was an indispensable condition to his forming a Cabinet. He had declared that Parliament, as constituted, was not representative and that there should be new and honest elections.

M. Maniu gained additional support today by his oath loyally to support the present monarchy and the Regency. Later he said:

"Our Government will confirm the legislation passed under former Premier Bratianu concerning Prince Carol, who by his childish act has forfeited his rights to the throne forever. Michael will be our King, to whom we shall be answerable through the Regency, whose powers are fixed by law to which we agree unreservedly."

M. Maniu is the first Roman Catholic to become Premier of this predominantly Greek Orthodox country. A Roman Catholic priest, therefore, shared honors today with Patriarch Miron Christea, the ecclesiastical member of the Regency, in swearing in the Cabinet.

A dramatic incident occurred during the investiture of the new Rumanian Cabinet today, when the Commissioner for the Banat Province, Dr. Heradu, refused to take the oath before the Regency Council with his colleagues, on the ground that he was a free thinker.

Despite the presence of the Regency and the entreaties of his associates, he declined steadfastly to take the customary oath, and it seemed for a time as if the swearing in of the entire Cabinet might be upset. The Regency finally decided to pass Dr. Heradu without the usual pledge, but there is some fear that this may give rise later to legal complications.

Demonstrations on a tremendous scale continued throughout all parts of Rumania. In Bucharest this afternoon 15,000 people demonstrated in front of the capital in favor of the new Government. In thousands of windows the Rumanian flag and M. Maniu's picture were displayed. Tonight the city was brilliantly illuminated.

M. Maniu is faced with a series of enormous internal tasks. By the end of the year the Government must pass urgent legislation, including the finance bill and measures for stabilization of the currency. According to the new Premier, the deficit for the current year amounts to nearly $40,000,000. A great part of the State's debts must be paid, including an Italian loan and other obligations amounting to $60,000,000.

There will be a complete reorganization of Rumania's diplomatic service and it is probable that the present Ministers at Paris, Berlin and other important capitals will be changed.

While events of vast importance are taking place in this country, King Michael, who has just celebrated his seventh birthday, is not worrying. He seems to have been more impressed by an experience he recently had at the hands of an American magician. The little King's amazement exceeded all bounds when the wizard told him to press an ace of hearts over his heart, and while doing so converted the card into Michael's own photograph.

### Transylvanians Rejoice

CLUJ, Transylvania, Nov. 10 (AP)—All Transylvania, the stronghold of the "National" wing of the National Peasant Party, is rejoicing over Julius Maniu's triumph. Street manifestations are being held in all the large towns.

Two million Transylvanian Rumanians, who were formerly under Hungary's rule, see in Vintila Bratianu's downfall the first prospect of their getting an equal share in the Government with their brother citizens in Old Rumania.

\* \* \*

**December 30, 1928**

## JUNE TRAGEDY BARS SERB-CROAT ACCORD

---

*Latters' Withdrawal Leaves No Parliamentary Contact of the Two Factions*

**MODERATION IS HOPED FOR**

*Trial of Ratchitch, Who Shot Leaders of Opposition, May Lead to Change in Attitude*

---

By CLAIR PRICE
Special Correspondence of The New York Times

BELGRADE, Dec. 13—The Serb-Croat conflict goes from bad to worse. The tragedy of last June led to the withdrawal of the Croat parties from Parliament and left the two sides without contact in Belgrade. The government's insistence on an official celebration of Yugoslavia's tenth anniversary on Dec. 1 resulted in rioting in the Croat capital of Zagreb. The rioting resulted in the appointment of a Serbian military governor in Zagreb. This step, which has no precedent outside the backward and turbulent provinces of Macedonia, led to a refusal of the Zagreb County Council to sit with a representative of the Governor in attendance. This in turn brought a decree from the government in Belgrade suspending the council, a decree without precedent anywhere in the country. The two sides are now without contact in Zagreb as well as in Belgrade, and the Croat aims are announced as independence within a Yugoslavian dual monarchy like the old Austro-Hungarian monarchy.

Conversations with party leaders here indicate a readiness to consider the revision of the present centralist constitution with a view to meeting the Croats. Providing a preliminary agreement can be reached, Father Anton Koroshetz, the Prime Minister, has expressed the government's willingness to dissolve the present Parliament and to hold new elections under a neutral Serb-Croat government on the issue of a constitutional revision extending home rule to all the provinces. In the government's view a preliminary agreement is necessary to prevent the shootings of last June from being used as a Croat election cry with the possible result of serious and widespread violence.

### Croats Maintain Boycott

To these advances the Croats have replied by refusing to depart from the boycott of the government which they have maintained ever since June 20 when five members of the Croat opposition, including Stephen Raditch himself, the Croat leader, were shot in Parliament by a government deputy from Montenegro. The Croats refuse to consider any conditions precedent to the dissolution of Parliament and the holding of new elections. While not departing from their allegiance to King Alexander, they have broken off relations with the King's present government and the government's reply has been to place the Croat capital under martial law.

A suggestion of an anti-dynastic movement exists at the moment in a Croat committee in Paris which is working for Prince Alexander Dabisha Kotromanitz, a Russian who until recently was a Berlin chauffeur, as the occupant of a new Croatian throne, but it is improbable that the committee gets any of its support in Zagreb. In this connection it is pertinent to remember that the Croats have been quick to seek cover under the Yugoslav umbrella whenever squalls have threatened from Italy. Italian aggressiveness, indeed, has been a powerful influence in the maintenance of Yugoslav unity and it is interesting to note that of late Italy has been conspicuously quiet. As far as Yugoslavia is concerned the Italian political skies could hardly have been bluer or more smiling than they have been since the Serb-Croat rupture of last June.

Meanwhile Punisha Ratchitch, the Montenegrin deputy who fired the five shots which cost the lives of three Croat deputies, has been lying in a Belgrade jail ever since and his trial for murder is now not far away. As this article was written, the date of the trial had been repeatedly set and as often postponed. Whether it was to be heard in the political or the criminal courts had not been announced. The primary courtrooms in Belgrade are too small to hold the witnesses who were to be summoned and the question of whether the trial was to be held in the hall of the university or even in an outdoor place was not decided. The conduct and the result of the trial, when it is held, will be political events of the first importance.

### Break Is Now Complete

Ratchitch's five shots, fired from the rostrum in the old cavalry barracks which serve as the temporary home of the Parliament, were by no means the beginning of the conflict between Serbian centralism and Croatian federalism. They were merely the spark applied to a too explosive atmosphere of bitterness and recrimination. The break has now become so complete that it has created a new danger point in a Europe to which the existence of a sound and healthy Yugoslavia is essential. No part of Europe has had a longer and fuller experience of the forcible repression of nationality, and nowhere has the use of force against national aspirations brought more disastrous consequences to Europe as a whole. The consolidation of Yugoslavia is a task which is inevitably reminiscent of Bismarck's consolidation of the old German Empire and of Cavour's making of modern Italy, but it has to be admitted at once that there are neither Bismarcks nor Cavours in Yugoslavia. The three long-lost brothers of the South Slav races have come together into their new home in the Kingdom of the Serbs, Croats and Slovenes as strangers to each other. In blood and in language, although not in script, they are one and the same people, but they have been brought up in different homes.

The Serb has come from a brief independence after 500 years of the tutelage of the Grand Turk, and there are traces of the Turk still visible upon him. He is as thoroughly a soldier as the Turk was, and he has fought his way to an independence of which he is justly proud. He is a big healthy Balkan peasant with simple democratic tastes, with no aristocracy and even a bourgeoisie whose growth is decidedly recent; an untutored person but ambitious and keen to learn; an Orthodox who is not a great churchgoer except on his feast days; a sturdy farmer who, if he ever thinks of the sea at all, is apt to think of it as something which occurs at Saloniki.

### The Croats Are Different

The Croat, on the other hand, has come direct from the old Hungary and is a highly civilized European who has been brought up under the European tutelage of Budapest and Vienna. He usually talks German as his second language and talks it so well that one has to look twice at him to make sure he is not a Viennese. He has retained many of his old aristocratic families, and there is never any doubt about who his townspeople are and who his peasantry. He is as Catholic as Cork, and his capital of Zagreb has grown in the way Central European cities usually grow, according to plan and not haphazardly as Belgrade has grown.

The Slovene has come direct from the old Austria. Like the Croat, he is a Catholic and a Central European who has discovered for himself on the Adriatic that the sea is both wet and deep. If Zagreb may be regarded as the Yugoslav Edinburgh, the Slovene capital of Ljubljana may perhaps be regarded as the Yugoslav Aberdeen. Compared to both of them, rough old Belgrade is a robust pupil. Civilization in Yugoslavia is highest in the north, decreasing as one goes south to reach its lowest point in Macedonia, and the greater part of the population lies toward the south. There are only about 1,200,000 Slovenes as compared with 3,000,000 Croats and 5,000,000 Serbs. The country as a whole is fortunate in having a comparatively homogeneous population. Eighty-five per cent of it is Slav, its small non-Slav minorities bringing its total population up to about 13,000,000.

To consolidate these three long-lost brothers into an enduring new state with a territory which stretches from Austria to Greece and from Rumania to the Adriatic—potentially one of the great powers of Europe—is a task which obviously calls for statecraft of a very high order. But far from revealing a master hand to cope with a situation which calls for master handling the Belgrade of today reveals in the impending trial of Punisha Ratchitch the full depth of the bitterness and short sightedness of which Balkan politics is capable.

### Belgrade an Apt Pupil

This is the more noticeable because the physical Belgrade is rising with an almost breathless rapidity to its new responsibilities as one of the important capitals of Europe. The Serbs used to be told that one of the dangers of union with the Croats was the hopelessness of attempting to raise the rough Balkan village of Belgrade to the splendors of Zagreb, but as a pupil in Europeanism the physical Belgrade surpasses the rosiest expectations. Ten years have accomplished an astonishing amount of de-Balkanization in its once straggling and shell-shattered streets. The old Serbian capital has trebled its population since it became the capital of Yugoslavia in 1918. Imposing government buildings and big blocks of offices have been pushed to completion along the Street of Milosh the Great.

Smooth asphalt has been laid in place of the old cobblestones on the central streets and Belgradians, whose sleep has been ruined by the noise of paving gangs working all night, can offer heartfelt testimony to the furious speed with which the transformation has been pushed through. Motor buses now ply the new streets and in the new suburbs bathrooms and elevators are taken as a matter of course. Ten years ago the water supply was so limited that, except in the riverside parts of the town, it was impossible to wash one's hands in the middle of the day. Today an ornamental fountain with a dozen jets plays in the large open space outside the Café Moscova, high on the ridge. Much of the roughness of ten years ago still remains on the slopes of the ridge and even in the newer parts it is possible to break one's leg by falling at night into an unlighted hole in a new sidewalk. But generally the higher and more central parts of the capital now contain new theatres, new banks, new hotels and new shops pushing in unbroken ranks to Kalemegdan Park behind the old Turkish fortress which overlooks the confluence of the Danube and the Save. Trailing its neo-Munich suburbs, the Belgrade of today thrusts itself imperiously into the junction of its majestic rivers and at its tip, high up in front of the historic old fortress, displays to the "European" side of the Danube Ivan Mestrovitch's heroic statue of Victory.

### Consolidation Is Difficult

The great domed parliament building beyond the gardens at the back of the royal palace is another reminder that this is the capital of a country conscious of its destiny. But it is perhaps easier to change the face of a city than to consolidate a country with as tangled a skein of provincial usages as Yugoslavia has inherited. The shirt-sleeved peasant parliament of today is still meeting in its temporary home, the low white building which used to be a cavalry barracks and is now almost lost amid the imposing new government buildings around it. The physical Belgrade is rising to meet the future, but its political parties appear thus far to have found it difficult to trouble themselves about a theoretical tomorrow. Two factors in the political life of the country appear to have made possible the present Serb-Croat conflict. One is the great figure of Nicholas Pashitch who, though dead, still casts his long shadow over Yugoslav politics. The other is the nature and the number of the parties, whose intricate permutations and combinations are so involved as to be almost unintelligible to the uninitiated.

The Serbs are a people so democratic that they used to constitute one large family with only the King and the white-bearded figure of the patriarchal Pashitch to look up to. In his earlier days the best known and one of the ablest of Balkan politicians, Pashitch was a centralist and a Greater Serbian at heart and his party, the Serbian Radicals, was the political home of the Serbian centralism which has been written into the Yugoslav Constitution. It is possible that Pashitch might have modified his centralism if the war had not made an old man of him. The longer he remained in power after the war, the more rapidly his power slipped into the hands of the lesser men who surrounded him.

It was the Pashitch clique during the latter days of the growing senility of the "Grand Premier," which made Serbian centralism perhaps more odious in practice than it need to have been in theory. The Pashitch clique consisted exclusively of Serbs from Old Serbia and the tales which are told of it today need to be viewed in the light of the fact that the present generation of Serbs has been through a fearful ordeal which has done nothing to abate its native qualities of shrewdness and tenacity. It should also perhaps be borne in mind that the army, of which the streets of Belgrade are as full as those of any other capital in Europe, is the one really well-organized institution in the country and is exclusively the work of Serbian hands and brains.

### A Successor Still Lacking

This formidable combination, the native assertiveness of the present generation of Serbs backed up by the strong Serbian Army, was at the disposal of the Pashitch clique, and it is hardly possible that all the tales which are told of its high-handedness and its corruption are sheer nonsense.

Pashitch is dead now and he has never had a successor. His party is still by far the largest in the Parliament, holding 111 out of 315 seats, but there are so many parties that no one party can hope to govern except in coalition. The Radicals were part of a four-party coalition at the time of the shootings last June and the then Prime Minister, Veija Vukitchevitch, a Belgrade high school teacher, may be regarded as the present party leader, although the central committee of the party does not now recognize him as such.

After the shootings the government was compelled to resign and the same four parties re-shuffled themselves into a new government with Father Anton Koroshetz, leader of the Slovenian Clerical Party, as Prime Minister. It was to the more chauvinistic wing of the Radicals that Punisha Ratchitch, the Montenegrin deputy, who is now awaiting trial for murder, belonged, but it ought to be added that the death of Pashitch has rid the party of the Pashitch clique and its excesses. The Radicals express themselves today as ready to consider a revision of the Constitution and Father Koroshetz has sought to reach an agreement with the Croats preliminary to dissolving Parliament and holding new elections on the issue of a constitutional revision extending home rule to all the provinces. The resulting deadlock and the dispatch of a Serbian military governor to Zagreb have already been mentioned.

### Politics Is Self-Sufficient

The Radicals have hitherto been the permanent constant in so rapid a succession of coalition governments as to bewilder the foreigner accustomed to more stable political forces. It will be easier to understand the whirling kaleidoscope of the parties if it is remembered that politics in Yugoslavia is self-sufficient and all-powerful. Thus far the economic and industrial life of the country has not succeeded in introducing into politics the sobering and stabilizing influences which it exercises in older countries. This is especially true of the regional parties of the new provinces which represent nationalities or religions, and are incapable of growing beyond their definite geographical boundaries. Thus the present coalition, which includes four of the six big parties, is such a coalition as under normal circumstances would be unthinkable in an older country. It unites the Radicals (or Conservatives), the Democrats (or Liberals), the Slovenian Clericals and the Bosnian Mohammedans. The other two big parties, the Raditchists and the Independent Democrats, who were both in opposition on June 20, withdrew from Parliament after the shootings and are still abstaining.

With sixty-one seats in Parliament the Democrats are the second largest of the parties, and in Ljubo Davidovitch they have one of the strongest leaders on the floor of the house. The Serbs are so democratic as to nickname their party leaders even in solemn official communications, and Dr. Davidovitch, who is now nearly 70 years old, is known to all Serbs either as "Uncle" Ljubo or as "Ant" Davidovitch, the latter because he used to be a professor of zoology in the university of Belgrade and once wrote a book on ants. Honest, straightforward and a good speaker, he is physically broad and squat, with short white hair standing up brush-like above his broad forehead. He was formerly one of the King's tutors, but his position in his party is toward the Left wing. His party is predominantly, although not exclusively, Serbian, and it is usually regarded as open-minded on the subject of the Croats.

The Slovenian Clericals, with twenty seats in Parliament and the Bosnian Mohammedans, with eighteen, are, as their names imply, regional parties from the new provinces in the west. Like the Conservative party in the present Austria, the Slovenian Conservatives are Clericals. The Slovenians were themselves Austrian subjects before the war, and their party leader. Father Koroshetz, was chaplain to the Empress Zita and a Deputy in the Vienna Parliament. The party has a home rule program for Slovenia, but at present its program has been shelved. The Bosnian Mohammedans, led by Dr. Mehmed Spaho, a former secretary of the Serajevo Chamber of Commerce, are Slavs who embraced Islam under Ottoman rule in order to save their lands.

### Opposition Stays Out

It is one of the weaknesses of the present political situation that both the opposition parties refuse to attend Parliament. Terrible as the shootings were, the government made every effort to dissociate itself from "the crime of a madman." It extended every inducement, even to offering Raditch himself the task of forming a government, in its effort to bring the opposition back to its seats in the house. But Raditch refused to have any dealings with any party of "the blood-stained government" and the seats of the opposition parties are still unoccupied. Raditch has since died from the effects of his wound, and the only man who could have led the opposition back into the house without loss of prestige has gone. He and his policies, however, will continue to dominate his party. Under the leadership of Dr. Vladimir Matchek, the party has acquired a broader basis in Croatia than was possible to it under its old name of the Croat Peasant party. Abstaining from the house, it is necessarily condemned to a negative policy. It holds sixty seats in the house and all five of the shot Deputies were its members.

The other opposition party, the Independent Democrats, who hold twenty-three seats, is the result of a split in the Democratic party five years ago. The drafting of the present centralist constitution was due as much to Svetozar Pribitchevitch as to any other one man, but when Raditch's opposition to centralism broke the Democratic party, Pribitchevitch left off denouncing the Croat leader as a Bolshevik and withdrew with a section of the party to form the Independent Democrats. Pribitchevitch is himself a Serb and his party is largely Serbian, although there are Croat and Slovene elements in it. Its program is a revision of the Constitution in the direction of a Yugoslavia as distinct from the triune kingdom of the Serbs, Croats and Slovenes, but in the present Serb-Croat conflict it ranges itself with the Croats.

This brief summary of the Yugoslav parties sounds confusing enough without adding to the confusion by listing the smaller political groups. It leaves the present deadlock an apparently hopeless one, but the fact is that there is an element of hope which remains to be mentioned. Until the tragedy of last June, the parties were gradually losing their regional characters. They were slowly broadening out to new national bases and were acquiring more definite social and economic programs. The Radicals and the Slovenian Clericals were coming together in a Conservative party, and the Democrats and Bosnian Mohammedans in a Liberal party. The powers of the provinces were being slowly extended and the worst features of centralism were being rapidly removed.

It was not a steady or a smooth progress, but it was nevertheless a real progress. It was during one of the intermittent setbacks, when both the anti-centralist parties happened to be in opposition, that the shootings occurred. It will take time to undo the enormous harm they have done, but when the trial of Ratchitch is ended and the tragedy of last June has been left behind, it is perhaps not too much to hope that a moderation of the attitudes of both sides will enable the new country to resume its work of consolidation.

*   *   *

January 7, 1929

## KING OF YUGOSLAVIA ASSUMES ALL POWER

*In Midnight Coup Alexander Abrogates Constitution and Dissolves Parliament*

**SETS UP HIS OWN CABINET**

**Establishes Dictatorship to End Heretofore Irreconcilable Dissensions in Triune Kingdom**

By EDWIN L. JAMES
Special Cable to The New York Times

PARIS, Jan. 6—One more European parliamentary system passed into the limbo of insufficiency today when King Alexander of Yugoslavia dissolved the Skuptchina and suspended the Constitution adopted on June 28, 1928, by the Serbs, Croats and Slovenes, who were thus welded into a new State as a result of the World War.

Tonight the young King rules his country of 14,000,000 people with the absolutism of a czar, working through a cabinet responsible to him alone. Alexander does not plan a dictatorship like that of Premier Mussolini, in Italy, nor even like that of General Primo de Rivera in Spain. For in theory his dictatorship is temporary.

No one who knows the affable Serbian monarch believes for one moment that he acted for personal aggrandizement. It must have been against his personal wishes that he was obliged to condemn that parliamentarism which was developed by his father in Serbia.

It is to the defects of the Yugoslav Parliament rather than the ambitions of the King that today's coup d'état is due.

Ever since the Serbs, Croats and Slovenes were self-determined into one country by the Paris Peace Conference, and that largely through the intervention of the American delegation, the different sorts of Slavs, who make up politically and culturally the kaleidoscopic state have failed to use their common Slavonic brotherhood to reach that state of harmony so ardently wished for by Alexander, who it will be recalled, was Regent at the time Yugoslavia came into being.

Having contended for many generations for independence the Croats vehemently and the Slovenes less vehemently, have never ceased to charge that the Serbs, under the work-

ings of the Constitution of 1921, have taken too preponderant a part in running the country, and that to the detriment of Croatia, and especially its politicians.

Since the shooting affray in Parliament about seven months ago, in which Stephen Raditch, the Croatian leader, was mortally wounded, the Croatian members of the Skuptchina have left Belgrade and sat in a rump Parliament at Zagreb. Repeated efforts by the King to restore the entity of Parliament failed and he took his heroic measures today only after a new series of conferences with the Croat leaders.

As he says in a proclamation, the parliamentary situation as it existed under the Constitution offered no way out. He found that the institutions of the country were in danger under parliamentarism and the country impotent and torn by blind political passions.

"Parliamentarism, as it exists," he said, "is beginning to provoke spiritual disorganization and national disunion."

### Doubt King Favors Federalization

It is scarcely believed that the King will go to the lengths asked by the Croats and establish in the country three or four States with separate Parliaments after the example of the State Legislatures in the United States or the State Parliaments in Germany. While it is believed he intends eventually to convoke a new constitutional Assembly, an announcement in his proclamation indicates that by royal decree he intends to solve many of the internecine problems which lack of Parliamentary harmony has kept in suspense. A royal power law proclaimed in Belgrade tonight gives the King complete power at home and abroad.

In other words, the King has taken upon himself the task of welding his country into a harmonious whole after the uselessly verbose Parliament failed to do so over almost a decade.

It is a task of difficulties both domestic and foreign. No country in the world has as many neighbors as Yugoslavia and with most of them she has troubles.

There is Greece, once the ally of Serbia, who abandoned her in the war.

There is Bulgaria against whom Alexander led his army in the Second Balkan War and who attacked Serbia in the World War.

With Rumania, Yugoslavia has good relations due largely to the French hold in both countries.

Hungary, encouraged by Mussolini's foreign policy, is regarded as a potential enemy of Yugoslavia.

Alexander has nothing to fear from powerless Austria, but on the south lies Albania, controlled by Premier Mussolini, and to the west lies Italy whose differences with Yugoslavia have formed a disagreeable chapter of post-war diplomacy.

In other words, of 80,000,000 neighbors of the 14,000,000 Yugoslavs, about 60,000,000 have no great friendship for Belgrade.

### Diversity of Populations

At home, it is true, all the inhabitants of Yugoslavia are Slavs. That denomination would appear today to be almost all they have in common except a joint respect for King Alexander. They are divided in religion, some being Moslems, some Catholics, and a large number belonging to the Orthodox Church.

There are some who write in Latin letters and others in Russian characters. There are the Serbs, who have maintained their independence for the last 100 years. There are Croats who used to be administered by Hungary, Slovenes and Dalmatians formerly governed by Austria, and Bosnians and Herzegovinians formerly governed in common by both Austria and Hungary since their liberation from the Turk.

In the north country, you will meet blond men and women of modern civilization, while in the south you will meet women wearing veils and men attired as the Turks dressed 100 years ago, faithful to their mosques where no Christian may enter. In the north you see tall mountains, while in the south you see warm valleys, where cotton and tobacco grow.

All these divergences of climate, nationalities, religion, customs and education have been faithfully reflected in the incessant quarrels which have now led the Skuptchina to abolition.

And so King Alexander has taken on himself one of the most difficult jobs in the world.

There is perhaps opened to Mussolini an opportunity to serve Alexander. For nothing would more quickly abolish the present divergences among the Serbs, Croats and Slovenes than a menace from the Roman peninsula.

However, there is small doubt that both England and France, and Germany as well, will use their influence to see that Alexander has a chance to work out the salvation of his country without interference from abroad.

It is recalled here that although the King is a sufferer from kidney trouble, which caused him to lose twenty pounds in the past year, he is now under treatment by a French specialist, under whose care he has regained nearly ten pounds since his visit last November to the French capital.

### How Coup d'Etat Was Effected

Special Cable to The New York Times

BELGRADE, Jan. 6—"There is no longer a constitution. There are no laws any more. Henceforth there is only the King and his people." These words, spoken figuratively by the great Croat chieftain, Stefan Raditch, on the shooting of Croat leaders in the Belgrade Parliament last June have been made literally true in Yugoslavia since midnight.

By a royal coup d'état executed in the course of a few hours last night King Alexander swept the inextricably muddied political pawns from the Yugoslav chessboard. A fresh game was begun, but played according to his rules, with himself as sole umpire.

The Serbs demanded that some one end what they called the treasonable separatist activities of the Croats. It has been done, but in the last way which the Serbs imagined possible. The Croats demanded abolition of the Centralist Constitution of 1921, abolition of the Serbian hegemony and the granting of new elections. They have get their first two

demands satisfied, but in a manner which not half a dozen of them ever dreamed of. None can tell when their last wish will be realized.

Throughout last night the streets of Belgrade in the neighborhood of the Royal Palace were thronged with bigger crowds than even at noontime. The people knew nothing except that behind the gates of the palace something momentous impended. At 3 o'clock this morning their curiosity was satisfied when heralds posted a royal proclamation on the walls of the palace and later throughout the city. It informed them that the Constitution of the country had been suspended and that Yugoslavia had passed from democracy to extreme absolutism while they were talking.

### King Appeals to the People

The proclamation was addressed "to my dear people, Serbs, Croats and Slovenes," and began: "The King feels it his imperative duty as a son of this land to turn to you, its people, and frankly and truthfully tell you what in this moment my conscience and love of the Fatherland compel me to say.

"The moment has come when no third person may stand between the people and their King."

His soul, said the King, was tortured by the cry for help which arose from the industrious, patriotic but tormented population, who were convinced most justly that things could not continue in the future as in the past. Political consolidation had not resulted as was hoped from the parliamentary system, which, on the contrary, by purely negative results was imperiling the whole structure of the State. It was even endangering foreign relations and the credit of the State abroad.

"Parliamentary government, which was always my own ideal as it was that of my unforgettable father," the proclamation continued, "has been so abused by blind party passions that it prevented every useful development in the State. The people have lost all faith in the institution. In the Parliament even the common decencies of social intercourse between parties and individuals have become impossible.

"It is my sacred duty to preserve the unity of the State by every means in my power. To seek to remove these abuses by fresh elections would have been a waste of time and valuable energy. By such methods we have already lost many precious years. We must try other methods and tread new paths.

"I am certain that in this solemn moment all Serbs, Croats and Slovenes understand these words from the heart of their King and that they will be my loyal fellow-workers in all my future efforts to do what the health of the State requires.

"I have, therefore, decided hereby to decree the Constitution of the kingdom of 1921 abolished. The laws of the land will remain in force unless canceled by my royal decree. New laws in future will be made by the same method. The Parliament elected Nov. 1, 1927, is hereby dismissed.

"In communicating my decision I command all the authorities and all my people to respect and obey my will."

### People Cheer the Proclamation

Thus passed Yugoslavia from a free but faction-torn people to subjects of an undisguised despotism established in the name of their salvation. Within five hours the people were cheering to the echo this proclamation of the King who with a stroke of the pen had deprived them of all constitutional rights.

A special edition of the Official Gazette today published four new laws which are such because they are the King's will. They complete the work of establishing an absolute monarchy and royal dictatorship.

The first law establishes the position of the King. It declares he is the sole source of power throughout the country. He issues laws and appoints officials and officers of the army. This law establishes the line of succession of the dynasty. Kara George settles the matter of a regency if required. The ministers are responsible to the sovereign alone, who may order their arrest and trial.

The second law deals with public security. After prohibiting communism and nihilism it declares that any political party of a nationalist or Chauvinist character will be instantly dissolved.

The third is a severe press law limiting freedom of comment.

The fourth abolishes all local elective and self-governing bodies. Belgrade, Zagreb and Laibach, though capitals, will receive municipal councils nominated by the King. In all other cases the only local authority will be a Governor.

### The New Cabinet

The composition of the Cabinet is as follows:

*Premier and Interior Minister*—General ZIVKOVITCH.
*War*—General HADZIC.
*Foreign Minister*—M. MARINKOVITCH.
*Justice*—Dr. MILAN SRSKITCH.
*Finance*—Dr. SVERLIUGA.
*Education*—MAXIMOVITCH.
*Religious Affairs*—Dr. ALUPOVITCH.
*Public Health*—Dr. KRULJ.
*Trade, Industry and Social Policy*—Dr.
    DRINKOVITCH.
*Agriculture*—Dr. FRAGES.
*Transport and Railways*—Dr. KOROSHETZ.
*Forests, Mines and Agrarian Reform*—M.
    RADIVOJEVITCH.
*Posts and Telegraphs*—M. SAVKOVITCH.
*Minister Attached to the Royal Court*—M. JEFTITCH.

The Cabinet is as representative of the King's personality as his new rule will be. A score of old enmities are buried at the King's command. Generals Zivkovitch and Hadzic are old rivals in the army which is now united in the person of the leaders of the two factions under the King's command. There are nine Serbs, four Croats, one Slovene and three Bosnians. The Peasant Democrat Croats are not represented, but Croatia

will be pleased to see Finance. Trade and Agriculture—the three departments where they always complained the Serbs exploited them—placed in their hands. Dr. Sverljuga is chairman of the Croatian Discount Bank and vice president of the Southern Slav Union Bank at Zagreb.

Particular satisfaction is given to the Croats by the King's dismissal overnight of the Minister attached to the court, M. Jankovitch, who was accused by the Croats of complicity in the Skuptchina assassinations and his replacement by M. Jeftitch, previously Minister at Vienna.

### Press Censorship Rigid

Immediately the Cabinet had taken oath, at 11 o'clock last night, a council was held, when a preventive censorship was imposed on the newspapers. All telegraph and telephone communication with abroad was cut and not restored until 8 this morning. As all newspapers have to submit everything to the censor before publication and are not allowed to publish anything regarding the coup d'état beyond official announcements, it is impossible to say what the true attitude of the country is toward the change. Foreign correspondents are under the same restrictions as the Yugoslav journalists.

With these reservations made it may be said that the country so far is not too stunned to realize what occurred and feels relief at seeing a strong hand come to the rescue. There is no doubt that the ship of state is as rapidly breaking up under the political and racial storms. Only the crown remained as a bond between the Croats and Serbs. Now everything but that bond has been swept away.

As the Sunday morning crowds in Belgrade caught sight of the placards they burst into loud shouts "Bravo! Bravo! Long Live the King! Long Live Yugoslavia!"

### President Barred From Chamber

There was a dramatic scene at 10 o'clock as several members accompanied the President of the Skuptchina, M. Mihailovitch, to the Parliament building, where he intended to collect his papers. At the doorway sentries were posted and they refused to let him enter. At midnight the Cabinet Council had dissolved Parliament and established guards outside as a symbol of the new order. The President and members were forced to depart without their belongings.

A second Cabinet Council was held at midday. As the Ministers emerged from the Foreign Office where they had met, they were surrounded by an eager crowd of newspaper men seeking information. General Zivkovitch said:

"We have nothing to say. We shall work, work, work—not talk. We leave that to you in your verdicts on our activities."

"But you have forbidden our verdicts by the censorship," retorted one journalist.

The newspaper man was told that within a few days the press would be called to an official discussion of the situation.

At this moment the gathering crowds caught sight of King Alexander looking down from a window of the Konak, as the royal palace on the opposite side of the street is called. A storm of cheering arose:

"Long live the King! Long live your Slav people!"

The King, smiling and looking thoroughly satisfied with his night's work, acknowledged the cheers.

### Croats, Too, Cheer Change

In Zagreb, where its reception might be expected to be less enthusiastic, many groups cheered the proclamation.

For the moment the Croats see only the hated Centralist constitution and exploitation of their land by a grasping band of professional politicians at an end, and what they call, as the scene of the murder of their leaders, the "bloody Skuptchina," swept away bag and baggage. Their hearts are filled with gratitude to the King, who effected so many of their desires in a few hours. Tomorrow may come realization that their dreams of autonomy vanished in that strong dictatorship having absolute disposal of their fates with the army to back its will.

That the dictatorship, anyway, is efficient is shown by the automatic precision of the coup d'état which, of course, was prepared long in advance and has been executed now at a most suitable moment, the beginning of the Orthodox Christmas holidays. When these are at an end the country will return to work with the new government arrangements complete.

Another thing every one realizes is that the national dictatorship is not a party one, as is the case in other countries which have lost their Parliamentarianism.

### Matchek Praises the King

Dr. Matchek, the Croat Peasant Democrat leader, declared in Zagreb this morning:

"The King acted in the spirit of Stefan Raditch when he said: 'There is no Constitution and there are no laws, only the King and his people.' On his own initiative the King has made a clean sweep in order to give Yugoslavia a chance to rebuild from the bottom up, according to the needs and desires of the people."

The Novosti, leading Croat paper, says:

"Like Alexander of Macedonia, Alexander of Yugoslavia cut through the Gordian knot."

This is a fair specimen of general Croatian press comment—of course under censorship.

That the Gordian knot has been cut is clear enough. What use will be made of the new order of things by those who swept away the débris of the past? An absolute régime will bring a period of much needed quiet, enabling Yugoslavia to present a strong, united front to her enemies abroad, who already are eagerly looking forward to her collapse. It will afford an essential breathing space enabling her many races to realize that as they are obliged by geographical, political and economic necessity to live in the same house, it is desirable that that house be well ordered and peaceful.

But when these beneficent results have taken place will it be possible for the King with equal ease to remove the men who will have grown accustomed to exercising absolute power under his authority and restore to his people the freedom which from what are believed unquestionably righteous motives was taken from them today?

That in their relief at finding some one acting instead of eternally talking and playing a game of political "grab" is a question the Yugoslavs are leaving until a more sober tomorrow.

\* \* \*

January 17, 1929

# TRIALS OF A DICTATOR

The apparent pessimism in dispatches about the effects of the dictatorship proclaimed in Yugoslavia by King Alexander need not be taken too seriously. Within the kingdom there is a censorship. Outside it, notably in the near-by countries, there are the usual rumors fathered by ignorance or prejudice. Both within and without Yugoslavia there are persons whose interest is to capitalize the troubles of the King and the differences between his subjects.

So far as Croatia is concerned, it is not surprising that doubt is expressed by some of the Croat leaders about the King finding a "satisfactory" solution. The Croatians are far from united as to what a "satisfactory" solution really would be. When the Croat representatives in the Yugoslav parliament withdrew from Belgrade last June, they swore that never again would they set foot in the King's capital. But they could not agree on the creation of an independent Croatian State, nor on a formula for binding it to Serbia through the person of the monarch. The Serbian elements within Croatia were opposed to separation. The different Croatian leaders were jealous of each other.

It is too early to contend that the King's dictatorship neither can nor will effect better relations between the Croats and the other peoples in the kingdom. He has hardly had time to begin the difficult task of settling complex problems. Despite the racial and historical differences between the Croats and the other South Slavs the principal inciters of antagonism are not peasants but politicians. The latter stand to gain by creating a situation in which they can obtain most from the King.

Whatever danger is latent in the situation lies in the political threat if one or other of Yugoslavia's foreign enemies were to endeavor to force a crisis in this period of internal embarrassment. Fortunately, the ramifications of Balkan politics are in themselves sufficiently far-reaching to make it unlikely that this will happen. Furthermore, the League of Nations is in close touch, ready at the first sign of danger to the peace of the Balkans to use its influence in order to prevent trouble.

The King is facing serious difficulties. These are administrative rather than political. He is also sure to be bitterly criticized. But it will be weeks before the outside world can decide whether his policies will heal or open wounds. The dangers of a dictatorship lie in weakness or stupidity. In proportion to the King's wisdom and strength will he succeed. In his favor is his record of intelligent and devoted service to his country.

\* \* \*

January 18, 1929

## BELGRADE FORESEES DICTATORSHIP'S END

*Yugoslav King Orders New Constitution Prepared to Take Place of Military Decrees*

**MARINKOVITCH TO DRAW IT**

*Court for Judging Offenses Against the Security of the Realm is Formed*

BELGRADE, Jan. 17 (AP)—Indications that King Alexander is already planning an end of the dictatorship became apparent today. The monarch arranged to have Vojislav Marinkovitch, Foreign Minister, draw up a new Constitution to take the place of the present military decree. This work will be undertaken as soon as the Minister returns from his convalescence in Switzerland.

M. Marinkovitch is an accomplished lawyer. It was believed, therefore, that he would be able to formulate a Constitution based on democratic principles yet giving full opportunity for development of the nationalism which the King desires to foster.

The new court for judging offenses against the security of the realm was constituted today. It is composed of eight judges, four deputy judges and a public prosecutor, the last named being under the immediate control of General Peter Zivkovitch, Premier and Minister of the Interior.

The directorate issued orders today forbidding boys and girls in the secondary schools from dancing in public. Sixty additional government officials were dismissed. It was stated that the government found so many surplus public employes that in some departments there were not even enough desks and chairs to go round.

\* \* \*

March 10, 1929

## ALEXANDER TELLS YUGOSLAVIA'S WOES

*Mischief of Politicians, He Says, Forced Him as King to Set Up the Dictatorship*

**SAW IT AS PATH TO UNITY**

*"The Country Is at Peace, Everybody is at Work and My People Will Support Me"*

By JAMES A. MILLS
*Associated Press Staff Writer*

BELGRADE—Sprawled along the Adriatic Sea for 450 miles and sewed in between Austria, Italy, Hungary, Rumania, Bulgaria, Greece and Albania, like a crazy Oriental patch-quilt, is the Balkan Kingdom of Yugoslavia, whose diverse racial elements would furnish first-class material for an ethnographical museum. This heterogeneous mass, which is mostly of Slavic origin, is composed of Serbians, Cro-

atians, Slovenians, Dalmatians, Bosnians, Herzegovinians, Mohammedans. Macedonians and Montenegrins who at one time or another were vassals either of Turkey or Austria-Hungary.

They vary as much in mentality and religion as they do in costume and appearance. For instance, the Croatians of the north, who are the most enlightened, educated and progressive element in the entire triune kingdom, are Roman Catholics, while the Serbs of the old kingdom, who have more political experience, but far less culture, are members of the Greek Orthodox Church. Again, while most of the people in Dalmatia, Montenegro and Macedonia are Christians, those in Bosnia and Herzegovina are Moslems, their men wearing the Turkish fez and the women the veil.

Since 1919, when the old Kingdom of Serbia, as a reward for its services in the World War, was doubled in area and quadrupled in population, the medley of races composing the newly formed Kingdom of Serbs, Croats and Slovenes have quarreled among themselves for political power. In that period Yugoslavia has had no fewer than twenty-one governments. As the country produced no statesman of sufficient popularity and sagacity to bring permanent peace among the peoples of the various provinces. King Alexander himself was called upon constantly to arbitrate their disputes and pour oil upon the troubled political waters.

### The Murders in Parliament

The youthful Slav King had measurable success as a peacemaker among his 12,000,000 subjects until a few months ago, when a half-crazed member of the dominant Serbian political party assassinated three prominent members of the Croatian Peasants' party, including Stephan Raditch, its leader, in open Parliament. This act precipitated such a grave crisis between the Serbs of the old kingdom and the Croatians of the former Austrian provinces that it threatened the very unity and existence of the kingdom.

It was at this point that King Alexander, distinguished alike for his fairness and fearlessness, stepped in and, scrapping Parliament, the Constitution, all existing political parties and most of the present laws, set up a modern dictatorship as the only means of bridging the chasm. This absolutist regime, says General Peter Zikovitch, its head, will endure until the King feels the people are fitted for a return of real parliamentary government.

What manner of man is this young King who had the courage to tear down the existing political edifices, built at the cost of so much blood, toil and money, and prepare the way for a better, more unified and enduring structure, which may serve as a house in which all the quarreling units in his kingdom will at last live in peace? The Associated Press correspondent had the privilege recently of seeing King Alexander at the royal palace in Belgrade and conversing with him for an hour. It is from that conversation, held informally over coffee cups and cigarettes, that the following impressions of the sovereign are based.

### Descendant of "Black George"

The great-grandson of the famous peasant-warrior, Kara George ("Black George"), who could neither read nor write, but who led the Serbs against the Turks in their war of independence, King Alexander inherits the courage and independence of his humble but sturdy forebear. In addition to this he inherits, on his mother's side, the boldness and dash of the fearless, patriotic mountaineers who upheld Serbia's independence in her days of greatest adversity, for Alexander is the grandson of the doughty King Nicholas of Montenegro, who with his predecessors kept the cross of Christianity shining above the mountains of his rock-bound country, instead of the star and crescent of Turkey.

The King is of small stature and is not of robust physique. He possesses great simplicity and charm of manner. Although a man of distinct courage and strong convictions, he is intensely shy. He has none of the austerity or aloofness of a monarch. He makes the visitor feel immediately "at home." He is a careful listener rather than a communicative talker. He has the typical dark features of his Slav countrymen, with whom he is probably more closely connected, by birth, blood and breeding, than any King of any people in the world.

The King's large, prominent nose, firm mouth and dark eyes denote the firmness of the soldier, but there is no suggestion either of the autocrat or the dictator. He is mild-mannered and soft-spoken. His rimless eyeglasses and his engaging smile soften his dusky features. He has jet black hair and a closely cropped mustache. He dresses habitually in the uniform of a General, which offsets his somewhat undersized frame to better effect than civilian dress. He has just passed his fortieth birthday.

### Constantly in Poor Health

Throughout all the recent months of political stress and trial, when King Alexander tried by might and main to bring peace between the dominant but less advanced Serbs of the old kingdom and the virile, progressive and politically ambitious Croats of the north, the sovereign was afflicted constantly with poor health. He suffered intermittently from colds and fever. He was also tormented with tooth trouble, which was relieved only when he sought the services of an American dentist.

Notwithstanding his physical distress, the King remained at his desk day and night, trying still to calm the surging political waters, which literally had become so turbulent that they threatened to submerge his kingdom. The Serbian and Croatian political leaders remained inflexible and irreconcilable to the end. It was then that the King stepped in and virtually created a new Yugoslavia overnight.

King Alexander dislikes publicity and rarely talks for publication, but his views regarding the crisis that confronted him may be summed up briefly as follows:

"It was one of your great Americans, Abraham Lincoln, I think, who said that a house divided against itself cannot stand. The politicians attempted to divide our people. They sought individual privileges for their provinces which we could not grant. I could not allow them to undermine the foundations of unity and solidarity which it had taken so many years to build up. I labored hard to avoid taking the drastic steps I took, but it was the only solution. Desperate situations demand desperate remedies.

"My patience exhausted and my strength taxed to the breaking point by the irreconcilable and unreasonable demands of the leaders of the various political parties, I decided I would abolish Parliament, although I have profound confidence in and respect for true parliamentary government, and that I would deal directly with the people. My people are of one heart and mind, and I knew they would support me. Although in the new regime they will preserve their individualities, they all belong to the one family and have one common ideal—the unity of the southern Slav race.

"I think the results have justifed the measures. The whole country is at peace. Everybody is at work. Those mischievous persons and organization who sowed seeds of discord have been silenced. By hard work and honest deeds we must make up for the idle political discussions and inattention to the nation's real interests of the last ten years. We shall return to a normal regime as soon as the work of reorganization and production warrants it. I am sure that, after a period of freedom from political discord and party strife, a new better and stronger Yugoslavia will emerge."

\*   \*   \*

**October 4, 1929**

## 'YUGOSLAVIA' DECREED AS COUNTRY'S NAME

---

*Popular Choice Becomes Official—Nine New Divisions Will Replace 33 Provinces*

---

Special to The New York Times

BELGRADE, Oct. 3—By a royal decree signed today the name of this country, until now known as the "Kingdom of Serbs, Croats and Slovenes," will officially become that which has long been applied popularly—the "Kingdom of Yugoslavia."

A second decree destroys any historical memories, for it wipes out such historical names as Croatia, Slavonia, Old Serbia, Bosnia, Herzegovina, Dalmatia and Montenegro by establishing new provinces or banats to replace the old divisions.

This reorganization is designed to obliterate all traces of its varied origin and to emphasize the idea of unity. It was recently reported that this measure was about to be decided upon and that a return to parliamentary government was likely to follow soon after.

Thirty-three provinces of the old kingdom are now erased and replaced by nine banats which, with the new capitals, are as follows: Save, capital Zagreb; Danube, capital Neusatz; Vardar, capital Skoplje; Drina, capital Sarajevo; Morava, capital Nisch; Drave, capital Ljubljana; Vrbas, capital Banjaluka; Coastal Banat, capital Spalato and Zeta, capital Cetinje. Each banat will be governed by banus appointed by the King.

The new names correspond generally to those of the great rivers of Yugoslavia and the frontiers roughly conform to those of the old provinces.

It is doubtful whether the majority of the Croats will be satisfied by this regulation of frontiers, which runs entirely counter to their desire for autonomy.

\*   \*   \*

October 13, 1929

## TO BROADEN YUGOSLAV RULE

### King Alexander's Constitution Will Provide for Parliament

Wireless to The New York Times

BELGRADE, Oct. 12—It is authoritatively stated that King Alexander has solved the problem of how to be dictator with parliamentary sanction. Political circles are now busily discussing the details of the forthcoming Constitution, which it is believed the Premier, General Zhivkovitch, will make public on Jan. 6, precisely twelve months after the suspension of the Constitution and the assumption of the dictatorship by King Alexander.

It is not expected that there will be any return to unfettered democracy, such as prevailed prior to Jan. 6 last. It is believed that the King intends to introduce transition conditions to last for a few years. During this time Parliament will be composed of persons elected by the Diets, to be formed in nine new banats, or provinces. But if, as anticipated, the Diets themselves are not elected but nominated by the central government, it is clear that the new form of parliamentary government is going to be very different from the old.

In addition to the projected "Chamber," the King is considering the nomination of a "Senate" which should sit at Zagreb, instead of Belgrade. But the crux of the whole scheme is that neither house would have powers of law-making, but would merely sit in an advisory capacity to the King.

Limited freedom will probably be restored to the ordinary citizen in such matters as expression of opinion through press publication.

\*   \*   \*

May 22, 1930

## ANTI-JEWISH RIOTS RECUR IN RUMANIA

### Outbreaks Follow Return of Dr. Cuza to Parliament—Defense Being Organized

### STUDENTS LEAD IN CLASHES

### 'Iron Guard' In Galatz Makes Attack In Streets—Cemeteries Profaned In Bessarabian Cities

Wireless to The New York Times

BUCHAREST, Rumania, May 21—Since Professor Alexander Cuza, the anti-Semitic leader, was returned to Parliament in a recent by-election there has been a recrudescence of minor anti-Semitic disturbances in Rumania which appear to be supported by the anti-Semitic wing of the Liberal party.

In Galatz an anti-Jewish "Iron Guard" has been organized and has frequently attacked Jews in the open streets. In some Bessarabian cities Jewish cemeteries have been profaned and gravestones destroyed.

Jewish pedestrians have been molested by Cuzist supporters in the streets of the capital.

The government has ordered suppression of the riots and arrest of the rioters, but local authorities have not shown much energy in carrying out these orders. In several cities, therefore, the Jews have decided to establish their own defense organizations.

#### Clash in Seizure of Papers

BUCHAREST, May 21 (Jewish Telegraphic Agency)—A number of Jews were attacked and injured today in the streets of Bucharest. Cuzist students utilized clashes between gendarmes and dealers in confiscated Oppositionist papers as an opportunity for a new outbreak against the Jews. The clashes followed the Maniu Government's decision to confiscate all papers that advocate a return of Prince Carol.

This evening, after a speech by Professor Cuza at the Capitol, a number of his student followers attempted to organize a parade. A police cordon was immediately formed, but a number of students managed to break through into the Strada Roseti, shouting: "Death to the Jews!"

It is reported that two of the nine Targufromos Jews arrested a fortnight ago after a clash with students were released from the Jassy prirson when they were able to prove that they were not in the town when the incident happened. The others are still being detained.

New details regarding the Targufromos incident have been reported by the Dimineatza, which sent a special correspondent to investigate the incident. He asserts that when the students arrived with Professor Cuza on his return from his victorious election campaign they shouted, "Out with the Jews! Kill the Jews!" and then opened a bombardment on Jewish houses.

The correspondent says the crowd stormed the house of Moise Lazar, a Jewish banker, and beat an aged Jew, Selig Herschcu, breaking his arm, and injured his wife. The

Dimineatza's correspondent also says that the students then proceeded from house to house, smashing windows, breaking up the shop of the septuagenerian bootmaker, Hirsch Leizer, and injuring the proprietor. The students then proceeded to the centre of the city with no apparent effort on the part of the police to check them.

The correspondent also reports that at the Central Market a number of Jews resisted the attack and a fight followed. When the students saw that the resistance was likely to become serious they fled. The police began an investigation by examining eighty-three Jews, of whom nine were arrested.

* * *

June 8, 1930

## CAROL WILL BE KING TODAY BY VOTE OF PARLIAMENT; RUMANIAN CABINET RESIGNS

### PEOPLE HAIL PRODIGAL PRINCE

*Immediate Proclamation Urged by Deputies, but Delay Is Necessary*

### PREMIER LOYAL TO MICHAEL

*Five Ministers Vote for Carol as Regent, Seven Demanding That He Be Monarch*

### DIVORCE MAY BE ANNULLED

*Papers Expect Reconciliation With Princess Helen—Queen Marie "Very Pleased"*

Special Cable to The New York Times

BUCHAREST, June 7—The Maniu Government has resigned to make way for the proclamation of former Crown Prince Carol as King of Rumania.

The Maniu Government has been succeeded by a Cabinet headed by Professor George Mironescu, ex-Premier Maniu's Foreign Secretary, and composed of the same members with the exception of three representatives of the National Peasants' party—Dr. Julius Maniu, his Minister of Interior, Dr. Alexander Vayda-Voevod, and his Minister of Trade, Virgil Madgearu. The new Cabinet has already taken the oath and has called a meeting of the National Assembly for 11 o'clock tomorrow morning.

The Assembly, which consists of both houses of Parliament, will, according to all present probabilities, make Carol King. It also is likely that its next act will be to pass a resolution of no confidence in the Mironescu Cabinet, which will then resign and make way either for a concentration Cabinet or for a new government headed by Dr. Maniu.

### Maniu Loyal to Boy King

Dr. Maniu's resignation is understood to be grounded on his refusal to compromise his loyalty to King Michael, although that nine-year-old ruler would doubtless be glad to be excused at the moment from the cares and restrictions of sovereignty. Dr. Maniu resigned after an all-day Cabinet council had broken

up without reaching an agreement as to whether Carol should be a member of the Regency Council, succeeding his brother Prince Nicolas, or be made King over the head of his son.

Five Ministers voted for Carol as regent, while seven wanted him proclaimed King. Dr. Maniu then proposed that Ton Mihailache, Minister of Agriculture: Gregory Junian, Minister of Justice, or Professor Mironescu should succeed him. The first two refused and Professor Mironescu stepped into the office of Premier.

Thus Carol, who made such a dramatic re-entry into Bucharest last night after five years' exile, has been received as Rumania's prodigal son. The newspapers announce that application has already been made to the court to set aside his divorce from Princess Helen, so as to permit resumption of his life with her. The dethronement act is to be annulled, to allow him to ascend the throne which he renounced, and a new government is to be formed to meet his wishes.

### Parties Fall Into Line

A report that George Bratianu, son of Rumania's former dictator, Jon Bratianu, had been summoned to Bucharest to be offered a post in the proposed Cabinet makes it evident that Carol's homecoming has made ducks and drakes of the inner organization of the Liberal party, which under the present leader, Vintila Bratianu, has violently opposed Carol's return. The People's party, a minor faction headed by ex-Premier Averescu, also has fallen into line with remarkable celerity, as has the still more negligible National party, headed by Professor Jorga, Carol's former tutor.

The return of Prince Carol was carefully organized by his friends in cooperation with a number of leading army officers. Ten days ago Colonel Precop went to Paris and bought an airplane and a few days later left by automobile with Prince Carol, their passports being made out to Sigmaringen, Germany.

At Munich they left the automobile for the airplane, Carol being equipped with a passport giving a false name. Rumanian frontier posts had been warned to give the fliers every possible assistance if necessary, and precautions had been taken for a forced landing in Hungary. However, with the exception of a minor halt at Arad, just inside the frontier, to get more gasoline, the trip to Cluj was made without incident. It is certain Premier Maniu knew of Prince Carol's intention to return, although the actual arrival may have taken him by surprise.

That Carol's return was popular with citizens of the capital was evident from the manner in which the streets were belagged, and according to reports the Bucharest example has been followed in this by other Rumanian cities. Huge crowds had assembled before Parliament today in expectation of a meeting of the National Assembly and others surged restlessly through the main streets cheering for Carol and the boy King Michael. When it was discovered that the offices of the Liberal newspaper Vlitorul, unlike its neighbors, bore no flag in honor of Carol's return, a crowd of demonstrators pressed into the building, hoisted a flag by force and affixed a huge placard with the inscription, "Long live King Carol II."

### Secretary Precedes Prince

Prince Carol flew to Cluj, Rumania, in a French airplane piloted by the Yugoslavian flier Pibernik. At Cluj he was received by Secretary Gatosky and the three generals commanding the local forces. The Prince changed from civilian clothes to the uniform of a Rumanian general. Secretary Gatosky entered a Spad military machine and, arriving at Bucharest two hours earlier than the Prince, quickly spread the news that his royal master was en route.

While Parliament was sitting, Secretary Angelescu entered the chamber and informed Voicu Nitzescu, the only Minister present, that Carol had come back. M. Nitzescu told the president of the chamber, who immediately adjourned the sitting. Some one cried, "Prince Carol has arrived," and the announcement quickly filled the corridors with buzzing groups of members. A Cabinet council was summoned, but while it still was deliberating the Prince arrived at the Baneasa Airdrome.

The airdrome was dark and besides a few representatives of the Cidna Company, in whose airplane the Prince had flown from Munich to Cluj, the only other person present was this correspondent. When the clatter of the airplane motor was heard a searchlight was switched on, three rockets flew in the air and the machine landed. Carol jumped into an automobile and hastened to Cotrocent Palace, where Prince Nicolas awaited him. Two regimental bands marched up and enlivened the occasion with martial airs, while a guard of honor stood watch before the palace.

Premier Maniu hastened to greet the Prince, who received him cordially. While they were conversing, military detachments were sent to the postoffice and telegraph offices and to patrol the main streets. Their presence was unnecessary, however, the capital receiving the news of Carol's return with the utmost calm. That he commanded the support of the army was demonstrated at 10:30, when he took the salute of two regiments which paraded before him in front of Cotroceni Palace.

### Two Regents Reported Out

Special Cable to The New York Times

BELGRADE, June 7—According to reports from Bucharest, the Regents, Patriarch Miron Cristea and Judge Saratzeanu, handed in their resignations at 11:30 tonight. It is expected Prince Nicolas will resign tomorrow.

### Carol Explains Return

BUCHAREST, June 7 (AP)—In the first conference between Carol and Premier Maniu, respecting Carol's return, Carol said he had come back to Rumania because of the bad economic situation of the country. His previous renunciation, he said, had occasioned grave uncertainty concerning Rumania at home and abroad. He then told the Premier that his work would be to restore Rumania's prestige and welfare.

"I have come to conciliate and to calm the minds of the people," Carol said in an interview. "I have no thought of hate or vengeance; on the contrary, I have come to facilitate union in the interests of the country."

Through the intervention of Prince Nicholas with Princess Helen, Prince Carol spoke this afternoon to his little son for the first time in several years. Both showed emotion.

The boy king always had believed his father was on a long trip. When he viewed a film showing a shipwreck recently, he asked with tearful voice if his father had gone down with the ship.

Tomorrow Prince Carol will deposit a wreath on the grave of his father, the late King Ferdinand.

Professor Mironescu will be both Premier and Foreign Minister. General Condesco is Minister of War. Other new Cabinet members are Minai Popovici, former Finance Minister, who becomes Minister of the Interior, succeeding Dr. Alexander Vayda-Voevod, and D. R. Joanitescu, who succeeds Virgil Madgearu as Minister of Labor. The others of the old Cabinet remain, and it is believed that former Premier Maniu may re-enter the government after Carol is proclaimed.

The general expectation is that Prince Carol will assume the name Carol II when proclaimed.

At present Carol is quartered in the wing of Cotroceni Palace occupied by Prince Nicolas. He was visited today by his sister, the former Queen Elizabeth of Greece, whom he warmly greeted.

\*     \*     \*

June 9, 1930

# CAROL PROCLAIMED KING AMID RUMANIA'S CHEERS; CORONATION IN OCTOBER

### BANISHMENT IS CONDEMNED

*Ex-Tutor Tells Chamber Exile Was Forced by Prince's Enemies*

### BRATIANU SOLE OPPONENT

*Annulment of the 1926 Decree Erases Boy's Reign Under Regency Council*

### PRISONERS GET AMNESTY

*New Monarch Says He Harbors No Vengeance Against Those Plotting Against Him*

By G. E. R. GEDYE
Special Cable to The New York Times

BUCHAREST, June 8—By a brief act of Parliament the Rumanian people today wiped out the history of the last five years. The act by which the late King Ferdinand's son renounced his right to the throne and agreed to live in exile was declared null and void and Carol was stated to have been the de jure ruler under the title of Carol II from the date of his father's death. Carol's little son, Michael, thus loses the right to the title of ex-King, being instead established as heir apparent, with the title of Grand Voivode (nearly equivalent to Duke) of Alba Julia.

Bucharest exceeded today the wildest moments of yesterday's enthusiasm. Crowds gathered outside Cotroceni Palace

Times Wide World Photo

King Carol II.

early in the morning, cheering King Carol, who did not appear.

### Renunciation is Annulled

The Senate and Chamber met this morning in separate sittings to pass a bill annulling Carol's act of renunciation of Jan. 4, 1926. Professor Jorga, Carol's former tutor, after criticizing Michael's new title, Grand Voivode, as being taken from a Viennese operetta, spoke movingly in the Chamber in favor of the proclamation of Carol as King of Rumania through passing the act of annulment.

"Carol has been the victim of discreditable intrigues," said Professor Jorga. "On the late Jon Bratianu, on Prince Stirbey rests the shame of having persuaded the unwilling King Ferdinand to pronounce a sentence of banishment against his beloved son. It was in vain that Dr. Maniu, Ton Mihailache and Dr. Vayda-Voevod joined me in counseling King Ferdinand to refuse to banish his son."

Raising his voice, he cried:

"At last the day has come to repair the wrong then done."

Professor Jorga made a moving appeal for peace in the land, urging the parties which united today in welcoming Carol to maintain this amity and refrain from political demonstrations.

"We hope the army, which played a great part in Carol's return, will now quietly resume its normal duties and avoid all participation in politics," he said, adding:

"I trust another reconciliation will shortly delight us all— that of our King with his wife Helen. Nothing now stands in the way of such a step."

This speech produced a sharp rejoinder from Gregory Junian, former Minister of Justice, who declared Carol had not been brought back by the army or any individual, but had returned in obedience to the call of his people.

### Maniu Assures Support

Former Premier Maniu, who received prolonged applause, declared the vast majority of the country stood behind him and his policies. His party welcomed Carol back, he said, and placed itself at the service of the Mironescu Cabinet for the proclamation of Carol as King.

Professor Mironescu then declared a new chapter was opened in the history of Rumania by Carol's return.

The laws canceling Carol's abdication was passed, 310 votes against 1, in the absence of all the Liberal party members except Theodore Florescu; who recently dissociated himself from the anti-Carol campaign of the Liberals.

Immediately after the laws were passed in the Senate and Chamber of Deputies both houses met as the National Assembly to proclaim Carol as King. Gregory Junian, former Minister of Justice, moved that Carol be recognized as the successor of King Ferdinand and that the National Assembly install him in his rights. Leaders of every party except the Liberals, who were absent, agreed, and the proposal was adopted, 485 votes against 1.

A storm of applause from the Deputies and the packed galleries greeted the result. At precisely 2:40 P. M. Carol was proclaimed King of Rumania.

While the negotiation of the decision of the National Assembly was being conveyed to the royal palace elaborate preparations were made for the reception of Carol before the National Assembly. The table of the president was removed and in its place an altar was raised covered with red brocade and bearing two silver candlesticks. Between the candles were placed a Bible and a crucifix. Two priests with long black beards, tall velvet caps, golden embroidered robes and purple shoes, assisted the Metropolitan of the Orthodox Church, who, wearing a golden Byzantine crown and carrying the apostolic staff was a dignified figure with his long gray board.

### Carol Takes the Oath

At 2 o'clock the King accompanied by his brother, Prince Nicolas, left Cotroceni Palace. Although they had to go only two miles to Parliament, the irrepressible enthusiasm of the crowds was so great that they did not arrive until 3:15. The roar of cheering from the street became even louder within Parliament until the doors were flung open and President Poppociceo announced:

"The National Assembly has to take the oath of the king."

The members rose, cheering wildly for fully eight minutes, when Carol entered in the uniform of a general in the flying corps, his breast decorated with orders and medals. Nicolas accompanied him. Bowing and smiling in acknowledgment of the cheers "Long live Carol the Second," the King made his way to the altar.

Premier Minonescu handed him the written oath. With a firm voice Carol read aloud the declaration of fealty to the Constitution and kissed the crucifix. A new storm of cheering broke out, which lasted fifteen minutes. When quiet was restored Carol gazed around the house for some seconds and then drew a paper from his pocket and began his speech.

Carol declared that despite his years of exile the spiritual unity of himself and the Rumanian people had never been interrupted. By their intrigues, he said, his enemies had succeeded in keeping him outside the country, but he had neither hatred nor resentment for them in his heart.

"I do not wish death to those who sinned against me, but I rejoice over every one who returns to the fold from which he never should have strayed," said Carol quoting from the Orthodox version of the Scriptures.

### Happy to Be With Son

Carol then adopted a personal vein:

"At last I can return to my dear son whom I will protect with all the love of a father and whom I will bring up to love his fatherland. I thank my brother and his colleagues in the regency who have guarded the country for me while I was away."

Carol said he had not come to seek revenge, but to cooperate with all who sought the welfare of Rumania.

"I have always shared the ideals and sufferings of my Rumanian people" he exclaimed.

There was room, said Carol for every one without distinction of religion or race, who wished to cooperation in the restoration of the fatherland.

"In this hour" he continued, his voice breaking with emotion, "my father's last wish was fulfilled."

It was noticeable that Carol did not refer to his mother, Queen Marie, or his ex-wife Princess Helen with a single word. At the conclusion of the speech the Assembly burst into a wild storm of applause, in which the gallery joined.

For a quarter of an hour it was impossible to silence the frenzied plaudits. Carol fought hard with his emotions but finally tears were seen welling in his eyes. After the President of the Assembly had declared the whole nation stood behind Carol the new King embraced his brother Nicolas.

The Assembly adjourned at 4:45 and Carol walked out through a double row of Generals. As the new King moved toward the door showers of roses fell ahead of him. Outside the guard of cavalry again gave the royal salute.

Through crowds still wild with enthusiasm, although they had been awaiting his appearance since 7 in the morning, Carol passed with his escort to the grave of the Unknown Soldier, where he laid a wreath.

As soon as Carol left the Parliament Building all parts of Bucharest were placarded with manifestoes in terms of the royal speech.

### Mironescu Cabinet Resigns

Later, when Carol had returned to the palace he received the resignation of the Mironescu Government but asked the Premier to continue to conduct affairs pending the formation of a new Cabinet. The King then received Professor Jorga and will see Dr. Maniu tomorrow.

Throughout the day the flying corps was particularly prominent. This was only natural as throughout it had been Carol's strongest ally. During the proceedings in Parliament airplanes continually wrote the letters of Carol's name in smoke across the sky to the delight of the multi-colored throngs in national dress.

### Helen Says She Will Stay

The relations between King Carol and Princess Helen still are very obscure. At a long audience which Professor Jorga had with her this morning she told him she would never leave Rumania but would educate Michael herself.

It was reported tonight that Carol had sent his brother Nicolas to the palace where Princess Helen resides with Michael, asking her to send their son to see him. Nicolas returned, it was stated, with Helen's sister Elizabeth and with a message that she loved her son too much to part with him for an hour. Carol is believed to have gone then to the palace, and after some difficulty to have seen his son.

It is impossible to ascertain whether these details are accurate but under the Rumanian common law Michael belongs to Carol. Sons of divorced parents in Rumania are in the father's custody after they are 6 years old.

When King Carol received Professor Jorga tonight the former tutor advised him to form a coalition government under General Presan, commander of the Rumanian Army in the World War. Professor Jorga added that he would never serve any government headed by Dr. Stantu.

Meanwhile the Liberal party threw away its chance of reconciliation with the new King. Premier Mironescu had a long interview with Princess Helen this morning before Parliament assembled and subsequently saw the leaders of all political parties, including Vintilla Bratianu, Liberal leader. The latter brusquely told him that he declined to discuss for one moment the "Carol question." The Liberal party's attitude toward Carol, he declared, would remain as hostile as ever.

When George Bratianu later visited his Uncle Vintilla, the latter burst out.

"I am disgusted to see a son of Jon Bratianu acting as an errand boy for Carol."

He ordered George out of his house, demanding an explanation of his attitude toward the Liberal party. George later wrote to Vintilla that he would do whatever the Liberal party decided.

M. Hiott, Minister to the Court and trusted adviser of Princess Helen, has resigned his post. M. Diammanti, Minister to France, also has resigned because of Carol becoming King.

### King Carol's Address

BUDAPEST, June 8—King Carol II spoke as follows after taking the oath before the National Assembly today.

"The touching reception you have given me deeply moves me. I am happy to perceive in your voices the feelings of those who send you here, and to confirm once more the intimate bonds which have united me and will unite me always with my people.

"The oath which I have taken today before the representatives of the people will have an effect beyond the walls of this historic hall. In my soul it has become a sacred pledge between me—the King—and my people: it is a sacred pledge taken before the Almighty to become a father full of solicitude and zeal for his son.

"An exile of more than four years, far from the people among whom I was born and nurtured, was inflicted upon me by certain persons who by their words filled with sorrow the soul of their great King my dear father and whose object it was to break the bonds between me and the Rumanian nation.

"The sublime demonstration of today clearly shows that these persons did not achieve their aims, and that the unshakable love which I have borne in my heart for Rumania has been abundantly rewarded in the affection shown me by the nation and its representatives.

"I come today, with uplifted heart, into the midst of my people, without the least trace of resentment even toward those who by their unthinking action sought to break the indissoluble bonds which unite me and all those who feel themselves to be true Rumanians.

"In keeping with the words of the Gospel, I wish not the death of the guilty but their return to the right path, which they should never have left. I have not come to take vengeance against anybody. It is with all the warmth and affection of my soul that I desire to gather under one shield all those who have the will and power to elaborate for the progress of the country.

"Deeply moved, my thoughts turn toward those who before me took here the same oath and consecrated their whole lives to the welfare of the country they were destined to rule.

### Father's Wish Realized

"The shades of the great King Carol I and Ferdinand the Faithful stand over me today and the soul of my well-beloved father rejoices at seeing realized his last wish and most ardent desire. The example which my predecessors have given me of their infinite love for their country and defense of its interests will be followed to the full by me."

The King then alluded to the 800,000 who sealed with blood the union of their nation, saying that their sacrifice deter-

mined him more than ever to preserve inviolate the integrity of the national territory. He added that he needed for this purpose cooperation of all the living forces of the country and an army organized on the most modern lines. He was convinced that everybody, regardless of religious or political opinion, would unite around the throne to assure the country the place it is destined to occupy in the comity of civilized nations.

One of the chief features of the King's proclamation was the granting of amnesty to all political prisoners.

After mentioning his joy at being reunited with his son and thanking his brother, Nicolas, and the other Regents who worked for the progress of the country, King Carol concluded.

"I most earnestly appeal for all to work together for the good of the country. Rumanians unite in your thoughts, in your feelings. Now to work."

From Parliament the King went to the grave of Rumania's Unknown Soldier, where he laid a wreath. Then he visited the royal palace from which he had been banished, and was deeply moved by the emotion of the old servants who cared for him as a child. They kissed his garments and wept, while the King warmly shook their hands, but was unable to speak.

The proclamation ceremony was broadcast by radio. Tonight the inhabitants of Bucharest danced in the streets.

The festival of the coronation will take place in October at Alba Julia, where King Ferdinand was crowned.

The first King Carol preceded King Ferdinand, Carol II's father.

\* \* \*

**June 10, 1930**

## CAROL'S SUCCESSFUL COUP

The return of Rumania's prodigal King has been hailed in traditional style. His past vagaries have been forgiven and the best of everything is offered him on silver platters. Even his stern and disapproving mother, conveniently out of the country during the coup d'état, is reported to have sent him her blessing. It must be assumed that her maternal instinct outweighed her ambition to continue as Dowager Queen in Rumania.

International implications of the episode do not promise to amount to much. Talk of a union with Hungary is, to put it mildly, premature. Hungarians are as bitter toward the Rumanians as ever, and the other countries of Eastern Europe, not to mention the Western nations, would be loath to see Rumania further enlarged at this time. In the other Balkan capitals there will be gossip and speculation, and doubtless we shall hear wild rumors of strange plots for some time to come. But Carol is, after all, heir to the Rumanian throne, whose abdication in favor of his son was the result of family and local politics, not of international pressure.

The internal consequences of his return are more important. Carol succeeds his father after a stormy career. Although his contacts have necessarily been limited by the horde of social parasites, climbers and intriguers that always surround royalty in exile, he has had occasion to see more of the world than if he had succeeded directly to the throne on his father's death. This may help him if he decides to take up seriously his new profession of being a King.

A danger lies in his prejudices against the political leaders who were responsible for his banishment. In Rumania political affairs are in the hands of a few families and their followers. Despite the growth of the political influence of the peasants and the rise to power of intellectuals like Professor Jorga or of self-made men of the type of Maniu, a few political cliques still rule the political roost. Will the new King yield to a desire for revenge, or will he carry out his formal promise to forget and forgive?

A general impression is that King Carol is not a man of force. While he has undoubtedly suffered from unfavorable publicity, he has also the handicap of coming from a branch of the Hohenzollern family that has not been distinguished for virile character. Yet from his mother he has inherited the strain of Queen Victoria. Bred in the unsavory environs of the Rumanian court and social life, the odds have been against him from the beginning. For the sake of the Rumanian people it is to be hoped that his new responsibility will bring out his mettle, and that he will be able to use a strong guiding hand in leading his country out of its present troubles and establishing it on the firm foundations of its peasant stock.

\* \* \*

March 4, 1933

## ARREST BALKS FIRST ATTEMPT AT HITLERISM IN RUMANIA

Wireless to The New York Times

BUCHAREST, March 3—The first attempt to introduce Hitlerism in Rumania resulted in the arrest of Ion Ciolak, a Deputy belonging to Professor Cuza's anti-Semitic party, today. He arrived in the Chamber wearing an imitation of the Nazi uniform, with the swastika emblem on his arm, but a storm of protest arose during the sitting and he was arrested when he left the hall.

The ground for the arrest was the strict prohibition of the wearing of uniforms under the existing martial law, parliamentary immunity not protecting a Deputy detected in such an act. The Deputy was released later when he promised not to repeat the offense.

\* \* \*

March 12, 1933

## REDS RELEASE PRISONERS

Special Correspondence, The New York Times

SOFIA, Feb. 23—Friday was the occasion for a Communist demonstration in the village of Ugurchin, near Plevna. The village is "all red," and the demonstration was in honor of Lenin, Liebknicht and Clara Luxemburg. The police locked up the chief organizer and the villagers, armed with

sticks, broke into the station and released their leader. When police reinforcements arrived they found a deserted village, the entire population having taken to the woods.

\* \* \*

April 10, 1933

## 23 BULGARIAN SOLDIERS HELD AS COMMUNIST PROPAGANDISTS

Wireless to The New York Times

SOFIA, April 9—Following the recent arrest of two Communist Deputies on suspicion of organizing Communist cells in the Bulgarian army, nine cavalry troopers of the Rahovo garrison, near the Danube, were arrested on charges of engaging in Communist agitation. Fourteen soldiers suspected of being in correspondence with the two Communist lawyers in Sofia were arrested at the Danubian garrison at Nikopol.

A special session of the War Council was held today to consider the situation created by the formation of Communist cells in the army. The question of the expulsion of Communist Deputies from Parliament and dissolution of their so-called Labor party was considered by the Cabinet.

\* \* \*

October 31, 1933

## KING BORIS VISITS CAROL AT FRONTIER

*Yugoslav and Rumanian Rulers, With Premiers, Confer on Balkan Problems*

**PEACE STIMULUS IS SEEN**

*Each Sets Foot on Territory of the Other—Rumors of Carol's Betrothal Are Denied*

Wireless to The New York Times

BUCHAREST, Oct. 30—King Boris of Bulgaria spent seven hours with King Carol of Rumania today.

Although most of the time was spent on King Carol's yacht in the neutral waters of the Danube, the two monarchs crossed the frontier twice to set foot in each other's territory. The conference thus was turned into a State ceremony which seems likely to improve relations between the two countries.

Neither it nor a long private conversation between the two Kings and their respective Prime Ministers, however, heralds Bulgaria's adherence to the Little Entente. The difference between the plan of the Little Entente for a regional pact and Bulgaria's desire to confine herself to bilateral treaties is too great to be bridged so easily.

The newspapers of the three Little Entente capitals and Sofia were unanimous today, however, in predicting an improvement in relations between the countries concerned as a result of the conference and the royal visits which preceded and will follow it. Only the Belgrade Politika comments critically on speeches made by Premiers Muschanoff of Bulgaria and Goemboes of Hungary in the course of a visit to Sofia by General Goemboes last week, when both recalled their brotherhood in arms during the World War. General Goemboes's declaration in his speech to Macedonian youth that it might soon be necessary once more to don uniform is condemned as ill-calculated to further peace.

An announcement in the newspaper Calendarul that a marriage between King Carol and King Boris's sister, Princess Eudoxia, is under consideration has been promptly denied in government circles. A communiqué says merely that "both governments declared themselves ready to consider current questions and work for peace in a spirit of hearty friendship." Semi-officially it was intimated that Bulgaria had expressed readiness to prevent further Macedonian raids on Rumania and had requested amnesty for 400 Bulgarians sentenced in Dobrougja for political offenses.

An official visit by King Boris to Bucharest next January is considered likely and Belgrade advices speak of his spending some days in the Yugoslav capital with King Alexander in the near future before King Alexander leaves for Paris and London.

King Boris arrived at 10 o'clock this morning on a Bulgarian monitor in the Rumanian Danubian harbor of Giurgiu, where he was greeted by King Carol with a royal salute and by the Mayor of Giurgiu, according to old custom, with salt and bread.

Carol then crossed the river with his guest to the Bulgarian port of Rustchuk, where he was received with a similar ceremony. The two Kings, Premier Muschanoff of Bulgaria, Premier Vaida-Voëvod of Rumania and Foreign Minister Titulescu of Rumania then boarded King Carol's yacht and spent the next five hours in discussion while it cruised up and down the Danube.

\* \* \*

**December 30, 1933**

# DUCA IS SHOT DEAD BY RUMANIAN NAZI AT A RAIL STATION

---

*Premier, Foe of Anti-Semitic Iron Guard, Slain After a Conference With Carol*

### THREE YOUTHS ARE HELD

*Assassin Calmly Says He Has No Regret for Killing of 'Friend of Jews'*

---

By EUGENE KOVACS
Wireless to The New York Times

SINAIA, Rumania, Dec. 29—Rumania's recently named Premier, Ion G. Duca, leader of the Liberal party, was assassinated at 10:30 o'clock tonight on the platform of the Sinaia station as he was waiting for a return train to Bucharest after having had an audience with King Carol.

The assassin, a former student who gave his name as Radu Constantinescu, denied membership in any party, but it is

SLAIN BY ASSASSIN: Premier Ion G. Duca

believed established that he was a member of the Rumanian Nazi organization, the anti-Semitic Iron Guard.

The New York Times correspondent reached here within a couple of hours of the murder and obtained an exclusive interview with the assassin, who revealed himself frankly as a whole-hearted devotee of the doctrines of Hitlerism. Speaking with complete calmness and satisfaction, the youth said he had no regret for having destroyed the "friend of the Jews."

Premier Duca arrived early this morning at Sinaia—a two-hour railway journey from the capital—to report to King Carol on the results of the elections and on his own political plans. After his audience he drove to the station. Had the train been punctual he would in all probability have returned to Bucharest uninjured. He was obliged to wait however, because the train had been delayed by snowdrifts.

### Bomb Exploded on Platform

As the Premier was walking up and down the platform three young men approached him. One of them threw a smoke bomb. At almost the same moment, the youth later identified as Constantinescu drew a pistol and at close range discharged its contents into the face of the Premier. M. Duca, without uttering a word, sank to the ground dead. Four bullets had pierced his skull.

In the shooting Mayor Costescu of Bucharest, who was with the Premier was slightly injured.

Gendarmes and detectives rushed forward and disarmed and arrested the three youths.

King Carol, apprised immediately of the deed, ordered the body of his Premier brought at once to his royal castle, not far away in the mountains above the Sinaia station.

The ruler waited at the gates of the castle for the arrival of the body of M. Duca, from whom he had parted only an hour before. He was greatly moved as the body was carried past him into the castle.

King Carol at once telegraphed to Bucharest an order to Dr. Constantine Angelescu, Minister of Public Instruction and Deputy leader of the Liberal party, to rush to Sinaia. At the same time he called on Nicolas Titulescu, Foreign Minister, to return quickly from St. Moritz.

The two accomplices of the assassin said they were John Calimachy, a café owner, and John Doradu-Belimache, a student. Both are said to be members of the Iron Guard, although, like the actual assassin, they deny formal connection with any party. Doradu-Belimache is believed by the police to have been the organizer of the outrage. It was from a pistol owned by him that the fatal shots were fired.

In Bucharest the news of the murder came as a complete shock to the crowds in the streets, who were making their way home from cafés. Extra editions of the newspapers were already sailing heavily before bodies of troops and fully armed gendarmes began to patrol the streets and disperse the gathering crowds.

It is expected that King Carol, who is determined to pursue his policy of checking the reactionary anti-Semitic movement, will proclaim martial law. It is feared he may have to take refuge in a military dictatorship by his trusted army friends to preserve order.

Premier Duca was regarded tonight as a victim of his own courageous efforts to stem the rising anti-Semitic tide in Rumania and of his indifference toward the most outrageous threats. As this correspondent cabled on Dec. 12, General Cantacuzenu, member of one of the greatest Rumanian families and an aspirant to dictatorship, wrote to M. Duca, saying:

"As a result of the dissolution of the Iron Guard I will shoot you down on sight like a dog."

At the same time General Cantacuzenu telegraphed to King Carol demanding an audience to explain the necessity for murdering the Premier. M. Duca ignored the threat.

M. Titulescu, Rumania's most astute statesman, was reported that same day to have said privately that the dissolution of the Iron Guard would cost Carol his throne. It was only after long consideration that M. Titulescu signed the Cabinet Council's decree pronouncing the dissolution of the Iron Guard. He left the country the same night and the edict was not published until he had gone.

### Carol's Decision Awaited

What Rumanians are asking now is whether Carol will have the courage of his convictions and stand firm or whether he will be intimidated by the murderous policy of the Iron Guard. Zelea Codreanu, leader of the organization, escaped arrest when the Iron Guard was dissolved. He did not face the consequences with his followers, hundreds of whom were arrested because of their participation in street fighting against the police, but fled, it is believed, to Germany, whence since the beginning of the Hitler régime has come the greater part of the funds for the support of the Iron Guard.

From Belgrade it is reported that news of the assassination created a painful sensation. It is believed one result necessarily will be postponement of the meeting of the Little Entente planned for Jan. 8.

M. Codreanu's Iron Guard has for the last two years quite outdistanced the old-fashioned anti-Semitism of the aged Professor A. C. Cuza. It has adopted German Hitlarism's anti-democratic slogans and its amazing showmanship. Its leader constantly rode around the country among his followers on a white horse. Members of the Iron Guard courted peasant support by working on farms without payment except supplies of food. The Iron Guard contends that had it not been dissolved it would have obtained more than 200,000 votes in the recent election and some thirty seats in Parliament, entitling it to claim a Ministerial post.

### Body Lies in State

Sinaia, high in the Carpathians and deeply buried in snow, had a strange aspect tonight. Across the snow the lights of the royal castle, where the Premier lay in state, were ablaze while King Carol was conferring with Dr. Angelescu. Troops and gendarmes were gathered around campfires. At the gates and on the turrets of the castle stood smoking censers for the murdered Premier.

Among the population it is feared this is the beginning of a terroristic campaign by the Iron Guard along regular Nazi lines. The German news agencies are already sending out reports of the assassination, glorifying the activities of the Iron Guard.

### Iron Guard Members Seized

By The Associated Press

SINAIA, Dec. 29—The Rumanian Cabinet met in extraordinary session tonight shortly after the assassination of Premier Duca and ordered a round-up of known members of the Iron Guard. By midnight word from Bucharest said 1,300 had been jailed in that city alone.

The Premier's body will lie in state in the Athenaeum, which will be open to the public until the state funeral on Sunday afternoon.

### A Defender of Liberalism

Ion G. Duca, after a long and rather stormy political career, had come to stand out as a defender of liberalism against fascism and communism. He was one of the youngest Ministers in Rumania when he first entered the Cabinet in 1916.

He rose to the office of Premier only six weeks ago, succeeding Alexander Vaida-Voevod. A week ago M. Duca's

Liberals won a sweeping victory in the national elections, gaining 300 of the 389 Parliamentary seats.

M. Duca was born in 1879, the son of George Duca, one of the builders of the Rumanian Railway. He was a descendant of an ancient Rumanian family, a branch of which included the Bratianus. He attended the universities of Bucharest and Paris, for a time was a newspaper man and was first elected a deputy in 1907.

Subsequently he held the posts of Minister of the Interior, Minister of Foreign Affairs and Minister of Public Instruction.

Anti-Semitic and Fascist elements were the first to feel the whip when, after he became Premier, he decreed the dissolution of the anti-Semitic league of Professor Cuza and of the Iron Guard, which had been responsible for many anti-Semitic outbreaks. Zelea Codreanu, the leader of the Iron Guard, was outlawed as "dangerous to the State," and several Nazi newspapers were suppressed.

Three years ago, M. Duca succeeded the late Vintilla Bratianu as the leader of the Liberal party. For many years before that, however, he had been one of the most powerful men within his party and he had been one of the outstanding public men in Rumania.

After the return of King Carol, the Liberals had been unwilling to link their fortunes with Premier Jorga because they thought the number of seats offered to them was not a fair price. The King peremptorily ordered M. Duca to conclude an election pact with M. Jorga. Unable to resist the direct order, M. Duca complied and was immediately rewarded with the highest Rumanian decoration. M. Duca had been reputedly opposed to the return of Carol from Paris in 1930, and this was supposed to have caused coolness between them.

\* \* \*

December 31, 1933

# 1,400 IRON GUARDS SEIZED TO PREVENT RUMANIAN TERROR

---

*Assassination of Premier Duca Reveals Plot to Slay Others—Martial Law Decreed*

### RELATIVE FIRES AT KILLER

*Body is Taken to Bucharest for Funeral—Angelescu Heads Government*

---

By EUGEN KOVACS
Wireless to The New York Times

BUCHAREST, Dec. 30—Fourteen hundred leading members of the Iron Guard were arrested today in the government's efforts to curb the anti-Semitic Nazis who were responsible for yesterday's assassination of Premier Ion G. Duca.

Among the prisoners is General Cantacuzenu, a prominent Rumanian Nazi, who recently wrote an open letter to Premier Duca threatening to shoot him "like a dog" because of his tolerant attitude to Jews and his opposition to the Iron Guard.

General Cantacuzenu was deputy leader of the whole Iron Guard after the flight of Corneliu Z. Codreanu to Germany to escape arrest.

It was reported that Codreanu's father, himself an Iron Guard leader, also had been arrested at a railroad station where General Cantacuzenu was seized just as he was entering a train. A brother of Codreanu was seized.

**Attempts to Kill Assassin**

Premier Duca's brother-in-law, Radu Polizu, attempted to avenge the murder of the Premier today. As the train which was to convey the body of M. Duca to Bucharest drew up at the Sinaia station M. Polizu left the ranks of the mourners and dashed into the station's police office where the assassin, Nicholas Constantinescu, was sitting in chains. He fired two revolver shots at the prisoner, but both missed. M. Polizu was disarmed and escorted from the building.

The arrested accomplices of the assassin are as cold-blooded as he. They said that Premier Duca could not have escaped because they had placed themselves in position to cut off his retreat, and each had an automatic pistol with sixteen rounds ready to fire at him.

When the assassin was approached by press photographers he proudly struck an attitude, throwing back his head and placing his hands on his hips as he posed for pictures.

Last night King Carol twice visited Premier Duca's body as it lay in State in the royal castle at Sinaia. On each occasion he placed flowers by the bier.

**Bucharest Honors Victim**

The body reached Bucharest at 4 P. M. and was received by a big military escort. M. Duca had been declared in a proclamation to have fallen in the service of his country. The body was escorted by several squadrons of cavalry and detachments of King Carol's personal bodyguard past hundreds of thousands of mourners who had assembled in a violent rainstorm to see the procession to the Athenaeum.

The body will lie in state in the National Hall of Honor until Monday, when the funeral will be held. M. Duca's will requested that the body be taken to the farmhouse where he was born and then be buried in the grounds of the neighboring Urseni Monastery.

The severity of the Winter makes the preparation of a grave at the monastery almost impossible, so the body will be buried temporarily in a Bucharest cemetery. A vault has been presented by the Bratianu family, which M. Duca succeeded as leader of the Liberal party.

Premier Constantine Angelescu, who was summoned to Sinaia last night and took the oath at dawn today, met with the Cabinet for several hours this morning. It adjourned without issuing a communiqué. After meeting again tonight the Cabinet proclaimed martial law applicable to all the principal cities of Rumania and decreed a strict press censorship.

All military leaves have been canceled. The official New Year festivities have been canceled by King Carol, and unofficial celebrations have been dropped. There will be four day of national mourning. All members of the Liberal party will wear mourning for one year.

### Murder Plot Is Charged

The police announced tonight that they had evidence of an Iron Guard plot to kill many government leaders. They said that when dissolution of the Iron Guard was decreed thirty university students swore to assassinate every one responsible for the dissolution. Apart from the three held for the Duca murder only one member of the group has been identified, a student named Florescu.

At the head of the list of intended victims stood M. Duca. The second was Foreign Minister Titulescu. Five other Ministers and State Secretaries were on the list, among them King Carol's secretary, M. Dumitrescu.

At the time of the murder conspiracy Corneliu Z. Codrianu, Iron Guard chief, issued an open letter to members in which he made all persons on the list responsible for any blood shed. This was printed by the Iron Guard newspaper Calendarul, the editor of which was arrested today.

There was a second explosion in the Sinaia station at noon today which damaged the royal waiting room. A boy received severe injuries. At first it was believed to be a new terrorist attack, but later the police said the bomb had been dropped by one of the assassins last night and had been picked up by the injured boy.

Bucharest newspapers revealed that the slain Premier had in his pockets only a small amount of money. He had intended to purchase a third-class ticket to Bucharest so as to travel with a group of young sportsmen who could not afford to travel better.

M. Duca's will was published today. It leaves all his property, which is very little, to his son, who is secretary of the Tokyo Legation. Most of the income will go to the widow.

Condolences were received by the government today from the foreign offices of all countries with which Rumania had friendly relations.

*    *    *

May 20, 1934

## BULGARIA TURNS FASCIST IN COUP AIDED BY THE KING; SOCIALIST LEADERS SEIZED

### TROOPS CONTROL COUNTRY

*Stationed at Strategic Points in All Cities to Prevent Disorders*

### WIDE REFORMS PLANNED

*Trade, Farm and Cultural Program Set—Russia to Be Recognized*

### GUEORGUIEFF IS PREMIER

*Yugoslavia Is Reported to Be Concentrating Border Force to Bar Bulgarian Radicals*

Wireless to The New York Times

SOFIA, Bulgaria, May 19—A Fascist régime was set up in Bulgaria today with the approval of King Boris and after troops had occupied public buildings and strategic points in this capital and elsewhere throughout the country.

During the last few weeks it had been widely declared that the end of parliamentary government in Bulgaria had come, and for many months agitation had been afoot, led by former Premier Alexander Tsankoff, in favor of the establishment of a national non-party government and corporative Parliament.

This movement succeeded in persuading King Boris to replace the Muschanoff Cabinet by an "authoritarian" government led by Kimon Gueorguieff and to dissolve Parliament. The King, who hitherto had endeavored to preserve neutrality in matters of internal politics, issued the necessary orders early this morning and a coup d'état was carried out without serious disturbance of the public order.

### Machine Guns Set Up

At 1 o'clock this morning the Sofia garrison was concentrated in the barracks and at 2:30 the troops occupied public buildings and railway stations. Machine guns were put in position in the squares and at other strategic points while military airplanes flew over the city.

Martial law was proclaimed, and no one was permitted to leave his home. Telephone exchanges were occupied by the police, and no international telephonic communications were possible. The streets were empty, while large forces of troops circulated along the boulevards. The new government issued a manifesto explaining that these measures were necessary to enable the Cabinet to repress any disorders.

"The King has appointed this Cabinet," the manifesto said, "to give the country a strong, stable government, which will solve Bulgaria's difficult political and economic problems. The previous system of party government paralyzed efficient administration and by eternal party quarrels had created an atmosphere of general distrust and uneasiness. We mean to do our best for Bulgaria and for Bulgaria only."

About 800 persons were arrested in Sofia and transferred to the police prison. They were said to be mostly Communists. Socialists and other radicals. It is rumored that among

The King Being Borne by Some of His Soldiers at a Recent Review.

the political prisoners are also a certain number of Macedonian extremists, but this report could not be verified.

### Former Cabinet Kept in Homes

Members of the previous Cabinet were forbidden to leave their homes. Nicolas Muschanoff, although warned of the possibility of a coup d'état, had not abandoned hope even this morning that his attempts to reconstitute a Cabinet would meet with success. Early today he tried to telephone to the former Minister of War, but he was unable to get connected with him. When he angrily shouted in the telephone, "Premier Muschanoff speaking here!" a harsh voice answered, "You are not Premier any more."

News from the provinces shows that military measures like those taken here were carried out throughout the country and that the coup d'état did not meet armed resistance anywhere. Socialist and Communist leaders were arrested also in the provinces and martial law was proclaimed there. Official reports emphasized this afternoon that the new government had been welcomed by the great mass of the public.

King Boris signed a decree removing from their posts all Mayors in Bulgaria. They will be replaced by men appointed by the government. Directors of railways and of the public health service also were removed. All political parties will be dissolved. Nearly all high officials with party affiliations will be replaced by non-party men or by pensioned officers.

### To Reduce State Employes

A plan of administrative reform that will reduce the number of State employes has been issued by the government, thus answering one of the main demands of the Fascist movement for reduction in the cost of the State administration.

Unverified reports tonight said Fedor Mikhailoff, famous leader of the Imro, Macedonian revolutionary organization,

was among those arrested today. This rumor indicates anti-Macedonian tendencies on the part of the new régime.

One of the fundamental principles laid down by the new government is the "establishment of governmental authority throughout the country." This statement evidently affects the situation in the district of Petrich, which is virtually administered by the Imro. It collects taxes, punishes traitors and controls the authorities in all the towns and villages in that part of Bulgaria.

MM. Tsankoff and Gueorguieff are said to favor a policy of rapprochement between Yugoslavia and Bulgaria, even against Macedonian opposition. The reported imprisonment of Mikhailoff would indicate the government intends to repress the Imro, in which case a Macedonian terrorist campaign against the new government would inevitably follow.

The frontiers of Bulgaria were closed today. Telephone and telegraph service to foreign countries was suspended this morning Rumors circulated in Belgrade and Budapest regarding an alleged attempt to assassinate King Boris were promptly denied by Bulgarian authorities. At noon the King issued a decree dissolving Parliament.

Telephone communications with other countries was resumed at 8 o'clock this evening, but telegrams still were held up. All local newspapers published this afternoon were confiscated on account of their comments on the coup d'etat. The government intends to suppress all party papers and to permit only papers of Fascist and nationalist organizations.

The new Premier, M. Gueorguieff, was a partisan of M. Tsankoff in his successful revolution against the peasant dictator Stambuliski in 1923. He was Minister of Railways in the Liaptcheff Cabinet in 1926. In 1927 he founded the political club Zveno which became the centre of Bulgarian Fascism and advocated the establishment of a corporative State and authoritarian government.

### Backed by the Military

His Cabinet is supported by the army and its generals and the powerful Reserve Officers' Association. In the new Cabinet the Premier will hold the portofolio of Foreign Affairs temporarily. M. Batoloff, who at present is the Bulgarian Minister to Paris, is said to be likely to receive the Foreign Affairs portofolio later.

The tentative Cabinet list follows:

KIMON GUEORGUIEFF—Premier and Foreign
PETER MIDILEFF—Home and Justice.
YANKI MOLOFF—Public Education.
PETER TODOROFF—Finance.
General PETKO ZLATEFF—War.
KOSTA BOYADJIEFF—Commerce.
NICHOLAS ZACHARIEFF—Railways.

M. Moloff has not yet definitely accepted his portfolio.

Premier Gueorguieff told the writer tonight that Bulgaria's foreign policy would remain unchanged. He said:

"Our aim will be peace and understanding with everybody, especially our neighbors. I am glad to be able to tell you that the establishment of the new régime has been carried out without the slightest disturbance. I hope to be able to lift in a few days the extraordinary measures we were forced to take today.

"The majority of the Bulgarian people certainly welcome the downfall of the party system and its replacement by a strong national government, the only aim of which is to work for the benefit of the country. We will not copy Italian fascism but will reorganize our political life and Constitution in accordance with the special needs of Bulgaria and the Bulgarian people."

### Program of New Régime

Copyright, 1934, by The Associated Press

SOFIA, Bulgaria, May 19—The program of the Bulgarian dictatorship set up today, as outlined in a manifesto issued by the government, involves the following points:

Organization of a disciplined State, with fusion of some Ministries and a reduction in the number of political divisions in the public services.

Creation of a stable local administration, with the Mayors named by the central government.

Re-establishment of the credit and authority of the State by balancing the budget and creating new sources of revenue.

Provisions to make credit more accessible, especially to farmers and artisans.

Raising of the cultural level in villages.

Regulation of industrial production with respect to the real needs of the country, and the lowering of prices of industrial goods.

Reduction of unemployment through measures to provide work by strict application of social legislation.

Creation of new markets.

A fundamental reorganization of the educational system.

Reforms expediting justice.

Maintenance of peace and good relations with all powers, particularly neighboring countries, and establishment of relations with Soviet Russia.

The streets were crowded tonight and the cafés and clubs were well patronized.

### Yugoslavia Is Favorable

Special to The New York Times

BELGRADE, May 19—The Bulgarian coup d'état was received with satisfaction in Yugoslavia official circles today, because several members of the new Bulgarian Government are regarded as partisans of rapprochement between Bulgaria and Yugoslavia.

Uncertainty reigns, however, about the attitude of Alexander Tsankoff, adviser to the new régime, who is known as a friend of the Macedonians. But there are reports that M. Tsankoff changed his mind following the Imro's Terrorist campaign and is now favorably inclined toward a policy of reconciliation between Belgrade and Sofia.

### Yugoslav Concentration Rumored

BELGRADE, Yugoslavia, May 19 (AP)—Unconfirmed rumors today said Yugoslav troops of the Vardar and Morava divisions were concentrating as a result of the coup d'état in Bulgaria.

A general mobilization of armed forces was considered possible since the new Bulgarian dictatorship was interpreted here as directed by King Boris against the Macedonian revolutionary committee, an anti-Yugoslav organization.

It was reported that 700 arrests had been made in Sofia alone.

### Austrian Fascists Pleased

VIENNA, May 19 (AP)—Supporters of Chancellor Dollfuss were gleeful over the establishment of a new dictatorship in Bulgaria, which they interpreted as a further extension of the ideas incorporated in their own government.

A radio message dispatched from Sofia at 3:20 P. M. Vienna time indicated that there was no interference with that type of communication in Bulgaria.

### Expulsion of Radicals Possible

Official confirmation of Yugoslav troop mobilization was not immediately forthcoming, but if true, it was regarded as an indication that the Yugoslav Government was concerned over the likelihood that Bulgaria now would begin expelling radicals.

These radicals, whom King Boris of Bulgaria has sternly suppressed, are highly anti-Yugoslav. Hence, any military mobilization in Yugoslavia would be interpreted more as a police act than as a gesture of opposition to the new Bulgarian regime.

\*   \*   \*

**May 24, 1934**

## COUP BY MACEDONIANS FORESTALLED IN SOFIA

*Istanbul Hears Mihailoffists Planned One for Yesterday—Many Arrests Reported*

Wireless to The New York Times

ISTANBUL, May 23—News has reached here from a trustworthy source that Saturday's coup in Sofia forestalled one planned for today by the Mihailoffist section of the Macedonian revolutionary organization as a counter-stroke to the rapprochement between Bulgaria and Yugoslavia.

With the exception of Vantcho Mihailoff, who cannot be found, all the members of the Mihalloffist section of the Macedonians are reported arrested and all their organizations dissolved.

Wireless to The New York Times

SOFIA, May 23—The president of the Macedonian National Committee has denied to your correspondent rumors abroad regarding the alleged imprisonment of Macedonian leaders by the new Bulgarian régime. He added that the Macedonians had not the slightest reason to complain about the change in government.

This unusually mild and conciliatory statement direct from Macedonian leaders who used to control Bulgarian governments is surprising as one of the first declarations made by the new Premier, Kimon Gueorgueiff, emphasized the necessity for "re-establishing the government's sovereignty in all parts of the country."

Every one in Bulgaria knew that the Premier meant the Petrich district, which until a few days ago was entirely controlled by the Imro, the Macedonian revolutionary organization. Recent reports from Petrich indicated that troops and gendarmerie had already taken energetic measures against local members of the Imro, warning them against continuing their terroristic methods against political opponents.

Party newspapers are still suppressed and their reappearance is doubtful, as the government has prepared a decree dissolving political parties altogether.

\* \* \*

June 3, 1934

# BULGARIA CRUSHES FACTIONAL STRIFE

*Cabinet Suppresses Parties, Curbs Macedonians and Prunes Official Payrolls*

**KING'S HAND SEEN IN COUP**

*Boris Believed by Some to Have Dismissed Army Leaders to Leave Them Free to Act*

Wireless to The New York Times

SOFIA, June 2—There is a saying that every nation gets the government it deserves. Bulgaria unquestionably has needed a government which would suppress political parties, and now she has just that. The new Gueorguieff government, which carried out a military coup d'état on May 19, is assured of popular support, provided it refrains from abusing its powers.

The chief cause of the coup was the chaos into which party quarrels had plunged the nation. The Muschanoff government, to satisfy its followers, had filled posts with its own partisans, regardless of qualifications. It had expanded administrative machinery until 2.5 per cent of the population were officials whose salaries absorbed half the budget. Corruption was rife, and inefficiency characterized every department. The condition of the country drifted from bad to worse while party leaders conspired against each other.

## Military Demanded Reform

The military insisted that party interests be subordinated to those of the country. The people agreed, but the parties were powerless because none would undertake the weeding-out task. The establishment of a non-party government

was difficult, for King Boris wished to adhere to the Constitution, although rebuking the partisans.

It appears that preparations for the coup began last Fall. Its organizers were Colonel Georghieff, retired; General Zlateff, and Colonel Veltcheff, supported by many members of the Zveno, founded six years ago, with a non-party government, suppression of Macedonian influence and a Yugoslav entente as its aim.

King Boris was aware of these preparations but had his own plans, should parliamentary government collapse, as seemed inevitable. On May 9 the Minister of War, General Alexander Kissieff, resigned, his successor being Colonel Vateff, who symphathized with the Zveno.

On May 14 it was announced General Bakardjieff, chief of staff; General Solaroff, commander of the Sofia garrison, and Colonel Georghieff were resigning because they objected to the appointment of Colonel Vateff, their junior. Now some persons suggest the King connived in the coup d'état and dismissed these officers to facilitate the plan. There is evidence against this theory, however.

### Officers Urged a New Deal

On May 18 eighty senior officers held a secret meeting and resolved to petition the King to appoint a non-party government. The same afternoon Generals Yoveff and Bossilkoff were appointed respectively chief of staff and commander of the Sofia garrison. It is reported one of their first acts to have been to arrest the organizers of the pending coup.

Palace events are still a mystery. It is believed that when Colonel Georghieff and General Zlateff went to the palace the King declared he would abdicate rather than accept an unconstitutional change, but Premier Muschanoff persuaded him to bow to the inevitable. The unprecedented demonstration of loyalty to King Boris, when thousands passed in a procession through the palace grounds and cheered him loudly, was reassuring.

The new government has made a promising beginning. The Ministers have halved their own salaries. Two Ministries have been suppressed, and provincial administrative staffs have been reduced more than half. Officers opposed to the coup have been dismissed.

Bulgarian Macedonia, hitherto ruled by Mihailoff law, is now divided between the Prefectures of Plovdiv and Sofia. Local officials nominated by the Mihailoffists have been superseded. The Protogueroffists make no secret of their satisfaction, for they have many friends among the new officials.

The Imro (Macedonian revolutionary organization) will not die for want of funds. Italy, Greece, Hungary and disgruntled elements in Bulgaria are eager to encourage hostility to the government, which is committed to an alliance with Yugoslavia.

The government has shown the will and the capacity to drive the revolutionaries from power. The latter dare not resist while the nation is behind the army.

The government intends to renew relations with Russia, opening a fresh market for Bulgarian goods and a fresh source of cheap supplies. This step and the proposed alliance with Yugoslavia may have far-reaching consequences.

\*   \*   \*

June 14, 1934

## BULGARIA SEIZES MACEDONIAN ARMS

*Fascist Regime Sets Today as Deadline for Surrender, With Court-Martial as Penalty*

**PROPAGANDA ALSO TAKEN**

*Macedonian Bodies Forbidden to Collect Taxes—All the Parties Are Dissolved*

Wireless to The New York Times

SOFIA, June 13—Kimón Gueorguieff, Bulgaria's dictatorial Premier, has evidently decided to suppress once and for all the Macedonian revolutionary movement which for the last fifteen years has been the keystone of Bulgarian domestic and foreign policy.

A governmental order yesterday prohibited the collection of taxes by the Macedonian organizations in certain southern districts of the country, as has been their wont. Another decree ordered that all arms and ammunition must be delivered to the authorities before today and threatened to court-martial any one found possessing a rifle or revolver afterward.

Carloads of arms and ammunition have already been collected by governmental agents, and similar quantities of Macedonian propaganda material have also been delivered. Arms and ammunition have been found in the streets of cities, evidently thrown away by owners afraid to deliver them personally. In Sofia and other large cities a house-to-house search for arms is expected within a few days, similar to the action taken last year.

The only report of resistance has come from the town of Belitha, where the Mayor, who was also the leader of the local IMRO, or Internal Macedonian Revolutionary Organization, fired on gendarmes conducting a search and was killed by them.

Twenty leaders of the IMRO were brought to Sofia yesterday and then confined in small villages in Eastern Bulgaria far from their Macedonian comrades.

The whereabouts of the Macedonian leader, Ivan Mikhailoff, is unknown. There are rumors that he has succeeded in escaping to Italy, while other reports say he is still in the country preparing resistance by the Macedonians against the new régime, which is held to have abandoned the cause of Macedonia in favor of understanding with Yugoslavia.

Premier Gueorguieff has continued the fascistization of Bulgaria by issuing an order dissolving all political parties and forbidding any kind of party activities. Newspaper publishers were ordered to apply for governmental permits to assure further publication. The permits, however, will be refused to all party newspapers, which means that eleven of the twenty-one Sofia journals will disappear. Newspaper editors must be at least thirty years old.

The commander of the royal bodyguard, Colonel Mekeff, has resigned. He was arrested on the night of the coup of May 28 by the conspirators because he was a notorious opponent of the Gueorguieff group and its Fascist tendencies. He has now been released, reportedly at King Boris's request, but he is leaving the army altogether.

One hears the opinion expressed in foreign diplomatic circles that the dissolution of all political parties is a grave mistake on the part of the new régime. The Bulgarian people are greatly devoted to politics, and with all political life suppressed they are expected to turn to subterranean activities together with the Macedonians, who have long experience in plotting, dating from the period of Turkish domination over Bulgaria.

\*   \*   \*

October 10, 1934

## YUGOSLAV KING AND BARTHOU ASSASSINATED BY CROATIAN AS RULER LANDS IN MARSEILLES; EUROPE SHOCKED, FEARS GRAVE COMPLICATIONS

**GUNMAN FIRES INTO CAR**

*Shoots General as Well as Alexander and the French Minister*

**IS KILLED AFTER ATTACK**

*Beaten by Crowd Assembled to Welcome Monarch on Arrival for State Visit*

**DOZEN IN THRONG WOUNDED**

*Crime Dims Hope for Accord of Italy and Yugoslavia, an Aim of Journey*

By P. J. PHILIP

Wireless to The New York Times

PARIS, Oct. 9—Within a few minutes after having stepped ashore at Marseilles today on an official visit to France, King Alexander of Yugoslavia was shot dead by an assassin—apparently one of his own subjects who had obviously come to France for this express purpose.

The French Foreign Minister, Louis Barthou, who had been sitting beside the King in an automobile, was wounded and died less than two hours later after a blood transfusion had failed to arrest a hemorrhage.

Tonight there is not only personal but also political dismay in France and in all Europe over the outrage. For King Alexander, whose eldest son, Peter, 11 years old, is a student in England, not only reigned but ruled over his country. His personality, more than any other single factor, has held together the collection of peoples who were joined under the Serbian crown into the modern Kingdom of Yugoslavia after the World War.

### High Hopes Held for Visit

King Alexander's visit to France was planned months ago when Foreign Minister Barthou went to Belgrade. It was to have been a delicate affair. For while France and Yugoslavia are allies, there was, at least on the French side, an intention to make the visit an occasion for a reconciliation between Yugoslavia and Italy and an attempt to harmonize the aspirations and policies of the three countries.

Now all is lost. The King and M. Barthou are dead and the future is darkly uncertain.

The assassination was the work of one man, or at least only one man participated in it, although many may have planned it. He was Petru Kalemen, a Croat born in Zagreb, and he was killed by the police and the infuriated crowd. His passport, found on his body, showed he had entered France on Sept. 28, having come direct from Zagreb. His crime was carefully planned to the last detail, for as he rushed toward the King's car he shouted "Vive le Roi!" and so gained a few seconds of time while those whose business it was to protect the King hesitated as to whether they had to deal with an assassin or a drunken loyalist.

There was another death—that of Policeman Celestin Galli, who had rushed forward to try to seize the murderer and was shot down in the volley fired by the assassin.

In the fusillade a dozen persons were wounded, including two police inspectors, several women and a press photographer.

### King Arrives on Cruiser

The assassination took place at 4:10 o'clock in the afternoon. Less than an hour before the King, aboard the Yugoslav cruiser Dubrovnik, had steamed into Marseilles Harbor accompanied by a French fleet from Toulon. The ancient port and the city were ablaze with bunting and flags. Hundreds of thousands had massed along the two miles of streets through which the King was to pass on his way to the railway station and Paris.

Telephone messages from two witnesses of the tragedy at Marseilles to your correspondent give the following account of the events.

The King had just landed from a launch at the Quai des Belges in the old port amid immense cheering and the playing of the national anthems of both countries. A few minutes were taken up with the customary inspection of the guard of honor. Then the procession of dignitaries formed, with the King and M. Barthou in an open automobile, accompanied by General Alfonse Joseph Georges, a member of the Superior War Council. Theirs was the third automobile in the procession. Mounted guards and cyclist gendarmes accompanied the procession. Every balcony and window was crowded with cheering people.

It was the intention to drive along the famous Canebière to the Prefecture, where there would be a formal reception. As the procession passed the Bourse, where there is a garden on one side of the road, a man lurched forward out of the crowd with a cheer for the King.

For a moment the King's chauffeur hesitated, trying to decide whether or not to run him down. Then the man, described as heavily built, thrust his hand into a pocket and leaped to the running board of the car. The chauffeur struck out at him with his hand, but instantly a fusillade of shots rang out.

The King sank forward. M. Barthou was hit. So was General Georges. One of the King's attachés swung his saber at the assassin with all his force. The man fell and tried to shove a pistol into his mouth. The police dashed at him. The crowd poured in. There was pandemonium.

While some tried to hold the assassin to protect him from the crowd, others sought vainly to disengage the car with its tragic burden. It was obvious that the King was dying, if not dead. M. Barthou seemed only slightly wounded. He was seen to try to succor the King.

Then even those who were watching from windows and balconies could see nothing of what was happening. More shots were fired, but they were probably blanks fired by the police in an effort to keep the crowd back. In an instant the police were overwhelmed and the assassin was seized. He was beaten, trampled on, crushed and struck at with sabers and sticks.

In the assassin's pockets were found a bomb and a second pistol.

Slowly, amid infinite confusion, the King's body was carried to the Prefecture and M. Barthou and General Georges were placed in another car.

The King was mortally wounded by two bullets, one through the chest and the other through the groin. Death was almost instantaneous, according to the physicians who made the first brief examination at the Prefecture.

M. Barthou was wounded in the leg and the right arm, which was broken. He was conscious when taken to the Prefecture. But, although two blood transfusions were performed, a strong hemorrhage set in and at 6 o'clock the veteran French statesman, who had gone so joyously, as he always lived, to meet the King, was dead beside him, while over the building the flags of Yugoslavia and France hung at half-staff.

Half an hour later erroneous news came out that General Georges, one of the most prominent younger Generals of France, who had been attached to the King's person for the duration of the visit, had also succumbed to a bullet wound. His condition is grave.

[General Georges underwent an operation early today, according to The Associated Press.]

Amid great emotion the King's body was laid in the Prefect's office, where it later was clothed in a new uniform jacket with the scarlet ribbon of the Grand Cordon of the Legion of Honor laid across his chest. Diplomats, Generals, journalists and all those who had been admitted wept.

Among them was Marine Minister Francois Pietri, who had welcomed the King on board the cruiser only a short time before. His grief was equal for his colleague M. Barthou. As he had been driving in another carriage he had himself escaped the assassin's bullets.

Associated Press Photo

King Alexander of Yugoslavia.

Times Wide World Photo

Louis Barthou, French Foreign Minister.

### Slayer 34 Years Old

So far as it has been possible to establish the facts it appears that the murderer, Kalemen, was a Yugoslav subject, born in Zagreb on Dec. 20, 1899, when Zagreb was in the Austro-Hungarian empire. According to the passport description, he was a merchant and received the passport in Zagreb last May 30. On Sept. 28 he crossed the French frontier at Vallorbe. His actions since then have not yet been traced.

A message from Zagreb to the Petit Parisien seems to throw suspicion on the validity of Kalemen's passport. The French Consulate there declares no visa was granted on May 30 or at any time before or later to any one of the name Kalemen. It is further said that neither Kalemen nor Petru is a common Croat name and that no one of the name Kalemen is known to the Zagreb police. The name Kalemen is common on the Magyar frontier.

During the past few days detectives of the French Sureté Nationale have been combing Paris for undesirables and especially for two foreigners reported to have come here to assassinate Alexander.

The Sureté agents, it is learned, visited many hotels on the Left Bank frequented by political refugees from foreign lands showing photographs of the two suspects. These men were identified by one hotel proprietor and the police today had just succeeded in tracing them to Marseilles.

\*   \*   \*

**October 11, 1934**

# KING'S DEATH HALTS YUGOSLAVS' STRIFE

*Demonstrations in Favor of His Policy of Unification Take Place in Croatian Cities*

### WHOLE COUNTRY MOURNS

*Parliament to Proclaim Peter Ruler at Session Today—Slayer Called Bulgarian*

By G. E. R. GEDYE

Wireless to The New York Times

BELGRADE, Oct. 10—Political assassinations has proved in Yugoslavia as it did four months ago in Austria to be a boomerang that recoils and strikes its wielders.

The internal outbreaks upon which those who inspired the murder of King Alexander doubtless reckoned have not only failed to occur but the crime in Marseilles seems to have silenced political dissension momentarily at least. Those who opposed Alexander's policy express the same abhorrence at his murder as his warmest supporters.

In Zagreb and other Croat cities great demonstrations took place today in favor of the late King's policy of a unified Yugoslavia.

Belgrade seems stunned by the horror of the shooting in Marseilles and hushed into uneasy silence by its apprehensions. In the quiet streets the only sound audible is the slanging of an occasional street car. Small groups stand everywhere discussing in hushed voices yesterday evening's tragedy.

### Shops Are Closed

Every shop has been closed all day except for a few food stores, and from each one a small square of black crepe hangs from a roughly carved flagstaff.

The ordinary bustle of daily life is stilled, but every five minutes between 4 and 6 P. M. the silence was broken by the crashing of two guns, fired in token of mourning for the murdered monarch.

Your correspondent saw crowds from the humblest classes in Yugoslavia passing reverently in spontaneous tribute before the Dedinje Palace, on the outskirts of Belgrade. Peasant women weeping in silent grief wiped away their tears

Associated Press Radio Photo

A picture snapped at the moment of the assassination. The Yugoslav King can be seen in the rear of the car, at left. M. Barthou is behind the chauffeur and the assassin is at the side of the car, on the left.

with the corners of the black kerchiefs with which their heads were covered.

The impressive regulations for the official mourning will not produce such a moving effect as did today's spontaneous tribute of a grieving people.

It was remarkable in Belgrade how many of those who in the past had criticized King Alexander and his policy of forcible unification today maintained a determination that this policy should be realized.

Every hour throughout the day bells tolled in all places of worship of all denominations, and Roman Catholics, Orthodox Church members, Mohammedans and Jews uttered simultaneous prayers throughout the kingdom for the repose of the King's soul.

### Peasants Won't Believe News

Serbian peasants in their hamlets refused to believe the news that their beloved King was dead. They went in procession to near-by towns to obtain official information.

A national committee of mourning was formed to make arrangements for the funeral, the date of which is still unfixed. It will be attended by the boy King Peter and his mother Queen Marie, who will both arrive here shortly but it cannot take place before Sunday at the earliest. If the present intention of having one day of lying in state in Zagreb and one day in Belgrade is realized, the funeral cannot be held before Tuesday.

It is not yet certain whether the body will be landed at Dubrovnik, Split or Bocce di Cattaro.

Deep national mourning has been decreed for three days before the funeral and three days afterward. During this period all theatres and places of amusement will be closed. During the ensuing six weeks of general mourning all dances and public festivities will be forbidden.

During the State mourning, which will last for six months, government officials will wear crepe armlets, all official letters and documents will be written on stationery with broad black borders and all letters will be sealed with heavy black seals.

### Monarchs to Attend Funeral

It is reported this evening that King Carol of Rumania, King Boris of Bulgaria, and the Duke of York as the godfather of Alexander's children will attend the funeral.

Throughout the day telegrams from abroad have been pouring in expressing horror at the crime and sympathy with Yugoslavia in her loss. The warmth of the telegrams of condolence received from Bulgaria and Rumania has been particularly appreciated.

The Zagreb Municipal Council held a commemorative session today at which the councillors took the oath of allegiance to Peter. The appointed Mayor of Zagreb declared that all Yugoslavia would henceforth feel that its sacred duty was to maintain the deals that Alexander had pursued, at such cost to himself but with such determination, for many years. A similar session was held this afternoon by the Belgrade Municipal Council.

At tomorrow's memorial session of the combined Chamber and Senate the three regents will take the oath of allegiance to Peter and the Constitution and Parliament will proclaim Peter King of Yugoslavia. The government today notified foreign powers of Peter's accession to the throne and the nomination of the regency council.

It is impossible to say at the present time what will be the final political outcome of the measures taken in consequence of Alexander's assassination. It is at least possible to say that grave shock has been caused to the Serbians of the old kingdom by their exclusion from the regency. At the same time, the names of those appointed by the late King for the regency are taken by his friends as an indication of his determination that his policy of appeasement should be pursued even after his death.

### Complete Order Prevails

There is a general feeling of anxiety, but it does not appear justified by the news. "All bad things, even war may now come," were the words with which your correspondent was greeted on landing at the Belgrade airdrome, but from all parts of the kingdom it is reported that complete order prevails.

In Zagreb, Sarajevo and elsewhere in Croatia however the big loyalist demonstrations this morning had to be dispersed when they eventually became demonstrations against Italy. The nation is infuriated and anxious to blame some one, but it does not quite know whom.

The newspaper Politika reported today that the assassin was not a Croat but a Bulgarian and bore tattooed on his arm the badge of the IMRO Macedonian revolutionary organization and its motto, "Liberty or Death." Italy, Hungary, Austria and Bulgaria are blamed for fomenting the discontent of the Yugoslav emigrés.

At the moment there seems to be no danger of internal trouble. In the face of the Marseilles crime political discord has died down for the time being.

Your correspondent talked today with men who were bitter enemies of King Alexander and his policy, and they have the same feelings of horror at his murder as his strongest supporters. Every one recognizes that the strong hand has been violently snatched from the tiller of the ship of state and feels that there is none fit to replace it.

Feverish activity continued all night in the government departments. In the small hours of this morning a proclamation was issued announcing Alexander's death and Crown Prince Peter's succession. It declared the King's last words were "protect my country" and called on "every loyal subject to help fulfill his dying wish."

Under the Constitution Peter will not come of age until seven years from now, when he will be 18.

At midnight Prince Paul, cousin of Alexander, summoned Premier Nikola Uzonovitch, the commander of the Belgrade garrison and other notables to the royal palace to open the King's political testament. The Prince handed the Premier an envelope on which was written in the King's own handwriting, "This contains my last political dispositions in my own hand, in accordance with the Constitution."

Inside was a piece of blue official paper dated "Bled, Jan. 15, 1934." In Alexander's handwriting was written:

"Of my own free will and in the conviction that it is in the interest of my beloved Yugoslav country, my subjects and my royal house, I ordain that if the Crown Prince is called on to ascend the throne of Yugoslavia under circumstances such as are detailed in the Constitution, which would make it impossible for him to rule the country himself, he shall be assisted by a Regency Council.

"I nominate as its members Prince Paul Karageorgevitch, former Minister Dr. Stankovitch and the Ban [Governor] of Zagreb, Dr. Perovitch. Their deputies are General Tomich and Senators Banjanin and Zetz.

"I have written this testament in duplicate, one copy for the Premier and the other for Her Majesty the Queen."

### Only One Regent Prominent

The names of the Regents, with the exception of Prince Paul, whose appointment was expected, have come as a great surprise, because aside from Paul none of them is of great prominence. Dr. Stankovitch's name is known as that of a former Minister of Public Instruction. He is a Free Mason, as was Alexander himself, and was the King's personal physician.

The Regency list should be very popular in Croatia, as it foreshadows an attempt to settle the Croatian problem on fresh lines. Several of the names are those of Croats or other inhabitants of the so-called new Yugoslav territories formerly ruled by the Austro-Hungarian monarchy.

There is, however, a general uneasy feeling that the Regency Council is anything but a strong one. The fact that it does not include leading generals is commented upon anxiously in a country where the army is of such supreme importance as it is in Yugoslavia.

\* \* \*

**November 16, 1934**

# DRIVE HUNGARIANS OUT OF YUGOSLAVIA

*105 Farmers Expelled Tell of a 'Reign of Terror' Along the Frontier*

**AUSTRIANS MAY BE NEXT**

*Action is Linked to Alleged Complicity in the Slaying of King Alexander*

Wireless to The New York Times

BUDAPEST, Nov. 15—One hundred and five Hungarian refugees from Yugoslavia crossed the Yugoslav frontier yesterday. They are mostly so-called double landowners—that is, persons whose estates or farms are situated partly in Hungary and partly in Yugoslavia.

They complain that they had been threatened by Yugoslav Comitajis and told that their houses would be burned down if they did not go and that there was a regular reign of terror against Hungarians along the Yugoslav frontier. Yugoslav frontier guards were employing bloodhounds, they asserted, to prevent any irregular crossing of the border.

### Appeal to League Talked Of

There is a great deal of excitement here as a consequence of these expulsions, but no official figures were available. In Parliament the government is to be asked by a prominent Deputy to bring before the League of Nations Yugoslav allegations of Hungarian complicity in the assassination of King Alexander.

There is a general feeling that Yugoslavia has been warned by France not to make any open complaints about Italy's alleged complicity in the assassination and that Yugoslavia is concentrating public anger against Hungary.

The rôle of Germany in this situation is curious. It is remarked here that the official German news agency manages to combine messages asserting Hungary's innocence and virtue with others containing warnings to Yugoslavia to distrust France and her desire to keep Italy uninvolved.

### Yugoslavia Explains

Wireless to The New York Times

BELGRADE, Nov. 15—In reply to Hungarian complaints about expulsions from Yugoslavia, it is declared in official circles that figures given in some Hungarian sources of 5,000 intended expulsions are exaggerated. In all Yugoslavia, it is asserted, there are not 3,000 Hungarians.

The official view of what has happened is that, under the law concerning employment, foreigners are liable at the expiration of a two-year period after passage of the law to be refused a renewal of their permit to remain if they are replaceable in their jobs by Yugoslavs.

The two-year period expired in September. Now, as a result of the refusal of Hungary and Austria to comply with the French demand for extradition of alleged Croat terrorists, the law is being put into force against Hungarians employed here, and if Austria persists in her refusal it will probably also be put into force against Austrians.

As the permits of Hungarians, most of which are for twelve months, expire they are not being renewed, and in consequence Hungarians have to leave the country, but no steps have been taken to cancel any valid permits.

In addition, a great many Hungarians who there is reason to suspect have been supporting Croat terrorist schemes are being expelled, officials state. They assert that altogether the number of expulsions cannot possibly exceed 500 and will probably fall far short of that figure.

### Yugoslav Charges Predicted

Wireless to The New York Times

SOFIA, Bulgaria, Nov. 15—The Bulgarian press reports that Prince Paul, Yugoslav Regent, is planning big changes, to be put into effect forty days after the death of King Alexander. [He was assassinated Oct. 9.] Prince Paul is constantly negotiating with party politicians who were banned from public life under the dictatorship.

On the day fixed Prince Paul, say Bulgarian correspondents, intends to form a new government, release the Croat leader, Vladko Matchek, from prison, proclaim a general amnesty and issue an appeal to Yugoslav émigrés to work in the future for a united Yugoslavia.

Only the terrorists group headed by Dr. Pavelitch and Communists will be exempted from this amnesty, it is said. They will be declared public enemies of the State.

A memorial from 200 prominent Croat and Serb politicians for the restoration of parliamentary government has been presented to Prince Paul.

### Yugoslav Plan Told to French

Wireless to The New York Times

PARIS, Nov. 15—Kosta Fotich, Yugoslav delegate to the League of Nations, had a long conversation tonight with René Massigli, head of the French League delegation, concerning international responsibilities for the Marseilles assassinations.

M. Fotich came to Paris after a visit to Belgrade, and his purpose is to enlighten the French regarding a memorandum that Yugoslavia intends to submit to the League Council asking for an investigation.

\* \* \*

**December 23, 1934**

# YUGOSLAVIA FREES LEADER OF CROATS

*Country Hails the Release of Matchek, Peasant Party Head—
Democratic Regime Seen*

Wireless to The New York Times

BELGRADE, Dec. 22—The new Yugoslav Cabinet decided this evening to set free Vladko Matchek, leader of the Croat Peasant party. This decision was approved immediately by the Regency Council and caused the greatest satisfaction in Croatia and most other sections of Yugoslavia.

Zagreb and Belgrade newspapers promptly issued extras with this news, which tends to indicate that Premier Yeftitch is striving to conciliate the Croats and other opposition groups.

M. Matchek was sentenced a year ago to a three-year term by an extraordinary court in Belgrade for an alleged offense against the honor of the Yugoslav State. Because of ill health he was transferred several months ago from the Zagreb prison to a hospital. His release was actually effected yesterday, but the condition was made that M. Matchek should remain in his home until tonight.

Another extraordinary event today was an audience given by Prince Paul, Regent, to M. Davidovitch, leader of the oppositional Serbian Democratic party, who has often been mentioned as a possible candidate for the Premiership in case the constitutional régime were revived.

M. Matchek's release and the audience given to M. Davidovitch are viewed as signs that Premier Yeftitch intends sincerely to endeavor to restore the democratic form of government and settle the Croat question once and for all. There is no doubt that behind his endeavors is Prince Paul's desire to settle all of Yugoslavia's inner differences in order to present a united front on foreign problems.

\* \* \*

**March 2, 1935**

# ARMY AND NAVY ARE IN REVOLT IN GREECE; REBELS, QUELLED IN ATHENS, HOLD 4 WARSHIPS

Special Cable to The New York Times

ATHENS, Saturday, March 2—A revolt led by Venizelist army and navy officers broke out at three places in Athens at 6:30 last night. Martial law was declared throughout Greece at 9:20 P. M.

Troops loyal to War Minister George Kondylis subdued the revolt at the Officers' School without bloodshed.

An infantry lieutenant was killed and ten persons were wounded when Loyalist guns blasted a battalion of revolutionists from a position on the southern shoulder of the Acropolis. The surrender of the Acropolis garrison at 1 o'clock this morning gave the government control of the capital.

At 3 A. M. the naval arsenal on the Island of Salamis, with five destroyers and one cruiser, was in the hands of revolutionaries. They lacked munitions, however, and were besieged by government artillery on all sides.

The civilian population is orderly. The provinces are unaffected.

Two seized destroyers have been recaptured, and the remainder are expected to surrender soon.

The trial of sixteen participants in the attempt in June, 1933, to assassinate former Premier Eleutherios Venizelos began on Feb. 22 last. In the attempted murder, M. Venizelos's chauffeur was killed and four bullets struck Mme. Venizelos, seriously wounding her.

During the trial and the preliminaries leading up to it military precautions unprecedented except in times of revolution have been applied. Bombs planted in the Piraeus court house by political sympathizers of the assassins caused considerable damage during the hearings last Fall.

M. Venizelos unsuccessfully opposed the re-election of President Alexander Zaimis last October.

\* \* \*

March 4, 1935

## GREEK REVOLT SPREADS;
## REBELS NOW HOLD CRETE;
## RESERVES ARE MOBILIZED

### CIVIL WAR GRIPS COUNTRY

*Planes Bomb Home of Venizelos and One of Cruisers at Crete*

### REBELS CLAIM BIG SUPPORT

*Macedonia and Thrace Are in Revolt—Athens Quiet Under Martial Law*

### SHIPS HELD AT PIRAEUS

*Revolutionaries Assert They Aim to Prevent Restoration of Monarchy*

Wireless to The New York Times

ATHENS, March 3—The revolt in Greece has spread to Macedonia and other areas, and, with the entire Island of Crete in the hands of the revolutionaries, it has assumed the dimensions of civil war.

The uprising, it has been clearly established, is the action of Republicans headed by Eleutherios Venizelos, who is at Canea, Crete, and General Nicholas Plastiras [who is reported by The Associated Press to have left Cannes, France, for an undisclosed, destination]. The rebels aim to forestall the threat to the Greek Republic that they frequently have warned is implicit in the monarchist-minded Tsaldaris government's policies.

Premier Panayoti Tsaldaris has always replied he would remain loyal to the interests of the State but the Venizelists hold that his actions more and more have belied his promises. The monarchists aimed at placing the exiled former King George, now living in London, back on the Greek throne.

### Rebels Gain Strength

Republican rebels now have the support of a considerable proportion of the army and most of the naval units. Most of the rebel warships are reported today to be at the Island of Crete, where they have placed themselves at the disposal of M. Venizelos, who is 71 years old today. The revolutionaries in Crete have seized wireless stations and all public buildings and they have imprisoned the Governor.

Four bombing planes, the government says, accomplished three objectives during a five-hour flight this afternoon. They attacked with machine guns the villa of M. Venizelos at Halepa, a half-mile from Canea, in Crete. The Athenian Government believes the former Premier is directing the rebellion from that villa. Machine-gunners inside the villa drove off the government planes.

From a height of 150 feet bombs were dropped upon the bridge of the rebel flagship, Averoff, causing damage. As a third objective the government airplanes overtook two rebel destroyers and bombed them.

Coastal traffic has been forbidden to prevent rebels in Crete from capturing transport vessels.

Admiral John Demestichas, who is still the only authority signing rebel dispatches, sent a radio message to the Italian station at Bari, which three times a week broadcasts Greek programs, asking the Italians to tell the Greek people that "400 officers are supporting the Cretan revolution," and also asking the Italian station "not to broadcast false news."

According to governmental reports the revolutionary movement has been thwarted in the northern cities of Alexandropholos and Drama. Newspapers appear with gaping wide deletions due to police censorship. Male relatives of Venizelist officers are being arrested on sight.

M. Venizelos was reported to have issued a proclamation against the government and to have convoked Senators and Deputies of Crete to meet him in convention.

### Three Military Classes Called

The government issued another proclamation today declaring the revolt would be crushed with all the means at its disposal and would show no mercy to any rebels. Mobilization of three military classes also has been ordered. The government declares it is master of the situation in Athens and the mainland generally, but it was reported tonight that the garrison of Godeazatsch declared for M. Venizelos and that the revolt is under way in Greek Macedonia.

All government military planes and even some commercial airplanes have been mobilized for the fight on the rebels. The government has called up the naval reservists of the 1932 class to replace the sailors who have gone over to the revolutionaries.

The Athens victory of the government in the preliminary engagements with the rebels and the enforcement of martial law have given Premier Tsaldaris undisputed control of Athens and the surrounding country. The government also is said to have mastery over the Salonika situation.

Only governmental reports, however, are available from the two sectors. Furthermore, they are emasculated by police censorship, which allows only government communications to appear in the press.

Thirty-five former Venizelist officers, who were cashiered under the Tsaldaris regime, were arrested at Salonika during the night, and all editors of Venizelist newspapers were imprisoned. Loyalist agents prevented Venizelist leaders from boarding trains going to Salonika.

According to General George Kondylis, Minister of War, the entire army at the present moment is loyal to him. It is doubtful whether the revolutionaries possess airplanes, but they have all the serviceable units of the fleet, having sabotaged the three destroyers which they left at Salamis.

### Submarine Cut From Fleet

The largest radio station in the country has been listening in on communications from the Averoff, rebel flagship, as the conspirators had not arranged a code. One rebel submarine became separated from the fleet during the night after having been bombed by government airplanes.

The Venizelos home in Athens was searched today. The Venizelist leaders, Alexander Papanastassiou and M. Caphandaris, were arrested during the search. The government says arms and hand grenades were found there.

M. Tsaldaris strengthened the Cabinet's hold over the anti-Venizelist elements by persuading General John Metaxas to become Minister without portfolio. General Metaxas is known as one of the leaders of Greek fascism and a partner in the Tsaldaris-Kondylis coalition. He had not been a member of the Cabinet previously because he was not sympathetic to republican methods.

Government circles say M. Venizelos would be unable to lead a revolution, if such was his intention, without help from a foreign power.

General Metaxas has taken over command of the Athenian headquarters, though General Kondylis remains the strategical dictator.

The government asserts many volunteers are enlisting. The funeral of the victims in fighting for the Acropolis was held today under heavy guard. All theatres and cinemas are closed in Athens and taxicabs are forbidden on the streets unless in possession of special permits. The police and troops enforced a 10 o'clock curfew.

*   *   *

**March 6, 1935**

# NEIGHBORS ARMING AS GREEKS BATTLE

*Bulgaria, Reinforcing Border, Hopes Turkish Concentration Is Not Directed Against Her*

**ATHENS LISTS VICTORIES**

*Loyal Forces Split the Rebels in Macedonia as Flanking Movement Is Successful*

Wireless to The New York Times

ATHENS, March 5—From the confusion resulting from interrupted communications and government censorship the fact emerged that the government of Premier Panayoti Tsaldaris still held the upper hand in the Greek civil war today but was undoubtedly hard pressed, while the concentration of troops by Greece's neighbors on their frontiers gave the situation a graver aspect than the purely local revolts Greece has had in the past.

[In Sofia the Bulgarian Foreign Minister expressed alarm lest a large concentration of Turkish troops on the Bulgaro-Turkish border might be directed against Bulgaria, which has also heavily reinforced her frontier garrisons.]

For the government the danger points are Thrace, Macedonia and of course Crete, where the supporters of former Premier Eleutherios Venizelos are in full control. The government is making every possible effort to convince the rebels that they have lost the day.

Victories were reported all along the line by the government, but the reports failed to carry full conviction. Athens was quiet for the most part and the government canceled decrees limiting the repayment of deposits by the banks, but there were riots between Venizelist and Tsaldarist students, which caused Athens University to be closed indefinitely. Saloniki harbor has been protected by mines against rebel ships.

**To Arrest Rebels' Relatives**

The government today ordered the arrest of all male and female relatives of rebels and their internment in concentration camps in order to compel the rebels to surrender.

Unconfirmed reports say that an artillery battle near Drama today ended in the rebels' favor.

Reports from Crete say that M. Venizelos is still confident of final victory and is planning to capture the Cyclades Islands preliminary to an attack on Athens and Southern Greece.

With General George Kondylis, the Minister of War, commanding, loyal troops crossed the Struma River in Macedonia early this afternoon. The cooperation of General Kondylis with the loyal General Yalistras resulted, according to an announcement from the government in a completely successful flanking movement that cut communications between the main rebel body and frontier troops belonging to the same dissident army corps. At 5 P. M. General Yalistras reported that he was controlling the River Nestos.

When the weather cleared General Kondylis sent airplanes to drop leaflets on the rebel infantry exhorting them to desert their officers and freeing them from the obligation of obeying their superiors.

The proclamation read:

"We have 100,000 soldiers ready and Venizelos has four disabled battleships. We have sixty airplanes and Venizelos has none. He has lost the game and in a few days he will desert you and go abroad.

"I have the power to crush you, but I do not want to shed the blood of Greek soldiers because of an insane old criminal who wants to play the despot. Throw down your arms or I will throw against Macedonia all the terrors of war. You will face all of Greece's airplanes, cavalry and artillery.

"Every private soldier who surrenders has my word as an officer that he will go unpunished because it was his officers who led him astray. Those who surrender will be sent to their homes at once.

"If you do not surrender Macedonia will be stained with the blood of brothers and a national curse will fall on Venizelos."

The government reports many desertions.

The rebels were also bombarded by planes with another proclamation issued by General Kondylis from Saloniki, which resembles an armed camp in the days of the World War. The proclamation read:

"Venizelos has gone mad. Because he wants to be continually in power he has forced you to revolt against the government. The government has been obliged to mobilize

Greek mutineers being led to prison by loyal soldiers. This photograph was telephotoed to London and then transmitted to New York by radio.

in order to save the nation. We know that Venizelos tricked you with a handful of officers who showed you the false side of the situation.

"The government's power is limitless, but the government is unwilling to kill Greeks and allows you until tomorrow to surrender. Afterward you will have no chance. We shall throw against the rebels the Eastern Macedonian corps and the entire military aviation forces.

### To Hold Venizelos Responsible

"Venizelos will be held responsible for everything that has happened. You have only a few hours in which to change your mind. The great disaster will overtake you. An honest soldier who has never lied warns you."

The government declares that the rebels have been repulsed near Poroi, one officer and two soldiers being killed.

Ultimatums sent to the rebel leader General Kamenos nightly urging him to surrender before morning have been futile. After the expiration of the government's ultimatum at 10 o'clock this morning advance detachments of loyal troops crossed the Struma River with artillery near the point where an American drainage company recently completed land-drying operations.

Across grassless plains that a short time ago were marshes, the government troops marched forward toward the advanced rebel headquarters in Seres, intending to retake the town. From Larissa engineers were ordered up to replace other bridges over the Struma which had been destroyed.

Twenty-one bombing planes helping the government forces were obliged to land because of storms from the direction of Larissa.

General Kamenos was overheard calling on the radio to the rebel light cruiser Helli asking for reinforcements. The Helli replied that it was impossible to help him. It is believed, however, that both messages were tricks.

This afternoon M. Venizelos's chief political ally, Alexander Papanastassiou, the founder of the Balkan conference and a prominent party leader in the Venizelist coalition, telephoned Premier Tsaldaris that he had returned home after the police had been unable to find him for five days. George Caphandaris, another Venizelos leader, is still in hiding.

Andreas Michalokopoulos, Senator from Patras, has published a message asking M. Venizelos as a former comrade to abandon the revolt. Efforts at mediation here have shown no progress thus far.

The newspapers quote at length French criticism of M. Venizelos as having been guilty of the double crime of thwarting the Balkan pact and then declaring a pointless revolt.

Patrol boats steam back and forth in the gulf before Athens, but seaplanes have been moved to the Phaleron base. Foreign planes have been barred from flying over Greece.

When your correspondent asked the United States Legation concerning the safety of fourteen American men, women and children—American engineers employed by a company in the Greek Government's projects on the Struma River and their families—it was said that they were receiving every consideration from the Greek authorities in Saloniki.

The Americans have their headquarters in Seres, the town that the rebels retook after loyal troops had ousted them yesterday. The legation said that, without being able to supply definite information, it was confident the rebel troops would likewise do their utmost to protect the lives of all American citizens.

\* \* \*

March 10, 1935

## TOPICS OF THE TIMES

### Cannon Against Athens

It is hard to believe that the insurgent Venizelists will go so far as to throw shells into Athens, or, for that matter, that the present government will let it come to that. But if the shooting does begin, they will be shots heard very much round the earth. You can't raise a really loud noise in a place called Athens without starting up echoes in all the corridors of the world.

Shells dropping in the vicinity of the Parthenon will sound exceptionally loud to the American School of Classical Studies in Athens. Gunfire from the Venizelist cruisers may spoil the fine repair job which the Greek archaeologists carried out about a half a dozen years ago with the aid of a special fund raised in this country. It consisted in setting up again half a score of the broken columns of the Parthenon on the north portico.

### Parthenon Once Intact

The architects of the Parthenon did not originally design it as a ruin, as a good many generations of schoolboys may have been tempted to suspect. Nor was the wrecked Parthenon, as we all know it, the work of the ancient Greeks themselves in one of their civil wars or local uprisings. The famous shattered columns are really a Venetian masterpiece of the late seventeenth century. In the year 1687 the Parthenon was a Turksh powder magazine and a Venetian shell dropped into it. It was as simple as that.

Today it is not a question of one set of barbarians from Venice firing upon another set of barbarians calling themselves Turks. If the Parthenon suffers new hurt it will be from Greeks throwing high explosives against Greeks. The thing, of course, is not impossible. In 1914 the human race showed what it can do when it really gets going. And the old Greeks were always at each other's throats, literally. They had to be at each other's throats because gunpowder had not been invented.

Still, if the beauty of Hellas which is reverenced by barbarians in the United States should be marred by Greek cannon, things will have come to a pretty pass; as Leonidas might have grimly remarked at Thermopylae.

### Voted and Quizzed

One reason why Athens means so much to modern men everywhere is that the Greeks had a word for it. That is to say, they had a word for pretty nearly everything that is of intimate concern to the heart of man, with the exception, perhaps, of automobiles and crooners.

It is amusing to think that when a man wants to say that something has no meaning to him he says "It is Greek to me." He will say it of the language which has given us the word Politics. He will say it of the language which has given us Democracy and Demagogue and Despot and Tyrant, together with the frogs' chorus from Aristophanes for the special benefit of Yale. What would we in the newspaper headlines do when we needed a short word for members of the Albany Legislature if the Greeks had not produced a Solon? But there was a Solon in Athens and so the headlines can now say "Solons Vote Quiz," or something of the sort.

For that matter the Greeks started the voting habit and, necessarily, the quiz habit. First people vote and then they start an inquiry into why they voted the way they did. But the Greeks went still further in the pioneering line. They started the habit of voting against. If, for instance, you didn't like a man named Aristedes because everybody called him honest, you voted against him by casting a small seashell, called in the Greek language *ostra*. If enough shells were cast against Aristedes then he was declared ostracized and he had to go and live abroad, the Riviera or Sussex or somewhere.

### Highly Flexible Language

The old Greeks had a great many words for a great many things, and that was largely because they discovered or invented so many things. They discovered or invented or named such things as politics, democracies, demagogues, oligarchs, despots, debts and how to get rid of them, drama, philosophy, science, poetry, art, oratory, public debate, &c.

The principal reason why the Greeks had so many words is, of course, that they were a gifted people. But they were greatly assisted by the peculiar genius of their language, which lent itself to all sorts of flexible combinations. Thus the Greeks had a two-letter word *ge,* pronounced gay, for "earth," but they used to call an ascetic monk, as a few surviving readers of Kingsley's "Hypatia" may recall, an old "heautontimoroumenos," or "self-tormentor."

It is this special genius of the Greek language which enabled good old Samuel Johnson to get the better in a debate with a Billingsgate fishwife whom he called an old parallelopipedon, so that the poor woman burst into tears. It also permitted the Puzzlers League of America only the other day to provide themselves with a new champion word, pneumonoultramicroscopisilicovolcanokoniosis, meaning some form of a dust disease. The Greek language can do this, just as it can sum up an entire natural philosophy by saying "panta rei," "everything flows."

### Quite at Home

The old Greeks invented demagogues, Olympic Games, science and the letters for Greek letter fraternities, among many other things; so they would be quite at home with us today. Huey Long is in the great line of descent from Thersites in the Iliad and Cleon in Aristophanes. But lined up with the Huey Longs are the Millikans, the Einsteins, the Rutherfords, the Mendels, the T. H. Morgans. For if these gentlemen need a word for it they go to the Greeks—atoms, electrons, cosmoses, positrons, genes, hormones.

Yes, the old Greeks would not be lost in our modern world. The sound of gunfire against Athens might puzzle them for a little while, but the spirit behind it they would understand. The old Greeks knew what it is to tear a civilization to pieces in strife.

*   *   *

**May 10, 1935**

# OLD FEUD FLAMES IN GREECE'S CIVIL WAR

*Venizelos and the Republicans Fight a Government Allied With Monarchists and Ambitious Politicians and Soldiers*

## By NICHOLAS S. KALTCHAS

The civil war that is raging in Greece is much more than a mutiny of disaffected army and navy officers and the soldiers and sailors who may have been duped or coerced into following them. Though by far the grimmest affair of its kind in the history of modern Greece, it is not without precedent. For the army and navy have played a decisive part in initiating every change of political régime effected by extra-constitutional means during the last hundred years.

It would be a mistake to attribute this meddling in politics merely to motives of professional self-interest or to the inability of the average Greek to divest himself of his inveterate political-mindedness even after he has donned a uniform. Rebellious officers and men have always claimed to epitomize the nation and to express the general will.

### A Long-Standing Quarrel

If the armed forces of Greece have been at best the interpreters of the national will and at worst the shock-troops of political faction, what is the alignment behind their present fratricidal struggle? Its origins can be traced back to the conflict between Mr. Venizelos and King Constantine over the participation of Greece in the World War, a conflict which, in the ideological garb of republicanism and monarchism, has been the leitmotif of Greek politics during the last twenty years. But today there are important differences epitomized by the presence in the government camp of General Condylis and (until a week ago) Admiral Hadjikyriacos, two men with lurid anti-monarchist records, who, though still professing to be republicans, have turned upon Mr. Venizelos and their former comrades with as much fury as they expended in the past upon the King and the monarchy.

### A Culmination

Hence on its personal side the rebellion is the culmination of the feud between the Condylis and the Venizelos-Plastiras factions of republican officers, many of whom have been removed or demoted by General Condylis, in his capacity of War Minister, in favor of his own friends or monarchist sympathizers. But the rebels have rationalized their personal grievances into the conviction that they are the sword of the hard-pressed republic against the menace of monarchical restoration or military dictatorship.

How real is this menace? Mr. Venizelos believes that the policies of the Tsaldaris Government during the past three years have systematically undermined the republican régime. He accuses his opponent of having thwarted the foundation of a coalition government which would have removed the issue of form of government from politics. He maintains that the Prime Minister, despite his formal pledge of adherence to the republic, has purged the administration of republican office-holders and has favored increasingly violent monarchist agitation while denying equal freedom to the republicans. He caps the indictment with the charge that the government is determined upon the abolition of the Senate (where it does not have a majority), in order to remove the most important constitutional obstacle to more basic changes.

In appraising the validity of this indictment we must consider the Prime Minister's personality and political position. Mr. Tsaldaris is temperamentally a moderate man and an orthodox constitutionalist. Though originally a monarchist and a disciple and successor of Gounaris, whose memory he reveres, he has been sincerely converted to the republic because it seemed to him to be the régime that promised to divide the Greeks least. But despite his considerable authority he is not the complete master of his party. Its right wing under John Rallis is avowedly monarchist, and among the many factors that have enhanced its influence not the least potent have been the blunders of the republicans.

The most flagrant of these blunders was Plastiras's abortive coup in March 1933. This placed Mr. Venizelos in an extremely awkward position and not unlikely precipitated the attempt upon his life which has poisoned Greek politics ever since.

### A Greek Enigma

Moreover Mr. Tsaldaris has to consider another friend, but potential rival and successor, John Metaxas, the most enigmatic figure in Greek politics. As Minister of Communications in the Zaimis coalition (1926–28), he displayed great initiative and administrative talent, combined with a tendency to favor big business and high finance, and impatience with parliamentary processes. His anti-democratic bias is possibly due in part to his successive electoral defeats.

Though completely lacking the mass magnetism of a Mussolini or a Hitler, Metaxas is the only man in Greece who has the stature and the temperament of a Fascist dictator. To offset his influence Mr. Tsaldaris has leaned more and more heavily on General Condylis, whose presence in the government not only served as a counter-weight to Mr. Metaxas's influence, but also shielded the Prime Minister against the suspicion of plotting the overthrow of the republic.

### Role of Condylis

But is General Condylis still a republican? Until he threw in his lot with Mr. Tsaldaris his career had been distinguished by single-minded devotion to the republican ideal. But, like many other Greeks, he came by his republicanism by way of nationalism. An assiduous reader of history, and particularly of Plutarch's Lives, he has served the republic in the past with Catonian disinterestedness, but may just as conceivably aspire to liquidate it in Caesarean or Napoleonic fashion. Hence a great deal will depend upon the effect which the outcome of his campaign against the rebels will have upon his prestige and power.

What, then, is the immediate outlook for Greece? If the rebellion proves more formidable than has so far been admitted by the government, a compromise settlement may be reached on the basis of the elimination from the political scene of the protagonists of the present struggle. If, on the other hand, the government crushes the rebellion, the fate of the republic will depend on the sincerity of Mr. Tsaldaris and General Condylis, who, supported by the large republican element in the country, can be trusted to checkmate Mr. Metaxas and the monarchists.

### Question of Monarchy

But there is a third possibility which, though remote, should not be entirely excluded from speculation. The restoration of the monarchy cannot be considered apart from the candidates. George II, precisely because he has displayed statesmanlike reserve and lack of vindictiveness during his years of exile, does not arouse the passionate loyalty which attached the Greek people to his father. But a few months ago the daughter of his uncle, Prince Nicholas, the shrewdest of the Gluecksburgs, married into the British royal family.

A Greek Princess on the throne of Greece with an English Prince as her consort is a prospect calculated to reawaken the almost atavistic faith of the Greek people in the beneficent omnipotence of Britain and possibly reconcile many republicans who would otherwise be unshakably opposed to restoration. But apart from international objections to such a solution, intradynastic rivalry, namely, the opposition of the legitimate King and his faction, is equally conceivable; and the Greek Republic may gain a respite from such rivalry, much as the Third French Republic benefited from the conflict between the legitimist and the Orleans branches.

\* \* \*

**October 20, 1935**

## GREECE TURNS TO A KING

*The Recent Coup Is a Symptom of the Nation's Political Unrest, and Reflects Social and Economic Change*

### By EMIL LENGYEL

A walk in Athens while shadows creep from behind Mount Hymettus, cautiously climb the Acropolis and then plunge headlong into Salamis Bay, starts a train of thought concerning the perennial problems of Greece. It was in this violet-crowned city that democracy, tyranny, republic and

Where Politics Is a Passion—A Demonstration In Athens.

monarchy first found the forms which have survived until the present day. Here change has succeeded change; here change persists, for only recently a military coup d'état liquidated an eleven-year-old republican régime and re-established monarchy.

At the foot of the Acropolis, where excavators are at work exposing the remnants of the ancient Agora, western man ventured his first halting steps on the road to political self-determination. Here Solon formulated laws that have inspired many commonwealths. Here was argued whether Pericles was a man of the people or a tyrant. Here citizens plotted to overthrow Pisistratus, father of the modern dictator-demagogue. Here Demosthenes arraigned Philip of Macedon before the bar of civilization.

To the modern Athenian yesterday is part of today. In this setting of never-dying glory, politics is a heritage to which the citizen of contemporary Greece feels he must remain loyal. His passion for politics is partly responsible for the fact that in Greece, as a Greek statesman has put it aptly, there are public opinions but there is no public opinion. This fact has contributed to political unrest.

The passion for the history of the moment is evident upon a first acquaintance with Athens. Not only broad University Street but even the darkest alley is swarming with people engaged in rapid-fire talk. They are discussing not the afternoon's football match or an approaching boxing match, but the speech of the Prime Minister, the pronunciamento of a political general, or an editorial on the national budget.

Guests in sidewalk cafés drink innumerable small cups of coffee, eat tiny slices of toasted bread spread over with Hymettus honey; but their interest is in the newspaper they are reading. They read not only the papers which present their own views but also those of the Opposition. In Athens alone, including its suburbs, about twenty daily newspapers are published. They are avidly read.

The Greek is full of good advice for the government, and is generally critical of all authority. His distrust of it has been attributed to the Greek's sad experiences with government under the Turkish régime. For more than four centuries the Turk squeezed the country dry, giving no value in return. The Greek watched his moves with suspicion.

The Turkish heritage also works in another direction. So long did the nation consider itself the prize of the political ruler that the ancient spoils system was perpetuated after the declaration of independence. The party in power feels entitled to fill government jobs with its own adherents, making short shrift of the hangers-on of the old régime. Distrust for the government has been increased by such practice.

In the Greek political system the army plays a heavy rôle. Wherever one turns in Athens there are soldiers and marines. The Evzones attract particular attention because of their exotic uniform of Albanian origin; pleated and starched kilts, white tights and turned-up shoes with large pompons. Their officers wear heavily embroidered jackets and the Turkish scimitar. There is an army of some 70,000 officers and men in a country of 6,500,000 inhabitants.

This corner of the world is constantly calling upon its soldiery. Greece is exposed to trouble not only because she forms part of the Balkans but also because she occupies a strategic position in the Mediterranean. Here wars last longer and are, if possible, even more ferocious than they are in the West. For Greece the World War lasted ten years, ushered in by two Balkan wars and brought to a close by disastrous fighting in Asia Minor.

In this area of dynamic changes, inherent in nature and national character, the army has become a fixed point to which the spirit of independence is anchored. But other hopes have attached themselves to it also. It was first in 1909 that a group of army officers overthrew a Greek Government, and political success has given the army a new field of action. Since then the armed force has been an instrument of coups and revolutions.

Although Athens is The City of Greece, in which the governmental power is centralized, the village has also a story to tell. Athens enjoys life's latest comforts, has been moving into houses that are the last word in modernity, is sophisticated and cultured. The village, on the other hand, is primitive, poorly sheltered, cut off from the world; its people suffer from malaria and tuberculosis.

As the capital beautifies itself, the village foots the bill and vainly tries to obtain its share of power. The eternal struggle between town and country was intensified by the influx into the country of 1,500,000 Greeks from Asia Minor a little more than ten years ago.

The refugees were the heirs of an old city civilization and insistent on their rights, and their coming has produced not only widespread social but important economic consequences.

They brought with them into the country a modest amount of prosperity. A loan from the League of Nations and other foreign moneys fertilized the capital market. Building houses for the enormous mass of newcomers drained the unemployment market so that for a time there was even danger of a labor shortage. They also brought with them many new industries, such as carpet-making, coppersmithing, silk and glass-making.

They made the Greek countryside factory conscious. In their peasant neighbors they injected the virus of discontent.

Greece has not only her domestic but also her highly exacting diplomatic problems. Once the centre of the world, then for centuries a land of little account among the nations, she is again assuming a position of importance. Commercially the Piraeus now outranks all Italian seaports, and is the second harbor of the Mediterranean.

In diplomacy Athens sees eye to eye with London— Greece believes she has no better friend than Great Britain. England's interest in Greece is conditioned upon her strategic importance, and it is fairly obvious in the present crisis how great this importance can be for the British Navy. The Greek island of Corfu is well situated to keeping an eye on Italy, across the narrow strait.

If Britain is the friend, Italy is the foe for the average Greek. He has not forgotten the Corfu incident of twelve years ago, when an Italian fleet shelled that island, violating its neutrality and killing several hospitalized Greek refugees and Armenian orphans. Although the League made Italy withdraw, the memory of the bombardment still smarts.

Nor has Greece resigned herself to the loss of the Dodecanese, the Twelve Islands, in the easternmost Mediterranean, off the Anatolian coast. Italy ultimately took those islands, although it was one of her statesmen, Premier Giolitti, who had refused to annex them on the ground that they were Greek.

But Greece has friends besides Britain. She is linked by a treaty of friendship to Turkey, her proverbial enemy, and a similar treaty binds her to Yugoslavia. She also looks hopefully toward Bulgaria and Albania.

Popular dislike of Italy and gratitude to Great Britain have assigned the place of Greece in the conflict involving Ethiopia. In the Balkans there has been much speculation in recent months about Downing Street's alleged interest in a monarchist restoration as an aid to stabilizing political conditions in Hellas.

Let us see, so far as we can, what forces lie back of the change from republic to monarchy.

The royalists of Greece took their cue from the army leaders, who held that parliamentary democracy, which was identified with the republic, was outmoded, while monarchism, a system of the strong hand, belonged to the future.

They advocated the dynamic State, which was free to take initiative without being impeded by a dilatory and wrangling Parliament. The army men also popularized the argument that a country with a talkative Parliament was in a more unfavorable position from the point of view of defense than a country without it.

The general trend away from democracy, according to these critics, has been demonstrated throughout the Balkans. In neighboring Bulgaria King Boris has been forced to concentrate authority in his hands by muzzling a recalcitrant Parliament. In Albania King Zog has developed into a full-fledged dictator. In Yugoslavia King Alexander had assumed quasi-autocratic powers before an assassin's bullet put an end to his career last year. Even King Carol of Rumania was shown as treading the way that leads to concentrated power.

The military people seem to have played skillfully on the jealousies of the politicians of "Old Greece" in their fight against the politicians of "New Greece," the million and a half refugees from Asia Minor. The new Greeks had become predominantly republican; they considered the dynasty which had been forced upon the country as anything but Greek. Besides, they had fallen under the spell of the ablest statesman of Greece, Eleutherios Venizelos, who had been strongly republican since King Constantine refused to follow his lead into the Allied camp.

The republic's chances of survival decreased with the loss of prestige suffered by Venizelos in the revolution of last March. Instead of taking the battle into the enemy's territory, Venizelos remained at home in Crete and when all seemed to be lost took refuge on the soil of the very power which the Greeks dislike most—Italy. To make things worse, he landed on one of the Dodecanese Islands, Greek ethnically but ruled by Rome. On that day the fight between monarchism and republicanism in Greece was ended.

The general economic depression, the waves of which reached the shores of Greece, facilitated the labors of the monarchists. The trade balance of Greece showed a downward trend, the remittances from overseas declined, while wholesale prices and the cost of living rose. The government was forced to take radical measures by appointing a Superior Economic Defense Committee to cope with the crisis.

Then the monarchists took the offensive. Pro-republican newspapers were harassed and high public officials broke an agreement to let the country judge the issue, by coming out with strong monarchist statements. Lower-placed government officials were given to understand that it would be in their interest to carry on some monarchist propaganda.

So great was the royalist pressure that three months ago Premier Tsaldaris resigned. Although the Premier professed monarchistic sympathies, he opposed a coup d'état and favored a plebiscite. He even offered the government to Field Marshal Kondylis, who, however, refused it either because he thought the time not yet ripe for it or because he preferred to take title to power by strong-arm methods.

Finally, it should be remembered that although the monarchy has been proclaimed it is by no means certain that it is supported by a majority of the people. Rather it is reasonable to suppose that the restoration represents the will of the generals instead of the popular will. But Kondylis, who calls himself Regent, will attempt to confirm the monarchy at a plebiscite next month. There is little reason to doubt that he will succeed.

\*   \*   \*

November 4, 1935

# GREECE'S KINGDOM RESTORED BY VOTE

*Overwhelming Majority Given for Return of George II— Republicans Shun Polls*

**NO DISORDER IN PLEBISCITE**

*Crete, Venizelos Stronghold, Reported to Have Given 95% of Total for Monarchy*

By GEORGE WELLER
Wireless to The New York Times

ATHENS, Greece, Nov. 3—Minister of the Interior Schinas stated tonight that the vote in Greece as a whole today was 98 per cent for the monarchy, and in Athens itself 99 per cent. The plebiscite silences those who have opposed the return of King George II to the throne and relegates the republic to Greece's turbulent past.

As republican leaders had instructed their followers to abstain from the plebiscite as a protest against methods used in engineering the Regency, no other result was to be expected. Returns from precincts in Athens gave the monarchy such margins as 700 in favor to 4 against and 980 in favor to 2 against.

The republic disappeared under overcast skies and without any signs or reports of disorder. The army, navy and air corps rested upon their arms in barracks and on warships throughout the day, except when the men marched to the churches, schools and court houses serving as polling places, where they uniformly voted for King George's return.

A tour of polling places revealed no pressure was being brought upon citizens who appeared at the ballot boxes to vote either way.

Ballots were openly deposited, whether blue, the national color for the monarchy, or scarlet, which signified allegiance to the republic. When a "Venizelo-Communist" (republican) appeared, officials almost welcomed him for increasing the general total of the vote.

Field Marshal Kondylis, who is Regent, Premier, Finance Minister and Minister of the Navy, voted here. Former Premier Panayoti Tsaldaris also voted in Athens, but required a special permit, because he is a Corinthian. General John Metaxas swept the Ionian Islands into the royalist fold by an eleventh-hour campaign.

### George Demanded Plebiscite

The plebiscite cannot really be considered as a vote by the Greeks for the monarchy or the republic since the monarchy was re-established by force through the recent coup d'état by Field Marshal Kondylis, and today's vote was a pure formality tolerated by the new government in view of King George's refusal to return before a plebiscite had taken place.

The voting began at sunrise and ended at sunset. The blue monarchist ballots bore the words, "For a crowned democracy." The red Republican ballot bore the words "For an uncrowned democracy."

Times Wide World Photo

RECALLED TO THRONE. King George II of Greece, who was restored by plebiscite.

As a measure of the inconclusive nature of the voting as an impartial test of the feelings of the people may be mentioned the fact that Regent Kondylis opened the plebiscite this morning with a proclamation calling on every one to vote for the monarchy "in order to put an end to anarchy in public life and inaugurate a new era for Greece."

### George II Declared King

By The Associated Press

ATHENS, Nov. 3—Greece voted today to bring King George II back to the throne he quit by request twelve years ago. Overwhelming majorities were reported in Athens and in the provinces—even in Crete, revolt hot-bed of other days—for the monarchy.

"As of tomorrow, King George II will be King of the Hellenes," said Regent Kondylis, head of the new government; "there will be no political parties. They have been broken up by the people themselves and a new epoch of reconstruction will start."

The regent predicted "the King will be here in fifteen days and will have full power." In fact, he added, the monarch, now in London, will have "absolute right of decision even from Nov. 4." Field Marshal Kondylis telegraphed news of the vote to the King.

Tonight the populace, soldiers and sailors paraded through the streets of Athens and church bells rang out. The city, with extra street lights gleaming, took on a gala appearance after a quiet day of voting.

Typical, apparently, of the general trend was this count from the village of Chalandri near Athens: For the monarchy, 1,980; against 5. In the city of Athens official results showed 138,885 for the restoration, 1,930 against; in Saloniki, 124,449 for, 2,877 against. In Peloponnesus the average was well over 90 per cent in favor of the monarchy.

M. Kirkos, a former member of the ousted Tsaldaris Cabinet, tried to persuade the people of Saloniki to abstain from voting, but it was reported his efforts were looked upon coldly. From Crete a 95 per cent majority in favor of the monarchy was reported. Crete is the birthplace of Eleutherios Venizelos, now in exile, and the stronghold of many of his supporters.

### George Notified in London

Special Cable to The New York Times

LONDON, Nov. 3—King George II of Greece heard the news of the plebiscite when he returned to his hotel here after a dinner party tonight. Major Dimitry Levidis, an old friend of the King who has shared his exile, handed the monarch a telegram. Both were smiling.

Afterward Major Levidis announced the King would return to Greece soon, but that the date had not been arranged.

\* \* \*

**November 26, 1935**

# KING GEORGE ENDS HIS 12-YEAR EXILE

*Thousands Pay Tribute as He Rides in Triumph Into the Greek Capital*

**WELCOMED BY KONDYLIS**

*Ruler Gets a Memorandum From Regent Recommending His Cabinet Be Retained*

By G. E. R. GEDYE
Wireless to The New York Times

ATHENS, Nov. 25—King George II of Greece today became the first of the monarchs who lost their thrones as the result of the World War to experience restoration when he ended his twelve-year exile at 10:05 this morning by setting foot on the soil of Greece. He landed at the Naval Airport in Phaleron Bay amid the ear-splitting din of sirens of the entire fleet and of yachts and merchant vessels anchored at Phaleron and Piraeus. He received a friendly if not exuberant welcome from a tremendous crowd that had awaited his arrival since dawn.

From aboard the Greek destroyer Thyella the writer, the only American reporter aboard, watched the royal flagship Helli steam slowly into the home waters of the Gulf of Athens at 5:45 this morning.

The Thyella weighed anchor at midnight Sunday. The ship crossed the Gulf of Athens to the mouth of the Corinth Canal at 3 A. M. Here were five destroyers and three cruisers at anchor with all lights ablaze. At 4 A. M. a rocket signaled the approach of the first escorting destroyer Hydra which slowly emerged from the canal followed a half hour later by the destroyer Psara.

After a long vigil in silence suddenly a red rocket illuminated the hills toward Corinth. The Helli slowly approached from the narrow exit of the canal. Across the waters came the sound of cheering from the distant crowds which stayed up all night waiting to welcome the returned exile. All the signal lights on the warships began twinkling. Sirens hooted while the towns of Isthnia and Kalanakia on either side of the canal became a mass of lights. The crew of the Thyella dressed ship and remained at attention. The ship moved up as warships formed in a double line with the Helli in the middle.

It was a scene of wonderful beauty which surrounded King George as the ships crossed the gulf with the dawn gradually lighting the sky. As the royal convoy approached Salamis at 7:30 a squadron of airplanes from Athens dipped in salute above the Helli while the flagship steamed toward the shore, still in the centre of the double line of escorting warships.

At 8:25 the Royal Standard was broken on the Helli's masthead followed by those of the entire fleet and the bunting was run up. The Helli's crew was visible standing at attention on the deck while King George appeared on the bridge in the uniform of a cavalry general—selected instead of a naval uniform as a token of his return as the leader of the army—accompanied by Prince Paul.

### Crowds Line the Shore

At 9 o'clock amid an ear-splitting din from sirens which suddenly rent the air, the Helli steamed in place at the right of the line and dropped anchor with its escort following suit. Along the shore of Phaleron Bay dense crowds stretched as far as the eye could see. At 9:15 the Helli's guns boomed out. King George was seen standing upright at the prow of a naval cutter heading for the shore. Guns ashore returned the salute of the Helli whose crew cheered wildly as King George left the ship.

All bells began pealing as King George set foot on the air base followed by his brother Paul. Massed bands went through the motions of playing the royal anthem, "Son of the Eagle," but in the din their strains were not audible. The first person to greet the King on the flower-strewn quayside was Marshal George Kondylis, dressed in civilian clothes.

"I am happy to welcome Your Majesty to the soil of the fatherland," was Marshal Kondylis's simple greeting, to which the King replied, obviously moved:

"I am really grateful to be able again to set foot on the soil."

After the Mayor of Phaleron's little niece presented a bouquet the King entered an open motor car with Prince Paul and drove along the four mile boulevard leading to Athens. He was preceded by a police car and escorted by a squadron of khaki-clad cavalry with crowds cheering enthusiastically as he passed. Police had difficulty in repressing them. Hadrian's Arch, the Gate of Athens, was barred by five Evzones who challenged.

### Given Keys to the City

On receiving the reply "I am the King of the Hellenes," they handed over to the King the keys to the city. The King, who had dismounted from the car, advanced to meet the Mayor of Athens, who read an address of welcome, to which the King replied. Enthusiastic crowds pressed forward. More than 100,000 must have seen the King during this halt from the open spaces on the hills leading to the Acropolis, which were packed as far as the eye could see.

From Hadrian's Arch King George and Prince Paul, both monocled and pale, King George's expression stern, proceeded along the boulevard. Repeatedly white-skirted Evzones forced back people with barred rifles. Military airplanes whipped past barely a hundred feet above the crowd while flight commanders scattered thousands of tiny paper flags in the Sovereign's path. King George's face never lost its resolute impassivity as he was driven past officers of all the armed forces awaiting him below the bronze battleshield on the Unknown Soldier's Tomb.

Swinging around Constitution Square King George's car and escort went to Athens Cathedral. Archbishop Chrysostomos, Marshal Kondylis and President of the National Assembly Balanys received King George at the church door. Archbishop Chrysostomos offered a crucifix to King George who bent slightly to kiss it.

At 1 o'clock at the palace King George received Marshal Kondylis, who without resigning gave the Sovereign a long memorandum recommending that the present Cabinet be maintained by the King until the election because it was this government that made the October revolution and carried through the plebiscite and alone commands the support of the armed forces.

"I will ask you to confer with me shortly," King George said.

"As Your Majesty wishes," Marshal Kondylis responded.

### King Issues Proclamation

King George's first message asserts that he was summoned by the people and that the responsibility for a successful reign is mutual. His proclamation is as follows:

"Greeks! Obeying your unanimous invitation I return to our beloved country after a twelve-year absence. My emotions are deep and my gratitude to the people is great. I hid in my heart the sorrow of our separation and my desire to see Greeks. I never ceased to watch with the greatest of interest your days of happiness or distress. Invited today to assume my highest duties I am ready to place all my experience and my energy in the service of my people with no exceptions. I discard the past and am determined to obtain absolute equality for all. I wish to establish national unity and close and firm cooperation of all Greeks under my leadership and guidance. I hope I will bring Greece happier days and glory like that my grandfather and noble father knew. Long live the nation!" signed "George Second."

The King lunched and dined with Prince Paul, keeping strict privacy because of the political crisis. He will first attempt to form a coalition government from the Deputies in the present Assembly plus the Republicans, but omitting all recognized leaders.

This afternoon the King walked in the royal gardens expressing pleasure for the care given them. This evening he spent examining congratulatory telegrams and conferring with Prince Paul.

Marshal Kondylis said that the King would inform him tomorrow when he should submit his formal resignation but today's memorandum was supposed to free the King's hands to decide whether he will maintain Marshal Kondylis.

\* \* \*

November 28, 1935

## KING AND CABINET AT ODDS IN GREECE

---

*Deadlocked on His Insistence Venizelos and Plastiras Be Included in Amnesty*

### KONDYLIS WOULD BAR FOES

*Ruler is Expected to Summon a New Government—Would Free 578 Political Captives*

---

Wireless to The New York Times

ATHENS, Thursday, Nov. 28—A serious conflict between King George and the Kondylis Cabinet developed last night over the question of an amnesty for participants in the Republican revolt of last March, and the issue is now deadlocked.

A proclamation of a general amnesty for all political offenders, including former Premier Eleutherios Venizelos and General Nicholas Plastiras, was submitted by George yesterday to a Cabinet meeting presided over by Vice Premier John Theotokis. Objections that Marshal George Kondylis, the Premier, raised in an audience with the King were mostly overruled by the sovereign.

According to the amnesty planned, 578 persons now in prison would be released and 400 fugitives living in foreign countries on funds from Mr. Venizelos would be allowed to return, but confiscated property and estates would not be restored and Venizelist officers would not be permitted to re-enter the army and navy, this being a concession to Marshal Kondylis.

During his conversation Marshal Kondylis insisted that his mortal enemy, Mr. Venizelos, and his chief military rival, General Plastiras, should not be included in the amnesty and

warned the King of the army's dissatisfaction if they returned, but the King refused to accept his proposals.

George was evidently induced to take this decision by the fact that the Republican leaders Alexander Papanastassiou and George Kaphandaris yesterday refused to visit the palace on his invitation. Neither Republican leader mentioned the amnesty in his refusal and Mr. Kaphandaris told this correspondent that the amnesty was only one among several demands made by the Republicans.

After many conversations the Cabinet finally unanimously demanded last night that Mr. Venizelos and General Plastiras be excluded from the amnesty. Marshal Kondylis and Mr. Theotokis then conferred at length with the King, the conversations ending only at midnight, but they were unable to satisfy the royal insistence that the amnesty be general.

It seems impossible, therefore, for the King to issue the general amnesty that he desires through the medium of the present Cabinet, and he will be obliged to do so through another government.

\* \* \*

December 2, 1935

## TERRORISM THRIVES AMID DICTATORSHIPS

---

*The Harvest of Political Outrages Has Been Large in Non-Democratic Lands*

---

By G. E. R. GEDYE

VIENNA—Yugoslavia's complaint that Hungary has harbored Croatian terrorists is only one of many signs that this has been a good year for terrorism in Europe. The harvest has been a rich one both for tyrannical governments enforcing their will on hostile subjects and for discontented subjects striking fear into the hearts of their real or fancied oppressors.

Terrorism expresses itself not only in killings, but also in demonstrative bomb explosions that merely destroy property and cause alarm. The governmental form of terror is exercised not alone by the hangman, the firing squad and those who cause secret deaths which are afterward listed as "suicide in the cell" or "slain while attempting to escape." There is the terror of long imprisonment, of indefinite internment without trial, of confinement behind the barbed wire of the concentration camp. There is the terror created among whole populations by the eavesdropping informer. Morally, the worst form of all is the economic terror, which threatens loss of employment and consequent starvation.

### Pre-War and Post-War Outrages

Pre-war terrorism was mostly the birth pangs of new nationalism; for example, the Serbian assassinations at Sarajevo, which Austria-Hungary answered with the terror of her ultimatum; or it was the expression of demand for freedom against despotism, as in the crimes of the early Russian nihilists, which brought on Czarist terrorism in retaliation. It remained for Lenin, cold-blooded methodical thinker, to sweep away in Russia the belief in the efficacy of terrorist outrages against individuals. He advocated mass terrorism instead. Probably eight out of ten of the authors of so-called "Communist outrages" in Europe at present know nothing of Communist doctrines or reject them utterly.

### Continuation of the War

Post-war terrorism is largely a continuance of the war by underground methods. The terrorism of the Nazis in Germany is fundamentally the refusal of German nationalist sentiment to swallow the dictated peace of Versailles. It was probably automatic reaction of the stream of propaganda from Germany depicting Dollfuss as the man who had sold the Austro-Germans to the opponents of the Anschluss, that made Otto Planetta draw his revolver and shoot down the escaping Chancellor.

The murder of King Alexander in Marseilles last October was, if one goes deep enough, the refusal of the "revisionist bloc" to accept the allocation of Croatia and Macedonia to Serbia. The nerves of the long-dead Hapsburg monarchy twitched at the spectacle of the triumphant Alexander and he died.

The Croat terrorists have always been closely connected with those who will not accept the destruction of Hapsburg rule in Central Europe. Both they and the Macedonian terrorists, formerly citizens of Bulgaria, have always found shelter and support in countries of the "revisionist bloc" that continue in peace the struggle against the victory of the Entente powers.

### Echo of the Past

The revolver shots at Marseilles were, in a sense, only the echo of those fired in the Belgrade Skupshtina on June 20, 1928, by the Serbian Deputy, Punisha Rahchitch, which killed the leader of the Croats, Stephen Raditch, and three of his supporters. Had the assassin been executed in accordance with law, this act of terrorism might have proved an isolated one. But the government of King Alexander protected the murderer, who was sentenced only to imprisonment. On Jan. 6, 1929, King Alexander proclaimed his dictatorship, the Croat Deputies having meanwhile boycotted Parliament "until it should be purged of the crime of June."

The publicist, Tony Schlegel, went over to the dictatorship and was shot dead in the street. Since then there has been a long chain of murders and counter-murders. There was a reign of police terror in Zagreb. Croats were arrested, beaten, tortured and "shot while attempting to escape."

Terrorism on the Croat side was encouraged from abroad. Two of Yugoslavia's neighbors had interest in fostering Croatian unrest against her. Italy would like to sever the Dalmatian littoral from Yugoslavia Hungary has never reconciled herself to the loss of Croatia after the war. In Austria, too, was a circle that dreamed of a reunion of Catholic Croatia with Catholic Austria under the Hapsburgs. Reactionary as this group was it was not terrorist, but it did much to secure for a time an asylum for the real terrorists on Austrian soil.

### Serbian Plots and Murders

The leaders of the Croat terrorists were members of the small reactionary group called the "Frank party"—Dr. Ante Pavelitch, Gustav Perchitch and Dr. Ivo Frank. They and their methods were repudiated by Dr. Vladko Matchek, who succeeded Stephen Raditch as leader of the Croat Peasant party, and by many notable Croatian emigrants and exiles.

Dr. Pavelitch ultimately established himself in Borgotaro, in Italy, and set up a camp in which Croatian émigrés received terrorist and military instruction. In 1932 his emissaries organized an uprising in the Lika Mountains of Croatia. The Yugoslavs said that men from his camp were smuggled across the border under supervision of Italian officers.

Last Christmas Pavelitch sent the Croat terrorists Oreb and Begovitch from Borgotaro to Zagreb to kill King Alexander. Oreb's nerve failed him. Before the two men could make a second attempt they were betrayed. After killing a police officer they were captured, tried and hanged.

Dr. Ivo Frank operated from Budapest, apparently acting as liaison officer between the Croat terror group and its Hungarian sympathizers. Gustav Perchitch came to Vienna, but spent much time in Hungary. He is believed to have directed the series of bomb outrages in Yugoslavia between 1929 and 1932, in which bombs were concealed in trains entering Yugoslavia, timed to explode after passing the border.

It was in 1930 that I first met Perchitch in Vienna. An unknown Croat telephoned that Perchitch would like to meet me and felt that he could rely on my discretion. I was told to be at the Café Astoria in the Alserstrasse 7 o'clock next evening and to place a handkerchief on the table before me. I was there on time and waited to see a single man enter before giving my sign. None had appeared at 7:15, and I put out my handkerchief on the chance. Immediately two young men approached from the next table

### A Terrorist Visited

They told me that Perchitch could not show himself in public. They took me in a closed car and drove me to an unnamed destination. They were two of his bodyguard and proudly they showed me that they carried two revolvers apiece.

We stopped in a dark street and I was taken into a first-floor flat, where an elaborate "high tea," with Croatian wines and schnapps, had been spread in my honor, Perchitch's very pretty niece acting as hostess. I had an hour's talk with the famous terrorist, a good-looking young man with a reddish, pointed beard. He already was under sentence of death.

Two months later I met him again and did not recognize him—his beard was gone. This time he made no mystery of the address where he would receive me, though it was not, of course, the house in which he lived. He gave a musical evening, attended by Austrian monarchists, Italians and Hungarians.

In 1930 the Yugoslavs presented the Austrian Government with proof of Perchitch's complicity in bombings, and the Austrian authorities expelled him, though rather reluctantly. Yugoslavia has since charged before the League of Nations that Hungary received him, gave him a passport in the name of "Emil Howarth" and allowed him to organize a training camp for terrorists on a farm six kilometers from the Croatian border. I was amused, when in Budapest a fortnight after the murder of King Alexander, to see a high Hungarian official solemnly note down Perchitch's real and passport names as if my mention of them had brought them to his attention for the first time.

It was only in April last that Hungary finally yielded to Yugoslavia's demands and broke up the camp. Apparently the inmates were not sent far away, for armed Croatian émigrés were boldly flaunting it at another Hungarian point close to the frontier even after the assassination.

### Macedonian Conspirators

Alexander's assassin, Georgieff, was actually a Macedonian, but that does not absolve the Croat terrorists from the charge of having organized the crime. Ante Pavelitch, after his flight from Yugoslavia, went to Sofia, then at daggers drawn with Belgrade, and had a great reception. He swore blood brotherhood with Ivan ("Vancha") Mihailoff, the all-powerful leader of the Macedonian terrorists, and from that day Macedonian and Croatian terrorists worked hand in hand against the Yugoslav régime.

The Macedonian group known as Imro (Internal Macedonian Revolutionary Organization) is one of the oldest in Europe. Until the Bulgarian military dictatorship tackled it eight months ago it seemed invincible. Formed in 1893 to fight the terror of the Turkish oppressor, it had a patriotic halo in the eyes of Macedonians and Bulgarians.

After the war a slice of Macedonia formerly Bulgarian was allotted to Yugoslavia. Its very name was obliterated by the new designation, "South Serbia," and the Serbs began a terrorizing "Serbianization" of the unwilling Macedonians, in the course of which 200,000 persons were driven into exile in Bulgaria. The Imro promptly took a new lease on life and got to work.

No Yugoslav frontier guard could keep out the Imro avengers. They picked off local Governors and military figures across the border. Their long arm reached to every corner of Europe, Todor Panitza, a Macedonian, "sold the pass" to the Communists. The hand of pretty Mencia Carmincia struck him dead in a Vienna theatre, and Mencia, acquitted as a "dying consumptive" by a sentimental Vienna jury, returned to Sofia to marry Vancha Mihailoff and to raise a healthy family for him. Mihailoff reigned until six months ago as head of a State within a State—the Imro.

In two Bulgarian Provinces the writ of the government did not rule; the law of Imro was supreme. Some Macedonian followers of General Protogeroff "sold the pass" to the Yugoslavs and began to take Yugoslav money, as Mihailoff took that of Fascist Italy. Two hundred Protogeroffists died at the sentence of Mihailoff. Protogeroff himself leading the list, within the ensuing four years.

Now that the Bulgarian dictatorship, desiring friendship with Yugoslavia, has apparently broken the Imro, Vancha and Mencia have fled to Turkey.

Terrorist assassinations in Europe since 1900 have removed fully thirty heads of States and politicians of the first rank. The "Fehme" murders of the German nationalist terror form a chapter in themselves. Considering all the obscure Socialists and Communists killed by the Nazis and the Nazis killed by members of other parties in the Nazi rise to power, Germany must easily have the post-war record for political assassinations.

Only Great Britain, Scandinavia, Holland, Belgium, France and Czechoslovakia, the remaining strongholds of democracy in Europe, have been virtually free from native terrorism of any kind.

\* \* \*

December 28, 1935

## FOUR FASCIST GROUPS IN YUGOSLAVIA UNITE

### 'People's Movement,' Headed by Dr. Lyotitch, Expected to Win Support of Yeftitch

Wireless to The New York Times

BELGRADE, Dec. 27—Another step toward consolidation of four individually weak Yugoslav Fascist movements, all of which demand a corporative State, was taken last night when the four united under the title of the Yugoslav People's Movement. They accepted the leadership of Dr. Demetrice Lyotitch, a former Minister of Justice.

The four groups are the Slovene Boyovniki (Yugoslav War Legion), the Yugoslav Action (Croat and Dalmatian Nationalist organizations), the Bosnian Zbor, or union, and the Serbian Peasant Movement, headed by Dr. Lyotitch.

Tomorrow the new Fascist party will ask the government for permission to carry on political activities. It is believed Premier Yeftitch intends to develop this movement and make it the backbone for a party of his own. His new Minister for Social Welfare, M. Marusitch, was the founder of one subgroup, the Boyovniki.

Like the Austrian Fascists the Yugoslav Fascists assert that they stand for "partial democracy," but actually their program is indistinguishable from that of pure Fascists.

\* \* \*

January 16, 1939

## CROATS BAR PARLIAMENT

### Deputies Refuse to Recognize Legality of New Body

Wireless to The New York Times

ZAGREB, Yugoslavia, Jan. 15—Under the Presidency of Dr. Vladimir Matchek, the Croat leader, the recently elected Croat members of the Skupshtina or Chamber of Deputies met today, as they did after the elections of 1935, and constituted themselves "the Croat National Representation."

They refused to recognize the legality of the new Parliament, which they said had been elected under an electoral law that permitted the police to coerce voters and allowed terror, corruption and false representation. The result, it was stated, was only a disguise for absolutism.

\* \* \*

February 21, 1939

## REVISION IS BARRED BY BALKAN PARLEY

*Rumania, Yugoslavia, Greece and Turkey in Talks Ban Discussion of Frontiers*

### COLDNESS TO RUSSIA SEEN

*Conference in Bucharest Is Expected to Consider Ways of Placating Bulgaria*

Wireless to The New York Times

BUCHAREST, Rumania, Feb. 20—The Balkan Entente conference opened here today with the participation of the four Foreign Ministers of the member States—Rumania, Yugoslavia, Greece and Turkey.

General John Metaxas, Greek dictator, speaking at a banquet here tonight, intimated that the entente members were determined to safeguard their territorial integrity and the inviolability of their frontiers and that they were convinced that the Salonika agreement concluded with Bulgaria would improve the relations between that State and the entente.

That statement was regarded as an indication that no revisionist demand by Bulgaria upon Hungary would be considered by the entente. The Black Sea pact envisaged by Turkey will not be discussed at this conference in view of General Metaxas' declaration that the outcome of the present meeting would not be the signing of any new commitments.

Yugoslavia, moreover, persists in opposing any agreement with Russia, while King Carol of Rumania, who refused to join the anti-Commintern pact, is reluctant to accept any combination in which the Soviet Union would join.

The conference will continue tomorrow, when it will consider de jure recognition of the Spanish Insurgent regime.

### Exclusion of Russia Seen

BUCHAREST, Feb. 20 (AP)—Informed quarters close to the four Balkan Entente Foreign Ministers meeting here said tonight the entente had decided to exclude Soviet Russia from immediate or direct participation in Balkan political affairs.

After the Ministers of Greece, Yugoslavia and Turkey had a preliminary discussion with Foreign Minister Grigore Gafencu of Rumania this afternoon, it was reported that plans for the formation of a Black Sea pact in which Russia was to have been a leading member had been dropped.

### Turkey Is Watched

Wireless to The New York Times

ISTANBUL, Turkey, Feb. 20—The Turkish press takes the occassion of the Balkan Entente meeting in Bucharest to voice its concern over the future of Balkan politics.

When the Balkan pact was signed it was realized that, while the interests of Rumania and Yugoslavia were primarily in Central Europe, Greece and Turkey were essentially Eastern European countries. This divergence of interests did not become conspicuous, however, until last year when events in Central Europe threatened to involve Rumania and Yugoslavia, while Greece and Turkey remained relatively unconcerned owing to their remoteness from the danger zone.

It is expected, therefore, that the positions of the four countries on their present problems will be defined at Bucharest. At the same time the Bulgarian question is likely to be discussed at some length. It is still hoped here that Bulgaria, which has now been freed from restrictions under the Treaty of Neuilly, will join the Balkan Entente, but it is realized some quid pro quo will be necessary.

The internal situation in Rumania and the recent Cabinet crisis in Yugoslavia have been giving Turkish statesmen some cause for anxiety. It is hoped here that Foreign Minister Sarajoglu's personal contacts at Bucharest will enable him to test the solidity of the ties linking the signatories of the Balkan pact and on his return give the Turkish Government the assurances held needed.

\* \* \*

February 22, 1939

## CAROL PRAISES WORK OF BALKAN ENTENTE

*Bucharest Conference Ends—Bulgaria May Join Group*

Wireless to The New York Times

BUCHAREST, Rumania, Feb. 21—The Balkan Entente conference here ended today. A communiqué will be issued tomorrow.

Tonight King Carol conversed at length with the delegates, to whom he expressed his satisfaction with the outcome of the conference.

De jure recognition of Generalissimo Francisco Franco's regime in Spain was accepted in principle, but it was left to the member States themselves—Rumania, Yugoslavia, Turkey and Greece—to choose what they considered a suitable moment to open official relations.

Rumania's reluctance immediately to recognize Burgos is ascribed to the fact that many Franco refugees are now harbored in the Rumanian legation in Madrid, which the Loyalists would refuse extraterritorial rights the moment Bucharest recognized Burgos, with disastrous consequences to those it is sheltering.

The conference abstained from proposing extreme measures against Bulgarian revisionism and refused to discuss similar Hungarian claims—on the ground that these problems did not affect all the member States.

The absence of Dr. Milan Stoyadinovitch, recently ousted as Yugoslav Premier, reportedly facilitated the negotiations.

The four Foreign Ministers stressed the value of the Balkan Entente, pointing out that the region formerly regarded as Europe's powder barrel was now constructively working for permanent peace.

Wireless to The New York Times

SOFIA, Bulgaria, Feb. 21—"Bulgarians will never allow foreign influence to interfere in the affairs of the Balkans, which can be arranged by a series of friendly pacts between the countries concerned." Premier George Kiosseivanoff told newspaper men today in his first definite statement on this country's foreign policy since Munich.

"I stand for a policy of 'Balkan countries for the Balkan peoples,' " he said.

"Our relations with the Balkan Entente are most friendly, and I am convinced our national problems can be solved among ourselves."

The Premier referred to Bulgaro-Turkish relations as particularly cordial, adding that Turkey might sponsor Bulgaria's admission to the Balkan Entente.

\* \* \*

April 3, 1939

## MATCHEK RECEIVES YUGOSLAV PREMIER

### *Formal Negotiations on Croat Demands Will Begin Today in Zagreb*

#### CONCESSIONS ARE LIKELY

*Cvetkovitch Has Full Power to Arrange an Understanding With United Opposition*

Wireless to The New York Times

ZAGREB, Yugoslavia, April 2—Premier Dragisha Cvetkovitch arrived in Zagreb this afternoon for the opening tomorrow of the often-postponed important conversations with Dr. Vladimir Matchek, the Croat leader.

Shortly after his arrival the Premier paid a courtesy call on Dr. Matchek who later returned the call at the City Hall, where the Premier is the guest of the Mayor. Both meetings were brief.

The Premier came here with full powers from Prince Paul, chief Regent, to negotiate a full understanding with the Croats and to make any concessions he deems necessary. Dr. Matchek will negotiate not only as the leader of the Croats but also, because of yesterday's full agreement between the Serb opposition and the Croat leaders, for the united Serb-Croat opposition.

In view of the obvious danger and difficulty of pursuing his "complete sovereignty" policy well-informed circles said tonight that Dr. Matchek was willing to make some concessions. The problems to be discussed include electoral reform and modification of the laws governing the press and political union.

\* \* \*

April 12, 1939

## BULGARIA DISSOLVES FASCIST PARTY; RUMANIA ASSURED ON DARDANELLES

### *Sofia Outlaws German-Aided Organization for Seeking the Overthrow of the Regime—Turkey Declares for Balkan Unity*

Wireless to The New York Times

SOFIA, Bulgaria, April 11—The Bulgarian Government ordered today the dissolution of the Bulgarian Nazi organization, which was supported by Germany. Although all political groups have been prohibited in Bulgaria for some time, this one escaped the ban owing to the impression that it was a patriotic association.

Recently, however, the Nazis had been actively campaigning for the overthrow of the regime. All government functionaries continuing their membership in the organization will be immediately dismissed.

Former Socialist Leader Pastouhoff, in an open letter today to Nicolas Muschanoff, President of Parliament, protested his plan to take part in his official capacity in the birthday festivities to be held in Germany for Chancellor Adolf Hitler on April 20, when the German leader will be 50 years old.

While Premier Dragisha Kiosseivanoff was receiving various diplomats, including the Soviet Chargé d'Affaires, other Cabinet members were still on vacation until tomorrow, when a Cabinet meeting will be held. Parliament has been convoked for Thursday.

In view of the international situation a latent Cabinet crisis will be overcome by means of one change—namely, the dropping of Spas Ganeff as Minister of Public Works and the replacement of him by M. Pecheff, Vice President of Parliament.

BUCHAREST, Rumania, April 11 (AP)—Diplomatic circles tonight indicated Turkey had granted Rumania's demand to open the Dardanelles, vital strait between the Aegean and Black Seas, for passage of military and other supplies to Rumania in case of war.

Seara, the mouthpiece of the Rumanian Press and Propaganda Department, gave the first hint of the full import of the conversations in Angora between the Turkish and Rumanian Foreign Ministers. It said friendship between Rumania and Turkey gave dynamic force to the Balkan Entente, which includes those two powers in addition to Greece and Yugoslavia.

It was pointed out by Seara that Rumania and Turkey had joint economic interests in peacetime and would cooperate in case of war to maintain each other's security. The propaganda mouthpiece declared the two nations loved peace but were ready to defend their independence with all their might.

### Carol-Boris Meeting Denied

Wireless to The New York Times

BUCHAREST, April 11—Wide rumors that a meeting between King Carol of Rumania and King Boris of Bulgaria was taking place were emphatically denied tonight in official quarters here, which said Carol was still resting at his Black Sea castle while Boris only today left his castle near Blovdib to return to Sofia, where he was expected tonight.

A meeting of the two Kings, however, is not entirely out of the question particularly since both rulers are the real directors of their countries' foreign policies and friendlier relations have existed between them since their meeting on the Danube in 1932.

While Foreign Minister Grigore Gafencu was busy conferring with various diplomats, M. Grazianu, Foreign Office Secretary, left here for Paris on a secret mission. It is believed the Foreign Minister wishes precise information before he makes his trip to Berlin on April 18 or 19.

M. Gafencu will not attend the Hitler birthday celebrations. Rumania will have three representatives—former Premier Alexander Vaida-Voevod and George Bratianu, who were privately invited, and M. Sidorovici, leader of a Rumanian youth organization. It is interesting that not a single representative of Alexander Cuza's anti-Semitic, party was invited.

### Gives Turkey's Position

Wireless to The New York Times

ISTANBUL, Turkey, April 11—Premier Refik Saydam after a declaration of Turkey's faith in herself, today received a unanimous vote of confidence for the new Turkish Government from the 389 Deputies in the Kamutay (National Assembly), in session at Angora.

Turkey, he said, was watching the heterogeneous development of the international situation with great attention and concern. He added:

"In the face of international troubles Turkey is maintaining and will continue to try to maintain her friendly relations with all powers, great and small. In these times, when 'ideas and interests conflict with such violence,' no ideology or passion of interests will make Turkey deviate from the path of peace.

"No act capable of imperiling the life or well-being of the Turkish nation will come first from your government unless our good-will and our sincere and friendly neutrality toward all States should be directly the object of an attempt at violation."

Premier Saydam emphasized that Turkey had given proof of her vigilance by taking measures against events that the Turkish nation might have to face.

"I am proud to say," he added, "that, thanks to her great army, Turkey is fully prepared to repulse any attack."

Istanbul newspapers reproduce without comment London news about negotiations for fresh guarantees for Greece and Turkey. Official circles are silent on the subject. Most of the newspapers take the view that the only measure that will now inspire confidence in the smaller countries is conscription in Great Britain.

What the Premier did not say was that Turkey considered that she occupied in the Balkan Entente what has become today a position of leadership. Her sympathies lie westward with Britain as a possible guarantor of her integrity; eastward, in conformity with the late President Kemal Ataturk's policies, she entertains cordial relations with Moscow.

### For Balkan Unity

On the other hand, her material interests are closely linked with Germany and Italy, especially the former, who is her best customer. In these conditions Turkey's leaders, while attaching due value to any British guarantee, seem convinced that the most important thing is that the Balkan countries show complete unity and cooperation.

This policy was patent at the recent Balkan Entente conference in Bucharest, in which Foreign Minister Shukru Saracoglu of Turkey played a leading part. Since then Premier George Kiosseivanoff of Bulgaria and Foreign Minister Grigore Gafencu of Rumania have come to this country successively to confer with him. In both cases, it is asserted, the outcome was satisfactory.

In the case of Rumania it is understood Angora will use its good offices in Moscow to improve relations between Rumania and the Soviet Union. In the case of Bulgaria the situation is less clear. It is believed there must be some quid pro quo if she is to be withdrawn from German and Italian influences, which are very strong dynastically, economically and otherwise.

Much faith is placed here in the Bulgarian Premier's cautious shrewdness, and it is believed he has seen eye-to-eye with Foreign Minister Saracoglu, so much so that Bulgaria's formal adherence to the Balkan Entente is considered possible in the relatively near future. Such adherence would be a great moral triumph for Turkey.

Of the two remaining entente members, Greece, because of her long seaboard and proximity to the Italian Dodecanes Islands and to Albania, naturally leans toward Britain and Turkey, while Yugoslavia presents a different problem because of her aversion to Moscow, but even that difficulty is not considered insuperable here.

The strategic key to the Balkans is the Dardanelles. The Montreux convention made Turkey the keeper of those straits. Therefore, it is argued here, Turkey is fully qualified to take the lead to insure Balkan unity.

\*  \*  \*

April 27, 1939

# BASIC AGREEMENT REACHED ON CROATS

### Matchek is to See Advisers Before Signing Yugoslav Autonomy Pact

Wireless to The New York Times

ZAGREB, Yugoslavia, April 26—The Croat problem was virtually settled today as a result of conversations here between Premier Dragisha Cvetkovitch and Dr. Vladimir Matchek, the Croat leader. It is probably the greatest political event since little Serbia after the World War became first the Kingdom of the Serbs, Croats and Slovenes and then Yugoslavia.

Details of the settlement are not known yet, but will probably be revealed in a communiqué. The accord, however, is known to be based on the federal idea, which a new coalition Cabinet will work out.

There will be a general feeling of relief throughout Yugoslavia, for the Croat problem had complicated and embittered every national issue during the past twenty years.

It is understood the Croats will obtain considerable concessions in that their future autonomous region will include not only Croatia proper but also Slovenia and Dalmatia.

### Bosnia Is Kept Intact

On the other hand, the proposal to divide Bosnia has been abandoned. That province will become an autonomous entity, as will also Serbia, of course. All will enjoy a large measure of administrative autonomy, but always within the framework of the present kingdom and the present Constitution, which dates from 1931. In point of fact this constitution contains the main lines of a federal kingdom, but the clauses relating to this have hitherto remained a dead letter.

It is not concealed that there will have to be much negotiating yet before the new system is applied. This will be the task of the new Cabinet, which will presumably continue to be headed by Premier Cvetkovitch.

It is expected such a Cabinet will be formed Friday. Alexander Cincar-Markovitch is likely to retain the Foreign Affairs portfolio. Other members will include representatives of the present Government party, the Croat Peasant party and the Old Serbian Opposition. It will thus represent Serb, Croat, Slovene and Moslem interests.

### Provinces to Have Cabinets

Control of foreign affairs, national defense and national finance will be concentrated mainly in Belgrade, but each autonomous province will have a sort of Cabinet of its own with its Ministers of Finance, Commerce, Education and Social Welfare. One knotty problem will be delimitation of the respective powers and authority of the provincial Ministers of Finance and the Federal Minister of Finance.

For the present there is no question of creating regional Diets, as this would necessitate modification of the Constitu-

NEW YUGOSLAV SET-UP: Under an agreement virtually completed yesterday Croatia is to enjoy autonomy, with Slovenia and Dalmatia included in the Croats' region. Serbia will form another autonomous entity and Bosnia will constitute a third.

tion. It is understood this matter will be discussed when King Peter comes of age.

Today's accord represents a compromise, both Premier Cvetkovitch and Dr. Matchek having approached the conference table in a statesmanlike mood with willingness to make reasonable concessions. Nor must Regent Paul's part be overlooked, for behind the scenes he has constantly acted as conciliator.

The tenseness of the European situation was also a factor in facilitating an agreement. There is an old Slav proverb: "If thou knowest not how to be thy brother's brother, thou deservest thy enemy as overlord." The negotiators doubtless had it in mind during their conversations.

### Matchek Defers Signing

ZAGREB, Yugoslavia, April 26 (AP)—Dr. Vladimir Matchek, Croat leader, refused today to sign an agreement with the government until the question has been referred Sunday to the Croat Assembly.

The Assembly is composed of forty Croats who won district majorities in elections last December but did not get seats, because Yugoslav election laws provide that the party winning a bare majority automatically gets two-thirds of the seats in Parliament. The Croats then formed an extralegal

Assembly which has served as a virtual Cabinet for Dr. Matchek in his fight for Croat autonomy.

The impression prevailed that Dr. Matchek and Premier Cvetkovitch had agreed in principle, although Dr. Matchek refused to bind the Croat party without reference to his advisers.

\*   \*   \*

April 28, 1939

## UNEASY YUGOSLAVIA

Italy on the west; Germany, Hungary and Rumania on the north; Rumania and Bulgaria on the east; Greece on the south—thus lies uneasy unhappy Yugoslavia. Serbs, Croats. Slovenians: with a "King" of less than 16 years, 14,000,000 of population, 95,000 square miles. After twenty years of discord these children of the Slavic race have reached an agreement whereby Croatia is to enjoy autonomy, with Slovema and Dalmatia included. Bosnia and Serbia are also to be autonomous. For many centuries the northern and southern portions of the elements which compose this country have been at odds. The Croats, then Austrians, fought for Austria in the war; the Serbians, for the Allies.

But external menace has now brought the quarreling elements into a degree of unity hitherto unattained. Together, they are threatened in many directions. Italy sees in the Dalmatian coast a remnant of the glories of ancient Venice. Bulgaria and Hungary have definite ideas of frontier revisions. And in the north sits Germany, which can at any time, have the deciding voice in any reorganization of or control over the country. Germany might, conceivably, one day wish to pass that way to the Adriatic. There are here, however, no sons of the Fatherland to be redeemed and Germany may have at present all the Slavs on her hands that she cares to have. Yugoslavia is now fairly united as regards externals, but no people in Europe is faced by more difficulties in the preservation of national entity.

\*   \*   \*

June 29, 1939

## RUMANIAN OUTLAY ON ARMS STRESSED

―――――――――

*Calinescu Tells the Chamber That the Nation's Frontiers Will Remain 'Immovable'*

**VOICES HOPES FOR PEACE**

*But Declares Minority Issue is an Internal Matter, Not a Territorial One*

―――――――――

Wireless to The New York Times

BUCHAREST, Rumania, June 28—In the Chamber of Deputies today Premier Armand Calinescu made his scheduled statement on domestic and foreign policy. It was a long, comprehensive, businesslike exposition of the present situation.

The Premier reiterated that Rumania did not claim anything beyond her frontiers and that her chief concern was the maintenance of peace.

M. Calinescu insisted that Rumania's partial mobilization during the March crisis had been neither a threat nor a provocation, but a precaution. He indicated that this partial mobilization had enabled the general staff to remedy certain deficiencies and that consequently the country today stood ready to defend its frontiers with all its resources in men and material.

From 1920 to February, 1938, he continued, Rumania spent 25,000,000,000 leu on armaments; between February, 1938, and February, 1939, 11,000,000,000 leu, and from the latter date to the present time another 25,000,000,000—an aggregate of 61,000,000,000 leu, of which about 40 per cent had been spent in the last four months [the leu is currently quoted at .72 cents].

The Premier stressed that the minority question remained an internal matter for Rumania and that in no case could it become a territorial problem.

In the Senate today Professor Nicolas Iorga made an appeal for a return to parliamentary government. Rumania, he said, "has never been and never will be a totalitarian State."

BUCHAREST, Rumania, June 28 (AP)—Declaring that Rumania was rearming on an unprecedented scale, Premier Armand Calinescu told the Chamber of Deputies today that large-scale fortifications were being built on the nation's borders, which Hungary and Bulgaria want to alter.

"Our frontiers will remain immovable as long as there remains a single Rumanian soldier able to hold a rifle in his hand," he declared.

\*   \*   \*

August 2, 1939

## FIREWORKS IN CROATIA

Not for the first time has Dr. Vladimir Matchek, Croat leader, threatened secession from the kingdom of Yugoslavia unless Croat demands for home rule are met by the Belgrade Government. But yesterday he indulged in a little extra dramatics in choosing for his latest threat the twenty-fifth anniversary of the general mobilization of 1914, the day on which the war between Austria and Serbia became a general war. No doubt he meant to add a few new shivers to the universal state of alarm by an anniversary reminder that the break-up of a state which he ominously compared to Czecho-Slovakia would probably usher in another world war.

For a long time the peasant leader, successor of the murdered Raditch, has been dropping dark hints that the Croats might find powerful support abroad for their claims to autonomy. Yesterday he mentioned Germany by name, but obviously with the idea of brandishing a club over the Serbs rather than with any thought of being taken at his word.

Negotiations for a long overdue settlement of the Croatian question have been going on for months between Matchek and the Yugoslav Premier, and disappointment that victory could not be announced at Kupinec, as was expected, was evidently responsible for the fireworks. This shrewd and intensely nationalistic Croat would be the last to exchange his right to explode for the lot of Slavs under German "protection," whether ostensibly invoked, as in Slovakia, or imperiously imposed, as in Bohemia-Moravia. Croatia, moreover, is separated from the German border by the province of Slovenia and impinges on Italy. Matchek is fully aware what the Italian reaction would be to a move to plant Germany on the eastern coast of the Adriatic.

He is fairly safe in swinging a club to bring Belgrade to terms. But his threat illuminates the ambiguous attitude of Yugoslavia in the line-up of opposing fronts. The Yugoslavs have insisted that they intend to remain neutral in the next conflict, and their position is only partly explained by the fact that they were the first battlefield in 1914 and are now wedged between the two horns of the Axis. Paralyzed by internal division, they reveal the real source of Hitler's power to terrify the Governments of Southeastern Europe. It is not his strength or Nazi dynamism so much as the inner weakness of the states he threatens.

\* \* \*

August 26, 1939

## YUGOSLAVIA SEEKS 4 CROAT MINISTERS

*Foreign Office Under Secretary Also Won by Matchek in Revision of Cabinet*

**COUNCIL APPROVES PACT**

*Many Changes Are Necessary in Carrying Out Autonomy for Enlarged Province*

Wireless to The New York Times

BELGRADE, Yugoslavia, Aug. 25—The new Cvetkovitch Cabinet, which will include four Croat Ministers and a Croat Under-Secretary for Foreign Affairs, is expected to be completed tomorrow night or Sunday morning. The revision meets the terms of the agreement between the government and the Croats.

The Croats have always manifested leanings toward the democracies but nevertheless have accepted a policy of strict neutrality for Yugoslavia, which policy is believed to have been fortified by the realignment of European powers after the conclusion of the German-Soviet non-aggression pact.

The new Cabinet became necessary when Premier Dragisha Cvetkovitch and his Ministers resigned on the definite conclusion of the Serb-Croat agreement yesterday when the Premier and Dr. Vladimir Matchek, Croat leader, conferred with Prince Paul, Chief Regent at Bled. M. Cvetkovitch was then requested by the Regent to form a new Cabinet. It is doubted that Dr. Matchek will become vice premier.

The text of the new accord has not been published but it is believed it gives wide autonomy in local affairs for the enlarged Province of Croatia. Foreign affairs and national defense will continue to be directed by Belgrade.

### Many Changes Are Necessary

BELGRADE, Aug. 25 (AP)—Premier Dragisha Cvetkovitch hurried to Belgrade today after his settlement with the Croat leader, Dr. Vladimir Matchek, had been approved by the Regency Council, and informed governmental circles of the new composition of his administration. He returned to Bled later to consult again with Regent Prince Paul.

Before Croatian home rule aims are realized many far-reaching changes must be put into effect, but it is expected they will be worked out in a new spirit of harmony.

The hero of his 5,000,000 followers is Dr. Matchek, who only a few weeks ago declared that the "Belgrade clique" must accept his idea of a United States of Yugoslavia, or Croatia would be forced to secede.

\* \* \*

August 26, 1939

## YUGOSLAVS REGAIN DEMOCRATIC RULE

*Decrees Given Out With Croat Accord Bring Freedom and Unity Against Pressure*

Wireless to The New York Times

BELGRADE, Yugoslavia, Aug. 26—Together with the details of the Serbo-Croat accord, a number of decrees were promulgated today which in effect tend to abrogate the dictatorial regime established by the late King Alexander in January, 1929. Briefly put, Yugoslavia rejoins the ranks of the parliamentary democracies.

Coming at the present juncture, this decision may have far-reaching consequences. At a time when German propaganda asserts that the Reich has Yugoslavia on its side, political circles here interpret these decrees as strengthening the country's unity and its capacity of resistance against any sort of foreign pressure.

The terms of the Serbo-Croat accord had been indicated and consequently caused no surprise. But no one had an inkling that the accord would be merely one of several decrees reestablishing a democratic form of government.

### Freedom of Press

These decrees comprise a restoration of freedom of the press and of association. This is tantamount to the removal of previous restrictions on political parties. The decrees, moreover, are supplemented by a new electoral law; both houses of Parliament are dissolved and their renewal will be conducted under new conditions.

As was expected, the new Croat province comprises the districts of Save and of the coast, together with several counties of the Dubrovnik district.

It will have its own Parliament, which will deal with cultural and economic matters, and will enjoy a certain measure of financial autonomy. The security of the State and the control of means of communication remain the privilege of the central authority.

The federal idea, which the Croats have been advocating for years, seems to have been accepted since the new decrees foreshadow the creation of other autonomous provinces, beginning with Slovenia.

Dr. Dusan Subutitch, son-in-law of the Croat leader Vladimir Matchek, will be the first Governor of autonomous Croatia.

The formation of a new Cabinet by Premier Dragisha Cvetkovitch was also announced today. It will have Dr. Matchek as Vice Premier and five other Croats holding portfolios. It is described as a "National Union Cabinet," which designation also has importance in the present tense European situation.

That the new government is really one of union is proved by the fact that it includes several members of the former Serb Opposition party.

Alexander Cincar-Markovitch retains the foreign affairs portfolio.

The news was received with great satisfaction throughout the country, both on the Serb and Croat sides. Much credit was given to Prince Paul, Chief Regent, for his patient and statesmanlike handling of a very delicate situation which on several occasions seemed likely to end in a deadlock.

Both Premier Cvetkovitch and Dr. Matchek received the grand cordon of the White Eagle order.

\* \* \*

**September 23, 1939**

## SCORES EXECUTED IN RUMANIAN PLOT

*Government Acts to Wipe Out Entire Iron Guard
After Murder of Premier*

By EUGEN KOVACS
Special Cable to The New York Times

BUCHAREST, Rumania, Sept. 22—Those remnants of the Iron Guard who had survived until today in concentration camps were executed wholesale by the Rumanian Government after yesterday's assassination of Premier Armand Calinescu by members of the outlawed fascist organization.

At least 100 and perhaps as many as 200 were killed today. It is believed that as many more face death tomorrow.

[The known dead numbered 161 last night, The United Press reported.]

The government is determined that this time there will be no Iron Guard left to cause trouble. But, unfortunately for the

success of this aim, the "men higher up" who presumably are Germans, have fled the country.

Before being sentenced, M. Calinescu's assassins revealed to the public prosecutor all details of the organization of the plot. As in all previous cases, the Iron Guards admitted their guilt with bravado, but gave no names of accomplices. Some of those who took part in yesterday's plot have not yet been captured.

It was learned that their leader was a lawyer named Dumitrescu. On Monday he met a student named Cesare Popescu who revealed that he and four other students from Ploesti had organized a plot to kill the Premier.

Details of the plot were discussed and the place where it would be carried out inspected. Dumitrescu took over command of the group. He was the man who paid all expenses and bought the car used in the murder.

Only one question still is unanswered—where did Dumitrescu obtain the money to defray the expenses? He had been an unemployed refugee since last February. Nevertheless, he spent more than 40,000 lei on the plot, a large sum in Rumania.

The police now are searching throughout the nation for the accomplices who supplied money for the murder. It is clear that despite the severe measures against the Iron Guard many members still are active and there is an organization obtaining money from some secret source.

The financiers of the plot, who undoubtedly are in contact with Iron Guards, are supposed to have fled from Rumania.

Recently important Rumanian personages have received postcard photographs showing a group of well-known Iron Guards at a seaside resort. On the back of the cards was written, "Don't forget we are still alive." These postcards came from Swinemuende, Germany.

### Thousands View Bodies

Until tonight the bodies of the assassins lay in the street where they killed M. Calinescu and where they themselves were executed. Scores of thousands of citizens came during the day to view the bodies. Beside them was a plaque on which was written in large letters: "From now on this will be the fate of all murderers. They were traitors."

An official communiqué says that during last night all the assassins, their accomplices and instigators were executed. In many parts of the country, Iron Guards who were connected in some way with Dumitrescu were also shot in public and their dead bodies exposed. In Ploesti two Iron Guards were shot and their bodies placed at the foot of the Goga monument.

All Iron Guards who were taken to concentration camps a year ago have been executed—between 100 and 200. Among them was the father of Corneliu Zelea Codreanu, Iron Guard leader who was shot last year with thirteen of his lieutenants.

The body of the Premier lay in state at the Atheneum today. Theatres, movies and music in public places have been forbidden. The Bucharest Stock Exchange closed today and will remain closed tomorrow. Officially, it was stated this measure was taken because the funeral service for M. Calinescu will occur during the hours in which the exchange normally would be open. The whole country is quiet, it was declared authoritatively.

It was learned that M. Calinescu was to have attended a dinner last night to be given by the United States Minister in Bucharest in honor of Anthony J. Drexel Biddle Jr., United States Ambassador to Poland.

[Mr. Biddle, accompanied by several members of his staff and Leon Noel, French Ambassador to Poland, left for Paris today, according to The United Press.]

### Frontiers Watched Anxiously

BUCHAREST, Rumania, Sept. 22 (AP)—The new government, headed by three generals, made full use of King Carol's dictatorial powers today to stamp out what had been feared was a widespread revolt after the assassination of Premier Calinescu.

Although the government declared the crisis was purely domestic, Rumanians nervously watched the frontiers. Troops and frontier guards were on the alert, heavily reinforced. Pedestrians were searched, motorists halted for identification.

Rumanians particularly watched the activities of Germany and Russia. Germany, they knew, wants Rumanian oil, and part of Rumania is former Russian territory. Troops of both nations were across the border in Poland.

All through last night men, women and children came to the scene of the assassination, where the bodies of the killers still lay, and today the stream of humanity continued. Around the roped-off, oblong area, under a dreary sky, hawkers were selling cakes and beer to a wide-eyed stream of Rumanians come to see an object lesson in swift Balkan punishment.

Meanwhile, the slain Premier lay in state after a mourning procession through the city's streets. King Carol headed the government and military officials who accompanied M. Calinescu's widow and son to the Atheneum. Houses and street lamps in the crowded thoroughfares through which the procession passed were draped with black crepe.

M. Calinescu's body was placed on a raised dais in an open coffin, draped in a Rumanian flag. There was a single spray of red flowers. Mourners passed by the coffin today in a steady stream, the line extending far into the street. Guarding the coffin was an honor guard of the King's Regiment; at the foot stood a black-robed Orthodox priest.

The funeral oration will be given Sunday morning, when the body will be taken to Arges for burial.

### Thousands Arrested

BUCHAREST, Rumania, Sept. 22 (UP)—The known number of Iron Guardists executed during the twenty-four-hour period of reprisals since the killing of Premier Calinescu stood tonight at 161. Guardist leaders and sub-leaders still are being weeded out from thousands of men seized in wholesale arrests.

### Instigated by Nazis, London Hears

Special Cable to The New York Times

LONDON, Sept. 22—Reports reaching representatives of Balkan countries here indicate Premier Calinescu was slain by Iron Guards who were smuggled back into Rumania from Germany ten days ago to carry out the assassination plot coincidentally with the expected arrival of Nazi troops on the frontier between Poland and King Carol's realm.

The plan was to throw Rumania into turmoil and provide Nazi agents with an opportunity for seizing power in key centers, apparently with the aim of crippling the country's resistance to invasion, it was said in diplomatic circles here.

The arrival of Russian troops prevented the German Armies from reaching the frontier, but it was said the assassins, having no contrary orders, went ahead with the killing anyway. These sources said the assassination was rendered easier because the Premier, learning of the Nazi plot to foment general disorders, sent all available police, including his own bodyguard, to the border to investigate and take the necessary counter steps.

[The British Broadcasting Company reports that the Rumanian Embassy in Athens has issued a call to all Rumanians of military age in Greece to return for service.]

### Germany Expresses Sympathy

BERLIN, Sept. 22 (UP)—The German Minister in Bucharest, Dr. Wilhelm Fabricius, today was instructed to express the "deepest sympathy" of the German Government in connection with the assassination of Premier Calinescu.

Baron Ernest von Weizsaecker, State Secretary and the chief Protocol Minister of the Foreign Office, called upon the Rumanian Minister here, Radu Crutzescu, and extended the condolence of Foreign Minister Joachim von Ribbentrop.

### Rumania Heeds Nazi Requests

BERLIN, Sept. 22 (AP)—It was disclosed tonight that the interning of Polish military officers and restrictions placed on Polish Government officials by Rumania were made at the request of Germany.

It was said Germans had desired to prevent the Poles from going to France and there operating or agitating against Germany.

Bank of Poland gold also was said to be blocked in Rumania, whose geographic position was said to have made her lean over backward to observe neutrality and to promise continued delivery of raw materials.

### Soviet-German Demand Reported

LONDON, Saturday, Sept. 23 (UP)—The Daily Mail said today that, according to reports reaching London, Germany and Russia jointly are sending a demarche to Rumania demanding that members of the Polish Government be interned. Refusal would be regarded as contravention of neutrality, it was said.

Consequently, according to the report, armed intervention by Germany and Russia automatically would become necessary.

\* \* \*

October 25, 1939

## LIQUOR A CROAT PROBLEM

*Germans Can't Buy Plums So They Are Turned Into Brandy*

By Telephone to The New York Times

ZAGREB, Yugoslavia, Oct. 24—Too much hard liquor has been the cause of a national headache in Yugoslavia's northern province of Croatia, which received partial autonomy last August.

This year Croatia had the best plum crop in half a century. At the same time, the German fruit importing market collapsed because of the war. The practical Croat peasants therefore used up most of the crop in brewing the powerful national drink, schlivovitza.

The price of this hard-hitting plum brandy fell to 16 cents a gallon, and there is a shortage of barrels and bottles. The result has been a mighty effort to drink up the surplus.

During the Autumn there have been many fights, some twenty murders and the mutiny of 3,000 reservists.

\* \* \*

November 27, 1939

## BALKAN WOMEN DEMAND VOTES

By Telephone to The New York Times

BELGRADE, Yugoslavia, Nov. 26—Balkan women suffragettes met today demanding votes in the forthcoming Parliamentary elections. A new electoral law is being prepared by the same committee of experts who drew up the successful accord between the Croat and Belgrade authorities last August.

# PART V

# WORLD WAR II, 1939–1944

## ITALY HASTENS TO UTILIZE ALBANIA'S ASSETS

### *Former Kingdom Seen As Bridgehead*

By HERBERT L. MATTHEWS
Wireless to The New York Times

ROME, June 24—Italy is losing no time in making of Albania as much a political, military and economic asset as possible. Ethiopia can be taken and consolidated slowly, for it is a huge morsel to swallow and its strategic importance in the European struggle is small. Albania, on the other hand, not only would play a great role in a future war but already counts for much in the struggle for power now going on.

The political organization of Albania has been just about completed under the energetic direction of Achilie Starace. The constitutional status was peremptorily settled on June 3 with a statute of fifty-four articles that effectively brought the Albanian governmental machinery under Rome's direction. On the same day the Albanian diplomatic services were taken over, and a week before that a customs union brought the little Balkan country's foreign trade into Italy's economic empire.

### Strengthening the Army

It remained only to absorb what military forces there were in Albania and then to make the new kingdom into the spearhead of Italian strength in the Balkans. That too is being accomplished in record time. First, the Albanian armed forces were told to ask to be incorporated in the Italian forces. This they did on May 29, and a few days later a delegation came to Rome, where King Victor Emmanuel graciously consented to grant their request.

Last week the Italian general staff announced the creation in Albania of two army corps, totaling about 60,000 men. Meanwhile those soldiers with their material had already been sent to Albania, where they were reported to be concentrated chiefly on the Greek border, much to the alarm of Athens. Now Marshal Badoglio has gone over to supervise the execution of plans which will make Albania into a powerful Italian "bridgehead across the Adriatic." Eight hundred million lire have been appropriated to build new roads, and Badoglio is going to say where they will be laid—which means that they are to be strategic roads.

So already Italy's military strength has been enormously enhanced by the absorption of Albania. It bids fair to make Rome the dominant military power in the Balkans, not only against the "democratic encirclers" but also vis-a-vis her axis partner, Germany.

All of that means a further financial drain, but it is hoped that by developing Albania's economic resources Italy will be repaid for her investment.

Albania is a poor country but it has far greater possibilities than its previous exploitation would indicate. Forests cover 36 per cent of the area, which means great scope for a lumber industry. The chief crop is Indian corn, of which about 100,000 tons annually are produced. Wheat amounts to about half that, while there are also some barley, oats and rice. Albania grows tobacco of high quality.

### Other Resources

One of the greatest riches is cattle, and hence skins and cheese. There are extensive mineral resources, particularly of bitumen, lignite and oil. Oil is fairly abundant, and there now are thirteen concessions, with Italians having the largest share. Needless to say, Italy's desperate need for oil will induce her to get the maximum yield in the coming years. It is estimated that 300,000 tons annually will be extracted.

Finally, there is much potential water-power, and the Italians are certainly going to develop it for irrigation as well as for power.

A first appropriation of 1,200,000,000 lire already has been made to develop Albania's economic resources, and there will be more coming. Considering that it is less than three months since Italy took over Albania, one cannot say that any time has been lost.

*   *   *

## BALKANS DISCUSS CHANCES OF PEACE

### *Press Studies Peril of War's Spreading—Soviet 'Menace' to Rumania Is Cited*

### ITALY CONTINUES ACTIVITY

### *Still Seeks Tie With Hungary and Yugoslavia—No Date Set for Entente Parley*

By C. L. SULZBERGER
Special Cable to The New York Times

BELGRADE, Yugoslavia, Dec. 30—The press of Central and Southeastern Europe is replete with speculations about the impending meeting of the Foreign Ministers of the four countries belonging to the Balkan Entente—Rumania, Yugoslavia, Greece and Turkey.

According to dispatches published in Prague and one in the Yugoslav papers, the conference would be held on Jan. 7. The Bulgarian press believes it will occur on Jan. 3.

How this report got started is not clear. The four Foreign Ministers meet traditionally each February and probably the locale of the next get-together will be Belgrade. But it is denied here that any January sessions are contemplated. Indeed, it is said in some quarters that because of the international situation the usual conference may be postponed.

It is pointed out that the first half of January is dedicated to the celebration of the orthodox Christmas and New Year's fetes observed by the Serbian Church and there is not the slightest indication that such a diplomatic conference is planned during the holiday season.

Under the terms of the Balkan pact the four Foreign Ministers are bound to confer annually but no set date is specified. February merely happens to be the custom. Grigore Gafencu, Rumanian Foreign Minister, this year holds the rotating Presidency and it will be up to him to convoke the Assembly. In Bucharest it was said tonight that no plans as yet have been made.

### Russian Threat Studied

There is no use in speculating on what the meeting will do if it is held. Obviously, the most imminent problems are those reflections of war which threaten to infringe upon Balkan peace. Number one in urgency is the possibility of a Russian threat against Rumania.

Under the terms of the pact the members are not bound to give military help to each other in case of attack by a non-Balkan power, but they are pledged to act against any Balkan nation which would throw in its lot with an aggressor. Put bluntly, this means that if Bulgaria moves against any Entente member, either alone or in concert with a non-Balkan power, the Entente will attack Bulgaria.

Bulgaria has never made any bones about realizing the purpose of the Entente, which, in this peninsula, operates in the way the Little Entente was supposed to operate against Hungary. Today's Sofia press seized the occasion of the rumored meeting to clarify once more Bulgaria's position.

In effect, the newspapers said that Bulgaria regards the pact as an instrument made against her and that she could only join a fuller Balkan bloc after her revisionist claims are satisfied. They suggest that there are no differences to settle, but Rumania for one, and Greece for another, hold radically opposite views. Bulgaria wants the Southern Dobruja Province from Rumania and a Mediterranean outlet through Thrace from Greece. She also has small claims against Yugoslavia.

Rumania would be inclined to negotiate the Dobruja question if all the members of the Entente were disposed to discuss the general satisfaction of Bulgarian claims on a based compromise. This would surely be the main topic of any meeting of the four Foreign Ministers.

### Diplomats Are Active

Meantime there are signs that the hubble-bubble of Balkan diplomatic activity continues in full force. Basil Stoica, Rumania's Minister to Turkey, returned to Bucharest yesterday. On the way he stopped off at Sofia and talked with Premier George Kiosseivanoff. Shortly after his visit the Yugoslav and Greek Ministers saw M. Kiosseivanoff.

At the same time Italy appears once more to be launching new trial balloons in this region. Thanks to Italian intervention, further negotiations regarding the Hungarian minority in Rumania were started. This time, Premier George Tatarescu was talking with the Transylvanian leaders instead of M. Gafencu, who was recently involved, in a sharp exchange with Hungary's Foreign Minister, Count Stephen Csaky.

It was also indicated that Rome's effort to build some sort of accord between Hungary, Italy and Yugoslavia was still going on. It was learned that Count Csaky will spend a ten-day vacation in Italy early in January. Although he is going to Cortina d'Ampezzo ostensibly for a rest, it is more than likely that he will see some Fascist officials. Count Csaky is a personal friend of Premier Benito Mussolini and Count Ciano, Italy's Foreign Minister.

Finally, Hungary is doing all she can to win Yugoslav sympathy, although she entertains little hope that Yugoslavia will desert the Balkan Entente and Rumania for a three-country Adriatic pact.

The well-known Budapest paper, Pester Lloyd, will soon devote a special issue to Yugoslavia.

\*    \*    \*

June 27, 1940

## BALKAN DIVISION BY AXIS REPORTED

*Rumanians Say Germany Will Rule Them, Poland, Hungary—*
*Turks Not to Enter War*

Wireless to The New York Times

BUCHAREST, Rumania, June 26—Germany and Italy are reported to have reached an agreement by which Slovakia, Hungary, Poland and Rumania will be placed under German influence and Yugoslavia, Greece and Bulgaria will be under Italian influence, according to Rumanian political leaders who arrived today from Berlin, where they conferred with prominent German officials.

They said all territorial claims of the Balkan countries and Hungary would be settled immediately. Bulgaria will receive territories from Rumania and Yugoslavia, they predicted, while Hungary's claims on Rumania will be satisfied only in a small degree.

Germany intends to establish peace in Eastern and Southern Europe for at least fifty years, it was stated.

It is evident the Germans and Italians will try to liquidate all French and British interests in this sector and will adapt the whole territory to their own economic needs.

The same circles said Germany intended to establish an independent Ukraine. Bukowinian-Ukrainian circles say the Ukrainians in Russian-occupied Polish Ukraine are preparing for political action.

The new Rumanian party has begun organization work. An order signed by the Chief of the General Staff today grants permission to all Rumanians more than 23 years old to apply for membership. Minorities wishing admittance will be registered separately, but Jews will not be admitted.

### Report Rumanian-Soviet Clash

BUCHAREST, Rumania (Thursday), June 27 (AP)—The Rumanian airlines today suspended all commercial service from Bucharest to Cernauti, Jassy, Cetatia and other Bessarabian cities today following a report from Cernauti that four Russian machines had been fired on near there, and one had been shot down. Others were said to have dropped bombs on a near-by village.

Bessarabia, Rumania's eastern province, formerly was ruled by Russia, but broke off and joined Rumania after the World War.

The Soviet Minister, Arkady I. Lavrentieff, who was recently sent to Rumania from Bulgaria in a move interpreted as an effort to strengthen relations between Bucharest and Moscow, still has not been received officially. He had asked for an immediate audience, but two tentative dates have been postponed.

That something may have gone wrong with King Carol's formation of a new totalitarian party to swing Rumania more into line with the Axis powers was seen in the announcement by Jon Mikhailache, close friend of Juliu Maniu, the leader of the National Peasants' party, that he was quitting his new post of Royal Councilor and retiring to private life. There was no public explanation of his decision, however.

The winning of M. Mikhailache was regarded as a great success at the time for the policy of internal unity.

The Rumanian maritime service announced today that Rumanian ships, held in their Black Sea ports for several weeks because of the European war, had resumed Mediterranean sailings.

### Turks Remain Aloof

ANKARA, Turkey, June 26 (AP)—Premier Refik Saydam of Turkey told Parliament tonight that his government has definitely decided not to enter the war.

Turkey, which once considered herself a non-belligerent ally of Great Britain and France, however, is "alertly continuing defense preparations," the Premier said.

The address, which was the first official announcement of Turkish policy since Italy entered the conflict, came amid grave concern over the future of French-protected Syria and the possibility of a Bulgarian attack on Turkey from the north.

"Our position, devoid of any provocation, is a guarantee of our own and our neighbors' peace," the Premier said.

He sought to justify Turkey's refusal to go to war on the side of the Allies when Italy entered the conflict by citing the section of the mutual assistance pact with Britain and France that stipulated that Turkey was required to take no action that would bring her into conflict with Soviet Russia.

Thus, Premier Saydam indicated that Moscow had told Turkey that Russia would regard Turkish entry into the war as a hostile act.

Foreign diplomats, however, believe that the French collapse was the real reason for Turkey's refusal to go to war.

ISTANBUL, Turkey, June 26 (UP)—Bulgarian press reports received here said that Vyacheslaff M. Molotoff, Soviet Premier and Foreign Commissar, had told Rumanian and Turkish Ambassadors that the time was ripe for negotiations on outstanding problems between Russia and those countries.

Turks interpreted the report to mean that Russia was ready to receive a Turkish delegation when the pro-British members of the Cabinet had been removed.

LONDON, June 26 (AP)—An agreement between Turkey and Iraq for the joint defense of Iraq and French-mandated Syria in collaboration with Great Britain was concluded today at Ankara, Exchange Telegraph [British news agency] reported today in a dispatch from Istanbul.

The accord was the fruit of consultations between the Iraq Ministers of Foreign Affairs and Justice, now in Ankara, and Turkish Cabinet members.

Since France surrendered to the Axis powers, both Iraq, which maintains close treaty relations with Britain, and Turkey, which had mutual assistance pacts with France and Britain, have shown increasing anxiety lest Syria become a battleground.

The Turks have feared that Italy might attempt to succeed France as the occupying power in Syria and make it a base for further expansion in the Near East.

\* \* \*

June 28, 1940

# BUKOVINA SLICED

*Part of Province, Ports on Black Sea and the Danube Also Ceded*

### HUNGARY IS WATCHED

*Carol Prepares to Resist Blow From That Nation—Will Meet Russians*

By The Associated Press

BUCHAREST, Rumania, Friday, June 28—Rumania bowed last night to a Soviet demand for great areas of her territory and moved nearly 2,000,000 men into Transylvania to meet an expected Hungarian attempt to get that province.

Despite earlier reports that Red troops already were on the march, it was disclosed late last night that Russia had agreed to hold back from the actual occupation of the ceded areas—Bessarabia and Northern Bukovina—until the last details of the cessions had been worked out. Diplomats labored at that

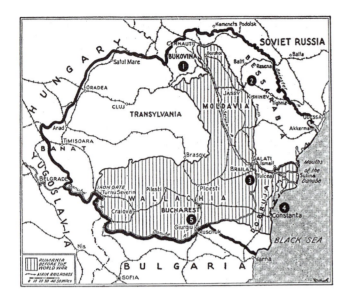

**RUMANIA FACES PARTITION AS RUSSIA MAKES DEMANDS**

In compliance with a Moscow ultimatum, Bucharest is understood to have agreed to surrender two northern districts of Bukovina (1) and the province of Bessarabia (2) and to have accepted Soviet supervision of the important Danubian ports of Galati, Braila and Tulcea (3)—one dispatch included Giurgiu (5) also. Another Russian demand was said to be for a naval base at Constanta (4). To block an expected Hungarian move to recover Transylvania, Rumania was declared to have moved troops to the Hugarian border. Bulgaria, southern neighbor of Rumania, is desirous of regaining Southern Dobruja which was lost after the World War.

task. It is expected to be completed today. Soviet troops then would cross the frontier.

[An authoritative diplomatic source in London said early today that Rumania had yielded to Russia on the cession of Bessarabia and Northern Bukovina and that King Carol had asked a conference with the Russians to bid for Russian aid in case of attacks by Hungary and Bulgaria, which also claim Rumanian territory, according to a dispatch to The New York Times.]

The capital was quiet. The officially censored press still was not permitted to publish a word of the Red ultimatum or of King Carol's acceptance.

### The Road From Munich

Whether she fights Hungary or not, whether Bulgaria presses her own territorial claim for Southern Dobruja or lets it lie, Rumania, World War heir to Balkan supremacy, was well on the road to dismemberment. It is a road that winds from Munich, through Czecho-Slovakia and Poland to Finland and back again to France.

Apparently Germany and Italy gave their consent to Russia's latest coup. Axis Ministers were in long and earnest consultation with King Carol in his hours of deliberation and decision.

Rumania, rich in oil and grain, but poor in strategic location and useful alliances, decided she must give in to Russia—that no calling into force of her months of military preparations could alter the final result. Hence she yielded just short of a 10

o'clock deadline last night for her peaceful assent and agreed to discuss details later.

She had invoked a virtually general mobilization while the Grand Council considered Russia's demands. The council first accepted them in principle, pleaded unavailingly for time to dicker and finally capitulated.

The decision disposed only of Russia's claims. Now will come Hungary, with the reported backing of Adolf Hitler, to ask for Transylvania. Bulgaria, a friend of Russia, may seek the return of Southern Dobruja.

All told, Rumania stands to lose nearly half of her 113,884 square miles and return to Balkan obscurity—a satellite wavering between the gravitational pulls of the Axis powers in the west and the Red empire in the east.

### The Reported Demands

Amid reports that Red Army planes were darkening the horizon and that Red troops, tanks and artillery were massing at her frontier, Rumania's Grand Council, under the presidency of the 46-year-old King, gave reluctant consent to demands that authoritative sources outlined as follows:

Return of Bessarabia, 17,146 square miles of fertile country, inhabited by more than 3,000,000 persons.

Cession of the northern part of Bukovina Province, but how much of Bukovina's 4,030 square miles, and 911,000 inhabitants Russia wanted was not known.

Control of Rumania's big Black Sea port, Constanta, as a Red naval base.

Supervision of Galati and Braila, two Rumanian ports controlling all navigation on the Danube, one of Germany's principal lifelines.

Railway bases at certain Rumanian ports along with certain other incidental concessions.

[Reports to Berlin said "control" of Tulcea, another Danube port, also was demanded.]

A Rumanian communiqué, issued shortly after 8 P. M. yesterday, signified the acceptance of the demands. Its reference to an invitation to Russian representatives to discuss the demands was merely a formal way of stating that consent, official quarters disclosed.

The communiqué said:

"The Crown Council, under the presidency of His Majesty the King, took note of demands of the Soviet to cede Russia Bessarabia and the northern part of Bukovina.

"With a desire to maintain good relations with the Soviet, the Rumanian Government asked the Soviet Government to discuss the Russian demands."

Foreign military attachés were then advised that most of Rumania's armed forces were en route to Transylvania. They were bolstered by truckloads and plane loads of reservists called to the colors only yesterday by Rumania. For while Rumania was still pleading with Russia for time to dicker, gendarmes went from house to house, farm to farm and factory to factory, calling up Rumanian reservists. Planes patrolled the Bucharest airport, and anti-aircraft guns were mounted on the capital's tall buildings.

But, so far as Russia was concerned, these were only precautionary gestures. Unrelenting on her ultimatum, Russia won Rumanian concessions apparently without firing a shot.

### Resistant Toward Hungary

As regards Hungary and her demands for 24,020-square-mile Transylvania, there was a show of resistance. It was learned officially that Rumanian troops were being concentrated in Transylvania, near the Hungarian frontier.

Official quarters expressed the belief that King Carol had decided to grant all Russia's requests in order to be able to throw his armed might against the expected Hungarian attempt to regain Transylvania, lost by Hungary in the World War settlements.

Bulgaria's claim on the southern part of 8,979-square-mile Dobruja remained a more undetermined factor in Rumania's future. There was no sign of extraordinary military activity in Bulgaria—or Hungary, for that matter—but foreign observers pointed out that both had strong forces on their borders with Rumania.

Responsible Bulgarian sources at Sofia expressed the belief that Russia's success was the long-awaited opening wedge for remaking the Balkan man.

A Bulgarian army of 250,000 remained on the Turkish frontier, in apparent preoccupation over Turkish aims rather than the winning of the historic Dobruja claim against Rumania.

### Claim to Giurgiu Reported

BUCHAREST, Friday, June 28 (UP)—It was understood here that among other territory demanded of Rumania by Russia, was the Danube port of Giurgiu, forty miles south of Bucharest on the Bulgarian border. The main oil line to Germany passes through Giurgiu, supplying the fuel for Germany's war machine.

King Carol changed six members of his Cabinet early today. Two new members of the Cabinet, both Ministers without portfolios, are Bessarabian leaders.

The Rumanian Premier kept his post, but Foreign Minister Ion Gigurtu was replaced by Constantin Argetoianu, a member of the Crown Council and former Premier. Other Cabinet shifts were relatively minor, except for the inclusion of the two Bessarabians.

Joseph Stalin chose to act, according to speculation here, because Germany and Italy are involved in preparations for a Blitzkrieg against the British Isles. For this reason, it was said, he chose to make extravagant demands.

Thousands of Russian troops, including new reinforcements, were reported opposite the borders of Bessarabia and Bukovina and scores of Russian planes, including large bombers, were in the air.

The Russian ultimatum was served on the Rumanian Minister in Moscow, G. Davidescu, because the new Russian Minister to Bucharest. Arkady I. Lavrentieff, had not yet presented his credentials to King Carol. Mr. Lavrentieff arrived here only recently from Bulgaria.

Some reports indicated that the Russian move was made with the advance knowledge and perhaps the collaboration of Bulgaria. These same reports, unconfirmed, said that Germany and Italy also had been fully informed by the Soviet Union.

In connection with the efforts to obtain an extension of the 10 P. M. deadline, King Carol was said to have asked that the Russians send plenipotentiaries to Bucharest from Moscow so that he might confer on the security of Transylvania and Dobruja.

During the day, as news of Russia's demands spread like wildfire across the nation, thousands of Rumanians started fleeing from Bessarabia. For more than a century Czarist Russia held Bessarabia, and since it was attached to Rumania in 1918 the Soviet Government persistently refused to recognize it as Rumanian. Russian maps still include it within the boundaries of the U. S. S. R.

### Soviet Officials Silent

MOSCOW, June 27 (UP)—Soviet officials tonight refused either to confirm or deny that an ultimatum had been served on Rumania.

### Reports Troops March In

BUDAPEST, Hungary, June 27 (UP)—Hungarian official quarters reported tonight that King Carol of Rumania had submitted to Russia's ultimatum and that Soviet troops already were marching into Bessarabia.

### Reports Oil Control Sought

LONDON, June 27 (AP)—The Swiss radio tonight said Russia, in addition to demanding Bessarabia, Northern Bukovina and certain port control from Rumania, also insisted upon control of Rumanian oil fields and a different political system in that country. Rumania agreed to the ultimatum, the radio report said.

\* \* \*

**July 3, 1940**

# RUSSIA IN THE BALKANS

Every day it becomes more evident that this is a war on a scale beyond all previous wars. In an increasingly literal sense it is a war not of nations but of continents, Reduced by the defeat of France to a clear-cut struggle between Britain and Germany, before this battle of giants begins it is already apparent that it is more than a fight for the mastery of Europe. The other Great Powers of the earth are inevitably involved in the contest. In the dark room in which the picture of the future is being developed we catch glimpses of new conflicts—a long series of vast and interlocking engagements where in the Battle of France, and even the Battle of Europe, may later seem to have been but episodes in an intercontinental war.

Such a forecast is pointed up by the entry of Russia into the Balkans. This marks the beginning of a new phase in the combat. It would be too much to assume that the Soviet occupation of Bessarabia implies a break between Stalin and Hitler, or that Russia means to challenge the German military machine, now or in the near future. But it is plain that the southward push of the Red Army has an entirely different significance from the Russian moves in the Baltic. True, both invasions serve to restore the old imperial frontiers, both represent a determination to strengthen Russia's position against attack from the west. Stalin is thoroughly aware that such an attack can come only from Germany, and every advance he makes proves this awareness. He is providing against the time when Hitler, if he finishes his Blitzkrieg against the Western Powers, will turn east and train all his forces on the Soviet Union, the great undeveloped empire at Germany's back door which he has always coveted.

But the thrust into Rumania means more than a fortification of Russian defenses. The immediate tremors set in motion throughout the Balkans, the turmoil in Rumania, the dismay in Berlin and Rome, the strong repercussions in Turkey and the Middle East, signify that the Soviet action has opened up another theatre of war.

Russia needs no more territory. She is in fact, the greatest land-possessing Power in the world, ruling over 27,500,000 square miles, against the 13,000,000 square miles of the entire British Empire and 3,780,000 square miles owned by the United States. She has no intention of risking a showdown with any strong military force. She seeks to check Germany by other means. The war is going too fast to suit the strategists in the Kremlin. They recognize that the subjugation of France is the end of a decisive campaign: Hitler today dominates the European Continent, and this tremendous upset in the balance, brought about within a few months, cannot fail to affect a Power which occupies the biggest single slice of Europe.

While the Red armies are reported to have been stopped by German pressure at the River Pruth, a tributary of the Danube defining the limits of Bessarabia, this is no guarantee that they will not move farther if Germany is fully engaged elsewhere. Russia's logical aim would be to slow up the war, to obstruct German expansion in the region where the Pan-Slav movement is gaining strength and to race the Nazis to the Dardanelles, the Mediterranean gateway, which Moscow cannot willingly see under the control of another Great Power. For the moment she waits at the Pruth, but her stand there shakes the Balkans and gives notice that Hitler is not alone in plotting the future shape of Europe.

\*   \*   \*

July 3, 1940

## TROUBLE IN THE BALKANS

### By HANSON W. BALDWIN

The Balkans, long the cockpit of Europe, again echoed to the tread of marching armies yesterday as troops of the Red Army completed the seizure of Rumanian Bessarabia and planted the hammer and sickle of the Soviet Union within forty to fifty miles of the Rumanian oil fields and close to the Carpathian mountain passes.

The Russian seizure of Bessarabia and Northern Bukovina, together with the other concessions extorted from Rumania, represents more than another event in a great game of grab. As a reclamation of territories lost in the World War the Russian move was not unexpected, but the latest Russian seizure has brought her strategic as well as territorial and economic advantages.

The Russian frontier in the south has now been advanced from the Dniester, which at places ran perilously close to the important Russian railroad to Odessa, to the Pruth River, which empties into the Danube. The Russian southern flank is therefore protected by the Black Sea, and the frontier runs along the northern mouth of the Danube, thence along the Pruth northward to the ridges of the Carpathians in Russian Poland; thence along the San, the Bug and the Narew Rivers in Poland to the Lithuanian frontier and the Baltic.

### Close to Main Oil Fields

This move not only puts Russia within easy reach by ground troops as well as by air forces of the main Rumanian oil fields, but also brings her closer to the passes through the Carpathians and the Transylvanian Alps than any other great power. By her seizure of Bukovina in North Rumania and her earlier seizure of Eastern Poland, Russia has put her frontier squarely upon some of these strategically important passes; her new position on the Pruth River and the Danube in the south puts her not far from the important Predeal Pass near Brasov and the Iron Gate where the Danube runs through the Transylvanian Alps—both important military routes for any force from Western Europe advancing against the fertile Danube-Black Sea plain.

Moreover, if early reports of the Rumanian-Russian agreement prove to be correct and the Rumanians do cede to the Russians naval base and other rights in the important Black Sea port of Constanta, Russia will also have a stranglehold on the terminus of the railroad and oil pipe line from the Rumanian oil fields to the Black Sea.

This advantage, coupled with the new Soviet grip upon the mouth of the Danube and the proximity of Red Army troops to the Rumanian oil fields, important to German military economy, gives to Russia a strategic position not only of potential defensive strength but also of considerable bargaining power, in case the marriage of convenience between Stalinist Russia and Hitlerian Germany should be ended by mutual jealousies.

### Strength Put at 750,000

Russia has probably thrown some thirty-five divisions, or more than 750,000 men, into her new territory, while Rumanian forces, taking up defensive positions along the west bank of the Pruth, are ready to resist any further invasion. But Rumania is squeezed between three foes—with Hungary threatening the rich province of Transylvania in the west and Bulgaria on the south, anxious to reclaim the territory she lost after the World War—Southern Dobruja.

The military forces of these three small Balkan powers follow:

### RUMANIA

Maximum effectives, 1,100,000; forty to fifty divisions. Indifferently trained and equipped, poorly led. Five hundred to 1,200 planes of many different types, mostly old; only about 300 to 600 combat ships. Four destroyers, one submarine, seven monitors, torpedo boats. Defense forces poorly organized, with a lack of most things, except numbers, that go to make a modern army. Diversified equipment a further handicap.

### HUNGARY

Maximum effectives, 425,000; seventeen to twenty-three divisions. Good soldiers but indifferently trained, lack much equipment. Four hundred to 600 planes, about two-thirds of them combat types, mostly Italian and German. A Danube River flotilla of slight strength.

### BULGARIA

Maximum effectives, 400,000; fifteen to twenty-one divisions. Good fighters, fairly well trained but poorly equipped, with a particular lack of heavy equipment. One hundred to 300 planes.

Rumania's Hungarian frontier is protected, not by natural obstacles but by a defensive noncontinuous line of field works, including tank traps and some concrete pillboxes of indifferent strength which extends from the vulnerable Muresul River Valley along the frontier to the Carpathians. Fortifications protect Bucharest and local field works guard the Arges River Valley and approaches across the Danube from Bulgaria.

The real defensive line of Rumania, however, is the Carpathian Mountain line plus the Danube; the rich province of Transylvania lies exposed to the west and north of this line; Southern Dobruja is more or less unprotected east of the curving Danube, and the whole line is now taken in the rear by the Russian colossus.

The Balkans are thus a logical place for serious trouble, and Rumania is threatened with partition. The three small countries—Rumania, Hungary and Bulgaria—have little voice in power politics, and the real issue of peace or war in the Balkans does not depend upon them but upon Russia and Germany and, secondarily, Italy. These great powers most certainly may be expected to try to avoid war in the Balkans at this time—the Axis powers because of their preoccupation in the campaign of Britain, Russia because of inherent military weaknesses. And if war comes in the Balkans, its coming can be advantageous only to Britain.

\* \* \*

August 12, 1940

## YUGOSLAVIA BANS RUSSIAN MOVIES

ZAGREB, Yugoslavia, Aug. 11 (AP)—A riot between Communist sympathizers and Croatian Peasant Leader Vladimir Matchek's guards in a theatre resulted today in a police order banning Russian motion pictures.

\* \* \*

August 18, 1940

## BULGARIA OBTAINS SOUTHERN DOBRUJA

*Rumania Agrees to Include the Towns of Silistra and Balcic in Cession*

### SIGNING IS DUE THIS WEEK

*Extensive Hungarian Claims to Transylvania Reported—Talks Resume Tomorrow*

Wireless to The New York Times

BUCHAREST, Rumania, Aug. 17—Negotiations with Bulgaria were declared today to have been concluded with the cession by Rumania of all the Southern Dobruja, including the towns of Silistra on the Danube River and Balcic on the Black Sea.

The Rumanian and Bulgarian delegates will meet Monday at Craiova to sign the general agreement, it was stated. Negotiations to arrange details of the transfer will continue.

Through this cession Rumania loses 7,726 square kilometers of territory with 378,364 inhabitants, among them 77,728 Rumanians.

A survey shows that 91,476 Bulgarians will still remain in Rumania, but their gradual transfer to Bulgarian territory on an exchange basis is likely.

Authoritative sources said Hungary's claims, set forth in a memorandum now before the Rumanians, cover all Northern Transylvania north of the Muresh Valley and the Seklar district. Neither the Rumanian nor Hungarian delegates think an exchange of population is feasible.

If Rumania ceded all the territory, she would lose 64,754 square kilometers with 3,730,000 inhabitants, of whom 1,675,111 are Rumanians. In Rumanian territory there would remain only 201,409 Hungarians.

The Hungarians now emphasize that Rumania has ceded to Russia and Bulgaria all territories Rumania got from them after the World War, while Hungary asks only two-thirds of the territory taken from her.

The negotiations will be resumed Monday at Turnu Severin, when a reply is likely to be made to the Hungarian memorandum. It is being studied by King Carol and members of the Cabinet over the week-end.

### Pomenoff Heads Bulgar Delegates

SOFIA, Bulgaria, Aug. 17 (AP)—A Bulgarian delegation headed by Svetoslaff Pomenoff, former Minister to Rome, is leaving tonight for Craiova for the Rumanian territorial discussions, it was officially announced.

### Loss of Danube Control Seen

Although the cession of Southern Dobruja had been foreshadowed in dispatches earlier this month, to the effect that under German and Italian pressure Rumania had agreed in principle to this lopping-off of her territory, it had not been expected that Silistra and Balcic would be included in the shift of lands.

Silistra, in particular, is of vital importance to Rumanian strategy, and the Rumanians wanted to keep the city. The town stands on hilly lands overlooking and dominating the Danube. Slightly beyond it, in the neighboring province of Oltenia, the river banks become low and marshy and of little strategical importance. This surrender of Silistra is the more important to Rumania because it had been agreed earlier that the ceded territory should include the town of Turtucaia, Rumania's other principal hope of control of the river.

Balcic, on the Black Sea, is of less practical importance, but of great sentimental interest to the Rumanians and to their ruler, King Carol, for it is in a little chapel at that point that the heart of Queen Marie, Carol's mother, was interred. Bucharest had indicated hopes of an arrangement to leave the chapel and its surrounding grounds, at least, under Rumanian control, guarded by Rumanian soldiers.

### The Dobruja Held Since 1913

The territory of the Southern Dobruja, forming a strip on the Black Sea, was lost by Bulgaria to Rumania as a result of the second Balkan war in 1913. Rumania then had a population of 6,500,000.

In the World War, which began in the following year, Rumania sided with the Allies and was over-run, during the period of the hostilities, by the armies of the Central Powers.

At the end of the World War she obtained still further territory from Bulgaria, together with other areas from Hungary and Russia. These acquisitions, brought to the country a population of 19,000,000, and boundaries now being drastically reduced.

\*    \*    \*

September 7, 1940

# CAROL'S ABDICATION WELCOMED BY AXIS

*Berlin and Rome Regarded Ex-King as Political Heir of Titulescu and Benes*

**ANTONESCU IS TRUSTED**

*New Premier Expected to Bring Rumania's Policy in Line With Reich's and Italy's*

By GUIDO ENDERIS
Wireless to The New York Times

BERLIN, Sept. 6—The abdication of King Carol of Rumania is appraised in authoritative German quarters as a definitive liquidation of British influence in Southeastern Europe.

Carol has been suspected as the habitual catspaw of the Western Powers. His disappearance, therefore, is welcomed with unconcealed gratification, especially as it represents, in the German view, a logical sequel to the recent arbitration award of the Axis powers in the Rumanian-Hungarian frontier conflict. It also signalizes, in German opinion, the complete elimination from Rumanian internal politics of those elements that have opposed closer cooperation with the Axis powers.

Speculation as to the further drift of developments in Rumania assumes that the new regime of Ion Antonescu will be constituted on Fascist lines, not unlike the Italian pattern. The new government's policies, it is assumed, will lead to intensification of Rumania's relations with the Axis powers and eventually in a quasi-political union completely in accord with Italo-German aspirations for Southeastern Europe.

The German press takes leave of Carol with a light heart. With the slaying of Zelea Codreanu, leader of the Iron Guard, Carol was promptly eliminated from further consideration in German quarters. It was accepted as a foregone conclusion that he would not survive ratification of the recent mandatory award of the Axis powers, which gave Hungary a big slice of Rumanian territory.

The new configuration of Continental Europe, left Carol as the last remnant of the Little Entente. As the avowed puppet of Great Britain and France, he was always viewed with deepest distrust in official quarters in Germany, where he was recognized as the political heir of Nicolas Titulescu and Eduard Benes.

The political course of the new Rumanian regime will be under the close surveillance of the Axis powers. It is suggested in a section of the German press that Premier Antonescu cannot escape the realities of the new situation. He is designated as a man who has no illusions on this score and who realizes his immediate problems are of an internal rather than a foreign political nature.

While repercussions of the Vienna award probably will continue to convulse the Rumanian domestic situation, it is expected that General Antonescu will assign the foreign political portfolio to Dinu Bratianu, who has openly championed a pro-Axis political orientation. German quarters assume the new Premier will avail himself of the collaboration of Horia Sima, the Iron Guard leader, with whom he is openly in sympathy.

### Rome Welcomes Abdication

Wireless to The New York Times

ROME, Sept. 5—The abdication of King Carol of Rumania is another victory for the Axis, and it is greeted as such by the Italian press today. A known friend and well-wisher of Great Britain and France has been driven out, and Rumania is to be run by a man as much under the control of the Axis as any of the long line of politicians, starting with Arthur Seyss-Inquart.

Moreover, the Vienna decision is now consolidated. In addition the Axis has a strong anti-Bolshevik friend in Bucharest.

So there is a feeling here today that all is well that ends well. There are no doubts here that the new Rumanian Premier, General Ion Antonescu, has the upper hand. If he did not have, he would be given it.

If the Russians had planned to do anything about it, they would have acted before this, it is believed. The Axis has every hope, therefore, of peace in the Danube area.

The usual "political circles" were reserved in their comments this morning. King Carol's abdication was described as primarily an internal affair.

"We have always had respect for the internal politics of other nations and for the delicate problems involved in domestic changes," it was stated.

The Rumanian State's progressive withdrawal from democratic principles has been viewed with "notable sympathy," it stated here.

"In the Vienna decision," it is added, "the Axis showed its concern for Rumania, which is now strengthened by an Axis guaranty of its territorial integrity and its assurances of friendship. Any consolidation of the order in Rumania will cause satisfaction in Rome."

Italian newspapers all point to Carol's leaning toward democracies, and above all they attack him for lack of continuity in his policies.

\* \* \*

September 7, 1940

## MAGYARS CHEERED IN NEW CEDED AREA

*Regent Horthy Leads Soldiers Into Oradea, Completing the Second Stage of Occupation*

### RUMANIANS CITE LOYALTY

*Passing of Carol Fails to Find Any Tears in Budapest—Iron Guard Moves Followed*

BUDAPEST, Hungary, Sept. 6 (UP)—Tens of thousands of cheering Hungarians jammed the streets of Oradea today as Hungarian forces led by the Regent, Admiral Nicholas Horthy, marched into the city, completing the second phase of the occupation of Transylvania.

Government and city officials mounted the speakers' stand erected in the public square to hear the leader of the Rumanian minority, Dr. Lengil, proclaim a pledge of loyalty to Hungary, "in the hope the fatherland will not suppress us."

The local Hungarian party leader said "the Hungarians want to forget the past and live in brotherly community with their Rumanian co-citizens."

The speeches were interrupted frequently by cries of "give them all back," referring to Hungarians still living in other parts of Rumania.

Meanwhile political informants said that Hungary's first reaction to King Carol's abdication was "good-bye without tears."

For Hungarians Carol's reign had been marked by complete resistance to all Hungarian demands, and by suppression of Hungarian minorities. Hence, it was said, nobody in Hungary regretted very much his departure.

There was the keenest interest in Iron Guard movements in Rumania and in Russia's reaction to developments.

Iron Guard cooperation, it was said, would be necessary for maintenance of order in Rumania. Guardists, it was asserted, had penetrated into the army and the bureaucracy.

\* \* \*

September 9, 1940

## ANTONESCU CURBS RUMANIAN GROUPS

*Dictator Resists Iron Guard's Bid for Control, but Delays Forming of Cabinet*

### ARMY REMAINS IMPARTIAL

*German Support Indicated—Carol's Wealth Sequestered in Purge Program*

By EUGEN KOVACS
Wireless to The New York Times

BUCHAREST, Rumania, Sept. 8—General Ion Antonescu, Rumania's military dictator, is still governing with the members of the former Cabinet who took the oath of allegiance to him. He will not form a government until the evacuation of Northern Transylvania is ended.

It seems that the constitution of a new Cabinet is more difficult than had been expected. Four possibilities are open to General Antonescu. He can build up his government with members from the former political parties and some representatives of the Iron Guard. In this connection it is interesting that General Antonescu has not yet annulled the standing prohibition of political parties, but the parties can publish their communiques in the press and have reopened their clubs, which were closed in February, 1938.

The second possibility is to form a government of men outside of politics, but with sufficient personal authority. The third possibility would be an Iron Guard regime and the fourth a military government.

### Iron Guard Is Divided

The Iron Guard can be divided into two groups. The first, whose present leader is Horia Sima, is that of the intransigents, who are not disposed to share power with any one else, and the second group is disposed to participate in a coalition government. These two groups are opposed. The situation thus can be compared with that of the Communist party in Russia in 1917, when the Mensheviki and Bolsheviks adopted similarly opposing positions.

The general is busy discussing his problem with the Iron Guard leader, M. Sima, but the results have remained unsatisfactory. He had intended to cooperate to some degree; but the group asked for a purely Iron Guard government. General Antonescu, primarily an army man, rejects the Iron Guard claim that it effected the change of regime and therefore should control the new government.

The Iron Guardists would like to dictate to General Antonescu, but the general, with his dictatorial powers, refuses to allow them to interfere in state affairs. He recognizes the present weakness of the Iron Guard movement, but there is no other element of driving force in the country, except the army.

It is significant that M. Sima forbade demonstrations in Bucharest, as his following in the capital did not permit an impressive exhibition of strength. He added that the legionnaires would receive orders in time for eventual manifestations.

### Party Leaders Withhold Aid

Leaders of the former political parties are only theoretically supporting General Antonescu and not giving him real help. They ask for return of a constitutional parliamentary regime, which again is possible now that the King's prerogatives are extremely reduced and his control of state affairs and the government eliminated.

The Liberals and National Peasants know, however, that for the present it is impossible to realize this full program, concerning either parliamentarianism or external politics, as Rumania is pledged to follow the Rome-Berlin Axis.

General Antonescu seeks a solution that would allow him to direct Rumania without the hampering intrigues of the Iron Guardists or the politicians. He is thus leisurely examining the situation and the temper of the army.

It is significant that during the Iron Guard demonstrations the army and the police cooperated in quelling the weakly organized risings. In no instance did the troops refuse to attack the demonstrators, proving that the army remains neutral and without political bias.

The army, especially the High Command, is with General Antonescu as against the Iron Guard. These circles are angry about the Iron Guard attack against the house of General Alexander Argeseanu, former Premier and Military Governor of Bucharest. Besides, the army does not wish to have a second military or part military organization built up by the Iron Guard or any one else.

For its part the Iron Guard would never consent to a government of generals. The moderate wing of the Iron Guard is therefore ready to cooperate with General Antonescu chiefly to avoid a military government, which would take strong measures against every one who attempts to oppose the dictator.

### Germans Favor Dictator

German circles are more inclined toward General Antonescu than the Iron Guard. The Germans are aware that after the real leaders of the Iron Guard were killed, the group's unity was destroyed and its political power became insignificant. The rebellions organized in Brasov, Bucharest and Constanta proved this. The Germans consider General Antonescu capable of restoring order in the country and quite disposed to satisfy Germany's economic demands.

Germany expects from Rumania foodstuffs, oil and big orders for German manufactured goods. Only a politically and economically well-organized country could fulfill this requirement, and the Germans trust General Antonescu's ability and energy more than that of the Iron Guard.

The Germans would like, however, a political organization built up on the Nazi model with its roots embedded in nationalism. Such an organization, conducted by General Antonescu with his excellent army following and authority among the population, would be created by Germany. Nevertheless the Germans declare they have no great interest in Rumanian internal policy as they know that at the moment only a pro-Axis policy is possible and they have the country in their hands.

The General's first aim is to restore order in the army, which has suffered much by the evacuation, and to reorganize it to have it ready for all eventualities.

### State Purge Under Way

He is conducting also a general State purge. He has ordered that everyone who has purchased shares belonging to Carol in the Rumanian Bank of Credit, the textile works of Buhushi & Scherg, the iron works of Reshitza & Malaxa, the gold mine Mica, the sugar factory of Lugani & Ripiceni, the Bank Marmorosch and the Rumanian Telephone Company must deposit them within five days with the Bucharest Court of Justice.

Another order issued today refers to control of the fortunes of former premiers, ministers and other statesmen who have held office in the last ten years. A second ordinance refers to the control of coal supplies delivered to the army and to the spending of funds for rearmament. There will also be an inquiry into the granting by the National Bank of foreign currencies at less than the normal rate. The privilege of special trains and saloon cars for ministers also is abolished.

The inquiry into deliveries to the State railways is directed openly against M. Malaxa, engineer and armament leader, who was an intimate friend and poker partner of Carol and Mme. Magda Lupescu.

A special commission will investigate all political trials during the last eight years and recommend necessary cancellation of sentences and punishment of the judges.

General Antonescu has prohibited the wearing of uniforms of the former Rumanian Renaissance Front and the Nation's party, as well as that of the youth organization. In the future each officer will have a single khaki uniform in place of six various uniforms.

### Michael Prays With Crowds

BUCHAREST, Rumania, Sept. 8 (AP)—By command of Premier Ion Antonescu, the populace of Rumania knelt today to pray for King Michael and to "curse those responsible for the nation's troubles."

The capital's churches were jammed. Traffic stopped for one minute throughout the city. Pedestrians even knelt in front of the palace. Michael, guarded by steel-helmeted soldiers, went to the cathedral to join in the service.

The Iron Guard Minister of Culture issued decrees requiring all subordinates to resign immediately from the Masonic organization and prohibiting Jews from "continuing their blasphemy" of selling religious art objects or having even the remotest connection with anything artistic—even serving as ushers in motion-picture theatres.

Both the capital's newspapers and government offices said King Michael's mother, Princess Helen, had not yet arrived in Rumania, but was expected tomorrow or Tuesday.

The ban on Bucharest theatres, movie houses and gypsy orchestras was lifted and the city began taking on a more normal aspect.

### Mussolini Thanks Dictator

LUGANO, Switzerland, Sept. 8 (UP)—About the time former King Carol's train was entering Italy today, Premier Mussolini sent a message to General Ion Antonescu of Rumania, who seized Carol's dictatorial powers and drove him from his throne and his country saying:

"I am grateful for your cordial wishes, which I reciprocate, and wish you success in your work and peace and prosperity for Rumania."

Upon assuming power, General Antonescu had sent telegrams to Premier Mussolini and Chancellor Hitler, pledging Rumania's fidelity to the Rome-Berlin Axis.

### Bulgarians Hail Cession

SOFIA, Bulgaria, Sept. 8 (AP)—Tens of thousands of Bulgarians, celebrating the cession of South Dobruja by Rumania, passed in review today before the Bulgarian royal family and the Cabinet and gave thanks in the nation's churches, where special services were held.

The government freed hundreds of political prisoners in commemoration of the occasion.

### YUGOSLAV REDS IN FIGHTS
#### Ten Reported Seriously Hurt in Demonstration in Zagreb

ZAGREB, Yugoslavia, Sept. 8 (AP)—Ten persons were reported seriously wounded today in a fight between police-

men and Communist demonstrators in the streets. More than 100 demonstrators were arrested.

Other outbursts were reported at Split, where many shops were sacked. Today's clashes were the third in the past few weeks.

The Communists demanded a military alliance between Yugoslavia and Russia and attacked the Government for its alleged Rome-Berlin Axis sympathies.

The Sokol athletic organizations at Sibenic and Zara were disbanded yesterday and a leader was arrested after Italy had protested against their anti-Italian demonstrations.

\*   \*   \*

October 27, 1940

## BALKANS FEARFUL OF WAR

*Their Interest in Its Outcome Overshadowed By Fervent Hope It Will Pass Them By*

By C. L. SULZBERGER
Wireless to The New York Times

SOFIA, Bulgaria, Oct. 26—After fourteen months of warfare in the world around him, during which time entire nations have lost their liberty, the Balkan peasant tends ever more to regard this struggle in the terms of his fundamental life—crops and prices.

In this part of the world, whose peripheries are still barely touched by its more shattering aspects, the conflict strikes deepest by its economic repercussions. Now a Bulgarian can receive in a week only as much of the national sheep-milk cheese as he previously consumed at one meal, and he grumbles.

The Montenegrin, amid his crags, discovers that, although he can get more dinars for sparse products of his soil, these dinars are worth only half their former value in terms of tools and clothing.

The seafaring Greek trader finds shrinking markets for his goods.

The Rumanian farmer sees the cost of living shooting ever higher in his badly warped land.

### Europe's Throes Are Blamed

Europe's convulsions are the cause of all this. Germany and Italy are draining off the life-giving foodstuffs of this region's agriculture to withstand the British blockade. Although they pay prices which on paper appear fair, the compensatory rise in the cost of the manufactured goods they barter forces the cost of living upward.

Britain, intent on crumbling the Axis and stopping all possible supply leaks, shuts off access to other sources of materials and again prices rise and factories close.

Finally, the need to prepare for possible self-defense, the necessity of buying arms and building fortifications, the constant mobilization, training and retraining of recruits, all push

A Topographical Map of the Balkan Peninsula

up prices and reduce the national labor supply, thus slowly causing the atrophy of national wealth.

These things are mysteries to most of the millions of peasants in this sector, and these mysteries are not completely clarified by the contradictory blasts of propaganda. The Communists, as ever, are on the alert, and their insistence in fixing the blame for this slow misery on "imperialistic war" is having its effect.

From the heights of Herzegovina to the Black Sea coast of Bulgaria this simple analysis worries the discontented Balkan Slavs. In Rumania for the first time expert Russian organizers are replacing local Communist party members in sowing the seeds of dissatisfaction.

### Hungarians Resent Germans

In Hungary there is grumbling as sugar becomes increasingly scarce and great food shipments move westward to the Reich. Despite able Nazi propaganda, which claims credit for enlarging Magyar territory, there is resentment at the Germans.

In Greece, on the other hand, the impressing of local shipping into British service and the growing roster of losses damage Britain's popularity.

Increasingly the attitude of the average Balkan toward the war is: "I wish to heaven it was over," and "May its terrors stay away from my door."

Graphic press reports of war's destructive capacity bewilder the simple mind. The Bosnian, who is confident that he can conquer the Italian, man for man, wonders whether Premier Mussolini can put his entire army in an airplane. The Greek fisherman prays that, since his new anti-aircraft gun is automatic, it will automatically dispose of aerial invasion.

The actual reality here is that of the stubborn. These people have not dropped their individualistic ideals which enabled them to win freedom in the last century.

### "Free Spirit Remains"

Among the peasants the free spirit remains, regardless of national policy. The only anti-democratic governmental philosophy that has made noticeable headway is the tantalizing Utopian version of communism that is dangled secretly before discontented eyes.

It is nearly a certainty that the overwhelming majority of Rumanians hope for a British victory. The Hungarians think more of preventing a Russian gain that would menace them than of the outcome between the present combatants.

The reserved and earnest Bulgarians are perhaps in their hearts the most neutral of the Balkan peoples. And, although they are fonder of Germany than of Britain, they generally hope only that the war will avoid them.

This last is unquestionably the fervent desire of all Balkans. No matter what the outcome of the present conflict may be, the growing desire of the Balkan peoples is that peace will soon be coming.

\* \* \*

**October 28, 1940**

## ITALY INVADES GREECE, STARTING BALKAN DRIVE, AS ATHENS REJECTS A THREE-HOUR ULTIMATUM; METAXAS ASKS GREEKS TO FIGHT TO THE DEATH

### BORDER IS CROSSED

*Italians Move In From Albania—Athens Has First Raid Alarm*

### PREMIER IS DEFIANT

*Appeal for Aid Is Sent to Britain—Attacking Force Put at 200,000*

By A. C. SEDGWICK
Wireless to The New York Times

ATHENS, Greece, Monday, Oct. 28—Full mobilization went into effect at 6 o'clock this morning after an ultimatum, served at 3 o'clock, to the Greek Government by Italy had expired.

The ultimatum was refused at 6 o'clock. Hence a state of war exists or is presumed to exist between this country and Italy, as the Axis starts its Balkan drive. The nation is on a wartime footing.

### Ten Divisions Attack

BELGRADE, Yugoslavia, Monday, Oct. 28 (AP)—Italy was reported today to have attacked Greece by land, sea and air, hurling at least ten divisions of 200,000 Italian troops across the Greek-Albanian frontier.

Reports from the Yugoslav frontier said troops of Greece's small army flung themselves into the path of the Fascist advance through mountain passes.

Italian warships and fighting planes were believed to have joined in the onslaught.

At the same time, British sources here declared that warships of the British Mediterranean squadron were steaming from their patrol posts to the assistance of Greece, who holds a British guarantee of aid in event of attack.

[There was no immediate confirmation of this report from London.]

Greek Minister Raoul Bibica-Rosetti declared today that a state of war existed between Italy and Greece and fighting had started at 6 A. M.

The Greek Minister said that he had learned in a telephone conversation with Athens that Italian troops pushed across the border from Albania just as a 6 A. M. Italian ultimatum expired.

### Greeks Appeal for Aid

Special Cable to The New York Times

LONDON, Monday, Oct. 28—In a formal statement telling of Italy's ultimatum to Greece and the Greek rejection the British Foreign Office announced this morning that the Greek Government had "applied to His Majesty's Government for certain assistance."

The Italian ultimatum not only fulfills the terms of the British guarantee to Greece, but also fulfills the terms under which Turkey had agreed to come to the assistance of Britain in the Mediterranean. Though Turkey was theoretically obligated to enter the war when Italy attacked France, she did not do so at that time.

Since Italian troops massed on the Greek frontier, the Turks and the Greek have been conferring and there is some reason for believing that Turkey may now decide to render some assistance to Greece.

### First Air-Raid Alarm

ATHENS, Greece, Monday, Oct. 28 (UP)—Greece early today rejected an unconditional surrender ultimatum by Italy and ordered general mobilization, determined to fight to defend her territory.

Athens had an air-raid alarm at 7 A. M.—one hour after the Italian ultimatum expired. Whether this indicated an attack or merely a test alert was not immediately known.

### Urges "Fight for Honor"

ATHENS, Greece, Monday, Oct. 28 (AP)—Rejecting an Italian ultimatum calling for surrender by Greece of part of her territory, Premier John Metaxas declared today "the moment has arrived for Greece to fight for her independence and honor."

Immediately after, a decree for general mobilization was signed.

Times Wide World, 1940

Premier John Metaxas of Greece

The Italian ultimatum was given to Premier Metaxas at 3 A. M. (8 P. M. Eastern standard time Sunday) and gave him three hours to comply or Italian troops would march in.

Premier Metaxas' message to the Greek people said:

"The moment has arrived for Greece to fight for her independence and honor.

"Though we have kept the strictest neutrality toward all, Italy, not recognizing ourselves as free Greeks, demanded of me at 3 o'clock this morning to surrender sections of national territory and that for their occupation her armies would start moving at 6 A. M.

"I replied to the Italian Minister I considered the demand and the method in which it was made as a declaration of war by Italy on Greece.

"Greeks, we shall now prove whether we are worthy of our ancestors and of the liberty which our forefathers secured for us.

"Fight for the Fatherland, your wives, your children and sacred traditions.

"Now, above all, the fight.

"METAXAS."

King George II announced today that Greece had been "compelled to go to war against an Italy coveting Greece's independence." The King's message said:

"The Prime Minister just announced to you under what terms we have been compelled to go to war against an Italy coveting Greece's independence.

"At this great moment I feel sure every Greek man and woman will do their duty to the end and show themselves worthy of our glorious history.

"With faith in God and in our destinies the nation as a body and disciplined as a man will fight for its hearths to final victory."

### Greek Minister Moved

WASHINGTON, Monday, Oct. 28 (UP)—A State Department spokesman said early today that no word has been received of the Italian ultimatum to Greece for unconditional surrender on the threat of invasion by Italian troops.

George S. Depasta, Minister-Counselor of the Greek Legation, was reached at his hotel apartment. His voice broke when he was advised of the news.

The legation, he said, had received no word from Greece since yesterday afternoon when the official Greek news agency cabled a statement asserting that shots were heard inside the Albanian border Friday and Saturday nights.

### Mussolini Off for Parley

ROME, Oct. 27 (AP)—Premier Mussolini was reported tonight to have left Rome for Florence for an important meeting—possibly with Chancellor Hitler, Marshal Henri Philippe Pétain, Chief of State of France, and General Francisco Franco of Spain.

[Adolf Hitler has arrived at Florence to confer with Premier Mussolini, it was announced officially today, the United Press reported.]

His departure took place as Rome opened the celebration of the anniversary of the Oct. 30, 1922, Fascist march into the ancient capital and in the midst of a new Greek-Italian crisis, whipped up by Italy's charges of Greek attacks on the Albanian frontier. Foreign observers believed the newly initialed French-German collaboration agreement probably would be discussed.

[There was no word from Vichy that Marshal Pétain had left the capital of occupied France, but Vice Premier Pierre Laval, who conducted the first negotiations with Herr Hitler in Paris last week, was to leave for Paris today.]

The meetings were expected to last a few days and to be of utmost importance.

A new series of episodes along the tense Albanian-Greek frontier, which the official Italian news agency Stefani said "deserved attention" was reported tonight by the Tirana newspaper Tomori.

In the last forty-eight hours at six points along the frontier numerous groups of armed persons had appeared and disappeared from view, Tomori said. One group was said to have entered nearly a mile of Albanian territory, where the frontier guard ordered a halt.

Airplanes, which the paper said presumably were British, loosed pamphlets in the Albanian language from high altitudes over Southern Albania, inciting the population to revolt.

Tomori also said that some hundred Greek students guided by their schoolmasters made an anti-Italian, anti-Albanian demonstration near Karvia, waving Greek banners and shouting insults and threats.

The newspaper said excitement created artificially among the populace by propagandists was based on a claim that British troops and planes were ready to enter into a conflict, helping the Greeks invade Albania.

### Italians Await 'Events'

By CAMILLE M. CIANFARRA
By Telephone to The New York Times

ROME, Oct. 27—Intense diplomatic activity was reported today between Rome and Athens following last night's communiqué containing allegations of Greek hostilities against Albania.

It was admitted in Italian circles that the situation was "fraught with unpleasant developments," but queries as to whether this meant that Italo-Greek relations were nearing the breaking point met with reserve. The only comment was that "events will speak for themselves in a few days."

The communiqué was printed by all the Italian newspapers, but the headlines were noncommittal. The Athens denial was ignored.

Italy's main charge against Greece is that the latter has been helping the British fleet. The emphasis laid on this point by officially inspired writers has been taken as a preparation for some move that would give Italy control over the Greek naval bases.

Italy, so runs the Italian thesis, is fighting a life-and-death struggle in the Mediterranean against superior naval forces. It is therefore obvious according to Italians, that she should attempt to secure for herself political as well as strategic positions to use against her enemy.

In Greece's case, many Italians argue that she is in no position to "defend" her neutrality against a "British imposition" and that some action should be taken to prevent what they term Greek weakness from placing Italy at a disadvantage before the enemy.

This view was stressed by the Messaggero today. It headlines a dispatch from Berlin discussing the British position in the war, "British Blackmailing Athens—Greece Forced into Insufferable Policy of Feverish Armaments—Athens the Last Base of British Intrigues."

\*   \*   \*

October 31, 1940

## BRITISH LAND ON GREEK ISLES AS ITALIAN FORCES PLOD ON; AXIS URGES ATHENS TO YIELD

### SEA BASES SEIZED

*Fleet Also Mines Coast as Metaxas Praises London's Aid*

### HIGHWAY TOWNS TAKEN

*Italians Capture Breznica and Open a Main Route Across Macedonia to Salonika*

Wireless to The New York Times

SALONIKA, Greece, Oct. 30—British marines landed on certain islands today while the British fleet mined the coast and British planes reportedly—but unconfirmedly—landed in Northern Greece.

[The Greek highway town of Breznica was reported captured yesterday by the Italians, opening a major route for the Fascist invaders toward the Aegean port of Salonika, the United Press reported from Belgrade. The Italians are said to be planning a major offensive. The Greeks were also said to have been driven from two other border towns.]

Premier John Metaxas received the heads of the Athens newspapers and told them that British help had been even better than expected and that everything else was going better than had been expected.

### London Reseals Mining

By ROBERT P. POST
Special Cable to The New York Times

LONDON, Oct. 30—Little news is reaching London of the Greek campaign and the British share in it. It was denied in military quarters today that any troops had been landed on either Corfu or Crete. There was no confirmation of reports that the Italians had landed.

An indication that the British fleet is active in protecting the sea road to Greece was contained in an Admiralty announcement of the mining of the Gulfs of Patras and Corinth and their entrances. Another field apparently has been laid between Cape Spadi and Cape Colonna, cutting off the Gulf of Aegina, on which lies Athens.

That is, the Admiralty announced that these waters were dangerous. This does not necessarily mean that a really effective mine field has been laid. It is not known whether the mines have been laid by ships or planes—the notice may merely mean that the British are preparing to mine.

### Middle East Force Stronger

London is not a good place from which to report operations in the Mediterranean. Both General Sir Archibald P. Wavell, Commander in Chief of the Middle East Army, and Admiral Sir Andrew Browne Cunningham, Commander in Chief of the Mediterranean fleet, are men of independent minds. It is believed quite possible that they will act first and tell London about it afterward.

An indication that the British forces in the Near East have recently been reinforced was given today by Minister of Shipping R. H. Cross, who said the biggest task of the merchant navy in recent months had been the reinforcement and maintenance of the troops in the Middle East. There were great quantities of tonnage for this purpose, the Minister said. Since the end of June 100,000 tons of stores have been shipped.

Harold Nicolson, Parliamentary Secretary to the Ministry of Information, said tonight that British responsibilities in the Mediterranean were heavy.

"We must not underestimate the power, skill, equipment and courage of the enemies with whom we are faced," he said.

Chancellor Hitler, Mr. Nicolson said, had not abandoned the idea of an invasion of Britain, but if it came now it would be "the suicidal fling of a desperate man." The object of the latest Axis move was not to win the war, but to keep from losing it, Mr. Nicolson said. The aim was to break the British grip in the Mediterranean by capturing both Greece and Spain and to relieve the Axis of the British blockade, he continued.

The Greek Legation had little information, but the Greek Minister in London, Charalambos Simopoulos, today said in a speech that his country would fight to the end for freedom, as it had fought before, and was confident it would eventually win.

Germany, the Ministry of Economic Warfare said, got much tobacco, figs and currants and a little Iron ore from Greece. The most important import to Germany, it was said, was chromium, which the Germans formerly got from Turkey, who now sells all her chromium to Britain.

### Italy's Gains Held Slight

LONDON, Oct. 30 (UP)—British military sources said today that the Italians had concentrated their drive near the Adriatic coast, where two infantry divisions operating from Konispolis had succeeded in occupying Philastronis [five miles inside the Greek frontier] by noon on Tuesday.

Greek outposts were said to have withdrawn ahead of the Italian advance, which had nowhere reached Greece's prepared defense positions.

"So far, the Italians have not used any armored divisions," an informant said. "Elsewhere on the front there have only been local skirmishes, for example at Kokovia, on the road from Argyrokastron, and in frontier regions in the vicinity of Florina."

British newspapers, while urging the government to do its utmost to aid Greece, intimated that the best course might be to concentrate on offensives on the African Continent, especially in Egypt. It was agreed that Italy was the weak link in the Axis and that if Britain moved cautiously but forcefully she might find a way to deliver a crippling blow without weakening important positions elsewhere and thus falling into a trap.

The British mine fields were intended to throw a protective barrier around the Isthmus of Corinth, the only land bridge between Northern Greece and the Peloponnesus, it was said in Admiralty circles. The isthmus, as well as the Corinth Canal [attacked this week by Italian bombers], is vital to Greece and it was believed Italy might have planned a surprise landing there or a bombardment from the sea.

Squadrons of British bombing planes have hammered incessantly at Italian air bases on the Dodecanese Islands since Italy declared war on Greece, causing great destruction at many bases there, reports from Athens said.

### British Positions Strong

CAIRO, Egypt, Oct. 30 (AP)—Britain's sea-borne aid to Greece will be able to flow through a maze of well-fortified points established in the Aegean islands and on the Greek mainland, Greek leaders disclosed tonight.

The Greek islands are so solidly ringed with guns that they can be held indefinitely and there are so many of them that there still would be plenty of ports of entry for the British even if some withdrawals were necessary, these informants said.

They declared the islands would be held to provide a solid triangle with Alexandria, Cyprus and Haifa in which the British can have complete sea control, thus erecting a formidable barrier between the Axis and the shores of Egypt and Asia Minor.

These leaders predicted that slow Greek withdrawal operations would hold up the Italians for several weeks, giving the British time to establish themselves in Greece.

\* \* \*

November 3, 1940

## GREEKS PLAY STAR ROLE IN THE MEDITERRANEAN

*Evidence of First Battles Indicates Italy Will Be Able to Overrun Mainland but Not Islands*

By HANSON W. BALDWIN

The long-expected Mediterranean campaign of the Axis powers was resumed last week in Greece.

The wild and tumbled mountains of Greece—with few roads or railroads, the valleys drenched in rain, the peaks bitterly cold—were the setting for the war's newest campaign, and the difficult terrain and lack of transportation and communication facilities obviously militated against a Blitzkrieg, even if the Italian Army were adequate in training, leadership, staff work and matériel for such technique—something that is doubtful. Greece is not a large country; air-line distances from point to point are short, but on the ground the miles are vertical; one climbs or descends. Greece is cut up by water—streams and rivers and arms of the sea; the land-bridge at Corinth forms the only link between the Peloponnesus and the north; it is a country in which mechanized and motorized equipment must operate at a disadvantage.

### Greek Forces Small

Greece commenced to mobilize her forces to full strength rapidly after the invasion, but the numbers and equipment available were not impressive. Probably no more than 150,000 effectives (fully equipped) plus supply and administrative troops can be maintained in the field simultaneously, though Greece has total reserves of about 600,000 indifferently trained.

Equipment is diverse and obsolescent, but there are plenty of rifles and considerable mountain artillery; the Evzones (mountain troops) and King's Guards are good troops and good marksmen, hardy, wiry and well adapted to mountain fighting. Like the Yugoslavs and many of the Balkan peoples, the Greeks find their morale and confidence is bolstered by their low opinion of the Italian fighting qualities. The Greeks have only some 100 to 200 planes, most obsolescent, and their navy consists of one obsolescent armored cruiser, ten destroyers, thirteen torpedo boats, six submarines and mine-layers, etc.

The Greeks have cadres for some thirteen infantry and two cavalry divisions, but at the week-end, dispatches had mentioned only some eight divisions as in process of mobilization. It is unlikely that more than that number can be put into the field for some weeks. Nor did the quality of this army lend much confidence in the Greek ability to resist long unaided.

### Italian Strength

The Italians apparently started the campaign with some 200,000 troops in Albania, who were immediately reinforced by troops transported across the Adriatic to Porto Edda, Durazzo and elsewhere. The largest number of divisions mentioned as used by the Italians was ten or eleven; apparently only two or three of these—Alpinists, Bersaglieri and Blackshirts—had seen action by the week-end. The Italians had available at least fifteen to twenty other divisions, 1,000 planes, and the strength of their very considerable navy, if they wanted to employ them.

The difficult nature of the terrain and the apparently small Italian forces used explain, therefore, in some part, the relative slowness of the Italian advance. The fighting has been limited to sharp skirmishing and sniping by the Evzones as they fought delaying actions with the Italian Alpinists and Bersaglieri and fell back on their prepared field fortifications embraced in the Metaxas Line.

This line—earthworks, concrete pillboxes, trenches and barbed wire—is backed up at the western end by the fortified town of Yanina in Epirus, west of the Pindus Mountains and gateway to the port and small naval station of Preveza farther south and to the important railroad town of Trikkala, east of the Pindus.

Even more important than the actual fighting, however, was the nature of the British riposte. The eyes of the world were on the Greek islands last week as the world waited to know whether or not, this time, Britain would be able to aid a small invaded neutral, or whether the fate of Greece was sealed.

### Aid Limited

Many thought Turkey and possibly Yugoslavia or Russia would aid Greece. But at the week-end Salonika had seen no British forces; the British aid, as officially described, had been limited to naval and air action; mines had been laid off Western Greece and south of Athens; British planes had bombed the Dodecanese and Naples, and though there was no confirmation, there was general belief that British marines and perhaps some troops had occupied some Greek islands, probably in the mouth of the Aegean Sea.

All of these developments seemed to point to certain conclusions—some of which are tentative only and which may be invalidated by this week's events or by more complete information:

(1) Greece, without help, is no match for Italy.

(2) The Italians apparently limited their effort in the first days of their invasion to relatively small forces, and their advance, made initially at the cost of few casualties to either side, though particularly pronounced in the west, was relatively sluggish.

(3) As Italian dispatches hinted, the Italians seemed at first to be depending upon Axis pressure upon the Greek Government almost as much as upon military force to accomplish the conquest of Greece. The latter, however, was supplanting the former at the week-end.

(4) The success of this manoeuvre depended first upon the capability of Greek military resistance; second, upon the help that Greece could expect from other powers.

(5) That help, it appeared, would be of strictly limited character. The threat of Germany kept, and probably will keep—until they are directly threatened—Yugoslavia, Turkey and Russia immobilized. The pattern of British aid was not yet clear, but it seemed likely that it would be limited to naval and air assistance, and that the British forces in the Near East would not be able to spare many troops and that air raids would be limited. It was expected, however, that small forces of marines (plus some army detachments), with the aid of the navy, might seize and hold certain Greek islands, such as Crete or some of the Cyclades.

### Fate of Greece

If these tentative conclusions are supported by later events, therefore, it seems likely that eventually Greece proper may come under Italian political and military domination, with certain parts of Greece used by the Axis as air and naval bases. Britain, on the other hand, may control Crete or other Greek islands, which would give her additional naval and air bases (though of limited capacity) at the mouth of the Aegean, from which British forces might operate against the Italian Dodecanese, against Albania and Italy and Italian Grecian bases, and particularly against the Italian sea supply lines across the Mediterranean from Taranto to Benghazi, the latter one of the principal supply bases of the Italian forces invading Egypt.

But it must be constantly remembered that the Grecian campaign is only the first scene in the drama of the Mediterranean, and in itself is in no sense conclusive. The Italians' Egyptian campaign, long stopped at Egyptian Sidi Barrani, far in the Western Desert, showed some signs of resumption last week and will very likely be pushed this Winter, but perhaps not until other threats to Britain's hold on the Mediterranean basin develop. These have been forecast many times—the neutralization of Gibraltar as a naval base with the help of Spain; perhaps the extension of German influence and military power down the African West Coast, with the help of Spain and France; perhaps a German push into Turkey and Syria as the final development of a great pincer move against Suez.

### Uncertainties Remain

It seems quite likely that some or all of these things may be tried; what is uncertain is whether or not the enormous military, diplomatic, political and economic problems incident to accomplishment can be resolved successfully. The British Fleet alone, still dominating most of the Mediterranean, is an obstacle that will not easily be surmounted, and behind that fleet stand the armies of Egypt and Palestine, the air forces of the Middle East and the resources of an empire which is just commencing to exert its great military strength.

\* \* \*

**March 2, 1941**

# NAZI TROOPS OCCUPY SOFIA AND KEY BASES AS BULGARIA ENTERS ALLIANCE WITH AXIS; BRITISH HINT BOMBING; U. S. TO FREEZE FUNDS

### GERMAN MARCH ON

*Forces Pour Into Bulgar Capital and Ports by Plane and Truck*

### PEOPLE WATCH IN SILENCE

*British Expect to Leave Soon—Air Defenses Increased— Blackout in Effect*

Special Cable to The New York Times

BELGRADE, Yugoslavia, March 1—The German Army and Air Force started what is apparently an occupation of all strategic bases in Bulgaria today when that country joined the Berlin-Rome-Tokyo pact in Vienna.

German bombers appeared over Sofia at dawn, according to reports telephoned to different sources here, and were followed an hour later by squadrons of light and heavy bombers, fighters and reconnaissance planes.

At the same time unconfirmed reports from Varna and Ruschuk declared uniformed German troops were entering Bulgaria at Black Sea ports and across the Danube. Other information from frontier sources said bridging operations had begun at other points on the Danube, including Nikopol, and that steel-helmeted Germans were crossing in trucks, accompanied by tanks and ammunition trucks.

#### Planes Thunder Over Sofia

Seventeen troop trucks were reported by foreign press sources at Sofia to have left Varna during the morning,

As the little Balkan nation signed on the dotted line in Vienna yesterday, German mechanized forces from Rumania swept across the Danube and into Sophia (1), accompanied by many war planes. Varna (2) and other ports on the Black Sea also were occupied by the Germans, and so were strategic bases throughout the country, including air bases near the Greek frontier, while more Bulgarian troops were sent to the Turkish border (3). The four smaller nations that have now joined the German-Italian-Japanese alliance are shown on the map in various degrees of shading, together with the dates of their adherence.

loaded with German soldiers and headed for the interior. Information this evening from foreign military and diplomatic sources said German dive-bombers were arriving at Southern Bulgarian air bases close to the Greek frontier. These reports could not be confirmed. Telephone communications with Sofia were refused in Belgrade tonight.

One Belgrade foreign journalist who talked with Sofia by telephone this morning was told that "hundreds" of German planes were then flying over the capital. Whether these planes landed at Bulgarian bases or returned to Rumania it was then impossible to ascertain.

The Belgrade journalist could hear the sound of planes in the receiver, and at one moment it was almost impossible to understand the Sofia correspondent because of the thundering noise in the transmitter. This was ascribed to the roaring of airplane engines, which Sofia said was "deafening," since the planes, flying in formation, were only a few hundred feet above the rooftops.

Late reports this evening said scores of German bombers and fighters had landed on airdromes south of Sofia and that other planes had passed low over the capital, headed for other air bases already occupied by German ground crews and anti-aircraft units.

#### Control Points Occupied

At 4 P. M. it was reported to foreign correspondents here that German troops had appeared in Sofia and marched through the main streets, parading before the German lega-tion. Last night's reports that the Germans had occupied all major railheads and highway intersections as well as tele-graph and telephone controls were reiterated by tonight's reports to foreign diplomatic sources here.

The British Minister at Sofia, George W. Rendel, is under-stood to have called the Foreign Office and the Presidency this morning and demanded a conference tomorrow with Premier Bogdan Philoff. Reports that Mr. Rendel would serve an ulti-matum tomorrow, requiring an immediate Bulgarian explana-tion of today's events and the government's intentions, could not be confirmed here, either from the Foreign Office or from Bulgarian or British sources.

It is known, however, that the British press office in Sofia was closed today and that several members of the staff were leaving tonight. All Britons in Bulgaria not attached to the legation have departed or are planning to leave tonight or tomorrow. Most of them, it is understood in British circles here, will leave for Istanbul.

It was reported late this evening that the Yugoslav-Bulgarian frontier would be "closed to all traffic." A Turkish diplomat is due here tomorrow aboard a train from Sofia and his embassy has been unable to learn whether he will be able to come or will be held up at the frontier.

Diplomats here, in the absence of positive information, held the opinion that the situation was worsening in the light of scantier reports from Sofia. Foreign military sources could learn little beyond the reports of flights of German planes over Bulgaria to unspecified bases and information that German troops were landing at Ruschuk, Varna and Vidin. There was no confirmation of reports that "three bri-gades" had arrived.

### Crowds Watch in Silence

An eyewitness telephoning from Sofia described the arrival of a dozen dust-covered German army cars, which went immediately to the German legation. Crowds gathered and eyed the German soldiers curiously, but there were no demonstrations. More curiosity was aroused, however, when a German travel agency unfurled a huge swastika banner.

German planes flew over the city most of the afternoon and many transports were sighted flying in a northeasterly direction. The police visited shopkeepers all day, ordering them to observe the strictest blackout beginning tonight. Additional anti-aircraft batteries were installed throughout the city, many of them reportedly manned by German crews. Unconfirmed reports said additional classes of reservists were called to the colors today and most of them were believed to be needed as aerial protection squads.

The general belief here, however, is that the British will not take aerial action until after the departure of the Minister and his staff, which is believed to be imminent.

British subjects have been leaving Yugoslavia for two days, now, while others are reported to be packing tonight. It is believed they will take the Athens route to Istanbul before a possible German offensive cuts communications at Salonika.

Several violations of the Yugoslav air space were reported today and one German bomber was forced down by heavy anti-aircraft fire. The crew was interned. The pilot announced that he had lost his way and was looking for Bulgaria. Six other German planes that came from Rumania encountered heavy anti-aircraft fire and one of them was believed damaged.

### Grave Questions Raised

SOFIA, Bulgaria, March 1 (AP)—Germany occupied Bulgaria today—the eleventh sovereign State she has overrun since 1938.

The coming of Reichsfuehrer Hitler's legions in gray-green battle dress by plane, armored car and truck raised grave questions as to the future of Greece in her war with Italy, of Turkey's future under her alliance with Britain and of Britain's attitude toward Bulgaria.

The military occupation extended even to the heart of Sofia almost before the ink of Bulgaria's signature was dry on a protocol of the German-Italian-Japanese military pact.

Official Bulgarian quarters admitted that Varna, strategic port on the Black Sea, was occupied by the Germans.

The British Minister to Sofia, George William Rendel, obtained an early evening audience with King Boris, and members of the legation expected him to notify the monarch that German occupation of Bulgaria left Britain no choice but to break off relations.

Mr. Rendel said recently that Britain probably would declare war on Bulgaria and bomb her communications if Nazi occupation was permitted.

The occupation of Bulgaria must have started at dawn today—hours before the Vienna signing ceremony. Bulgarians mutely watched German armored cars roll into their capital even before many had learned that the pact had been signed.

### Arrive Soon After Signing

The vanguard of the German mechanized forces reached Sofia this afternoon, only two hours after the Vienna pact signing. As the gray column filed into the traffic-cleared streets, fleets of planes—fighting craft and troop-carrying transports—roared low overhead.

Many German business houses promptly unfurled their swastika flags in welcome. The police cleared the main ave-nues, apparently for the approach of truck columns believed to be just outside the city.

Bulgaria showed concern over Turkey's intentions, now that the Nazis had been let in. The country approached general mobilization. Troops newly called from cities to the colors left Sofia in large groups—bound for the Turkish frontier. Thou-sands of peasant soldiers trudged along with them.

The German armies, naturally, were pointed south toward Greece in their occupation of Bulgaria, but none could say that was their destination.

Thus at long last Bulgaria joined the procession of States overrun by Germany since the annexation of Austria on March 13, 1938. Those that preceded her are, in chronological order, Austria, Czecho-Slovakia, Poland, Denmark, Norway, the

Netherlands, Belgium, Luxembourg, France and Rumania. Hungary, though not occupied, has provided railroads for Nazi armies moving into Rumania, whence they entered Bulgaria.

Still other territories to go under Nazi control include Memel, Britain's Channel Islands and the Free City of Danzig.

Thus, for the second time in twenty-five years, Bulgaria has cast her lot with Germany's fortunes of war. She was a World War comrade of the Central Powers. What persuasion it took, no one announced.

But Bulgaria was in the Axis debt for return from Rumania of Southern Dobruja, which added 2,883 square miles to the 39,825 of her former national territory and increased her population by 375,000 to nearly 6,500,000.

### Yugoslav Position Shaky

Yugoslavia's position appeared to be extremely shaky. The belief that Rome-Berlin-Tokyo diplomats now would put the squeeze on the Belgrade Government was strengthened by the words of German Foreign Minister Joachim von Ribbentrop, in Vienna for the pact signing, that Bulgaria would not be the last to join in the Axis campaign to destroy the British Empire.

A few hours after the Vienna ceremony, diplomatic quarters heard that British Foreign Secretary Anthony Eden, who has just completed talks with the Turks at Ankara, might fly from Cairo to Belgrade as well as to Athens. At Belgrade, presumably, he would attempt to steady Yugoslavia's wavering neutrality.

Premier Philoff's expression of friendship with Russia today in Vienna was viewed by observers as confirming reports that Joseph Stalin had given Herr Hitler the go-ahead in Bulgaria in return for territorial concessions elsewhere—such as in Finland or Rumania's province of Moldavia.

The attitude of Bulgaria's reputedly pro-British King, 47-year-old Boris III, remained a mystery. The monarch remained secluded in his big yellow palace in the heart of Sofia, while German troop trucks and armored cars rolled past the gates.

Bulgaria's World War partnership with Germany carried Boris's father, Ferdinand, into exile and his nation to partition at the World War peace-conference table. Ferdidand abdicated on Oct. 3, 1918.

### Sofia to Be "Open City"

SOFIA, Bulgaria, March 1 (UP)—As German motorized and airborne troops roared into Bulgaria tonight, a high Nazi source said German General Staff headquarters, from which future military moves would be directed, would be established at Chamkuria, forty-three miles from the capital.

The resort town of Chamkuria had been chosen, it was said, to avoid concentration of troops in Sofia, which would be declared an "open city" to save it from British bombing. It was reported that 200 villas had been requisitioned for the German staff.

Communication to and from Sofia was difficult. Thrice during the night United States Minister George H. Earle was pre-vented from crossing the border into Yugoslavia at Dragoman to advise Washington what was transpiring.

\* \* \*

March 21, 1941

## YUGOSLAV CABINET WEIGHS NAZI TERMS; REPORTED ASSENT THREATENS STRIFE; WAVES OF PLANES HAMMER PLYMOUTH

### BELGRADE IS TENSE

*3 Ministers Expected to Resign if Regime Signs With Axis*

### LIMITED PACT POSSIBLE

*Pro-British Peasantry Held Likely to Rebel at Alliance—Nazi Threats Seen*

By Telephone to The New York Times

BELGRADE, Yugoslavia, Friday, March 21—An emergency meeting of the Yugoslav Cabinet summoned last night to consider the German demands on the Belgrade government ended at 12:30 this morning after a three-hour session.

A semi-official spokesman declared ten minutes later that the Cabinet was called to consider "political questions concerning Yugoslav foreign policy." The editors of the official news agency indicated at about 1:30 this morning that there would probably be no further statement for the time being.

[Yugoslavia will sign a pact with Germany making the Belgrade government a passive but effective member of the Axis alliance, said a Belgrade Associated Press dispatch, which added that three Cabinet members and the Yugoslav Minister to Russia were expected to resign over the decision and that it remained a question whether the pro-British peasantry of Yugoslavia would accept any such move passively. A United Press dispatch from Belgrade said the Cabinet was reported to have approved a "special form" of adherence to the Axis alliance.]

### Reich's "Final Terms" Debated

Sources close to government circles declared during the course of the emergency session that Premier Dragisha Cvetkovitch had summoned his Ministers to debate the "final terms" for settlement of the Reich's demands upon Yugoslavia.

One neutral diplomat here, while noting that the emergency sessions of the Palace Council and Cabinet had fallen exactly one week apart and always on Thursday—on the sixth, thirteenth and twentieth of March—added that "this is simply a tribute to German efficiency operating in the diplomatic field and elsewhere."

Rumors continued to circulate long after midnight and this morning. Some British sources, expressing fears that intensive German pressure had forced the Cvetkovitch government into a position where a modified form of the tripartite pact would be the only peaceful solution, reported rumors from diplomatic sources that the Yugoslav-German agreement would be signed on Sunday.

The Belgrade morning press continues to emphasize the "friendly relations" among Germany, Yugoslavia and Greece. The newspaper Vreme repeats that "the position of Yugoslavia and Turkey will shortly be made generally known."

Widespread reports in Belgrade that a German ultimatum was served upon the Yugoslav Government yesterday were flatly denied by a trusted source close to the Foreign Office.

While the Yugoslav-German negotiations during the past few days have been conducted in an increasingly cooler atmosphere and German demands for Yugoslavia's signature to the tripartite pact, for passage of German troops and munitions trains through Yugoslavia and economic concessions have been phrased in sharper language, the informant assured this correspondent that nothing approaching an ultimatum had been received either in the Palace or the Presidency.

### Conversations in Two Capitals

The German demands were expanded and renewed, according to this information, through diplomatic channels at Berlin and by the German Minister to Yugoslavia, Viktor von Heeren, at Belgrade. This is substantiated by reports from other sources totally, disassociated from this informant.

Germany, it is understood, has offered to remove virtually every objectionable section of the tripartite pact through a series of "escape clauses" to induce the Regent, Prince Paul, and his government chieftains to sign. Yugoslavia's territorial integrity, for instance, would be "guaranteed" by the Axis and other co-signers of the Axis alliance. It would be specifically stated that no military clauses, published or secret, had been included in the framework of the pact. "An Aegean outlet," understood to mean Salonika, would be guaranteed to Yugoslavia for the duration of the war and thereafter by German military force and by any post-war peace conference.

In return, according to this information, Yugoslavia would have to permit the passage of German munition and hospital trains and also troop trains and grant special express privileges to German trains of any category upon German demand. Yugoslavia would agree to halt all anti-Axis activity, including propaganda, and, according to one report, to censor all news telephoned abroad and agree to "co-operate economically."

Economic cooperation would include the installation of technical production experts in Yugoslav agriculture and industry and the continuation of present cooperation with additional economic concessions to Germany during the April meeting of the Yugoslav Trade Commission.

Agency reports sent abroad to the effect that Yugoslavia already has initialed a version of the Tripartite pact guaranteeing all major German demands were labeled "pure guesswork" by authoritative circles here, who added that it was probably bad guessing. The companion report, which was traced directly to the German Legation here, that Premier Cvetkovitch and Foreign Minister Alexander Cincar-Markovitch would leave on Monday for Berlin appeared to have a trifle more substantiation, inasmuch as this visit already has been postponed three times and is still expected.

One German version reported that the pact—of the original non-aggression type agreed upon exactly two weeks ago—would be signed next Wednesday after the arrival in Berlin of the Japanese Foreign Minister, Yosuke Matsuoka.

### Plan to Join Axis Reported

BELGRADE, Yugoslavia, Friday, March 21 (AP)—Violent objections by Cabinet members who predicted serious internal disorder were reliably reported early today to have arisen from the Yugoslav Crown Council's approval of a program described as a passive but effective alliance with the German Axis.

Such an alliance, which would clear the way for Germany to attack Greece as soon as signatures are affixed in Berlin, possibly next week, was approved by the Council late last night. The Cabinet and military chiefs were asked to initial the scheme without discussion, but three Ministers were asserted to have raised vigorous objections. Their resignations were considered likely.

Political quarters pointed out that the Regent Prince Paul then would be free to find a Cabinet that would approve a German alliance, but they agreed that such action might well bring to a blaze the smoldering passions in this pro-British country. Such a reaction was predicted particularly among the peasant population.

The three objecting Cabinet Ministers were Dr. Srdjan Budisauljevitch, Minister of Social Welfare; Dr. Branko Kubrilovitch, Minister of Agriculture and leader of the Serb Peasant party, and Professor Mikhail Konstantinovitch, Minister of Justice.

Friends of Dr. Kubrilovitch said he probably would resign immediately in protest against the council's decision, and associates of Milan Gavrilovitch, first Yugoslav Minister to Soviet Russia, said a few days ago he had threatened to quit his post and not return to the country if an Axis agreement was signed.

Seemingly confirming that Yugoslavia would sign with the Axis, probably next week, one Cabinet Minister declared when the meeting broke up after midnight:

"Because of Yugoslavia's delicate foreign situation, it is necessary that her position of strict neutrality should be modified in some way so that she should become more closely connected with the Axis. Because she is surrounded on all sides by Axis troops, it is necessary for Yugoslavia to form a new foreign policy in order to maintain her independence and prevent her from being involved in war.

"Therefore, an agreement is being made with the Axis providing for more intimate relations."

These relations, as described by a responsible government leader, would involve an offer of economic and semi-military aid to Germany and the Axis, but another version said the program called for full Axis membership in everything except that Yugoslavia would not furnish active military aid to the Axis and troops would not cross Yugoslavia to get at the Greeks.

Greek quarters, stunned by the swift decision of the Yugoslav Crown Council after weeks of obscure bargaining, said the government solemnly assured Greece only a few days ago that nothing would occur.

In view of this, it was believed that Germany and Italy had put extreme pressure on Yugoslavia in the past few days, this speed-up possibly being linked with tidings last night of an Italian rout at Greek hands in Albania.

After the stormy Cabinet session, which ended this morning, a Yugoslav communiqué said merely that "questions of foreign policy" had been discussed for three hours. It was added semi-officially, however, that Yugoslavia would get a "guarantee" that no power that has signed the Axis pact would violate Yugoslav territory.

### Yugoslavs Hostile to Nazi Film

BELGRADE, March 20 (UP)—The approaching climax of German-Yugoslav diplomatic negotiations coincides with the showing of the Nazi propaganda film, "Victory in the West." At each performance the Yugoslav authorities deem it necessary to have at least 100 plainclothes detectives among the audience to suppress any possible hostile reaction.

\* \* \*

March 25, 1941

# BELGRADE YIELDS TO NAZIS, SIGNS LIMITED PACT TODAY; TURKS REASSURED BY SOVIET

### YUGOSLAVS ON WAY

*Nation Tense as Premier and Foreign Minister Go to Vienna for Signing*

### MILITARY CLAUSES BARRED

*Police Kept on 24-Hour Duty—Army Leaves Are Canceled—More Reservists Called*

### By RAYMOND BROCK
By Telephone to The New York Times

BELGRADE, Yugoslavia, March 24—The Yugoslav Premier and Foreign Minister left Belgrade by special train at 10:06 o'clock tonight en route for Vienna, where about 11 o'clock tomorrow morning they will sign the capitulation of the Yugoslav Government to the demands of Germany in a pact dictated from Berlin.

Viktor von Heeren, the German Minister, accompanied the Premier and Foreign Minister aboard the four-car special train, which also carried about twenty additional passengers, German and Yugoslav editors, journalists and secret police.

Until the moment of departure tonight, final details of the pact were a closely guarded secret. According to the most reliable information late tonight, however, from sources close

With Yugoslav statesmen en route to Vienna (1) to sign an agreement with the Axis, Sofia looked forward to the return to her of the territory known as "Westernland" (shaded areas at 2) and of Strumitza (shaded area at 3), which Bulgaria lost to Yugoslavia after the World War. In addition, Sofia hoped to regain an outlet to the Aegean Sea; after the Second Balkan War in 1913 Bulgaria had such an outlet (shaded area at 4).

to the Foreign Office, Premier Dragisha Cvetkovitch, and Foreign Minister Alexander Cincar-Markovitch will sign a pact that may be designated "tripartite" but, will bear little resemblance to the pact signed by Hungary, Slovakia, Rumania and Bulgaria.

It will contain no military clauses, published or secret. Germany, according to these sources, will receive permission to use Yugoslav railroads for transportation of munitions and hospital trains. The proposal for sealed trains, German railroad control posts and a hands-off policy by Yugoslav customs, it was said, was rejected.

### Economic Aspect Stressed

The most important section of the Belgrade-Berlin pact, aside from the political implications of the signing itself, is said to be economic. Germany, it is reliably reported, will be permitted to send industrial and agricultural technicians into Yugoslavia to increase factory and field production of foodstuffs and raw materials to help feed and clothe the German Army and the German people.

Germany will obtain increased surpluses of grains and meats where these exist and supervisors and technicians may be installed in Yugoslav mines and smelters to assist in the production of raw and finished copper, lead and lead concentrates so badly needed by the German war machine. The status of the British-owned and American-managed Trepcha lead mines is still unknown, although the German Supply Ministry is eager to secure control of the mines and foundries if possible.

The German demand that Yugoslavia demobilize her army was flatly rejected.

Further details about the pact to be signed before Adolf Hitler and Foreign Minister Joachim von Ribbentrop are necessarily vague. There is even reason to believe there are few other details, despite the enormous number of speculative stories abroad about them. The signature of the pact undoubtedly will be accompanied by a thundering acclamation in the controlled press of Germany and Yugoslavia about the mutual confidence and friendship and cooperation existing between these two countries.

### Premier Looks Haggard

A farewell party—if that is what it was—on the platform at the isolated Topchidersko station tonight radiated neither confidence nor friendship. There were no smiles and no handshakes. The Italian Minister, the Hungarian Minister, the Rumanian and Bulgarian chargés d'affaires, the Yugoslav Vice Premier, Vladimir Matchek, and a large group of journalists and about fifty special policemen solemnly stood about in a cold wind until the limousines arrived with M. Cvetkovitch and Dr. Cincar-Markovitch.

The Premier looked almost haggard. Dr. Cincar-Markovitch appeared tired, too. Both men were immediately surrounded by the police and escorted to the special train. The police were observed to be heavily armed. It is common knowledge in Belgrade that certain members of the government have been warned that they will be assassinated if they capitulate to Germany. These warnings are taken here in all seriousness.

M. Cvetkovitch and Dr. Cincar-Markovitch entered their private car and Herr von Heeren followed. The press delegation, including Predrag Milojevitch, the Yugoslav press chief, and the directors of the Belgrade Vreme and Politika, the Hrvatski Djnevnik of Zagreb and the Slovenech of Ljlubljana, and the Deutsche Volksblatt, then boarded the train and it pulled slowly out of the station, six minutes after the time scheduled for its departure.

Nobody even waved good-bye. A Serbian journalist remarked at this to a photographer.

"Would you wave good-bye at a funeral?" demanded the photographer.

M. Matchek, clearly bearing the marks of the long crisis that ended this morning, was the first to leave the station after the train's departure. Reports abroad that M. Matchek had also gone were disclaimed by a communiqué issued here tonight declaring he would remain in Belgrade during the journey of the Premier and the Foreign Minister. The other Ministers, several of whom are ordinarily genial and approachable, displayed no inclination to talk, but entered their cars and were driven away.

Mikhail Konstantovitch, whose resignation from the Ministry of Justice was still the subject of political debate tonight, was not at the station. He is reported to have withdrawn his resignation, thus filling up the Cabinet with the appointment of Charslav Nikitovitch to the Ministry of Agriculture and Dragonir Ikonitch to the post of Minister of Social Affairs and Public Welfare.

The last two are virtually unknown, and the communiqué announcing their appointments at noon today drew wrathful expletives from old Serbian politicians and business men. Their indignation, however, had cooled tonight.

"The relative importance of these two nobodies is rather academic now," said one Serbian attorney. "We are now concerned with a larger issue and the men responsible for it."

### British Deliver Note

Ronald Ian Campbell, the British Minister, delivered a note to the government today, the text of which was not disclosed here. It was learned, however that the note expressed British surprise at the "sudden drastic change" in Yugloslav policy.

Following a reference, according to diplomatic sources, to the "friendship existing between these two countries, sealed during the World War" the note declared that "the Yugoslav Government deludes itself if it considers that this change in policy will be condoned by His Majesty's Government."

The note, however, contained no reference to the intentions of the British Government should Yugoslavia follow the example of Rumania and Bulgaria, where British diplomatic relations were severed.

What reaction may be expected from the people to the government's capitulation appeared tonight to be indicated by reports from the provinces. The anti-German demonstrations at Kragujevac, Skoplje, Banja Luka and Berane were followed by similar protests at Cetinje, the Montenegrin capital, and the smaller villages of Bosnia and South and Central Serbia and Macedonia.

### Pamphlets Appear on Streets

In Belgrade pamphlets appeared on the streets denouncing the government and calling the signature of the pact "an act of treason." The pamphlets said:

"We 16,000,000 people want liberty and freedom. Sixteen members of the government want to sell us slavery. They must remember that those who risk the necks of others risk their own . . . we do not desire pacts, tourists, instructors or economic experts . . . we want only liberty and freedom!"

A delegation of Sokol leaders called at the White Palace today to plead with Prince Paul against tonight's journey. The Prince Regent refused to see them. Belgrade University students drew up a resolution today condemning the government and its policy.

The Serbian Patriarch, whose advice to Prince Paul against this pact was ignored today, summoned an emergency meeting of the Episcopal Council of the Serbian Orthodox Church of Belgrade on Thursday.

The Vice Governor of Croatia, Svetozar Ivkovitch; chief of the Croatian Internal Political Department, Bojan Bojkitch, and Milotin Kozanovitch of the Croat Government Public Health Department, resigned today in protest. They are Independent Democrats. All Agragrian party members have resigned their State posts. Information from high Agrarian political circles said that Milan Gavrilovitch, party president, has signified that he will resign as Yugoslav Minister to Moscow if the Cvetkovitch government signs the Tripartite Pact.

The Yugoslav Army remains the biggest unknown quantity. The entire force, officered almost universally by Serbs, is admirably disciplined and devoted to most of the elder generals. There is a rapidly growing dissatisfaction in the ranks, however, and among the younger captains, majors and colonels, some of whom might be expected to assume active command in general staff and divisional staff posts if Yugoslavia was forced into war.

"Of one thing you can be certain," an officer told this correspondent tonight, "if the people are against this thing there is no man on this earth who can lead this army against this people . . . ."

\*    \*    \*

**March 25, 1941**

## THE TIMETABLE OF A SURRENDER; WHAT HAPPENED TO YUGOSLAVIA

By Telephone to The New York Times

BELGRADE, Yugoslavia, March 24—The story of the Yugoslav crisis reads like the thrice-told tale of Hungary, Rumania and Bulgaria—German "power diplomacy" turned on and off like a water tap, generating storms of rumors, alarmist news, editorials in the controlled press and the German introduction of new demands at the psychological moment when all seemed beautiful and everything solved.

Germany began to "turn on" the crisis the first week in February. The German invitation to come to the Berghof was transmitted to Premier Dragisha Cvetkovitch and Dr. Alexander Cincar-Markovitch, the Foreign Minister, from the German Minister to Yugoslavia, Viktor von Heeren and Danilo Gregoritch, the Germanophile director of the Belgrade newspaper Vreme, who had just returned from one of his periodic trips into the Reich. When the journey was certain on Feb. 12 the German Legation "released" the story through its agents and journalists. M. Cvetkovitch and Dr. Cincar-Markovitch departed in secrecy the next day. From then on it might be told chronologically.

### Day-by-Day Story

Feb. 14—Herr Hitler and Herr von Ribbentrop presented the original German demands to the Yugoslav Premier and Foreign Minister at the Berghof. Germany desired the Yugoslav signature of the Tripartite Pact, permission to pass munitions and troops if necessary across Yugoslavia, immobilization of the Yugoslav Army when Bulgaria's occupation started and "economic cooperation," meaning more drastic concessions in foodstuff production and the clearing rate.

Feb. 15—The envoys returned and reported to Prince Paul. Prince Paul instructed M. Cvetkovitch to form a consolidation government to include the opposition party and negotiate with Germany. Various reports indicated that Germany would

reward Yugoslavia with stretches of Albanian and Greek territory "after the German victory."

Feb. 16 to 18—The press campaign started to woo Yugoslav cooperation. Germany finally obtained control of Yugoslavia's great Bor copper mines, a stop-gap concession by M. Cvetkovitch, who was playing for time.

Feb. 22—Trade Minister Ivan Andres held trade talks with German supply delegates at Belgrade to discuss the specific German economic demands.

Feb. 23 to 28—M. Cvetkovitch struggled vainly to lure opposition leaders into the government. German impatience increased. Herr von Heeren renewed his calls at the Foreign Office and the Presidency.

March 1—Germany marched into Bulgaria and simultaneously Berlin warned Prince Paul that time was running out—Yugoslavia must come to terms. Herr von Heeren left Belgrade for Zagreb, presumably to attend the Dresden Opera.

March 2—Prince Paul departed secretly for Slovenia, where he conferred at his Brdo lodge with Herr von Heeren and a special German envoy; still unidentified. The British Minister, Ronald Ian Campbell, departed secretly for Athens to confer with Anthony Eden, the British Foreign Secretary.

March 4—Mobilization posters appeared upon the streets of Belgrade and the provincial capitals. Prince Paul returned from Slovenia. Mr. Campbell flew back from Athens.

March 6—Prince Paul called a Palace Council of the government chieftains, the Army High Command and Regency, and presented the German demands, now slightly enlarged. Five Ministers threatened to resign. Prince Paul conferred with Herr von Heeren. The Tripartite Pact was thrown overboard. A nonaggression pact to be accompanied by a declaration of friendship was hit upon. Protesting, the Cabinet finally agreed.

March 7—Mr. Campbell saw Prince Paul, warning him that Great Britain was disturbed by the trend of things and would regard excessive Yugoslav concessions to Germany in the light of events that took place in Rumania and Bulgaria. M. Cvetkovitch, lunching with the American Minister, was informed that Washington hoped Yugoslavia would maintain her peaceful neutrality, shunning Axis pacts and anything dangerous to her integrity. The lease-lend bill, it was pointed out, would place arms at Yugoslavia's disposal if needed.

March 9 and 10—M. Cvetkovitch renewed his struggle to consolidate the government, but in vain. Soviet diplomatic pressure was reported and a Soviet friendship declaration was dangled if Yugoslavia held out for harmless concessions to Germany, M. Cvetkovitch's second proposed journey to Germany to sign the non-aggression pact was postponed upon German initiative.

March 11—Herr von Heeren called at the Foreign Office and presented the new German demands—and the real crisis was on. Prince Paul immediately summoned the Crown Council to meet the following day.

March 12—At the Crown Council meeting three Ministers offered their resignations on the spot. The government seemed about to fall and both Vice Premier Vladimir

Matchek and General Peter Pesitch, the Minister of War, were approached by the Prince Regent with the tentative office of the Premiership. Both refused. It was Yugoslavia's "M-day" and about 300,000 new men were called to the colors in all the provinces.

March 13 to 15—German pressure was turned on hard. Herr von Heeren beat a path to the Foreign Office and Presidency. The Italian Minister, Signor Mamelli, called to reinforce his Axis colleague. The Turkish Ambassador called too and Mr. Campbell made a second visit to Prince Paul. Opposition was growing in the army, the church and throughout the provinces against any concessions to Germany.

March 18—Ex-Premier Milan Stoyadinovitch was smuggled out of the country to asylum in Greece. "No Quislings for Yugoslavia," said his enemies.

March 20—Germany turned the pressure full on and the government crumbled. Herr von Heeren warned Prince Paul that Herr Hitler "calmly desired" settlement of the Yugoslav-German situation within eight days. M. Cvetkovitch summoned an emergency meeting of the Cabinet. He presented the "final" German demand. Three Ministers promptly resigned.

March 21, 22 and 23—The crisis rushed to its climax. Twenty-seven candidates rejected proffered Cabinet posts. A violent storm of opposition began to break in the provinces with demonstrations in Central Serbia, Montenegro, Bosnia and Macedonia.

March 24, today—Two minor politicians were finally induced to accept the portfolios of the two Ministries. M. Konstantinovitch, M. Cvetkovitch's long-time aide, was reported to have withdrawn his resignation from the Justice Ministry. The Cabinet met to initial a proposed Belgrade-Berlin pact. A few hours later the train pulled out with the uneasy Premier and his party, bound for Vienna and the sign-up.

\*   \*   \*

**March 26, 1941**

## SERBS STIR RISINGS AGAINST AXIS DEAL

*Fall of Cabinet Is Threatened as Yugoslav Anger Spreads—*
*Demonstrators Jailed*

By RAY BROCK
By Telephone to The New York Times

BELGRADE, Yugoslavia, March 25—The patchwork Cvetkovitch government, which capitulated to Germany in Vienna today and signed a pact with the Axis, already was disintegrating tonight in Yugoslavia under a wave of public anger. Its complete collapse is confidently expected in high political circles here soon after the Premier and Foreign Minister return from Germany.

Belgrade was dumfounded today by the resignation of the Germanophile Minister of Education, Dusan Pantitch. A sensation followed when usually reliable sources reported that

Mikhail Konstantovitch, the Minister of Justice, was maintaining his resignation despite its non-acceptance by the Prince Regent.

Prince Paul himself was scheduled to broadcast to the country late today in an effort to soothe the inflamed peasantry and find some support among the people for a government that defied the will and traditions of the Yugoslavs, most of whom seem to be clamoring for the downfall of the government and an opportunity to defend the country with arms against Germany.

The broadcast was repeatedly postponed and appeared tonight to have been canceled.

### More Resignations Likely

Additional resignations from the Cvetkovitch Cabinet, led by those of Milan Protitch, Minister of Supply, and Dr. Jurai Shutej, Finance Minister, seemed almost certain, according to well-informed political circles here.

Agrarian party circles here tonight said the party president, Milan Gavrilovitch, had filed his resignation with the Foreign Office today from his post as Yugoslav Minister to Moscow and was returning immediately to lead his party with the now fast-uniting opposition.

While reinforced squads of regular and special police guarded the German and Italian Legations, extra policemen were posted in public gathering places to maintain order in Belgrade. The huge public outcry against capitulation took shape in demonstrations throughout most of the provinces.

Two thousand shouting peasants bearing pitchforks and clubs stormed into Hadji Popovec in Central Serbia today. In Kragujevac, the old Serbian capital, the peasants and townspeople met in a protest meeting.

The management closed a textile factory in Belgrade late this afternoon when a workers' demonstration started. Nearly 300 boys between the ages of 14 and 19 went on strike in three Belgrade schools, marched downstairs and into the courtyard, where they upbraided the government and demanded, "Let us defend our country!" The olders leaders at the trade academy school obtained a British Union Jack, which they ran up the flagpole late this afternoon to the accompaniment of cheering by people in the streets.

### Belgrade Dissidents Jailed

The most important demonstrations took place in the capital itself and the ringleaders were jailed. There was no bloodshed. In the provinces, however, there were bloody riots, the principal ones being in Cetinje, the capital of Montenegro, and at Kragujevac, where there had been trouble yesterday.

In Cetinje the townspeople, who average a height of six feet three inches, gathered in front of a monument cheering the army and King Peter, but shouting down with all other government leaders, including the Prince Regent, and then marched through the streets to the house of the Army Commandant and demanded that he make a speech, which he refused to do.

Reports continued to come into the capital tonight of angry demonstrations throughout Bosnia, Montenegro, Serbia, South Serbia, Macedonia and Herzegovina. That there have been others in Slavonia was implied in a series of communiqués printed in Wednesday's Politika, declaring all was quiet in specified parts of the country, but not mentioning the above provinces or Slavonia, which adjoins Hungary.

There were reports of pro-German demonstrations at Dubrovnik, Zagreb and Sissak, but these were significantly quiet and orderly.

The British and Greek Legations were besieged by Serbian boys and young men, most of them demanding uniforms and transportation to the Albanian and African fronts. The waiting rooms of both legations and the Turkish Embassy were jammed with Britons and other foreigners pleading for visas immediately to leave the country.

The baggage checkroom at the central railroad station was inundated tonight with piles of baggage, golf clubs, skis and tennis racquets. The 11:40 P. M. train for Salonika and Istanbul was booked to capacity.

While the tide of evacuation reached a new high and gloom ruled in the foreign colony, church leaders, Yugoslav political opposition leaders, young army officers and common soldiers, the peasants and townspeople appeared to be uniting in an impressing and apparently spontaneous nation-wide determination to undo what has been done, unseat those who did it and confront Germany with an about-face of Yugoslav policy—made this time in Yugoslavia.

### Cabinet Overthrow Possible

The shortest route to an overthrow of the government is, of course, wholesale resignation of the Cabinet. Agrarian and Independent Democratic leaders hope to precipitate this by their wholesale resignations from all State posts and a common front in opposition. The Serbian Orthodox Church leaders, at their meeting tomorrow, will present to the Patriarch a formal resolution condemning the capitulation, according to information from church circles tonight.

Soldiers and young officers are making their pressure felt up through the ranks to the divisional and general staff leaders, who have the ear of War Minister Peter Pesitch. The people are already rising in widespread and still unorganized opposition, which probably will be the final factor.

The Serbian Komitajis, the irregular but tightly knit organization of guerrilla fighters, already have flung down their warning—that capitulation means death or exile for every man who participates.

Some observers here wondered whether M. Pantitch's resignation from his post as Education Minister was not partly inspired by receipt of a Komitaji letter. M. Pantitch's friends said the Germanophile Minister quit because a higher post had been promised justice or agriculture—during the tentative Cabinet juggling over the week-end and had been forgotten in the excitement.

Whatever the reason for M. Pantitch's resignation, the Komitajis are uniformly furious, resolute and determined that today's scenes at Vienna shall be obliterated, peacefully if possible, by violence if necessary, but obliterated. The Komitajis

include peasants and former peasants, business men, lawyers, doctors and kafana keepers, old men and young men from all walks of Serbian life. The emblem of the old veterans is a lapel button patterned after a Mills bomb.

### Serbs Seethe with Anger

It was a somewhat frightening experience to mingle today with Serbs of long acquaintance, observing what the events of last night and today had done to them. Some of the older men were in tears and could not talk at all, except in bitterly ejaculated words of profanity.

A few—very few—had taken refuge in slivovitz, drinking the hot Serbian brandy from noontime on until the huge headlines and pictures of the 1 o'clock special editions and the fanfare from Vienna faded into the background. Some of these business men and elderly editors were reminiscent of some of the Czechs known to this correspondent in Prague in 1938.

The younger men and most of the older ones who are still active Komitajis bore no resemblance to the Czechs and little resemblance to themselves as of the day before yesterday. There was not one smile, not one pleasantry or joke among men celebrated for their political wit. Not one laugh—even when it was reliably reported that M. Pantitch had gone straight from his office today to his home and to bed.

There was only an uninterrupted exchange of plans and ideas in the coldest imaginable manner, as if the subject under discussion were the Autumn slaughtering of the hogs. The German demands, the capitulation, the pact were all abandoned as topics of conversation. These men, like others sitting at other kafanas in other parts of Belgrade, were discussing ways and means . . .

In the streets there was a new blossoming of the lapel-button Union Jack and the crossed British and Greek flags that have become so popular here in recent weeks. Almost every Serb is wearing one, even some government office-holders, government party functionaries and men in uniform.

The freezing of Yugoslav credits in the United States brought home with painful suddenness to hundreds of persons just what today's events will mean to them in the future.

"Well, we knew it would happen if this thing came about," said a Serbian banker, "only we did not think this thing of today would happen."

### Strict Censorship Prevails

By Telephone to The New York Times

BERNE, Switzerland, March 25—Although diplomatic circles here discount much of the talk of assassination that seems to be the vogue throughout Yugoslavia, all—including some pro-Axis circles—considered the internal situation of that country as very disturbing tonight.

Reports received at a late hour gave details of peasant uprisings in some of the central and southern provinces and intimations of more to come. As far as is known here, order still reigns, but its duration is regarded as highly problematical.

Censorship was suddenly clamped down on telephone communications early this afternoon. It ceded nothing to the severity of that from a belligerent capital. Any reference to the pact, its signers, Vienna or the government provoked instant interruption. In fact, the censorship's efficiency smacked of the Germans in Rumania and Bulgaria.

### Envoy to Moscow Resigns

MOSCOW, March 25 (AP)—Milan Gavrilovitch, Yugoslavia's first Minister to Russia and a leader of the Agrarian party, which opposed alliance with the Axis, announced today that he had resigned his diplomatic post.

M. Gavrilovitch said he sent his resignation to Belgrade yesterday after the Cabinet was reorganized minus representatives of his party He did not announce his plans, but it was understood he expected to return to Belgrade. A prominent Serbian publisher and politician, he came to Moscow after Yugoslavia recognized the Soviet Government last May.

\*   \*   \*

**March 29, 1941**

## EUROPE

---

### *Courage to Be Free Impels Serbs to Defy Hitler*

---

### By ANNE O'HARE McCORMICK

It is strange—strange and exciting—to behold the lost features of Europe suddenly reappear in the one corner of the Continent most remote from the main currents of European life and culture. It is as if the faceless had shown its old face; as if the iron mask had lifted to reveal a man you recognize; as if you awakened from a nightmare of exile in an automatic new order to find yourself in a well-known room, with the same cracks in the ceiling, the same loose boards in the floor, topsy-turvy as ever but full of familiar objects and people behaving like human beings.

Europe is still Europe. Under the blanket that has smothered it all these months it continues to breathe and kick as usual. This is the first effect of the revolt of Yugoslavia: it makes Europe live again, restores the sense of its reality to us for whom the line of communication is broken. One break in the wall of fog and silence, and the illusion that it has changed because the Germans say so vanishes into thin air. The instant the Serbs begin to stir, one remembers them as they are. Dozens of impressions and episodes crowd into the mind to explain why they felt themselves betrayed by a government that sought to ally them to the Germans, why they are ready to fight again on the side of the British. The Serbs are a simple people who do not understand political strategy and diplomatic manoeuvres. They fought with the Allies against the Germans in the last war, and they are primitive enough to believe that the old conflict is still being fought, and the old lines hold.

Perhaps they do not understand modern war. General Simovitch, the head of the new government, is chief of the air force. He commands not more than 750 planes, of which at

least half are old models. The army, which could mobilize more than a million hardy fighters, is far better equipped than the Greeks were when they drove back the Italians, but its motorized units are few and much of its armament is out of date. It takes desperate courage for a nation so equipped to defy the Germans by refusing to ratify the Axis pact.

There is no question that the Yugoslavs would prefer, if they could, to return to the course of absolute neutrality. But if they must fight, they cannot fight with their foes, the enemies of their independence. That is the simple formula on which they have taken their stand. For that, ill-equipped as they are, they are ready to risk war with the greatest army in the world. They are ready to risk what they fear even more— the break-up of their country; for the extent to which armed resistance will be supported by the Croats and Slovenes, exposed as they are to the first onslaught of the Germans, is still an open question. Other grave questions plague a regime stepping overnight into the shoes of a government that piled new schisms and discontents on top of the old.

No country in Europe faces attack with so many handicaps, with the scales apparently weighted so heavily against it. This is what the Germans counted on. Probably Hitler has never been so astounded in his life as by the defiance of this encircled and divided State. What he did not count on is the strength of instinct in the people, their sense of loyalty, their power to love and hate. They cannot forget that they were allied to the French, that the British were their friends. Over and over the visitor to Yugoslavia has felt the pull of these ties. One recalls the embarrassment of Queen Marie when young King Peter was a child of 5 or 6 and refused to learn German or Serb. "He insists on speaking English," his mother sighed. "He is always telling everybody he intends to live in England." And the stationmaster at Nish, who entertained us for a long day with the saga of the prowess and generosity of the English, particularly of Lloyd George, who had clothed and schooled his son. On the lonely shores of Lake Ochrida there was the Orthodox Bishop who assured us that the only naturally religious people on earth, the only true Christians, were the British. In every town are teachers, officials and leading citizens who were taken to England during the war and educated there.

Admiration for the English, esteem for the culture of the French, enthusiasm for Americans, color the mind of the country. Yugoslavia does not want to fight with the British, but it will not fight against them. Yet this loyalty, strong and primitive as it is, is not the determining motive in its present attitude. The Yugoslavs are driven to take a desperate stand by sheer instinct—the instinct of self-preservation, the instinct that their own life as a free people is bound up with the fate of Europe.

No one would look to the black rocks of Montenegro for signs that "Europe" lives. No one would seek for the spirit that failed France in the primitive sheepfolds and pig farms of Old Serbia or the bleak uplands of Macedonia. One would not expect a people who have known little order to react instantly against Hitler's false order or to grasp at once the full significance of a pact of allegiance to his system. Yet it may be because these old peasants see things simply that they see them whole. And even if the Vardar Valley is overrun, there are signs—in France, in Norway, in Bulgaria—that the surge of instinct in Yugoslavia has roused Europe from its stupor and opened the way for nature to take its inevitable course.

\* \* \*

March 30, 1941

# A DIPLOMATIC VICTORY GOES SOUR ON HITLER

### Yugoslav Coup d'Etat After Signing Of Axis Treaty Puts a New Face Upon the Balkan Situation

### ARMY NOT TO BE DEMOBILIZED

By EDWIN L. JAMES

It is too early to measure exactly and completely the results of the coup d'état in Belgrade, but one thing is certain and that is that it marks a setback for German diplomacy. That being true, it complicates the Nazi position in the Balkans and serves to delay the projected onslaught of Hitler against the Greeks who have defeated his pitiable Axis partner named Mussolini.

On Tuesday Prince Paul, the then Regent, and his Ministers went to Vienna and signed a pact adhering to the tripartite Axis. Paul took this action despite strong evidences of popular disapproval, especially on the part of the Serbs. The next day his government was thrown out and General Simovitch set up a new government which appeared at once to have a strong popular support.

The important issue for the moment relates, of course, to the attitude of the new regime toward the treaty signed at Vienna. The Germans are awaiting impatiently for a declaration from Belgrade. The Simovitch government has made no direct statement, as this is written, regarding the Vienna pact. It says it will respect "open" obligations of the preceding government. For very good reasons that is not a complete statement, as the Germans know full well.

#### The Yugoslav Army

While little was said about it publicly, it is known that in the negotiations between the Germans and Prince Paul, the spokesmen for Hitler insisted on the demobilization of the Yugoslav Army, which had been placed on a war footing. Most of the army officers, who think well of their 1,200,000 men, were bitterly opposed to this move. Their argument was that, although Germany had made some apparent concessions relating principally to a Nazi promise not to send German troops through Yugoslavia, if Belgrade had no means of resistance there would be the danger that Hitler, as he had done before, might not be able, in a tight spot, to resist the temptation to break his promises. Therefore when Prince Paul drew up his proposals for the Vienna pact the German demand for the demobilization of the Yugoslav Army was not mentioned.

While Paul was in Vienna, the report spread among the army officers that he intended to sign a secret understanding with the Germans providing for the demobilization of the army. It is now reported by the new regime that he did make such a commitment, although it was not mentioned in the public terms given out. Apparently, this was what spurred the army leaders to resistance and when Paul got back they ousted him from power.

Therefore, it may be readily understood that the word "open" used by the Simovitch government in describing the commitments it will respect may have a very important meaning because Paul's promise to demobilize the army may well be regarded as not being an "open" commitment. In any event, it seems a very good surmise that the new Cabinet does not intend to send home the army, thus leaving the country at the mercy of the Germans without the ability to resist. Doubtless it feels that within or without the Axis family, the country will receive much more consideration if it has an army ready for defense.

#### Situation Is Not Clear

The new Belgrade regime proclaims its intention to remain "neutral." Yet the Vienna agreement, even without the secret understanding regarding the army, provides for the passage of German munitions through Yugoslavia. It would not be difficult to argue in useful circumstances that such permission would be unneutral.

That the Germans feel that some difficulty has been created for them is indicated by the Berlin press campaign alleging "atrocities" against Germans in Yugoslavia. This is reminiscent of the campaign that preceded the attack on Poland and it may well be that the Nazis feel that their position, on the face of it, is so weak that they must prepare a special case for use among the German people should Hitler decide to attempt to crush Yugoslavia.

It is easily possible that Berlin is hoping for a division between the Serbs and Croats which may take away from the Simovitch government the benefit of national unity. The Belgrade Government is engaged in intensive negotiations with the Croatian leaders in an effort to cement national unity.

Naturally if the Germans go at it hard enough they could defeat Yugoslavia in the long run. But nevertheless the existence of an army of more than a million men ready to resist invasion by the Germans complicates matters no little for the Nazis. In the first place they will hesitate to push down through the narrow Bulgarian approaches to Greece with the Yugoslavs on their flank, not to mention the Turks on the other flank. This means that their generals will wish to put much stronger forces in Bulgaria should the Yugoslav Army succeed in maintaining itself.

#### Factor of Delay

Should the Nazi General Staff decide to deal with Yugoslavia before attacking Greece there will develop an important delay, during which the British would be able to strengthen their position in Greece.

It would not be an overnight job to crush the Yugoslavs. Of course, with their Panzer divisions and air force the Germans should be able fairly quickly to drive the Yugoslavs from their northern frontiers. In fact, it is possible that the Belgrade generals would not attempt a serious defense of the northern quarter of their country. But further on the mountains begin and there may be a different story.

Across their country the Yugoslavs have a strong line of natural defense with mountain ranges crossed by few roads. Here the German tanks would find hard going as did Mussolini's tanks against the Greeks in similar terrain. Aviation is not as efficacious in mountain warfare as it is on flat ground. It is easily possible that it would take the Germans two months to go through Yugoslavia and consolidate their positions.

Having shown that they can hold back Italian attacks in Albania, even when directed by Il Duce himself, the Greeks must feel that the Belgrade developments are like manna from Heaven. A week ago, they faced the prospect of a quick German attack on Salonika, with a Yugoslav bargain with Germans which would keep Belgrade not only neutral but furnishing certain facilities to their would-be invaders. Now, suddenly, there is a row between Berlin and Belgrade, the outcome of which must give the Greeks a little surcease. It does not mean that the Greek situation has been saved, but it does help it considerably and to an extent which cannot yet be determined.

### A Sight for Matsuoka

If there is any room for humor in such a situation, it could be reflected in the German plans to show Matsuoka, the Japanese Foreign Minister, how they were sweeping everything before them and that if Japan wished to be in the Axis bandwagon she should get busy with some devilment in the Orient. That was the plan and it was even thought at one point that Matsuoka would attend the signing up of the Yugoslavs.

But, instead of that, the Tokyo Foreign Minister has been given the sight of a signal German diplomatic defeat. Following that, he is going to Rome tomorrow to visit Mussolini, whose Ethiopian empire has just been chewed to pieces by the British. The Japanese are noted for not saying all they think, but anyhow Matsuoka has been given something to think about, even if he keeps quiet about it until he sees his Emperor again.

\* \* \*

April 6, 1941

# GERMANS INVADE YUGOSLAVIA AND GREECE; HITLER ORDERS WAR, BLAMING THE BRITISH; MOSCOW SIGNS AMITY PACT WITH BELGRADE

### NAZI TROOPS MARCH

*Goebbels Reads Order to Germans to Rid Europe of All Britons*

### QUICK BLOW PLEDGED

*Greece Told She Invited It—U. S. Is Said to Share Blame*

By DANIEL T. BRIGHAM
By Telephone to The New York Times

BERNE, Switzerland, Sunday, April 6—At 5 o'clock this morning German forces attacked Yugoslavia and Greece in the long-awaited culmination of the Balkan war of nerves.

The news broke on the world with startling suddenness when a German radio station announcer with a triumphant blast this morning introduced Dr. Joseph Goebbels. Minister of Propaganda, who then read Reichsfuehrer Hitler's order of the day to "my forces in Southeast Europe."

"Since dawn this morning," said Dr. Goebbels, "the German Reich has been at war with Yugoslavia and Greece."

It was indicated that the friendship pact signed between Yugoslavia and Russia yesterday was one of the factors of which Germany complained. This was another version of the Nazi charges of "aggressive encirclement of Germany" which have been used since Herr Hitler's advent to power.

### Yugoslav Arming Held Cause

Another source of grievance, it would seem, was Belgrade's mobilization, a point that Herr Hitler mentioned in his order of the day as one of the chief reasons for the attack.

Immediately after Dr. Goebbels's broadcast, telephone communications to the eastward from this city—and south to Rome—were cut off.

[United States and British encouragement to the Yugoslavs in their resistance to German demands was also cited as grounds for Germany's attack, according to The Associated Press. Alleged American offers of material aid were also quoted.]

The German Army was told it would not lay down its arms until the "ruffians" and "plotters" in Belgrade had been deposed and the last Briton driven out of this territory.

### Friendship for Greeks

German soldiers have been fighting in Greece since dawn today, the proclamation stated. It was indicated that the battle in Greece was not directed against the population but only against the "world enemy," Great Britain, who had dispatched troops there for an attack against the interests of the Reich.

Germany, Herr Hitler was quoted as saying, does not consider herself at war with Greece and will not molest any Greek who does not take up arms against the German Army, but any who lends his support to the British will be crushed.

"Soldiers of the Southeast Front," the Reichfuehrer proclaimed, "your hour has now come."

He then told these troops that they must emulate their comrades in Poland, Scandinavia, the Lowlands and France. He added that the general mobilization in Yugoslavia was considered by the Reich as final proof that Britain had mixed into the internal affairs of Yugoslavia and would lead that country into hostile acts against Germany.

### Yugoslav Provocation Charged

BERLIN, Sunday, April 6 (AP)—The German radio, in broadcasting Reichsfuehrer Hitler's order to the German Army, quoted him as saying Germany was unable longer to endure the Yugoslav attitude. The Reich was said to be reacting to the mistreatment, "attacks and murdering" of Germans in the Serb Kingdom.

The order said the greatest patience had been exercised by Germany respecting Yugoslavia and Greece, but that now the moment for action had arrived.

It was said that Herr Hitler had frequently called attention to the dangers in the Southeast.

Now, it was said, Germany was obliged to recall her nationals and consuls from the Southeast.

It was stated that it was Germany's policy to strike her enemy wherever he shows his head. It was observed that Germany cannot tolerate the landing of British troops in Salonika.

The British, it was said, will learn to their sorrow that Salonika is for them another Dunkerque.

The Hitler order added that Yugoslavia had entered the Tripartite Pact on the most favorable terms and then repudiated the signature. It contended that no demands that touched on Yugoslav independence had been made.

At the end of Dr. Goebbels's broadcast, the German station broke into a program of sprightly dance music.

Foreign press correspondents were summoned at dawn to hear a statement by Foreign Minister Joachim von Ribbentrop.

In the Foreign Office, he and his Under-Secretaries presented a long statement justifying, in the German view, military actions against Yugoslavia and Greece.

The first statement by Herr von Ribbentrop said the months-long policy of Greece and Yugoslavia had been to aid Great Britain by all possible means.

It observed that lately the United States also had been encouraging the two Balkan nations to resist Germany in all possible ways.

### Germans Charge Plot

#### By C. BROOKS PETERS
By Telephone to The New York Times

BERLIN, April 5—An increase in the tension of existing relations between Germany and Yugoslavia was indicated today by a brief announcement in the press here that "Yugoslavia is preparing for war."

The mobilization proclamation by King Peter placed the entire armed forces of Yugoslavia, effective last Tuesday, on a footing of the fullest preparedness, it was explained.

Thus, while no declaration of policy from the new Belgrade government has been made, German quarters profess to see in the military preparations of Yugoslavia a further indication of the increasing seriousness of the present situation.

It is said in authoritative quarters here, moreover, that Germany has virtually no more diplomatic contact with the Yugoslav Government. Ivan Andritch, the Yugoslav Minister, is still in Berlin, but it was stated that he had not paid a call in the Wilhelmstrasse.

["Yugoslavia has ceased to be a nation," was the way some German commentators put it, according to The Associated Press.]

### Compared to Czecho-Slovakia

Editorials in several leading newspapers that are believed to represent authoritative views and whose statement tonight are emphasized by the semi-official Dienst aus Deutschland, declare that ethnologically Yugoslavia resembles former Czecho-Slovakia and after the latter State was and is the least consolidated nation in Europe.

It is composed of Serbs, Croats, Slovenes, Magyars, Albanians and Macedonians, these editorials assert, but the Serbs have always been the dominating factor in determining the policies of Yugoslavia. The Serbian military coup d'etat has always been a possibility in Yugoslavia, these comments continue, and the Serbian chauvinistic military clique fears that increasing autonomy of the Croats would nullify in the future their complete domination of the State and Serbian control not only of Yugoslavia's politics but also of her economy.

"That Vladimir Matchek, Vice Premier, has allowed himself to be induced to enter the government—who knows under what threats and with the help of what promises the worth of which is just as great as that of the Serbian signature on the documents of Vienna—is an episode," says the Deutsche Allgemeine Zeitung, "and changes the basic situation not at all. An uncontrollable circle of persons who are the descendants of those who unleashed the World War in 1914, and who are obviously determined to do any deeds from which they await an increase of power, wanted and had to prevent at any price the internal consolidation of the land."

The ink was not yet dry on the signature of the legal Yugoslav representatives who ratified the Tripartite pact, the comment adds, and thereby demonstrated their country's desire to become a factor for order and peace in Europe, when the chauvinistic Belgrade clique through its putsch demonstrated "that it is determined to fight against such a development."

If there had been any doubt as to the motives of the Belgrade coup, the German comments continue, it would have been dispelled by the reaction that the revolution evoked in Washington and London. That reaction, it is suggested, would indicate that the Anglo-Saxon powers, through Colonel William J. Donovan, President Roosevelt's personal envoy to Europe, and the British agents are not free of blame for what has happened in Belgrade.

"It is also from Britain and America," the Deutsche Allgemeine Zeitung says, "that the promises of assistance and of all the fine things that so often have been promised in this war and never kept, emanate."

\*   \*   \*

April 6, 1941

## YUGOSLAVIA FIGHTS

### Belgrade Has Air Raid as Armies Resist, Berne Hears

#### DRIVE FROM BULGARIA

### Greeks Announce Nazi Attack—Stukas Clear Path, Germans Say

By RAY BROCK
Wireless to The New York Times

BELGRADE, Yugoslavia, Sunday, April 6—At 3:25 o'clock this morning the air-raid sirens in Belgrade sounded an alarm. For the Yugoslavs it was the first indication that the nation was at war.

An hour later, at 4:32, two Yugoslav fighter planes appeared over the city, flying in an easterly direction. They came from the Zemun airdrome. Two more fighter planes appeared a short time later.

[At this point wireless connections with Belgrade were cut.]

#### Greeks Announce Attack

The Greek High Command announced in a communiqué broadcast from Athens that since 5:15 A. M., Athens time, the German troops had been attacking Greek troops on the Bulgarian border, the Columbia Broadcasting System announced this morning. No further details were in the communiqué as it was received here.

The German Propaganda Ministry announced in a broadcast from Berlin, according to CBS, that swarms of German planes, including Stuka dive bombers, were "pouncing like hornets" on Greek and Yugoslav airdromes and railways in an effort to cripple the resistance to the invading German armies. The Nazi Propaganda Ministry also asserted that the planes were clearing a path for tanks and infantry, and that parachute troops were landing at strategic points within the Greek-Yugoslav defenses. There was no confirmation of these claims, however.

#### Belgrade Has Second Alarm

By Telephone to The New York Times

BERNE, Switzerland, Sunday, April 6—The Belgrade correspondent of The New York Times reported at 5:30 o'clock this morning that naturally he had heard of the situation, but that "you wouldn't know the difference." Aside from two air-raid alarms in the capital early this morning, no incident had yet occurred. Reports as to the exact location of the fighting were very scant.

On the Greek frontier the invasion doubtlessly came from Bulgaria through the Struma Valley with a secondary attack down the Vardar Valley. This latter attack, however, would entail driving across the southeastern border of Yugoslavia—the Third Army region based on Skoplje under General Ilija Brasitch.

For some time before the Yugoslav crisis began to take on even faintly menacing tones, the Yugoslav High Command had been reinforcing that Third Army region, which was considered highly important, to remove any temptation on the part of the Axis to move through Yugoslav territory in a march against Greece.

The First Army, which probably also took a heavy first charge from troops advancing into the Dunava Plains from Hungary and Western Rumania, is based on Novi Sad. It is commanded by General Milan Radenkovitch. The role of this army, will be to fight a rear-guard action as it retreats to a line running roughly east and west some twenty miles south of Belgrade.

The Fifth Army, under General Zhivko Stanislavjevitch, based on Nish, is the third section of the front that doubtlessly was pounded heavily in any advance by the German forces.

#### Turks Guard One Route

In Greece military dispositions have long been taken to block an advance down the Struma or Mesta Valley through the Rhodope Mountains. The only other way around—down the Meritza Valley—is presumed to be guarded by the Turkish forces that Marshal Fevzi Cakmak. Chief of Staff, dispatched there around March 20.

Turkey's position, however, remains somewhat unclear, owing to the fact none of her statesmen has made a clear statement of policy, though many have been made implying that any attack on Greece through Bulgaria would automatically bring into play the terms of the Balkan Entente.

#### Attack on Greece Launched

BERNE. Switzerland, Sunday, April 6 (AP)—German armies smashed into Greece and Yugoslavia simultaneously at dawn today.

Reports reaching here said that of twenty-two German divisions [about 330,000 men] massed in Bulgaria, half were launched down the Struma River valley against Greece and the others set out west-ward across the Yugoslav frontier in the direction of the Vardar Valley, which leads to Salonika, Greece.

Bulgaria's army of 300,000 was reported to have joined the Germans in attacking Greece. Indications were that Hungary's forces were inactive, at least for the moment.

While there were unconfirmed rumors in Berne that Belgrade suffered a German air raid shortly after 6 A. M., efforts to reach Belgrade, Rome and Berlin met with the uniform response, "The lines are cut."

#### Hungary Reports Attack

The Hungarian radio early today charged that Yugoslav troops fired across the frontier at Hungarian troops with machine guns. The radio said Hungarian soldiers concentrated on the border were facing large Yugoslav motorized divisions across the frontier from Ecs, Hungary.

Reichsfuehrer Hitler's land and air armies were reported to have crossed the Yugolsav frontiers from Austria, Hungary, Rumania and Bulgaria, the German-owned or dominated countries almost surrounding the kingdom of the Serbs, Croats and Slovenes.

Whether the troops of the Nazis' satellite countries joined in the attack was not immediately clear, although earlier reports from Sofia said Bulgaria and Hungary had reached agreement on territorial claims to be presented to Yugoslavia.

Big German forces in Bulgaria also were reported fronting along the Turkish frontier near Adrianople as all Europe awaited Turkey's reaction to Germany's latest sensational military move.

### Government to Be Moved

By Telephone to The New York Times

BELGRADE, Yugoslavia, Sunday, April 6—The Yugoslavia Government was in emergency session early today while, with Yugoslav-Axis diplomatic relations at a standstill and peace hopes apparently abandoned, Premier Dusan Simovitch fought for time against the German invasion, which appears to some responsible sources here "a matter of hours."

The dean of the Belgrade diplomatic corps, Mgr. Ettore Felici, the Papal Nuncio, called the Ministers of all the legations together late yesterday to ask if they were prepared to evacuate the capital. All Belgrade legations, with the exception of the German and Italian skeleton staffs, and possibly the Bulgarian, will send representatives with the departing government when the attack comes.

Arthur Bliss Lane, United States Minister, will remain in Belgrade, according to authoritative sources. Robert B. Macatee, the United States Consul, will accompany the government to its new seat in Central Serbia or Bosnia. Eight American correspondents will travel with the Yugoslav Government and the General Staff in a motor caravan.

The final transmission of the Belgrade radio last night ended with a coded message addressed to the Yugoslav Legation in Sofia.

Toward the end of the Belgrade radio broadcast the announcer warned: "To the Yugoslav Legation at Sofia: Important! Stand by to take an urgent message at the end of this transmission." A few minutes later the warning was repeated. At the end of the transmission a new voice was heard reading a message, which began: "Cheteri, dva, cheteri, pet—four, two, four, five,'' and on through a series of coded numbers. The message was then repeated and the station signed off.

Belgrade again was plunged into darkness at 9:34 last night and at exactly midnight. By 12 o'clock the streets outside this correspondent's hotel were almost empty and only one taxi with blue lights passed during the twenty-two-minute blackout.

Across the street, in the dark gardens of the Kalemegdan Fortress, a soldier began to sing a plaintiff South Bosnian song: "Dusha Moia [My Soul]." The refrain was taken up by a woman's voice, then by several others. The song ended just before the lights came up again to reveal the head of an infantry column piling out of the Kalemegdan and down the long, winding street toward the railroad station.

A hurried taxi journey through central Belgrade and along diplomatic row disclosed the lights burning in the British Legation and press office, the Italian Legation and at the home of the Italian Minister.

A motor caravan of three cars was forming outside the British Legation toward midnight, bound for Greece with evacuees from the Budapest and Belgrade colonies. The hotels and kafanas, open after midnight since abolishment of the 12 o'clock curfew, were almost empty. But music still burst out through the open doors into the balmy Spring weather in the streets.

This correspondent saw some of the guerrilla Komitajis in the streets of Belgrade yesterday afternoon and last night for the first time since General Simovitch's army coup ten days ago. Two women members of the Cetnik irregulars' organization appeared last evening. One of them, young, pretty and unusually smart in gabardine skirt and tunic bearing the arm band, Karageorge emblem and cap emblazoned with the Komitaji skull and crossbones insignia, dined at the next table in the hotel.

The other, Ljubitchitch Andrijana, from Central Serbia, turned up in an out-of-the-way kafana. Mrs. Andrijana, 50 years old, wore her uniform and Cetnik cap and a pair of knives in her belt. She wore a dozen medals, including the Karageorge star, third degree, which she won for valor in the World War.

"I came up to Belgrade," she said, "because Belgrade apparently is to be the front line in this war. The government has declared it an open city and if 'they' respect it, then we can fall back to better positions. If they do not, then we shall be here to deal with them."

Mrs. Andrijana was wounded nine times by machine-gun and rifle fire in the Balkan and World Wars. The Komitajis, including their women members, have organized special anti-parachute squads to patrol the capital's outskirts and vital communication centers of the provinces.

\* \* \*

April 8, 1941

# ANXIOUS ITALY EYES EVENTS IN ALBANIA

### *Looks to Nazis to Relieve Army—Mussolini Gets Plea for Backing of Croats*

### ROUT OF GREEKS ALLEGED

### *Agency Reports Wiping Out of Division at Lake Ochrida—Claims 4 Ships Sunk*

### By HERBERT L. MATTHEWS
#### By Telephone to The New York Times

ROME, April 7—In the second day of the war against Yugoslavia, Italy today remained on the defensive while all Italian eyes turned anxiously toward besieged Albania.

A new source of worry is naturally Albania. Today's war bulletin merely records bombing raids by Italian planes on Spalato, Cattaro and a few other places; and since it says nothing of any land operations, one must presume that there were none.

[On the other hand, according to a Rome dispatch by The Associated Press, credited to Stefani, official Italian news agency, an Italian counter-attack near Lake Ochrida shattered a Greek division trying to effect a junction with Yugoslav forces, causing it to be withdrawn from the line. The sinking of two ships in Yugoslav ports and bomb hits on two destroyers was also claimed by the Stefani report.]

Without knowing anything about German plans or strategy one may conclude that there is just one thing for them to do, and that is to drive across Southern Yugoslavia as fast as possible to relieve the Italian Army in Albania. Italy, meanwhile, must stave off attack from three directions and prevent a junction of Yugoslav and Greek forces until the Germans can make a joining with the Italians. Such a manoeuvre would split the Allied forces in two and go a long way toward defeating them, according to observers here. The Germans are supremely confident that they can do it in a matter of days, and that, in turn, has given confidence to the Italians.

### Croat Asks Italian Aid

So far as the Italo-Yugoslav frontier is concerned, there is no news of any activity, and since the Italian forces there are very strong no anxiety is felt. Anyway, that is the frontier with Croatia, and the Axis has the highest hopes of detaching it from Serbia without a struggle.

The bread that Premier Mussolini cast upon the waters when he saved Dr. Ante Pavelitch from the punishment that France wanted to mete out for complicity in the assassination of King Alexander has now returned in the form of a cordial message, asking Italian soldiers to protect Croat independence.

"In this decisive hour," wrote Dr. Pavelitch to Signor Mussolini, "for which the Croat people, subjugated by the imposition of Versailles, by Serbian tyranny and by its pluto-democratic backers, have waited twenty-two years. I turn toward you and bring you the salutations of all the Croat nationalists.

"The whole of Croatia jubilantly awaits your glorious soldiers and all our nationalist forces will fight together with them for the liberty of our people and the independent State of Croatia for which we have struggled long and bloodily. We salute you as the great friend of small peoples and as the promoter of a new government of justice."

### U. S. Role Is Indicated

The problem of what to do about Yugoslav citizens in Italy and Italian citizens in Yugoslavia had not been solved late this evening. It is not even known what country will take over Yugoslav interests, although the expectation is that the United States will do so. The legation staff is packed and ready to go and so are journalists and other privileged persons who will be exchanged in accordance with recognized procedure. However, no one has figured out yet where they can go, since the frontiers are now war zones.

A determined effort is being made by newspaper and radio commentators to convince the Italian people that this conflict could not be avoided and that it was entirely Yugoslavia's fault, backed by Britain and the United States. Virginio Gayda devotes three heavy columns to his explanation, which ends up by saying that this is "truly a war of national and international defense against the aggressor who has launched himself on the maddest imperial undertaking."

The Popolo di Roma regretfully announces, that the Axis had to intervene "to restore peace, order and tranquillity to this delicate sector of the European Continent." All newspapers agree that the Serbians must be insane and, as the Tevere puts it, "tired of life." They, and political circles, point out significantly that "certain historically Italian zones in Dalmatia and the islands" had been renounced by Italy for the sake of peace.

### Soviet Pact Is Studied

Competent circles claim that the Russo-Yugoslav treaty of friendship is to be interpreted as Moscow's way of saying she wants to remain out of the European War. At the same time, most neutral observers see in the publication of this treaty a warning to the Italian public that trouble with Russia may yet arise.

Nothing is known here of the report that the Yugoslavs have begun their offensive against Albania, but naturally everybody expects them to. The Italians in Albania are caught through the pitiless operation of geographical factors that nothing could alter. It is up to the Germans to extricate them, since this particular conflict was certainly not sought by the Italians.

They have stood to suffer in their way just as much as the Yugoslavs and Greeks. The economic angle, alone, would have been enough to make this a very unhappy business, since quantities of meat, poultry, eggs, wheat, lumber and copper were coming from Yugoslavia while vital oil supplies and other products came through from Rumania and the Black Sea.

### Claim Rout of Greeks

ROME, April 7 (AP)—Premier Mussolini's hard-pressed legions developed a new war today with Yugoslavia and after a counter-attack on their old enemies, the Greeks, reported, a Greek division virtually wiped out.

Greeks, trying to drive through to a junction with Yugoslav forces near Lake Ohrida in Albania, were turned back in a two-day battle that started even before the Axis war with Yugoslavia opened, said Stefani, official Italian news agency.

The Greek division that launched the offensive was so shattered it had to be withdrawn from the line, Stefani added.

Violent bombing attacks against Yugoslav bases on the Adriatic marked the direct hostilities against Yugoslavia, Stefani said, while Italian dive bombers were reported to have hit "hard" several British mechanized formations located in Yugoslav and Greek territory.

The air force's onslaught followed up attacks yesterday in which the High Command said the naval bases at Spalato and Cattaro and an arsenal at Theodo, near Cattaro, and an air base at Mostar were pounded.

Two steamers at Spalato and one at Cattaro were declared sunk, while two destroyers, one at Theodo and the other at Cattaro, were hit.

The most damaging return blow acknowledged by Italy in the new phase of hostilities was at Scutari, in Northern Albania, which was bombed.

\* \* \*

April 11, 1941

## FREE CROAT STATE REPORTED FORMED

*New Leaders Involved in the Murder of King Alexander— Germans Enter Capital*

By The Associated Press

BERNE, Switzerland, April 10—German motor troops rolled tonight into Zagreb, the capital of old Croatia, and German news agency dispatches said the patchwork Kingdom of Yugoslavia had been ripped asunder by the formation of a separate Croat State.

[Hungarian troops were reported early today to have entered Yugoslav areas that had been taken from Hungary after the World War.]

The Croats, long a large and restless element of Yugoslavia, were declared to have established their own nation under Ante Pavelitch and another extremist named Egon Kvaternik, both once sentenced to death for complicity in the assassination of King Alexander in 1934.

Vladimir Matchek, mild bespectacled old Croat peasant leader who only last week accepted vice premiership of the Yugoslav Government, was portrayed as one of the prime movers of the new Zagreb Government. This is a sensational about face, if true, for M. Matchek long has been known as an enemy of Pavelitch and an outspoken critic of the many assassinations and terroristic plots laid to Pavelitch in his campaign against Yugoslav unity.

Times Wide World, 1935

Dr. Vladimir Matcek

It was M. Matchek, however, to whom the German news agency attributed announcement of the new Croat State in a radio address from Zagreb.

The German High Command announced merely that Zagreb was occupied and that the Croat population greeted the Nazi troops joyously. This conformed with M. Matchek's asserted advice to the public just before the occupation to hang German and Croat flags on their homes.

According to the news report, M. Matchek announced that Pavelitch would head the government, that he himself would participate and that "at this very moment" a Croat politician named Kvaternik had been appointed vice-premier and was "taking the administration in hand."

[D. N. B., official German news agency, carried in Berlin a slightly different account from Bratislava, Slovakia, to the effect that the Zagreb radio announced "General Sladko Kvaternik," as chief of state, had proclaimed Croatia an independent nation.]

This apparently is the same mysterious person, known variously as Egon Kvaternik and Egon Kramer, who with Pavelitch was sentenced to death in absentia by French courts for the Marseilles killing of King Alexander. Yugoslavia's present King Peter II is Alexander's oldest son.

Both Pavelitch and Kvaternik found sanctuary in Italy, which refused extradition.

Associated Press, 1934

Ante Pavelitch

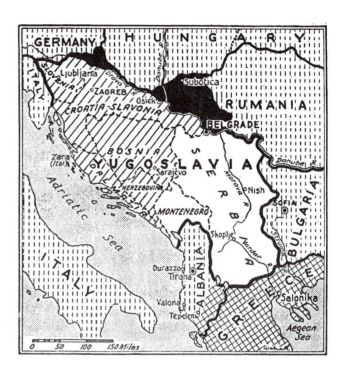

NEW BLOWS AGAINST TOTTERING YUGOSLAVIA
German sources announced the setting up of an independent Croat State with Zagreb (upper left on map) as its focus. The boundaries of the State are not specified. Simultaneously Regent Horthy of Hungary ordered troops into territories lost by Hungary after the World War. The diagonal shading shows what was taken from the Austro-Hungarian Empire and given to Yugoslavia, but it is presumed Hungary's present interest is in the Magyar areas, which are shown in black.

Only three days ago Pavelitch, still in Italy, telegraphed Premier Mussolini a pledge of support.

M. Matchek, chief of 3,500,000 Croats, has been with the fugitive Yugoslav Government of King Peter and Premier Dusan Simovitch at an undisclosed place in Central Yugoslavia, but reports here said he returned to Zagreb two days ago "to spend these decisive hours with my people."

It was to guard against just such a schism as the German sources now report that General Simovitch assigned Croat troops to South Serbia and Serb troops to Croatia before the war began. Apparently this device failed.

From the Axis point of view, Pavelitch the man of action and M. Matchek, the revered old scholar, would be an ideal team to head a Croat government.

Now 48 years old, Pavelitch is head of the Ustachi, a terrorist organization whose members for two decades have been blamed by the secret police of many lands for a score of political assassinations, poisonings and bombings in Southeast Europe.

Pavelitch himself has been sentenced to death three times. Members of the Ustachi were taught their arts at the Janka Puszta farm in Hungary, and the "students" declared Pavelitch often made speeches to them in praise of Adolf Hitler.

Testimony at the French trials of King Alexander's accused assassins included allegations that Italy, Germany and Hungary had meddled in the scheme.

### Hungarian Troops Enter Banat

By Telephone to The New York Times

BERNE, Switzerland, Friday, April 11—Answering reported appeals of Hungarian minority leaders of the Yugoslav Banat for protection and charging that the proclamation by Dr. Ante Pavelitch of a "legitimate government of independent Croatia" constituted de facto disintegration of the Kingdom of Serbs, Croats and Slovenes and hence constituted no violation of the Hungaro-Yugoslav amity pact, Admiral Regent Horthy early today announced he had put Hungarian troops in the Banat areas ceded to Yugoslavia under the Treaty of Trianon in 1919, "to protect their inhabitants."

The troops entered immediately, and since dawn have been digging in, and making all preparations to resist should "irregular bands of komitajis" attempted to drive them out, the statement by the Regent said.

He stressed that this measure was not to be interpreted as a hostile act directed against Yugoslavia, "with whom we wish to maintain friendly relations," but rather as a "temporary" measure to prevent Hungarian lives and property from being endangered in a zone where no proper authority existed.

A Hungarian broadcast, referring to the pact of "eternal friendship," signed in December with Yugoslavia, and its present relations with that country, said in part:

"Any group that overthrows the constitutional government of the State in order to assume power no longer has either the moral or the political right to interpret in its favor treaties which its evicted predecessors had signed with any other State."

This would seem both from the tone of the broadcast and its context to indicate that Hungary has, to her own satisfaction, dealt with her moral obligations under that treaty not to attack the "territorial integrity" of Yugoslavia.

When the Treaty of Trianon deprived Hungary of two-thirds of her territory, she became a revisionist power. In 1938 and 1939 she satisfied some of her claims by the acquisition of parts of dismembered Czecho-Slovakia; in 1940 she obtained Transylvania at the expense of Rumania: today she covets "her" one territorial claim still outstanding—the Yugoslav Banat.

Bulgaria's position harbors a latent threat when one couples her leaders' declarations of intentions to maintain an attitude of "watchful waiting" with the Yugoslav claims of Bulgarian troop intervention in the Strumitza offensive and the special "defense" budget of 2,200,000,000 leva passed without debate today.

Bulgaria is also a "revisionist" State with territorial aspirations on both Yugoslavia and Greece. Here, again, the tenuous position of Yugoslavia, according to the German version and the geographical fact that German forces are more than two-thirds of the way across the Southern Vardar Province, would appear to present the long-awaited occasion to satisfy these desires.

### Large Areas Lost

Under the Treaty of Trianon in 1920 Hungary lost perhaps 500,000 of her Magyar population to Yugoslavia in the Banat, Baranya and Medjumurje regions. The first district was divided between Yugoslavia and Rumania. The Baranya portion was that formed by the angle of the Drava and Danube rivers, and the other in the region between the Drava and Mur rivers.

Altogether the treaty took from Hungary and gave to her neighbors, 192,000 square miles of her 283,000 square-mile area: 10,782,000 of her population of 20,886,487, and thirty per cent, or 3,300,000 of the 9,945,000 pure Magyars.

\* \* \*

**April 16, 1941**

## CROAT 'STATE' WINS AXIS RECOGNITION

*Hitler and Mussolini Join in Messages of Congratulation to Independence Leaders*

**REICH PROTECTORATE SEEN**

*Structure to Be Based on That of Slovakia—All Parties Are Already Abolished*

By Telephone to The New York Times

BERLIN, April 15—The first harbingers of the recreated Balkans that are to issue from the war became manifest today when the Axis powers formally recognized the sovereignity of the newly reconstituted "independent Croatia."

Responding to the joint messages of Dr. Ante Pavelitch, the Croat leader, and General Sladko Kvaternik, [Dr. Pavelitch has been described as President and General Kvaternik as his Premier, in dispatches from Nazi-controlled Hungary] announcing the debut of the Croat State, Reichsfuehrer Hitler, for the Reich, and Premier Mussolini for Italy, informed the Croat leaders in the name of the Axis powers that the recognition sought not only was cheerfully granted, but that both powers "received with joy and satisfaction" the news that the Croat people had won their struggle for independence in an hour when the Axis powers said they had demolished the artificial creation which was Yugoslavia.

The concurring replies of the Axis powers stated that the questions involving the future frontiers of the Croat State would be discussed in the near future with what they called the Zagreb Government.

The proclamation of the new Croat State, it was said here, represents the first political sequel to the disappearance of Yugoslavia as a political entity, and it was designated as the initial step in the process of establishing order in the Balkans.

### Likened to Slovakia

Recognition of the sovereignty of the Croat nation was unconditional and absolute and it automatically identified the new State with the policies of the Axis powers in Europe and the Three-Power Pact.

No information was available in Berlin political circles as to the nature of the political structure that the Croat State was to receive, but it was said not to be improbable that it would resemble that of Slovakia and ultimately resolve itself into a protectorate under German military hegemony and be joined to the Reich by a customs and currency union.

The process of redrawing other Balkan countries which may be shattered by the war was said to be expected to get under way soon. Various national aspirations were said to await appeasement and the reshuffle to which the checkered political configuration of this sector of Europe was to be subjected.

It requires no prolific imagination to predict that the job of rolling up maps will be undertaken with less rhetoric than was applied to similar undertakings by the powers assembled at Versailles, and official comment indicated that along with the Croats, the aspirations of the Albanians, Macedonians and Montenegrins would also be adjusted in keeping with the "principles of justice and decency." Hungary, it was said here, is to receive redress for wrongs she claims to have suffered through the Treaty of Trianon.

### Parties, Meetings Abolished

BERLIN, April 15 (AP)—The official German news agency D. N. B. reported tonight in a dispatch from Zagreb, Yugoslavia, that among the first acts of Dr. Ante Pavelitch as chief of the new Croat State were the banning of all political parties and prohibiting all public meetings.

[The British news agency, Reuters reported hearing of these decrees yesterday from the Zagreb radio in an announcement by General Sladko Kzaternik, Commander in Chief in the Croat State.]

### Italy Welcomes New State

By Telephone to The New York Times
ROME, April 15—The "independent State of Croatia" has been recognized by Italy, it was made known in a telegram sent by Premier Mussolini to Dr. Ante Pavelitch, the Croat leader, and published in the newspapers today.

Referring to a message from Dr. Pavelitch, Signor Mussolini said he was "pleased to express to you the recognition of the independent State of Crotia on the part of the Fascist government, which will be glad to reach an agreement with the Croat national government in order to determine the borders of the new State, to which the Italian people wish all luck."

Signor Mussolini also expressed his "great satisfaction" regarding the new State, which he said "reacquires its much awaited and longed-for liberty now that the Axis powers have destroyed the artificial Yugoslav construction."

\* \* \*

**May 19, 1941**

## CROATS GET SPOLETO AS KING; DALMATIA IS GIVEN TO ITALY

### By HERBERT L. MATTHEWS

By Telephone to The New York Times
ROME, May 18—The ancient House of Savoy gave a new sovereign to Europe today when Aimone, Duke of Spoleto was designated King of Croatia. He goes to rule a race of Slavs, whose obstinate pugnacious will to independence and whose determined nationalism is even more ancient than Savoy's, and whose new kingdom comes to birth on a tortured Continent dominated by powers who even today made it clear that Croatia cannot exist alone.

Croatia not only received a king today but also entered the "new order" in Europe under the Italian sphere of influence. The new Kingdom of Croatia, in accordance with agreements

ITALY GETS SPOILS OF WAR IN YUGOSLAVIA

A German Transocean dispatch originating in Rome said yesterday that the Italo-Croatian frontier agreement fixing the western frontiers of Croatia gave to Italy the districts of Castus, Susak and Cabar and part of the district of Delnice (1). Italy also obtained the reef of San Marco, the islands of Veglia and Arbe, the smaller islands off Jablanac, all south of (1), and all the islands of the Zara archipelago (2).

Part of the line between the two countries is as follows: From Previaka to the Canal della Morlacca, then along a line following the islands to the Novogradska Sea; from there along the coast of this sea, including Bokovac, to the Kerka River in the vicinity of Podjene. The line then goes down the river, including the entire region of Sebenico, Trau (3) and the town of Spalato, including all the suburbs but excluding the islands of Brazza and Lesina.

Italy gets the islands of Bus, Zirona, Solta, Lissa, Bisevo, St. Andrea, Pomo and other small islands in this group, in the vicinity of (4). The islands of Curzola and Meleda and the entire district of the Bay of Cattaro (5) are also ceded to Italy.

The frontier leaves the coast between the towns of Cavtat and Vitaljina, then runs in a northeasterly direction, including the town of Gruda and the mountain range of Orjen, until it reaches the frontier of Montenegro.

While this agreement fixes the Adriatic frontier of Croatia, the eastern frontier of that country, bordering Serbia, has not yet been settled. Administration of the town of Spalato and suburbs and the isle of Curzola is to be regulated by special convention.

signed today, is carefully curbed, so far as its foreign or military and naval powers are concerned.

It is a country now fully dependent upon Italy and presumably Germany, for protection, self-defense and, indeed, for its very existence. Even its economy is clearly going to depend on links with Italy and Germany.

### Gets Long-Sought Dalmatia

Territorially, Italy received today one of fascism's greatest vindications—the part of the Dalmatian coast that she asked for in the Treaty of London of 1915 as the price of entering the World War, and that was refused afterward. One of the treaties signed made the so-called "Classic Dalmatia" part of the Kingdom of Italy, that is to say, the coast from Zara to Spalato, including those two ports, as well as Sebenico and Trau.

She received all the islands of the Dalmatian coast, which formerly belonged to Yugoslavia, except Pago, Brazza and Lesina. Susak, Yugoslavia's rival to Fiume, becomes Italian. Finally, and by no means least important, Italy got the former Austrian naval base of Cattaro and the coast down to Albania.

That left two important outlets to the new Croat Kingdom, one from Zagreb, which will include special facilities for the use of the port of Spalato and another from the rich mineral districts of Bosnia to the port of Ragusa. Italy's little enclave of Zara now becomes large, but it still remains detached from the metropolitan district.

The exact delimitation of the frontiers, including the province of Ljubljand, will be made by a mixed commission. Incidentally, it is to be noted that Croatia's eastern and southern frontiers have yet to be established.

### Coast Zone Demilitarized

After the territorial accord two more agreements were signed tying Croatia into a neat bundle. One was of a military character, concerning the Adriatic shore. Croatia undertakes not to institute or maintain any military fortifications or defenses, whether on land, sea or in the air, nor any base of operations or military installations susceptible of being used for bellicose purposes in the zone along the Adriatic. The Croat Government likewise declared that it had no intention of creating a navy.

The last agreement was a "treaty of guarantee and collaboration." By it Italy guarantees the independence and territorial integrity of the Kingdom of Croatia, and on its part the Croat Government undertakes not to contract international obligations that are not in conformity with the guarantees of the spirit of the treaty signed with Italy. This treaty is to last twenty-five years.

However, that is not all that the "Independent Kingdom of Croatia" undertakes to do. For she is going to "collaborate with the Italian armed forces in everything that concerns the organization of her army." Finally, there are going to be customs and monetary accords, agreements regarding railway and maritime traffic, the treatment of minorities and even cultural accords.

Giovanni Ansaldo puts the whole matter with more bluntness than diplomacy in the Telegrafo.

"All the races linked with the Adriatic," he writes, "are showing themselves more than ready to come to an understanding with us and to enter in some form into the orbit of our imperial power."

Political circles also spoke confidently of the new Croat State's "gravitating within the sphere of Italian influence," and Virginio Gayda completed the picture by writing that Croatia entered into the "Axis system in the new order in Europe."

### Rain Mars Colorful Fete

Rome went through all the ceremonies with that lack of concern that comes from having in the last 2,600 years seen innumerable kings, emperors and crowds. No people in the world are so blasé about the pageantry of history as the Romans and today, anyway, was a nasty, rainy day. However, the city was gay with Croat and Italian flags and there were thousands of persons in their proper places at the proper moment.

The Croat delegation was driven first to the Palazzo Madama in an automobile and went from there in royal coaches drawn by white horses to the Quirinal Palace. On the Via Flaminia the horses of one coach shied and balked, throwing the coachman and cracking his skull, which was considered a bad omen by some bystanders.

The actual designation of the new King in the throne room of the palace was a scene of great dignity and color. It was there that one felt the weight of the historic forces that have converged on Rome today. The King entered at 11:15, dressed in the uniform of a field marshal. Behind him came the Prince of Piedmont and other princes of the Royal House, including the Duke of Spoleto in his admiral's uniform.

Premier Mussolini and Foreign Minister Count Ciano followed to take up positions at the right of the throne. There were many high fascist, military and court officials, but no foreigners except newspaper men.

### Pavelitch Heads the Croats

The Croat delegation was headed by their Poglavnik [the Croat equivalent of Duce or Fuehrer], Dr. Ante Pavelitch. He and some others were dressed in the uniform of the Ustashi, the Croat irredentists, terrorists who worked for the independence of Croatia. Some of the Croats were in peasant costume and a few religious orders were represented.

The ceremony consisted of two brief speeches, one by Dr. Pavelitch, asking King Victor Emmanuel to designate a King and the other by the Italian monarch, naming the Duke of Spoleto. Victor Emmanuel's address was notable for its strong fascist terminology.

"The presence of a Prince of Savoy on the throne of the independent State of Croatia," he said, "testifies to the will of your people to collaborate with Italy in the spirit of closest friendship. We consider the rebirth of the Croat nation as a happy omen for the new order that is being affirmed in Europe."

Finally he said, "We designate our beloved nephew, His Royal Highness Aimone of Savoy-Aosta, Duke of Spoleto, to assume the crown of the kingdom of Croatia."

As the spectators walked out the Prince of Piedmont ostentatiously stepped back to allow the new King of Croatia to precede him, for his cousin was now of higher rank.

The Croat delegation then went to the Palazzo Venezia to sign the various accords. There the usual crowds shouted for Premier Mussolini and Dr. Pavelitch and they came out on the balcony many times. There was a luncheon at the palace and a banquet tonight in the Quirinal Palace. The delegation left Rome for Zagreb at 10 o'clock.

There was no announcement that any of the Croats saw the Pope despite yesterday's reports that they would but it is possible that the Bishop of Zagreb had an audience with the Pontiff.

It is believed that the new King will go to Zagreb within a week for the coronation. He is considered here what Americans call a good sport, figuratively and literally, for he is a pilot, polo player, automobile racer and explorer.

Although less famous than his soldier brother, he is well liked, and Italians are wishing him a better fate than his predecessor King Zvonimir of 800 years ago, the last King that the House of Savoy furnished. He was Amedeo of Savoy, who spent a few unhappy years trying to satisfy that independent, nationalistic people.

\* \* \*

May 20, 1941

## ITALY TO ENFORCE FASCISM ON CROATS

*Gayda Outlines Regime Form—Mussolini's Troops to Stay in Puppet State*

**POPE DENIES RECOGNITION**

*Vatican Paper Says King and Leader Were Received as Private Individuals*

By HERBERT L. MATTHEWS
By Telephone to The New York Times

ROME, May 19—The outlines of the new Kingdom of Croatia became somewhat clearer today, but the clarity only proves even more that the Croat State will be a helpless dependency of Italy and to a lesser extent of Germany. Even the Italian armed forces are not to be withdrawn from Croat territory. Italy has won a greater prize than she even demanded of the Allied powers in the Treaty of London of 1915.

Virginio Gayda puts the whole matter as uncompromisingly and as clearly as anybody. The territorial outlines, he says, were inspired by two principles—"to reconquer the regions and cities that always belonged to Venetian civilization and were always permeated by Italian culture" and, second, "to insure Italy's defense on the basis of the principle that all recognize: that the Adriatic is held and defended from the Dalmatian coast."

Fiume, which had been perched perilously on the edge of Italian territory, has received a hinterland and the whole Gulf of Quarnaro. The line, which includes the former Yugoslav rival port of Susak, swings as far back as Delnice and thence north to include Cabar.

The isolated port of Zara is now part of an enclave which includes Split, and Signor Gayda admits that this "greatly exceeds the zones once contained in the old Venetian frontiers of 1669." Then there are all the islands that go to Italy and "the vast Bay of Cattaro, with all its territory, which is the keystone of the Adriatic military system."

### Fascist Structure Foreseen

As for the new kingdom's political system, Signor Gayda makes no bones about that. "It goes without saying that it will express an identity of political aims with Italy," he writes. "This will find its intimate confirmation in an identity of political forms and institutions which the new Croat State is going to construct in resemblance to Fascist, with a single totalitarian party with a corporative regime with respect to agricultural policy and racial intransigence."

Meanwhile, Italian troops are to remain on Croat territory. This was made clear in an order of the day issued today by Premier Mussolini. It stated, first, that "all the civil powers that until now have been placed under Italian military occupation pass to the Croat authorities" and, second, that "the Italian armed forces now on territory of the Independent State of Croatia cease as of tomorrow to possess the character and prerogatives of an army of occupation and assume the character of troops stationed on the friendly and allied territory of the Independent State of Croatia."

### Pope Withholds Recognition

The Osservatore Romano in three brief official notices has made it clear to the world that Pope Pius XII has not recognized the new Croat Kingdom and only granted to its representatives the minimum of courtesy that the occasion demanded. He did receive the Duke of Spoleto, Dr. Ante Pavelitch and a Croat delegation, but in each case the reception was so arranged that it was deprived of any political or official character.

First came the request of the Duke of Spoleto to be received. The Pope naturally would not refuse such a request, but he simply told the Duke to come and see him at 7 o'clock on Saturday evening. Had he waited until yesterday the Pope would have been receiving the King of Croatia and by that gesture given official recognition to the new kingdom.

Just to make that clear, the Osservatore Romano today publishes this note:

"The Supreme Pontiff, Pius XII, granting the filial desire, received in private capacity His Royal Highness Prince Aimone of Savoy-Aosta, Duke of Spoleto. The audience took place on Saturday at 7 o'clock. The Holy Father received the august visitor in his private library, talking with him with paternal cordiality for more than forty minutes."

Then came the even more delicate problem of what to do about Dr. Pavelitch, who also made a formal request in advance to be received by the Pope along with the whole Croat delegation. There again, to accede to the request would have been to recognize the new kingdom. On the other hand, as they appeared in the role of Catholic leaders of a truly Catholic people, the Pope did not feel he should disappoint them. The problem was solved by dividing the delegation into two parts.

First Dr. Pavelitch was received alone—only a stenographer accompanied him—not as the head of the Croat Government but simply as Dr. Ante Pavelitch, a Catholic individual. This was made quite clear by the Osservatore Romano today in a second note, which said:

"His Holiness received Dr. Ante Pavelitch, who had made a devoted request, in a strictly private audience yesterday evening at 6 o'clock."

Finally came the turn of the whole Croat delegation. Of them, the Osservatore Romano simply says:

"The Holy Father deigned to admit to his august presence a group of Croat Catholics, accompanied by His Excellency, Mgr. Francis Salis-Sewis, Titular Bishop of Corico, Auxiliary of Zagreb. His Holiness gave his hand to each of those present to be kissed, comforting them with the Apostolic Blessing."

In other words, the delegation was received without special honors, just like any group of Catholic pilgrims. The Pope did not say a word to any of them, except to give his blessing.

### Pavelitch Crosses Border

ROME, May 19 (AP)—Dr. Ante Pavelitch and his Croat delegation crossed the northeastern Italian border into the newly created monarchy of Croatia today after arranging with Italy what observers considered a possible model for States to be set up under the Axis new order in Europe.

Whether a similar structure eventually would be received by what is left of Poland, Norway, Belgium, the Netherlands, Serbia and Greece after the Axis powers and their smaller friends annex territory they desire remained to be seen. But some persons thought Croatia might provide the pattern.

\*    \*    \*

June 5, 1941

## TERROR IN CROATIA AIMS AT LOYALISTS

*Wholesale Sedition Trials Laid to Anti-Pavelitch Feeling of King's Backers*

### GERMANS FIGHT DISSENT

*Their Drive Against Unrest Is Believed Made Necessary by Native Opposition*

Special Cable to The New York Times

JERUSALEM, June 4—Increasing terrorism in Croatia is reported in messages reaching authoritative loyalist Croat circles in the Middle East, to whom it is reported that four military tribunals recently were instituted to try hundreds of cases of alleged sedition, which really is loyalty to the Yugoslav kingdom.

While the Germans declare secret propaganda is being used in Croatia to stir up dissatisfaction, actually the latter is a genuine manifestation of the public feeling against the regime of Ante Pavelitch, President of the new Croat State. It is said that M. Pavelitch has not published the names of the members of the delegation that accompanied him to Rome to negotiate the Croatian "monarchy" because no men of public standing are supporting him.

Croat circles here consider that the creation of the Croat kingdom was agreed to by Reichsfuehrer Hitler as a sop to Italy to compensate for the loss of Ethiopia and for coveted territorial concession from France. Despite protestations that Croatia has entered an era of collaboration with the Axis, German and Italian troops continue to occupy the territory at the expense of the inhabitants, it is pointed out.

The recent monetary customs agreement is described here as another method of despoiling the country, since Italy has nothing that she can export to Croatia, but wants to deprive the latter of valuable timber and other natural resources.

\*    \*    \*

June 22, 1941

## YUGOSLAV BOY KING ARRIVES IN ENGLAND

*Peter, Accompanied by General Simovitch, Is Expected to Set Up London Regime*

### AIR ROUTE IS KEPT SECRET

*Officials Indicate, However, That Party Was Bombed and Machine-Gunned on Way*

By CRAIG THOMPSON
Special Cable to The New York Times

LONDON, June 21—King Peter of Yugoslavia arrived in London this morning with the intention of setting up his government here from which to give the British all possible aid and at the same time to become part of the third kingdom in exile to seek refuge in this monarchical democracy.

With King Haakon of Norway and Queen Wilhelmina of the Netherlands he becomes the third regal refugee seeking a haven in this island from the Nazi war machine. When established, his government will be the seventh of exiled peoples in Britain—at least in terms of those who represent them here—the other four being the Poles, Belgians, Free French and Czechs.

The young King was accompanied by Prime Minister General Dusan Simovitch, Minister of Foreign Affairs, Momcilo Nincitch and M. Knezevitch, who, before the flight from Belgrade, was Minister at Court. He landed in England during the late hours of this morning and came to London by train.

He received the usual courtesies extended to sovereigns. The Duke of Kent, who was on hand to receive him, presented greetings from King George. An attaché of No. 10 Downing Street presented the compliments of Prime Minister Winston Churchill.

On behalf of Foreign Secretary Anthony Eden, Sir John B. Monck, vice marshal of the diplomatic corps, presented the

Foreign Office's respects. Also present were ranking officers of the Yugoslav Legation here.

Young King Peter's ticket of re-establishment on foreign soil was written by Mr. Eden months ago when, acknowledging Yugoslav protests against the Nazi dismemberment, he wrote:

"I wish to avail myself of this opportunity to inform Your Excellency that these acts by the Italian and German Governments are held null and void by His Majesty's Government of the United Kingdom who are supporting, and will continue to support the government of King Peter II as being the only duly accredited representatives of Croatia, Slovenia and other parts of the Yugoslav States."

The exact route young Peter followed enroute from Belgrade to London was not made known. It was said to have been an adventurous journey on which he was followed by the German Air Force and bombed and machine-gunned at each place he touched. There was none in his party who had been injured, however.

King Peter's mother, Marie, has been here with her sons Tomislav, 13 years of age, and Andrej, 11, for some time.

\*   \*   \*

**September 2, 1941**

## YUGOSLAV LIBERTY DAY SET

Next Saturday, the eighteenth birthday of the exiled King Peter II of Yugoslavia, has been proclaimed Yugoslav Liberty Day by the Governors of New York, New Jersey, Michigan, Pennsylvania, Ohio and Illinois, it was announced yesterday by the American Friends of Yugoslav. A nation-wide celebration will be sponsored by the American Friends of Yugoslavia, with a two-way broadcast over the Columbia Broadcasting System at 2 P. M., with Wendell L. Willkie and Governor Lehman speaking from New York and King Peter from London.

\*   \*   \*

**September 7, 1941**

## BALKANS SEETHE UNDER NAZI RULE

*Old Tensions and New Decrees Reported Breeding Revolt All Through Southeast*

**SABOTAGE IS WIDESPREAD**

By RAYMOND BROCK
Wireless to The New York Times

BAGHDAD, Sept. 6—As if by prearranged signal, a series of isolated revolts and organized rebellions against Axis rule is igniting Southeastern Europe. Something approaching a revolution threatens the German and Italian front and rear at a period which historians may cite as the turning point of the second World War.

Within three weeks after the German invasion of Soviet Russia, Serbia's Chetniks began a series of sorties from the mountains of South Serbia, Herzegovina and Bosnia, attacking German and Italian supply routes and Axis army patrols themselves, beginning a revolt which has now spread almost the length and breadth of Yugoslavia. Reports confirmed by an Axis communiqué make it clear that the Bulgarian and Rumanian peasantry is increasingly dissatisfied with food shortages, the mobilization of younger men and German demands for the support of the war against the Soviets with foodstuffs and man power. The result has been outbreaks of sabotage, isolated but violent incidents and a general movement toward resistance to German domination.

### The Union of Hate

The rising Union of Hate in Europe's always troubled Southeast is not directed solely against the Nazis, however. An old Balkan proverb takes the form of a question, asking: "Does a Serb hate a Croat more than a Croat hates an Austrian, than an Austrian hates a Hungarian, than a Hungarian hates a Rumanian?"

Europe's Southeastern peoples are at once more united and more divided today than they have been in a quarter-century. The Serbs, betrayed, as they see it, by the Croats in their direst hour, are sworn to destroy the Croat leaders and Croat State forever. Croat Republicans, driven underground by the Axis troops are nursing an age-old hatred against the Germans and Hungarians at the same time they are hating and fearing the remorseless Serbs. The Hungarians, at present crushed by a complete German military, political and economic domination, are awaiting the moment when they may unseat the Horthy Government, cast out the Germans and battle the Rumanians for the precious remnants of Transylvania that are still Rumanian.

### Sick of the War

The Rumanians, for their part, are thoroughly sick of the Russian war and would be delighted to swivel their guns to the west in order to regain their World War prize, Transylvania, at the same time destroying their present despised and hated allies, the Hungarians. The Bulgars, beset by German demands that they join in the Russian war, stand ready to join in an invasion of Turkey, if necessary, and would be only too glad to strike a blow at the hated Turks. But they are fiercely resentful of the present necessity for belligerency against Russia, which is firmly tied to Bulgaria, ethnically and emotionally.

A passive war reigns meantime in Greece. While an estimated 20,000 British, Australian and Yugoslav fugitives are harbored in Greek sanctuaries, the Greeks are nursing an undying hatred for the Germans and a complete contempt for the Italians, and are preparing to join the Balkan revolution.

### Reports in Turkey

Reports from eyewitnesses arriving in Turkey and Syria almost daily indicate that something of enormous proportions is under way throughout the Balkans.

New German and Italian reinforcements in Yugoslavia, Rumania and Greece may be there only in preparation for a new Axis drive southeastward upon Turkey—or they may have been necessitated by reported imminence of rebellion in Greece, Rumania and Bulgaria similar to the Serbs' open warfare. Stern new military decrees in Greece, threatening death for the assembly of more than three persons and for listening to foreign radio broadcasts, may indicate the latter.

German and Italian occupation forces, whatever is the case in Southeastern Europe, today face the severest test for all conquerers—retaining the mastery of suppressed peoples and at the same time waging war against powerful enemies elsewhere. These suppressed peoples hate one another with a violence surpassing their anti-German feeling in most cases, but it is probable that they would unite at least temporarily against a common enemy.

\* \* \*

September 23, 1941

## EXILED GREEK KING ARRIVES IN LONDON

### *George II Brings Political Entourage to Establish Formal Government*

### TRAVELED A LONG ROUTE

### *Premier Issues Declaration That Greece Will Carry On Fight to Victory*

Special Cable to The New York Times

LONDON, Sept. 22—Five months to a day since he left his stricken country, King George II of the Hellenes, accompanied by his brother, Crown Prince Paul, and high officials of the Greek Government arrived today in London.

The royal party alighted from a special train at Euston Station that had brought them here from a northern port, where they landed this morning after a long journey by way of Egypt and South Africa. The King of Greece and his brother were welcomed in person by King George, Queen Elizabeth, the Duke and Duchess of Kent, Prime Minister Churchill and many other notables.

The party included Princess Alexandra, the Greek King's niece; her mother, Princess Astasia; Emanuel Tsouderos, President of the Greek Council, and a number of other Greek officials.

The Greek King's presence in Britain adds one more royal exile to the colony already here. The occupied countries represented by royalty in this country are Norway, the Netherlands, Yugoslavia, Luxemburg and Albania. In addition to these countries other governments have established themselves here.

This was the second time within seventeen years that King George II of the Hellenes had come to England as an exile from his country. In 1924 he was driven from his throne by his own people and spent eleven years here. He returned to

Athens in 1935 when he was restored to the throne. He also visited London in 1937 and again in 1938.

The arrival of the King and officials of his government will, of course, permit direct contact with the British Government. It is believed that the Greek Minister of Finance and the governor of the Bank of Greece will make their headquarters in London in much the same way that the Greek service Ministers have established themselves in the Middle East.

Premier Tsouderos issued a statement today declaring that it was impossible to say how long the party would stay, but he added:

"We are extremely happy to find ourselves here among the British people, where we intend to carry on to the very end of this struggle at the side of the British against the Nazi and Fascist tyrants of Europe. We are going to build up our resources to continue this fight to victory, of which I am confident."

\* \* \*

October 11, 1941

## MASSACRES LAID TO CROAT USTASHI

### *More Than 300,000 Serbs and Pro-Yugoslav Croats Reported Slain by Revolutionaries*

### 25 MORE CZECHS KILLED

### *Two Additional Frenchmen Are Executed by Germans—3 Doomed in Bulgaria*

Special Broadcast to The New York Times

ANKARA, Turkey, Oct. 10—The Croatian revolutionary Ustashi have killed between 300,000 and 340,000 Serbs and pro-Yugoslav Croats since last May, according to figures compiled by intelligence experts from agents operating in Croatia and Bosnia and released to this correspondent here today.

While some of the executions have been carried out by German Elite Guard units, the Gestapo and regular German Army officers and by Italians in Western Croatia, the bulk of the killings have been done by the Ustashi, according to this report.

One authenticated dispatch sent by short-wave radio from near Yatovo, in the Lika sector in Croatia, said that nearly 5,000 Serbs were slaughtered by Croatian Ustashi in a concentration camp outside Yatovo. Most of the Serbs, it is reported, were from the huge colony at Lika, called the "Serbian Island" in Croatia.

#### Report 700 Died in Boxcar

The same report said that more than 700 Serbs died or were killed in a railroad boxcar prison near Karlovatz. The entire Serbian population of Pihac in Bosnia has been destroyed, the report stated. At Banja Luka, Bosnian industrial center, documented reports said that there was no longer one Serb living in the city. The pre-war Serbian population of Banja Luka was 12,000.

Three political followers of the former Croatian political leader—Dr. Vladimir Matchek, president of the Croat Peasant party—were reported executed by the Ustashi when they refused to renounce allegiance to the imprisoned Dr. Matchek. The men were identified as "Kastanovitch, Frankovitch and Vradnechevitch."

More than 500,000 Serbian refugees, many of whom have joined the Serbian guerrilla Chetnik army, are reported to have made their way from Bosnia and Croatia to Serbia since last July.

Late reports tonight from Montenegro and Hercegovina, said that the Chetnik war against the Italian Army of occupation was increasingly audacious despite violent reprisals taken against captured Chetniks and Serbian hostages. Italian Army liaison was reported completely interrupted for three days this week between Cetinje. Trebinje and the Dalmatian coast by Chetnik units operating in the wild mountain country of Montenegro and Hercegovina.

After repeated ambushes, which wiped out several hundred Italians, the Italian command at Kotor is understood to have dispatched three battalions, which temporarily cleared the roads for staff cars and dispatch riders.

\* \* \*

**November 10, 1941**

## RUMANIAN PLEBISCITE CHECKS DISSIDENTS

### Voters Against Antonescu Rule Had to Reveal Intention

The national referendum on Rumanian foreign and home policies decreed by Premier General Ion Antonescu was held yesterday, according to a German Transocean broadcast recorded by The New York Times, but any one who wanted to express disapproval of his collaboration with the Nazis had to declare his intention to the authorities.

"Every one entitled to cast his vote was asked by the head of the polling station whether he was going to vote 'Yes' or 'No,' whereupon he was handed the corresponding ticket," the broadcast said.

None of the results were known but the German news agency had no doubt about the outcome, stating:

"No one in Rumania doubts that the outcome of this plebiscite will be an overwhelming demonstration of confidence in Antonescu and his work."

Early returns were expected this morning, last night's broadcast said, with the rural votes to come in later.

The dispatch, which already referred to Premier Antonescu as "Stateleader Antonescu" another augury of Rumania's impending change into a "new order" corporate State, said that

"citizens had formed long queues outside" voting stations hours before they opened at 8 A. M., "to pass judgment" on Premier Antonescu's policy.

\* \* \*

**December 18, 1941**

## FALSE ALIGNMENTS

Nothing better illustrates the utter unreality of some of the alignments in this conflict than the announcement that Albania has declared war against the United States. As far as this country is concerned, Rome's act of ventriloquism for its helpless little vassal is merely ludicrous, but for Albania it borders on the tragic. The Albanian people are grateful to American foundations and institutions for help in the fight against malaria, for the initial effort to teach trades to the boys from the primitive mountain villages, for nursing centers and schools. If they know what has happened, which is highly doubtful, these people will be bitterly resentful that their conquerors have committed the final treachery of representing them as the enemies of the country they look upon as their best friend.

The case of Albania is typical. Many of the small countries of Europe are lined up in ghastly masquerade of false faces. Even worse than the fate of being defeated or made captive— a misfortune which may overcome the bravest in a war against superior force—is this alignment on the side of their enemies against their friends. From their point of view, Hitler's supreme and intolerable presumption is that he dares to speak in the name of his prisoners, that he pretends to be the voice of the "Europe" he has clubbed and gagged and robbed.

And from our point of view it is of cardinal importance to remember that the subject countries which have declared war against us are not free agents. Their decisions are not their own. This goes for Bulgaria, Rumania and Hungary as well as Albania. The Governments of these states speak neither for their people nor, in most cases, even for themselves. Italy itself, for that matter, is about as helpless as Albania, and the declaration of war against the United States is no more representative of popular sentiment in one country than in the other.

Now that we are in the war to the finish, we can never afford to forget that the Axis "front" is largely forged and false. Its moral weakness is that it masks millions of friends—whole nations struggling behind the bars for our victory and Hitler's defeat. In the long run these allies behind the enemy's lines may be as useful in their way as our avowed allies, and one of our main tasks is to encourage them to believe in their own future.

\* \* \*

## SERBIAN PRELATE CHARGES KILLING OF 180,000 IN NAZI-INVADED CROATIA

***Archbishop Accuses 'Quislings' of Wholesale Massacre and Torture—Post-War Court Is Suggested to Punish the Criminals***

### By JAMES MacDONALD
Special Cable to The New York Times

LONDON, Jan. 2—The Yugoslav Legation here made public today a document prepared by the Archbishop of the Serbian Orthodox Church that said more than 180,000 persons were slaughtered in the Nazi puppet state of Croatia up to the early part of August.

The document was replete with grisly stories of the torture and mass murder of men, women and children. According to the Archbishop, the wholesale killings were carried out on orders of "Quisling" Pavelitch and members of the Ustashi, an organization of Croatian extremists. The Archbishop sent his original report to the Nazi commandant in Croatia, hoping that in consequence steps would be taken to prevent the continuation of the seeming attempt to exterminate the Serbs, but, according to the document made public today, the massacre still goes on.

A copy of the report has been sent to the Archbishop of Canterbury. Also the names of many alleged terrorists contained in the report are being kept on file for presentation to an international court of justice after the war in hope that the "Quislings" will be duly punished. The report also contains the names of scores of victims.

Giving what is described as "only a pale picture" of the ghastly reign of terror, the document says that at Korenica hundreds of persons were killed, but before they died many of them had their ears and noses cut off and then were compelled to graze on grass. The tortures most usually applied were beating, severing of limbs, gouging of eyes and breaking of bones. Cases are related of men, being forced to hold red-hot bricks, dance on barbed wire with naked feet, and wear wreaths of thorns. Needles were stuck in fingers under the nails and lighted matches were held under noses.

Of murders on a large scale, the Archbishop records that in the village of Korito 168 peasants were severely tortured, tied in bundles and thrown into a pit. When it was found some were still breathing, the Ustashi threw bombs among them "to finish them off." Sixty-three more bodies were brought to the scene and flung into the pit. Then gasoline was poured over all the bodies and ignited.

The report says that as a result of similar deeds in two other villages of the same area hardly one Serb remains in the region.

According to the Archbishop, over 600 people were killed in and around Krupa between July 25 and July 30. Many victims were thrown into a near-by stream. At another town "blood was shed in torrents and the murdered Serbs were cut to pieces so that it was impossible to identify them." In other villages every house was razed.

At still another place bombs were set off to make pits in which cartloads of bodies were dumped after the corpses had been stripped of their clothing by special detachments who had received this "right" in payment for carrying out the burials.

Among many specific instances of individual torture the Archbishop describes how four men were first crucified on the doors of their homes, then mutilated with knives.

Priests' beards were pulled out and their throats cut.

In one case a priest was forced to dig the grave for his own son, who was a student. The son was tortured to death before the father's eyes. Then the clergyman was ordered to read the burial service. During the ceremony the father fainted three times, but was revived each time and forced to continue the service. When he had finished he also was tortured and killed. The document adds that both the priest and his son "were killed by a Ustachi agent, Ivan Scheifer, a teacher by profession."

Families of some of the victims had to pay large sums of money for return of bodies for decent burial, the Archbishop said.

\* \* \*

## GENERAL LEADING YUGOSLAVS' FIGHT IS REWARDED WITH POST IN CABINET

***Mikhailovitch Made War Minister by Regime in London— Yovanovitch, a Jurist, Succeeds Simovitch as Premier***

### By DAVID ANDERSON
Wireless to The New York Times

LONDON, Jan. 12—General Draja Mikhailovitch, known here as the "Yugoslav Robin Hood," was appointed Minister of War today by the Yugoslav Government in London in recognition of his successful effort to keep up resistance within his country. At the same time it was announced that Dr. Slobodan Yovanovitch had succeeded General Dusan Simovitch as Premier.

The latter appointment was designed to strengthen the Yugoslav Cabinet in its dealing with postwar problems. The new Premier is a politician believed to be better able to cope with such issues than is the former soldier leader.

General Mikhailovitch has become an almost legendary character through his skill in maintaining a large force of men for a brilliant undercover campaign against the Germans and Italians. He is credited with having absolute control of 20,000 square miles in Southern Serbia, and tales of his exploits continue to grow in number and variety.

The general has made a great point of keeping in touch with the progress of the war elsewhere, often sending telegrams to the Yugoslav Government in this country and to the British in North Africa.

Dr. Yovanovitch is Yugoslavia's leading jurist and is known to be strongly pro-British. He has been rector of Belgrade University, president of the Yugoslav Royal Academy of Science and a professor of diplomatic history and constitutional law, as well as dean of the university's faculty of law.

### Statement by Cabinet

The Yugoslav Cabinet issued the following statement setting forth the reasons for the changes:

"The conclusion of the Atlantic Charter, the entry of the United States into the war and the recent success of the democratic powers against the Axis in Europe and Africa have made it necessary for all the Allied governments to turn their attention more and more to the question of the political and economic organization of Europe after the war.

"In handling these questions the Kingdom of Yugoslavia has an important but difficult part to play, and it is essential that the Yugoslav Government not only should be truly representative of the whole country and able to speak authoritatively for Serbs, Croats and Slovenes, but should be fully qualified to take its share in the political discussions that must henceforth take place on important problems that are likely to arise.

"At the time of its first constitution in 1941 the immediate problem facing the government was a purely military one. Today it is desirable that the leadership of the government should be in political rather than military hands. Dr. Yovanovitch, a former Vice Premier, commands the unqualified support of all the other Ministers and those whom they represent.

"The new government will continue to work for a steady development of relations and of close collaboration between Serbs, Croats and Slovenes, and for defeat of the persistent and cunning efforts of the Axis powers to sow discord between them."

A post of "high importance for the continuance and development of the war effort of Yugoslavia" has been offered to General Simovitch.

### Oath Will Be Broadcast

LONDON, Jan. 12 (U.P.)—It was disclosed today that within twenty-four hours General Draja Mikhailovitch would stand before the microphone of his powerful short-wave radio station in Yugoslavia to take the oath of office as Minister of War.

Yugoslav sources said that the general would pledge the following:

"I, Draja Mikhailovitch, promise to carry out the duties of my office until death or until my country is freed of the invader."

Dr. Milan Gavrilovitch, former Yugoslav Minister to Moscow, has been made Minister of Justice.

\*   \*   \*

## YUGOSLAV WOMEN JOIN FIGHT ON AXIS

*Reports From Secret Short-Wave Radio Station Tell of Stubborn Resistance*

**NAZIS, ITALIANS ATTACKED**

*Officials Say Guerrilla War Persists Despite Penalty of Death for Rebels*

With German and Italian troops increasing their pressure in an attempt to shatter the resistance of Yugoslavia to their occupation, detachments of women guerrilla fighters are taking up the fight under General Draja Mikhailovitch, leader of the revolt, according to word received here yesterday from a secret Yugoslav radio station.

The account of conditions in Yugoslavia was picked up in London and released here by the delegation of the Royal Yugoslav Government in the United States. Franc Snoj, Minister of State of Yugoslavia and a member of the delegation, said that many such women's detachments had been organized and were in action against the German and Italian invaders.

The radio report gave several specific instances of revolt against the Axis domination and of severe punishment meted out recently to Serbs, Croats and Slovenes.

The military tribunal in Ljublana, capital of Slovenia, which is occupied by the Italians, it was said, recently sentenced sixty-nine Slovenes for propaganda activities and attacks on military objectives and occupying soldiers. Eighteen were condemned to death, according to the report, and twelve were executed immediately. Forty-one others were sentenced to prison terms, some of them ranging up to life imprisonment at hard labor.

In recent weeks, according to the secret radio report, attacks have been made against the Italian garrison at Loz, near Ljublana, and against the railroad station at Verd, in the same district. In the Verd fighting the station was demolished, tanks of gasoline were destroyed and Italian soldiers killed. Thirty-nine Slovenes, accused of these attacks, have been shot.

In Bosnia, Yugoslav guerrillas recently attacked an Italian column on the railroad line from Bileche to Niksich, seized tanks, motor vehicles and munitions and tore up the railroad tracks. It was reported also that many Croats, forcibly mobilized and sent to the Russian front to fight for the Axis, had deserted and joined the Red Army.

"German and Italian punishment includes not only instant death, hard labor and life imprisonment, but forced emigration," Mr. Snoj explained. "Among Slovene counties completely evacuated are Litija, Brezice and Krsko, where Germans have already moved in and started to build new factories."

The Minister said the Axis was making a deliberate attempt by propaganda to foster the belief that Yugoslavs were not united in their revolt against the occupying troops.

He declared that all sections of the population, Serbs, Croats and Slovenes were participating in the fight.

A representative of the delegation said that sixteen "terrorists" who were executed recently at Ljublana on the orders of an Italian court-martial were Slovenes. In a headline, The New York Times, reporting their death in a Berne dispatch on March 12, referred to the victims as Serbs.

### YUGOSLAV RAIDS GROW
#### Attacks Are Reported Almost Daily in Newspapers

BERNE, Switzerland, March 14 (AP)—Despite recent official declarations that various parts of Axis-occupied Yugoslavia have been cleared of irregulars, Belgrade and Zagreb newspapers indicate increasing guerrilla activity.

Almost daily these newspapers report surprise attacks on pro-Axis government forces, raids on villages, sniping at trains and other disorders.

[General Draja Mihailovitch, who has resisted Germans, Italians and the Axis-sponsored governments alike since Yugoslavia was invaded last April, was reported Feb. 9 to be recruiting additional men for his guerrilla army of 20,000.]

The Belgrade press said 440 insurgents and 33 policemen were killed in a recent seven-day engagement near Toplica, about fifteen miles east of Valjevo.

D. N. B., German news agency, reported another important battle at Kursumlija, in Southern Serbia. It said a band that had hidden in the mountains during the Winter attacked the town, overpowered the police and slew residents, but was overwhelmed by a force of policemen and farmers several days later.

Seventy guerrillas were reported killed and 130 captured. Sentenced to death, the prisoners were seized and slain by farmers while they were being led to a place of execution, D. N. B. said.

Obnova, Belgrade newspaper, described another series of engagements in which 250 men were killed in a triangular area formed by Valjevo, Cacak and Uzice. The paper said seventy-five more were killed near Lebane and eighty captured near Alesinac.

\*   \*   \*

**March 26, 1942**

### HITLER'S WARS NEVER END

It is just a year since Hitler met his first check in Southeastern Europe. A year ago tomorrow the Yugoslavs rose in their anger and overthrew the Government that two days before had yielded in Vienna to German demands for passageway through their territory. The people contradicted the official "Yes" with a thunderous "No!" that opened their land to rapine and bombing and death. Yet this reckless but heroic decision of a peasant people, resolved like their ancestors "to die in honor rather than live in shame," may affect the course of history as much as the stand of the Serbs against Mohammedan invasion in 1389. Then they stood

against the barbarians from the East as now they resist the new barbarians from the West; in neither case in vain, for were it not for their defiance last Spring, the story of this Spring would be far different.

But for the unforeseen delay caused by Yugoslav resistance, Hitler's Russian campaign would have started earlier. He might well have taken Moscow before the Winter. He might have avoided the crushing losses in manpower that leave him today dependent on levies from his sullen satellites. He might have overcome the opposition of Turkey and beaten the British to Syria, Iraq and Iran. But for the time lost in subduing Yugoslavia and Greece, in a word, he might have crashed the gates of the Middle East and accomplished last year what he is forced to try this year.

Last March the Yugoslavs threw themselves across his path and upset the timetable of the conqueror—and this March they are still unconquered. They have fought fiercely and effectively ever since, in the villages, in the forests, in the craggy fortresses of their black mountains. The Serb Army remains in being under the command of General Draja Mikhailovitch, a national hero who represents the Government-in-exile as Minister of War. It remains as the most spectacular symbol of Hitler's failure. The example of Yugoslavia, resisting with an organized army nearly a year after it was overpowered and defeated by the Wehrmacht, is a living mockery of Nazi claims of victory and hopes of peace.

Hitler has overrun and occupied most of Europe. He has disarmed its garrisons, subdued its peoples, dispersed its Governments, robbed its banks and eaten up its food. He has not conquered a single country. He cannot leave unguarded a single door he has burst open. Until now he has gained nothing by his enormous efforts but new enemies. He has only to look at Yugoslavia after a year of "subjugation" to see that the business of conquest is always unfinished business. Hitler's wars never end.

\*   \*   \*

**May 4, 1942**

### YUGOSLAVIA CHAOTIC UNDER AXIS; NAZI REINFORCEMENTS FACE FIGHTS

By RAY BROCK
Wireless to The New York Times

ISTANBUL, Turkey, May 3—Yugoslavia is in chaos on the eve of Germany's expected Spring offensives and the anticipated general attack on the Axis occupying forces there by General Draja Mikhailovitch's Yugoslav troops, according to information given the writer today by a special agent who escaped from Yugoslavia last week.

The agent reported that the German High Command had sent fresh troops into Serbia in an attempt to quell the guerrilla warfare and sabotage that have been playing havoc with Germany's Balkan rear.

An additional German infantry division and a Nazi Elite Guard division have been moved into Belgrade to reinforce the

Elite Guard division that remained there after the Germans' general withdrawal last Winter.

The total Axis forces now engaged in fighting General Mikhailovitch's regulars and Chetniks, the Croat and Moslem revolutionaries and Communist saboteurs in the country include nine Italian and seven Bulgarian divisions, one Hungarian division and the entire Croatian Army of about 80,000 ragamuffin conscripts.

Half of a German tank regiment is billeted outside Belgrade and the rest of the regiment is expected to arrive from Hungary, according to detailed information given the writer. German field officers have been installed in command over the Hungarian, Bulgarian, Italian or Croat garrisons in every village and city of Serbia that was not devastated by Nazi dive bombers or artillery in the Germans' clean-up campaigns last Fall and Winter.

Despite wholesale destruction and mass executions in the Serbian towns, the people's resistance and sabotage are continuing and growing. When Yugoslav mines and factories manage to produce their estimated 10 per cent of capacity output, trains cannot be depended upon to transport the products to the Reich.

The confusion and disorder in Belgrade, which aids the night-raiding Chetniks, is heightened by the German bureaucracy, with four separate Nazi administrations besides the puppet Neditch government, now attempting to rule. They include the military governor, the Gestapo and the civil administrator—the notorious Franz Neuhausen.

The fourth regime is the Volksdeutscheburo, which is in itself a maze of beaureaucrats, Gauleiters and Nazi party ne'er-do-wells from Berlin.

The regimes override each other in a muddle of "efficiency." Last month Herr Neuhausen's department launched a clean-up of Belgrade's Chetniks and communists, in the course of which his police seized and held incommunicado for forty-eight hours Colonel Mischa Masalovitch, the Quislingist undersecretary of Premier Milan Neditch.

The Italian and Croat detachments stationed in Belgrade are treated with contempt by the Germans as well as by the Serbs. Many Croats are reported to be deserting daily rather than suffer the humiliation of boot-shining jobs and the danger of guard duty at suburban warehouses and on the Danube wharves after nightfall.

### Outbreaks After Hostage Seizures

The recent arrest by the Germans of members of General Mikhailovitch's family and of those of forty officers serving with the Yugoslav commander and War Minister, which the Nazis supposed would bring the general to a bargaining mood, instead is reported to have precipitated the wildest outbreaks of sabotage and resistance since last June.

The Germans have re-arrested eighty of the 430 Serbian officers who had been released to induce them to join the despised Neditch forces. That "army" now numbers fewer than 3,500 men, most of them members of the German minority of Slovenia.

The Yugoslav agent, who smuggled closely-written documents out of Croatia, told the writer of anarchy and disorders besetting Dr. Ante Pavelitch's "kingdom." More than 1,000 favored Croatian families were settled upon farms and estates seized from Serbs who had been executed or forced to flee. But the Croats are now clamoring for food, seed and live stock, because the Serbs carried out an effective "scorched earth" policy.

Marshal Kvaternik, Puppet Leader Pavelitch's Chief of Staff, has narrowly escaped assassination three times and travels in an armor-plated limousine similar to that used by Dr. Pavelitch, who received his from Adolf Hitler.

### Croatians Desert Pavelitch

Dr. Pavelitch's hold upon Croatia now exists in name only, according to a report from Zagreb. His Ustachi continue to rule in that Croatian capital but outlying cities such as Karlovatz and Banjaluka, a Bosnian industrial city now put in "Greater Croatia," are frequently terrorized by Chetnik raiders.

Dr. Pavelitch and Marshal Kvaternik have lost much of their former support by desertions. Since the departure of 25,000 Croat troops to the Russian front as "volunteers," their remaining army of about 80,000 has been ill-clad and short of arms.

Only 20 per cent of the original Croat officers remain, it is reported, the rest having been "removed" for suspected pro-Yugoslav feelings or having deserted.

\*   \*   \*

**May 5, 1942**

# BULGARIA TO SEGREGATE GYPSIES

By Telephone to The New York Times

BERNE, Switzerland, May 4—It was reported from Sofia that a decree would soon be promulgated ordering the segregating of Gypsies and prohibiting their marriage with Bulgarian nationals. The decree is also expected to assign definite residences to all Gypsies living in the country.

\*   \*   \*

**June 30, 1942**

# REIGN OF TERROR IN CRETE

LONDON, June 29 (UP)—Greek sources here reported tonight that German occupation authorities had launched a reign of terror in Crete, executing 102 Greeks in the last two weeks and seizing as hostages the families of many who fled into the mountains.

Reports reaching London said sixty-two Greeks were executed several days ago, among them a former mayor and the editor of a newspaper. They were accused of aiding guerrilla troops resisting the occupation forces. Forty more were shot later on charges of sabotage, the reports said.

\*   \*   \*

June 30, 1942

## ATHOS MONKS' BOAT BECOMES A SHRINE

---

*Tiny Craft in Which 3 Fled Pillaging Foe is Placed in the River Jordan*

**VOYAGE OF NINETY DAYS**

*They Report Enemy Looted Treasures of Church on the Holy Mountain*

---

By A. C. SEDGWICK
Wireless to The New York Times

JERUSALEM, June 29—On the River Jordan near Jericho lies a vessel that has become another shrine in this already hallowed land, and it will, it is believed, be an object of veneration for generations to come.

The vessel was carried to her present moorings from the seacoast near Halfa by order of the Greek Orthodox Church authorities in Palestine, who hold that in view of her being both the result and the token of a divinely wrought miracle, it is fitting that she should remain in the sacred stream.

The tiny craft, a combination sailboat and rowboat, no more than fifteen feet long, comes from near Mount Athos, or, as the faithful usually call it, the Holy Mountain, on the most easterly of the three massive promontories of Chalcidice that jut into the northern Aegean Sea.

Athos is to the Eastern Church the holiest of all holy places, where monks throughout the centuries have chosen to dwell in numerous monasteries perched on hilltops, and where, from Christianity's earliest days, hermits have lived in caves. It is a haven for the recluse in search of a spiritual life. Before the war it was nominally independent.

The vessel's crew, three monks inexperienced as seamen, embarked on a perilous expedition that lasted some ninety days, because, they said, they could no longer suffer life in holy precincts that had been defiled by enemy occupying forces, made up mainly of Bulgarians and some Rumanians and a few Nazis, who were charged with directing pillage and with lending German efficiency to vandalism.

The monks told how the bells that had sounded matins and vespers throughout peaceful ages had been removed from belfries half hidden among tall, guardian cypress, presumably to be melted down for war purposes. They told how ecclesiastical treasures that had been heaped on altars and shrines in vast profusion, and had constituted the church's principal wealth, had been placed in trucks and taken northward; how ikons of enormous value and historical interest had been stolen; how libraries containing rare volumes and some of the world's most-famous illuminated manuscripts, together with many other priceless objects, had been added to the loot.

The monks believe that their little vessel would have been wrecked on reefs or would have foundered in one of the many storms that they encountered but for Divine protection.

They said that, in numerous sequestered ports where they put in, food and water had been provided for them by Greek men, women and children, in defiance of the orders of the enemy occupying authorities.

\*   \*   \*

July 23, 1942

BERNE, Switzerland, July 22 (AP)—Countries under Axis domination are taking measures designed to force Jews to increased labor in behalf of the German war effort.

The police of Salonika have registered more than 6,000 Jews between the ages of 18 and 45 for compulsory labor. About 80,000 Jews of Warsaw, all skilled workers in their own ghetto workshops, have been assigned to tasks by Germans through a special liaison office. Similar regulations were reported throughout Poland.

The Bulgarian Government announced establishment of a ghetto in Sofia.

Rumania added another to its many decrees regulating the lives of Jews. A new order stipulated that all property of Jews, except synagogues and cemeteries, might be "transferred" to other owners.

\*   \*   \*

September 27, 1942

## THE ONE AND ONLY MIKHAILOVITCH

By RAY BROCK

ISTANBUL (By Wireless)—In the swiftly gathering gloom of a chill Spring evening in 1939 a dun-colored Yugoslav Army staff car, speeding northward from Belgrade, came to a sudden halt as the chauffeur jammed on his brakes near the outskirts of the Northern Yugoslav city of Novisad. The beam of the headlamps caught khaki-clad figures of young men and boys in a marching column blocking the highway.

From the back seat of the car, as the machine halted, a square-jawed, bespectacled face poked through the curtains and a crisp voice demanded:

"What passes here?"

"Hitler Jugend," a loud voice answered.

The owner of the voice, a strapping Storm Trooper, pushed his way through the ranks and stared brazenly at the dim outlines of the face peering at him from the car.

"Hitler Youth," the trooper repeated. "Heil Hitler!"

The car door whipped open, a stocky figure bounded into the highway, and there was a sharp crack as a fist smashed against the Storm Trooper's jaw. The big German collapsed upon the asphalt. The husky assailant from the car wheeled upon the German's followers. They broke ranks and gave way.

The angry figure advancing upon them in the glare of the headlamps was that of a Yugoslav Army colonel.

"Get out!" he snapped. His pale blue eyes flashed furiously in the lights. "*Brzo* quickly! Get out!"

He moved toward a sullen-faced peasant in the front ranks of the crowd. The man turned and fled, and the mob fled after him toward Novisad.

The officer strode back to his car, readjusting his shell-rimmed spectacles. He climbed in. "Drive on Milosh," he ordered.

"Da, Colonel Mikhailovitch," declared the delighted chauffeur, and he stepped on the gas.

The Draja Mikhailovitch legend is long. Tales about Yugoslavia's 45-year-old War Minister and Generalissimo have multiplied a hundredfold in the fourteen months since he assumed supreme command of Serbia's Chetniks, Yugoslavia's disbanded troops, freedom-loving peasants and tough mountaineers, and launched against the astounded Axis armies the fiercest, most vast guerrilla war in history. Those tales inevitably include many popular inaccuracies about this extraordinary man.

Mikhailovitch seems undersized when compared to the majority of strapping Serb officers, some of the tallest fighting men in Europe. Actually, he stands just over 5 feet 8 inches. Extraordinarily broad shoulders and great depth of chest make him seem shorter. Under close-cropped, reddish-sandy hair is a broad brow with heavy eyebrows arching cold, light blue eyes habitually squinted through shell-rimmed spectacles. A reddish, rather thin mustache shades a straight-lipped mouth which is supported by an aggressively outthrust chin on the point of a heavy, squarish jaw.

Casual inspection of the man leaves one feeling that he is taciturn and humorless; but among his intimates he is gay and companionable and he has a deep-throated, infectious laugh. He rarely smokes, almost never drinks.

Although he rose from obscurity to command, he is well-equipped. He had long and practical service with the Serb Chetniks and in the Serbian Army in the First World War. He has a sound staff college training, intermixed with tireless study of Balkan and Central European political relations.

The strategy and tactics of Mikhailovitch's armies are modeled on the classic lines of the 40-year-old Chetnik organization, founded to fight the Turks and Bulgars. But Mikhailovitch has drilled his Chetniks to precision in 1942-model warfare against armored forces and air power arrayed against him in the terrifying ratio of almost twenty to one.

The fundamentals of Chetnik warfare are surprise, speed, sabotage—highly refined Blitzkrieg tactics made possible by the shrewdest planning and unfailing intelligence about enemy forces and distribution. Mikhailovitch's intelligence service is nothing short of breath-taking to those who have been privileged to see some of its operations and the results; it is nerve-wracking, infuriating, maddening to the enemy.

The name chete comes from the Turkish and means simply "company." Chetnik companies, however, range from three men to 500 or more, depending on the operation in view. The Chetniks have evolved a combination of knife and brass knuckles similar to the celebrated Commando weapon, and for minor operations the men may be armed only with Chetnik knives. A minor operation may call for removal of an enemy patrol in order to penetrate enemy lines for specific information; or it may be a preliminary to a larger operation. Three to six men may be sufficient for such a task.

For full-scale attack, such as the outburst of offensive actions last June, Mikhailovitch uses a chete numbering upward of 1,500 men. This chete in turn is broken up into smaller units of 100, 50, 10, or 3 men, each unit with a specific assignment such as knocking out pillboxes, mopping up patrols, dynamiting bridges and barracks, or laying down a deadly fire with machine guns to cover the Chetniks as they strike.

The raid upon the Kragujevach arsenal in the June operations was a masterpiece in which Mikhailovitch, leading a picked chete of 1,500, killed more than 2,000 Germans, captured 800 more and stripped the arsenal of badly needed rifles, machine guns, ammunition and shells for mountain batteries which later wiped out a column of more than 2,000 Germans west of Visegrad. The Nazi prisoners were shot when the Nazi command ordered reprisal bombings of Shabtz and Uzice and staged the Kragujevach massacre.

Much has been written—too much, including guesswork and downright invention—about Mikhailovitch's so-called air force. In fact, the few antiquated planes at his disposal are rarely off the ground of their secret airdromes, and then only in bad weather for the shortest reconnaissance flights, when they are absolutely necessary.

There are only two known instances when planes were used for offensive purposes, against German armored columns in Western Serbia and during the December retreat of the Germans to Belgrade last Winter. Mikhailovitch's main arm is, and must continue to be—until he is reinforced with more powerful arms and Allied Commandos from the outside—the small chete of a handful to 1,500 men, springing from nowhere to blast bridges and roads, to destroy transport and tie up communications, to wipe out as many as possible of the enemy, and to disappear as quickly as they came, leaving disorder and confusion in the ranks of the enemy.

So long as Mikhailovitch can maintain his incredible liaison among his scattered forces, using short-wave radio, signal fires, smuggled micro-printed dispatches, carrier pigeons and a score more devices which have baffled and infuriated the Germans, so long as he can out-think and outmanoeuvre the enemy in his superb war of movement, so long as he can isolate and wipe out Italian garrisons guarding vital supply routes to the Dalmatian coast and smuggle in more munitions by air and submarine, so long the war in Yugoslavia will go on.

Mikhailovitch knows his country first hand, and Chetnik warfare is in his blood. He was born at the Serb village of Ivanitza, about fifty miles south of Chachak in Serbian Shumadiya. His father was an obscure peasant, but his grandfather had made himself a legend throughout Javor Planina as a Chetnik leader in the endless war against the Turks. Reared in the hard life of the Serbian peasantry through his earliest years, young Draja grew tough and wiry.

At 17 he enlisted under the Chetnik Voyvoda of Javor Planina and fought through a cruel Winter campaign against the Turks until he was wounded, in 1913. Having decided on a military career, he entered the Serbian Military Academy, and when Austria attacked Serbia the next year, precipitating the First World War, he became a noncommissioned officer in the regular army.

He was a hardened veteran leading a company when the war ended. He received the Karageorge Star with crossed swords, Serbia's highest decoration, and was promoted to captain. And he went to the Ecole Supérieure de Guerre, and from there to the General Staff School, graduating with the rank of major.

After service in Serbia and Bosnia he was selected in 1931, for King Alexander's Royal Guard, but jealous older officers intrigued until he was sent to Sofia as military attaché, later going on to Prague. There the Germans complained that he was in league with anti-Nazi operatives, and he was called home and put in command of an infantry regiment at Selje. When Nazi agents poured into Slovenia in 1938, Mikhailovitch demanded action from Belgrade, was ignored, and took matters into his own hands. He doffed his uniform and led tough Slovene Sokols against the Nazi groups, driving them back to Austria. When the German Legation at Belgrade objected, Mikhailovitch was called in, kicked upstairs into a colonelcy and made Chief of Inspection of defense fortifications.

His investigation revealed lack of arms and inadequate fortification, but his request for action was ignored by Minister of War Neditch—present Quisling Premier of Serbia. Then Mikhailovitch submitted a fifth-column memorandum exposing Cabinet Ministers and General Staff officers as pro-German. The upshot was Mikhailovitch's military arrest for "disloyalty," which later was canceled and Mikhailovitch was sent to Mostar in Herzegovina. From there he watched the slide toward the Axis and secretly renewed his Chetnik alliances. He plotted a guerrilla campaign and issued secret orders to his loyal officers for operations from mountain bases when and if the government surrendered. When Prince Paul capitulated on March 25, 1941, Mikhailovitch was ready.

When the Germans smashed through and the Simovitch government took flight, Mikhailovitch led his guerrilla armies into the mountains. After nine weeks of preparation, they launched their war on the night of June 25, starting a relentless campaign which has ranged through the length and breadth of Yugoslavia.

Today Mikhailovitch's armies fight on from their encircled strongholds in Western Bosnia, Herzegovina and Montenegro. And General Draja Mikhailovitch leads them as Minister of War, named by the proud Yugoslav Government in Exile at London in a struggle which undoubtedly will go down in history as one of the most remarkable and soul-stirring chapters in the Second World War.

*   *   *

October 24, 1942

### KING PETER SALUTES SLAV EXHIBIT HERE

*Masaryk, Also From London, Asks Unity of Two Nations*

With a brief message of greeting from King Peter of Yugoslavia and a stirring appeal for a speedy United Nations victory by Jan Masaryk, Foreign Minister of Czechoslovakia, by short wave from England, an exhibit of the history and the fight for freedom of their countries was opened formally yesterday at Freedom House, 32 East Fifty-first Street.

Because he was suffering from a cold, King Peter's address was delivered by Vladimir Milanovich, chargé d'affaires of the Yugoslav Embassy in London. The youthful monarch said the "interest and sympathy which the people of the United States feel for my martyred country" was reaching even into Yugoslavia "despite the thickness of the dungeon walls in which the Axis forces tried to enclose us."

Mr. Masaryk pleaded for cooperation between the two Slav nations as "terribly necessary" and said that when it was torn apart by "short-sightedness, stupidity, wishful thinking and cowardly complacency, Europe became one concentration camp." Replying to the speakers from abroad were Geoffrey Cox and Leigh White, newspaper correspondents.

The exhibit, titled "Agony and Courage," symbolizes the universality of the menace to the democracies. Native Czech artists arranged the Yugoslav story and the Yugoslavs created the Czech exhibit. The show will continue through Nov. 27. William Agar, educational director of Freedom House, welcomed the guests at the opening.

*   *   *

January 14, 1943

### BALKAN SYMPTOMS

The reports from Central Europe and the Balkans, coming as they must through roundabout channels, are vague and sometimes contradictory, but they leave no doubt that there is serious unrest verging on open revolt in Bulgaria, Rumania and Hungary, and that guerrilla warfare of substantial proportions continues in Yugoslavia and Greece. As long as the German armies remain intact, it would be dangerous to overestimate the importance of these developments, but they are further symptoms of the turn in the tide. They hamper Hitler's supplies and drain his manpower at a time when the Nazis themselves are forced to admit a shortage of manpower on the Russian front. And they are likely to increase as the Winter progresses and the food situation grows worse—and the Russian steamroller continues to roll nearer to the Axis lands.

The collapse of the Balkan front in 1918, said Ludendorff, "sealed the fate of the Quadruple Alliance"—the Axis of that day. There is no Allied battle-front in the Balkans now, but there is the Third Front, and, after his failure to capture the

Russian oil fields, Hitler is far more dependent on Rumanian oil than ever was the Kaiser. It is premature to compose an epitaph for the Axis of today, but the Balkans will be well worth watching for further developments.

\* \* \*

**January 29, 1943**

## BITTER CIVIL WAR RENDS YUGOSLAVIA

*Ten Armed Groups Fight Each Other for Control,*
*Incited by Axis Intrigue*

**BRITAIN AND SOVIET SPLIT**

*London Backs Mikhailovitch's Chetniks, Moscow Actively*
*Aids Partisans*

By C. L. SULZBERGER
Special Cable to The New York Times

LONDON, Jan. 27—Unfortunate Yugoslavia, after experiencing a shattering military defeat and partitioning among the Germans, Italians, Hungarians and Bulgarians, followed by savage slaughter and waves of brutality, is now being ravaged by a widespread bitter civil war. In this thousands of guerrillas are participating, urged on by Axis agents, and the subjugated peasant population is experiencing untold misery.

The situation in many ways parallels the anarchy that reigned in the Ukraine between the start of the Soviet revolution and the culmination of Russia's civil wars with the establishment of Communist authority.

### Schisms on Several Bases

Stewing in this turbulent cauldron, continually warmed by Axis intrigue, are various elements of patriotism, national spirit, sectional differences, especially between the Serbs and Croats; political jealousies, religious antipathies, ideological cleavages and the basic ingredients of social revolution.

Unfortunately for the harmony of the United Nations' cause, the Yugoslav Government in London and its small army in the Middle East are inextricably mixed up in the repercussions of this sad confusion and the British and Soviet policies have been flatly at odds over this most difficult situation.

There is no sign as yet of any coordinated effort on the part of the exile Yugoslav Government, the Soviet Union and Great Britain to patch up this scrambled affair, which, indeed, it is probably quite impossible to do from the outside. In the meantime, from the Slovenian mountains to the forests of Macedonia intermittent waves of turmoil are sweeping over the unhappy land and the misery-stricken peasants are caught up like chaff in battles between various factions.

In Yugoslavia today there are ten distinct organized types of fighting men, in addition to the German, Italian, Hungarian and Bulgarian armies of occupation, which are believed to total more than twenty divisions. The Yugoslav forces are the Shumari, Ustachi, Domobranci, Village Guards, White Guards, the Chetniks of Kosta Pechanatz, the Chetniks of

Jan. 29, 1943

Enemy-occupied Yugoslavia, which is a scene not only of internal political battles but also of international complications.

General Draja Mikhailovitch, the Fascist Blackshirts of Ljuba Ljotitch, the puppet Serbia's army under Premier Milan Neditch and the People's Liberation Army, commonly known as the Partisans.

### Two Main Control Centers

The main centers of control are as follows:

First, capital of puppet Croatia, from which Poglavnik (Leader) Ante Pavelitch directs his Ustachi, the equivalent of Adolf Hitler's Schutzstaffel [Elite Guard] and the National Militia, which includes the Domobranci, the Croatian equivalent of the Hitler Youth, plus the Brownshirts.

Second, Belgrade, from which Marshal Neditch directs his small Serbian Army, used for policing purposes, and the Serbian Fascist Ljotitch runs a Blackshirt organization that assists the Germans to hunt down guerrilla patriots.

There also resides Kosta Pechanatz, who heads the Society of Chetniks, a sort of American Legion with Fascist leanings.

Made up of veterans of previous wartime Chetnik groups, it has nothing to do with General Mikhailovitch's Chetniks, so-called for the small bands or chetas in which they operate. Pechanatz, who went over to Marshal Neditch immediately after the collapse of Yugoslavia, also uses his Chetnik Society to hunt down guerrilla patriots.

Those are all the Slav factions that might be called unpatriotic, working against the United Nations' cause, and hence against their country's salvation. All other groups, it may be assumed, are sincerely patriotic but are bitterly divided on objectives and methods and are engaged in violent campaigns to exterminate each other.

The main centers of these patriotic groups are Bihac, in Northwestern Bosnia due south of Zagreb and theoretically a part of Poglavnik Pavelitch's Croatian domain, and an area in Southern Bosnia under the sway of General Mikhailovitch.

### Partisan Regime Set Up

In Bihac, a town on the Una River captured last year by the Partisans, an independent political regime has been established under the leadership of Ivan Ribar, former President of the Belgrade Skupshtina [Yugoslavia's National Assembly], or possibly his son.

That regime maintains constant liaison with the various Partisan units associated in the Peoples Liberation Army under the direction of four chief military leaders: Kosta Nagy, Milosh Duditch, a mysterious figure alleged to be a Russian named Tito, and Petko Diptchevitch.

The Bihac republic claims to control a free area of 30,000 square miles and to maintain constant radio communications with the outside world, especially with Moscow, by secret transmitters.

Further south at the bottom of Bosnia and in Sanjak is a large region where General Mikhailovitch has established what might be called a Chetnik state. He acts as a sort of regent for the exiled King Peter II, now a student at Cambridge University.

Also in the country are smaller bands, most of which appear to be lined up with the main Partisan or Chetnik organizations.

These include large numbers of Shumari [forest men] in Croatia, who seem to be supporting the Partisans, and the so-called White Guards in Slovenia, who owe allegiance to General Mikhailovitch, as well as the Partisans there. In Slovenia there is also an organization called the Village Guards, which represents the Clerical party and apparently is close to General Mikhailovitch but possibly not directly aligned with him.

### Chetnik Factions Clash

Bitter strife raged between the powerfully organized Mikhailovitch and Bihac groups. In recent months Bihac partisans have been far more active than Marshal Mikhailovitch, who has adopted a policy of quiet reorganization, awaiting the day when the second front may reach the Balkan states. Ruthless killings continue between these two factions, and the Axis busily incites one against the other in an effort to reduce the southern Slavs to the point where they can be conquered from the outside.

The British-Russian divergence comes over the Chetnik-Partisan dispute. The British so far have strongly supported General Mikhailovitch, who is War Minister in the Yugoslav Cabinet. It is now no secret that some British officers serve with him and that his radio is in continual touch with United Nations headquarters.

Moscow, on the other hand, equally strongly supports the Partisans, who it feels are more representative of popular Yugoslav opinion and a stronger, more active force in actually combating the Axis and helping win the war.

The Partisans frankly proclaim their sentimental attachment to Moscow. Many, although by no means all, of their leaders are Communist. Last April they secretly dispatched envoys to the Ukraine, where they met chiefs of the Ukrainian partisans guided by the Red Army.

It is this split that causes such a stream of utterly contradictory news and propaganda concerning Yugoslavia from Moscow and London. There does not appear to have been any progress yet toward altering this situation, although Alexander P. Bogomoloff, Soviet envoy to the London émigré governments, recently visited Moscow to discuss the problem. Moscow is convinced that it is backing the right horse. London, while perhaps not as convinced as it was a year ago that General Mikhailovitch is the right choice, is now standing by him because there is little else it can do, having for so long held him up as a symbol of Yugoslav resistance. The émigré Yugoslav Government is firmly anti-Partisan and pro-Mikhailovitch.

\*   \*   \*

January 30, 1943

## YUGOSLAV GUERRILLAS SEND PLEA FOR REVOLTS THROUGHOUT EUROPE

*Russian Said to Be Leader of Army That Set Up Regime Opposed to Mikhailovitch and to Emigre Officials in London*

### By C. L. SULZBERGER
#### Wireless to The New York Times

LONDON, Jan. 29—An independent "people's government" with its own Chamber of Deputies is now established in Bihac, Northern Bosnia, and its armies have liberated 30,000 square miles of territory from Axis domination, according to information made available here by sympathizers with the Yugoslav partisan movement.

A considerable part of the knowledge here regarding the Bihac government was obtained from Soviet broadcasts, repeating communiqués by the Free Yugoslavia station. The partisans' supporters say this station is in the area under Bihac control or in Montenegro. Members of the émigré government here, which opposes the partisans, say the Free Yugoslavia station is in Tiflis, Russia.

According to the partisans the Bihac government was established last month following the election of a Chamber, including all political factions and priests, professors and peasants. An executive committee was named under the presidency of Dr. Ivan Ribar, former president of the Yugoslav Chamber of Deputies. Mikhailovitch men here say the head of the committee is Dr. Ribar's son, who has Leftist sympathies.

Two vice presidents of the committee are reported to be Nurija Pozderats, a Moslem politician and former Senator from Bosnia, and Dr. Pavle Savitch, professor of Belgrade University.

## Third Partisan Government

This was the third partisan central government to be set up in Yugoslavia. The first, with its capital at Uzice, was expelled westward by opponents of the partisans more than a year ago. Another similar State existed for a time around Kocevje, Slovenia.

The first political act of the new government was the staging on Dec. 27, 28 and 29 of an anti-fascist youth congress, which was said to have included delegates from various Yugoslav regions and from the partisans. The congress published an appeal to the youth of Russia, Britain, the United States and occupied Europe.

This appeal, later broadcast by the Moscow radio, attacked Adolf Hitler, Benito Mussolini, the Croat Ustachi and General Draja Mikhailovitch's Chetniks with equal vigor. It claimed that within six months the partisans had slain 17,535 Germans, Italians, Ustachi and Chetniks, had taken 27,000 prisoners, had captured forty-five guns, sixty mortars and 531 machine guns and had destroyed nineteen tanks and six planes. It said the partisans had smashed Axis communication lines by constant sabotage.

The appeal called on European youth not to wait for a second European front but to arise to battle the Axis now.

"Freedom is not served on a gold platter," it said. "It is won with arms in hand. This is a lesson of the history of the liberation struggle of our peoples, a lesson of reality today.

"Young Poles and Czechs, we have one common enemy. Follow the example of the free youth of Russia.

"The hour has struck for the final reckoning with bloody fascism. The people will never forget any one who is guilty of inaction, cowardice or treachery in these days. Forward to the offensive! Our cause is just! Victory will be ours!"

## Russians Guide Regime

Dominating the Bihac government as it did the short-lived Uzice republic is the Yugoslav Army of Liberation or partisans. There is little doubt that this army is directed by Russians, because partisans who escaped from a German prison told the writer that the Liberation Army's Chief of Staff was a Russian and that partisan delegates met secretly with Soviet partisans in the Ukraine last April.

The Yugoslav Army of Liberation was said to be organized under a unified command into divisions, brigades, battalions and groups. The smallest detachments have 120 to 200 men. In each province the groups are commanded by a provincial general staff which is subject to the direction of the central command.

The units generally bear the name of a Yugoslav province, mountain, river or partisan hero. Among the heroes claimed by the partisans are Father Vladimir Zechevitch, a Serbian priest; Dragljlo Duditch, a peasant writer; his son Milosh, a Yugoslav regular army lieutenant; Peko Daptchevitch, a veteran of the Spanish civil war, who now heads the Montenegro partisans, and his Chief of Staff, Colonel Savo Orovitch of the Yugoslav Army, who was ousted before the war after political disputes.

According to a partisan veteran here the principal figures in the High Command of the Army of Liberation are Kosta Nagy, Daptchevitch, Lieutenant Duditch and a mysterious man called Tito. Tito, according to this partisan, is a Russian. Some partisans believe he is Vassily Lebedieff, who was counselor of the Soviet Legation in Belgrade when Yugoslavia was invaded.

Mikhailovitchists here say Mr. Lebedieff had a large sum in United States dollars—the writer has heard estimates of $13,000,000 and to $35,000,000—to finance guerrillas.

But Alexander P. Bogomoloff, Soviet Ambassador to the émigré governments in London, said Mr. Lebedieff was working in the Moscow Foreign Office and might come to London soon. Mr. Bogomoloff said he saw Mr. Lebedieff during his recent visit to Moscow. Whoever he is, the mysterious Tito is said to be the Chief of Staff of the Army of Liberation. The actual field commanders appear to be Kosta Nagy, Daptchevitch and Lieutenant Duditch, of whom Nagy probably is the most important because he is in charge of the most active area, Bosnia.

According to the partisan, who served under him, Nagy comes from a good Belgrade family and is a Serb, not a Hungarian as Mikhailovitchists allege. He said Kosta Nagy, which means Big Kosta in Hungarian, is a nom de guerre, that his first name is Peter, but his surname is a secret.

He described Nagy as a short stocky man of about 40 with black hair, hawk nose and long mustache. He does not smoke or drink, is very serious minded and an unusually strict disciplinarian.

By the end of August, 1941, when the escaped partisan began serving under Nagy the latter commanded the Sava division of partisans, which included three brigades totaling 6,000 men. A Soviet type of organization is indicated by the fact that the division had a political commissar, Boro Markovitch. Nagy later reorganized the division, splitting it into smaller units to facilitate guerrilla sorties.

## Wear Communist Emblem

Nagy's men were distinguished from others by their badge, a five-pointed star bearing the Communist hammer and sickle emblem. Their military equipment depends largely on what they capture from the enemy and factories for small arms. Large quantities of arms were hidden by the Yugoslav Army at the time of its capitulation.

When the Uzice republic was at its peak, the partisans were said to have had 190 tanks. These were captured from Italians in battles or in mountain traps and repaired by partisan mechanics in Uzice workshops. The partisans also captured 800,000 gallons of gasoline. When Uzice was evacuated the machinery was hidden or placed on trucks and taken westward.

### BOOK DESCRIBES PARTISANS
#### Yugoslav Guerrillas Said to Be Always on Offensive

Wireless to The New York Times

MOSCOW, Jan. 29—Details of the formation of the Yugoslav partisan army are given in a new book published by the

State Publishing House entitled "Yugoslavia in the Fire of Partisan Warfare," written by I. Klakhovitch, a young Yugoslav who participated in the Spanish civil war and now resides in Moscow.

Mr. Klakhovitch says the partisans always employ offensive tactics and that following their reorganization under a single command they were more successful and learned how to shift reinforcements, at one time marching 6,000 men nearly 200 miles.

He says the partisans are using pigeons for interfront communications.

The shock brigades, which are often mentioned in the Free Yugoslavia radio station communiqués, are said to have political commissars, of whom one is a young woman, Andzha Rankovitch. The writer stresses the broad character of the partisan movement, embracing representatives of all anti-fascists.

The book lists partisans' newspapers, the principal one of which has a circulation of 10,000 to 15,000.

\* \* \*

February 4, 1943

# BALKAN PUSH NEEDS YUGOSLAV ACCORD

*Any Allied Plan of Attack on Nazis Through Area Seen Hampered by Strife*

**PARTISAN ISSUE RAMPANT**

*Details of Mikhailovitch's Troubles Show Problems for London and Moscow*

By C. L. SULZBERGER
Wireless to The New York Times

LONDON, Feb. 3—Prime Minister Winston Churchill's conference with President Ismet Inonu of Turkey, combined with the constant German nervousness voiced in official Berlin propaganda about the possibilities of a United Nations attack in the Dodecanese Islands as preliminary to the potential opening of a second front in the Balkans, has focused public attention on the necessity of cleaning up the dreary Yugoslav situation as soon as possible.

If there is any thought in the Allied High Command about getting at Germany through the back door of the Vardar and Danube valleys, as was done in World War I, it is essential to seek urgently for an end to the civil war now going on between the patriot Chetniks and patriot partisans of Yugoslavia to insure the greatest support of the vigorous peasant population of Southeastern Europe.

At present, with Britain still strongly backing General Draja Mikhailovitch's Chetniks, Soviet Russia standing by the partisans and the United States not knowing much what is going on, the situation remains unfortunate and pregnant with disaster.

It would be small comfort to try to push up the narrow communications channels of the mountainous Balkan Peninsula with a large portion of the population hostile.

The partisan-Chetnik war commenced in 1941.

The Mikhailovitchists allege that the partisans' movement was launched by Victor K. Lebedieff, former Soviet Chargé d'Affaires in Belgrade, with a special fund in United States dollars, but this charge appears ill-founded, especially in view of the circumstantial denials transmitted by The New York Times correspondent at Moscow from that Russian official.

### Charges of Russian Activity

The Mikhailovitchists assert that the partisans began to organize after the collapse of Yugoslavia, but remained quiescent until the Russo-German pact was shattered by the Nazi invasion of the U. S. S. R. According to the Mikhailovitchists, during the partisans' organizational period, a certain Csarist Russian Colonel Makin, who had been a social revolutionary and was in Yugoslavia, got wind of a Nazi plan to arrest him and fled to the mountains where he joined the partisans, along with another mysterious Russian leader, whose existence certainly cannot be proved and who may be a product of the imagination of the Goebbels Ministry at Berlin.

After considerable territory had been liberated by coordinated Chetnik and partisan action, the first quarrel between the Chetniks and partisans developed in August, 1941. Pro-Chetniks say the fighting continued sporadically through that October, when General Mikhailovitch telegraphed the Yugoslav Government in London asking intervention with both the Russians and the British to obtain unity.

The dispute apparently arose over which group should establish authority in liberated communities. The partisans, according to pro-Chetniks, wished loyal Communists placed in control. They say General Mikhailovitch insisted no political considerations should be taken into account and that the authorities should be military men of assured patriotism.

When General Mikhailovitch received no indication of any change, he again requested the Yugoslav Government to arrange the broadcasting of simultaneous appeals for cooperation from Moscow and London In that message, which the writer has seen along with others, General Mikhailovitch said the situation was becoming extremely serious and that the partisans were beginning to "slaughter" on a wide scale and were seeking "to start a revolution in a glass of water." He charged that some of the best patriots and local leaders in Yugoslavia were being slain by the "Communists."

### Killings Laid to Partisans

Major clashes between the partisans and Chetniks began in Western Serbia around Uzice, Pozega and Ivanica, all in Uzice Department, according to Yugoslav officials here and the Mikhailovitchists.

They say the partisans killed many of the peasants and small bourgeoisie, enabling partisan delegates to take control of the district. This is their explanation of the origins of the Uzice Republic which has been mentioned in previous dispatches.

The partisans in the meantime complained that the Chetniks were cooperating with the Axis against them and slaughtering harmless Croatian peasants.

Whether either story is correct, the first period of fighting ended temporarily after the collapse of the Uzice Republic, which the partisans say was put down by a combined Chetnik-Axis force. General Mikhailovitch reported to London that he had arranged a temporary working agreement with the partisan Chief of Staff, one Tito. However, after an uneasy period, new troubles began, including attacks in reprisal.

General Mikhailovitch sent by radio long lists of men whom he said had been slain by the partisans, emphasizing their respectable status in the community. For example, one list of 171 names was sent here in September, 1942, with a statement that the majority of the alleged victims were peasants, as well as priests, servants, clerks, gendarmes and ex-officers.

This list referred entirely to Montenegro and represented, according to General Mikhailovitch, the partisans' effort to eliminate community leaders.

According to General Mikhailovitch, the partisans were trying to supersede the national revolution with a Communist revolution and the Yugoslav peasants could not understand the procedure. He reported that various groups had appealed to him to save them.

In November, 1941, the Yugoslav Government formally requested the Kremlin to intervene and begged Moscow to instruct the partisans to work with General Mikhailovitch against the Axis.

The Yugoslavs state that they again complained to the Russians in December, 1941, and that a brief armistice period ensued between the partisans and Chetniks, which delighted the London Government so much it sent wireless congratulations to General Mikhailovitch. Then, according to General Mikhailovitch, in March, 1942, the partisans broke the prevailing agreement and the fighting was resumed. The General accused the partisans of collaborating with the Axis.

In this connection it is noteworthy to report that this same charge of collaborating with the Axis is a principal complaint by the partisans against General Mikhailovitch. It is the opinion of some observers that both sides have been so steamed up that it is probable each has stretched the moral code for the sake of vengeance.

According to General Mikhailovitch the partisan movement in Serbia proper was completely liquidated in the early part of 1942. He reported that groups headed by Simo Miloshevitch escaped to Montenegro, where they began to work among the semifeudal tribal organizations of the hinterland. Finally, he said, the Vassolevitchi tribe under three local leaders, Djurashitch, Djukanovitch and Stanishitch, rose near Rijeka and soon all Montenegro was caught up in civil war.

General Mikhailovitch said that Italian garrisons in Montenegro, seeing the spread of an anti-communist movement, joined his Chetniks and peasant levies against the partisans, and the partisans complained to Moscow that he, Mikhailovitch, was collaborating with the Axis. General Mikhailovitch reported to London that some Slovenes in the Italian Army aided him in smuggling out arms.

The government and pro-Chetniks assert that, after the Montenegrin civil war, the partisans withdrew to Hercegovina and to North Dalmatia, Croatia and Slovenia. They say that, before quitting Montenegro, the partisans sent a resolution to Moscow signed by 180 persons accusing General Mikhailovitch of collaborating with the Axis and naming him a traitor. This was broadcast by the Moscow radio.

The Yugoslav Government sent the text of this resolution to General Mikhailovitch by wireless and received the reply:

"They must have to search about for people to sign such proclamations. I have no need for signatures, because the people are with me."

\* \* \*

**February 4, 1943**

## GREEK WOMEN'S HEROISM RECALLED AS UNDERGROUND PLEADS FOR AID

An appeal to women of the United Nations to intensify their war efforts, issued yesterday through the Greek Office of Information at 30 Rockefeller Plaza, disclosed that Greek women in the homeland and throughout the United States had seized the opportunity nearest at hand to make their force felt in the war.

The appeal was from the 10,000 women who are members of the Greek underground, risking their lives in organizing resistance and committing sabotage within Greece. The letter, smuggled out of Greece, presumably reached Cairo in the hands of a young patriot who dared the Mediterranean Sea in a small boat to join the Allies. It read:

"Thousands of our brothers and husbands have been victims of mass executions before our very eyes and have been made to dig their own graves. Tens of thousands of our men folk now rot in concentration camps.

"Now homeless, starving and unprotected, with babies in our arms, we drag our weary footsteps up the seemingly endless road of our Calvary. Our knees may bend, tears run from our eyes, our souls may be torn—but we do not submit. We may starve. We may have become human shadows, we may see our children gradually pining away—but we do not give in.

"Many of us have watered the tree of liberty with our life blood, and many of us are rotting in jail."

### Girl Shot Down Nazi Planes

Mrs. Dimitri Negroponte, who has charge of the Friends of Greece shop at 52 East Fifty-seventh Street, reported that accounts reaching this country of underground activity disclosed Hellenic women's bravery.

"We know now that whatever task falls to Grecian women, they perform it," said Mrs. Negroponte. "And we are assured that they have been of great aid to their men folk in putting up the heroic resistance that they have shown against the Axis.

"In Crete, during the battle of May, 1941, women took up primitive farm implements and plowed deep furrows into every field where enemy planes might have tried to land. And many German planes that did undertake to come down crashed in doing so."

Mrs. Negroponte recounted the story of Georgina Anyfantis. Only a girl of 20, she escaped alone to Crete after her family had been destroyed. Donning a uniform she took charge of a machine-gun post close to an airdrome. As German troop carriers approached, flying low, Georgina crouched, waiting. When the planes came within range, she fired, and the stream of lead she directed at them felled two planes before her eyes. She is now serving with the South African Women's Air Force.

### Mountain Women Help

Mountain women have their jobs to do, too, Mrs. Negroponte added.

"We have learned that during the recent dynamiting of the Gorgopotamos Bridge in Central Greece, a few women of the underground lured its guards away. In the meantime, guerrillas descended from their hiding places nearby and destroyed the bridge.

"When the Italian Venezia Division penetrated into the heart of the Pindus Mountains, they were surrounded by Greek mobile units. Officers of the mobile units say their success was due largely to the steady stream of supplies and ammunition carried to them by volunteers, many of whom were women."

Throughout the United States, women of Grecian ancestry are everywhere active in the war effort, Mrs. Negroponte said.

\* \* \*

February 14, 1943

# GERMANS COMBAT RUMANIAN SCHISM

*400,000 Casualties in Russia Swell Tide of Defeatism in Region Vital to Nazis*

## ANTONESCU IS COERCED

*Hitler Is Reported Using Rivals of Dictator to Enforce His Demand for New Aid*

By C. L. SULZBERGER
Wireless to The New York Times

LONDON, Feb. 13—Rumania, Adolf Hitler's most important puppet ally in Eastern Europe, has already suffered an estimated 400,000 casualties on the Russian front and the Germans are doing their utmost to combat the rising tide of defeatism and war weariness gradually filtering into the country.

These losses have temporarily, and in a large proportion permanently, put out of action almost 80 per cent of the maximum force ever believed to have been supplied by Rumania as cannon fodder for the Wehrmacht. It is believed that twenty-two divisions, including two of cavalry, were in Russia at the peak last year. A Rumanian infantry division, with its auxiliary services and artillery, numbers about 25,000 men on a war footing.

These losses, while severe, are far from crippling, but Rumania—already amputated by German dictates in 1940—is not particularly united or anxious to continue what appears increasingly to be a hopeless struggle, despite the traditional anti-Russian sentiments that have been cleverly drummed up by the Nazis and their tool dictator, Field Marshal Ion Antonescu.

### Worried About Transylvania

At present Marshal Antonescu is keeping twenty-two divisions, including two of cavalry, at home and is equipping four additional divisions with German aid. Four divisions are stationed on the Hungarian frontier. Herr Hitler is demanding new units to combat the Red Army, but the populace not only is fed up with the Russian adventure but ever worried about the defenses of the cockeyed Transylvanian border in the event that an Axis collapse is followed by anarchy.

Already Rumania's highest authorities, if not yet the people, are becoming aware of the gravity of their position. All the population that has moved into Bucharest since the start of the war is being ordered evacuated. The official excuse given is the fear of increasingly heavy air raids but there is some reason to believe that the officials are making room for new German staff quarters and that it is intended to use the Rumanian Capitol as a behind-the-lines seat of operations for the defense of the Ukraine in case the Russians manage to reach the Dnieper Line.

Rumania's rulers have suddenly begun to talk out of the other side of their mouths since the reversal of the tide of Axis military fortunes. Marshal Antonescu even last year pompously orated on Rumania's historic mission to defend Europe on the banks of the Volga. It is interesting to note that he permitted young King Michael to say in his New Year's message last month:

"The Rumanian people can await with confidence the fulfillment of destiny's decisions . . . in so far as they will not covet what belongs to others and they will be satisfied with their own."

### Insurgents Look to Soviet

Opponents of Antonescu, headed by the Transylvanian leader, Dr. Juliu Maniu, who apparently has managed to maintain not only his prestige but also a certain amount of contacts despite intermittent spells of house arrest, are busily working on the disillusioned feelings of the population. Messages from Dr. Maniu, smuggled out of the country, urge Rumanians abroad to "unite for defense of the cause of Rumania" and intimate a realistic desire for friendly relations with the Soviet Union after the war. In this connection it is believed that former Foreign Minister Grigore Gafencu, now residing in Berne, is privately favoring Dr. Maniu's efforts.

The stage as being set, perhaps, for some form of intervention by United Nations diplomacy, though it is still far too early for active expectations. It is curious to note the British effort to play down criticisms of Marshal Antonescu, who certainly is an archenemy of the Allied cause.

Marshal Antonescu was bitterly disappointed over his meeting with Herr Hitler last month despite the Axis soft soap since. The Germans are eager to get both more fighting men and more production from Rumania, especially of oil; all hopes of production from Russian fields to be conquered obviously have evaporated.

The Reichsfuehrer now has allowed Marshal Antonescu's enemy, Horia Sima, Iron Guard leader, to proceed to Rumania by way of Italy to threaten an Iron Guard plot if the dictator does not produce the goods. He also has invested Col. Gen. Alexander Loehr with full responsibility for maintenance of order in Rumania and has ordered Elite Guard leader Pohme to take over control of the Rumanian security services.

Thus Rumania is assuming the status of France, with Marshal Antonescu as Pétain and General Loehr as von Rundstedt. Herr Hitler is believed to have informed Marshal Antonescu that Rumania's "new mission" is no longer on the Volga, but is to produce oil and soldiers. The latter are to be used not only in Russia but also for defense of the Balkans in the event of a United Nations attack. This view is more or less confirmed by a recent broadcast from Rome by Aldo Valori, who said:

"Marshal Antonescu's visit calls attention to the undoubtedly flattering position Rumania has acquired in this war, in which she took up a decided stand and from a military viewpoint, has performed wonders. This is not an insignificant fact, especially now that the conflict on the Eastern front has assume such importance, while Rumania might be called on to fulfill a delicate and vital task in the near future should the enemy coalition really think of attacking Europe by way of the Balkans and hence the Danube.

"There can be no doubt that Marshal Antonescu discussed these matters, and it is equally certain that the new Rumania's task was enlarged."

\*   \*   \*

March 2, 1943

## BULGARIANS WARY OF FULL AXIS ROLE

*Decline of Enthusiasm Traced to Churchill-Inonu Talks and Recent Allied Gains*

**TURKISH PACT RECALLED**

*Rumor Also Links Officials to Appeasement Gestures to the United Nations*

Wireless to The New York Times

LONDON, March 1—The only Slav country on the side of the Axis—except such subject and sub-divided States as Slovakia and Croatia—is Bulgaria, which finds herself in the paradoxical position of being at war with Britain and the United States whom she cannot fight and at peace with Soviet Russia with whom Reichsfuehrer Hitler would like to see her at war.

Nevertheless, it is clear that Herr Hitler has not yet given up hope of dragging the Bulgars into the war, possibly against Turkey, and his Gestapo is busily doing its best to stir up persecutions among the Turkish minority in Kazanlik in the south. Since the Churchill-Inonu conference at Adana, however, and the United Nations gains, the Bulgarians are evincing a decreasing enthusiasm for entry into a more active war than their fights against guerrillas in the areas they have occupied in Greece and Yugoslavia.

Officials at Sofia appear now to be recalling the existence of the two-year-old Turko-Bulgarian non-aggression pact and stating that "Bulgaria is just as anxious as Turkey to see peace in the southeast preserved." There have been rumors of Bulgarian envoys secretly striving to arrange post-war terms with Britain and America.

The Germans in Bulgaria, as elsewhere in the Balkans, are preparing against a possible United Nations landing and a Nazi military mission, headed by Field Marshal General Fritz Erich von Mannstein, is reported to be inspecting the country and supervising fortifications, especially the Burgas and Varna regions.

### True Attitude Obscure

The true attitude of Bulgaria is difficult to ascertain. While numerous officers are apparently still ardently pro-German, many in the ranks, as well as the peasants and intellectuals, are pro-Russian, and there is a sizable Communist movement and probably a stronger and sympathetic left wing agrarian bloc.

Some politicians have been surprisingly outspoken against the government. Former Premier Nicolas Mouchanoff some weeks ago sharply protested against the dictatorship and the many arrests and he was threatened by Peter Gabrovski, Minister of the Interior.

Other politicians are sympathetic but quieter, excepting the "Zveno" and the Communist party. The old leader, Athanase Buroff, has spoken out against the government's pro-German policy. M. Fitcheff and other right wing agrarians are reticent and two of their members—Dimitri Kousheff and Nicolas Zahariev—have accepted office in the Bogdan Philoff government. Some members of the "Stamboulisky" wing are active in resistance and several of their leaders, including General Nicola Petkoff, are in custody.

### General Shot for Treason

The "Zveno," which is composed mostly of reserve officers, has been uncompromising in its opposition to the government and several of their more prominent leaders, such as Colonel Damian Veltcheff and Simon Georgieff, are under police supervision or in prison. One—General Zaimov—was shot for treason. Several members of the "Pladne," an agrarian group of political and refugees, are abroad, including Georgi Dimitroff, Kosta Todoroff and D. Matzankieff. They are ardently attacking King Boris and the government.

Several members of the Communist party have been arrested and shot and it would appear that the party is leading the active opposition to the Boris regime. Undoubtedly, it is in close touch with Moscow and is helped by efficient wireless apparatus and clever propaganda.

Russian propaganda is extremely well informed on events in Bulgaria and sticks mainly to concrete topics, giving slight prominence to ideology. It is always emphasized that Bulgaria is being starved to feed the Fascists, and King Boris and Premier Philoff are represented as having sold the pass to Germany so as to safeguard their personal position, class privileges and fortunes.

The Germans continue to use Bulgaria in other ways than economic and it is reported that three Nazi divisions are quartered there now for rest. One Bulgarian division is rumored to have gone to Yugoslavia to relieve Germans fighting the guerrillas for service in Russia and there are reports that a Bulgarian patrol was wiped out by Yugoslav guerrillas near Kraljevo, with the result that the Bulgarian commanders warned that fifty Yugoslavs would be shot for each Bulgarian lost.

There have been numerous arrests of officers and students accused of plotting with Russia and more active troubles in territories taken from Yugoslavia and Greece. One mixed German-Bulgarian division that recently entered Macedonia has begun a campaign of ruthless repression.

\*   \*   \*

March 4, 1943

# ALBANIA PREPARES FOR POST-WAR DAY

*No Single Group Is Regarded as Official, but Principle of Independence Is Accepted*

### 3 GROUPS OF GUERRILLAS

*They Are Making the Italians in the Country Uncomfortable— Jews Suffer Greatly*

By C. L. SULZBERGER
Wireless to The New York Times

LONDON, March 3—Tiny Albania, which has the briefest independent history of any European nation and which has been constantly embroiled with her neighbors—Greek, Italian and Yugoslav—since she was liberated from the Ottoman Empire, is once again seeking to prepare her post-war liberation. Since no émigré government of Albanians has been recognized by the United Nations, this is an exceedingly difficult task, but the principle of Albanian freedom has been recognized by the United States, Britain and the Soviet Union.

Refugee Albanians—some of whom are aiding the Allied cause by propaganda work in their exceedingly difficult language—are by no means all agreed on the objectives and personnel of the future government. Former King Zog, who dwells near London with his family and some retainers, has been unable to obtain any political recognition from the powers, but has not abandoned hope.

Albanians are worried that, instead of a chance to participate as a free State in an Eastern European federation, they may be partitioned among the Greeks and Serbs, but these fears have been considerably assuaged by recent great power declarations. Some Greeks are most anxious to obtain South Albania, which they call North Epirus and which contains a sizable number of Greeks in the Gjinoncastro and Korea areas, as well as strategically important mountain ranges and lateral communications. Many Yugoslavs desire to obtain the northern lake city of Scutari.

### "Greater" Albania Under Axis

At present Albanians under an Italian puppet government have extended the areas under their pseudo-control to include a large portion of Greek Epirus as well as parts of Yugoslavia. The government is headed by Ekrem Libohova, the new Premier, who used to be King Zog's Foreign Minister. Premier Libohova is known as a pro-Italian of a prominent feudal family of the south. He is a tricky, clever man—as this correspondent knows well from numerous poker games with him when he conducted Zog's diplomatic affairs—without much popular support.

Premier Libohova came into power after the Allied pledge of Albania's future freedom, which incited popular support to such a degree that the previous government of Merlika Kruja was forced out. This declaration, which was emphasized in broadcasts from Moscow and London, stimulated guerrilla resistance, which is fairly effective in that mountainous but disorganized, extremely poor and illiterate land.

There are three principal guerrilla-patriot groups in Albania. In the northeast there is the band of Colonel Muharrem Bajraktari; near Tirana, in the center, there is the band of Myslim Peza; in the south there is the band of Colonel Bilal Nivica.

There have been numerous clashes with Italian authorities in the districts of Tirana, Korca, Scutari and Valona, and last Autumn one Italian general was killed in one of these forays. Guerrillas largely control the Kurvelesh and Martanesh districts and have liberated Skrapar for a second time.

The active guerrilla movement is reported demoralizing many Italian soldiers—which are not the best that Premier Mussolini has mobilized—and there have been occasional mutinies. Some weeks ago an Italian battalion at Durazzo was disarmed and sent back to Italy under escort.

### Raid Made in Tirana

Probably the most formidable band is led by Peza. It has been raiding along the Tirana-Durazzo road and actually fought in the capital once, killing several Fascist officers and men. The Italians call Peza a Communist. Colonel Bajraktari, ex-commander in the British-trained gendarmerie, who is known to have been in contact with the Yugoslav patriot and War Minister, General Mikhail Mikhailovitch, has been raiding and sabotaging near the Montenegrin-Macedonian frontiers.

Another former gendarmerie officer is leading a smaller band in the neighborhood of Kruka, birthplace of the Albanian hero, Skanderbeg. That band, led by Colonel Nivica, frequently attacks the important oil wells of Kuchova and the pipeline running thence to Valona.

It is clear, despite the morale-building efforts of the Fascist veteran Giovanni Giro, who probably is the most important Italian official connected with Albania, that Signor Mussolini never has been able to popularize the occupation. The Italians have sought to raise an Albanian legion to fight in Russia, but not a single man volunteered.

Last Summer the Italians forced contributions of wool to make Winter uniforms for Russia, but Albanians burned the Durazzo warehouse before it could be used. Guerrilla chieftains have forbidden all Albanian drivers to transport Italian soldiers under penalty of death. The underground organization has attacked some Albanian Quislings. One patriot, sentenced to death for refusal to give up names of a secret oppositionist list, kicked the hangman in the stomach and shouted:

"Down with Italy! Down with the Quislings!"

Then he deliberately upset the chair on which he was standing and hanged himself.

As elsewhere under the Axis, the Jews are suffering cruelly, although there are only about 1,000 in Albania. Most of them are in a concentration camp at the Yugoslav town of Pristina, where, it is reported, hundreds have died of cold, hunger and disease.

\*   \*   \*

July 22, 1943

## SERB PARTISANS GET BRITISH AID; TITO PRAISED FOR HARRYING AXIS

*Statement Welcomes Group's Help to Allies—Coolness Toward Mikhailovitch Seen in Stand on Yugoslav Fighting*

### By C. L. SULZBERGER
By Wireless to The New York Times

CAIRO, Egypt, July 21—The British Government has established military liaison with the Yugoslav Partisan movement led by the chieftain who bears the nom de guerre Tito, it was officially revealed today at the General Allied Headquarters for the Middle East, which, while faithfully reporting the activities of Gen. Draja Mikhailovitch's Chetniks, also for the first time took official cognizance of the existence of his past enemies, the Partisans. It had been known for a long time that the British had liaison with General Mikhailovitch.

This certainly cannot be called an act tantamount to recognition of the Partisan movement and its civilian government, but it indicates that the British are trying to conciliate the rival forces of patriots. The Partisans, who by their policy of quick disbandment, disappearance and reappearance survived German efforts to eliminate them during the drive that ousted them from their Croatian and Bosnian strongholds around Bihac, have reappeared along the frontier between Montenegro and the Sanjak, just west of General Mikhailovitch's main headquarters.

"In Eastern and Central Bosnia the Partisan army under the leadership of Tito, the Partisan commander, has taken the offensive and captured a number of important towns, including Kladanj and Viasenica, from their Axis garrisons," it was announced.

### Allied Cause Aided

According to the statement, "this is welcomed here as proof that the German claim to have wiped out the main body of the Partisan army is false. It is known that the three Partisan divisions, which were engaged against more than double their number in Montenegro, have now largely escaped to carry on their unceasing war against Axis communications. At a time when the Axis must switch troops to Italy, this military success is considered to be of particular value to the Allied cause."

This important headquarters announcement then continued with a discussion of the patriot forces of General Mikhailovitch, which have been consistently at odds with the Partisans since late in 1941.

"More good news," it said, "is that the forces united under the leadership of General Mikhailovitch in Serbia have now denounced the Quisling 'Chetniks' who for long claimed to form part of the Mikhailovitch movement and under this cover accepted military help from the Axis in order to fight against the Partisans. General Mikhailovitch's forces are now playing a gallant and honorable part in the joint fight against the occupiers.

"As in other parts of Europe, Yugoslav resistance is closely linked with the Allied offensive and invasion plans. British military liaison with the forces of General Mikhailovitch and with the Partisans insures that the guerrilla activity is not carried out on a haphazard hit-and-miss basis, but systematically so as to achieve the greatest effect at a given place and moment.

"Some indication of the success of Yugoslav resistance is shown by the well-substantiated claim that the Partisans in Croatia have attacked and destroyed about 250 Axis trains passing over Croat railways since the spring of 1942."

To the best of this writer's knowledge this represents the first British statement published on the guerrilla operations in Yugoslavia. It further represents the first official British admission that direct liaison has been established by the British with the Partisans. It has been common knowledge ever since the Mikhailovitch resistance movement began that the British have had liaison with his forces. However, although for some time the British have had means of contact with the Partisans, this is the first time they have admitted it publicly.

Furthermore, this is the first official British recognition that Tito is the commander of the Partisan troops. Actually, Tito is chief of staff of the People's Liberation Army, which serves under a civilian Partisan government headed by Ivan Ribar, erstwhile president of the Yugoslav Skupshtina in Belgrade.

Furthermore, this is the first news from any source that General Mikhailovitch has "denounced the Quisling Chetniks." That statement frankly does not make much sense to this writer.

The term "Chetnik" means a member of a band and is derived from an old Turkish word, "chete," or band. It is an old Balkan word and there were Chetniks in the first Balkan liberation wars against the Turks. After the last war a Society of Old Chetniks was formed in Yugoslavia that had semi-political, semi-veteran connotations, somewhat like the American Legion.

The president of this society when the Yugoslav war broke out was Kosta Pechanac, who consistently since the armistice has passively aided the Axis and General Neditch's Quisling government. General Mikhailovitch never worked with this group, but always against it, sometimes even fighting it, so he certainly could not have denounced it.

### Denunciation Is Obscure

General Mikhailovitch's own movement received the name Chetnik in the world's press because it was a guerrilla group organized in bands. It is still popularly known as the Chetniks, so just who was denounced and by whom it is difficult to understand. Some renegade followers of General Mikhailovitch, led by some of his senior officers, deserted many months ago and were then denounced by him and by King Peter in London, but that is an old story.

As this correspondent has written many times, there has been evidence from time to time that both the Partisans [Tito's] and Chetniks [Mikhailovitch's]—there are still other patriot groups in Yugoslavia—have been so embittered against each other that they have accepted Axis aid in an effort to exterminate each other. There is reason to believe that this tendency has ceased.

Until about last March the British consistently backed General Mikhailovitch and the Yugoslav Government in exile and the Russians consistently backed the Tito Partisans. There have been efforts to straighten out this situation, but their success has been limited.

The wording of today's statement certainly indicates confirmation of a belief by many persons who have been following the British propaganda broadcasts to the Yugoslavs that Britain has considerably cooled off in her affections for General Mikhailovitch and is at least equally backing the Partisans now. This is bound to irritate many Serbs, since they provide the greatest backing for General Mikhailovitch's movement, but it will please many others. The British apparently are trying to be just and fair. At any rate, it is certain that the Soviet Union will be pleased, because Moscow has been adamantly pro-Partisan and anti-Chetnik since early in 1942.

\* \* \*

August 1, 1943

## CROATIAN 'KING' QUITS; NEVER VISITED REALM

By Wireless to The New York Times

ISTANBUL, Turkey, July 31—The Duke of Aosta, designated by Mussolini as King Tomislav of the Fascist State of Croatia, has resigned on orders from King Victor Emmanuel of Italy. The Croatian puppet Premier, Ante Pavelitch, has accepted the resignation, according to reports reaching usually well informed Balkan sources.

Members of the official Italian Fascist delegation to Zagreb have demanded and obtained the right of asylum in Croatia, it is reported, and that State will soon be proclaimed a "republic" under German protectorate, similar to Slovakia.

The Duke of Aosta is reliably reported not to have wanted the Croatian throne, and he never visited the State from the time of its founding as a result of a Ustashi revolt in Yugoslavia in April, 1941. Formerly Duke of Spoletto, he succeeded his late brother as Duke of Aosta.

\* \* \*

August 1, 1943

## NEW YUGOSLAV PREMIER IN EXILE ANNOUNCES HIS KING'S BETROTHAL TO PRINCESS OF GREECE

By Cable to The New York Times

LONDON, July 31—Formal announcement of the engagement of King Peter of Yugoslavia and Princess Alexandra of Greece was made here today by Milos Trifunovitch, the Yugoslavia Premier.

Actually the couple became engaged fully a year ago, but official sanction was withheld as a matter of policy. Even now the date of their marriage cannot be fixed for the same reason. Princess Aspasia, mother of the bride-to-be, explained:

"We want to hear good news of the war before anything else. Princess Alexandra feels this is not a time for rejoicing."

Princess Alexandra is 22 years old and has dark hair and a vivacious manner. Her time in exile in London is spent working mornings at St. James's Palace for the relief of prisoners of war and lending a hand afternoons at a canteen for Allied nurses, officers and men run by Mrs. Anthony J. Drexel Biddle, wife of the United States Ambassador to the exiled Governments.

Princess Alexandra is a niece of King George of the Hellenes, a daughter of the late King Alexander of Greece and a great-great-granddaughter of Queen Victoria.

Her engagement ring is a family heirloom in King Peter's possession. It has a blue diamond set in white diamonds.

\* \* \*

**August 2, 1943**

# BIG RUMANIAN OIL FIELD BOMBED BY 175 U.S. PLANES IN LONG FLIGHT; BADOGLIO PACIFIES NORTH ITALY

### PLOESTI SMASHED

*300 Tons Rain on Major Gasoline Source of Reich Air Force*

### RAID MADE AT LOW LEVEL

*Delayed-Action Bombs Enable 2,000 Fliers to Get Away, Leaving Great Fires*

By A. C. SEDGWICK
By Cable to The New York Times

CAIRO, Egypt, Aug. 1—A daylight air attack that "may materially affect the course of the war" smashed the oil refineries and dependent installations at Ploesti, Rumania, where fully one-third of the Axis' petroleum supplies for use in aircraft, tanks, transport vehicles, submarines and surface ships is believed to originate.

[The area produces 90 per cent of the German Air Force's gasoline, according to The United Press. The distance flown by its attackers was believed to have set a record for serial warfare.]

The raiders, numbering more than 175, were all Liberators of the Ninth United States Air Force. The 2,000 men in their crews had been trained especially for this all-important mission and the machines were equipped with special low-altitude bomb-sights.

### 300 Tons of Bombs Dropped

The planes were over their target at about 3 P. M. today. They remained not more than a minute and then were off, having dropped their great load of bombs with what, judging by first reports, seemed to have been highly satisfactory results. The pilots reported that, according to every indication, many fires and explosions had been caused. In all, some 300 tons of high-explosive bombs, mostly of the delayed-action type, were dropped. Clusters of incendiaries by the hundreds were also dropped, all from altitudes of less than 500 feet.

Brig. Gen. U. G. Ent led the formations. His plane was among the first to return. All the aircraft had been expected about an hour earlier and there had been a period of the greatest tension. Lieut. Gen. Lewis H. Brereton, American Commander in the Middle East, was among the anxious crowd. He was the first to welcome General Ent and to hear reports from a number of officers.

Col. Keith Cropton said, "We got them completely by surprise." Capt. Harold A. Wickland, who also took part in the recent Rome raid, said: "I saw a lot of smoke and we did some damage, but it all happened so quickly I don't know what it was we hit." Many others gave testimony that tended to show the general impression that widespread damage had been done.

### Rumanians Seem Friendly

Particularly interesting at this time was the testimony of several of the air crews. They said that the Rumanian peasantry had shown the greatest friendliness. Rumanian girls were said to have waved "a great welcome." A Rumanian soldier, gun on shoulder, was described as completely unconcerned.

It was said at Ninth Air Force headquarters that months of planning and preparation had gone into this attack on Ploesti. Not only military specialists but authorities on oil refining were consulted.

It was explained that, for several reasons, no large-scale bombing of the Ploesti refineries had been attempted before. The nature of the target makes it particularly invulnerable to attack by small formations.

There were too few long-range heavy bombers based within striking distance of Ploesti. The distance to the target from any Allied airdromes rendered it impossible to attack with large forces of medium bombers.

As soon as it appeared feasible to the Allied commanders to destroy Ploesti, a plan for doing so was formulated and its execution fell to General Brereton, the first commander of heavy bombers in the United States Army Air Forces to see action in this war. General Brereton supervised all phases of training and practice for the raid.

Repeated high-level attacks on Ploesti would undoubtedly have accomplished its destruction, but such a process would have meant heavy losses to the attacking force. It would also have enabled the enemy to protect his installations.

### Extremely Vital Target

The city of Ploesti, with its adjoining oil fields, refineries and transportation facilities, is generally conceded to be one of the most vital targets in Europe. Perhaps as much as half the entire German war machine would be halted if it were obliterated.

In 1941 the Russians realized its importance but were unable, in two raids, to do more than a modicum of damage. In June, 1942, a small force of Ninth Air Force Liberators attacked but had little success, largely because of foul weather.

Ploesti and its vicinity have thirteen refineries, seven of which are said to produce almost 90 per cent of all Rumania's oil. The rest are all small and some are obsolescent. The Ploesti refineries can produce annually approximately 11,500,000 tons, but, since the German occupation, the flow of crude oil from the ground has dropped to a point at which it can supply scarcely more than half the capacity of the refineries.

Nevertheless, it is estimated that the Ploesti area still supplies at least 35 per cent of Germany's petroleum demands, including, besides aviation fuel, ordinary gasoline for motor transport and lubrication and Diesel oils. Including its refineries and pump stations, which encircle the city, the Ploesti area approximates nineteen square miles. Most of it is an enormous rail ganglion.

### Greatest Low-Level Raid

CAIRO, Aug. 1 (AP)—Today's raid on the Ploesti oilfields was the "biggest low-level mass raid in aviation history," General Brereton announced tonight, praising the gallantry of the American airmen who participated.

Returning fliers said that they had concentrated on the seven largest refineries. Storage tanks, distilleries and cracking plants were bombed. Other installations were wrecked by machine-gun fire.

The raiders met heavy ground and air opposition. While there were no immediate figures on the number of enemy planes downed, it is safe to say that dozens were destroyed. Returning crews said that combats had been joined well before the target was reached and for some distance on the homeward run.

\* \* \*

August 9, 1943

## ATHENS OF TODAY IS SHOWN IN FILM

*Movie of City's Axis Rule, Its Starvation and Deaths Taken Out to Cairo*

### CHILDREN HUNT MORSELS

*Photographer Secretly Caught Nazi and Italian Officers and Crippled Greek Youth*

By A. C. SEDGWICK
By Cable to The New York Times

CAIRO, Egypt, Aug. 8—A motion picture that might be entitled "Athens Under the Axis" has been shown privately to a small audience here, including members of the Greek Government and may, it was said today, be widely shown later.

The film was taken by an amateur photographer who was obviously in minute to minute danger of being caught. German and Italian officers strut past and men in plain clothes, whose appearance seems to mark them for Axis secret agents, pause a moment, apparently in suspicion, and then go on.

The scenes are ill-assorted and there is no artistry, yet the film is an historical document of the Axis occupation of the Greek capital.

### Reduction of Greek Life

It is a pictorial indictment of the Nazi, Fascist and Quislingist rule of Greece. It is ocular proof of devastation and the reduction of humanity to a subhuman state.

The lesson is that unless the people of Athens who are actors unaware before the camera are not relieved soon, they will surely perish. Those who saw the film here know this.

The cameraman simply filmed what he could. He took the everyday life of Athens.

There is almost no traffic except military cars. Motor vehicles are shown that do not run, having been stripped of their parts and all tires. Horses, mules and donkeys were killed long ago for food. Occasionally a street car with people riding even on the roof creeps, along a familiar boulevard.

There are shops. The plate-glass windows of some are broken. There is nothing in those shops. One serves as a soup kitchen and there is a seemingly endless queue extending from its door.

### The Near-Dead and the Dead

Women and children with cups in their hands turn expressionless faces toward the camera, attempt to smile and shuffle a step farther along.

Here is a flash of a street in a residential quarter. Refuse—it is impossible to say what—is piled along the edge of the street and little creatures, who resemble dwarfs more than children, together with emaciated dogs, probe and search in it. One child finds something that looks like a bit of orange peel and puts it in his mouth while others beg for a morsel.

Here is a shot of one of the smaller hospitals—the large city hospitals are used exclusively for the Germans and Italians—and from its door several dead are carried on stretchers.

Heaps of dead elsewhere are pictured, to their number the bodies from the hospital will be added for collective burial as soon as graves can be dug in the hard soil.

Here is a flash showing the end of a procession of wounded men. They are young Greek soldiers who fought in Albania and lost their legs by frostbite. They are still young men but they look very old. Some crawl on the ground, others hobble along on wooden stumps and sticks.

There is a shot of the Acropolis with the swastica flying over it.

\* \* \*

August 29, 1943

# SOFIA RULER REPORTED SHOT ON HIS RETURN TO ABDICATE

*Boris Said to Have Planned to Quit to Avoid Giving More Help to Hitler—Six-Year-Old Son Takes Throne*

By DANIEL T. BRIGHAM

By Telephone to The New York Times

BERNE, Switzerland, Aug. 28—King Boris of Bulgaria died shortly after 4 o'clock this afternoon in Sofia after four days of suffering following a reported shooting at a small railway station just outside of the capital last Tuesday night.

He was returning to Sofia en route to Plovdiv from a visit to Adolf Hitler's field headquarters. According to Hungarian sources he was shot in the abdomen by one of the police inspectors charged with his protection.

His wife, Queen Ioanna, was with him when he died. His 6-year-old son, Simeon, Prince of Tirnovo, ascended to the throne as Simeon II.

News of the King's death was broadcast in two proclamations read by Premier Bogdan Philoff over the national radio at 7 o'clock tonight. At the end of the 4 o'clock broadcast it had been announced that all Bulgarian radio stations would close for three hours.

The Premier's proclamation read: "His Majesty, King and Czar Boris III, the uniter of Bulgaria, surrounded by his family, died at 4:22 this afternoon after a brief but grave illness. The sorrow of the nation and the Bulgarian people is immeasurable. We now all have the sacred duty of carrying out his last wishes and continuing united on the path he traced out for us."

Following this proclamation a second one signed by members of the government was read to the nation. It said:

"Bulgarians: This twenty-eighth day of August, 1943, His Royal Highness Crown Prince Simeon of Tirnovo, beloved child and hope of Bulgaria, ascended to the throne under the name of Simeon II in accordance with Article 34 of the Constitution. Under the terms of Article 151 of the same Constitution the Council of Ministers will assume the direction of the country until such time as the question of the regency will have been settled.

"We call upon all Bulgarians to tighten their ranks behind the King in the conviction of a happy future for Bulgaria and united to continue on the path already entered as we confide ourselves to God. Long live the King! Long live Bulgaria!"

United in sorrow but divided in support of the government, the country received this news with stupor, but scarcely two hours later, before the cutting of telephonic communications with Sofia, reports from the capital indicated Bulgaria would not long remain on the chosen path if it were in its power to change.

According to reliable Balkan sources, if King Boris had survived he had until midnight tonight to answer Hitler on three main demands, the acceptance of any one of which would spell the end of Bulgaria as an "independent" Axis ally. The demands King Boris brought back, according to these reports, were:

1. The immediate and total military and economic mobilization of Bulgaria for the furtherance of the war.

2. The creation of a second line along the Turkish frontier that would be manned by German forces and "technicians."

3. The granting of "full powers" to German political police in Bulgaria to repress further manifestations and terroristic acts.

### Abdication Was Expected

Diplomatic quarters here believe that if he had survived, the King would have abdicated rather than accept any of these demands. The question of abdication was understood to have been one of the main topics during the Cabinet meeting late Thursday night.

Today Premier Philoff was "unable" to tell the German Minister what turn events might take when the envoy called to present his condolences to the government.

That the Premier may be able to give any answer appeared increasingly unlikely in view of reports of a coalition of the Pan-Slav pro-Communist party, which is ostensibly the author of all recent terrorist outbreaks, with the Democratic party of Nicolas Mouchanoff, leader of the "tolerated" opposition, who was present at yesterday morning's talks.

This coalition is reported tonight to have sent an "ultimatum" to the Queen demanding her support for the creation of a "nonpartisan Bulgarian nationalist" regency commission of three to "lead the country to a more constructive path."

\* \* \*

August 29, 1943

# BORIS WAS PUPPET OF HITLER'S ORDER

*But Pro-Russian Sentiment in Country Barred His Sending Troops Against Soviet*

### LONG ASSASSINS' TARGET

*Three Attempts Made on His Life in 1921–29—Sofia Kept Under Martial Law*

King Boris III assumed the throne of Bulgaria as a result of his father's abdication after the defeat of the Central Powers in the First World War, and it was his ambition to restore his country to the position and the territory it had occupied before the German alliance.

Signing the Axis pact in 1941 and throwing open Bulgaria to the German troops that crushed the resistance of Greece and Yugoslavia, he was rewarded with Greek lands in Macedonia and Western Thrace and with permission to control the Skoplje region in the Vardar Valley of Yugoslavia.

Adolf Hitler, in March, 1941, congratulated him on his decision and expressed his "deepest wishes for the happy future of Bulgaria."

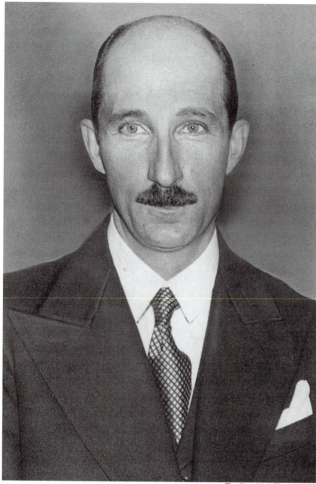

King Boris of Bulgaria

All this King Boris gained without supplying the Axis with a single fighting man—the military police force in the occupied territories excluded—but the future proved less happy than Hitler had hoped.

### Pressed for Fighting Men

Germany pressed constantly for a Bulgarian contingent on the Russian front, such as the satellite Hungarians and Rumanians had been forced to furnish.

Bulgaria, faced with an apparent eventual repetition of the events of 1918, rioted under King Boris' government. Martial law was declared in Sofia on May Day, 1943, when anti-Axis, pro-Russian demonstrations reached an unprecedented height, and it was reported that the King was forced to flee the city temporarily.

Sometimes called "the most cunning diplomat in Europe," King Boris was born with a foot in both camps of the present war. A member of the Saxe-Coburg family, he was, on his mother's side, a descendant of Louis Philippe of France. His wife was a daughter of King Victor Emmanuel of Italy, giving him a link with fascism. His people, however, were generally Slavic in their sympathies and descent. King Boris signed a pact of "eternal" friendship with Yugoslavia under

King Alexander and even after joining the Axis maintained some diplomatic relations with Russia.

### Had No Love for His Office

Left to his own devices, it was said, he would rather have been a zoologist, a botanist or a locomotive driver than have attempted to resolve the contradictions of his ancestry and office.

He said once that if his people demanded it he would abdicate and find himself a position as a professor in some far-away college. America seemed to be his aim, and in 1922, after the overthrow and assassination of Premier Stambulisky, he said:

"While I do not expect to lose my throne as a result of revolution, it would not frighten me if I did, for I would go right to America and get a job. I know lots of trades, including those of a locomotive engineer and racing automobile driver and, if mechanics fail, there is no reason why I should not get a place as a university professor. There ought to be work somewhere in America for an ex-King."

When Boris became King, on Oct. 3, 1918, he was 24 years old. Bulgaria had given up the struggle; the country was in a chaotic state. The politics that his father had followed ended in national disaster, and there were plenty who demanded a republic. By his autocratic methods Ferdinand had offended many of his subjects; rarely had a King ascended to a throne under such painful and difficult circumstances.

### Lost Much Territory

Under the Treaty of Neuilly, Bulgaria was disarmed, condemned to a heavy indemnity, and lost the southern Dobrudja to Rumania, Carlbrod and Strumica to Yugoslavia, part of Macedonia to Greece and her Aegean coastline to the Allies and associate powers, who assigned it to Greece at the Conference at St. Remo in April, 1920.

The Government now became a semi-dictatorship, under Alexander Stambulisky, peasant leader, but it was known as an Agrarian Government. It lasted from 1920 to 1923 and ended in a revolt. Stambulisky was murdered in the night of June 8, and the Tsankoff Government came into power. But from 1923 to 1925 Bulgaria was on the verge of civil war.

The tense situation culminated on April 14, 1925, when an attempt was made on the life of King Boris. Another attempt to assassinate King Boris was made in 1921, when he was watching a parade at Sofia. In 1929 two bombs were exploded under the King's private railway car, but little damage was caused.

Boris III, whose full name was Boris Clement Robert Marie Pius Louis Stanislas Xavier, was born at Sofia on Jan. 30, 1894. His mother was Czar Ferdinand's first wife, Marie Louise of Bourbon, who was the eldest daughter of Robert, Duke of Parma.

He was educated in the Military Academy at Sofia and was a major in the first Balkan War in 1912. He again saw service in the second Balkan War (1913), and during the World War he was on the staff of his father.

When he became King he was a general and commander of the Fourth Infantry, Fourth Cavalry and Third Artillery Regiments.

He was an excellent linguist and spoke eight languages fluently. The young King was fond of going for long rambles in the countryside, generally unaccompanied. He collected rare flowers and had a splendid assortment in his palace at Vrania.

Many stories were told of King Boris in connection with his bent for mechanics. He once narrowly escaped being tipped by American tourists, whose automobile he had repaired after it had broken down on a lonely mountain road in Bulgaria.

### Monarch Far From Wealthy

King Boris was far from wealthy. Indeed, he was often described as the poorest monarch in Europe, unlike his father, who possessed a huge fortune. In 1928 Boris received a 50 per cent increase in his allowance, bringing his income to 6,000,000 leva, or about $43,000 a year.

King Boris remained a bachelor until he was 36 years old. Rumors of marriage were almost daily, with princesses and grand duchesses from all countries mentioned as his future queen. But he met Princess Giovanna, and from the start it was a real love match.

Boris was born in the Roman Catholic faith, but for political reasons he became Orthodox and had been of that faith since Feb. 14, 1896, when he was 2 years old. The marriage with a Catholic princess presented many difficulties, but papal dispensation was finally obtained and the couple were married in the ancient church at Assisi on Oct. 25, 1930, with much pomp. Queen Ioanna, as she was called in Bulgaria, was Giovanna, Princess of Savoy, who was born in Rome on Nov. 13, 1907. A daughter, Princess Marie Louise, was born to them at Sofia on Jan. 13, 1933, and a son, Crown Prince Simeon of Tirnovo, was born June 16, 1937.

In May, 1934, Bulgaria turned Fascist by a coup d'état. King Boris approved of the new régime.

### Political Activity Stopped

The new government of Khimon Gheorghieff, based upon the Zveno, an association of former officers and Ministers, fixed its program: dissolution of the political parties, prohibition of all political activity, suppression of the Macedonian influence and an entente with Yugoslavia. The Gheorghieff Cabinet resumed diplomatic relations with Russia and dissolved and prosecuted the IMRO, the Macedonian terroristic-revolutionary organization.

For eight months the King was virtually the prisoner of the government. Gheorghieff and the officers behind him prepared to deprive the King of all influence and convert him into an ornamental appendage of the Fascist regime.

Colonel Damian Veltcheff, the leader of the group, organized the officers' association and took the lead in demanding that the King be shorn of his power. They asked particularly that Boris should no longer be in a position to appoint and dismiss Ministers. The King refused to surrender his prerogatives and with military circles supporting him, got rid of the Gheorghieff Cabinet in June, 1935.

King Boris then appointed General Petko Zlateff as Premier. This was a personal government of the King. The new Premier arrested Colonel Veltcheff and rid the administration and the army from all adherents of the former government.

### Andrew Techoff Appointed

The King, taking advantage of the split among the officers, dismissed General Zlateff and appointed Andrew Tocheff, a former diplomat, who promised to aid the King. The Premier and the Foreign Minister, Georgi Kiosseivanoff, were friends of the King.

Later, in October, 1935, the new government arrested most of the members of the Zveno group, including Colonel Veltcheff, who tried to cross the Bulgarian-Yugoslav border.

The Tocheff Cabinet resigned on Nov, 21, 1935, and the King appointed Georgi Kiosseivanoff Premier. The Kiosseivanoff government was completely under the King's influence, and Boris found time to go abroad and get in touch with the leaders of European politics. His trips to Belgrade, Paris, London and Berlin were of capital political importance. The negotiations between his country and Yugoslavia for a pact of non-aggression and friendship were carried out by him personally.

In September, 1938, he visited Hitler and Goering, after a visit made in London. In October of the same year, the Macedonians, by killing General Peyeff, the Chief of the General Staff, tried a coup d'état, but were prevented and thousands were arrested.

After the outbreak of war, King Boris tried to keep his country out of war and to realize Bulgaria's territorial claims by peaceful means.

On Feb. 15, 1940, the Kiosseivanoff Cabinet resigned. The King then appointed Professor Bogdan Philoff Premier and Ivan Popoff Foreign Minister.

The pro-Axis policy of Bulgaria won back Northern Dobrudja from Rumania in September, 1940.

### Gave Aid to Germany

That October King Boris, in a speech delivered in Parliament underscored Bulgaria's friendship with Germany and Italy and in November, during an interview with Hitler in Berlin, he granted Germany the right of passage of troops through Bulgaria.

King Boris had to pay for Hitler's support in getting back some parts of former Bulgaria from the Rumanians, Yugoslavs and Greeks, for he had to join the satellites in declaring war on the United States on Dec. 13, 1941. Although Boris introduced all the Nazi measures against democrats and Jews, he refused to declare war against Russia.

Prince Cyril, the younger brother of King Boris, and one of his sisters, the Princess Eudoxia, are living in Bulgaria. Another sister of the late King, the Princess Nadejda, was married to Duke Albert Eugene of Wuerttemberg. King

Boris' father, the dethroned King Ferdinand, is living at his castle in Slovakia.

\* \* \*

September 5, 1943

# CROAT TROOPS JOIN ARMY OF PATRIOTS

*London Hears Puppet Forces Go Over to Mikhailovitch as Yugoslavs Await Allies*

**SLOVAK SOLDIERS MUTINY**

*15,000 Reported Seized After Battle With Nazis Over Transfer to Germany*

LONDON, Sept. 4 (U.P.)—Hundreds of Croat soldiers, including an entire artillery regiment, have deserted the Axis puppet regime and joined the guerrilla forces of Gen. Draja Mikhailovitch, information reaching the emigré Yugoslav Government said tonight.

The reports said Axis Balkan leaders were anticipating that the Allies, following up the Italian invasion, would drive into southeastern Europe.

General Mikhailovitch, the Yugoslav War Minister who heads the Balkan patriot armies, was reported watching the situation in southeastern Europe, ready to unleash his fierce guerrillas in a major campaign the moment he received the word from the Allied command.

Reports reaching the Greek and Yugoslav Governments said news of the invasion of Italy had been received with great enthusiasm in the Balkans, and that the patriot forces believed that they, too, would soon be able to strike a blow for liberty against the Axis.

### Croat Resistance Spreads

A Yugoslav spokesman said he believed the Allied invasion was causing the forces of Croat puppet Premier Ante Pavelitch to desert. He said the Croat artillery regiment joined General Mikhailovitch after its leaders had made contact with the Thirteenth Guerrilla Division at Varazdin, where the Croat barracks had been under guerrilla fire for three days.

Other small Croat units were reported switching over to the side of General Mikhailovitch in other parts of Croatia.

The reports reaching here said heavy fighting had been in progress between General Mikhailovitch's men and those of Pavelitch for three weeks. Heavy fighting also was reported along the Montenegrin-Albanian frontier between guerrillas on one side and German Elite Guard troops and Italians on the other.

The Berlin radio reported that units of the Rumanian and German naval fleets were strengthening the Rumanian and Bulgarian coastal defenses against possible Soviet operations in the Black Sea.

A dispatch from Cairo said there was growing alarm among the Germans in Athens. In the Larissa area of Greece the Germans were reported threatening the Greeks with machine guns to make them perform forced labor.

### Slovak Mutiny Put Down

LONDON, Sept. 4 (Reuter)—Fifteen thousand Slovak troops have revolted against their Commander in Chief. The revolt broke out in a garrison at Trnava in central Slovakia this week, according to a first-round account that reached London today.

The men refused to carry out an order by Gen. Ferdinand Catlos, Quisling Minister and Commander in Chief of the Slovak Army, to put on German uniforms and join Elite Guard anti-aircraft units in the Reich.

General Catlos then ordered troops from a neighboring garrison and an Elite Guard detachment to quell the revolt. A sharp engagement occurred and there were casualties on both sides until late at night. The resisting troops were captured. Not a word has been heard of these troops since they were taken away to Germany.

This is the latest symptom of Slovak opposition to Adolf Hitler that has flared up recently. The Slovaks are especially incensed against fighting the Russians. A complete unit of Slovak troops surrendered to the Red Army and five Slovak pilots, ordered to fly their bombers to the Russian front, were reported from abroad to have flown instead to Turkey, explaining when they landed that they did not want to fight against the Russians.

### Link With Balkans Awaited

The view that the capture of southern Italy will enable the Allied armies and their mighty fleet to establish a large-scale direct contact with Yugoslav fighters was expressed by the Yugoslav Prime Minister and Foreign Minister, Bozidar Pouritch.

"Then the Balkan front, where the Yugoslavs have been pinning down numerous Axis divisions, will become one of the most dangerous ones for Hitler's European fortress," he said.

"The fact should not be forgotten that the Allied offensive in the Balkans in 1918 marked the beginning of final military collapse of the Central Powers. The Yugoslav people are anxiously awaiting the time when Allied armies will proffer them their brotherly hands and assistance for the liberation of the Balkans."

\* \* \*

September 10, 1943

## BALKAN PATRIOTS ACT UNDER BRITISH

---

*They Accept the Direct Orders of General Wilson—Await Signal for Uprising*

**ITALIANS ALSO AFFECTED**

*Question of High Command is Posed in Event of the Allies Striking Across Adriatic*

---

By Wireless to The New York Times

CAIRO, Egypt, Sept. 9—The Balkan guerrilla movement, numbering many thousand of Yugoslav, Greek and Albanian patriots, is now under the direct command of Gen. Sir Henry Maitland Wilson, Allied Commander in Chief in the Middle East, who has likewise assumed command of the defeated Italian troops in that area who are subject to his orders regarding steps toward their return home.

Thus an actual United Nations army is in being and exists on enemy-held territory awaiting the future decisions of the Allied combined chief of Staff in Washington regarding its next field of operation.

Even if the Germans manage to establish a new defensive line in northern Italy the Allies will nevertheless be established along the Adriatic coast opposite Greece, Albania, Yugoslavia and Dalmatia.

The question then will be whether, if operations across the Adriatic are contemplated, they will be commanded by Gen. Dwight D. Eisenhower in Italy or General Wilson, who commands the Middle East.

This question will shortly be decided by Prime Minister Churchill and President Roosevelt and their staffs.

In the meantime the Balkan guerrillas, aided by their British liaison in Greece and Yugoslavia, are ready for the signal for a general uprising which General Wilson promised them they would receive when the proper moment came.

In Albania where the patriot forces are smaller than in either Greece or Yugoslavia, bands are headed by a colonel operating in the northeast, another operating in the center of the country and another operating in the south.

In Greece there are three main guerrilla organizations that have united under central general headquarters at which a British general representing General Wilson is present.

Both the Allied Nations and German military plans will depend to a certain degree on the immediate effects of the Italian collapse on the Balkans.

If the Allies are able to take over the Dodecanese easily, that would pierce the German "iron ring" defenses of the Balkans and outflank Crete, giving access to island-hopping stepping stones to the mainland of Greece. If the Italians in Albania give up without trouble—and there are very few German troops there—the Allies might be able to establish a foothold in that country—a hundred miles west from Salonika—with ease.

In either case, such developments, or a surrender by Hungary, Bulgaria or Rumania, which cannot yet be counted upon, might force a hurried German evacuation of the Balkans. That is what Turkey is counting on and should it come about Turkey is believed ready to permit Allied troops to cross her domain and to employ her own army as an "occupying force to avert chaos."

There are many who feel that Hungary, Rumania and Bulgaria may soon be forced out of the war as a result of the Italian example. The Horthy Government has been trying to secure terms from the United Nations for some months, but unconditional surrender still prevails as the formula. However, Admiral Nicholas Horthy has more or less guaranteed that his troops will not fight the Allies when they reach the Danube valley.

Premier Emmanuel Tsouderos of Greece issued a statement today saying:

"Italy's collapse constitutes the beginning of the end of the Fascist systems. Italy is being punished severely but justly, because she initiated fascism from which nazism is the perfected continuation and because she attacked France from behind and because she treacherously attacked small countries like Greece, whose national integrity she strove to smash."

\* \* \*

September 17, 1943

## MIKHAILOVITCH'S TROOPS DESTROY NAZI UNIT SENT TO REPLACE ITALIAN OCCUPATIONAL FORCES

By Wireless to The New York Times

*The following dispatch was sent to The New York Times by the Democratic Yugoslavia news agency from station YTG "in the free mountains of Yugoslavia." The agency is the organ of the committee supporting General Mikhailovitch.*

SOMEWHERE IN YUGOSLAVIA, Sept. 16—While great excitement is growing up all over the country as a consequence of the greatest possible attention paid by all sections of our people to the heroic fightings of the Allied armies, especially in Italy, news concerning the ever-growing resistance of the people and the movements of the Yugoslav troops under the command of Gen. Draja Mikhailovitch is reaching us.

Besides the fighting that is taking place on the Adriatic shores of Montenegro against the Germans, we have just received the details of a successful attack by General Mikhailovitch's units against a German detachment in eastern Bosnia, not far from the town Zvornik. Owing to a skilled calculated maneuver, the Yugoslav soldiers succeeded in splitting this detachment in two groups and pushing them toward the Drina River. Forced to swim the river, the Germans were attacked and annihilated on the right bank.

It was understood here that the Germans were a Hitler Elite Guard formation dispatched to the Adriatic shores to replace the Italian units.

As a means of repression against the peasant population who offered fierce resistance to the German soldiers who came in the village Zvizdar near the small town of Ub on the right bank of the Sava River to rob the peasants' houses, a punitive expedition was sent there that gave new evidence of the German barbarian methods. They stole everything that had any value for them. They set fire to six houses, causing the deaths of all occupants, including seven children.

Next they gathered all males more than 15 years of age and sent them to a concentration camp.

In the neighboring village of Bukovica the Germans entered the church to arrest the priest during his services, but he succeeded in escaping.

WASHINGTON, Sept. 16 (AP)—A Free Yugoslavia radio station has been sending dispatches to Press Wireless, Inc., of New York, it was disclosed today with the filing of tariff schedules with the Federal Communications Commission.

Press Wireless filed schedules covering delivery of dispatches to New York, Washington and Los Angeles. The communication apparently is only one way, as no schedules were filed for transmissions to Yugoslavia.

After filing of the schedules, the State Department confirmed that the Yugoslav station was operated by forces of Gen. Draja Mikhailovitch. The Yugoslav Embassy said General Mikhailovitch had been sending direct messages to Washington for about ten days.

The Yugoslav Embassy, an official said, also has received two messages from a newly formed Yugoslav news service, the Democratic Telegraphic Agency. It was presumed that the Press Wireless application referred to dispatches from this agency.

\* \* \*

**October 4, 1943**

## PATRIOTS IN BULGARIA URGE TIE TO ALLIES

### Manifesto Urges People to Break With the Germans

ISTANBUL, Turkey, Oct. 3 (AP)—A manifesto from the Patriotic Front of Bulgaria, which calls on the Bulgarian people and army to break with the Germans and, on the basis of the Atlantic Charter, to collaborate with other Balkan nations and the United States, Britain and Russia, has just been smuggled out of Bulgaria.

The manifesto bears a strong resemblance to the phraseology often used by Bulgaria's "Black Radio," presumed to be Soviet-directed, which nightly breaks in on Sofia news broadcasts with advice to Bulgarians to get out of the war. The manifesto, however, is remarkable for its advice to Bulgarians to be friendly with the United States and Britain as well as Russia and its indication that Bulgaria's future will be decided within the framework of the Atlantic Charter.

Most important among the manifesto's twelve points were: prevent Bulgarian entry into Hitler's war; break the Bulgarian alliance with Germany and recall Bulgarian armies fighting against neighbor states and Serb patriots; restore political rights and freedom of the press; remove control of the army from the Fascist clique.

The Bulgarian Air Force is reported to be helping the Germans to patrol the Aegean because the Germans in the Balkans are short of aircraft, the British radio said yesterday in a broadcast recorded by the Columbia Broadcasting System.

\* \* \*

**October 30, 1943**

## NEW ALLIED BLOWS IN NORTHERN ITALY AND THE BALKANS

The Allies, pushing ahead across Italy (1), bombed landing fields near Rome, Orvieto and Foligno (2). A force of 30,000 Italians was reported fighting the Germans in the Verona area (3). Yugoslav Partisans severed the Zagreb-Belgrade railroad (4) in 130 places, attacked Brod and captured many fortified villages south of the Sava. A second German force attempting to land on Brac (5) was wiped out, but the enemy got ashore on the peninsula on which Ston (6) is located. The Partisans took Rogatica (7) but were on the defensive in Montenegro (8). General Mikhailovitch's men cut the Belgrade-Salonika railroad at Leskovac (9). Allied planes bombed the Candia airfield on Crete (10) and an airdrome on the island of Rhodes (11).

\* \* \*

November 2, 1943

## GREEK GUERRILLAS AGAIN IN CONFLICT

### *Popular Army Battles Zervas Group, Which Is Also Being Attacked by Nazis*

### TITO'S MEN GET AIR FORCE

### *Planes Will Support Partisan Troops in Yugoslavia—Foe Active in Montenegro*

By Wireless to The New York Times

CAIRO, Egypt, Nov. 1—The most recent information from Greece indicates that the Popular Liberation Army, which is the military organization of the Communist-led Greek National Liberation Front political body, has reopened its attack against the forces of Col. Napoleon Zervas in the general area south of Metsovo. General Zervas, at the same time, is being attacked by three German columns. One German group is coming from the north, the other from the west and the third from the southwest.

Apparently there is heavy fighting, according to persons in a position to follow the military situation in Greece and to appraise the political trends in a country where a state of civil strife has existed for almost a month.

### Partisans Form Air Corps

LONDON, Nov. 1 (U.P.)—The Yugoslav People's Army of Liberation today announced the formation of a Partisan Air Force to aid its 180,000 ground troops, and appealed to all former military and civilian pilots and ground crews to register immediately, for service against the Germans.

Gen. Josip Broz's [Tito] headquarters, in a broadcast over the free Yugoslav radio, reported that some units of the newly organized air force already had gone into action in support of guerrillas who were holding down an estimated dozen or more German divisions in Yugoslavia. There was no indication how many planes the Partisans had at their disposal or by whom they had been supplied.

Meanwhile, Geneal Tito's ground troops were locked in heavy battles against two German offensives in Slovenia and Montenegro.

### Fratricidal War Continues

The growing dissension between General Tito and his rival, Gen. Draja Mikhailovitch—with accusations and counter accusations of treason—swelled today as General Tito, reporting fighting on the Sanjak-Serbian frontier at Mount Belo Brdo and near Prijob, fifty-five miles southeast of Sarajevo, said the enemy forces included Mikhailovitch troops.

The Partisan communiqué also reported that Partisan units had clashed with Serbian Quislings and Chetniks at Zhivkovci, thirty-one miles south of Belgrade and near Guberevatz, south of Kragujavac in the Belgrade region.

In Cairo, meanwhile, semi-official Yugoslav Government sources accused the Partisans of assassinating General [Milo] Djukanovitch, a leading patriot and strong supporter of General Mikhailovitch.

During the coup d'etat in March, 1941, when Yugoslavia sided with Britain, General Djukanovitch was appointed Governor of Montenegro. He was captured by the Partisans a few days, ago in the Montenegro fighting, accused of treachery. Yesterday's communiqué said he had died of wounds received while fighting "with the Germans."

\*   \*   \*

November 2, 1943

## BALKAN PROBLEM PLAGUING ALLIES

### *Internal and External Affairs of Greece and Yugoslavia Pose Perplexities*

By C. L. SULZBERGER
By Wireless to The New York Times

CAIRO, Egypt, Nov. 1—One of the critical problems that the Allies must solve when Europe is liberated is the future of Greece and of Yugoslavia. Those nations—the only Balkan members of the United Nations bloc—serve as a link between the Soviet sphere and that of western Europe and between any conceivable Danubian federation.

Despite the bravery displayed by the guerrillas within those lands their political situations, both internally and externally, are unwholesome. Their futures, at best, are vague. United Nations plans and policies regarding methods of straightening out this situation have been marked by a shifting and unsteady course. But that something must be done everyone agrees. If nothing is done, it is felt trouble may well loom ahead. The last war began in the Balkans, and this one might well have done so. Care must be taken that the next one does not.

At this moment civil war, in varying stages, is raging in both devitalized and occupied lands between patriot organizations of undoubted courage but of differing political ideals. Simultaneously, their émigré Governments in Cairo have been undergoing a continuous series of Cabinet crises, and their small refugee military units are discontented.

Inside Greece the Communist-led organization, fearing the Germans might evacuate before it had established its full powers, ordered its armed Elas forces to attack rival guerrilla units with the purpose of seizing control and thereby present to the Allied armies, when they arrive, a fait accompli. Both the Communist-led group and its rival, led by Col. Napoleon Zervas, are republican-minded and wish to prevent the return of King George.

The bulk of the Greek population are war-weary and tired of politics. They hope only for liberty and are united, in all probability, only behind its National Orthodox Church. But numerous people, even in this frame of mind, definitely oppose the return of the King until after a plebiscite to be held in the future. Many fear that the King's return before such a vote were held would aggravate the situation.

With Yugoslavia the questions are in some senses parallel. Civil war between Gen. Draja Mikhailovitch and the Partisans of Gen. Josip Broz [Tito] has been going on since early 1942. At first Great Britain supported General Mikhailovitch exclusively and the Soviet Union, General Tito. The United States, apparently, had hardly any policy of its own.

General Tito's power, nevertheless, continued to grow, until he is now reported to be ten times stronger than General Mikhailovitch. Earlier this year Anglo-American liaison missions were sent to him, and now he is receiving from us more aid than is General Mikhailovitch.

But fratricidal strife continues, and it is almost certain that a full-fledged civil war will scourge liberated Yugoslavia, unless there is a big Allied force to stop it. The position of King Peter is uncertain. General Mikhailovitch is for him, and General Tito never has said anything against him. There is some likelihood that he still is quite popular with large elements of his country. But the King has been consistently hampered by quarrels in his successive Governments, whose members certainly cut a very small figure back home.

*    *    *

November 5, 1943

# AID FOR ALBANIANS CITED BY CHURCHILL

### *Prime Minister Reveals Britons Are Serving as Liaison Aides With the Guerrillas*

## YUGOSLAVS SCORE GAINS

### *Partisans Capture Town Near Sarajevo Railroad—Allies Bomb Nazis in Greece*

LONDON, Nov. 4 (U.P.)—Prime Minister Churchill revealed today that British liaison officers were aiding thousands of guerrillas fighting the Germans in Albania and confirmed that British officers had also been sent into Greece and Yugoslavia.

At the same time, it was announced that Partisan troops of Gen. Josip Broz [Tito] had occupied Priboj, south of the Sarajevo-Sofia railroad.

The Allies, Mr. Churchill said, were looking to the Albanian guerrillas to "play their part, with their ancient warlike traditions, in future military developments in the Mediterranean area." He added:

"The Germans are employing the usual methods by which they seek to subdue all warlike peoples," Mr. Churchill said. "Already they have bombed Albanian villages, killed Albanian women and children, but the Albanian guerrillas continue to harass the enemy and attack his communications."

The British Premier, replying to a question in the House of Commons, reiterated that the British Government wished to see Albania's independence restored, with consideration for her frontiers at the peace settlement.

### Partisans Win Town

A Partisan communiqué broadcast by the Free Yugoslav radio said that Priboj, sixty miles southeast of Sarajevo, had been occupied after several days' fierce fighting with Germans. Serbian Quislings and Chetniks allegedly aligned with Gen. Draja Mikhailovitch, Yugoslavia's War Minister.

In a counter-offensive in Montenegro the Partisans said they had regained another town. Berani, which the Germans took by a tank and infantry onslaught a few days ago, and pursued the Nazis back from the interior. The German offensive in this region appeared to have been halted.

In Croatia the Partisans said they were firmly holding four towns thirty to fifty miles northeast of Zagreb under repeated attacks by German forces that had swept into northern Yugoslavia from Italy.

Croatian Partisans who penetrated into Hungary between the Drava and Mura Rivers last week were reported to have carried out a number of "successful operations."

### Partisan Gains Confirmed

*By Wireless to The New York Times*

CAIRO, Egypt, Nov. 4—Various claims to victories that have bulked large in their guerrilla warfare of the Partisans last month appeared to be substantiated today by reports from other sources. Sixty kilometers [thirty-seven miles] double-track railroad between Zagreb and Belgrade and a bridge thirty meters [ninety-eight and one-half feet] long at Dubski Potok, together with two trains and sixty cars laden with German troops and electric pylons, and twenty culverts were destroyed. Two hundred Germans were said to have been killed.

A communiqué issued here by the Yugoslav office of information says that, according to German sources, general large-scale mopping up operations have been ordered throughout Yugoslavia. German troops are said to have begun the process in the hope of clearing resistance before winter comes. The Germans are also reported to be mustering available manpower in Croatia and Serbia.

### Fight in Greece Continues

No new developments have been reported on the fighting in Greece, and it is assumed the situation remains the same, with German columns pressing in on Col. Napoleon Zervas, who, in turn, appears to be attacked by Elas troops of the Communist-led Opposition party.

RAF planes attacked warehouses and shipping of Syros Harbor Tuesday night and the air-field at Candia, on Crete. The following night the British again attacked Syros, setting fires.

### Zara and Araxos Bombed

*By Wireless to The New York Times*

ALGIERS, Nov. 4—Allied air forces had another busy day across the Adriatic yesterday, although the heavy bombers of the new United States Fifteenth Air Force did not operate.

The trans-Adriatic raids were carried out by Mitchells with Lightning escort, which bombed the airfield at Araxos [Pappas], Greece, while Boston light bombers flew to the harbor at Zara, Yugoslavia, a German supply port, the night before.

Fragmentation bombs tore up parked aircraft at Araxas, while at Zara bombs hit both sides of the harbor area.

\* \* \*

**November 17, 1943**

## YUGOSLAVS PUT 35 CENTS ON HEAD OF PAVELITCH

Yugoslav Partisans have countered a rich reward posted by the Nazi puppet regime of Croatia for the capture of Gen. Josip Broz (Tito) by offering approximately 35 cents for the head of the Croatian Quisling, Ante Pavelitch, the British Broadcasting Corporation reported yesterday.

BBC, in a broadcast to Turkey recorded by the Federal Communications Commission said that the Pavelitch regime had announced a reward worth more than $21,000 for the head of Tito, leader of the Partisan forces in Yugoslavia.

In posting the 35-cent offer on signs at many places in Yugoslavia, the Partisans added to their grim humor by promising that the person bringing Pavelitch's head to their headquarters would be "protected from the crowd that will try to snatch it away," BBC said.

\* \* \*

**December 5, 1943**

## PARTISANS SET UP YUGOSLAV REGIME

### Tito Faction Elects Parliament That Ignores Government of King Peter in Cairo

By The Associated Press

LONDON, Dec. 4—The strongly pro-Russian Yugoslav Partisan movement announced over the Free Yugoslav Radio today that it had set up a provisional regime in opposition to the existing exiled government now sitting in Cairo and recognized by the Allies—including Russia.

The development thrust before the United Nations the sharpest Balkan political problem to arise since Hitler's ouster from that area became a reasonable military prospect.

The Partisans announced that 140 delegates had created a Parliament and governing body for territory already wrested from the Nazis. The government is headed by Dr. Ivan Ribar, first President of the Constitutional Assembly formed in Yugoslavia after the last war and a former member of the Serb Democratic party.

Gen. Josip Broz [Tito], military leader of the Partisans, has been elevated to the rank of field marshal and made chairman of a new Committee for National Defense, the broadcast continued. General Tito was officially identified as a former underground labor leader who had fought in the Spanish Civil War against Generalissimo Franco's forces.

Three Vice Presidents were elected by the delegates, Mosa Pidje, a Serbian journalist; Ivan Augustinitch, Croat sculptor, and Josip Rus, a Slovene.

Vlado Ribnikar, a Serb, and Bozidar Magovas, a Croat journalist, were named assistant defense commissioners, and Josip Smodlaka, former Yugoslav Minister to the Vatican, was appointed Minister of Foreign Affairs. The conference also set up Ministries for Home Affairs, Reconstruction and Forestry and Mines.

Nothing was said in the broadcast of the Government of Dr. Bozhidar Puritch at Cairo, of Gen. Draja Mikhailovitch, Chetnik leader, and Dr. Puritch's Minister of Defense, or of the youthful King Peter.

The war bulletin issued from Tito's headquarters said 300 Nazis had been killed in heavy fighting between Glina and Petrinja in western Croatia, and that bitter fights were going on along the Croat-Slovene border. It reported a reverse in Macedonia, where Partisans evacuated the town of Debar near the Albanian border after a sharp fight with German units.

Yugoslavs here said the personnel of the new Government ran from Extreme Leftist to Liberal Democratic. The choice of Serbs, Croats and Slovenes for subordinate officers appeared to be an effort to give the Ribar Government a country-wide flavor.

While the followers of General Mikhailovitch have implied they considered Tito's followers as being mainly Communist, the best available information here indicated his movement had been primarily nationalistic, although its friendship with the Soviet Union had been close and marked. Tito's followers, fighting the Germans savagely in a campaign of attrition, number about 200,000 compared to Mihailovitch's 30,000, it is believed.

The timing of the Free Yugoslav announcement caused disconcerting surprise in some quarters here, since the decision to confront King Peter and the Allies with an open contest for national leadership came just at a moment when the world was whispering of impending heavy-scale military action in Europe to follow the Roosevelt-Churchill-Stalin meeting.

It also came coincident with reports here that King Peter had been trying to shake up his Cairo Government and seemed likely to delay his projected marriage to Princess Alexandra of Greece.

Whatever the effect of Tito's emergence into public identity and public office as a claimant to the War Ministry of his country, the fact remained that his operations afield were wasting and bleeding large German forces.

#### British Decline to Comment

LONDON, Dec. 4 (U.P.)—British diplomatic circles here declined comment, saying they had no information on the new Yugoslav Government aside from the radio broadcast, which they considered insufficient for a statement.

The followers of King Peter and General Mikhailovitch said the move was a deliberate plot to prevent the Allies, especially the United States, from carrying out any plan to allow rations freed from the Axis yoke to choose their own form of government.

The Yugoslav radio listed other members of the Partisan Government as:

Minister of Interior—Vlado Zecevitch.

Minister of Reconstruction—Rade Pribicevitch.

Minister of Forestry and Mines—Sulejman Filipovitch.

### Allied Planes Hit Balkans

ALGIERS, Dec. 4 (U.P.)—Four attacks were made by B-25's yesterday on the Yugoslav port of Sebenico, south of Zara. The American Mitchells scored several direct hits on the railway yards and main quay, hit one vessel squarely and dropped bombs among smaller craft in the harbor, it was announced officially today.

P-40 Warhawks of the USAAF and RAF Bostons joined in the attack on the Yugoslav coast. They attacked Spalato as well as Sebenico. The Warhawks damaged a vessel at Spalato in daylight and the Bostons bombed docks and warehouses at Spalato and motor transport at Sebenico during darkness.

British Spitfires strafed road transport in Albania and the Greek island of Corfu.

\* \* \*

**December 10, 1943**

## U. S. TO HELP TITO IN YUGOSLAV FIGHT

*Hull Says We Will Assist All in the Country Who Are Trying to Oust the Germans*

### PARTISANS SEE VICTORY

*London Spokesman Says Group in Cairo, Backing Mikhailovitch, Will Be Ousted*

Special to The New York Times

WASHINGTON, Dec. 9—The United States will aid the Partisans in Yugoslavia as well as the forces of General Draja Mikhailovitch, according to indications given today by Secretary of State Cordell Hull.

When his attention was called to reports that the Partisans were going to ask for American lend-lease help, Mr. Hull said the policy of the Allies was to aid any group in Yugoslavia that was effectively fighting the Germans. This Government, he added, has not come to the question of the mechanism so far as lend-lease was concerned but he did not consider that material.

It was clear that the American Government's attitude toward aid to various forces in Yugoslavia was based primarily in the practical question of their resistance to the Germans and that it was felt internal political questions in Yugoslavia could wait until later.

This attitude was understood not to be out of line with the British policy of supplying more aid to the Partisans than to the forces of General Mikhailovitch on the grounds that the Partisans were more active against the Germans.

Russia is supporting the Partisans but has also recognized King Peter. The United States from the first has supported King Peter and the exiled Government of Yugoslavia, which is now established in Cairo.

In general the attitude of Washington can be set forth as follows:

The Yugoslav people have demonstrated to the whole world their determination to regain their independence and to drive the Axis forces from their country. With inhuman cunning the Nazis strove to divide this people against itself, by partitioning its territory, by establishing conflicting authorities maintained by violence and terror and by incitement to the lowest passions of civil strife.

It is natural that in repelling an enemy operating with every method of violence and deception, the organizers of Yugoslav resistance should also seek to utilize every regional advantage, every social group and every skillful and daring leader. Whatever their differences may be, their ultimate purpose is to drive out the enemy and to restore the institutions of free government.

The king and the government of Yugoslavia, now temporarily established in Cairo, are recognized by all the United Nations as the authority conducting Yugoslavia's participation in the general conduct of the war. Within the country resistance movements under diverse leadership have grown into forces of undoubted military value.

In the circumstances it is natural that political factors should also play a part. It is our intention to assist in every possible way the resistance forces from the point of view of their military effectiveness, without, during the fighting, entering into discussions of political differences.

In line with our consistent policy we consider that political arrangements are primarily a matter for the future choice of the Yugoslav people.

Meanwhile every means is being utilized to obtain factual and objective information on all aspects of the situation in Yugoslavia for use in the prosecution of the war.

### Partisans Announce Plans

LONDON, Dec. 9 (U.P.)—Marshal Josip Broz's [Tito's] Yugoslav Partisan Government announced over its radio today that it had decided to ask lend-lease aid to carry on its fight against the Germans and to seek representation on the Allied Advisory Commission for Mediterranean Affairs.

Mihailo Petrovitch, spokesman for the South Slav Committee here, predicted that the Partisan government would eventually replace the Yugoslav Government in exile at Cairo as the legal Government of the country.

[Gen. Draja Mikhailovitch, recognized by the Yugoslav exile Government as the leader of guerrilla forces, retorted in a dispatch received by The United Press in New York that the Broz regime was a "so-called Communist government" and that the place of Yugoslav patriots was with the Mikhailovitch forces.]

It was indicated that as the result of the series of Allied conferences, America, Britain and Russia were about to put strong pressure on refugee governments, especially Yugoslavia's, to end internal fighting and get organized for the promised attack on Germany. No doubt remained that the Allies were leaning increasingly toward Marshal Broz as the No. 1 Yugoslav.

### Blow to Peter's Government

CAIRO, Egypt, Dec. 9 (AP)—The feeling prevailed here tonight that King Peter's Yugoslav Government in Exile suffered a body blow in Britain's newly announced policy of sending greater support to the guerrilla warriors of Marshal Josip Broz [Tito], than to the government forces under Gen. Draja Mikhailovitch.

\* \* \*

**December 11, 1943**

## BOMBERS HIT BULGARIAN CAPITAL

### SOFIA ROCKED ANEW

*Planes, Believed to Be American, Strike 3d and Hardest Blow*

### BULGAR CRISIS DEEPENED

*Attack Seen Adding to Pull Away From Axis Caused by Teheran, Cairo Parleys*

By DREW MIDDLETON
By Cable to The New York Times

LONDON, Dec. 10—The city of Sofia, shabby capital of Bulgaria, was heavily bombed by Allied planes today, according to German and Bulgarian reports, as affairs in that least helpful of Germany's Balkan satellites moved toward another crisis brought about by the struggle within the country between Teuton and Slav.

Although the Teheran and Cairo conferences appear to have caused the current crisis in Bulgaria, well informed quarters here felt they were only contributing factors to a situation that has been moving toward the boil for many months. Bulgaria's position is too complex to be dismissed as the result of any single action.

Into this internal upheaval Allied bombers, apparently based in the Mediterranean area, dropped a considerable load of explosives, according to the Sofia radio.

[Balkan dispatches reaching Stockholm said extensive damage occurred around rail and troop barracks areas, and that members of the Bulgarian Parliament interrupted their session to take shelter, The Associated Press reported. Meanwhile the Bulgarian Government was said to have clamped rigid restrictions on rail travel, suggesting troop moves.

[American planes were believed to have made the attack, and it was indicated that the target again was the railroad district; which was hit hard Nov. 24 by United States Liberators of the Northwest African Command, after an American medium bomber blow at Sofia Nov. 14.]

### Blow at Bulgar Axis Ties

The attack, like so many of those directed against Axis targets in the Balkans, had a political as well as military objective, in this case to make the Bulgarian people realize that the less happy aspects of war will be visited upon them in increasing fierceness if they continue within Germany's orbit.

This lesson will not be lost on the workers and farmers in Bulgaria, who long have been pro-Russian and who will see in the attack another proof of the strength of the forces aligned against their country.

These Bulgar elements have contended for almost fifteen years against the strongly pro-German industrial and social aristocracy that has dominated Bulgaria's army.

The Roosevelt-Stalin-Churchill conference at Teheran, which sealed the unity between Russia, the United States and Britain, and the subsequent Cairo conference, which edged Turkey, Bulgaria's strongest neighbor, toward war on the Allies' side, increased the political pressure within Bulgaria.

Aside from the fact that they emphasize the growing unrest within the country, Continental reports about Bulgaria are contradictory.

On the one hand, Stockholm relays word to the effect that Berlin has told the Bulgarians they could not back out of the fight. Another Balkan report through Stockholm says there have been "incidents" on the Turkish-Bulgarian frontier that would indicate a willingness on the part of Bulgarian forces to fight rather than drop out of the German system in Europe.

The Germans are expected to make every effort to force the divided Bulgarian Army into strong defensive measures on the Turkish frontier.

### Rail Yard Seen Major Target

BERNE, Switzerland, Dec. 10 (AP)—Sofia was blasted for an hour and 45 minutes this afternoon by several waves of Allied planes, whose explosives caused great destruction and killed many persons, the Sofia radio said tonight.

Hungarian reports said the Sofia rail center was heavily pounded.

The Sofia rail yards are a mile from Parliament, scene of fervid Bulgarian deliberations of political and military import following the tri-power announcement at Teheran and the subsequent "closest unity" council among President Roosevelt, Prime Minister Churchill and President Ismet Inonu of Turkey.

The heavy air attack, the third in a month, began at 11:40 A. M. and Sofia was under an alert for two hours or more, a Budapest radio announcement said.

Premier Dobri Boshiloff of Bulgaria interrupted a later address to Parliament at 5 P. M., asking his legislators to rise in silent tribute to those who had died, the Sofia radio said.

### U. S. Warnings to Bulgars Cited

The Sofia radio announced late yesterday that the Bulgarian Regency Council had called Lieut. Gen. Nikola Mikhoff, the

War Minister, into conference, the Federal Communications Commission reported.

The reported bombing of Sofia yesterday followed a Budapest dispatch in the day's issue of the Swiss newspaper Basler Nachrichten saying that United States planes had repeatedly dropped leaflets over Bulgaria in recent days warning that previous bombings of Sofia had been "only a warning" and that much heavier attacks would follow.

The Nachrichten dispatch, reported to the Office of War Information, said that the leaflets had called on Bulgarian troops to evacuate Macedonia as not belonging to Bulgaria and had warned them not to participate in punitive expeditions against Yugoslavs and Greeks.

\* \* \*

December 15, 1943

## BULGARIAN PEACE FEELERS REJECTED BY U. S. AND BRITISH GOVERNMENTS

### By C. L. SULZBERGER
### By Wireless to The New York Times

CAIRO, Egypt, Dec. 14—Germany's most powerful Balkan satellite, Bulgaria, has officially communicated peace feelers to the Allied Governments in an effort to get out of a war that both the Bulgarian Government and the population now realize is lost.

These feelers have been sent separately through the Russian Government and to Britain and the United States, and they have been turned down. Premier Dobri Boshiloff said that Bulgaria would be willing to negotiate a peace on the basis of the Atlantic Charter, in return for guarantees that Bulgaria might keep those territories that she seized from Yugoslavia and Greece. These, she is prepared to argue, are ethnically Bulgarian.

Thus far, the only response that has been received at Sofia is continued Anglo-American bombing and the reiteration that the sole terms that will be considered are unconditional surrender. This means the evacuation of the stolen territories.

As a result, a major crisis is rapidly developing in Bulgaria. Three Cabinet Ministers—Ivan Vasoff, Ivan Betshkoff and George Shishmanoff—have resigned. The Germans are reported to have warned Sofia that any further efforts to desert will be met with strong German action and the unhappy state of Italy is cited as evidence of what may happen.

The Turkish Government is seeking to induce Bulgaria to get out of the conflict by combined suasion and threats. Turkey recently defeated a German-inspired effort to form a Turkish-Bulgarian-Rumanian bloc.

The Russian influence in Bulgaria is growing daily. It was announced a few days ago that a Russian military attaché had been sent to Sofia, and a Bulgarian attaché will soon be sent to Moscow. Nine months ago these attachés were recalled. One of Russia's ablest envoys, V. G. Dekanozoff, is the Minister in Sofia.

The arrival of the new Russian attaché could greatly benefit the western Allies if he could find out enough about the disposition not only of the Bulgarian forces but of Germany's Balkan troops. Bulgaria is not at war with Russia, and her position vis-à-vis Moscow is similar to Finland's vis-à-vis Washington. Bulgaria is thus even now of great use in some ways and the Russian Legation in Sofia can pass on for rebroadcasting by the powerful Tifis station the dim broadcast of the Free Yugoslavia radio.

The anti-Government and pro-Russian Partisan movement in Bulgaria has now grown so strong that the Minister of the Interior, Dmitri Christoff, has been forced officially to admit its existence, although he minimizes its membership at about 1,000. Actually it is considerably larger and is based on the Balkan and Rhodope Mountains north and south of Plovdiv. It is well known that these groups are supplied, on and off, with leaders and materials sent from Russia by air.

The Bulgarian Government realizes the extent and growth of the traditional Russophilism that was the sole force barring Bulgaria's declaration of war on Russia. Premier Boshiloff now confers with M. Dekanozoff after almost every Cabinet meeting.

Trouble is gradually spreading over various sections of the country. Mr. Christoff has admitted conflicts between the old kingdom and the Macedonian and Thracian possessions seized from Greece and Yugoslavia. The Yugoslav Partisans are gradually seeking to work their way into the latter and, if they succeed, a large penetration may have a considerable effect in encouraging desertions among Bulgarian troops, 80 per cent of whom are reservists. There is increasing evidence of popular Bulgarian support for the idea of a South Slav federation including all Yugoslavs. This idea is not only sponsored by Marshal Tito (Josip Broz) but likely to receive Russian approval.

\* \* \*

December 19, 1943

## TITO REGIME ASKS FOR RECOGNITION

*Yugoslav Partisans Urge Allies to Repudiate King Peter and Emigre Cabinet*

### By C. L. SULZBERGER
### By Wireless to The New York Times

CAIRO, Egypt, Dec. 18—Marshal Tito (Josip Broz), leader of the Yugoslav Partisans, has formally requested that the Allies withdraw recognition from young King Peter and his émigré Cabinet and acknowledge the Partisans' newly created temporary Yugoslav Government as the sole representative of sovereignty among the southern Slav peoples.

This urgently worded request was broadcast this morning by the Free Yugoslav radio after insisting that the émigré Government be deprived of all rights to represent the country. Marshal Tito pledges, furthermore, that a democratic Federal

State will be established after the war. The Tito Government, however, reserved the right to review all treaties and obligations signed by King Peter's Cabinet in exile, and said it would definitely not recognize any future commitments that Cabinet made.

This dramatic and, for the United Nations, extremely complex demand was formulated at the same anti-Fascist Yugoslav congress late last month that announced the creation of the temporary government.

The declaration broadcast today actually was agreed upon Nov. 29 and was signed by Ivan Ribar Sr., President of Parliament.

This development, while not unexpected, has served to precipitate a diplomatic problem. There is a tendency even among some Tito admirers to wish that he had not been in such a hurry. Anglo-American diplomacy has been striving to find some formula that would unify some of the divergent elements, in Yugoslavia and preserve the position of the young King.

It is felt by some here that King Peter himself has been wrongfully attacked by the Tito movement and blamed for some things for which he is by no means responsible.

That Soviet diplomacy apparently is working in conjunction with Great Britain and America is indicated by the fact that only a few weeks ago the new Soviet Ambassador presented his credentials to King Peter.

When Marshal Tito angled for Allied recognition a few days ago in telegrams to Premier Stalin, President Roosevelt and Prime Minister Churchill, Moscow's reply was an announcement that a military mission would be sent to him. The dispatch of such a mission merely places Russia in the same position with respect to Marshal Tito as Britain and America occupy. There was no indication of any political move to recognize him.

For better or worse, a first-rate Balkan political crisis has now been initiated. Clearly, an immediate consultation with the Soviet Union is now indicated. It would seem unlikely yet that the Allies were prepared to abandon King Peter's cause entirely, and the best guess would be that they will try to postpone that issue until after the war.

Nevertheless, there is so much disappointment with the activities of the King's War Minister, Gen. Draja Mikhailovitch, that it is possible that, unless he mends his ways, Allied support for General Mikhailovitch, even verbal, may be withdrawn entirely.

The document signed by Mr. Ribar, who, as President of the Partisans' Anti-Fascist Council, serves as chief of the legislative branch, thanks the Allies for the food and supplies sent to the Partisans. It also praises the results of the Allied conference.

\* \* \*

December 20, 1943

## BALKAN SENTIMENT SEEN COOL TO KINGS

*Belief Grows That Exiled Rulers Will Not Retrieve Crowns—Democracy in Ferment*

By JOSEPH M. LEVY
By Cable to The New York Times

ANKARA, Turkey, Dec. 19—The birth of liberal movements throughout Balkan Europe is seriously disturbing the peace of mind of those Kings and politicians who hope to re-establish after the war the old regimes in their respective countries.

In this neutral observatory, polemical earthquakes in Europe register as soon as they occur, and there have been many since Germany was thrust upon the defensive.

This correspondent has just learned that 16,000 Bulgars have deserted from the army, taking their rifles and large quantities of ammunition. They have become guerrillas, creating havoc for the Germans, as well as for their own puppet government, which they hope to overthrow. Recently 5,000 of them joined the Yugoslav forces of Marshal Tito (Josip Broz).

Well informed circles here in Ankara are betting ten to one that neither King George of Greece nor King Peter of Yugoslavia will ever again sit on his throne. This belief has been fostered not only by the creation of the newly established regime of Marshal Tito but also by the news coming out of those parts of Greece and Yugoslavia where the Nazis are still masters. It would hardly be considered a blunder to forecast that there will be no crowned heads in the Balkans after the war.

It has been virtually substantiated that, with the exception of Hungary, where the legitimists are advocating a monarchy under Otto of Habsburg, that all the peoples of south, east and central Europe are stanchly republican and vehemently opposed to royalty. They are aiming for government of the people, by the people and for the people—government that will endeavor to raise the standard of living of workers and peasants.

Many of the movements for the reform of Europe have a Socialist platform. The people's tendencies are perhaps best illustrated by a passage from a letter received here from Poland:

"For the past three years I have been living and working with a type of men who were looked upon by you and me as the scum of the earth and parasites that continually grumbled they were underpaid and exploited by us. After my first few weeks with them I realized what fools we were. No, they are not scum; they are the cream of the earth and the backbone of our nation.

"I vow that if I survive the war I shall devote the rest of my life working for a just distribution of our country's wealth among all its inhabitants. If you consider this socialism, you must make up your mind that I am a Socialist."

The writer of this letter was a big industrialist in Poland and is now one of the leaders of the underground.

From all over Europe, except from Hungary and Scandinavia, come reports that the people are as eager for social reform as to throw off the Nazi yoke. They believe that it is imperative to establish a new kind of government, totally different from the one that ruled their respective countries before the war.

This state of affairs appears most displeasing to the governments in exile, as well as to their satellites. In their anxiety of losing their jobs after the war, they have searched for a scapegoat and found an ideal one—communism.

From now on it must be expected that in their life-and-death struggle to retain power the exiled and satellite governments will claim that a Soviet conspiracy exists behind all the liberal movements of Europe. It is a common belief here that, although living in exile and considered members of the United Nations, the Governments of Poland, Yugoslavia and Greece have never been, nor are now, great sympathizers of democracy. Their hope of being restored to office is commonly regarded as their only reason for staying in the Allied camp.

\* \* \*

**January 8, 1944**

## TITO EXPELLED FROM BANJA LUKA
## BY STRONG NAZI REINFORCEMENTS

*Foe's Losses Reported Large in 7 Days' Street Fighting;*
*Partisans Reported Veering Toward Peace With the King*

LONDON, Jan. 7 (U.P.)—Yugoslav Partisans, after seven days of bloody street fighting in Banja Luka, have been forced to withdraw from the strategic Bosnian communications center after inflicting heavy casualties on the German garrison, Marshal Tito (Josip Broz) announced today.

At the same time, Marshal Tito's broadcast communiqué reported that other Partisan units had carried out a successful attack on Bosanska Gradiska, twenty-five miles north of Banja Luka.

Simultaneously, units of the Sixth Slavonian Corps, operating near the Sava River, attacked Stara Gradiska, suburb of Bosanska Gradiska, and another detachment raided Nova Gradiska, astride the Zagreb-Belgrade railroad.

German reinforcements were rushed from Dalmatia to Banja Luka and on Wednesday night a Nazi counter-thrust, spearheaded by tanks, ousted the Partisans.

Besides killing 680 Nazi soldiers and wounding 700, Marshal Tito's soldiers reportedly captured seventy-two prisoners, including twenty-six Nazi officers. In addition, they seized large quantities of war materials and destroyed German installations and gunpowder mills and mines in the vicinity.

German broadcasts asserted that more than 2,000 Partisans had been killed in severe fighting before Banja Luka

The New York Times

Yugoslav Partisan girl soldier in the uniform of a captured German. On her cap is a Red Star, insignia of the People's Liberation Army.

was emptied by its attackers. Off the Croatian coast the crew of the grounded German minelaying vessel was taken prisoner, and in Slovenia a railway line was destroyed at several points, causing a German military train to crash into the Drava River, the communiqué said.

[The Berlin radio, heard in New York, said Friday that the secret central bureau of the Slovenian Communist party had been discovered, revealing the scope of its membership and of the underground movement in northern Yugoslavia. The broadcast said that "files with names of roughly 20,000 inhabitants to be liquidated" had been found.]

On the Yugoslav political front a source in London said today that King Peter of Yugoslavia might soon obtain an opportunity to make a deal with Marshal Tito in which the exiled monarch would be appointed head of a committee representing the National Liberation Movement and Yugoslavs abroad.

Partisan sources said the liberation movement was not completely opposed to the re-establishment of the monarchy, despite the Partisan leader's recent declaration that the youthful King would not be permitted to return until after post-war elections. They said an agreement might be reached if the Yugoslav Government-in-Exile in Cairo were dissolved and its War Minister, Gen. Draja Mikhailovitch, disavowed.

\*   \*   \*

January 22, 1944

## TITO'S PARTISANS RETAKE BOSNIAN CAPITAL; ENEMY CLAIMS CAPTURE OF ISLAND OF BRAC

LONDON, Jan. 21 (U.P.)—Yugoslav Partisans announced today they had recaptured Jajce, their capital, which Axis troops had entered nine days ago. The Partisans added they had ripped through enemy lines into the railway city of Tuzia, in a sudden counter offensive against strong German forces in Bosnia.

But assertions from Zagreb, capital of the Croat puppet state, said that crack German marine units had swept the Partisans from the island of Brac, commanding the entrance to the important harbor of Spalato on the Adriatic, and had isolated other Partisans holding the strategic island of Hvar, whose northern coast is but three miles south of Brac.

In breaking into Jajce, reported headquarters of Marshal Tito (Josip Broz), the Partisans put to flight two German divisions between Mrkonicgrad and Glamoc, southwest of Jajce. The Partisans had not formally admitted the loss of Jajce.

Partisan units in eastern Bosnia battled the Germans successfully along a forty-eight-mile front northwest of Sarajevo, extending from Doboj to Tuzla to Zvornik, and seizing two towns northwest of Doboj. They also took two mines in the area, the Partisan communiqué disclosed.

The Germans were offering stubborn resistance in Tuzla, and street fighting raged there. The Partisans turned back a German column that was attempting to reinforce Tuzla by a drive from Brcko, twenty-five miles to the north.

A temporary reverse was admitted in the Rama River sector of western Bosnia, where the Germans managed to gain a brief hold on Prozor, forty miles southeast of Jajce, before the Partisans rallied and drove them out. More than 300 Germans were killed and many wounded, the Partisans said.

### Wounded Tito Eludes Trap

AT A YUGOSLAV PARTISAN REFUGEE CAMP, in the Middle East, Jan. 18 (Delayed) (U.P.)—A German bullet winged Marshal Tito in the upper left arm but failed to prevent the commander of the Yugoslav Partisans from leading his forces out of a trap set by 35,000 enemy troops in the mountains of Montenegro last June, a wounded guerrilla leader who had participated in the battle said today.

The New York Times

Marshal Tito (Josip Broz) and his general staff somewhere in the mountains of their native country.

The story was told by Dushan Alac, a 26-year-old machine gunner, who is one of the five-man committee that operates this camp. Alac said he had battled the Nazis in all five of their major offensives against the Partisans, and he bore wounds in both arms. Three fingers of his right hand are paralyzed.

"It was Tito's greatest military triumph to break through that trap," Alac said. "The Germans threw five rings composed of parts of seven divisions of Germans and Ustashis (Croat irregulars) around us.

"Tito personally led his troops through the enemy lines and was wounded in the upper arm. But the Germans failed to stop him. The fighting was the toughest I saw in two years of battling the Nazis."

\*   \*   \*

March 5, 1944

## GREEK HYMN

The "Hymn of the Greek Guerrillas," the words of which have recently arrived in America, has become during the past year the national fighting song of the "Antartes," or guerrillas. It has spread all over Greece, and has become such a symbol of Greek resistance to German occupation that within one month five Greeks were condemned to death by the Germans for singing it. The name of the Greek author is as yet unknown. This translation was made by Warren E. Blake, Professor of Greek at the University of Michigan.

*Loud the thunder from Olympus; bright Giona's*
*lightning flame;*
*Agrapha rolls back the echoes, midst the quaking of*
*the Main!*
*"Arms! To arms!" resounds the summons, "Forward!*
*Forward to the fray!*
*Liberty, our dearest treasure, is the prize we win*
*today!"*

*Spirit of the Revolution, living, breathing once again*
*Gives to arms the steel to conquer, wraps in flame*
*the souls of men.*
*See, the foreign wolves are cringing; fear and*
*trembling fills their hearts.*
*Well they know what vengeance waits them from the*
*freeman's deadly arts!*

*Hear Spercheios' rushing waters proudly hail our*
*patriot band,*
*Prophesying by their triumph peace and freedom for*
*our land.*
*Greet our day of Resurrection with the bells of*
*Eastertide!*
*Tell to all our new Salvation, won by those who fought*
*and died!*

\* \* \*

**March 30, 1944**

## MOSCOW DEMANDS SATELLITE RISING

*Rumania, Bulgaria and Finland Warned They Must Resist Hitler*
*to Escape War*

**HUNGARY'S LESSON CITED**

*Nations Urged to Use Their Own Armed Forces—Sofia Said to*
*Rebuff Soviet*

### By W. H. LAWRENCE
By Cable to The New York Times

MOSCOW, March 29—A plain warning was delivered today to the peoples of Finland, Rumania and Bulgaria that the only way they can save their countries from becoming battlegrounds is to break immediately with Adolf Hitler, using their own armed forces to resist any attempt by him to occupy their territories as he did Hungary.

Significance is given to the declaration—published as an editorial in Izvestia—by the fact that the Red Army now has powerful forces poised at the borders of Rumania and Finland, but, so far as known here, without orders as yet to invade territory beyond the Soviet Union. In the case of Bulgaria, the Soviet Union is not at war with her.

[Russia's pre-1941 boundary with Rumania was at the Prut River.]

As has been the case since Soviet armistice conditions were tendered to Finland at her request, the editorial was a restrained argument for leaving Hitler's camp and joining that of the United Nations, without denunciations of the "satellite countries" for their previous collaboration with Germany.

### Hungary an Object-Lesson

Hitler's occupation of Hungary, an "ally," is an object-lesson to Finland, Rumania and Bulgaria, especially the last two, which, Izvestia points out, have sizable armies that give them every possibility of resisting attempted German occupation. Foreign press reports are cited as basis for the information that Bulgaria has twenty divisions.

Izvestia put the problem to these countries bluntly as follows:

"Either to be completely occupied without resistance by the Germans with the inevitable prospect of making their territories a theatre of war operations and in the final analysis sharing the fate of Germany, or to break with Germany, joining with the democratic countries, firmly and decisively rising in defense of their sovereignty and the very existence of their State."

Izvestia disputes the arguments being put forward inside the "satellite countries" by "servants of Hitler" and joined by some people inside the democratic countries, that it is dangerous for such countries as Rumania, Bulgaria and Finland to break with Hitler because such an act would cause the Germans to transform their countries into a destructive, bloody battleground.

Such arguments are offered, Izvestia said, not only to "move to pity some 'tender-hearted people,'" but also to hide first of all the fact that it is not breaking away from Germany but on the contrary retaining union with Germany that inevitably entails catastrophe for the satellite countries."

Hungary's experience is a good answer to this argument, Izvestia argued, contending that the only help the satellites can expect from Hitler would be "treachery, violence and banditry."

The restrained tone of the editorial and the arguments it put forward are regarded here as confirmation that the door to early peace with Finland is not firmly shut despite the Soviet Government's announcement last week that Finland must bear responsibility for all consequences of her refusal to accept what are generally considered generous terms.

It is also regarded as explanation why the Soviet Government has not yet reported any advance across the Rumanian border by Marshal Ivan S. Koneff's troops now at the Prut River on an eighty to 100 mile front.

### Ploesti Destruction Expected

By Wireless to The New York Times

BERNE, Switzerland, March 29—Private reports through neutral channels from Bucharest tonight said German technicians in the Ploesti oil fields had begun dismantling mobile equipment and were preparing the total destruction of the wells and such equipment as could not be moved should the Russian drive take a sudden turn "for the worse."

Simultaneously, German forces, which have replaced Rumanian police in the oil field area, proclaimed a state of siege and ordered the evacuation of Rumanian civilians in a twenty-five mile radius from Ploesti. Other preparatory measures include transport to the Reich of all available petroleum reserves.

Forty-eight hours behind events, the Rumanian people received an inkling of the gravity of the situation in a semi-official broadcast referring to artillery barrages across the Prut.

### Bulgarian-Soviet Accord Seen

By Cable to The New York Times

ANKARA, Turkey, March 28 (Delayed)—There have been unconfirmed reports here that the Soviet Union has informed the Sofia Government it would consider it an unfriendly act if Bulgaria extended any kind of military aid to Rumania. Recently Alexander Lavrideff, Soviet Minister to Sofia, went to Moscow and his departure was interpreted as a warning to Bulgarians that the Kremlin would declare war against them if they gave military assistance to the Rumanians or the Germans.

However, competent quarters here discredit these reports, contending the Russians are so sure of pro-Soviet sympathies among the Bulgarian masses that they can afford to ignore the puppet government.

Ever since March, 1941, when Bulgaria joined the Axis and German divisions marched into the country, the Germans have exerted every effort to uproot pro-Russian Bulgarian sentiments, but have failed. The only price Bulgaria agreed to pay for the large territories acquired from Greece, Yugoslavia and Rumania was to serve as an army of occupation in the two former countries, relieving Nazi troops for other fronts, but not one Bulgarian was sent to the eastern theatre. It is considered significant that just when the Germans are receiving deadly blows from the Red Army, Sofia's quislings find it expedient to prove to the people that the Government is not unfriendly toward Russia.

\*   \*   \*

April 3, 1944

### GREEK UNDERGROUND DRAFTS NEW CONSTITUTION TO PROVIDE STRONGER PARLIAMENTARY RULE

Determined "that the political future of Greece shall not be planned by groups abroad," Greek underground forces have formed a united political front and drafted a new Constitution to eliminate the weaknesses of the country's old parliamentary system, André Michalopoulos, former Minister of Information, said yesterday in a radio speech on the Columbia Broadcasting System network.

Mr. Michalopoulos said that the document had been framed by distinguished parliamentarians and jurists and that they intended to submit it "to the representatives of the nation as soon as the enemy is driven out."

The proposed new Constitution provides for the election of Parliament for periods of four years. The Premier would be chosen by Parliament, not appointed by the majority party, as in the case of most European Governments.

"One of the disadvantages of the present European parliamentary system," Mr. Michalopoulos said, "is that the party which has the majority in the legislature forms the Government. If the largest party in opposition has a membership only slightly inferior in numbers to the Government party, by combining with a very small minority group of, let us say, Communists or Fascists, it can quite legally overthrow the Government. This procedure gives excessive power to small groups and therefore deviates from the principles of true democracy. It also often results in a rapid succession of widely divergent Governments, and therefore creates instability. This has been particularly noticeable in France in the recent past."

Other important points in the proposed Constitution, Mr. Michalopoulos said, included judicial machinery to insure the democratic functioning of trade unions on the basis of majority rule, and a permanent labor-dispute arbitration board composed of representatives of workers, employers and Government officials, headed by a judge of the Supreme Court. The proposed Constitution also calls for social-security legislation and a supreme political court to check all abuses by Ministers of State and high officials.

The draft, Mr. Michalopoulos said, did not specify whether the head of the state would be a King or a President, "for the leaders of the underground are agreed that the question of the monarchy is to be referred to the free decision of the people by plebiscite."

\*   \*   \*

April 8, 1944

### POST-WAR DEMOCRACY

One of the greatest problems of the post-war period will be the restoration and maintenance in Europe of stable democracies. It would be a tragedy if the terrible lessons of the last quarter century were still unlearned, and if Europe were to return to the type of unstable democracies that fell prey to internal dissensions and proved such easy victims for fascism and dictatorship. Primarily, of course, the maintenance of democracy after the war will be possible only with a healthy public opinion; but a determining role will also be played by the kind of Constitutions that are set up.

It is gratifying to learn that even in the midst of terror and chaos men in the occupied countries are thinking seriously and sanely on this subject. Nothing could be more heartening than the radio talk made a few days ago, for example, by André Michalopoulos, the former Greek Minister of Information, concerning a proposed new Greek Constitution drafted by "distinguished parliamentarians and jurists" representing a united political front of the underground. The mere fact that the men in such a position would have the heart and hope to draft any Constitution would alone be remarkable; but what is even more encouraging is the evidence that these men, whose suffering is in part due to the mistakes of pre-war democracy, see clearly what some of the basic faults of the prewar democratic Constitutions were, and are determined not to repeat them.

The principal provision in the proposed new Constitution is described by Mr. Michalopoulos as follows:

The people will elect the Parliament for periods of four years, and the Prime Minister will be chosen by Parliament—not appointed by the party of the majority. The Prime Minister in turn appoints his Government and in the event of a radical dissension between Parliament and Prime Minister, Parliament is dissolved, a new Parliament is immediately elected by the people and this new Parliament elects its Prime Minister.

This system is calculated to make for stability, because when the legislature knows that it cannot, as heretofore, change the Government as often as it chooses, by internal maneuvers, but that 3it too, has to go with the Government, its members will be more cautious and will not be likely to sacrifice their seats and authority by opposing the Government on trivial issues. In the case of a major issue a direct appeal is made to the people. Thus, it seems to me, both stability and democracy are safeguarded.

Though there are differences in details, basically this is the kind of parliamentary Government that exists in Great Britain. Wherever the Prime Minister has the real power of dissolution, there is stable and responsible Government. Wherever he does not have this power, as in the Third French Republic there is instability and intrigue, and a change in the Ministry every few months. It has been the great mistake of many sincere democrats to believe that the best protection against dictatorship is a weak Executive. On the contrary, the best protection against dictatorship is a strong Executive—provided that the latter is always made accountable to the people, and that the Government can be changed promptly and in a peaceful manner when it no longer has public support.

The political history of Greece in the last twenty years has been a particularly unhappy one, oscillating from monarchy to republic to dictatorship. But whatever the rate of the proposed new Greek Constitution, what is important is that men in the occupied countries of Europe recognize that the alternative to despotism is not a weak democracy that drifts from one parliamentary crisis to another, but a strong and stable democracy whose leaders can speak with force and authority.

\*   \*   \*

April 27, 1944

# VENIZELOS RESIGNS AS GREEK PREMIER

*Succeeded by Papandreou at King's Request—Views of Allies at Variance*

By C. L. SULZBERGER
By Wireless to The New York Times

CAIRO, Egypt, April 26—The Greek political crisis accompanying the recent serious mutiny that was crushed early this week was temporarily solved by the appointment of a new government, it was disclosed today.

Sopohocles Venizelos, who served as Premier for barely a fortnight, and his interim Cabinet resigned late last Sunday and, after a series of consultations, King George requested George Papandreou to serve as Premier. He was sworn in yesterday and will serve as his own Foreign Minister.

Mr. Papandreou is a rather well known politician and one of the leaders of the remnants of a liberal and basically republican party. He recently escaped from Greece and is certainly the best known political figure among those who have found refuge abroad in a long time. Mr. Papandreou is favorably looked on by both the British and the American Embassies.

### Must See Emissaries

The first important task awaiting the new Cabinet will almost certainly be an important conference with the emissaries of the various guerrilla and political factions within Greece with a view to achieving some form of compromise and to working out the salvation of the country, still ravaged by intermittent civil war. Any solution of the present crisis, both within and without the country, among politically minded Greeks will certainly be difficult, but it is regarded as imperative that concrete decisions be made soon to prepare a basis for the country's eventual liberation.

The attitude of the great powers is showing some signs of crystallizing. For a long time there was a paradoxical situation in which the British military authorities, following the precept of aiding all groups fighting the Germans, gave considerable assistance to the left Wing and Communist-led Elas, the guerrillas of a political organization called the EAM, without troubling about future political results while the Foreign Office adamantly opposed a short-term policy pregnant with the danger of a Communist dictatorship.

### British Policy Untried

Now it is clear that the British policy has been unified and, although it hopes for a complete compromise among all factions, it will not tolerate dictation over the others by the Eam. The American policy does not permit backing any faction and is purely moral in its effect, since the Eastern Mediterranean is obviously a British sphere of influence, but it is evident that the State Department is inclined to look with equal disfavor on any Eam aspirations to control Greece.

Russia, on the other hand, has recently, for the first time, evinced a definite interest in Greek affairs and, through her press and radio, she has indicated her support of the Eam. Russia has also indicated her sympathy with the mutineers who have just been crushed and attacked many loyal factions as "Fascists" in her propaganda.

While no further details may yet be given regarding the revolt in the Greek Army because of the strictest censorship, it may be said that in subduing the naval mutiny nine men, including two officers, were killed and thirty-five were wounded. A one-hour battle with small arms occurred aboard the corvette Saktouris. The destroyer Israx was subdued within fifteen minutes and a second corvette in ten minutes.

\* \* \*

**April 27, 1944**

## BRITAIN HARASSED BY WOES OF ALLIES

*Greeks' Internal Dissension is Latest Problem—Linked to Yugoslav Question*

By Cable to The New York Times

LONDON, April 26—Britain is suffering from an embarrassment of riches in the matter of allies.

The country that once fought Germany alone is finding it increasingly difficult, as victory becomes more certain, to keep small nations' attention focused on the common enemy. As the prospect of liberation brightens and external pressure is removed the temptation to engage in civil strife increases and the exiled Governments that were welcomed so eagerly in 1940 and 1941 are beginning now to prove something of a problem, although few would be so impolite as to put it quite that way.

Now the Greeks are proving difficult. Their trouble is the same one that besets other exiled Governments in one form or another—that ideas and movements have been brewing at home under the German occupation that tend to make the exiled Government somewhat anachronistic. To a somewhat greater extent, the same thing is true of Yugoslavia, where Britain, which has recognized a Government loyal to King Peter, finds itself forced by military necessity to provide practical support to Marshal Tito while denying it to Gen. Draja Mikhailovitch, who takes his orders from the recognized Government, at least in theory.

### French Also a Problem

The Netherlands and Norway have not proved problem-children of the grand alliance, but Gen. Charles de Gaulle and the French Committee of National Liberation have raised issues that remain to be ironed out between Washington and London. President Eduard Benes and the Czech Government have not raised any serious problems, but there is a group of Slovaks in London who challenge its authority. The Poles have caused this country considerable

embarrassment, by lambasting Russia in unofficial publications, by their diplomatic break with Russia and finally by the airing of charges of religious persecution against Jews and Orthodox Ukrainians and White Russians in their army.

The Poles have had their difficulties for some time and the British have come to accept them as part of the burden that they have to bear. The Yugoslav troubles have been difficult. But now it is becoming apparent that a situation similar to that of Yugoslavia, but different enough to preclude the possibility of a common formula, is shaping up in Greece.

### Backed by Britain

The King of Greece has declared his intention of forming a government "as representative as possible, made up of all trends of patriotic opinion, to the exclusion only of those who have collaborated with the enemy against their fellow countrymen in the common cause."

"The British Government," Mr. Churchill said, "is in full agreement with this policy and will give the King and his Government all possible support in its execution."

At that time, Premier Sophocles Venizelos held about all the portfolios. A few hours later, however, it was announced that Mr. Venizelos' Government had resigned and George Papandreou, leader of the Social Democrats, had been sworn in as Premier and Foreign Minister.

The Greek and Yugoslav problems are linked up in some ways, because King George is a sort of protector of King Peter of Yugoslavia and there are marked points of similarity between the rise of the leftist Eam movement in Greece and the growth of Marshal Tito's organization in Yugoslavia. Both have a strong Communist slant.

The official British attitude is that the Eam has been expending more energy in fighting Greeks than in fighting Germans. Leftist circles here say that the Government is as badly misled on this score as it was on Marshal Tito for a long time.

\* \* \*

**May 14, 1944**

## 15,000 MOSLEMS JOIN TITO

*2 Brigades Formed by Partisans—Recruits Prove Their Worth*

BARI, Italy, May 8 (delayed) (AP)—Nearly 15,000 Moslems now are fighting in the ranks of the Yugoslav Liberation Army, a spokesman for the Partisan mission in Italy reported today.

After streaming into liberated territories from the occupied sections of Bosnia and Macedonia they have been placed in two all-Moslem brigades and in some smaller detachments assigned to the various corps of Marshal Tito's armies.

They share supplies and equipment on an equal basis with other Partisan outfits and their ability to travel swiftly and lightly has made them invaluable to the guerrilla warfare being waged in many sections of the Yugoslav hinterland.

The first Moslem brigade was formed four months ago and it has particularly distinguished itself in western Bosnia, the spokesman said.

\* \* \*

May 15, 1944

## TITO, IN INTERVIEW, CITES NAZI TACTICS

### Allied Newsmen Have Dinner With Yugoslav Leader in Mountain Fastness

By JOHN TALBOT
Reuter Correspondent
For the Combined Allied Press

MARSHAL TITO'S HEADQUARTERS in the Yugoslav Mountains, May 10 (Delayed)—High up in the Yugoslav mountains, less than twenty miles from where the Partisans are putting up a magnificent fight against the Germans, Marshal Tito has the most impregnable headquarters of any commanding general in the world.

The Germans have tried to get it.

Some time ago fifteen German dive-bombers tried to blast the Yugoslav marshal from his eyrie. They failed completely.

The headquarters are a series of natural caves running in a gallery straight into the sides of a deep ravine.

Last night my American colleague, two Allied cameramen and I had dinner with Tito in his incredible lair. Also present were Gen. Arsu Yvanovitch, his chief of staff; M. Chokalovitch, secretary of the Anti-Fascist Council, and M. Kardelz, Vice President of the Yugoslav National Committee.

To reach Tito's headquarters our guards, who were changed three times during the journey from our billets, led us along a rough path cut out of the rock and up the side of a ravine. Beside us, for part of our journey, a great waterfall plumed down in a thundering white cascade into the dim, moonlit valley far below. At times we clung to rocks as the path twisted and turned round jutting spurs and ledges.

At length we arrived at the top to find the Marshal waiting to welcome us. He led us into the study of a small, simply furnished apartment.

A long dining table stands against a wall facing two windows which look directly down over the ravine and out into the valley. The chairs are all simple, wooden affairs. On three walls are maps, including a large-scale one of Yugoslavia.

### Calls Ustashis Good Soldiers

The meeting with the marshal was completely informal, and we discussed a variety of topics. The marshal does not like to talk in English as he does not consider himself sufficiently fluent. He can, however, read it easily. We spoke with him mostly through the American correspondent, Stoyan Pribichevich (Time and Life correspondent), who is a Serbian by birth.

The marshal wore the blue-gray uniform of the National Army of Liberation, with his marshal's insignia on his sleeves and collar. He is some 5 feet 8 inches tall, very strongly built and has an exceedingly strong face, which at first strikes one as being stern until one sees the lines of laughter at the corners of his eyes and mouth.

I asked him if he thought that German and Quisling troops had any plans for another offensive against the Partisans.

"No," he answered. "I do not think they have.

"The main German concern at the moment is to keep the forces of the National Army of Liberation split into groups throughout the country.

"German tactics at present consist of minor thrusts in various localities, with the idea of making the Partisan soldiers use up their scanty stores of ammunition and thus immobilize them.

"We are finding now that the German soldier is deteriorating as a fighter and is not what he used to be a year ago. By far the best soldier the enemy has is the Ustashi (Yugoslav puppet troops). I think one Ustashi is two Germans against us. Chetniks definitely are bad soldiers."

### Allied Censorship Assailed

LONDON, May 14 (AP)—The British weekly Reynolds News, commenting on the suppression of an Associated Press interview with Marshal Tito, said editorially today that "once again censors of the Allied military command in the Mediterranean have acted as a political gag."

"The interview given by Marshal Tito to an Associated Press correspondent has been stopped.

"Tito is the acknowledged war leader of the Yugoslav people. To ban a statement by him is tantamount to banning a statement by Stalin or de Gaulle, Churchill or Roosevelt," it declared.

\* \* \*

May 21, 1944

## MIKHAILOVITCH OUT IN YUGOSLAV SHIFTS

### King Drops Tito Rival as War Minister, Directs Subasitch to Form New Cabinet

By The United Press

LONDON, May 20—King Peter of Yugoslavia announced today that Gen. Draja Mikhailovitch, who Partisan leaders assert has collaborated with the Germans against them, had been relieved of his post as Minister of War in the Yugoslav Government in Exile.

The youthful monarch followed this announcement with an emphatic denial of press reports that he would form a regency or a committee of three to replace the Cabinet of Prime Minister Bozidar Pouritch.

[An Associated Press dispatch from London Saturday said that the Pouritch Cabinet was dismissed Friday and that King Peter had directed Dr. Ivan Subasitch, former Governor of Croatia, to form a coalition cabinet.]

It was understood that General Mikhailovitch would remain commander in chief of the Royal Yugoslav Army, which now is reported to consist of a skeleton force of 20,000. It appeared that a strong new attempt would be made to effect a reconciliation between him and Marshal Tito, head of the National Liberation Army, to unify Yugoslavia before the Allies strike against Germany in the east and west.

The successor to General Mikhailovitch as War Minister, Peter said, will not be an army man. This silenced speculation that the post might be offered to Gen. Dusan Simovitch, former Premier, or Gen. Vladimir Velebit, head of Marshal Tito's military mission now in London.

Reports that a regency would be formed instead of a new Cabinet were carried in dispatches by the Exchange Telegraph Agency, which said that the regency would offer a chance to establish contact with the provisional government of Marshal Tito. The Yugoslav Partisan Government previously refused to recognize any government formed outside the country.

King Peter denied rumors that the new Cabinet would be formed by General Simovitch, who led Yugoslavia's revolt against the Germans when they invaded the Balkans.

The King explained that he was attempting to form a "neutral" government which would have the best interests of the country at heart and which would not be prejudiced in any way, indicating that any person who openly declared loyalty to General Mikhailovitch or Marshal Tito would not be included.

"Reports concerning the establishment of a regency or a committee of three are pure nonsense," Peter declared in an interview with The United Press. "If there is to be anything, it will be a government. I have already accomplished something toward establishing a new government. It is succeeding quite satisfactorily and I hope to be able to announce the composition of the Cabinet soon. It will be a neutral government."

It was understood that Peter had conferred with Prime Minister Churchill twice within the last two weeks. Usually reliable quarters said they understood that the King had refused a suggestion by the British Prime Minister that he make a public declaration promising a plebiscite after the war whether he should return to the country.

\*    \*    \*

**June 3, 1944**

## TITO AND CHURCHILL'S SON ESCAPE AS AIRBORNE NAZIS CAPTURE BASE

By The Associated Press

BARI, Italy, May 29 (Delayed)—German paratroopers, supported by glider-borne infantry, swarmed down and captured the Bosnian headquarters of Marshal Tito on May 25

but failed to catch the wily Yugoslav leader, Partisan sources disclosed today.

Field Marshal Erwin Rommel, whose whereabouts had been a mystery for weeks, was said to have directed the attack personally.

Marshal Tito escaped to the mountains along with Major Randolph Churchill, son of the British Prime Minister, and virtually all Allied officers attached to Marshal Tito's staff.

Two Allied correspondents, Stoyan Pribichevich of Time, Life and Fortune magazines, John Talbot of Reuter, and two photographers were captured in the Nazi stroke, but Mr. Pribichevich escaped later during a Partisan attack on the Nazis.

A blistering Stuka dive-bombing attack at 6 A. M. preceded the airborne assault on the headquarters, situated in a vast grotto near Drvar, seventy miles north of Spalato. Paratroopers and gliders followed quickly, coordinating their attack with a powerful ground assault in which tanks led the way.

With bitter fighting raging over a wide area and vantage points changing hands numerous times, German transports and additional gliders poured in more men, field pieces and supplies throughout the afternoon, night and following day.

Marshal Tito's Partisans regained much ground the first night but on the second day the enemy managed to push an armored column into Drvar, meanwhile taking the important airport of Petrovac, fourteen miles north, and bombing several Partisan towns in the vicinity.

Planes of the United States Fifteenth Air Force and the Royal Air Force went to the aid of Marshal Tito's men. Flying Fortresses pounded the big German supply operations center at Bihac on May 26, Liberators roared across the Adriatic twice and plastered troop concentrations at nine different points.

At the same time P-38's and Spitfires beat up the area thoroughly, attacking transports, troops and airfields from which the paratroopers took off. One formation caught a troop train near Podjice and left it in flames with more than 100 Nazis hanging from the windows and strewn along the tracks.

Ground troops employed in the Nazi effort to trap Marshal Tito were estimated unofficially here at four divisions at least. Striking from Bihac, forty miles northwest, from Banjaluka, forty-eight miles northeast and Livno, fifty miles southeast, they sought to envelop the Yugoslav High Command and members of Allied missions. In addition a full air-borne division was believed to have landed.

Withdrawing into the Dinaric Alps where the Partisans know every goat trail, Marshal Tito and his staff had been gone an hour before the first enemy troops reached the stronghold from where the Marshal had directed Partisan operations for more than a year. Headquarters was so organized that it could move on thirty minutes notice.

Members of the British mission, taking note of recent strengthening of German forces in the vicinity, had moved to the outskirts of the area several days before the attack. American and Russian groups likewise were well removed, but the correspondents and two cameramen were billeted in the center of town and had less opportunity to escape.

### Nazis Open Wide Attacks

LONDON, June 2 (AP)—The Germans, apparently alarmed at the seriousness of the situation in Yugoslavia and the growing strength of the Partisan army, have launched a large-scale offensive against liberated territory, Marshal Tito declared today.

A communiqué broadcast from his headquarters said the offensive was begun several days ago in western Bosnia with more than three Nazi divisions participating.

\* \* \*

August 24, 1944

# BREAK IN BALKANS

*King Proclaims Nation's Surrender and Wish to Help Allies*

### NAZIS IN AREA FIGHT

*New Bucharest Regime Asks United Nations Aid
Against Hungary*

By DANIEL T. BRIGHAM
By Telephone to The New York Times

BERNE, Switzerland, Aug. 23—In a brief proclamation to the Rumanian people broadcast from Bucharest at 9:25 o'clock this evening, King Michael of Rumania ordered his armed forces to cease fire against the forces of the Allies, saying he had accepted their terms of unconditional surrender in the name of the nation.

The youthful King called on the nation to take up the fight immediately by the side of the Soviet forces on Rumanian soil against their common enemy, Germany.

Dramatic and apparently sudden as was the entire announcement the Germans were obviously forewarned, for when the home broadcast service at Bucharest interrupted its regular transmission at 9:24 P. M., within thirty seconds the two powerful Bucharest transmitters were shrouded by interference from a battery of German jammers of all varieties.

[Moscow, which broadcast the Rumanian surrender—beaming it especially to Germany—soon after the Bucharest announcement, reported later in the night that German troops were fighting Rumanian forces that were withdrawing from the Red Army front.

### Bulgaria Expected to Quit

[Bulgaria's withdrawal from the war was believed to be imminent, according to reports from Cairo, which said the Allies were insisting on the return of territory seized in the war.]

King Michael, who had until recently been virtually a prisoner of the Gestapo, has overthrown the pro-Nazi dictatorship, ousting the Premier and Commander in Chief, Marshal Ion Antonescu. [The Berne radio, heard by Columbia Broadcasting System, said early Thursday that Antonescu had fled to Germany.]

He named as Chief of Government and Marshal of Rumania the master of his military household, Gen. Constantin Sanatescu. He announced a new Cabinet that constituted a Government of national union.

The new Cabinet includes Peasant party leader Juliu Maniu, as Minister of State Without Portfolio, and the leader of the Liberal party, Dinu Bratianu, in a similar post.

[Lucretiu Patrascanu, a Rumanian Communist party leader, and Constantin Petrescu, a Socialist leader, were also named Ministers of State, said a Bucharest broadcast recorded by the Federal Communications Commission.]

### War With Hungary Evident

The new Rumanian Government is made up of a wide grouping of forces from the liberal, independent center to the extreme left.

King Michael's proclamation announced the denunciation by Rumania of the Treaty of Vienna of Aug. 30, 1940, by which the Nazis gave Transylvania to Hungary. It made it plain that Rumania is now at war with Hungary to recover Transylvania and seeks Allied backing in that effort.

A new Rumanian General Staff, as well as the country's political leaders, met at the King's palace, all approaches to which were being heavily guarded lest some of the numerous Gestapo agents still in Bucharest attempt to intervene.

A German garrison in Bucharest, which earlier attempted to surround the King's place, has been disarmed and interned, pending further disposition, by the Rumanian Army.

The first announcement of Rumania's surrender, barely audible over the racket caused by the German attempts to join the Bucharest broadcast, came as the voice of a person, identified by Rumanians here as the King himself, read the proclamation firmly.

The King's speech and proclamation were rebroadcast at least four times in the course of the night, but receivers here have not been able to get the full text.

The King was heard to repeat at one point in his address that the nation's new leaders after careful consideration had deemed the time now arrived for Rumania to take her fate into her own hands.

Still further was a passage seemingly announcing that Rumanian forces were deployed along the Hungarian frontier of ceded Transylvania and had begun their entry into that territory to recapture it, supported on their right flank by the advancing Russians.

### First Balkan Satellite to Quit

By Cable to The New York Times

LONDON, Thursday, Aug. 24—Rumania deserted the Axis and joined the United Nations last night.

King Michael told his people that they had changed sides and not very long afterward the Moscow radio announced that the retreating Rumanian forces were being attacked by their former German comrades in arms.

The news from Bucharest of the formation of a Government friendly to the Allies and hostile to the Nazis will take quite some explaining by Reich Propaganda Minister Joseph Goebbels. Rumania is the first Axis satellite to desert Germany. The Bulgarian situation is in a state of flux.

These are the first fruits of Turkey's severance of diplomatic relations with the Reich.

The Balkan countries that cast their lot with Germany in the first flush of Nazi success are beginning to second-guess themselves. Rumania's action confirms reports that the one thought of the Balkan countries is to finish the war on the winning side and salvage what they can from the wreckage of Hitler's promises to them.

With the Peasant party leader, Juliu Maniu, and the Liberal leader, Dinu Bratianu, in King Michael's new Cabinet, a national-unity regime has been formed for the transition period between Axis satellite and member of the United Nations.

### Molotoff Stated Russia's Policy

The armistice terms accepted by Rumania are based on the statement by Soviet Foreign Commissar Vyacheslaff M. Molotoff at the time the Red Army crossed into Rumanian territory last spring, reaffirming Russian claims to Bessarabia and northern Bukhovina, but assuring Rumania that the Soviet Union had no further territorial claims and would not interfere in the social or economic affairs of Rumania.

Rumania hopes that by being the first satellite to desert the Axis she will be allowed to recover Transylvania, which was given to Hungary under Hitler's Vienna award of August, 1940. In that award Hitler as arbiter gave half of Transylvania and border provinces inhabited mostly by Magyars to Hungary. Rumania lost more than 2,500,000 citizens, including more than 1,000,000 Rumanians.

Politically and militarily Rumania's desertion of the Axis is a major triumph for the Allies.

What military force Rumania's surrender will release to the Allies is not known. Military observers here say it means that Allied forces can be brought to the borders of eastern Yugoslavia and the Bulgarian frontier and that it will deprive the German war machine of the output of the Ploesti oilfields, which the Germans have needed badly since 1941.

But, more important, Rumania's new political orientation and her new military direction endanger the German Army group fighting to hold the Galati gap between the Carpathians and Black Sea.

Two main strategic consequences of Rumania's surrender can be expected logically. They are that something approaching thirty Red Army divisions are freed, with the road to Bulgaria, eastern Yugoslavia and Hungary open to them, and that the rear of the German group between the Carpathians and the Black Sea is threatened.

### NEW RUMANIAN CABINET
#### Bucharest Declares Amnesty and End of Concentration Camps

The Bucharest radio, in a late broadcast yesterday, reported by the Federal Communications Commission, said that Gen. Constantin Sanatescu had been named to head the new Rumanian Cabinet and that a new Army Chief of Staff and mayor of Bucharest had also been appointed.

Gen. Gheorghe Mikhail was named Chief of Staff and Brig. Gen. Victor Dongorschi as mayor and prefect of the Rumanian capital.

Besides Premier Sanatescu, the broadcast listed the members of the new Rumanian Cabinet as follows:

Ministers of State—Juliu Maniu, of the Peasant Party; Dinu Bratianu, of the Liberal Party; Lucretiu Patrascanu, a Communist leader; Constantin Petrescu, a Socialist leader.

National Defense—Gen. Michael Racovita.

Foreign Affairs—Grigore Niculescu-Buzesti.

Interior—Gen. Aurel Aldea.

National Economy and Finance—Gen. Gheorghe Potopeanu.

Labor and Public Health—Gen. Dr. Nicolae Marinescu.

Agriculture and Domains—Dimitrie Decutescu.

Public Works and Communications—Gen. Dimitrie Dumitru.

National Education—Gen. Ion Voiceanu.

Under-Secretaries of State—Air, Gen. Ilie Gheorghiu; Navy, Vice Admiral Ion Georgescu; Interior, Gen. Gheorgo Iuteanu and Col. Dumitru Damaceanu.

Premier Sanatescu late in the night broadcast a declaration of the new Government, also reported by the FCC, saying it included National Liberal, National Peasant, Communist and Social Democrat representatives and would constitute "a democratic regime in which public freedom and the rights of citizens will be guaranteed and respected."

Of the Allies' armistice terms, the declaration said:

"With the intermediary of authorized representatives, the Governments of the Union of Soviet Socialist Republics, Great Britain and the United States have guaranteed the independence of Rumania and, while respecting her national sovereignty, they will refrain from any interference with the internal affairs of our State. . . . As from today onward Rumania considers the United Nations as friendly nations."

### Concentration Camps Ended

The new Government of Rumania "has already broadcast its first two decrees: these are an amnesty for political crimes since 1918, except certain cases such as assassinations; the closure of all concentration camps and the restoration of full liberty of the internees," the London radio reported last night in a broadcast recorded by Columbia Broadcasting System.

In another broadcast recorded by the FCC the British radio said there was no official comment in London on the Bucharest announcement of Rumania's surrender, but it recalled that Prime Minister Churchill had declared in the House of Commons on Aug. 2 that "Russia has offered generous terms to Rumania."

The British broadcast also recalled that later in the Commons debate Foreign Secretary Anthony Eden had told the House that Russia's terms for Rumania had been approved by Britain before they were submitted to Bucharest.

Three and a half hours before the Bucharest broadcast of the proclamation by King Michael the German Foreign Office's NPD agency transmitted a wireless dispatch to Nazi diplomats and agents abroad declaring that all was "calm" in Rumania.

### Nazis Broadcast Denounciation

The German radio, broadcasting in Rumanian to Rumania early today, denounced the small clique of traitors who have put aside Marshal Antonescu and appealed to the people to obey only the orders of a Nazi-puppet "Rumanian National Government," which Berlin said, "has been formed to continue fighting together with the Germans against Russian Bolshevism."

The German broadcast, beamed over Nazi propaganda transmitters in the Balkans and reported by the FCC, gave no indication as to where the alleged pro-German Government had been formed nor the names of the persons forming it.

Immediate reactions elsewhere in southwestern Europe were indicated. A broadcast by the Hungarian Telegraph Agency, heard by the FCC, said that the Budapest Cabinet of Premier Doeme Sztojay had conferred on "current questions."

The Associated Press from London reported an announcement by the Bratislava radio saying that the puppet government of Slovakia had "held a meeting and discussed urgent problems" and that "important decisions had been taken." A part of Czechoslovakia, Slovakia was declared an independent state under German "protection" in March, 1939. Dr. Joseph Tiso is its puppet president.

Rumania joined the Axis in November, 1940, and when Germany attacked Russia on June 22, 1941, she followed with a declaration of war against the Soviet Union. Rumania declared war against Britain Dec. 6, 1941, and against the United States on Dec. 12, 1941.

\* \* \*

September 1, 1944

# BULGARIANS BEGIN SURRENDER TALKS

---

*Representatives Reported in Conference With Briton—Soviet Press Hits Sofia*

---

By C. L. SULZBERGER
By Wireless to The New York Times

CAIRO, Egypt, Aug. 31—The first parleys in final armistice negotiations between Hitler's satellite Bulgaria and the Allied representatives were held here this morning, according to apparently reliable reports. Lord Moyne attended as British representative. Lincoln MacVeagh, United States representative, has not yet arrived and late this afternoon it was believed he would not get here today as scheduled.

Although it has been said officially that negotiations might take a little longer than originally thought, this writer believes they will be pretty swift once all the Allied emissaries and all the Bulgarian delegates show up. There are only five main points to the terms and the Bulgars had a pretty good idea what they were before they came here.

Rumors are going around today that the final signature may after all be arranged elsewhere, but this correspondent is informed that this is most unlikely.

### Bulgaria Seals Frontier

ISTANBUL, Turkey, Aug. 31 (AP)—Bulgaria sealed the Turkish-Bulgarian frontier today.

The closing of the border to all traffic was taken to mean that German diplomats awaiting exchange in Turkey, which recently severed diplomatic relations with Germany, would be unable to leave this country.

### Rumanians Study Terms

MOSCOW, Aug. 31 (AP)—Seven Rumanian delegates accompanied by a woman newspaper reporter studied at the official Soviet guest house tonight the terms by which their kingdom would be allowed an armistice with the Allies.

The Soviet Foreign Office consulted the British and American Embassies today before the negotiations began, it was learned. The possibility arose that the three powers might join in a declaration concerning Rumania's claim to northern Transylvania, annexed by Hungary in 1940 with Hitler's approval.

### Soviet Press Assails Bulgaria

MOSCOW, Aug. 31—The Soviet press, whose Government is not at war with Bulgaria, accused the Bulgarian Government today of violating its newly announced policy of "complete neutrality" by harboring German ships and submarines fleeing from the Russians in the Black Sea, by permitting the escape of German forces with their material from Bulgaria and by accepting German equipment that cannot be removed to Germany in payment of German debts to Bulgaria.

All Moscow newspapers feature a series of sharply worded articles today in which it is stated without qualification that the Bulgarian Government does not really intend to make a basic change in its pro-Hitlerite policy, despite the fact that the Red Army now has driven virtually to the Bulgarian frontier.

\* \* \*

September 10, 1944

# SOVIET ENDS WAR WITH BULGARIANS

*Sofia Forms a New Cabinet—Veteran Communist Becomes One of the Regents*

By SYDNEY GRUSON

By Wireless to The New York Times

LONDON, Sept. 9—Bulgaria, rapidly ridding herself of the men who tied the country to Germany during the last four years, got her second new Government in two weeks tonight and an armistice in the four-day-old war with Russia.

Col. Kimon Georgieff, who headed the Government for a short time in 1934, was installed as Premier, succeeding Constantin Muravieff's short-lived administration, with Prof. Petko Stoyanoff as Foreign Minister and Col. Damien Veltcheff, the strong man behind the Georgieff Government of 1934, as War Minister.

The new Cabinet, which has a military cast, probably will act only until the peace terms, now being drawn up by the Allies, are accepted, when it is expected in London that a leftist Government will take the helm.

The Russian decision to grant an armistice to Bulgaria was announced by the Moscow radio, which a short time later broadcast an order of the day from Marshal Stalin declaring that by her actions of the last two days "Bulgaria has ceased to be a center of German influence in the Balkans, which she had formerly been for the last thirty years."

Completing the break-up of the Regency established with German connivance after the death of King Boris, the new Government deposed the old Regents, Prince Cyril and Gen. Nikola Mikoff, and arrested all Cabinet Ministers of the Government in power on January, 1941, and all members of Parliament who voted for its pro-Axis policy. A third Regent, Bogdan Philoff, resigned last night.

A veteran leader of the Communist party, Todor Pavloff, is one of the two new Regents appointed by Premier Georgieff. He had been held in a concentration camp recently during Nazi-inspired oppressive action against Communists. The other Regent is Prof. Venelin Ganeff, a Professor of constitutional law, who has no political connections.

In cooperation with the Russian Black Sea Fleet the Red Army occupied Burgas, a big port fifty miles south of the port of Varna, the capture of which was announced yesterday. The Germans admitted today that the Russian Fleet holds supremacy in the Black Sea. Although the Germans claimed they had scuttled their ships, the swiftness of the Russian advance to the coast is believed to have netted more than 100 German vessels.

A Bulgarian delegation appointed by the new Government will discuss with Gen. Fedor I. Tolbukhin, commander of the Soviet Third Ukrainian Army, terms for the re-establishment of relations with Russia and questions of Russian-Bulgarian cooperation against Germany, the Sofia radio reported tonight.

Kimon Georgieff

### The New Cabinet

LONDON, Sunday, Sept. 10 (U.P.)—The new Bulgarian Cabinet, as announced by Sofia, is:

Premier and Minister Without Portfolio—Kimon Georgieff.

War—Col. Damian Veltcheff.

Foreign—Prof. Petko Stoyanoff.

Without Portfolio—Nikola Petkoff.

Justice—Khristo Neytsheff.

Finance—Prof. Petko Stoyanoff.

Trade—Dimiter Neykoff.

Agriculture—Vasil Pavloff.

Public Works—Boris Bumbaroff.

Railways—Angel Derzhansky.

Public Health—Dr. Rayko Raysheff.

Social Affairs—Gregor Fetfadzhieff.

Propaganda—Dimo Kazakoff.

### Bulgarian Quisling Cabinet

The Berlin radio announced last night the formation of a Bulgarian "National Government," at the head of which is a former Bulgarian Prime Minister, Prof. Alexander Tankoff, who fled to Germany and whom the Berlin radio calls "a friend of the German nation and an advocate of close and sincere collaboration between Germany and Bulgaria."

The German broadcast was recorded by the Columbia Broadcasting System.

* * *

September 10, 1944

# RUSSIA EXTENDS HER SWAY OVER THE BALKAN COUNTRIES

---

*She Now Holds the Place of Power Which Her Statesmen Have Long Sought*

---

### By C. L. SULZBERGER
By Wireless to The New York Times

CAIRO, Egypt, Sept. 9—Russian influence in southeastern Europe, embracing, roughly, that area from Trieste to the Carpathians and the Danube delta, is today at a zenith never before attained in the complicated history of that area.

Russia's military prestige is unsurpassed. Her psychological impact is enormous in the chaos from the German disaster. Her proximity is immediate.

Along the South Slav belt from the Adriatic to the Black Sea there is no doubt that the Soviet Union is the great power among the United Nations in the average peasant mind, and this feeling is enhanced by a certain individual pride of many Montenegrins, Croats, Serbs and Bulgars in the prowess of Grandfather Ivan, who, as their proverb has always stated, would, in times of trouble, "come up the river to help us."

## Long Russian Tradition

Russia has a long tradition in the Balkan Peninsula. It was there that the Czar conducted the European part of that enormous pincer move through the Caucasus and Trans-Danubia designed to compress the Turkish Sultan's domain ever to the south.

On the other hand, intellectually and politically, although in every Balkan country it was forced to work underground, communism as a political force has been an exceedingly important, if usually silent, factor. The principal independence movements that mushroomed to importance under fascist hegemony in the Balkans were led by members of this veteran secret Communist force: Marshal Tito's Yugoslav Partisans, Greece's EAM and ELAS, and Bulgaria's Fatherland Front.

## Interest of Great Powers

What bearing the actual situation of the moment will have on the future of southeastern Europe can still only be guessed at, but probably with a certain amount of accuracy. Before entering the realms of speculation one must gauge the attitude of other great powers vis-a-vis this extremely important but traditionally misunderstood and mishandled portion of the Continent. France, which was the dominant power in southeast Europe in the wake of the last war's Austro-German collapse, had already abdicated that position before the start of the present conflict and it is highly improbable that she can ever regain it.

Britain has always had strong ties and influence with and in the Mediterranean States and the general Balkan region—Greece and Turkey—for both commercial and strategic reasons in times of peace and war. This still prevails and can be considered an element of London policy.

But in its strongest and most crystallized sense Britain would appear vitally concerned only with the area between the two narrows entering into the Mediterranean and the area lying between them: Otranto and the Dardanelles.

Boiling these great power interests down to their essentials, only four large powers are really intimately concerned with the Balkans as border States, either to their actual domains or to their imperial arteries—Germany, Italy, the U.S.S.R. and Britain. The first two are defeated powers whose influence is not to be reckoned with for some years to come.

As far as Moscow and London go, some clue as to the modus vivendi can be seen in the terms of the military agreement between the two which was arranged as a preliminary to the present Balkan offensive.

## Zones Already Agreed Upon

Initial steps toward outlining zones of "initiative" in the Balkans were agreed on by the British and Soviet Governments some months ago. Greece was definitely recognized by Moscow as Britain's military sphere of influence and Rumania was likewise recognized by London as within the Soviet's military sphere of influence. Thus, just as the Rumanian armistice parleys were under Soviet guidance, any future surrender of the Germans from Greece would have to be extended through the British. It would be a likely enough guess that the same reasons making for such military arrangements might carry on into a world at peace. In between lie Slavic States, and the magnetic pull of the mystical racial concepts prevailing among these peoples at this moment cannot be exaggerated.

Excluding these great power pulls and confining oneself to an analysis of the tendencies prevailing in the Balkans now, it is beginning to look as if Left Wing agrarian democracy is the prevailing fashion of thinking for future government modes. Certainly, at this moment in Yugoslavia, despite vigorous and dynamic opposition, large blocs of sturdy Serbs of the Tito movement claiming to desire something along those lines are in the ascendancy. In Bulgaria it is a likely solution when the shards of the Boris system are swept up.

## Future of the Balkans

Moscow is not believed to be particularly interested whether a king or a president heads future Balkan States and has professed itself as not desirous of altering the governmental forms desired by the peoples themselves. Thus, it is certainly within the realm of possibility that a monarch may continue to rule in Bucharest, Sofia and even—although it is less probable—in Belgrade. As far as Greece is concerned the people seem pretty well fed up with any sort of dynasty.

In its essence it would seem as if in the future the Balkans will have Left Wing democracy governments, at least in respect of their pre-war regimes, and will all be politically closely aligned to Moscow, which is determined to forestall any efforts to create an anti-Soviet cordon sanitaire in eastern Europe.

In the predominantly farming areas of small holdings, such as Bulgaria and Yugoslavia, politics and economics of Stambulisky's agrarianism appear increasingly influential. And one thing can be certain: now that the veteran active and experienced Communist parties of southeast Europe can work in the open without fear of repression and in the shadow of the Red Army's glory, they will have very powerful influence in all political thinking south of the Danube.

\*    \*    \*

**September 13, 1944**

# ARMISTICE GRANTED RUMANIA BY ALLIES

### *Russia, Britain and U. S. Act on Behalf of United Nations— Bulgars Fight Nazis*

By The Associated Press

LONDON, Wednesday, Sept. 13—The Moscow radio announced today that an armistice had been concluded with Rumania. Russia, Great Britain, and the United States acted on behalf of all the United Nations.

The broadcast, recorded by the Soviet monitor, said that the United States Ambassador, W. Averell Harriman; the British Ambassador, Sir Archibald Clark Kerr, and the Soviet Foreign Commissar, Vyacheslaff M. Molotoff, had participated in the negotiations, which continued two days and terminated yesterday.

The armistice was signed by Marshal Rodion Y. Malinovsky, whose army had swept through Rumania, on behalf of all three powers and the United Nations. General Damatcanu Stirby signed for Rumania.

Details of the terms were not made known immediately, but were expected to be announced later today.

The armistice announcement came as Russian and Rumanian troops were fighting side by side in the liberation of Transylvania—the province taken from Rumania by the Germans and handed to Hungary.

### Bulgars Fight Germans

A Bulgarian communiqué yesterday said fighting was taking place between Bulgarian troops withdrawing from Greece and German troops still stationed there. The Bulgars claimed they were fighting in full agreement with Yugoslav Partisan Marshal Tito and in collaboration with the Soviet Union, Britain and the United States.

Available reports indicated the Germans still were disengaging generally throughout the southern Balkans.

Meanwhile, the Czechoslovak press bureau in London announced that Slovak Partisans and regular Czech forces had destroyed the only two rail bridges east of Zilina, important Slovak junction eighty miles southwest of Cracow, Poland.

King Peter of Yugoslavia called on all Serbs, Croats and Slovenes tonight to unite and join the National Liberation Army under Marshal Tito.

### King Calls for Unity

In an address in Serbo-Croat prepared for a broadcast by the British Broadcasting Corporation, the young King said that with the gathering of Allied armies on the Yugoslav frontiers, the day of liberation was dawning, and that the time had arrived to unite in the struggle.

"My Government, under its Prime Minister, Dr. Ivan Subasitch, has with my full knowledge and approval concluded substantial and advantageous agreements with this, our National Army," King Peter said.

Bulgaria's new pro-Allied Government was energetically cleaning house today as Sofia prepared to welcome the Red Army.

A Moscow radio broadcast reported by the Soviet monitor quoted Premier Kimon Georgieff as having announced in Sofia that in forty-eight hours the Council of Regents had been abolished and all members of former governments in power since 1941 had been jailed.

A majority of the Members of Parliament were reported arrested. Many newspapers have been suppressed, fifteen diplomats recalled from foreign posts and "a purge of State administrative apparatus" has been launched, it was added.

The Sofia radio's home service, heard by the British Ministry of Information, carried appeals of labor unions and the "provisional central administration" to chauffeurs to place themselves and their cars and trucks at the disposal of the new Government.

A newly formed committee of journalists announced a democratic press was to be established, with "disruptive elements to be removed and punished," and "liaison with our colleagues of the Soviet press to be established."

The Ankara radio said Sofia was decorated with red flags and reported "civilians and Communists who have come down from the mountains are all armed" and singing Communist songs.

\*    \*    \*

# LENIENT ARMISTICE GIVEN TO RUMANIA

*Allies Scale Down Reparations Payable to Russia in Return for Active War Aid*

By The Associated Press

LONDON, Sept. 13—Rumania has pledged to fight on the Allied side until final victory over Germany, to pay $300,000,000 worth of reparations to Russia, to restore all United Nations property and to adhere to the 1940 frontier that gave Russia Bessarabia and northern Bukovina, the Soviet Government announced tonight in broadcasting the terms of the Rumanian armistice.

In return, Rumania is to get back the Transylvanian territory that the Germans had handed to Hungary in 1940 and is to maintain her own civil administration in non-combat zones.

Commenting in the twenty-point armistice, formally signed today, the chief Rumanian negotiator in Moscow, Lucretiu Patrascanu, declared, "We don't have a right to be dissatisfied with the terms."

These first published armistice terms of the war were signed by Marshal Rodion Y. Malinovsky on behalf of Russia, Britain and the United States, with Russia "acting in the interest of all the United Nations," and by the Rumanian delegation, which has been dealing in Moscow while Rumanian troops already were fighting under Red Army direction against the Germans and Hungarians.

Italy received the first armistice of this war from the United Nations, but its terms never have been made public. Terms for Bulgaria have been drafted by the European Advisory Commission, but not yet signed.

Acknowledging defeat at the hands of Russia, Britain and the United States, Rumania agreed formally to fight for the restoration of her own "independence and sovereignty," providing at least twelve infantry divisions and reinforcements, to be under Soviet supreme command, and to place her naval and air forces under similar command. Transport, food and industrial needs of the Red Army are to be met as the Soviet command shall direct.

Rumania agreed to abolish racial discriminatory laws and to intern all German and Hungarian nationals on her soil except Jews. All Allied war prisoners and interned persons are to be repatriated at Rumanian expense and persons interned for favoring the Allies must be freed.

Rumania also must return all property taken from the Soviet Union and all property in Rumania of the United Nations.

The biggest reparation item was the equivalent of $300,000,000, with American dollars specified as the yardstick, to be paid by Rumania to Russia in goods, industrial equipment and foodstuffs over a six-year period.

The armistice specifically declared that this was acknowledged to be only a part payment of the damage done to Russia by Rumanian troops, but was scaled down by virtue of Rumania's active participation in the war against Germany and Hungary.

Damage to property of other Allied nations and their citizens is to be paid in amounts to be fixed later.

Domestically, Rumania promised a clean sweep of fascism, abolishing any Hitlerite or fascist parties and militaristic organizations.

The armistice is to be supervised by an Allied Control Commission.

### Hull Reserves Comment

Special to The New York Times

WASHINGTON, Sept. 13—Secretary of State Cordell Hull reserved comment today on the terms of the armistice with Rumania pending study. Some time will be required for the study in view of the length of the terms. They were not received from the American Embassy in Moscow until late in the day.

\*    \*    \*

# RUMANIA'S ARMISTICE

It is a token of the tremendous change in the war situation wrought by Allied triumphs on all fronts that all interest is now centered on final victory in Europe and the surrender of the main enemy, Nazi Germany. The capitulation and change of sides by Germany's former satellites arouse only passing notice. Yet a development such as is taking place in the Balkans in the south and in Finland in the north would have been tremendous news before D-day, and it is still important both for the further course of the war and even more so for the future peace, in which all these states must find their appropriate place if peace is to endure. For these reasons the armistice concluded between the United Nations and Rumania, which will be taken as a pattern by other satellite states seeking similar escape, deserves attention.

Clearly the most important thing about it is that it was concluded at all and in a manner which has ranged Rumania on the Allied side with all her forces. The Allies may not need a further stimulant to their victorious mood, but Rumania's turnabout must be a further blow to Germany's fighting morale, and any such blow must be of help to all the Allied armies now storming the "walls" of Fortress Germania. Moreover, though negotiated in Moscow and signed by a Russian marshal, it was concluded in the name of the three "Allied Powers," Russia, Great Britain and the United States, acting in the interest of all the United Nations. That is a further demonstration, already made in the armistice with Italy, that these three Powers, and for that matter the United Nations, make war and peace together. This fact should dispel whatever hopes Hitler may still have of gaining a separate peace, east or west.

As for the armistice terms themselves, they are perhaps best described in the remark of the chief Rumanian negotiator that Rumania "doesn't have a right to be dissatisfied with

with them." Rumania again loses Bessarabia and northern Bukovina, which Russia took from her in 1940, but she regains all or most of Transylvania, which she acquired in the last war and which Hitler had given to Hungary. She will have to pay $300,000,000 in reparations to Russia and an amount still to be fixed to the other Allies in compensation for damages. She must suppress all Fascist organizations; but she retains her civil administration under an Allied control commission.

Considering all the circumstances, these are not harsh terms. In fact, they might well prove to be more lenient than those granted Italy. But they have been granted in consideration of the important fact that Rumania has agreed to "work her way home" by fighting on the Allied side with at least twelve infantry divisions under Russian command. That is much more than the Italian King, or Badoglio, or the Italian underground, was able to deliver at the time of the surrender. And it is one more warning to others who would save themselves that "working their way home" means more than a profession of good intentions.

\*   \*   \*

**September 19, 1944**

## ANTONESCU SEIZED

*Russians Also Hold Dr. Clodius as Likely War Criminal*

**EIGHT AIDES TAKEN**

*5 Nazis, 5 Rumanian Leaders Captured in Ex-Satellite's Coup*

By The United Press

LONDON, Sept. 18—Russian troops, in the first Allied bag of major Axis war criminal suspects, have arrested ten Rumanian and German military and political leaders in Rumania, including former Premier Ion Antonescu and Dr. Karl Clodius, Germany's ace economic expert in the Balkans.

The prisoners—five Rumanians and five Germans—represented the cream of the Axis representatives in Rumania trapped by the overthrow of Antonescu's government by King Michael and the quick entry of the Red Army.

"In view of the fact that the group headed by Marshal Antonescu and representatives of the German Command in Rumania may appear as suitable candidates for entry into the list of war criminals, the command of Soviet troops in Rumania" made the arrests, a Soviet communiqué broadcast by Moscow announced.

Indicating the importance that the Russians attached to the development, the announcement was included in the regular military communiqué.

### Key Officials Captured

In addition to Antonescu, who was Premier, Chief of State, Foreign Minister and Defense Minister before his removal, and Dr. Clodius, Hitler's No. 1 economic trouble

shooter and head of the German Trade Commission, the following were under arrest:

A former Rumanian Deputy Premier and Foreign Minister, Michael Antonescu, not related to the former Premier.

A former Rumanian War Minister, Gen. Constantine Pantazi.

A former Inspector General of Rumania's inner security police, Vasiliu.

A former prefect of the Bucharest police, Col. George Elefterscu, who also was Antonescu's adjutant.

General Hansen, a cavalry officer, chief of the German military mission to Rumania.

Admiral Tillessen, chief of the German naval staff in Rumania.

Lieut. Gen. Gerstenberg, commander of the Luftwaffe in Rumania.

Maj. Gen. Stahel, who was commandant in Warsaw this year.

### Trial Status Is Obscure

There was no immediate indication whether the ten still remained in Rumania, where they presumably were seized by the Government of Premier Sanatescu after Rumania's break with Germany. Nor was there any hint when or where they might be put on trial, either by the Russians or the Allies in concert.

Prior to his recent departure from Moscow after the signing of the Russo-Rumanian armistice, Lucretiu Patrascanu, Minister of State and chief of the Rumanian delegation, said he believed the Russians had every right to demand that the Axis leaders be turned over to them.

Marshal Antonescu, popularly known as "the red dog," was a close friend and admirer of Corneliu Codreanu, founder of the anti-Semitic Iron Guard. When King Carol, prior to his flight to Mexico, began shifting to complete cooperation with Berlin, he invited Antonescu to become Minister of War, but the marshal refused because he felt the new Cabinet was not 100 per cent pro-Nazi.

Antonescu's subsequent entry into the Government led to Carol's departure under a rain of bullets, and within a few months Antonescu took over complete control as dictator.

\*   \*   \*

**September 22, 1944**

## BULGARS ANNOUNCE 3 SOCIAL REFORMS

*Equal Rights, Separation of Church and State and Free Worship Promulgated*

By JOSEPH M. LEVY
By Telephone to The New York Times

SOFIA, Bulgaria, Sept. 17 (Delayed)—The present Fatherland Front Government has no intention of establishing a Communist regime in Bulgaria, Anton Yugoff, Communist Minister of Interior in the Georgieff Cabinet, reiterated today. Mr. Yugoff was one of five Ministers who addressed a large mass meeting this morning when Premier Kimon Georgieff outlined his Government's program and announced many reforms that the Government had decided to introduce at once.

Outstanding among the reforms promulgated were equal rights for women, separation of church and State and freedom of religion, religious tolerance and civil marriage. Heretofore all marriages in Bulgaria had to be performed by the church.

Mr. Georgieff also announced the immediate restoration of the original democratic Constitution and said free elections for a new Parliament would be held soon.

Mr. Yugoff, an outstanding Communist leader in Bulgaria, said:

"Our enemies are trying to create the impression throughout the world that the Fatherland Front Government has brought about chaos in Bulgaria. This Government, of which I am a member and on whose behalf I speak, categorically denies that it has any intention of establishing a Communist regime in Bulgaria.

"There is no truth in rumors that the Government intends to nationalize any private enterprise in the country. The Government's aim is to help the people and establish a Government of the people, by the people, for the people. But this Government cannot realize these aims by itself. It needs and relies on the help and control of the people.

"The Government not only promised to do so but has actually restored the rights and liberties of the people. Speaking of forces on which the Government relies, much praise is due to our army, without whose help the change of regime and the achievement of liberty would not have been possible."

The Georgieff Government, which includes four Communists, is exerting every effort to establish a liberal, democratic regime in Bulgaria, and unless unpredicted events come it is most unlikely that this country will be subjected to Communist rule. The Georgieff Cabinet represents the vast majority of Bulgarian people, who are strongly opposed to fascism. The Cabinet includes all liberal, democratic and leftist elements that organized the Fatherland Front.

Bulgaria cannot be judged by Sofia alone, whose inhabitants, mostly workers, contain a growing Communist element. More than 80 per cent of the Bulgarians are agrarians, who, though opposed to communism, are great believers in farm cooperatives and would support any liberal Government that would help develop the cooperative system.

### Russia Arrests More Bulgars

LONDON, Sept. 21 (AP)—The Moscow radio tonight announced the arrest of two former Premiers of Bulgaria, Prince Cyril, former Bulgarian Regent, and the German Ambassador to Sofia.

Ex-Premier Bogdan Philoff and Dobri Boshiloff were the two former Government heads reported held.

The High Command of the Soviet troops in Bulgaria made the arrests, the radio said in a broadcast heard by the Soviet monitor.

\* \* \*

September 28, 1944

## OUST AMERICAN OFFICERS

### Russians Send Britons Also From Bulgaria to Turkey

SOFIA, Bulgaria, Sept. 26 (Delayed) (Reuter)—Some twenty British and American officers who had been in Sofia for about ten days left by car for Turkey on Monday night after receiving a direct order from the Soviet military command in the Sofia area to leave Bulgaria within twenty-four hours. Russian officers traveled in a separate car with the British and American officers to the Turkish frontier.

Reuter's diplomatic correspondent learns that certain British and American officers, who were in Sofia before the Russians arrived, have left Sofia at the request of the local Russian military authorities. These officers did not form any part of the official missions which, it is hoped, will eventually go to Bulgaria as the British and American sections of the inter-allied control commission to be established there.

\* \* \*

October 14, 1944

## ATHENS REPORTED HELD BY PATRIOTS

### Greek Government and British Generals Herald Approach of Allied Liberating Force

By HERBERT L. MATTHEWS
By Wireless to The New York Times

ROME, Oct. 13—Three proclamations announcing the approach of an Allied force and pleading for unity and order were broadcast by radio and planes tonight to the Greek people, whose capital, Athens, is reported now to be in the hands of patriots.

[An Allied expeditionary force joining Greek Partisans captured Athens, The United Press reported, citing an Ankara dispatch, which said British, Greek and Polish forces had captured a large number of German troops in the capital.

[The Rome radio broadcast an "official announcement" Friday that Athens had been evacuated by the Germans, The Associated Press reported. The Allied-controlled radio said its report came from Allied headquarters. A Cairo dispatch earlier announced that the Germans had declared Athens an open city. Unofficial reports said the Greek flag was flying over the Acropolis in the capital and that the Athens radio was in Allied hands.

[The French radio in Algiers said Piraeus, Athens' port, also had been liberated.]

This was the first time in the war that the existence of an Allied force had been announced while it was still on its way to its destination, but events precipitated themselves in Athens and Piraeus and it was considered imperative to try to prevent civil strife.

The proclamations were issued by the Greek exile government, Gen. Sir Henry Maitland Wilson, Allied Supreme Commander in the Mediterranean, and Lieut. Gen. Ronald M. Scobie, commander of British forces in Greece.

"The great hour of freedom has come," began the Government's proclamation. "Guerrilla and clandestine patriotic organizations, police forces, officers and noncommissioned officers of every arm, both regular and territorial, are particularly called upon to obey the Government and its representatives in an exemplary manner.

"All civil servants must remain at their posts and await orders from the Government. Those among them who during the period of occupation conducted themselves in a manner contrary to the national conscience will be removed. Just punishment of those as well as of every person who collaborated with the enemy will be swiftly imposed by the Greek State. Any punitive action attempted against such persons by isolated individuals or organizations, but not guaranteeing a dispensation of real justice, would constitute an arbitrary usurpation of the function of the State."

After asking the populace to remain where they are and avoid confusion, the proclamation goes on:

"At this critical hour, avoid political disputes and everything that could disturb the spiritual unity of Greeks. The Greek people, which has suffered so much, is regaining its liberties, and it alone possesses the sovereign right to decide freely on a constitution, social order and government of its choice. As soon as possible it will be called upon to do so. The time has also come for us to achieve our national restoration. In fulfillment of this aim we have the support of our Allies."

General Wilson's proclamation begins by reminding the Greeks that "for the second time in this war a force under my command is about to land in Greece, but I am thankful to say under very different conditions."

"When we were forced to leave Greece in April, 1941, you called on us to 'come back again,' and we are now responding to that call," the proclamation continued.

The General also pleaded for unity. "I call on you all to work together both amongst yourselves and with us," he said.

General Scobie's proclamation was that of a soldier handling practical problems. He asked the Greeks "to behave in an orderly manner and keep the roads clear." He ordered, "Public officials and servants, stay at your posts."

"I appeal for the cooperation of all Greeks, whatever their political opinions, in preserving order and hastening the work of relief," General Scobie added.

His proclamation ends with these two sentences, which will be capitalized on leaflets dropped over Athens and Piraeus:

"We are not here to interfere in any way in the internal affairs of Greece. Our only wish is to see her, as soon as possible, happy, prosperous and united."

### Contrast With Earlier Blow

ROME, Oct. 13 (AP)—General Wilson's broadcast indicated an Allied landing in force was imminent, contrasted with the comparatively small forces employed in the Peloponnesus.

Late in September, the British landed in the Peloponnesus, large southern peninsula of the Greek mainland, and with Greek patriots cleared the Germans from most of that area, captured Patras, Pyrgos and Corinth.

Allied planes operating over the Greek coast in close cooperation with the Land Forces of the Adriatic heavily bombed large concentrations of small enemy craft, and British naval aircraft sank a heavily loaded enemy landing craft, Allied headquarters announced today.

The communiqué made no mention of land forces in Greece, last reported holding Corinth on the road to Athens.

British naval planes carried out heavy attacks against German shipping off the eastern coast of Greece yesterday; and swept inland to destroy two locomotives and an ammunition train on the Athens-Salonika line. A communiqué said five enemy landing, craft were heavily damaged and severe losses were inflicted on enemy troops.

### Government Set to Leave

Premier Papandreou and his Cabinet "are about to leave for Athens by air from their present seat of government in Italy," the British radio, heard by the Columbia Broadcasting System, reported yesterday.

\* \* \*

**October 18, 1944**

# ATHENS UNHARMED, ANCIENT ART INTACT

*Port of Piraeus Wrecked by Germans—Wild Celebration Goes On for Days*

By A. C. SEDGWICK
By Wireless to The New York Times

ATHENS, Oct. 15 (Delayed)—This city is now free of German domination, which lasted more than three and a half years. The oppression, perhaps unequaled elsewhere and designed to humble and humiliate its citizens and rob them of every vestige of freedom and self-respect, is at an end.

The Germans' mission, which was to destroy the people's spirit, has failed, but its undertaking to reduce the people to a state of physical weakness had largely succeeded. The Germans have been the accomplices of disease and famine.

At long last some modicum of humaneness, which may be attributed to General Felny, German corps commander in charge of Athens, averted demolitions that were previously planned. The Marathon dam was not blown up, hence a water shortage has been avoided. No works of art in any of the museums were stolen and in the end it was decided that the city whose civilization gave light to the world be declared open. Preliminary reports indicate that no damage was done to the Parthenon or any of the other temples.

### An Order to an Ex-Painter

As soon as the hated enemy was gone, however, out came paint pots and sign painters began to cover the walls of the city and even some monuments with the slogans of all ninety-two political parties that sprang into existence. One addressed to Hitler said:

"Adolf, go back to your original occupation and start trying to paint out all these signs."

Greek Orthodox priests entered every place formerly occupied by the Germans, exorcized their diabolical influence and blessed the buildings that they might become habitable again for Christians.

Maj. Gen. George Tsolakoglou and Jean Rhallis, former Premiers and alleged quislings, and others accused of having collaborated with the enemy were taken off by the police before the liberation had been completed, and lodged in a prison that the Germans had previously used.

There was bloodshed when armed youths of the Communist Elas and the Edes who had taken part in a great victory parade started shooting at one another. At the same time came news from Sparta and elsewhere of civil strife resulting in deaths and injuries.

### Exit Is Far Different

Early last Wednesday a British patrol entered the city. At about 10 A. M. a German flag was taken from the Acropolis by a German guard of honor, which proceeded to the Tomb of the Unknown Soldier in the center of the city. A German junior officer perfunctorily set down a wreath. As he did so Athenians turned away. The officer then got into a car and drove off toward the port, Piraeus, with cyclists as outriders.

The cortege had not gone more than 100 yards when Athenians removed the wreath, savagely tore off its black, white and red ribbons and destroyed it. From then on Athens was the scene of an unrestrained celebration and pent-up passions found tumultuous expression. There is no diminution in the shouting after three days.

Piraeus was not declared an open city. It is on the outskirts of the seaport, which is almost completely destroyed, that the main power station providing the Athens area with electricity is situated. The Germans left a contingent of almost 100 strong there to blow it up, but succeeded only partly, largely because of the resistance put up by workers who had managed to bring rifles in with them.

### Own Grenade Kills Germans

German prisoners indicated that the commander who had ordered the destruction of the plant had had no expectation of the men's avoiding capture or death. When a group of belea-guered German soldiers attempted to surrender they were kept from doing so by a noncom who hurled a grenade in their midst, killing some.

Another rearguard detachment blew up various installations, including runways on an airfield.

The Germans' progress along the main escape route toward Thebes was slow. The last elements proceeding westward along the "Sacred Way" to Eleusis passed through Scaramonga at 4 o'clock Friday morning.

Shortly afterward other British patrols which had landed at several places made their way to the capital. As soon as they were spotted they were carried shoulder high by the crowds amid a deafening welcome.

On Saturday a larger British force made up of "commandos," many of whom had participated in the 1941 operations in Greece, arrived. They, too, were almost pulled apart by the Athenians demonstrating their affection and gratitude.

Recently issued Communist directives were to show the greatest consideration to the British and Americans, and the party members did not disobey. This is not to imply that the greatest share of the welcome the Communists accorded the British troops was anything but genuine.

### WOMEN, CHILDREN HELD
### Fleeing Germans Slay Hostages as Threat to Guerrillas

ROME, Oct. 17 (AP)—Greek women and children are being used as hostages by German troops fleeing northward, authentic reports said today.

The enemy warned the Greeks that ten hostages would be killed in retaliation for each guerrilla attack. Reports said the first group of civilians taken along had been slain.

German troops fleeing toward Larissa took fifty women and children, but their fate is not known.

Reports from Ankara said the Germans had started evacuation of their important base and communication center at Salonika, where about 50,000 Germans are concentrated. Greeks in Ankara expressed the belief that only a few thousand would escape.

About 6,000 Germans were reported still on Rhodes and 12,000 on Crete. No shipping is available to move them and Allied navies have clamped a blockade on the Aegean Sea islands.

British troops, landed from a huge fleet of 150 Allied warships yesterday at Piraeus, patroled Athens after having broken up clashes between Greek factions.

During the last week of German occupation more than 500 civilians were reported machine-gunned by the Germans.

General Kleemann, commander of the German garrison at Rhodes, was reported to have committed suicide after he was ordered to hold the island and not evacuate the garrison to the mainland. There was no confirmation of the report.

Members of the Greek Cabinet are expected to arrive in Athens aboard a Greek cruiser tomorrow, an official said.

Huge stores of supplies were being unloaded from the fleet.

**Koropi Razing Confirmed**

The London radio said last night it had been confirmed that the Germans "have completely destroyed the Greek town of Koropi, thirty-two kilometers southeast of Athens," according to The Associated Press.

\*   \*   \*

October 27, 1944

## BALKAN 'SPHERES' DECIDED IN MOSCOW

*Russia Will Have Predominant Influence in Rumania, Bulgaria and Hungary*

By PERTINAX
North American Newspaper Alliance

WASHINGTON, Oct. 26—The new set-up in the Balkans and in central Europe, as gradually built by military events and endorsed by Prime Minister Winston Churchill, Foreign Secretary Anthony Eden and Marshal Joseph Stalin during their recent Moscow conversations, can be described as follows.

Russian influence is sure to predominate in Rumania and, above all, in Bulgaria. A general of the Red Army heads the commission of armistice that for some weeks has been at work in Bucharest. Another general of the Red Army will preside over the Sofia commission of armistice in the very near future, as soon as the convention putting an end to hostilities has been signed with representatives of the Bulgarian Government. And all the probabilities are that, in accordance with the claim of the Soviet Union, the Hungarian commission of armistice is also to be presided over by a Russian military leader.

**Russia to Occupy Three Areas**

This state of affairs need not cause any surprise. It derives from the fact that Rumania, Bulgaria and Hungary were, or are, being redeemed by Russian exertions and that Russian troops are going to remain in occupation. Had the British and American general staffs found it possible to undertake a campaign of their own in the Balkans, the picture might be different. But British and American military power, notwithstanding its tremendous expansion, was not able to cope with the Balkans.

North Africa, Italy, Western Europe, the Pacific, Burma, etc., did not leave any surplus that could be applied to eastern Europe.

Besides, these commissions of armistice, under their Russian presidents, will not be the only channel available to Britain and America for conducting their relations with the Governments in Sofia; Bucharest and Budapest. Contrary to the Allies' practice in Italy, independent diplomatic missions will be on the spot very quickly.

Here is the important point that Mr. Churchill is believed to have made secure while in the Russian capital. In Yugoslavia the Russian Government does not intend to get for itself any special position by the means of treaties of alliance, etc. In the judgment of Russian diplomacy, Yugoslavia does not fall in the same category as Czechoslovakia, Rumania and Bulgaria. In regard to Yugoslavia, the Governments in Moscow, London and Washington will thus be placed on a footing of equality.

But what would happen if, for instance, Bulgaria were to enter a Yugoslav federation? That problem may well be left to the future. However, were Bulgaria and Macedonia to be included in a state of the Southern Slavs, is it so sure that Croatia and Dalmatia could be induced for any length of time to continue their membership? They might be attracted toward the new Austrian state that bids fair to emerge from the reshuffle at the termination of the war. It is well known that, in London, a revival of the Austrian state within territorial limits less restricted than those of 1919, has long been favorably considered.

There is reason to believe that in Moscow Marshal Stalin did not raise any objection to the re-establishment of a common frontier between Greece and Turkey. Thus from Anatolia to the Adriatic it is not difficult to see the areas where British and American moral influence and where British and American economic contributions will make themselves felt.

All this must not be interpreted in terms of zones of influence. Anyone who readily assumes that between Britain and Russia no true spirit of cooperation comes to play is bound to forecast an era of rivalry and opposition between great powers, to speak of antagonistic blocs and the like. But in Moscow Mr. Churchill and Mr. Eden stood by the principle from which they have never departed—that Britain and Soviet Russia are pledged to a twenty years' alliance. The essential condition of success is that the lasting enforcement of the eventual armistice with Germany should keep the victorious powers in close solidarity.

\*   \*   \*

October 29, 1944

## BULGARIA ACCEPTS ARMISTICE TERMS

*Agreement Signed in Moscow With United Nations—Text May Be Known Today*

By W. H. LAWRENCE
By Wireless to The New York Times

MOSCOW, Oct. 28—Bulgaria today signed an armistice with the United Nations. Representatives of the former German satellite state, which has now declared war on Hitler, signed the terms this afternoon in the presence of representatives of the Soviet Union, the United States and the United Kingdom. Marshal Fedor I. Tolbukhin signed for the Soviet Government and Lieut. Gen. J. A. H. Gammell signed for the Allied Supreme Command in the Mediterranean Theatre.

It is expected that the terms of the armistice, which were worked out in part by the negotiations of Premier Stalin and Prime Minister Churchill during the recent Moscow conference, will be made public tomorrow.

The Bulgarian Government declared war on the United States and Great Britain on Dec. 13, 1941, but never declared war on the Soviet Union, although Bulgaria's resources were employed by the Germans in waging war against Russia. The Soviet Union declared war on Bulgaria on Sept. 5 of this year but announced the cessation of military operations ninety-nine hours later, when Bulgaria asked for an armistice and broke with Hitler. Armistice negotiations between Bulgaria and the Western Allies were in progress in Cairo at the time the Soviet Union declared war.

The signing of the Bulgarian armistice left Hitler with only one ally in the European war—Hungary—and that country has already been entered by the Red Army.

Foreign Minister Petko Stainoff, who signed the armistice on behalf of his recently established Government, said the present regime had admitted the mistake committed by its predecessors in waging a "completely unjustified war on the great Western democracies" and violating the neutrality affecting the Soviet Union. This "grave crime," he said, "lies on the conscience of the whole people," but he added that the world little knew the sacrifices the Bulgarian people had made to overthrow their own Government and to free the country from Nazi occupation.

He pointed out that the Patriotic Front Government already had begun to punish those Bulgarian authorities responsible for his country's recent policy and said he could assure the Allies that those persons would be punished.

Discussing the fact that Bulgarian troops now are marching with Tito's Partisan Army against the Germans in Yugoslavia, Mr. Stainoff said:

"The Bulgarian people wish to show to the whole world, and primarily to the great Allies that it is ready to wash away in its own blood the stain thrown onto its forehead by its former criminal rulers."

### Most Terms Already Fulfilled

MOSCOW, Oct. 28 (AP)—The Bulgarian Foreign Minister declared today that his country's armistice delegation "regards it as its duty to inform representatives of the Allied Governments that the new Bulgarian Government of the Patriotic Front has been able to carry out a considerable part of the conditions provided for in the draft terms of the Allied Governments."

He asserted that the Bulgarian Government "considers it its fundamental duty to implement the armistice terms in a most conscientious manner.

"This armistice will assist the Bulgarian Government to establish relations between Bulgaria and the peoples of the United Nations, and will inaugurate a policy of cooperation with these nations."

The "whole people" of his country backed the Government in the realization of this policy, he added.

Negotiations for the armistice agreement opened Thursday and ended with the formal signing today.

\* \* \*

November 17, 1944

## GREEK EXTREMISTS KEEP UP AGITATION

*Left-Wing Factions Resisting Efforts to Disarm Them—Reds Losing Support*

By A. C. SEDGWICK
By Wireless to The New York Times

ATHENS, Nov. 16—Requests made by the Greek Government to political factions to refrain from further demonstrations, on the understanding that all will receive a sympathetic hearing later, have re-party slogans on Athen's walls and in greater vociferating of political doctrines on street corners by Communist party members or by persons taking their side.

Other factions remain comparatively undemonstrative and silent, but they harbor a noticeable resentment against the methods adopted by extreme leftist elements, which are often accused of taking advantage of the nation's disrupted state to further their own ends.

The fact that the Elas is officially opposed to the Government's program of disarming all resistance groups by Dec. 10 has aggravated the situation considerably. The Elas' attitude is that it is unfair to disarm its elements while the National Army and the official police constabularies remain armed. Present indications are that the Elas is determined to give no ground on this vital issue affecting the personal security of all citizens.

The Government's announced intention is to call up one military age group for duty outside the Athens area, which will act as a Provincial police force until a regular constabulary may be formed to take the place of the now disbanded "horophilaki," whose record may, in some cases, have been tainted by collaboration.

Outside the Athens area the "politophilaki," which is the Elas' own police force, continues, meanwhile, to enjoy full powers, reserving the right to arrest whomever it chooses on charges of collaboration, charges seldom possible to substantiate. It controls the movements of all citizens and can continue the present practice of the Elas to levy taxes and to distribute food stocks only to those selected to receive them.

With the exception of a relatively small area, Epirus, including Yanina, where Gen. Napoleon Zervas, leader of the National Democratic front, controls, the situation is that the armed force of Elas, with full Communist party sanction, remain supreme in the provinces, and it is clear that Elas has no intention of giving up any of its power.

Within recent days the circulation of the Communist daily Rizospastis has sharply risen in relation to the Eam's official journal Apoliftherotis, which would indicate a tendency on the part of left-wingers to follow the extreme element. At the same time, secret balloting held among the personnel of the banks, Ministries and guildlike organizations, such as butchers and grocers, indicates an overwhelming turnabout from communism.

\*   \*   \*

## ALBANIAN CAPITAL FREED OF GERMANS

### *Partisans Battle Rear Guards After Foe Quits Tirana—Escape Route Harried*

By JOHN MacCORMAC
By Wireless to The New York Times

LONDON, Nov. 18—The Albanian Army of National Liberation, led by a young former school-master now known as Col. Gen. Enver Hoxha, has driven the Germans out of Tirana, the capital, the Germans admitted tonight.

Earlier announcements by the Yugoslav radio had claimed merely that fierce fighting was raging in the Albanian capital and that the Town Hall, the officers' home, the radio station and the prison had been captured by the National Liberation Army.

Fighting, it was said, continued in Skandor Beg Square, near the palace of former King Zog. On the entire Durazzo front the Liberation Army was reported to be engaged in fierce fighting in trying to block the retreat of the Germans westward into Montenegro.

In Tirana the Germans were said to be still holding the barracks on the River Shkruba and at Zog's palace, but in the country area as a whole they were described as retaining only Durazzo, Scutari and Kirkush.

The communication lines between these towns, it was announced, were being ceaselessly attacked by the Liberation forces.

The German DNB news agency, however, said that heavy fighting had developed around the barracks in Tirana "while the German troops were evacuating the city." In the course of the fight, it was added, the German rear guards managed to avoid encirclement and to link up with the main body of German troops.

Fighting in the suburbs of the capital began a fortnight ago. The Liberation army numbers about 30,000 hardened guerrilla fighters.

The Albanian Partisans and their leader, General Hoxha, have not been officially recognized by the Allies, although their military activities have received some assistance. General Hoxha's relations with Marshal Tito, head of the Yugoslav National Army of Liberation, are reported to be friendly. They are not so friendly with Greece, which is claiming southern Albania.

Albania, it is said, has no more use today for former King Zog than for the Italian invaders who drove him into exile. The political program of the Partisans calls for federation with other Balkan countries for agrarian reform and for recovery of Albania's mineral resources from Italian interests, which have exploited them since 1925.

### 15th Capital Freed Since June

LONDON, Nov. 18 (U.P.)—Tirana, capital of a country that was enslaved by the Italians and Germans for five and a half years, is the fifteenth European capital freed from Axis domination since June 4.

Albania, 10,629 square miles in area, was invaded by Benito Mussolini's Italian troops on Good Friday, 1939. Swiftly overrunning the country, the Italians named Victor Emmanuel of Italy King of Albania. King Zog fled into exile.

In April, 1941, the Germans in Yugoslavia poured into Albania to help Italians expel Greek troops who had thrown Italian forces out of Greece. The Germans remained to garrison the revolt-torn kingdom.

The Albanians then launched a reign of sabotage and organized resistance. During the last year four guerrilla groups have liberated the major area of Albania.

Capitals still controlled by Germany are Budapest, Warsaw, The Hague, Oslo, Copenhagen, Prague, Vienna and Berlin.

\*   \*   \*

## TITO PROCLAIMS AMNESTY

### *Acts to Have Chetniks and Croats Join United Yugoslavia*

LONDON, Nov. 22 (U.P.)—Marshal Tito of Yugoslavia, in a sweeping move to consolidate his war-shattered country, has granted full general amnesty to thousands of Yugoslavs who supported Gen. Draja Mikhailovitch, Serb leader and Marshal Tito's enemy, as well as to members of the Croat Regular Army, the Free Yugoslav radio said today.

The move—interpreted as an effort to enlist every Yugoslav in the task of rebuilding the almost liberated nation— specifically excludes the Ustashi, the Croat Fascist followers of the German puppet, Ante Pavelitch, and persons guilty of criminal acts such as plunder, looting, assassination and torture.

The amnesty terms specify that the Mikhailovitch Chetniks and Croat soldiers surrender by Jan. 4, 1945, to Marshal Tito's National Liberation Army or to local liberation committees at present acting as civil authorities. It was not clear whether General Mikhailovitch himself was included in the amnesty decree.

# PART VI

# THE RISE OF COMMUNISM, 1944–1949

December 9, 1944

## BROWDER ASSAILS BRITAIN ON GREECE

### Calls Her Intervention 'First Serious Departure From the Teheran Concord'

Britain's intervention in Greece was attacked last night by Earl Browder, president of the Communist Political Association, as "the first serious departure from the Teheran Concord" in an address before 3,000 Communists at a meeting of the association at the Manhattan Center, Thirty-fourth Street near Eighth Avenue.

The British policy in Greece, Italy and Belgium are ill-considered attempts to improve Britain's position so she can demand more consideration from America in arrangements concerning post-war markets, the Communist leader asserted. Saying that British recognition of the need for collaborating with the United States to restore her trade outlets was "sound policy," he said that Americans should warn Britain that such collaboration was not possible unless she abandons political intervention on the Continent.

### Praises Stettinius Stand

He praised the statement of Secretary of State Edward R. Stettinius Jr., "laying down the principle of nonintervention in the internal evolution of Italy and, even more emphatically, in the countries of the liberated allies."

This, he said, "is fully in the spirit and the letter of the Teheran Concord." The principle, he said, "is receiving the enthusiastic welcome of all the peoples of Europe who have been praying for American initiative in this direction."

Mr. Browder spoke at the end of the meeting, which adopted unanimously a resolution protesting against "the British policy of interfering in the internal affairs of liberated countries and bolstering discredited regimes, specifically in Greece, Belgium and Italy." Another resolution, also adopted unanimously, commended the State Department under Secretary Stettinius "for its hands-off policy of non-interference in the internal affairs of liberated countries and for continuing President Roosevelt's foreign policy."

### Says EAM Got Allied Blessing

Mr. Browder, in his remarks, which were an elaboration of a column he had written for tomorrow's edition of The Worker, Communist Sunday newspaper, said that the Greek Liberation Front, the EAM, which Prime Minister Churchill characterized yesterday as the spearhead of gangster rule, had received the blessing of the Allied chiefs at Teheran.

"This was what was firmly envisaged at Teheran as the channel for the peaceful internal development of Europe after its liberation from the Nazis," the Communist spokesman declared. "It has a program which differs in no essential respects from that of the de Gaulle government in France or the Tito government in Yugoslavia.

"If it can be crushed by British arms under the pretext that it is a Communist dictatorship, then the whole perspective for peaceful evolution of the new Europe is black, indeed."

Charging that Mr. Churchill's policy contemplated "arming the Quislings and the Royalists against the people," he said that the British Prime Minister's claim that he was opposing a "Communist dictatorship" in Greece was a slogan coined by the Nazis. He added, "And it is a bald lie."

He asserted that Eam was the real democratic force in Greece, and its armed partisans had driven out the Nazi invaders and made it possible for the British to land in that country. The British, he asserted, did not engage any considerable body of Nazis.

Mr. Browder presided at the meeting, which was under the auspices of The Daily Worker and The Worker, Communist publications.

\* \* \*

December 15, 1944

## ELAS REOPENS FIRE AFTER A BRIEF LULL

### Greek Government Insists on Unconditional Surrender—Help of Bishop Sought

By The United Press

ATHENS, Dec. 14—Artillery of the anti-Government Elas forces opened fire on the center of Athens this afternoon, ending a lull in the fighting that had extended through the morning, and Greek Government sources reported they would insist upon the unconditional surrender of forces in arms against the regime of Premier George Papandreou.

For a time before noon not a gunshot was heard in downtown Athens for the first time since the civil war began.

But at about 3:35 P. M., the guns again opened up. Sharp fighting began around Omonia Square near the heart of the city, and British-manned tanks rumbled to the scene. The Elas forces were throwing mortar and heavy machine-gun fire against the lines held by British and Greek Government troops, who yesterday repelled the sharpest Elas thrust yet.

Intermittent Elas shellfire continued in Athens well into the evening. Three shells slammed into central Athens shortly after 10 P. M.

During the relatively quiet period there were reports from Elas sources that their leaders had decided to inform Lieut. Gen. Ronald M. Scobie, British commander in Greece, that they would accept his terms for ending the conflict and withdraw armed forces from Athens provided that certain guarantees were given.

Elas sources said that the central committee of the Eam, the National Liberation Front directing the Elas, had decided to advise General Scobie that his terms would be accepted if he could guarantee amnesty for Elas troops and make sure that a National Government would be formed with a proper proportion of Leftists.

Commenting upon these reports—which were not confirmed by official sources—Greek Government quarters said they would insist upon unconditional surrender. They said they could not accept such "political" terms as the Eam reportedly had suggested.

Harold Macmillan, British Resident Minister for the central Mediterranean, conferred twice today with Mr. Papandreou, it was learned, and the British Ambassador to Greece, Rex Leeper, began a series of conferences with leaders of the Greek political parties.

Military liaison quarters said today that much of the Athens population was approaching the starvation level rapidly. Equipment and supplies of dried food have been assembled for opening soup kitchens as soon as it is considered safe for Athenians to gather around them.

### Prelate's Help Requested

By Wireless to The New York Times

ATHENS, Dec. 14—In the port of Piraeus area, an Elas attempt to win back territory on the peninsula came to nothing, while the British increased the cleared area, which will facilitate the unloading of ships. There has been a comparative lull, in fact, except for sniping, which continued in all parts of Athens.

Further steps have been taken to guard against Elas infiltrations into the perimeter lines, where civilians are restricted except for two hours at midday. This measure is to prevent the further distribution of weapons.

Meanwhile, Alexander Svolos, former Minister of Finance, has indicated his willingness to put out peace feelers, according to persons in position to know. His conditions, however, are based on anything but an immediate clearing out of all Elas forces from the Attic peninsula, and it is not likely that they will be considered.

Many persons believe that Mr. Svolos and a host of other Eam supporters are opposed to violence and do not sympathize with the extremists, many of whom are said to be committed to a war to the finish.

According to British sources the bulk of prisoners so far captured in the Athens area represent the purely urban element and have divergent political views.

Gen. Nicholas Plastiras, the veteran revolutionary, who arrived here yesterday after some twelve years of exile, has been in touch with the Archbishop of Greece, with the result that there has been some speculation about setting up a new Government, with such constitutional changes that, it is believed, would serve to diminish the suspicions entertained by many Leftists.

Archbishop Damaskinos, whose record shows him to have been habitually friendlier to the Left than to the Right, appears now as a figure of leading importance and the man of the hour. Many consider that the tremendous prestige derived from his frequent stands against the German occupying authorities and his hostility to authoritarianism put him in unique position to lead his country out of the present turmoil.

### Elas Called Anti-Monarchist

By Cable to The New York Times

STOCKHOLM, Sweden, Dec. 14—The Elas Partisans are more anti-monarchist than Communist, and it is almost certain that they are not receiving help either from the Russians or the Germans, says Dr. Christian Callmer, a member of the Swedish Commission for Aid to Greece, who has just returned from Athens.

The Left-Wing Greeks are fed up with the pre-war dictatorship and want to run the country themselves on their own principles, Dr. Callmer said. The Germans who are fighting with the Partisans are few in number, he added. All of them are Germans who deserted from the army and abandoned their units as soon as the civil war broke out.

"I have myself spoken to one of these Germans," said Dr. Callmer, "and that's what he told me."

The Elas groups represent all social layers of various ages, including women. They are led by former regular army officers, and their equipment consists of arms smuggled in by the British as well as older models of Greek Army weapons.

\* \* \*

December 17, 1944

## BRITAIN ENJOYS MAJOR ROLE IN BALKANS BY U. S. CONSENT

By C. L. SULZBERGER

By Wireless to The New York Times

ROME, Dec. 16—The chaotic bloodshed in the Balkans, which has reached its most tragic stage to date in the Greek civil war, is distinctly connected with a series of great-power diplomatic maneuvers. These, by their signal lack of success, have provided fertile ground for the dragon's teeth sown by the retreating German armies. This is the opinion of qualified officials who have been closely connected with events in southeastern Europe and with American, British and Russian negotiations concerning them.

The background of the unfortunate situation dates back to 1941, before the United States entered the war and when Britain, already planning for the then distant future, was discussing the general possibilities of opening a new assault on German-held Europe when the Allies' forces were strong enough.

### Supported Mikhailovitch

In Yugoslavia Britain was wholeheartedly supporting Gen. Draja Mikhailovitch's cause and approved his general strategic concept of organizing a widespread secret army that would conduct certain sabotage and guerrilla operations, but would basically limit itself to a potential army in being designed to cooperate with the Allies' landings in the Balkans at a future date.

When Marshal Tito's Partisan movement developed in Yugoslavia, it followed the fundamental Russian military idea of guerrilla strategy—to fight all the time everywhere in order to mess up enemy communications and, although at a great sacrifice, give continual active assistance to the Allies' armies fighting the Axis.

The idea of an eventual Allied front in the Balkans had been a pet of Prime Minister Churchill since 1940. During the Beaver-brook-Harriman conferences in Moscow in September, 1941, when the "second front" idea was first formally broached by the Russians, Premier Stalin asked the British to open another front in either Scandinavia or the Balkans; or, as a poor third, in Libya. The British replied that they were in a position to move only in Libya, but they promised an offensive there that materialized unsuccessfully in November.

Meanwhile guerrilla movements in the Balkans continued to operate on a limited scale. Those in Yugoslavia were the only bands of importance, since the Greek guerrillas were not yet organized on any large scale except in Crete. The active civil war between Marshal Tito's and General Mikhailovitch's movements had already commenced. The reasons have often been publicized in the past.

### Truce With Italians Sought

In 1942 General Mikhailovitch, who by that time was entirely confined to defensive operations against the Italians and Germans, and, quite often, offensive and defensive operations against the Partisans, informed the British through a British mission stationed with him that, to protect his flank and conserve his strength for the Allies' eventual landings, it would be desirable for him to work out some form of truce with the Italians. He received reluctant but definite British approval.

This was the beginning of General Mikhailovitch's so-called collaboration with the Axis. There is no doubt that he exchanged liaison officers with certain Italian units in Yugoslavia, as well as receiving arms. Naturally this infuriated the Partisans.

British military and diplomatic thinking continued to consider the future in terms of a Balkan offensive—a subject very dear to Mr. Churchill's heart and definitely to be linked mentally with the Dardanelles campaign of the first World War, which he sponsored. At the Casablanca conference in early 1943, steps were taken toward the preparation of a possible diplomatic background for this. In a direct face-to-face session, President Roosevelt and Mr. Churchill thrashed out certain vital subjects. They were accompanied only by Harry Hopkins and a British adviser believed to have been Sir Alexander Cadogan. Foreign Secretary Anthony Eden, at this stage of the talks, was slightly indisposed and not present.

Mr. Roosevelt ardently urged the adoption of an "unconditional surrender" policy by the Allies; Mr. Churchill was reluctant to support such an out-and-out statement, especially on the advice of Air Chief Marshal Sir Robert Brooke-Popham. It was felt that this would tend to negate the moral effect of the Allies' serial bombings of Germany by stiffening the Germans' resolve.

### Churchill Sets Price for Accord

Finally, however, Mr. Churchill agreed to accept and endorse this policy. As a quid pro quo he insisted that, as between Britain and the United States, Britain have complete charge of the Allies' military operations and corollary diplomatic policy in the Middle East and the Balkans. This was accepted by Mr. Roosevelt.

The State Department was not advised of this agreement for some time. In fact, the first time that Secretary Cordell Hull heard about it was when the United States was preparing to ship some lend-lease materials for Turkey and the Earl of Halifax told him that this must be cleared through Britain under the Casablanca agreement.

In April, 1943, before the end of the Tunisian campaign, the idea of a Balkan offensive was raised by the British and flatly turned down by the American planners. One month later the first British mission was sent to Marshal Tito's Partisans under Lieut. Col. William Deakin, a former Oxford don.

This mission was later amplified and placed under a new leader, Brig. Fitzroy MacLean in September, 1943. Very soon afterward Mr. Eden, en route to Moscow for his conference with Foreign Commissar V. M. Molotoff and Mr. Hull, informed King Peter in Cairo that he feared that should the subject of Yugoslavia arise in the Kremlin talks he would find it very difficult to defend General Mikhailovitch.

The Partisan movement, which had been fighting courageously against great odds, received enormous new strength with the collapse of Italy and seized considerable quantities of munitions and arms. There became little doubt that it was the dominant movement in Yugoslavia, and it now began to receive strong propaganda and moral backing from Britain—and eventually the United States.

The British ceased sending any supplies at all to General Mikhailovitch and somewhat accelerated the supplying of the Partisans. Later they formed special Commando teams, supported by small special American outfits, operating off the Partisan-held island of Vis.

In Greece, meanwhile, during 1943 special British demolition teams and liaison missions increased their activities to such a degree that the nervous Germans sent in new troops in fear of landings.

The Greek Communist movement had formed the wide-spread Eam, or National Liberation Front, based on political and popular support of various trends. Outbreaks of fighting between this organization's army—the Elas—and the more conservative anti-Communist Edes, as well as other organizations that have now disappeared, occurred intermittently, but, through the efforts of the British liaison mission, a truce was signed and a united front was obtained in July, 1943. Unfortunately, it was only temporary.

### Foreign War Offices at Variance

British military thinking and War Office policy consistently backed the Elas throughout the summer of 1943, while the Foreign Office, worried about Britain's favored position in Greece, consistently backed the Edes. Thus both rival organizations felt that they were officially supported by London and open civil war flared out between them in September, 1943.

After a series of conferences between various officials and Mr. Eden and Mr. Churchill British policy began to veer increasingly toward the Edes inside Greece and continued to work with the Government outside. Efforts to achieve internal harmony in Greece crystallized at a conference in Lebanon last spring when, officially speaking, all Greek groups agreed to function together under Premier George Papandreou who had just arrived from Greece.

It was already evident, however, that, should this accord break up, Britain would wholeheartedly support Mr. Papandreou, the regular Greek Army and the Edes and would equally strongly oppose what it felt were the Eam's attempts to seize power in a dictatorial manner.

### Balkan Front Again Urged

As the Allies' military successes advanced, the final stages of planning for the invasion developed. For the last time the idea of a major Balkan offensive was turned down by the United States last February. Britain's political strategy in the Balkans had already veered sharply from its original concepts.

The United States was playing a relatively negligible role of a secondary nature in Balkan affairs. Although—late in the game—American special officers and men were sent into various Balkan countries, they usually started under British auspices and for a long time their information was sent out through British channels. Major Linn M. Farish, who headed the first regular American mission to Marshal Tito, served for a long time as a member of Brigadier MacLean's staff.

Thus, in effect, American military and especially diplomatic policy in the Balkans, by faithfully adhering to the Casablanca agreement, became to all intents and purposes a zero. Several important American diplomats and other officials tried to interest the White House in taking a more active role in the Balkans because of America's moral interest in her small Allies, Greece and Yugoslavia, as well as her eventual, although seemingly distant, potential direct interests. These failed.

### Russia Takes a Hand

Thus, as far as the great powers went, policies in these regions became a matter virtually for bipartite negotiation between Moscow and London, and the United States was deliberately placed in a position where it could hardly say very much about them. Last April, when the Greek mutiny broke out in Egypt under undoubted Eam leadership, Moscow propaganda, which in the past had strictly laid off Greece, suddenly commenced to support the mutineers and Russia seemed to be developing a rapid interest in Greek affairs.

Mr. Churchill called this to Mr. Molotoff's attention and expressed urgent disapproval of Russia's support of the mutineers. Mr. Molotoff replied that he would request the press and radio to ascertain the facts more carefully. The propaganda stopped.

Soon thereafter the Russians complained about certain activities of Britain's secret mission in then enemy Rumania. The result of this was an agreement between Britain and Russia under which Rumania was regarded as a Russian sphere militarily and Greece was regarded as a British sphere militarily. Although the word "military" was specifically used and the operative time of the accord was limited, nevertheless some observers feared that the usual great-power tendency to divide the Balkans had again commenced.

As at Casablanca, America had in effect given Britain more or less carte-blanche in the Balkans as far as the western powers went. At Teheran the basic Russian policies there were approved by Mr. Churchill and Mr. Roosevelt.

### Bombings Damage Position

Officially, the American policy in the Balkans remains one of non-intervention and hoping for popular national solutions under the Atlantic Charter's concepts. Nevertheless, it has been impossible to avoid interference. American aircraft, by bombing Belgrade on the Orthodox Easter, considerably damaged our position in Serbian eyes. American aircraft have several times attacked targets described in briefings as "enemy strong-holds" on information provided by Brigadier MacLean's mission and they have turned out to be General Mikhailovitch's centers.

From a military viewpoint this may well have been desirable, but nevertheless it amounted to direct interference in Balkan politics and direct support of one of the contending sides. The statement by Secretary of State Edward R. Stettinius Jr. on non-interference in the Greek civil war is being strongly used by the Eam as propaganda evidence of Washington's support. This may or may not be desired by Washington but it is a fact and Americans in Greece have not yet shared Britain's unpopularity with the Eam. Only the other day a British general, going into Athens from an American airfield in an American jeep bearing the Stars and Stripes and not wearing his British general's hat, was embraced enthusiastically by an Elas guerrilla shouting: "Zito Roosevelt!"

As a result of the lack of an over-all and clear-cut great-power understanding and a united public policy in the Balkans, there is no reason to believe that the situation will show any basic improvement as long as this root of confusion lasts. The Germans deliberately sowed discord before their retreat. They started schools in Greece teaching how to foster civil war. At least three German officers have been captured from the Elas ranks, according to British sources, who also say that some Elas artillery is now shelling Athens from Lykabettus Hill and is manned by German gunners. For all that anyone knows, there may be disguised Germans on the other side, too.

At this stage unilateral action has apparently become fashionable. Many fair-minded Englishmen sharply deplore the action in Italy concerning Count Carlo Sforza. They say that it was a dangerous precedent for Mr. Stettinius' statement, which they also consider a unilateral action, although of a theoretically impartial nature.

In Yugoslavia four Greek brigades are being organized in Macedonia under Marshal Tito. Brigadier MacLean has protested to Marshal Tito, who has given assurances that the Partisans do not intend to interfere in the civil war. But suspicions prevail.

*   *   *

**December 19, 1944**

## BALKANS' LEFTISM NO PAN-SLAV SHIFT

---

*Swing Held Due to Political, Not Ethnological, Factors— Albania Also Veers*

### ALLIES' REPORTS DIFFER

*Tito Is Believed to Consider Yugoslavia Without Any Obligations to Britain*

---

By C. L. SULZBERGER
By Wireless to The New York Times

ROME, Dec. 18—The ascendency of Left-Wing movements sympathetic to the Soviet Union is now clearly discerned in liberated Balkan areas from the Aegean Sea to the Danube River.

Not only in Greece, where most of the strife-torn land is in the hands of the Elas, but also in Albania, Bulgaria, Yugoslavia and Rumania the Partisan movements or liberation fronts, strongly influenced by veteran Communists, have emerged on top in the chaos following the German withdrawals.

This cannot be explained simply by traditional pan-Slavism's seeking to emulate Moscow. Pan-Slavism not only does not exist in Albania, Greece and Rumania but, on the contrary, the history of these areas has always been marked by a degree of Slavophobia. Furthermore, although the Red Army penetrated Rumania, Bulgaria and Yugoslavia it has not entered Greece or Albania, where similar tendencies are evident.

In some regions the Governments have not moved swiftly enough toward the left to suit local leaders. The Communist Mayor of Constanta, Rumania, has, in a manner of speaking, established a regional dictatorship of his own. Rumors that the Russians were laying down large fortifications in Constanta seem untrue, however.

### Albanian Government Leftist

In Albania the Government of Enver Hoxha is patterned along the pro-Communist, pro-Russian lines evolved in the Balkan Partisan movements. Although the movement led by Premier Hoxha and Mehmet Shehu was closely connected from time to time with Marshal Tito's Yugoslav Liberation Army, the only great support it received was from Britain, which helped supply and organize the Shehu Brigade.

A few days ago Premier Hoxha conferred at Tirana with a Soviet mission which had flown in suddenly. Shehu has made it clear that he is not only anti-British but that he entirely sympathizes with the Greek Elas.

Greece has been traditionally Anglophilic and Slavophobic. The Soviet Union has agreed to recognize the British military sphere in Greece and has ceased propaganda backing of the Eam and Elas. The Kremlin still recognizes the Government of Premier George Papandreou and King George.

The confusion in large Balkan areas even apart from Greece is magnified by mutual suspicions of the great powers and the disagreements in reports made available to the capitals of the three great Allies.

In Yugoslavia there is no similarity in American and British reports on the overshadowed Mikhailovitch movement, its alleged remaining forces and claims as to its popular backing.

Long after the British withdrew their entire mission from the head-quarters of Gen. Draja Mikhailovitch—who, incidentally, is still in Yugoslavia despite reports that he had been taken out by American special forces—the United States sent in a special group of observers, who emerged strongly impressed by his strength and popular backing. This took place only a few weeks ago.

American observers say that General Mikhailovitch still has a considerable but poorly armed force of 100,000 fighters and wide popular backing. This force calls itself the "national" movement and vehemently asserts that Marshal Tito's Partisans did not attack the Germans until after the invasion of the Soviet Union.

British observers contend that General Mikhailovitch's forces are finished and are now a myth.

### Churchill Backs Tito

It has been evident that since September, 1943, Prime Minister Churchill has put all his eggs in Marshal Tito's basket, so far as Yugoslavia is concerned.

In the opinion of competent observers, the Tito movement secured its present power mainly through its own efforts, however, and not because of British support or of the Red Army sweep along Danubia. For this reason Marshal Tito probably feels entirely independent and under no obligation to make concessions to his British allies.

The Communist direction of the Tito movement and his temporary Government is strong and open; there is no attempt to disguise it. In the words of one expert on this subject, the result is that "officials of any great power who have illusions of winning Yugoslavia from its developing ties with the Soviet Union or who think that arrangements can be made to share this country's attentions with the Kremlin would seem at this moment to be dreaming a fantasy."

\* \* \*

December 21, 1944

# TITO'S PROPAGANDA COMBATS HIS FOES

*Youth Groups and Children Are Organized to Back Regime—Secret Police Curb Critics*

By C. L. SULZBERGER
By Wireless to The New York Times

ROME, Dec. 20—To establish his provisional government on the widest possible popular basis, since it is no secret that there have been various groups in Yugoslavia strongly opposing him, Marshal Tito is paying considerable attention to propaganda.

Various organizations have been formed to instruct the young. Youth groups have been formed under the United Alliance of Anti-Fascist Youth of Yugoslavia. Children have been organized in Pioneer formations similar to Soviet Union groups.

Much emphasis appears to be placed on parades, displays, slogans and posters. Soviet Union authorities have supplied a number of loudspeakers, which have been installed on street corners in Belgrade to reach the people with national programs because there are few radios. Many large pictures of Marshal Tito and Premier Stalin are on display as well as a considerably smaller number of Prime Minister Churchill and President Roosevelt.

### Four Papers in Belgrade

Four daily papers are appearing in Belgrade. Borba is the Communist party organ and is edited by General Djilas, perhaps the most active Communist leader. Glas is the organ of the National Liberation Front. Omladins represents the United Alliance of Anti-Fascist Youth. Politika Yugoslavis, leading pre-war paper, has resumed publication under its old editor, Vladislav Ribnikar, who serves Marshal Tito as Minister of Information.

There is a strict censorship and criticism of the new regime is not countenanced, but this is not a new phase in the history of the Balkans. The contrast between the papers can be seen in the fact that Politika prints more foreign news emanating from the Western Allies than from Soviet sources, while the reverse is true in the case of Borba.

A state trust is being organized for the distribution of movies. Because of the puritanical moral standards of the Partisans, it is possible that Hollywood's usual output will not do too well.

A new secret police, the Section for the Defense of the People, also known as Ozna, has been formed under the leadership of a Serbian priest, Lieut. Col. Pop [Father Zechovitch]. Collaborationists are being rounded up and early this month it was stated that 105 had been executed, while 5,000 were in prison awaiting trial. Marshal Tito's enemies say the real figures are considerably larger.

Many persons, especially in the provinces, fear the new regime and believe they face arrest if they criticise it. Perhaps this has caused untrue reports of mass arrests and executions.

### Poor Field for Reds

Marshal Tito's most ardent Communist supporters admit that Yugoslavia has none of the usual prerequisites for a Communist regime. Some recall that Lenin predicted that Serbia would be the last country in Europe to become Communist. There are few large financial interests, and the land is well divided in small peasant holdings.

Endre Hebrang, Acting Minister of Commerce, recently said: "Industry in the new Yugoslavia will be organized on the basis of private initiative and private ownership." In the view of some observers, Marshal Tito seems to be developing a State-controlled, State-planned economy, not unlike Russia's, but at the same time private small trading continues and there is no talk of the collectivization of land.

At present Marshal Tito's movement favors private enterprise, religious freedom and cultural and nationalities' equality. Despite undoubted areas of opposition Marshal Tito enjoys a good deal of popular support, and it is the opinion of many observers that this is not a regime imposed from outside but represents the desires of a large portion of the unhappy Yugoslav people.

### Eden Gets Yugoslav Plan

By Wireless to The New York Times

LONDON, Dec. 20—Dr. Ivan Subasitch, Premier of the Royal Yugoslav Government, who is seeking British endorsement of a plan already approved by Premier Stalin for a Federal Government for Yugoslavia, outlined his proposals to Foreign Secretary Anthony Eden this week. He hopes to see Prime Minister Churchill soon and then return to Belgrade to form a Government.

As a result of his conversations with Mr. Eden, Yugoslav quarters said today, no complications are expected in obtaining British approval of the Government that was agreed upon by Premier Subasitch and Marshal Tito.

British diplomatic sources seem to expect that the Subasitch-Tito proposal for the creation of a regency pending a plebiscite on the future of the monarchy will be adopted despite objections by King Peter and his supporters.

\* \* \*

**December 29, 1944**

## BRITAIN AND GREECE

Mr. Churchill and Mr. Eden are on their way home from Athens with a plan for a regency in Greece which they will submit, with due regard to the proprieties of the situation, to the Greek King, who is in London. This plan is reported to have the unanimous approval of all the factions whose representatives attended the conferences in Athens. Time alone will show whether its acceptance can provide a basis for establishing enough peace in Greece to make possible a free and fair election. But at least the record shows that Mr. Churchill has made a good try at solving this problem, and that his trip across Europe for this purpose is, and was intended to be, a gesture of British good-will.

Doubtless it will continue to be charged, especially by those who find pleasure in suspecting the worst of British policy, that Mr. Churchill's primary interest in Greece is not consultation of the real wishes of the Greek people, but the maintenance of Greece safely within the orbit of what is described as Britain's "sphere of influence." This phrase has many meanings. If it is intended to mean that Britain seeks to dominate Greece politically and commercially, close Greece off from other markets, exploit Greek resources for Britain's benefit, then there is nothing in the record of British relations with Greece to substantiate such a charge. If it means, on the other hand, that the lifeline of the British Empire runs through the Mediterranean, and that the British have a natural interest in wishing a country so close to that lifeline as Greece to be orderly and prosperous and democratic, then we may remind ourselves that we have a similar interest in small countries bordering on the Panama Canal. This interest of ours does not necessarily bode ill for the people of these countries. It may well serve to their advantage.

If we think realistically enough about lifelines, we may even remind ourselves that we sometimes take an interest in the kind of government possessed by countries no nearer to the Panama Canal than Argentina.

\*   \*   \*

**January 1, 1945**

## GREEK PREMIER OUT, REGENT IS SWORN IN

*Damaskinos Takes Over Power—Eam Asserts It Accepts Basis for Armistice*

By A. C. SEDGWICK
By Wireless to The New York Times

ATHENS, Dec. 31—Archbishop Damaskinos of Greece was sworn in as Regent at a simple but impressive ceremony at the Foreign Office at noon today. Chiefs of the Greek Army and Navy and diplomatic corps were present.

Earlier Premier George Papandreou and his Cabinet resigned. The new Regent accepted the resignations.

Monsignor Damaskinos took the oath "on my own sanctity." Spiridon, Bishop of Yannina, and ten other bishops were witnesses.

There was a lull in the fighting, but shortly afterward mortar fire was directed from distant suburbs and there was some sniping. In the twenty-four hours before the British troops had succeeded in clearing up stretches north of the cemetery of Piraeus and their artillery had silenced mortars that had been firing on populous areas of Athens.

During the night the Elas [forces of the Eam, or National Liberation Front] attacked the cable and wireless transmitting station at Pelini, fourteen miles from Athens. Though they were repulsed, they cut the cable. One result is a cessation of complete press messages on this route.

### Eam Pictured as Conciliatory

ATHENS, Monday, Jan. 1 (AP)—Archbishop Damaskinos, in his oath as Regent, said:

"I swear in the name of the Holy and Indivisible Trinity to be loyal to the King, protect the religion of the Greek nation, maintain the Constitution and preserve national independence."

Fighting continued in Athens and Piraeus, although the visit of an Elas delegation to the British commander, Lieut. Gen. Ronald M. Scobie, to discuss a truce and surrender terms was reported reliably last night.

Alexander Svolos, former Finance Minister, representing the Eam, returned from Elas territory and said that the Left-Wing group was conciliatory concerning the formation of a new Cabinet, insisting that the Ministries of War and the Interior be given to persons of common confidence. The Eam, he reported, also named George Kafandaris as a candidate for the Premiership.

British troops continued to clean out Elas forces in the Athens-Piraeus area and reported Elas forces had landed on Meganisi Island and were concentrating on the mainland opposite the island of Levkas. Gen. Napoleon Zervas, leader of the Rightist forces, continued to evacuate his remaining troops to Corfu from Preveza, which is just north of Levkas.

### Bid to U. S., Russia Reported

ATHENS, Dec. 31 (U.P.)—The newspaper Free Greece, organ of the Eam, reported that the Eam had invited the United States Secretary of State, Edward R. Stettinius Jr., and Soviet Foreign Commissar Vyacheslaff M. Molotoff to form a United Nations commission for Greece with British cooperation.

### EAM Blames Right

By Cable to The New York Times

LONDON, Dec. 31—An Eam memorandum expressing admiration today for Prime Minister Churchill placed the blame for the continued fighting in Attica squarely on the parties of the Right, whom British troops have been jockeyed into supporting. The memorandum said:

"You will permit us to believe that there is no justification for the extension of hostilities, especially since the Left has accepted the basic points in General Scobie's memorandum and by its conciliatory proposals in the political field is rendering much easier the finding of a solution for all outstanding questions."

The two basic points in General Scobie's ultimatum were:

1. The Elas must carry out his orders as troops placed under his command by the Caserta agreement.

2. The Elas is to withdraw from Attica, hand in its arms and disband.

General Scobie's reply, released by the Foreign Office tonight, said that it remained to be made clear that the Elas had really accepted his two conditions of a truce. The statement said:

"If the central committee of the Eam and Elas will confirm their acceptance of these conditions and will send an officer or officers with full power to this headquarters, arrangements can be made forthwith for the execution of these conditions and the cessation of hostilities."

\*    \*    \*

January 9, 1945

## ITALY FEARS LOSS OF TRIESTE, FIUME

*Granting of Yugoslav Demand Held Tragic Strategic and Psychological Blow*

By HERBERT L. MATTHEWS
By Wireless to The New York Times

ROME, Jan. 8—Yugoslav Foreign Minister Josip Smodlaka's demand in London yesterday that Trieste and Fiume be given to Yugoslavia brings officially into the open one of the most delicate problems that Europe is going to face in the final peace settlement.

The loss of Trieste would be so crushing a blow to Italy that it may be taken as certain that it would be the powder keg in the Europe of the future. The Italians fought in the first World War to get Trieste from Austria and they gave up 600,000 dead in the process. Slovenes make up half the population, but they are mainly agriculturalists.

Strategically, the loss would greatly weaken Italy, for every invasion on that side, including the one that resulted in the battle of Caporetto, was made down those valleys in Trieste's hinterland for which the Yugoslavs now ask. The Istrian coast is Italian and the late President Wilson recognized it as such.

Fiume too is Italian, but it is realized that its unsavory connection with the late Gabriele d'Annunzio and the beginnings of Fascism weaken the Italian claims. Zara is a little Italian enclave.

This is the Italians' case that they are frantically presenting to the British in particular because of Britain's long connection of aid to Marshal Tito, but so far they have had nothing but chilly silence in reply and one finds much discouragement in official circles.

It is realized that Benito Mussolini's regime oppressed and tyrannized the Slavs in that region, but the Italians point out that they did nothing to the Serbs as bad as the Croats under Ante Pavelitch did later. The Croats killed about 600,000 Serbs and 60,000 Jews—after Maldonek, the worst massacre in Europe. It is asked whether the Croats are to be rewarded and the Italians are to be punished on such bases.

One thing that makes Italians nervous is the fact that marshal Tito is almost certainly going to get to Trieste before the Allies' armies in Italy. He has Italians fighting for him, but carefully keeps them down in Bosnia. Hence, it is feared that Europe will be faced with another fait accompli. The Italian colonies in Trieste and Fiume are said to fear that they are going to be massacred, if not at first, then in time.

Italians ask that the whole question be deferred until after the war, when it can be considered calmly and coolly by all the United Nations. Count Carlo Sforza and others have made it clear that they would welcome seeing Trieste turned into an autonomous international port.

But no Italian can contemplate, except with grief and rage, the possibility of the loss of Trieste. No Italian Government that agreed to such a loss could survive one moment. These are simple facts to which anyone who knows Italy and the Italians can certify.

\*    \*    \*

January 14, 1945

## BULGARS REPORTED UNDER RED CONTROL

*Observer Says Population Is Disappointed by Too Slow Advent of Democracy*

By JOSEPH M. LEVY
By Wireless to The New York Times

ISTANBUL, Turkey, Jan. 10 (Delayed)—The people of Bulgaria are disappointed and feel that they are being cheated by the Allies. The average Bulgar believed the promises made over the Allied radio from London, Moscow and New York that when his country was liberated from the Germans, he, too, would be liberated and eventually enjoy President Roosevelt's Four Freedoms.

He hoped that as soon as the dictatorial fascist regime in Bulgaria was overthrown, the Allies would assist his country to establish a true liberal and democratic government. But instead, he feels, Bulgaria today, four months after liberation from the Nazi yoke, is subjected to a Bulgarian dictatorial regime as unbearable and distasteful to the vast majority of Bulgars as was the former Nazi-inspired fascist government.

The present government is composed of representatives of the four major parties, but only the Communists exercise real power. When, on Sept. 9, a group of Army officers headed by the present Minister of War, Gen. Damian Veltcheff, staged a coup d'etat and overthrew the Muravieff Cabinet, the Fatherland Front formed a new government under the Premiership of Kimon Gueorgieff, which is still in office.

### Reds Control Militia

The Fatherland Front is composed of representatives of the Agrarian, Zveno, Socialist and Communist parties. Although the Communists represent hardly more than 2 per cent of the people of Bulgaria, their party is well organized while the others are not. The Minister of the Interior, Anton Yugoff, a Communist, has full control of the militia, which is the only police force in Bulgaria.

During the period of the Nazi regime, of a total population of about 6,000,000, there were from 12,000 to 15,000 Partisans roaming the Bulgarian mountains, resisting the local police and military authorities, and occasionally staging acts of sabotage to German supply dumps. Nearly all these Partisans were Communists. Under the Fascist Philoff-Boshiloff and Bagrianoff Government, the most barbaric and inhuman methods were employed against the Partisans. Not only were they killed and their bodies left lying naked in village or town squares—to intimidate the population—but all their relatives, including women and children, also were executed by firing squads, burned alive or hanged to the nearest telegraph pole.

After the coup of Sept. 9, the Partisans came down from the mountains and nearly all of them were enrolled in the militia. With rifles and revolvers placed at their disposal, these young Partisan militiamen are in absolute control of Bulgaria.

For about a fortnight after the coup they were extremely well-behaved and disciplined and did not act vengefully. During that period the majority of Bulgars believed it probable that the Fatherland Front would create a genuine democratic government in which Communists would participate and cooperate. It soon became apparent, however, that the Fatherland Front committees had become the tools of the hitherto insignificant Communists, who had never been a political power in Bulgaria.

### Terrorism Is Charged

With the militia under their control, the Communists have asserted themselves and now are driving fast to gain a full hold on the country's administration. The methods they employ are often barbaric, and certainly undemocratic.

A case in point is that of George Kissiloff, a close associate of former Premier Dobri Boshiloff. All agree that his arrest was fully justified, but even the most ardent anti-Nazis fail to understand why his wife and 14-year-old son were sent to a concentration camp. The only charges against his wife, who incidentally is Jewish, and their son is their relationship to Kissiloff.

A virtual reign of terror prevails in Bulgaria, in which ordinary civil rights are almost non-existent. Such elementary democratic principles as free speech and free press criticism are taboo. The writer, having just returned from a six-week stay in Bulgaria, is convinced that the vast majority of the people in that country are bitterly disillusioned over the present situation They ardently are hoping for early Allied action to establish a democratic regime. The Bulgarian people are confused and hurt, but are clamoring for democracy.

\* \* \*

February 6, 1945

## BLACKOUT IN THE BALKANS

An Associated Press dispatch to this newspaper yesterday from Rome reported that "prolonged negotiations" on the part of Allied officials in that city "have failed to gain access for American and British correspondents as a group to any of the Balkan countries except Greece." One Reuter man who formerly lived in Belgrade has been permitted to return there. But no other correspondent has been permitted to go from Italy into Yugoslavia, and efforts to arrange for the sending of a group of correspondents into Rumania and Bulgaria have been "fruitless." As a source of news the Balkans are blacked out.

Questioned in Washington yesterday about this Associated Press dispatch, Under-Secretary of State Grew "made it clear that Moscow policies and Moscow administrators control the area to which correspondents have not been admitted freely." He also said that our Government "vigorously supports" the applications of American correspondents "to go into the Balkans and report what is going on there."

We hope that in the course of its vigorous support our Government has told the Soviet authorities frankly and with the emphasis which such a warning merits that nothing could possibly do more harm to Russian-American relations than a policy which, whatever its purpose, encourages in this country a belief that the Soviet Government is blacking out the Balkans because it does not want the outside world to see what is happening in the area under its control. Such a policy will merely feed suspicion, rumor and resentment. If there is any subject that deserves plain speaking between allies, this is it.

\* \* \*

February 11, 1945

## ALBANIA VOICES PLEA

### Ask Allies to Recognize Present 'Democratic' Government

Declaring that the meeting of the Big Three had been received "with great enthusiasm by the Albanian people," the Tirana radio said in a domestic broadcast reported yesterday by the Federal Communications Commission that in connection with the conference the "Albanian people raises its voice once again" asking that the Government of Col. Gen. Enver Hoxha be recognized by the Allies.

The broadcast said that the Albanian people had denounced all traitors who had collaborated with the enemy and had placed at the head of the Government those men who "enjoyed its confidence, those persons who had emerged out of this war of liberation, those persons who were able, faithful, industrious and who were from the people."

It declared that recognition should come now for the sake of the war the Albanian people had waged and "is still waging in Yugoslav territory" and "for the sake of the contribution it has given."

\* \* \*

February 12, 1945

## GREEKS SIGN PACT ENDING CIVIL FIGHT

*Government, Eam Delegates Reach Accord After Long Parley, Aided by British*

By The United Press

ATHENS, Monday, Feb. 12—The Greek Government and leaders of the Eam faction have signed a peace protocol, it was announced early today.

The settlement, came after ten days of negotiations of problems that caused the Greek civil war. The date of the termination of martial law in the country was believed the final issue to be settled.

Earlier the conferees had called in British Ambassador Reginald Leeper and Harold MacMillan, British Resident Minister in the Mediterranean, to sit during the final phase of the negotiations.

Both sides had agreed on details for separation of political from common crimes committed during the period of turmoil that followed so swiftly on the country's liberation from the German yoke. This had been one of the main obstacles, the Eam having insisted on amnesty for those charged with political offenses.

The Government of Archbishop Damaskinos and Premier Nicholas Plastiros had delivered what it called its final views prior to a six-hour conference ending Sunday morning in which fresh disagreements developed. British advisers attended this meeting, which was reported to have produced sharp argument. Foreign Minister John Sofianopoulos obtained adjournment of the session until later in the day. In talks that ran after midnight the settlement was made.

\* \* \*

February 13, 1945

## PACT GIVES ELAS 2 WEEKS TO DISARM

*Leftists to Oversee Collection—Plebiscite on King, Vote on Greek Regime Reported Set*

### BOTH SIDES PRAISE ACCORD

*Eam Leader Explains Excesses as Due to Collaborators, Promises Investigation*

ATHENS, Feb. 12 (AP)—Elas forces have agreed to stack their arms within fourteen days, it was announced today, under terms of the pact reached by the Left Wing Eam [National Liberation Front] and the Government of Premier Nicholas Plastiras.

Under the peace agreement, signed early today after weeks of negotiation, the arms of the Elas, fighting force of the Eam, will be turned over to Elas guards in thirty-seven localities within Elas territory. The Elas will remain custodian of the arms for the Greek Government.

The agreement stipulates the minimum of arms to be accounted for, including at least 41,500 rifles, 1,000 light machine guns, 168 mortars, sub-machine guns, heavy machine guns, thirty-two pieces of assorted artillery and fifteen radios.

A National Guard call-up by age groups will go into effect in each area as that body takes over for the Government. This appeared to indicate that Elas members in appropriate age groups would be mustered as national guards.

[The British radio said that its Athens correspondent had reported that the agreement provided for a plebiscite on the monarchy and a general election this year. The broadcast was recorded by the Office of War Information.

[A British broadcast from Athens, heard by the Columbia Broadcasting System, quoted Harold Macmillan, British Resident Minister in the Mediterranean, as having said that he considered the agreement "a fair and honorable settlement," whose results would be fruitful for Greece.]

### ANNOUNCEMENT OF PACT

The communiqué on the agreement:

The conference between representatives of the Greek Government and the Eam delegation which was convened on the initiative of his beatitude, Archbishop Damaskinos, Regent, has been brought to a conclusion.

At 4:30 A. M., Feb. 12, agreement was reached on all points under discussion without exception.

As it was late, it was not possible for a detailed statement to be signed and representatives of either side were satisfied with the signing of a brief protocol.

In a subsequent statement to the press, its first since the civil war began, the Eam said through its secretary general, Dimitrius Partsalides, that the agreement would "contribute to the pacification of the country because it will enable the economic rehabilitation necessary to Greece in its present plight.

"The Eam will continue to exist after the agreement," he added, "with the view of securing the people's rights."

Mr. Partsalides said that the Eam had asked for a general amnesty "because the differentiation between various types of crimes (political and criminal) is difficult and dangers may arise." He added that the Eam agreed that there had been cases where Eam supporters took the law into their hands, but declared that "such things are inevitable when collaborators are circulating freely."

Concerning the executions of certain prominent persons not identified with collaboration. Mr. Partsalides asserted that "nobody can justify these crimes, but as soon as we can get back we shall investigate the matter, as we feel sure they were committed by anarchists and reactionaries."

Questioned about the presence of Germans and Bulgarians in the Eam-Elas ranks, he said, "if there have been a few, we cannot be blamed, because they served on ideological grounds."

### Communist Traces Conflict

George Siantos, secretary general of the Communist party and spokesman for the Eam, said that he was pleased with the agreement.

Speaking at his first formal news conference, Mr. Siantos added, "Our policy always has been to insure popular liberty and democratic evolution. For this we will continue to struggle."

"In such a conflict as this," he said, referring to the civil war, "the fruits will be obvious later on. It was a conflict between opposing currents—one the popular movement that seeks a new and better future, and the other the Old World, which considers power in our country a God-given something never to change. It was these two currents that clashed."

He emphasized that in his view the clash did not originate from the Left. He denied that the Eam-Elas attempted a coup d'etat Dec. 3 and said that the trouble arose from former Premier George Papandreou's order of that day prohibiting a demonstration.

An Eam statement disclosed that the organization had made no demand to be permitted to participate in the Greek Government.

\* \* \*

cent of the seats in his Cabinet, seems likely to afford the first test of the new Yalta formula for the tri-partite solution of internal conflicts in liberated countries, it was said here today in diplomatic circles.

According to reports received in London there is a strong resemblance between the present situation in Rumania and that in Greece before the recent civil war.

The Moscow newspapers, in fact, have accused General Radescu of provoking a state of affairs that would justify him in taking "Greek" measures. The analogy is imperfect in that the measures taken by former Premier George Papandreou, and after him by Gen. Nicholas Plastiras in Greece, received the support of the major power within whose sphere of influence Greece lay—Great Britain. But Rumania was liberated by the Red Army, and if the Teheran rather than the Yalta formula were to prevail, it would be Soviet Russia that would be expected to call the tune there, in a manner unfavorable to General Radescu.

### Pre-Election Control Possible

Will the Yalta formula be applied? What the Moscow press has been demanding is that the growing strength of the National Democratic front be recognized at the expense of the Peasant party of Julius Maniu, whose supporters still hold the most important Government posts.

It is understood in London that the Inter-Allied Control Commission in Bucharest, in which Soviet Russia, the United States and Great Britain are represented, has already recommended that the Radescu government, or one similarly constituted under a different leader, should administer Rumania's affairs until elections can be held.

The position is that Rumania is still a chief military base for Russian operations against the German Army in Hungary, and that the Allies therefore do not want civil war or even a too embittered political conflict there if it can be avoided. The best chance of avoiding it—according to present indications—is to set up a provisional government in which Left and Right will be equally represented under a Premier less suspect to Moscow.

General Radescu, it is said, has a reactionary background and is in close touch with former Fascist Army leaders.

\* \* \*

**February 27, 1945**

# RUMANIAN IMPASSE HELD A YALTA TEST

*Radescu's Struggle Likened in Part to Greek Conflict—*
*Allies May Yet Step In*

By JOHN MacCORMAC
By Wireless to The New York Times

LONDON, Feb. 26—The dispute between the Rumanian Prime Minister, Gen. Nicolai Radescu, and the Communist-inspired National Democratic Front, which holds 40 per

**March 4, 1945**

# PLOT TO BALK YALTA IN RUMANIA IS SEEN

*Leftists Held Trying to Seize Power Before Crimea Plan*
*Can Be Implemented*

By FRANK O'BRIEN
Associated Press Correspondent

ANKARA, Turkey, March 3—Disorders in Rumania which preceded the resignation of Premier Nicolae Radescu this week were apparently led by Leftists in the hope of seizing power before the Crimea Conference decisions could be put into effect.

There is no indication here that any Russians are taking a hand in the settlement of the important problems raised by the bid for power by Rumania's Communists in the name of the National Democratic Front.

I have information that as late as last Wednesday no new instructions based on the Yalta conference had reached American quarters in Rumania, and my informant said that he believed that none had reached the British or the Russians.

It seems that the left wing in Rumania forced the crisis with all possible speed after the Yalta meetings, hoping that concerted action would enable them to seize power before the decisions could filter down in the form of executive orders to the relatively lesser Soviet authorities ordinarily in charge of Rumania.

### 2,000 Members Claimed

It remains to be seen whether an impartial advisory or control board will hand the Rumanian Government over to the Communists. I asked the supposed head of the Communist party, Lucretiu Patrascanu, in September how many members his party had. He answered 2,000. [M. Patrascanu was made Minister of Justice in November.] His answer would indicate that a Communist government in Rumania would mean rule by a small minority and could survive only with outside help, either direct or indirect.

According to information available here, Gheorghe Gheorgiu-Dej, Minister of Communications in the Radescu government, went to Moscow early in January with one of the two real heads of the Rumanian Communist party, Anna Pauker, a Rumanian who became a Soviet citizen in the Thirties.

They returned the same month and are said to have spread the word that:
(1) Peasant Leader Juliu Maniu had to be eliminated.
(2) An effort had to be made to win the peasants by forcing land reforms.
(3) The workers had to stay at their benches in factories.
(4) Rumania would get United Nations standing if a National Democratic Front Government came to power.

### Splinter Groups Formed

The National Democratic Front was formed last October by Left Wingers who grouped themselves into six parties, giving them a claim to six Cabinet seats, instead of the one or two that the Communist party alone might claim and get.

In a platform published after the formation of the front it was announced immediately that only control of the government by the Front would satisfy the Left, and since then agitation against all other elements has been steady.

Shortly after the Front's formation I witnessed a National Peasant party demonstration in front of the Royal Palace in Bucharest, at which King Michael and M. Maniu were cheered. The demonstration was broken up by Communist intervention with shouts of "Down with the

King," "Down with the army" and "Let's get the Red Army to protect us."

The Soviet censor refused to pass my eye-witness account or any account at all.

The following day Communist papers in Bucharest declared that the Peasant party demonstrators had shouted slogans in favor of Horia Sima, former leader of the Rumanian fascist Iron Guard. The papers also accused M. Maniu of being a Fascist.

### Maniu Forced Out

Shortly afterward M. Maniu, who was Minister of State, was forced out of the government, and the Leftists insisted on General Radescu as Premier. Now he is attacked as a Fascist.

General Radescu in a recent speech blamed the Left for the first of the current disorders, particularly Anna Pauker and her coleader of the Communist party, the Hungarian Laszlo Luca. This was followed by an abrupt end to his career as Premier.

### Sovietizing Aim Denied

MOSCOW, March 3 (AP)—The Moscow News, English-language newspaper, denied today foreign newspaper statements that the demands of the National Democratic Front in Rumania would "Sovietize" the country.

Accusing former Premier Radescu of "political banditry" and "the shooting of peaceful demonstrators in Bucharest on Feb. 24," the Moscow News continued:

"What is strange is that the correspondent of such a substantial newspaper as The New York Times should be credulous enough to believe the provocative fiction invented by Radescu and should be now attempting to assure the American reader that carrying out of the demands of the National Democratic Front would mean 'sovietizing' Rumania."

The newspaper said further that "every unprejudiced objective observer who studies the ten points of the program of the Rumanian National Democratic Front will have no difficulty seeing that not one of them extends beyond the framework of the armistice terms presented Rumania by the three Allied powers."

\*   \*   \*

April 12, 1945

## TITO SIGNS SOVIET PACT

*Binds Yugoslavia to 20-Year Alliance With Moscow*

LONDON, Thursday, April 12 (U.P.)—Russia and Yugoslavia yesterday signed a pact of friendship, providing for an alliance of twenty years duration, the Moscow radio announced early today.

The pact was signed in Moscow by Marshal Tito and Soviet Foreign Commissar Vyacheslaff M. Molotoff, it was announced.

\*   \*   \*

**May 23, 1945**

## BALKAN REDS GET CONTROL BY RUSE

*Run Governments Through Ministries of Justice and Interior—
Purges Bloody*

By Wireless to The New York Times

ISTANBUL, Turkey, May 22 (London Times dispatch)—
Developments in the Balkans point to the existence of a plan
carefully preconceived and systematically applied to establish
a Communist regime, or one like it, in every country in the
peninsula.

The principle seems to be that a political organization,
however small the number of its original members, can, if it
possesses determined, well-disciplined and "dynamic" elements, easily acquire political ascendancy and finally impose
its will on a country.

The first step is to get hold of such key positions as the
Ministers of Justice and the Interior, with the control of the
police and gendarmerie. The second is to exterminate political opponents and to break up kindred parties that might
become rivals.

### Minority Wields Control

When the process is completed the strength of the party
seizing power is increased by the adherence of people who
are prompted to join by fear or opportunism, and thus it has
a following of 25 to 30 per cent of the electorate, a figure
considered sufficient for wielding political control. This
technique is now being applied in the Balkans.

When the German collapse in the Balkans began there was
formed in Bulgaria the Patriotic Front, composed of the
Communist, Agrarian, Social-Democrat and Zveno parties,
and the present Georgieff Government was put into power.
The Communists took the Ministries of Justice and Interior.
They displaced the police and gendarmerie by a militia under
their control. Thus, in spite of official appearances, Bulgarian
public life today is under complete Communist sway.

The first consequence of this Communist ascendancy has
been the extermination of political opponents through trials
in "people's courts" and by other means. Between 1,500 and
2,000 politicians, administrators, professors and journalists
have been sentenced to death and executed. No doubt some
of them deserved punishment, but the guilt of many of them
was, to say the least, open to question—so much so that these
wholesale killings revolted the more moderate elements
among the Communists and the trials were stopped.

Apart from these official executions, some 15,000 or 20,000
persons have been murdered, a figure based on the knowledge
that at least two persons, a local policeman and a tax collector,
have been put to death in each of 8,000 Bulgarian villages.

### The Method in Rumania

The method used in Rumania is almost the same, with the
difference that the number of Rumanian Communists is small

and the pace is slower than in Bulgaria. The diamissal of
Gen. Nicolae Radescu, the Prime Minister, and the advent of
Petru Groza gave the Communists the Ministries of Justice
and Interior and control of the police.

The official program is to punish collaborationists and
eradicate the Iron Guard. The National Peasant party and its
leader, Jutiu Maniu, are also targets for violent attacks, aiming
at breaking the party up and compelling most of its supporters
to join the Communists.

The activity of the British and American missions with the
Allied Control Commissions in Bulgaria and Rumania has so
far been purely formal. The real power was in the hands of
Russian Commanders in Chief while the war lasted.

### Serbs Await Their Day

Conditions in Yugoslavia are rather different because of
the personality of Marshal Tito, who has emerged as the only
real war leader in the Balkans. Moreover, Yugoslav political
issues, grave as they are, are overshadowed by national and
confessional differences. The vast majority of Serbs are
maintaining an attitude of sullen opposition to the present
regime. Conscious of the sacrifices that Serbia has made during the past thirty years for the liberation and unification of
Yugoslavia, they refuse to accept the partition of their country at a time and under conditions that render a free expression of the popular will impossible.

Reports from Albania are so confusing that it is impossible to form a clear idea of the situation there.

\* \* \*

**May 25, 1945**

## BUFFER IN BALKANS CALLED SOVIET AIM

*Lend-Lease and UNRRA Aid Reported Used by Moscow in
Establishing Cordon*

By C. L. SULZBERGER
By Wireless to The New York Times

LONDON, May 24—The problems of eastern Europe
have posed the first seriously difficult set of inter-Allied
questions, because it is across this area that rival ideologies
and diplomatic policies of the Soviet Union and of Britain
and the United States initially meet.

It would seem that eastern Europe in Soviet eyes includes
that area east of a rough line extending northward from Trieste
and Italian Gorizia to Stettin on the Baltic on the west bank of
the Oder.

This takes in a good piece of Austria, which is therefore
involved in toto. Furthermore the present impermanent
demarcation line between Anglo-American and Red Army
troops in Germany is also affected. That this may be shifted
farther westward is widely rumored.

The Soviet Union regards eastern Europe proper as a
security zone where in the past western powers have built

up cordons sanitaires that have been turned against the Soviet system. Therefore, with frequently tactless haste, Moscow has sought to establish in that area governments and social systems that it can consider truly and reliably friendly. Many toes have been stepped upon in the process, but the Soviet feels its strong interests justified.

### Treaty Aimed at All Attackers

The net result has been, if anything, to develop a cordon sanitaire in reverse—one that points west. Some observers see confirmation of this in the wording of the unilateral treaties between the U.S.S.R. and the three western Slavic states of Yugoslavia, Czechoslovakia and Poland.

This correspondent asked Prime Minister Edward B. Osubka-Morawski of the Polish Provisional Government: "Does the new Soviet-Polish treaty apply to any potential enemies of either Poland or the Soviet Union or just to Germany or allies of Germany?"

The bushy-haired, dynamic little Premier and Foreign Minister replied, "For the present moment the treaty is intended only against Germany, but if any other country attacks our territories it will be applied against them also." Emphasis to this determination is given by the prominent role devoted to the rapid rearmament of all three west Slavic countries.

Marshal Michal Rola-Zymierski told the writer that already his forces included the following: Two armies comprising ten infantry divisions, one tank corps, one aviation corps and "several" infantry divisions completing their training in Poland now.

He said that at this moment Poland could mobilize 500,000 men, except for a lack of officers and a shortage of uniforms. The Lodz textile factories are now working overtime to make uniforms.

The following officers' schools have been opened: Three for infantry officers, two for artillery officers, two for aviation officers, one for tank officers, one for liaison officers, one for engineering officers and last, but far from least, one for "political education officers."

Marshal Rola-Zymierski expressed confidence that this would permit him not only to replenish his officers corps but to form new units.

Similarly great efforts are being made in Czechoslovakia and Yugoslavia to build up again an armed strength from their ravaged lands to face the danger, it is emphasized, of any potential future German aggression. These steps are being taken quickly.

The Soviet Union is implementing its treaties with these lands by granting arms, munitions, transport and other assistance to facilitate this effort to regain strength. Even lend-lease trucks are being employed to accomplish this and in some cases, as in that of Trieste, United Nations Relief and Rehabilitation Administration materials.

There should be no concern about such development if, as popular sentiment insists, a brave new world of global security is constructed from the shambles of the old. Unfor-

tunately, at times, there are indications of the lack of inter-Allied harmony.

The Soviet Union is furthermore trying to assist its new allies in eastern Europe, as well as in former enemy countries, by strengthening trade relations. From certain defeated lands, such as Rumania, huge quantities of machinery, such as refinery equipment, were removed to the U.S.S.R., but this tendency has now ceased.

The U.S.S.R. would like to develop markets in eastern Europe and especially Danubia. It can use Polish cloth, metal and glass from Silesia, arms and consumers' goods from Bohemia, Czechoslovakia, and copper, lead and zinc from Yugoslavia.

Some of these items can be obtained in exchange in the near future for assistance already granted, including food and armaments and some on credits. And, in the more distant future, it is certain that a more soundly coordinated commercial system can and will be established to a large degree, at least replacing the regions' formerly absolute dependence upon Germany—a development facilitated by the liberation of Austria and Bohemia and the improvement of their economic ties with Moscow.

\* \* \*

September 9, 1945

## GREECE HELD ISSUE TESTING BIG FIVE

*Peace in Southeastern Europe Seen Resting in Council's Ability to Find Solution*

**RHINELAND ALSO FACTOR**

*Problems of Far East, Coming Sooner Than Expected at Potsdam, Also Thorny*

By C. L. SULZBERGER
By Cable to The New York Times

LONDON, Sept. 8—The Soviet Union's Foreign Commissar and the Foreign Ministers of France and China are expected to arrive here tomorrow, together with their delegations, to attend the Big Five Council meeting of Foreign Secretaries. On Monday the United States party, headed by Secretary James E. Byrnes, will land, and the following day Ernest Bevin, director of Great Britain's foreign policy, will open the initial session of the biggest diplomatic event that London has seen in years.

Already a whole series of international discussions, some open and some secluded, are taking place in the battered British capital, which for weeks to come will serve as a proving ground for statesmen seeking to win the peace made possible by the military victory of their armies.

The problems already under discussion are numerous, but they are likely to be overshadowed by those brought here within the next forty-eight hours by the Big Five's delegates.

The main subject on the diplomatic front at week's end was Greece. The Greek Regent, Archbishop Damaskinos, who already has had a long meeting with Mr. Bevin, will resume his talks after the Foreign Minister has had a chance to take up the burden of the prelate's visit with Prime Minister Clement R. Attlee and the Cabinet.

### Socialist Flavoring Possible

As far as can be ascertained, the British are eager to shift their policy in Greece by postponing the scheduled popular decision on the King's return. This would more or less freeze the Regency status for a year or eighteen months, which the British now may advocate in view of the uneasy conditions in Greece today and the unsettled East European diplomatic situation.

Should this move be decided on, it is a good guess that Archbishop Damaskinos, upon returning to Athens, would terminate the Voulgaris service Cabinet and install a political Government with large Socialist participation, a political flavoring equally pleasing to Mr. Bevin and to the Regent, who himself reputedly has socialistic leanings.

King George of Greece has been conveniently got out of the way to Scotland during Regent Damaskinos visit, and if he does get called back it is possible it would be to hear the tactful suggestion that he might ease the tension by offering to abdicate—something to which he is not in the least likely to agree.

The present Government in Britain does not differ much in this policy from that of Winston Churchill during the past year. Mr. Churchill himself prevailed upon the Greek King not to return last December. Now, because the large Leftist opposition in Greece would boycott popular ballotting under present conditions, thus giving the monarchists a majority and promising a first-class crisis, the British are eager to postpone things.

### Peace in Southeast at Stake

They hope to obtain American backing in this aim so that they can act jointly. Archbishop Damaskinos is eager to see Mr. Byrnes, but since Greece was not on the original Council agenda, it is uncertain whether the Secretary of State, who is a stickler for form, will care to mix in this business now.

On the success or failure of these discussions will depend to a certain extent the entire Southeast European diplomatic situation and Allied policy in that area, Yugoslavia, Rumania and Bulgaria are all current sore spots, and when the Big Five Council meeting was planned at Potsdam, it was not exactly clear how they would figure in the sessions, aside from discussions concerning the eventual peace treaties with the defeated powers, such as the latter two.

But things are taking their own course. Young Peter of Yugoslavia slipped over to Paris incognito for two days this week and saw Dr. Vladimir Matchek, émigré Croatian Peasant leader, because the British would not give him a visa.

Dr. Matchek agreed to back Peter, and the King in turn has promised the little Peasant politician his full support. If the British still balk on giving Dr. Matchek a visa, he may go to the United States, for which he already has an entry permit, and the King might decide to go there also.

As Yugoslavia prepares for the eventual elections, nasty stories of dictatorship are echoing out from there. King Peter, whose revenues with which to pay his personal staff have just been cut off by Marshal Tito, hopes to be able to obtain Anglo-American intervention in his country, at least as strong as the recent slap at Bulgaria.

### Balkans Not Ignorable

Marshal Tito's Government is seeking to get into the diplomatic scramble here and has applied for visas for a Yugoslav delegation "to the peace conference." The British have advised Yugoslavia that this is not a peace conference but just a Big Five meeting, and no visas were issued.

Meanwhile, the Big Powers are calling each other mild names over neighboring Rumania. While Generalissimo Stalin entertained Petru Groza, Rumania's Premier, Moscow accused Britain and America of prompting King Michael to complain about his Government. British sources rebutted that this was not only untrue but that the Foreign Office had warned King Michael that he had better not get into any hot water just now because he could not rely on London's support.

Whether the Big Five planned it that way or not, the Balkans are going to intrude into a schedule that is quite packed anyway.

Obviously the Balkans are involved up to their ears in two of the biggest subjects on the agenda—the question of administering waterways, such as the Dardanelles and the Danube River, and the question of drafting peace treaties with Italy, Hungary, Rumania, Bulgaria and Finland.

It is obvious that no quick decisions can be made on either topic. The Big Five will be doing well if they settle a few major points on treaty proposals and then leave it to the expert commissions to draw up the drafts. These commissions may well not have the proposed treaties ready for presentation for six months.

### Trieste Bristles With Thorns

The Soviet Union, Britain and the United States are likely to run head-on into one another on the question of Trieste. Moscow wants Yugoslavia to have it, and the English-speaking lands do not. Furthermore, the Renner Government in Austria, as was expected, has just filed a claim to southern Tyrol.

The Greeks are going to get the Dodecanese Islands from Italy, and it is possible that, because of their internal difficulties, they may be advised not to claim any continental lands from Albania and Bulgaria, which might slightly simplify treaty-making on the Balkan mainland.

It is almost certain that the French Foreign Minister will bring another man-sized problem with him—French desire to separate the Rhineland from Germany by one means or other. This is the first topflight meeting in which the French have been included, and Georges Bidault can be expected to use it as a forum to demand not only this drastic weakening of the Reich, but also to raise the subject of Indo-China and the Levantine States.

Far Eastern problems, which had not been planned for this session when it was conceived at Potsdam because nobody knew that the Japanese war would be over, are bound to arise. For this reason, the British Dominions have been invited to send observers who may be called in for special sessions.

Furthermore, the British have their own private sideshow— a full-dress gathering of their diplomatic envoys to Middle Eastern lands, where plenty of post-war trouble is likely to pop. The Anglo-Egyptian treaty expires next year. There is heated feeling in Cairo, Egypt, about all foreigners and much suspicion that London plans to strengthen its hold on the Sudan.

\* \* \*

September 10, 1945

## BALKAN DEMOCRACY IS FOUND BY PRAVDA

*Moscow Newspaper Assails The Times for Views, Denies Regimes Are Totalitarian*

By BROOKS ATKINSON
By Wireless to The New York Times

MOSCOW, Sept. 9—The Sabbath morning peace was disturbed today by sharp words about The New York Times in the newspaper Pravda's "International Notes." After a general discussion of "reactionary" journalists who characterize the political regimes of Rumania, Bulgaria and Hungary as totalitarian, the article says:

"With a stubborness worthy of other uses, The New York Times frequently declares that totalitarian instead of representative regimes have been establishd in Bulgaria, Rumania and Hungary. It would be futile to try to get The New York Times to offer arguments in proof of this position. It prefers to make the statement dogmatically.

"But this is clear: one does not need to know the history of the internal political situation of these countries, but one has deliberately to close one's eyes to the spring-tide of democracy in these countries and one has to be completely lacking in respect for the national initiative and creative democratic force of the masses to call modern Bulgaria, Rumania and Hungary countries of totalitarian regimes.

"The New York Times avoids arguments because they are against the policy of this newspaper. But murder will out. The New York Times cannot conceal the anti-democratic attitude of some of its correspondents."

### Atomic Bomb's Role

According to Pravda, The New York Times thinks that democratic development of the Governments in question can be promoted on one hand by "the strength of American democracy, which was revealed by the part that the United States played in the victory in Europe and Asia, the crowning achievement of which was the atomic bomb," and on the other hand, by the fact that "the world hopes to get help from the United States."

Then Pravda exclaims:

"So the atomic bomb and future help from the United States are to be the means of influencing the peoples of the Balkan countries! At last here is where The New York Times stands."

In Pravda's estimation, this is "turning the great cause of freedom and independence of people into a simple commercial transaction, into common business."

### View on Journalists

Elsewhere in the polemic Pravda declared that the journalists who describe the political regimes of Rumania, Bulgaria and Hungary as totalitarian are the same who want to restore the political parties that acted as fascist agents and the same ones who are not excited about the regime in Greece, "where a fascist clique oppresses all democratic elements."

The method that these journalists use, according to Pravda, is the same that Herbert Hoover used when he described President Franklin D. Roosevelt's regime as totalitarian and when Conservatives in Britain tried to prove that election of a Labor Government would be equivalent to the suicide of British democracy.

Today's article is further proof of the increasingly obvious fact that Russia's use of the word "democracy" is not identical with its use by the Western democracies. Our whole conception of democratic procedures differs radically. In Russia democracy has a much more specific political connotation, as does the use of the word "people."

For some time this correspondent has requested the proper authorities for a definition of "democracy" as the Russians understand the word, but so far without success.

\* \* \*

October 17, 1945

## U. S. AND RUSSIA TILT ON EASTERN EUROPE

*America and Britain Weigh the Advisability of Recognizing Hoxha, Albanian Premier*

**YUGOSLAV FERMENT RISES**

*Democratic Elements Aided by Our Stand for Freedoms— Trend Toward West Grows*

By C. L. SULZBERGER
By Wireless to The New York Times

LONDON, Oct. 16—The diplomatic contest between the Soviet Union, on the one hand, and America, on the other, that has been taking place in eastern Europe is now intensifying as the Balkan elections impend and as the great powers prepare their positions for what must be the inevitable, if not imminent, resumption of post-war peace talks.

Two distinct types of competition are going on—a rivalry for ascendancy in particular countries; a contest in other countries in which the Western powers are clearly giving their support to the numerous but not politically powerful opposition as against Communist-dominated governments supported by Moscow.

It is learned here tonight that the United States and Britain are preparing to recognize Premier Enver Hoxha's Albanian Government, although the move has not yet positively been decided upon. This fits into the over-all Balkan tug-of-war picture.

### Tito Asks Albanian Allegiance

Some time ago Marshal Tito secretly invited Albania to join Yugoslavia. The idea was to incorporate it as an autonomous, federated "Slavic" province. The bait for this offer, which was conveyed through diplomatic channels, was a proposal that if Albania submitted to Belgrade, Tito would award it the territory of the old Turkish Kossovo vilayet, famous in Serbian history but now largely inhabited by Albanians. Tito has also been giving Premier Hoxha open support in his quarrel with Greece.

Premier Hoxha turned down Tito's offer with, it is believed, British and American encouragement. He is asserting Albanian independence on the basis of the pre-occupation 1939 frontiers.

The American view of Premier Hoxha is that he is not what he has been accused of being—a "stooge of Moscow." Washington is thought to believe that he is more of a French Socialist than a Russian Communist and that he is more eager to get Western support as a balance against the Slavic mass than to tie up with the latter.

This opinion, right or wrong, seems to be the policy basis behind the contemplated recognition move. While there is only one Comintern-trained Communist in Premier Hoxha's Cabinet, Sejfullag Malleshova, it is noteworthy that in the projected elections only one party—the usual Balkan Patriotic Front combination—is offering candidates.

### Churchill Disappointed

It may be a risky thing to gamble that recognition is going to mean that Premier Hoxha is going to become a pal, because Winston Churchill found out that it did not work the way he thought it would in the case of Tito. However, it seems there is a hope that Albania, which controls the Otranto Strait leading out of the Adriatic, will look more to the West as a result and that it may help to stabilize things a bit in Greece.

The trouble is that the Greeks are certainly going to suspect that recognition of a country insisting on its 1939 borders means the Allies will not back Greek claims on the Koritza-Argyrokastron area of South Albania and that is not going to make them any too happy. Meanwhile, as a balancing move in Yugoslavia, Marshal Tito is stepping up the propaganda campaign for revisionist claims on Greece. In this he clearly has the mute backing of Moscow.

Internally Tito's situation is increasingly uneasy. Western diplomatic pressure is encouraging a stiff attitude by the very sizable opposition within the country. Dr. Milan Subasitch, it may be recalled, resigned as Foreign Minister after consultation with the British Ambassador.

The American Ambassador Richard C. Patterson, has Washington's full approval to make a battle for democracy as America knows it, and not only is he withholding all economic aid from Tito and insisting on the implementation of the four freedoms but he is employing the potential threat of withdrawal of recognition.

### Report on Yugoslavia

The Yugoslav opposition within the country is keeping close liaison with King Peter, and the politicians grouping around him, including Dr. Vladimir Matchek. Mr. Stoh, a Serbian diplomat who went back to Yugoslavia after the Tito-Subasitch agreement, but who has just slipped out of the country to join this group, has made a disconcerting report on the internal situation. It is understood that he told Dr. Matchek:

"There is general discontent and no real collaboration between Communists and the other parties of the Liberation Front, which serves as a powerless camouflage in the name of democracy.

"The Croats are 90 per cent against the regime and Dr. Matchek is their undisputed leader. His popularity is increasing as he is attacked. More than 120,000 persons are still in prison despite the recent amnesty.

"All important posts are held by Communists, including the local positions, such as the presidency of the Serbian, Bosnian and Croation federated governments, all of whom are local party secretaries who enforce strict controls and suppress individual liberties.

"The Russians have lost their traditional popularity, and the regime could not last without their support, although 700,000 soldiers remain under arms and the Ozna (secret police) are everywhere. If they had a chance the vast majority would vote against the government."

Of course, Dr. Matchek, who is in violent opposition to Tito was delighted at such a report, especially from a Serb, and, of course, Tito's supporters vigorously deny its accuracy. But the matter transcends local political importance and enters directly into the realm of Big Three relationships since London and Washington are displeased with Tito's current rule.

In neighboring Bulgaria the situation is becoming tense on the eve of elections, with the parties outside the Fatherland Front counting on Western support and refusing to take part in the vote. This creates a situation parallel to that of Aug. 26, when American warnings caused postponement of the balloting and the disappearance—so far—of Georgi Dimitroff, former Comintern leader, who was en route back to Sofia.

Maynard Barnes, the American representative in Bulgaria, feels very strongly on the situation and is believed to have obtained Washington's backing when he visited London during the meeting of the Foreign Ministers' Council. Mr. Barnes had actually saved the Agrarian opposition leader, whose name is also Georgi Dimitroff, from arrest and got him out of the country.

### King Michael Looks to Us

In Rumania King Michael is awaiting a reply to a new note to Washington and London asking what he should do next, having broken with the Groza Government on State Department advice and having heard nothing since. However, the easing of censorship in Bucharest is clearly a victory for Burton Y. Berry, American representative there. The situation remains more or less that the Western Powers are backing the King and keeping his father Carol away while the Russians are endorsing Premier Petru Groza.

In Hungary London and Washington were pleased by the election results won by the moderates. However, Communist demonstrations have begun in the provinces, and a coup is not to be excluded at a future date. American recognition has been pledged to Austria and Hungary, and the British will give partial recognition, such as they have accorded to Italy.

In Poland private reports are leaking out that the Beirut support is waning fast and that the Russians, who are now sending in special forces to clean out "bandits," are suffering from the same trend. Neutral observers estimate that Premier Boleslaw Beirut has as little as 10 per cent of the vote behind him now and that Stanislaw Mikolajczyk privately claims 60 per cent, a probable exaggeration.

All over Europe east of the Stettin-Trieste line the cleavage between existing Governments friendly to Moscow and opposition movements leaning on the West is growing. This is an uneasy and potentially dangerous situation.

\*   \*   \*

**October 20, 1945**

## GREEK RIGHT GETS BRITISH WARNING

*Foreign Office Says It Would Oppose Coup—Election Put Off, Athens Official Asserts*

By Wireless to The New York Times

LONDON, Oct. 19—Britain would oppose any Rightist attempt in Greece to seize power just as she opposed the Eam [National Liberation Front] and its army, Elas, last December, Hector MacNeil, Parliamentary Under-Secretary of the Foreign Office, said in Parliament today. Meanwhile the British are not seeking to intervene or influence the composition of the present Greek Government, according to him.

Mr. MacNeil said that the British Government was investigating allegations that members of the Communist party, others in the resistance movement and those who took part in the December fighting had been in prison for considerable periods though no charges had been brought against them.

By implication, he let it be understood that these charges were correct. He said that "considerable influence had been used to oppose these tendencies" and that when the Regent, Archbishop Damaskinos was in Britain representations had been made to him to declare a "wide amnesty from which only collaborators would be excluded."

### Patras Rioting Reported

LONDON, Oct. 19 (U.P.)—A Greek Government spokesman asserted today that elections scheduled for Jan. 25 had been postponed.

The subject of Greece came up in the Commons as dispatches from Athens told of rioting and a general strike call at Patras, in the northern Peloponnesus.

Rome reports have said that United States troops were scheduled to be sent to Greece as "observers" for the elections. Royalists had sought to postpone them until after a plebiscite on return of the monarchy.

An Athens dispatch said that two persons were killed yesterday and several others injured in Patras when police clashed with a crowd returning from the funeral of a worker.

### Tension Still High

By A. C. SEDGWICK
By Wireless to The New York Times

ATHENS, Greece, Oct. 18 (Delayed)—The political crisis that ended yesterday with the assumption of the Premier's duties by the Regent, Archbishop Damaskinos, was apparently followed by tension as great as that before his accession and Greeks who are studying all signs of inflation, food shortages and soaring living costs realize the dangers of a complete national collapse.

It was noted that Senator Claude Pepper of Florida in a press conference last night said that aid from the United Nations Relief and Rehabilitation Administration for an additional year would depend on the Greek people's ability "to establish foundations of political and economic stability."

Following repeated efforts to find a suitable person to form a Government, it appeared that the Regent had no alternative to descending into the arena of party strife, as bitter now as ever in the country's history. Having done so, however, it is contended, he lost the prestige attendant on the Vice-regal office and is now open to political criticism and efforts to undermine his good intentions.

As a year ago moderates saw extremists of the Left manipulating, so now they view with much the same alarm the extremists of the Right, particularly of royalist organizations allegedly addicted to terroristic methods, military cliques and small but influential groups of industrialists, steering the weight of conservative opinion—some think to violence.

It is the Regent's main preoccupation, according to persons close to him, that violence must be avoided at all costs. Any attempt at a coup would be quelled by British arms, probably with international complications.

The reported utterances of Philip J. Noel-Baker, Minister of State, in the British Parliament, to the effect that Britain was opposed to a continuation of the Greek monarchy drew sharp criticism here from many who have hitherto been opposed to royalty but who none the less hold that if the will of the people were manifested in favor of King George II's return then democrats should be the last to interfere with the democratic process.

\* \* \*

October 26, 1945

## BIG POWERS' SPLIT MARS OCCUPATION

### Stalemate Reached in Germany—Balkans Virtually Zone of Russian Interest

By C. L. SULZBERGER
By Wireless to The New York Times

LONDON, Oct. 25—The split among the great powers in the Council of Foreign Ministers has injected confusion into the operations of the Allies' machinery erected in conquered enemy countries. The situation has continued crystalizing into phases varying from a stalemate in the functions of the Allied Control Council in Germany to the de facto existence of a Russian zone of interest in Rumania, Bulgaria and Hungary and of an Anglo-American sphere in Italy.

Certainly this cannot be considered a healthy situation. Furthermore, there is little doubt that the political factions in these conquered populations are fully aware of it. Reports from The New York Times' correspondents in six zones governed by Allied Control Council or commissions—Germany, Austria, Hungary, Italy, Rumania and Bulgaria—indicate the following situation:

In Germany the ACC faces serious problems, the foremost of which is what should be done about France. France was not a party to the Berlin Conference and is refusing to implement the decisions taken there.

### Possible Solutions Listed

Since the procedure demands unanimous ACC decisions for Germany and the Berlin Kommandatura, the French attitude has created a stalemate in such questions as administration, taxation and communications. The possible solutions presented are French acquiescence to be sought diplomatically—most unlikely, since the French elections gave Gen. Charles de Gaulle's foreign policy an incentive to press harder for the further partition of Germany—the ousting of the French from participation in the ACC of the revision of the Potsdam agreement.

Additional sources of friction in the German ACC are Russia's suspicions about the Anglo-American hesitation to implement the reparations promises and the personal pique between Marshal Georgi K. Zhukoff and Field Marshal Sir Bernard L. Montgomery that Gen. Dwight D. Eisenhower is forced to soothe, while in the meantime all three parties are becoming irritated with what they consider French obstinacy and vice versa.

In Rumania the ACC is functioning with a minimum of friction by comparison with its inception, but the Russians are making it clear that they consider that they are running the show. The Americans and the British, without admittedly yielding their rights, are being treated as observers rather than active participants. The Russians head all the ACC's sections as well as the plenary sessions.

### Personal Relations Cordial

While this situation prevails, personal relations remain cordial among the Big Three's representatives. This is not so true in Bulgaria, where the Russian attitude is basically similar but psychologically stiffer. The need to settle fundamental problems and differing interpretations of aims does not contribute to harmony, but at any rate the councils in these two countries function as well as might be expected under the circumstances.

In Italy the "control" has dropped from the Allied Commission, and the Allied Military Government is functioning only in Piedmont, Liguria and the three Venezias. All but Venezia Giulia will be handed over to Italian administration any day, so the Allied Commission is a sort of lame duck ready to pass its job over to the United Nations Relief and Rehabilitation Administration and the economic missions except in territory disputed with Yugoslavia.

The Russians have had little to do with the ACC itself but their liaison and displaced-persons missions have been getting in a lot of spadework with Italian Communists and Yugoslav expatriates.

In Hungary the ACC has not been so successful as in Austria. It is reported Marshal Klementi Voroshiloff is courteously but insistently running rather a one-man show and the American and British representatives are limited largely to extra-mural influence.

\* \* \*

November 9, 1945

## 5 RUMANIANS SLAIN; REDS SMASH FETE

### Troops Fire Into Crowd of 40,000 Hailing King's Birthday— Communists Charge Masses

BUCHAREST, Rumania, Nov. 8 (AP)—Rumanian troops fired machine guns point-blank into crowds at the royal palace today until a Russian general intervened, silenced their fire, and halted a furious riot between Communists and supporters of King Michael.

At least six persons fell when the troops machine-gunned a crowd at one entrance to the Royal Square. First estimates said at least five persons were killed and nearly 100 wounded.

Soviet General Susaikoff, head of the Allied Control Commission in Bucharest, ordered the Rumanian troops to cease firing, thus breaking up the bloodiest part of a six-hour riot between Communists and demonstrators holding a forbidden celebration of the King's birthday.

### Shout "Down With Terror!"

Lines of armed troops tonight guarded the Royal Square, scene of the riots, but demonstrators still marched on the outskirts of the square shouting, "Long live the King" and "Down with terror!"—the same fight-provoking slogans that they had hurled at the Communists during the day's street brawling.

The demonstration had been banned by the Soviet-supported government of Premier Petru Groza, long at odds with young King Michael.

[The Groza Government in a broadcast communiqué Thursday night charged the riots were "a blind for a revolutionary plot directed against the government" by Dr. Juliu Maniu, Peasant party leader, and George Bratianu, Liberal party leader, the British Broadcasting Corporation said. The broadcast, recorded by NBC, charged that the Peasant and Liberal parties "have during recent weeks prepared acts of disorder and mobilized well-known fascist and reactionary elements, under cover of monarchist demonstrations."

[It quoted the Rumanian Minister of the Interior as saying he had decided "to take the most severe and urgent measures to preserve order."]

Guns barked, fists flew and several trucks were overturned in the milling riot that started when Communists charged the crowds celebrating the King's twenty-fourth birthday.

### Reds Roar Into Square

Fifteen truck loads of Communists, waving clenched fists and shouting, "Long live the Groza Government!" roared into the square. They tried to disperse between 40,000 and 50,000 supporters of Michael.

The first shots were fired by unknown persons from the direction of the Ministry of the Interior, which faces the Royal Square. Troops guarding the entrances to the square fired at the demonstrators shortly afterward, but one witness said the officer in charge had ordered his men to shoot over the demonstrators' heads.

At 3:55 P. M. the troops fired again, and it was this time that the six persons were seen to fall to the pavement. Two were killed and four were wounded.

The troops involved on both occasions were members of the Tudor Vladimirescu Division formed in Russia from among Rumanian troops captured in the Stalingrad area.

After the troops fired General Susaikoff who, witnesses said, just happened to be passing by, ordered the shooting stopped. Russian troops in Bucharest remained aloof throughout the day, although well-armed Russian patrols moved about the city tonight pushing in closer to the Royal Square as night fell.

In addition to the Groza Government's forbidding the demonstrations today, a Government-controlled radio broadcast warned all persons to stay at home. Yesterday's newspapers said any celebration would be suppressed. Despite the warnings, the crowds began to gather peacefully before the palace early today. They shouted, "Long live the King!" and waved Rumanian flags and pictures of Michael, who was reported out of the city at Slanio, ninety miles to the north.

Then the Communist trucks sped into the square, weaving through the crowds. For a time it appeared the Communists would break up the demonstrations. Suddenly the crowd converged on two of the trucks and overturned them, dumping out the Communists. The trucks were set on fire.

Then guns fired from the direction of the Ministry of the Interior. The other Communist trucks withdrew, and the Communists fired back at the demonstrators, who scurried for cover.

The rioting, which broke out during a solemn Te Deum in honor of the King's birthday, contrasted with yesterday's peaceful Communist observance of the Soviet October Revolution. That observance was sponsored by the Groza Government. The Government also had announced that the schools, traditionally closed on a Rumanian monarch's birthday, would remain open today.

\* \* \*

November 9, 1945

## BULGARS FETE DIMITROFF AS RED HERO; REICHSTAG FIRE TRIAL FIGURE STEALS SHOW

By Wireless to The New York Times

SOFIA, Bulgaria, Nov. 7 (Delayed)—Celebrations in Sofia marking the twenty-eighth anniversary of the Soviet revolution were turned today into a great manifestation for Georgi Dimitroff, famous Bulgarian Communist, who has just returned from Moscow after twenty-two years exile.

Mr. Dimitroff, hero of the Reichstag fire trials in 1938, at which he made a fool of Hermann Goering, has returned to take part in the general elections scheduled for Nov. 18. He is the first candidate on the single combined Fatherland Front list for the first Sofia district.

An official performance in the National Theatre this afternoon ended with a speech by Mr. Dimitroff, who asserted that the elections would take place as scheduled, despite opposition efforts. He insisted that the present Government would carry them out as the only lawful regime, a Government that really represents Bulgaria and one that is needed at a historic time.

Mr. Dimitroff pledged that he would spend the rest of his life "in service to my own country."

After referring to his role as a defendant in the Reichstag trials he asserted that Nikola Mushanoff, present Democratic leader and then Premier, refused to grant his urgent request for restitution of Bulgarian citizenship following the acquittal in Berlin. In a trembling voice Mr. Dimitroff stressed that it was Premier Joseph Stalin who saved him by granting him Soviet citizenship.

Mr. Dimitroff escaped from Bulgaria in 1923 after the September revolution had been suppressed by Alexander Tsankoff's Government.

\* \* \*

November 13, 1945

## OPPOSITION VOTES CAST IN YUGOSLAVIA

*Tito's Majority Expected to Be Less Than 90–95 Per Cent Previously Predicted*

By Wireless to The New York Times

BELGRADE, Yugoslavia, Nov. 12—Though only the most fragmentary results have begun to come in from yesterday's voting, it is believed that the assured Government majority will prove less than the 90 to 95 per cent that was widely predicted. The actual figure will probably be unavailable for several days.

The percentage of registered voters actually voting is expected to be about 90, but there is no way of knowing how many absentees deliberately abstained. The voting was completely secret and there were no signs of intimidation or violence, at least in Belgrade or the surrounding area visited by press and diplomatic observers. None was reported from elsewhere.

It is safe to say that these were the most honest elections in Yugoslavia's history as far as the electoral machinery was concerned. Even in the 1938 elections, voters were required to ballot openly and violence to opposition voters was far from unknown.

Undoubtedly the opposition would have polled many more votes if the preliminaries had been different. Because of the impossibility of any real campaign, the opposition refused to present candidates. A vote for the opposition meant merely a vote against the Government without any hope of electing somebody else—and still in a polling place where I watched the count the opposition polled 19 per cent, and 17 per cent of the registered voters did not vote. If one considers half the latter group as deliberate abstainers, there is already a respectable opposition vote.

The population is largely ignorant and easily overawed. At the same time, Marshal Tito is a national hero and few would want to vote against him as a person. Aside from a few real reactionaries, the opposition is based on either or both of two factors, according to the individual—opposition to communism and resentment of the coercive measures of Marshal Tito's supporters.

It was the first Yugoslav elections in which women and all classes of men could vote. It would be incorrect to call it a free election, because certainly the opposition had no opportunity to present its case and many voters were afraid to follow their consciences, but it is not only not worse but better than any previous election here.

\* \* \*

November 20, 1945

## FATHERLAND FRONT VICTOR IN BULGARIA

SOFIA, Bulgaria, Nov. 19 (U.P.)—The results of yesterday's nationwide elections, announced today, showed that a high percentage of voters had participated and that the candidates of the Fatherland Front, which supports Premier Kimon Georgieff's Government, had piled up a huge majority.

[The Moscow radio, crediting a statement by the Bulgarian Information Bureau, said that 85 to 90 per cent of the electorate had voted. In the Sofia region, Moscow said, 75 per cent for the Fatherland front.]

Typical results in early returns showed that 32,523 voters in the town of Aitos had given 30,000 votes for the Fatherland Front and that 21,991 had voted for the Fatherland Front in Razlog, where 22,197 voters cast ballots. Approximately 70 per cent of the electorate voted before midafternoon in the Sofia region and neighboring villages. The polling was orderly and no incidents were reported.

Supervisory committees were composed mostly of school teachers. They were appointed to each district by regional judges.

LONDON, Nov. 19 (U.P.)—The Sofia radio said tonight that the five-party Fatherland Front had polled 88 per cent of the total vote cast despite the opposition of the Agrarian party, which allegedly boycotted the elections. Sofia said that the Fatherland Front had received 3,407,355 of 3,862,492 votes cast by a potential electorate of 4,504,732.

\* \* \*

November 30, 1945

## YUGOSLAVS OUST KING PETER, PROCLAIM FEDERAL REPUBLIC

*Belgrade Radio Says Dynasty Has Forfeited All Rights— Monarch Charges Fraud, Tyranny—Official Britain Silent*

By HERBERT L. MATTHEWS

By Cable to The New York Times

LONDON, Nov. 29—Yugoslavia was proclaimed a republic today by the Constituent Assembly meeting in Belgrade. The news was learned here from the Belgrade radio and Peter Karageorgevitch—still considering himself King Peter II—promptly issued a statement expressing his grief and refusal to accept this decision.

At the British Foreign Office it was calmly stated that some such result had been expected ever since the elections, and that there was no intention to get too excited about it. It is realized, however, that Great Britain and the United States, as allies of Yugoslavia, will have to consult one another as to the official stand that they will take.

The British Government is no longer headed by Winston Churchill, but by a group of Laborite Ministers who recently advised Greece to put off the plebiscite on the monarchy until the spring of 1948. They are not likely to feel too upset about the deposition of King Peter, but a study will be made of what obligations may still exist to the young monarch.

The new republic takes the name of "Federal People's Republic of Yugoslavia."

It will be a "unified people's state with a republican form of government, a community of equal peoples who have freely expressed their will to remain united within the Yugoslav State," said the proclamation read over the radio.

"By this decision, the monarchy has been finally abolished, and Peter Karageorgevitch, together with the entire Karageorgevitch dynasty, is deprived of all rights vested in him and his dynasty."

The same proclamation denounced the "national oppression, as well as brutal social reaction, brought about by reactionary circles headed by the monarchy."

The proclamation also accuses the King of failing to organize the resistance against the Fascist invasion and of fleeing the country and of "abandoning the peoples of Yugoslavia to their own fate."

During the four years' struggle of liberation, says the proclamation, "the monarchy was the greatest obstacle in the creation of a new Yugoslavia."

This decision was taken exactly two years after the Avnoj [Resistance party] had met in Marshal Tito's mountain stronghold of Jajce and voted for a republic. In between, in November, 1944, came the Tito-Subasitch agreement, which pledged a plebiscite on the monarchy, which obviously will not necessarily be held.

### Plebiscite Seen in Elections

The elections of a few weeks ago evidently have been taken by Marshal Tito and his followers as the equivalent of a plebiscite, and that is the legal problem that the Allies will have to solve. Dr. Radenko Stankovitch, former Regent, in fact, told the Skuptschina [Parliament] after the proclamation had been read, that those elections represented a plebiscite for the Republic.

Belgrade citizens gathered outside the Assembly building, cheering, while in the distance, salvos fired by Yugoslav soldiers could be heard, said the broadcast.

King Peter, who is in London, immediately got together with his advisers and issued his statement. It charged that Marshal Tito had taken the decision out of the hands of the people and claimed that it was a violation of the Tito-Subasitch agreement.

"The Tito Government simply trampled down all their obligations, destroyed the agreement and organized a totalitarian form of government in most striking contrast to the ideals of the United Nations' Yalta resolution and the promises that they themselves had made," King Peter said.

He referred to letters, which never had been made public, of Mr. Subasitch, Milan Grol, former Vice Premier, and Dr. Juraj Sutej, former Minister, charging Tito's regime with deceit. He denied the validity of the recent elections.

"My conscience is shocked when I look at the sufferings of my people, who are subjected to a merciless violence, without freedom or justice," Peter continued.

He told how his dynasty had begun and how his father and grandfather had fought to unify the Croates and Slovenes, and how his father had fallen as "the first victim of fascism."

The King ended by repeating that he would accept the free decision of his people, but until that had been made, he would follow the dictates of his conscience "to liberate Yugoslavia from tyranny—no matter whence it comes."

The broadcast, which apparently ends the reign that began on Oct. 9, 1934, when King Alexander was assassinated, was made at 4:30 o'clock this afternoon Belgrade time.

### TEXT OF PROCLAMATION

*LONDON, Nov. 29 (Reuter)—The text of the proclamation approved by the Yugoslav Constituent Assembly declaring Yugoslavia to be a republic, as broadcast by the Belgrade radio:*

During the twenty-two years' existence of the Yugoslav State before the war, the peoples of Yugoslavia were unable to achieve their age-long aspiration—national equality and social justice. Instead of realizing brotherly unity by granting equal rights, the former anti-popular regimes, striving as they were for hegemony, sowed discord and caused disunity.

This policy of national oppression, as well as the brutal social reaction brought about by reactionary circles headed by the monarchy, weakened our state both internally and in its relations with foreign countries, leading to catastrophic results at the time of the Fascist aggression in April, 1941.

During the invasion by the armed forces of Germany, assisted by Fascist elements inside the country, Peter Karageorgevitch [King Peter II] had neither the ability nor the necessary will to organize the people's resistance to the invader. They fled abroad, abandoning the peoples of Yugoslavia to their own fate.

### King Accused of Aiding Enemy

By his actions during the struggle for liberation, Peter II undermined the resistance of the people against the occupation forces. By all means at his disposal, he assisted the traitors who since 1941 fought against the Liberation Army and against the People's Liberation Movement and collaborated with the enemy.

The peoples of Yugoslavia rose against the Fascist occupiers and the traitors, firmly resolved to defend their independence and freedom and to contribute with all their strength to the victory of the United Nations against the common enemy.

In the course of the four years' struggle, the peoples of Yugoslavia achieved their union and brotherhood. By the blood they have shed and the hundreds of thousands of lives they have laid down, the peoples of Yugoslavia duly defeated the enemy and his collaborators inside the country and firmly decided to install an order that would allow their peaceful development and the realization of a better future.

During the four-year struggle for liberation, as well as during the period that followed it, the peoples of Yugoslavia have reached the conclusion that the monarchy was the greatest obstacle in the creation of a new Yugoslavia of a fraternal community of equal peoples.

They are convinced that the monarchy also bears the guilt for the activities of the anti-popular regimes before the war and for all they have suffered at the hands of traitors.

On the strength of this and in accordance with the freely expressed will of all the peoples of Yugoslavia, the Constituent Assembly (Skupshina) have decided in the name of the people and in the name of legal decisions taken by both Houses:

(1) The democratic federal Yugoslavia is proclaimed a people's republic under the name of the Federal People's Republic of Yugoslavia. The Federal People's Republic of Yugoslavia is a unified people's State with a republican form of government, a community of equal peoples who have freely expressed their will to remain united within the Yugoslav State.

(2) By this decision the monarchy has been finally abolished and Peter Karageorgevitch, together with the entire Karageorgevitch dynasty, is deprived of all rights previously vested in him and in his dynasty.

Made in Belgrade, capital of the Federal People's Republic of Yugoslavia, this 29th day of November, 1945.

### KING PETER'S STATEMENT

By Wireless to The New York Times

LONDON, Nov. 29—King Peter of Yugoslavia issued the following statement in London tonight:

The Constituent Assembly has declared Yugoslavia a republic. This decision has been arrived at as a result of a series of acts by Marshal Tito, which have had the effect of removing such a decision from the hands of the people themselves and placing it entirely within his own and those of the "National Front."

In the first place, the Tito-Subasitch agreement concluded under the auspices and guarantees of the great Allies, and with which I complied on their explicit wish and advice, was intended to serve as a pact binding both contracting parties.

The aim of the agreement was to regulate conditions inside Yugoslavia.

The Tito Government simply trampled down all their obligations, destroyed the agreement and organized a totalitarian form of government, in most striking contrast to the ideals of the United Nations, the Yalta resolutions and the promises they themselves had made.

The letters relating to the resignations of Dr. Subasitch, Foreign Minister and co-signatory of the Tito-Subasitch agreement, Dr. Grol, Vice Premier, and Minister Sutej, which charged Tito's regime with deceit and the non-execution of the agreement, tell their own story. These letters have never been made public by Tito.

#### Free Election Disputed

Further, the results of elections just concluded could in no way convince anyone that the will of the people had been tested and freely expressed. The world is only too familiar with the swollen figures used by the "National Front" to demonstrate their popularity. It is common knowledge, and impartial reports compiled by those whose duty it has been to administer relief within the country make it abundantly clear, that whole sections of the population are displaced and in no position to record a true vote, and that there is an equally large displaced population living outside the country who have not had any opportunity of expressing an opinion on the future government of their country.

There is only one conclusion to be drawn, and that is that the elections have been rushed through long before the life of the country has reached any degree of freedom and stability.

My grief is profound that my loyal officers, non-commissioned officers, men and civilians, although liberated from the Germans, are not able to return to their families as they do not wish to fall victims to slavery within the country. In a similar spirit, Yugoslav refugees are forced to flee the country and seek hospitality beyond their own frontiers.

A tyranny unworthy of the great victory of the Allies reigns in Yugoslavia. A totalitarian regime odious to the moral loftiness and the Christian traditions of the Yugoslav people is introduced. My conscience is shocked when I look at the sufferings of my people, who are subject to merciless violence without freedom or justice.

#### Calls Father Fascist Victim

My dynasty began its historical life in the struggle for national liberation. The peasants' home out of which the Karageorges dynasty rose to lead the insurrection against the Ottoman Empire still stands.

My family has been connected with all their struggles for independence and liberty. My grandfather, Peter the First, conducted the wars for liberation and unification of all Serbs, Croats and Slovenes.

My father, Alexander the First, fell as the first victim of the Fascist and Nazi criminal plans against Europe on the threshold of Allied France just as he was about to strengthen the ties with Western Europe.

I did not take upon me, following the summons of the major Allies, the huge responsibility on March 27, 1941, to call the Yugoslav people to arms against Nazi-Fascist totalitarianism in order that my freedom-loving people should fall after heavy struggles and ultimate victory into another and similar slavery, namely that of Josip Broz (Tito).

The major Allies are justly insuring that even the defeated enemy peoples of Austria, Hungary and Bulgaria attain their rights as free citizens in democratically governed States.

Therefore it is justified to suppose that they will even desire more fervently to promote freedom and democracy in Yugoslavia, which sacrificed all for the common victory. The collapse of democracy in Yugoslavia and the ensuing catastrophe will not confine itself to that country alone.

I said before and will again repeat now that if my people freely decide on a different system of government I shall be prepared to accept their will. In such an event I should be a loyal subject of Yugoslavia which is my native country.

I am fully conscious of my duties toward my country and, despite all steps taken against me by the present regime, shall continue to follow their clear dictates of my conscience in order to liberate Yugoslavia from tyranny—no matter whence it comes.

\*   \*   \*

December 1, 1945

## SOVIET TILTS SCALE AS BALKANS WAIT

### U. S., Britain's Act in Delaying Recognition in Rumania and Bulgaria Held Awkward

By SAM POPE BREWER
By Wireless to The New York Times

BUCHAREST, Rumania, Nov. 30—The departure of Mark Ethridge as special State Department representative in the Balkans leaves this part of Europe in a state of tense expectancy, waiting to see what the next move will be. Political developments in the past three weeks have put the United States and Great Britain in an awkward spot, with the next move clearly up to them while nobody has yet made any workable suggestion as to what they can do that would have any practical effect.

Mr. Ethridge's report on the present Bulgarian Government is already known to be unfavorable, but despite the refusal of the American to recognize it, the Administration went ahead with elections since the Russians did not oppose them.

The United States' views of the Tito Government are equally unfavorable, but the Yugoslav's Government, too, went ahead with the elections and won them under conditions that Americans and British disapproved of. There, however, the Government was already recognized, and it is difficult to see what can be done except to break relations—which would immediately be represented by the Tito Government as a mark of "fascism" instead of as a protest against its own unrepresentative measures.

### U. S. Recognition Still Doubtful

There is no reason to believe that Mr. Ethridge's report will be of a nature to produce United States recognition of the Government of Premier Petru Groza because there has been no change in the conditions that resulted in the American note in August that the United States did not consider the Government entitled to recognition.

The contrast in the Bucharest press between the treatment of Mr. Ethridge's arrival and of his departure is striking. It seems to indicate that Government supporters have lost the hope they had proclaimed before his arrival that he was really coming just to white-wash the Groza Government and to give the Americans an opportunity to back down on their previous refusal to recognize it. Before he came, the press was greatly preoccupied with him, and while he was here the entire city buzzed with interest in everything he did or said. When he left, all papers published polite accounts without comment, and most had a picture of him. One or two gave prominence

to the fact that he had talked with leaders of the factions they represented—and that was all.

### U. S., Britain Seen in Impasse

In the past two weeks this correspondent has talked with several American and British representatives in Belgrade, Sofia, and Bucharest and has found a general willingness to acknowledge that the refusal of Yugoslavia. Bulgaria and Rumania to live up to the promises of the Yalta Agreement, and the support given to them by the Soviet Union in that attitude has left the Anglo-Saxon Allies pretty well up against a blank wall.

Recognition of the present Governments and acceptance of their methods, it is remarked, would simply scrap the Yalta Agreement and the spirit of the Atlantic Charter. On the other hand, if they persist in their present refusal to recognize them, it is a pretty feeble gesture as long as the Soviet Union approves their conduct, these observers feel.

\*   \*   \*

December 5, 1945

## HOXHA PARTY IN SWEEP

### Captures All Assembly Seats in Albanian Election Triumph

TIRANA, Albania, Dec. 4 (AP)—Premier Gen. Enver Hoxha's Democratic Front party, the only ticket in last Sunday's elections, won all eighty-two seats in the voting for Albania's constituent Assembly, official returns disclosed today. The Democratic Front polled more than 95 per cent of all votes.

Of the 603,556 persons eligible to vote in the first Albanian elections in twenty-four years, 555,271 cast ballots. No date yet has been set for the first meeting of the Assembly which will draft a new Constitution and determine the method of selecting the chief of state.

At a press conference General Hoxha said that Albania demanded the right to participate in international organizations.

\*   \*   \*

December 24, 1945

## TITO'S RECOGNITION

The United States, together with Great Britain, has extended formal recognition to the Government of Marshal Tito and the Yugoslav Republic which he proclaimed, thereby recognizing that history has cast another royal dynasty into the discard. In that respect the recognition will undoubtedly find the approval of many Americans. But there is another side to it, and that is expressed by the declaration of the State Department accompanying the recognition which convicts the Tito regime of breaking all its pledges to extend the basic freedoms to its people, and of holding power by virtue of an election which did not express the free choice of the Yugoslav people. And that declaration makes the recognition an act of special significance.

It curtly brushes aside all the specious propaganda about the "democracy" of the Tito regime. But it does not alter the fact that it marks a repudiation of both the Yugoslav Government which took its country into war at the side of the Allies in a desperate moment of their affairs, as well as the coalition regime of both factions which Britain labored so hard to create. And that will not encourage the creation of similar coalition regimes elsewhere. Moreover, the reports from Washington plainly suggest that this recognition is the first fruit of the second Moscow Conference among the Big Three Powers, and that it may be followed by recognition of similar regimes in Rumania and Bulgaria, despite a supposedly adverse but still unpublished report on them by Mark Ethridge, Secretary Byrnes' personal investigator.

The declaration which accompanied it makes it evident that the American Government is not very enthusiastic about Tito's recognition and makes no pretense of liking him. In fact, it puts Tito very much in a class with Franco, whom the American Government also recognizes despite similar strictures on his regime. But it is also a fact that the United States, while holding high the principles for which it fought and while seeking to implement them wherever possible, is under no commitment to crusade for their imposition on other nations by force at the cost of interfering in their internal affairs and possibly at the risk of new war, unless its own vital interests and security are endangered.

Even the Atlantic Charter expresses only the "wish" to see sovereign rights and self-government restored to those who have been forcibly deprived of them. It obligates the United Nations to "respect" the right of all peoples to choose the form of government under which they will live. And though, in his Navy Day speech, President Truman declared that we shall refuse to recognize Governments imposed on other nations by force, there is a question whether that provision applies to Tito. Certainly if Tito came to power with foreign aid, that aid was first extended to him by Great Britain and the United States, which makes it difficult for them now to disavow him. They can only hope that by directing the light of pitiless publicity on him they will not only encourage the democratic elements within Yugoslavia to assert themselves, but will also subject Tito himself to the pressure of world opinion to effect reforms.

At the same time, since it is far easier in diplomacy not to do something than to do it, the recognition of Tito and possibly other Balkan regimes is a measure of the distance which our Government is willing to go to achieve agreement with Russia, the sponsor of these regimes. It is another concession in the interest of peace the importance of which should not be overlooked at Moscow.

\* \* \*

December 25, 1945

## END OF MONARCHY IN BULGARIA SEEN

### *Yugoslav Step Viewed as Part of Project for a Union of South Slav States*

By C. L. SULZBERGER
By Wireless to The New York Times

LONDON, Dec. 24—Now that the largest South Slav state, Yugoslavia, has changed to a republic and this step has been accepted by the big powers, it can be taken as more than probable that Bulgaria will liquidate its monarchy, which has been losing steadily in the popular imagination since the death of King Boris.

The ground has been prepared. Georgi Dimitroff, former head of the Communist newspaper Borsa, said recently that the Bulgarian Parliament intended to amend the Constitution and that "this means the removal of conservative and harmful institutions such as the monarchy."

George Popoff, Minister for Social Welfare, is also on record as having said that the Bulgarian Social Democratic party intended "to liquidate the monarchy as soon as possible."

The boy King Simeon and his mother are living in the royal castle of Vrana. It is reported that Queen Ioanna recently wished to visit her father, King Victor Emmanuel of Italy, with her son, but the Soviet authorities on the Allied Control Commission felt that such a visit might be unwise and that Bulgarian émigrés might choose the moment for political intrigues.

#### Emigrés Now in Italy

Several such émigrés, including George M. Dimitroff (an Agrarian leader, not to be confused with the former Comintern chief), are now in Italy. Mr. Dimitroff was flown out by Maynard Barnes, United States diplomatic representative in Sofia.

The creation of a Bulgarian republic would remove an obstacle from a scheme that has been the fancy of many Balkan Slavs for some time and that is said to be gathering favor now: the union of Bulgaria and Yugoslavia in one big state stretching from the Black Sea to the Adriatic.

The prospects that this will be implemented depend largely on Moscow. Marshal Tito talked about such a federation in his days as a guerrilla champion. If Moscow likes the idea, it is logical to expect that it will be carried out and that those old Comintern veterans, Mr. Dimitroff and Josip Broz [Marshal Tito], will work the problem through.

Yugoslav-Bulgarian unification, which was nearly carried out last March, when various difficulties were encountered, will, it is thought likely, await two developments: liquidation of the Bulgarian monarchy and signing of a peace treaty between Bulgaria and the Allies.

Mr. Dimitroff recently expressed the view that the removal of the monarchy would not only improve the internal situation of Bulgaria, but also pave the way for closer relations and harmony of the southern Slavs.

### Important Strategically

The ousting of the Karageorgevitch dynasty in Belgrade will accelerate this process in Sofia. It is a pretty good bet that by the end of next year Bulgaria and Yugoslavia will be a single country of approximately the strength of Poland, and with considerable strategic importance.

This is likely to come about despite British and United States distaste for the methods of the Sofia and Belgrade Governments and will, de facto, alter the whole Balkan picture, causing nervousness particularly in Italy, Turkey and Greece.

It is believed probable that to facilitate such a development Bulgaria and Yugoslavia will contribute territory to the formation of a Macedonian republic within the federation, enlarging the present Yugoslav Macedonian republic. This would produce even greater pressure on Greece for revision of the Greek Macedonian border.

There have been efforts by Marshal Tito to bring Albania into this scheme, but so far they have been hesitantly resisted by Premier Enver Hoxha, whose Government was recognized by London and Washington partly to forestall such a move.

Bulgaria is full of rumors that when the big day comes for South Slavdom, Mr. Dimitroff will stand for the Presidency of a Bulgaro-Yugoslav-Albanian union.

\* \* \*

December 26, 1945

## MANIU, BRATIANU FACE TRIAL IN 'PLOT'

*Accused as Anti-Jewish and Fascists by Rumania's Red-Dominated Regime*

### By SAM POPE BREWER
By Cable to The New York Times

BUCHAREST, Rumania, Dec. 25—An inquiry into the Nov. 8 disturbances here, which has dragged on ever since, is virtually completed, it is learned, and according to apparently authentic sources the Government has decided to bring accusations of responsibility for the disorders against Dr. Juliu Maniu, chief of the National Peasant party, and Constantin Bratianu, National party chief.

According to reliable sources, the questioning to which both leaders were subjected during past weeks was directed toward proving that they organized anti-Jewish and pro-Fascist manifestations on Nov. 8.

This correspondent and others who witnessed the incidents at close range can testify that there were no signs of either pro-Nazi or any other form of political manifestations except by Government opportunists who attempted to break up the demonstration in King Michael's honor before the palace. The disturbance developed when the crowd, angered at being forced to jump for their lives as trucks came through, overturned and burned three of them.

Something was begun shortly afterward from the corner of the square where the Ministry of the Interior stands.

Government witnesses at the preliminary inquiry are reported to have said they saw banners with the swastika and anti-Jewish slogans and that the crowd cheered Hirohito and Hitler. This correspondent and others who were present saw no banners of any kind except the Rumanian national flag, signs saying, "Long live King Michael!" and the King's portrait. Talk of cheers for either Hirohito or Hitler at that point is considered obviously preposterous by all observers here.

Emil Bodnaras, secretary general of the Prime Ministry and reputed head of the political secret police, informed this correspondent that an anti-Jewish demonstration occurred under Dr. Maniu's direction. When asked whether he really believed such a statement, he said in any case that Dr. Maniu and M. Bratianu were "spiritually responsible."

If he believes that there was an anti-Semitic demonstration, however, all available testimony from other sources shows that he must have been misinformed.

\* \* \*

January 3, 1946

## BRITISH SEEK CHECK ON GREEK AFFAIRS

*Aid Plan is Said to Call for Behind-the-Scene Officials in Key Administrative Posts*

By Wireless to The New York Times

LONDON, Jan. 2—The British are tentatively proposing that the installation of British officials in key behind-the-scenes positions in the Greek Administration should be a condition attached to any substantial financial aid to Greece from this country, it was learned today.

Current discussions between Greek representatives led by Emmanuel Tsouderos, Deputy Premier, and British officials are seeking a solution to Greece's chronic financial crisis in a general program for economic stabilization and administrative reform.

The broad nature of the conversations is indicated by the participation of United Nations Relief and Rehabilitation representatives, led by Bruce Maben, American chief of the UNRRA's mission to Greece. The UNRRA is still the only source of outside supplies for the country and Greek officials have nothing but praise for its work both in furnishing supplies and in assisting the Greek Administration with the work of distribution.

### Little Success So Far

In spite of a complete conversion of the Greek currency in the fall of 1944 designed to provide the basis for stabilizing prices and exchange rates, recent developments indicate that little success has been achieved in either direction.

One object of the present talks will be to seek ways of resuming exports of currants and tobacco. Greece's principal pre-war exports, to provide a means of paying for imports as UNRRA's aid inevitably tapers off.

Until a beginning is made toward putting normal trade back on its feet, experts foresee little prospect that recurrent financial crisis can be avoided, whatever outside financial assistance may be given the poverty stricken country.

Particular urgency attaches to the present discussions because of the elections scheduled for March in which United States and British representatives will participate as observers in an effort to insure fair balloting. An atmosphere of financial instability is considered to be particularly unhealthful for the elections in Greece where political tension has come to be associated with recurring currency crises.

\* \* \*

**January 12, 1946**

## ASSEMBLY DECREES ALBANIA REPUBLIC

*Action Terminates Monarchy Launched in 1938—*
*'To Be Expected,' King's Aide Says*

By Cable to The New York Times

LONDON, Jan. 11—Albania was proclaimed a republic today by the Constituent Assembly, the Tirana radio announced, and a two-day holiday has been decreed to celebrate the event that put an end to the monarchical system voted in 1928 to supplant the previous republic.

The Tirana broadcast said the proclamation had been accompanied by a 101-gun salute to signalize the new path chosen by the people under Premier Enver Hoxha's Government.

There was no mention of King Zog who ascended the throne after having been President of the previous republic. He has been living in England since he fled Albania after the Good Friday invasion by Benito Mussolini's troops in 1939.

Today's action, following a similar Yugoslav step overthrowing the monarch there last November, came the day after the arrival in Tirana of the new Soviet Ambassador, Stepanovitch Shuvakin, who was greeted at the airport by Premier Hoxha. The Hoxha Government is also recognized by the United States and Britain.

It was expected in London tonight that the change in the regime would be recognized by the Big Three powers, just as that in Yugoslavia has been.

The Albanian action, it was noted, had been expected for some time. In fact, the only comment from King Zog's entourage tonight was a statement by one of its members that "it was to be expected."

LONDON, Jan. 11 (Reuter)—Late tonight King Zog's secretary issued this statement:

"The King cannot consider these elections (establishing the new regime) as free. It would have been our desire, after this long and tragic period, that the people of the country should be free to re-establish the situation as they wanted, but for us Albanians there is a more serious and important question than that of the regime, and that is the question of national and territorial integrity."

\* \* \*

**January 22, 1946**

## RIGHT-WING GREEKS SLAY 14 HOSTAGES

*Martial Law Is Proclaimed in Peloponnesus as Royalists*
*Ignore Ultimatum*

**LEFT WING URGES A STRIKE**

*Regime Hastens Troops and a Warship to Quell Uprising of*
*2,200 Armed Men*

ATHENS, Jan. 21 (AP)—Fourteen hostages have been killed by members of an extreme Right-Wing group who barricaded themselves in a mountain village ten miles northwest of Kalamata after having rejected a surrender ultimatum, the Greek Government said tonight.

The ultimatum had given the insurgents until 4 P. M. tomorrow to surrender or be attacked by Government troops.

Meanwhile, the political bureau of the Left-Wing EAM (National Liberation) party issued a statement accusing the British of responsibility for "Monarcho-Fascist terrorists in Greece" by directly supplying weapons to Right-Wing elements.

The announcement called upon the people to proclaim a general strike and take up arms.

In Kalamata itself, order was restored fully, the Government said, after the arrival of substantial reinforcements, but skirmishing was reported on the outskirts of the city between Government forces and rebel Monarchist groups.

### Martial Law Proclaimed

The Minister of Public Order, Stamatis Mercuris, ordered troops and gendarmerie to rescue 150 hostages who he said were held in the barricaded mountain position by the Right Wing insurgents. The Bishop and Mayor of Kalamata appealed without success for release of the hostages, taken in a raid yesterday.

Mr. Mercuris said earlier that a state of near-anarchy had inflamed the area of Kalamata and that martial law had been proclaimed in southern Peloponnesus. The Greek destroyer Crete opened fire on forces of the Royalists in Kalamata.

The Monarchists, reported to number about 2,200 men, were said to be well equipped. Most of them were uniformed, the Minister said.

Mr. Mercuris dispatched a battalion of motorized troops and 200 police to the port city after armed members of the Monarchist organization, identified by the symbol "X," had seized 200 civilians in a raid yesterday.

Centering their attacks on police headquarters, the raiders freed thirty-two suspects who had been held in the slaying of four supporters of the EAM last week.

Mr. Mercuris said 700 of the insurrectionists had marched on the public prosecutor's office in Kalamata but had been driven off by police and National Guardsmen, who had barricaded themselves in the prison and other public buildings. No estimate of casualties for either side was available.

### Reprisal Uprising Indicated

The police and guardsmen, Mr. Mercuris said, were under orders to protect all public buildings, but particularly the prison, where a number of EAM supporters are held.

Apparently the rebels had swiftly seized control of the southern Peloponnesus port. Leaflets announcing the imposition of martial law had to be dropped on Kalamata and neighboring towns from planes. The captain of the destroyer that opened fire on the rebels said the Monarchists were attempting to capture Kalamata civilians.

The prefect of Kalamata, in a telephone report to Athens, said the revolt had broken out in reprisal for the slaying by Communists last week of one of the leaders of the "X" group, his 2-year-old son and two other Royalists.

\* \* \*

February 2, 1946

## TITO REVISES CABINET

By Wireless to The New York Times

LONDON, Feb. 1—Marshal Tito, naming the new Yugoslav Government today, also kept the office of Defense Minister and named Stanoje Simitch, Yugoslav Minister in Washington, as Foreign Minister, the Belgrade radio reported. Edvard Kardolj, Vice Premier in the last Cabinet, retains that post and is also president of the Control Commission. Jasa Prodanovitch, formerly Minister for Serbia, becomes second Vice Premier.

Other appointments are Dr. Vlado Zecevitch as Minister of Construction, formerly Minister of the Interior; Nikola Petrovitch, now as Minister for External Trade; Dr. Drago Marusitch, Posts, Telegraphs and Telephones; Dr. Todor Vujasinovitch, Communications; Andrija Hebrang, Industry and chairman of the committee for drawing up an economic plan; Bano Andrejev, Mines; Dr. Vasa Chubrilovitch, Agriculture and Forestry.

\* \* \*

February 4, 1946

## RUSSIAN-BRITISH CLASH IN UNO TRACED TO SOVIET EMPIRE BID

*Moscow Said to Seek Subservient Greece as Link to Red Sea-Mediterranean Interests—Tripolitania and Eritrea Tied In*

By JAMES B. RESTON

By Wireless to The New York Times

LONDON, Feb. 3—The Anglo-Russian clash over the presence of British troops in Greece will be continued in the Security Council tomorrow. Soviet Vice Foreign Commissar Andrei Vishinsky spent today preparing an answer to British Foreign Secretary Ernest Bevin's defense of British policy in that country.

Meanwhile leading delegates at the UNO meeting agree that the Greek dispute is just one phase of a basic cleavage between Moscow and London over the future of the Mediterranean and they see it in relation to the following fundamentals of Soviet and British foreign policy:

First, the Soviet Union is trying to get strategic bases from Tripoli in the western Mediterranean to the shores of the Red Sea in order to protect her warm water communications routes through the Dardanelles to the rest of the world.

Russia fears that if the forthcoming Greek elections are held under the supervision of American, British and French observers and order is maintained by British troops the Greek people will elect a government that will maintain Greece's present alliance with Britain, give the British bases in the Greek islands and deny strategic bases to the Soviet Union.

Second, the British fear that if they withdraw their troops from Greece civil war would break out in that country again. This, they feel, would help Communist elements establish what Mr. Bevin on Friday called a minority government that would grant the Soviet Union strategic bases astride Britain's vulnerable Mediterranean Sea route to India.

Third, in pursuit of their objective of getting out into the Mediterranean the Russians are not only seeking bases in the Greek islands but have asked for partial control of Tripoli, have sought trusteeships under the UNO for Tripolitania and Eritrea, have asked Turkey for strategic bases at two or three points in the Straits connecting the Black Sea with the Aegean and have indicated their desire for bases in the Dodecanese Islands, which belonged to Italy but which will go to Greece in the peace treaties if the United States and Britain have their way. As to this latter point, the Russians are willing, provided Greece has a government that is willing to recognize Russia's aims in the Mediterranean.

Neither Mr. Vishinsky nor Mr. Bevin has mentioned these things in the Security Council debate. They have talked about the confused political situation in Greece, the Russians asserting it is a threat to peace and security and the British denying that it is anything of the sort.

## Reported Like a Prize Fight

They have used language that makes the exchanges on Capitol Hill seem meek and courteous, and as a result the meetings of the past week have been reported like a prize fight.

The cloistered main committee room at Church House, where the Security Council meets, has been seen as a sort of peace arena. Mr. Bevin and Mr. Vishinsky, both heavyweights, have been presented as the chief gladiators and admittedly their tone and appearance have suggested the comparison.

But it is generally admitted here that this is no common dispute over the mysteries of Balkan politics or a clash of personalities. It is seen instead as a clash of empires, a new phase in the old Anglo-Russian struggle for influence in the Mediterranean and the Near and Middle East. And it is seen as the beginning of a showdown before the Paris Peace Conference redrafts the map of the Mediterranean area.

The historical background of the case is remarkably similar to the pattern evolving in the Security Council and in the discussions in the Soviet and British papers.

In 1844 Czar Nicholas I, whom Tennyson, in familiar modern journalese, called the "icy Muscovite" and "the overgrown barbarian from the East," called in the British Ambassador in St. Petersburg and explained the Russian desire for an outlet to the Mediterranean.

When the British were in desperate difficulties during what somebody has called the "next to the last war," they made a secret treaty with the Russians to give them the Dardanelles and Istanbul, but when the war was won and the Soviets came to power the British reconsidered their magnanimity and retired into their traditional policy of keeping Russia away from Britain's communications lines.

It is precisely those same policies that are being picked up by a new generation of British and Russian diplomats and being fought out in the Security Council of the new world organization. The great difference is that the balance of power has shifted, but, as Mr. Bevin said when he came to the Foreign Office and as he is proving every day, socialism has not changed geography.

Nor has communism in Russia changed the long-range objectives of the foreign policy of the Czars.

"Britain and the Soviet Union," the Russian Embassy's new bulletin says this week (in language remarkably similar to that used by Czar Nicholas to the British Ambassador exactly 102 years ago) "have an equal interest in keeping the Mediterranean open.

"What is wanted is a clear recognition of the strategic needs of the U.S.S.R. in the Mediterranean and the Near and Middle East. The rest of all the trouble between Britain and the Soviet Union today is directly traceable to the fact that, contrary to all expectations, the present British Government has embraced in full the British policy of the nineteenth century vis-a-vis Czarist Russia."

The fact that the UNO is the scene of a new phase in this traditional struggle for influence between Britain and Russia has not, however, produced any marked despondency or cynicism among the delegates to this first meeting in London.

On the contrary, the general feeling among observers here is that the UNO was never expected to put an end to power politics—what other kind of politics are there? they ask. Nor is there any future for the organization, they feel, in trying to protect it from the very problems it was created to solve or minimize.

Moreover, they conclude that the UNO has done a pretty good job in ventilating the Greek problem and the Iranian problem and has a chance of reconciling the conflicting interests between the two great powers in this part of the world.

Across the park from Central Hall, where the UNO is meeting, the Deputy Foreign Ministers of the big powers are discussing the future of the Italian overseas empire. Here again the Russians are pressing for the right to trusteeship over Tripolitania. British oppose this and so do we, but the outcome is likely to be that it will be placed under joint trusteeship of all the big powers plus Italy, so that Russia's interest in the Mediterranean will be recognized, and Moscow will receive an opportunity to start exerting her influence in areas from which she has been barred for a century.

\*   \*   \*

**February 27, 1946**

# NAZI SADISM SHOWN IN WAR TRIAL FILM

### *Soldiers Grinned as Yugoslavs Were Beheaded and Torn to Pieces by Animals*

NUREMBERG, Germany, Feb. 26 (AP)—Photographs of German soldiers laughing while one swung an axe to behead helpless Yugoslavs, of Elite Guards swinging corpses after hangings and of ferocious dogs and starving hogs devouring victims were shown today on a motion picture screen to the International Military Tribunal.

The film, prepared by the Yugoslav Government and flown here for its first showing, was made up entirely of the Germans' own snapshots. Most of the pictures had been taken from captured soldiers.

One view showed grinning Elite Guards posing beside the hanged body of a young blond Bosnian school teacher, Darinka Stanitch, who was executed for having joined Marshal Tito's patriot army.

Another Nazi had photographed the bare body of a beheaded child, the head resting beneath an arm. Yugoslavs said copies of that snapshot were circulated widely throughout Bosnia.

Several of the twenty-one defendants shuddered and turned away as the projector showed grinning Germans posing for a photographer with two large shepherd dogs and then its sequel, the dogs ripping a Yugoslav victim to shreds.

Earlier the Russian prosecution introduced over bitter defense objections a British report charging that Hermann

Goering, Wilhelm Keitel and Ernst Kaltenbrunner, all defendants, had sanctioned the execution of fifty recaptured Royal Air Force prisoners of war.

A German, Major General Westhoff, was quoted in the British report as having said that Keitel, in a Berlin interview with him, had complained that he, Keitel, "had been blamed by Goering in the presence of Himmler for having let the prisoners of war escape."

"Gentlemen, these escapes must stop," the report said Keitel told Westhoff and General von Graevenitz, German prisoner-of-war inspector. "We must set an example. We shall take very severe measures. I can only tell you that the men who have escaped will be shot. Probably a majority of them are dead already."

When von Graevenitz objected, the report said, Keitel shouted, "I don't care a damn. We discussed it in the Fuehrer's presence, and it cannot be altered."

\* \* \*

**March 25, 1946**

## TITO'S MEN SEIZE GEN. MIKHAILOVITCH IN YUGOSLAV CAVE

*Arrest of the Chetnik Leader and 11 Guards Announced in Belgrade Parliament*

**HE FACES TREASON TRIAL**

*Former War Minister in Royal Regime Accused in Capital as Collaborator of Nazis*

By The Associated Press

BELGRADE, Yugoslavia, March 24—Gen. Draja Mikhailovitch, wartime leader of the Chetniks who has been hunted for nearly two years in the hills of Yugoslavia by Marshal Tito's forces, was captured on March 13. Lieut. Gen. Alexander Rankovitch, Minister of the Interior, told the Yugoslav Parliament today.

The Interior Minister said General Mikhailovitch was arrested in a mountain cave guarded by only eleven soldiers of his once-large force.

General Rankovitch made the announcement during an address to a joint session of the Federal Council, or Parliament, on internal security in the country. There had been reports that General Mikhailovitch, King Peter's former War Minister, might rally his forces for a revolt against the Tito regime this spring.

### Reported Taken at Vishegrad

Although General Rankovitch did not disclose the locale of the capture, it was rumored that Yugoslav Army forces trapped the former Chetnik leader at Vishegrad, Bosnia, near the Serbian border.

The Belgrade radio said General Rankovitch's announcement was greeted with cheers by the Parliament members.

"Mikhailovitch, guarded by eleven soldiers, was sitting in a cave," General Rankovitch said. "These men were all that was left after his disastrous defeat of May, 1945.

"There is no doubt that Mikhailovitch was the last hope of all reactionaries, both in this country and abroad, who are working, openly or secretly against the Yugoslav Federal Republic."

General Mikhailovitch, accused by the Belgrade Government of traitorous collaboration with the Germans during the war, is listed by Yugoslavia as a war criminal.

### Statement Calls Him "Traitor"

The official statement made over the Belgrade radio said:

"At a joint session of the Federal Council, Lieut. Gen. Alexander Rankovitch announced that the traitor Mikhailovitch had been in the hands of the people's authorities since March 13."

General Mikhailovitch faces swift trial at the hands of the Yugoslav Government. Former Foreign Minister Ivan Subasitch said last May that the Chetnik leader "will be shot" when captured. He said General Mikhailovitch would get "a fair trial, but we have enough legal evidence now to convict him."

The Yugoslav High Commission on war crimes of Nazis and their collaborators published last September a 600-page book that contained what it said were original documents, pictures and facsimiles to support charges that the Chetniks practiced open treachery.

The commission said the documents proved General Mikhailovitch collaborated with the Nazis while issuing orders in the name of the Yugoslav Army and while serving as War Minister in King Peter's Cabinet.

### Mikhailovitch's Career Recalled

Gen. Draja Mikhailovitch, now 49 years old, was born of peasant parents in Ivanitsa, Serbia, The Associated Press notes.

A professional soldier, he held the rank of colonel and was specializing in the perfection of guerrilla warfare at a station in the Dinaric Mountains when the Germans swarmed into Yugoslavia in April, 1941.

He took command of a guerrilla force, estimated at various times to number from 30,000 to 200,000 men, and was so successful at repelling German attacks that for a year he was looked upon as one of the great heroes of the Allied cause. He was promoted to general in December, 1941, and a month later King Peter appointed him Minister of War, the Navy and Air Force.

In February, 1943, the Soviet Union first accused General Mikhailovitch of collaborating with the Axis. His guerrillas were reported still waging war against the Germans, and his family was in a German concentration camp.

His wife died in a concentration camp in August, 1944, and later his daughter joined the Partisans. Then his son, Branko, accused his father of treachery and joined Marshal Tito.

The total disintegration of the Mikhailovitch forces came in May, 1945, when about 20,000 men, women and children remaining from his tattered army crossed the border into an Italian concentration camp in the British Eighth Army lines.

\* \* \*

**April 1, 1946**

## GREEK ROYALIST LEAD SLIGHT IN BIG TURNOUT IN ELECTIONS

*Communist-Eam Boycott Fails in 70% Poll—Liberals and Republicans Nearly Match Populists in Athens—Clashes Kill 20*

### By A. C. SEDGWICK
By Cable to The New York Times

ATHENS, Monday, April 1—Greece held her first elections in ten years yesterday in an atmosphere that was generally tense. With hundreds of Allied observers watching the polling, twenty-one parties of various combinations and political shades contested the elections, which the Communists and their associates in the left-wing coalition, Eam, and other leftist bodies tried to boycott.

During the evening Premier Themistocles Sophoulis announced his intention to resign as soon as the election results were known.

Reports early today on the count throughout Greater Athens indicated a working majority for the Populist (Royalist) party, led by Constantin Tsaldaris.

Groups in the center Republican combination headed by former Premier George Papandreou, Sophocles Venizelos and former Premier Panayoti Caneliopoulos, together with Premier Sophoulis' Liberal party, which apparently gained many left-wing votes at a late hour, got considerably more than was anticipated. They matched the Populists in many districts.

The boycott order of the Communist party and other left-wing groups was largely disregarded—in some areas completely. The size of the poll for the center parties surprised observers as the Populists had been expected to sweep Athens. [A turnout of about 70 per cent of registered voters was reported throughout Greece, said news agency dispatches.]

An outcome of the voting may be that the Populists are not strong enough throughout Greece to hold a plebiscite at an early date to decide upon the return of King George II, which they favor. It is possible a coalition Government will be formed.

[Clashes of extreme Left and Right groups with Greek police over the week-end killed twenty persons, news agencies stated.

[The American, British and French chiefs of the Allied observer mission in Greece announced through the British Foreign Office in London that its report on the Greek elections would be issued April 10, after time for study of data from local observer teams.]

A considerable number of voters was reported to have turned up just at sundown at the polling places in the Kaisariani suburb, known during the period of civil strife here as the "Stalingrad" district of Athens.

Associated Press Radiophoto

Constantin Tsaldaris, Populist Head.

The Government ordered the polls to remain open another three hours.

### Worst Clash in Thessaly

The most serious incident so far reported is from the village of Litochoro in the Mount Olympus area of Thessaly, where six gendarmes and two Greek Army sergeants were said to have been killed and eight gendarmes were missing Saturday night in a fight with Communists. The official report said 100 Communists armed with mortars and machine-guns attacked the village police station, which they destroyed, trapping some of its occupants.

Toward the end of the day the voting was generally reported far heavier than officials had expected, with a very substantial turnout in Macedonia, Crete, the Peloponnesus and Thessaly, except in the district of Verroia, which is regarded as a Communist stronghold.

Later reports from the Greek Press Ministry indicated only 30 per cent abstention in the port of Pirseus, reported to have been largely Communist. Out of fifteen electoral sections checked in Athens, five of which were believed largely Communist, 25 per cent abstention was recorded.

The writer visited a number of polling places in Greater Athens during the day, and found no justification of Leftist allegations of a "white terror."

In some working class sections there were rumors that factory owners had insisted upon their employes' voting, and elsewhere, according to police, Communists had stopped many voters on their way to polls in efforts to dissuade them from taking part in what the Reds termed a "right-wing electoral coup d'etat."

The writer is prepared to believe there may have been irregularities of one kind or another, although at every balloting place he visited in schools, shops and churches the authorities and participating party representatives were found to be eager to be visited by observers of the allied mission to forestall any possible charges of faking.

### Turnout Looks Bigger Than in 1936

The writer, in watching the voting, gathered the impression that the poll would be considerably larger than ten years ago, except perhaps in strongly Communist districts such as Kaisariani. There in one polling place only fifty of a registered 750 had voted by noon.

However, at another polling booth in an older part of the same suburb half the eligible persons had voted by 11:45 A. M.

In nineteen electoral districts of Greater Athens, including the Communist district of Galatsi, 9,634 out of a possible 10,590 voters had cast ballots when the polls closed.

A possible sample of the way Communist followers may have disregarded party orders not to vote may be seen in the strong Communist area of Ghyzis, in northeast Athens, where out of 600 registered and believed to be preponderately of the extreme Left, 85 voted for Premier Sophoulis' Liberals, 76 voted Populist and 56 for the Venizelos-Papandreou-Canellopoulos coalition.

Communist and other Left-Wing circles said that a large part of the difference that had been expected between the count of voters and the 2,211,791 on the electoral register would represent those who abstained.

On the other hand, abstention on a large scale has been a feature of previous Greek elections—the poll in 1936 was 62 per cent.

\*   \*   \*

**April 2, 1946**

# GREEK RIGHT SEEKS RULE BY COALITION

*Populists, With Bare Election Margin, Look to Venizelos, Liberalist, as Premier*

### VOTE COUNT IS SUSPENDED

*Sophoulis' Carry-On Ministry Stops Tally After Royalist Charges Bias in Figures*

### By A. C. SEDGWICK
By Wireless to The New York Times

ATHENS, April 1—Premier Themistocles Sophoulis handed his resignation today to the Regent, Archbishop Damaskinos, who, while accepting it, asked the Premier to continue his duties for a day or so until the full results of yesterday's elections were known.

The Regent will press tomorrow discussions with the chiefs of the Populist party, which from present indications won a 60 to 65 per cent majority in the newly-elected Chamber.

This majority is not overwhelming, mainly because of the heavy vote for the National block of moderate Republicans led by former Premiers George Papandreou, Panayoti Canellopoulos and Sophocles Venizelos.

Therefore it is thought most likely the Regent will advise the formation of a coalition Government, possibly taking in some elements of Mr. Sophoulis' Liberal party. The Liberals, running third in the count of the elections, represent considerable strength, having the support of such left-wing groups as took part in the balloting.

Some political circles tonight suggested the choice for Premier might be Mr. Venizelos in view of his probable acceptability to all parties.

[Mr. Venizelos, leader of one group using the Liberal party designation, was put forward for the Premiership by Greek Royalist circles in London, The United Press reported. From Athens a United Press dispatch said Messrs. Sophoulis and Papandreou had rejected a Populist request that they join a Populist-led coalition.]

Because the Populist party, which together with some lesser groups supports the monarchy, has not received the wide mandate it had expected, its chances of inviting King George II to return to his throne seem to be slender.

### Tally Halted After Bias Charge

ATHENS, April 1 (AP)—The Ministry of the Interior suspended tonight the counting of votes in yesterday's national elections after a leader of the Populist party, which claimed a victory at the polls, declared the Government's figures were biased.

Before stopping the count, the Ministry reported that 510,445 persons had voted in 1,550 of Greece's 3,2000 voting stations. [The Ministry announced with the halting of the count that it would discontinue its previous practice of reporting the number of registrants in each district when returns were made public, The United Press stated. It reported the last returns counted from the provinces showed an increasing rate of abstention.]

The Populists received 269,498 votes in the latest count, the Ministry announced; the National block, 118,740; the middle-of-the-road Liberals, 72,390, and the Zervas party of extreme Rightists, 22,907.

The Populists also claimed the defeat of the Communist-Left Wing campaign to boycott the voting. By unofficial estimate 65 to 75 per cent of the total electorate voted Sunday, which would be a heavy turnout compared with the 62 per cent that voted in the last Greek elections in 1936.

Constantin Tsaldaris, chief of the Royalist division of the Populists, said he believed the Government's figures were biased and that the Populists would announce their own figures. He did not elaborate.

Observers said Mr. Tsaldaris' charge of bias might have resulted from a 7 P. M. official revision of the noon figures released by the Government. Although the noon bulletin covered 499 precincts and the 7 P. M. announcement 900, the latter bulletin shaved about 20,000 votes from the Populist total,

3,000 from the Nationalist bloc, and about 2,000 from the Liberals.

The Ministry said the noon and 7 P. M. reports were from different sets of returns.

The Communist newspaper Rizopastis took issue with the unofficial estimates of the percentage of the electorate that voted and claimed that abstentions in some districts had exceeded 50 per cent of the eligible voters.

The Communist and left-wing groups had refused to put up candidates or participate in the election.

### Moscow Charges Forced Voting

LONDON, April 1 (Reuter)—The Moscow radio in its first comment on the Greek elections asserted tonight that in Athens suburbs people had been arrested merely for urging others to abstain from voting. The broadcast quoted a Tass correspondent in Athens as saying the elections took place "in an atmosphere of extraordinary terror."

"To maintain order the entire police and national guards were mobilized," said the Tass account. "Even in Athens and Piraeus, not to mention the provinces, many cases of forcible 'heading' to the ballot boxes were observed.

"In estimating the returns it should be remembered that in the present situation abstention from voting is impossible because the Rightists have declared in advance that all absentees will be regarded as 'dangerous Communists.' An identification document without the stamp of the polling station becomes a yellow ticket—that is to say, a certificate of unreliability. Persons who decided to risk the boycott were risking not only their employment but in certain cases even their lives."

\*   \*   \*

June 11, 1946

## U. S. AIDE, BRITON ACCUSED AS MIKHAILOVITCH CASE OPENS

*Prosecution Says Chetnik Met Nazi Officer While American Colonel Looked On—Order to Kill Reds Laid to Briton*

By The Associated Press

BELGRADE, Yugoslavia, June 10—The Yugoslav Government's indictment of Gen. Draja Mikhailovitch charged today that the Chetnik leader had been told by a British officer in 1943 to "liquidate the Communists" in Yugoslavia, and that in 1944 an American officer had taken part in conferences between General Mikhailovitch and a German commander.

Referring to another British message, purportedly sent from the British Command in Cairo in 1941 and relayed by a British liaison officer, the indictment said Mikhailovitch had been told "that Yugoslavs are to fight for Yugoslavia and not transform the fight into a rebellion of Communists on behalf of Soviet Russia."

The indictment was read at the opening of Mikhailovitch's trial on charges of treason and collaboration in a floodlighted court room packed with more than 1,000 spectators

Observers noted that the prosecutor did not mention the death penalty, but said he "will expect the court to pass severe and just sentence over these traitors and criminals." The prosecution asked the court to "pronounce such verdict as each accused deserves, according to the gravity of his criminal acts; severe and just punishment—cruel and merciless punishment—for those who committed cruel crimes."

Drawn up by Marshal Tito's Government, the indictment said that in August 1944, an American colonel named McDowell, identified in the document as chief of a United States mission to the Mikhailovitch headquarters, met the Chetnik chief and a German named Neubacher, identified as chief of the administration staff of the Nazi military commander in Serbia. It said that a month later Colonel McDowell also attended a meeting with General Mikhailovitch and Neubacher's deputy.

[In Washington the War Department identified the United States officer as Col. Robert H. McDowell and said he was a teacher of Balkan history at the University of Michigan. The War Department did not know his whereabouts and was unable to say whether he was still in the service.]

The grizzled Chetnik leader entered the courtroom unaided, despite recent reports that his near-sightedness had grown almost to blindness. With him in the dock were thirteen co-defendants accused of treasonable relations with the Germans. Ten others are being tried in absentia.

General Mikhailovitch, with a quiet dignity, replied to preliminary questions in a firm voice. When asked his occupation, he said "General of the Army." He gave his birth date as April 17, 1893.

About 100 foreign and Yugoslav journalists were in the courtroom, the auditorium of an infantry school in a Belgrade suburb, to report the trial of the man King Peter left behind in Yugoslavia for the announced purpose of waging underground war against the Nazi invaders. General Mikhailovitch had been Peter's War Minister.

The indictment, relating what purported to be an account of Colonel McDowell's visit to Chetnik headquarters, said the American told General Mikhailovitch on his arrival:

"We Americans are not interested in your fight with Germany. They must go out of Yugoslavia by action of the Allies. It is up to you to remain among the people. . . . America is helping exclusively you and your movement in Yugoslavia."

The indictment said that in 1943, in what was called the fourth offensive of the Axis against Marshal Tito's Partisan National Army of Liberation, General Mikhailovitch personally or through an aide "commanded all Chetnik units, which were armed with Italian or German munitions, and took part with the Germans and Italians in operations aimed at the destruction of the forces of the National Liberation Army."

### King Peter Also Accused

"At that time," the charge continued, "British Colonel Bailey, who was attached to the Mikhailovitch supreme command, and who was fully acquainted with the plan and development of operations carried out by General Mikhailovitch, said that the Allies were preparing an invasion for the spring of 1943 on the Adriatic coast, and that 'it is necessary to liquidate the Communists' to have a clear hinterland that would enable his forces to take up a position unhindered on the Dalmatian coast."

In the course of these operations, the indictment continued, Mikailovitch "received full collaboration" from King Peter's Government in Exile in London.

The indictment said the Government in Exile had been informed "that Mikhailovitch collaborated with the occupier in the struggle against the National Liberation Army," but that it "denied all news that Mikhailovitch was collaborating with the occupier and spread invented news about the struggle of Mikhailovitch against the occupiers, giving him their agreement for such collaboration in ciphers through the British Broadcasting Corporation."

Referring back to 1941, the indictment said General Mikhailovitch had launched an offensive against the Partisans, planned in accordance with a message to him from the British Cairo Command, conveyed by a Captain Hudson, who was identified as a liaison officer. The message said, the indictment continued, "that Yugoslavs are to fight for Yugoslavia and not transform the fight into a rebellion of Communists on behalf of Soviet Russia."

This attack failed, the indictment said, adding that General Mikhailovitch continued to fight the Partisans with the encouragement of "radio broadcasts of the Yugoslav emigré Government."

The document said General Mikhailovitch held his first meeting with German commanders about that time, "in the greatest secrecy, under the protection of German armored cars."

"Mikhailovitch informed the emigré Government by radiogram through the British Intelligence Service of this meeting, both before and after the meeting was held," the indictment said.

### Pro-Nazi Accord Charged

The Government charged General Mikhailovitch's detachments had fought under Italian command in 1942, "mixed with Italian forces," and that the Chetniks received special rewards in money or flour for every slain Partisan, and in addition to this the Italians supplied them with arms, ammunition and food, helped in operations with their artillery and treated wounded Chetniks in Italian hospitals.

The charge said further that the fourth offensive in 1943 had been planned personally by Hitler to annihilate the Partisans and free German divisions for service against the Red Army in the East.

It said that after Italian capitulation to the Allies in 1943, all General Mikhailovitch's forces in the former Italian occupation zone, "carrying out his instructions and orders, entered into open collaboration with the Germans."

The indictment said General Mikhailovitch had reached an agreement with the Vice Premier of the puppet Yugoslav Government, Milan Neditch, in August, 1944, under which Neditch gave him financial aid and General Mikhailovitch promised that the arms furnished "would under no conditions be used against, the Germans," Neditch, who was facing trial, committed suicide in a leap from his prison cell last January.

The indictment also listed specific acts that it charged as atrocities to Mikhailovitch Chetniks. Constantin Fotitch, former Yugoslav Ambassador to the United States, who is being tried in absentia was charged with organizing abroad "large-scale propaganda, fully aware that Mikhailovitch and his Chetniks, with their organization, were collaborating with the occupiers."

\* \* \*

**July 3, 1946**

## YUGOSLAVIA, ALBANIA ANNOUNCE NEW PACT

By Wireless to The New York Times

LONDON, July 2—Yugoslavia and Albania have concluded an agreement of friendship and mutual assistance confirming "the resolution of both nations in the future jointly to defend their freedom and independence," the Belgrade radio announced tonight.

Full agreement was also reached on economic cooperation between the two countries, according to the broadcast, which said that "the conversations have not only displayed complete mutual confidence but also a realization of the indentity of interests of both countries."

The Belgrade announcement said that the accord resulted from conversations in the Yugoslav capital between Col. Gen. Enver Hoxha, Albanian Premier, and Marshal Tito. The decision to enter into such collaboration, it was asserted, was prompted by a determination to forestall any future encroachments by invaders such as "the German imperialist aggressors" at whose hands both countries had suffered.

A similar announcement was broadcast from Tirana. A later Belgrade broadcast said that General Hoxha and his party, who had been in Yugoslavia since June 23, left for Tirana today. General Hoxha was quoted as having said in a broadcast to the Yugoslav people from the airfield:

"Albania will always treasure Yugoslavia's friendship as the main guarantee for her freedom and independence."

\* \* \*

July 16, 1946

# DEATH IS DECREED FOR MIKHAILOVITCH

*10 Others Also to Be Shot for Treason and War Crimes—13 Get Lighter Sentences*

### By SAM POPE BREWER
By Wireless to The New York Times

BELGRADE, Yugoslavia, July 15—Gen. Draja Mikhailovitch and all twenty-three of his co-defendants were found guilty of treason and war crimes by the Military Section of the Peoples' Supreme Court here today after a thirty-five-day trial. General Mikhailovitch and ten others were sentenced to death by shooting. Constantin Fotitch, former Ambassador to the United States, was sentenced in absentia to twenty years at forced labor with the loss of all civil rights for ten years, confiscation of all his property and loss of citizenship.

The death sentences were imposed in absentia on the former Premier and War Minister, Gen. Peter Zivkovitch, who is now in Rome, and on Mladen Zuyovitch, former Chetnik commander and a Mikhailovitch delegate abroad, who now is in Paris.

### Judge Speaks 3½ Hours

General Mikhailovitch and the others sentenced to death had until 8 o'clock tonight to appeal for clemency to the Presidium (Executive Committee) of the Peoples National Assembly, the court announced. Otherwise, the judge said, "sentence will be carried out immediately."

Extra guards surrounded the courtroom as the verdicts were announced and no one was allowed to loiter in the vicinity of the building, despite a double cordon of guards on all approaches.

As each death sentence was announced, the spectators applauded vigorously, and when the prisoners—all of whom apparently were completely unmoved by the sentences—filed out of the courtroom with their guards, the crowd, in complete disorder, climbed onto the seats and struggled with each other to get a better view.

The court president, Col. Mihail Georgevitch, devoted three and a half hours to his delivery of the verdict and explanation of the decision and the sentences. He spent most of the first two hours reviewing the indictment in some detail to emphasize the charges on which the men were convicted after he had announced that all were found guilty. He then announced the sentences, and finally again went over the points he considered particularly telling, although their relative importance seemed to have little relationship to the evidence on which they were based.

The court declared that the contention that General Mikhailovitch had represented the legal authority of the Royal Yugoslav émigré government in Yugoslavia was invalid because he had collaborated with the enemy and had tried to destroy not only Communists but everyone who tried to fight against the enemy occupation forces.

The heavy sentence on M. Fotitch was no surprise, as he is particularly disliked by the present regime. The judge said that in general he was charged, "like all the absentee defendants," with aiding General Mikhailovitch from abroad, "instigating criminal acts against the people" and with making or directing broadcasts to deceive both Yugoslav and world opinion as to the real state of affairs in Yugoslavia.

### Mikhailovitch Charges Accepted

Colonel Georgevitch accused the absentees of knowledge and approval of "Chetnik crimes."

In the case of General Mikhailovitch the court accepted all the charges as proved, even to the assertion that he had organized a rebel force, although the defense attorney, Dragitch Yoksimovitch, pointed out in the course of his summation that on the basis of official documents General Mikhailovitch was the only legal representative of the only recognized Yugoslav Government up to the signature of the Tito-Subasitch agreement of March, 1944.

Of the seven co-defendants directly associated with him, only Radoslav Raditch, Milosh Glishitch and General Zuyovitch received the death sentence, and the extra severity in their cases apparently was the result of the charge that they actually helped organize the Chetnik forces.

Neither of two associates, Slavoljub Vranyeshevitch, a former Chief of Staff to Raditch, and Djuro Vilovitch, a former member of the National Committee, who pleaded guilty, was condemned to death. The former received twenty years and the latter seven.

All six defendants accused of direct collaboration with the Germans as members of the quisling regime of the late Field Marshal Milan Neditch were condemned to death. This was the only sign of recognition that the motives of General Mikhailovitch and his associates might have been patriotic in their own eyes, although their actions were regarded as treasonous to Yugoslavia's allies.

When sentence on Dragomir Yovanovitch, who was head of the security forces and the terror of the Communists, was announced, the crowd applauded more heartily than for any other.

### Military Phase Stressed

Whereas the sentences were based primarily on alleged actual war crimes, rather than military action, it was the military side that the judge emphasized in reviewing the charges against General Mikhailovitch. Briefly, these were that he had not, as generally supposed abroad, begun by fighting the Germans, progressed to fighting both Germans and Communists and finally had devoted himself to defense against the Partisans, but that he had collaborated actively from the first.

General Mikhailovitch's defense on this score was that although he had gone through the forms of collaboration, he really was duping the enemy into helping him, without giving anything in return.

He was accused of devoting the period from the emergence of the Partisans in June—when Russia was attacked—

Gen. Draja Mikhailovitch

until November in making contact with Chetnik groups throughout the country, bringing them under his command and from then on fighting the Partisans at every opportunity, with constantly increasing collaboration with the Germans.

General Mikhailovitch was accused of having made an agreement with Neditch as early as Sept. 5, 1941, and of having made and broken two truce agreement with Marshal Tito's forces in 1944.

He said he never kept nor intended to keep the Neditch agreement and that all truces with the Partisans were violated first by the Partisans.

He was said to have made an agreement with the Germans on Nov. 13, 1941, not to fight German forces, but he declared the meeting was only to discuss the surrender of the Chetniks, which he refused.

Another agreement with the Germans—under United States auspices—was said to have been sought late in 1944 and early in 1945, but his defense was that he and the American Col. Robert McDowell merely were trying to talk the Germans into surrender.

### Never Linked Directly

Although accused of general responsibility for war crimes and atrocities allegedly committed by his subordinates, he never was directly and personally connected with them by really reliable evidence, and his conviction rested principally on the points mentioned above, which were summed up by the judge today with the statement: "Through the whole war, he maintained collaboration with the enemy to establish a regime of international oppression."

Colonel Georgevitch also accused General Mikhailovitch of having broken up the unity of the Serbian people under false slogans of Serbdom, of having collaborated with all anti-democratic groups against the Yugoslav people and of having organized terrorism and sabotage in his country.

Those sentenced to death, now in Yugoslav hands, were:

Raditch, 56 years old, a burly illiterate who commanded the Chetniks in Bosnia and was accused of direct responsibility in many war crimes; Glishitch, 36, who commanded the Chetniks in the Sandjak district; Yovanovitch, 44, former head of all police and security forces under the Neditch government; Tanasiye Dinitch, 55, former Minister of the Interior under Neditch; Dr. Velibor Yonitch, 54, Minister of Education under Neditch who organized "forcible education camps"; Gen. Djuro Dokitch, 72, who was Minister of Communications under Neditch; Kosta Kushitski, 49, commander of the Serbian State Guards, accused of organizing terrorism, sabotage and espionage, and Boshko Paviovitch, 54, a hulking giant who was chief inspector of Belgrade police and was accused of helping the Germans organize the massacre of 7,000 Serbs at Kragujevac in 1941.

### U. S., Britain Attacked

In reviewing the accusations and the evidence on which the convictions were based, Colonel Georgevitch took the occasion to attack the United States and British Governments, saying that Colonel McDowell and the British liaison officers with General Mikhailovitch "in pushing him to fight the Communists were instigating him to aid the occupier. They were expressing the policy of reactionary circles abroad without regard for the interests of the Balkan peoples."

One of the points the three judges—Colonel Georgevitch and Lieut. Cols. Milya Lakovitch and Mihail Yankovitch—considered proved was that General Mikhailovitch and Colonel McDowell had conferred with Dr. Herman Neubacher, Adolf Hitler's special representative for southeastern Europe, in an effort to obtain arms for the Chetniks. General Mikhailovitch always has affirmed—and no evidence to disprove it was produced during the trial—that Neubacher did not attend the meeting and that the meeting's sole purpose was to ask the German surrender, although admittedly they insisted on the surrender of arms to the Chetniks rather than to the Partisans.

The heaviest sentence other than death was twenty years' forced labor, plus ten years' loss of civil and political rights and loss of all property. Besides M. Fotitch, this was imposed on his military attaché, Maj. Zhivan Knyezhevitch, 40, former Chief of the War Cabinet of the Yugoslav exile Government; Dr. Zivko Topalovitch, 60, former Mikhailovitch delegate abroad, who now is in Rome; Dr. Slobodan Yovanovitch, former Premier of the exile Government, who now is in London, and Dr. Stevan Moleyvitch, 58, General Mikhailovitch's former chief political adviser, who is a prisoner here. All absentee defendants lost their Yugoslav citizenship in addition to all the other penalties.

### The Lightest Sentences

The lightest sentences were on Lazar Markovitch, former Minister of Justice, who received six years at forced labor and loss of property, and Kosta Kumanudi, a former Cabinet Minister, who received eighteen months' forced labor, the additional loss of civic rights for two years and the loss of all property. Both were accused of morally supporting both Neditch and General Mikhailovitch, and of having taken part in the organization of the "Belgrade Representative Committee" to welcome the Western Allies. This, according to the court, was inspired by the Germans.

Other sentences on absentees included Dr. Milan Gavrilovitch, first Yugoslav Minister to the Soviet Union and later Minister in the émigré Government fifteen years; Radye Knyezhevitch, former Minister in the émigré Government, who now is in London, ten years forced labor; Bozidar Pouritch, a former Premier, sixteen years forced labor, and Momchilo Nincitch, émigré Minister of Foreign Affairs, who now is in Switzerland, eight years at forced labor.

### FOTITCH APPEALS TO U. S.
#### Begs Truman to Aid Mikhailovitch—Warns of Effect on the Peace

Special to The New York Times

WASHINGTON, July 15—Constantin Fotitch, former Yugoslav Ambassador to the United States, appealed to President Truman in a message today to intervene in an effort to save General Mikhailovitch from execution.

"I appeal to you and implore you," said M. Fotitch in his message to the President, "to use all your authority with the Government in Belgrade that this monstrous sentence not be carried out.

"I feel sure that the peoples of Yugoslavia, and especially the Serbs, have all their hopes directed toward this great democracy with the conviction that it will do everything in its power to prevent this crime."

He warned: "If this sentence is carried out, it will greatly affect the tranquility and internal peace of Yugoslavia and, consequently, the peaceful consolidation of this part of Europe."

### First to Fight Occupiers

The sentence passed on General Mikhailovitch, he declared, will "be deeply resented by the Serbian people for whom he was, and will remain, the symbol of their traditional fight for democracy and against any dictatorship, no matter from which side it comes."

The former Ambassador emphasized that General Mikhailovitch's force was the first in Europe to "rise against the occupiers." He recalled that the general "waged an unrelenting war against the occupation forces under most adverse conditions, fighting for the liberation of his country and for democratic ideals."

By his action, M. Fotitch said, General Mikhailovitch "contributed considerably to the Allied cause," and "his services were recognized and praised by the highest Allied military leaders." He also stressed the rescue of hundreds of United States airmen by General Mikhailovitch and his forces.

In spite of this record, M. Fotitch said, General Mikhailovitch has been condemned "under the infamous accusation of treason and collaboration with the enemy by a court whose verdict was motivated by a partisan spirit of revenge."

He asserted that the judgment was rendered "even before the court proceedings," and quoted in support of this assertion the Yugoslav note rejecting the United States appeal for American airmen to testify in General Mikhailovitch's behalf. This note said, "Mikhailovitch's crimes are far too big and horrible to even permit the discussion of whether he is guilty or not."

### Attlee's Aid Also Asked

The Committee for a Fair Trial for Mikhailovitch appealed yesterday to President Truman and Prime Minister Atlee to use their influence to save the life of General Mikhailovitch. The committee characterized the death sentence imposed on the Chetnik leader as a travesty of justice and a crime against the United Nations.

The appeals to the President and Mr. Atlee noted the contributions of General Mikhailovitch to the Allied causes and stressed his rescue and evacuation of almost 500 American airmen. General Mikhailovitch was described as a faithful ally of the democracies whose only "crime" was his opposition to a political regime that tolerated no opposition.

"It would forever dishonor America," the telegram to President Truman stated, "if our government were to permit the execution of Mikhailovitch, after a trial which was a travesty of justice, without using every diplomatic resource at its command."

### King Prepares an Appeal

LONDON, July 15 (U.P.)—Exiled King Peter's Yugoslav National Committee decided today to cable urgent appeals to the United States, Great Britain and France to intercede with Yugoslavia to prevent the "legal assassination" of General Mikhailovitch.

### Tito Hails "Reaction's" Defeat

LONDON, July 15 (Reuter)—Marshal Tito declared tonight "the sentence pronounced on Mikhailovitch was a sentence on international reaction," the Belgrade radio reported tonight. Speaking at Centinje, Montenegro, he added:

"The trial showed there is not only unity among reaction but also among all democratic forces. Mikhailovitch associated with all forms of reaction at home and abroad. He did not shrink from having connections with the Catholic Church, with the Croat Peasant party. It was a coalition of reaction and this coalition was defeated.

"Now reaction tries to take its revenge in denying us Istria, Trieste and the Julian provinces. Reaction would make an alliance with the devil himself."

\*    \*    \*

**July 24, 1946**

## HE HELPED SAVE MOSCOW

The fingers of history, rustling through the pages of the Second World War, may provide an ironic postscript to the scene that took place at dawn yesterday somewhere in the vicinity of Belgrade when Gen. Draja Mikhailovitch crumpled before the bullets of a Yugoslav firing squad. The record is fairly obvious now. A more complete search and study of the files of the German General Staff, and a historical assessment of the various factors that entered into the successful defense of Moscow by the Red Army during the fall and winter of 1941, may show that the one most important factor was the time that was bought for the Russians in the spring of 1941 by Yugoslavia and Mikhailovitch. On the record written thus far, the Russian-controlled Tito Government has taken the life of a man to whom Russia owes a great debt.

The recorded facts of the German attack on Yugoslavia and Soviet Russia in 1941 are these, as testified to by von Paulus, the German commander at Stalingrad, and by Jodl, the former German Chief of Staff, before the Allied Tribunal at Nuremberg:

Hitler drew his plan for the attack on Russia in December, 1940. At that time he hoped to absorb the Balkans without a fight. This would secure his right flank for the attack on Russia. Mikhailovitch, then a colonel, was among an influential group in Yugoslavia that resisted an alliance, with Germany, overthrew the pro-Nazi Government and installed one favorable to the Allies. When it became evident that Yugoslavia would not yield without a fight, von Paulus tells us, Hitler set the date of the drive on Yugoslavia for March and that against Russia for five weeks later. The attack on Yugoslavia actually was launched on April 6, 1941.

While Hitler was preparing his move against Yugoslavia, the new Yugoslav Government at once sent emissaries to Moscow seeking a mutual assistance pact. The best that it could get was, first, a promise to remain neutral, and then a treaty of friendship. The Ribbentrop-Molotov non-aggression pact still was in force then.

The initial German attack on Yugoslavia made swift progress. The Government was driven from Belgrade. In the hills, however, a new Yugoslav hero emerged. Mikhailovitch, fighting a gallant delaying action, rallied the remnants of the Yugoslav Army and began an open and effective guerrilla resistance to the German Army. Because of this unexpected resistance, the German Army's timetable of five weeks between the attack on Yugoslavia and the drive on the Soviet stretched to ten weeks. When it began June 22, it was weakened by the necessity of maintaining several divisions in Yugoslavia to hold that flank.

Everyone knows the rest of the story. Delayed three months beyond the time originally set for the attack, the German Army failed to reach Moscow before the dreaded Russian winter had set in. With the help of winter, the Red Army held the line in front of Moscow. Hundreds of thousands of Germans who had expected to garrison in the shelter of the Russian capital died instead in the icy trenches a few miles away. There is good reason to believe that this—even more than the defense of Stalingrad—was the turning point of the German-Russian conflict.

History may decide that it is not Tito—who was in safety while Mikailovitch was fighting in the hills in those early days—but the executed Chetnik leader whose statue should stand in Red Square in Moscow. But Mikhailovitch fell yesterday in Belgrade.

\*    \*    \*

September 29, 1946

## KING BACK IN GREECE
## AS DANGERS INCREASE

*British Hope Independence of the Last Balkan Outpost*
*Can Be Saved*

By HERBERT L. MATTHEWS
Special to The New York Times

LONDON, Sept. 28—King George returned to Greece on Friday—to a Greece divided by civil strife and, as the world has come to realize this past week, in an extremely dangerous position.

There are few things more ironical in recent history than the parallel in Greece—in reverse—to the Spanish civil war. Here it is totalitarian communism instead of fascism which is charged with intervening with material and technicians, and it is the Communists who are accused of providing the fifth column. The distorted reflection of international brigades is to be found in Albanian, Yugoslav and Bulgarian partisans who are, by Athens accounts, aiding and helping to train Elas guerrillas and bandits or their own nationals in that hopelessly mixed ethnic zone which runs along northern Greece.

The western democracies once again have their official sympathies tied on the whole to a legitimate Government which, unfortunately in this case, is monarchist, Rightist and reactionary. However, it is a Government that won the clear majority in the recent plebiscite, as the Spanish Popular Front did in February, 1936; and, as democracy goes in the Balkans, it is far ahead of any of its northern neighbors.

### Greeks Oppose Intervention

And then in the background are the Greek people who, like the Spaniards, have shown that they want to be left alone in peace and do not like foreigners intervening. Only the Eam, of all the political parties in the past week, has refused to rally round the Government in defense of Greek independence. The Greeks, again like the Spaniards, are a proud, fierce, courageous and xenophobic people.

Spain never became a casus belli, but it was the rehearsal for the second World War. Even the British, who feel very deeply about what is happening in Greece from what might be called sincerely sentimental as well as imperialist reasons, do not conceive of its leading to a third World War.

However, there still are British troops in Greece and if raids into Greek territory, gun-running attacks on Greek frontier posts and barracks, banditry and the like should get continued encouragement from Greece's northern neighbors and, above all, should increase in intensity and territorial scope, it is inevitable that British soldiers will be involved in the fighting.

### British to Remain

It is officially stated here that there is no present intention of withdrawing any troops unless the Greek Government requests it. There is no intention of reinforcing these units

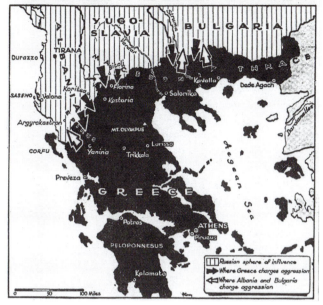

**TROUBLED AREAS IN THE EASTERN MEDITERRANEAN**

Tensions within Greece and between Greece and her northern neighbors have been highlighted by clashes at a number of points along the frontier. Greece charges that Leftist attacks on Government forces originate in or are supported by her neighbors; Albania and Bulgaria have accused Greek forces of making forays into their territory. Further tension in the area has been caused by Bulgarian demands for Thrace and Soviet demands at the Dardanelles.

either, for the British continue to believe and hope that the Greek Army and gendarmerie will be able to handle the situation. By making believe, as in Spain, that this is an internal problem, it is hoped that a major international conflict can be avoided. Yet this is very obviously a part of the whole great clash of East and West.

Behind Bulgaria, Yugoslavia and Albania is the Soviet Union. It is Manuilsky of the Ukrainian Government, for instance, who represents the Soviet bloc at the Paris peace conference and at the Lake Success Security Council in attacking Greece and championing the territorial claims of Bulgaria to Thrace. The campaign is aimed first at getting an outlet to the Aegean for Bulgaria, with Salonika playing a role similar to that of Trieste, and, above all, at moving the "iron curtain" forward to include the only Balkan country still left outside.

In short, Greece fits into that whole picture of Russian expansion on one hand and the attempts of the western democracies to block it on the other.

Some would say that she is the last bridgehead of the west or at least of the British, in the Balkans, but, whatever she is called, the point of major importance is that she should remain "free and independent" in the western sense of the words.

### American Naval Force

That was the meaning which everyone and especially the Greeks read into the visit of the American naval force in Greek waters a few weeks ago. As stated before, nobody feels that Greece is worth another world war. At the same time, there are the strongest possible reasons for not abandoning her to a fate which the majority of the Greek people would obviously hate.

Moreover, Greece is a European country which western democracies cannot help looking upon in a different light from that for instance, in which they view Iran.

The latter country is a very grave potential danger to world peace because of events which in some ways resemble what is happening in Greece, but the British recognize that it would be a bad thing to fight a war over oil. Despite some beliefs abroad, Britain is not that imperialistic.

At the same time the Greeks, as well as the British, expect that the United States will at least do what it can in the United Nations. There is no confidence whatever in the ability of the Security Council to do anything, in view of its record and of the Russian veto, but the British would be surprised and dismayed if the United States saw Greece being dragged behind the iron curtain and did nothing about it.

\* \* \*

October 1, 1946

## TITO'S 'PROPAGANDA' STIRS U. S. PROTEST

*Note Charges Yugoslavs Make 'Mischievous' Statements and Ignore AMG Rules in Trieste*

By WALTER H. WAGGONER
Special to The New York Times

WASHINGTON, Sept. 30—The United States, in a strong and impatient note, today accused the Yugoslav Government of ignoring Allied military regulations in Trieste and issuing "mischievous propaganda without any foundation in fact."

With this message, which betrayed mounting annoyance at Yugoslav complaints against Allied military authorities, William L. Clayton, Acting Secretary of State, in effect deflected and turned against Yugoslavia a formal protest by that Government against the arrest by United States military police of six Yugoslav soldiers.

Mr. Clayton asserted that the soldiers had been detained and then expelled from Zone A of Venezia Giulia "for violations of the standing orders against carrying weapons."

A full report on the incident, said Mr. Clayton, confirms the arrest to which Marshal Tito's Government had objected, but it also points out that the soldiers were searched and "found to be carrying hand grenades concealed in their clothing, contrary to standing instructions that UNRRA guards were not to be armed." This discovery was made, he added, at a point in Trieste near which a large explosion had just occurred.

### Prior Release Pointed Out

In addition to the arrest of the six soldiers, the note also referred to the "alleged detention" of a Captain Segota and his escort at Trieste on Sept. 9.

"The Government of the Federal Peoples Republic of Yugoslavia must have been aware at the time its protest was addressed to this Government," wrote Mr. Clayton, "that the six Yugoslav soldiers had been released to the Yugoslav military authorities in Zone A despite their violations of Allied military orders, and this Government is therefore unable to see any basis for a Yugoslav protest in this case.

"Instead, it appears that this Government must protest once again the disregard shown by officers and men of the Yugoslav detachment in Zone A for Allied military regulations in that area."

In addition to citing the findings of a board of officers as justifying the detention of Captain Segota, the State Department note declared that it wished the Yugoslav Government to know that the United States Government "resents the charges that Allied military authorities took no steps in this matter and that they inspired a 'fascist' press to give a 'false' account of the incident."

The State Department asserted that the board of officers, in discussing the arrest of the six soldiers with an American desk sergeant, said Captain Segota assumed a "menacing" attitude and his escorts surrounded the sergeant.

The discussion, which terminated with the brief detention and searching of the captain and his escort by other military police, was made difficult by the language barrier, said the report, and there was no way of determining that "disrespectful remarks or profane language" had been used against the Yugoslav military personnel.

The note said the findings of the board had the "full support" of the United States Government.

\* \* \*

October 1, 1946

## STEPINATZ DENIES GUILT AT HIS TRIAL

*Zagreb Archbishop Rejects Defense Counsel— Bishop Hurley is Spectator*

**VATICAN PAPER IS CRITICAL**

*L'Osservatore Romano Says Verdict and Sentence Have Already Been Decided*

ZAGREB, Yugoslavia, Sept. 30 (U.P.)—Archbishop Aloysius Stepinatz, head of the Roman Catholic Church in Yugoslavia, was brought to trial today on charges of collaborating with the enemy and subversive activities, and throughout three hours on the witness stand today insisted: "I do not consider that I have ever betrayed my country."

Before he started to testify, Archbishop Stepinatz, dressed in a simple black clerical frock, pleaded not guilty and refused, "for reasons of principle," to name his own defense counsel.

The four-man People's Court, which has the power to sentence him to death, appointed Dr. Ivo Politico and Dr. Ivan Katicio, two prominent Zagreb attorneys, to defend him.

He repeatedly said, "I refuse to answer" or "I have nothing to say" when the prosecutor asked him about alleged political activities of the Catholic church.

Among the 500 spectators in the courtroom, brilliantly lighted for photographers, was Bishop Joseph Hurley of St. Augustine, Fla., representing Pope Pius XII.

Since the Archbishop refused to answer so many questions, his examination was mainly a monologue by the Chief Justice, who read numerous magazine and newspaper articles and reviewed many questions and answers from the Archbishop's preliminary examination.

"It is my holy duty to ask God to help the enemy too," he said when the president of the court accused him of "acting without conscience" in not trying to keep people from joining the Fascist Ustashi movement.

### Stresses Conscience Is Clear

"My conscience is clear," he added.

"Which of your consciences, that of the priest or the man?" the Justice asked.

"My conscience as a man," the Archbishop said.

Then the Justice showed the Archbishop photographs of him attending Ustashi functions in the company of Dr. Ante Pavelitch, Premier of the Croat puppet state.

"I see no reason not to go to ceremonies when I am asked," the Archbishop said. "We all know what such ceremonies mean."

Most of the spectators hissed when the court read an article describing the Archbishop's blessing of the Ustashi "crusaders."

"I give my blessings to all who ask," he said.

When the court asked whether that included "criminals," he replied: "Everyone has the right to get blessings."

The scene of the trial is a sports auditorium. There are fifteen defendants beside Archbishop Stepinatz, who appeared No. 2 in the prisoners' dock next to Col. Erik Lisak, a notorious member of the Ustashi.

The indictment against the Archbishop contained a statement allegedly made by the Archbishop during his preliminary examination and at one point included these words:

"There exists a dispute between the church and the state, a fight of ideologies and principles in which he cannot give up religion and canonic principles."

At another point, the indictment said:

"The accused said no court in any other country could sentence him and the priests, neither after international nor divine and natural law . . . he is going to maintain in all his conscience, to which he frequently refers, that such clergymen are prosecuted without reason and that this is a persecution of the church and faith, not a prosecution of criminals.

"This no longer is an archbishop but the most responsible terroristic conspirator, . . . Consequently, there is no question of a persecution of the Catholic Church and its priests, but criminal proceedings against Stepinatz, who, as a traitor to our people, helped the occupiers, closely collaborate with Pavelitch and the Ustashi against the national liberation struggle . . . and aided Ustashi remnants after the liberation."

The indictment also charged that he was responsible for "forced conversions" to Catholicism "to strengthen Papal interests in the Balkans and secure the penetration of Italian imperialism."

\*   \*   \*

October 5, 1946

## CONSTITUTION DRAFT IS ISSUED IN BULGARIA

Special to The New York Times

SOFIA, Bulgaria, Oct. 4—The draft of the new Bulgarian Constitution was published this morning. A special committee of representatives of the five Fatherland Front parties drafted it.

The draft asserts that the Constitution is based on the equality of the people and freedom of press, assembly and speech. The first article says: "Bulgaria is a People's Republic with a representative government."

The head of the State will be an elected president with a four-year term. He can be elected only for two successive terms.

There will be a National Assembly, elected for a four-year term. The Assembly will elect the head of the State and the Premier and will have full control of State affairs.

Private enterprise and belongings earned by labor and savings will be protected by the State. The land belongs to those who work on it, the Constitution declares.

\*   \*   \*

October 7, 1946

## YUGOSLAVS CLEARED CHURCH, POPE SAYS

*Cites 1942 Exoneration of Its Hierarchy in Croatian Forced Conversions*

Special to The New York Times

ROME, Oct. 6—In a speech delivered at his summer residence, Castel Gandolfo, to the Sacred Tribunal of the Roman Rota, which resumes its activities tomorrow, the Pope declared today that Yugoslavia had acknowledged as long ago as 1942 that neither the Holy See nor the Roman Catholic Episcopacy had had any part in the "so-called forced conversions" in Croatia. He categorically rejected the charges made at what he called the "very sad trial" of Archbishop Aloysius Stepinatz that he himself had approved such conversions.

The Pope began by explaining what the church meant by "freedom of conscience" and by tolerance toward other religious confessions. He dwelled particularly on the article of the Canon Law saying that "nobody must be obliged against his will to embrace the Catholic faith."

Referring directly to Monsignor Stepinatz' trial, the Pope continued: "If, therefore, a few days ago, according to news appearing in the press, the public prosecutor in a very sad trial affirmed that the Pope himself had approved the so-called 'forced conversions' and moreover—what would be even graver—that he had done so for reasons of national imperialism, we have the right and the duty to reject such a false accusation. In order that our assertion may be duly documented, we consider it fitting to read to you a memorandum of the Secretariat of State, dated Jan. 25, 1942, in reply to a question submitted to it by the Yugoslav legation to the Holy See about the movement of conversion, in which Yugoslavia herself expressly acknowledged that neither the Holy See nor the Catholic Episcopacy in Croatia had had any part whatsoever." The Pope read the memorandum, making it quite clear, that if any forced conversions were occurring in Croatia, they certainly did not have the approval of either the Vatican or the local Catholic hierarchy.

\* \* \*

October 12, 1946

## STEPINATZ DECLARED GUILTY; HE GETS 16 YEARS IN PRISON

By ARTHUR M. BRANDEL
Special to The New York Times

BELGRADE, Yugoslavia, Oct. 11—Archbishop Aloysius Stepinatz, Roman Catholic Primate of Yugoslavia, was sentenced in Zagreb today to sixteen years imprisonment and deprived of his civil rights for five years. The sentence included confiscation of all the Archbishop's property. The prelate was found guilty on fourteen counts.

The first twelve counts against the Archbishop related to alleged activities during the Ustashi regime in the puppet Croat state of Ante Pavelitch, foremost Yugoslav quisling, in which Msgr. Stepinatz was charged with active collaboration with Pavelitch and the Axis powers.

The last two counts concerned his activities since the end of the war, when he was said to have supported Ustashi leaders and Crusaders, alleged Ustashi terrorist bands. He issued a pastoral letter before the elections last year in which he charged official persecution of the church and condemned the political changes in the country.

The Archbishop received his sentence calmly, remaining immobile, as he did through most of the trial.

Erik Lisak, former colonel and police chief of the Pavelitch regime, who was sentenced to death by hanging, leaped up shouting, "I will die for the independent State of Croatia." Lisak, notorious during the Ustashi regime, returned to Yugoslavia and was alleged to have made contact with the Zagreb prelate after the war to continue violent opposition to the present Yugoslav Government. He was captured in Zagreb.

Pavle Gulin, an alleged terrorist, was sentenced to death by shooting. Another civilian, Josip Crnkovitch, was sentenced to eleven years' imprisonment and five years' loss of civil rights.

Three of the rest, all of whom are priests or Franciscan Friars, were acquitted. Eight received sentences ranging from five months to fourteen years.

The sentences were broadcast by radio throughout Yugoslavia in public squares where loudspeakers had been set up. In the main squares of Belgrade several hundred persons listened but showed no reaction since it was expected the Archbishop would be found guilty. The only question was regarding the sentence.

One of the biggest factors against the Catholic churchman was the forced conversion of thousands of Serbian Orthodox church members in Croatia. Ustashi leaders felt that such actions would strengthen the regime in the country, which is 90 per cent Roman Catholic.

The prelate maintained that he had raised his voice against massacres and conversions by force, stressing to the court that such things were against canon law. Atrocities were committed, however, and the Orthodox and Moslem populations throughout Yugoslavia feel particularly bitter.

### Court Lists Charges

ZAGREB, Yugoslavia, Oct. 11 (U.P.)—Before sentencing Archbishop Stepinatz today the presiding justice said the Archbishop had been guilty of urging the Catholic clergy to collaborate with the Croat puppet regime, of writing "actively in a fascistic way" as president of the Bishops' conference and president of the Catholic press, of serving the Ustashi in provoking racial hatred; of in many ways giving signs of his collaboration with and sympathies for the Ustashi; of serving as president of a group of three men who directed forcible conversions to Catholicism; of joining in 1944 and 1945 with Croat puppet Premier Pavelitch and "other traitors" to link "all enemies of the country in a plan to secure foreign intervention to save the independent state of Croatia," and of influencing priests to organize Ustashi and Crusader units in terroristic activities against the present regime.

Other convicted defendants and their sentences were:

Ivan Shalitch, a priest and Archbishop Stepinatz's secretary, twelve years at forced labor and the loss of all citizenship rights for five years.

Josip Simecki, a clergyman accused of blessing the Crusaders' banner and working with the Ustashi, fourteen years.

Djuro Maritch, a clergyman and Ustashi captain, five years.

Modesto Martinitch, provincial of the Franciscan Friars in Croatia, five years. He was a witness against the Archbishop and the prosecutor asked leniency for him.

Kriso Klemen, superior of the Franciscan Monastery, three years.

Mamerto Margetic, a Franciscan monk, thirteen years.

Frankjo Pavlek, a Franciscan monk, one year.

Josip Crnkovitch, Ustashi terrorist, eleven years.

Mikro Kolednjak and Josip Vidovitch, monks, six months each.

The Franciscans were charged collectively with hiding Ustashi gold and jewels in their monastery.

Two thousand Yugoslavs crowded into Zagreb cathedral tonight to pray for the Archbishop. The Yugoslav radio broadcast the sentence throughout the country, and repeated it at intervals throughout the day.

Bishop Patrick Hurley of St. Augustine, Fla., acting Papal Nuncio, said he had not been permitted to see the Archbishop despite daily requests since the trial opened, and he could not comment. It is understood that Bishop Hurley sent daily reports to the Vatican during the trial and that he will return to Belgrade in a few days.

\*  \*  \*

## "HUMAN RIGHTS" AT ZAGREB

No one in or out of Yugoslavia can have been surprised by the conviction of Archbishop Aloysius Stepinatz in a Zagreb court on fourteen charges of collaboration with the Axis Powers and with anti-Tito rebels. The surprise lay in the comparatively light sentence of sixteen years' imprisonment. This was clearly a political trial, of such a nature, as Acting Secretary of State Dean Acheson said on Friday, as to cause "concern and deep worry" in this country. The political trial is as definite a procedure in Communist and Communist-dominated nations as an election is in democratic nations. It always looks beyond the question of immediate guilt or innocence. General Mikhailovitch was convicted and shot as part of a campaign to prove that American and British wartime policy in Yugoslavia had been reactionary. Archbishop Stepinatz has been convicted and will be imprisoned as part of a campaign against his Church, which is guilty of unfriendliness toward communism and which for historic reasons can hardly help nourishing the spirit of Croatian patriotism.

Just as the Archbishop was convicted for political reason, so for political reasons his life was spared. Marshal Tito did not feel quite strong enough to make a new martyr. He was influenced by popular opinion in Croatia, if not in the outer world. As Mr. Acheson said, the United States drew Tito's attention to what we considered an "undesirable situation" in the field of civil rights when we recognized his Government. Under the United Nations Charter, Yugoslavia is pledged, like other nations, to respect "human rights and fundamental freedoms for all without distinction as to race, sex, language or religion." A political trial, with conviction foreordained, violates this pledge. It is our Government's right, as a member of the United Nations, to point out this fact. Beyond this we are not likely to go, but it is important to make this appeal from the court at Zagreb to the court of world opinion.

\*  \*  \*

## YUGOSLAVS DRIVE RUTHLESSLY TOWARD COMMUNIST STATE

### By C. L. SULZBERGER
Special to The New York Times

ATHENS, Nov. 10—Marshal Tito's Communist Government, which completely dominates Yugoslavia behind only the thinnest facade of all-party cooperation, is firmly in the saddle. The Opposition is massive but disorganized and generally mute. It has neither national leaders nor a concrete program as an alternative to the Premier's.

Overcoming the handicap of an extreme shortage of skilled civil servants and technicians, the new regime is making considerable headway, vastly assisted by the United Nations Relief and Rehabilitation Administration, in reconstructing its war-torn land. Railways are being built, bridges repaired, roads resurfaced and buildings restored. Inflation has been skillfully avoided.

No thoroughgoing social or economic revolution has yet been accomplished, however. A peasant economy remains. That will change. Regardless of official statements noting that private enterprise still exists in Yugoslavia side by side with state socialism, the former is clearly doomed, and it is only a matter of time.

The Soviet Russian model is being followed as carefully as possible in economy, diplomacy, police methods, anti-clericalism and, above all, political theory. A tiny minority regime made up of stringently disciplined Communist cadres is dictating its will to the Yugoslav people on the philosophical assumption that this direction is good for the majority in the long run.

Marshal Tito's regime is accomplishing excellent things. The marshal's personal popularity is considerable despite a dislike of communism in large sections of the population. The Government has a specific plan and knows where it is going. It is receiving strong support in every way from Russia. In every village and town Generalissimo Stalin's picture can be seen posted beside Marshal Tito's.

These accomplishments are registered at a cost. Personal liberty, never at a premium under the prewar dictatorships in Yugoslavia, is at a new low ebb. Fear reigns. It is a fear now more implicit than actual: a fear of the midnight rap on the barred door by the dread secret police.

### Rankovitch Has Vast Power

Maj. Gen. Alexander Rankovitch, impassioned Communist Minister of the Interior once called by foreigners "the wizard of Ozna" until his secret police changed its name from Ozna to UDB (State Security Administration), is in a position to control the individual fate of every inhabitant.

That control is used emphatically by those who are guiding Yugoslavia down what they sincerely believe is the road of justice, prosperity and success.

On Sept. 28 Marshal Tito told a delegation of international students: "We arrested [Archbishop Aloysius] Stepinatz and we will arrest everyone who resists the present state of affairs, whether he likes it or not."

Specially in Serbia and Croatia the new regime is widely disliked. On the other hand, there seems every reason to believe it is supported by a large number of persons in poorer Montenegro, Bosnia and, above all, Macedonia. For the first time the Slavic Macedonians can govern themselves with great autonomy under the heel of neither Turk nor Bulgar nor Serb.

These are the basic impressions of this correspondent after a trip by jeep across Yugoslavia from the Morgan Line in Venesia Giulia through Slovenia, Croatia, Slavonia, Serbia and Macedonia, with stops in Ljubijana, Zagreb, Belgrade, Nish, Skoplje and Bitolj.

### No "Iron Curtain" Visible

There was no "iron curtain" visible. Everywhere the writer was received with courtesy; in Government circles, from Marshal Tito's residence down, and, more discreetly, in Opposition circles.

At no time did the writer have to register with the police, apart from the routine registrations by hotel concierges as is customary throughout Europe. Road blocks were few, aimed obviously against black marketers, and easily passed.

On the surface the people appeared cheerful and, compared to their miserable past since 1941, prosperous. There is plenty of food.

Even in military zones such as Slovenia or Macedonia there was neither suspicion nor any effort to restrict movement. My jeep was the first vehicle to cross into Greece through the Monastir Gap since 1944, when the Germans retreated in the opposite direction.

A Yugoslav military patrol at a frontier post—there were no customs officials—gravely examined my papers and waved the jeep on. At the Greek border nervous Greek guards dived into trenches and machine-gun positions at the astonishing sight of the vehicle and, finally, cautiously sent out a tommy-gun patrol to investigate after it had ground to a halt.

### A Heterogeneous Country

This dispatch seeks to describe with impartiality what is going on in a confused situation within a traditionally complex land made up of many peoples: Serbs, Croats, Slovenes, Bosniaks, Macedonians, Montenegrins, Turks, Albanians, Bulgarians, Gypsies and Vlachs.

Any reader who dislikes communism for itself will naturally detest Marshal Tito's Government and the program it is seeking to effect. Pro-Communists will admire it.

It is not democracy.

It is remarkable how normal life appears on the surface throughout Yugoslavia, if one can except the omnipresent posters, Communist Yugoslav and Russian slogans, portraits of Generalissimo Stalin and Marshal Tito and the ubiquitous red stars.

This writer found that a huge ratio of the rumors fomented outside Yugoslavia and even in the main Yugoslav cities, such as Zagreb, Belgrade and Skoplje, appear to be untrue.

Although some armed oppositionist hands are certainly functioning, it is on the most limited scale. Tales of marauding Krizhari (Crusaders) in Croatia and Chetniks in Serbia are immensely exaggerated.

On the basis of my experience, a traveler can go about in Yugoslavia about as easily as before the war provided he has the necessary papers.

### Misery Below the Surface

If one scratches below the surface, however, one finds darker shadows of dictatorship. The regime's ruthless devotion to its program echoes subterranean misery, in police jails, state prisons and court rooms and behind shuttered windows of those who disagree with communism—and they are many. The misery is mirrored in the eyes of hungry holders of the most meager ration cards, who cannot obtain jobs because their political orientation is found wanting.

As an important Yugoslav, whose identity cannot be revealed, described the situation, "Marshal Tito told me once confidentially that the Yugoslav Communist party is the only real Communist party in Europe, not the French, nor the Italian, nor the Czech, nor the Bulgarian. The Yugoslav Communist party is secret, disciplined, conspirational.

"Its discipline is Jesuitical. And it is illegal in the country it governs because it is the only party that is not forced to register its officers and organization.

"It is my belief that communism is a noble doctrine like Christianity. But here Tito and his supporters have brought bolshevism."

After his country's liberation, in which Marshal Tito's partisan movement played a fanatical and heroic role, the Marshal told a politician that the Yugoslav Communist party did not aim to be a party of the masses but was rather one of officers or cadres. Its membership is probably not more than 100,000 or 150,000.

It governs from the top down through the dictatorship of a ruling clique. This dictatorship is convinced it is working for the people's ultimate happiness.

Many opponents concede that Marshal Tito saved Yugoslavia as a country, that he held together embittered, frantricidal regional forces. Racial feuds have been ended or discouraged as firmly as possible, though some Serb opponents describe the regime as a "Red Croatian dictatorship" and some Croats as "another Belgrade tyranny." Those are slogans.

This strength is pitiless, however. In a speech six weeks ago in Tuzia, Marshal Tito said: "Those who will persist in hindering the creation of a better future, the reconstruction of our country, the creation of something better and new, will have to disappear from the face of this earth.

"We will have no pity toward them and we will behave toward them as against our worst enemies. We cannot stop halfway. Our road is already marked."

That road is the road of communism as mapped by Moscow. Those on whom no pity will be wasted are opponents of communism, regardless of the clean patriotic records they may have.

Men like Dragoljub Iovanovitch, left-wing Agrarian leader, who before the war was continually persecuted by the Yugoslav Government as "a Red" and "a recipient of Russian rubies" and gladly joined the Tito regime, are now in the opposition. He ventured to criticize developments in Parliament.

He has been expelled from the Serbian Assembly. He will be expelled from the Yugoslav Assembly when it reconvenes. He has been discharged from his position as a Belgrade University professor. He is called "reactionary" and "a recipient of American dollars" by those who were in prison with him seven years ago. Young Communist claques hurl vegetables at him.

### Macedonian Partisan in Jail

Men like Metodi Andonovn, who as "Cento" fought as a Partisan in Macedonia and was the first Vice President of the Federated Macedonian Government, are in prison, victims of a smear campaign as they await trial.

It would seem as if the Government felt that it was easier to rule than to govern. Moshe Piade, a veteran Communist and a member of the seven-man central committee of the party, whose identity has never been officially revealed, once said: "The altar lamp of the terror must never be extinguished. The people must have fear."

As a Serb, by no means a Conservative, put it, "A long night of terror has descended over Serbia. The whole country of Yugoslavia is a prison camp from which none can escape."

A Communist leader accused two opposition leaders of being jackals smelling evil. A Serb in whose blood runs the people's traditional poetry replied, "There is death about."

Above and beyond the bitter passions on all sides, however, the regime is grimly determined to carry out its ideas of good. One must not forget that in Croatia and Serbia, the greater part of Yugoslavia, no Government has been truly popular and grumbling is a heritage and a pastime. Neither prisons nor the secret police are new to Yugoslavia, but never were they so effective or so wholesale as now.

### Free Election Not Held

There are many in the country who hoped for more than they are getting, for spiritual freedom as well as economic democracy. Article 6 of the Constitution guarantees free elections. Even Communist leaders privately acknowledge, however, that they have not yet been held. But a Montenegrin party member remarked, "Marshal Tito could win even a free election because he would have a huge majority in Montenegro, Bosnia and Macedonia."

Privately, Marshal Tito does not deny that there is a lack of freedom. It is understood that Ambassador Richard C. Patterson Jr. once told Premier Tito that he hoped the Marshal would continue as personal leader of the country on the condition that the Four Freedoms would be implemented but that under present conditions Yugoslavia should not expect to receive a dime or a pair of shoes from the United States.

Marshal Tito was said to have replied that he regretted that help would not be forthcoming, but explained that his Government must take strong action against those seeking to upset it, sometimes aided by the Western powers.

He did not dispute that freedom was incomplete. He explained that the new regime was only a year and a half old and wondered if the Ambassador realized how conditions were in the United States a century ago. He said that in forming a new state it was necessary to employ more severe measures than in normal conditions, that freedom of the majority was more important than freedom of a minority.

Article 18 of the Constitution guarantees private property and private initiative if it does not interfere with "the common interest." Nevertheless, private businesses have been expropriated and their owners jailed as collaborators in innumerable instances when they were out of the country during the war and could not have collaborated.

### Drive on Church Is On

Article 25 guarantees freedom of religion, but an obvious campaign is under way to smash the Catholic Church. The old Serbian Orthodox hierarchy fears it will soon encounter a similar drive.

Article 27 guarantees freedom of the press, speech and assembly. This is a joke. No opposition paper appears. Milan Grol's Demokratija was feverishly circulated for a few days, but then the compositors' union, under strict Government control, as are all unions, refused to set further issues. In Zagreb, Marika Raditch, widow of the Croat Peasants' first leader, Stepan Raditch, began to edit Narodni Glas, which the compositors' union refused to set and which the Government, to make doubly certain, officially banned. A bomb exploded in Mme. Baditeh's bookshop.

The extent to which the opposition is muzzled can be seen in a joint announcement by the Serb Democratic and Radical parties, distributed Oct. 10 in typewritten copies to be passed on among party members, as this was the only way of reaching them. The announcement follows:

"The decrees of executive law and the circumstances under which they are being applied have determined the parties outside the People's Front [Communist-controlled all-party "coalition"] not to participate in the elections to the Constituent Assemblies of the Federated Republics."

Even their determination not to participate could not be announced in the Government-controlled press, perhaps so the world would be under the illusion that the elections would be open and free. This announcement, stressed the "absence of a free press."

### Full Opposition Boycott Claimed

The statement asserted that all opposition parties had agreed to boycott the elections.

Article 28 of the Constitution guarantees the inviolability of person and states that no one can be detained more than three days without a written decision of the public prosecutor or a law court. But jails are full and cases of persons imprisoned for months without having been charged are common knowledge throughout the country.

Although the Government is supposed to be a workers' and peasants' paradise, it is curious that no strike has occurred in Yugoslavia since her liberation. In theory strikes are permitted, but since all employes and employers are in a united syndicates organization, headed by an earnest and able Communist, Djuro Salaj, it is easy to see that the Government machine controls labor totally.

It is not unnatural or illogical that Russia should be reflected everywhere. Shops are full of Russian books, most of them published after the 1917 Bolshevik revolution. The Yugoslav Army is receiving new uniforms like that of the Soviet Army and new Russian equipment. Soviet artists and actors frequently tour the country. Soviet newspapers are in all cafes.

Although British and United States military missions, composed largely of parachutists who had fought alongside the partisans, were abruptly ordered to leave in June 1945, a Soviet military mission remained until last month. There is a military mission for special instruction with the Yugoslav Army, much like the British mission in Greece, which is distinct from the British Army in Greece. The NKVD, Soviet secret police, is said to have a mission to the UDB. There are reports, impossible to confirm, that each Ministry includes Russian experts to "check up" on Yugoslav technicians and bureaucrats.

### Secret Police Checks Russians

All Russian émigrés, of whom there were thousands in Yugoslavia, have been ordered to take out Soviet citizenship. A special NKVD mission has virtual extraterritorial rights in cases involving Russian soldiers with the military training mission and Russian citizens, including former émigrés.

The NKVD has its own prison near Belgrade. Last month there was a jail break there. Russian soldiers cordoned off the entire area, taking over the search without Yugoslav help. Yugoslav citizens are occasionally arrested by the NKVD and sent to Russian prisons.

It was rumored that liaison between Marshal Tito and Generalissimo Stalin had been conducted by Major General Kisselev and Lototsji who headed the military mission. They left only on Oct. 5 and were seen off at the airport by General Rankovitch.

The Soviet Union gets precedence in everything. Even the Belgrade paper Politika said editorially that next to the Soviet Union, Yugoslavia contributed the greatest proportional effort to victory in the war.

Certainly the loss of Yugoslav life was incredibly high—it was estimated at 1,400,000—but at least 1,100,000 were probably slaughtered in internal strife.

The Russians and Yugoslavs resent any suggestion that they are giving or receiving orders. Liaison of the two air forces is so great, however, that a Soviet officer was running the Ljubijana airport when American planes were recently forced down. The Soviet Ambassador still refuses to admit this.

### Envoy Forced to Seek House

Last year an American aircraft was forced down in Yugoslavia and not permitted to depart. During a recent discussion Maj. Gen. Vladimir Velebit, Under-Secretary for Foreign Affairs, said "This is a Russian operational field."

When Ambassador Patterson arrived in Belgrade a certain house was promised for his residence. The owner wished to rent to him. Three rooms were occupied by three Russian officers. They refused to move. The Belgrade Foreign Office was powerless to oust them. It then said the Soviet Ambassador intended to take it but the Russian envoy denied this to Mr. Patterson.

Mr. Patterson then asked Marshal Tito to evict the three officers. General Velebit and Colonel Bakitch, a high official, called on the United States envoy two days later and apologized but said Mr. Patterson could not have the house.

Mr. Patterson said, "You mean they won't leave even if Marshal Tito requests it?" General Velebit replied he was afraid not. Mr. Patterson added, "You mean the Prime Minister of Yugoslavia issues orders that three junior Russian officers should quit a house and they won't leave?" General Velebit sheepishly said that was the case.

A month later Col. Mihail Sergeichik, Russian head of the UNRRA mission, moved in.

Economic benefits granted to the Soviet Union can only be guessed. Yugoslavia is supposed to be self-supporting in sugar, but despite large UNRRA shipments she is still short because of exports to the Soviet Union.

### Called Chief Soviet Ally

Yugoslav supporters of Marshal Tito boast that Belgrade is the important western Slav capital to Moscow, that Poland is too divided and Czechoslovakia still too bourgeois.

It was reported that in a conversation with Marshal Tito Mr. Patterson complained that although the Premier talked of good-will to the United States, in his speeches he mentioned only Russia and Premier Stalin, never the United States and President Truman. Marshal Tito replied that his references to Russia and America were in direct proportion to the amount of aid received from them.

Mr. Patterson referred to the preponderant United States contribution to UNRRA. The Marshal acknowledged his country's indebtedness to UNRRA but stressed that it was an international organization of the United Nations designed to aid countries wrecked by the war.

Yugoslavia was in chaos when the Tito Government took over. A strong hand was needed.

Many leftist political thinkers in the country object that because of a lack of skilled government agents or by cynicism those who are in the saddle in Belgrade are betraying many of the revolution's causes. Some say the corrupt gang of pre-war politicians has been replaced by a new gang of politicians of the left who are rapidly becoming corrupt.

The fancy bourgeois villas of Dedinje have been largely taken over by Communist leaders. Only M. Piade among the leaders lives simply, sleeping in his office when tired and following the hermit-like regime he learned during his many years in jail.

When Vice Premier Edvard Kardeij took over the former house of former Premier Milan Stoyadinovitch he found it too small for his needs and moved, taking with him the entire staff of servants.

The grand living of some Communists has become a joke in Belgrade. Marshal Tito presented to Mitra Mitrovich, wife of Lieut. Gen. Milovan Djilas, whom the opposition has dubbed the "mad dog" of the regime, a gaudy solitaire diamond.

Belgrade gamins now sing a ditty. "I am Mitra the proletariat, I wear only diamonds."

Discouraged as many elements in the country are, the more intelligent concede that it was the Tito regime that saved Yugoslavia as an entity. They will further stress that, large as the opposition is numerically, it is completely split and lacks not only leaders of national scope but a real program.

The country as a whole almost certainly would never freely agree to the return of King Peter or the old regime, although in some sections of Serbia the King remains popular. The Croats and Slovenes as well as the Macedonians, Montenegrins and Bosnians would oppose him.

As a result, it appears certain that Marshal Tito and the Communist party are in Yugoslavia to stay a long time; they are firmly in power with considerably more popular support, especially in the poorer areas, than the outside world has perhaps realized. The opposition is being crushed by a ruthless juggernaut.

\*   \*   \*

**November 24, 1946**

## RUMANIA FORMALLY LINES UP WITH SOVIET BALKAN BLOC

*Election Gives the Communists Control There as in Neighboring States*

By JOHN MacCORMAC
Special to The New York Times

VIENNA, Nov. 23—The Government bloc of "democratic" parties won a clear majority in Rumania this week. That the Government would win was as certain as that dogs will continue to bite men and the most unexpected feature of the voting was that its majority was not greater.

Roughly speaking, all Balkan Governments have won all elections ever since they first began to imitate parliamentary practices. The only exceptions were the result of really revolutionary changes of public opinion; and with the Soviet Army at hand nothing of that sort could be expected to show itself in Rumania.

Rumania was the latest Danubian country to go to the polls since the war and Tuesday's election was the first ostensibly free expression of public opinion since 1938.

Of the six general elections in the Danube Valley since the war ended, four have been held in Russian-occupied coun-

tries. Russian troops had occupied Yugoslavia and Czechoslovakia also but had left them before the polling took place. This helped rather than harmed Moscow, for whose policy Soviet Army soldiers had not been good ambassadors.

### No Russian Interference

The Austrian Communist party would certainly, and the Hungarian Communist party would probably, have been considerably stronger today had those two countries not been occupied by Russians when polling took place. In neither country did the occupying forces make the slightest attempt to interfere with voting and it was an ironic fact that the election in November, 1945, in which Hungary returned a largely conservative Government, was the first really free expression of popular will in the country's history.

The Austrian elections, where the conservative-minded People's party and the Social Democrats divided 95 per cent of the vote with only about 10 per cent difference between them, and the Czechoslovak elections, in which Communists were returned as the strongest single party, were also conducted in accordance with democratic practice and the result was representative of the popular will.

### Czech Communists Win

In both countries Communists had enjoyed equal representation and held key positions in provisional governments which ruled before the elections. Czechoslovakia's Communists made good use of their opportunities, and of the obvious expediency of maintaining good relations with Moscow, to gain the largest single party vote and with it the Premiership. Austria's Communists—mostly because labor remained true to social democracy—gained only 5 per cent of the vote and four seats.

In Yugoslavia Marshal Tito obtained an overwhelming majority in the national general elections and another endorsement in the local elections a few weeks ago.

In Bulgaria after the referendum had turned the country from a monarchy into a republic the general election returned the Communists as by far the strongest party. And now Rumania has re-elected the National Democratic Front of Premier Groza.

### Dimitrov for Premier

The Bulgarian elections will probably end the political career of ex-Premier Kimon Georgiev, who, after faithfully serving the interests of the Soviets, was not even re-elected. On Thursday, he resigned and was promptly succeeded by Georgi Dimitrov, Bulgarian hero of the Reichstag fire trial, former chief of the Comintern and present head of the Bulgarian Communist party. At the moment the Bulgarian Communists are coquetting with the idea of discarding the Fatherland Front now that it has served their purpose and they have purged the Government and the army with its aid.

The victorious Government bloc in Rumania also may prove the beginning of the end for Premier Peter Groza, who has hitherto led it. He, too, sooner or later, will probably be succeeded by a Communist. For a capitalist, Groza played the Communist game skillfully. But though a rich man may enter the Communist heaven none has stayed there long.

Now that it has its puppet Governments in Yugoslavia, Rumania and Bulgaria and a highly reliable regime in Czechoslovakia, it remains for Russia to reverse the popular verdict in Hungary. There, too, by practically absorbing socialism and forcing the People's party to discard its "reactionary" members, communism has been making steady progress.

\*   \*   \*

**February 11, 1947**

# 5 TREATIES SIGNED IN PARIS CEREMONY

### Drive for Revision Is Started by 4 Ex-Enemy Countries, Yugoslavia and Greece

By C. L. SULZBERGER
Special to The New York Times

PARIS, Feb. 10—The first treaties of peace following World War II were signed today. They will formally terminate the state of war between the Allies and Germany's five European satellites.

Paris, already surfeited with the laborious negotiations that made today's ceremony possible and more concerned with its own economic and political problems, was indifferent. Although the weather was unseasonably warm, few curiosity-seekers assembled at the gates of the French Foreign Ministry on the Quai d'Orsay as, throughout the day, diplomatic cars whisked past idling clusters of gendarmes.

As a result of today's most undramatic proceedings, Italy, Rumania, Hungary, Bulgaria and Finland are now conditionally no longer at war with the powerful Allied coalition that developed to defeat them.

The condition is that of ratification. In all cases except that of Italy this should not be problematic. But there is so much dissatisfaction in the Italian peninsula that a critical argument is expected to develop when the Constituent Assembly faces the problem in Rome.

With the exception of Rumania, not one of the enemy states has professed much satisfaction with the conditions laid down today in the red-sealed and beribboned document that it was called upon to sign. Rumania is pleased to affirm that her possession of Transylvania—already unilaterally assured by Premier Stalin of Russia, in March, 1945—is accepted as permanent, and is keeping blinders carefully adjusted to the lost provinces of Bessarabia, Northern Bukovina and Southern Dobruja.

However, Rumania was one of the four former enemy states that delivered formal protests against the treaty terms today. Only Finland, of the defeated nations signing the treaties, did not protest. The protests of the others, along with objections entered by Yugoslavia and Greece, showed that the fight for revision had already started.

### Italian Incident Causes Flurry

Today's program was run off without a flaw, although behind the scenes a crisis had developed that for a brief time threatened to prevent the signing of the Italian treaty, by far the most important. This crisis almost forced a delay in the planned timetable.

What happened, as pieced together from various diplomatic sources here, was this:

Yesterday evening, to the astonishment of the Italian Government, the British Ambassador to Rome sent a note to the Italian Foreign Ministry stating that, in the view of the British Government, Italian signature of the treaty today would be tantamount to ratification.

This caused a wild flurry in Rome. At 10 P. M. Count Carlo Sforza, Italian Foreign Minister, telephoned to his plenipotentiary here, Marchese Antonio Meli Lupi di Soragna, and told him to ascertain from the peace conference secretariat whether such an attitude prevailed among the Big Four.

The Italian Embassy here immediately telephoned Jacques Fouques-Duparc of the French Foreign Ministry, who served as secretary general of last summer's peace conference. After the urgency of the situation had been explained to M. Fouques-Duparc, he agreed to get dressed and call upon Foreign Minister Georges Bidault.

### Bidault Consults Allied Envoys

It is understood that M. Bidault expressed the opinion in a conference late at night that signature by Marchese Lupi di Soragna would not be the same thing as ratification—a most important point.

However, M. Bidault was not in a position to decide as an arbiter, and after breakfast today he summoned the United States, British and Soviet envoys to reach a hasty decision on this point. Article 90 of the treaty states that "it shall also be ratified by Italy," and it was decided that the Italian Constituent Assembly retained this right.

Meanwhile, Marchese Lupi di Soragna, who had been instructed not to sign until this point had been cleared up, was nervously awaiting the verdict in the Italian Embassy. He had told this correspondent in an interview last night something of Italy's views on the treaty, describing it as a series of conditions imposed upon the Italians and stating that his Government expected to seek peaceful revision as soon as possible after its admission to the United Nations—either through that body or by bilateral agreements.

At the request of the Italian Embassy this correspondent removed Marchese Lupi di Soragna's name from the statement and attributed it to a responsible Italian source. The reason for this request is, presumably, now clear, since the story of the eleventh-hour crisis has become known.

Today's ceremonies, which proceeded without a hitch, began when the delegates of the Allied states assembled in the Salon de la Paix, just inside the doors of the Quai d'Orsay, and waited about a long, green-covered table until M. Bidault arrived to address them in the adjoining Salle de l'Horloge (Clock Room). Then, at intervals, the plenipotentiaries of the defeated states were invited to appear.

### Table With a History

In the Salle de l'Horloge a famous seventeenth century table stood on a Savonnerie carpet of Gobelin's manufacture. This table had belonged first to Louis XV and then to Louis XVI. The wounded Robespierre was laid on the table before he was guillotined. Today it was furnished with inkpots, six ordinary pens of Moroccan onyx with differing points and a series of documents on heavy white parchment paper. These were the peace treaties.

The treaties were signed with dispatch and without incident. Everybody except Marchese Lupi di Soragna used the equipment supplied; he preferred his fountain pen.

Stanoje Simitch, Yugoslavia's tall, gray-haired Foreign Minister, signed under protest. Thus, the last doubts about the adherence of Yugoslavia and Italy to the treaty were dispelled.

Alexander E. Bogolomov led the Big Three's Ambassadors in the process of counter-signing because Foreign Minister Molotov of Russia had been the last of the Big Three Ministers to sign in their respective capitals. Mr. Bogomolov wrote with deliberate care, as did Alfred Duff Cooper of Britain; Jefferson Caffery of the United States signed with verve.

Outside not more than three dozen idlers stood at the Quai d'Orsay gates listening to loud-speakers calling for delegation cars. At 11:35 A. M. Italy was at last at peace (subject to ratification), and at 6:10 P. M. Finland was eligible to join the comity of nations.

In midafternoon a young man strolling beside the Seine with his girl, oblivious to what was occurring a few yards away, said:

"Ah! The newspapers are promising fresh meat this week."

\* \* \*

**March 13, 1947**

# TRUMAN ACTS TO SAVE NATIONS FROM RED RULE; ASKS 400 MILLION TO AID GREECE AND TURKEY; CONGRESS FIGHT LIKELY BUT APPROVAL IS SEEN

### NEW POLICY SET UP

*President Blunt in Plea to Combat 'Coercion' as World Peril*

### PLANS TO SEND MEN

*Goods and Skills Needed as Well as Money, He Tells Congress*

By FELIX BELAIR Jr.
Special to The New York Times

WASHINGTON, March 12—President Truman outlined a new foreign policy for the United States today. In a historic message to Congress, he proposed that this country intervene wherever necessary throughout the world to prevent the subjection of free peoples to Communist-inspired

Associated Press Wirephoto

President Truman addressing Congress yesterday.

totalitarian regimes at the expense of their national integrity and importance.

In a request for $400,000,000 to bolster the hard-pressed Greek and Turkish Governments against Communist pressure, the President said the constant coercion and intimidation of free peoples by political infiltration amid poverty and strife undermined the foundations of world peace and threatened the security of the United States.

Although the President refrained from mentioning the Soviet Union by name, there could be no mistaking his identification of the Communist state as the source of much of the unrest throughout the world. He said that, in violation of the Yalta Agreement, the people of Poland, Rumania and Bulgaria had been subjected to totalitarian regimes against their will and that there had been similar developments in other countries.

### Cardinal Points of Departure

As the Senate and House of Representatives sat grim-faced but apparently determined on the course recommended by the Chief Executive, Mr. Truman made these cardinal points of departure from traditional American foreign policy:

"I believe that it must be the policy of the United States to support free peoples who are resisting attempted subjugation by armed minorities or by outside pressures.

"I believe that we must assist free peoples to work out their own destinies in their own way.

"I believe that our help should be primarily through economic and financial aid which is essential to economic stability and orderly political processes."

In addition to the $400,000,000, to be expended before June 30, 1948, the President asked Congress to authorize the detail of American civilian and military personnel to Greece and Turkey, upon the request of those countries. The proposed personnel would supervise the use of material and financial assistance and would train Greek and Turkish personnel in special skills.

Lest efforts be made to cast him in the role of champion of things as they are, the President recognized that the world was not static and that the status quo was not sacred. But he warned that if we allowed changes in the status quo in violation of the United Nations Charter through such subterfuges as political infiltration, we would be helping to destroy the Charter itself.

### Aware of Broad Implications

President Truman said he was fully aware of the "broad implications involved" if the United States went to the assistance of Greece and Turkey. He said that while our aid to free peoples striving to maintain their independence should be primarily financial and economic, he reminded Congress that the fundamental issues involved were no different from those for which we fought a war with Germany and Japan.

The standing ovation that marked the close of the President's address was echoing through the Capitol corridors as he left the building to motor to the National Airport, where he left by plane for Key West, Fla., for a four-day rest on orders of his personal physician, Brig. Gen. Wallace Graham.

The President appeared tired from the ordeal of his personal appearance before the joint session, but evidently satisfied that the specific recommendations of his message, with its delineation of the implications of a new policy, had temporarily discharged the obligation of the Executive. It was the turn of Congress to make the next move.

That move was not long in the making. Senator Arthur H. Vandenberg, chairman of the Foreign Relations Committee, called a meeting of his group for tomorrow morning to consider the President's proposals. The House Foreign Affairs Committee was to consider the kindred $350,000,000 appropriation for destitution relief in liberated countries.

In the sharp and conflicting reaction to the President's program, many voices were raised on each side of the Capitol in approval and in criticism. However, there was little doubt that the vast majority in both houses would reflect the wishes of their leaders and go down the line for the new policy and the added financial responsibility it implied.

### Would Bar Any Coercion

Apparently conscious of the advance demands by Senator Vandenberg and others that he set forth the full implications of his recommendations, President Truman explained that one of the primary objectives of our foreign policy had been the creation of conditions in which this and other nations would work out a way of life free from coercion by outside influences.

It was to insure the peaceful development of nations; free from coercion, that the United States had taken a leading role in the establishment of the United Nations, Mr. Truman went on. And the United Nations was designed to provide a lasting freedom and independence for all its members.

But these objectives could not be attained, said the President, "unless we are willing to help free peoples to maintain their free institutions and their national integrity against aggressive movements that seek to impose upon them totalitarian regimes."

Anticipating criticism, not long in developing, that his proposals to lend $250,000,000 to Greece and $150,000,000 to Turkey would "by-pass the United Nations," Mr. Truman explained that, while the possibility of United Nations aid had been considered, the urgency and immediacy were such that the United Nations was not in a position to assist effectively.

The President made it clear that the responsibilities he asked Congress to face squarely had developed suddenly because of the inability of Great Britain to extend help to either the Greek or Turkish Government after March 31. He said the British withdrawal by March 31 foreshadowed the imposition of totalitarian regimes by force in both countries unless the United States stepped in to support the existing Governments.

The President reiterated that it was a serious course on which he was asking Congress to embark. But he said he would not ask it except that the alternative was much more serious. The United States contributed $341,000,000,000 toward the winning of World War II, the President recalled.

Although there was a note of apology for the present Greek Government, which the President conceded had made mistakes, it was described as a freely elected one.

The Greek Government, he said, represents 85 per cent of the members of the Greek Parliament. He recalled that 692 American observers had been present in Greece when the Parliament was elected and had certified that the election represented a fair expression of the views of the Greek people.

Although the President did not specify the allocation of the $400,000,000, it has been generally understood that the Administration intends to use $250,000,000 for Greece and $150,000,000 for Turkey. He asked further authority to permit the speediest and most effective translation of the funds into "needed commodities, supplies and equipment," which was taken to refer to the supply of surplus war equipment to the Greek Army out of United States Army supplies in Europe.

\* \* \*

June 6, 1947

# PETKOV HELD IN SOFIA

### Bulgaria Arrests Opposition Chief on Conspiracy Charges

SOFIA, Bulgaria, June 5 (U.P.)—Nicolas Petkov, leader of the opposition to Bulgaria's Communist-dominated Fatherland Front Government, was arrested tonight on charges that he was involved in two military conspiracies.

M. Petkov, who was formerly Minister Without Portfolio, is secretary of the Agrarian National Union, which holds ninety of the ninety-nine Opposition seats in the National Assembly.

His arrest was ordered by the Assembly after a six-hour debate airing charges that M. Petkov participated in the alleged conspiracies.

\* \* \*

## Independent Socialists Curbed

he basis of the unfavorable comment on the present
n, M. Tatarescu proposed the realization of his pro-
ntaining fifteen points that represented "a new course
ning."

ply inspired by Communist-party leaders stressed that
ce Premier himself has a great share in the responsi-
f the Government's general policy."

Government Social Democratic party representatives
terday for Zurich, Switzerland, to participate in the
ional socialist conference, but the independent Social
ratic party's delegates were prevented from leaving
stantin Titel Petrescu, leader of the independent
sts, in a protest to Zurich, asserted that his party "can-
present at the conference, being considered Public
No. 1 by the dictatorial regime which governs the
in close cooperation with the communistic Social
ratic group."

letter declared that "the working masses of Rumania
mained loyal to the Socialist ideology and the demo-
actics" and that therefore "they contest the right of that
mental opportunistic faction to represent them."

he same time, the independent Social Democrats for-
to Zurich an appeal asking an end to the "oppres-
imprisonments and the indignities of treatment to
members of the Socialist party are subject."

\*　\*　\*

**July 16, 1947**

# EK ARMY CLOSES TRAP ON ATTACKERS
# YANINA; U. S. ASKS SWIFT U. N. ACTION

### REBELS ARE HALTED

Athens Brigades Pen 2,500 Guerrillas North of Epirus City

**EARLY SHOWDOWN IS SEEN**

N. Security Body Agrees to Long Session Tomorrow—
Balks on Meeting Today

By The Associated Press

HENS, July 15—Airborne Greek Army reinforcements
abruptly halted a drive by 2,500 savagely fighting guer-
oops nineteen miles from their objective, the Epirian
of Yanina in northwestern Greece, and enveloped
n a trap from which they "cannot escape," a Cabinet
er said tonight.

e guerrilla drive, which the Greek Government con-
originated in Albania, was stopped short at the village
grades, nineteen miles north of Yanina, during the first
etween Government troops and the insurgent band.

e Government Minister said it had not been determined
w large a scale the battle at Negrades had been waged,
at the Government was confident the threat to Yanina
population of 20,000 had been dissipated.

[The United Nations Security Council failed to agree to the
request of the United States that two sessions on the Greek situation be held Wednesday, but will meet morning and afternoon on Thursday. Russia opposed the motion and ridiculed
the Greek charges after the United States had warned that the
situation "might burst into an explosion any day."]

War Minister George Stratos said that two Army brigades
of 1,500 men each moving down on the guerrilla forces from
the north and a third brigade moving against them from the
opposite direction had halted the menace to Yanina.

### Forced to Stand and Fight

The guerrillas "cannot escape and they have to give battle." Mr. Stratos declared.

A source close to the Greek General Staff said a "showdown" battle between the Army and the guerrillas, who
began a surprise offensive Sunday, moving against the village
of Konitsa with military precision and full war equipment
probably would take place soon in the region of the village of
Yeroplatanos, twenty-five miles north of Yanina.

Guerrillas in the area of Yeroplatanos and near-by
Vasilikon, a few miles to the north, now are surrounded, he
said, while nine miles west of Yeroplatanos the insurgents
who were repulsed at Konitsa now are trapped by two Greek
brigades.

[Navy Minister Sophocles Venizelos said savage fighting
continued at St. Nicholas, five miles northwest of Konitsa,
The United Press reported. Regulars and rebels also were
engaged in heavy skirmishes in the Mount Grammos area, to
the northeast.

[It quoted Gen. Napoleon Zervas, Minister of Public
Order, as saying at Yanina that guerrilla reinforcements were
pouring across the Albanian frontier.]

Mr. Stratos said his Government had ascertained that there
were large concentrations of arms and military supplies at
three points in Albania just over the Greek frontier and at
three points in Yugoslavia.

### "Foreign" Support Reported

He added that twenty guerrilla prisoners admitted that the
"invasion" force included contingents of an "international
brigade." [The Government said the guerrillas were "supported by foreign elements," Reuters reported.]

The War Minister said that members of the United Nations
Balkan investigation subcommission, currently studying
Greek border incidents, returned to Salonika today after
viewing some battle grounds "convinced" the current attacks
in northwest Greece were launched in Albania.

The subcommission, he said, would return to Konitsa,
which he described as now entirely "free," to question guerrilla
prisoners.

Despite Government victories at Konitsa and Negrades,
there was some speculation here that those guerrilla attacks
had been diversionary operations to screen even greater
actions planned in the Florina and Kastoria regions, just
south of the Yugoslav border.

**June 6, 1947**

### THE TREATIES RATIFIED

The first four peace treaties to follow the Second World War have now been ratified by the Senate with much more than the necessary two-thirds majorities. They will become effective as soon as the documents are deposited by the United States, Britain, Russia and—in the case of Italy—France. In contrast to our action after the First World War, when we repudiated the peace treaties and thereby contributed to the conditions which led ultimately to the outbreak of the greater war, this is a convincing demonstration that the United States is determined this time to carry out the obligations it assumed both toward its allies and its former enemies. We may be thankful also that peace has at last been established between this country and at least four European nations—Italy, Hungary, Rumania and Bulgaria—with a combined population of more than 77,000,000.

But it is significant both of the deteriorating international situation and of the nature of the treaties themselves that yesterday's ratification, despite its approach to unanimity, was undertaken with grave misgivings and justified only on the principle of choosing the lesser of two evils. For the treaties are unsatisfactory, and those with Rumania, Bulgaria and Hungary have already been violated in decisive respects by Russia and the puppet regimes she has set up in these countries—in the case of Hungary in a manner which President Truman has just characterized as an outrage. Moreover, there is ample basis for the fear that once American and British troops are withdrawn from Italy, in conformity with the treaty, attempts will be made to upset the provisions agreed upon for that country as well.

These misgivings apply not only to the questions of boundaries, disarmament, reparations and other such things, but to the integrity and sovereignty of the four nations concerned. The treaties provide that all four of these countries shall take all measures necessary to secure to all persons under their jurisdiction "the enjoyment of human rights and the fundamental freedom of expression, of press and publication, of religious worship, of political opinion and of public meeting." They thus go considerably beyond the democratic provisions of the wartime agreements, and by providing for specific rights and freedoms patently exclude the "democracy" of a "proletarian dictatorship." Furthermore, they make the enforcement of these provisions mandatory upon the Italian, Hungarian, Rumanian and Bulgarian Governments, and upon all signatory Governments, our own included.

Despite this, under Russian domination and with Russian help, all these rights and freedoms are being abrogated in the three Balkan countries, and Communist forces are preparing to follow suit in Italy. In this respect Russia merely pursues a now established practice. In contrast, in the Truman Doctrine the United States takes its stand against further direct or indirect aggression against any nation, either by pressure from the outside or by armed minorities on the inside, and the new peace treaties both extend the scope of that Doctrine and pro-

vide it with new legal instruments, enforcing both Doctrine and treaties

As regards the Doctrine, a begin been made through aid to Greece ar directed against any nation or any rather against aggression, already Nations Charter. The nature of the m for this purpose were outlined yester shall in his speech at Harvard. We sha but shall oppose any government, p which seeks to perpetuate human mis and we shall do our best to cooperate to join us in the task of restoring th Europe and the world.

Such a program cannot, of course, b of the United States, and Secretary Ma pean nations to take the initiative in dr which we can support. The aim of this quickest possible restoration of the str Western Europe.

\* \* \*

### CHANGE IN POLICY SOUGHT

*Vice Premier Offers 15-Point Plan for ;
Cites 'Wave of Disconte*

Special to The New York  
BUCHAREST, Rumania, June 5—Ge Premier, Minister of Foreign Affairs ar dissident National Liberal party, has urge other parties in the Government" to st proposal he has just made for "changing external policy" of Rumania.

The proposal, contained in a memora tarescu circulated privately, was the late the growing tension in the interior politic caused much comment.

M. Tatarescu asserted in the memorandu wave of discontent, all over the country, a; ment, discontent that grows from day to da the causes of this unrest include:

"The negative economic results, because governing [by the present regime], general sents scarcely 48 per cent of 1938's output, w charges represent 50 per cent of the states' in

"That is what has brought about inflati cost of living and excessive taxation."

M. Tatarescu asserted that the situation als by "excesses concerning preventive arrests," "completely innocent men are arrested, whic ation of the legend that the regime is main force and terror because it is unpopular and un

The Cabinet praised the Greek Air Force tonight for its part in moving reinforcements into the battle areas under difficult conditions. Greek veterans also were rushed from Yanina to Kalpaki, twenty-five miles to the west, where regulars and guerrillas joined battle last night.

A report from the Second Army Corps said the regulars and gendarmerie had dislodged guerrillas from passes and heights in the Kalpaki region, ten miles east of the Corfu channel.

Unconfirmed reports said the Government was strengthening its forces at Kastoria and Florina, both opposite the Yugoslav frontier, in case any "invasion" should be staged from that direction.

The Royalist newspaper Estia said a squadron of British warships was scheduled to arrive Saturday at Piraeus, the port of Athens, and that United States vessels, including an aircraft carrier, might arrive sooner than expected because of developments here.

### Navy Tells of Placement

Special to The New York Times

WASHINGTON, July 15—The Navy Department denied the report that United States warships might arrive in Greek ports soon. Its units are in the Salerno, Italy, area and at Venice, the Navy said, and there is no plan to move any of them to Greece. There are none in or near Grecian waters. [The spokesman said the Navy had four light cruisers and six destroyers in the Mediterranean, press services reported.]

### International Conflict Feared

By DANA ADAMS SCHMIDT

Special to The New York Times

ATHENS, July 15—In the first official allegation that members of an "international brigade" were participating in the guerrilla invasion, Minister of War Stratos stated tonight that the Greek Government would ask the United Nations subcommission to interrogate twenty prisoners at Konitsa.

The development of the guerrilla warfare into international conflict was threatened, in the opinion of Greek Government quarters, by a virtual declaration of war against the Americans and British in Greece issued by the guerrilla chief, Gen. Markos Vafthiadis, in an article published in Paris.

Citing ten alleged acts of United States and British participation in the conflict, he stated:

"Following these acts, we are obliged to abolish any discriminations, and confront the British and Americans who take part in the campaigns against us in the same way as against the forces of monarcho-fascism and therefore as our enemies. For whatever ensues, the British and Americans and their Governments will be responsible."

### The Way Seen as Paved

The statement, in Government opinion, prepared the ground for the participation of Albanian or other Balkan troops as well as an "international brigade" in the fighting.

Contrary to some reports, there had been no "second invasion" by guerrillas from Albania up to tonight, but Greek

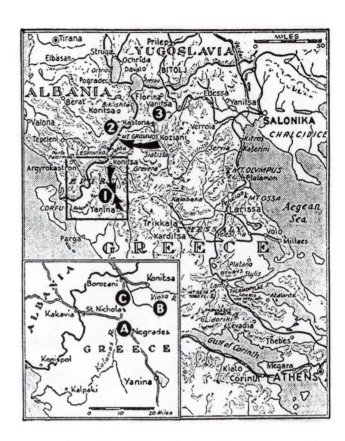

Troops driving south from Konitsa and northwest from Yanina were said to have surrounded 2,500 guerrillas in the area (1) shown in detail on the inset map. The rebel units that had crossed the Albanian border to attack Yanina were reported encircled at Negrades (A) and at a point twenty-five miles north of Yanina (B). The guerrilla force repelled at Konitsa was also surrounded (C). Skirmishing continued in the Mount Grammos region (2). Five thousand rebels were reported massing across the border from the towns of Kastoria and Florina (3).

intelligence was worried by reports of strong concentrations of enemy forces at six points along the border, particularly bands totalling 5,000 opposite Florina and Kastoria.

Considering the Mount Grammos area still the main center of operations and the most likely location of the Communists' proposed "free government," intelligence officers interpreted the attack on Konitsa as a diversion. The road running along the Albanian side of the frontier northward round Lake Prespa to Monastir, they pointed out, gave the guerrillas means of rapid deployment of forces and scattered, darting incursions.

Communist quarters—still publishing newspapers and operating freely in Athens—boasted that there soon would be a fighting front stretching from Florina to the sea opposite Corfu.

For the first time a meeting of the Greek National Defense Council, presided by Premier Demetrios Maximos, was attended tonight by the chiefs of the United States military and naval missions, Maj. Gen. William G. Livesey and Rear Admiral John A. Snackenberg, and the chiefs of the British military, naval and police missions.

Dwight P. Griswold, director of the United States aid program, consulted with Premier Maximos and the permanent

Under-Secretary for Foreign Affairs, Pakis Pipinellis, this afternoon. While Mr. Griswold maintained a discreet silence, Greek sources said he had recognized the priority of re-establishing order and hence of equipping the Greek Army over all other objectives of his mission.

### British Squadron Due

The British Embassy announced tonight that a British naval squadron, including the cruiser Liverpool and the aircraft carriers Ocean and Triumph, would visit Piraeus over the week-end. Other British naval units will call at Salonika; Candia, Crete, and Leros at the end of July, while another Mediterranean squadron will visit Nauplia in the Peloponnesus in the first week in August.

General Zervas, in a telephone call from Yanina to Premier Maximos, reported that many of the guerrillas wore red jackets, others red armbands with the hammer and sickle, and yet others the Soviet star.

Members of the Greek General Staff said they had reason to believe there were Germans, Italians and Albanians among the invaders.

\* \* \*

**July 16, 1947**

## RUMANIA ARRESTS MANIU AND AIDES

*Peasant Chief Incommunicado in Sanitarium—*
*Others at Airport When Seized*

By The Associated Press

BUCHAREST, Rumania, July 15—Several leading members of the Government's principal opposition, the National Peasant party, were arrested yesterday at an airport just outside Bucharest while trying to flee to another country, it was announced tonight.

Among them were Ion Mihalache, vice president of the party; Nicholae Penescu, its secretary general, and Dr. Constantin Gafenko, a prominent member. Dr. Juliu Maniu, president of the party, is being held incommunicado in a sanitarium here that he entered six days ago for treatment.

The arrests were confirmed tonight by the Ministry of Internal Affairs, which issued a communiqué saying:

"Full of hate for the popular democratic regime and wanting to overthrow the regime; being implicated in the criminal actions of elements hostile to the people and afraid of the responsibilities before justice and the people's anger at the illegalities they have committed, several leaders of the National Peasant party, at the direct order of Juliu Maniu, attempted on July 14 to escape to a foreign country.

"For that purpose they bribed several pilots of the military air force.

"State security police, on July 14 at 7 o'clock, arrested at Tamadau Airport . . . as they tried to escape by boarding a plane the following leaders of the National Peasant party and their accomplices:

"Ion Mihalache, vice president of the National Peasant party.

"Nicholae Penescu, secretary general of the party.

"Elena Penescu, wife of the secretary general.

"Ile Lazar, member of the central committee of the party.

"Nicholae Carandino, former editor of the party newspaper.

"Lily Carandino, his wife and well-known Rumanian actress.

"Dr. Constantin Gafenko, prominent member of the party.

"George Popescu, engineer and party member."

The arrests apparently preceded a raid on party headquarters staged by police last night. Several party members found on the premises were also arrested.

The National Peasant party opposes the policies of the six-party pro-Government Leftist bloc.

### Other Balkan Arrests Cited

LONDON, July 15 (Reuters)—The latest wave of arrests of Rumanian Opposition politicians was considered by London observers tonight to be the most drastic and most significant that had taken place since the pro-Communist National Democratic Front Government of Petru Groza was placed in power by the Russians in 1945.

Several hundred members of the Opposition National Peasant party were reported to have been arrested during the last few months, but they were not the leaders of the party.

Now that the party's president, Juliu Maniu, has been arrested, together with his chief party officials, it is believed that the Government has decided to eliminate its chief opposition.

During the war M. Maniu's prestige was so great that, although he was known by the Germans to be maintaining contacts with the Western Allies, he was never arrested, presumably because the Germans feared the dangerous effects of such a step on Rumanian public opinion.

His arrest today follows the arrest last month of Bulgaria's chief Opposition leader, Nikola Petkov, and the arrest in Yugoslavia of the leader of the Serbian Peasant party, Dragoljub Yovanovitch, a few weeks earlier. The developments in Rumania seemed to observers here to be part of a general drive to paralyze or eliminate all active opposition movements in the Balkans.

\* \* \*

**August 6, 1947**

## BULGAR 'CONFESSIONS' LINK PETKOV TO COUP

Special to The New York Times

SOFIA, Bulgaria, Aug. 5—The trial of the opposition Agrarian leader, Nikola Petkov, began here today with two of the four high-ranking army officers indicted with him on a charge of attempting to overthrow the present regime by a military coup confessing guilt and naming Mr. Petkov as the instigator of their crime.

The confessions came from Major Athanas Athanassov and Colonel Boris Gergov who shared the dock with Colonel Marko Ivanov, Dimiter Ivanov and Mr. Petkov.

A request by Mr. Petkov's counsel for a postponement of the hearing for three or four days was rejected by the court. The court's president read the eighteen-page indictment which concluded: "Nikola Petkov used all the means of spoken and written propaganda, for criminal purposes, for preparing a coup d'état and for the overthrow of the Government by violence."

SOFIA, Aug. 5 (U.P.)—The American diplomatic observer, Jack Horner, was barred from the treason trial of Nikola Petkov today. He immediately accused the Bulgarian Government of "bad faith." Mr. Horner said he was informed that the trial was closed to all foreigners except correspondents.

He immediately called on Foreign Minister Kimon Georgiev and accused the Government of "bad faith" in view of Prime Minister Georgi Dimitrov's pledge that Mr. Petkov would get a fair and open trial.

Associated Press

Nikola Petkov

\*    \*    \*

**August 17, 1947**

## SOFIA SENTENCES PETKOV TO DEATH

*Four Aides in Alleged Plot to Overthrow Government Get 5 to 15 Years in Prison*

By The United Press

SOFIA, Bulgaria, Aug. 16—Nikola Petkov, leader of the Opposition Agrarian party, was sentenced to death today on a charge of having conspired to overthrow the Communist-dominated Fatherland Front Government.

He also was found guilty on four minor counts and received jail sentences aggregating forty-five years. He was fined 500,000 leva and was deprived of his citizenship.

He had pleaded not guilty to all charges, and the court announced that the sentences could be appealed within two weeks. No date was set for the execution.

Four co-defendants, all of whom pleaded guilty and gave testimony aimed at linking M. Petkov with plans for a revolution, were sentenced as follows:

Col. Marko Ivanov, the alleged contact man between M. Petkov and the "conspirators"—Fifteen years' imprisonment and twenty years' deprivation of rights.

Col. Boris Gergov and Maj. Athanas Athanassov, both alleged members of an army conspiracy group—Ten years' imprisonment and fifteen years' deprivation of rights.

Dimiter Ivanov, a minor official in the Agrarian party and alleged director of sabotage for M. Petkov—Five years' imprisonment and eight years' deprivation of rights.

**Cameras Record Sentencing**

Presiding Judge Naiden Raichev of the Sofia District Court read the sentences "in the name of the National Republic of Bulgaria." He mumbled and was frequently drowned out by the noise of newsreel cameras.

The courtroom was tense and silent throughout. There were no demonstrations inside or outside the marble-walled room, where for eight days the prosecution had paraded sixty-five witness, and M. Petkov stood alone to defend himself.

Diabetic and generally in ill-health, the Agrarian party secretary stood rock-like, betraying no emotion of any kind as Judge Reichev read his sentence.

Leaflets with excerpts from the prosecutor's speech demanding the death penalty were distributed in Sofia streets this morning. The Government controlled press played up resolutions demanding the death sentence, adopted by organizations throughout the country. Newspapers declared that inasmuch as "the court represented the people," it had no choice but to inflict the death penalty.

In the final summation M. Petkov's counsel had appealed to the court to realize that it represented the people.

When the defense presented its summary there were no camera men present. On other days, camera men swarmed over the room.

M. Petkov was jailed June 6 on a charge that he had been "conspiring" against the Government for twenty-three months. When his trial opened Aug. 5, the four co-defendants began testimony charging M. Petkov was the leader of the plot.

### Petkov Said to Seek Rule

M. Ivanov told the court that M. Petkov had informed him that the Allies would never permit Bulgaria to be "communized." He said M. Petkov had fancied himself the leader of a regime sponsored by the United States and Britain that would replace the Fatherland Front.

M. Petkov denied the charge and the allegations of the co-defendants. He said he wanted "to rouse the people to fight the Fatherland Front at the ballot box."

M. Petkov was named Minister Without Portfolio Sept. 9, 1944. He resigned in July, 1945, under pressure. He had urged Allied supervision of elections in his country, in accordance with the Yalta Agreement.

\* \* \*

**November 12, 1947**

# MANIU CONVICTED, GETS LIFE SENTENCE

*Rumanian Opposition Chief to Serve in Solitary—18 Others Guilty in Treason Plot*

By W. H. LAWRENCE
Special to The New York Times

BUCHAREST, Rumania, Nov. 11—Dr. Juliu Maniu, leader of the Opposition Peasant party and a former Premier, and Ion Mihalache, vice president of the party, were convicted of treason tonight by a Bucharest military tribunal and sentenced to life imprisonment.

The New York Times, 1938

Dr. Juliu Maniu

The two Peasant heads, considered the most dangerous politically because of their popularity with the masses in this country, received the maximum penalty along with two Rumanian politicals who now are abroad—Grigore Nicolescu-Buzesti, former Foreign Minister, and Alexander Gratianu, once Minister to Turkey. The death penalty is not permitted by the Rumanian Constitution.

Col. Alexander Petrescu, the presiding judge, who used to be Minister of Justice and in charge of prison camps when the Germans were in power here, read the unanimous decision to a hand-picked throng that filled the courtroom and that burst into applause when he finished.

None of the nineteen on trial was acquitted. Even Vasile Serdici, Dr. Maniu's former press chief, whose confessions and angry denunciations of his one-time leader sounded like something out of Arthur Koestier's "Darkness at Noon," drew ten years at hard labor, confiscation of his property and a 50,000 lei fine [about $338].

Baron Ion de Mocseny-Styrcea, former marshal at King Michael's court, who was accused only of not informing the authorities that he had been a spectator when the alleged conspiracy was planned, received two years in a correctional institution and a 50,000-lei fine, but escaped confiscation of his land and property holdings.

The other sentences were: Victor Radulescu-Pogoneanu, former Foreign Ministry official, twenty-five years at hard labor, confiscation of his property and a 50,000-lei fine.

Dr. Ili Lazar, of the Peasant party central committee and formerly a Cabinet member, twelve years at hard labor and confiscation of property.

Nicolae Carandino, editor of the Peasant newspaper, six years and confiscation of property.

Nicolae Penescu, Peasant general secretary, five years and confiscation of property.

Camil Dimitrescu, former official of the Foreign Ministry, fifteen years at hard labor, confiscation of property and 50,000-lei fine.

Radu Nicolescu-Buzesti, of the Peasant central committee and brother of Grigore, ten years, confiscation of property and a 50,000-lei fine.

Col. Stefan Stoica, eight years and a 50,000-lei fine.

Florin Roiu, another former Foreign Ministry official, five years, confiscation of property and a 10,000-lei fine.

Emil Oprisan, former code officer of the Foreign Ministry, three years and a 500-lei fine.

Emil Lazarescu, once a Foreign Ministry official, two years in a correctional institution and a 100-lei fine.

Lieut. Col. Dimitru Statescu, one year and a 5,000-lei fine.

Two others who are abroad—Grigore Gafencu, former Foreign Minister and once envoy to the Soviet Union, and Constantin Visoianu, another former Foreign Ministry official—received twenty and fifteen years, respectively, for their part in the alleged plot to overthrow the present pro-Communist Government of Premier Petru Groza.

\* \* \*

**November 12, 1947**

## GUILTY, AS PLANNED

From the moment Dr. Juliu Maniu was charged with high treason in Bucharest it was a foregone conclusion that the Russian-dominated government of Rumania would find him guilty. The verdict given yesterday comes at the end of a trial which, like the recent trial of Nikola Petkov in Bulgaria, follows a made-in-Moscow pattern, with evidence that was a little too pat for credence, judges who leaned over forward to aid the prosecution, and confessions from alleged co-conspirators that read like something lifted bodily from the pages of Arthur Koestler's "Darkness at Noon." Maniu, however, unlike Petkov, will not die on the gallows. Because of his advanced age (he is seventy-five) he will escape with the assertedly lenient sentence of solitary confinement for life instead of hard labor.

Here is a man who, more than any other Rumanian, has stood for years as the symbol of his country's independence. This was no "Fascist reactionary" [i.e., middle-of-the-road democrat]. This man was the leader of the great popular left-of-center political party in Rumania, the National Peasant party—a man so rugged in his leadership, and so secure in his hold on the loyalty of great numbers of devoted followers, that his arrest was something that even the Nazis at the peak of their power in occupied Rumania could not force the Antonescu regime to accomplish. Why has Moscow marked this man for political extinction? The ready answer is that Moscow is now determined to destroy all vestiges of political opposition in Rumania. But if this highly practical objective is the goal, what sense does it make to give the predominantly peasant population of Rumania a cause for bitter grievance against Moscow which it will nurse for years to come? We are left with the explanation that this is a case of Russian jitters; or that Moscow, despite the resentment among the peasants which this verdict will arouse, believes in the efficacy of shock treatment; or that this is primarily and deliberately an act to widen as far and for as many years as possible, the cleavage between East and West in Europe.

Perhaps the motivation is a combination of several of these factors. In any case, Maniu has been found guilty. Guilty, as planned.

\* \* \*

**December 5, 1947**

## BULGARIA ADOPTS CHARTER

---
### Opposition Joins to Make Vote on Constitution Unanimous
---

Special to The New York Times
SOFIA, Bulgaria, Dec. 4—A salute of guns proclaimed tonight the National Assembly's adoption of the new Constitution of the People's Republic of Bulgaria. All 365 Deputies, including nine Opposition Social Democrats, unanimously

approved the Charter on third and final reading, and signed the text.

Vassil Kolarov, President of the Republic, presided over the session, which was attended by Premier Georgi Dimitrov, the entire Cabinet, foreign diplomats and high officials. A large crowd outside the chamber cheered M. Dimitrov and the Deputies.

The new Constitution is Bulgaria's second since her liberation from Turkish rule seventy years ago. Its basic principle is that "the entire power comes from the people and belongs to the people" and that "the National Assembly is representative of national sovereignty and is the supreme organ of the state." The Assembly is empowered to elect a Presidium of a President, two Deputy Presidents and fifteen members.

\* \* \*

**December 28, 1947**

## TRUD HAILS 'FREE GREECE'

---
### Soviet Trade Union Paper Prints Moscow's First Comment
---

MOSCOW, Dec. 27 (AP)—The Soviet trade union newspaper Trud, in the first published comment in Moscow on the proclamation of the Communist state of "Free Greece," said today the undertaking was "noble" and represents the desires "of all Greek patriots."

Trud's commentary by L. Simin was carried under the headline, "Greek People Hate Interventionists."

"The war of imperialists against the Greek people has lasted over the years," the article said. "English and American interventionists seek to convert Greece into their colony, under the disguise of aid, to make her into a beachhead in the Balkans. All their efforts suffer failure and are smashed against the heroic stoicism of Greek patriots defending their freedom and the independence of their country."

\* \* \*

**December 31, 1947**

## KING OF RUMANIA ABDICATES; 'PEOPLE'S REPUBLIC' SET UP

---
### Michael Quits Suddenly— Presidium Is Chosen to Rule Provisionally
---

By W. H. LAWRENCE
Special to The New York Times
BUCHAREST, Rumania, Dec. 30—King Michael of Rumania abdicated today and the Communist-dominated Government immediately proclaimed a "People's Republic."

Michael, last surviving monarch behind the Iron Curtain, made his decision to quit the throne suddenly, and the decision was announced by radio to the Rumanian people without

The New York Times (London Bureau)

King Michael

warning at 6 o'clock this evening. Why he had abdicated was not announced.

The King returned to Rumania only nine days ago from his first trip abroad since the war. He was then apparently determined to fight for retention of his throne and for Communist permission to marry Princess Anne of Bourbon-Parma, to whom he became engaged while attending the wedding of Princess Elizabeth in London.

[A Government official said, according to The Associated Press, that Michael was free to live in Rumania and marry Princess Anne. Other agency dispatches reported that Michael had been arrested, that he had gone to Turkey on his way to Switzerland, and that he was still in Bucharest.]

The Communist sweep in Eastern Europe is now complete, and the bloc of Poland, Czechoslovakia, Hungary, Yugoslavia, Albania, Bulgaria and Rumania is under the influence of Communist governments subservient to the Soviet Union, without even the handicap of passive resistance such as King Michael put up.

While Michael is undoubtedly beloved by his people, it is a certain fact that as of late tonight there have been no publicly known demonstrations against his removal, and the Government radio has reported demonstrations by Communists in favor of his leaving the throne. It is equally true, of course that Juliu Maniu, Opposition leader, now serving a life sentence, had a great hold on the affections of the Rumanian people, but he went to jail without a single popular demonstration in his favor and against the Government.

The Rumanian Parliament received the King's abdication in a specially convoked session at 5:15 P M and immediately elected a five-member Presidium headed by Mahai Sadoveanu, President of Parliament and a novelist. Parliament will meet again at 10 o'clock tomorrow morning, and it is probable that M. Sadoveanu will be named Provisional President of the Republic.

Michael's abdication decree said that because of the great political, economic and social changes effected in Rumania since the war the institution of the monarchy no longer corresponded to the present conditions of state and thus represented a serious obstacle to the country's future development.

Michael, who took the throne for the second time in 1940, when his father, King Carol, was forced to abdicate by Field Marshal Ion Antonescu, pro-Nazi dictator, renounced the throne not only for himself but for all members of his family. He declared that the Rumanian people were free to choose their own future form of government.

The Government of Premier Petru Groza followed immediately with the proclamation of a "People's Republic," declaring that the removal of the monarchy opened great opportunities for the advancement of popular democracy and for increasing the welfare of workers, peasants and intellectuals.

Heading the new republic provisionally as members of the presidium, in addition to M. Sadoveanu are Ion Miculi, Gheorghe Ster, Nicolai Parhon, and Stefan Voitec who until today was Minister of Education. M. Sadoveanu was elected to Parliament as an Independent, and M. Voitec is a Social Democrat. The others are Communists.

As soon as the King had abdicated and the Presidium had been chosen, the Groza Government offered its resignation en masse. The presidium reappointed all the present members of the Government with the exception of M. Voitec, who renounced his portfolio to become a member of the presidium. His post as Minister of Education was assumed temporarily by a fellow-Social Democrat, Lotar Radaceanu, Minister of Labor and Social Security.

The King's decision obviously came with great speed. Members of his Court, who had been questioned as recently as midday, offered no information of the potential development and it was felt then that the King would, as usual receive all members of the foreign diplomatic corps on New Year's Day.

When or if Michael will leave Rumania was not disclosed tonight. Efforts to establish contact with members of his staff by telephone or in person were unavailing, but more news may be forthcoming after tomorrow's sitting of Parliament.

\*   \*   \*

March 7, 1948

## RUMANIA PUBLISHES DRAFT CONSTITUTION

Special to The New York Times

BUCHAREST, Rumania, March 6—Rumania will nationalize her mines, oil and mineral rights, transport, telegraph, telephone and radio services under a draft constitution published today. The draft is expected to be approved by the Constituent Assembly early in April.

A section dealing with democratic rights guarantees "liberty of the press, of speech, of assembly and of demonstration" only for "those who work." Under the Constitution "any association having a Fascist or anti-democratic character is forbidden and punished by the law."

The published draft retains the clauses of the former Constitution concerning individual liberties and the inviolability of domiciles.

The Constitution contains 110 clauses and begins with the affirmation that "the republic sprang from the fight carried on by the people, headed by the working class, against fascism, reaction and imperialism."

Private property and the right of inheritance are retained, except for industries to be nationalized but a provision is made for the state to take over industrial property "when public interest demands."

Twenty-one clauses establish the citizens' rights and obligations. The Rumanians attain their legal majority and have right to vote at the age of 18. Minorities have the same rights as Rumanians.

Religious liberty is guaranteed but religious bodies will lose the right to maintain their own schools except for the training of priests.

\* \* \*

**May 5, 1948**

## 2,000 SEIZED IN BUCHAREST IN WIDE RUMANIAN PURGE

Special to The New York Times

LONDON, May 4—A political purge, that had resulted in the arrest of more than 2,000 persons in the Bucharest area alone last week, is now under way throughout Rumania, according to reports reaching diplomatic quarters here.

The purge is being conducted by the Communist-dominated Government against Liberal political leaders and against "bourgeois" elements in the Armed Forces, the clergy, industry and Government.

Among those arrested, it was reported, is Mihai Romniceanu, National Liberal party leader who joined Rumania's first postwar administration in 1945 with the approval of the Tripartite Allied Commission.

Constantine Tataranu, former Governor of the Bank of Rumania, was also reported to be in custody.

\* \* \*

**June 24, 1948**

## CATHOLICS CHARGE TERROR IN ALBANIA

*Declare Persecution Has Left Only One Bishop—*
*Murder Reported Widespread*

By CAMILLE M. CIANFARRA
Special to The New York Times

ROME, June 23—The Catholic Church in Albania has been virtually suppressed by what Vatican circles describe as the methodical murdering and jailing of members of the episcopate and clergy.

A report by the Fides agency on religious conditions in Albania, published today in l'Osservatore Romano, stated that religious persecution under the Communist Government headed by Premier Enver Hoxha had left Albanian Catholics with only one bishop and a handful of priests.

Fides said that two of Albania's five bishops had been executed—Msgr. George Volai, Bishop of Sappa, last Feb. 3 and Msgr. Gjini of Alessio on March 11. Msgr. Gaspare Thaci, Archbishop of Scutari, died in May, 1946, while in jail, Fides said, and Msgr. Vincenzo Prennushi, Archbishop of Durazzo, has been sentenced to twenty years. Surviving is the 73-year-old Bishop of Pulati, Bernard Shlaku, who is confined in the mountainous northern region, the agency reported.

Of seventy members of the secular clergy, twelve were executed, Fides said. Many others, the agency continued, are in jail and three have escaped to Italy, "while those still free are watched so closely that they cannot preach or teach the catechism, because if they did they would immediately be arrested."

Of fifty-five Jesuits, three were executed, seven were jailed and thirty-one others, who were of Italian nationality, were expelled, according to Fides, and those remaining are scattered throughout the country. Of fifty Franciscans. Fides said twelve were killed—two of them by Yugoslavs and one by Montenegrins—many are in jail and others missing.

Of the seminarists in Albania, one was executed, two are in jail and all those considered able-bodied have been forcibly drafted into the Albanian Army, Fides reported. The few remaining were evicted from their seminary and warned not to wear priestly garb, it was said.

Italian nuns have been expelled from the country, while the nuns who are Albanian have been evicted from their convents and forbidden to wear the dress of their institutions, the Fides account stated.

"Virtually all religious orders and institutes have been suppressed and their property confiscated," Fides said. "Even a certain number of prominent lay Catholics were forced to flee the country to avoid violent death. Many of those who remained have been killed or jailed. All Catholic schools are closed. Catholic Action has been declared illegal and Catholic printing shops confiscated."

\* \* \*

June 24, 1948

# GREEKS CONTINUE TO PRESS REBELS

*Pace of Drive Is Slowed, but Wedge Seems to Be Driven Between Two Red Forces*

By A. C. SEDGWICK
Special to The New York Times

ATHENS, June 23—The advance of the Greek National Army in the Grammos mountain area continued during the last twenty-four hours, but at a slower pace, a military spokesman said tonight.

There were, however, several important developments in the military situation, according to messages reaching here from various fronts. Elements of the First and Fifteenth divisions operating among mountain peaks near Nestorion made progress in a northward movement toward the Albanian border and appeared to have driven a solid wedge between rebel forces in the Grammos mountain mass proper and other large rebel concentrations in the mountains just south of Lake Presba.

Other thrusts, however, were seriously contested. According to military opinion here any signs that the rebels choose to give battle rather than to flee are welcome because in standing to fight the rebels offer a fixed target that can be destroyed.

## Mountain Bombarded

Mount Ammounda, a few miles northwest of Nestorion, was constantly bombarded by army artillery and the Greek Air Force but there were no indications that the thousand-strong guerrilla concentration there meant to surrender a key position. This feature had been carefully fortified with ingeniously camouflaged blockhouses and mines strewn about its approaches.

In the Konitsa sector there were clashes north and east of the town, tonight's general staff communiqué said. It added that twenty-six of the enemy had been killed and a quantity of arms and ammunition seized.

Rebel forces, some of whom fled into Albania during the last few days, recrossed the border in the vicinity of Amarantos, some ten miles north of Konitsa and attacked the National Army's left flank. According to all accounts reaching here the attackers were beaten and pursued, but the pursuit had to cease at the Albanian border. The accounts mentioned the "anger of the soldiers" when they were told that they must stop short.

The military command at Konitsa immediately summoned the United Nations observation team to bear witness to the use of foreign soil as a base for attack and a haven for retreat.

The Markos radio referred to a message sent to the United Nations though the "American League for Democracy in Greece" in which he sought to justify the abduction of children from northern Greece "to protect them from starvation due to the blockade of Free Greece and the danger of Monarchofascist air raids."

That the United Nations should have any dealings with the unrecognized rebel regime caused indignation in the local press, sections of which published reprints from the Swedish newspaper Svenska Morgenbladet alleging maltreatment of Greek children in the satelite states.

Another Markos radio broadcast picked up near Athens mentioned the fighting in the Grammos area for the first time. It asserted that the "Monarcho-Fascist Army" had been badly beaten at all points except in the vicinity of Kastoria where certain Army gains were conceded.

## Defense Line Pierced

ATHENS, June 23 (AP)—Greek Army troops pierced a guerrilla defense line along the Albanian border today and mounted a heavy assault against the southern portion of the semi-circular front, field dispatches said.

A general staff communiqué said that guerrilla resistance was broken in the Kastanohorion area southwest of Nestorion. There the Communist-led rebels had slowed one prong of the pincers that American-advised Greek commanders are seeking to close around the entire rebel force of 7,000 in the Grammos mountains area.

Front accounts said that units of the crack Ninth Division had seized Vourbiani in the drive through guerrilla positions near the frontier. There the Ninth, which makes up the southwestern arm of the pincers, was closer to a junction with troops of the First and Fifteenth Divisions, advancing from the Nestorion sector. Sweeping into the Sarandaporos River valley, the Ninth Division liberated a number of villages.

Second and Tenth Division troops established full contact with guerrilla forces in the drive against the southern section of the front. The Second Division, advised by Lieut. Col. Henry C. Davall of Jamesburg, N. J., advanced from Grevena toward Pentalophon and Eptakhorion, a strong point in the guerrilla defense positions.

Farther west the Tenth Division struck hard against guerrilla units holding slopes of the Pindus range northeast of Metsovo.

Lieut. Gen. James A. Van Fleet, head of the United States Military Mission, told reporters at the front that he was satisfied with the progress made by Greek troops.

He predicted that major fighting in the Grammos area would end within four weeks and that mopping up would be complete by Aug. 1.

King Paul I reached Koziani on a commercial airliner and proceeded to the front for an inspection.

\*   \*   \*

**June 29, 1948**

# COMINFORM DENOUNCES TITO, CHARGING HE LEANS TO WEST; HIS EXPULSION THREATENED

### SOVIET RIFT BARED

*Yugoslav Leaders' Acts Termed 'Hateful' and 'Slanderous' of Russia*

### VIEWS HELD TROTSKYIST

*Belgrade Accused of Retreat From Leninism and Straying From Cominform Fold*

By The Associated Press

PRAGUE, June 28—The Communist Information Bureau denounced today Marshal Tito's leadership of Yugoslav Communists. The international Communist organization declared that Belgrade's Premier and other top members of the party must hew to the Moscow line or get out.

The Yugoslav leaders were accused by the Moscow-blessed bureau of pursuing a hateful and slanderous policy toward Russia and of leaning toward Western methods.

The blast came in a 3,000-word statement adopted at a meeting in Rumania this month of the Cominform, a meeting at which Yugoslav Communists, among the Cominform's founders, were not represented. The statement was published here today. According to the statement, the Yugoslav Communist leaders had placed themselves outside the Cominform ranks.

Marshal Tito and his top aides were accused of retreating from Marxism-Leninism by "undertaking an entirely wrong policy on the principal question of foreign and internal politics."

### Confidence in Party Expressed

The statement called for "either a true return to Marxist policy or a change of Communist leaders in Yugoslavia."

One section of the declaration indicated that Marshal Tito and his chiefs might get a chance to change their ways before final action was taken. It said:

"The aim of . . . sound elements of the Communist party of Yugoslavia is to force their present leaders to confess openly and honestly their faults and correct them; to part from nationalism, to return to internationalism and in every way to fix the united Socialist front against imperialism: or, if the present leaders of the Communist party of Yugoslavia prove unable to do this task, to change them and to raise from below a new internationalistic leadership of the Communist party of Yugoslavia. The Information Bureau does not doubt that the Communist party can fulfill this task."

### Kardelj Among Four Named

Singled out for criticism were Marshal Tito, Vice Premier Edvard Kardelj, a founder of the Cominform: Milovan Djilas, Minister for Montenegro, a Yugoslav state, and Col. Gen. Alexander Rankovitch, who as Minister of the Interior has bossed Yugoslavia's police force.

There was speculation that such a blast would have been issued only after specific action had been taken against Marshal Tito, but there was no confirmation of this. Dispatches from Belgrade said Marshal Tito was believed to be at his summer home in Bled.

Col. Gen. Andrei A. Zhdanov, a member of the Soviet Union Communist Politburo and often rated one of the three most powerful men in Russia, attended the Cominform meeting and signed its official statement. As published in Rude Pravo, official newspaper of the Czechoslovak Communist party, the statement said that the Yugoslav Communist leaders had "created a hateful policy in relation to the Soviet Union and to the All-Communist Union of Bolsheviks."

An "undignified policy of underestimating Soviet military specialists was allowed" by the Yugoslavs and members of the Russian Army were discredited by them, it said.

Russian "private specialists" in Yugoslavia were put under guard of the organs of state security and were watched, the statement added. It said that the Soviet Union's delegate to the Cominform in Belgrade also had been under surveillance.

The Cominform contended that a slander propaganda campaign "borrowed from the arsenal of counter-revolutionary Trotskyism" had been conducted against Russia. This campaign, it said, pictured Russia as "degenerate."

"All these facts," the statement said, "prove that the leading persons in the Communist party of Yugoslavia took a standpoint unworthy of Communists."

In wooing Western states, Yugoslavia's leaders, according to the declaration, strove toward a capitalist ideology. The statement said:

"Yugoslav leaders, orienting themselves badly in the international situation and frightened by extortionate threats of the imperialists, think that by a series of concessions to imperialistic states they can gain the favor of these states to make an agreement with them about the independence of Yugoslavia and gradually to implant in the Yugoslav people the orientation of these states; that is, an orientation of capitalism."

The statement said that the accused Yugoslavs had begun to identify Russia's foreign policy "with that of the imperialistic powers" and to treat Russia "in the same manner as they treat the bourgeois states."

Inside Yugoslavia, the statement went on, Communist leaders "are retreating from positions of the working class and are parting from the Marxist theory of class war." The declaration said "capitalist elements in their country are growing," and added:

"The Cominform believes that the present leadership of the Yugoslav Communist party is revising the Marxist-Lenin theory of the Communist party. Whereas this theory says that the Communist party stands for the leading and guarding strength in a country, in Yugoslavia the People's Front, not the Communist party, is considered the main, principal strength. This means devaluating the Communist party."

The statement condemned the "purging and arresting" of two Yugoslav Communists "because they had dared to criticize the anti-Soviet conceptions of the leaders and to express themselves for the friendship of Yugoslavia with the Soviet Union."

Sreten Zujovitch was dismissed last month as Finance Minister and Andrija Hebrang as Minister of Light Industry in a Government shake-up.

According to the statement, Yugoslav delegates "refused to defend their actions before the Cominform and to listen to criticism and reproaches from other Communist parties." It went on: "This may be considered as a violation of equality among Communist parties and as calling for creation of a privileged attitude of the Yugoslav Communist party in the Cominform."

The Cominform was set up by Russia and eight other Eastern European nations last year. Its headquarters is in Belgrade.

Marshal Tito long has been regarded as one of the staunchest leaders of communism outside the Soviet Union. He catapulted to the head of Yugoslavia's Government from command of that country's wartime partisans. He has had many conferences in the Kremlin. His Government once was described by Senator Styles Bridges of New Hampshire as "a Red puppet dancing to Joe Stalin's tune."

\*    \*    \*

June 29, 1948

## TITO'S GRIP ON NATION FIRM; REPLY TO CHARGES DUE TODAY

By M. S. HANDLER
Special to The New York Times

BELGRADE, Yugoslavia, June 28—Marshal Tito and his deputies in the Politburo and Central Committee of the Yugoslav Communist party were in complete control of the situation tonight. Judging by the calm prevailing at party headquarters and government offices, they are likely to retain this hold against the powers of the Communist Information Bureau.

There were no special military or police precautions at any of the party or Government buildings to reinforce normal security measures. Means of entry and exit to these buildings were no more complicated than they had been before the Cominform's action (denouncing the Yugoslav leaders). The calm aspect of Belgrade indicated that Marshal Tito and his deputies had no fears that the Cominform had the backing of a Yugoslav group to challenge their power or was likely to find one.

The secretariat of Milovan Djilas, propaganda and agitation chief of the Central Committee of the Communist party said that a statement would be issued tomorrow afternoon.

The rift between the Yugoslav Communist party and the Cominform and between Yugoslavia and the Soviet Union is not interpreted here to mean a complete reversal of the Yugoslav position on essential domestic and foreign policies but rather as a split of historic importance in the Communist front. No one in Belgrade who has been watching the development of the struggle would predict the repercussions of the Cominform's action.

The news of the Cominform's denunciation of Marshal Tito and his party leadership did not reach the Yugoslav public. Keeping of the news from the country reflected the high degree to which Marshal Tito and his deputies had established their control not only over the party but also over the country.

Certain facts in the history of the Yugoslav Communist party appear to have been overlooked abroad in assessments of the degree of independence of the party compared with other Communist organizations.

That independence is part of the record of Marshal Tito and his lieutenants since the early days of the German occupation of Yugoslavia. The Communist party membership in the country had declined to 14,000 when World War II began. Marshal Tito and his chief aides had spent much time in Moscow during their exile from Yugoslavia between the two World Wars but were in Yugoslavia when she was invaded and occupied.

Unlike Communist leaders now in power in other Eastern European countries, Marshal Tito and his deputies did not return to their country with the conquering Soviet Army. While other Eastern European leaders were laying their plans in Moscow and organizing their teams, the Yugoslav chieftains were in the mountains organizing partisan detachments and placing their handful of party survivors in key positions to rally support among the people.

### Helped Liberate Nation

They raised large armies, won the support of a substantial section of the population and, perhaps most significantly, built up the party during the fighting. The party leadership, with a few exceptions, is composed of the body of men that organized and led the partisan war against the Germans. They pinned down and engaged German forces estimated at ten to twenty-two divisions. They did not wait for the Soviet or other Allied armies to liberate their country; they did not operate as auxiliaries of foreign armies but did the main job before Russian troops entered Yugoslavia.

The Central Committee of the Yugoslav Communist party, in the absence of elections, is composed of twenty-six appointees of Marshal Tito and his deputies. The party leaders in every echelon who hold key party and Government positions belong to the Tito school and it is believed that for some time they have given only lip service to Moscow. It is considered that the Yugoslav Communists look to Moscow as an anchor to the wind but that their first loyalty has been to Marshal Tito and his lieutenants and their party.

The rank-and-file Communists who grew up in the partisan struggle are cognizant of their country's war record and of their war contribution. There has therefore been less adulation here of the Soviet Union than in other Eastern European Communist parties that owe so much to the Soviet Army.

The first straw in the wind of the undercurrent of difficulties between the Yugoslav and Soviet Union Communist parties was noted in the last May Day parade. Portraits of Marshal Tito and his deputies dominated the walls along the line of march and along the Terasiye, the principal street in

Belgrade. Marchers carried thousands of portraits of Marshal Tito and his deputies and Generalissimo Stalin's portraits were noticeable for their modest size and small number.

### Praise of Soviet Restrained

All the slogans on the banners were in praise of the Yugoslav leaders and of the achievements of the Yugoslav Communist party. Those addressed to the Soviet Union were modest and the praise addressed to the Soviet Army was significant for its moderate tone.

All these portents aroused the speculation of observers versed in Communist affairs.

Five days after May Day the newspapers announced without explanation the dismissal from office of two outstanding Communists, Andrija Hebrang, former chairman of the State Planning Commission, and Sreten Zujovitch, Minister of Finance. The struggle between the Yugoslav and Russian leaders was well advanced, but, like an iceberg, only a fragment of the edifice showed above the surface.

The struggle broke the surface again several weeks after the dismissal of the two men when Edvard Kardelj, Deputy Premier, denounced the Ministries headed by M. Hebrang and M. Zujovitch. He said they had sabotaged the peasant policy of the Yugoslav Communist party and of the Government. M. Kardelj said, for example, that M. Zujovitch had withheld funds from the program to develop the cooperative movement as a vehicle to bring about the eventual collectivization of farming.

The two men were held guilty of deviation from the Yugoslav party's viewpoint because the party felt that caution and time must be used to attack the peasant problem. The peasants form 75 per cent of the population and a frontal attack on their land ownership would have provoked an upheaval.

Finally M. Zujovitch was stripped of his reserve army rank, colonel general. In view of the Cominform's defense of M. Zujovitch, it is possible that the dismissal from the army was unforgivable.

The struggle broke the surface again on June 15 when the semimonthly Cominform publication attacked unidentified Communist leaders as conceited, arrogant and over-publicized. No Serbian language edition of the June 15 issue was published, and it is not likely to be. This was the first instance of Yugoslav censoring or suppression of the Serbian edition of the Cominform publication.

### Belgrade Rumors Spread

The attack by the Cominform stirred rumors and added weight to an incident in Belgrade concerning the Danubian conference. The United States Government had suggested to the Soviet Government a postponement of the conference from May 30 to July 30. Moscow acceded to the request but suggested that the conference be held in another Danubian city because, it said, the Yugoslav Government had informed it that it would be difficult to accommodate the conference in Belgrade then.

Shortly thereafter, Stanoje Simitch, Yugoslav Foreign Minister, invited the United States chargé d'affaires and the British and French Ambassadors to visit him. M. Simitch informed them he had made an error in having informed the Soviet Government that Belgrade could not accommodate the conference and that, on the contrary, the Yugoslav Government would be happy to have the conference meet in Belgrade.

Foreign observers interpreted this triple-play as further evidence of a rift between Belgrade and Moscow. A final act in the drama was played last week. Its chief protagonist was Moshe Piyade, veteran Communist leader, who had spent much of his life in Yugoslav prisons, where he translated the principal Marxist literature from Russian into Serbo-Croat.

As if in answer to the unprinted charges, M. Piyade asserted in a long newspaper article that the Yugoslav Communist party had perfected the machinery of the dictatorship of the proletariat as defined by Lenin and outlined by Premier Stalin. He tried to demonstrate that the Yugoslav Communist party had extended the base of mass organization, considered to be a prerequisite for a dictatorship of the proletariat.

M. Piyade seemed to be reviewing charges made by an unidentified accuser, and his method was to attempt to demonstrate that the Yugoslav Communist party had gone far beyond other Communist parties in establishing and maintaining power and that it had closer ties with the people than were prescribed in Communist strategy and tactics.

\* \* \*

**June 30, 1948**

## YUGOSLAVIA DEFIES CHARGES OF COMINFORM AS SLANDERS; REJECTS DICTATION BY RUSSIA

### TITO STRIKES BACK

*Party Charges 'Fascist Forces' Led Attack—Insists on Equality*

### OUSTED AIDES 'TRAITORS'

*2 Ex-Ministers Called Ustashi—Soviet Press Accused of Malevolence, Distortion*

By M. S. HANDLER
Special to The New York Times

BELGRADE, Yugoslavia, June 29—The Central Committee of Yugoslavia's Communist party tonight defied the Communist Information Bureau powers led by the Soviet Union and called upon party members to close their ranks around this country's leaders headed by Marshal Tito.

The Central Committee, in a point-by-point refutation of the Cominform charges, virtually accused the Cominform of conspiracy with intent to undermine and overthrow the Yugoslav party. The committee made it clear that it would not submit to the dictate of the Soviet Union and other Cominform powers and would discuss the dispute only on a "basis of equality."

The Central Committee said it was ready to participate in the Cominform but that the charges against the Yugoslav party came from "Fascist forces." The only conciliatory note in the committee's harsh reply to the Cominform was that "direct contact was needed."

### Two Called Ustashi Traitors

The Central Committee announced that Andrija Hebrang and Sretan Zujovitch, former Cabinet Ministers, had been expelled from the Yugoslav Communist party as traitors, Ustashi agents and saboteurs—this despite the Cominform's support of the two men. The Central Committee went a point further and said that in view of the unsubstantiated charges and "insults," it no longer could consider itself bound in the future to remain silent on issues at stake.

The committee struck back hard at the accusation that it did not tolerate free criticism inside the party with its own charge that free criticism did not exist inside the Communist party of the Soviet Union.

At 7 o'clock this evening and every ten minutes thereafter, a Belgrade radio speaker interrupted programs and alerted the people to listen to the very important news that would be broadcast at 8 o'clock by all Yugoslav radio stations.

Four statements were broadcast. The first was the Central Committee's refutation of the Cominform charges, followed by the decisions on M. Hebrang and M. Zujovitch.

### Innocence and Scorn Expressed

The Central Committee's defiant spirit was best reflected in the dramatic phrase "this people, which has looked death in the eyes, behaved in that way." The implication was clear: persons with the record of achievement and sacrifice of the Yugoslav Communists would not be guilty of the accusations against them, nor were they fearful.

The Central Committee warned the Cominform that its charges "spread a lack of confidence, and there could be no discussion on this basis."

For perhaps the first time, the Communist party of one country accused the press of another Communist state of malevolence and distortion. The Central Committee charged that the Soviet press had not published a single item of news favorable to Yugoslav achievements and had used material out of context.

The Central Committee, making another serious charge that only the Western countries heretofore had been leveling against the Soviet Government, asserted that the Russians had been recruiting agents in Yugoslavia to undermine the Yugoslav leaders.

Giving the genesis of the dispute, the Central Committee said that the Communist party of the Soviet Union, without the knowledge of the Yugoslav party, had sent a letter on March 27 to the Cominform making serious charges. This was followed by letters from the Hungarian and other Communist parties, and again the Cominform did not notify the Yugoslav party.

The Russians sent a second letter on May 22. The Central Committee said that the Cominform's communiqué constituted a "rehash" of the charges in that letter.

### Charges Called Inaccurate

After summarizing the Cominform's accusations, the Yugoslav Central Committee said it would not discuss charges made from calumny until the real facts had been established. It said the Cominform's communiqué was inaccurate and represented an attempt to undermine the authority of the Yugoslav party and that the Communist party of the Soviet Union had even refused to verify the charges on the spot.

Defending its peasant policy, the Central Committee said that it was not only limiting but also eliminating the capitalist elements in the villages.

The Central Committee said that the Cominform was completely misinformed on conditions in Yugoslavia and replied to criticism of the People's Front policy with the stand: "The Communist party gives directives to the front, and not vice versa." The Central Committee then proclaimed that the Yugoslav party had the confidence of the Yugoslav people.

The Central Committee expressed amazement that the Cominform would protect M. Hebrang, former Minister of Light Industry, and M. Zujovitch, former Minister of Finance, whom the committee denounced as traitors.

Touching on a very delicate subject, the Central Committee said in effect that the Soviet Union, had given Yugoslavia little or no material assistance, adding: "Nobody denies that Yugoslavia needs help from the other peoples' democracies, but it must point out that the collaboration necessary for success must include help from the Soviet Union."

### Troubles in the 5-Year-Plan

In this connection, the Central Committee denounced M. Hebrang for allegedly having sabotaged the five-year plan and said that if the plan for 1948 should fall, it would be his responsibility. This allusion to difficulties in the five-year plan would tend to confirm reports that the authorities were facing many unforeseen obstacles.

It was reported tonight that Palmiro Togliatti of Italy and another prominent Communist leader from abroad had visited Marshal Tito some time before the rupture in an effort to convince him to change the policy of the Yugoslav party as required by the Cominform powers. This visit was reported to have been followed by two similar letters from Premier Stalin.

It is believed that the Cominform powers, particularly the Soviet Union, were critical of the great amount of personal power vested in Marshal Tito and were determined to make the Yugoslav party more amenable to control. Charges of personal dictatorship were flung at Marshal Tito; it was felt that his position was becoming far too strong compared with that of the other Communist leaders in Eastern Europe.

It also was said tonight that dissatisfaction with Marshal Tito's conduct of Yugoslav foreign policy was one of the principal reasons for the dispute. According to one source, Marshal Tito steered his Government's foreign policy in a manner that did not conform with the general pattern and objectives of the foreign policy of the Eastern European coalition.

Greece, Trieste and Austria were mentioned as sources of disagreement between Marshal Tito and the Soviet Government.

The exact nature of the difficulty could not be determined tonight, but the course Marshal Tito pursued was of a sort to warrant Russia accusing him of not aiding her "peace policy."

It has been fairly well established that Marshal Tito steered cleared of any course of action that would have resulted in any serious involvement for Yugoslavia. His policy was largely, restricted to strong propaganda offensives against the Athens Government and the Anglo-American authorities in Trieste and Austria, but it would be quite impossible to prove a single act since the beginning of this year that could be interpreted as preparation for forceful intervention.

The Yugoslav Government, for example, has studiously refrained from recognizing Gen. Markos Vafiades, the guerrilla leader in Greece. Such recognition, de facto or de jure, could have given the Yugoslav Government the possibility of openly supplying him.

Yet the question arises: why did not the Yugoslavs commit themselves to such a policy? The answer seems quite clear: Such a policy would have involved Yugoslavia not only with the Athens Government but with the Western powers.

The attitude of the Yugoslav Government during the recent Italian election required re-examination in the light of the Cominform's accusations. It was clear during the weeks preceding the balloting that the Yugoslav Government conceivably could have influenced the outcome to a certain extent with an aggressive policy, rather than the passive one it actually pursued.

It would have sufficed to send reinforcements to the Yugoslav Army along the Trieste and Italian border. Publicizing that fact would have aroused grave concern among many Italians and would have made them hesitate to vote for the Christian Democrats.

Instead, the Yugoslav Government not only refrained from any demonstrative action but also reduced its propaganda attacks against the de Gasperi Government.

It follows from the above that Marshal Tito was not and is not prepared to use Yugoslav power on strategic positions occupied by Yugoslavia for any political adventure that might result in unpredictable consequences for the security of his country.

The Central Committee's allusion to the fact that little or no economic assistance had come from the Soviet Union threw additional light on the schism. The Yugoslav Government has embarked on a five-year plan to industrialize the country. The plan requires a very heavy capital expenditure that could be made only through heavy exports of raw materials so as to pay for imports of machinery.

Lacking any material assistance from Eastern Europe, Yugoslavia found herself exporting considerable quantities of raw materials, thus bringing about a reduction in the standard of living. At the same time, trade relations with the Western powers, principally the United States and Great Britain, were brought virtually to a stand-still because the Yugoslav Government could not or would not participate in the European Recovery Program.

The result has been that the five-year plan is being put through with considerable hardship.

\* \* \*

June 30, 1948

## U. S. COMMUNIST LEADERS DENOUNCE YUGOSLAV MOVE

William Z. Foster, chairman of the National Committee of the Communist Party of the United States, and Eugene Dennis, general secretary, issued a statement yesterday denouncing the Communist party of Yugoslavia, which, they said, had begun "to pursue a policy which could only result in the restoration of a capitalist state in Yugoslavia under the domination of imperialism."

"The United States imperialists, through their press and the State Department, are distorting the meaning of the Communist Information Bureau statement and the situation out of which it arose," the party leaders' statement said.

Mr. Foster and Mr. Dennis asserted that the Cominform communiqué had demonstrated that the leading forces "in the world camp of peace and democracy" are alert to every danger. "Their timely action," the statement said, "dooms to failure the efforts of the Marshall planners to split and disorient the anti-imperialist camp of peace and social progress."

\* \* \*

July 1, 1948

## TITO DEMANDS BALKAN BLOC IN NEW BLOW AT COMINFORM; MARSHAL APPEARS IN PUBLIC

**FEDERATION URGED**

*Bid Made to Bulgaria, Albania Regarded as Defiant Gesture*

**SOVIET ATTITUDE IGNORED**

*Belgrade's New Party Line Lays Claim to Pure Marxism and Disregards Charges*

By M. S. HANDLER
Special to The New York Times

BELGRADE, Yugoslavia, June 30—The Central Committee of the Communist party of Yugoslavia today struck another blow at the Communist Information Bureau [Cominform] with a demand for a Balkan federation consisting of Bulgaria, Albania and Yugoslavia.

This demand was inserted in the party's new program, which is being sent to party organizations of all levels for discussion in preparation for the fifth party congress, which is scheduled to meet in Belgrade on July 21. The Politburo approved the new party program on June 14 and the central committee has sent it to all party organizations with a request that their comments and proposals reach Belgrade before July 18.

The demand for federation with Bulgaria and Albania was phrased in this manner.

"The Communist party of Yugoslavia will strive for the closest ties of cooperation with the People's Republic of Bulgaria and the People's Republic of Albania and work for the establishing of conditions of unity of the Bulgarian, Albanian and Yugoslav peoples on the principle of national equality."

"National equality" is the principle on which the Yugoslav Federal Republic of Serbians, Croatians, Macedonians, Slovenes and Montenegrins is constituted.

### Faces Soviet Opposition

The resurrection of the idea of a Balkan federation in the face of declared Soviet opposition can mean only that the Yugoslav Communist party is determined to retain its independence concerning the basic objectives of this country. It indicates further that the Yugoslav Communist party is satisfied that its offensive political power is not inconsiderable.

The fairly moderate statement of the Bulgarian Fatherland Front endorsing the Cominform communiqué but pledging non-interference in Yugoslav internal affairs warrants the belief here that the Yugoslav Communist party has reached a point of maturity at which it can confidently hold its own in political warfare.

The new party program placed the stamp of legality upon the policies pursued by the Yugoslav Communist party until the rupture with the Cominform. In asking the party congress to oppose this program when it convenes on July 21 the central committee is seeking to counter the Cominform's charges of illegality.

The program was so constructed as to ignore the Cominform's action. It attributes every act in the policy of the Yugoslav Communist party to the doctrinal and tactical principles laid down by Marx and Lenin. Never once referring to the Cominform's charges, the Yugoslav party's new program bases itself squarely on Marxism and Leninism and thus lays claim to being the faithful interpreter and follower of the two Communist founders.

Slight attention is paid to the Soviet Union. On one occasion the program said that Premier Stalin had elaborated the principles laid down by Marx and Lenin. But this reference is lost in two columns of historical survey of the Yugoslav party demonstrating that at every turn the Yugoslavs have adhered to the principles of the Communist founders.

At another point in the program it was said that the Soviet Army had made the principal war contribution. This was counterbalanced, however, by columns of historical analysis demonstrating that the Yugoslav revolution was accomplished on the field of battle and that the new Yugoslav state was born at the very time when the Partisans were fighting the Germans.

The New York Times

Crisscross shading indicates the region of the Balkan federation proposed by the Yugoslav Communists despite Moscow's opposition. Vertical shading designates the other Soviet countries.

### Peasant Policy Stated

The program makes concrete the peasant policy pursued by the Yugoslav Communist party and outlines the steps to be taken to make the cooperative movement the instrument for the eventual establishment of Socialist agriculture. Ignoring the Cominform's criticism on this question, the party's new program said that it was essential to eliminate all capitalist elements from the villages and to make the maximum effort to induce the peasants to join the cooperative movement.

Clinging to the letter of Communist orthodoxy, the party's new program said that the industrialization of Yugoslavia could not be accomplished without the introduction of Socialist agriculture. The program then went on to endorse the party's Five-Year Plan to industrialize Yugoslavia and prescribed a series of measures to be taken in this field.

The first section of the 30,000-word program contains 10,000 words of historical analysis of the present state of capitalism, such as can be found in any of the standard works of Marxist authors. It gives the classic Communist analysis of finance capital and concludes with the Marxist view that imperialism is the last stage of capitalist development and, is doomed to extinction.

### Revolution Called "Historic"

The authors of the new program said that the Yugoslav revolution was part of the world historic events that began with the October Socialist revolution in Russia. It related how the party had purged its ranks of "Trotskyites" and other opposition elements—apparently an allusion to the Cominform's communiqué.

The program said that the aim of the Communist party of Yugoslavia was to construct a classless Communist society where everyone would work according to his ability and be paid according to his needs.

In a backhanded thrust, the program's authors said that the Yugoslav party had been guided, not only by the teachings of Marx and Lonin, but also by the experience of the Communist party of the Soviet Union, as well as its own considerable experience.

The section of the program on "the Independence of the Federal Republic of Yugoslavia" outlines most of the same standard foreign policy shared by all the Cominform powers. The one exception to this rule is the demand for a Balkan federation.

The Yugoslav party reiterates every well-known plank of Communist foreign policy as if the Cominform incident had never occurred. Thus, it makes clear that no matter what the Cominform may think the Yugoslav party will continue to travel along the well-marked road.

### 'Cries Against Imperialists'

The party program declared, for example, that "the national independence of Yugoslavia is a condition for the road to socialism and progress in general; that is why the Communist party of Yugoslavia will unswervingly struggle against all attempts of imperialists who would in any form try to plunder the Socialist Fatherland of the peoples of Yugoslavia."

The party program said that the party would seek to strengthen the political and moral unity of the Yugoslav peoples and, second, that it would strive to strengthen and develop close cooperation with the Soviet Union and close cooperation with other "people's democracies."

But in comparison with striving for "close" cooperation with the Soviet Union, the party program demands the "closest" cooperation with Bulgaria and Albania for purposes of federation. The distinction is unique.

The program goes on to say that the Yugoslav party favors "peace-loving cooperation with all countries who desire cooperation with Yugoslavia on a basis of respecting its independence and equality within the framework of the United Nations Charter."

### "Warmongers" Cited

Yugoslavia will cooperate in a "democratic anti-imperialist front" against "imperialist warmongers," it says, and will support countries and movements struggling for peace against interference.

The party program not only does not depart from the Communist objectives but prides itself on adhering to them in the strictest sense. Far from retreating from positions to satisfy the Cominform, the party program restates every basic detail of the past program and then adds the new element of the Balkan federation.

Instead of accomplishing a complete revolution of the clock, the party program makes it clear that the Yugoslav Communist party considers that it is on "the line" and intends to travel in a parallel position with the Cominform powers whether they like it or not.

\* \* \*

**July 4, 1948**

## ALBANIA CUTS OFF YUGOSLAVS' TRADE, EXPELS MISSIONS

*Belgrade Foreign Office Gives Details of Reply— Charges Bad Faith, Illegality*

### ACTION IS NOT RECOGNIZED

*Unilateral Treaty Abrogation Held Invalid— Support for Tito Is Recorded*

Special to The New York Times

BELGRADE, Yugoslavia, July 3—The Yugoslav Government announced tonight that the Albanian Government had ordered the expulsion of all Yugoslav advisers, technicians and teaching staffs and had canceled by unilateral action two long-term trade agreements and the trade protocol integrating the economies of the two countries.

Albania also dissolved the customs union with Yugoslavia.

The effect of Albania's action was to complete the quarantining of Yugoslavia by the Communist Information Bureau. Yugoslavia had enjoyed a special position in Albania.

The thirty-year trade agreement and customs union gave Yugoslavia a paramount position in Albania and Yugoslav Army instructors were advisers to the Albanian Army. Besides heavy capital investments for the development of Albanian mines, the Yugoslav Government had contributed heavily to the equipment of the Albanian Army.

### Action Is Denounced

The Yugoslav Government denounced the Albanian Government's action as illegal and demanded the repayment of 2,000,000,000 dinars ($40,000,000).

The Yugoslav announcement did not indicate whether the colony of Yugoslav advisers, technicians and teachers had already departed from Albania as demanded by the Albanian Government. The Yugoslav note said that the Albanian Government would be held responsible for the consequences of its unilateral act. Copies of a special edition of the newspaper Glas, which contained news of the Albanian Government's action, were snatched up by pedestrians in Belgrade tonight. They walked along the streets reading the news.

BELGRADE, July 3 (AP)—Yugoslavia today retorted to Albania's rupture of relations with an acid note, terming Albania's action "unprecedented," "brutal" and "grossly insulting" and a violation of international law.

The Belgrade radio recounted this latest episode in the Yugoslav-Albanian feud. The note said that Albania:

(1) "By a unilateral act . . . contrary to all fundamental principles of international law" had denounced "all economic agreements and protocols" with Yugoslavia.

(2) Expelled Yugoslav trade, cultural and military experts, giving them forty-eight hours to leave.

(3) Violated the Yugoslav-Albanian treaty of alliance by expelling the Yugoslav military mission.

The note, dated July 1, said that Yugoslavia had "in a friendly spirit warned representatives" of Albania to "remove obstacles which stood in the way of correct fulfillment of obligations" under the terms of the economic pact.

It said that up until June 29—three days after the Russian-led Communist Information Bureau made its attack upon Yugoslavia, Albania had not made a single protest against Yugoslavia's performance under the pact's terms.

It said that the economic agreements, signed in November, 1946, were drafted for a thirty-year period with a provision that they could not be terminated without notice in writing at least one year in advance.

"The act on the part of Albania, therefore, is a gross and illegal violation of existing agreements," the Yugoslavs charged. Although the text of the Albanian note on its action was not disclosed, the Yugoslav reply said that Albania's assertions that Yugoslavia had failed to carry out obligations under the pact "are incorrect and arbitrary."

Yugoslavia therefore will refuse to recognize Albania's action in declaring the cultural and economic agreements "null and nonexistent," the note said.

### Tito Wins Backing

BELGRADE, Yugoslavia, July 3 (UP)—The Yugoslav Communist newspaper Borba today reported the words of Marko Velicitch, Croatian Communist committeeman, at a mass meeting that, the paper said, "turned into a manifestation for Tito, for the Yugoslav Communist party, and for the Soviet Union."

The newspaper printed dozens of similar messages, most of them expressing hope that the situation would be clarified soon.

Except for the ominous Albanian situation, Yuglloslavia seemed to be getting on well with most of her Communist-dominated neighbors despite the fact that most of them had indorsed the Cominform attack.

The Government announced today that a Bulgarian cultural delegation arrived here yesterday.

Preparations also were continuing for a scheduled soccer game between Yugoslavia and Bulgaria in Sofia—the Bulgarian capital—tomorrow. The Yugoslav team was named only yesterday.

### Hungarian Action Reported

PRAGUE, July 3 (UP)—Reliable but unofficial reports said today that Hungary had stopped shipments to Yugosla-via, the Soviet satellite nation recently denounced by the Communist Information Bureau.

At the same time it was learned that preparations had been halted for an official Hungarian publication dealing with Eastern European trade. A notice said the publication would have to be "rewritten."

### Sofia Supports Cominform

SOFIA, Bulgaria, July 3 (UP)—The nation's leaders and press rallied today behind the Communist Information Bureau's attack on Marshal Tito of Yugoslavia.

A number of cross-country meetings were held at which influential speakers clarified the Cominform's report of shortcomings within the Yugoslav Communist party.

Sofia's morning newspaper devoted 7,000 words to a report from Vulko Chervenkov, Minister of Arts and Communist party secretary here, in which he supported the "truthfulness" of the Cominform's accusation. Mr. Chervenkov is Bulgaria's Cominform delegate.

\* \* \*

**October 3, 1948**

# OTHER SATELLITES SNAP AT YUGOSLAVIA'S HEELS

*Tito's Relations With Neighbors Are Embittered by Cominform Row*

By M. S. HANDLER
Special to The New York Times

BELGRADE, Yugoslavia, Oct. 2—Three general patterns of conflict have emerged in the continuing struggle which has rent the Soviet bloc since the Cominform's resolution of June 28 attacking Marshal Tito's "line" in Yugoslavia.

The first pattern involves the principles which generated the struggle between the Yugoslav and Soviet Communist parties. The second concerns the relations of the smaller Cominform states—Bulgaria, Rumania, Czechoslovakia, Hungary, Albania and Poland—with Yugoslavia. The third pattern establishes the relationship of these smaller Cominform states with one another and with the Soviet Union.

### Summary of Views

In considering the conflict, such Yugoslav theoreticians as Milovan Djilas insist on: firstly, Yugoslav equality with the Soviet Communist party in all problems affecting Yugoslav national interest; secondly, free and equal discussion of all problems affecting the Cominform world as opposed to dictation; thirdly, acceptance of the moral leadership of the Soviet Union in the struggle against "imperialists," but not that kind of leadership which would transform Yugoslavia into a pawn.

Comparisons of the Communist pattern in Yugoslavia with the pattern of other Cominform states establish clearly that the Yugoslavs are far in advance of the others on the road to achieving Soviet socialism in their country. In the fields of nationalization of industry, trade and commerce, of the agrarian problem and of new civil services, Yugoslav Communists are found at least six months further along the road than their rivals of eastern Europe.

The role of smaller members of the Soviet bloc in this quarrel between Yugoslavia and the Soviet Union is clear and well-defined. In a military sense they constitute an advanced attacking force to test the strength of Yugoslav resistance and to harry its defenders with nuisance raids in an effort to demoralize them.

To date we have witnessed a gradual dissolution of treaties of friendship, cooperation and mutual assistance binding Yugoslavia with her neighboring states of the Soviet bloc. This was brought about through a series of inimical acts in an effort to intimidate the Yugoslavs through a sense of isolation. Albania, Bulgaria, Rumania, Hungary and Czechoslovakia have terminated all forms of cultural cooperation through acts which have included expulsions of Yugoslav teachers, assaults upon headquarters of the Yugoslav cultural societies; intimidation of Yugoslav minorities and—in the case of Albania—scrapping of trade treaties and expulsion of Yugoslav engineers and teachers.

### Relations in Czechoslovakia

In Czechoslovakia, relations between some 3,000 Yugoslav apprentices studying in that country and the Czechoslovak Communist party became so envenomed that the Yugoslav Government had to repatriate its students. Intensive nuisance attacks upon Yugoslavs in the Soviet bloc countries bordering Yugoslavia were obviously designed to rattle the confidence of the Yugoslav Communist party, but so far as can be judged the maneuver has failed to achieve its intended results.

States in the Soviet blocs bordering Yugoslavia have also become "firing points" of Cominform propaganda barrages against the Yugoslav Communist party's leadership. Propaganda attacks and methods of psychological warfare used by the Cominform states have not had the desired effect.

The states of the Soviet blocs also serve as collecting points for disaffected Yugoslavs who have either resigned their official positions abroad or have escaped from Yugoslavia. Thus far, the Cominform states have not been able to gather many anti-Tito Yugoslavs or any Yugoslavs distinguished for their position in the Yugoslav Communist party.

### Leadership Is Stronger

It is obvious that the Cominform states hope to gather a sufficient number of anti-Tito Yugoslavs so that they may eventually establish a strong émigré organization, but two and a half months of intensive warfare have not been fruitful. The political scene in Yugoslavia has not been disturbed by the strivings of the Cominform states. If anything, the present Yugoslav leadership is in stronger position than it was at any time before June 28.

The weeding out of anti-Tito or uncertain elements of the Yugoslav Communist party has been paralleled by purging of

elements which were unreliable from the Cominform point of view in states of the Soviet blocs. The movements are parallel but in opposite directions and are intended for opposite reasons. The Yugoslav leadership has stripped the party down to its hard core in the struggle with the Cominform, while the Cominform states are eliminating unreliable elements who might undermine those states in their loyalty to the Soviet Union and weaken the fight against the Yugoslav Communist party. The purge of parties in the Soviet bloc indicates greater political integration with the Soviet Union's policy—a stand which Yugoslavs oppose and which was a fundamental cause of the rift with the Soviet Union.

### Purges Among Satellites

In Bulgaria, Traiche Kostov, principal party lieutenant of Premier Georgi Dimitrov warned the party on the eve of its Liberation Day celebration, Sept. 9, that complacency in view of the situation in Yugoslavia was dangerous because party opponents had viewed the Yugoslav example with hope.

The Bulgarian party will be rid of unreliable elements at the next party congress, which convenes in Sofia Oct. 31. In Hungary Matyas Rakasi, the Communist leader, announced as long ago as June 1 in the official Cominform publication that purging of the Hungarian party was under way and that too many suspect and unreliable elements had gained admission to membership. In Poland, the purge is affecting the Socialist party, which is being stripped of hostile elements before fusion takes place with the Communists. In Czechoslovakia, party memberships are being "verified." According to reports from Rumania, the party in that country is also being carefully scrutinized.

Tightening of control, in a sense, blind loyalty to the Soviet Union and submergence of national interests to Soviet interests, is growing apace in states of the Soviet blocs. The movement is part of the general Soviet drive to mend Russia's fences and establish greater unity of command. Advent of the Yugoslav question accelerated the urgency of this movement because of repercussions of Tito's independent stand upon more independently-minded individuals and groups of Eastern Europe.

### Yugoslav Attitude

This unity of command was manifest at the recent Danubian conference, where in hundreds of votes taken the Soviet bloc voted as one man on resolutions submitted by the Soviet delegation. The Yugoslav delegation cooperated.

The same is now occurring at the United Nations Assembly meeting in Paris. Yugoslavs persist in their attitude that no matter what the Soviet bloc thinks or does, the Yugoslavs are members of that bloc and their foreign policy is primarily based on that of the Soviet Union.

The Yugoslav Communist leadership still maintains the keystone of its foreign policy is "anti-imperialist." It must vote with the Soviet, it asserts, but that voting is not automatic. Yugoslavia supports the Soviets on the general concept of identity of views, but votes are not cast automatically and discussions of tactics occur. Therein lies the exceptional position of Yugoslavia with reference to the Soviet bloc in matters of concepts, strategy and tactics.

\* \* \*

October 31, 1948

## SERBIAN REGION GETS AUTONOMY

BELGRADE, Yugoslavia, Oct. 30 (Reuters)—Serbia's National Assembly decided today to grant autonomy to the two regions of Vojvodina and Kossovo-Methuia, the Yugoslav news agency Tanyug reported.

\* \* \*

January 26, 1949

## ECONOMIC AID UNIT FORMED BY MOSCOW AND SATELLITES

*Organizers Charge U. S. and Britain Block Trade With East—Yugoslavia Left Out—Others Asked to Join and Spurn ERP*

By The Associated Press

MOSCOW, Jan. 25—Organization of a Council for Economic Mutual Assistance by the Soviet Union and five of its neighbors was announced today. It was viewed by foreign diplomats here as the East's answer to the West's European Recovery Program.

Bulgaria, Czechoslovakia, Hungary, Poland and Rumania joined the Soviet Union in forming the economic council at a Moscow conference earlier this month. Yugoslavia was not mentioned.

The announced aim of the new council was "the exchange of experience in the economic field, the rendering of technical assistance to each other, and the rendering of mutual assistance in regard to raw materials, foodstuffs, machinery, equipment, etc."

[Washington economists said the program appeared to be designed to improve Russian living conditions at the expense of the peoples in the satellite state. They doubted Moscow could meet the cost necessary to implement the program.]

The Soviet Union obviously is going to be the key nation in the council.

"Other countries of Europe that share the principles of the council and wish to participate in broad economic cooperation with the afore-mentioned countries" may join, a communiqué announcing the council said.

The communique declared that one of the reasons for the establishment of the council was that the United States, Britain and "certain other countries of Western Europe" were boycotting the six nations in trade.

Another was that the Marshall Plan interfered with the sovereignty of nations.

To become a member of the new Eastern Council then, an applying country must at least view the Marshall Plan and the present economic policy of the United States and Britain as they are regarded by the council.

Diplomats speculate that Albania and Finland, the Soviet zone of Germany and the Soviet zone of Austria may be included.

The fact Yugoslavia was not among the organizing nations was still another step in the isolation of Premier Marshal Tito's nation from other Eastern European countries in the last six months. Cut off politically by the Communist Information Bureau's denunciation of Marshal Tito and his aides, Yugoslavia is now all but cut off economically.

The Soviet Union still has a trade agreement with Yugoslavia, but it was curtailed seven-eighths in 1949 because of what the Russians described as "the unfriendliness of the Yugoslav Government."

### Marshall Plan Believed Aim

The announcement did not say that nations now participating in the European Recovery Program would be barred from membership in the Eastern Council. But it was obvious that any countries seeking to join the council first would be obliged to renounce Marshall Plan aid.

The Soviet Minister of Foreign Trade, A. I. Mikoyan, is destined to play an important role in the council's work.

A curly-haired Armenian, Mr. Mikoyan is regarded as one of the best economic thinkers in the Soviet Union. He has taken part in talks on all trade agreements the Soviet Union has made with the other five members of the new economic council.

Nothing official was announced on when the council would hold its first business meeting or where, but there were indications that a session would be held soon. Inasmuch as the Eastern council was formed in Moscow, the first session may be held here. If alphabetical order were followed, the first would be held in Bulgaria.

### Economist Cites Barter Trade

PRAGUE, Jan. 25 (AP)—Moscow has given its barter baby a name with the establishment of the new Eastern economic council. A veteran observer on economics here commented:

"The council represents nothing more than what they have been doing for months. They have given a name to the trade pacts they have been promoting among themselves. Trade pacts are a fine thing, but for a country like Czechoslovakia how will they get them the raw materials necessary to keep their production machine going?"

The observer said this was how Germany once had tried to line up Central Europe in her economic grasp.

\* \* \*

March 18, 1949

# PRESIDENT REPORTS UPTURN FOR GREECE

*Military Program of U. S. Aid Now Making Progress Against Communist-Led Guerrillas*

By FELIX BELAIR Jr.
Special to The New York Times

WASHINGTON, March 17—President Truman reported to Congress today that since the first of the year the tide of battle had been running against the Communist-led guerrillas in the Greek civil war. At the same time he cautioned against any expectation of "a quick and easy victory."

In his regular quarterly report to Congress on the Greek-Turkish aid program, President Truman said that since the first of the year "there is growing evidence of discouragement and dissension within the Communist guerrilla leadership" in Greece.

President Truman spoke of the last quarter of 1948 as "a period of stalemate" in the battle for the independence of Greece, but he added that, "since the beginning of 1949, there are signs that the balance is shifting against the guerrillas as a result of the training, regrouping and tenacious holding operations of the Greek armed forces."

A recent declaration of the Greek Communist party promising autonomy for the "Macedonian people" was cited in the report as "tacit admission that the guerrilla movement is approaching bankruptcy in the eyes of the Greek people and as an excellent example of the subservience of the Greek Communist party to the dictates of international communism."

Among encouraging military developments the report mentioned that the Greek Army offensive in the Peloponnesus, started in the last week of 1948, was "making excellent progress."

No mention was made in the report of the Administration's intention to ask Congress for additional funds to carry the program of economic and military aid to Greece and Turkey through June, 1950. Estimates of the amount required range from $150,000,000 to $300,000,000.

The President estimated active guerrillas now in Greece at 23,000 or about 1,000 more than reported last Sept. 30. Since then, according to the report, more than 6,000 casualties had been inflicted on the rebel forces but an estimated 7,000 additional persons had been recruited or forced into the rebel ranks in the same period.

The Presidential report said Turkey "has made a sincere effort fully to utilize United States assistance in improving the efficiency of its armed forces." Large-scale maneuvers held during October displayed "a high degree of skill" in using American equipment said the report.

\*   \*   \*

April 5, 1949

# BULGARIA ARRESTS HER VICE PREMIER

*Kostov Stripped of His Posts—Yugoslavs Again Say Sofia Is Purging Communists*

SOFIA, Bulgaria, April 4 (Reuters)—Traicho Kostov, Vice Premier and chairman of the Bulgarian Committee for Economic and Financial Questions, has been relieved of his posts and placed under arrest, the Bulgarian official news agency reported tonight.

M. Kostov's arrest, first reported on the Belgrade, Yugoslavia, radio Thursday, was ordered at a plenary session of the central committee of the Bulgarian Communist party on March 26 and 27, according to a communiqué in the party's official newspaper.

The committee discussed the political errors he had committed and "his errors in relation to the party," the communiqué said.

The session also decided to exclude M. Kostov from membership in the Politburo.

### Removed From Politburo

SOFIA, Tuesday, April 5 (AP)—The central committee of the Bulgarian Communist party announced today that Deputy Premier Kostov had been removed from the Politburo and as Deputy Premier.

The announcement said he had been removed for "gross political and anti-party errors," "incorrect methods of leadership," "insincere and unfriendly policy regarding the Soviet Union," and "nationalistic deviations."

BELGRADE, Yugoslavia, April 4 (UP)—The Belgrade radio said tonight that the purge of Bulgarian Communists had been intensified and that a total of 300, including Deputy Premier Kostov, had been arrested.

M. Kostov is Bulgaria's leading Communist next to Premier Georgi Dimitrov. He directed Communist activities in Bulgaria until M. Dimitrov returned from Moscow at the end of World War II.

The Yugoslav press service reported last Thursday for the first time that about 100 Bulgarian Communists had been swept from office and taken into custody on charges of espionage for "imperialist powers."

At the time a spokesman for the Bulgarian Foreign Office denied the report as a "cock-and-bull invention."

Tonight's broadcast referred indirectly to the Sofia denials. Belgrade said that Bulgarian authorities had given "false and tendentious information" to foreign press representatives.

\*   \*   \*

**April 6, 1949**

## GREEK REBELS GAIN 6 GRAMMOS PEAKS

*Government Discloses Defeat as Battle Continues—*
*New Guerrilla Cabinet Set*

By A. C. SEDGWICK
Special to The New York Times

ATHENS, April 5—Guerrilla forces steadily reinforced during the day pressed home a series of attacks mainly between the Albanian border and the Sarantoporos River today. The guerrillas announced the formation of a full new "Free Greek" Cabinet.

The Greek General Staff said it had positive information the several-pronged attack was based on Albania. Observers of the United Nations Commission for the Balkans already have been invited to witness the large-scale military operations, allegedly carried out in violation of international law.

Tonight's communiqué stated the battle in the Grammos Mountains was continuing with "undiminished" vigor. It acknowledged the loss of a number of heights, including Mounts Steno and Pyrgos and the withdrawal of Government garrisons at several adjoining points.

[The United Press reported that the communiqué said the guerrillas had captured snowcapped Mount Tabouri fifteen miles east of the Albanian border: Mounts Kardhari, Voliana and Yiftissa, and several villages. All these points are in the area of the Albanian frontier and all were defended tooth and nail by the guerrillas last summer. Six Government divisions spent all last summer wresting these peaks from the "Free Greek" guerrillas.]

### Some Nationalist Gains

In some instances, however, Government forces were reported to have recaptured lost positions and were said to be "clearing" areas wrested from their hands.

On the Government side published casualties indicate sixty-seven killed, 132 wounded and forty-eight missing up till last night, while guerrilla losses were 114 killed, eighteen captured.

The number of guerrilla troops engaged now is believed to be nearing 5,000.

Today, the guerrilla radio announced the formation of a new "Provisional Government of Democratic Greece."

This junta, the whereabouts of which is unknown, significantly includes as window-dressing persons not of the Communist party proper. Still more significantly two portfolios have been placed in the hands of representatives of the Macedonian National Liberation Front.

### Partsalides Heads Junta

Dimitrius Partsalides is now the Premier. During war and liberation he was Secretary General of the EAM, a position he still holds, and he was a signatory of the Varkiza agreement that brought one phase of the war between the Com-

The New York Times

Dmitrius Partsalides

munist-led guerrillas and Government forces. John Ioannides who was appointed Premier after Gen. Markos Vafiades was removed, is now Vice Premier. He represents the Greek Communist party as do others, including Petros Rousos, rechosen Minister of Foreign Affairs; Lieut. Gen. Kostas Karagiorgis, formerly editor of the Athens Communist organ Rizospastis, now Minister of War Supplies; Lieut. Gen. Vassilios Barzotas, Minister of the Interior; and Leonidas Striggos, Minister of Finance. Miltiades Porphyrogenis retains the post of Minister of Justice.

The Greek Agrarian party, regarded as merely an annex of the Communist party, is represented by M. Papadimitris, appointed Minister of Agriculture; by Stephanos Savides, Minister of Trade Unions; and several others.

An organization referred to as the "General Federation of Labor" is represented by A. Grozos. The Macedonian Liberation Front is represented by Paskal Mitrofsky, Minister of Supply and Vengeli Koichev, Deputy Minister "in charge of minorities." The guerrilla radio said that the new Government, described as "representing all classes of people," had appointed a "Supreme War Council." Heading this group is Nicolas Zachariades, Secretary General of the Communist party.

\*　\*　\*

**May 20, 1949**

## SOVIET BACKS MOVE TO END GREEK WAR

*Tass Says Moscow Is Ready to Meet West on Plan, Which*
*Gromyko Discussed Here*

By The Associated Press

LONDON, Friday, May 20—Tass said today the Soviet Union was willing to talk over settlement of the Greek civil war on the basis of the recent peace bid of the Greek guerrilla Government.

The official Soviet news agency in a statement distributed by the Soviet Monitor here said Soviet Deputy Foreign Minister Andrei A. Gromyko expressed Russia's willingness in talks with United States and British representatives at the United Nations General Assembly on April 26.

Tass issued the statement under a Moscow dateline. It said that United States Assistant Secretary of State Dean Rusk and British Minister of State Hector McNeil had "proposed unofficially" to discuss steps to settle the war in Greece.

Tass said Mr. Gromyko replied that if their Governments should propose that the Soviet Government "take part in the matter of stopping the civil war . . . the U.S.S.R. would not refuse to take part in this matter and that for a settlement of the situation in Greece it would be best to utilize the recently published peace declaration of the Provisional Greek Democratic Government on the desire to end the civil war."

The Communist-led Greek guerrillas broadcast an appeal in April that the United Nations mediate the Greek civil war. They reportedly sent their terms for such an agreement to United Nations officials.

### TEXT OF SOVIET STATEMENT

The text of the Tass statement follows:

In American newspapers in the last few days and later in other foreign newspapers reports have appeared to the effect that talks on inclusion of the Greek question in the agenda of the forthcoming Paris session of the Foreign Ministers Council had been held between Mr. Gromyko, U. S. S. R. representative at the United Nations General Assembly in New York, on the one hand and United States Assistant State Secretary Rusk and Minister of State of Great Britain McNeil on the other. Tass considers it necessary to report this information does not correspond to the facts.

In reality the matter stands as follows: On April 26 Rusk and McNeil when meeting Gromyko proposed unofficially to discuss the question of steps for settlement of the situation which had arisen in Greece and cessation of the civil war.

In reply to this proposal of Rusk and McNeil, Gromyko declared that if the British and American Governments proposed to the Soviet Government to take part in the matter of stopping the civil war and establishing peace in Greece the U.S.S.R. would not refuse to take part in this matter and that for settlement of the situation in Greece it would be best to utilize the recently published peace declaration of the Provisional Greek Democratic Government on a desire to end the civil war.

### Proposal for Greek Election

In reply to the proposal of Rusk and McNeil that he expound the views of the Soviet Government on measures to normalize the situation in Greece, Gromyko named as measures which could be adopted

in this regard: (a) an appeal to the belligerent sides by representatives of the (three) Powers to end military operations: (b) a declaration of general amnesty: (c) holding of general free parliamentary elections in such a way that the supreme Greek organ for conducting elections in Greece include representatives of Greek democratic circles headed by the Peoples Liberation Movement in Greece.

Gromyko further pointed out that it would be expedient (d) to establish observation over the correct conduct of elections in Greece by representatives of the powers, including the U.S.S.R., and (e) formation of a joint commission with participation of the U.S.S.R. for controlling the borders of Greece with the neighboring northern states.

Gromyko declared that with introduction of this control, announcement should be made on ending of military aid by foreign powers to the Greek Government in personnel and materials and that a date be fixed for evacuation of foreign troops from Greece.

Rusk and McNeil on their part declared Gromyko's views on measures for normalizing the situation in Greece would be studied by them and that at their next meeting they would expound the views of their governments.

\* \* \*

October 17, 1949

## GREEK REBELS SAY THEY HAVE CEASED FIGHT; KEEP FORCES

*Communist Broadcast States They Seek Peace—Points to Soviet Position in U. N.*

### STEP TIED TO TALKS HERE

*Conciliation Body to Report This Week—Athens Charges Border Threat Persists*

By Reuters

LONDON, Oct. 16—The Greek guerrilla army tonight announced it had ceased operations "in order to avoid the total destruction of Greece"—but had not disbanded.

The announcement, made over the so-called Free Greek Radio in a proclamation from the "Provisional Free Greek Government" [the Communist directed rebel regime] came about forty-eight hours before the United Nations Balkan Conciliation Committee was due to report back to a General Assembly committee at Lake Success.

At the same time, the Greek General Staff in Athens alleged that the guerrilla forces, defeated in recent battles, were now reorganizing in Albania.

The Greek rebel proclamation denounced what it called the role of the "Anglo-American imperialists and their agents, the monarcho-fascists" in the operations that have torn Greece internally since the end of World War II.

"They have brought untold misery to the Greek people since they pushed it into civil war three and a half years ago," said the broadcast proclamation.

### Peace and Bread Called Aim

The proclamation said a peaceful solution of Greece's problems was now being sought in the United Nations "with the participation of the Soviet Union."

"Athens is speaking about amnesties and agreements," the Communists statement went on, "but, in fact, the monarcho-fascists [the guerrillas' term for the Greek Government in Athens] go on persecuting democrats wherever, they find them in Greece."

After asserting that the interests of the Greek people were the paramount consideration of the guerrillas, the proclamation said the Greek people needed peace and bread.

"Greece is now in ruins and hunger reigns everywhere," it declared.

But, the proclamation asserted, the "temporary cessation" of military operations did not mean the "Provisional Greek Government and the people" renounced the fight for the rights of the Greek people.

"The monarcho-fascists are mistaken if they think that the struggle is ended and the Democratic Army has ceased to exist," it said.

The declaration ended with an appeal to the Greek people to be united and to continue the struggle for "peace, bread and liberty," with the assurance that all true democrats were with them and that they belonged to the same camp as the "truly democratic countries and the Soviet Union, the champion of peace and democracy in the world."

The Greek General Staff said tonight that the guerrilla forces defeated in recent battles in the Grammos and Vitzi Mountain regions were now reorganizing in a camp in Albania.

This camp, the statement said, was in a wooded region near the Skoumbi River about six miles from the southern Albanian town of Elbasan. Existence of the camp was reported by George Tzoumas, a sergeant in the rebels Eighth Division who entered Greece from Albania on Sept. 24 to gather information and carry out sabotage, the General Staff statement said. He surrendered to a Greek Army detachment five days later.

Vassili Bartzotas, Minister of the Interior in the Greek guerrilla government, was alleged by the General Staff in Athens to have said in a speech last month at the camp: "We are organizing among the Albanian people for the attack that will give us final victory."

Sgt. Tzoumas was reported in the statement to have said there were from 2,500 to 3,000 guerrillas in the Elbasan camp. Most of them had entered Albania with their arms and were undergoing military training, using Albanian military equipment.

\*   \*   \*

## LOOKING FORWARD IN GREECE

In a colorful ceremony the last British military units have made their farewell to Greece. Their going is the symbol of the passing of a phase in modern Greek history. It recalls the heroic and ill-fated stand is the peninsula against the German onslaught. It recalls the return of the Britons for the campaign of liberation and the firm stand that was made to forestall a Communist coup. It is a reminder, also, that Britain's obligation was too heavy longer to be borne alone and that the United States was able to step in with the Truman Doctrine and substantial assistance to the freedom of Greece.

With that freedom now more firmly assured than at any time since the German attack it is now possible to turn our attention away, in part, from military problems and desperate defenses. It is possible to look to a revival and strengthening of those firm spiritual bonds between the Greeks and ourselves that made our assistance imperative. In our community of culture lies an enduring basis for understanding and a common devotion to profound aspects of our civilization.

As Greece again looks forward, therefore, it is only natural that these feelings should have outward expression. Columbia University is establishing a center of Greek studies for expanded work in the fields of language, literature, culture history and economics. Greek Foreign Minister Tsaldaris graciously said just what we would have expected when he declared that the Greek Government would "contribute significantly" to this project. At approximately the same time comes the news that a combination of efforts on the part of the Rockefeller Foundation, the American School of Classical Studies in Athens and the European Cooperation Administration is bringing forth a restoration of the Stoa of Attalos in Athens as a great new museum.

Projects of this sort express the ties that bind us to Greece more accurately than do grants of money and the dispatch of military missions. The Greeks and ourselves, jointly, are interested in far more than the physical preservation of certain territorial limits. What has been endangered is a mode of life, a totality of culture, a wealth of wisdom and beauty that we could not afford to loss. If, with President Truman, we rejoice in the military victories in Greece, it is because they make possible the wider triumphs of the mind and spirit.

\*   \*   \*

## KOSTOV CHARGE SET IN BULGARIA PURGE

---

*Indictment Alleging Tito Link and 'Spying for U.S.'*
*Follows Pattern of Rajk Case*

---

Special to The New York Times

SOFIA, Bulgaria, Nov. 30—An indictment was published today accusing Traicho Kostov, long a leader of the Bulgarian Communist party and former Deputy Premier, of having plotted to overthrow the present regime, in association with Premier Marshal Tito of Yugoslavia and United States and British agents.

The main charge against Mr. Kostov and ten other top Communists in the long indictment, printed in all newspapers here, was that they conspired against Bulgaria's Communist-directed Government, to murder the late Premier Georgi Dimitrov and to annex Bulgaria to Yugoslavia.

[An Associated Press dispatch said the indictment was "almost identical to charges for which Laszlo Rajk, former Hungarian Foreign Minister, was hanged Oct. 15 after trial in Budapest." The Kostov purge has been viewed as part of the Cominform fight on Marshal Tito.]

Some of the specific charges leveled against the eleven defendants now awaiting trial are conspiracy, treason, espionage, betrayal of the fatherland and sabotage. For eight of the accused, the indictments indicate, the maximum penalty upon conviction is death—and, under a recently adopted law, there would be no appeal from the sentence.

The prosecution will call fifty-one witnesses. The date of the trial has still to be announced. The arrests in the Kostov case were carried out last April.

The published indictment listed the accused as:

Traicho Kostov Diunev, former Deputy Premier and former secretary of the Bulgarian Communist party's Central Committee.

Ivan Stafanov Hadji Mateev, former Finance Minister.

Nikola Pavlov Kolev, former administrative secretary of the Politburo and former Deputy Minister of Public Works.

Nikola Nachev Petkov, former deputy president of the State Economic and Financial Commission.

Tsoniu Stafanov Tsonchev, former governor of the Bulgarian National Bank.

Boris Andonov Khristov, former commercial representative of Bulgaria in the Soviet Union.

Ivan Slavov Gegrenov, former director of the rubber industry.

Ivan Georgiev Toutev, former director of the Foreign Trade Ministry.

Blagoi Ivanov Hadjipansov, a native of Yugoslav Macedonia who became a Bulgarian subject; he was counselor of the Yugoslav Embassy in Bulgaria.

Vasil Atanasov Ivanovski, native of Yugoslav Macedonia, but now a Bulgarian subject, former instructor in the Propaganda Department of the Communist party's Central Committee and former president of the Macedonian Cultural Societies in Bulgaria.

Ilia Ivanov Bayaltseliev, a native of Salonika, Greece, now a Bulgarian subject, a former official of the Sofia municipality.

The indictment, said to be based on written confessions of the accused, set forth alleged intrigues with the Yugoslav, American and British intelligence services.

M. Kostov allegedly made a long confession, in which he was said to have quoted extensively from conversations with Marshal Tito, who purportedly advised him, to have Premier Dimitrov assassinated.

The indictment said Mr. Kostov, "with the knowledge and consent of the British Intelligence Service, entered into secret criminal relations with the Yugoslav leaders Tito, Kardelj, Djilas and Rankovitch, with whom he agreed on joint action to deprive Bulgaria of her national sovereignty, her integrity and independence through her annexation to Yugoslavia and above all, to detach the Pirin (Macedonian) region from Bulgaria and annex it to Yugoslav Macedonia."

[The Yugoslav leaders cited with Marshal Tito are the Tito lieutenants most frequently under Cominform attack—Foreign Minister Edvard Kardelj, Propaganda Chief Milovan Djilas and Col. Gen. Alexander Rankovitch, Interior Minister.]

The name of Donald R. Heath, the United States Minister to Sofia since 1947, is mentioned in the indictment. Mr. Kostov is alleged to have admitted that he had made contact with and received instructions from Mr. Heath to collaborate with Marshal Tito for the detaching of Bulgaria from her association with the Soviet Union.

The indictment quotes an alleged written statement in which Mr. Heath was represented as telling Mr. Kostov at the end of 1947 that "advices" Mr. Kostov had received from Titoists should be considered as coming also from the Americans because "in this respect complete agreement exists between Marshal Tito and the United States."

The name of Col. William S. Bailey, described as head of the British Secret Service in the Balkans, and of a Stanley Brown and a Comdr. Frank Gosling are mentioned as among those of British Intelligence agents from whom Mr. Kostov received instructions.

\* \* \*

**December 17, 1949**

## KOSTOV EXECUTED; 'CONFESSED' ANEW

*Sofia's Former No. 2 Red Said to Have Retracted 'Not Guilty' Plea at Last Moment*

### ISSUE IN BULGAR ELECTION

*'Anglo-American,' 'Tito' Charge Aired as Yugoslavs See Rift Open in Communist Party*

Dispatch of The Times, London

SOFIA, Bulgaria, Dec. 16—Traicho Kostov, former Deputy Premier who was the principal defendant in the Sofia treason trial, was executed here today, after a last-minute appeal for mercy had been sent by Mr. Kostov to Premier Vassil Kolarov.

Mr. Kostov's petition said that his written confession, submitted at the beginning of the trial last week, was correct and that if his life was spared he would devote the remainder of his days to the Communist party in which he had until last spring been second in Bulgaria to the late Georgi Dimitrov.

On the first day of the trial Mr. Kostov had denied most of the incriminating statements in the written confession.

A few hours after Mr. Kostov was executed by hanging, Premier Kolarov, addressing a large election meeting, said that, although there were still elements of traitors among the Communist party, these would soon be all rooted out.

### Premier Uses Case in Speech

SOFIA, Dec. 16 (UP)—Premier Kolarov told 100,000 cheering, singing Bulgarians in the central square of the city tonight that the Kostov trial had wrecked Anglo-American plans to "enslave" the Balkans.

The Premier's address was part of an intensive campaign by the Communist-led Fatherland Front Government to assure 100 per cent support for its unopposed candidates in the election Sunday, when 4,500,000 Bulgarians are expected to go to the polls to choose a National Assembly and fourteen regional councils.

Vice Premier Vulko Chervenkov, Secretary General of the Communist party, also addressed the rally. Both speakers bitterly assailed "Anglo-American imperialists" and Premier Marshal Tito of Yugoslavia.

The official news agency announced the Kostov execution as follows:

"The Presidium of the National Assembly at its session of Dec. 15, 1949, considered the request for clemency of Traicho Kostov, who was condemned to death by the Supreme Court of Bulgaria for treason, espionage and sabotage, and found no reasons to attenuate the sentence pronounced against the traitor.

"Traicho Kostov was executed today, Friday, Dec. 16, 1949."

### Bulgarian Party Rift Seen Wider

Special to The New York Times

BELGRADE, Yugoslavia, Dec. 16—Evidence that exists in Belgrade indicates the arrest, trial and execution of Traicho Kostov have accentuated a split among Bulgarian Communist leaders over the question of whether Bulgaria is to continue as a dependency of the Soviet Union or fight to recover her independence.

The only portion of such evidence that can be reported today involves a high Bulgarian official who committed suicide just before the Kostov trial began.

The man in question was named Parmatarov, one of the chief public prosecutors, who was briefed by the Communist party to prosecute Mr. Kostov. According to a reliable source, Mr. Parmatarov received the prepared indictment against Mr. Kostov at the headquarters of the central committee and was ordered to take charge of the prosecution.

Mr. Parmatarov is said to have found himself in disagreement with many points in the indictment and, although a disciplined party member, he found he could not undertake to prosecute Mr. Kostov. A street car was almost abreast of the building when Mr. Parmatarov emerged and in a moment of despair he threw himself under it and was killed instantly. His death was announced as accidental.

The Parmatarov suicide is regarded as indicative of the degree to which violent passions have been aroused inside the party leadership over the question of Bulgaria's independence since Georgi Dimitrov's death last July 2. Mr. Kostov's decision to repudiate his prison confession and enter a plea of not guilty to major charges against him was not the result of caprice nor was it accidental. The Bulgarian court and the Bulgarian party were clearly taken by surprise.

It is believed in Belgrade that the developments of the Kostov case will only intensify the struggle between the two factions in the Bulgarian Communist party and will be followed by an even more violent purge.

It also believed that the hunt will be directed almost exclusively against those of Mr. Dimitrov's followers who openly or secretly supported the late Bulgarian Premier's sympathetic views concerning close association with Yugoslavia and the establishment of a strong South Slav federation.